Warman's Americana & Collectibles

8TH EDITION

EDITED BY ELLEN T. SCHROY

Published by

700 E. State Street • Iola, WI 54990-0001
Telephone: 715/445-2214

Please call or write for our free catalog.
Our toll-free number to place an order or obtain a free catalog is 800-258-0929
or please use our regular business telephone 715-445-2214
for editorial comment and further information.

Library of Congress Catalog Number: 84-643834

ISBN: 0-87069-752-8

Printed in the United States of America

Table of Contents

Part 1

Part 2

Part 3

One of the new categories in this year's guide is thermometers.

Introduction

Welcome to *Warman's Americana & Collectibles*. In 1984, the first edition of *Warman's Americana & Collectibles* introduced the collecting community to category introductions featuring collecting hints, history, references, periodicals and reproduction and copycat information, complemented by detailed, accurate listings and values. As a result of the enthusiastic acceptance of this format, it was extended to *Warman's Antiques and Collectibles Price Guide* and other Warman's titles.

Warman's Americana & Collectibles was a pioneering work, the first general price guide to mass-produced 20th century objects. It helped define and solidify the modern collectibles market. As the collectibles market has matured, so has *Warman's Americana & Collectibles*. If you have a copy of the first edition, compare the categories listed in it to those found in this eighth edition. Times *have* changed. Perhaps this is why so many individuals find the collectibles market so exciting.

Collectibles are the things with which your parents, you and your children have played and lived. The things that belonged to your grandparents are now *antiques*. The evolution of an object from new to desirable to collectible to antique within one's lifetime, i.e., an approximately 50-year span, is difficult for some to accept. However, it is reality.

Warman's Americana & Collectibles takes you on a nostalgic trip down memory lane. Do not get angry about the things you or your parents discarded. Be thrilled by the value of the things that were saved. Do not hesitate to buy back the things from your childhood that evoke pleasant memories. As you do, you will find that the real value of objects is not monetary, but the joy that comes from collecting, owning and, most importantly, playing and living with them once again.

Finally, do not ever be embarrassed by what you collect. *Warman's Americana & Collectibles* is based on the premise that it is acceptable to collect anything you wish. Remember one simple fact: All of today's antiques were collectibles in the past.

What is a Collectible?

As the 20th century nears its end, the definition of an antique remains clear while what constitutes a collectible has become more confusing. Part of the confusion rests within myself—I am not yet ready to admit that I am an antique.

For the purpose of this book, an antique is anything made before 1945. A great many individuals in the antiques and collectibles field disagree with this definition, but with each passing year it becomes harder and harder to deny this premise. The key is the war years of 1942–1945. During this period, production switched from domestic to wartime products. When the war ended, things were different. American life and expectations were very different in 1948 than in 1938. New war technology modified for productive civilian use was partially responsible. However, the most-telling fact of all is that well over half the population living in America today was born after 1945 and approximately two-thirds grew up in the post-1945 era.

Keeping this in mind and seeking technical definitions, a collectible then becomes an object made between 1945 and 1965 and a "desirable" an object made after 1965. The difference between a collectible and a desirable is that a collectible has a clearly established secondary market while a desirable exists in a market rampant with speculation.

Actually, the post-1945 era is broken down into three distinct collecting periods: 1945–1965, 1965–1980 and post-1980. Goods from the 1965 to 1980 period are moving out of their speculative mode into one of price stability.

Warman's Americana & Collectibles is the volume designed to deal with objects from the 20th century. Three criteria are applied when preparing the book: Was the object mass produced? Was it made in the 20th century, preferably after 1945? Do the majority of the items in the category sell for less than $200? The ideal collectible fits all three qualifications.

Since collecting antiques became fashionable in the early 20th century, there have been attempts to define certain groups of objects as the "true" antiques, worthy of sophisticated collectors and to ignore the remaining items. Most museums clearly demonstrate this attitude. Where do early 20th century tin toys, toy soldiers, or dolls fit? Those made before 1915 are antique. No one argues this any longer. Those made between 1920 and 1940 are in transition. We designate them "prestige" collectibles, objects changing in people's minds from collectible to antique.

To clarify the distinction between antique and collectible, consider Webster's definition of collectible: "an object that is collected by fanciers, especially one other than such traditionally collectible items as art, stamps, coins, and antiques."

International Market

Collectibles began to draw worldwide interest at the end of the 1980s. All of a sudden, American buyers found themselves competing with buyers from Europe and Japan on their home turf. In head-to-head competition, the American buyers frequently lost. How can this be explained?

The largest portion of the 1990s collectibles market is made up of post-World War II material. During this period, the youth of the world fell under three dominant American influences: movies, music and television. As the generations of the 1950s, 1960s and even 1970s reached adulthood and started buying back their childhood, many of the things they remember and want have American associations.

America is the great mother lode of post-war collectibles. At the moment, it is packages and boxes of American collectibles that are being sent abroad. It will not be too much longer before the volume reaches container loads.

American collectors also are expanding their horizons. They recognize that many objects within their favorite collectible category were licensed abroad. They view their collections as incomplete without such examples. Objects are obtained by either traveling abroad or by purchasing from foreign sources through mail or auction.

Price Notes

Prices in the collectibles field are not as firmly established as in the antiques area. Our pricing is based on an object being in very good condition. If otherwise, we note this in our description. It would be ideal to suggest that mint, or unused, examples of all items do exist. In reality, objects from the past were used, whether they be glass, china, dolls, or toys. Because of this, some normal wear must be expected.

The biggest problem in the collectibles field is that an object may have more than one price. A George Eastman bubblegum card may be worth $1 to a bubblegum card collector but $35 to a collector of photographic memorabilia. I saw the same card marked both ways. In preparing prices for this guide we have considered the object in terms of the category in which it is included. Hence, a girlie matchcover may be valued at 25 to 50 cents in the matchcover category and $2 to $5 in pinup art. However, for purposes of making a sale, if all you can find are matchcover collectors, take the quarter and move on.

Organization of the Book

Listings: We have attempted to make the listings descriptive enough so the specific object can be identified. Most guides limit their descriptions to one line, but not *Warman's*. We have placed emphasis on those items which are actively being sold in the marketplace. Nevertheless, some harder-to-find objects are included to demonstrate the market spread. A few categories in this book also appear in *Warman's Antiques and Collectibles Price Guide*. The individual listings, however, seldom overlap (except for a few minor instances). We've tried to include enough objects to give readers a good basis for comparison. After all, that is what much of the collectibles marketplace uses to establish prices: comparables. To properly accomplish this task, some overlapping between books is unavoidable. It is our intention to show objects in the low to middle price range of a category in *Warman's Americana & Collectibles* and the middle to upper range in our main antiques guide, *Warman's Antiques and Collectibles Price Guide*, thus creating two true companion lists for the general dealer or collector.

Collecting Hints: This section calls attention to specific hints as they relate to the category. We note where cross-category collecting and nostalgia are critical in pricing. Clues are given for spotting reproductions. In most cases, we just scratch the surface. We encourage collectors to consult specialized publications.

History: Here we discuss the category, describe how the object was made, who are or were the leading manufacturers and the variations of form and style. In many instances, a chronology for the object is established. Finally, we place the object in a social context—how it was used, for what purpose and so on.

References: Many general references are

listed to encourage collectors to learn more about their objects. Included are author, title, most recent edition, publisher and a date of publication. If published by a small firm or individual, we have included the address when known.

Finding many of these books may present a problem. The antiques and collectibles field is blessed with a dedicated core of book dealers who stock these specialized publications. You may find them at flea markets, antiques shows or through their advertisements in leading publications in the field. Many dealers publish annual or semi-annual catalogs. Ask to be put on their mailing lists. Books go out-of-print quickly, yet many books printed more than 25 years ago remain the standard work in a field. Also, haunt used-book dealers for collectible reference material.

Collectors' Clubs: The large number of collectors' clubs adds vitality to the collectibles field. Their publications and conventions produce knowledge which often cannot be found anywhere else. Many of these clubs are short-lived; others are so strong that they have regional and local chapters.

Periodicals: In respect to the collectibles field, there are certain general monthly periodicals to which the general collector should subscribe:

Antiques & Collecting Hobbies, 1006 S. Michigan Ave., Chicago, IL 60605.

Antique Trader Weekly, P.O. Box 1050, Dubuque, IA 52001; http://www.csmonline.com.

AntiqueWeek, P.O. Box 90, Knightstown, IN 46148; http://www.antiqueweek.com.

Maine Antique Digest, P.O. Box 358, Waldoboro, ME 04572; http://www.maineantiquedigest.com.

Several excellent periodicals relating to the collectibles marketplace are published by Krause Publications, 700 E. State St., Iola, WI 54990-0001; http://www.krause.com. Check out these interesting publications: *Coin Prices, Coins, Goldmine, Numismatic News, Sports Cards, Sports Collectors Digest, Toy Shop* and *Warman's Today's Collector.*

Many of the categories included in *Warman's Americana & Collectibles* have listings of specialized periodicals and newsletters. Please refer to your specific collecting interest for these additional references.

Museums: The best way to study any field is to see as many documented examples as possible. For this reason, we have listed museums where significant collections are on display. Special attention must be directed to the Margaret Woodbury Strong Museum in Rochester, NY, and the Smithsonian In-stitution's Museum of American History in Washington, DC.

Reproduction Alert: Reproductions are a major concern, especially with any item related to advertising. Most reproductions are unmarked; the newness of their appearance is often the best clue to uncovering them. Where the words "Reproduction Alert" alone appear, a watchful eye should be kept on all objects in the category.

Reproductions are only one aspect of the problem; outright fakes are another. Unscrupulous manufacturers make fantasy items which never existed, e.g., a Depression glass Sharon butter dish reproduced in Mayfair blue.

Research

Collectors of objects in the categories found in this book deserve credit for their attention to scholarship and the skill with which they have assembled their collections. This book attests to how strong and encompassing the collectibles market has become through their efforts.

We obtain our prices from many key sources— dealers, publications, auctions, collectors and field work. The generosity with which dealers have given advice is a credit to the field. Everyone recognizes the need for a guide that is specific and has accurate prices. We study newspapers, magazines, newsletters and other publications in the collectibles and antiques fields. All of them are critical to understanding what is available in the market. Special recognition must be given to those collectors' club newsletters and magazines which discuss prices.

Our staff is constantly monitoring the field, paying attention to all parts of the country. We accomplish this by reading trade publications and using the Internet and its vast resources to reach many places. Frequent visits to several different Web sites yield valuable information as to what is being offered for sale and what people are looking for, as well as insights into collecting clubs and new collecting interests. Our Board of Advisors provides regional as well as specialized information. More than 100 specialized auctions are held annually and their results provided to our office. Finally, private collectors have worked closely with us, sharing their knowledge of price trends and developments unique to their specialties.

Buyer's Guide—Not a Seller's Guide

Warman's Americana and Collectibles is designed to be a buyer's guide, a guide to what you would have to pay to purchase an object on the open market from a dealer or collector. **It is not a seller's guide to prices.** People frequently make this mistake and are deceiving themselves by doing so.

If you have an object mentioned in this book and wish to sell it, you should expect to receive approximately 35% to 40% of the value listed. If the object cannot be resold quickly, expect to receive even less. The truth is simple: Knowing to whom to sell an object is worth 50% or more of its value. Buyers are very specialized; dealers work for years to assemble a list of collectors who will pay top dollar for an item.

Examine your piece as objectively as possible. If it is something from your childhood, try to step back from the personal memories in evaluating its condition. As an antiques appraiser, I spend a great deal of my time telling people their treasures are not "gold," but items readily available in the marketplace.

In respect to buying and selling, a simple philosophy is that a good purchase occurs when both the buyer and seller are happy with the price. Don't look back. Hindsight has little value in the collectibles field. Given time, things tend to balance out.

Where to Buy Collectibles

The collectible has become standard auction house fare in the 1990s. Christie's East (219 E. 67th St., New York, NY 10021) and Sotheby's (1334 York Ave., New York, NY 10021) conduct collectibles sales several times each year. Specialized auction firms, e.g., Lloyd Ralston Toys (447 Stratfield Rd., Fairfield, CT 06432) in toys; and James Julia, Inc. (P.O. Box 830, Fairfield, ME 04937) and Bill Bertoia Auctions (1881 Spring Rd., Vineland, NJ 08360) in advertising, toys and a host of other categories, have proven the viability of the collectible as a focal point.

The major collectibles marketing thrust continues to be the mail auction, either with material on consignment or directly owned. Hake's Americana & Collectibles (P.O. Box 1444, York, PA 17405) is the leader in mail auctions. More and more collectible mail auctions are sprouting up all across the country. Add to this the excitement of buying online and even participating in online auctions and you can see why so many expand their collections using these venues.

Direct-sale catalogs abound. Most major categories have one or more. These dealers and many more advertise in periodicals and collectors' clubs' newsletters. Most require payment of an annual fee before sending their catalogs.

Of course, there is an unlimited number of flea markets, estate and country auctions, church bazaars and garage sales. However, if you are a specialized collector, you may spend days looking for something to add to your collection. If you add in your time, the real cost of an object will be much higher than the purchase price alone.

All of which brings us to the final source—the specialized dealer. The collectibles field is so broad that dealers do specialize. Find the dealers who handle your material and work with them to build your collection.

Board of Advisors

Our Board of Advisors are dealers, authors, collectors and leaders of collectors' clubs throughout the United States. All are dedicated to accuracy in description and pricing. If you wish to buy or sell an object in their field of expertise, drop them a note. Please include a stamped, self-addressed envelope with all correspondence. If time permits, they will respond.

We list the names of our advisors at the end of their respective categories. Included in the list at the front of this book are mailing address for each advisor and, when available, phone number and/or e-mail address.

Comments Invited

Warman's Americana & Collectibles is a major effort dealing with a complex field. Our readers are encourages to send their comments about this book and suggestions for new categories in upcoming editions to P.O. Box 392, Quakertown, PA 18951-0392; or via e-mail to schroy@voicenet.com. We're also interested in hearing from you if you if you are an expert in a particular category and would like to become an adivsor.

Acknowledgments

By now, you've noticed that *Warman's Americana & Collectibles* has been through a few changes with this edition. First, it's grown to the same size as its big brother, *Warman's Antiques and Collectibles Price Guide*. This change allows more information to be offered to you in a larger type face and also accommodates more photographs in a larger format.

The second big change is the new publisher, Krause Publications from Iola, WI. This change is a wonderful one for the whole Warman's series, giving new energy to the dusty old pages. With the support of Krause's great staff, *Warman's Americana & Collectibles* promises to be a great new edition. Krause editor Jon Brecka is getting settled into his new position and this edition offers him a new challenge. His support over the last few months, along with the others in the Krause family, have been important to me.

The third change to this edition of *Warman's Americana & Collectibles* is the new name on the cover—mine. To some of you I'm an old friend, to others mine may be a new name; but let me assure you that I've been involved with *Warman's Americana & Collectibles* since its very creation. I have fond memories of helping to plan the first edition, discussion on how it was to be different from its big brother, how it would react to the collectibles marketplace. Well, since its birth in 1984, we've both grown, changed a little to stay "with it" in the 1990s. Sometimes *Americana* has been the launching pad for new categories, some of which have sprouted wings and flown off to *Warman's Antiques and Collectibles Price Guide*, like Morgantown Glass, while others have proven to be of less interest to today's collectors and have been quietly retired. Perhaps if the collecting interests for those categories warms again, they will reappear. As you flip through the pages of this latest edition, you'll see some new categories, such as Dr. Seuss Collectibles and some expansion into areas where the market is hot.

No edition of Warman's would be complete without a special thanks to the members of the Board of Advisors, a wonderful, dedicated group. Like the categories covered in this edition, a few have chosen not to return and some new names have been added, helping to give this edition a very up-to-date and wide geographical flavor. Through the mail, telephone and now e-mail, I've been in contact with each and every one, heard about what's important to their collecting interests as well as what's new in their lives. Through these conversations and their warm wishes of support, we've created an even better *Warman's Americana & Collectibles*. Add to this Board a very talented lady by the name of Harriet Goldner, who's a trusted and valued friend and assistant. Harriet keeps the feathers from ruffling, keeps track of all new books, collectors' clubs and many of the details. This edition was a first *Americana* experience for Harriet and she did a wonderful job.

Perhaps it's this beautiful sunny day, the fragrance of lilacs coming in my window; perhaps it's the hope that you'll enjoy the end result; but I think it's time to let this new creation fly so it may enjoy a long and happy life.

— Ellen Tischbein Schroy
May 1997

Editorial Staff

Ellen T. Schroy, Editor

Board of Advisors

Gary L. Miller & K.M. Scotty Mitchel
Millchell
2112 Lipscomb
Fort Worth, TX 76110
(817) 923-3274
Electrical Appliances

Jocelyn C. Mousley
137 S. Main St.
Quakertown, PA 18951
e-mail: gammajae@voicenet.com
Dog Collectibles

Joan Collett Oates
685 S. Washington
Constantine, MI 49042
(616) 435-8353
Phoenix Bird China

Clark Phelps
Amusement Sales
127 N. Main
Midvale, UT 84047
(801) 255-4731
Punchboards

Evalene Pulati
P.O. Box 1404
Santa Ana, CA 92702
Valentines

Julie P. Robinson
10 Colonial Dr.
Davidsville, PA 15928
(814) 479-2212
Plastics

Jim & Nancy Schaut
Box 10781

Glendale, AZ 85318
(602) 878-4293
e-mail: nschaut@aztec.asu.edu
Horse Collectibles

Kenneth E. Schneringer
271 Sabrina Ct.
Woodstock, GA 30188
(707) 926-9383
Catalogs

Susan Scott
882 Queen St. West
Toronto, Ontario, M6J 1G3, Canada
(416) 657-8278
e-mail: scottca@ibm.net
Chintz China

Virginia R. Scott
275 Milledge Ter.
Athens, GA 30606
(706) 548-5966
Candlewick

Richard Shields
The Carolina Trader
P.O. Box 769
Monroe, NC 28112
(704) 289-1604
Scouting

Judy Smith
702 Lamont St. NW
Washington, DC 20010
(202) 332-3020
e-mail: judy@quilt.net
Reamers

Lissa Bryan-Smith/Richard Smith
Box 208, RD1

Danville, PA 17821
(717) 275-7796
e-mail: Lissabryan@aol.com
Christmas Items; Holiday Collectibles; Santa Claus

Connie Swaim
P.O. Box 331
Carthage, IN 46115
e-mail:TheLorax50@aol.com
Dr. Seuss Collectibles

George Theophiles
Miscellaneous Man
Box 1776
New Freedom, PA 17349
(717) 235-4766
Posters

Dixie Trainer
The Souvenir Building Network
P.O. Box 70
Nellysford, VA 22958-0070
(804) 325-9159
Souvenir Buildings

Lewis S. Walters
P.O. Box 8178
Turnersville, NJ 08012
(609) 589-3202
e-mail: lew69@erols.com
Radios

Maret Webb
4118 E. Vernon Ave.
Phoenix, AZ 85008-2333
Swarovski Crystal

Auction Houses

The following auction houses provided catalogs of their auctions and price lists which were used in preparing this edition of *Warman's American & Collectibles*. Their support is truly appreciated.

Albrecht & Cooper Auction Services
3884 Saginaw Rd.
Vassar, MI 48768
(517) 823-8835

Sanford Alderfer Auction Company
501 Fairgrounds Rd.
Hatfield, PA 19440
(610) 368-5477
web site: http://www.alderfer
company.com

email: auction@alderfercompany.com

Andre Ammelounx
The Stein Auction Company
P.O. Box 136
Palantine, IL 60078
(847) 991-5927

The Armans Collector's Sales and Services
P.O. Box 4037
Middletown, RI 02842
(401) 849-5012

Arthur Auctioneering
RD 2, P.O. Box 155
Hughesville, PA 17737
(717) 584-3697

Aston Americana
2825 Country Club Rd.
Endwell, NY 13760-3349

(607) 785-6598

Aution Team Köln
Jane Herz
6731 Ashley Ct.
Sarasota, FL 34241
(941) 925-0385

Bailey's Antiques
102 E. Main St.
Homer, MI 49245
(517) 568-4014

Noel Barrett Antiques & Auctions
P.O. Box 1001
Carversville, PA 18913
(610) 297-5109

Robert F. Batchelder
1 W. Butler Ave.
Ambler, PA 19002
(610) 643-1430

Bill Bertoia Auctions
1881 Spring Rd.
Vineland, NJ 08360
(609) 692-1881

Biders Antiques Inc.
241 S. Union St.
Lawrence, MA 01843
(508) 688-4347

Brown Auction & Real Estate
900 E. Kansas
Greensburg, KS 67054
(316) 723-2111

Butterfield & Butterfield
7601 Sunset Blvd.
Los Angeles, CA 90046
(213) 850-7500

Butterfield & Butterfield
220 San Bruno Ave.
San Francisco, CA 94103
(415) 861-7500

C.C. Auction Gallery
416 Court
Clay Center, KS 67432
(913) 632-6021

W.E. Channing & Co., Inc.
53 Old Santa Fe Trail
Santa Fe, NM 87501
(505) 988-1078

Chicago Art Galleries
5039 Oakton St.
Skokie, IL 60077
(847) 677-6080

Christie's
502 Park Ave.
New York, NY 10022
(212) 546-1000
web site: http://www.
sirius.com/~christie/

Christie's East
219 E. 67th St.
New York, NY 10021
(212) 606-0400

Cincinnati Art Galleries
635 Main St.
Cincinnati, OH 45202
(513) 381-2128

Mike Clum, Inc.
P.O. Box 2
Rushville, OH 43150
(614) 536-9220

Cohasco Inc.
Postal 821
Yonkers, NY 10702
(914) 476-8500

Dargate Auction Galleries
5607 Baum Blvd.
Pittsburgh, PA 15206
(412) 362-3558
web site: http://www.dargate.com
email: awkshun@aol.com

Marlin G. Denlinger
RR3, Box 3775
Morrisville, VT 05661
(802) 888-2775

Dorothy Dous
1261 University Dr.
Yardley, PA 19067-2857
888-5 HUMMEL

William Doyle Galleries, Inc.
175 E. 87th St.
New York, NY 10128
(212) 427-2730
web site:
http://www.doylegalleries.com

Dunbar Gallery
76 Haven St.
Milford, MA 01757
(508) 634-8697

Dunning's Auction Service
755 Church Rd.
Elgin, IL 60123
(847) 741-3483

Early Auction Co.
123 Main St.
Milford, OH 45150
(513) 831-4833

Ken Farmer Realty & Auction Co.
105A Harrison St.
Radford, VA 24141
(703) 639-0939
web site: http://kenfarmer.com
email: info@kenfarmer.com

Fine Tool Journal
27 Fickett Rd.
Pownal, ME 04069
(207) 688-4962
web site: http://www.wow
pages.com/FTJ/

Steve Finer Rare Books
P.O. Box 758
Greenfield, MA 01302
(413) 773-5811

William A. Fox Auctions Inc.
676 Morris Ave.
Springfield, NJ 07081
(201) 467-2366

Freeman/Fine Arts Co. of Philadelphia, Inc.
1808 Chestnut St.
Philadelphia, PA 19103
(215) 563-9275

Garth's Auction, Inc.
2690 Stratford Rd.
P.O. Box 369
Delaware, OH 43015
(614) 362-4771

Greenberg Auctions
7566 Main St.
Sykesville, MD 21784
(410) 795-7447

Green Valley Auction Inc.
Rt. 2, Box 434
Mt. Crawford, VA 22841
(540) 434-4260

Guerney's
136 E. 73rd St.
New York, NY 10021
(212) 794-2280

Hake's Americana & Collectibles
P.O. Box 1444
York, PA 17405
(717) 848-1333

Gene Harris Antique Auction Center, Inc.
203 S. 18th Ave.
P.O. Box 476
Marshalltown, IA 50158
(515) 752-0600

Norman C. Heckler & Company
Bradford Corner Rd.
Woodstock Valley, CT 06282
(203) 974-1634

High Noon
9929 Venice Blvd.
Los Angeles, CA 90034
(310) 202-9010

Leslie Hindman, Inc.
215 W. Ohio St.
Chicago, IL 60610
(312) 670-0010

Michael Ivankovich Auction Co.
P.O. Box 2458
Doylestown, PA 18901
(215) 345-6094

Jackson's Auctioneers & Appraisers
2229 Lincoln St.
Cedar Falls, IA 50613
(319) 277-2256

James D. Julia Inc.
Rt. 201, Skowhegan Rd.
P.O. Box 830
Fairfield, ME 04937
(207) 453-7125

Lang's
30 Hamlin Rd.
Falmouth, ME 04105
(207) 797-2311

Leonard's Auction Company
1631 State Rd.
Duncannon, PA 17020
(717) 957-3324

Howard Lowery
3818 W. Magnolia Blvd.
Burbank, CA 91505
(818) 972-9080

Joy Luke
The Gallery
300 E. Grove St.
Bloomington, IL 61701
(309) 828-5533

Martin Auctioneers Inc.
P.O. Box 477
Intercourse, PA 17534
(717) 768-8108

McMasters Doll Auctions
P.O. Box 1755
Cambridge, OH 43725
(614) 432-4419

Wm. Frost Mobley
P.O. Box 10
Schoharie, NY 12157
(518) 295-7978

Wm. Morford
RD #2
Cazenovia, NY 13035
(315) 662-7625

New Hampshire Book Auctions
P.O. Box 460
92 Woodbury Rd.
Weare, NH 03281
(603) 529-7432

Richard Opfer Auctioneering
1919 Greenspring Dr.
Timonium, MD 21093
(410) 252-5035

Pacific Book Auction Galleries
133 Kerney St., 4th Fl.
San Francisco, CA 94108
(415) 989-2665

Pettigrew Auction Company
1645 S. Tejon St.
Colorado Springs, CO 80906
(719) 633-7963

Phillips Fine Art Auctions
406 E. 79th St.
New York, NY 10021
(212) 570-4830

Postcards International
P.O. Box 5398
Hamden, CT 06518
(203) 248-6621

Poster Auctions International
601 W. 26th St.

New York, NY 10001
(212) 787-4000

David Rago
333 S. Main St.
Lambertville, NJ 08530
(609) 397-9374

Lloyd Ralston Toys
173 Post Rd.
Fairfield, CT 06432
(203) 255-1233

Mickey Reichel Auctioneer
516 3rd St.
Boonville, MO 65233
(816) 882-5292

Sandy Rosnick
15 Front St.
Salem, MA 01970

Thomas Schmidt
7099 McKean Rd.
Ypsilanti, MI 48197
(313) 485-8606

L.H. Selman Ltd.
761 Chestnut St.
Santa Cruz, CA 95060
(408) 427-1177
web site: http://www.selman.com
email: lselman@got.net

Sentry Auction
Frank Trunzo
113 School St.
Apollo, PA 15613
(412) 478-1989

Skinner, Inc.
Bolton Gallery
357 Main St.
Bolton, MA 01740
(508) 779-6241

Skinner, Inc.
The Heritage on the Garden
63 Park Plaza
Boston, MA 02116
(617) 350-5429

C.G. Sloan & Company Inc.
4920 Wyaconda Rd.
North Bethesda, MD 20852
(301) 468-4911
web site: http://www.cgsloan.com

Smith House Toy Sales
26 Adlington Rd.
Eliot, ME 03903
(207) 439-4614

R.M. Smythe & Co.
26 Broadway
New York, NY 10004-1710

Sotheby's
1334 York Ave.

New York, NY 10021
(212) 606-7000
web site: http://www.sothebys.com

So. Folk Pottery Collectors Society
1828 N. Howard Mill Rd.
Robbins, NC 27325
(910) 464-3961

Michael Strawser
200 N. Main St., P.O. Box 332
Wolcottville, IN 46795
(219) 854-2859

Swann Galleries Inc.
104 E. 25th St.
New York, NY 10010
(212) 254-4710

Theriault's
P.O. Box 151
Annapolis, MD 21401
(301) 224-3655

Toy Scouts
137 Casterton Ave.
Akron, OH 44303
(216) 836-0668
email: toyscout@salamander.net

Treadway Gallery, Inc.
2029 Madison Rd.
Cincinnati, OH 45208
(513) 321-6742
web site: http://www.a3c2net.com/
treadwaygallery

Vintage Cover Story
P.O. Box 975
Burlington, NC 27215
(919) 584-6900

Bruce and Vicki Waasdorp
P.O. Box 434
Clarence, NY 14031
(716) 759-2361

Web Wilson Antiques
P.O. Box 506
Portsmouth, RI 02871
800-508-0022

Winter Associates
21 Cooke St., Box 823
Plainville, CT 06062
(203) 793-0288

Wolf's Auctioneers
1239 W. 6th St.
Cleveland, OH 44113
(216) 362-4711

Woody Auction
Douglass, KS 67039
(316) 746-2694

Abbreviations

The following are standard abbreviations which are used throughout this edition of *Warman's Antiques & Collectibles Price Guide.*

3D: three dimensional
4to: 8" x 10"
8vo: 5" x 7"
12mo: 3" x 5"
ADS: Autograph Document Signed
adv: advertising
ALS: Autograph Letter Signed
approx: approximately
AQS: Autograph Quotation Signed
attrib: attributed
b&w: black and white
C: century
c: circa
chlth: chromolithograph
cov: cover
CS: Card Signed
d: diameter or depth
dec: decorated
dj: dust jacket
DQ: Diamond Quilted
DS: Document Signed
ed: edition, editor
emb: embossed
ext.: exterior

Folio: 12" x 16"
ftd: footed
gal: gallon
ground: background
h: height
horiz: horizontal
hp: hand painted
illus: illustrated, illustration, illustrator
imp: impressed
int.: interior
irid: iridescent
IVT: inverted thumbprint
j: jewels
k: karat
l: length
lb: pound
litho: lithograph
ls: low standard
LS: Letter Signed
MBP: mint in bubble pack
mfg: manufactured
MIB: mint in box
MIP: mint in package
mkd: marked
MOC: mint on card
MOP: mother of pearl
n.d.: no date

No.: number
NRFB: never removed from box
opal: opalescent
orig: original
oz: ounce
pat: patent
pc: piece
pcs: pieces
pg: page
pgs: pages
pr: pair
PS: Photograph Signed
pt: pint
qt: quart
rect: rectangular
Soc: Society
sgd: signed
SP: silver plated
SS: sterling silver
sq: square
TLS: Typed Letter Signed
unp: unpaged
vol: volume
w: width
yg: yellow gold
#: numbered

A

Abingdon Pottery

Collecting Hints: Like wares from many contemporary potteries, Abingdon Pottery pieces are readily available in the market. The company produced more than 1,000 shapes and used more than 150 colors to decorate their wares. Because of this tremendous variety, it is advisable to collect Abingdon Pottery with particular forms and/or colors in mind.

Abingdon art pottery, with its vitreous body and semi-gloss and high-gloss glazes, is found at all levels of the market, from garage sales to antiques shows. For this reason, price fluctuations for identical pieces are quite common. Study the market carefully before buying. Learn to shop around. Price listings for Abingdon Pottery can now be found in all the general antiques and collectibles price guides, as well as in several of the specialized ceramic and pottery guides. Pieces regularly appear for sale in classified advertisements in most trade papers, providing a good basis for pricing Abingdon wares.

Collectors and dealers are still in the process of defining the market relative to the most desirable shapes and colors. At the moment black (gunmetal), a semi-gloss dark blue, a metallic copper brown and several shades of red are the favored colors. Decorated pieces command a premium of 15% to 20%.

History: The Abingdon Sanitary Manufacturing Co., Abingdon, Ill., was founded in 1908 for the purpose of manufacturing plumbing fixtures. Sometime between 1933 and 1934, Abingdon introduced a line of art pottery. In 1945, the company changed its name to Abingdon Potteries, Inc. Production of the art pottery line continued until 1950 when fire destroyed the art pottery kiln. After the fire, the company once again placed its emphasis on plumbing fixtures. Eventually, Abingdon Potteries became Briggs Manufacturing Co., a firm noted for its sanitary fixtures.

Reference: Susan and Al Bagdade, *Warman's American Pottery and Porcelain*, Wallace-Homestead, 1994; Joe Baradis, *Abingdon Art Pottery*, Schiffer Publishing, 1996.

Collectors' Club: Abingdon Pottery Collectors' Club, 210 Knox Hwy. S., Abingdon, IL 61410.

Bookends, pr
    Horse Head, black, #441 ....60.00
    Quill, black and white 125.00
Bowl, 12" d, low, blue,
    floral decals, #518 ....30.00
Candlesticks, pr,
    scalloped, white, #575 ....15.00
Console Set, 11-1/4" l center bowl,
    4-1/4" h candlesticks with double
    arms, yellow-green glaze 35.00
Cookie Jar
    Daisy, 8" h................................40.00
    Hobby Horse 250.00
    Jack-O-Lantern, #674 ....225.00
    Little Miss Muffet, #622 ....200.00
    Little Old Lady, green, #471..195.00
    Pineapple, 10-1/2" h..................75.00
    Sunflower.................................30.00
    Windmill, #678 ....245.00
Cornucopia
    7" h, green, #565......................18.00
    8" l, pink, #569 ....18.00
Drippings Jar, Daisy, #679 ....40.00
Figure
    4-1/2" h, pouter
    pigeon, white, #388.................70.00
    5" h, goose, blue, #571 ....40.00
    7" h, peacock, pink,
    price for pr...............................35.00
Flowerpot, 5" d, Cattails, #151 ......30.00
Geranium Bowl, #543...................45.00
Planter
    6-1/2" h, Mexican and cactus,
    hand dec, #616D.....................60.00
    7-1/4" h, raised sailing ship, imp rope
    handles, sea green glaze.........20.00
Salt and Pepper Shakers,
    pr, Little Bo Peep.....................45.00
String Holder, 8-1/2" d, mouse.....85.00
Vase
    5-1/2" h, box,white, #402 ....65.00
    6" h, Betz, blue, #110...............40.00
    7" h, 2-3/4" w, 6-1/2" l, ship, #494
        Blue......................................35.00
        Pink.......................................35.00
    8" h, 9-1/2" w, Alpha, antique
    white, handles, #105 ....25.00
    9" h, quilted top, rope-twist handles,
    white, #599..............................20.00
    10" h
        Art Deco style,
        dusty rose, #114 ....35.00
        Classic, blue, handles, emb scroll
        top, ribbed bottom, #115......30.00
        Pink.......................................30.00
    10-7/8" h, 7-1/8" w, Acanthus,
    pink, #486 ....30.00
    11" h, swirl, rose decals,
    gold flowers.............................95.00
Wall Pocket
    Book...45.00
    Butterfly, #601 ....65.00
    Calla Lily, #586D......................50.00
    Cookbook, #676D 50.00
Window Box
    3" h, 3-1/8" w, 10" l,
    pink, #476 ....25.00
    4-1/4" h, 4-1/2" w, 11-3/4" l, Alpha,
    antique white, #576..................20.00

Action Figures

Collecting Hints: This is one of the hot, trendy collecting categories of the 1990s. While there is no question that action figure material is selling—and selling well—much of the pricing is highly speculative. Trends change from month to month, as one figure or group of figures becomes hot and another cools off.

The safest approach is to buy only objects in fine or better condition and, if possible, with or in their original packaging. Any figure that has been played with to any extent will never have long-term value. This is a category with off-the-rack expectations. Be extremely cautious about paying premium prices for figures less than 10 years old. During the past decade dealers have made a regular practice of buying newly released action figures in quantity, warehousing them and releasing their stash slowly into the market once production ceases.

Also, examine packaging very closely. A premium is placed on a figure in its original packaging, i.e., the packaging that was used when the figure was introduced into the market. Later packaging means a lower price.

History: An action figure is a diecast metal or plastic posable model with flexible joints that portrays a real or fictional character. In addition to the figures themselves, clothing, personal equipment, vehicles and other types of accessories are also collectible.

Collectors need to be aware of the following attempts to manipulate the market:

Limited production—a deliberate act on the part of manufacturers to hold back on production of one or more figures in a series.

Variations—minor changes in figures made by manufacturers to increase sales (previously believed to be mistakes, but now viewed as a deliberate sales gimmicks).

Prototypes—artists' models used during the planning process. Any prototype should be investigated thoroughly—there are many fakes.

The earliest action figures were the hard-plastic Hartland figures of popular television Western heroes of the 1950s. Louis Marx also included action figures in a number of playsets during the late 1950s. Although Barbie, who made her appearance in 1959, is posable, she is not considered an action figure by collectors.

G.I. Joe, introduced by Hassenfield Bros., (Hasbro) in 1964, triggered the modern action figure craze. In 1965, Gilbert introduced action figures for James Bond 007, The Man from U.N.C.L.E. and Honey West. Bonanza figures arrived in 1966, along with Ideal Toy Corporation's Captain Action. Ideal altered the figures by simply changing heads and costumes. Captain Action and his accessories were the hot collectible of the late 1980s.

In 1972, Mego introduced the first six super heroes in what would become a series of 34 different characters. Mego also established the link between action figures and the movies when the company issued series for Planet of the Apes and Star Trek: The Motion Picture. Mego's television series figures included CHiPs, Dukes of Hazzard and Star Trek. When Mego filed for bankruptcy protection in 1982, the days of 8- and 12-inch fabric-clothed action figures ended.

The introduction of Kenner's Star Wars figure set in 1977 opened a floodgate. Action figures enjoyed enormous popularity and manufacturers rushed into the market, with Mattel quickly following on Kenner's heels. Before long, the market was flooded, not only with a large selection but with production runs into the hundreds of thousands.

Not all series were successful—just ask companies such as Colorform, Matchbox and TYCO. Some sets were not further produced when initial sales did not justify the costs of manufacture. These sets have limited collector value. Scarcity does not necessarily equate with high value in the action figure market.

References: John Bonavita, *Mego Action Figure Toys*, Schiffer Publishing, 1996; Paris & Susan Manos, *Collectible Action Figures*, 2nd Edition, Collector Books, 1996; Carol Markowski and Bill Sikora, *Tomart's Price Guide to Action Figure Collectibles*, Revised Edition, Tomart Publications, 1992.

Periodicals: *Action Figure News & Review*, 556 Monroe Tpk., Monroe, CT 06468; *Tomart's Action Figure Digest*, Tomart Publications, 3300 Encrete Ln, Dayton, OH 45439.

Collectors' Clubs: Captain Action Collectors Club, P.O. Box 2095, Halesite, NY 11743; Captain Action Society of Pittsburgh, 516 Cubbage St., Carnegie, PA 15106.

Additional Listings: G.I. Joe Collectibles, Super Heroes, Star Wars, Star Trek.

Alien

Lasershot Predator	12.00
Swarm Alien	11.00

A-Team, 6" h, Galoob

Amy Allen	30.00
Hannibal, MOC	20.00
Murdock, MOC	25.00
Templeton Peck, MOC	20.00

Batman, animated

Killer Choc	12.00
Phantasm	25.00
Phantasm, foreign card	22.00

Batman, Legends of

Catwoman	13.00
Joker	13.00

Batman Returns

Catwoman	12.00
Robin	12.00

Cooperstown Convention

Harmon Killebrew	22.00
Pat LaFontaine	15.00
Pistons Grant Hill	23.00
Richie Ashburn	20.00
Rod Carew	20.00
Steve Carlton	20.00

Fantastic Four

Human Torch, flame-on sparking action	6.00
Medusa	6.00
Mr. Fantastic	8.00
Silver Surfer	8.00
The Thing, Clobberin Time Punch	7.00

Marvel

Beast, 10" h	10.00
Mystique, 10" h	14.00
Rogue, 10" h	11.00
Sabretooth, metallic	9.00
Spiderman, super posable, 10" h	9.00
The Thing, 10" h	11.00
Venom, original	10.00

Mask, Kenner, MOC

Betty Bustin	18.00
Chompin Milo	15.00
Dorian	15.00
Heads Up	15.00
Killing Time	15.00
Quick Draw	15.00
Toronado	15.00
Wild Wolf	15.00

Planet of the Apes, Cornelius

8" h, Mego, 1974	20.00

Savage Dragon, She Dragon

Long hair	22.00
Mohawk hair	20.00

Spawn

Air Cycle	25.00
Badrock	12.00
Barrasso, 1994, MIP	25.00
Maxx-4tzz, FAO	23.00
Overkill, gold	16.00
Pilot Spawn, black	13.00
Tremor	12.00
Troll	15.00
Twitch and Sam	13.00
Vampire	15.00
Vertebreaker	12.00
Violator, chrome card	15.00
Werewolf, brown	19.00

Spider-Man

Alien, Slasher	5.00
Carnage Unleashed	8.00
Peter Palmer	8.00

Spider-Man Web Racer....................5.00
The Lizard, red shirt 5.00

Starting Lineup

Alonzo Mourning, 1996 ....12.00
Brett Hull, 1994................................8.00
Cal Ripken......................................42.00
Deion Sanders, 1996.....................12.00
Dennis Rodman,
    1996, orange hair, MIP 20.00
Dream Team, 1996 Basketball,
    Set 1 or 2.................................35.00
Eric Lindros, 1996 ....13.00
Eric Metcalf, 1996...........................8.00
Grant Hill.......................................35.00
Arturs Irbe, 1994, MIP 30.00
Jim Carey, 1996 ....16.00
Joe Montana..................................42.00
Joe Sakic, 1996.............................13.00
Johnny Unitas, 1989......................20.00
Kevin Greene, 1996 ....12.00
Mark Messier, 1996.......................13.00
Marshall Faulk, 1995.....................35.00
Nolan Ryan....................................60.00
Reggie Jackson.............................25.00
Ron Francis, 1996 ....10.00
Steve Bono, 1996............................8.00
Willie Mays 20.00

Star Trek

Borg...8.00
Cochrane..8.00
Communicator...................................1.00
Hunter of the Tosck.......................10.00
Lily...8.00
Picard, space suit............................8.00
Set, Lt. Sulu, LCDR Scott,
    30th Anniversary....................140.00

Star Wars

Amanaman....................................110.00
ATST Driver, MIP 15.00
Barada...55.00
Ben, Yz photo, MIP 25.00
Boba Fett, 2 circles, MIP 25.00
Chewbacca.......................................8.00
C-3PO 7.00
Darth Vader, short saber 8.00
Dash Rendar's Outrider, MIP 40.00
Death Star Commander 8.00
Greedo, MIP 20.00
Hammerhead, green card, MIP 15.00
Hans Solo, Carbonite, #1 ....130.00
Jades, long saber, MIP..................10.00
Jawa...9.00
Jedi Luke, 1st print,
    gray vest, MIP........................30.00
Lando Cairissian, MIP 15.00

Leia

Coushh disguise............................12.00
Organa 20.00

Luke Skywalker

First issue, 12" h, MIP 35.00
Hoth gear, MIP 15.00
Jedi Knights, MIP 12.00
Long saber, MIP 10.00
Stormtrooper 150.00
Obi Wan Kenobi, 12" h, MIP 45.00
R5-D4, green card, MIP 15.00
Snaggletooth 8.00
Snowspeeder, MIP.........................40.00
Stormtropper 15.00
Taoonie Trooper, MIP 20.00
TIE Pilot...15.00
Walrus Man 8.00
Yak Face, staff 160.00
Zuckuss...8.00

WILDC.A.T.S.

Mr. Majestic..................................10.00
Slag...10.00
Void...10.00
Voodoo..10.00

X-Men

Clear Iceman.................................23.00
Deadpool #1..................................23.00
Sabretooth #1...............................10.00
Wolverine #2 ....10.00

Advertising

Collecting Hints: Many factors affect the price of an advertising collectible—the product and its manufacturer, the objects or persons used in the advertisement, the period and aesthetics of design, the designer and illustrator of the piece and the form the advertisement takes. In addition, advertising material was frequently used to decorate bars, restaurants and other public places. Interior decorators do not purchase objects at the same price level as collectors.

In truth, almost every advertising item is sought by a specialized collector in one or more collectible area. The result is diverse pricing, with the price quoted to an advertising collector usually lower than that quoted to a specialized collector.

Most collectors seem to concentrate on the period prior to 1940, with special emphasis on the decades from 1880 to 1910. New collectors should examine the advertising material from the post-1940 period. Much of this material is still inexpensive and likely to rise in value as the decorator

trends associated with the 1950s through the 1970s gain importance.

History: The earliest advertising in America is found in colonial newspapers and printed broadsides. By the mid-19th century manufacturers began to examine how a product was packaged. The box could convey a message and help identify and sell more of the product. The advent of the high-speed, lithograph printing press led to regional and national magazines, resulting in new advertising markets. The lithograph press also introduced vivid colors into advertising. Simultaneously, the general store branched out into specialized departments or individual specialty shops. By 1880, advertising premiums such as mirrors, paperweights and trade cards arrived on the scene. Through the early 1960s, premiums remained popular, especially with children.

The advertising character developed in the early 1900s. By the 1950s, endorsements by popular stars of the day became a firmly established advertising method. Advertising became a lucrative business as firms, many headquartered in New York City, developed specialties to meet manufacturers' needs. Advertising continues to respond to changing opportunities and times.

References: Bob Alexander and Mike Bruner, *Collectors Guide to Telephone, Telegraph & Express Company Advertising*, Guard Frog Books, 1992; Miles Beller and Jerry Leibowitz, *Hey Skinny: Great Advertisements from the Golden Age of Comic Books*, Chronicle Books, 1995; A. Walker Bingham, *Snake-Oil Syndrome: Patent Medicine Advertising*, Christopher Publishing House, 1994; Michael Bruner, *Encyclopedia of Porcelain Enamel Advertising*, Schiffer Publishing, 1994; Leslie and Marcie Cabarga, *Trademark Designs of the Twenties*, Dover Publications, 1991; Douglas Collins, *America's Favorite Food: The Story of Campbell Soup Company*, Harry N. Abrams, 1994; Douglas Congdon-Martin, *America for Sale*, Schiffer Publishing, 1991; ——, *Tobacco Tins*, Schiffer Publishing, 1992; Douglas Congdon-Martin and

Robert Biondi, *Country Store Antiques*, Schiffer Publishing, 1991; —-, *Country Store Collectibles*, Schiffer Publishing, 1990; Fred Dodge, *Antique Tins*, Collector Books, 1995; Ted Hake, *Hake's Guide to Advertising Collectibles*, Wallace-Homestead, 1992; Sharon and Bob Huxford, *Huxford's Collectible Advertising, 3rd Edition*, Collector Books, 1996; Jerry Jankowski, *Shelf Life: Modern Package Design*, Chronicle Books, 1992; Jim and Vivian Karsnitz, *Oyster Cans*, Schiffer Publishing, 1993; Ray Klug, *Antique Advertising Encyclopedia, Vol. 1* (1978, 1993 value update), *Vol. 2* (1985, 1990 value update), L-W Book Sales; John Margolies and Emily Gwathmey, *Signs of Our Time*, Abbeville Press, 1993; *1992 Catalog of Cigarette & Other Trade Cards*, Murray Cards (International) Ltd., 1992; Gerald S. Petrone, *Tobacco Advertising*, Schiffer Publishing, 1996; Dawn E. Reno, *Advertising*, Avon Books, 1993; Joleen Robison and Kay Sellers, *Advertising Dolls*, Collector Books, 1980, 1994 value update; B.J. Summers, *Value Guide to Advertising Memorabilia*, Collector Books, 1994; Robert Sloan and Steven Guarnaccia, *A Stiff Drink and a Close Shave*, Chronicle Books, 1995; David L. Wilson, *General Store Collectibles*, Collector Books, 1994; David Zimmerman, *Encyclopedia of Advertising Tins*, published by author (6834 Newtonsville Rd., Pleasant Plain, OH 45162), 1994.

Periodicals: *Advertising Collectors Express*, P.O. Box 221, Mayview, MO 64071; *Let's Talk Tin*, 1 S. Beaver Ln., Greenville, SC 29605; *National Association of Paper and Advertising Collectors* (P.A.C.), P.O. Box 500, Mt. Joy, PA 17552; *Paper Collectors' Marketplace* (PCM), P.O. Box 128, Scandinavia, WI 54977; *Tin Fax Newsletter*, 205 Brolley Woods Dr., Woodstock, GA 30188; *Tin Type Newsletter*, P.O. Box 440101, Aurora, CO 80044; *Trade Card Journal*, 143 Main St., Brattleboro, VT 05301.

Collectors' Clubs: Advertising Cup and Mug Collectors of America, P.O. Box 680, Solon, IA 52333; Antique Advertising Association of America, P.O. Box 1121, Morton Grove, IL 60053; Ephemera Society of America, P.O. Box 37, Schoharie, NY 12157; Inner Seal Collectors Club, 6609 Billtown Rd., Louisville, KY 40299; Tin Container Collectors Association, P.O. Box 440101, Aurora, CO 80044; Trade Card Collector's Association, Box 284, Marlton, NJ 08053.

Reproduction Alert.

Ashtray

Ames Heating Pumps, metal, figural pump 15.00

Baker's Cocoa 90.00

Blue Diamond Coal Co., 6" d, metal 20.00

Chesterfield, MIB 20.00

Crook Paper Box Co., Kansas City, MO, cast iron, cowboy-hat shape ... 50.00

Dobbs Hats, black glass, hat shape 25.00

Firestone, tire, copper 20.00

First National Bank of Florence, Florence, TN, 3-1/2" sq, glass, Smokey Bear center 38.00

Grants Scotch Whiskey, cobalt blue glass 15.00

John Deere, deer jumping over log, 3-1/4" d, galvanized metal 30.00

Levy's Jewish Rye Bread, milk glass, black boy eating bread, Art Deco 75.00

KMO Radio Station, brass, 5" x 6-1/2", c1930 .... 20.00

Nash Depot Store 30.00

National Foundry, Brooklyn, NY, cast iron 30.00

New York City Seafood, fish in whirlpool, figural, bronze 50.00

Pyrene Fire Extinguisher, figural, Bakelite 50.00

Security National Bank, Trenton, NJ, brown glaze, c1927 .... 20.00

Twin Bears Store, chalkware, dated 1931, 4-1/2" 45.00

Universal Studios, emb cameras and crew, metal 20.00

Blotter

Carver Hydraulic Equip, Summit, NJ, Paul Webb Mountain Boys cartoon illus,

Ashtray, Westinghouse, 6-7/8" x 5-3/4" x 1-1/8", $26.

4" x 9" 3.00
Colonial Salt, Akron, multicolored salt boxes, 4" x 9" 7.50
Eagle White Lead, York Hardware, 3" x 6" 5.00
Kahley & Swartzbaugh Furniture, York, PA, 3-1/2" x 6" 5.00
Kohr Insurance, York, Electoral Chart for 1960, 4" x 9-1/2" 9.00
Morton's Salt, 3-1/2" x 6-1/8" 5.00
National Liberty Insurance, Whistler's Mother image, 3-1/2" x 6" 5.00
Optimist Week, Nov. 1955, yellow, 4" x 8" 4.00
Riggs, Rossman and Hunter Insurance, Baltimore, 4" x 9" 5.00
Schaefer Flower Shop, York, diecut, lily shape, 3" x 5-5/8" 5.00
Wampole's Preparation, 9 multicolored birds, 3-1/2" x 6" 8.50

Box

Argo Starch, unopened, 1930s 10.00
Baker's Chocolate, 12 lb, wood ... 20.00
Bossie's Best Brand Butter, 1 lb 5.00
Candy's Faultless Powdered Dance

Mirror, cat, White Cat Union Suits, Cooper Underwear Co., Kenosha, WI, oval, black ground, white letters, Parisian Novelty Co., Chicago, 2-3/4", $25.

Box, Fairy Soap, Gold Dust Corp., 2-3/8" x 3-7/8" x 1", $9.50.

Floor Wax, cardboard, 3-1/4"..10.00
Churn Baking Soda, woman churning
   butter, unused, 1920s.............12.00
Daylight Soap, wood 25.00
Eagle Asbestos Stove
   Lining, cardboard....................10.00
Fairies Bath Perfume,
   unopened, 1920s....................10.00
Gnagey's Ice Cream,
   red and white 7.00
Honor Bright Soap, cardboard........8.50
Jessop's Cough Drops 5.00
Jewel T, Skipper, soap,
   12 oz, full, c1960 ....67.50
Ladies Favorite Polish,
   paper label, 4" 8.50
Metropolitan Life Insurance,
   black, wood lid 40.00
National Lead Co., paint-chip
   sample box 20.00
Quaker Puffed Rice, 1919 ....20.00
Pennsupreme, green and red,
   white lettering 4.00
Regal Underwear, cardboard 20.00
Royal Baking Powder,
   wood, 1880s 150.00
Soapine, Kendall Mfg. Co..............30.00

Blotter, Sugar Creek Creamery, blue and yellow, white ground, 3-1/4" x 6", $12.

Sugar Cane Cigars, 1893,
   5 black boys in tree 200.00
V.J. Dotterer Waxed Butter,
   1 pint, 1925.............................6.00
Ward Baking Co., wood 100.00
White Swan, oatmeal, 4 oz 30.00

Brochure

American Range 7.50
Arm & Hammer, Cleansing Help for the
   Housewife, 1922......................3.00
Bon Ami, The Chick That
   Never Grew Up......................12.00
Brown & Williamson Tobacco, How to
   Care for Pipe, 1930 ....7.00
Burma Shave, jingles, 1942 ....7.50
Chase & Sanborn, Famous Dates in
   History, 1929 ....5.00
Electrol Automatic Oil
   Heating, 1937 ....4.00
Enterprising Mfg. Co.,
   kitchen utensils, 1898..............32.00
Georgia Marble,
   4 pgs, 1941.............................3.00
Grandpa's Wonder Soap................5.00
Hire's Merry Rhymes...................15.00
Imperial Furniture, early 1920s 7.50
International Harvester, 1910........20.00
Larkin Soap, 1885 ....18.00
Magic Yeast, 3" x 5" 7.00
Moore Paint, fortune teller, 1941.....6.00
Oldsmobile, 8 pgs, 1948 ....10.00
Parks Air College, St. Louis,
   64 pgs.................................15.00
Peter Puppet, Howdy,
   c1950, 6 pgs...........................6.00
Philco Radio, foldout, 1936 ....7.50
RCA Radio, Power Tube
   Fittings, 1951 ....5.50
Seymour-Smity & Son,
   Pruning, 1935 ....6.00
Steuben Glass, 1972, photos..........3.00
Studebaker, 1934.......................50.00
Waverly Country Club 195.00
Westinghouse, Today's Ben
   Franklin, 1943..........................3.00
Youngstown Kitchens,
   multicolored, 1956 ....5.00

Mirror

ABC Bread, acetate over textured gold
   paper, inscribed in red
   and blue, Kansas City's
   Favorite Bread, c1930 ....40.00
American Line, ship, multicolored .75.00
Angelus Marshmallows, cherub 48.00
Beautifier of Homes, Reading, PA,
   red, white, blue and gold,
   patriotic theme.........................40.00
Beehive Overalls,
   woman in overalls...................75.00

Booklet, *Wrigley Mother Goose*, 1915, 4" x 5-7/8", $20.

Bell's Coffee, green bell trademark,
   mocha and java specialties, JH
   Bell & Co., Chicago 60.00
Buckwheat Flour, For Best Cakes,
   c1900, 1-7/8" l 25.00
Clothiers & Hatters, tinted pastel tones,
   men's clothing items,
   2-3/4" l, oval 50.00
Coast Fir Lumber Co.,
   Portland, OR 35.00
Globe A1 Flour............................20.00
Haines Shoe Wizard 30.00
I Wear Kleinert's, photo of woman, multi-
   colored, celluloid 30.00
Lady Laurel Stoves, woman and bread,
   wall type, oval........................175.00
Mascot Tobacco...........................35.00

Miscellaneous, spinner, Davis Hat Factory, Philadelphia, hand, flesh-colored ground, blue letters, 2-3/4", $15.

Morton's Salt, Morton's Salt/When It Rains— It Pours, blue and white, c1930, 1-3/4" 50.00

Ohio Blue Tip Matches, multicolored product and factory illus.........125.00

Opening of Maud Boltz Department Store, Pottsville, PA, c1920, aluminum cap 20.00

Parisian Novelty Co., Chicago, 3-1/2" 40.00

Rock Island Stove Co....................35.00

Schaeffer Piano, yellow.................50.00

Scranton Stove Works, Scranton, PA, b&w illus of ornate cast-iron Dockash cooking range 50.00

Shawmut Rubbers, multicolored product and birthstones 35.00

Shoe Worker's Union, c1910.........38.00

Traveler's Insurance, train, multicolored, oval..................125.00

Weingarten 5¢ Cigars....................35.00

Whirlpool Washer..........................25.00

Miscellaneous

Account Book, Pierce's Medicines, 48 pgs, 1923............5.00

Almanac
 Doan's Pills, Birthday Directory, 32 pgs, 1906, loose covers 8.00
 L&M Associated Press, 384 pgs, 1975 ....5.00
 Peruna Drug Co., Lucky Day Almanac, 32 pgs, 1907 ....7.50

Banner, Holsum Bread, illus by Howard Brown, 58" w 125.00

Bill Clip, Peacocks Condoms 30.00

Billhook
 Ceresota Flour 48.00
 Red Goose Shoes, 1949............5.00

Book
 Chase & Sanborn Coffee & Tea Importers, 1889 ....26.00
 Exxon Travel Club ValueBook,40 pgs of coupons, 1981 ....4.00
 Jell-O Presents the Willow Activity Book, 1988.....................3.00
 John Byrne Co. Insurance, quiz book, 74 pgs, 1905 ....10.00
 Kellogg's
  Funny Jungleland Moving Picture Book, 1932............................16.00
  When the Great Were Small, 54 pgs, 1935 ....12.50
  Pan-American Coffee Bureau, 18 pgs, 1949, activity type ...10.00
  Story of Knott's Berry Farm, 34 pgs, c1940 ....15.00
  Tip-Top Bread Horoscope Book, 24 pgs, 1940s 10.00

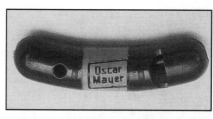

Whistle, Oscar Mayer, wiener, plastic, $10.

Utica Trust Co., Fruit Jar Markers, sticker type, 1930s.................5.00

Bottle, Old Tub Whiskey, moonshining black boy, 1938 ....120.00

Bowl, Birds Eye, General Foods ...26.00

Bridge Sore Book, Betoline Richfield, Sherwood Service 4.00

Bridge Tally, Otto Milk, diecut 15.00

Broom Holder, JF Owens, Fairbury, NE, 1930s 12.00

Bucket
 Chicken in the Rough, 3-1/2" h 35.00
 Clark's Sweet Chocolates, metal 42.50

Cabinet, Diamond Dye, rough condition 80.00

CB Radio Card, Burnt Hills Fur Shop, photo, 1960s..............................3.00

Change Keeper, wall mount, Diamond Fertilizer, 3 slots, butterscotch Bakelite 45.00

Children's Books, Loeser Dept. Store, miniatures, price for set of four 22.00

Clip, 7/8" brass spring clip Fine Shoes, Petersburg, VA, dealer's name and address, shows detailed black shoe 40.00

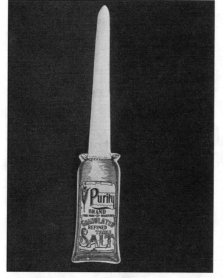

Letter Opener, celluloid, Purity Brand Salt, International Salt Co., of NY, Whitehead and Hoag, Newark, NJ, 7-3/4", $20.

Lehman's Clothes, dealer's name in red, black letters, white ground, c1904 ....25.00

Coat Hanger, San Francisco Cleaning & Drying Works, wood 10.00

Cook Book, Gold Medal Flour, 1917 ....25.00

Coloring Book, Ben Franklin Stores, Bicentennial, 1974, 16 pgs........8.00

Crayons, Red Goose Shoes, MIB.15.00

Crock, Hoosier Creamed Cottage Cheese, lip and front stamped, pottery 60.00

Cup and Saucer, Bowey's Chocolate 30.00

Diecuts, Fisk Tires, circus, 1929 ...40.00

Display
 Pearson's Snuff, easel display with containers.............50.00
 Sunshine Biscuits, four rusty racks 75.00
 Whitman's Candy, man, 1920s 365.00

Doll, Eskimo Pie Man....................12.00

Door Push, porcelain
 Junge's Bread 40.00
 Salada Tea, yellow and red 70.00

Drink Mixer, Ovaltine, woman holding can of Ovaltine, ceramic, English, c1935......................150.00

Emery Board, Wead's Bread 20.00

First-Aid Folder, Guardian Trust, 22 pgs, 1942 ....8.50

Funnel, Rippey's Extract of Vanilla, tin................................25.00

Game, Welch's, India Game, uncut 3-pkg carton 50.00

Hot Pad, 6" x 8-1/2", Levi's Jeans, front is orange cloth with Levi's XX label, blue denim back, Now Designs, San Francisco 85.00

Key Chain, Princess telephone.......3.00

Map
 Dial, Soap Map of the Moon, 18" x 24", 1958 ....5.00
 Kroeger Foods, Ohio State Fair, schedule and map, 32 pgs, 1980 ....4.00
 McCormick Spices, Map of the World, 23" x 24", c1960 ....30.00

Match Holder
 Buckwalter Stoves, celluloid 15.00
 Zephyr Flour, wall type 50.00

Memo Book
 Penney's Work Clothes, 1951-52 calendars 5.00
 Reese's Corn Remover, 1936-37 calendars 4.50

Mending Kit, Real Silk Hosiery.......................4.00

Menu
 Blue Moon Tea Room,

card type 4.00
Coon Chicken Inn....................100.00
Hot Shoppes,
place-mat type, 1952................4.50
Lost Stirrup Riding
Club Banquet, 1948 ....4.00
Model, Eatmore Village Bakery,
orig envelope 20.00
Mug, Carter Carburetor,
stoneware 20.00
Palm Puzzle, Holsum Bread, tin rim,
plastic cov, full-color paper image,
red, yellow and blue wrapped bread
loaf, yellow ground, blue lettering,
3 balls, c1960...........................30.00
Paper Soap, General Soap Co.,
Lather Leaves, c1940 ....4.00
Peanut Butter Pail
Bayle, 3-1/4" h, multicolored,
slant sided, Boy Scout and Girl
Scout at campground, minor
scratches and dents 275.00
Climax, 3-1/2" h, straight sided, red
ground, blue and white letters, emb
"Sococn" on lid, Newark, NJ,
minor scratches........................80.00
Monarch, 3-3/4" h, 1 lb, straight
sided, lion's face on front, policeman
overlooking Chinese laborers
on reverse, emb lid.................165.00
Monopole 150.00
Ontario, 3-3/4" h, straight sided, blue
letters, cream ground, oceanfront
scene, emb lid, minor dents,
slight lid wear 125.00
Squirrel Brand, 3-1/2" h, slant sided,
litho tin, gold ground, red letters,
squirrel profile, slight dent
and minor lid wear.................175.00
Sultana, 4" h, slant sided, litho tin,
orange ground, girl and boy,
pry-off lid, wear.........................80.00
Pencil Clip
Diamond Crystal Salt 9.00
Morton's Salt 5.00

Paperweight, glass, J.S. Hoskins Lumber Co., Baltimore, MD, blue lettering, white ground $25.

Sign, Kraft, I Get the Milk Bank Boost from Kraylets, figural pig, metal, 11-1/2" h, 18-1/2" l, $90.

Ritz Crackers, litho tin, yellow, blue
and red, company logo, c1930...7.50
White House Coffee, celluloid, de-
tailed illus of White House, dark blue
ground, white lettering, c1920..12.00
Pencil Sharpener, Baker's Cocoa Girl,
figural..30.00
Pennant, McFadden's Electric
Brand Coffee, 37" l 145.00
Pin, Red Raven Splits, thin diecut brass,
figural, red metallic-wash raven,
brass luster inscription band....50.00
Pin Holder, Prudential,
mother and baby 12.00
Plate
General Telephone,
china, 9-3/4" d 25.00
Quick Service Laundry,
tin, c1900 ....30.00
Playing Cards, Bluebird Bus System,
1947 ....25.00
Pocket Knife, Star Brand Shoes,
orig case...................................60.00
Poster, Bull Durham, 19-1/2" x 13-1/2",
includes cow figure.................375.00
Recipe Cards, Towle's Log Cabin Syrup,
set of 24 cards.........................35.00
Ruler
Clark Bars, wood.......................7.50

Pinback Button, McLaughlin Brothers, Horse Importers, Kansas City, MO, Columbus, OH, St. Paul, MN, white ground, black, 1-1/4", $10.

G Felsenthal & Sons, Chicago, celluloid, inch and metric rules, listing of
other celluloid novelties, 1" x 6"25.00
Glory Soap Chips, folding, celluloid,
blue and orange trademark for Swift
& Co., logo for Keystone Laundry
Soap, monthly calendars for first 6
months of 1919, 5-1/2" l..........20.00
Hartford, painted tin,
ornate, 1906.............................15.00
Northwestern Terra Cotta Co., Chicago, celluloid, b&w illus of factory, dark
orange logo, Chicago skyline on reverse, c1900, 1-3/4" x 12"........45.00
Western Union, diecut, silver and
blue logo, telegraph and cable rates,
1905 patent, 7-1/4" l 25.00
Salesman's Sample, cotton handkerchiefs, book form, Freeport Manufacturing Co., Brooklyn, 1920s ...190.00
Seed Package, Chlorodent, flower
seeds, 1950s, orig contents 3.00
Soap, Sinclair Heating Oils, figural, oil
truck, perfumed, 1940 ....10.00
Spoon
Hot Dan's French Mustard, figural
handle, Beetleware 7.50
Soronitz Chocolates.................25.00
Stickpin, State Blend High Grade Coffee,
3/4" brass oval, "Orr Mizell & Co" on
back, early 1900 ....15.00
Tape Measure
Fab...35.00
Lewis Lye & Piano Co..............25.00
Teapot
McCormick's, china, maroon ...65.00
Salada Tea 20.00
Thermometer
Crescent Products,
Terre Haute, IN 80.00
King Cole Tea & Coffee, tin, 1940s,
Canadian, French 50.00
Tile, McCormick Spices,
ceramic, 1955...........................12.00
Tip Tray
Red Cross Stoves and Ranges,
Greencastle, PA adv 20.00
Simon Pure, red, white and black,
hanger on back, 3-1/2" d..........15.00
Tobacco Tag, diecut litho tin
Butler's Old Peach, full-color
image of peach, 2 green
leaves on stem.........................20.00
Full Bloom, red and black, yellow
ground, tobacco plant illus, L Ash,
Statesville, NC 18.00
Golden Slipper, yellow image, red
ground, Whitaker-Harvey Co., Win-
ston-Salem...............................15.00
Red, White and Blue Tobacco, red,
white and blue, FM Bohannon .15.00
Rich and Ripe, yellow inscription, red
ground, Taylor Brothers,

Winston-Salem...........................15.00
WN Tinsley, extra fine..............10.00
Toothpicks, Diamond Match Co.,
unopened box of 1,500, birch
trees illus 35.00
Top
Betsy Ross Bread, litho tin, yellow,
red spinner, c1935 ....35.00
Poll-Parrot Shoes, litho tin, red, yel-
low and black, c1930................30.00
Tastykake, celluloid, red, white
and blue, Parisian Novelty Co.,
maker 35.00
Toy, Jewel T Delivery Van, front axle,
windows and doors missing.....27.50
Trivet, The Cleveland Foundry Co.,
cast iron 38.00
Tumbler
Coon Chicken Inn.....................15.00
Small Grain Distilling, Louisville,
etched, paneled sides, 4" h......55.00
Wallet, Rock Island Plow, cloth 20.00
Whetstone, Lavacide, For Fumigation,
Innis, Speiden & Co., NY,
celluloid....................................30.00
Window Decal, unused
Butter Nut Bread 9.00
Koesters Bread, brightly colored
litho, twin baby girls..................17.50
Wrapper, Huskey Ice Cream Bar,
snow dog 15.00
Yardstick
Kaiser Automobile 15.00
Smith's Furniture Store 10.00

Paperweight

American Glass & Construction Co.,
Rochester, NY, glass reinforced with
wire, rect, 3" x 4-1/2" 20.00
Bell System, bell shape,
glass, blue 95.00
Columbia Coal, brown and white
celluloid, mirror insert, coal
chunks filing railroad car, tracks
visible at extreme corners, yellow
accent tint, 1920s 70.00
Columbia National Bank, glass 20.00
Crane Co., Chicago, 75th Anniversary,
brass, round, 2-3/8" d 35.00

**Sign, Little Mommie Brand Sox, met-
al, white, red, and black lettering, 14"
x 17", $20.**

Doughnut Corporation of America, Opti-
mist Creed, silver mirror ground, rim
inscription for 25th anniversary Silver
Jubilee of doughnut promotion,
Oct. 1953 ....75.00
Elgin Watches 35.00
Hanover Safe Deposit Co. 25.00
Haskell Implement & Seed Co., sepia
celluloid, mirror insert, store building,
title above front door in yellow letters,
blue sky tint, 1920s..................65.00
Holt Motors, iron, figural 25.00
John Bird Co., black, white and red celluloid, mirror insert, b&w trademark
of 3 crows on fence rail, 1920s 35.00
Kellogg's Vitrolite, girl
holding box, c1905 ....475.00
MacBeth-Evans Glass Co.,
Pittsburgh, PA, rect 20.00
Matthew's Decorative Glass Co.,
New York, NY, domed hemisphere,
decorative trademark logo,
early 1900s 60.00
Mo-Lyb-Den-Um Car, ivory, b&w celluloid disk revolves to show weekly
and monthly dates for 1916 to 1926,
diecut openings in disk, individual car
adv with lettering "Pride of the Automotive World," mirror insert lightly
smoked around edges.............50.00
National Surety Co., bronze, spread
eagle on world globe 55.00
New York Telephone Bell System,
bell shape, glass, blue.............95.00
Purdue Foundry,
cast iron, Kewpie 40.00
Quick Service Express, mirror
insert, 4" x 2-1/2" 35.00
Renown Stoves, cast iron,
alligator, painted brown 25.00
Smith Bros. Cough Drops,
cast iron, emb 40.00
Wurtz Auto Garage, Degenhart.....40.00

Pinback Button

Aunt Jemima Pancake
Flour, c1896 ....90.00

**Tin, Teaberry Chewing Gum, D.L. Clark
Co., Pittsburgh, PA, yellow ground, red
letters outlined in blue, 6-7/8" x 5-1/4" x
2-3/8", $35.**

Banner Lumber & Building Co., blue
banner, yellow lettering, yellow
ground, red inscription, 1920s .20.00
Benzine-Ated Soap, multicolored,
detailed image of wrapped soap
bar, wrapper slogan "Will Not
Hurt the Hands," pale blue shaded
to white background, red letters,
early 1900s..............................60.00
Boston Leading Clothiers, Continental
Clothing House, black on yellow,
image of Revolutionary War
soldier, c1896 ....20.00
Ceresota Flour, trademark figure,
early 1900s, 1-3/4" 25.00
Derby Refining Co., Petroleum
Products, star, red, white
and blue, c1930.......................12.00
Dogongood Hosiery, black, white, red
and tan image of setter dog striding
across black stocking, red rim lettering "The Best Children's Hose That
Money Can Buy," early 1900s .35.00
Dustbane, Sanitary Sweeping Compound, black image, yellow ground,
early 1900s...............................30.00
Dutch Java & Santos Coffee,
multicolored, Dutch children,
early 1900s...............................75.00
Haslam Land Co., Canada Lands,
St. Paul, MN 15.00
Hostess Cake, red, white
and blue, 1940s.......................20.00
Karma Biscuits, multicolored, portrait of
young lady holding bright red, white
and yellow box, Ontario Biscuit Co.,
1900, 1-1/4" 55.00
Koester's Bread, red, white,
blue and gold, 1930s...............25.00
Liberty Four, multicolored, copyright
1903, 1-1/4"..............................40.00
Los Angeles, May 1906, comical man
riding dressed-up camel, ring of
roses on bottom mkd "La Fiesta de
Las Flores" 55.00
Maypo, b&w illus, slogan, 1960s...25.00
Palmolive Health Club, red, white, blue
and flesh tones, youngster drying
himself with towel, 1930s 40.00
Peerless Biscuit Co., b&w logo, bright
red ground, light blue tulips, c1912,
1-3/4" 25.00
Prisco Lanterns, 2" 25.00
Rainbow Packing, multicolored
scenic vista, white clouds, blue sky,
rainbow arc, white lettering, blue
serial number, Peerless Rubber Mfg.
Co., early 1900s 20.00
Red Cross Macaroni, red, white
and blue, Long Mac cartoon,
1930s, 1-1/4"............................35.00
Sherwin Williams Paint, S.W.P., S.W.V.
Brighten/Up Club....................35.00
S.O.S. Magic Bunny, black, white and

yellow litho, c1940 ....25.00
Studebaker, star 25.00
Van Camp's Pork & Beans............10.00
Wiemann's Java Tea, multicolored
    container, white ground,
    1911-20, 7/8" 25.00

Sign

Admiration Coffee Co.,
    cardboard, 23" x 33" 35.00
Bartholomay Carbonated Ice Cream,
    diecut Santa, early 1930s 200.00
Berkley Knit, stand-up type, man with tie,
    1925, 8" x 10" 35.00
Borax Dry Soap,
    red and white, metal 45.00
Brown's Mule Tobacco, mule reaching in
    window pulling cover off 195.00
Butternut Bread, tin 30.00
Carhartt Overalls, emb tin,
    c1920, 10" x 24" 35.00
Cloverdale, emb tin, 1930s,
    12" x 10" 30.00
Cork Distilleries Co., hp, framed..175.00
Crest Flour, cardboard,
    c1920, 5" x 8" 10.00
Diamond Dyes, diamond shape,
    cloth swatches under glass,
    10" x 14" 175.00
Dixon's Stove Polish,
    paper, 6" x 8" 65.00
Eckhart & Becker, celluloid............45.00
Fisk Tire, porcelain, 36" x 28"........45.00
Goody Headache Powder, cardboard,
    pretty girl, 1940s 15.00
Hanna Prints, emb tin,
    c1940, 3" x 12" 12.00
Hommel Wine, Sandusky, OH, stone
    litho, factory, grapes and bottles,
    1896, 19" x 26" 165.00
Iceman's Snow Scraper, painted brass,
    1928, 6" x 16" 35.00
Ismert-Hincke Flour Co., emb tin.100.00
KC Baking Powder, 2-sided tin, 1930s,
    12" x 28" 60.00
Kibber's Candies, brass, 9" x 8" 50.00
Lutz Funeral Home, cast-brass corner-
    stone type, 10" x 15"................65.00
Master-Visa-Discover, 2-sided metal,
    16" x 31" 40.00
Mikado Pencils, paper,
    1930, 20" sq 85.00
Mother Dexter's Bread,
    blackboard type 40.00
Munsingware, cardboard, woman illus,
    24" x 36" 95.00
New York Daily News, litho paper,
    newsboy, delivery wagon and
    NY skyline, 1890.....................35.00
Norwich Suntan Oil, litho tin,
    c1930, 10" x 16" 85.00
Oh Boy Gum, emb tin, c1930,
    17" x 10" 90.00

Overland Motors, porcelain, whippet,
    24" x 36" 195.00
Parker's Cold Cream, stand-up,
    Victorian woman, 1905,
    7-1/2" x 11-1/2".....................100.00
Pfeffer Bros. Pianos, Seneca, IL,
    emb tin, 8" x 24" 35.00
Portland Cement, Middle Branch, OH,
    round porcelain........................95.00
Purity Flour, porcelain, white, yellow and
    dark blue, 36" x 24" 95.00
Red Jacket Tobacco, cardboard, base-
    ball scene, 22" x 28" 150.00
Rhinelander Butter,
    emb tin, 2 pkgs illus 85.00
Salada Tea, figural tea box, porcelain,
    Canadian, French, 1940s 125.00
Schuler's Chips, emb tin 60.00
Sherman-Williams—Covers the
    Earth, die stamped, raised,
    porcelain, red, green, yellow, white
    and black, 36" h....................395.00
Steven's Pharmacy, emb tin, black on
    white, 11-1/2" x 24" 25.00
Stickney Poor Spice Co.,
    orig wood frame....................265.00
Sunbeam Bread, emb tin 65.00
Time Plug Tobacco,
    cardboard, 12" sq 25.00
White Rose Bread, baker boy
    carrying loaves 315.00

Tin

Coffee
    Acme Coffee, 6" h, cylindrical,
    flowers, red and white polka
    dot band on front, coffeepot
    and cup on reverse 135.00
    Bliss Coffee, key wind, orig top 25.00
    Blue Ridge Coffee, key wind, some
    minor scratches........................35.00
    Boscul Coffee, key wind,
    orig top 25.00
    Butternut Coffee,
    key wing, orig top 30.00
    Golden Sheaf Coffee, 6-1/2" h, cylin-
    drical canister, knob finial, litho tin,
    farmer plowing wheat field, some
    wear and scratches...............175.00
    Hatchet Brand Coffee 35.00
    Martinson Coffee,
    key wind, orig top 25.00
    Old Judge Coffee, key wind, multicol-
    ored graphics 35.00
    Sanka Coffee, key-wind,
    unopened 30.00
    Sunshine Coffee, 6" h, cylindrical,
    litho tin, blue ground, child with um-
    brella and slicker on front and back,
    minor scratches.....................200.00
    Universal Coffee, 7" h, cylindrical,

Tray, beer, Steigmaier Brewing Co., Wilkes-Barre, PA, 12" d, $25.

    litho tin, Uncle Sam, flag, rising
    sun on front, quality medallion
    on back 145.00
    Van Dyk, screw top,
    some paint loss 45.00
    WGY Coffee, 6-1/4" h, cylindrical,
    litho tin, coffeepot, cup and saucer
    on front and back, slight wear and
    damage 90.00
Condoms, Gold Circle
    Condoms, full 10.00
Cream, Hygienic Cutigiene
    Toilet Cream............................17.00
Food
    Campfire Marshmallows 25.00
    Golden Bear Cookies,
    black and orange 25.00
    Jolly Time Popcorn 40.00
    Kohrs Crown Lard, red............20.00
    Morris Fine Confectionery........20.00
    Ovaltine, 1921.......................25.00
    Planters Blanched Almonds,
    unopened................................70.00
    Sunshine Fruit Cake,
    Egyptian woman dec 12.00
    Towle Molasses 35.00
    Y&S Licorice Lozenges,
    glass front 75.00
Household
    Bee Brand Insect Powder 15.00
    Bell Tower Phonograph
    Needles, red 12.00
    Old Griffin Sterling
    Paste Shoe Polish 15.00
    Wizard Carpet Clean, 1901 .....45.00
Oyster
    Huitres, clear plastic top,
    bottom missing........................15.00
    M&V Brand, Salt Water Oysters,
    Crisfield, MD, chartreuse and
    dark green...............................15.00
    Singleton Oysters, 9 oz, oyster and
    oyster boat graphics 20.00
Salve
    Boyol Salve for Drawing 5.00
    Cloverine..................................5.00
    Dr Hobson's Arnica Salve,

orig contents...............................7.50
Pickmore Gall Salve................12.00

Spice

Allspice, red and gold................5.00
Cinnamon,
red and gold 12.00
Rich's Crystallized Canton Ginger,
yellow and black...................15.00
Sauer's Selected Spices, cream, red
and dark blue 7.50
Vantine's Canton
Crystallized Ginger..................7.50

Talc

Dream Girl Talc.......................35.00
Gardenia Talcum......................7.50
Johnson & Johnson
Baby Powder.........................20.00
Lander's Lilacs and Roses.......20.00
Maxim's Talcum Powder
Nelson's Baby Powder, Penslar Co.,
Detroit, blue ground, clouds,
frolicking babies 15.00

Tobacco

Bagley's Tobacco,
Silver Old Colony Mix.............225.00
Bayuk Perfecto.........................22.00
Dill's Best, round,
humidor type 20.00
Eight Brothers 50.00
Gloriana....................................25.00
Golden Sceptor 30.00
Hickey Nicholson......................15.00
Just Suits, 4" x 6"....................35.00
Kentucky Club, pocket 12.00
Myrtle Tobacco, Isley, 1890 .....55.00
Penn's Quality Tobacco 40.00
Prince Albert Tobacco, round...15.00
Princess Royal 150.00
Tuxedo, pocket.........................15.00
Yale...15.00

Trade Card

A&P Tea Co. 17.50
Acme White Lead & Color Works,
Granite Floor Paint 7.50
Alden's Vinegars, blacks illus........10.00
Bazin & Sargent's Face Powder......4.00
Bell's Cocktail Bitters, puzzle type, black
on white 7.50
Berry Brothers Hard Oil Finish, emb,
Uncle Sam, 7" x 4"..................50.00
Brown's Dentifrice 15.00
Burdock Blood Bitters,
3 kittens in basket....................4.00
Cashmere Bouquet Toilet Soap,
Colgate & Co. 5.00
Clark's ONT Spool Cotton, black young-
ster with fishing pole seated on
spool of thread.........................10.00
Coderre's Infants' Syrup, Elliott.......7.50
Colton's Nervine
Strengthening Bitters 9.00

Conqueror Clothes Wringer,
fold-up 15.00
Crown Prince Coffee,
baby in picnic hamper 7.50
Davis Sewing Machine,
lady sitting on bench.................5.00
Emerson Piano Co., black on green4.00
Espey's Fragrant Cream 5.00
Eureka Health Corset, adv on back 4.00
Extract of Roots Cures
Dyspepsia...............................17.50
Garland Stoves & Ranges..............9.00
Globe Cocktail Bitters,
black on white...........................6.00
Gypsy Queen Cigarettes, 1896.......4.00
Hands Remedies, Rochester, children
and chickens, dated 1886 ....7.50
Howard's Lotus Flower Cologne 5.00
Hoyt's German Cologne, 1892......15.00
JP Coats Thread, mechanical,
spools to be added as wheels,
c1920, mint.............................15.00
Judsons's Mountain Herb Pills........7.50
Koch Bros., Maud Humphrey illus, Allen-
town, PA, clothier 10.00
Lothrops & Pinkham Pharmacists ...4.00
Luca's Co., Paints and Varnishes,
factory scenes both sides..........7.50
Mack's Milk Chocolate 4.00
Merrick Thread Co., woman
and child at beach 3.00
Moline Wagon Co., Moline,
IL, couple in wagon 4.00
National Wax Thread Sewing Machine,
diecut, horse, black on yellow ...5.00
Northern Pacific Railroad Baked Potato,
dated 1909 ....10.00
Pear's Soap, baby........................12.00
Pillsbury's Best, blacks illus 10.00
Pratt Food Co.................................4.00
Quaker Bitters, girl in barrel 5.00
Quakermaid Stockings, Young, Knight,
Field & Co., Philadelphia, c19304.00
Red Rose Tea, Rockwell, 1958.......7.50

**Tray, beer, Steigmaier Brewing Co.,
Wilkes-Barre, PA, 12" d, $25.**

Remington Sewing Machine 5.00
Soapine, girl and doll 7.50
Solon Palmer,
diecut, flowers in bowl 5.00
Sterners, Quakertown, PA, sailing ship,
black on green...........................4.00
Swan Soap, Victorian
woman, 5" x 7-1/2" 15.00
Todtman Clothier, diecut,
black child in wash tub 15.00
Wheat Bitters, man and women in boat,
lake scene, black on white 5.00
Wilcox & White Organ Co., sailboat 7.00
Willimantic Thread, cupid tying thread
around world 4.00

Tray

American Brewery & Malting Co., Great
Falls, MT, roses, 12" d 45.00
Beamer Shoes, Victorian
woman, c1900 ....65.00
Buffalo Brewing, Scaramento, Ca,
Hawaiian girl playing
ukulele, c1910 ....295.00
CD Kenny Coffee Co.,
Santa Claus, 9-1/2" d 65.00
Cold Spring Moeschlin, Sunbury,
PA, nickel plated 85.00
Croft Ale, round, red and white,
black ground............................45.00
Diamond Wedding Rye, woman wearing
large hat, c1900 ....215.00
Donaldson's Dept Store 45.00
Fairy Soap, 13" d 125.00
Germania Brewing, stag 145.00
Heck's Capudine Medicine 215.00
I&GN, Wood and Coal Yard, vase
with roses, oval, 17" l 45.00
Kaiser Wilhelm Magic Bitters 215.00
Lomax's Celery Tonic, black, gold let-
ters, oval, 10" x 13" 85.00
Ogdens St. Julien Tobacco Cool &
Fragrant, 13" d 25.00
Resinal Soap For Skin Diseases, girl
with roses 45.00
Schmauss Garden and Cafe,
Milwaukee, 6" 75.00
Simon Pure Ale and Beer,
Buffalo, green, ground.............45.00
Staley's Flour,
horse and girl, 1905 ....45.00
Teaberry Gum, glass, amber 110.00
Wolverine Toy Co., c1920, 4" x 6" 95.00

Whistle

Atwater Kent Radios 15.00
Buster Brown Shoes, litho tin, full-color
image of Buster and Tige, brown
ground, yellow border, yellow
lettering "Tread Straight
Feature," 1930s 65.00
Endicott Johnson Shoes, green litho tin,
biplane shape, red lettering, mkd

"Made in Germany," c1930......25.00
Erna's Portraits, orange and black ..5.00
Golden Royal Milk, yellow
    and black 5.00
Leo R Cox Insurance,
    red and white, 2-1/2" l................5.00
Old Reliable Coffee 8.00
Oscar Mayer Wiener, hot dog shape,
    red, c1950...............................10.00
Poll Parrot Shoes, yellow litho tin, red
    and green trademark, made by Kir-
    chof Co., 1930s 35.00
Red Goose Shoes, yellow litho tin, yel-
    low and red symbol, made by Kirchof
    Co., 1930s 35.00

Advertising Characters

Collecting Hints: Concentrate on one advertising character. Three-dimensional objects are more eagerly sought than two-dimensional ones. Some local dairies, restaurants and other businesses developed advertising characters. This potential collecting area has received little attention.

History: Americans learned to recognize specific products by their advertising characters. In the early 1900s, many immigrants could not read but could identify the colorful characters. Thus, the advertising character helped to sell the product. Some manufacturers developed similar names for inferior-quality products, like Fairee Soap vs. the popular Fairy Soap. Trade laws eventually helped protect companies by allowing advertising characters to be registered as part of a trademark. Trademarks and advertising characters are found on product labels, in magazines, as premiums and on other types of advertising. Popular cartoon characters also were used to advertise products.

Some advertising characters, such as Mr. Peanut and the Campbell Kids, were designed to promote a specific product. The popular Campbell Kids first appeared on streetcar advertising in 1906. The illustrations of Grace G. Drayton were originally aimed at housewives, but the characters were gradually dropped from Campbell's advertis-ing until the television industry expanded the advertising market. In 1951, Campbell redesigned the kids and successfully reissued them. The kids were redesigned again in 1966. Other advertising characters (e.g., Aunt Jemima) also have enjoyed a long life; some, like Kayo and the Yellow Kid, are no longer used in contemporary advertising.

References: Douglas Collins, *America's Favorite Food: The Story of Campbell Soup Company*, Harry N. Abrams, 1994; Warren Dotz, *Advertising Character Collectibles*, Collector Books, 1993; ——, *What a Character*, Chronicle Books, 1996; Mary Jane Lamphier, *Zany Characters of the Ad World*, Collector Books, 1995; Joyce Lindenberger, *Planters Peanut Collectibles*, Schiffer Publishing, 1995; David Longest, *Character Toys and Collectibles*, 1st Series (1984, 1992 value update), 2nd Series (1987, 1990 value update), Collector Books; Joleen Robison and Kay Sellers, *Advertising Dolls*, Collector Books, 1980, 1994 value update.

Collectors' Clubs: Campbell Kids Collectors, 649 Bayview Dr., Akron, OH 44319; Campbell's Soup Collector Club, 414 Country Ln. Ct., Wauconda, IL 60084; Peanut Pals, 804 Hickory Grade Rd., Bridgeville, PA 15017; R.F. Outcault Society, 103 Doubloon Dr., Slidell, LA 70461.

Reproduction Alert.

Additional Listings: Advertising, Black Memorabilia, Cartoon Characters, Fast Food, Planter's Peanuts.

Aunt Jemima
    Badge, Breakfast Club premium, tin, fold-over tab, "Eat a Better Breakfast," 1940s 8.00
    Bell, 1940s 90.00
    Pinback Button,
        7/8" l, portrait, c1900...............40.00
    Place Mat, Aunt
        Jemima's Kitchen.....................20.00
Buster Brown
    Booklet, 5" x 7-1/4", Buster Brown's Latest, Buster Brown Hosiery Mills, Chattanooga, TN, 1909, R.F. Outcault signature on cover art, 3 different stories 95.00
    Calendar Plate, 7" d, 1907 ....50.00
    Cup and Saucer 50.00

Lapel Stud, 1-1/4" d, white metal, silver finish, Buster with hand on Tige's head, c1900 ....45.00
    Pinback Button, "Vote for Buster Brown," red outfit, tugging black stocking held by brown Tige, white ground, c1970......................25.00
    Shoe Box, Buster
        Brown Shoes 15.00
California Raisins, bank 30.00
Campbell Kids
    Book, *Campbell Kids at Home*, wear on bottom corner.....................15.00
    Bowl, baby feeding type, ceramic, Buffalo Pottery...........85.00
    Doll, 7" h, painted soft rubber, squeaker, much orig paint, late 1940s 200.00
    Jigsaw Puzzle, frame-tray type 15.00
    Money Holder, steel, fold-out nail file and knife, Imperial Co..............27.00
    Mug...15.00
    Pinback Button, Campbell's Kid Club, multicolored weight-lifter image, 1930 ....150.00
    Postcard, "Campbell Kids Thrive on Campbell Soups 10¢ a Can"....35.00
    Print, "The Elopement," artist sgd, dated 1906, framed, 13" x 14-1/2" 60.00
    Salt and Pepper Shakers, pr, F&F, figural, orig box 75.00
    Sign, porcelain, soup-can shape, gold medallion "Campbell's Condensed Vegetable Soup," 14" x 22-1/4" 2,420.00
    Soup Bowl, Campbell Girl on inside, alphabet and "Christine" on bottom, c1940 ....30.00
Casa Gallardo, figure, coyote 19.00
Charlie the Tuna
    Clock, 4" d, 6" h, brass, windup, red, orange and blue Charlie on dial, mkd "Lux Time Div of Robertshaw Controls Co," 1969...................60.00
    Doll, 7-1/2" h, vinyl 30.00
    Lamp, 10" h, painted plaster 75.00
Chiquita Banana, doll, uncut cloth, 1944 ....35.00
Coty, Tuxedo Bunny 15.00
Dutch Boy Paint
    Hand Puppet, 11" h, vinyl head, fabric body, orig cellophane bag, 1960s 45.00
    Paint Book, Dutch Boy illus, 1907, unused 25.00
Elsie the Cow
    Badge, 1-3/4" x 2-3/4" oval, Try Our Egg Nog, cream-colored celluloid pinback, Elsie with sprig of green holly, inscription in red letters, c1950 ....50.00
    Color-In Drawings Kit, 7-3/4" x 11"

mailing envelope, cover letter from Elsie, 7" x 7-1/2" sheet with full color illus of Elise preparing Beulah for school, 15 identical 7" x 9" picture coloring sheets to be finished, story continues on reverse about school and Borden's quality, manual with 1941 Borden's copyright, sheets browned but unused, slight damage to envelope 75.00

Cookbook, 1939 World's Fair ... 30.00

Cookie Jar, Elsie in barrel, small inner-rim chip 265.00

Ice Cream Cup, 4" h, tulip shape, multicolored Elsie logo 25.00

Pin, figural, white plastic, brown and black accents, pink tongue, c1940 .... 60.00

Ring, dark gold luster plastic, center clear plastic dome over multicolored Elsie image, 1950 .... 35.00

Salt and Pepper Shakers, pr, Elsie and Elmer, china, 4" h Elmer as chef, 3-1/2" h Elsie with fuchsia hat, simulated feather plume, c1940 ..... 125.00

Watch Charm, white plastic pocket watch, clear plastic dome over raised head image, red tongue, yellow daisy collar, brown printed hour numerals and hands, 1950s 30.00

Eveready Cat, bank 8.00

Gold Dust Twins

Calendar, 1933 .... 25.00

Fan, 7-1/2" d, diecut cardboard, multicolored litho, Twins at 1904 World's Fair, wood handle 175.00

Pinback Button, 7/8" l, Twins in washtub, 1898 .... 75.00

Johnny, Philip Morris

Pinback Button, black, white, red and flesh tone, 1930s 35.00

Place Card, figural 15.00

Sign, emb tin, well worn, 12" x 14" 92.50

Johnny Walker Red, mug 15.00

Joy Detergent, lemon 8.00

Kool Cigarette Penguin

Match Holder, tin, wall, penguin smoking 20.00

Pinback Button, 1" d, Willie between donkey and elephant, 1930s 25.00

Munsingwear Penguin, figure 40.00

Nipper, RCA Victor

Charm, 1-1/2" brass disk, "His Master's Voice" on front, phonograph and Nipper, back inscribed "RCA Victor, Div. of Radio Corp. of America" 25.00

Coffee Mug, plastic 7.50

Pinback Button, 1-1/4" l, diecut

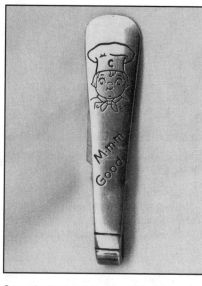

Campbell Kid, bib clip, SP, $15.

celluloid, red, white and blue, dealer's name on back 35.00

Snowdome 40.00

Old Crow, statue, metal on wood .. 50.00

Oscar Mayer

Weinermobile, bank, plastic 30.00

Weinermobile, Hot Wheels car .. 2.00

Pillsbury Dough Boy

Bank 20.00

Cookie Jar 45.00

Figures, standing, Poppin' and Poppie, each 30.00

Salt and Pepper Shakers, pr 20.00

Poll Parrot

Top, litho tin, red, yellow and black, c1930 .... 30.00

Whistle, yellow litho tin, red and green trademark, made by Kirchof, Co., 1930s 35.00

Red Goose Shoes

Bank 145.00

Store Display, 11" h, plaster 45.00

Reddy Kilowatt

Ashtray, glass, red and white image, 1960s 15.00

Figure, 6" h, diecut red plastic, ivory features, glow-in-the-dark type, 1961 .... 45.00

Matchbook Cover, 1-1/2" x 4-1/2", red, black, white and silver, cardboard, Reddy and electric range, Niagara Hudson Power Co., c1930 .... 20.00

Pinback Button, 7/8" d, red image, white ground, c1930 .... 25.00

Shoney's Bear, comic book, No. 5, 1986, cover tear 4.00

Smokey the Bear, blotter, USDOA & PA, orange, 1953, 2-1/2" x 6-1/4" 8.00

Stork Club, statuette 55.00

Nipper, salt and pepper shakers, pr, Lenox China, mkd "RCA Victor 'His' Master's Voice" and "Lenox" around base, black and white, 3" h, $38.

Speedy Alka-Seltzer

Figure, 5-1/2" h, plastic, 1960s 18.00

Sign, 10" w 60.00

Susie Q, pinback button, 1-1/4" d, Norcross Greeting Cards 55.00

Tony the Tiger

Radio 30.00

Spoon, SP, emb "Kellogg's" 8.50

Akro Agate Glass

Collecting Hints: The Akro Agate mark—"Made in USA"—often includes a mold number. Some pieces also have a small crow in the mark. Akro Agate glass is thick; therefore, collectors should buy only mint pieces. The marbleized types of Akro Agate were made in many color combinations. The serious collector should look for unusual combinations.

History: The Akro Agate Co., was formed in 1911, primarily to produce marbles. In 1914, the owners moved from near Akron, Ohio, to Clarksburg, W.V., where they opened a large factory. The firm continued to profitably produce marbles until after the Depression. In 1930, the competition in the marble business became too intense and Akro Agate decided to diversify.

Two of its most successful products were the floralware lines and children's dishes, first made in 1935. The children's dishes were very popular until after World War II, when metal dishes captured the market. Akro Agate also made special containers for cosmetics firms, such the Jean Vivaudou Co., and Pick Wick bath salts (packaged in the Mexicali cigarette jar). Operations continued successfully until 1948. The factory, a victim of imports and the increased use of metal and plastic, was sold to Clarksburg Glass Co., in 1951.

References: Gene Florence, *Collectors Encyclopedia of Akro Agate Glassware*, Revised Edition, Collector Books, 1975, 1992 value update; Roger and Claudia Hardy, *Complete Line of the Akro Agate*, published by author, 1992; Ellen T. Schroy, *Warman's Glass*, 2nd Edition, Wallace-Homestead, 1995.

Collectors' Clubs: Akro Agate Art Association, P.O. Box, 758, Salem, NH 03079; Akro Agate Collector's Club, 10 Bailey St., Clarksburg, WV 26301.

Reproduction Alert: Pieces currently reproduced are not marked "Made In USA" and are missing the mold number and crow.

Ashtray
    2-7/8" sq, blue and red marble ...8.00
    4" x 2-7/8" sq, red marble...........8.00
    4-1/2" w, hexagon,
    blue and white 35.00
Basket, 2 handles,
    orange and white 35.00
Children's Play Dishes (small unless otherwise noted)
    Cereal Bowl
        Concentric Ring,blue, large..25.00
        Interior Panel, green,
        transparent, large...............15.00
        Stacked Disk Interior Panel, blue,
        transparent, large.................45.00
    Creamer
        Chiquita, cobalt blue,
        baked-on...............................9.00
        Interior Panel, blue,
        opaque, large.......................42.50
        Octagonal
            Blue, large...........................15.00
            Sky blue, large,
            open handle 22.50
        Stacked Disk,
        green, opaque.......................6.00
        Stippled Band, green,
        transparent, 1-1/4" h 25.00
    Creamer and Sugar
        Chiquita, cobalt blue 20.00
        Interior Panel, turquoise.......50.00
        J. Pressman, cobalt blue,

Child's dish, sugar, Concentric Ring, yellow, $7.25.

        baked-on..............................12.00
        Stacked Disk Interior Panel,
        turquoise 50.00
        Stacked Disk, medium blue .12.00
    Cup
        Chiquita
            Cobalt Blue 7.00
            Green, opaque 6.50
        Concentric Rib,
        green, opaque.......................4.50
        Concentric Ring
            Green, opaque 7.00
            Periwinkle........................30.00
            Rose, large......................35.00
        Interior Panel
            Blue, medium 6.00
            Pumpkin 35.00
        J. Pressman, lavender 30.00
        Octagonal, green, large 10.00
        Stacked Disk,
        green, opaque.......................5.00
        Stacked Disk Interior Panel
        Blue, transparent,large 40.00
        Pumpkin...............................35.00
        Stippled Band, green, large .20.00
    Cup and Saucer
        Chiquita, cobalt blue,
        transparent...........................18.00
        Interior Panel, green
        and white marble 35.00
        Stacked Disk Interior Panel, green
        and white marble 35.00
        Stippled Band
            Cobalt Blue, large 35.00
            Topaz 28.00
    Demitasse Cup, J. Pressman
        Green 9.75
        Pink.................................30.00
    Demitasse Saucer, J.
    Pressman, green.......................8.00
    Pitcher
        Interior Panel, green,
        transparent...........................30.00
        Stacked Disk,
        green, opaque.....................10.00
        Stacked Disk and Panel,blue,
        transparent...........................50.00
        Stippled Band, green,
        transparent...........................15.00

Plate
    Concentric Rib, opaque
        Green 2.50
        Yellow 3.00
    Concentric Ring
        Dark blue 5.00
        Light blue 5.00
    J. Pressman, 3-3/4" d, green,
    baked-on..............................4.00
    Octagonal
        Blue, large..........................10.00
        Green, opaque, large...........4.00
        Lime..................................5.00
    Stacked Disk Interior Panel, blue,
    transparent, large 18.00
    Stippled Band
        Green, transparent, 4-1/4" d 6.00
        Topaz, large......................9.00
Saucer
    Concentric Rib, yellow 2.50
    Concentric Ring
        Green, opaque 3.00
        Ivory 3.00
        Pink 4.00
        White.................................2.00
        Yellow 3.00
    Interior Panel, green 3.00
    Octagonal
        Pink, dark..........................6.00
        White, large.......................10.00
    Stacked Disk Interior Panel, blue,
    transparent, large 15.00
    Stippled Band, green,
    transparent, 2-3/4" d 3.00
Set
    Interior Panel, yellow,
    opaque, white teapot lid,
    large, 21-pc set 350.00
    Octagonal, green cups and plates,
    white saucers and lids, yellow
    creamer and sugar, blue teapot,
    closed handles, large,
    17-pc set 100.00
Sugar
    Chiquita, cobalt blue,
    transparent 9.00
    Interior Panel, lemonade
    and oxblood 40.00
    Stacked Disk, white 6.00
    Stacked Disk Interior Panel
        Blue, medium 15.00
        Cobalt Blue 30.00
Teapot, cov
    Interior Panel, blue marble ..45.00
    Octagonal, medium blue, green
    lid, large, open handle 20.00
    Raised Daisy, blue...............60.00
    Stacked Disk,
    pumpkin, beige lid...............25.00
    Stacked Disk Interior Panel
        Blue, transparent, large 85.00
        Green with white 45.00
    Stippled Band, amber 10.00

Teapot, open
   Chiquita, green, opaque.........8.00
   Concentric Rib,
   light blue, opaque..................8.00
   Interior Panel
     Green, luster 10.00
     Green, transparent, large ...15.00
     Oxblood marble..................28.00
     Pink, opaque 9.75
   J. Pressman, cobalt blue,
   baked-on..............................8.75
   Octagonal, turquoise, large..15.00
   Stacked Disk, medium blue ...7.00
Tumbler, 2" h
   Stacked Disk, white...............6.00
   Stacked Disk Interior Panel
     Blue, transparent...............20.00
     Green, transparent............10.00
Water Set, Stippled Band, green,
   pitcher and 6 tumblers............105.00
Demitasse Cup
   Blue and white marble..............12.00
   Green and white marble...........12.00
Demitasse Cup and Saucer
   Green, dark, marble 20.00
   Orange and white marble.........20.00
Flowerpot
   2-1/4" h, ribbed,
   green and white...........................9.00
   2-1/2" h, Stack Disk
     Green and white...................11.00
     Orange and white.................15.00
   4" h, Stacked Disk,
   green and white.......................22.00
   5-1/2" h, scalloped top, blue.....30.00
Lamp
   12" h, brown and blue marble,
   4" d black octagonal top,
   Globe Spec Co.........................75.00
   13" h, green and
   brown marble, round
   5-1/4" d ribbed base, Houzex...95.00
Marbles, Chinese Checkers,
   orig box of 60............................125.00
Mexicalli Hat, blue and white.........20.00
Mexicalli Jar, orange and white.....40.00
Planter, rect, wire cart holder,
   orange and white.....................35.00
Powder Jar, Colonial Lady, white..60.00
Vase
   2-3/8" h, red, white,
   green streaks 5.00
   3-1/4" h, cornucopia,
   multicolored..............................15.00
   3-3/4" h, green, marble,
   smooth top 18.00
   4-1/4" h, lily, marble 15.00
   6-1/4" h, tab handle, marbled...35.00

Aluminum, Hand Wrought

Collecting Hints: Some manufacturers' marks are synonymous with

Cigarette Holder, blue and white marbleized, 8-sided, 2-3/4" h, 2-7/16" d, $10.

quality, e.g., "Continental Hand Wrought Silverlook." However, some quality pieces are not marked and should not be overlooked. Check carefully for pitting, deep scratches and missing glassware.

History: During the late 1920s, aluminum was used to make many decorative household accessories. Although manufactured by a variety of methods, the hammered aluminum with repoussé patterns appears to have been the most popular.

At one time, many companies were competing for the aluminum giftware market. To be more competitive, numerous silver manufacturers added aluminum articles to their product lines during the Depression. Some of these aluminum objects were produced strictly as promotional items; others were offered as more affordable options to similar silver objects. Many well-known and highly esteemed metalsmiths contributed their skills to the production of hammered aluminum. With the advent of mass-production and the accompanying wider distribution of aluminum giftware, the demand began to decline, leaving only a few producers who have continued to turn out quality work using the age-old and time-tested methods of metal crafting.

References: Marilyn E. Dragowick (ed.), *Metalwares Price Guide*, Antique Trader Books, 1996; Everett Grist, *Collectible Aluminum*, Collec-

tor Books, 1994; Frances Johnson, *Aluminum Giftware*, Schiffer Publishing, 1996; Dannie A. Woodard, *Hammered Aluminum Hand Wrought Collectibles, Book Two*, Aluminum Collectors' Books, 1993; ——, *Revised 1990 Price List for Hammered Aluminum*, Aluminum Collectors' Books, 1990; Dannie Woodard and Billie Wood, *Hammered Aluminum*, published by authors, 1983.

Periodical: *Aluminist*, P.O. Box 1346, Weatherford, TX 76086.

Collectors' Club: Aluminum Collectors, P.O. Box 1346, Weatherford, TX 76086; Wendell August Collectors Guild, P.O. Box 107, Grove City, PA 16127.

Ashtray
   4" x 6", Wendell August Forge,
   adv, Quaker State Motor Oil, dogwood dec 9.50
   6" d, Hand Forged/Everlast Metal,
   berry dec, straight sides.............7.50
Basket
   7-1/4" d, Continental
   Silver Co., Chrysanthemum
   pattern, #1088...........................20.00
   12" d, Hand Forged, Harvest pattern,
   flared sides, scalloped handle . 18.00
   13" d, Milcraft, Intaglio Wheat pattern, flat, double-strand handle 20.00
Bowl
   6-1/2" d, Palmer-Smith,
   stalks of wheat 42.00
   8" d, Wendell August Forge, Pine
   Cone pattern 45.00
   10" d, Rodney Kent, tulip dec, flower-ribbon handles, #450 ....45.00
   11-3/4" d, Continental Silverlook,
   Chrysanthemum pattern, applied
   leaves, #715 ....28.00
   14" d, West Bend, grapes dec,
   hammered ground 28.00
Butter Dish, Buenilum, round,
   domed cov, double-loop
   finish, glass insert....................35.00
Candleholder
   2-1/2" sq base, Everlast Forged Aluminum, arrow shape, corners form
   feet, handle, #1020 ....12.00
   6" h, Buenilum, beaded-edge base,
   aluminum stem with wood ball. 10.00
Candy Dish, cov, 4-1/2" d,
   dogwood dec, glass base..........7.50
Casserole Holder, cov
   7-1/2" d, Everlast
   Forged Metal, rose dec,
   beaded knob 25.00

10" d, ftd ring, wheat and vegetables dec, fan-shaped handles and knob, glass baking dish.......................18.00

Coaster, Wendell August Forge

3-1/4" d, Edison Institute Museum Entrance.......................5.00

4-1/4" d, State of Texas, various symbols 6.00

Cocktail Shaker, Buenilum, straight sides, grooved Art Deco top, clear plastic knob lid 20.00

Compote, 5" h, Continental Hand Wrought Silverlook, wild rose dec, #1083................15.00

Creamer and Sugar, Continental Hand Wrought Silverlook, Chrysanthemum pattern, grooved handles, applied leaves, matching tray...............25.00

Crumb Tray, Faberware, hammered shiny finish.............10.00

Desk Set, Everlast Forge, Bali Bamboo pattern, price for 3-pc set.........40.00

Goblet, 8-1/2" h, D. Miller, aluminum cup supported by brass Art Moderne base, mkd "Don (Dan) Miller" in script, price for set of four 195.00

Hot Pad, 11" x 8" oval and matching 9" d round, Wendell August Forge, Pine Cone pattern, cork bottom, price for pr 25.00

Ice Bucket, cov, 11-1/2" h, handles, plastic knob 35.00

Ladle, 14-1/2" l, Argental Cellini Craft................25.00

Lazy Susan, 16" d, Rodney Kent, cov glass dish, ribbon and flower trim 32.00

Napkin Holder, fruit dec, trefoil shape, ftd 18.00

Pitcher, Buenilum, ovoid, slender neck, twisted handle..........................35.00

Salad Set, Buenilum Hand Wrought, 13" d bowl, tulip dec, matching serving utensils........................20.00

Silent Butler, 6" x 8", Henry Miller, oval, floral bouquet..........................10.00

Tray

6" x 8", roses 15.00

7-1/2" x 14-1/2" d, Farber & Schlevin, zinnia dec, spiral handle...........25.00

10" x 16", Arthur Armour, gold anodized, chessman dec 28.00

14" x 20", Rodney Kent, tulip dec, handles, #425...........................30.00

23" x 13-1/2" d, Wendell August Forge, Pine Cone pattern, dark finish................................95.00

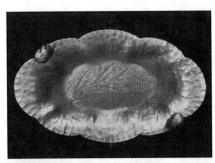

Bread tray, chrysanthemum, Continental, #572, 13-1/4" x 7-3/4", $20.

Water Set, World Hand Forged, pitcher, eight 20-oz tumblers, applied flowers, sq knob handle 75.00

American Bisque

Collecting Hint: When searching for American Bisque products, look for a mark consisting of three stacked baby blocks with the letters "A," "B" and "C." This common mark is readily found.

History: The American Bisque Co., was founded in Williamstown, W.V., in 1919. Although the pottery's original product was china-head dolls, it quickly expanded its inventory to include serving dishes, cookie jars, ashtrays and other decorative ceramic pieces. B.E. Allen, founder of the Sterling China Co., invested heavily in the company and eventually purchased the remaining stock. In 1982, the plant was sold and operated briefly under the name American China Co. The plant closed in 1983.

Sequoia Ware and Berkeley are two trademarks used by American Bisque, the former used on items sold in gift shops and the latter found on products sold through chain stores. Cookie jars produced by this company are marked "ABC" inside blocks.

References: Susan and Al Bagdade, *Warman's American Pottery and Porcelain*, Wallace-Homestead, 1994; Mary Jane Giacomini, *American Bisque*, Schiffer Publishing 1994; Lois Lehner, *Lehner's Encyclopedia of U.S. Marks on Pottery, Porcelain & Clay*, Collector Books, 1988.

Periodical: *Pottery Collectors Express*, P.O. Box 221, Mayview, MO 64071.

Ashtray, Fred Flintstone 45.00
Bank, Little Audrey 550.00
Cache Pot, 4-1/2" h, mushroom and stump 14.00
Cookie Jar, cov
 Candy Cane Babies...............195.00
 Carousel 50.00
 Cowboy Boots.......................235.00
 Donald Duck, pastel, flake 325.00
 Girl, with lamb, eyes closed 85.00
 Ice Cream Freezer.................460.00
 Mr. Rabbit 185.00
 Mrs. Rabbit 300.00
 Poodle, gold trim 275.00
 Spool of Thread 275.00
 Yogi Bear 500.00
Dinnerware,
 Ballerina Mist, painted
 Cereal Bowl 5.00
 Plate, dinner............................6.00
Lamp, Billy the Kid 195.00
Planter
 Duck, wearing flower hat 25.00
 Kitten, waiting 20.00
 Parrot, burgundy and green.....18.00
 Rooster, 5" h 20.00
Salt and Pepper Shakers, pr, churn 65.00

Animation Art

Collecting Hints: A very specific vocabulary is used when discussing animation cels. The differences between a Courvoisier, Disneyland, master, key production, printed, production and studio background can mean thousands of dollars in value. Sotheby's and Christie's East, the two major auction houses selling animation art, do not agree on terminology. Carefully read the glossary section of any catalog.

A second of film requires over 20 animation cels. The approximate number of cels used to make that cartoon can be determined by multiplying the length of a cartoon in minutes times 60 times 24. The question that no one seems to be asking as prices reach the ten- and hundred-thousand dollar level is "What happened to all the other animation cels?" Vast quantities of cels are in storage.

There is no doubt that Walt Disney animation cels are king. Nostalgia, legend and hype drive pricing more than historical importance or workmanship. The real bargains in the field lie outside the Disney material. Although animation art has a clearly established track record, it also is an area that has been subject to manipulation, representational abuse and shifting nostalgia trends. It is not the place for the casual collector. Avoid limited-edition serigraphs—color prints made by silk screening. Although they may appear to be animation cels, they are not.

History: According to film historians, the first animated cartoon was Winsor McCay's 1909 "Gertie the Dinosaur." Early animated films were largely the work of comic-strip artists. The invention of the celluloid process (a "cel" is an animation drawing on celluloid) is attributed to Earl Hurd. Although the technique reached perfection under animation giants such as Walt Disney and Max Fleischer, individuals such as Ub Iwerks, Walter Lantz and Paul Terry—along with studios such as Columbia, Charles Mints and Screen Gems, MGM, Paramount/Famous Studios, UPA and Warner Brothers—did pioneering work.

Leonard Maltin's *Of Mice and Magic: A History of American Animated Cartoons* (A Plume Book/New American Library, Revised and Updated Edition, 1987) is an excellent source for historic information.

References: Jeff Lotman, *Animation Art: The Early Years*, Schiffer Publishing, 1995; ——, *Animation Art: The Later Years*, Schiffer Publishing, 1996; Jerry Weist, *Original Comic Art*, Avon Books, 1992.

Periodicals: *Animation Film Art*, P.O. Box 25547, Los Angeles, CA 90025; *Animation Magazine*, 4676 Admiralty Way, Ste. 210, Marina Del Ray, CA 90292; *Animato!*, P.O. Box 1240, Cambridge, MA 02238; *In Toon!*, P.O. Box 217, Gracie Station, New York, NY, 10028; *Storyboard/The Art of Laughter*, 80 Main St., Nashua, NH 03060.

Collectors' Club: Greater Washington Animation Collectors Club, 12423 Hedges Run Dr. #184, Lake Ridge, VA 22192.

Museums: Baltimore Museum of Art, Baltimore, MD; International Museum of Cartoon Art, Boca Raton, FL; Museum of Cartoon Art, Rye Brook, NY; Museum of Modern Art, New York, NY; Walt Disney Archives, Burbank, CA.

Bugs Bunny, Mutiny on the Bunny, 1992, showing Yosemite Sam as captain trying to get lazy Bugs to mop up, sgd by Friz Freleng, limited ed of 178/750, unframed, 14-1/2" x 17" 365.00

Cinderella and Her Fairy Godmother, 1950 ....36,800.00

Donald Duck, orig layout drawing, swinging ring on his finger, wearing straw hat 600.00

Fantasia, Walt Disney, Mickey Mouse as Sorcerer's Apprentice, 1940 ....15,000.00

Fat Albert and the Cosby Kids, Filmation Studios, 1970s, tempera background sheet, framed 900.00

Fred and Wilma Flintstone, Barney and Betty Rubble, orig production cel, multi-cel setup mounted on full celluloid, mounted, framed, glazed, 16" x 19" 400.00

Jimminy Cricket, from Pinocchio, orig copy background, smiling, 13" x 18", unframed 1,650.00

Jungle Book, Walt Disney, 1967, Baloo, 6-1/2" x 4" gouache on celluloid, cel trimmed, unframed...........900.00

Lady and The Tramp, Walt Disney, Belle Notte scene, 1955 ....57,500.00

Peter Pan and Tinkerbelle, Walt Disney, 1952 ....21,850.00

Pocahontas, Walt Disney
John Smith helping Pocahontas out of her canoe, Flit and Meeko looking on, 4-cel setup 13,225.00

Pocahontas glaring at surprised John Smith, nose to nose, 12-1/2" x 17" 12,000.00

Pocahontas, Meeko and Flit looking out into the distance atop branches of Grandmother Willow, 12-1/2" x 17" 17,250.00

Pocahontas paddling canoe, Meeko seated in front of her, Flit beating wings alongside to keep pace, 12-1/2" x 17"............20,700.00

Pocahontas paddling canoe toward bend in river, huge trees, 20" x 25".............................10,900.00

Pocahontas paddling canoe with Flit, mountain background, colorful rainbow, 12-1/2" x 17".............18,400.00

Pocahontas peering through misty sky in search of John Smith, 3-cel setup 13,225.00

Pocahontas, running with Meeko, dwarfed by trunks of trees, 12-1/2" x 17" 14,375.00

Pocahontas superimposed on the cliff as John Smith was to die, 12-1/2" x 17" 18,400.00

Sleeping Beauty, from 1939 release, princess in front of castle ...3,950.00

Snow White and the Seven Dwarfs, Walt Disney, 1937
Grumpy 17,250.00
Snow White and 3 dwarfs, inside cottage....................85,000.00

Sylvester, orig production cel, gouache on full celluloid, accompanied by orig layout drawing, c1960, mounted, framed, glazed, 17" x 32" 400.00

Tom and Jerry, from Tom and Jerry The Movie, orig production multi-cel setup, reproduction background, gouache on full celluloid, unframed, sgd by Bill Hanna and Joe Barbera, 11" x 14"................................250.00

Winnie the Pooh with Rabbit and Piglet, from 1960s orig film...............300.00

Yellow Submarine, John Lennon and Ringo Starr, Heinz Edelman, King Features, 1968, 7-1/2" x 9" gouache on celluloid 2,500.00

Autographs

Collecting Hints: The condition and content of letters and documents significantly influences value. Signatures should be crisp, clear and located so that they do not detract from the rest of the item. When possible, obtain a notarized statement of authenticity, especially for pieces worth more than $100.

Drawing, Woody Woodpecker, crayon and ink, framed and matted, 10-5/8" x 12-1/2", $95.

Forgeries abound; copying machines compound the problem. Furthermore, many signatures of political figures (especially presidents), movie stars and sports heroes were signed by machine (autopen), rubber-stamped or signed by a secretary rather than by the individuals themselves. Photographically reproduced signatures resemble originals. Use a good magnifying glass or microscope to check all signatures.

Presentation material, something marked "To...," has less value than a non-presentation item. The presentation personalizes the piece and often restricts interest to someone with the same name.

There are autograph mills throughout the country run by people who write to noteworthy individuals requesting their signatures on large groups of material. They in turn sell this material on the autograph market. Buy an autograph of a living person only after the most careful consideration and examination.

History: Autograph collecting is an old established tradition. Early letters were few, hence, treasured in private archives. Municipalities, churches and other institutions maintained extensive archives to document past actions.

Autograph collecting became fashionable during the 19th century. However, early collectors focused on the signatures alone, clipping off the signed portion of a letter or document. Eventually collectors realized that the entire document was valuable.

The popularity of movie stars and sports, rock 'n' roll and television personalities brought about changes in the way autographs were collected. Fans pursued these individuals with autograph books, programs and photographs. Collectors requested that autographs be signed on everything imaginable. Realizing the value of their signatures and the speculation that occurs, modern stars and heroes are often unwilling to sign material under certain circumstances.

References: Mark Allen Baker, *All Sport Autograph Guide*, Krause Publications, 1994; ——, *Collector's Guide to Celebrity Autographs*, Krause Publications, 1996; George S. Lowry, *Autographs*, Avon Books, 1994; Susan and Steve Raab, *Movie Star Autographs of the Golden Era*, published by authors, 1994; Kenneth W. Rendell, *History Comes to Life*, University of Oklahoma Press, 1996; George Sanders, Helen Sanders and Ralph Roberts, *1994 Sanders Price Guide to Autographs, No. 3*, Alexander Books, 1994; ——, *Sanders Price Guide to Sports Autographs*, Scott Publishing, 1993.

Periodicals: *All-Star Celebrity Address Book*, P.O. Box 1566, Apple Valley, CA 92307; *Autograph Collector*, 510-A S. Corona Mall, Corona, CA 91720; *Autograph Dealer's Price Guide*, P.O. Box 63, Umpqua, CA 97486; *Autograph Quarterly & Buyers Guide*, P.O. Box 55328, Stockton, CA 95205; *Autograph Review*, 305 Carlton Rd., Syracuse, NY 13207; *Autograph Times*, 2302 N. 44th St., #225, Phoenix, AZ 85008; *Autographs & Memorabilia*, P.O. Box 24, Coffeyville, KS 67337; *Celebrity Access Directory*, 20 Sunnyside Ave., Ste. A241, Mill Valley, CA 94921; *Collector*, P.O. Box 225, Hunter, NY 12442; *John L. Raybin's Baseball Autograph News*, 527 Third Ave. #294-A, New York, NY, 10016.

Collectors' Clubs: Manuscript Society, 350 N. Niagara St., Burbank, CA 91505; Universal Autograph Collectors Club, P.O. Box 6181, Washington, DC 20044.

Libraries: New York Public Library, New York, NY; Pairpoint Morgan Library, New York, NY.

Abbreviations: The following are used to describe autograph material and size.

Materials

ADS	Autograph Document Signed
ALS	Autograph Letter Signed
AQS	Autograph Quotation Signed
CS	Card Signed
DS	Document Signed
FDC	First Day Cover
LS	Letter Signed
PS	Photograph Signed
TLS	Typed Letter Signed

Joe DiMaggio baseball, $125.

Sizes (approximate)

Folio	12" x 16"
4to	8" x 10"
8vo	7" x 7"
12mo	3" x 5"

Autograph Letters Signed (ALS)

Fred Astaire, handwritten 3-pg letter, c1958, accompanied by 8" x 10" b&w still from 1951 MGM movie "Royal Wedding" 165.00

Marlene Dietrich, 10 autographed letters to Stanley Hall, 1966 to 1978 165.00

John Drew, actor, Hotel Ponchartrain stationery, early 1900s, 4 single pgs, 6" x 9" 150.00

Adelina Patti, Italian opera singer, signed as Baroness Ledenbrun, 1 pg, 12mo, letterhead of Craig-Y-Nos Castle, Breconshire, South Wales, England, orig envelope addressed to American woman, March 30, 1904, thank you note 285.00

Gene Stratton Porter, author and poet, 1919, 8" x 10" 200.00

Cards Signed (CS)

Humphrey Bogart, framed with Warner Bros. promotional photo 820.00

Barbara Bush, First Lady, Blair House stationery, 3" x 2" 60.00

Katherine Cornell, American author, calling card, bold signature 25.00

Florence Kling Harding, First Lady, black-ink signature, engraving of White House, 6" x 4" card 60.00

John Philip Sousa, card mounted to album pg 125.00

George Takei, Star Trek, 3" x 2" white card, dark blue Star Trek imprinted at top, blue Enterprise image 65.00

Document Signed (DS)

Julie Andrews, 2 sgd checks 82.00

Thomas A. Edison, minutes from Board of Directors meeting, 12" x 16", 2 pgs, c1920 .... 295.00

Andrew Jackson, President, land grant

to Palmer Eliot,
IL, Jan. 3, 1832......................60.00
David Niven, 2 sgd checks.........164.00
Ronald Reagan, partially printed bank
check, sgd and filled in by Reagan,
1 pg, 5" x 7", Los Angeles,
Oct. 8, 1948........................550.00
Rod Sterling, writer and producer, bank
check, June, 1968.................295.00

Equipment

Hank Aaron, baseball bat............120.00
Keith Allen, hockey puck..............18.00
Roberto Alomar, baseball.............35.00
Richie Ashburn,
baseball cap.........................40.00
Paul Azinger, gold cap.................30.00
Ernie Banks, baseball cap............60.00
Yogi Berra, baseball cap..............50.00
Wade Boggs,
baseball bat.........................100.00
Earl Campbell, football................125.00
Jim Carey, hockey puck................32.00
Roger Clemens,
baseball bat..........................90.00
Jim Colbert, golf club.....................75.00
Fred Couples, golf cap..................45.00
Andre Dawson, baseball................25.00
Joe DiMaggio,
baseball cap.........................300.00
Steve Elkington,
golf cap, U.S. Open..................35.00
Glenn Hall, hockey puck................18.00
Reggie Jackson,
baseball cap..........................90.00
Jim Kelly, football.......................125.00
Joe Namath,
official Jets helmet..................400.00
Arnold Palmer, golf club..............250.00
Ken Stabler, football...................100.00
Allen Stanley, hockey puck...........25.00
Payne Stewart, golf cap...............45.00
Lawrence Taylor,
official Giants helmet.............425.00
Fuzzy Zoeller, golf club.................90.00

First Day Covers (FDC)

Fred Astaire and Ginger Rogers,
honoring the 50th Anniversary of
Talking Pictures, canceled
Hollywood, 1977.....................195.00
Otto Griebling, hp watercolor cachet of
clown, sgd on blank.................45.00
Prince Rainer of Monaco, honoring
Great American Presidents, Wash-
ington, Lincoln, FDR and Eisenhow-
er, canceled 1966, blue-ink
signature..............................50.00
Chuck Yeager, and Scott Crossfield,
honoring Glenn Curtiss, canceled
NY, 1980..............................50.00

Letters Signed (LS)

John Sherman, Secretary of State,
lined personal stationery, 1
886, OH, 5" x 8"......................50.00
D.H. Vinton, Chief QM in
Mexican War, light blue
stationery, aged, 8" x 10".........45.00

Photograph Signed (PS)

Hank Aaron, b&w glossy, 8" x 10".25.00
Troy Aikman, b&w glossy,
11" x 14"..............................48.00
Muhammad Ali, b&w glossy,
8" x 10"................................45.00
Michael Andretti, b&w glossy,
8" x 10"................................25.00
Brigette Bardot, b&w glossy,
8" x 10"................................30.00
Berra, Ford and Rizzuto,
sepia, 11" x 14".....................90.00
Christie Brinkley, b&w glossy,
8" x 10"................................50.00
Nicholas Cage, b&w glossy,
8" x 10"................................55.00
Mary Chapin Carpenter,
b&w glossy, 8" x 10"..............35.00
Cher, b&w glossy, 8" x 10"........50.00
Eric Clapton, b&w glossy,
8" x 10"................................55.00
Harry Jr. Conick, b&w glossy,
8" x 10"................................35.00
Courtney Cox, b&w glossy,
8" x 10"................................50.00
Cindy Crawford, b&w glossy,
8" x 10"................................55.00
Robert DeNiro, b&w glossy,
8" x 10"................................55.00
Neil Diamond, b&w glossy,
8" x 10"................................95.00
Joe DiMaggio, b&w glossy,
11" x 14"..............................125.00
George Foreman, b&w glossy,
8" x 10"................................40.00
Vince Gill, b&w glossy,
8" x 10"................................35.00
Ken, Jr. Griffey, b&w glossy,
11" x 14"..............................60.00
Whitney Houston, b&w glossy,
8" x 10"................................60.00
Helen Hunt, b&w glossy,
8" x 10"................................50.00
Elizabeth Hurley, b&w glossy,
8" x 10"................................35.00
Jimmy Johnson, b&w glossy,
8" x 10"................................22.00
Winona Judd, b&w glossy,
8" x 10"................................40.00
Jack Kemp, b&w glossy,
16" x 20"..............................60.00
Lisa Kudrow, b&w glossy,
8" x 10"................................45.00
K.D. Lang, b&w glossy,
8" x 10"................................40.00
Joe Montana, b&w glossy,

8" x 10"................................50.00
Herman Moore, b&w glossy,
8" x 10"................................25.00
Willie Mosconi, b&w glossy,
8" x 10"................................50.00
Kate Moss, b&w glossy,
8" x 10"................................35.00
Jack Nicholson, b&w glossy,
8" x 10"................................60.00
Greg Norman, b&w glossy,
8" x 10"................................30.00
Al Pacino, b&w glossy, 8" x 10"....55.00
Arnold Palmer, b&w glossy,
8" x 10"................................40.00
Dolly Parton, b&w glossy,
8" x 10"................................35.00
Drew Pearson, b&w glossy,
8" x 10"................................20.00
Ginger Rogers, b&w glossy,
8" x 10"................................70.00
Spielberg, Scheider, Dreyfus, Jaws,
b&w glossy, 8" x 10".............140.00
Rod Stewart, b&w glossy,
8" x 10"................................60.00
Y.A. Tittle, b&w glossy,
8" x 10"................................15.00
Travolta, Thurman, Jackson, Willis, Pulp
Fiction, b&w glossy, 8" x 10".150.00
Shania Twain, b&w glossy,
8" x 10"................................60.00
Robin Williams, b&w glossy,
8" x 10"................................35.00
Bruce Willis, b&w glossy,
8" x 10"................................55.00
Tiger Woods, b&w glossy,
8" x 10"................................45.00
Billy Zane, b&w glossy, 8" x 10"....30.00

Typed Letter Signed (TLS)

Calvin Coolidge, President,
MA Governor stationery,
1918, 8" x 10".......................200.00
Edsel B. Ford, fund-raising letter,
8" x 10"................................85.00
EG Grace, President of Bethlehem
Steel, business stationery, to son,
1932, 8" x 10".......................85.00
Katherine Hepburn, 1-pg 8" x 10",
Oct. 18, 1973, thank you note,
orig envelope.........................185.00
Sandra Day O'Connor,
Supreme Court Justice,
Supreme Court stationery, orig
envelope, 8" x 10", 2 pcs.........65.00

Aviation Collectibles

Collecting Hints: This field developed in the 1980s and is now firmly
established. The majority of collectors
focus on personalities, especially

Charles Lindbergh and Amelia Earhart. New collectors are urged to look at the products of airlines, especially those items related to the pre-jet era.

History: Most of the income for the first airlines in the United States came from government mail-carrying subsidies. The first non-Post Office Department flight to carry mail was in 1926 between Detroit and Chicago. By 1930, there were 38 domestic and five international airlines operating in the United States. A typical passenger load was 10. After World War II, four-engine planes with a capacity of 100 or more passengers were introduced.

The jet age was launched in the 1950s. In 1955, Capitol Airlines used British-made turboprop airliners for domestic service. In 1958, National Airlines began domestic jet passenger service. The giant Boeing 747 went into operation in 1970 as part of the Pan American fleet. The Civil Aeronautics Board, which regulates the airline industry, ended control of routes in 1982 and fares in 1983. Major American airlines include American, Delta, Northwest, Pan Am, TWA, United and USAir. There are many regional lines as well. As a result of deregulation, new airlines are forming; some lasting longer than others.

References: *Air Transport Label Catalog*, Aeronautica & Air Label Collectors Club of Aerophilatelic Federation of America, n.d.; Stan Baumwald, *Junior Crew Member Wings*, published by author, n.d.; Lynn Johnson and Michael O'Leary, *En Route*, Chronicle Books, 1993; Richard R. Wallin, *Commercial Aviation Collectibles*, Wallace-Homestead, 1990.

Periodical: *Airliners*, P.O. Box 52-1238, Miami, FL 33152.

Collectors' Clubs: Aeronautica & Air Label Collectors Club, P.O. Box 1239, Elgin, IL 60121; C.A.L./N-X-211 Collectors Society, 226 Tioga Ave., Bensenville, IL 60106; Gay Airline Club, P.O. Box 69A04, West Hollywood, CA 90069; World Airline Historical Society, 3381 Apple Tree Ln., Erlanger, KY 41018.

Commercial

Baggage Sticker, Pan American,

blue and white, wing over glove emblem, "The System of The Flying Clippers" 5.00

Cup and Saucer

American Airlines, mkd "Mayer China" 25.00

TWA, white, gold emblem, mkd "Rosenthal, Germany".............30.00

Employee Badge

American Airlines, red, white and blue, center logo, 1930s...........45.00

Continental Aviation, metal frame inscribed with company name, tiny winged propeller symbols, insert paper for temporary worker, c1930 ....50.00

Eastern Airlines, 1-1/2" x 2-1/4", silvered brass frame, tinted photo portrait, name on paper insert, worn silver luster, 1930s..........................60.00

Fan, Air India, litho, blue and orange, cream ground, route map, four stylized figures, c1960 ....10.00

Lapel Stud, 1/2" d, TWA, brass, red enamel...................20.00

Plate, Conair Corp., mkd "Vernon Kilns".......................25.00

Pencil Chip, celluloid, wings and propeller illus, TWU AFLCIO Transport Workers 25.00

Pinback Button, celluloid, You've Got First Class Legs! So Fly Western 8.00

Postcard, Flying Hostesses of Eastern Air, c1950 ....7.50

Poster, Air France Nordafrika, 25" x 40", airliner swooping over North African setting, c1946............265.00

Puzzle, American Airlines, 707 jet in flight, frame tray, Milton Bradley, 1960 ....17.50

Schedule, Air France, 4" x 9" paper folder, opens to 9" x 20" sheet, air route of Europe, 3 major routes, int b&w photo of Golden Clipper, c1930......................................25.00

Tableware, United Airlines, fork 7.50

Toy

American Airlines Flagship, orig propellers, Fisher-Price 195.00

Capital Airlines Viscount, airplane, 14" w wingspan, Linemar, c1950 ....95.00

General

Book

Air Piloting, A Manual of Flight Instruction, Ronald Press, NY, 1938, 8vo, 284 pgs 30.00

The American Heritage History of Flight, American Heritage, 1962 ....16.00

Book of Modern Warplanes, Harold H Booth, author and illus, 1942, 9-1/2" x 12", hard cover, 28 pgs, orig dj 35.00

The Modern Airliner, Peter W Brooks, Putnam, London, 1961, 1st ed. 14.00

Safety in Flight, Assen Jordanoff, Funk & Wagnalls Co., NY, 1941 ....25.00

The Story of the Airship (Non-Rigid), H Allen, 1942, 6-1/4" x 9-1/4", 74 pgs 30.00

War Birds, Diary of an Unknown Aviator, illus by C Knight, 1926, 277 pgs 7.00

Cigarette Lighter, 6", chrome-plated metal, desk type, propeller opens lighter compartment in wing, c1937 ....95.00

Coloring Book, Airplanes to Color, 10" x 14", 24 pgs, Saalfield, 1930 ....60.00

Guide Book, *American Airlines Picture Guide Book,* Whitman, 1940, 3-1/2" x 6", full-color illus and text 20.00

Lapel Pin, Curtiss-Wright, miniature wings, centered blue enamel name, c1940 ....20.00

Magazine

Aero Digest, June 1935, 9" x 12", 88 pgs, b&w photos, articles 10.00

Airships Transatlantic Transportation Magazine, 1936, U.S. Naval Air Station, Lakehurst, NJ, includes *Hindenburg* plans, 9" x 12", 36 pgs.........................28.00

Battle Planes, 1941, Dell Publications, 40 pgs, full-color cover art by Charles Rosner, illus of war aircraft 30.00

Popular Aviation, March 1936, 8-1/2"

Sheet Music, *Wait Till You Get Them Up in the Air Boys*, words by Lew Brown, music by Albena Von Tilzer, published by Broadway Music Corp., 8-7/8" x 11-7/8", $10.

x 11-1/2", 70 pgs, full-color cover art by Herman R Bollin 18.00

Palm Puzzle, silvered rim holding plastic cover, full-color paper playing surface, primitive "Voisin" box aircraft in flight, inscription "1908 80 Kahem/Frankreich," German, c1970......................................35.00

Patch, 7-1/2" x 9", yellow, red and blue, Boeing, Wichita Division, c1940 ....20.00

Pinback Button
7/8" d, Megow Contest, red, white and blue member button 12.00
13/16" d, Planes and Pilots series, China Clipper, black and gray litho 15.00
1-1/4" d, Chicago Endurance Flight, red, white and blue litho, August 1929 event, illus aircraft and slogan "We Will," top rim inscribed "Junior Sponsor"...................................30.00

Planter, 7" h, hot-air balloon shape, ceramic.....................................35.00

Plate, 10-1/2" d, Martin Aviation, Vernon Kilns, brown illus of 5 aircraft, titles, c1940 ....55.00

Pulp Magazine, *Dare Devil Aces*, 7" x 9-1/2", May, 1943, 98 pgs...........20.00

Sign, White Flyer Armour Laundry Soap Makes Dirt Fly, white Bleriot plane, 1912, tin.................................275.00

Tie Clip, Curtiss-Wright, winged symbol, inscribed "Buffalo Plant No. 2 Dedication Aug. 14, 1941" 40.00

Watch Fob, 1-1/4" x 1-1/2", silvered white metal, single-wing passenger plane, c1920 ....20.00

Personalities

Book
Alone, account of Richard Byrd in Antarctica, 1934, autographed 125.00
Lindbergh, His Story in Pictures, Frances Trevelyan Miller, Putnam's, 1929, 1st ed, dj........................17.00
That's My Story, Douglas Corrigan, published by E P Dutton & Co., 1938, 5-1/2" x 8-1/4", hard cover, 221 pgs, 56 sepia photos......................20.00
"We" The Famous Flier's Own Story of His Life and His Transatlantic Flight, Charles A Lindbergh, GPP/Knickerbocker Press, 1927, photos, 318 pgs, 1st ed............45.00

Christmas Light Bulb, 3" h, Charles Lindbergh wearing aviation uniform 65.00

Film, Lindbergh's Paris Flight, Pathex Motion Pictures........................50.00

Game, Howard Hughes Game, 11" x 17" x 3", Family Games, Inc., thick brown plastic box designed as attaché

case, orig cardboard label and shrink-wrap, copyright 1972 ..100.00

Money Clip, Spirit of St. Louis, silvered brass, spring clip, finely detailed illus of Lindbergh aircraft, Anson Co..............................125.00

Pinback Button
7/8" d, Welcome Lindbergh, blue and white.........................75.00
1-1/4" d
Atlantic, Newfoundland to Wales, Amelia Earhart and passengers Lou Gordon and William Stultz, 1928.....................325.00
Bond Bread, Spirit of St. Louis, dark red, black and white, c1930.................40.00
Captain Lindbergh, b&w photo..........................25.00
General Balbo portrait, sepia, leader of Italian air fleet visitation to Chicago World's Fair, 1933............................50.00
Welcome Wiley Post, black and white, aviator with patch over blinded eye, 1930s.............150.00
1-3/8" d, red, white and blue litho, photo of Lindbergh, eagle, Spirit of St. Louis, Statue of Liberty and Eiffel Tower, American flags 120.00
2" d, Orville Wright, black, white and buff litho, "Orville Wright-American/First Man to Fly," 1930s 20.00

Photograph, 31" x 41", Wright Bros. first flight, 1903, framed.................165.00

Plate, 8-1/2" sq, Lindbergh commemorative, yellow ground, multicolored transfer center, mkd "Limoges China, Sterling, Golden Glow" 35.00

Pocket Mirror, 2-1/4" x 3-1/2", celluloid, Lindbergh and plane in flight, maroon and white.................125.00

Post Card, 3-3/4" x 5-1/2", air mail, b&w, issued to welcome Lindbergh, Milwaukee, August 1927, back text endorses air mail 30.00

Sheet Music, 9-1/4" x 12-1/4", *Lindy, Lindy*, Wolfe Gilbert and Abel Baer, copyright 1927, black, white and orange cov...............................25.00

Tape Measure, 1-3/4" d, black and white celluloid, Wright Bros., 1910 Trenton St. Fair 95.00

Watch and Fob, 2" diecut silvered pocket watch, 1-1/2" x 2" diecut silvered metal fob, commemorating Richard Byrd's 1929 flight...................300.00

Avon

Collecting Hints: Avon collectibles encompass a wide range of objects,

including California Perfume Co., bottles, decanters, soaps, children's items, jewelry, plates and catalogs. Another phase of collecting focuses on Avon Representatives' and Managers' awards.

Avon products are well marked with one of four main marks. There is a huge quantity of collectibles from this company; collectors should limit their interests. Although they may be harder to find, do include some foreign Avon collectibles. New items take longer to increase in value than older items. Do not change the object in any way; this destroys the value.

History: David H. McConnell founded the California Perfume Co., in 1886. He hired saleswomen, a radical concept for that time. They used a door-to-door technique to sell their first product, "Little Dot," a set of five perfumes; thus was born the "Avon Lady." By 1979, Avon Ladies numbered more than a million. In 1929, California Perfume became the Avon Co. The tiny perfume company grew into a giant corporation. Avon bottles began attracting collector interest in the 1960s.

References: Bud Hastin, *Bud Hastin's Avon Products & California Perfume Co. Collector's Encyclopedia*, 13th Edition, published by author (P.O. Box 9868, Kansas City, MO 64134), 1994; ——, *Bud Hastin's Avon Collectible Price Guide*, published by author (P.O. Box 9868, Kansas City, MO 64134), 1991.

Periodical: *Avon Times*, P.O. Box 9868, Kansas City, MO 64134.

Collectors' Clubs: National Association of Avon Collectors, Inc., P.O. Box 7006, Kansas City, MO 64113;

After Shave, Windjammer, Volkswagen, aqua, 4 oz, $4.

Shawnee Avon Bottle Collectors Club, 1418 32nd NE, Canton, OH 44714; Sooner Avon Bottle Collectors Club, 6119 S. Hudson, Tulsa, OK 74136; Western World Avon Collectors Club, P.O. Box 23785, Pleasant Hills, CA 94523.

Museums: Hagley Museum and Library, Wilmington, DE; Nicholas Avon Museum, Clifton, VA.

Reproduction Alert.

Note: Prices quoted are for empty mint-condition bottles in their original boxes.

Awards and Representative Gifts

Charm Bracelet, silver,
   6 charms, 1959 .... 200.00
Necklace, SS, acorn, velvet pouch, Tiffany box and card, 1980 .... 90.00
Order Book, 1968, Charisma,
   red pen 7.50
Pin, Manager's, diamond
   crown, guard, 1961 .... 175.00
Tie Tac, telephone,
   gold tone, 1981 .... 15.00

California Perfume Co.

Almond Meal, Violet,
   8 oz, glass jar, 1893 .... 150.00
Bath Salts, Ariel, ribbed
   glass jar, 1903 .... 135.00
Perfume, White Rose, clear glass jar,
   orig neck ribbon, 1918 .... 145.00
Soap, Dr. Zabriskie's, brown,
   orig blue box, 1915 .... 50.00
Talcum, California Rose,
   3-1/2 oz, 1921 .... 115.00
Toilet Water, Lily of the Valley, 2 oz,
   ribbed glass jar, 1923 .... 115.00

Children's Items

Baby Lotion, bear, 10 oz, pink, matching
   pump dispenser, 1981 .... 7.50
Bank, Humpty Dumpty,
   5" h, ceramic, 1982 .... 18.00
Bubble Bath
   Freddy the Frog, mug, 5 oz, white
     glass, red top, 1970 .... 9.00
   Mickey Mouse,
     plastic, 1969 .... 7.50
   Snoopy, snow flyer,
     plastic, 1973 .... 6.00
Comb and Brush Set, Hot Dog, yellow
   and red plastic, 1975 .... 5.00
Nail Brush, Happy Hippo,
   3" l, pink, 1973 .... 2.50
Set
   Cowboy Set, white box, 2 red
     leatherette cowboy cuffs, cream hair
     dressing/toothpaste and

toothbrush, c1950 .... 50.00
Hair Trainer, 6-oz bottle,
   blue cap, red and white label, plastic
   comb, 1967 .... 25.00
Shampoo, Jet Plane, red,
   white and blue plastic tube, white
   plastic wings, 1965 .... 3.00
Soap
   Easter Bonnet, soap on
     a rope, yellow, 1970 .... 6.00
   Tub Racer, 3 speed boats, red, blue
     and yellow, 1970 .... 5.00
   Toothpaste, Toofie, 3-1/2 oz, white
     tube, raccoon, pink cap, pink
     toothbrush, 1968 .... 4.50

Men's Items

After Shave, figural
   Corncob Pipe, decanter, 3 oz, amber
     glass, black plastic stem 5.00
   Eight Ball, decanter, 3 oz, black and
     white, black cap 3.00
   Golf Cart, green glass,
     5-1/2" l, 1973 .... 5.00
   Guns, set of seven 35.00
   Pony Express, brown glass, copper
     man, 1971 .... 6.00
   U.S. Mail Truck, plastic and glass,
     red, white and blue 6.50
Body Splash, tennis ball,
   3 oz, light green flocking,
   green cap, 1977 .... 4.00
Chess Piece, 3 oz, amber glass,
   silver-colored top
   King, 1972 .... 6.00
   Pawn, 1975 .... 5.00
   Queen, 1973 .... 6.00
   Rook, 1974 .... 5.00
Hair Lotion, figural
   Bowling Pin, 4 oz, white
     plastic, red trim, c1960 .... 17.50
   Tractor, amber glass,
     amber plastic, 1974 .... 8.50
Set
   Commodore, maroon and white box,
     4-oz after shave, 2 white handkerchiefs, maroon paper talc box,
     1943 .... 75.00
   Valet, maroon and ivory box,
     4-oz after shave, shaving cream
     tube, talc can, smoker's tooth powder, 1945 .... 85.00

Miscellaneous

Bowl, 6" d, American Heirloom, Independence Day, 1981,
   black plastic base 20.00
Hostess Bell, SP, 1978 .... 20.00
Vase, bud, ruby red 15.00

Women's Items

Bubble Bath, Christmas
   Sparkler, red, 1969 .... 10.00
Candle

Cologne, Swan Lake Charisma, 8" h, 3 oz, 1972-76, $5.

   Fostoria, clear glass holder,
     perfumed, 1973 .... 7.50
   Gingerbread House, brown and
     white, 1977 .... 8.00
   Plum Pudding, 4" h, brown, green
     and white, 1978 .... 6.00
   Snowman, 5-1/2" h, white, green
     trim, 1981 .... 5.00
Christmas Ornament, rocking horse,
   clear glass, 1979 .... 7.50
Cologne
   Betsy Ross, glass, white, 1976 15.00
   Flower Maiden, glass,
     yellow, 1974 .... 9.00
   Library Lamp, 4 oz,
     gold-plated base, 1976 .... 6.00
Decanter, Skin So Soft, 5-3/4 oz,
   cylindrical carton, 1962 .... 20.00
Foaming Bath Oil
   Cruet, amber, ribbed, 1973 .... 6.00
   Victorian Washstand, buff, simulated
     marble top, blue pitcher and
     bowl cap, 1973 .... 5.00
Hand Lotion, rooster, 6 oz, milk glass,
   red plastic head, 1973 .... 6.00
Lip Gloss, Lucky Penny,
   2" d, compact type, 1978 .... 4.00
Perfume Glace
   Cameo Ring, 1970 .... 20.00
   Owl Pin, gold metal, green eyes, gold
     and green box, 1968 .... 9.00

B

Banks, Still

Collecting Hints: The rarity of a still bank has much to do with determining its value. Common banks, such as tin advertising banks, have limited value. The Statue of Liberty cast iron bank by A.C. Williams sells in the hundreds of dollars. See Long and Pitman's book for a rarity scale for banks.

Banks are collected by maker, material or subject. Subject is the most prominent, focusing on categories such as animals, food, mailboxes, safes, transportation and world's fairs. There is a heavy crossover of buyers from other collectible fields. Banks are graded by condition. Few banks are truly rare. Therefore, only purchase examples in very good to mint condition—those which retain all original paint and decorations.

History: Banks with no mechanical action are known as still banks. The first still banks were made of wood or pottery or from gourds. Redware and stoneware banks, made by America's early potters, are prized possessions of today's collectors.

Still banks reached their golden age with the arrival of the cast-iron bank. Leading manufacturing companies include Arcade Mfg., Co., J. Chein & Co., Hubley, J&E Stevens and A.C. Williams. The banks often were ornately painted to enhance their appeal. During the cast-iron era, banks and other businesses used the still bank as a form of advertising. Tin lithograph banks, again frequently a tool for advertising, were at their zenith from 1930 to 1955. Tin banks were an important premium, whether a Pabst Blue Ribbon Beer can bank or a Gerber's Orange Juice bank. Most tin advertising banks resembled the packaging of the product.

Almost every substance has been used to make a still bank—diecast white metal, aluminum, brass, plastic, glass, etc. Many early glass candy containers also converted to a bank after the candy was eaten. Thousands of varieties of still banks were made and hundreds of new varieties appear on the market each year.

References: Savi Arbola and Marco Onesti, *Piggy Banks*, Chronicle Books, 1992; Don Cranmer, *Collectors Encyclopedia: Toys-Banks*, L-W Book Sales, 1986, 1994-95 value update; Don Duer, *A Penny Saved: Still and Mechanical Banks*, Schiffer Publishing, 1993; Dick Heuser, *Heuser's Quarterly Price Guide to Official Collectible Banks*, Heuser Enterprises, 1992; Earnest and Ida Long and Jane Pitman, *Dictionary of Still Banks*, Long's Americana, 1980; Andy and Susan Moore, *Penny Bank Book*, Schiffer Publishing, 1984, 1994 value update; Tom and Loretta Stoddard, *Ceramic Coin Banks*, Collector Books, 1997; Vickie Stulb, *Modern Banks*, L-W Book Sales, 1997.

Periodicals: Glass Bank Collector, P.O. Box 155, Poland, NY 13431; Heuser's Quarterly Collectible Bank Newsletter, 508 Clapson Rd., P.O. Box 300, West Winfield, NY 13491.

Collectors' Club: Still Bank Collectors Club of America, 1456 Carson Ct, Homewood, IL 60430.

Museum: Margaret Woodbury Strong Museum, Rochester, NY.

Reproduction Alert.

Advertising

Atlas Storage, litho tin	20.00
Bremen, IN, cast metal, rock shape	20.00
Citizens Federal Savings, metal, cable car, key	25.00
Drydock Savings, pottery	15.00
Gulf Oil, oil tank	27.50
Hamm's Beer, 16" h, bear with calendar	40.00
Harris Trust and Savings, Chicago, pot metal, lion	30.00
Imperial Life Insurance Co., Ashville, NC, pot metal, Ben Franklin	40.00
Lucas Paint, litho tin	20.00
Lucky Charms, plastic, plays Lucky Charms theme song when coin is deposited	25.00
Ocean Spray Cranberry Juice, litho tin	20.00
Old Dutch Cleanser, litho tin	25.00
Pittsburgh Paints, glass, log cabin shape, paper label	35.00
Prudential Insurance Co., 7" h, dime register, cast iron, nickel plated, book shape	115.00
Rival Dog Food, litho tin	20.00
Seaman's Savings, pottery	20.00
Swank, pottery	18.00
Triangle Shoes, litho tin	20.00
Alligator, 5" h, diecast, gilt paint	40.00
Bank Building, litho tin, cupola, blue, red roof, c1870	65.00
Barrel, Happy Days, litho tin, Chein	25.00
Baseball Player, cast iron, c1900	90.00
Batman, 7" h, glazed ceramic, 1966	20.00
Bear, 7" h, cast iron, stealing honey from beehive, c1908	195.00
Boy Scout, 6" h, cast iron	115.00
Buffalo, 4-1/2" l, cast iron, Arcade	95.00
Bugs Bunny, pot metal	55.00
Buster Brown and Tige, 5-1/2" h, cast iron, c1910	150.00
Camel, cast iron	95.00
Captain Marvel, dime register, litho tin, Fawcett Publications, 1948	75.00
Cat, 2-1/2" h, cast iron, with ball	175.00
Charlie McCarthy, pot metal, black and white paint, natural face, Charlie standing by trunk, 7-3/4" h, trap missing	95.00
Chick, yellow, glass eyes, Lefton	20.00
Clock, cast iron, emb "A Money Saver," Arcade, c1910	60.00
Clown	150.00

Dog

Boxer, bobbing head, fuzzy coat	30.00
Mother and 2 puppies, Lipper & Mann	20.00
Pointer, cast iron, 18" l	120.00
Scottie dog, 5-1/2" h, in barrel, composition	24.00
St. Bernard, ceramic, leaning on keg	20.00

Drum, litho tin, 3" d, trap with key	20.00
Eagle, Emigrant Industrial Savings Bank, pottery	15.00
Elephant, 4" h, cast iron, red blanket, wheels	90.00
Fred Flintstone, 12-1/2" h, vinyl	18.00
Horse, cast iron, black,	

Advertising, Tootsie Roll, cardboard and tin, 11-1/4", $3.50.

Globe, Chein, tin, c1930, 4-1/4" h, $10.

emb "Beauty" 65.00
Indian, 5" h, cast iron, bust 70.00
Jack and Jill, 5" h, diecast, dark bronze
    finish, holding pail 30.00
Laurel and Hardy, 14" h,
    plastic, figural 45.00
Liberty Bell, glass, emb "1919" 30.00
Lincoln Bank, 9" h, glass, bottle shape,
    orig top-hat cap, paper label 50.00
Lion, brass, 8" l 70.00
Owl, 7" h, chalkware 60.00
Parking Meter 75.00
Pig
    Republic Pig 110.00
    Seated 85.00
    Wise Pig 125.00
Rabbit
    Napier 45.00
    Nicodemus,
        green mottled, 4" h 95.00
Rocking Horse, 4-1/2" h,
    bronze finish 25.00
Safe, cast iron, combination lock, black,
    emb "Security Safe Deposit" 95.00
Savings for Baby, metal, boot shape,
    toys, stork holding baby 60.00
Suitcase, litho tin, printed labels, key
    lock, mkd "Marx" 30.00
Superman, litho tin, dime register, opens
    at $5, DC Publications 75.00
Swiss Chalet, wood, 5" x 2-1/2" x 4",
    emb metal dec, key lock 25.00
Top Hat, cast iron, emb
    "Pass Around the Hat" 90.00
Turkey, cast iron 50.00
Woodsy Owl, pottery 45.00

Barbershop Collectibles

Collecting Hints: Many barbershop collectibles have a porcelain finish. If chipped or cracked, the porcelain is difficult, if not impossible, to repair. Buy barber poles and chairs in very good condition or better. A good appearance is a key consideration. Many old barbershops are still in business. Their back rooms often contain excellent display pieces.

History: The neighborhood barbershop was an important social and cultural institution during the 19th century and first half of the 20th century. Men and boys gathered to gossip, exchange business news and check current fashions. "Girlie" magazines and comic books, usually forbidden at home, were available for browsing, as were adventure magazines and police gazettes.

In the 1960s, the number of barbershops dropped by half in the United States. Unisex shops broke the traditional men-only barrier. In the 1980s, several chains began running barber and hairdressing shops on a regional and national basis.

References: *Barbershop Collectibles*, L-W Book Sales, 1996; Keith E. Estep, *Shaving Mug and Barber Bottle Book*, Schiffer Publishing, 1995; John Odell, *Digger Odell's Official Antique Bottle and Glass Collector Magazine Price Guide Series, Vol. 1*, published by author (1910 Shawhan Rd., Morrow, OH 45152), 1995; Robert Sloan and Steven Guarnaccis, *A Stiff Drink and a Close Shave*, Chronicle Books, 1995.

Collectors' Clubs: National Shaving Mug Collectors' Association, 320 S. Glenwood St., Allentown, PA 18104; Safety Razor Collectors' Guild, P.O. Box 885, Crescent City, CA 95531.

Antiseptic Container, 8" h,
    plated brass 45.00
Ashtray, 5" d, Wm. Marvy
    Supply giveaway 12.00
Barber Bottle, glass
    Advertising, Le Varns
        Hair Tonic 70.00
    Amber, floral, dot pattern 80.00
    Bristol, bell shape, hp, cherubs,
        scene, gold trim 165.00
    Clambroth, 8" h, "Witch Hazel" in red
        letters 75.00
    Milk Glass, sq, orig top 70.00
Barber Bowl, brass, c1820 .... 250.00

Blade Bank
    Barber, china 25.00
    Shaving Brush, 6" h, china 25.00
    Treasure Chest, Ever Ready adv,
        litho tin 20.00
Blade Tin
    Challenge, c1898 .... 25.00
    Yankee, c1900 .... 60.00
Bobby Pins, dozen on orig card, picture
    of Bob Hope, Paramount Star ... 5.00
Business Card, 6" x 3-1/4", man cutting
    hair "The Newest and Most Sanitary
    Shop in Providence" 12.00
Catalog
    Biedermeier, German barber supply,
        48 pgs, German text, c1910 .... 25.00
    Cattaraugus Cutlery Co.,
        81 pgs, 1925 .... 75.00
    J.E. McBrady & Co., Chicago, 48
        pgs, 1938, 6" x 9" 25.00
Chair
    Oak, 1890 .... 500.00
    Pedestal base, round seat, Theo
        Kochs Manufacturer 400.00
Clippers, Andis, c1940 .... 25.00
Comb Holder, Barbacide 30.00
Counter Mat, 9" x 8", Wardonia Razor
    Blades, rubber 18.00
Display Case, 4" h, Gillette, wood and
    glass, c1940 .... 45.00
Hair Net, blond, orig envelope 3.00
Lamp, 9" h, barber pole 40.00
License, framed, c1930 .... 45.00
Neck Duster, cherry handle 30.00
Newspaper,
    Barber's Journal, 1881 .... 12.00
Paperweight, Norvell-Shapleigh
    Hardware Co. 25.00
Playing Cards, Gillette,
    1905, unused 150.00
Pole
    28" h, wood, red, white and blue,
        round top with stars 125.00
    42" h, stained glass and
        porcelain, wall mount, Theo Kochs
        manufacturer 900.00
    84" h, porcelain and glass,
        rotating top, floor-mount
        electric motor 800.00
Poster, Packer's Tar Soap,
    9" x 12", scene of barber shaving
    customer, 1900 .... 40.00
Razor Hone, Keen Kutter, E.C.
    Simmons, cardboard box 30.00
Safety Razor, Gillette,
    SS blade 125.00
Scuttle, scene of men, women, girl and
    cherub in oval reserve, royal blue
    ground, gold trim 65.00
Shaving Brush, aluminum handle, emb
    design, c1910 .... 10.00
Shaving Mirror

7" h, celluloid, folding, German silver trim, milk glass insert................25.00

14" h, SP, Colonial Silver, beveled mirror, c1920 ....30.00

Shaving Mug

Ancient Order of United Workers, gold trim, monogram 175.00

Astra Castra Numen Lumen...110.00

Baker, delivery scene, gold trim 225.00

Banker, gold trim, monogram.165.00

Floral, pink and blue flowers, gold trim 65.00

Milkman, milk wagon..............365.00

Plumber, bathroom scene 425.00

Woodmen of America, gold trim, monogram 65.00

Shaving Mug Rack, 38" h, pine, 24 mugs 160.00

Sign

10" x 14", Leukroth's Oriental Hair Tonic, cardboard, color litho, beautiful woman................................225.00

19" l, Andis Clippers, plastic, light-up 30.00

Sterilizer, 12" h, wood cabinet, glass door, United Beauty Co. 60.00

Storage Cabinet, wood-grain litho tin, shelves and racks, Safetee Brand..........................35.00

Strop, 9" x 2-1/2" x 2", leather, 2-sided, mkd "Horse Hide Burl Finish" ..20.00

Stropper, metal, Rundel, c1920.....25.00

Tin, Sweet Georgia Brown, 1-1/8" d, black, white and red, Hair Dressing Pomade, stylish male and female young blacks, instructions for use on back, Valmor Products Co., c1930 ....25.00

Towel Steamer, nickel-plated copper, porcelain over steel base.......325.00

Trimmer, Quick Trimmer Inc., plastic 5.00

Shaving brush, Ever Ready, blue box, black celluloid handle, dark bristles, $15.

Sign, Klondike Head Rub, emb, blue letters, cardboard, 11" x 8-3/8", $20.

Barbie

Collecting Hints: Never forget that a large quantity of Barbie dolls and related material has been manufactured. Because of this easy availability, only objects in excellent to mint condition with original packaging (also in very good or better condition) have significant value. If items show signs of heavy use, their value is probably minimal.

Collectors prefer items from the first decade of production. Learn how to distinguish a Barbie #1 doll from its successors. The Barbie market is one of subtleties. You must learn them. Recently, collectors have shifted their focus from the dolls themselves to the accessories. There have been rapid price increases in early clothing and accessories, with some of the prices bordering on speculation.

History: In 1945, Harold Matson (MATT) and Ruth and Elliott (EL) Handler founded Mattel. Initially, the company made picture frames but became involved in the toy market when Elliott Handler began to make doll furniture from scrap material. When Matson left the firm, Elliott Handler became chief designer and Ruth Handler principal marketer. In 1955, Mattel advertised its products on "The Mickey Mouse Club," and the company prospered.

In 1958, Mattel patented a fashion doll. The doll was named "Barbie" and reached the toy shelves in 1959. By 1960, Barbie's popularity was assured. Development of a boyfriend for Barbie (named Ken, after the Handlers' son) began in 1960.

Over the years, many other dolls were added. Clothing, vehicles, room settings and other accessories became an integral part of the line.

From September 1961 through July 1972, Mattel published a Barbie magazine. At its peak, the Barbie Fan Club was second only to the Girl Scouts as the largest girls' organization in the United States. Barbie is now a billion-dollar baby, the first toy in history to reach this prestigious mark—that's a billion dollars per year, just in case you're wondering.

References: J. Michael Augustyniak, *Collector's Encyclopedia of Barbie Doll Exclusives and More*, Collector Books, 1997; Sibyl DeWein and Joan Ashabraner, *Collectors Encyclopedia of Barbie Dolls and Collectibles*, Collector Books, 1977, 1994 value update; Sarah Sink Eames, *Barbie Fashion, Vol. I* (1990, 1995 value update), *Vol. II* (1997), Collector Books; Laura Jacobs, *Barbie*, Artabras, 1994; M.G. Lord, *Forever Barbie*, Avon Books, 1995; A. Glenn Mandeville, *Doll Fashion Anthology & Price Guide*, 4th Edition, Hobby House Press, 1993; Paris and Susan Manos, *Wonder of Barbie*, Collector Books, 1987, 1994 value update; ——, *World of Barbie Dolls*, Collector Books, 1983, 1994 value update; Marcie Melillo, *Ultimate Barbie Doll Book*, Krause Publications, 1996; Lorraine Mieszala, *Collector's Guide to Barbie Doll Paper Dolls*, Collector Books, 1997; Patrick C. Olds and Myrazona R. Olds, *Barbie Doll Years*, 2nd Edition, Collector Books, 1997; Margo Rana, *Collector's Guide to Barbie Exclusives*, Collector Books, 1995; Jane Sarasohn-Kahn, *Contemporary Barbie*, Antique Trader Books, 1996; Beth Summers, *Decade of Barbie Dolls and Collectibles*, Collector Books, 1996; Kitturah B. Westenhouser, *Story of Barbie*, Collector Books, 1994; Craig Yoe, *Art of Barbie*, Workman Publishing, 1994.

Periodicals: *Barbie Bazaar*, 5617 6th Ave., Kenosha, WI 53140; *Barbie Fashions*, 387 Park Ave. S., New York, NY 10016; *Barbie Talks Some More*, 19 Jamestown Dr., Cincinnati, OH 45241; *Collector's Corner*, 519 Fitzooth Dr., Miamisburg, OH

45342; *Miller's Price Guide & Collectors' Almanac*, West One Summer #1, Spokane, WA 99204.

Videotapes: Joe Blitman, *Oh, You Beautiful Doll!*, available from producer (5163 Franklin Ave., Los Angeles, CA 90027), 1994; Those Swell Doll Guys, *Swell Dolls, Vol. 1*, TSDG Holdings, 1994.

Beach Bus, 1974 ....30.00
Beauty Kit, 1961, MIB..................27.50
Book

  Barbie's Adventures Read-Aloud Series, Wonder Books, #2048, paperback, 1964, 129 pgs................10.00
  Barbie's Easy-As-Pie Cookbook, Cynthia Lawrence, Random House, 1964, 114 pgs, 1st printing.......14.00
  Barbie's Fashion Success, Mary Lou Maybee, Random House, 1962, 188 pgs 18.00
  Portrait of Skipper, The Story Book of Skipper—-A New Doll, Wonder Books, 1964, 48 pgs 14.00

Car

  Corvette, 1968, MIB 60.00
  Dune Buggy, Irwin, MIB 75.00

Christmas Ornament, Hallmark

  1993, red dress, 1st ed 125.00
  1994, gold dress........................45.00
  1995, green dress 35.00

Clothing

  Air Force Bomber Jacket, #1....60.00
  Arabian Nights, #0874, 1963....35.00
  Ballerina, #989, 1961 ....25.00
  Busy Gal, #981, 1958...............40.00
  Check the Suit, #1794, 1970....15.00
  Fur Stole, 1960s........................20.00
  Garden Tea Party, #1606, 1964 ....30.00
  Panties, pkg of three, Premier Co. 1960s, MIP 3.25
  Ship Ahoy, #1918, 1964...........25.00
  Tennis Anyone, #941, 1962 ...320.00

Colorforms Set 10.00
Diary, 1963, unused 20.00
Doll

  Barbie

    #1, brunette, orig ponytail, red lips, hoop earrings, white-rimmed sunglasses with blue lenses, finger and toe paint, black and white 1-pc knit swimsuit, hair slightly frizzy, some touch-ups, discoloration to body 4,100.00
    #3, brunette, orig ponytail, blue eyeliner, full red lips, pearl earrings, finger and toe paint, black and 1-pc knit swimsuit, black open-toed shoes, #3 pedestal stand, pink-covered booklet, neck insert, some discoloration, 2 holes in swimsuit, worn box......1,700.00
    #4, brunette, orig ponytail, full red lips, finger and toe paint, black and white 1-pc knit swimsuit, hair slightly frizzy, some light staining, swimsuit loose 235.00
    #5, blond, orig ponytail, full red lips, finger and toe paint, black and white 1-pc knit swimsuit, black wire stand, box insert, yellow-covered booklet, slight staining and scratching, age discoloration on box 180.00
    1961-62, Bubble Cut, blond, light pink lips, finger and toe paint, Let's Dance dress........................105.00
    1964, Bubble Cut, blond, coral lips, pearl earrings, finger and toe paint, red 1-pc swimsuit, red open-toed shoes, orig box with insert, box worn 200.00
    1966, Color Me Magic Barbie, raised-letter issue, dark red hair, barrette, bright pink lips, faint cheek blush, finger and toe paint, swimsuit, belt and scarf, aqua mules, orig plastic closet box, purple plastic hanger, closet bracket, barrettes and ribbons, netting, color changer A and B, brush, Color Magic booklet, Exclusive Fashions Book 1, hair is slightly frizzy, box worn 800.00
    1970, Living Barbie, brunette, rooted eyelashes, pink lips, orig silver and gold metallic swimsuit, some fading 70.00
    1971, Walk Lively Barbie, NRFB 165.00
    1973, Live Action Barbie, blond, rooted eyelashes, pink lips, orig outfit, wrist tag, orig plastic baggie pkg 155.00
    1979, Italian Barbie, International Series, NRFB.....................175.00
    1981, India Barbie, International Series, NRFB.....................125.00
    1985, Greek Barbie, International Series, NRFB.......................55.00
    1986, Blue Rhapsody Barbie, Porcelain Series, No. 03220, stand, certificate and Styrofoam insert in box, box worn 350.00
    1987, Enchanted Evening Barbie, Porcelain Series, No. 0044986, stand, certificate and Styrofoam insert in box, box worn.......175.00
    1988, Happy Holidays Barbie, first issue, red dress, gold glitter, NRFB 575.00
    1989, Happy Holidays Barbie, white dress, fur trim, ornament, NRFB 200.00
    1990, Gold Barbie, Bob Mackie Series, complete, cardboard shipping box 650.00
    1990, Happy Holidays Barbie, fuchsia dress, silver design, ornament, NRFB...............100.00
    1991, Happy Holidays Barbie, green velvet dress, sequins, NRFB.................................160.00
    1992, Blossom Beautiful Barbie, Sears, orig outfit, stand, shoes and no box.........................265.00
    1992, Empress Bride, Bob Mackie Series, complete, cardboard shipping box 750.00
    1992, Happy Holidays Barbie, silver dress, pearls, sequins, glitter, NRFB..........95.00
    1992, Satin Nights Barbie, Service Merchandise, NRFB 115.00
    1993, Happy Holidays Barbie, red dress, gold trim, sequins and glitter, NRFB 85.00
    1994, Queen of Hearts, Bob Mackie series, complete, cardboard shipping box 200.00
    1996, Easter Basket 20.00
    1996, Pretty Hearts..............20.00
    1996, Target Valentine 30.00
    1997, Hallmark Valentine 65.00

  Francie, Growing Pretty Hair, 1970 ....75.00
  Julia, Twist 'n' Turn, 2-pc uniform, 1969 ....30.00
  Ken

    1979, #1930, white pants, striped shirt 20.00
    1980, #1932, beach

Birthday card, c1995, 50 cents.

#2 Doll, brown ponytail, pearl earrings, orig stand, 11-1/2", $500.

cover-up, salmon 20.00
Doll Case, 12" x 10" x 2-1/2",
    pink vinyl, 1985, used 5.00
Easter Ornament, 1995,
    Hallmark 25.00
Game, Prom Game 20.00
Gift Set, 35th Anniversary, 1993, Keep-
    sake Collection, blond, replica of
    Easter Parade and Roman Holiday
    outfits, NRFB 100.00
Lunch Box, blue, Thermos brand, 1990,
    no thermos.................................8.00
Magazine, *Mattel Barbie Magazine*, Mar-
    April, 1969, 8-1/2" x 10-1/2".....15.00
Make-Up Case,
    1963, unused...........................20.00
Paper Dolls, Golden Barbie, uncut
    1989 ....7.00
    1992 ....6.00
Pendant, Sweet 16 ....16.00
Salt and Pepper Shakers, pr, ceramic,
    Barbie and Ken, 3-1/2" h, Enesco,
    1994, MIB 25.00
Sewing Pattern, Simplicity, doll clothing,
    blouse, pants, shorts, dresses,
    jackets, used, worn orig
    envelope, 1965 ....15.00
Stand, black wire, mid 1960s 12.50
Sticker Fun Book, Golden
    Barbie, 1988, unused 6.00
Stocking, Hallmark, orig tags.........12.00
Suitcase, Ken, 1962 ....20.00
Wristwatch, 1963...........................50.00

Baseball Cards

Collecting Hints: Condition is a key factor—collectors should strive to obtain only cards in excellent to mint condition (and mint condition only on post-1980 cards).

Concentrate on the superstars; these cards are most likely to increase in value. Buy full sets of modern cards. In this way you have the superstars of tomorrow on hand. When a player becomes a member of the Baseball Hall of Fame, the value of his cards and other memorabilia will increase significantly.

The price of cards fluctuates rapidly, often changing on a weekly basis. Spend time studying the market before investing heavily. Reproduced cards and sets have become a fact of life. Novice collectors should not buy cards until they can tell the difference between the originals and reproductions. The latest, highly speculative trend is collecting rookie cards, i.e., those from a player's first year. Limited edition "insert" or "chase" cards are also highly speculative.

History: Baseball cards were first printed in the late 19th century. By 1900, the most common cards, known as "T" cards, were those made by tobacco firms such as American Tobacco Co. The majority of the tobacco-related cards were produced between 1909 and 1915. During the 1920s, American Caramel, National Caramel and York Caramel candy companies issued cards identified in lists as "E" cards.

During the 1930s, Goudey Gum Co., of Boston (from 1933 to 1941) and Gum Inc. (in 1939) were prime producers of baseball cards. Following World War II, Bowman Gum of Philadelphia (B.G.H.L.I.), the successor to Gum, Inc., lead the way. Topps, Inc., (T.C.G.) of Brooklyn, followed. Topps bought Bowman in 1956 and enjoyed almost a monopoly in card production until 1981 when Fleer of Philadelphia and Donruss of Memphis became competitive. Since then, many other companies, such as Score and Upper Deck, have joined the fray.

References: *All Sport Alphabetical Price Guide*, Krause Publications,

1995; *Baseball Card Price Guide*, 10th Edition, Krause Publications, 1996; James Beckett, *Official 1996 Price Guide to Baseball Cards*, 15th Edition, House of Collectibles, 1995; Tol Broome, *From Ryan to Ruth*, Krause Publications, 1994; *Charlton Standard Catalogue of Canadian Baseball & Football Cards*, 4th Edition, The Charlton Press, 1996; Gene Florence, *Standard Baseball Card Price Guide*, 6th Edition, Collector Books, 1994; Allan Kaye and Michael McKeever, *Baseball Card Price Guide*, Avon Books, 1995; Troy Kirk, *Collector's Guide to Baseball Cards*, Wallace-Homestead, 1990; Jeff Kurowski and Tony Prudom, *Sports Collectors Digest Pre-War Baseball Card Price Guide*, Krause Publications, 1993; Mark Larson (ed.), *Baseball Cards Questions & Answers*, Krause Publications, 1992; ——, *Sports Collectors Digest Minor League Baseball Card Price Guide*, Krause Publications, 1993; ——, *Sports Collectors Digest: The Sports Card Explosion*, Krause Publications, 1993; Bob Lemke (ed.), *Sportscard Counterfeit Detector*, 3rd Edition, Krause Publications, 1994; Roderick A. Malloy, *Malloy's Guide to Sports Cards Values*, Wallace-Homestead, 1995; Michael McKeever, *Collecting Sports Cards*, Alliance Publishing, 1996; ——, *Confident Collector: Baseball Card Price Guide*, Avon Books, 1996; *101 Sports Card Investments*, Krause Publications, 1993; ——, *Premium Insert Sports Cards*, Krause Publications, 1995; Alan Rosen *True Mint*, Krause Publications, 1994; *Standard Catalog of Baseball Cards*, 6th Edition, Krause Publications, 1996.

Periodicals: The following appear on a monthly or semi-monthly basis: *Baseball Update*, 220 Sunrise Hwy., Ste. 284, Rockville Centre, NY 11570; *Beckett Baseball Card Monthly*, 4887 Alpha Rd., Ste. 200, Dallas, TX 75244; *Beckett Focus on Future Stars*, 4887 Alpha Rd., Ste. 200, Dallas, TX 75244; *Card Trade*, 700 E. State St., Iola, WI 54990; *Diamond Angle*, P.O. Box 409, Kaunakakai, HI 96748; *Old Judge*, P.O. Box 137, Centerbeach, NY 11720; *Sports Cards*, 700 E. State

St., Iola, WI 54990; *Sports Collectors Digest*, 700 E. State St., Iola, WI 54990; *Your Season Ticket*, 106 Liberty Rd., Woodsburg, MD 21790.

Collectors' Clubs: There are many local card collecting clubs throughout the United States. However, there is no current national organization.

Reproduction Alert: The 1952 Topps set, except for five cards, was reproduced in 1983 and clearly marked by Topps. In addition, a number of cards have been illegally reprinted including the following Topps cards:

1963 Pete Rose, rookie card, #537
1971 Pete Rose, #100
1971 Steve Garvey, #341
1972 Pete Rose, #559
1972 Steve Garvey, #686
1972 Rod Carew, #695
1973 Willie Mays, #100
1973 Hank Aaron, #305
1973 Mike Schmidt, rookie card, #615
1984 Fleer Update Roger Clemens
1984 Fleer Update Kirby Puckett

Notes: The prices below are for cards in near mint condition. The listings for cards after 1948 show the price for a complete set, common player and superstars. The number of cards in each set is indicated in parentheses.

Sports Cards Language: As in a dictionary, new terms and abbreviations are added to various antiques and collectibles categories. Here are some commonly used Sports Cards terms:

American Card Catalog (ACC): Edited by Jefferson Burdick, Nostalgia Press, 1960. Lists alphabetical and numerical designations as it identifies card sets. A set of sub-abbreviations, such as F for food inserts, has been devised. The one-, two- or three-digit number which follows the letter prefix identifies the company and the series.
All Star Card (AS): A special card for players of the all-star teams of the National League or American League.
AU: Card with autograph.
Blank Back: Card with no printing at all on the back.
Borders: Space (generally white although sometimes colored) which surrounds the picture, used in establishing grading.
Brick: Wrapped group of cards, often representing only one year.
Centering: Refers to requirement that the player be centered on the card with even borders; an important grading factor.
Chipping: Wearing away of a dark-colored border.
Combination Card: Shows two or more players but not an entire team.
Common Card: Ordinary player, lowest-value card in a set.
CO: Abbreviation for coach.
COR: Corrected card.
CY: Cy Young award.
Ding: Slight damage to the edge or corner of a card.
DP: Double-quantity print run.
DR or DP: Draft choice or draft pick.
Error card (ERR): Card with a known mistake, misspelling, etc. Error cards are only valued more highly when a corrected version of the card is issued. Sometimes, there are more error cards than correct cards produced, sometimes vice versa.
First Card (FC): First card of a player in a national set, not necessarily a rookie card.
Foil: Foil-embossed stamp on card.
F/S: Father and son on card.
Gloss: Amount of shine on a card; again, a value determination.
Grade: Condition that helps determine value.
Key Cards: Most important cards in a set.
Reverse Negative: Common error in which picture negative is flipped so the picture comes out backwards.
ROY: Rookie of the Year.
SP: Single or short print, printed in smaller quantity than rest of series.
Team Card: Card showing entire team.
Wrapper: Paper wrapper surrounding wax packs.
YL: Yellow letters, Topps, 1958.

Pre-Bowman/Topps Period

Honus Wagner, T209,
    1909-1911 .... 160,000.00
Jimmy Collins, #39, T205, 1911 .. 500.00
Ty Cobb, #9, T3, 1911 .... 10,000.00
Joe Tinker, #35, T3, 1911 .... 325.00
Jimmy Foxx, #29, Goudey, 1933 600.00
Dizzy Dean, #6, Goudey, 1934 ... 900.00
Lou Gehrig, #61,

Bowman, 1953, #10 Richie Ashburn, $90.

    Goudey, 1934 .... 3,200.00
Jackie Robinson,
    #79, Leaf, 1948 .... 750.00
Babe Ruth, #3, Leaf, 1948 .... 2,250.00

Bowman Era

1948 Bowman, black and white
    Complete Set (48) 3,500.00
    Common Player (1-36) 20.00
    Common Player (37-48) 28.00
    6 Yogi Berra 475.00
    36 Stan Musial 675.00
1949 Bowman
    Complete Set (240) 12,500.00
    Common Player (1-36) 16.00
    Common Player (37-73) 16.00
    Common Player(74-144) 16.00
    Common Player (145-240) 56.00
    84 Roy Campanella RC 700.00
    100 Gil Hodges 135.00
    229 Ed Lopat 100.00
1950 Bowman, color
    Complete Set (252) 6,500.00
    Common Player (1-72) 30.00
    Common Player(73-252) 12.00
    6 Bob Feller 155.00
    217 Casey Stengel 120.00
    248 Sam Jethroe 16.00
1951 Bowman, color
    Complete Set (324) 15,000.00
    Common Player (1-252) 9.50
    Common Player (253-324) 6.50
    134 Warren Spahn................. 110.00
    143 Ted Kluszewski................. 30.00
    305 Willie Mays................... 2,500.00
1952 Bowman, color

Complete Set (252) 9,000.00
Common Player (1-216)...........12.00
Common Player (217-252).......25.00
4 Robin Roberts 55.00
8 Pee Wee Reese 100.00
14 Cliff Chambers 17.00
22 Willard Ramsdell 17.00
44 Roy Campanella................190.00
53 Richie Ashburn...................50.00
100 Sibby Sisty 14.00
200 Ken Silvestri 14.00

1953 Bowman, color
Complete Set (160) 10,000.00
Common Player (1-112)...........24.00
Common Player (113-128).......57.00
Common Player (129-160).......45.00
40 Larry Doby.........................35.00
57 Lou Boudeau 50.00
59 Mickey Mantle 2,500.00
125 Fred Hatfield.....................55.00
153 Whitey Ford.....................450.00

1954 Bowman, color
Complete Set (224) 4,200.00
Common Player (1-112).............8.00
Common Player (113-224).......12.00
1 Phil Rizzulo 125.00
50 George Kell 25.00
74 Jim Gillam 16.00

1955 Bowman, color
Complete Set (320) 4,200.00
Common Player (1-96)...............6.00
Common Player (97-224)...........6.00
Common Player (225-320).......16.00
25 Minny Minoso 17.00
103 Eddie Mathews.................50.00
202 Mickey Mantle 550.00

Topps Era

1951 Topps, blue backs
Complete Set (52) 1,800.00
Common Player (1-52).............30.00
3 Richie Ashburn....................110.00
37 Bobby Doerr 70.00
50 Johnny Mize 125.00

1951 Topps, red backs
Complete Set (52) 875.00
Common Player (1-52)..............10.00
1 Yogi Berra 90.00
31 Gil Hodges 40.00
38 Duke Snider 65.00

1952 Topps
Complete Set (407) 53,000.00
Common Player (1-80)..............45.00
Common Player (81-252).........25.00
Common Player (253-310).......50.00
Common Player (311-407).....225.00
33 Warren Spahn 200.00
48 Joe Page, ERR 325.00
88 Bob Feller.........................150.00
400 Bill Dickey......................225.00

1953 Topps
Complete Set (280) 13,500.00
Common Player (1-165)...........18.00
Common Player (166-220).......20.00
Common Player (221-280).......50.00
1 Jackie Robinson..................425.00
10 Smokey Burgess................50.00
62 Monte Irvin 50.00
100 B. Miller 22.00
149 Dom DiMaggio 32.00

1954 Topps
Complete Set (250) 7,000.00
Common Player (1-50).............12.00
Common Player (51-75).........25.00
Common Player (76-250).........12.00
17 Phil Rizzuto 65.00
30 Eddie Mathews 70.00
36 Hoyt Wilhelm 40.00

1955 Topps
Complete Set (210) 6,700.00
Common Player (1-150)...........11.00
Common Player (151-160).......20.00
Common Player (161-210).......28.00
31 Warren Spahn.....................70.00
100 Monte Irvin 25.00
123 Sandy Koufax RC 850.00

1956 Topps
Complete Set (340) 6,500.00
Common Player (1-100)............9.00
Common Player (101-180).......11.00
Common Player (181-260).......15.00
Common Player (261-340).......11.00
33 Roberto Clemente.............375.00
180 Robin Roberts 35.00
226 Giants Team 60.00

1957 Topps
Complete Set (407) 7,000.00
Common Player (1-176)............8.00
Common Player (177-264).........6.00
Common Player (265-352).......17.00
Common Player (353-407).........8.00
18 Don Drysdale RC 190.00
20 Hank Aaron 190.00
120 Bob Lemon.......................24.00
154 Red Schoendienst............17.00

1958 Topps
Complete Set (495) 5,200.00
Common Player (1-110).............8.00
Common Player (111-198).........7.00
Common Player(199-352)..........5.00
Common Player (353-474).........4.50
Common Player (475-495).........5.00
2 Bob Lemon YL 35.00
71 Dodgers Team 40.00
115 Jim Bunning 20.00
420 Vada Pinson RC 30.00

1959 Topps
Complete Set (572) 4,500.00
Common Player (1-110).............5.00
Common Player (111-506).........3.00

Topps, 1973, #615 Rookie card, includes Mike Schmidt, $350.

Common Player (507-572) 13.50
8 Phillies Team 30.00
102 Felipe Alou RC.................30.00
317 Ashburn/Mays..................40.00
467 Hank Aaron HR................22.00

1960 Topps
Complete Set (572) 3,800.00
Common Player (1-440) 3.50
Common Player (441-506) 5.00
Common Player (507-572) 13.00
28 Brooks Robinson 40.00
109 Clete Boyer 5.50
386 Neal WS............................5.00

1961 Topps
Complete Set (589).............4,500.00
Common Player (1-446) 2.75
Common Player (447-522) 5.00
Common Player (523-589) 27.00
2 Roger Maris 145.00
35 Ron Santo RC.....................50.00
98 Checklist 7.50

1962 Topps
Complete Set (598).............4,500.00
Common Player (1-370) 3.50
Common Player (371-446) 5.00
Common Player (447-522) 7.50
Common Player (553-598) 20.00
5 Sandy Koufax 105.00
73 Nellie Fox............................8.00
530 Bob Gibson 150.00

1963 Topps
Complete Set (576).............5,000.00
Common Player (1-283) 3.00
Common Player (284-446) 4.00
Common Player (447-522) 15.00
Common Player (523-576) 11.00
54 Dave Dubusschere RC 5.00
169 Gaylord Perry RC 240.00
233 Casey Stengel 15.00
380 Ernie Banks 60.00

1964 Topps
Complete Set (587).............2,500.00
Common Player (1-370) 3.00
Common Player (371-522) 6.00
Common Player (523-587) 10.00

5 Koufax/Drysdale...................12.00
125 Pete Rose.......................145.00
300 Hank Aaron.....................90.00

1965 Topps
Complete Set (598)............3,500.00
Common Player (1-283)............2.25
Common Player (284-370)........3.50
Common Player (371-522)........6.00
Common Player (523-598)........7.00
24 Twins Team.......................4.00
207 Pete Rose.......................125.00
500 Eddie Mathews.................30.00

1966 Topps
Complete Set (598)............4,000.00
Common Player (1-196)............1.50
Common Player (197-370)........2.00
Common Player (371-446)........4.00
Common Player (447-522)........8.00
Common Player (523-598).......16.00
100 Sandy Koufax...................85.00
172 Mets Team.......................6.00
288 Don Sutton RC..................85.00

1967 Topps
Complete Set (609)............5,000.00
Common Player (1-196)............1.25
Common Player (197-370)........1.75
Common Player (371-457)........3.00
Common Player (458-533)........6.00
Common Player (534-609).......12.00
103 Mantle Checklist................10.00
480 Willie McCovey.................35.00
609 Tommy John.....................70.00

1968 Topps
Complete Set (598)............3,200.00
Common Player (1-457)............1.25
Common Player (458-598)........2.50
110 Hank Aaron......................62.00
205 Juan Marichal....................8.00
257 Phil Niekro........................4.50

1969 Topps
Complete Set (664)............2,500.00
Common Player (1-218)............1.25
Common Player (219-327)........2.00
Common Player (328-512)........1.25
Common Player (513-664)........2.00
82 Pirates Rookies..................10.00
260 Reggie Jackson RC........375.00
410 Al Kaline..........................18.00

1970 Topps
Complete Set (720)............2,100.00
Common Player (1-372)............1.00
Common Player (373-546)........1.50
Common Player (547-633)........3.00
Common Player (634-720)........6.00
140 Reggie Jackson.................85.00
210 Juan Marichal...................12.00
537 Joe Morgan......................10.00
712 Nolan Ryan......................500.00

1971 Topps
Complete Set (752)............2,200.00

Topps, 1982, #210 Keith Hernandez, 50 cents.

Common Player (1-393)............1.00
Common Player (394-523)........2.00
Common Player (524-643)........3.50
Common Player (644-752)........4.50
26 Bert Blyleven......................25.00
55 Steve Carlton.....................25.00
709 Don Baylor.......................90.00

1972 Topps
Complete Set (787)............2,150.00
Common Player (1-394)...............75
Common Player (395-525)........1.00
Common Player (526-656)........2.00
Common Player (657-787)........6.00
37 Carl Yastrzemski.................10.00
595 Nolan Ryan......................250.00
695 Rod Carew.......................75.00

1973 Topps
Complete Set (660)............1,200.00
Common Player (1-396)...............40
Common Player (397-528)...........70
Common Player (529-660)........2.00
31 Buddy Bell RC.....................4.00
193 Carlton Fisk......................30.00
245 Carl Yastrzemski...............15.00
615 Mike Schmidt RC...........425.00

1974 Topps
Complete Set (660)...............600.00
Common Player (1-660)..........30.00
80 Tom Seaver.......................15.00
283 Mike Schmidt....................75.00
456 Dave Winfield...................200.00

1975 Topps
Complete Set (660)...............900.00
Common Player (1-660)...........30
61 Dave Winfield.....................70.00
70 Mike Schmidt......................65.00
223 Robin Yount RC...............125.00
228 George Brett RC............200.00
370 Tom Seaver......................12.00

1976 Topps
Complete Set (660)...............400.00

Common Player (1-660)..............25
19 George Brett......................60.00
98 Dennis Eckersley RC..........35.00
340 Jim Rice............................6.00
480 Mike Schmidt...................30.00

1977 Topps
Complete Set (660)...............400.00
Common Player (1-660)..............20
110 Steve Carlton....................8.00
400 Steve Garvey.....................3.00
473 Andre Dawson RC............65.00

1978 Topps
Complete Set (726)...............300.00
Common Player (1-726)..............10
36 Eddie Murray......................90.00
72 Andre Dawson....................20.00
360 Mike Schmidt....................15.00

1979 Topps
Complete Set (726)...............250.00
Common Player (1-726)..............15
39 Dale Murphy........................4.00
116 Ozzie Smith......................90.00
650 Pete Rose..........................4.00

1980 Topps
Complete Set (726)...............230.00
Common Player (1-726)..............12
70 Gary Carter.........................1.25
77 Dave Steib RC......................1.00
482 Rickey Henderson RC......65.00

1981 Topps
Complete Set (726).................65.00
Common Player (1-726)..............06
315 Kirk Gibson RC...................2.50
479 Tim Raines RC....................7.00
700 George Brett......................5.00

1982 Topps
Complete Set (792)...............140.00
Common Player (1-792)..............05
21 Cal Ripken Jr......................90.00
254 Jorge Bell..........................1.00
668 Dale Murphy......................1.00

1983 Topps
Complete Set (792)...............140.00
Common Player (1-792)..............05
49 Willie McGee........................1.00
83 Ryne Sandberg...................25.00
163 Cal Ripken Jr....................22.00

Baseball Collectibles

Collecting Hints: Baseball memorabilia spans a wide range of items that have been produced since baseball became the national pastime more than 100 years ago. This variety has made it more difficult to establish reliable values, leaving it to the individual to identify and determine what price to pay for any particular item. This "value in the eye of the beholder" approach works well for the experienced collector. Novices should solicit the advice of a reliable dealer or an advanced collector before investing heavily. Fluctuating market trends are compounded by the emerging interest in—and inordinately high prices paid for—unique pieces, especially items associated with superstars such as Ty Cobb, Babe Ruth and Mickey Mantle.

Because of the unlimited variety of items available, it is virtually impossible to collect everything. Develop a collecting strategy, concentrating on particular player(s), team(s) or type of collectible(s), such as Hartland Statues or Perez-Steele autographed postcards. A special emphasis allows the collector to become more familiar with the key elements effecting pricing within that area of interest, such as condition and availability and permits building a collection within a prescribed budget.

History: Baseball had its beginnings in the mid 19th century; by 1900, it had become the national pastime. Whether sandlot or big league, baseball was part of most every male's life until the 1950s, when leisure activities expanded in a myriad of directions.

The superstar has always been the key element in the game. Baseball greats were popular visitors at banquets, parades, and, more recently, at baseball autograph shows. They were subjects of extensive newspaper coverage and, with heightened radio and TV exposure, achieved true celebrity status. The impact of baseball on American life has been enormous.

References: Gwen Aldridge, *Baseball Archaeology*, Chronicle Books, 1993; Mark Allen Baker, *All Sport Autograph Guide*, Krause Publications, 1994; ——, *Sports Collectors Digest Baseball Autograph Handbook*, 2nd Edition, Krause Publications, 1991; ——, *Team Baseballs*, Krause Publications, 1992; Don Bevans and Ron Menchine, *Baseball Team Collectibles*, Wallace-Homestead, 1994; ——, *Sports Equipment Price Guide*, Krause Publications, 1995; David

Photo, Hazen "Ki Ki" Cuyler, silvered-wood frame, autographed, 3-1/2" x 5-1/2", $35.

Bushing and Joe Phillips, *Vintage Baseball Bat 1994 Pocket Price Guide*, published by authors (217 Homewood, Libertyville, IL 60048), 1994; ——, *Vintage Baseball Glove Pocket Price Guide, No. 4*, published by authors (217 Homewood, Libertyville, IL 60048), 1996; Bruce Chadwick and David M. Spindel authored a series of books on Major League teams published by Abbeville Press between 1992 and 1995; Douglas Congdon-Martin and John Kashmanian, *Baseball Treasures*, Schiffer Publishing, 1993; Mark Cooper, *Baseball Games*, Schiffer Publishing, 1995; Bruce Kronnick, *Baseball Fan's Complete Guide to Collecting Autographs*, Betterway Publications, 1990; Mark Larson, *Complete Guide to Baseball Memorabilia*, 3rd Edition, Krause Publications, 1996; Mark Larson, Rick Hines and Dave Platta (eds.), *Mickey Mantel Memorabilia*, Krause Publications, 1993; Roderick A. Malloy, *Malloy's Sports Collectibles Value Guide*, Wallace-Homestead, 1993; Michael McKeever, *Collecting Sports Memorabilia*, Alliance Publishing, 1996; Ron Menchine, *Picture Postcard History of Baseball*, Almar Press Book Publishers, 1992; Joe Phillips and Dave Bushing, *Vintage Baseball Glove Price Guide*, published by authors, 1992; Don Raycraft, *Collecting Baseball Player Autographs*, Collector Books, 1991; M. Donald and R. Craig Raycraft, *Val-*

ue Guide to Baseball Collectibles, Collector Books, 1992.

Periodicals: *John L. Raybin's Baseball Autograph News*, 527 Third Ave., #294-A, New York, NY 10016; *Sports Collectors Digest*, 700 E. State St., Iola, WI 54990; *Tuff Stuff*, P.O. Box 1637, Glen Allen, VA 23060.

Collectors' Clubs: Glove Collector, 14057 Rolling Hills Ln., Dallas, TX 75210; Society for American Baseball Research, P.O. Box 93183, Cleveland, OH 44101, members receive *Baseball Research Journal The SABR Bulletin* and *National Pastime*.

Museum: National Baseball Hall of Fame and Museum, Cooperstown, NY.

Reproduction Alert: Autographs and equipment.

Autograph
    Whitey Ford, canceled check...30.00
    Frank Thomas, black
    batting gloves, Reebok, game
    used, sgd in silver 185.00
Badge
    Cincinnati Reds, 3-1/2" celluloid figural baseball, National League Champs in red letters, white ground, black simulated stitching, 1961 ....30.00
    Milwaukee Braves, 3" d, red, white and blue litho, Home of the Braves above tiny pennant banner reading "1957 National League Champions," blue civic slogan "Baseball Capital of the World" 45.00
Bank, baseball shape, glass 40.00
Baseball, autographed
    Leo Durocher,
    Smith & Smiths, 1947 .... 100.00
    Harmon Killebrew 30.00
    Mickey Mantle 300.00
    Joe Nuxhall and teammates of D farm team, Lima, OH, 1945 ...295.00
    Red Sox, AL Champs, 1986, 24 dark signatures 400.00
    Enos Slaughter 20.00
    Ted Williams 200.00
Bat
    Autographed, Hank Aaron, 1973 home run record, H&B Pro Model Bats Clemente 80.00
    Game-used
        Edgardo Alfonzo, Louisville Slugger, cracked..................60.00
        Jay Bell, Louisville Slugger, cracked 590.00
        Rod Carew,H&B, uncracked,

autographed 550.00

Ken Griffey Jr., Louisville Slugger, uncracked, autographed 595.00

Al Martin, Louisville Slugger, cracked 50.00

Mike Piazza, Rawlings by Asics, cracked 475.00

Dale Sveum, Louisville Slugger, cracked 30.00

Frank Thomas 1996 Adirondack, cracked, autographed 450.00

Book, *Inside Baseball for Little Leaguers*, Wonder Book, 6" x 8", paperback, 1958, 64 pgs, black, white and blue, portraits and playing tips from 30 well-known Major League stars 40.00

Bottle Opener, figural, 3" h, silvered brass, figural key chain opener, pitcher, engraved sponsor name "The Coffee Pot" plus street address, 8-16-14 patent date 35.00

Cigar Box Label, 5-1/2" x 9", glossy paper inner lid label, 4-1/2" center image of white baseball, gold letters, black ground, American League Hand Made Perfectos, inscription "Title and Design Registered by Alfonso Rios & Co," early 1900s.40.00

Figure

Set, Hartland, set of 16 orig 8" h statues, 13 autographed, 1958 to 1963 players 5,350.00

Set, LL Rittger, 3 players 275.00

Game, tin, Roger Maris, colorful, 1962 ....85.00

Glove, softball, Sears Roebuck & Co., 1933, orig box.............150.00

Jersey, game-used

Billy Ashley, 1996 Los Angeles, road jersey 395.00

Yogi Berra, 1973 New York Mets, road, autographed...............1,295.00

Brian Downing, 1988 California Angels, road jersey.....................250.00

Steve Garvey, 1985 San Diego Padres, road jersey, autographed 495.00

Gregg Jeffries, 1990 NY Mets, home jersey......................................395.00

Dick Schofield, 1987 California Angels, road jersey 225.00

Magazine

Baseball Magazine, Nov. 1939, DiMaggio, Walters..................100.00

Dedication Shea Stadium Souvenir, New York Mets, 8-1/2" x 11", official program for April 17, 1964, dedication, full-color cover with Mets emblems and 1964-1965 NY World's Fair, 48 glossy pgs 35.00

Sporting News, Babe Ruth cover, at bat for last time........................32.50

Sports Life, Nov. 1948, Ted Williams 40.00

Menu, Chicago White Sox, 5" x 6-1/2" velveteen cardboard folder, cord binding holding 4-pg menu by Chicago and Alton Railroad for Chicago White Sox passengers en route to spring training in San Antonio, TX, Feb. 21, 1931, inside cover lists all players, menu options, back cover with schedule of exhibition games, dark green cover with silver and black design 150.00

Mug, baseball shape, figural handle, batter holds bat, fielder holds glove, pottery, price for pr 120.00

Nodder, 7-1/2" h, Oakland A's, 1974, orig box....................................45.00

Pass, Chicago Cub's, child's, 2-1/2" x 4" black on pink paper slip, 1950, Wrigley Field, 1" bright red, white and blue litho pinback button, inscribed "Chicago Cubs Junior Booster Club" 30.00

Pen and Pencil Set, Brooklyn Dodgers, "National League" in oval on barrel, facsimile Pee Wee Reese signature, 1940s....................150.00

Photograph, autographed, Mickey Mantle, color, rookie 450.00

Pinback Button

Baltimore Orioles, red, white and blue litho, 1960s..............................20.00

Brooklyn Dodgers, blue and white, 1950s 25.00

Chicago Cubs/Brown, Sweet Caporal Cigarettes, brown and white, orig back paper, c1910-11, 7/8" d...18.00

Chicago White Sox/1959 Champs, red, white and blue litho, American League championship..............25.00

Leroy "Satchel" Paige, early photo portrait....................................150.00

Longest Game Played, red, white, blue, yellow litho, Big League Leader series, text for game Boston vs. Brooklyn/26 Innings/May 1, 1920, 13/16"..............................45.00

Milwaukee Braves/World Champs, red, white and blue litho, 1957 World Champs banner 25.00

New York Giants, blue and red bands, 1950s 20.00

New York Giants/Bridwell, Sweet Caporal Cigarettes, brown and white, orig back paper, c1910-11, 7/8" d......................18.00

Our Bums, nickname for Brooklyn Dodgers, black letters, white ground, red rim, 1930s, 2-1/2" d............85.00

Peach Baseball Scores, blue-rimmed litho, white letters, blue-tone portrait of Grover Cleveland Alexander over-

laid on peach-colored fruit image, mid-1920s 85.00

Philadelphia Phillies, red, white, blue, flesh tones, 1960s....................25.00

Pittsburgh Pirates/Camnitz, Sweet Caporal Cigarettes, brown and white, orig back paper, c1910-11, 7/8" d, design off-center 15.00

Sherlock's Henline-Catcher, Toledo, Mrs. Sherlock's Home Made Bread, black and white, red letters, 1933 ....30.00

Washington Nationals, red, white and blue litho, early 1960s..............15.00

Washington Senators/Street, Sweet Caporal Cigarettes, brown and white, orig back paper, c1910-11, 7/8" d......................18.00

Program

All Star Game, Houston, 1986 ...3.00

Cleveland-Boston World Series, 1948, 9" x 12", official program, Cleveland Indians home game, 32 pgs, individual player black-and white-photos and profiles, center scorecard blank 90.00

Plate, Mickey Mantle, dinner size .65.00

Scoring Tablet, 2" x 3-3/4", Spaulding, white celluloid mechanical scorer, hits, runs, errors, innings, outs for both teams, reverse has baseball-like logo of AG Spaulding & Brothers, late 1890s................................80.00

Silhouette, boys baseball game, framed, 1927 ....30.00

Tab, on orig card, Baseball Hero series, 2" x 2-1/2" card, 7/8" litho tin tab, blue, white and flesh tone

Pinback button, Los Angeles Dodgers, celluloid, blue letters, white ground, blue and white ribbons, 1-3/4" d, $2.50.

Hank Greenberg,
Detroit Tigers.............................30.00
Irving "Bump" Hadley,
New York Yankees....................25.00
Ticket Stub, World Series,
Yankee logo...........................295.00
Yearbook
Brooklyn Dodgers, 1954, 8-1/2" x 10-3/4", authorized yearbook, Big League Book series, front cover cartoon art by Williard Mullin, 48 pgs, orig envelope............................75.00
The Reds, 1947, 8-1/2" x 11", official club yearbook, b&w cover photo of Cincinnati Reds pitching stars Bucky Walters and Ewell Blackwell, 40 pgs, worn spine..................25.00

Basketball Collectibles

Collecting Hints: The NBA is trying hard to make collectors out of all their fans. Enjoy the hoopla as more and more collectibles are being generated. Save those programs, promotional pieces and giveaways. Collectors should pay careful attention to the growing interest in women's collegiate basketball and the enthusiasm t's creating, as well as the new women's professional leagues.

History: The game of basketball originated in Springfield, MA, in 1891, under the direction of Dr. James Naismith of the YMCA. Schools and colleges soon adopted the game and it began to spread worldwide.

Basketball was added to the Olympic games in 1936. The National Basketball Association was founded in 1949 after professional teams became popular. Today, the NBA has nearly 30 teams. Basketball is generally considered to be an indoor game, but almost every town in America has some place where locals gather to shoot a few hoops.

References: Mark Allen Baker, *All Sport Autograph Guide*, Krause Publications, 1994; James Beckett, *Official Price Guide to Basketball Cards*, 6th Edition, House of Collectibles, 1996; David Bushing, *Sports Equipment Price Guide*, Krause Publications, 1995; Roderick A. Malloy, *Malloy's Guide to Sports Cards Values*, Wallace-Homestead, 1995; ———, *Malloy's Sports Collectibles Value Guide*, Wallace-Homestead, 1994;

Michael McKeever, *Collecting Sports Memorabilia*, Alliance Publishing, 1966; *Standard Catalog of Football, Basketball & Hockey Cards*, 2nd edition, Krause Publications, 1996.

Periodicals: *Sports Collectors Digest*, 700 E. State St., Iola, WI 54990.

Advertisement, 6-3/4" x 11", b&w glossy, proof sheet for Larry Bird's first McDonald's endorsement 25.00
Autographed photo
Charles Barkley........................50.00
Larry Bird 55.00
Wilt Chamberlain.....................60.00
Juwon Howard 25.00
Magic Johnson.........................75.00
Michael Jordan......................110.00
Jamal Mashburn 30.00
Gary Payton 25.00
David Robinson.........................35.00
Badge, Harlem Globetrotters, 3-1/2" d, celluloid, full-color team photo, white ground, blue letters, small gold stars, c1970 ....20.00
Basketball, autographed
Walt Frazier,
indoor/outdoor ball 70.00
Shawn Kemp,
official game ball 100.00
Jason Kidd,
synthetic Spalding ball 80.00
Magic Johnson,
official game ball 250.00
O'Neal, Shaw 160.00
Canceled check, Bob Cousy 50.00
Jersey, autographed
Magic Johnson......................325.00
Michael Jordan, red 895.00
Magazine
Basketball Digest, Nov. 1980, Larry Bird on cover.............................15.00
NBA Hoop Today, Nov. 1984, Larry Bird in Celtic warm-up on cover 15.00
Spectacular Magazine, Oct. 1979, Terre Haute, IN, Larry Bird illus cover 35.00
Sports Illustrated
Bird and Cheerleaders, Nov. 1977 ....45.00
Willis Reed, Pete Maravich on cover, 1970 ....2.00
Magnet, Larry Bird retirement, 4" x 8" picture of Bird shooting, facsimile autograph, 1993 ....18.00
Program
Boston Globe Basketball Clinic, directed by Red Auerbach, instructions by Bob Cousy, John Havlicek, Sam Jones and Clyde Lovellette, 14 pgs, autographed 20.00

Harlem Globetrotters, 1964 .....45.00
NBA All-Star Game, Philadelphia, Wilt Chamberlain 225.00
Retirement, Kevin McHale, Jan. 1994, McHale vs. Lakers cover, full ticket, mini replica banner 50.00
Shoes, game used, dual autograph
Marcus Camby, Nike Air Force, Jan. 25th game 150.00
Patrick Ewing, "Ewing" embroidered on back 395.00
Tim Hardaway, Nike Air Flight, "M.E.E." written on each 125.00
Larry Johnson, Converse.......195.00
Shawn Kemp, Reebok 395.00
Alonzo Mourning,
Nike Air Force 300.00
Bryant Reeves, Warner Brothers, "50 BC" sewn on 95.00
Steve Smith, Reebok 150.00
Yearbook
Boston Celtics, 1974-75, Silas/Chaney cover, Dick Raphael photos 35.00
Chicago Bulls, 1984-85, 160 pgs, Orlando Woolridge and Michael Jordan on cover 95.00
World Champion Boston Celtics, 1981-82, Larry Bird jump shot vs. Julius Erving cover..................25.00

Battery Operated Automata

Collecting Hints: Prices fluctuate greatly, but operating condition is a key factor. Many pieces were originally made with accessory parts; these must be present for full value to be realized. The original box, especially if it has a label, adds 10% to 20% to the price. Also, the more elaborate the action, the higher the value. Many collectors live in Japan and dealers must allow enough margin to ship pieces overseas.

History: Battery-operated automata began as inexpensive Japanese imports in the 1950s. They were meant for amusement only, many ending up on the shelves of bars in the recreation rooms of private homes. They were marketed through five & dime stores and outlets. The subjects were animals—bears being favored—and humans. Quality of pieces varies greatly, with Linemar items being among the best made.

Reference: Don Hultzman, "Battery

Operated Toys," in Richard O'Brien's, *Collecting Toys*, Krause Publications, 1997.

Balloon Vender, 4-1/2" x 7" x 12", litho tin, vinyl, clown-type face, body moves, hand shakes metal bell, holds 4 plastic balls on wire rods, Yone, Japan 100.00

Brewster the Rooster, Marx..........45.00

Bubble Blowing Monkey, Wolverine, orig box................150.00

Burger Chef, 6" x 6-1/2" x 9", litho tin, fabric, plush, dog cooking hamburger, brick-grill litho base, red plastic burner which lights up, 1 hand cooks and flips hamburger, other holds salt shaker, eyes move up and down, brown plush ears move, Yone, Japan 125.00

Electric Open Car, lever on dash makes car go forward and back, litho on dashboard, tin body, rubber wheels, 2 seats, MIB...........................195.00

Fire Chief Car, blinking red light on top, MIB.....................120.00

Fireman, 4-1/2" x 6-1/2", multicolored litho tin, 3 metal ladder sections extend to 25", 4 metal wheels, center with bright red and orange scene of 8 firemen fighting fire, 7" litho tin fireman climbs up and down ladder, Sonsco, Japan, c1950 ....160.00

Gypsy Fortune Teller, 6" x 7" x 11", fabric, black outfit, red trim, pearls, molded vinyl face and hands, holds sheet of red fabric, white plastic ball, black and red printed fortunes, dark-red tin base, coin inserted, gypsy nods head, eyes light, arm moves and delivers card, multicolored orig box, Ichida, Japan 900.00

Haunted House Mystery Bank, 7" x 9" x 8", multicolored house, gray plastic roof and base, litho tin sides, coin goes in doorstep, light goes on above door, door opens, ghostly figure appears and retrieves coin, Brumberger, Brooklyn, c1960 375.00

Highway Patrol Police Car, blinking red light on top, MIB.....................75.00

Horse Racing, 6-1/2" x 19-1/2" x 3", plastic, 6 small brown horses ridden by multicolored tin jockeys, tin and cardboard "Horse racing" sign post, orig box, Shinsei, Japan, c1970 .....45.00

Lincoln-Continental Mark V with Retractable Roof, 4" x 11" x 13", litho tin, multicolored detailed int, black, white and red wheels, tin grills and bumpers, red plastic cov wire to remote-control battery box, multicolored orig box, Cragston Toys, Japan 475.00

Magic Snowman, 5" x 7" x 11-1/2", white fabric, bright red facial accents and gloves, light brown scarf, holding tin-handled broom and brass bell, stream of air blows out top of hat and keeps small Styrofoam ball in air, eyes light, broom waves, orig instruction sheet, gold-colored box with cellophane window, black lettering, orig foil sticker, Modern Toys, Japan, c1960 ....225.00

McGregor, puffs lighted cigar, stands up and sits down on tin trunk, MIB 195.00

Mercedes Benz, tin, red, blinking rear window, logo on front and wheels, MIB......................95.00

Merry Go Round, white action, 3 children in teacups on saucers 175.00

Miss Friday, The Typist, 5-1/2" x 8-1/2" x 7-12", litho tin, vinyl, fabric, secretary seated at tin desk, vinyl hands move up and down on tin typewriter, roller moves to left and right with bell sound, tin upper body, vinyl head and arms, rooted blond ponytail, black, white and pink fabric skirt, Japan, MIB 275.00

Musical Rabbit, litho metal, beats drum, orig box, Japan.........................45.00

Piggy Cook, flips tin ham and egg from pan over stove, pours pepper from other hand, MIB.....................225.00

Police Car, Highway Patrol, blinking red light on top, MIB 120.00

Poodle, 4" x 11" x 10", white plush, bright red, gray and yellow plaid body, pink neck box, walks and wags tail as eyes light up, c1950 ....95.00

Robot, monster, helmet opens and closes, growing red-lighted dragon, MIB..............................95.00

Santa, ringing bell, Alps, orig box..75.00

Squirrel, 3" x 5" x 6", litho tin, brown and yellow, blue and white apron, moves forward to bring metal walnut to mouth, mouth opens, large black, white and brown eyes move, brown rubber ears, brown plush tail, multicolored orig box, Stone Mountain, Japan, distributed by Cragston, c1950 ....75.00

Taxi Cab, doors open and shut, passengers inside, red light on top, moving meter 120.00

Weaver, Charlie, shakes cocktail mixer, pours and takes drink, smacks lips, smoke comes from ears, MIB 120.00

Bauer Pottery

Collecting Hints: Bauer pieces range in style from Art Deco to Streamlined Modern. Focus on highly stylistic, designer forms; interest in utilitarian redware and stoneware pieces is minimal.

Remember that jiggered and cast production pieces were made in large quantities. Unfortunately, hand-thrown pieces by Matt Carlton and Fred Johnson, which were made in limited numbers, are not marked. Learn to identify them by studying photographs of known examples. Among the more desirable shapes are oil jars—the taller the jar, the higher the price.

Some colors of dinnerware are more highly prized than others. Premium prices are paid for burgundy, orange-red and white pieces in all patterns.

History: In 1885, John Bauer founded the Paducah Pottery in Paducah, KY, to manufacture stoneware and earthenware utilitarian pieces such as crocks and jugs. Bauer died in 1898 and John Andrew Bauer continued the business in Paducah until 1909, at which time the plant was moved to Los Angeles. Bauer's initial California production consisted of redware flowerpots. Stoneware production did not resume immediately after the move to California because of the difficulty of locating suitable stoneware clay. Utilitarianware such as bean pots and mixing bowls remained a company staple.

In 1913, Matt Carlton, an Arkansas potter, and Louis Ipsen, a Danish designer, developed an art-

Captain Blushwell, litho tin and cloth, fuzz hair, mfg by "Y," Japanese, orig box, 11" h, $50.

ware line of glazed bowls, jardinieres and vases. The company won a bronze medal at the Panama-California Exposition of 1915-16, but within a short time period, the firm's artware was replaced by a line of molded stoneware vases.

In 1922, John Andrew Bauer died. Just prior to his death, he established a partnership with Watson E. Brockmon, his son-in-law. The firm prospered under Brockmon's leadership. In the early 1930s the company introduced a line of popular dinnerware designed by Ipsen and covered with glazes developed by Victor Houser, a ceramic engineer. In 1931, "Ring" ware was introduced to contrast with the plain ware of the previous year. Eventually, more than 100 different shapes and sizes were manufactured in table and kitchenwares. Brusche Contempo (1948-61), La Linda (1939-59), Monterey (1936-45) and Monterey Moderne (1948-1961) were some of the more successful tableware lines. Ipsen's Aladdin teapot design was part of the Glass Pastel Kitchenware series.

The company continued operations during World War II, reformulating the glazes to correspond to wartime restrictions. Wheel-thrown artware featuring the designs of Carlton and Fred Johnson was made and cast forms were kept in production. Tracy Irwin, a designer, developed a modern line of floral containers. Following the war, the company faced stiff competition in the national, as well as in the California market. A bitter strike in 1961 signaled the end; in 1962, W.E. Brockmon's widow closed the plant.

References: Susan and Al Bagdade, *Warman's American Pottery and Porcelain*, Wallace-Homestead, 1994; Jack Chipman, *Collector's Encyclopedia of California Pottery*, Collector Books, 1992, 1995 value update; Lois Lehner, *Lehner's Encyclopedia of U.S. Marks on Pottery, Porcelain & Clay*, Collector Books, 1988.

Artware
    Model, cowboy hat, yellow 125.00
    Vase
        9" h, gold trim 45.00
        10" h, Matt Carlton 395.00

Atlanta
    Mixing Bowl, cobalt blue,
      No. 24 ....65.00
Cal-Art, vase, 12" h,
    No. 508, white 65.00
Cookie Jar, cov, Pink Fish..........225.00
Kitchenware, Gloss Pastel
    Bowl, 11-1/2" l, 2-3/4" h,
      light green 25.00
    Casserole, cov
        1 qt......................................45.00
        1-1/2 pt................................35.00
La Linda
    Ashtray, 4" sq, cobalt blue 25.00
    Tumbler, chartreuse,
      price for set of six.....................95.00
Moderntone, sugar, no cov 12.00
Monterey
    Butter Dish, cov
        Ivory 65.00
        Red 85.00
    Teapot, cov, yellow 145.00
Ring-Ware
    Batter Bowl, yellow................35.00
    Bowl, 10" d, green....................50.00
    Butter Dish, cov
        Delph, light blue 135.00
        Green................................130.00
        Red 165.00
    Candleholder, yellow................20.00
    Canister, wood lid, oval,
      orange, "Coffee" 80.00
    Casserole, cov, individual size
        Green..................................55.00
        Red, wood frame 60.00
    Chop Plate
        12" d, red 75.00
        14" d, green 75.00
        17" d, greed 225.00
    Coffee Server, red,
      copper handle 65.00
    Cookie Jar, cov, red 695.00
    Creamer
        Delph, light blue 35.00
        Ivory 125.00
        Red 35.00
    Mixing Bowl
        5" d, No. 36, yellow..............15.00
        7" d, No. 24, blue 20.00
        8" d, No. 12, turquoise 40.00
        10" d, No. 9, black..............250.00
    Mug, barrel
        Jade 300.00
        Yellow 300.00
    Plate
        7-1/2" d, salad, mixed
        colors, set of six.................100.00
        9" d
          Red 20.00
          Yellow 15.00

        10-1/2" d, dinner
          Black 75.00
          Red 50.00
          White..................................75.00
    Salt and Pepper Shakers,
      pr, black, short 95.00
    Sherbet, ftd, yellow 35.00
    Spice Jar, red, 3 qt................595.00
    Sugar, cov, ivory 125.00
    Sugar Shaker, jade 350.00
    Teapot, cov
        Cobalt blue 135.00
        Cobalt blue, 6 cup.............350.00
        Red 150.00
        Rust, Hi-Fire line.................60.00
    Tumbler, black, 6 oz,
      wood handle 60.00
    Water Set, carafe and 6 tumblers,
      wood handles, red and yellow tumblers, price for set 250.00

Beatles

Collecting Hints: Beatles collectibles date from 1964 to the present. The majority of memorabilia items were produced from 1964 to 1968. The most valuable items are marked "NEMS." Most collectors are interested in mint or near mint items only, although some items in very good condition, especially if scarce, have considerable value.

Each year, Sotheby's holds one or two auctions that include Beatles memorabilia, primarily one-of-a-kind items such as guitars and stage costumes. The average collector generally does not participate in these sales since the items command high prices.

History: The fascination with the Beatles began in 1964. Soon the whole country was caught up in Beatlemania. The members of the group included John Lennon, Paul McCartney, George Harrison and Ringo Starr. The group broke up in 1970, after which the members pursued individual musical careers. Beatlemania took on new life after the death of John Lennon in 1980.

References: Jeff Augsburger, Marty Eck and Rick Rann, *Beatles Memorabilia Price Guide*, 3rd Edition, Antique Trader Books, 1997; Perry Cox and Joe Lindsay, *Official Pride Guide to the Beatles*, House of Collectibles, 1995; Michael Stern, Barbara Crawford and Hollis Lamon, *The Beatles*, Collector Books, 1994.

Periodicals: *Beatlefan*, P.O. Box 33515, Decatur, GA 30033; *Instant Karma*, P.O. Box 256, Sault Ste. Marie, MI 49783.

Collectors' Clubs: Beatles Connection, P.O. Box 1066, Pinellas Park, FL 34665; Beatles Fan Club, 397 Edgewood Ave., New Haven, CT 06511; Beatles Fan Club of Great Britain, Superstore Productions, 123 Marina, St. Leonards on Sea, East Sussex, England TN38 OBN; Working Class Hero Club, 3311 Niagara St., Pittsburgh, PA 15213.

Reproduction Alert: Records, picture sleeves and album jackets have been counterfeited. Sound quality may be poorer on the records and printing on labels and picture jackets usually is inferior to the original. Many pieces of memorabilia have been reproduced, often with some change in size, color or design.

Animation Cel, *Yellow Submarine,* goatee on celluloid, group of eight, certificates of authenticity, King Features Studio, 1968 ....2,600.00
Apron, paper, white, black pictures, name and song titles 75.00
Autograph, 4" x 4-1/2", ink and pencil signatures of each Beatle, inscribed "XXX Beatles" in McCartney's hand...............1,265.00
Bag, 9-1/2" x 10", textured vinyl, red, portraits, black inscription and signatures, cord carrying strap, 1964...............165.00
Bank, 7-1/2" h, plastic, Yellow Submarine, bust figures of each Beatle, 1960s, price for set of 4, minor damage.....................1,400.00
Banner, printed nylon, black images of 4 Beatles, blue printed "The Beatles," Memphis, 1966...................1,150.00
Beach Towel, 34" x 57", terry cloth, Beatles in bathing suits, c1960 .....115.00
Billfold, red, 4 white signatures on 1 side, picture on other........................90.00
Blanket, 62" x 80", wool, tan, printed black and red bust figures and instruments, "The Beatles" center, mfg by Whitney............................165.00
Book, *Yellow Submarine*, Signet Book, Oct. 1968, paperback, 128 pgs20.00
Button, cartoon type, price for set of four 15.00
Calendar, 12" x 12", spiral bound, 1969, Golden Press, orig brown paper

envelope....................................65.00
Cake Decorating Kit, figurals, playing instruments, set of 4, MIB 195.00
Christmas Tree Ornament, 7" h, blown glass, figural, 3 in red, 1 in blue, 3 plastic guitars, c1960............925.00
Coaster, 4" sq, Yellow Submarine, cardboard, set of 12 ....65.00
Coat Hangers, Yellow Submarine, set 295.00
Coin Holder, 3" x 2", plastic, red, faces and names on front, squeeze to open......................12.00
Coloring Book, 8-1/4" x 11", Saalfield, Nems 1964, includes 8 b&w photos, unused..65.00
Drum, 14" d, red sparkle finish, "The Beatles Drum" on skin, metal stand, mfg by Mastro....................325.00
Figure, 6-1/2" h, painted and glazed plaster, set of four, 1960s......150.00
Game, Flip Your Wig, Milton Bradley, 1964 ....90.00
Handkerchief, 8-1/2" sq.................20.00
Lunch Kit, Yellow Submarine, metal, matching thermos, King-Seeley, 1968 ....220.00
Magazine Cover and Story
   Life, August 6, 1981, Yoko story 13.00
   Saturday Evening Post, Aug. 27, 1966, Beatles in matador costumes, 6-pg spread, full-page photos, British Empire medals.........................35.00
   Sixteen, Aug. 1966...................15.00
   Teen World, July 1965.............15.00
   Time, Dec. 22, 1980, John Lennon 10.00
Mug, 4" h, 3" d, ceramic, bust photos of group wearing blue jackets, England, c1964.......................................85.00
Nodder, 8" h, light blue suits, standing on

Record Case, Disk-Go-Case, plastic, olive green ground, black figures, white handle, black base, "1966 by NEMS Enterprises, Ltd.," Charter Industries, Inc., NY, 8-1/4" h, $75.

gold base, sgd on base, c1964, price for set of four 370.00
Notebook, three-ring binder, red vinyl cover, Standard Plastic Products 135.00
Paddle Ball Game 100.00
Pencil Case, 8" x 3-1/2", vinyl, blue, group picture and facsimile autographs, zipper top, Standard Plastic Products 35.00
Pennant, 23" l, felt, white, red and black, printed illus and facsimile signatures, red trim and streamers, Official Licensee, 1964 ....80.00
Photograph, 20" sq, Sgt. Pepper's Lonely Hearts Club Band cover shot, Beatles in different poses, image of Bowery Boy Leo Gorcey 400.00
Pin, guitar shape, 1964, set of 4, MOC 65.00
Print, Shea Stadium, canvas, 1965..........................55.00
Program, tour, Beatles pictured on playing cards, 1964 British tour, minor folds...........................230.00
Puzzle, Yellow Submarine, MIB....55.00
Record, "Got to Get You into My Life," 45 rpm 10.00
Ring, flasher type, 1960s, set of 4 ....25.00
School Bag, 12" x 9" x 3-1/2", tan, "The Beatles" printed on flap, handle and shoulder strap 215.00
Scrapbook, NEMS, 1964 ....50.00
Sheet Music, *Day Tripper*, 1964 ...20.00
Soap Container, 10" h, plastic, Ringo, removable head, Colgate-Palmolive Co., 1965 Nems 85.00
Sunglasses, plastic, black, green lenses, Solarex 25.00
Sweatshirt, white, NEMS, 1963 ..150.00
T-Shirt, Beatles '65, size large 17.00
Tile, 6" sq, ceramic, group picture, "The Beatles," mfg by Carter Tiles...85.00
Window Card, Hard Days Night, band performing 150.00

Beer Bottles

Collecting Hints: Beer bottles often are found by digging in old dumps or wells. Although these bottles may be discolored and flaked, the key is whether or not they are broken. Damage to the bottle is of greater concern in pricing than the discoloration. Concentrate on the bottles from one brewery or area. When an example is sold in the area in which it originated, it is likely to command more money than when sold outside that local region

Over the years, breweries usually changed bottle styles several times. This also is true for the paper labels found on later bottles. Early bottles had special closures and a bottle is worth more if the closure is intact. Presence of the metal caps is not critical to the value of later bottles. However, collecting metal caps is a growing field.

History: Breweries began in America shortly after the arrival of the first settlers. By the mid-19th century, most farmsteads had a small brewery on them. Local breweries dominated the market until the arrival of Prohibition. The majority of breweries closed although a few larger ones survived. When Prohibition ended, a much smaller number of local breweries renewed production. The advertising, distribution and production costs of the 1950s and 1960s led to the closing of most local breweries and the merger of many other breweries into a few national companies.

In the 1960s, imported beers from Europe entered the American market. Some companies signed licensing agreements to produce these foreign labels in the United States. In more recent years, beers brewed in Canada and Mexico have been gaining popularity.

Pilser Brewing Co., Inc., Bronx, NY, Pilser's Maltcrest Brew, 12 oz, $7.

References: Ralph and Terry Kovel, *Kovels' Bottles Price List*, 10th Edition, Crown Publishers, 1996; Jim Megura, *Official Price Guide to Bottles*, 11th Edition, House of Collectibles, 1991; Michael Polak, *Bottles*, Avon Books, 1994.

Collectors' Club: American Breweriana Association, Inc., P.O. Box 11157, Pueblo, CO 81001.

Embossed
    Buffalo Brewing Co.,
    Sacramento, CA, emb buffalo jumping through horseshoe, 12" h, amber, blob top 20.00
    Callie & Co., Limited,
    emb dog's head, St. Helens below center, 8-1/4" h, dark green, ring-type blob top 20.00
    Cumberland Brew Co.,
    Cumberland, MD, amber..........10.00
    Excelsior, 9-1/4" h, aqua..........18.00
    Hand Brew Co.,
    Pawtucket, RI, aqua.................15.00
    Iroquois, Buffalo, Indian's
    head, amber.............................12.00
    McCormick Brewery, Boston,
    1897, clear 12.00
    Piel Bros., East New York Brewery, fancy logo, aqua......................18.00
    Royal Ruby, ABM, 9-1/2" h 24.00
Painted Label
    Augusta Brewing Co.,
    Augusta, CA, 7" h, aqua...........15.00
    Cock 'n' Bull Ginger Beer,
    7" h, crow top 6.00
    Rolling Rock Extra Pale,
    blue and white label, green label, unopened 20.00
    Schlitz Brewing Co.,
    9-1/2" h, amber 10.00
Paper Label
    Central Brand Extra Lager Beer,
    9-1/4" h, aqua............................6.60
    Cooks 500 Ale, 9-1/2" h, aqua ...5.00
    Diamond Jim's Beer,
    9-1/4" h, aqua............................6.50
    Grand Prize Beer, Gulf Brewing Co., Houston, 9" h, clear, crown top ..9.00
    Pabst Extract, amber, 2 labels .12.00
    Southern Brewing Co., machine made, 9-1/2" h, green 4.00
Stoneware
    Biscomb's, 8-1/2" h,
    brown and tan 15.00
    Ginger Beer, c1915..................35.00
    Russell's...................................40.00

Beer Cans

Collecting Hints: Rusted and dented cans have little value unless they are rare examples. Most collectors remove the beer from the cans. Cans should be opened from the bottom to preserve the unopened top. As beer can collecting became popular, companies issued special collectors' cans that never contained beer. Many were bought on speculation; value has been shaky.

History: Before Prohibition, beer was stored and shipped in kegs and dispensed in returnable bottles. When the Prohibition Act was repealed in 1933, only 700 of 1,700 breweries resumed operation. Expanding distribution created the need for an inexpensive container that would permit beer to be stored longer and shipped safely. Cans were the answer. The first patent for a lined can was issued to the American Can Co., on Sept. 25, 1934, for their Keglined process. Gotfried Kruger Brewing Co., Newark, NJ, was the first brewery to use the can. Pabst was the first major company to join the canned-beer movement.

Continental Can Co. introduced the cone-top beer can in 1935; Schlitz was the first brewery to use this type of can. The next major change in beer can design was the aluminum pop-top in 1962.

References: Bill Mugrage, *Official Price Guide to Beer Cans*, 5th Edition, House of Collectibles, 1993; Thomas Toepfer, *Beer Cans*, L-W Book Sales, 1976, 1995 value update.

Collectors' Clubs: Beer Can Collectors of America, 747 Merus Ct.,

Left: Croft Champagne Ale, Crown Brewing Co., Cranston, RI, $75; right: Genessee Ale, Genessee Brewing Co., Rochester, NY, $50.

Fenton, MO 63026; Capitol City Chapter of the Beer Can Collectors of America, P.O. Box 287, Brandywine, MD 20613; Gambrinus Chapter of the Beer Can Collectors of America, 985 Maebelle Way, Westerville, OH 43081.

Museum: The Museum of Beverage Containers and Advertising, Goddlettsville, TN.

Note: Listings follow this order: name, type of beer, brewery location, top identification, price.

Abbreviations: The following abbreviations are used in the listings:

CR: Crowntainer-type cone top

CT: cone type

FT: flat top

ML: malt liquor

PT: pull top

7 oz

Ace Hi ML, Ace, Chicago, IL FT ..115.00
Lucky Lager, Lucky Lager,
    San Francisco, CA, FT 12.00
Olympia Light, Olympia,
    Olympia, WA, PT 8.50
Rolling Rock, Latrobe,
    Latrobe, PA, PT 4.50

8 oz

Bantam, Goebel, Detroit, MI, FT ...27.50
Colt 45 ML, National, 4 cities, PT 2.00
French 76 ML, National,
    Baltimore, MD, PT 50.00
Goebel Ale, Goebel,
    Detroit, MI, FT 35.00
Tech Premium, Pittsburgh,
    Pittsburgh, PA, FT 60.00

10 oz

Budweiser, Anheuser-Busch,
    7 cities, PT 5.00
Fabacher Brau, Jackson,
    New Orleans, LA, PT 12.00
Schaefer, Schaefer, 3 cities, PT 3.50

11 and 12 oz

ABC Ale, Wagner,
    Columbus, OH, PT 4.00
Acme, Acme,
    Los Angeles, CA, FT 18.00
Atlas, National, Detroit, MI, FT 40.00
Balboa, Southern,
    Los Angeles, CA, FT 150.00
Ballantine, P Ballantine,
    Newark, NJ, PT 5.00
Berghoff, Berghoff,
    Ft Wayne, IN, FT 75.00
Brau Haus Premium Lager, FT ...100.00

Breuing's, Rice Lake,
    Rice Lake, WI, FT 7.50
Butte Special, Butte,
    Butte, MT, FT 25.00
Chief Oshkosh, Oshkosh,
    Oshkosh, WI, FT 12.00
Crown Darby, Westminister,
    Chicago, IL, FT.....................215.00
Drewry's Oldstock Ale, Drewrys, South
    Bend, IN, FT 40.00
Dutch Treat, Dutch Treat,
    Phoenix, AZ, PT 2.50
Eastside Old Tap, Pabst,
    Los Angeles, CA, FT 15.00
Fisher Light, General,
    2 cities, PT 2.00
Gablinger's, Forrest,
    New Bedford, MA, PT 6.50
Gettleman, Gettleman,
    Milwaukee, WI, FT 25.00
Hamm's, Hamm, St. Paul,
    MN, PT 4.00
Heidelbrau, Heileman,
    LaCrosse, WI, PT 2.50
Horlacher Pilsner, Horlacher, Allentown,
    PA, FT 10.00
Kentucky ML, Fehr,
    Louisville, KY, FT 45.00
Manheim, Reading,
    Reading, PA, FT 12.00
Milwaukee's Best, Miller,
    Milwaukee, WI, PT 6.50
National Bohemian, National,
    Detroit, MI, FT 15.00
North Star, Associated,
    3 cities, PT 4.00
Old Crown Ale, Centilgre,
    Ft Wayne, IN, FT 50.00
Pearl Draft, Pearl, 2 cities, PT.........1.00
Queens Brau, Queen City,
    Cumberland, MD, FT 55.00
Red Top, Drewrys, South Bend,
    IN, PT 10.00
Royal Amber, Heileman,
    4 cities, PT 2.50
Schiltz Light, Schlitz, 6 cities, PT 1.00
Stein Haus, Schell,
    New Ulm, MN, PT 4.00
Tavern Pale, Atlantic,
    Chicago, IL, FT 30.00
Topper, Eastern, Hammonton,
    NJ, PT 4.00
Tudor Ale, Cumberland,
    Cumberland, MD, PT................2.00
Utica Club Pale Ale, West End,
    Utica, NY, FT 50.00
Valley Forge, Valley Forge,
    Norristown, PA, FT 20.00
Walter's Light, Walter,
    Pueblo, CO, PT 4.00
West Virginia Pilsner, Little Switzerland,
    Huntington, WV, PT 5.00

Yuengling, Yuengling,
    Pottsville, PA, PT 5.00

12 oz, Cone Top

Aero Club Pale Select, East Idaho,
    Pocatello, ID 125.00
Breuing's Lager, Rice Lake, Rice Lake,
    WI 65.00
Dawson's Pale Ale, Dawson, New
    Bedford, MA 45.00
Falstaff, Falstaff, 3 cities 30.00
Grain Belt Golden Premium, Minneapolis, Minneapolis, MN 40.00
Menominee Champion, Menominee-
    Marinette, Menominee, MI 65.00
Rahr's, Rahr's Green Bay,
    Green Bay, WI.........................55.00
Stag Premium Dry, Griesedieck-
    Western, 2 cities......................35.00
Ye Tavern, Lafayette,
    Lafayette, IN 95.00

15 and 16 oz

Altes, National, Detroit, MI, PT........5.00
Burger, Burger,
    Cincinnati, OH, PT 30.00
Champagne Velvet,
    Associated, 3 cities, PT 12.00
Eastside Old Tap, Pabst,
    Los Angeles, CA, FT 18.00
Hamm's Draft, Hamm,
    3 cities, PT 5.00
Mustang Malt Lager, Pittsburgh,
    Pittsburgh, PA, PT 25.00
Old German, Easter,
    Hammonton, NJ, PT.................5.00
Piels Light, Piels,
    Brooklyn, NY, FT 25.00
Spur Stout ML, Sick's Rainer, Seattle,
    WA, PT 50.00
Whale's White Ale, National,
    4 cities, PT 35.00

Bicycles

Collecting Hints: Collectors divide bicycles into two groups—antique and classic. The antique category includes early high wheelers through safety bikes made into the 1920s and 1930s. Highly stylized bicycles from the 1930s and 1940s represent the transitional step to the classic period, beginning in the late 1940s and running through the end of the balloon-tire era.

Unfortunately, there are no reliable guide books for the beginning collector. A good rule is that any older bike in good condition is worth collecting. Restoration is an accepted practice, but never pay a high price for a bicycle that is rusted, incomplete or repaired with non-original parts. Replacement of leather seats or rubber handle bars does not effect value since these have a short life.

Make certain to store an old bicycle high (hung by its frame to protect the tires) and dry (humidity should be no higher than 50%). Do not forget all the secondary material that features bicycles, e.g., advertising premiums, brochures, catalogs and posters. This material provides important historical data for research, especially for restoration. Bicycle collectors and dealers gather each year on the last weekend in April at the Saline/Ann Arbor Swap Meet and Show in Michigan.

History: In 1818, Baron Karl von Drais, a German, invented the Draisienne, a push scooter, that is viewed as the "first" bicycle. In 1839, Patrick MacMillan, a Scot, added a treadle system; a few years later, Pierre Michaux, a Frenchman, revolutionized the design by adding a pedal system. The bicycle was introduced in America at the 1876 Centennial.

Early bicycles were high wheelers with a heavy iron frame and two disproportionately sized wheels with wooden rims and tires. The exaggerated front wheel was for speed, the small rear wheel for balance. James Starley, an Englishman, is responsible for developing a bicycle with two wheels of equal size. Pedals drove the rear wheels by means of a chain and sprocket. By 1892, wooden rim wheels were replaced by pneumatic air-filled tires; these were followed by standard rubber tires with inner tubes. The coaster brake was developed in 1898. This important milestone made cycling a true family sport. Bicycling became a cult among the urban middle class—as the new century dawned, more than four million Americans owned bicycles.

The automobile challenged the popularity of bicycling in the 1920s. Since that time, interest in bicycling has been cyclical, although technical advances continued. The 1970s was the decade of the 10-speed. The success of American Olympiads in cycling and the excitement of cycle racing, especially the Tour d'France,

have kept the public's attention focused on the bicycle. However, the tremendous resurgence enjoyed by bicycling in the 1970s appears to have ended. The next craze is probably some distance in the future.

References: Fermo Galbiati and Nino Ciravegna, *Bicycle*, Chronicle Books, 1994; Jim Hurd, *1991 Bicycle Blue Book, Antique,* 1991; Neil S. Wood, *Evolution of the Bicycle, Vol. 1* (1991, 1994 value update), *Vol. 2* (1994), L-W Book Sales.

Periodicals: *Antique/Classic Bicycle News*, P.O. Box 1049, Ann Arbor, MI 48106; *Bicycle Trader*, P.O. Box 5600, Pittsburgh, PA 15207; *Classic Bicycle & Whizzer News*, P.O. Box 765, Huntington Beach, CA 92648; *National Antique & Classic Bicycle*, P.O. Box 5600, Pittsburgh, PA 15207.

Collectors' Clubs: Cascade Classic Cycle Club, 7935 SE Market St., Portland, OR 97215; Classic Bicycle and Whizzer Club, 35769 Simon, Clinton Township, MI 48035; International Veteran Cycle Association, 248 Highland Dr., Findlay, OH 45840; National Pedal Vehicle Association, 1720 Rupert, NE, Grand Rapids, MI 49505; The Wheelmen, 55 Bucknell Ave., Trenton, NJ 08619.

Museum: Schwinn History Center, Chicago.

Advertising
   Brochure, Schwinn-Built Bicycles, 3-1/4" x 6", illus of 9 bicycles, c1948 ....55.00
   Mirror, Bakersfield Cyclery and Novelty Works 20.00
   Trade Card, Clark Bicycle Co., Christmas, Santa on high wheeler, 1880s..........................25.00
Badge
   L.A.W. 18th Annual Meet/Philadelphia/Aug. 4-7, 1897, diecut brass link, "Souvenir," pendant in shape of victory wreath around star symbol centered by logo of League of American Wheelman 65.00
   YMCA Bicycle Club/New Brunswick, NJ, 1896, gold luster metal link, inscribed "Mileage" hanger bar, pendant with victory wreath motif and YMCA inscription around triangle logo, back professionally engraved "Century-1896 YMCA Bicycle Club/New Brunswick, NJ" 75.00

Game of Bicycle Race, McLoughlin Bros., boxed board game, 6 pieces, multicolored litho, wood box, 1895, $285.

Bicycle
   Ace Cycle and Motor Works, metal label reading "George Tenby-Cycling champion of Wales-retired, 1879-1889," as-found orig condition 150.00
   Ames and Frost Co., Model #36 Imperial 500.00
   Cleveland, lady's drive shaft model, 20" frame 290.00
   Columbia
      Expert, 1887, 54" wheel, orig condition 2,500.00
      Fire Arrow 300.00
      5 Star Superb, 75th Anniversary edition 375.00
      Standard, 1883, 48" front wheel, restored condition 2,700.00
      Twinbar..........................3,200.00
   Elliot, hickory safety, wooden spokes and fellows, c1898, as-found condition, needs re-tiring 470.00
   Excelsior, man's motor, orig olive drab, no tires......................1,050.00
   High Wheeler, Scottish, 42" h front wheel, primitive, excellent condition 3,100.00
   Huffy, Radiobike 2,000.00
   Monark
      Holiday..............................950.00
      Silver King, hexagonal tube 900.00
   Olmstead Co., Boneshaker, c1869.............3,400.00
   Overman Wheel Co., Victor Light, safety, man's, 25" frame, butterfly handlebars, c1894 ....395.00
   Pope Mfg. Co., Columbia Model #50, drive-shaft, orig condition.......400.00
   Roadmaster, Luxury Liner 600.00
   Rollfast, Custom Built, Model V200.........................2,750.00
   Schwinn
      Aerocycle, Model 34 ....8,500.00
      Autocycle, B-107 ....1,750.00
      Corvette 300.00
      Hornet................................400.00
      Mark II Jaguar...................750.00

Panther,
  Model D-77, girl's 900.00
  Phantom, Model D0-27 ......900.00
  Starlet, Model D0-67 ....500.00
Sears, Elgin
  Bluebird..........................7,000.00
  Robin..............................3,500.00
  Skylark 2,000.00
  Twin 30 ....700.00
Shelby, Donald Duck...........2,000.00
Springfield Roadster,
c1888, 50" to 100" ratchet drive, orig
condition..............................5,100.00
Sterling, tandem, lady's front 3-gear,
c1897, orig condition 1,200.00
TRB Alenax, ratchet drive, nice
condition.................................110.00
Unknown Maker, hard-tired safety
type 700.00
Western Wheel Works, Chicago, Ot-
to, boy's, c1900, late high wheel,
wooden spokes 1,350.00
Book
  Around the World on a Bicycle, Fred
  A. Birchmore, autographed 30.00
  Riding High, A. Judson
  Palmer, autographed................82.00
Business Documents, Worcester Bicycle
Co., foreclosure papers 90.00
Cabinet Card, man with
  high wheeler 120.00
Catalog
  Coventry Machinist Co. 55.00
  Eclipse, Elmira, NY 46.00
  G.W. Stevens Bike Suits,
  orig fabric swatches 100.00
  Imperial 25.00
  Indian Bicycle...........................90.00
  Iver Johnson, 1914.................120.00
  NSU Motorcycle 110.00
  Rollfast 70.00
  Springfield Roadster...............110.00
Victor
  Bicycle, 1898.......................200.00
  Overland, Binghamton,
  NY, rice paper 45.50
China, partial service,
velocipedes motif, Portmierion, price
for 120 pcs 450.00
Display, Dunlop Cycle, repair display
and repair outfit 70.00
Lamp
  Argonaut...................................45.00
  Lucas, Silver King, petroleum ..95.00
  Majestic Lamp 25.00
  Neverout Safety Lamp, U.S. Army
  Bicycle Corps 47.00
  P&H Ltd., The Winner 15.00
  Solar Model S...........................55.00
Lapel Stud, 7/8" d, celluloid on metal,
  c1896

America, red letters on
white "Buy the America and You
Can't Go Wrong" 20.00
Bicycle Saddles, red and white,
winged gargoyle trademark,
Muller Mfg. Co., NY.................25.00
Colonial Bicycles, red, white and
blue, patriot-shield symbol 20.00
Columbia Bicycles, black and white,
nameplate inscribed "You See Them
Everywhere"..............................20.00
Conroy Bicycle, Willard & Conroy,
Co., NY, black, white and red ..15.00
Crescent Bicycles,
red lunar crescent, white ground,
black letters..............................20.00
Dey's Bike, red, white
and blue figural wheel 20.00
Falcon, olive green and pink logo,
tiny falcon image 20.00
The Fowler Bicycles, white
letters, plum ground 20.00
Frontenac Bicycles,
brown and white.......................15.00
The Liberty, black letters, peach
ground, tiny slogan "American's
Representative Bicycle" 25.00
Northampton Bicycles, olive green,
black and white 15.00
Oquaga, white letters,
rose pink ground 15.00
Phoenix Bike, black,
white and red, trademark Phoenix
bird rising from ashes, slogan "It
Stands the Racket" 20.00
Richmond Bicycle Company,
black and white 15.00
Spaulding, black,
white and red 10.00
Sylph Cycles Run Easy,
black and white 15.00
The Winton, white letters,
deep purple ground.................15.00
Yellow Fellow, black letters, orange
ground, "Trans-ontinental Relay Sou-
venir," sponsored by NY Journal
Examiner..................................30.00
Lap Robe, cycling motif..............320.00
Magazine
  Cycling Magazine,
  6 bound volumes...................400.00
  Wheelman, 1882-84,
  4 bound volumes...................500.00
Membership Cards,
  L.A.W., 1886 to 1907.............130.00
Photo Album, 2 cabinet cards, 10 tin-
types of bicyclists 700.00
Photograph, William Witaschek,
  The Great Calvert, 1937, 30th year
  on road 60.00
Pinback Button, 7/8" d, celluloid, c1896
  Bellis Bicycles, multicolored.....25.00
  Ellsmore Bicycles, multicolored, red

and black lettering...................30.00
Mak-Nu, Expressly
For Bicycle Use......................15.00
Member Bicycle
Riders Thrift League 23.00
Ride a Pope Bicycle, black, white and
blue, green Tribune model.......25.00
Stewart's Cycle Brake, blue image,
red letters, white ground 15.00
Superb Ajax Cycles, white
letters, blue ground 15.00
Playing Cards, Monark,
  King Cooper, 1895 ....300.00
Quadracycle, leather seat and fenders,
  tiller steering,
  handles for pumping..........1,000.00
Ribbon, Clerk of
  the Course, 1896....................45.00
Seat
  DeLuxe Messenger, leather, balloon-
  tire-type bicycle 20.00
  Monarch, twin 30.00
Stickpin, 7/8" d celluloid, Lovell Diamond
  Cycles, black and white,
  diamond logo, c1896...............30.00
Tire Setter, Improved Peerless ...150.00
Tricycle
  Boy's, butterfly handlebar, leather
  padded seat 190.00
  Gendron, c1900, tiller steering,
  20" wheel, restored 370.00
  Girl's, tiller steering, 28" rear wheels,
  front treadle drive...................270.00
  Homer Benedict, invalid type .325.00
  Streamlined,
  c1940, as-is condition 220.00
  Victor, 25" wheels, c1890 ...1,000.00
Truing Stand 160.00

Big Little Books

Collecting Hints: Ongoing research on Big Little Books is a factor in shifting values. Condition always has been a key. Few examples are in mint condition since the books were used heavily by the children who owned them. Each collector strives to obtain copies free from as many defects (bent edges on cover, missing spine, torn pages, mutilation with crayon or pencil, missing pages, etc.) as possible.

The main character in a book will also determine price since collectors from other fields vie with Big Little Book collectors for the same work. Cowboy heroes (currently experiencing renewed popularity), Dick Tracy, Disney characters, Buck Rogers, Flash Gordon, Charlie Chan and The Green Hornet are a few examples of this crossover influence.

Until recently, little attention was given to the artists who produced the books. Now, however, books by Alex Raymond and Henry Vallely command top dollar. Other desirable artists are Al Capp, Allen Dean, Alfred Andriola and Will Gould. Personal taste still is a critical factor. Little is known about production runs for each book title. Scarcity charts have been prepared but constantly are being revised. Books tend to hit the market in hoards, with prices fluctuating accordingly. However, the last decade has witnessed price stabilization.

The introduction to Larry Lowery's book includes an excellent section on the care and storage of Big Little Books. He also deserves credit for the detailed research evident in each listing.

History: Big Little Books, although a trademark of the Whitman Publishing Co., is a term used to describe a wealth of children's books published from the 1930s to the present day. Whitman and Saalfied Publishing Co., dominated the field. However, other publishers entered the market. Among them were Engel-Van Wiseman, Lynn Publishing Co., Goldsmith Publishing Co., and Dell Publishing Co.

The origins of Big Little Books can be traced to several series published by Whitman in the 1920s. These included Fairy Tales, Forest Friends and Boy Adventure. The first actual Big Little Book appeared in 1933. Ten different page lengths and eight different sizes were tried by Whitman prior to the 1940s. Whitman also deserves attention for the various remarketing efforts it undertook with many of its titles. It contracted to provide Big Little Book premiums for Cocomalt, Kool Aid, Pan-Am Gas, Macy's, Lily-Tulip's Tarzan Ice Cream and others. Among its series are Wee Little Books, Big Big Books, Nickel Books, Penny Books and Famous Comics.

In the 1950s, television characters were introduced into Big Little Book format. Whitman Publishing became part of Western Publishing,

owned by Mattel. Waldman and Son Publishing Co. under its subsidiary, Moby Books, issued its first book in the Big-Little-Book style in 1977.

References: Larry Lowery, *Lowery's Collector's Guide to Big Little Books and Similar Books*, privately printed, 1981; Norman E. Martinus and Harry L. Rinker, *Warman's Paper*, Wallace-Homestead, 1994; *Price Guide to Big Little Books & Better Little, Jumbo, Tiny Tales, A Fast-Action Story*, etc., L-W Book Sales, 1995.

Collectors' Club: Big Little Book Collector Club of America, P.O. Box 1242, Danville, CA 94526.

Notes: Prices are for books in very fine condition: cover and spine intact, only slight bending at the corners, all pages present, only slightest discoloration of pages, a crisp book from cover color to inside pages. No effort has been made to list variations and premiums published by Whitman.

Additional Listings: Cartoon Characters, Cowboy Heroes, Disneyana, Space Adventurers.

Big Little Books

Buck Jones, Roaring West.......45.00
Buffalo Bill and the Pony Express.....................20.00
David Copperfield, Whitman #1148, 4-1/2" x 5-1/4", 1934, movie edition, W.C. Fields, Freddy Bartholomew..............100.00
Don Winslow USN,

Buffalo Bill and the Pony Express, Leon Morgan, Hal Arbo, illus, Whitman, 713, 1934, $20.

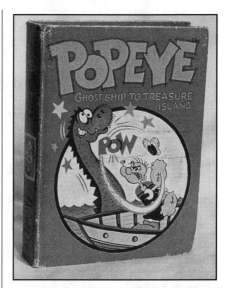
Popeye Ghost Ship to Treasure Island, Paul S. Newman, Whitman, 2008, 1967, $8.

Whitman #1107, 1935..............50.00
Ella Cinders and the Mysterious House, Whitman #1106, 1934 .50.00
Mickey Mouse and Bobo the Elephant, Whitman #1160, 1935 ....75.00
Pluto the Pup, Whitman #1467, 1938 ....65.00
Powder Smoke Range, Harry Carey and Hoot Gibson 45.00
Skeezix at the Military Academy, Whitman #1408, 1938 ....30.00
Smilin Jack and the Stratosphere Ascent, Whitman #1152, 1937 ....30.00
Snow White and the Seven Dwarfs, Whitman #1460, 1938 ....60.00
Treasure Island, Whitman #1141, 4-3/4" x 5-1/4", 1934, movie ed, Jackie Cooper, Wallace Berry 100.00

Better Little Books

Brer Rabbit from Song of the South, Whitman #1426, 1947 ....75.00
Bugs Bunny and the Pirate Loot, Whitman #1403, 1947 ....40.00
Donald Duck Lays Down the Law, Whitman #1449, 1948 ....60.00
G-Men Breaking the Gambling Ring, Whitman #1493, 1938 ....40.00
Ghost Avenger, Whitman #1462, 1943 ....30.00
Inspector Charlie Chan, Whitman #1424, 1942 ....60.00
Little Orphan Annie in the Den of Thieves, Helen Berke, 1948....25.00
Mickey Mouse and the Pirate Submarine, Whitman #1463, 1939 .....50.00
Mickey Mouse in the World of Tomorrow, Whitman #1444, 1948 ....75.00
Mr. District Attorney, Whitman #1408, 1941 ....50.00

Radio Patrol, Whitman
#1496, 1939............................30.00
Smiling Jack Flying High with Downwind,
Whitman #1412, 1942 ....65.00
Tailspin Tommy All-Pictures Comics,
Whitman #1410, 1941 ....25.00
Tim Tyler's Luck,
Whitman #1479, 1939 ....25.00
Uncle Sam's Sky Defenders, Whitman
#14612, 1941...........................30.00

Black Memorabilia

Collecting Hints: Black memorabilia was produced in vast quantities and variations. As a result, collectors have a large field from which to choose and should concentrate on one type of item or a limited combination of types.

Outstanding examples or extremely derogatory designs command higher prices. Certain categories, e.g., cookie jars, draw more collectors, resulting in higher prices. Regional pricing also is a factor. New collectors frequently overpay for common items because they mistakenly assume all Black collectibles are rare or of great value. As in any other collecting field, misinformation and a lack of knowledge leads to these exaggerated values. The Black memorabilia collector is particularly vulnerable to this practice since so little documentation exists. New collectors should familiarize themselves with the field by first studying the market, price trends and existing reference material. Seeking out other collectors is especially valuable for the novice. Black memorabilia has developed into an established collecting field and continues to experience increasing public attention and interest.

History: The term "Black memorabilia" refers to a broad range of collectibles that often overlap other collecting fields, e.g., toys and postcards. It also encompasses African artifacts, items created by slaves or related to the slavery era, modern Black cultural contributions to literature, art, etc., and material associated with the Civil Rights Movement and the Black experience throughout history.

The earliest known examples of Black memorabilia include primitive African designs and tribal artifacts. Black Americana dates back to the arrival of African natives upon American shores. The advent of the 1900s saw an incredible amount and variety of material depicting Blacks, most often in a derogatory and dehumanizing manner that clearly reflected the stereotypical attitude held toward the Black race during this period. The popularity of Black portrayals in this unflattering fashion flourished as the century wore on.

As the growth of the Civil Rights Movement escalated and aroused public awareness of the Black plight, attitudes changed. Public outrage and pressure during the early 1950s eventually put a halt to these offensive stereotypes. Black representations are still being produced in many forms, but no longer in the demoralizing designs of the past. These modern objects, while not as historically significant as earlier examples, will become the Black memorabilia of tomorrow.

References: Patiki Gibbs, *Black Collectibles Sold in America*, Collector Books, 1987, 1993 value update; Douglas Congdon-Martin, *Images in Black*, Schiffer Publishing, 1990; Kenneth Goings, *Mammy and Uncle Mose*, Indiana University Press, 1994; Dee Hockenberry, *Enchanting Friends*, Schiffer Publishing, 1995; Kyle Husfloen (ed.), *Black Americana Price Guide*, Antique Trader Books, 1997; Jan Lindenberger, *Black Memorabilia around the House*, Schiffer Publishing, 1993; Jan Lindenberger, *Black Memorabilia for the Kitchen*, Schiffer Publishing, 1992; ——, *More Black Memorabilia*, Schiffer Publishing, 1995; J.L. Mashburn, *Black Americana Postcard Price Guide*, Colonial House (Box 609, Enka, NC 28728), 1996; Myla Perkins, *Black Dolls, Book I* (1993, 1995 value update), *Book II* (1995), Collector Books; Dawn E. Reno, *Encyclopedia of Black Collectibles*, Wallace-Homestead, 1996; J.P.

Memo holder, mammy, plastic, red, yellow turban, scarf, and broom, 10", $65.

Thompson, *Collecting Black Memorabilia, A Picture Price Guide*, L-W Book Sales, 1996; Jean Williams Turner, *Collectible Aunt Jemima*, Schiffer Publishing, 1994.

Periodicals: *Black Ethnic Collectibles*, 1401 Asbury Ct., Hyattsville, MD 20782; *Blackin'*, 559 22nd Ave., Rock Island, IL 61201; *Fabric of Life*, P.O. Box 1212, Bellevue, WA 98009.

Collectors' Club: Black Memorabilia Collector's Association, 2482 Devoe Ter., Bronx, NY 10468.

Museums: Black American West Museum, Denver, CO; Black Archives Research Center and Museum, Florida A&M University, Tallahassee, FL; Center for African Art, New York, NY; Great Plains Black Museum, Omaha, NE; Jazz Hall of Fame, New York, NY; John Brown Wax Museum, Harper's Ferry, WV; Museum of African American History, Detroit, MI; Museum of African Art, Smithsonian Institution, Washington, DC; National Baseball Hall of Fame, Cooperstown, NY; Robeson Archives, Howard University, Washington, DC; Schomburg Center for Research in Black Culture, New York, NY; Studio Museum, Harlem, NY.

Reproduction Alert: The number of Black memorabilia reproductions has increased during the 1980s. Many are made of easily reproducible materials and generally appear new. Collectors should beware of any item offered in large or unlimited quantities.

Note: The following price listing is based on items in excellent to mint condition. Major paint loss, chips, cracks, fading, tears or other extreme signs of deterioration warrant a considerable reduction in value, except for very rare or limited production items. Collectors should expect a certain amount of wear on susceptible surfaces.

Advertising
    Ashtray, Levy's Jewish Rye Bread, Art Deco styling, milk glass, black boy eating bread dec 75.00
    Box, 11-1/2" w, Masons Challenge Blacking, paper label, wood box 85.00
    Doll, Cream of Wheat, 18" h, stuffed, chef, 1960s 60.00
    Fan, 14" h, cardboard, Jamup and Honey, b&w illus 40.00
    Hat, Aunt Jemima Breakfast Club, paper, fold-out style 20.00
    Puzzle, Amos and Andy, Pepsodent, 1932 .... 90.00
    Recipe Booklet, Knox Gelatin, black child on cover, 1915 .... 10.00
    Tin
        3-3/4" h, Delites Cocoa, paper label 50.00
        7-1/4" h, Sunny South Peanuts 75.00
        11" h, CD Kenney, Mammy's Favorite Brand Coffee, Mammy carrying coffeepot and cup 150.00
    Tip Tray, 4" d, Cottolene Shortening, litho tin 60.00
    Trade Card
        Globe Shoe & Clothing Co., Negro boy 9.50
        Sanford's Ginger, Potter Drug and Chemical Co., Boston, black girl with child in watermelon cradle, multicolored litho, mfg by Forbes, Boston 10.00
    Tray, 12" d, Green River Whiskey, black man and horse 95.00
Ashtray
    3" d, bisque, boy in outhouse while other boy waits, mkd "Japan" ... 35.00
    3-1/2" d, bisque, boy and crow, beside match holder shaped like tree trunk, mkd "Japan" 45.00
    4-1/2" w, ceramic, black boy with head in alligator's mouth, FL souvenir 75.00
Badge, Aunt Jemima Breakfast Club, 4" d, litho tin, sepia face, pink lips, yellow and red-checkered bandanna,

red ground, white letters "Eat a Better Breakfast," bar-pin fastener, c1960 .... 50.00
Bank, mechanical
    Jolly Nigger, place coin in hand, press lever on back, arm moves up, eyes roll back, tongue moves in
        Butterfly tie, cast iron, John Harper & Co., England 135.00
        Ears move, aluminum, designed by Robert Eastwood Starkie, England 115.00
    Little Joe, cast iron, place coin in hand, press lever behind shoulder, raises arm and swallows coin, eyes roll back, tongue flips in, attrib to John Harper & Co., Ltd, c1910 .... 200.00
Bank, still, cast iron
    4-1/4" x 4", Save and Smile, England 395.00
    5-1/8" x 4-7/16", Pickaninny, painted red shirt, blue bow tie, England 440.00
    5-1/4" h, Darky Sharecropper, painted, A C Williams, c1901 .... 150.00
    5-1/2" h, Mammy 90.00
Bell, Mammy 45.00
Book
    Little Black Sambo, 1932 .... 75.00
    Minstrel Joke Book, 1898 .... 25.00
    Turkey Trot and The Black Santa, 1940s 75.00
Bottle Opener, 7" h, figural, minstrel, painted wood 40.00
Butter Dish, Someone's in the Kitchen 125.00
Christmas Card, 1930s 8.00
Cigar Box
    6-1/4" l, Sir Jonathon Brand 45.00
    11" l, Old Plantation Brand, emb 60.00
Cigarette Box, donkey pulling cart 75.00
Cigarette Holder, 5-1/2" l, ceramic, boy with melon, melon bowl for ashes 35.00
Comics Page, Kemple Duke of Dahomey, 1911 .... 45.00
Cookie Jar, Mammy
    Mosaic tile, yellow 495.00
    Pearl China 650.00
Creamer and Sugar, Black Clown, stacking type 75.00
Cutout Sheet, 8" x 10-1/2", stiff paper, full-color printed caricatures of jazz band members, intended to be used as table place cards, band members have brown faces, matching red, blue and yellow marching band uniforms, each playing different instrument, Mayfair Novelty Co., c1930, unused 60.00

Dish Towel, Mammy illus 30.00
Doorstop, 13-1/2" h, cast iron, Mammy, painted, Littco label 265.00
Figure
    2" h, diecut painted metal, porter, carrying suitcase, birdcage, golf clubs and bat, 1930s 65.00
    3-1/2" h, celluloid, man carrying cane, triangular tin base, mkd "Germany" and "W" in circle, 1920 .. 60.00
    4-1/2" h, bisque, woman, native clothing, mkd "Occupied Japan" 20.00
    6-1/2" h, bisque, accordion player, mkd "Japan" 30.00
Game
    7" x 10" x 1-1/2", Chocolate Splash, cardboard box, paper label, target game, Willis G Young Mfg., Chicago, 1916 .... 150.00
    13" x 13" x 1-1/2", The Game of Hitch Hiker, Whitman, 1937 .... 75.00
    24" l, Three Black Crows, bean bag, painted wood standing frame, swing-out targets 195.00
Magic Lantern Slide, Black playing banjo 20.00
Match Holder, 5-3/4" h, ceramic, woman, scalloped collar and sleeves ... 45.00
Mug, grotesque male face 70.00
Nodder, 4-1/4" h, painted metal, boy in yellow hat, smoking cigar, mkd "Occupied Japan" 55.00
Notepad Holder and Pencil Holder, 6" x 10-1/2", painted hard plastic, wall hanger, 3D Mammy image, insert pencil as broomstick in 1 hand, orig paper tablet, yellow and black accents, 1950s 150.00
Palm Puzzle, tin rim holding glass over emb glossy paper image

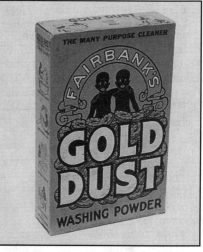

Caricature black face, blue shirt, green ground, dark red mouth slot, 5 tiny balls serve as teeth, German, c1920 ....150.00

Caricature black youngster eating slice of watermelon, 2 tiny balls serve as eyes, 1930s 85.00

Party Favor, 3-1/2" d, diecut, expandable colored paper ovals, boy eating watermelon 40.00

Pencil Holder, 5-1/2" l, celluloid, alligator with black boy's head in mouth, c1930 ....40.00

Pennant, 25" l,. NY Black Yankees, felt...........................195.00

Photograph, 4-1/4" x 6-1/2", cabinet photo

Girl holding black-faced doll, long white outfit, photographer Warren, Lowell, MA................................30.00

Young lad seated on packing crate, eating watermelon slide, photographer F.W. Legg, Woburn, MA, late 1800s................................35.00

Pillow, 18" x 19", embroidered, man walking with chicken, "If the Man in the Moon Were a Coon," faded......................................400.00

Pinback Button

7/8" d, full color, Ten Days—Smoke Up, caricature of black man standing before judge, art by Tep, c1912 ....25.00

1-1/8" d, full-color, litho, inscribed "Factory No. 30, 2nd District, New York" on reverse

Don't You Love Me No Mo'?, black girl in pigtails wearing skimmer hat, daisy flower, art by Tad.25.00

I Raise You, black man in uniform holding cable with word "elevator" next to him, art by Goldberg..30.00

1-3/4" d, Decatur Corn Carnival and Exposition, yellow and black, Negro youngsters enjoying ears of corn, Oct. 1899, Decatur, IL............225.00

Pincushion, sitting black baby, movable arms and legs, tape measure ..85.00

Pipe Rack, 12" l, figural, male head with large hat, brass......................225.00

Pitcher, Mandy, Omnibus 160.00

Planter, 4-3/4" h, ceramic, black boy next to stump, brown, blue and green, Japan Orion Co. 75.00

Pot Hanger, 7-1/2" x 5-1/2", chalkware, black boy and girl, wire hook, c1935 ....115.00

Program, Penn Wheelman Frolic, 1927, Minstrels, Orpheum Theater, 64 pgs 40.00

Range Shakers, Mammy and Chef, yellow, gold trim................80.00

Salt and Pepper Shakers, pr

Boy lying in alligator's mouth .115.00

Butler and Mammy, flowers on dress.....................125.00

Jonah and Whale 85.00

Kids in Basket 80.00

Leapfrog Boys.........................90.00

Native and Hut 65.00

Native and Watermelon Slice....................45.00

Native on Hippo 210.00

Porter and Suitcase 185.00

Rockingham Couple, standing 70.00

Salty and Peppy, Pearl China 225.00

Seal and Trainer 90.00

Valentine Couple, gray hair....195.00

Sheet Music

A Warmin' Up in Dixie, 1899 ....35.00

Aunt Jemima's Picnic Day, 1914 ....25.00

Little Alabama Coon, 1893.......30.00

My Sugar Coated Chocolate Boy, 1919................15.00

Sam the Accordion Man...........15.00

When the Coons Are on the Move, 1901, 13-1/2" x 17", matted and framed..................65.00

Sign, cardboard, Out to Lunch, Sappy's Barbershop, Colored Only, Pittsburgh, 1929 ....15.00

Soda Bottle, emb "Mammy" 70.00

Souvenir, A Present from Hastings, 4-1/2" h, porcelain, black potty boy and girl, black, white, light orange luster, 1930s, Germany 195.00

Stove-Pipe Vent Cover, 9-1/2" d, multicolored, black youngster with straw hat, holding banjo, looking at 2 others driving car made out of corn ear, watermelon wheels, passenger with pink plumed hat, brass frame and hanging chain, asbestos backing, c1900 ....125.00

String Holder

Boy, bending beside watermelon...................35.00

Mammy 40.00

Tobacco Tag, Alabama Coon, tin, black man holding top hat and cane.70.00

Toothpick Holder, metal, cotton bale with 2 blacks 145.00

Toy, painted wood

5" h, Wakouwa Boxing Champs 75.00

8" h, Trapeze Artist, squeeze type 40.00

11" h, Dancing Dan, orig board and instructions...............................65.00

16" h, Dancing Tap Dancer, wearing tuxedo 75.00

Tumbler, native, price for 4-pc set 35.00

Wall Pocket, Blackamoor, mkd "Royal Copley".................30.00

Water Sprinkler, Mammy 165.00

Postcard, mkd "Margret Boriss," $12.

Blue Ridge Pottery

Collecting Hints: Blue Ridge patterns are among the most established of the collectible American dinnerwares. Collectors pay a premium for artist-signed pieces. The Talisman Wallpaper dinnerware pattern, because of its original failure to attract buyers, is the most difficult dinnerware pattern to find. Among the harder to find shapes are the China demi-pot and character jugs.

Patterns and forms made in the 1940s are the most popular. As in most dinnerware patterns, hollowware pieces command higher prices than flat pieces. Demi-sets that include the matching tray are considered a real find. Blue Ridge collectors must compete with children's dish collectors for miniature pieces. Because the wares were hand decorated, identical pieces often contain minor variations. Develop a practiced eye to identify those that are most aesthetically pleasing. Minor color variations can change a pleasing pattern into one that is ordinary.

History: In 1917, the Carolina Clinchfield and Ohio Railroad, in an effort to promote industry along its line, purchased land along its right-of-way and established a pottery in Erwin, Tennessee. Erwin was an ideal location because of the availability of local white kaolin and feldspar, two of the chief ingredients in pottery. Workers for the new plant were recruited from East Liverpool and Sebring, OH, and Chester, VA.

In 1920, J.E. Owens purchased the pottery and received a charter for Southern Potteries, Inc. Within a few years, the pottery was sold to Charles W. Foreman. Foreman introduced hand-painting under glaze and trained girls and women from the nearby hills to do the painting. By 1938, Southern Potteries was producing Blue Ridge "Hand Painted under the Glaze" dinnerware. The principal sales thrust contrasted the Blue Ridge hand-painted ware with the decal ware produced by most other manufacturers.

Blue Ridge maintained a large national sales organization with 11 showrooms scattered nationwide. Few catalogs were issued and trade advertising was limited. As a result, researching Blue Ridge is difficult. Most of the patterns used on Blue Ridge originated at the plant. Lena Watts, an Erwin native, was chief designer. Eventually, Watts left Blue Ridge and went to Stetson China Co. Blue Ridge also made limited-production patterns for a number of leading department stores.

As the 1930s came to a close, Southern Potteries was experiencing strong competition from inexpensive Far Eastern imports, but World War II intervened and changed the company's fortune. Southern Potteries' work force increased tenfold, production averaged more than 300,000 pieces

Platter, blue, pink flowers, yellow center, green leaves, 12-1/2" l, $12.

per week and the company experienced a period of prosperity that lasted from the mid-1940s into the early 1950s. By the mid-1950s, however, imports and the arrival of plastic dinnerware once again threatened Southern Potteries' market position. The company tried half-time production, but the end came on Jan. 31, 1957, when the stockholders voted to close the plant.

References: Susan and Al Bagdade, *Warman's American Pottery and Porcelain*, Wallace-Homestead, 1994; Jo Cunningham, *Collector's Encyclopedia of American Dinnerware*, Collector Books, 1982, 1995 value update; Lois Lehner, *Lehner's Encyclopedia of U.S. Marks on Pottery, Porcelain & Clay*, Collector Books, 1988; Betty and Bill Newbound, *Collector's Encyclopedia of Blue Ridge Dinnerware*, Collector Books, 1994; ——, *Southern Potteries, Inc.*, 3rd Edition, Collector Books, 1989, 1995 value update.

Periodicals: *The Daze*, P.O. Box 57, Otisville, MI 48463; *National Blue Ridge Newsletter*, 144 Highland Dr., Blountville, TN 37617.

Collectors' Club: Blue Ridge Collectors Club, Rt. 3, Box 161, Erwin, TN 37650.

Museum: Unicoi Heritage Museum, Erwin, TN.

Advertising, plate, United
   Wallpaper, produced by Southern
   Potteries 500.00
Apple, spoon rest 45.00
Applejack, Skyline shape
   Coffeepot, Ovide 235.00
   Plate
      6" d 6.50
      9" d 16.00
   Platter 28.00
   Vegetable Bowl, divided 36.00
Appleyard, teapot, cov 95.00
Artist Sgd, plate
   Flower Cabin, sgd
     "Mildred T. Broyles" 650.00
   Quail scene, sgd
     "Mildred T. Broyles" 900.00
Becky
   Eggcup 30.00
   Plate
      8" d 8.00
      10" d 12.00
Betsy Jug

   China, tulips dec 175.00
   Earthenware 98.50
Big Apple, cereal bowl, 6" d 5.00
Black Edge
   Bonbon Tray 82.50
   Chicken Shakers 85.00
   Chocolate Pot 190.00
   Powder Box 135.00
Blossom Top, salt and pepper shakers,
   pr 35.00
Bluebell Bouquet
   Gravy Boat 25.00
   Plate, 9" d 7.50
Calico
   Candy Box 175.00
   Teapot, Colonial shape 165.00
Carnival
   Creamer and Sugar 25.00
   Mixing Bowl, 9-1/2" d 20.00
   Platter, 13" l, oval 18.00
Carol, 62-pc set 300.00
Carol's Roses, vegetable
   bowl, open, oval 12.00
Cassandra, pie plate,
   maroon border 25.00
Champagne Pinks, teapot, cov 95.00
Character Jug
   Daniel Boone 700.00
   Pioneer Woman 650.00
Cherry Bounce
   Platter, 11" l, oval 18.00
   Vegetable Bowl, open, round ... 20.00
Cherry, Cherry, platter, 12" l 18.00
Chevron, teapot 145.00
Chick, pitcher, figural, 6" h, all white,
   vitreous china 75.00
Chickory, teapot, Colonial shape,
   crazed inside 45.00
Chintz
   Bonbon 82.50
   Cake Plate, maple-leaf shape,
   loop handle, molded grape
   cluster, 10" l 50.00
   Chocolate Pot 295.00
Christmas Doorway, plate 115.00
Christmas Mistletoe, plate 85.00
Christmas Packages
   Cup and Saucer 87.50
   Plate 87.50
Christmas Tree, dinner service, 8 place
   settings, cup, saucer and plate,
   price for-24 pc set 850.00
Chrysanthemum, platter 18.00
Clara, pitcher, Galore 70.00
Cock O' the Morn
   Cup and Saucer 20.00
   Fruit Bowl 9.00
   Plate, 10" d 20.00
   Snack set, plate and cup 30.00
Cocky Locky, platter 135.00
Colonial Rose, 61-pc set 480.00

Crab Apple
    Dinner Service, 6 place settings,
    dinner plates, bread and butter
    plates, cups and saucers, berry
    bowls, creamer and sugar, platter
    and round vegetable bowl, price for
    40-pc set 395.00
    Plate, 6" d...............................2.50
    Platter, 11" l, oval 25.00
Cumberland, platter, 13" l, oval 25.00
Dahlia, creamer 12.00
Darcy, plate, 8" sq 10.00
Dazzle, bowl, tab handle 12.50
Delphine
    Cigarette Box 75.00
    Vase 95.00
Duck in Hat
    Children's Feeding Dish 55.00
    Teapot, child's size 125.00
Dutch Bouquet, Colonial shape
    Cereal Bowl, 6" d 11.00
    Cup and Saucer 12.00
    Plate
        6" d, bread and butter 9.00
        9-3/8" d, dinner 16.00
Easter Parade
    Bonbon 65.00
    Chocolate Pot 175.00
    Creamer and Sugar, open 85.00
    Relish Dish, round 75.00
Elegance, chocolate set,
    cov chocolate pot, creamer,
    open sugar, tray......................600.00
Evening Flowers, 22-pc set 100.00
Festive, creamer...........................6.00
Flower Bowl, plate, 8-1/2" d 25.00
French Peasant
    Bonbon...................................165.00
    Butter Pat 75.00
    Candy Box, cov 160.00
    Chocolate Pot.........................480.00
    Creamer 75.00
    Demitasse Cup
    and Saucer..............................50.00
    Plate, 10" d............................95.00
    Server, center handle..............95.00
Fruit Fantasy, cake plate, maple-leaf
    shape, loop handle, molded grape
    cluster, 10" l...........................50.00
Fruit Punch, plate, 10-1/2" d,
    dinner, Colonial shape.............16.00
Gladys, boot, backstamped
    in script, "Boot 310/1" 85.00
Grace, pitcher, green/blue.............95.00
Grapes, salad set,
    bowl, 4 plates........................135.00
Grape Wine, teapot, snub nose...225.00
Helen, pitcher 90.00
Hibiscus, Milady pitcher..............175.00
Hilda, 55-pc set 430.00
Irresistible, Martha snack tray 100.00

Jane, pitcher................................110.00
Jigsaw, child's feeding dish...........90.00
King's Ransom,
    vegetable bowl, cov.................85.00
Lyonnaise, demitasse cup............75.00
Mallard
    Box, cov 395.00
    Salt and pepper
    shakers, pr 395.00
Mardi Gras
    Creamer 10.00
    Pie Baker, Candlewick shape ..25.00
    Plate, 9" d, Colonial shape.........8.00
    Teapot....................................175.00
Millie's Pride, chocolate pot.........175.00
Language of Flowers,
    plate from salad set 85.00
Maple Leaf, cake tray...................50.00
Mexican, bowl 150.00
Mountain Cherry, 20-pc set.........175.00
Nocturne
    Cup and Saucer, Colonial shape,
    red edge..................................12.00
    Plate, sq 12.50
Nove Rose, Bonbon,
    flat shell shape 55.00
Orinda
    Cereal Bowl, 6" d,
    Colonial shape 10.00
    Cup and Saucer,
    Colonial shape 12.00
Pansy Trio, pitcher, 7" h,
    Spiral shape 65.00
Petit Point
    Child's, tea set 300.00
    Coffeepot, cov.........................145.00
Petunia Party
    Cup 20.00
    Plate..20.00
Pixie, bonbon tray 165.00
Poinsettia
    Creamer 8.00
    Cup and Saucer,
    Colonial shape 10.00
    Fruit Bowl, 5" d..........................5.00
    Plate
        6" d, bread and butter 3.00
        8-1/2" d, luncheon,
        Colonial shape.......................4.50
Provincial Farm Series,
    6" sq plate...............................85.00
Ridge Daisy
    Sugar, cov................................16.00
    Vegetable, round......................18.00
Ridge Rose Martha, snack tray...110.00
Rooster, cigarette set, cigarette box
    and 4 ashtrays 175.00
Roseanna, demitasse
    cup and saucer 30.00
Rose Marie, chocolate pot 175.00
Rustic Plaid, snack set, plate and cup,

price for set of six 30.00
Rutledge, dinner service, Candlewick
    shape, service for 4 plus serving
    pieces, price for 22-pc set 230.00
Sculptured Fruit
    Pie Server 32.00
    Pitcher, 7" h, 40 oz..................80.00
Seaside, box, cov,
    3-1/2" x 4-1/2"..........................98.00
Sherman Lily, cov, box, raised figural lily
    on cov....................................995.00
Spiderweb, pink and charcoal gray
    Cereal Bowl 8.00
    Cup and Saucer.......................12.00
    Fruit Bowl.................................6.00
    Plate
        Bread and Butter 9.00
        Dinner 9.00
    Vegetable Bowl
        Oval 18.00
        Round 18.00
Spindrift, pie baker 28.00
Spring Blossom,
    creamer, piecrust 20.00
Spring Hill Tulip, teapot, cov 110.00
Square Danish, snack set,
    plate and cup..........................125.00
Stanhome Ivy, plate, 9-1/2" d, dinner,
    Skyline shape 6.00
Strawberry, fruit bowl, 5" d.............3.00
Strawberry Patch
    Creamer....................................6.00
    Cup and Saucer......................10.00
    Plate
        6" d, bread and butter...........5.00
        8" d, luncheon......................5.00
        10" d, dinner 7.00
    Soup Plate, flanged rim 9.00
    Sugar Bowl, cov......................10.00
Strawberry Sundae, vegetable bowl,
    open, round 25.00
Summertime, celery tray,
    leaf shape...............................42.00
Sunfire, creamer, Colonial shape, teal
    edge..20.00
Sunflower, Colonial shape
    Creamer...................................20.00
    Soup Plate, 8" d, flat 15.00
Thanksgiving Turkey, plate,
    10-1/4" d, dinner.....................65.00
Tic-Tac
    Set, 22-pc set.........................275.00
    Teapot....................................150.00
    Vegetable, round 20.00
Tropical, plate, 9" d,
    Skyline shape 12.00
Turkey with Acorns, platter, oval, Sky-
    line-Clinchfield shape 135.00
Verna, maple leaf tray..................40.00
Vintage, plate, 11-1/2" d,
    Colonial shape 28.00

Virginia, pitcher.............................85.00
Weathervane
    Fruit Bowl 18.00
    Plate
        6" sq, cock 60.00
        9" d...................................48.00
        10-1/2" d 40.00
    Saucer.....................................14.00
Wild Rose, pitcher, 7" h,
    Spiral shape...........................75.00
Wild Strawberry, sugar...............135.00
Wrinkled Rose, teapot..................95.00

Bookends

Collecting Hints: Since bookends were originally designed to be used in pairs, make sure you've got the proper set. Check for matching or sequential numbers as well as damage or loss of decoration. Single bookends are sometimes marketed as doorstops or shelf sitters; a careful eye is needed to find one-of-a-kind items.

History: No formal history of bookends is available, but it is not too difficult to imagine those eager for knowledge who began to accumulate books searching for something to hold them in an orderly fashion. Soon, decorators and manufacturers saw the need and began production of bookends. Today bookends can be found in almost every type of material, especially metal and heavy ceramics, which lend their physical density to keep those books standing straight.

    Bookends range from artistic copies of famous statuary to simple wooden blocks, offering collectors an endless adventure.

Anchors, bronze 40.00
Bear, 4-1/2" h, clear glass,
    New Martinsville 100.00
Cat
    Cheshire, brass, c1930 ....135.00
    Full figure,
        Rookwood, c1923 ....250.00
Charles Lindbergh, 1929, bronzed
    metal....................................195.00
Conestoga Wagons.......................80.00
Cornucopia, 5-1/4" h, opal glass,
    New Martinsville 65.00
Dice, figural white, black and red dice
    mounted to marble squares.....35.00
Dogs, Goebel, crown mark..........130.00
Dolphin, Abingdon Pottery, #333...65.00
Donald Duck, 7" h, carrying school-
    books, chalkware....................45.00

Eagle, Frankart, bronzed
    metal finish 50.00
Elephants, ivory, teakwood base 165.00
End of the Trail, cast iron 115.00
Fish, clear glass, Heisey 160.00
Fleur-de-Lis, 10" x 5", copper,
    Roycroft orb mark..................115.00
Flowers in Basket, multicolored painted
    flowers, blue basket, cast iron .60.00
Fraternal, B.P.O.E., elk in high relief,
    bronzed cast iron....................75.00
Garfield and Odie, 5" h, 4" w,
    paper label, glazed ink stamp mark
    "Enesco," 1983 ....245.00
Irish Setters, chalkware, c1940 .....35.00
Kissing Children,
    Hubley, cast iron....................165.00
Lady's Heads,
    New Martinsville 265.00
Let 'er Buck, cowboy motif,
    painted plaster.......................632.50
Lincoln Memorial, plaster,
    bronze finish 40.00
Monk, reading books, cathedral shape,
    "Solitude" written
    on base, Art Pottery...............150.00
Nude Lady, chalkware, c1940.......45.00
Owl, sitting on books,
    matte green and gray glaze, Mon-
    mouth Pottery 225.00
Peony, Roseville,
    yellow floral dec....................135.00
Racehorse and Jockey, bronzed white
    metal, Art Deco........................90.00
Racing Horses, molded brass 65.00
Rectangular, Catalin, brown with
    dramatic marbling..................285.00
Rook, olive green, Rookwood
    Pottery, c1928 ....425.00
Scotties, cast iron..........................30.00
Sentries, 7-1/2" h, on orb mounted base,
    Bakelite trim, imp mark, Chase
    Chrome and Brass Co..........175.00
Setter, 4-1/2" x 7-1/2",
    cast iron, black, c1920.............95.00
Ships, mkd "Galleon at the time of
    Elizabeth," brass......................65.00

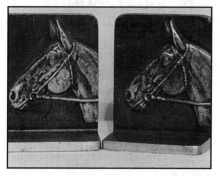

Horse's head, aluminum, sgd by noted thoroughbred artist Bruce Cox, $100.

Sailing ship, 3-masted, metal, *Constitution*, 5" h, 5" w, $35.

Sunbonnet Girls, green with gold,
    fine crystalline streaking,
    Cowan Pottery......................450.00
Terrier Dog, 4-1/2" h, chrome plated,
    round back and base, c1920.110.00
Tom and Jerry, 8" h,
    Gorham, 1980 ....45.00
Tooled Design, 6" x 6", leather, wood
    base, Roycroft mark..............190.00

Bookmarks

Collecting Hints: The best place to search for bookmarks is specialized paper shows. Be sure to check all related categories. Most dealers do not keep bookmarks together but rather file them under subject headings, e.g., Insurance, Ocean Liners, World's Fairs, etc.

History: Bookmark collecting dates back to the early 19th century. Bookmarks—any object used to mark a reader's place in a book—have been made in a wide variety of material including celluloid, cloth, cross-stitched needlepoint in punched paper, paper, sterling silver, wood and woven silk. Heavily embossed leather markers were popular between 1800 and 1860. Advertising markers appeared after 1860.

    Woven silk markers are a favorite among collectors. T. Stevens of Coventry, England, manufacturer of Stevengraphs, is among the most famous makers. Paterson, NJ, was the silk weaving center in the United States. John Best & Co., Phoenix Silk Manufacturing Co., and Warner Manufacturing Co., produced bookmarks. Other important United States companies that made woven silk bookmarks were J. J. Mannion of Chicago and Tilt & Son of Providence, RI.

Recently, collectors have discovered the colorful folk art quality of cross-stitched bookmarks created between 1840 and 1920. These were a popular handicraft made by young women who followed the design imprinted on pre-punched paper strips. Plain strips were available for those wishing to design their own bookmark. Most have a religious theme, but examples have been found commemorating birthdays or Christmas or depicting temperance (anti-drink) or other themes. Most were attached to colorful silk ribbons.

Periodical: *Bookmark Collector*, 1002 W. 25th St., Erie, PA 16502.

Collectors' Club: Antique Bookmark Collector's Association, 2224 Cherokee St., St. Louis, MO 63118.

Aluminum, Eberhart & Miller, Shoes & Rubbers, Warren, PA, emb floral design, attached silk cord 7.50

Beadwork, 8-1/4" l, 1-3/4" w, rect, navy blue ground, rose flowers, 3 beaded tassels terminating in floss green, rose and ecru tassel, leather top and thong, some loss to tassels ... 125.00

Brass, United States Fidelity & Guarantee Co., etched logo and "Home Office Baltimore USF&G" 5.00

Celluloid

Disney characters, Mickey Mouse, Goofy and Daisy Duck, fish shape, Walt Disney Productions, c1950 .... 15.00

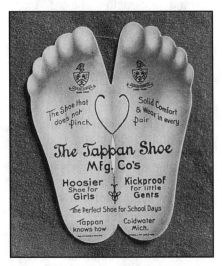

Advertising, The Tappan Shoe Mfg. Co., feet, flesh tone, black letters, $25.

Leaf Cluster, diecut thin celluloid, bouquet of late-summer green leaves to fall red and yellow leaves, small celluloid loop to hold bookmark string, early 1900s 50.00

Maltine, diecut thin celluloid, multicolored image, brown and white owl, lengthy text on reverse 45.00

Shriner, diecut thin celluloid, full color, caricature of costumed Shriner with fez, symbol, early 1900s ... 50.00

Universal Exposition of Paris, Standard Mfg. Co., Pittsburgh, diecut thin celluloid, multicolored, finely detailed lady preparing for bath, Victorian fixtures, crossed flags of France and U.S., 1900 .... 150.00

Cloisonné, Arizona, Grand Canyon State, deep blue, gold and white design 3.00

Cross-Stitched, on punched paper, attached silk ribbon

Florals, c1890 .... 5.00

Love, 6-1/4" l, beige, salmon and green dec 7.50

Merry Christmas, red and green holly dec 25.00

So-Far, 8" l, red and silver 12.00

Metal, shield shape, R K Company

Balance Rock, Pittsfield, MA, burnished-copper-type finish 8.00

The Flue of Franconia Notch, White Mountains, NH 4.50

Paper, diecut

Climax Catarrh Cure, woman with fur coat, multicolored 10.00

Daggets Chocolates, Clapsaddle girl, emb butterfly, multicolored 10.00

James Fitzgerald, Bookseller & Stationer, MA, rural scene 6.50

Sterling Silver, etched lace design, multicolored silk string and thread, mkd "Sterling, R&G Co." 12.00

Wood, souvenir, Ireland, hand-carved clover leaves and "Erin," swivel design, imp "Blarney," painted black 12.00

Books, Travel Related

Collecting Hints: Many types of travel-related books can be found in the antiques and collectibles marketplace. Watch for well-illustrated, complete and clean copies. Condition is always a key to prices. Keep an eye open for autographed copies, as well as first editions.

History: Before the advent of television and the remote control, people

more frequently read books for enjoyment and personal fulfillment, traveling around the world from the comfort of their favorite armchair. Some of these books were illustrated by famous artists while others display the works of famous photographers. Some travel books contain interesting accounts of the author's visit to a special land. Others may include stories collected from various sources in an area of interest. Diaries, accounts and photo albums all are interesting to readers.

References: Allen Ahearn, *Book Collecting: A Comprehensive Guide*, G.P. Putnam's Sons, 1989; Allen and Patricia Ahearn, *Collected Books, The Guide to Values*, G.P. Putnam's Sons, 1991; *American Book Prices Current*, Bandcroft Parkman, published annually; *Huxford's Old Book Value Guide*, 9th Edition, Collector Books, 1997; Marie Tedford and Pat Goudey, *Official Price Guide to Old Books*, House of Collectibles, 1994; John Wade, *Tomart's Price Guide to 20th Century Books*, Tomart Publications, 1994; Nancy Wright, *Books: Identification and Price Guide*, Avon Books, 1993.

Periodicals: *Book Source Monthly*, 2007 Syosett Dr., P.O. Box 567, Cazenovia, NY 13035.

A Buckeye Abroad or Wanderings in Europe & in the Orient, Follet, Foster & Co., 1860, 444 pgs 24.00

Anson, George, *A Voyage round the World in the Years MDCCXL,I,II,III,IV*, 4to, comp by Richard Walter, London, 1748, rebacked, 1st ed 1,495.00

Atwater, Caleb, *Remarks Made on a Tour to Prairie du Chien thence to Washington*, Columbus, 1831, 12mo, contemporary sheep, rebacked with dark calf 285.00

Baker, Sir Samuel W, *Eight Years Wandering in Ceylon*, Lippincott, 1873, gilded edge, 323 pgs 30.00

Bartram, William, *Travels through North and South Carolina, Georgia, East and West Florida*, James & Johnson, Philadelphia, 1791, 8vo, 8 engraved plates, folding map, modern calf, bookplate and signature of American zoologist Amos Binney 2,530.00

Blanchard, Robert G, *Northeast Lights, Lighthouses and Lightships*, Norwalk, 1989, 422 pgs.................22.00

Blane, William Newnham, *An Excursion through the United States and Canada during the Years 1822-33*, London, 1824, 8vo, 2 folding maps, linen backed, bookplate of Hermon Dunlap Smith, 1st ed 255.00

Bradshaw, M, *The Maine Land: A Portfolio of Views Taken in Vacationland*, July 1945, sgd by author, 149 illus 36.00

Bryant, William Cullen, ed *Picturesque America; or, the Land We Live In*, 2 vol, New York, 1872-74, 4to, blind- and gilt-stamped morocco 460.00

Bumpus, T. Francis, *Cathedrals of England & Wales*, London, 1928, 8 color plates, 48 photos, 344 pgs, gilt dec cover, dj.......................17.50

California, Grand Canyon, Yellowstone Park, John Stoddard's lectures, Vol X, 1898, 304 pgs 25.00

Capital of Our Country, Washington, DC, National Geographic Society, 1923, color illus, 7" x 10", 154 pgs, ...35.00

Champeny, Elizabeth W., *Romance of Old Belgium*, Putnam's, 1915, 90 photos, 432 pgs 15.00

Chapin, Frederick H, *Mountaineering in Colorado*, Boston, 1889, 8vo, pictorial cloth, plates and illus 258.00

Charlevoix, Pierre Francois Xavier de, *Journal of a Voyage to North America*, 2 vol, Chicago, 1923, 8vo, folding map, 1/4 cloth, 1 of 200 issued by Caxton Club..........................230.00

Clark, Thomas D., ed *Travels in the Old South,1527-1860: a Bibliography*, 3 vol, Norman, 1956-59, 8vo, cloth, dj 285.00

Crane, Charles Edward, *Let Me Show You Vermont: A Handbook on Everything Vermontish*, Charles Edward Crane, Knopf, NY, 1937, 347 pgs, dj 20.00

D'Urville, M. Dumont, *Voyage Pittoresque Autour Du Monde* (*Voyage Around the World*), Paris, 1834, 2 vol, maps 125.00

Darby, William, *A Tour from the City of New-York, to Detroit, in the Michigan Territory*, New York, 1819, 8vo, 3 folding maps, original boards, rebacked, 1st ed 290.00

Eggleston, G., *Tahiti--Voyage Through Paradise*, Devin-Adair, 1953, photos, maps, 10", 252 pgs, 1st ed 20.00

Ellis, William, *Narrative of a Tour through Hawaii, or Owhyhee*, London, 1826, 8vo, 7 plates, folding map, contemporary 1/2 calf........................230.00

Endurance: Shackletons Incredible Voyage, 1959, photos, 282 pgs 16.00

Fessenden, Blanchard and William

Stone, *Cruising Guide to the Chesapeake*, Dodd Mead & Co., 1968, illus, charts, dj....................................7.50

Fison, Lorimer, *Tales from Old Fiji*, London, 1907, illus, maps, 176 pgs 25.00

Florida: A Guide to the Southernmost State, American Guide Series, Federal Writers Project, Oxford University Press, 1939, 3rd printing, foldout map, 60 pgs, dj 17.50

Fuch, Vivian, *Antarctic Adventure: The Trans-Antarctic Expedition,1955-58*, Dutton, 1961, maps, photos, 190 pgs, 1st ed, dj..................17.00

Hall, Basil, *Travels in North America*, 3 vol, Edinburgh, 1829, 12mo, bookplates 150.00

Howe, De Wolfe, *Boston: The Place and the People*, Macmillan, 1912, 12mo, 397 pgs......................17.00

Hulett, T.G., *Every Man His Own Guide to the Falls of Niagara*, Buffalo, 1846, small 12mo, frontispiece map, wrappers 115.00

Hutton, Edward, *Highways and Byways in Wiltshire*, Macmillan, London, 1928, drawings by Nelly Erichsen, 463 pgs....................10.00

James, George Wharton, *The Grand Canyon of Arizona: How to See It*, Little Brown, 1910, small 8vo, photos, illus, map, 265 pgs............50.00

Johnson, Martin, *Camera Trails in Africa*, Grosset & Dunlap, 1924, photos, 342 pgs....................................15.00

Kentucky: A Guide to the Bluegrass State, American Guide Series, Federal Writers Project, Oxford University Press, 1939, 3rd printing, foldout map, 48 pgs, dj 16.00

Knox, Thomas W., *The Boy Traveler in Levant: Adventures of Two Youths in a Journey Through Morocco, Algeria, Tunis, Greece & Turkey*, Harper & Bros., 1895, engravings, b&w sketches 15.00

Knox, Thomas W., *The Boy Travelers— Japan and China*, 1880, engravings, 421 pgs, 1st ed 38.00

Lucas, E.V., *A Wanderer in Holland*, Macmillan, 1911, 20 color plates, 35 illus, gilt dec cover 15.00

Lyell, Charles, *Travels in North America*, 2 vol, London, 1845, 12mo, map, ...315.00

Marco Polo's Voyages and Travels, Springfield Armory, Jacob Abbott, 1853, 192 pgs, 16mo, juvenile 25.00

McLaughlin, Daniel, *Sketch of a Trip from Omaha to Salmon River*, Gordon Martin, 1954, 18 pgs.........25.00

Meyers, William H., *Journal of a Cruise to California and the Sandwich Is-*

lands, Book Club of California, San Francisco, 1955, plates, folio, cloth, 1 of 400 copies printed by Grabhorn Press 200.00

Michaux, Francois, *Travels to the Westward of the Allegheny Mountains, in the States of the Ohio, Kentucky and Tennessee*, London, 1805, 8vo, engraved folding map, original boards, 1st English ed.......................285.00

Moore, Joseph West, *Picturesque Washington, D.C.*, Reid Publishing, 1888, 309 pgs 25.00

Muir, John, *Gentle Wilderness: The Sierra Nevada*, Promontory Press, 1981, photos by R. Kauffman, ed by D. Brower, 14" x 10".....................18.00

Nordoff, Charles, *California: A Book for Travellers and Settlers*, Harpers, 1873, 255 pgs 70.00

North Carolina: A Guide to the Old North State, University of North Carolina, 1939, photos, maps, 635 pgs..12.00

Nutting, Wallace, *New Hampshire Beautiful, Old America Co,MA,1923*, small 4to, 302 pgs, 1st ed, dj...........68.00

Picturesque Tour in Picturesque Lands, L. Sequin, 1881, illus, 12" x 15-1/2", 312 pgs 135.00

Porter, Eliot, *Down the Colorado, John Wesley Powell Diary of the First Trip Through the Grand Canyon,1869*, E.P. Dutton, 1969, folio, 168 pgs 18.00

Reynolds, James, *Panorama of Austria*, Putnam's Sons, 1956, illus by author 10.00

Roberts, Adolphe, *Lake Ponchartrain: A Story of the Mississippi Delta and the City of New Orleans*, Bobbs-Merrill, 1946, 8vo, American Lakes Series, 376 pgs, dj................................30.00

Routes and Resorts of the Chesapeake & Ohio Railway, 1878, 9" x 7", 82 pgs 25.00

Smart, Ted, *Scotland: A Picture Book to Remember Her By*, 1978, 64 pgs, dj.......................15.00

Spears, Raymond, *Camping on the Great River*, Raymond Spears, Harper Brothers, 1912.............13.00

Sutcliff, Robert, *Travels in some Parts of North America, in the Years 1804, 1805, & 1806*, Philadelphia, 1812, 12mo, original boards, 1st American ed 80.00

Svinin, Paul and Avraham Yarmolinsky, *Picturesque U.S. of America 1811, 1812, 1813,Containing Excerpts from Account of Travels in America*, NY, 1930, small folio, 13" x 10", 46 pgs 45.00

Taylor, Bayard, *Library of Travel, Exploration and Adventure: Japan in Our*

Day, Scribner, 1872, illus, black and gilt emb dec.............17.00

Thornborough, Laura, *The Great Smoky Mountains*, Thomas Y. Crowell, 1937, sgd by author, 147 pgs ..17.50

Tissot, Victor, *Switzerland, Reminiscences of Travel*, James Pott, NY, 1900, gilded edge, 5-1/2" x 8-1/8", 371 pgs, dj 35.00

Townsend, John K., *Narrative of a Journey Across the Rocky Mountains, to the Columbia River and a Visit to the Sandwich Islands, Chili...*, Philadelphia, 1839, 8vo, publisher's cloth, 1st ed.....................................400.00

Turner, George, *Slim Rails Through the Sands, Carson & Colorado-Southern Pacific Narrow Gauge*, Trans-Anglo, 1964, 4to, 104 pgs, 3rd ed.......30.00

Verne, Jules, *Five Weeks in a Balloon*, Jules Verne, Vincent Parke, NY, 1911, 1 of 600 serially numbered and sgd editions, 404 pgs...............45.00

Wagner, Henry and Charles Camp, *The Plains & the Rockies: A Critical Bibliography of Exploration, Adventure and Travel in the American West 1800-1865*, San Francisco, 1982, 8vo, cloth, 4th ed 140.00

William Spence Robertson, ed, *Diary of Francisco DeMiranda 1783-1784*, Tour of United States, Hispanic Society of America, 1928, 206 pgs.30.00

Wortley, Emmeline Stuart, *Travels in the United States, etc. during 1849 and 1850*, New York, 1851, large 12mo, publisher's cloth, 1st American ed 70.00

Yankee Nomad, A Photographic Odyssey, *David Douglas Duncan*, Holt, Rinehart & Winston, 1967, 4to, 480 pgs...................25.00

Yee, Chiang, *Silent Traveller in New York: A Visitor's View in Words and Chinese Style Art*, Chiang Yee, John Day Co., NY, c1945, 8vo, 281 pgs............................25.00

Young, Hazel, *Islands of New England*, Little Brown, 1954, illus, 1st ed....................10.00

Bottle Openers, Figural

Collecting Hints: Condition is most important. Worn or missing paint, repainted surfaces, damage or rust result in lower value.

History: Figural bottle openers were produced expressly to remove a bottle cap from a bottle. They were made in a variety of metals, including cast iron, brass, bronze and white metal. Cast iron, brass and bronze openers are generally solid castings; white metal openers are usually cast in hollow blown molds. The vast majority of figural bottle openers date from the 1950s and 1960s. Paint variations on any particular figure are common.

References: Donald Bull, *Price Guide to Beer Advertising, Openers and Corkscrews*, published by author, 1981; *Figural Bottle Openers*, Figural Bottle Opener Collectors Club, 1992.

Collectors' Clubs: Figural Bottle Opener Collectors Club, 3 Ave. A, Latrobe, PA 15650; Just For Openers, 3712 Sunningdale Way, Durham, NC 27707.

Reproduction Alert.

Bear, 3-7/8" x 3-1/16", brass, wall mount, head, black highlights, John Wright Co........................65.00

Black Boy with alligator 2-5/8" h, hands down, green alligator, Wilton Products 145.00

    3" h, hand in air, green alligator and base, John Wright Co. 175.00

Black Man, 4-3/8" x 3-3/4", wall mount, smiling, red, bow tie, Wilton Products 95.00

Cathy Coed, 4-1/8" h, cast iron, preppy girl holding stack of books, green base, white front, sgd "L&L Favors"...................350.00

Clown, cast iron, wall mount, polka dot tie, minor paint loss 100.00

Cockatoo, 3-1/4" h, cast iron, orange and yellow chest...................125.00

Donkey, white metal, painted, 3-5/8", $22.

Cowboy with Guitar, 4-7/8" h, cast iron, yellow, brown and gray guitar, green cactus, black shoes, red bandanna, John Wright Co. 110.00

Dinky Dan, 3-1/4" h, cast iron, preppy boy, hands in pockets, green base, sgd "Gadzik, Phila" on back ..245.00

Do Do Bird, 2-3/4" h, cast iron, cream, black highlights, red beak......175.00

Drunk with Sign Post, 3-7/8" h, white sign, black post, wearing tux and hat.................25.00

Elephant, 3-1/16" h, sitting, trunk in circle, gray, pink nostrils, white toe nails, Wilton Products..............40.00

Four Eyes, 4" x 3-7/8", man with 2 sets of eyes, black hair and mustache, John Wright Co. 35.00

Grass Skirt Dancer, 5" h, cast iron, black native girl, white sign and post, green base, sgd "Gadzik, Phila" on back 275.00

Mademoiselle, 4-1/2" h, cast iron, streetwalker by lamp post, black, flesh-colored face, hands and legs, yellow light, John Wright Co. 25.00

Parrot, 5" h, standing, cast iron, orig paint, some loss on beak 110.00

Pelican, 3-3/4" h, cast iron, head up, cream, orange beak and feet, green base, John Wright Co............150.00

Rooster

    3-3/16" h, bronze, yellow, orange, black and white body, orange-yellow feet, green base, tail opener, Wilton Products........................40.00

    3-7/8" h, metal, black body, red comb, orange-yellow beak and feet, green base, opener under tail, John Wright Co. 55.00

Sailor, 3-3/4" h, hitchhiking, white uniform, blue tie and shoes, white sign with black trim, John Wright Co. 45.00

Sea Horse, 4-1/4" h, brass, green, white highlights, green base with blue and black highlights.................75.00

Skunk, cast iron 145.00

Boxing Collectibles

Collecting Hints: Collectors of boxing memorabilia might wish to limit their collections to specific fighters. Today's fighters often retire and re-enter the ring and new collectibles are being generated at a rapid rate.

History: Boxing, also known as prize fighting, is an old sport. The Romans enjoyed boxing competitions and the sport was revived in the early part of the 18th century in England. The marquees of Queensberry introduced rules for the sport in 1865 and required the used of boxing gloves. Boxing became an Olympic sport in 1904.

Boxing was illegal in America until 1896, when New York became the first state to legalize it. Every state has a boxing commission or athletic organization to regulate the sport. Competition, limited to timed three-minute "rounds," takes place in a ring, which is usually 20 feet square. Professional boxers are divided into eight weight classes, ranging from flyweight to heavyweight.

References: Mark Allen Baker, *All Sport Autograph Guide*, Krause Publications, 1994; David Bushing, *Sports Equipment Price Guide*, Krause Publications, 1995; Roderick A. Malloy, *Malloy's Guide to Sports Cards Values*, Wallace-Homestead, 1995; ——, *Malloy's Sports Collectibles Value Guide*, Wallace-Homestead, 1994; Michael McKeever, *Collecting Sports Memorabilia*, Alliance Publishing, 1966.

Periodicals: *Boxing Collectors Newsletter*, 59 Bosson St., Revere, MA 02151; *Sports Collectors Digest*, 700 E. State St., Iola, WI 54990.

Collectors' Clubs: Boxiana & Pugilistica Collectors International, P.O. Box 83135, Portland, OR 97203.

Arcade Card, John Consalves, green-
tone real photo, 1940s.............10.00
Autograph
  Boxing Trunks, Muhammad Ali, white
    trunks, black border, framed and
    matted...................................350.00
  Check, canceled
    Dempsey, Jack,
      matted and framed.............200.00
    Jake and Vikki LaMotta........60.00
  Menu, Jack Dempsey's Restaurant,
    7-3/4" x 12-1/4" cardboard folder
    menu from Dempsey's Corner res-
    taurant, 50th St. and 8th Ave., NY,
    sgd twice in black ink on cover, plus
    autograph by "Al," c1940........100.00
  Photograph, Rocky Marciano, 4" x 6",
    b&w, bold blue ink signature, matted
    and framed...........................995.00
Badge, Mayor Tommie Smith—Ali Char-
  ity Fight, 3" d, b&w celluloid, illus of
  Mayor Smith, Jersey City, NJ, as "Ur-

ban Fighter" vs. Muhammad Ali,
  illus of Jersey City Armory, June 29,
  1979 ....40.00
Book
  Boxing Record Reference, 5" x 7-
    1/4", paperback published by Ever-
    last Sports Publishing Co., 1929, 392
    pgs, fighter profiles and portraits,
    green, b&w cover.....................35.00
  Jack Dempsey/The Idol of Histiana,
    1936 revised ed, Nat Fleischer, 158
    pgs, inked autograph 35.00
Bottle Cap, Joe Louis Punch, red and
  white tin cap, c1940.................30.00
Boxing Gloves, Rocky
  Graziano, orig box 145.00
Bust, John Sullivan,
  Red Top Beer 250.00
Cartoon Art, Sharkey Is Thinking
  of a Comeback!, 13" x 13" stiff
  white art sheet, black pencil
  and ink orig art by Phil Berube,
  scheduled for newspaper sports
  section May 13, 1935, central
  pencil portrait of Jack Sharkey,
  some wear and damage, Bell Syndicate, Inc., stamp on back 75.00
Charm, Jack Dempsey, bright gold luster
  plastic, boxing glove, inscribed name
  on top, early 1950s..................35.00
Game, Muhammad Ali's Boxing Ring,
  mechanical, Mego Corp., 1976,
  Herbert Muhammad Enterprise Inc.,
  orig box..................................65.00
Magazine, *Sports Illustrated*, June 18,
  1973, George Foreman
  on cover..................................18.00
Photograph
  Ali-Ellis, 8" x 10" glossy b&w, 10 dif-
    ferent Muhammad Ali facial expres-
    sions and contortions explained by
    photo-release caption "Actor, Fighter
    or Both—A Study in Many Faces of
    Muhammad Ali," lists live closed-
    circuit telecast, July 26, 1971,
    Houston Astrodome 40.00
  Dempsey-Loughran, 7" x 9" glossy
    b&w, press release caption by Asso-
    ciated Press attached to rear, March
    23, 1938, release date, Jack Demp-
    sey in left, Tommy Loughran at right,
    attending Philadelphia dinner honor-
    ing State Boxing Commissioner Jules
    Aronson pictured in center 25.00
  Dempsey, U.S. Army Signal Corps,
    8-1/4" x 10" glossy b&w, Dempsey in
    military dress uniform, other military
    personnel and civilians,
    Signal Corps stamp dated Jan. 19,
    1944, on back 30.00
Pinback Button
  Marcel Cerdan, b&w photo, Europe-
    an middleweight who held U.S.
    championship, c1948 ....35.00

  Frazier-Ali, b&w, March 8, 1971,
    Madison Square Garden..........35.00
  Jake LaMotta, b&w, c1949 ......30.00
  Archie Moore,
    gray and black, c1956.............15.00
Poster, Koncert King Promotions presents Farewell to a Legend, Muhammad Ali in His Last Ring Appearance,
  March 12, Providence Civic Center,
  Providence, RI, also features fight
  with Marvelous Marvin Hagler
  in 10-bout round 180.00
Press Badge, octagonal diecut cardboard, inked authorization for "H&E
  Photog" for "Loughran vs. Walker"
  bout March 29, 1929, Chicago Stadium, pink silhouettes of boxers under
  inked name, printed "24" serial number, grommet for hanging........85.00
Record Book, Blue Book, 1922.....60.00
Toy, Bing 'n' Bang, 4" x 7-3/4" blue and
  white card, plastic mechanical-action
  novelty toy, Gala Plastics Corp.,
  c1950, solid yellow and red boxer figures, 1 arm swings freely, tan plastic
  front bar, pink plastic boxing ring
  ropes and corner posts 50.00
Trade Card, T9, Turkey Red,
  Abe Attell 125.00

Sascha Brastoff

Collecting Hints: When collecting items made by Brastoff, take special note of the signature. Pieces made exclusively by Brastoff are marked with his full name. A "Sascha B" signature indicates he only supervised the production.

History: Internationally known designer, artist, sculptor and ceramist Sascha Brastoff began producing ceramic artware in 1953. His hand-painted china originally commanded prices ranging from $25 to thousands of dollars for a single item. He also designed a full line of dinnerware.

References: Jack Chipman, *Collector's Encyclopedia of California Pottery*, Collector Books, 1992; Lois Lehner, *Lehner's Encyclopedia of U.S. Marks on Pottery, Porcelain & Clay*, Collector Books, 1988; Leslie Pina, *Pottery, Modern Wares 1920-1960*, Schiffer Publishing, 1994.

Ashtray
  5-1/4" d, round, domed 20.00
  5-1/2" l, leaf shape, enamelware,
    brown bones, sgd 25.00
  7" d, Eskimo.............................60.00

8" l, kidney shape, house 34.00
Basket, 17" h 150.00
Candleholders, pr, 8" h, walrus 75.00
Charger, 17" d 150.00
Cigarette Box, cov, 5-3/8" l, 3-7/8" w, 1-
    3/4" h, grapes, gold ext, black int,
    sgd "Sascha B" 35.00
Coffeepot, 10" h, 11" w, gold and black
    ext, white, pink and gold int, sgd
    "Sascha B" 45.00
Compote, 12" h, striped white 85.00
Conch, 9-1/2" l, 6-1/2" w, 4-1/2" h, white,
    gold, blue and brown, sgd "Sascha
    B" 55.00
Figure, 9" l, poodle,
    crackle glaze, sgd 115.00
Fruit Bowl, Surf Ballet, gold dec, emerald
    green ground, ftd 40.00
Mug, 6" h, Eskimo and walrus 75.00
Place Setting, 4 pc, marbleized, tur-
    quoise and silver top, white bottom,
    full signature, gold rooster
    trademark 65.00
Plate
    8-3/4" d, Surf Ballet, gold dec,
        emerald green ground..............35.00
    12" d, pagoda design,
        curled lip....................................85.00
Platter, 17-3/4" l, 14" w, rect, wavy rim, 1
    large green and white leaf,
    shaded deep-green ground, glossy
    finish 250.00
Smoker Set, 13-1/2" l, 5-1/8" w, #08 ash-
    tray, houses dec, 9" x 8-3/4", #F40
    bicycle-seat-shaped candy dish, 2-
    3/4" h #61 lighter, 2-3/4" h #61 match
    holder, multicolored, gold trim, roost-
    er trademark, for set 50.00
Vase
    9-1/2" h, rearing stallion 95.00
    12" h, Alaskan 250.00

Breweriana

Collecting Hints: Many collectors concentrate on items from one specific brewery or region. An item will bring slightly more when it is sold in its original locality. Regional collectors' clubs and shows abound.

History: Collecting material associated with the brewing industry developed in the 1960s when many local breweries ceased production. Three areas occupy the collectors' interest—pre-Prohibition material, advertising items for use in taverns and premiums designed for an individual's use.

References: George J. Baley, *Back Bar Breweriana*, L-W Book Sales, 1992; Jack McDougall and Steve Pawlowski, *United States Micro/Brew Pub Coaster Guide*, published by authors, 1995; Herb and Helen Haydock, *World of Beer Memorabilia*, Collector Books, 1996; Steve Pawlowski and Jack McDougall, *New Jersey Brewery Coasters*, published by authors, 1995; Robert Swinnich, *Contemporary Beer Neon Signs*, L-W, 1994; Dale P. Van Wieren (ed.), *American Breweries II*, East Coast Breweriana Association, 1995; *Westcott Price Guide to Advertising Water Jugs*, Globe Press, 1991.

Periodicals: *All About Beer*, 1627 Marion Ave., Durham, NC 27705; *Barley Corn News*, P.O. Box 2328, Falls Church, VA 22042; *Suds 'n' Stuff*, 4765 Galacia Way, Oceanside, CA 92056.

Collectors' Clubs: American Breweriana Association Inc., P.O. Box 11157, Pueblo, CO 81001; East Coast Breweriana Association, 3712 Sunningdale Way, Durham, NY 27707; National Association of Breweriana Advertising, 2343 Met-To-Wee Ln., Wauwatosa, WI 53226.

Museum: The Museum of Beverage Containers & Advertising, Goodlettsville, TN.

Reproduction Alert: Advertising trays.

Backbar Bottle, James Garfield,
    b&w image of Garfield in front of red,
    white and blue shield, gold
    borders, 1880 ....2,860.00
Badge, American Brewers Association
    Convention, 1899, "ABA" inscription,
    enamel and brass plated 18.00
Beer Tray,
    Yosemite Lager 750.00
Bell, Sterling Beer, girl...................72.50
Blotter, 3" x 7-1/2", Bergdoll Brewing
    Co., 60th Anniversary, black and yel-
    low Louis Bergdoll portrait,
    Christmas holly design,
    1909, unused...........................48.00
Bottle Opener
    Fritz's Corner,
        Coeur D'Alene, Idaho.................8.00
    Miller Beer, 1955.....................35.00
Calendar, 1907, Yuengling & Son
    Brewers & Bottlers, Pottsville,
    PA, 4 puppies at the bar, 34" x 26"
    frame 1,700.00
Clicker, Gunther's Beer, white litho tin,
    red letters "The Beer That Clicks,"
    Kirchof Co., 1930s...................25.00

Clock
    Busch, electrical, horse-and-rider
        scene, crossing valley near
        mountains of Busch 35.00
    Lord Calvert, "Custom Distilled for
        Men of Distinction," black wood case,
        11" x 12", 1940s......................70.00
    Piels Beer, 15" x 11" 85.00
    Schlitz, lights, 1959.................60.00
Coaster, 4" d
    Acme Beer, Cereal & Fruit Ltd., Ho-
        nolulu, red and black letters.......7.00
    Brugh Brau Beer, McDermott, Chica-
        go, black and gold letters.........18.00
    Champagne Velvet Beer, Terre
        Haute Brewing, IN, man
        holding up glass of beer, red,
        blue and black......................12.00
    Golden Age Beer, Fernwood Brew-
        ing, PA, center glass of beer, red,
        blue and yellow 50.00
    Gunther's Beer, Gunther Brewing,
        Baltimore, bear holding beer bottle,
        red, black and yellow 15.00
Cribbage Board,
    Drink Rhinelander Beer...........25.00
Decanter, Old Crow 30.00
Display Bottle, Old Grand-Dad,
    28" h, full 200.00
Doorstop, Hanley's Ale,
    cast iron, bulldog 565.00
Fishing Lure, Schlitz, bottle shape ..8.00
Foam Scraper, celluloid
    Goetz Brewery 18.00
    Meister Brau 20.00
Glass
    Best, Philip,
        Milwaukee, etched 395.00
    Colorado Three Star Beer, Trinidad,
        CO, enameled......................310.00
    Fox Head 400, Waukesha,
        WI, barrel shape 725.00
    F.W. Cook Brewing Co., Evansville,
        IN, pre-Prohibition.................185.00

Tray, Famous Manayunk Beer and Ale, Liebert and Obert Brewers of Fine Beer Since 1873, Manayunk, Philadelphia, PA, round, 12" d, $45.

Northwestern Beer, Superior, WI,
enameled 270.00
Silver Bar Beer,
Tampa, enameled 150.00
Ice Pick, Empire Lager,
Black Horse Ale 30.00
Key-Chain Fob, Schlitz Beer,
brass charm, beer-keg shape,
Schlitz trademark script name,
early 1900s 20.00
Lapel Stud, 3/4" x 7/8", Bert and Harry
Fan Club, diecut brass, blue paint,
cartoon figures, National Bohemian
Brewery Co., Baltimore, c1950 20.00
Map, Champagne Velvet,
battle map of the Pacific 20.00
Medallion, bronze,
Stroh's Run for Liberty 20.00
Memo Book, Pearl Beer,
1960-61 calendars 3.00
Menu, Old German Beer, Cafe Bischoff,
York, PA, 1940 ....10.00
Mug, pre-Prohibition
Genesee Brewing Co.,
Rochester, NY 230.00
Hafemeister Brewing Co., Green
Bay, WI................................98.00
Schlitz, Milwaukee, salt glaze ..45.00
Patch, Lucky Lager, 7-1/4" x 6-1/2",
large red X, white ground, yellow and
red letters...............................18.00
Peanut Dispenser, Miller Beer.......15.00
Pinback Button
Budweiser Month, red letters,
white ground, Anheuser-Busch
logo, c1950.............................25.00
Pabst/Milwaukee, 1/2" d, multicol-
ored, "B" grain-leaf symbol trade-
mark, early 1900s.....................30.00
Rupperts Beer/Ale, dark blue and yellow, c1930 ....25.00

**Sign, Silver Top Beer, cardboard, Du-
quesne Brewing Co., bottle, top, and
owl, 15-3/4", $20.**

Radio, Bud Can, MIB 50.00
Shot Glass
Henry Schnelten's Whiskeys,
Quincy, IL, etched 20.00
Penn State, blue enamel logo....2.00
Peoria Co., Club Whiskey,
Peoria, IL, etched.....................25.00
Shawhan Whiskey,
Weston, MI, etched..................25.00
Sign
Adam Scheidt, Norristown, PA, Val-
ley Forge Special, diecut, woman
holding bottle standing behind case
of beer, cardboard, 11" x 20" ...90.00
Ballantine, Newark, NJ, Ballantine
Bear, diecut, 1960s pro-football
schedule, cardboard, 12" x 20" 20.00
Falstaff Beer, blacks in bar setting,
lights, 11-1/2" x 18" 85.00
Old Dutch Bock Beer, Eagle,
Catasaqua, PA, referee holds up
hand of standing ram prize fighter,
cardboard, 13" x 19" 85.00
Schlitz, lighted 85.00
Wunder Beer, Oakland, CA, card-
board, hanging type 65.00
Stein, Budweiser
Hamburg, Germany,
cov, CS16 ....550.00
Label Logo, CS18 ....455.00
Pilque, German, CS5 ....310.00
Tab, litho tin, Ballantine slogan,
white litho, red letters, three-ring
symbol, 1970s 10.00
Tin, Chickencock Pure Rye,
multicolored 225.00
Tip Tray
Ballantine & Sons,
back hanger 25.00
Octavio Bumadez, red border, blue
center, liquor bottle
image, 4-1/2" d.........................15.00
Red Raven, 4" x 6", some damage
from use 100.00
Token, Hamm's Beer 20.00
Tray
Berghoff Beer...........................70.00
Falstaff, round, metal,
maiden pouring beer 115.00
Muehlebach Beer......................20.00
Schaefer Beer 10.00
Silver Bar Ale, Tampa, round...70.00
T-Shirt, Budman,
dated 1988, Jostens 10.00
Watch Fob, 1-1/2" d, diecut
silvered brass, Anheuser-
Busch, enameled red, white and
blue trademark 60.00

Bubblegum Cards, Nonsport

Collecting Hints: Don't buy individual cards; buy full sets. The price of

a set is less than the sum of its individual cards. Any set should contain
a sample of the wrapper plus any
stickers that belong to the set. Because these cards are readily available (except for pre-1970 cards),
make certain the sets you buy are in
mint condition. Collectors should
store cards in plastic sleeves.

History: The predecessors of the
modern bubblegum (trading) cards
are the tobacco insert cards of the
late 19th century. From 1885 to
1894, there were more than 500 sets
issued, with only about 25 devoted
to sports. Trading cards lost their
popularity in the decade following
World War I. However, in 1933 "Indian Gum" came out with a product
containing a stick of bubble gum and
a card in a waxed-paper package. A
revolution had begun.

Goudey Gum and National Chi-
cle controlled the market until the arrival of Gum, Inc., in 1936. Gum,
Inc., issued The Lone Ranger and
Superman sets in 1940. From 1943
to 1947, the market in cards was
again quiet. In 1948, Bowman entered the picture; a year later, Topps
Chewing Gum produced some non-
sports cards. The ensuing war between Bowman and Topps ended in
1956 when Topps bought Bowman.
Although Topps enjoyed a dominant
position in the baseball card market,
it had continuous rivals in the non-
sports field. Frank Fleer Company,
Leaf Brands and Philadelphia Chewing Gum provided competition in the
1960s; Fleer, Upper Deck and a host
of other companies provide the modern-day assault.

References: John Neuner, *Checklist & Prices of U.S. Non-Sport Wrappers*, Wrapper King Inc., 1992;
Robert Reed, *Collector's Guide to
Trading Cards*, Collector Books,
1993; Stuart Wells III, *Comic Cards
and Their Prices*, Wallace-Homestead, 1994.

Periodicals: *Non-Sport Report* (catalog from The Card Coach, but loaded with articles), P.O. Box 128,
Plover, WI 54467; *Non-Sport Update*, 4019 Green St., P.O. Box
5858, Harrisburg PA 17110; *Non-
Sports Illustrated*, P.O. Box 126, Lin-

Look N See (R714-16), 2-1/16" x 2-15/16", 135 cards, Topps; top left: #40 Stonewall Jackson, $1; top right: #37 George A Juster, $1; bottom left: 3#5 Matthew B. Ridgway, 50 cents; bottom right: #39 George Smith Patton, $1.

coln, MA 01773; *Wrapper*, P.O. Box 227, Geneva, IL 60134.

Collectors' Club: United States Cartophilic Society, P.O. Box 4020, St. Augustine, FL 32085.

Note: Prices are for cards in excellent condition.

Bowman

1948, Movie Stars, 2-1/16" x 2-1/2", 36 cards, set 350.00
1950, Wild Man, 2-1/16" x 2-1/2", 72 cards...........................1,200.00

Donruss

1964, Combat, Series 1, 66 cards, #1-66......................150.00
1964, Combat, Series 2, 66 cards, #67-132..................230.00
1966, Green Hornet, 44 cards.....300.00
1968, Flying Nun, 66 cards..................................290.00
1970, Odder Odd Rods, 66 cards 250.00
1973, Osmonds, 66 cards 120.00
1976, Bionic Woman, 44 cards 40.00
1978, KISS, first series, 66 cards..................................50.00
1979, Rock Stars, 66 cards 45.00
1983, Magnum PI, 66 cards 12.00

Fleer

1959, Three Stooges, 66 cards...900.00
1960, Casper, 66 cards...............475.00
1963, Goofy Gags, 55 cards 75.00

1965, Gomer Pyle, 66 cards 90.00
1971, Official Drag Champs, 63 cards..................................250.00
1972, Drag Nationals, 70 cards...200.00
1979, Gong Show, 66 cards, 10 stickers 40.00
1980, Pac Man, 28 cards-54 stickers 30.00
1981, Here's Bo, 72 cards, 12 posters..................5.00
1983, MAD, 128 stickers 125.00
1984, Dragon's Lair, 63 stickers, 30 rub-off games 45.00
1994, Marvel, 200 cards...............25.00
1995, Marvel Flair Annual, 150 cards...............................55.00

Leaf

1966, Good Guys & Bad Guys, 72 cards...............275.00
1967, Garrisons' Gorillas, 72 cards..................................275.00

Philadelphia Chewing Gum Co.

1965, James Bond, 66 cards 250.00
1966
   Green Berets, 66 cards...........70.00
   James Bond, Thunderball, 66 cards 325.00
   Tarzan, 66 cards 175.00
1969, Dark Shadows, Series II, 66 cards, green 365.00
1972, Happy Horoscopes, 72 cards..................................35.00

Skybox

1992, Garfield, 100 cards-9 stickers 13.00
1993, Nightmare Before Christmas, 100 cards..............................15.00
1994, Lion King, 90 cards 12.00
1994, Lion King II, 80 cards 12.00
1995, Gargoyles, 90 cards 16.00

Topps

1959, Fabian, 115 cards 115.00
1961, Crazy Cards, 66 cards 200.00
1962
   Casey & Kildare, 110 cards ...200.00
   Mars Attacks, 55 cards 1,600.00
1963
   Beverly Hillbillies, 66 cards 375.00
   Flag Midgee, 99 cards 80.00
1964, Outer Limits, 50 cards.......600.00
1965
   Daniel Boone (test), 55 cards 6,800.00
   Kookie Awards, 44 cards 450.00
1966
   Batman, Riddle back series, 38 cards......................230.00
   Flipper (test), 30 cards 1,750.00

Television and Radio Stars of NBC (R701-14), 2-1/2" x 3-3/4", 36 cards, Bowman, 1952; left: #1 Gertrude Berg, 90 cents; right: #22 Bess Myerson, 90 cents.

Lost In Space, 55 cards 500.00
1969, Brady Bunch, 88 cards......900.00
1970, Comic Cover, 44 stickers 325.00
1974, Evel Kneivel, 60 cards 200.00
1975
   Bay City Rollers, 66 cards 150.00
   Good Times, 55 cards, 21 stickers...............................75.00
1976
   Happy Days, Series 1, 44 cards, 11 stickers...............................35.00
   King Kong, 55 cards 45.00
   Shock Theater, 50 cards........250.00
1977, Charlie's Angels, Series 1, 55 cards 90.00
1978
   Battlestar Galactica, 132 cards, 22 stickers.............35.00
   Close Encounters, 66 cards, 11 stickers...............................24.00
1979
   Black Hole, cards and stickers.13.00
   Buck Rogers, cards and stickers..............................21.00
1980, Empire Strikes Back, Series 1 ....32.00
1983
   A-Team, 66 cards, 12 stickers ...8.00
   Dukes of Hazzard, Series 1, 66 cards....................50.00
1985, Rambo, 66 cards, 22 stickers 16.00
1987, Max Headroom, 33 cards-11 stickers 17.00
1993, Last Action Hero, 88 cards-11 stickers 10.00

C

Calculators

Collecting Hints: Mechanical calculators found at flea markets are often in very poor condition. Look for models in working order with no missing parts. Crank- or lever-operated machines are desirable, but 110-volt electro-mechanical machines have not attracted collector interest, perhaps because they are still so common.

Slide rules made of wood or metal are widely collected, but plastic models are not. Most slide rules are 6 to 12 inches long. Longer rules and circular models are less common and more valuable.

Electronic calculators have no moving parts. Battery-operated or pocket models are desirable, while desktop printing machines generally are not. Like early transistor radios (1955-1965), the first pocket calculators (1970-1980) have become an exciting collectible. But unlike transistor radios, early pocket calculators are still easy to find at thrift stores and flea markets. Best of all, thrift stores often sell 1970s models for less than $5. Models with display numbers that light up (LED type) were made only during the 1970s and are obsolete and collectible. Almost all pocket calculators made since 1980 have liquid crystal (black) display numbers. With the exception of novelty types, these newer models are not currently collectible. A very easy way to identify the early (1970s) models is to look for a socket (hole) for an adapter plug. Almost all early pocket calculators have an adapter socket while newer pocket models do not. Collectors generally don't care if the adapter and cord are missing as long as the calculator has a socket. Fortunately for the collector, almost every pocket calculator has both the manufacturer's name and the model number printed clearly on the front or back of the case.

History: Although the abacus has been used for over a thousand years, the first mechanical calculating devices were not invented until the 1600s. Few early machines survived; those that did are now in museum collections. A very early handmade brass calculating device recently sold for several million dollars.

Calculators were not manufactured on a commercial scale until the early to mid 1800s. By the late 1800s, mechanical calculators were being produced by many companies and some models, such as Felt's comptometer, are still found in flea markets today. Electric motors were added at the turn of this century and these "electromechanical" calculators were still in common use in the 1960s. During the 1960s, transistorized desktop calculators began to appear but initially cost thousands of dollars.

In the early 1970s, thanks to the invention of the integrated circuit, which packed thousands of transistors onto a microchip, the first affordable electronic calculators began to appear. Pocket-sized electronic calculators came onto the market in 1971-1972 for $200 to $400. This was the end of the line for mechanical calculator and slide rule companies. Competition to produce cheaper electronic calculators soon reached a frenzy and dozens of companies either went bankrupt or were quickly forced out of the calculator business—bad news for calculator manufacturers, but good news for collectors! By 1973, the price of a basic pocket calculator had fallen to the incredibly "low" price of $100 (about $300 in terms of today's adjusted currency). Today, a similar four-function calculator sells for about $5. Note that some manufacturers, like Texas Instruments and Unisonic, made dozens of different models. The first models made by a given company are generally the most sought after. Only two American companies—Texas Instruments and Hewlett-Packard—still produce pocket calculators.

References: William Aspray, *Computing before Computers*, Iowa State University Press, 1990; Bruce Flamm and Guy Ball, *Collector's Guide to Pocket Calculators*, Wilson/Barnett Publishing (14561 Livingston St., Tustin, CA 92680), 1997; Thomas F. Haddock, *Collector's Guide to Personal Computers and Pocket Calculators*, Books Americana, 1993; Geoffrey Tweedale, *Calculating Machines and Computers*, Shire, 1990; Michael R. Williams, *History of Computing Technology*, Prentice Hall, 1985.

Collectors' Clubs: International Association of Calculator Collectors (IACC), P.O. Box 70513, Riverside, CA 92513; The Oughtred Society (slide rules), 2160 Middlefield Rd., Palo Alto, CA 94301.

Museums: Cambridge University Science Museum, Cambridge, England; National Museum of American History, Smithsonian Institution, Washington, DC.

Advisor: Bruce L. Flamm.

APF Mark 21	25.00
Bohn Instant	30.00
Bohsei 3000	10.00
Bomar 901B	65.00
Busicom Handy LE	250.00
Calcupen	150.00
Canon Pocketronic	150.00
Commodore	
887D	30.00
MM1	70.00
MM2	45.00
MM3	25.00
Corvus 411	30.00
Craig	
4501	50.00
4502	55.00
4509	35.00
Crown CL 130	150.00
Facit 1140	45.00
Heathkit IC2006	50.00
Hewlett-Packard	
35	100.00
55	80.00
Hp-01	
Calculator	20.00
Calculator and watch	750.00
Keystone	
390	50.00
2030	40.00
Kings Point	
8412	40.00
SC20	35.00
Litronix 2220	25.00
Lloyds 303	20.00
Miida 838	45.00
National	20.00
Semiconductor 600	15.00
Omron 606	35.00
Radio Shack EC 425	45.00
Rapid Data 800	35.00
Rockwell 76	35.00
Royal 90K	25.00
Royal Digital 3	100.00

Sanyo ICC 804D 100.00
Sharp EL 8 ....75.00
Sinclair Sovereign 110.00
Summit KO9V..............................45.00

Calendars

Collecting Hints: Value increases if all monthly pages are attached. Most calendars are bought by collectors who are interested in the subject illustrated on the calendar rather than the calendar, per se.

History: Calendars were a popular advertising giveaway in the late 19th century and during the first five decades of the 20th. Recently, a calendar craze has swept bookstores throughout America. These topic-oriented calendars contain little or no advertising.

Reference: Rick and Charlotte Martin, *Vintage Illustration: Discovering America's Calendar Artists*, Collectors Press (P.O. Box 230986, Portland, OR 97281); Norman E. Martinus and Harry L. Rinker, *Warman's Paper*, Wallace-Homestead, 1994.

Collectors' Club: Calendar Collector Society, 18222 Flower Hill Way #299, Gaithersburg, MD 20879.

Additional Listings: Pinup Art.

Reproduction Alert.

1893, Hoods Sarsaparilla 95.00
1889, Buckeye Fire Insurance,
    color illus of Victorian woman,
    28" x 20" 295.00
1890, Success Horse Collars,
    14" x 24" 360.00
1894, Hatfield and Kearney, children,
    folding, 12-1/2" x 7-1/2" 85.00
1898, Fairbanks Fairy Floral Calendar,
    6 pgs, orig string holder,
    12" x 8-1/2" 85.00
1899, Youth's Companion 45.00
1901, Grand Union Tea, 4 pgs,
    12" x 8-1/2" 35.00
1905, Rock Crystal Salt, Chicago,
    celluloid, memo pad................35.00
1907, Capewell Horse Nails, horse, buggy, horseless carriage and blacksmith, J. Kerner and Shop, matted and framed, 13" 150.00
1913, Gross Druggist, Harrisburg, PA,
    multicolored, celluloid 35.00
1914, Ashland Brewery, WI..........75.00
1916, Metropolitan Insurance........20.00
1918, American Glass Co., Cincinnati, celluloid, ruler and blotter, black

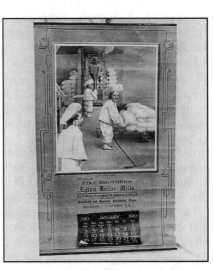

1910, Fike Brothers, Eglan Roller Mills, Eglan, WV, 1908, 14" x 22-1/4", $35.

    and white illus 20.00
1921, DeLaval, little boy fishing 70.00
1922, Minnehaha Falls, Fox,
    4-1/2" x 10" 35.00
1926, Mary Pickford, Pompeian....50.00
1927, Wrigley's Double Mint Gum,
    3-1/2" x 6" 30.00
1928
    American Book Co.,
    school type..............................15.00
    Maas-Steffen Fur Co.............275.00
1929, Historical Art........................21.00
1930, Peter's Cartridges 265.00
1931, DeLaval, illus by
    Norman Priss........................165.00
1934, Ramon's Brownies,
    6-pg flip-type, newsprint paper,
    12-1/2" x 19", metal top edge ..35.00
1936, Oliver Tractors....................75.00
1937, Traveler's, Currier and
    Ives illus..................................40.00
1938, Mt. Airy Milling,
    Gold Medal Flour....................25.00
1939, Johnson Winged Gasoline ..20.00
1940, American Book Co., school type,
    American Firsts 15.00
1941, When Winter Comes,
    Maxfield Parrish....................195.00
1942, Onawa Lodge, Poconos, blotter
    type, 3-1/2" x 6-1/8" 5.00
1943, Esquire, illus by Vargas,
    orig envelope 50.00
1944, Stem Brothers, Skyesville
    AMOCO....................................18.00
1945, American Book Co., school type,
    Pacific scenes 15.00
1946, Bathing Beauty, titled "I'll Say So,"
    illus by Rolf Armstrong 75.00
1947, Hercules Powder..............175.00
1948, First Dates, 8" x 11" 25.00
1950, Welsh Florists, Reisterstown,

    MD, flower pictures 12.00
1951, Four Seasons, illus by
    Norman Rockwell 35.00
1954, Elgren, "Some Help!" pinup girl
    painting Scottie......................75.00
1955, Farmer's Supply, 24 pgs,
    orig envelope............................8.00
1956
    Rock City Lookout
    Mountain, TN 4.00
    Sealtest, 24 pgs, hanging type ..7.50
1957, Jewish Art, color pictures,
    9-1/2" x 16"..............................7.50
1963, Pasadena Tournament
    of Roses 20.00
1969, Union Pacific
    RR Centennial........................20.00
1975, Arizona Highways 5.00
1976
    Girl Scouts 6.00
    Maryland, Bicentennial,
    b&w photos 6.00

Cameras and Accessories

Collecting Hints: Because of the sheer numbers of antique and classic cameras available, collectors often concentrate on specific eras, types, models, manufacturers or country of origin.

Leica has been the top name in 35mm photography since the German company of Ernst Leitz introduced its landmark camera in 1925. Although prices are relatively stable, Leica cameras are generally expensive. Demand for them exists worldwide. Kodak has been American's favorite camera since the introduction of the low-cost Brownie in 1900. As a result of the company's mass production and marketing, there is a surplus of many common models, both antique and modern.

The commercial success of Polaroid's instant-picture cameras has resulted in a surplus in the marketplace. Introduced in 1948, Polaroid cameras are not widely collected and prices for most models remain low. The few exceptions are Polaroid cameras outfitted with superior optics.

Condition is of utmost importance unless the camera in question is particularly scarce. Shutters should function properly. Minimal wear is generally acceptable. Avoid cameras that have missing parts, damaged bellows or major cosmetic problems. In addition to precision instruments, camera collectors look for the odd and unusual models. Examples run the gamut from an inexpensive plastic camera that looks like a can of soda to a rare antique camera disguised to look like three books held together by a leather strap.

History: Of all the antique and classic cameras available, the most prized are those that took the earliest photographs known as daguerreotypes. The process was successfully developed by Louis-Jacques-Mandé Daguerre of Paris in 1839. These photographic images, made of thinly coated silver on copper plate, have a legion of collectors all their own. However, few of the cameras that photographed daguerreotypes have survived.

Edward Anthony became America's first maker of cameras and photographic equipment by founding E. Anthony in 1842. The company later became Ansco. Stereoscope photos were shown at London's Great Exhibition in 1851 and soon became the rage in Britain and Europe. Stereo cameras are recognized by their horizontally mounted twin lenses. Tintype photographs were introduce in 1856.

George Eastman's introduction of the Kodak camera in 1888 made photography accessible to the general public. Made by Frank Brownell for the Eastman Dry Plate & Film Co., it was the first commercially marketed roll-film camera. The original Kodak camera was factory loaded with 100 exposures. The finished pictures were round and 2-1/2 inches in diameter. Eastman Kodak's No. 2 Brownie, a box camera made of cardboard, became a best-seller shortly after it was introduced in 1902.

After manufacturing microscopes and optical equipment for 75 years, Ernst Leitz of Wetzlar, Germany, introduced the first Leica 35mm camera in 1925. Japanese companies entered the photography market with Minolta (Nifca) cameras circa 1928, Canon (Kwanon) in 1933 and Nippon Nogaku's Nikon rangefinder cameras in 1948.

References: Michael McBroom, *McBroom's Camera Blue Book 1993-1994*, Amherst Media, 1993; Jim and Joan McKeown (eds.), *Price Guide to Antique and Classic Cameras 1997-1998*, Centennial Photo Service, 1996; Douglas St. Denny, *Hove International Blue Book Guide Prices for Classic and Collectable Cameras*, Hove Foto Books, 1992.

Periodicals: *Camera Shopper Magazine*, P.O. Box 1086, New Canaan, CT 06840; *Classic Camera*, P.O. Box 1270, New York, NY, 10157; *Shutterbug*, 5211 S. Washington Ave., Titusville, FL 32780.

Collectors' Clubs: American Society of Camera Collectors, 4918 Alcove Ave., N. Hollywood, CA 91607; International Kodak Historical Society, P.O. Box 21, Flourtown, PA 19301; Leica Historical Society of America, 7611 Dornoch Ln., Dallas, TX 75248; National Stereoscopic Association, P.O. Box 14801, Columbus, OH 43214; Nikon Historical Society, P.O. Box 3213, Munster, IN 46321; Photographic Historical Society, P.O. Box 39563, Rochester, NY 14604; The Movie Machine Society, 50 Old Country Rd., Hudson, MA 01749; Zeiss Historical Society, 300 Waxwing Dr., Cranbury, NJ 08512.

Museum: International Museum of Photography at George Eastman House, Rochester, NY.

Advisor: Tom Hoepf.

Cameras

Ansco (Birmingham, NY); merged with Agfa in 1928
    Buster Brown Box, No. 2A, c1910-23, 2-1/2" x 4-1/4 on 116 rollfilm 12.00
    Pioneer, c1947-53, plastic eye-level, 2-1/4" x 3-1/4 exposures on PB 20 film 5.00

Agfa Paramat, half frame, 35mm, zone focusing, $30.

Readyset Royal, No. 1, c1931-32, folding 120 rollfilm camera, textured leather covering resembling fur 25.00

Agfa (Munich, Germany)
    Paramat, c1963, 35mm half frame, Color-Apotar f2.8/30mm lens, automatic metering 30.00
    Selecta, c1962-66, 35mm rangefinder camera, Color-Apotar f2.8/45mm lens, Prontor-Matic shutter 25.00

Argus (Ann Arbor, MI)
    Argus Model M, c1939-40, small streamlined Bakelite camera, 828 film, Argus anastigmat 6.3 lens in collapsible mount 40.00
    Argus V-100, c1958-59, 35mm rangefinder, made in Germany for Argus, Cintagon II f2/45mm lens . 33.00
    Autronic C3, c1960-62, heavy 35mm rangefinder camera, Cintar f3.5/50mm lens, metered automatic exposure 20.00
    Ciro-Flex Model D, 1940s, common twin-lens reflex camera...........30.00

Clarus Camera Mfg. Co., (Minneapolis), Model MS-35, 1946-52, 35mm rangefinder camera, interchangeable f2.8/50mm Wollensak Velostigmat lens (plagued by erratic shutters) 40.00

Eastman Kodak (Rochester, NY)
    Anniversary Box Camera, No. 2 Hawk-Eye Model C camera, tan with foil seal, given away on 50th anniversary of Eastman Kodak in 1930...........30.00
    Bantam f8, 1938-42, Bakelite body, rectangular telescoping front instead of bellows 15.00
    Cartridge Kodak, No. 4, 1897-1907, 4" x 5" exposure on 104 rollfilm, leather-covered wood body, polished wood int, red bellows 150.00
    Medalist II, 1946-53, 2-1/4" x 3-1/4 frames on 620 rollfilm, Kodak Ektar f3.5/100mm lens, Flash Supermatic shutter 160.00
    Retina Reflex III, 1961-64, German-made single-lens reflex camera, f2.8/50mm Retina-Xenar lens, Synchro Compur shutter, coupled exposure meter 90.00

Eiko Co., Ltd (Taiwan), Can Camera, c1977-83, plastic, shaped like beverage can, various product labels......................................30.00

Konishiro Kogaku (Japan), Pearlette, c1946, "Made in Occupied Japan," trellis-strut folding camera, 127 rollfilm, Rokuosha Optar f6.3/75mm lens, Echo shutter 35.00

Toakoki Seisakusho (Japan), Gelto D III, c1950, half-frame 127 film camera, postwar chrome body, f3.5/50mm

Grimmel Anastigmat lens 90.00

Unknown Manufacturer (China)
  Empire State View, c1895, folding field camera, polished wood, brass fittings, 5" x 7"...............100.00
  Where's Waldo 110 camera, c1992, painted red and white stripes, premium for Quaker Oats Life cereal ..5.00

Voigtlander (Braunschweig, Germany),
  Vitessa, c1950-57, distinctive 35mm rangefinder, "barn-door" lens cover, rapid winding system operated by plunger extending from top of camera...................120.00

Zeiss Ikon (Jena, Germany), Contessa, c1950-55, folding 35mm rangefinder, Tessar f2.8/45mm lens, Synchro Compur shutter......................100.00

Camera-Related

Advertising
  Cooler, Kodak Disc Cameras and Film, vinyl, shoulder strap, 14" x 8" x 9"...............................8.00
  Trade Card, T.P. Stiff, The Photographer, Brockton, MA, chlth, 3-1/3" x 4-1/4".................15.00
  Sign, Kodak Film
    10" x 3-1/2" x 3-1/2", Kodak film box shape, lights up.............40.00
    18" x 14", two-sided, enamel on steel, no hanger...................65.00

Catalog, Kodak and Kodak Supplies, 1927, 64 pgs...........................18.00

Display Case
  Camera, glass, wood frame and base, "This is an ANSCO Camera" on metal plate, 11" x 10" x 7-1/2"..75.00
  Film, Agfa, glass, blue logo, 4 shelves, open back, 22" x 7-1/2" x 4-1/2"...............125.00

Exposure Meter, Zeiss Ikon Ikophot, clear-plastic case, instruction booklet....................................18.00

Magazine, *Kodakery—Magazine for Amateur Photographers*, 1919-21 ....7.00

Kodak Medalist II, 620 rollfilm, Ektar f3.5/100 mm lens, $160.

Candlewick

Collecting Hints: Select pieces without chips, cracks or scratches. Learn the characteristics, shapes and types of pieces Imperial made. Many items that are similar to Candlewick have been made by other companies and are often mixed with or labeled "Candlewick" at shops and shows. Learn to identify look-alikes and reproductions

History: Candlewick, Imperial Glass Corporation's No. 400 pattern, introduced in 1936, was made continuously until October 1982 when Imperial declared bankruptcy. In 1984, Imperial was sold to Lancaster-Colony Corp., and Consolidated Stores International, Inc. Imperial's assets, including inventory, molds, buildings and equipment, were liquidated in 1985. Imperial's Candlewick molds were bought by various groups, companies and individuals. At the liquidation sale, the buildings and site were purchased by Anna Maroon of Maroon Enterprises, Bridgeport, Ohio, with the intent of developing the site into a tourist attraction, Imperial Plaza. The Imperial glass outlet, The Hay Shed, the Bellaire Museum and a few small businesses moved into the building, but the project failed and the Imperial building deteriorated and was demolished in July 1995. The Hay Shed outlet relocated to a building near the Imperial site and operates as a consignment shop for Imperial and other glass. At its 1996 convention, the National Imperial Glass Collector's Society started a drive to establish an Imperial museum and preserve the heritage of glassmaking that took place at Imperial for more than 80 years.

Candlewick is characterized by the crystal-drop beading used around the edges of many pieces; around the bases of tumblers, shakers and other items; in the stems of glasses, compotes and cake and cheese stands; on the handles of cups, pitchers, bowls and serving pieces; on stoppers and finials; and on the handles of ladles, forks and spoons. The beading is small on some pieces, larger and heavier on others.

A large variety of pieces were produced in the Candlewick pattern. More than 650 items and sets are known. Shapes include round, oval, oblong, heart and square. Imperial added or discontinued items as popularity and demand warranted. The largest assortment of pieces and sets were made during the late 1940s and early 1950s. Candlewick was produced mostly in crystal. Viennese Blue (pale blue, 1937-1938), Ritz Blue (cobalt, 1938-1941) and Ruby Red (red, 1937-1941) were made. Amber, black, emerald green, lavender, pink and light yellow pieces also have been found. From 1977 to 1980, 4 items of 3400 Candlewick stemware were made in solid-color Ultra Blue, Nut Brown, Verde Green and Sunshine Yellow. Solid-black stemware was made on an experimental basis at the same time.

Other decorations on Candlewick include silver overlay, gold encrustations, cuttings, etchings and hand-painted designs. Pieces have been found with fired-on gold, red, blue and green beading. Blanks, i.e., plain pieces, were sold to many companies which decorated them with cuttings, hand paintings and silver overlay or fitted them with silver, chrome or brass bases, pedestals or lids. Shakers sold to DeVilbiss were made into atomizers. Irving W. Rice & Co. purchased Candlewick tray handles and trays, assembled boudoir sets and sold Candlewick clocks.

References: National Imperial Glass Collector's Society, *Imperial Glass Encyclopedia, Vol. I: A-Cane*, The Glass Press, 1995; Virginia R. Scott, *Collector's Guide to Imperial Candlewick*, 4th Edition, available from author (275 Milledge Ter., Athens, GA 30606); Mary M. Wetzel, *Candlewick: The Jewel of Imperial, Book II*, Walsworth Publishing Co., 1995.

Videotapes: National Imperial Glass Collectors Society, *Candlewick, at Home, in Any Home*, Vol. I, Imperial Beauty (Candlewick display), *Vol. II*, Seminar by Mary Wetzel and Virginia Scott, 1993 National Imperial Glass Collectors Society Convention (P.O. Box 534, Bellaire, OH 43528).

Collectors' Clubs: Candlewick Crystals of Arizona, 2430 E. Sheridan, Phoenix, AZ 85008; Maryland Imperial Candlewick Club, 23 Ashcroft Ct., Arnold, MD 21012; Michiana Association of Candlewick Collectors, 17370 Battles Rd., South Bend, IN 46614; National Candlewick Collector's Club, 275 Milledge Ter., Athens, GA 30606; National Imperial Glass Collector's Society, P.O. Box 534, Bellaire, OH 43528; Ohio Candlewick Collector's Club, 613 S. Patterson, Gibsonburg, OH 43431; Texas Regional Imperial Glass Group, P.O. Box 911, Decatur, TX 76234; Fox Valley Northern Illinois Imperial Enthusiasts, 38 W. 406 Gingerwood, Elgin, IL 60123.

Museum: Bellaire Museum, Bellaire, OH 43906.

Reproduction Alert: When Imperial Glass Corp. was liquidated in 1985, all the molds were sold but no accurate records were kept of all the buyers. It is known that Mirror Images, Lansing, MI, purchased more than 200 of the molds and Boyd Crystal Art Glass, Cambridge, Ohio, purchased 18 small ones. Other molds went to private individuals and groups. Since the late 1980s, Boyd Crystal Art Glass has used Candlewick molds to make items in various slag and clear colors. Boyd has marked their reproductions with their trademark, a "B" inside a diamond, which is pressed on the bottom of each article.

In 1985, Mirror Images had Viking Glass Co., New Martinsville, WV, make the 6-inch Candlewick basket, 400/40/0, in Alexandrite and a four-piece child's set (consisting of a demitasse cup and saucer, 6-inch plate and 5-inch nappy) in pink. In 1987, Viking produced clear plates, bowls, saucers, flat-based sugars and creamers (400/30 and 400/122) and the 400/29 tray for Mirror Images in crystal. These pieces have ground bottoms, are somewhat heavier than original Candlewick pieces and are not marked. Shapes of items may differ from original Candlewick.

In late 1990, Dalzell-Viking Corp., successor to Viking, began making Candlewick in Mirror Image's molds. They made five-piece place settings in crystal, black, cobalt, evergreen and red. Most of these are marked, either "DALZELL"

for the first-quality pieces or "DX" for seconds. In January 1991, Dalzell added handled plates, bowls and a five-section 400/112 center-well relish in crystal. A new pastel shade, Cranberry Mist, was added in 1992. Since late 1995, Dalzell Viking has offered Candlewick Gold, clear with gold beads; Candlewick Pastels, also called Satins, in azure, crystal, green, yellow and cranberry; 8-, 10- and 12-inch plates, cups and saucers and 6-inch bowls were made, all marked only with a paper label.

In 1996, Dalzell added a punch bowl set with gold beads and also began to make Candlewick with silver beads. The Pastel Satin production has been extended to include the following: 400/231 three-piece square bowl set; 400/161 butter dish; 400/154 deviled-egg tray; 400/68D pastry tray with a heart center handle; 400/87C and /87F vases; a 6-inch bowl on an 8-inch oval tray; and a 4-ounce sherbet, similar to 400/63B compote. Dalzell also added Candlewick Frosts, dark amber, plum, blue and sage green with frosted finish. All of the above are marked only with a Dalzell Viking paper label.

Advisor: Virginia R. Scott.

Salt and pepper shakers, pr, 400/190, $90.

Ashtray
    4-1/4", oblong, large beads,
    400/134/1 .... 6.00
    6", round, large beads, 400/150
        Caramel slag 14.00
        Cobalt blue 30.00
        Crystal 8.00
        Pink 14.00
    Nested set, 4", 5" and 6"
        Crystal, 400/450,
        price for set 20.00
        Pink, 400/550, price for set
          Patriotic dec 70.00
          Undecorated 32.00
        Red, white and blue, patriotic dec,
        400/550, price for set 175.00
Atomizer
    400/96 shaker, atomizer top, made
    by DeVilbiss 125.00
    400/167 shaker, atomizer top, aqua
    or amethyst 75.00
    400/247 shaker, atomizer top, aqua
    or amethyst 65.00
Banana Stand, 11" d, 2 turned-up sides,
    4-bead stem 800.00
Basket
    6-1/2", turned-up sides, applied
    handle, 400/40/0 .... 35.00

    11", applied handle,
    400/73/0 .... 130.00
Bell, 4", 4-bead handle 50.00
Bonbon, 6", heart shape,
    curved-over center handle,
    beaded edge, 400/51T
    Crystal 25.00
    Light blue 75.00
    Ruby red, crystal handle 200.00
Bowl, beaded edge
    6", nappy
        400/3F 10.00
        400/52, divided 15.00
    9", sq, crimped, 4 ball toes, 400/74SC
        Black or red 200.00
        Crystal 50.00
        Light blue 100.00
    10-1/2", 400/75B 32.00
    11", float bowl, cupped edge,
    400/92F 35.00
    14", belled, large beads on sides,
    400/104B 70.00
    Nested set, 4-3/4", 6", 7" and 8-1/2",
    400/4272B, price for set 60.00
Buffet Set, 14" plate, 400/92D; 5-1/2"
    cheese compote, plain stem,
    400/66E; 2-pc set, 400/9266 ... 50.00
Butter Dish
    1/4 lb, graduated beads on cover,
    400/161 .... 25.00
    5-1/2", cov, round,
    2-bead finial 30.00
    6-3/4" x 4", California, 400/276
        Beaded top, c1960 .... 95.00
        Plain top, c1951 .... 115.00
Cake Stand/Plate
    10", 1-bead stem
        Dome ftd, wedge marks on plate,
        400/67D, c1939 .... 80.00
        Flat ftd, c1943 .... 65.00
    11", 3-bead stem, 400/103D 75.00
    14", round, birthday plate,
    72 candle holes, 400/160 .... 300.00
Candleholder
    3-1/2"
        Dome ftd, small beads, round handle, 400/81 .... 50.00

Rolled saucer, small beads,
400/79R 12.50

5", round bowl, beaded or fluted,
vase insert, 2-pc, 400/CV.........75.00

5-1/2", ftd, 3 sections of arched
beads on stem, 400/224...........75.00

6-1/2", 3-bead stem
400/175 ....70.00

400/1752, adapter, prisms .125.00

9"

400/115, oval, beaded base,
3 candle cups.....................100.00

400/115/1-2, 2 eagles 250.00

Candy Dish, cov
5-1/2", cov, 2-bead finial,
400/59 ....35.00

6-1/2", cov, round bowl, sq cov,
2-bead finial, 400/245.............125.00

7", 3 sections, 2-bead finial,
400/110 ....50.00

8", 1-bead stem, 400/140
Flat, c1944 ....140.00

Footed, beaded-foot dome,
c1943 ....225.00

Celery Tray
11", oval, scalloped edge,
400/46 ....50.00

13-1/2", oval, 2 curved beaded
handles, 400/105.....................30.00

Cheese and Cracker Set, 5-1/2" ftd
cheese compote, 400/88; 10"
handled plate, 400/72D;
2-pc, 400/88...........................40.00

Cheese, Toast or Butter Dish,
7-3/4" plate with cupped
edge, domed cover with bubble
knop, 400/123........................200.00

Cigarette Set, cigarette holder, dome ftd,
small beads, 3", 400/44, c1941; 4
ashtrays, nested, 2-3/4", 400/64; kidney-shaped tray, 400/20; 6-pc set,
400/29/64/44 or 400/29/6 ....60.00

Clock, 4", large beads, uses 400/440
ashtray, New Haven works....400.00

Coaster, round
3-1/2", spoon rest, 400/226......12.00

4", 10 rays, 400/78 ....7.00

Cocktail Set, 6" plate with 2-1/2" off-center indent, 400/39; 1-bead cocktail
glass, #111; 2-pc set, 400/97 ..30.00

Compote, beaded edge, ftd
5", 3 sections, arched
beads in stem, 400/220............90.00

8", 4-bead stem, 400/48F.........65.00

9", large bead stem
Dome ftd, ribbed bowl, 400/67B,
c1937 ....75.00

Flat foot, 400/67B, c1943.....65.00

Console Set, bowl, pr of
candleholders 12" float bowl, cupped
edge, 400/92F; 2-light
candleholders, center circle of
large beads, ftd, 400/100.........75.00

13" mushroom bowl, 400/92L,
on 400/127B 7-1/2" base; mushroom
candleholders, 400/86;
set, 400/8692L 200.00

Condiment Set
Jam Set, 2 cov marmalade jars,
400/89; 3-bead ladles on 400/159
oval tray; 5-pc set, 400/1589....95.00

Oil and Vinegar Set, two 400/164 and
400/166 beaded foot cruets;
kidney-shaped tray; 400/29;
3-pc set, 400/2946 ....85.00

Cordial Bottle, 15 oz, beaded foot,
handle, 3-bead stopper, 400/82
Crystal, c1938 ....195.00

Crystal with red stopper and base,
c1938 ....275.00

Crystal, no handle,
400/82/2, c1941 ....175.00

Creamer and Sugar Set
Flat base, beaded question-mark
handles, 400/30; 7" tray, 400/29;
set, 400/29/30 ....25.00

Footed
Beaded foot, plain handles, c1937,
400/31
Crystal................................40.00

Light blue 60.00

Plain foot, question-mark handles,
400/31, c1941 ....30.00

Cup and Saucer Set, beaded
question-mark handles
After Dinner, small, slender, 5-1/2"
beaded saucer; set 400/77 ......18.00

Coffee, slender, 400/37; saucer
400/35; set, 400/37 ....15.00

Tea, round cup, 400/35; saucer,
400/35; set, 400/35 ....12.00

Decanter, beaded foot, round stopper,
400/163
Crystal...................................195.00

Crystal with red foot and stopper,
c1938 ....250.00

Deviled-Egg Tray, 11-1/2", 12 indents for
eggs, heart-shaped center handle,
400/154 ....95.00

Dresser Set, I. Rice Co., round mirrored
tray, 400/151; powder jar, beaded
base, 3-bead cov; 2 round perfume
bottles, beaded base, 4-bead
stoppers, 1940s, 4-pc set 185.00

Epergne Set, 9" ftd crimped flower candleholder, 1-bead stem, 400/196FC;
7-3/4" 2-bead peg vase, beaded top,
peg to fit into candle cup;
set, 400/196..........................175.00

Jelly Server
4-3/4", ftd, 1-bead stem, 2-bead cov,
400/157 ....50.00

6", divided dish, beaded edge,
handles, 400/52 ....15.00

Lamp, Hurricane, 3-1/2" saucer
candleholder, 400/79R, 9" chimney,

2-pc set, 400/79/R
Bohemian, cranberry-flashed
chimney, gold bird
and leaves 125.00

Crystal 75.00

3-pc set, including 400/152 Candlewick adapter, 400/152R ..90.00

Lemon Tray, 5-1/2" plate, center handle
of 3 sections of small arched beads,
large bead on top, 400/221 .....30.00

Marmalade Jar 400/18, old-fashion
tumbler, beaded notched cov with
2-bead finial, 3-bead ladle,
400/130; set 400/8918 ....60.00

400/89, round, beaded cov with
notch, 2-bead finial
Without ladle.......................25.00

With 3-bead ladle, 400/130..35.00

Mayonnaise Set, bowl, plate and ladle,
7-1/2" plate with indent
400/23D; 5-1/4" bowl, 400/23B;
3-bead ladle, 400/135; set,
400/23.....................................30.00

400/52D, handled; 2-handled 6-1/2"
bowl, 400/52B; ladle, 400/135;
set, 400/52/3 ....40.00

Mint Dish, 5", round, applied handle,
400/51F 20.00

Mint Tray, 9" heart-shaped center
handle, 400/149........................30.00

Mirror, domed beaded base like 400/18,
brass holder and frame, 2-sided
mirror flips on hinges, made for I.
Rice Co., 1940s......................85.00

Mustard Jar, beaded foot, notched
beaded cov with 2-bead finial,
3-1/2" glass spoon, fleur-de-lis
handle, 3-pc set, 400/156........35.00

Nappy, 6", beaded edge, 400/3F ..10.00

Pastry Tray, 11-1/2" beaded plate,
center heart-shaped handle,
400/68D..................................30.00

Pitcher
Beaded question-mark handle, plain
base

**Hurricane lamps, 400/79, hp Western
Rose dec, each, $125.**

16 oz, 400/16 ....125.00
80 oz, 400/24 ....135.00
Plain handle, beaded base
16 oz, Lilliputian, 400/18 ....200.00
80 oz, 400/18 ....185.00
Plate, beaded edge
6", bread and butter, 400/1D......6.00
8-1/2", salad/dessert, 400/5D...10.00
9", luncheon, 400/7D................14.00
10", 2 handles,
crimped, 400/72C 25.00
10-1/4", dinner, 400/10D 30.00
12", 2 open handles, 400/145D30.00
14", torte..................................40.00
17", torte, cupped or flat edge,
400/20V or /20D 50.00
Punch Set
6 qt, 13" bowl, 400/20
10" belled base, 400/128; 12
punch cups, 400/37, ladle, 400/91;
crystal, 15-pc set................250.00
17" plate, 400/20V; 12 punch
cups, 400/37; ladle, 400/91;
15-pc set, 400/20 ....225.00
10 qt, 14-1/2" bowl, 400/210; 9"
belled base, 400/210; 12 punch cups,
round beaded handles, 400/211;
ladle, 400/91; set, 400/210.....450.00
Relish Dish, beaded edge
6-1/2", 2-part,
2 tab handles, 400/54...............12.00
8-1/2", oval,
pickle/celery, 400/57 ....20.00
10-1/2"
2-part, oval, 2 tab handles,
400/256..................................20.00
3-part, 2 tab handles, also called
Butter 'n Jam (center section holds
stick of butter), 400/262 .....100.00
12", rect, 3 sections on side, long
section other side, tab handles each
end; 400/215 ....50.00
Relish and Dressing Set
10-1/2" round, 5-part relish, 400/112;
400/89 jar fits center well; long
3-bead long ladle, c1941;
4-pc, 400/1112, c1942 ....75.00
10-1/2" round, 5-part relish, 400/112;
400/289 jar fits center well; 3-bead
ladle, 400/130; 4-pc set,
400/1112, c1945 ....70.00
Salad Set
9" handled heart-shaped bowl,
400/73H; fork and spoon,
400/75 set, 400/735 ....110.00
10-1/2" beaded bowl, 400/75B; 13"
cupped plate, 400/75V; fork and
spoon set, 5-bead handles,
400/75; set, 400/75B 70.00
Salt and Pepper Shakers, pr, beaded
foot
Bulbous

8 beads, chrome tops,
400/96, c1944 ....12.00
9 beads, flat bottom, plastic tops,
400/96, c1941 ....30.00
Individual, chrome tops,
400/116 ....12.00
1-bead stem, no beads on foot,
plastic or metal tops, 400/116 ..70.00
Trumpet foot, chrome tops,
400/190 ....90.00
Sauce Boat Set, oval gravy boat with
handle, 9" oval plate with indent;
2-pc set, 400/169...................125.00
Stemware
400/190 Line, bell-shaped bowl, hollow
trumpet-shaped stem with beads
around foot, crystal
Cocktail, 4 oz 14.00
Goblet, 10 oz 15.00
Seafood icer,
1-pc coupette 50.00
Sherbet, 5 oz 12.50
Wine, 5 oz............................20.00
3400 Line, flared-bell top
Four graduated beads in stem,
crystal
Cordial, 1 oz......................25.00
Goblet, 9 oz.......................15.00
Sherbet/champagne,
tall, 5 oz.............................12.50
Wine, 4 oz 20.00
1-bead stem, crystal
Parfait, 6 oz.......................35.00
Sherbet, low, 5 oz 12.00
Tumbler, iced drink, 12 oz..15.00
Ruby Red bowls, crystal foot, any
3400 item, each 100.00
Solid colors, Verde Green, Ultra
Blue, Sunshine Yellow, Nut
Brown, goblet, iced tea, sherbet,
wine, 1977-1980, each 35.00
Tidbit Server, 2 tiers, 7-1/2" and 10-1/2"
plates joined by metal rod, round
handle at top, 400/2701
Crystal....................................55.00
Emerald green 350.00
Tidbit Set, 3-pc nested, heart shaped
4-1/2", 5-1/2", 6-1/2", beaded edges,
400/750
Crystal....................................40.00
Milk Glass 50.00
Tumbler
400/18, domed beaded foot, rounded
top
Dessert, 6 oz........................30.00
Iced tea, 12 oz 40.00
Water, 9 oz 30.00
400/19, beaded base, straight sides
Dessert/sherbet, 5 oz...........12.00
Iced tea, 12 oz 15.00
Juice, 5 oz...........................11.00
Old fashion, 7 oz.................20.00

Water, 10 oz 11.00
Vase
3-3/4", bud, beaded foot, ball shape,
crimped top, 400/25 ....35.00
5-1/4", bud, beaded foot, large
beads, crimped top, 400/107 ...45.00
7", rolled beaded flange top, solid
glass arched handles with small bead
edging, flat foot, 400/87R.........35.00
8"
Crimped beaded top, graduated
beads down sides, 400/87C 25.00
Fan shape, beaded top, solid glass
arched bead handles 25.00
8-1/2", bud
Beaded ball bottom, narrowed
top slants, applied handle,
400/227..................................95.00
Trumpet-shaped top,
crimped, beaded ball bottom,
400/28C 50.00

Candy Containers

Collecting Hints: Candy containers with original paint, candy and closures command a high premium, but beware of reproduced parts and repainting. The closure is a critical part of each container; its absence detracts significantly from the value. Small figural perfumes and other miniatures often are sold as candy containers. Study all reference books available and talk with other collectors before entering the market. Watch out for reproductions.

History: One of the first candy containers was manufactured in 1876 by Croft, Wilbur and Co., confectioneries. They filled a small glass Liberty Bell with candy and sold it at the 1876 Centennial Exposition in Philadelphia. Jeannette, PA, was a center for the packaging of candy in containers. Principal firms included Vic-

Glass, Army bomber, clear, $30.

tory Glass, J.H. Millstein, T.H. Stough and J.C. Crosetti. Earlier manufacturers were West Bros. (Grapeville, PA), L.E. Smith (Mt. Pleasant, PA) and Cambridge Glass (Cambridge, OH). Candy containers, which usually sold for 10 cents, were produced in shapes that would appeal to children. The containers remained popular until the 1960s when they became too expensive to mass produce.

References: *Candy Containers*, L-W Book Sales, 1996; George Eikelberner and Serge Agadjanian, *American Glass Candy Containers*, revised and published by Adele L. Bowden, 1986; Jennie Long, *Album of Candy Containers*, published by author, 1978; Robert Matthews, *Antiquers of Glass Candy Containers*, published by author, 1970.

Collectors' Club: Candy Container Collectors of America, P.O. Box 8707, Canton, OH 44711.

Museums: Cambridge Glass Museum, Cambridge, OH; L.E. Smith Glass, Mt. Pleasant, PA.

Reproduction Alert.

Bisque
   Pumpkin, 3" h, man..................40.00
   Witch, 5-1/2" h,
   holding vegetables...................40.00
Cardboard, duck, nodding head....15.00
Chalk, turkey,
   metal feet, Germany.................30.00
Cotton Batting,
   birds in nest, Japan..................65.00
Glass
   Airplane, passenger, painted wheels and wings, screw-on cap with tin propeller.....................................225.00
   Ambulance, Red Cross, paper label printed with Red Cross symbol, gold screw cap, printed "T.H. Stough"............................95.00
   Automobile
      Model T................................20.00
      Sedan..................................37.50
   Barney Google, by barrel.......495.00
   Bath Tub, emb "Dolly's Bath Tub," open top, painted white..........315.00
   Battleship, 4 guns, cardboard closure, printed "Victory Glass Inc.".....................45.00
   Bear...30.00
   Bulldog, sitting, orig paint.........85.00
   Chick, standing, painted yellow, tin closure..................................95.00

Dog, blue..................................12.50
Duck on nest, milk glass..........60.00
Fire Engine, Little Boiler No. 1...65.00
Flapper, round base,
paper mask.............................25.00
Gun
   Pistol....................................35.00
   Revolver, emb "Indian Chief" on one side of grip, running horse emb on other side, screw cap closure.........................95.00
Hanging Basket, attached chain, emb grape and vine dec, gold paint..........................35.00
Hen on Nest, Millstein..............15.00
Horn...25.00
Jeep...27.50
Lantern, large...........................35.00
Locomotive, blown, cardboard tube, tin whistle, emb "E3," Stough...40.00
Owl, 4-3/8" h, stylized feathers, gold tin screw cap...........................90.00
Pipe, 10-1/4" l, Bavarian style, wicker bowl, amber mouthpiece, cork closure.....................................45.00
Rabbit, holding carrot, 1947, Stough............................35.00
Rooster, crowing, gold screw-cap closure...................................125.00
Scottie Dog...............................9.00
Ship...30.00
Telephone.................................50.00
Vase...7.50
Papier-Mâché
   Apple, singing........................200.00
   Black Cat, sitting on pumpkin, mkd "Germany"........................75.00
   Chick, red comb, Germany......65.00
   Irishman, top hat and pipe.......10.00
   Rabbit, standing, glass eyes....40.00
   Reindeer, metal antlers, glass eyes, mkd "Germany".......................200.00
   Santa's Boot............................20.00
   Skull, mkd "Germany"..............75.00
Tin
   Building, 4 pcs, West Bros., c1913, 2-3/4" x 2"...............................50.00
   Football, Germany...................15.00

Papier-Mâché, rabbit pulling basket, pasteboard wheels, 9" l, $55.

Candy Molds

Collecting Hints: Insist on molds in very good or mint condition. The candy shop had to carefully clean molds to insure good impressions each time. Molds with rust or signs of wear rapidly lose value.

History: The chocolate or candy shops of Europe and America used molds to make elaborate chocolate candy items for holiday and other festive occasions. The heyday for these items was 1880 to 1940. Mass production, competition and the high cost of labor and supplies brought an end to local candy shops.

   Chocolate mold makers are often difficult to determine. Unlike pewter ice cream molds, makers' marks were not always on the mold or were covered by frames. Eppelsheimer & Co., of New York marked many of their molds, either with their name or a design resembling a child's toy shop and "Trade Mark" and "NY." Many chocolate molds were imported from Germany and Holland and are marked with the country of origin and, in some cases, the mold-maker's name.

References: Ray Broekel, *Chocolate Chronicles*, Wallace-Homestead, out of print; Eleanore Bunn, *Metal Molds*, Collector Books, out of print; Judene Divone, *Anton Reiche Chocolate Mould Reprint Catalog*, Oakton Hills Publications, 1983.

Museum: Wilbur's Americana Candy Museum, Lititz, PA.

Reproduction Alert.

Chocolate Mold

Clamp Type, no hinge, 2 pcs
   Copper, Indian, 7-1/2" h, mkd "Germany"...............................45.00
   Pewter, dancer, 6-3/4" h, mkd "Anton/Reichet/Dresden".........35.00
   Tin
      Basket, 1-1/2" x 4"...............40.00
      Bulldog, seated, 3" h............45.00
      Cigar, 9-3/4" l.....................25.00
      Felix the Cat, arm raised.......5.00
      Rabbit, 6-1/4" h, standing, mkd "Made in Germany"..............20.00
      Rooster, 6-1/4" h...................45.00
      Teddy Bear, 11" h, mkd "2644"........................165.00
      Turtle..................................25.00

Clown and dancer, pewter, clown #17515/#5/Anton/Reichet/Dresden, dancer #17514/#2/Anton/Reichet/Dresden, 6-3/4" h, each, $40.

Witch 40.00

Frame or Block Type, hinged, tin
Chicks, 5" h, wearing bonnets, 2 cavities, mkd "Made in Germany" .. 40.00
Cowboy, holding lasso 45.00
Heart, emb cupid,
double hinges 65.00
Jenny Lind, 3 part 95.00
Lamb, small 50.00
Lion 50.00
Rabbit, eyeglasses, paint brushes and pail, 3 part 115.00
Rooster, 10" h 100.00

Tray Type
Car, 4-door sedan, 3" x 5" 15.00
Egg, 9 cavities, 15" l 20.00
Leaf, 30 rect bars,
2-1/2" x 10-1/2" 45.00
Santa, 4 cavities, 4-1/2" h, 9-1/4" l,
mkd "Dresden/U.S. Distributor/TC Weyland, NY" 95.00

Hard Candy

Chicken on Nest, clamp type,
2 pcs, pewter 65.00
Rose Lollipops, 6 cavities,
clamp type, tin 55.00
Maple Sugar
Dog's head, tin, clamp type,
2 pcs 65.00
Elephant, clamp type, 2 pcs 45.00
Girl and dog, buff clay, 4-1/4" w,
4-1/2" h 35.00
Rabbit, wood, 1-3/4" w, 2" h, mkd "Germany" 40.00

Cap Guns

Collecting Hints: Condition is crucial to pricing. A broken spring that can be replaced is far less critical than a crack that cannot be repaired. Many older cast-iron cap pistols rusted and suffered other ravages of time. While restoration is acceptable, an unrestored gun in fine condition is more valuable than a restored example.

Beware of restrikes, reproductions and new issues. Recasts often have a sandy or pebbled finish and lack the details found on the original pieces. Several of the molds for cast-iron cap pistols have survived. Owners have authorized restrikes as a means of raising money. New issues are frequently made with the intention of deceiving and the restrikes are sold to the unknowing as period examples. Two prime examples are the Liberty Bell cap bomb and the Deadshot powder keg cap bomb.

It is important to know the full history of any post-World War II cap pistol, especially if it is one of a pair. Toy guns associated with a character or personality sell better than their generic counterparts. Some of the price difference is negated for products from leading manufacturers, e.g., Hubley. The presence of the original box, holster, and/or other accessories can add as much as 100% to the value of the gun.

History: Although the first toy gun patents date from the 1850s, toy guns did not play an important part in the American toy market until after the Civil War. In the 1870s, the toy cap gun was introduced. Cast-iron cap pistols reached their pinnacle between 1870 and 1900, with J&E Stevens and Ives among the leading manufacturers. Realism took second place to artistic imagination. Designs ranged from leaf and scroll to animal and human heads. The use of cast iron persisted until the advent of World War II, although guns made of glass, lead, paper, rubber, steel, tin, wood and zinc are known from the 1920 to 1940 period.

Stevens Comet, 1885, $145.

In the 1950s, diecast metal and plastic became the principal material from which cap guns were manufactured. Leading manufacturers of diecast guns were Hubley, Kilgore, Mattel and Nichols. Many of the guns were associated with television cowboys and detective heroes. Often, the guns were part of larger sets that consisted of a holster and other accessories.

Collecting cap and other toy guns began in the 1930s with the principal emphasis on cast-iron examples made between 1875 to 1915. In the mid-1980s the collecting emphasis shifted to the cap pistols of the post-World War II period.

Reference: Samuel H. Logan and Charles W. Best, *Cast Iron Toy Guns and Capshooters*, published by authors, 1990.

Periodical: *Toy Gun Collectors of America Newsletter*, 312 Starling Way, Anaheim, CA 92807.

E.J. Cossman Co., Hollywood, CA,
Speed Gun, No. 504, metal,
6-1/2" x 3-1/8" l 45.00
Flyright Products, Atom
Water Gun, die cast,
orig box, tear in flap, 1940s 75.00
Hubley
Cowboy, gold plated, black grips,
12" x 5-1/4" 200.00
Midget, flintlock, all metal, engraved all over, 5-3/4" x 2-1/4" 45.00
Mountie, automatic, engraved
all over 125.00
Rodeo Patrol, cowboy on bucking horse, red, white and blue, 8-1/4" x 1-1/2" x 1-1/8", orig box 145.00
Texan, revolving cylinder, lever on side, 10-1/4" x 4-1/4" 165.00
Texan Jr., gold plated, black grips,
9" x 4-1/2", c1940, played-with condition 60.00
Western Cap Pistol, white grips,
black steer, 9-1/2" x 4-1/2" 50.00
Ideal, Yo Gun, red and yellow, plastic,
6-1/2" x 7", 1950s 35.00
Kelmar Corp., Milwaukee, Pow's Pop,
automatic, Bakelite, maroon,
6-1/2" x 4-1/4" 40.00
Kilgore
Buck, No. 407, red, navy
and white, black grips, 7-1/4" x 3-5/8" x 1-1/4", orig box with illus of buck deer 120.00
Deputy, single holster, 2-1/4"
wide fancy felt 200.00
Hawkeye, automatic, Indian head and eagle on barrel,

4-1/4" x 3-1/8" 45.00
Ranger, cast iron......................75.00
Leslie Henry
   Gene Autry Flying A Ranch,
   double-leather holster set,
   two .44s, complete with bullets,
   tan and black..........................600.00
   Wagon Train, #48, pistol, antique
   bronze, 16" x 9-1/2" x 1-7/8" shallow
   box, 6 bullets 425.00
   Wild Bill Hickok, double-leather
   holster set, 2 Marshall guns, bronze
   grips, tan leather, felt lining 500.00
Mattel
   Bandolier, Winchester, leather,
   32 all-metal play bullets, belt,
   1958, minor damage to box ...125.00
   Shoot N Shell 40.00
   Winchester Saddle Gun, stock No.
   544, 33-3/4" x 3/4" x 1-1/2",
   orig box 500.00
Nichols
   Civil War Period Model 1861, revolv-
   er, shell firing, Model 61, orig
   10-1/2" x 16" x 2-1/8" shadow box,
   6 shells, 18 bullets, mint gun,
   near mint box 600.00
   Dyna-Mite Derringer,
   #2782, 3-1/2" x 4-7/8" x 3/4"
   presentation box......................45.00
   Spit Fire Rifle, 8-1/2" l 75.00
Remco, Okinawa Pistol, Monkey
   Division, 1964, 13" l..................40.00
Stevens, J&E, Buffalo Bill, repeating,
   1920s, orig box 300.00
Unknown Maker
   Automatic, .45, chrome, steel,
   4-1/2" x 6-1/2" 50.00
   Big Scout, cast iron, white grips,
   7-1/2" x 3-1/2" 100.00
   Cowboy Pistol, tin, red, black, gold
   and white, cowboy riding horse,
   11" x 4-1/2", 1940s..................40.00
   Hero, cast iron, cowboy on-cast
   iron grips 45.00
   Pistol, metal, cork stopper, red,
   black and silver, 9-3/4" l 35.00
   Police, automatic, steel picture
   of policeman on both sides,
   8" l, c1940 ....45.00
   Scout, cast iron, cowboy on metal
   grips, 3" x 6-1/2"......................95.00
   Wells Fargo, pistol, brown and white
   grips, horse's head, designs on
   barrel, 11-1/2" x 4-1/2" 125.00

Carnival Chalkware

Collecting Hints: Most chalkware
pieces appear worn, either because of
age or inexpensive production techniques. These factors do not affect the
value, provided the piece is whole and
has no repairs. Some pieces are decorated with sparkly silver. This adds
nothing to the authenticity of the piece
nor to its value. This category includes
carnival chalkware banks.

History: Carnival chalkware pieces,
cheerfully painted plaster of paris figures, were manufactured as a cheap,
decorative art form. Doll and novelty
companies mass-produced and sold
chalkware items for as little as $1 a
dozen. Many independents, mostly
immigrants, molded chalkware figures
in their garages and sold them directly
to carnival-booth owners. Some pieces are marked and dated; most are
not. The soft nature of chalkware
means it can be easily chipped or broken. Although some carnival chalkware was marketed for a nominal
price at dime stores, it was predomi-
nately given away as prizes at games
of chance along carnival midways.
Concessionaires awarded small prizes called "build ups." As you won, you
accumulated smaller prizes with the
option of trading them for a larger
prize, often a piece of chalkware.

Chalkware pieces, which range
in size from 3 to 24 inches, are usually three-dimensional. However,
some flat plaques and figures up to a
half-inch thick were also made. Colors were chosen by the individual
decorators. A variety of animal, character and personality figures were
made in chalkware. You can find
Betty Boop, Sally Rand, Mae West,
Shirley Temple, Charlie McCarthy,
W.C. Fields and Mickey Mouse, to
name a few. However, you will not
find the names on the figures or in
the advertising literature of the company which made them. Shirley
Temple was the "Smile Doll"; Mae
West was the "Mae Doll." Most character dolls were bootlegged, i.e.,
made without permission. Although
some carnival chalkware was made
before the 1920s, its peak of popularity was in the 1930s and 1940s.
The use of chalkware prizes declined in the late 1950s and ceased
in the 1960s.

References: *Carnival Chalkware,*
L-W Book Sales, 1995.

Alice the Goon, 10" h, King Features
   Syndicate, c1945.....................65.00
Bonzo Bulldog, 6" h, cap, bottle in
mouth, English, c1930.............80.00
Buddy Lee, 13-1/2" h, hp, cotton cap,
   c1930 ....65.00
Bugs Bunny.................................65.00
Captain Kiddo, pirate, 1929 ....65.00
Captain Marvel, 14-1/2" h, c1950..60.00
Cardinal, 1940s...........................20.00
Cat, 10" h, bank, c1940...............25.00
Circus Horse, 10" h, c1930 ....25.00
Collie, 18" l, c1940 ....20.00
Cowboy, ashtray, 1950s 60.00
Donald Duck, long bill 65.00
Dopey, 6" h, c1937......................45.00
Elephant, bank, c1930 ....20.00
Fan Dancer, 16" h, mkd "Portland
   Statuary Co," c1935 ....65.00
Felix the Cat, 12-1/2" h 65.00
Flapper, 10" l, reclining girl, painted,
   bobbed hair, red pants and top,
   c1920 ....125.00
Gigolo, string holder.....................30.00
Hula Girl, 17" h, grass skirt, c1940 25.00
Johnny, Philip Morris mascot, 12" h,
   mkd "Jenkins, 1934"...............65.00
Lamb, 7" l, flat back, mkd "Rosemead
   Novelty Co," c1940 ....15.00
Lone Ranger 75.00
Majorette, 12" h, mkd "El Segundo
   Novelty Co," 1949 ....27.50
Mickey Mouse 75.00
Miss America, 15" h, wearing bathing
   suit, c1940 ....25.00
Monk, playing violin......................25.00
Pig, 10" h, standing, carrying tray, wear-
   ing jack and hat, mkd "JY Jenkins,
   1937" 25.00
Popeye, 18" h, King Features Syndicate,
   c1930 ....95.00
Singing Cowboy, 1950s 65.00
Snow White.................................65.00
Squirrel, 12" h,
   eating corn, c1940...................15.00
Stripper, 13-1/2" h, heart-shaped
   medallion, c1935 ....45.00
Sweater Girl, 11-1/2" h, c1930......30.00
Terrier, 8" h, black and white, rhinestone
   eyes, c1940 ....20.00
Tex, cowboy, old paint. 1950s 130.00
Rudolph Valentino, 15" h, sheik
   costume, c1925......................125.00
George Washington, 12" h, mkd " Incroc-
   ci, Pittsburgh, PA," c1940........65.00
Wimpy, 18" h, c1940 ....45.00

Cartoon Characters

Collecting Hints: Many collectible
categories include objects related to
cartoon characters. Cartoon characters appeared in advertising, books,
comics, movies, television and as a

theme in thousands of products designed for children. Concentrate on one character or the characters from a single comic or cartoon. Most collectors tend to focus on a character that was part of their childhood. Another collecting strategy is to concentrate on the work of a single artist. Several artists produced more than one cartoon character.

The most popular cartoon characters of the early period are Barney Google, Betty Boop, Dick Tracy, Gasoline Alley, Li'l Abner, Little Orphan Annie and Popeye. The movie cartoons produced Bugs Bunny, Felix the Cat, Mighty Mouse, Porky Pig and a wealth of Disney characters. The popular modern cartoon characters include Garfield, Peanuts and Snoopy.

History: The first daily comic strip was Bud Fisher's Mutt and Jeff, first appearing in 1907. By the 1920s, the Sunday comics became an American institution. One of the leading syndicators was Captain Joseph Patterson of the News-Tribune. Patterson, who partially conceived and named Moon Mullins and Little Orphan Annie, worked with Chester Gould to develop Dick Tracy in the early 1930s.

Walt Disney and others pioneered the movie cartoon, both as shorts and full-length versions. Disney and Warner Brothers characters dominated the years from 1940 to 1960. With the advent of television, the cartoon characters of Hanna-Barbera, e.g., the Flintstones, added a third major force. Independent studios produced cartoon characters for television and characters multiplied rapidly. By the 1970s, the trend was to produce strips with human characters, rather than the animated animals of the earlier period.

Successful cartoon characters create many spin-offs, including comic books, paperback books, Big Little Books games, dolls, room furnishings and other materials which appeal to children. The secondary market products may produce more income for the cartoonist than the drawings themselves.

References: Bill Blackbeard (ed.), *R.F. Outcault's Yellow Kid*, Kitchen Sink Press, 1995; ——, *Comic Strip Century*, Kitchen Sink Press, 1995; Bill Bruegman, *Cartoon Friends of the Baby Book Era*, Cap'n Penny Productions, 1993; *Cartoon & Character Toys of the 50s, 60s, & 70s*, L-W Book Sales, 1995; Ted Hake, *Hake's Guide to Comic Character Collectibles*, Wallace-Homestead, 1993; Maurice Horn and Richard Marshall (eds.), *World Encyclopedia of Comics*, Chelsea House Publications, out of print; Chip Kidd, *Batman Collected*, Little, Brown, 1996; David Longest, *Character Toys and Collectibles*, 1st Series (1984, 1992 value update), 2nd Series (1987, 1990 value update), Collector Books; Alex G. Malloy and Stuart Wells III, *Comic Collectibles & Their Values*, Wallace-Homestead, 1995; Freddi Margolin and Andrea Podley, *Official Price Guide to Peanuts Collectibles*, House of Collectibles, 1990; Robert M. Overstreet, *Overstreet Premium Ring Price Guide*, Gemstone Publishing, 1994.

Periodical: *Frostbite Falls Far-Flung Flier* (Rocky & Bullwinkle), P.O. Box 39, Macedonia, OH 44056.

Collectors' Clubs: Betty Boop Fan Club, 6025 Fullerton Ave., Apt. 2, Buena Park, CA 90621; Peanuts Collector Club, 539 Sudden Valley, Bellingham, WA 98226; Pogo Fan Club, 6908 Wentworth Ave. South, Richfield, MN 55423; Popeye Fan Club, Ste.151, 5995 Stage Rd., Barlette, TN 38184; R.F. Outcault Society, 103 Doubloon Dr., Slidell, LA 70461.

Museum: The Museum of Cartoon Art, Port Chester, NY.

Additional Listings: Disneyana; also see the index for specific characters.

Andy Panda, Walter Lantz, artist

Big Little Book,*Andy Panda and the Mad Dog Mystery*, Whitman, #1431 ....45.00

Pinback Button, 1-1/4" d, New Funnies/Andy Panda, black, white, red, bright yellow ground.........25.00

Plaque, 7" h, ceramic, figural, multicolored, mkd "Napco Ceramics," 1958 ....60.00

Archie, Bob Montana, artist

Doll, cloth, 18" h 30.00

Figure, 5" h, Sirocco, painted, brown military uniform and hat, 1944 ....20.00

Pinback Button, 1-1/2" d, Member Archie Club, blue, white and orange, 1950s 20.00

Barney Google, Billy deBeck, artist

Book, *Barney Google and Spark Plug*, Cupples & Leon, 1925, 10" x 10" cardboard cover, black and white comic strips 95.00

Doll, 17" h, Snuffy Smith, stuffed felt, movable head, black floppy hat, orange shirt, green pants and felt suspenders, amber and black eyes, 1930s 175.00

Game, Barney Google an' Snuffy Smith, Milton Bradley, 1963, 16" sq board, full color, boxed 40.00

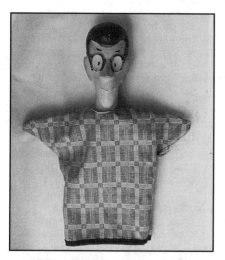

Dennis the Menace, Henry (his father) puppet, Hall Syndicate Inc., 1959, 10" h, $10.

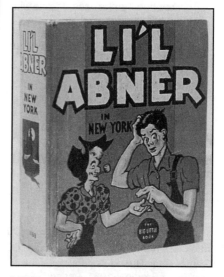

Li'l Abner in New York, Al Capp, Big Little Book, Whitman Publishing Co., No. 1198, $20.

Pinback Button, 13/16" d, multicolored litho, Kellogg's Pep, Barney Google 20.00

Toy, 4" h, 5" l, Spark Plug, wood figure, 1925, deBeck signature 185.00

Betty Boop, Max Fleischer, artist

Cel, 8-1/4" x 10-3/4" acetate, well-centered full-color 2-1/4" x 3-1/2 image of Betty, red dress, putting brown leash on yellow puppy, price for 3-cel set 150.00

Charm, 1" h, celluloid, tinted, Japanese, 1930s......................................45.00

Figure, 4-1/2" h, ceramic, Vandor 10.00

Perfume Bottle, glass 35.00

Picture Frame, 3" x 4", figural........12.00

Pinback Button, 1-1/4" d, Roxy Theater, NYC, b&w, late 1960s 15.00

Playing cards...............................75.00

Valentine, 3-1/2" x 4-1/2", mechanical, diecut round eyes, 1940 ....40.00

Wall Hook, ceramic, figural..............8.00

Bringing Up Father, George Mc-Manus, artist

Figure, bisque, 3-1/4" h Jiggs, black suit, green vest, red tie, smoking brown cigar, brown cane in left hand, 3-1/4" h Maggie in yellow and red dress, red headband, brown hair, black shoes, right hand on hip, 75% complete paint, c1920, price for pr........100.00

Newsboy Apron, 13-1/2" x 18" canvas, red and black text "Read America's Greatest Comics 12 Full-Size Pages *Sunday Ledger*," 5-1/2" h black and white smiling profile bust of Jiggs, c1930......................................100.00

Promo Card, 3-1/2" x 5-1/2", b&w graphics, red and orange accents, one with Jiggs thinking about working, other with Katzenjammer Kids laughing as goat butts Captain, reverse promotes "16 Full Pages of Colored Comics," New York American Sunday, c1930, price for pr 50.00

Salt and Pepper Shakers, pr, 2-1/2" h, figural, Maggie and Jiggs, orange china holder, mkd "Made in Japan," 1930s......................................75.00

Bugs Bunny, Leon Schlesinger, artist, Warner Bros.

Animation Cel, 10-1/2" x 12-1/2", acetate sheet, full-color 6" x 7-1/2" art, gray and white body, Warner Bros., 1970s......................................95.00

Bank, pot metal 65.00

Game, Bugs Bunny Adventure Game, Milton Bradley, 1961, unused ..25.00

Glass, Pepsi Collector series, 1973, copyright Warner Bros. Inc. 8.00

Lamp, 13" h, figural, copyright 1970 Warner Bros. Holiday Fair Mfg., paper label...............................85.00

Pinback Button, 1-5/8" d, litho, b&w, red nose, solid black background, bright red trim, copyright 1959 Warner 50.00

Dennis the Menace, Hank Ketcham, artist

Book, Hank Ketcham, *Dennis The Menace*, Holt & Co., 1952, 1st ed, single b&w cartoon panel, 6-1/4" x 9-1/4", full-color hardcover, 62 pgs.....................................35.00

Creamer, mkd "F&F Mold & Die Works" 25.00

Kit, 24 Ashtrays or Coasters of Aluminum Foil Kit, 24 different illus, orig box, 1950s, unused 55.00

Lamp, figural 50.00

Pin, figural, enamel dec................30.00

Production Cel, 9" x 10-1/2" clear acetate sheet, well-centered image of smiling Dennis, blue and white striped shirt, red overalls, accompanied by 9-1/2" x 10-1/2" paper sheet with matching lead-pencil drawing, number notations in margin Bic Studios, 1980, price for 2-pc set .300.00

Dick Tracy, Chester Gould, artist

Big Little Book, *Dick Tracy Encounters Facey*, Whitman, #2001, Paul S. Newman, 1967 ....10.00

Brush...50.00

Candy Bar Wrapper, color picture, premium offer, 1950s 10.00

Game, Dick Tracy Master Detective Board Game, Selright, 1961 ....25.00

Magazine, *Argosy*, June 1974.........5.00

Toy, two-way radio set, 1950, MIB 40.00

Felix the Cat, Pat Sullivan, artist

Advertising Brochure, 10-1/2" x 16-1/2", glossy paper, color ad, text for Kodatoy Film Projector and Theater, Eastman Kodak Co., late 1920s 75.00

Rocky and His Friends game, Milton Bradley, 1960, $10.

Figure, 4-3/4" h, plaster, left hand to ear, right hand at tummy, red and white areas professionally repainted, late 1920s...............................125.00

Pencil Box, 2-1/2" x 4-3/4" x 3/8", cardboard, American Pencil Co., black and white Felix, full-color ground, copyright Pat Sullivan, full-color scene of children doing artwork of peacock near Washington Monument on reverse, early 1930s..60.00

Record, 7" x 7-1/2" sleeve, smiling Felix face looking over fence, 7" d, 45 RPM black vinyl Peter Pan record, 4-part Felix story, copyright 1959 King Features Syndicate, Inc. .30.00

Foghorn Leghorn, Warner Brothers

Flicker ring, blue plastic, color image...............................20.00

Garfield, Jim Davis, artist

Bookends, pr, Garfield and Odie, 5" h, 4" w, paper label, glazed ink stamp mark "Enesco," 1983 ....245.00

Rug, 22" sq, full-face image 45.00

Telephone, figural 45.00

Gasoline Alley, Frank King, artist

Doll, oilcloth 25" h Walt wears red shirt, black pants and shoes, yellow hair, 12-1/2" h Skeezix wears red shorts and shirt, black shoes, yellow hair, King creator name printed on reverse, Skeezix with patent date Feb. 27, 1928, played-with condition, some wear and thin spots, price for pr 125.00

Pinback Button, 1-1/4" d, I Like Skeezix Sweaters, color image, Skeezix wearing bright yellow sweater with red trim, artist King facsimile signature, early 1930s 60.00

Toothbrush Holder, 1-3/4" x 2-1/4" x 3-3/4" d, bisque, figural, Walt wearing yellow shirt, red tie, blue pants, gray shoes, brown hair, holding hands of Skeezix who wears orange shirt, red shorts, brown shoes and neckerchief, orange hair, pink accent background, names incised on reverse with copyright F.A.S., 1930s, 80% orig paint 80.00

Jetsons, Hanna-Barbera

Animation Cel, 10-1/2" x 12-1/2" sheet, 3-1/2" x 4-3/4" h image of George, Jane and Judy Jetson walking, black-ink production notations, c1986....................250.00

Colorforms Set, copyright 1963 Colorforms and Hanna-Barbera, orig box, complete 40.00

Doll, 12" h, orig tags, Applause.....30.00

Little Golden Book, *The Jetsons*, 7" x 6-1/2" d, copyright 1962 ...15.00

Record, The Jetsons, First Family on the

Moon, 33 RPM, 1977, Columbia
label 65.00

Toy
Hopping Elroy,
litho tin windup 225.00
Ramp Walker, Astro and George,
hard plastic, Marx, copyright Hanna-
Barbera, early 1960s.............115.00

Watch, lunch-box type,
Fossil, MIB..............................75.00

Krazy Kat, George Harriman, artist

Doll, 18" h, stuffed, felt, blue, diecut
white felt face, white felt feet, tail
missing, orig tag mkd "Manufactured
Under Special Arrangement with
Geo. Harriman," patent application
Averill Mfg. Co., NY, c1920 ...475.00

Mask, paper, Einson-Freeman Co.,
1930s......................................85.00

Pin, 1-1/4" h, enameled, 1930s
Seated pose, colored stones
for eyes, blue bow....................65.00
Walking pose, playing banjo,
copper and white detailing,
black enamel body 75.00

Pinback Button, 7/8" d, Charles Mintz's
Krazy Kat-Columbia Pictures, black,
white and red litho, 1930s........35.00

Lil Abner, Al Capp, artist

Barrette, 2-1/8" l, oval, brass,
diecut, 1940s 20.00

Charm, 1" h, Shmoo, bright silver-
colored plastic, 1940s.............18.00

Flicker Ring, blue plastic, 1950s, full-
color flicker
Abner characters, Indian,
mountain man 25.00
Lil Abner and Daisy 30.00
Mammy and Pappy 25.00

Glass, 5" h, clear, enameled
image of Lil' Abner running with
2 Shmoos, 1949 ....15.00

Magazine Ad, *Life*, May 11, 1951..10.00

Planter, 2-1/2" x 4" x 3-1/2", Mammy
Yochum, white face, black eyes,
glossy black cap, mfg by Pearce,
copyright 1952 Al Capp 60.00

Tab, 1-5/8" d, black and white, red
ground, litho tin, Sealtest Shmoo
Club, late 1940s, unbent..........35.00

Moon Mullins, Frank Willard, artist

Advertising, transfer picture,
5" x 7", Kayo Chocolate, full-color
diecut of Kayo, 1930s.............37.50

Marble, 5/8" d, glass, Kayo portrait
center, white, dark green spot,
name in black, 1930s.............125.00

Nodder, 3-7/8" h, bisque, Moon Mullins,
mkd "Made in Germany"..........65.00

Pinback Button, 1-1/4" d, black, white
and flesh tone, *Los Angeles Evening
Express* contest 45.00

Mutt and Jeff, Bud Fisher, artist

Bank, cast iron 150.00

Blotter, 4" x 9", black, white and red,
cardboard, adv silent film cartoons,
1920s......................................25.00

Book, *Mutt & Jeff*, Cupples and Leon,
1922, Bud Fisher, artist, Famous
Comic Book Series #8, 10" x 10", 48
pgs, b&w comic strip reprints ..40.00

Figure, bisque, 3-1/4" h Jeff walking,
waving left hand, black coat, top hat
and shoes, brown mustache, yellow
vest, blue pants, 3-1/4" Mutt with
brown hat and mustache, black suit
and shoes, 95% complete paint,
c1920, price for pr 125.00

Pinback Button, 1-1/8" d, full-color litho,
Good Night, Jeff blowing
out gas light, art sgd by
Bud Fisher, c1912 ....25.00

Ozark Ike, Ray Gotto artist

Christmas Card, 1951, unused 12.00

Peanuts Gang, Charles Schultz, artist

Animation Drawing, 10-1/2" x 12-1/2"
animation paper, lead- and blue-
pencil 1-1/2" x 1-3/4 image of
Snoopy playing with man and baby
doll hand puppets, 2-3/4" h image of
Charlie Brown holding bag of
groceries, price for pr 150.00

Bank
Dog House, Bank of America,
early 1970s 50.00
Ferris Wheel, wheel spins and music
plays when coin is inserted,
Schmid, 1972 ....195.00
Peppermint Patty, Lucy, Linus, all
wearing baseball outfits,
Determined, 1973 ....50.00
Snoopy sitting on chicken,
Determined, mid 1970s............45.00

Book, pop-up, *The Peanuts
Philosophers*, Charles Schultz,
Hallmark, 1972 ....60.00

Card Game, Snoopying Around,
Hallmark, Snoopy wearing
Sherlock cap............................15.00

Clock, alarm, 3-1/2" x 5-1/2",
Snoopy illus..............................30.00

Music Box, Snoopy with Christmas tree,
plays "O' Tannenbaum,"
Schmid, 1986 ....275.00

Mug, ceramic.................................4.00

Nodder, 5-1/2" h, Charlie Brown,
Lego, 1959 ....65.00

Pinback Button
1-3/4" d, Happy Birthday
America, red, white and blue
design, yellow Woodstock
and flames of birthday cake candles,
bicentennial dates 25.00
2-1/2" d, Get Newsday for
Peanuts, bright orange, white

Tillie the Toiler, puzzle set #915, diecut
cardboard, 4-puzzle set, 50 pcs each
puzzle, Saalfield Publishing Co., Akron,
OH, 1935, 9-3/4" x 8", cardboard box,
guide picture, $65.

ground, c1965 ....20.00

Punching Bag, 34" h, Charlie Brown,
Determined, 1970s..................40.00

Rhythm Set, Peanuts Kindergarten
Rhythm Set, small drum,
triangle, tambourine, cymbals,
J. Chein, 1972 ....125.00

Pogo, Walt Kelly, artist

Book, *Positively Pogo*,
Simon & Schuster,
190 pgs, 1957, 1st ed..............30.00

Figure, plastic, Pogo and swamp friends,
movable heads and arms, copyright
1969 Walt Kelly, inscribed with name
on base, price for 6-pc set.......95.00

Mug, 4-1/8" h, plastic, full-color character images, copyright Walt Kelly,
c1960, price for 6-pc set..........75.00

Pinback Button, 1-3/4" d Pogo, black and
white, bright yellow ground, Walt
Kelly signature, 1968..............25.00
Pogo for Pres!, black silhouette,
orange ground 35.00

View-Master Reel, set of 3, story booklet, unopened pkg, copyright 1980
Possom Productions, Inc. 35.00

Popeye, E.C. Segar, artist

Bank, 3" x 4" x 4-1/2", multicolored litho
metal, mkd "Popeye Daily Quarter
Bank," Kalon Co., 1950s 115.00

Card Game, 5" x 6-1/2" x 1",
Whitman, 1937 ....45.00

Flashlight, figural,
King Features, early 30.00

Flicker Ring, silvered plastic, colored im-
ages, 1960s, vending-machine type
Popeye and Olive 25.00
Popeye and Swee' Pea 25.00
Popeye and Wimpy..................35.00

Magazine, *Children's Playmate*, Dec.
1958, 2-pg comic strip by Sims &
Saboly, 62 pgs 25.00

Pinback Button, 1-1/4" d, multicolored,

Evening Ledger, Philadelphia,
mid 1930s..............................100.00
Tile, Swee' Pea, 4-1/8" x 3",
hanging type, multicolored, emb
image, 1960s, Italy.................45.00
Valentine, 1943 ....7.50
Wallpaper, 10-ft roll,
1940, unused......................135.00

**Porky Pig, Leon Schlesinger, artist,
Warner Bros.**

Animation Cel, 8" x 10-1/4", Porky in
Robin Hood outfit, holding ball over
head, 1940s............................75.00
Big Little Book, *Porky Pig And His Gang*,
Whitman, #1404 ....50.00
Ring, brass, diecut flesh-tone figure,
black and white accents, red hat and
bow tie, black and gold foil tag reads
"Hand Painted/J.R.S. copyright
Warner Bros., 1970" 20.00
Soakie, 9-1/2" h, molded vinyl, plastic
body, hard-plastic removable head,
1960s....................................24.00
Toy, 5-1/2" h, rubber,
mkd "Sun Rubber Co."..............60.00

Regular Fellars

Pinback button, 7/8" d, black,
white and red, 2 young boys at
center, reads "Drovers Telegram
Kansas City/Reg'lar Fellars
and Girls Too"..........................30.00

**Rocky and Bullwinkle, Jay Ward,
artist**

Charm, figural................................15.00
Coloring Book, Bullwinkle and Dudley
Do-Right, Saalfield, copyright 1971
Ward, 160 pgs, unused 30.00
Doll, plush body, molded soft-vinyl head
13" h, Rocky, green felt aviator's cap,
Ideal tag, 1960s.......................75.00
15-1/2" h, Bullwinkle, felt hands, red
and yellow fabric outfit, "B" on chest,
1961, copyright Terry Toons 75.00
Jigsaw Puzzle, Rocky and His Friends,
63 pcs, Whitman, copyright Ward,
1960s......................................35.00

Skippy, Percy Crosby, artist

Display, 19" h, smiling Skippy, blue
outfit, orange tie, yellow cap, neatly
cut from larger cardboard sign,
slight damage 60.00
Mug, whistle handle, SP, drawings
and dialogue on side 55.00
Pinback Button, 1-1/8" d, blue, white and
orange litho, *Sunday Herald and
Examiner*, 1930s.....................30.00

Smitty, Walter Berndt, artist

Book, *Smitty*, Cupples & Leon,
1928, Walter Berndt artist,
7" x 8-1/2", 32 pgs, full-color cover,
comic strip reprints 60.00
Marble, 5/8" d, glass, portrait center,

yellow, light green streak, name
in black, 1930s 125.00
Pinback Button, 1-1/4" d, multicolored,
Evening Ledger, Philadelphia,
mid 1930s..............................100.00
Wristwatch, gray aged dial, black, white,
red and green figure, New Haven
Clock Co., 1935, orig case 250.00

**Speed Racer, Tatsunoko Studios,
Japan**

Magnet, 2" x 3" 4.00
Sticker 1.50

Steve Canyon, Milton Caniff, artist

Christmas Card, 1951, unused 12.00
Pinback Button, 3/4" d, Steve Canyon—
Comic Togs, full-color litho,
1947 Field Ent. 55.00

Tom and Jerry, Hanna-Barbera

Pinback Button
1" d, ABC Minors/MGM's Tom and
Jerry, brown and light green characters, bright yellow accents, light blue
ground, English, 1960s 35.00
1-1/8" d, Tom and Jerry Go for
Stroehmann's Bread, black, red
and white litho, 1950s 25.00

**Woody Woodpecker, Walter Lantz,
artist**

Book, *Woody Woodpecker's Peck of
Trouble*, Whitman, 1951,
6" x 6-1/2", hardcover..............10.00
Kazoo, 7" l, plastic, red, orig instructions,
1950s, MIB 15.00
Night-Light, 20" h, hard plastic,
figural, vivid colors, copyright
1974 Walter Lantz 50.00
Toothbrush Holder,
4" h, pottery 225.00
Wall Plaque, 5-1/2" x 7-1/2", glazed
plaster, multicolored, holding yellow
hat in 1 hand, white suitcase in other,
1956 Walter Lantz 65.00

Yellow Kid, R.F. Outcault, artist

Cigar Box, 5-1/2" x 9" x 4", wood, hinged
lid with lightly engraved portrait of
Kid, other images, orig red label
"Smoke Yellow Kid Cigars, Manuf'd
by DR Fleming, Curwensville, PA,"
early 1900s.............................325.00
Ice Cream Mold, 4-3/4" h, hinged,
full figure 200.00
Pinback Button, High Admiral
Cigarettes, c1986
No. 3, Kid standing in barrel, Mrs.
Murphy mends clothes.............35.00
No. 14, Kid with large white collar,
dressed to go to ball.................40.00
No. 24, Kid as accountant, pencil
behind ear, large strip of adding-
machine tape 35.00

Yosemite Sam, Warner Bros.

Ring, brass, diecut flesh-tone
figure, colorful accents,
black and gold foil tag reads
"Hand Painted/J.R.S. copyright
Warner Bros., 1970"...............20.00

Catalina Pottery

Collecting Hints: Many dinnerware
patterns, in addition to a wide variety
of decorative pieces, were produced
under the Catalina name. From 1937
to 1947, many of the artware lines
were made by Gladding, McBean
and Company. Although the island
plant was closed, many pieces made
during this period were still marked
"Catalina Island." To distinguish between pieces made before and after
the Gladding, McBean takeover, collectors must learn the subtle differences in the various marks used.

History: The Catalina Pottery began
producing clay building products in
1927 at its original location on Santa
Catalina Island. In 1930, the pottery
expanded its inventory to include decorative and utilitarian pieces. Dinnerware was added in 1931. Gladding,
McBean and Co., bought the firm in
1937 and closed the island plant, limiting production to the mainland. Ownership of the trademark reverted to the
Catalina Island Co., in 1947.

References: Susan and Al Bagdade,
*Warman's American Pottery and Por-
celain*, Wallace-Homestead, 1994
Jack Chipman, *Collector's Encyclo-
pedia of California Pottery*, Collector
Books, 1992; Steve and Aisha Hoefs,
Catalina Island Pottery, published by
authors, 1993.

Periodical: Pottery Collectors Express, P.O. Box 221, Mayview, MO
64071.

Ashtray
Fish, blue, small 55.00
Outdoor, red...........................125.00
Sleeping Mexican,
matte green, cold paint 275.00
Cigarette Box, cov,
horse's head, ivory 450.00
Console Bowl, frog,
green, small, minor damage..125.00
Cup and Saucer, green.................50.00
Flower Frog, Toyon Red, 3 tier 85.00
Head Vase
Aqua satin..............................145.00
Terra-cotta and turquoise 145.00

Jug, red, handle............................75.00
Plate, Sailfish
    Descanza Green 1,300.00
    Ivory 1,100.00
Plate and Bowl, Flare, 6" plate 100.00
Tray, 13-1/2" d, Catalina blue......125.00
Vase
    Burnt Orange, matte, 6-1/2" h,
    grinding base flake 95.00
    Descanza, green, #300 ....85.00
    Island Mold, aqua, 12" h 95.00
    Mantel, aqua, #600, 1 with hairline,
    price for pr 125.00
    Terra Cotta, C801 ....145.00
    White, #1610 ....175.00
Wine Cup, Toyon Red...................35.00

Catalogs

Collecting Hints: The price of an old catalog is affected by the condition, data, type of material advertised and location of advertiser.

History: Catalogs are excellent research sources. The complete manufacturing line of a given item is often described, along with prices, styles, colors, etc. Old catalogs provide a good way to date objects. Sometimes old catalogs are reprinted so that collectors can identify the companies' specialties. Such is the case with Imperial and The Cambridge Glass Co.

References: Ron Barlow and Ray Reynolds, *Insider's Guide to Old Books, Magazines, Newspapers and Trade Catalogs*, Windmill Publishing (2147 Windmill View Rd., El Cajon, CA 92020), 1996; Don Fredgant, *American Trade Catalogs*, Collector Books, out of print; Norman E. Martinus and Harry L. Rinker, *Warman's Paper*, Wallace-Homestead, 1994; Lawrence B. Romaine, *Guide to American Trade Catalogs*, Dover Publications, 1960, 1990 reprint.

Advisor: Kenneth Schneringer.

A.C. Gilbert Co., New Haven, CT, toys, 62 pgs, 5-1/4" x 6-3/4" 17.00
Abercrombie & Fitch Co., New York, NY, 1920, 166 pgs, 6-3/4" x 9-3/4" .59.00
Allis-Chalmers Tractors, 1936, Milwaukee, 16 pgs, 8-1/2" x 11" 30.00
American Brewers Supply, Pittsburgh, c1925, 138 pgs, 9" x 12".........76.00
American Cabinet Co., Two Rivers, WI, 1905, 68 pgs, 5-3/4" x 8-3/4" ...63.00

Sears, Roebuck & Co., Color Perfect Wallpaper, portfolio with samples, 7-1/4" x 9", 1940, $12.

American Rug & Carpet Co., New York, c1929, 24 pgs, 7" x 9" 27.00
Atlas Shoe Co., Boston, 1912, 120 pgs, 7-1/2" x 10-1/4" 24.00
Atwater Kent Mfg. Co., Philadelphia, 1929, radios, 30 pgs, 6" x 9" ...48.00
Baldwin Locomotive Works, Philadelphia, 1907, 32 pgs, 6" x 9" 58.00
Bausch & Lomb Optical Co., Rochester, NY, 1919, microscopes and accessories, 112 pgs, 6-1/2" x 9-3/4" 52.00
Bausch & Lomb Optical Co., Rochester, NY, 1921, 12 pgs, 6-1/2" x 9-1/2" 21.00
Bell & Howell Co., Chicago, c1929, Filmosound Projector, 36 pgs, 5-1/2" x 8" 16.00
Black & Decker Mfg. Co., Towson, MD, 1931, electric tools, 44 pgs, 8-1/2" x 10-1/2"........................18.00
Brown-Morse Co., Muskegon, MI, 1922, 32 pgs, 8-1/2" x 11" 23.00
C.P. Barnes & Bros., Louisville, 1884, jewelry, 192 pgs, 6-1/2" x 3-1/2" 92.00
California Perfume Co., New York, c1929, 14 pgs, 3-3/4" x 8-3/4"..........................14.00
Caterpillar Tractor Co., Peoria, IL, 1937, 8 pgs, 8-1/4" x 10-3/4"............29.00
Chicago Mail Order Co., Chicago, 1927, 104 pgs, 6-3/4" x 9-1/2"............9.00
Crown Hair Goods Co., New York, c1920, Beauty Hints for the Beauty Salon, 48 pgs, 8" x 10-3/4"......82.00
Cundy-Bettoney Co., Inc., Boston, 1940, clarinets and flutes, 12 pgs, 8" x 11" 43.00
Eimer & Amend, New York, 1903, chemical and physical apparatus,

418 pgs, 6-1/2" x 10" 98.00
Encyclopedia Britannica, 1929, 30 pgs, 9" x 12" 16.00
Enterprise Mfg. Co., Philadelphia, household goods, 138 pgs, 5-3/4" x 8-3/4"..........................72.00
Estate Stove Co., Hamilton, OH, c1910, 64 pgs, 3-1/2" x 5-3/4" 28.00
Fiske & Co., Inc., Boston, 1911, brickwork, 40 pgs, 8" x 10-1/2" 26.00
General Electric Co., Schenectady, NY, 1919, The Electric Ship, 39 pgs, 8" x 10-1/2"............................68.00
Groome & Co., Philadelphia, 1912, wine merchant's price list, 24 pgs, 4" x 8-5/8"..............................34.00
International Harvester Co., Chicago, 1938, 32 pgs, 6" x 9" 34.00
Iron City Sash & Door Co., Pittsburgh, 1939, 68 pgs, 5-1/2" x 8-1/4"...32.00
J.L. Mott Iron Works, New York, 1895, 40 pgs, 9-1/2" x 11-3/4"...........46.00
J.R. Wood & Sons, Brooklyn, NY, 1922, jewelry, 208 pgs, 6-3/4" x 10" 110.00
John Deere, Moline, IL, 1956, Modern Farming with John Deere Quality Farm Equipment, 92 pgs, 7" x 10" 32.00
Jordan Marsh & Co., Boston, 1885, spring and summer catalog, 120 pgs, 9" x 11-3/4" 52.00
Kenneweg & Co., Cumberland, MD, 1891, wholesale groceries, 11 pgs, 8-1/4" x 10-3/4" 14.00
Lake Submarine Co., Bridgeport, CT, 1906, 49 pgs, 6-3/4" x 10" 92.00
Larkin Co., Buffalo, NY, 1914, 16 pgs, 5" x 8" 25.00
Mahler Bros., New York, 1900, spring and summer clothing, 88 pgs, 7-3/4" x 10-3/4" 46.00
Mead Cycle Co., Chicago, 1918, Ranger bicycles, 64 pgs, 8-1/2" x 11-1/4" 83.00
Montgomery Ward
    1912, No. 80 ....85.00
    1942, Spring And Summer 30.00
Morgan Sash & Door Co., Chicago, 1921, 96 pgs, 3-1/2" x 8".........19.00
National Cloak Co., New York, 1902, 28 pgs, 7-1/2" x 10".................34.00
National Trading Co., Chicago, 1924, Emma Post Barbour's New Bead Book, 28 pgs, 8-1/2" x 11".......23.00
Ormond Manufacturing Co., Baltimore, 1878, sewing machines, 96 pgs, 4-1/2" x 5-3/4"..........................73.00
Pabst Brewing Co., Milwaukee, c1896, 16 pgs, 3" x 5" 110.00
Paige-Detroit Motor Car, Detroit, 16 pgs, 6" x 8-3/4".............................46.00
Parker Brothers, Inc., Salem, MA, 1929, games, 12 pgs, 6" x 9" 39.00
Patton Paint Co., Milwaukee, c1900,

14 pgs, 3-1/2" x 5-1/2" 58.00
Philco Radio Corp., c1938, 12 pgs,
   3-1/4" x 5-1/2" 21.00
Piedmont Red Cedar Chest, Statesville,
   NC, 1912, 56 pgs, 6" x 9" 43.00
Proctor & Gamble Co., Cincinnati, 1918,
   Approved Methods for
   Home Laundering, 68 pgs,
   5-1/2" x 7-1/4" 32.00
Sears Roebuck
   1910, March-April, Colored
      Book of Carpets, Rugs,
      Curtains, 77 pgs 40.00
   1917, July and
      August, 120 pgs 10.00
   1927, Spring and Summer,
      1,076 pgs 28.00
   1932, Fall and Winter,
      1,035 pgs 40.00
   1951, Christmas 35.00
Spiegel, Chicago, Stern Co., 1936,
   48 pgs, 9-1/2" x 13-1/2" 19.00
Shear, Packard & Co., Albany, NY,
   1867, Improved American Hot Air
   Gas Burning Cooking Stove,
   42 pgs, 5-1/4" x 8-1/2" 63.00
Standard Mail Order Co., New York,
   c1924, men's and women's clothing,
   64 pgs, 6-1/4" x 8-1/2" 16.00
Star Motor Co., of NY, New York, c1915,
   The Star Car, built by W.C. Durant,
   24 pgs, 4" x 6" 63.00
Stetson Paint & Varnish, Chicago, 1934,
   42 pgs, 11" x 12" 68.00
Steuben Glass, New York, 1947,
   24 pgs, 6" x 8" 32.00
Studebaker Corp., of America, Detroit,
   1914, 32 pgs, 5" x 8-1/2" 93.00
Sutcliffe Co., Louisville, 1923, sports
   equipment, 64 pgs, 6" x 9".......48.00
U.S. Playing Card Co., Cincinnati, 1900,
   138 pgs, 4-1/2" x 7" 97.00
Westfield Mfg., Westfield, MA,
   1922, Columbia bicycles, 16 pgs,
   8" x 11-1/4" 76.00
White Hall Pottery Works,
   Stone Hall, IL, c1930, 44 pgs,
   10-1/4" x 13-1/2" 26.00
Wilson Furniture Co., Louisville, 1912,
   24 pgs, 4" x 9-1/4" 30.00

Cat Collectibles

Collecting Hints: Cat-related material can be found in almost all collecting categories—advertising items, dolls, figurines, folk art, fine art, jewelry, needlework, linens, plates, postcards and stamps, to name just a few. Antique cats are scarce but modern objects d'feline are plentiful. The better ones, the limited editions and pieces created by established artists, such as Lowell Davis the now-deceased Thaddeus Krumeich, are future collectibles.

The cat collector competes with collectors from other areas. Chessie, the C&O Railroad cat, is collected by railroad and advertising buffs; Felix, Garfield and other cartoon characters, plus cat-shaped toys and cat-related games, are loved by toy collectors. And cat postcards are collected by postcard collectors. Because cat collectors are attracted to all cat items, all breeds and realistic or abstract depictions, they tend to buy many items. It is best to specialize. Popular categories are fine art, crystal/glass cats and antique porcelain cats. Up-and-coming collecting categories include first-day covers, phone cards and dolls. Kliban's cats, especially the ceramic examples, art by Louis Wain, good Victorian paintings and cartoon cats are best-sellers in the secondary market.

History: The popular view of cats has been a roller coaster of opinion, from peaks of favoritism to valleys of superstition. Cats were deified in ancient Egypt and feared by Europeans in the Middle Ages. Customs and rituals resulted in brutal treatment of felines. Cats became associated with witchcraft, resulting in tales and superstitions which linger to the present. This lack of popularity adds to the scarcity of antique cat items.

References: Pauline Flick, *Cat Collectibles*, Wallace-Homestead, 1992; Marbena Jean Fyke, *Collectible Cats*, Collector Books, 1993; J.L. Lynnlee, *Purrfection: The Cat*, Schiffer Publishing, 1990.

Collectors' Club: Cat Collectors, 33161 Wendy Dr., Sterling Heights, MI 48310.

Museums: British Museum, London, England; The Cat Museum, Basel, Switzerland; Metropolitan Museum of Art, New York, NY.

Reproduction Alert.

Advisor: Marilyn Dipboye.

Art
   Cel, "The Aristocats," featuring Duchess, Walt Disney animated film, 1970, gouache on full celluloid,

Beadwork, heart with hump, five 3-fold dangles, silver, pink, white, green, gold-lilac, and blue beads, Indian souvenir, $95.

   11" x 14-1/2" 1,725.00
   Print, "Goderie des modes et
      Costumes," 1912 restrike by Paul
      Cornu, curator of Muse de Arts
      Decoratifs, 7-1/2" x 11" 100.00
   Oil painting, "Woman with Cat,"
      by Vittoria Corcos (1859-1953),
      35" x 38" 24,150.00
Book
   Old Possum's Book of Practical Cats,
      T.S. Eliot, Faber & Faber, Ltd,
      London, 1957 ....40.00
   With Louis Wain to Fairyland,
      described by Nora Chesson,
      Raphael Tuck & Sons, Ltd., London,
      1903, 1st ed, large 4to 2,650.00
Bookends
   Ceramic, pr black cats with gold trim,
      mkd "Japan," c1950, 5-3/4" h...25.00
   Composition material, antique white
      wash, mkd "Universal Statuary Corp.
      Original Sculpture B/W Marlotta,"
      6-1/4" h, 4-1/2" w, 4-1/2" d.......50.00
Bottle
   Avon
      Felina Fluffles, white cat in blue
         skirt, holding fan, 1976 ....15.00
      Kitten's Hideaway, white kitten in
         brown basket, 1974 ....7.00
   Clear blown glass, cat shape, filled
      with green creme de menthe, "1/2 pt"
      on paper label, 4-1/2" h...........50.00
   Ezra Brooks, cat-shaped pottery
      bottle, orange tabby with paw on blue
      ball, 8-3/4" h............................55.00
Clock
   Art Deco desk clock, marble base,
      metal cat beside clock, non-original
      battery-operated mechanism,
      6-1/2" l, 5-1/2" h 150.00
   White ceramic cat holding clock,
      plastic cat second hand, Sessions
      Clock Co., 1950s, 9" h 50.00
Cookie Jar
   Coalby, laughing black cat sitting
      upright..................................350.00
   McCoy

Kitten on pink basketweave 75.00
Two Kittens in a Basket,
white and black kittens
in yellow basket......................700.00
Figurines
Beswick Pottery, Cheshire cat,
Graham Tongue designer, 1973-82,
1-1/2" h..................................650.00
Ceramic cat band, 6 white
cats in blue jackets playing
gold instruments, Japanese,
1-1/2" h, each..........................50.00
Hedi Schoop, Turnabout Cat, contemporary design, cocoa brown with
silver details, 11" h.................110.00
Lowell Davis
Cat Napping Too?, black and
white cat curled on chair, mouse at
base, introduced in 1984, discontinued, 4-1/4" h.....................98.00
Country Christmas, cats
among Christmas presents,
1984, LE2500.....................525.00
Royal Doulton, Siamese, #2660,
#2662 and #2655, Chatcull Range,
1960-85, each.........................155.00
Tiffin Glass, Sassy Susie,
1929-41, milk glass or black
satin glass, 11" h....................165.00
Linens
Handkerchiefs, excellent condition,
price for 14 ....75.00
Tea towels, colorful, near-mint
condition, each..........................10.00
Metal
Calling card tray, cat's face,
emb "The Cat's Meow" between
the ears, "A. Everett & Son
Pattern Letters Auburn, NY' emb
under chin, c1915.....................85.00
Thermometer, hammered
aluminum, white metal cat on
base, 5-1/4" h...........................40.00
Miscellaneous
Coin, Isle of Man Manx cat, 1 crown
1970, uncirculated...............15.00
1975, proof...........................25.00
Comic Book, Felix the Cat "All Pic-

**Bookends, ceramic, black cats with gold
trim, mkd "Japan," c1950, 5-3/4" h, $25.**

**Toy, Felix the Cat, wood, jointed, mkd
"Pat Sullivan, patented June 23, 1925,"
4" h, $200.**

tures Comics," 1945.................50.00
Creamer, pottery, green with and
black spotted cat looking over side of
creamer, mkd "Erphila Fayence
Germany," 4-1/2" h...................50.00
Pinochle cards, with cat,
blue background, c1950,
fine condition, box.....................5.00
Pitcher, cat shape, tail forms
handle, clear class, incised "WMF
Germany," 8-1/4" h..................25.00
Record Album
78 RPM, "Classical Cats," London
Records, 1982 ....20.00
33-1/3 RPM, "Puss 'n' Boots,"
record with script, Madge
Tucker, c1942......................30.00
Wall plaque, mother cat and 3
babies, Miller Art Studio, OH, 1950s,
original box..............................30.00
Planter
Blue Willow,
earthenware, Japanese 230.00
Pottery
Beckoning Cat, black Shafford-
type paint quality, "Elvin Japan" on
paper label, 4-3/4" l..............32.50
Brown and white cat, blue bow,
standing upright with 1 paw raised,
6-1/2" l, 5" h 10.00
Stein, .5 L
Porcelain, Cat on Book, mkd "E.
Bohne Sohne".....................3,190.00
Stoneware, Student Cat, blue salt
glaze, mkd "Gerz #061" 575.00
Toy
Cup and saucer, child's set, cat on
twig of pussy willows, mkd "Made
in Japan" 11.00
Felix the Cat, wood, jointed, mkd "Pat
Sullivan, patented June 23, 1925,"
4" h..200.00
Tin cat, push tail down and cat moves
forward, yellow and red cat, red ball
and wheels, leather ears, mkd "MAR

Toys Made in USA," 6" l..........95.00
Salt and Pepper Shakers, pr
Ceramic Arts Studio, Thai and
Thai-Thai, Siamese cats 95.00
Porcelain, black and white cats, blue
bows, mkd "Czechoslovakia,"
2-1/4" h 15.00
Shawnee, original
paper labels, 3" h....................26.00

Ceramic Arts Studio

Collecting Hints: Collectors should
seek pieces which are free of damage and defects. Since this collecting area is relatively new, it
behooves collectors to buy the best
quality they can while prices are low.
A careful eye should be used to find
those unique pieces by designers
such as Harrington. A single firing
process was used to make Ceramic
Arts Studio wares. The pieces were
fired after decorations were applied
to the soft greenware. The firm's
specially developed glazes have remained stable with little discoloration
or crazing.

History: The Ceramic Arts Studio,
Madison, WI, was originally formed
by Lawrence Rabbit in 1940, while
he was a student at the University of
Wisconsin. He researched Wisconsin clay for a class project and later
produced hand-thrown pottery. By
January of 1941, he went into partnership with fellow University of Wisconsin Student Reuben Sand. Sand
became responsible for the administration, distribution, marketing and
management of the Studio.

Betty Harrington, who began
her career in 1942, designed more
than 600 figures and other items for
the Studio through her 14-year career. She was influenced by Martha
Graham's modern dancers. In addition to her theater series, she created storybook character and nursery
rhyme series. These series included
figures, head vases, salt and pepper
shaker sets, shelf sitters and wall
plaques. Harrington trained other
designers but was responsible for
most of the designs until the Studio
closed in 1956.

During peak production years in
the late 1940s, more than 100 peo-

ple produced 500,000 pieces a year. The molds were sent to Japan after the studio closed. Japanese pieces are sometimes found in the marketplace, but the depth of the color and clarity does not equal that of the originals. Ceramic Arts Studio wares were inexpensive—in the $2 to $3 range—and were marketed through department stores and by catalog sellers such as Montgomery Ward.

Collectors' Club: Ceramic Arts Studio Collectors Association, P.O. Box 46, Madison, WI 53701.

Candleholder, Speak No Evil	50.00

Figure
Arabesque, white	75.00
Attitude and Arabesque, green, price for pr	145.00
Beth, green	40.00
Budgie and Pudgie, price for pr	110.00
Chipmunk	40.00
Collie Pup	35.00
Columbine	80.00
Colt	85.00

Couples, price for pr
Blythe and Pensive, 6-3/4" h	300.00
Gypsy	155.00
Nip and Tuck	75.00
Oriental Couple	
Sitting	75.00
Standing	75.00
Pioneer Sam and Susie	110.00
Spanish	115.00
Water Couple	350.00
Fighting Leopards, price for pr	250.00
Harlequin	80.00
Lioness	135.00
Loreli on Shell	225.00
Panda	95.00

Skunk
Baby, 2" h	35.00
Mother, 3-1/4" l, 3" h	35.00
Wee Scotch Girl, 3-1/4" h	35.00
Winter Belle, 5-1/2" h	80.00
Head Vase, Lotus and Manchu, price for pr	295.00
Lamp, Zorina, Lucite base	275.00
Mask, Tragedy and Comedy, dark green, price for pr	185.00

Pitcher
Adam and Eve	55.00
Diana	55.00
Planter, Chinese girl	20.00

Salt and Pepper Shakers, pr
Brown Bear Mother and Baby	60.00
Calico Cat and Gingham Dog	90.00
Chinese Boy and Girl	40.00
Dokie on Leaf	175.00
Monkey Mother and Baby	75.00
Mouse in Cheese	35.00
Mushroom and Frog	35.00
Oakie on Leaf	175.00
Pink Elephant Couple, 3-1/2" h, sgd	80.00
Siamese Cat and Kitten	85.00
Wee Dutch	30.00

Shelf Sitter
Cat	35.00
Oriental Couple, price for pr	45.00

Wall Plaque
Cockatoo	50.00
Shadow Dancers, price for pr	110.00

Ceramics, Miscellaneous

Collecting Hints: The majority of ceramics included in this category were made in vast quantities, with long production runs. Condition is the key element. Don't settle for anything less than perfect. Prices for individual dinnerware pieces, especially hollowware serving pieces, are higher than prices for pieces sold as a set. The reason for this phenomenon, which is common to all dinnerware—European or American—is that many people have a basic set and are looking for filler pieces.

During the 1980s, collectors discovered wares from various West Coast potteries, some of which are included here. Part of the excitement about these pieces comes from the fact that many of the them reflect the style trends of the 1940s through the 1960s. What California collectors kept secret for more than a decade is now drawing nationwide attention—collecting California potteries is "in," as reflected in high prices and rampant speculation. No one is quite certain how much is available and prices vary regionally. Pieces are scarcer on the East Coast than on the West Coast. Collectors generally concentrate on items from a particular firm or period or on a specific pattern.

References: Susan and Al Bagdade, *Warman's American Pottery and Porcelain*, Wallace-Homestead, 1994; ——, *Warman's English & Continental Pottery & Porcelain*, 2nd Edition, Wallace-Homestead, 1991; Diana and John Callow and Marilyn and Peter Sweet, *Charlton Price Guide to Beswick Animals*, 1st Edition, Charlton Press, 1966; Jack Chipman, *Collector's Encyclopedia of California Pottery*, Collector Books 1992; Jean Dale, *Charlton Standard Catalogue of Royal Doulton Beswick Jugs*, 3rd Edition, Charlton Press, 1966; ——, *Charlton Standard Catalogue of Royal Doulton Beswick Storybook Figurines*, 2nd Edition, Charlton Press, 1966; David D. Dilley, *Haeger Potteries Through the Years*, L-W Book Sales, 1997; David Edwin Gifford, *Collector's Encyclopedia of Camark Pottery*, Collector Books, 1997; Kyle Husfloen (ed.), *Pottery and Porcelain Ceramics Price Guide*, 2nd Edition, Antique Trader Books, 1997; Dorothy Kamm, *American Painted Porcelain*, Collector Books, 1997; Lois Lehner, *Lehner's Encyclopedia of U.S. Marks on Pottery, Porcelain & Clay*, Collector Books, 1988; Richard Martinez, Devin Frick and Jean Frick, *Collectible Kay Finch*, Collector Books, 1996; Mike Nickel and Cindy Horvath, *Kay Finch Ceramics*, Schiffer Publishing, 1996; Mike Schneider, *Grindley Pottery*, Schiffer Publishing, 1996; Jim and Kaye Whitaker, *Josef Originals*, Schiffer Publishing, 1996.

Periodical: *Pottery Collectors Express*, P.O. Box 221, Mayview, MO 64071.

Collectors' Club: Royal Winton International Collectors' Club, 600 Columbia St., Pasadena, CA 91105.

Additional Listings: Cookie Jars; see also various named potteries by category.

Note: Included in the listings are several small companies for which little documentation exists.

Beswick: Since the 1890s, the father-and-son team of James Wright Beswick and John Beswick have been well known for their ceramic figures of horses, cats, dogs, birds and other wildlife. Animals from children's literature, such as Winnie the Pooh and Beatrice Potter books, have also been modeled. Royal Doulton Tableware, Ltd., bought the company in 1969.

Beatrix Pottery, Peter Rabbit, 100th Anniversary, orig box	55.00

Creamer and Sugar, matching tray,
 Cottage 35.00
Figure
 German Shepherd, U.S.
 Ulrica of Brittas 80.00
 Horse....................................150.00
 Hunca Munca #2 ....250.00
 Mr. Benjamin Bunny #2..........650.00
 Susie Jamaica........................200.00
Vase, 8" h, blue-yellow dribble glaze,
 pinched sides 50.00

Brayton Laguna: Brayton Laguna Pottery operated in South Laguna Beach from 1927 until 1963. The pottery was founded by Durline E. Brayton, who started making pottery in his home. The company produced lamps, cookie jars, figurines, tiles and salt and pepper shakers, in addition to hand-crafted dinnerware. Following Dublin's death in 1951, employees operated the company until it closed in 1963, a victim of an abundance of inexpensive Japanese imports.

Bowl
 4" d, handmade,
 wavy lip, burgundy 65.00
 19-1/2" l, 6" w, 4-1/2" h, black,
 incised dec 20.00
Creamer and Sugar, Calico Cat and
 Gingham Dog 85.00
Figure
 Blackamoor with cornucopias,
 gold trim, price for pr 195.00
 Gay '90s Men, bar....................80.00
 Prairie Lady 375.00
Hatpin Bonnet..............................45.00
Salt and Pepper Shakers, pr
 Calico Cat and Gingham Dog ..55.00
 Circus Clown and Dog 225.00
 Peasant....................................65.00
Teapot, cov, Provincial, brown,
 tulip stand 125.00
Vase, 8" h, Atlanta, spiral 95.00

Camark: Samuel Jack Carnes founded the Camark Pottery in Camden, AR, in 1926. The pottery employed well-known professional potters and artists to design and produce earthenware art pottery and decorative accessories. The plant was sold in 1966.

Candlesticks, pr, 5" h,
 double swirl, white 40.00
Console Set, center bowl with
 bird flower frog, matching
 candleholders 120.00
Figure
 Lion 35.00
 Squirrel, wall mounted, brown and
 albino, price for pr 140.00
Lily Vase, white glaze,
 orig foil label 50.00
Planter

Elephant, 11" x 8" 60.00
Swan, double, 7-1/2"................50.00
Vase
 6" h, matte,
 brown and mustard, 811 ....75.00
 7-1/2" h, shell finish, white,
 tassel handles 50.00
 10" h, matte, royal blue, 640 ....50.00

Carleton Ware

Bowl, 9-1/2" d, Lily of the Valley....45.00
Compote, Oak Leaf 115.00
Dish, Oak Leaf,
 lettuce-leaf type 50.00
Jug, Oak Leaf,
 green and yellow 65.00
Lobster Dish, 9-1/2" l, oblong........45.00
Marmalade
 Buttercup................................36.00
 Oak Leaf 48.00
Pitcher, Foxglove 95.00
Plate, Buttercup............................60.00
Salt and Pepper Shakers,
 pr, Oak Leaf.............................30.00
Spoon, Buttercup 15.00
Toast Rack, Foxglove 155.00

Copley

Bank, piggy, 5-3/4" h,
 blue coveralls 40.00
Figure, Oriental girl, open basket ..20.00
Pitcher, 8" h, pink and yellow,
 mkd "Royal Copley"................35.00
Planter
 6" h, Oriental boy,
 green and yellow planter..........16.00
 7-1/2" h, Chinese boy,
 big hat, wall type 22.00
Vase
 8" h, Floral
 Beauty pit..............................24.00
 Blue and gray........................20.00
Bear, Yellowstone label 48.00
Wall Pocket, bonnet, red..............15.00

Deforest

Condiment Jar, cov, jam, relish,
 onions or BBQ sauce, each.....50.00
Garlic Holder, Mr. and Mrs. 35.00
Wall Plaque, poodle,
 rhinestone trim.........................75.00

Dee Lee

Figure
 Cuban Dancer, woman 275.00
 Girl 50.00
Flower Frog, girl 125.00
Match Holder,
 Destinker, 5-1/8" h...................32.00
Planter
 Henny Penny, 6" h 45.00
 Kitty, 4-1/4" h, sitting, white......18.00
Spaghetti Poodle 70.00
Wall Pocket, Dee Stinker 30.00

Glidden: Glidden Parker founded a pottery about 1940. Marion L. Fosdick was his assistant. The factory employed 55 people during its peak years of producing dinnerware and some accessories.

Charger, 14-1/2" d, blue, #68........95.00
Vase, Desert Sand, #4 ....40.00
Wall Pocket, 6" x 9" 95.00

Goebel

Bank, Chimney Sweep.................125.00
Cigarette Snuffer, Friar Tuck..........60.00
Cookie Jar, cov, owl 135.00
Cruet, Friar Tuck, oil and vinegar, 3-line
 mark, price for pr 250.00
Figure
 Cat, 4" h, 9" l black wood tail,
 red body, mkd "Goebel W.
 Germany"................................50.00
 Country Boy Doctor 95.00
 Sheep, ram 55.00
 Snow White and the Seven Dwarfs,
 Germany mark 450.00
Inkwell, soldier, 2 pc, crown mark,
 small chip on hat 140.00
Pitcher, 5-1/4" h, Friar Tuck, fully glazed,
 #516/0, crown mark, chip 165.00
Salt and Pepper Shakers,
 pr, lobsters 25.00

Haeger: In 1871, David H. Haeger bought an interest in the Dundee Brick Yard in Dundee, IL. Eventually, he expanded his interests to include two other brick and tile factories. In 1900, his sons took over management of the company; in 1912, they began producing flowerpots. With the introduction of glazed pottery in 1914, Haeger Potteries, Inc., was founded.

Basket, 8" h, brown 12.00
Figure
 Indian Girl with Basket 25.00
 Mermaid, 14" h......................100.00
Lamp, pagoda, orig shade, finials,
 1950s, price for pr 175.00
Planter, Madonna and Child 18.00
Vase
 6-1/2" h, matte blue, orig label ...8.00
 10" h, ivory, brown and rust 20.00
 15" h, double leaf, dark green,
 #4101 ....25.00

Hedi Schoop: Hedi Schoop Art Creations was incorporated in 1942 in North Hollywood, CA. The pottery produced highly detailed figurines, lamps, wall plaques, planters and decorative accessories. In the mid 1950s, a line of television lamps was introduced, but a fire at the plant in 1958 brought an abrupt end to production. The pottery was not rebuilt, although Schoop did some design work for other companies for a short period of time.

Box, cov, boxer.............................150.00
Cookie Jar, Darner Doll,
blue and green 325.00
Figure
Claudette Colbert 95.00
Crowing Rooster, 15" h 125.00
Dutch Girl 75.00
French Maid, 10" h...................80.00
Greek Couple, 14" h..............125.00
Poodle, pink,
black and white, 12" l 125.00
Woman with dog 75.00
Pencil Box, cov, 4-1/2" x 7-1/2" d,
teal and gray, painted feather
on cov 75.00
Plate, apple, pr 70.00
Vase
Butterflies, resting,
gold, price for pr 150.00
Dancers, swirling dresses, arms
raised, white ground, speckled gold,
13" h, price for pr.....................85.00
Rooster, 13" h, forest, chartreuse,
red, figural 125.00

Holt Howard

Lady Head Vase, Christmas..........85.00
Salt and Pepper Shakers,
pr, bunnies 40.00
String Holder, cat...........................55.00
Tape Measure, cat, pincushion 55.00

Josef Originals: In 1946, Muriel Josef
George started production of her Birthday Girls figurines in Arcadia, CA. Within
a few years, companies in Japan, Korea
and Taiwan were marketing less-expensive copies. To compete, George relocated to Japan in 1955 and expanded
her line to include Christmas items, animals and other utilitarian ceramics.
Items produced in Arcadia between
1946 and 1955 are marked "California,"
those produced in Japan are marked
"Josef Originals."

Animal
Kangaroo with baby 75.00
Ostrich, large............................70.00
Swan, large 30.00
Cookie Jar, owl, green.................110.00
Figure
April Girl 20.00
Baby in cradle 30.00
Belle 55.00
Birthday Girl, orig box................32.00
Days of the Week, each...........65.00
February, lavender....................15.00
Island..35.00
July, Japanese doll...................40.00
Mama 150.00
Penny 75.00
Rose Morning,
Noon and Night 65.00

Simone...85.00
Sugar and Spice 30.00
Sweden..30.00
Wee Ching 60.00
Wu Fu and Wha Cha,
price for pr...............................125.00
Yvette...85.00
Nodder, Dalmatian 60.00

Kay Finch: Kay Finch Ceramics began
operating in a studio in Corona Del Mar,
CA, in 1935. All pieces were hand decorated and designed by either Kay Finch or
her son George. The company ceased
operations in 1963.

Bank, sassy pig 125.00
Candleholder, 14" h, white flower..30.00
Candy Bowl, swan.......................135.00
Figure
Cat
Jezebel, #179 ....450.00
Mutt & Puff, #182 and #183,
gray and blue 245.00
Cherub 150.00
Doves, #1502.........................375.00
Elephant, #4804
Jumbo 225.00
Mumbo 225.00
Grumpy Pig, #150 ....450.00
Lamb, #136 ....75.00
Mr. & Mrs. Bird,
#454 and #453 ....325.00
Peasant Boy...........................65.00
Peep, duck..............................35.00
Squirrels, #108A and #108C..225.00
Toot, owl 95.00
Mug, Santa, #4950 ....125.00
Planter
Baby Block, bear......................95.00
Booties 75.00
Stork...75.00
Salt and Pepper Shakers, pr,
turkeys, white 195.00
Wall Pocket, Santa.......................75.00

Pfaltzgraff: Known for their redware and
stoneware production, Pfaltzgraff is the
oldest family-owned pottery in America.
It was founded in 1811 to make redware.
Several different family members operated factories in different areas. The
name became Pfaltzgraff Pottery Co., in
1896. Production of art pottery took
place from 1931 to 1937. Kitchenware
was introduced in the 1930s and dinnerware about 1940.

Bowl, Gourmet, 5-1/2" d 10.00
Cheese Shaker, Village.................12.00
Cigar Jar, 6-3/4" h,
Handy Harry.............................350.00
Coffeepot, cov, Heritage 25.00
Cup and Saucer
America 8.50

Gourmet.......................................12.00
Village..5.00
Flowerpot, 3-3/4" h, attached saucer,
glossy yellow glaze 10.00
Plate
America, 10-1/4" d 15.00
Tea Rose, dinner 5.00
Village, salad 3.50
Sprinkler Bottle, Myrtle...............125.00
Vase
5-1/2" h, Sunburst, handle, Sunburst
noted on base, ink mark 140.00
6" h, #136, Spanish Tile...........65.00
7" h, cobalt, #117 ....75.00
7" h, blue, handle, ink mark ...125.00

Rosemeade: The Wahpeton Pottery
Company/Rosemeade Pottery operated
in Wahpeton, ND, from 1940 to 1961.
Laura Hughes, the potter, incorporated
wildlife themes in the design of her novelty and utilitarian wares. The pottery's
salesroom closed in 1964.

Ashtray, Pine Ridge Sioux,
geometric 70.00
Banana Bowl, 7" d,
pink and white 50.00
Cowboy Boots
4" h, bronze..............................45.00
6-3/4" h, tan 65.00
Creamer and Sugar,
Tulip, yellow 85.00
Figure
Cocker Spaniel, pink................95.00
Elephant, gray, miniature.......125.00
Flower Frog, fish shape 45.00
Incense Burner, Teepee 165.00
Rose Bowl
Black, metallic..........................45.00
Green, matte.............................45.00
Pink, matte................................45.00
Salt and Pepper Shakers, pr
Cattle 195.00
Cucumbers 75.00
Goose Goslings 95.00
Mallard Ducks 125.00
Palomino Horses' Heads 110.00
Pheasants
Crouched 185.00
Golden 235.00
Strutting, male 205.00
Tail down 165.00
Tail up 70.00
Skunks
Large 45.00
Medium 75.00
Teepees....................................150.00
Tulips, pink................................65.00
Turkeys 125.00
Spoon Rest, elephant, pink.........175.00
Vase
4-1/2" h, caramel, orig label 30.00

4-3/4" h, bud, pink 25.00
5-3/8" h, wheat 55.00
7" h, fan, pink and white 45.00
7-1/2" h, bud, bronze 45.00

Cereal Boxes

Collecting Hints: There are two keys to collecting cereal boxes. The first is graphics, i.e., the box features the picture of a major character or personality or a design that is extremely characteristic of its period. The second hinges on the premium advertised on the box.

Cereal boxes are divided into vintage boxes (those dating before 1970s) and modern boxes. Hoarding of modern cereal boxes began in the mid-1980s. Beware of paying premium prices for any boxes made after this date.

More desirable than cereal boxes themselves are large countertop and other cereal box display pieces. Cereal box collectors actively compete against advertising collectors for these items, thus driving up prices. Many cereal box themes also cross over into other collecting categories. In many cases, these secondary collectors are responsible for maintaining high prices for some boxes. Once the outside demand is met, prices drop. Carefully study which market component is the principal price determinant.

History: Oatmeal and wheat cereals achieved popularity in the 19th century. They could be purchased in bulk from any general store. The first packaged, ready-to-eat breakfast cereals appeared around 1900. Initially, the packaging pitch contained an appeal directed to mothers.

Everything changed in the late 1930s and early 1940s. Companies such as General Mills, Quaker, Post and Ralston redirected the packaging appeal to children, using as a hook the lure of premiums sent in exchange for one or more box lids or coupons. Many of these promotions were geared to the popular radio shows of the period. However, television advertising was most responsible for establishing a firm link between cereal manufacturers and children.

In the 1940s, General Mills successfully used the premium approach to introduce Cheerios and Kix. In the 1950s, sugar-coated cereals were the rage. By the 1960s and 1970s, cereal manufacturers linked the sale of their brands to licensed characters. As the popularity of characters faded, boxes—but not the cereal contents—were changed. Today, an endless variety of cereal brands parades across supermarket shelves, some brands lasting less than a year.

References: Scott Bruce, *Cereal Box Bonanza*, Collector Books, 1995; Scott Bruce and Bill Crawford, *Cerealizing America*, Faber and Faber, 1995; Tom Tumbusch, *Tomart's Price Guide to Radio Premiums and Cereal Box Collectibles*, Wallace-Homestead, 1991.

Periodical: *Flake*, P.O. Box 481, Cambridge, MA 02140.

Collectors' Club: Sugar-Charged Cereal Collectors, 92B N. Bedford St., Arlington, VA 22201.

Aunt Sally Quick Cooking Oats, 10" h, cylindrical, yellow and red, 1940s 40.00
Batman, bank, Michael Keaton face, shrink-wrapped, flat 50.00
Cap'n Crunch, island map, flat 50.00
Cheerios
    Lone Ranger Frontier Town, 1948, flat 150.00
    Muppet Movie, 1980 ....18.00
Fairway Oak Flakes, 10" h, cylindrical, boy and girl illus, c1910 ....90.00
George Washington Corn Flakes, unopened 60.00

Jersey Corn Flakes, 1920s, multicolored box with family eating cereal illus, unopened 45.00
Kellogg's
    Corn Flakes
        Superman, 1956, flat 350.00
        Vanessa Williams, 1984 ......50.00
    Frosted Flakes, Tony the Tiger spoon offer on back, 1975 ....40.00
    Pep, Superman, radio, 1945, flat 1,250.00
Nabisco
    Shredded Wheat, 1942 ....65.00
    Space Explorers, flat 40.00
Post
    Buck Rogers, 1946, flat 450.00
    Super Sugar Crisp, 1974 ....35.00
Quaker
    Sgt. Preston Yukon Trail, Puffed Wheat, complete set 2,500.00
    Temple, Shirley, Puffed Wheat, c1930 ....110.00
Ralston
    Addams Family 30.00
    Bill & Ted's Excellent Cereal, phone booth cassette tape case, 1991, MIP 10.00
Wheaties
    Cal Ripken, 2-1/2" x 7-1/2" x 11", unopened, issued as commemorative for breaking record, front panel with error print that omits shirt emblem, back panel with dramatic twilight color photo, yellow-lettered text, side panel text regarding Ripken and Lou Gehrig 75.00
    Minnesota Twins, 1987 ....8.00
    Reggie Jackson 10.00
    World Series, 1985 ....6.00
White Swan Oatmeal, 4 oz 30.00

Cereal Premiums

Collecting Hints: The rising collectibility of cereal premiums reflects the shift of emphasis from collectibles of the 1920-1940 period to those of the post-1945 era. The radio-premium generation is getting older. They have watched the price of scarcer examples of their childhood treasures rise beyond the point of affordability. Further, these collectors are reaching an age when selling, rather than buying, dominates their mindset. It is time for a new generation to enter the picture—herald the arrival of the cereal premium.

At the moment, collectors do not differentiate between premiums that were found in the box and those that were obtained by sending in the requi-

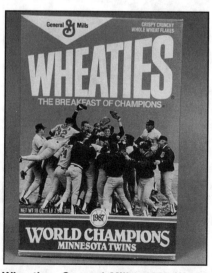

Wheaties, General Mills, 1987 World Champions, Minnesota Twins, 8-1/4" w, 2-3/4" d, 12" h, 18 oz, $7.

site number of box tops. As collectors become more sophisticated, look for this distinction to occur. The cereal premiums of most interest in the current market are those associated with a fictional advertising, cartoon or television character. As a result, much of the pricing in this category is being driven by the non-cereal premium collector. This does not appear likely to change in the decade ahead.

Collectors of cereal premiums narrow their collecting by focusing on the premiums found in a single brand or those of one particular manufacturer—variables dependent on whether the concentration is on the 1945-1962 or post-1962 period. The lack of a comprehensive list of manufacturers, brands and premiums often makes attribution a problem. When buying a cereal premium with which you are unfamiliar, insist that the seller indicate the manufacturer, brand name and date on the sales receipt.

The importance of original packaging—much of which was nondescript—is unclear at the moment. Current collectors tend to leave sealed any unopened packages. Most examples on the market have not retained their original packaging. At the moment there is little enthusiasm for generic pieces. However, anyone who compares the history of Cracker Jack premium collecting with that of cereal premiums will quickly see the long-term potential for generic material.

History: Cereal premiums were introduced in the 1930s when manufacturers such as General Mills, Post, Quaker and Ralston offered premiums to individuals who sent in the requisite number of box tops or coupons. Many of these premiums had a radio show tie-in. Although the use of in-the-box premiums and on-pack promotions dates from the 1930s, this approach achieved its greatest popularity in the post-1945 period. Buildings, dolls, games, masks and puzzles were just a few of the many items that a child could cut out by carefully following the directions on the back of a cereal box. Many in-box and on-pack promotional premiums related to a popular television program or movie.

When sugar-coated brands were introduced in the mid-1950s,

advertising characters were developed to assist in the merchandising effort. Characters such as Captain Crunch, Sugar Bear, Tony the Tiger and Toucan Sam achieved widespread recognition. Often in-box and on-pack promotions tied in directly with these characters.

In the 1970s, tie-ins were often more short-lived. Cereal manufacturers responded almost immediately to the latest movie or television craze and local and regional promotions became prominent. One result of this trend is the shift in emphasis from the premium to the box itself as the important collectible unit. Cereal box collecting is now a separate category. The value of most boxes now exceeds any value for the premium associated with it.

References: Scott Bruce, *Cereal Box Bonanza*, Collector Books, 1995; Scott Bruce and Bill Crawford, *Cerealizing America*, Faber and Faber, 1995; Tom Tumbusch, *Tomart's Price Guide to Radio Premiums and Cereal Box Collectibles*, Wallace-Homestead, 1991.

Periodical: *Flake*, P.O. Box 481, Cambridge, MA 02140.

Baseball Cards, Kellogg's, 1970 set, 75 cards 225.00
Baseball Cards, Kellogg's, 1975 set, 57 cards 125.00
Baseball Cards, Kellogg's, 1980 set, 60 cards 22.00

Nabisco, Straight Arrow Injun-uity Manual, Book 3, cardboard, green letters, 3-7/8" w, 7-3/8" h, Shredded Wheat, 1949, $30.

Basketball, Michael Jordan, Wheaties 25.00
Binoculars, Private Eye, Kellogg's 15.00
Book, *Dick Tracy*, Quaker Oats, c1939 .... 35.00
Calendar, Michael Jordan, Wheaties 25.00
Camera, premium 110, Kellogg's 1970s 15.00
Character Set, Disney Afternoon, 2" h plastic figure, copyright Disney, Kellogg's, Made in China, 1991, set of four
  Duck Tales 8.00
  Gummy Bears 8.00
  Rescue Rangers 8.00
  Tail Spin 8.00
Charm, figural, bright gold luster, Snap-in baker's hat, tiny Kellogg's inscription on crown, c1970 ..... 25.00
Children's Feeding dishes, plate, bowl and milk cup, General Mills, Cheerios Kids and Bullwinkle, Cheerios boy and girl on each pc, Melmac dinnerware, Boontown Molding Co., Inc., copyright Jay Ward Prod and GMI, price for set 45.00
Coloring Map, Captain Crunch, copyright Quaker Oats Company, 1983, MIP 15.00
Coloring Paper, Captain Crunch, early 1980s, MIP 10.00
Comic Book, *Baseball Facts & Fun*, 52 pgs, Post Sugar Crisp 35.00
Cut-Out, Rocket Firing Star Fighter Jet and Exploding Light Tank, Cheerios, 1950s 15.00
Doll, Quaker Oats, stuffed, 1960s . 30.00
Eraser, 2" h, Yogi Bear, Kellogg's, 1960s 20.00
Figure, 2-1/2" h, thin pressed plastic
  Boo Berry, glow in the dark 12.00
  Count Chocula, stand 12.00
  Frankenberry, stand 12.00
Frisbee, Ghostbusters, glow-in-the-dark, Ralston 35.00
Game
  Rin-Tin-Tin Bead in Hole Game, circular casing, Nabisco, 1956 . 15.00
  Space Match Card Game, color illus, Quisp, 1968 .... 25.00
Golf Ball, Ultra, Michael Jordan, Wheaties 25.00
Mask, Teenage Mutant Ninja Turtles, Ralston 40.00
Mug, plastic, white and black, 3 different illus, Cheerios, 1950s 30.00
Party Kit, Singing Lady Party Kit, masks, Kellogg's, 1936, uncut 65.00
Pencil Top, blue Count Chocula, red Frankenberry and white Boo Berry, set of 3 .... 5.00
Picture, Sgt. Preston framed portrait prize, color photo of Sgt. Preston and Yukon King, orig wood frame, 1950 .... 200.00

Pin
  Dennis the Menace 15.00
  Roy Rogers, Grape
    Nut Flakes, 1953 ....10.00
  Tony Astronaut Breakfast Game,
    Kellogg's Frosted Flakes,
    mkd "Made in USA"..................10.00
Pinback Button, Kellogg's Toasted Corn
  Flakes, multicolored, blond toddler
  holding cereal box, c1930........60.00
Plate, 8" d, plastic, white, Bullwinkle
  jumping off diving board, Cheerios
  Kid watching, General Mills 25.00
Post Card, 3-1/2" x 6", Cheerios Kid with
  Donald Duck, Huey, Louie and
  Disneyland, black and white,
  Cheerios, 1957 ....12.00
Puppet
  Banana Splits, Bingo, plastic,
    Kellogg's, 1969.........................12.00
  Cap'n Crunch, plastic, 1960s ...25.00
  Trix Rabbit, 12" h, cloth and vinyl,
    1960s 30.00
Puzzle
  Crunchberry Beast, Quaker Oats,
    early 1980s, MIP 15.00
  Jean Le Foot, Quaker Oats, early
    1980s, MIP 15.00
Record, 33-1/3 RPM, Archies, Jingle-
  Jangle, Post Cereal, c1968 ....7.50
Ring Game, features Captain
  Crunch on one side,
  Jean Le Foot on other 20.00
Secret Decoder, Toucan Sam,
  Kellogg's Fruit Loops, 1983 .....12.00
Song Card, Mr. Ed, Kellogg's........10.00
Spoon, Dennis the Menace,
  SP, Kellogg's 25.00
Stamp Album, house pets, copyright The
  Quaker Oats Company, 1982..10.00
Stamper, Chip 'n' Dale, Kellogg's..20.00
Toy, plastic
  Car, Chitty Chitty Bang Bang,
    two-tone, cardboard wings,
    Post, 1968 ....30.00
  Rickshaw, So-Hi figure pulls cart,
    Rice Krinkles, Post, 1965 ....90.00
  Wacky Races Bi-Plane,
    Muttley, Kellogg's, 1969 ....65.00
Whistle, Bo'sun, white front, yellow back,
  Quaker Oats 12.00
Wings Glider, Kellogg's 20.00

Character and Promotional Glasses

Collecting Hints: Contemporary character and promotional glasses are usually produced in series. It is important to collect the full series, including any color variations. This is not as easy as it sounds. Sports team glasses are frequently issued region-ally, i.e., Philadelphia Eagles glasses may appear just in the Philadelphia market while San Diego Charger glasses may be available only in the area around San Diego. Before paying a great deal of money for a recent glass, ask yourself if what may be rare in your area is common somewhere else. Any serious collectors needs this sense of perspective.

Some early examples were decorated with lead-based paint. They should not be used for drinking purposes. Collectors place a premium on glasses with out-of-the-box luster. The mere act of washing a glass, in a dishwasher or even by hand, can lessen its value. Avoid examples with any evidence of fading. Because of their wide availability, character and promotional drinking glasses should be collected only if they are in excellent to mint condition. Pay premium prices only for glasses that pre-date 1980. After that, glasses were hoarded in quantity by distributors, dealers and collectors.

History: Character and promotional drinking glasses date to the movie premier of "Snow White and the Seven Dwarfs" in December of 1937. Libbey Glass and Walt Disney designed tumblers with a safety edge and sold them through variety stores and local dairies. The glasses proved extremely popular. Today collector glasses can be found for almost every Disney character, cartoon and movie theme.

In 1953, Welch's began to package their jelly in decorated tumblers that featured Howdy Doody and his friends. Once again, the public's response was overwhelming. Welch's soon introduced tumblers with other cartoon characters, such as Mr. Magoo. In the late 1960s, fast food restaurants and gasoline stations started to use drinking glasses as advertising premiums. Soft drink manufacturers like Coke and Pepsi saw the advertising potential and developed marketing plans focused on licensed characters and movies. Sport's team licensing also entered the picture.

By the early 1980s, hundreds of new glasses were being issued each year. As the 1980s drew to a close, plastic drinking cups replaced glasses, although the use of licensed images continued. While most collectors still prefer to collect glass, a few far-sighted individuals are stashing away pristine plastic examples.

References: John Hervey, *Collector's Guide to Cartoon & Promotional Drinking Glasses*, L-W Book Sales, 1990, 1995 value update; Carol and Gene Markowski, *Tomart's Price Guide to Character & Promotional Glasses*, 2nd Edition, Tomart Publications, 1993.

Periodical: *Collector Glass News*, P.O. Box 308, Slippery Rock, PA 16057.

Animal Crackers, 1978
Dodo 8.50
Lyle 9.00
Annie and Sandy,
  Swenson's, 1982 ....7.50

Arby's
BC Ice Age, riding on wheel, 1981..9.00
Bullwinkle, Crossing the Delaware,
  11 oz, 1976 ....9.00
Charlie Chaplin, Movie Star series..7.50
Rocky, In the Dawn's Early Light,
  11 oz, 1976 ....9.00

McDonald's, Snoopy, Camp Snoopy Collection, "Civilization Is Overrated!," 1983, 6" h, $3.

Wizard of Id, 1983 ....12.00

Archies, 1971, 8 oz

Archie Takes the Gang for a Ride ...4.50
Betty and Veronica Fashion Show ..4.00
Hot Dog Goes To School 4.00

Battlestar Galactica, 16 oz, Universal Studios, Inc., 1979

Commander Adama 15.00
Cylon Warriors...........................15.00
Starbuck 15.00

Burger Chef

Endangered Species,
    Bengal Tiger, 1978 ....6.50
Jefferson, President Series 6.00
Washington, Bicentennial Series.....7.00

Burger King

Burger King, 1989 ....10.00
Denver Broncs, Moses 8.00
Shake A Lot, 1979.........................9.00

Burger King/Coca-Cola, Star Wars

Empire Strikes Back, 16 oz, copyright
    Lucasfilm, 1980
        Darth Vader..............................15.00
        Lando Calrissian 18.00
        Luke Skywalker.........................15.00
        R2-D2 and C-3PO....................15.00
Return of the Jedi, 16 oz, copyright
    Lucasfilm, 1983
        C-3PO at the Ewok Village.......15.00
        Jabba, Leia and the Rebo Band,
            slightly faded 12.00
        Luke & Han,
            Fighting on Tatooine 15.00
        Luke Fighting Darth
            in the Throne Room 17.50

Chipper-Up Soda, Galena, IL,
    Aquaman 46.00

Coca Cola

Betty, tray girl 12.00
Heritage Collector Series,
    Patrick Henry 6.00
Holly Hobbie, Good Friends
    Are Like Sunshine 6.50
Outdoor Scene, buttered corn.........5.00
Santa and Elves 7.50

DC Comics, Pepsi

Aquaman, 16 oz, 1978 ....15.00
Batman, 1966...............................7.50
Green Lantern 8.50
Superman, 1975............................7.50

Domino's Pizza, 1988

Noid, beach chair 2.00
Noid, tennis 2.00

Dr Pepper

Hot-Air Balloon 9.00
Star Trek, Mr. Spock, 1976 ....8.00

Hanna Barbera Productions, Inc.

Hair Bear mug,
    blue plastic, 1971 ....10.00
Larosa Pizzaria Parlor, 16 oz, Fred
    and Wilma, Yogi and Mr. Ranger,
    Scooby, Luigi, 1973.................30.00
Square Bear mug,
    yellow plastic, 1971 ....10.00

Hardee's, Flintstones, The First 30 Years—1964, 16 oz, 1991

Going to the Drive-In 5.00
Little Bamm-Bamm..........................5.00
The Blessed Event 6.50
The Snorkasaurus Story 6.00

Marvel Comics

Amazing Spiderman, 1977..............5.00
Howard the Duck, 1977..................4.00
Hulk, 1978 ....3.50

McDonald's

Big Mac, McVote, 1986 ....5.00
Camp Snoopy, Civilization
    Is Over-Rated 3.00
Mayor McCheese Taking Pictures ..5.00
McDonald Action Series, 16 oz, 1977
        Captain Crook 5.00
        Hamburglar, slightly faded 4.00
        Mayor McCheese........................5.00
Ronald McDonald Saves the Falling
    Star, 1977 ....6.00

Mobil, football, 10 different logos,
    price for set...............................20.00

National Periodical Publications

Batman...15.00
Robin, 6 oz, 1960s 25.00
Superman, Fighting the Dragon,
    5-1/4" h, 1965 ....12.00
Wonder Woman 10.00

Paramount Pictures

Gulliver's Travels, 1939.................40.00
Happy Days—Fonzie, "Hey!" 16 oz,
    1977 ....15.00

Pepsi

Batman, 16 oz, 1978,
    minor paint loss 15.00
Bugs Bunny, 1973,
    copyright Warner Bros. Inc........8.00
Bullwinkle 30.00
Daffy Duck and
    Tasmanian Devil, 1976............15.00
Dudley Do-Right,
    black lettering, 16 oz 30.00
Flash, 16 oz, 1976,
    minor mispaint 15.00
Foghorn Leghorn, 16 oz,
    1973, slightly faded 10.00
Natasha, 12 oz, copyright P.A.T. Ward,
    slight fading 35.00
Robin, 16 oz, 1978 ....18.00
Simon Bar Sinister, 12 oz.............40.00
Superman, 1975, slightly faded.....15.00

Tweety, 16 oz, thin glass,
    white lettering, 1973................15.00
Woody Woodpecker, 16 oz, 1977.15.00

Pizza Hut

Bullwinkle, blue truck 8.00
Care Bears, Funshine Bear, 1983 ..9.00
Dudley Do-Right, helicopter 8.00

7-Up, Indiana Jones and the Temple of Doom, 16 oz, 1984

High Priest Mola Ram 10.00
Indy Fighting 12.00
The Spiked Boom 10.00

Sunday Funnies

Gasoline Alley, 16 oz, copyright Chicago
    Tribune, Uncle Walt, Nina, Judy,
    Skeezix, 1976, slight paint loss15.00
Little Orphan Annie, 16 oz, copyright
    New York News, Orphan Annie,
    Sandy, Daddy Warbucks, ASP,
    Punjab, 1976 ....15.00
Moon Mullins, 16 oz, copyright New York
    News, Lord Plushbottom, Kayo,
    Willie, Lady Plushbottom and
    Moon Mullins, 1976 ....18.00
Smilin' Jack, 16 oz, copyright
    New York News, Rev Bob, Jack,
    Sizzle, Cindy, Sable, The Head,
    Fat Stuff and Jim S.................15.00

Taco Bell, Star Trek III, 16 oz, copyright Paramount Pictures Corp., 1984

Lord Kruge 12.00
The Search for Spock Enterprise
    Destroyed 15.00

Tommy Tucker Kola,
    Omaha, NE 40.00

Walt Disney

Goofy
    1937......................................140.00
    1978, Goofy and Pluto on back,
    16 oz, Pepsi, copyright Walt Disney
    Productions 12.00
Minnie Mouse...............................30.00

Warner Bros., Pepsi

Beaky Buzzard, 16 oz,
    thin glass, 1973 ....15.00
Cool Cat and Beaky
    Buzzard, 16 oz, 1976 ....15.00
Daffy Duck, 4 oz, 1976.................15.00
Elmer Fudd, 6 oz, 1976................15.00
Speedy Gonzales, 16 oz, 1973.....12.00

Welch's, 8 oz

Archies 4.50
Flintstones....................................6.00
Howdy Doody, 1953....................48.00

Children's Books

Collecting Hints: Most collectors look for books by a certain author or illustrator. Others are interested in books from a certain time period, such as the 19th century. Accumulating the complete run of a series, such as Tom Swift, Nancy Drew or the Hardy Boys, is of interest to some collectors. Subject categories are popular, too, and include ethnic books, mechanical books, first editions, award-winning books, certain kinds of animals, rag books, Big Little Books and those with photographic illustrations.

A good way to learn about children's books is to go to libraries and museums where special children's collections have been developed. Books on various aspects of children's literature are a necessity. You also should read a general reference on book collecting to provide you with background information. Eventually, you will want to own a few reference books most closely associated with your collection.

Although children's books can be found at all the usual places where antiques and collectibles are for sale, also seek out book and paper shows. Get to know dealers who specialize in children's books; ask to receive their lists or catalogs. Some dealers will try to locate books for your collection. Most stores specializing in used and out-of-print books have a section with children's books. Regular bookstores may carry the most recent works of authors or illustrators who are still working.

When purchasing books, consider the following: presence of a dust jacket or box, condition of the book, the edition, quality of illustrations and binding and prominence of the author or illustrator. Books should be examined very carefully to make sure that all pages and illustrations are present. Missing pages will reduce the value of the book. Significant bits of information, particularly details of the book's edition, can be found on the title page and verso of the title page. Try to buy books in the best condition you can afford. Even if your budget is limited, you can still find very nice inexpensive children's books if you keep looking.

History: William Caxton, a printer in England, is considered the first pub-

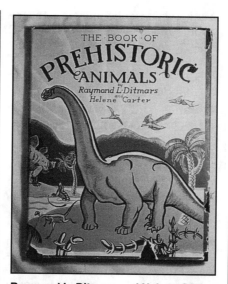

Raymond L. Ditmars and Helene Carter, *The Book of Prehistoric Animals*, $15.

lisher of children's books. *Aesop's Fables*, printed in 1484, was one of his early publications. Other very early books include John Cotton's *Spiritual Milk for Boston Babes* in 1646, *Orbis Pictis* translated from the Latin about 1657 and *New England Primer* in 1691.

Early children's classics were *Robinson Crusoe* (1719), *Gulliver's Travels* (1726) and Perrault's *Tales of Mother Goose* (translated into English in 1729). The well-known "A Visit from St. Nicholas" by Clement C. Moore appeared in 1823. Some of the best-known children's works were published between 1840 and 1900, including Lear's *Book of Nonsense*, Andersen's and Grimm's *Fairy Tales*, *Alice in Wonderland*, *Hans Brinker*, *Little Women*, *Tom Sawyer*, *Treasure Island*, *Heidi*, *A Child's Garden of Verses* and *Little Black Sambo*.

During the late 1800s, novelty children's books appeared. Lothar Meggendorfer, Ernest Nister and Raphael Tuck were the best-known publishers of these fascinating pop-up and mechanical or movable, books. The popularity of this type of book has continued to the present and some of the early movable books are being reproduced, especially by Intervisual Communication, Inc., of California.

Series books for boys and girls were introduced around the turn of the century. The Stratemeyer Syndicate, established about 1906, be-

came especially well known for series such as Tom Swift, the Bobbsey Twins, Nancy Drew and the Hardy Boys. After the turn of the century, biographies, poetry and educational books became popular. Van Loon's *Story of Mankind* received the first Newbery Medal in 1922. This award, given for the year's most distinguished literature for children, was established to honor John Newbery, an English publisher of children's books.

Picture books became a major part of the children's book field as photography and new technologies for reproducing illustrations developed. The Caldecott Medal, given for the most distinguished picture book published in the United States, was established in 1938. Dorothy Lathrop's *Animals of the Bible* was the first recipient of this award which honors Randolph Caldecott, an English illustrator from the 1800s.

Books that tie in with children's television programs, e.g., "Sesame Street," and toys, e.g., Cabbage Patch dolls, have become prominent. Modern merchandising methods include multimedia packaging of various combinations of books, toys, puzzles, cassette tapes, videos, etc. There are even books which unfold and become a costume to be worn by children.

References: E. Lee Baumgarten, *Price Guide and Bibliographic Check List for Children's & Illustrated Books 1880-1960*, published by author (Note: all the Baumgarten books are available from 718-1/2 W. John St., Martinsburg, WV 25401), 1996; ——, *Price List for Children's and Illustrated Books for the Years 1880-1940, Sorted by Artist*, published by author, 1993; ——, *Price List for Children's and Illustrated Books for the Years 1880-1940, Sorted by Author*, published by author, 1993; David and Virginia Brown, *Whitman Juvenile Books*, Collector Books, 1996; Diane McClure Jones and Rosemary Jones, *Collector's Guide to Children's Books*, Collector Books, 1997; *Price Guide to Big Little Books & Better Little, Jumbo, Tiny Tales, A Fast-Action Story, etc.*, L-W Book Sales, 1995.

Periodicals: *Book Source Monthly*, 2007 Syosset Dr., P.O. Box 567,

Cazenovia, NY 13035; *Martha's KidLit Newsletter*, P.O. Box 1488, Ames, IA 50010; *Mystery & Adventure Series Review*, P.O. Box 3488, Tucson, AZ 85722; *Yellowback Library*, P.O. Box 36172, Des Moines, IA 50315.

Collectors' Clubs: Louisa May Alcott Memorial Association, P.O. Box 343, Concord, MA 01742; Horatio Alger Society, 4907 Allison Dr., Lansing, MI 48910; International Wizard of Oz Club (L. Frank Baum), 220 N. 11th St., Escanaba, MI 49829; Thorton W. Burgess Society, Inc., P.O. Box 45, East Sandwich, MA 02537; Burroughs Bibliophiles (Edgar Rice Burroughs), Burroughs Memorial Collection, University of Louisville Library, Louisville, KY 40292; Randolph Caldecott Society, 112 Crooked Tree Trail, Moultrie Trails, RR #4, Saint Augustine, FL 32086; Lewis Carroll Society of North America, 617 Rockford Rd., Silver Spring, MD 20902; Dickens Society, 100 Institute Rd., Worcester Polytech, Dept. of Humanities, Worcester, MA 01609; Kate Greenaway Society, P.O. Box 8, Norwood, PA 19074; Happyhours Brotherhood, 87 School St., Fall River, MA 02770; Kipling Society (Rudyard Kipling), c/o Dr. E. Karim, Dept. of English, Rockford College; Rockford, IL 61107; New York C.S. Lewis Society, c/o J.L. Daniel, 419 Springfield Ave., Westfield NJ 07092; Melville Society (Herman Melville), c/o D. Yannella, Dept. of English, Glassboro State College, Glassboro, NJ 08028; Mystery and Detective Series Review, P.O. Box 3488, Tucson, AZ 85722; Mythopoetic Society, P.O. Box 6707, Altadena, CA 91003; National Fantasy Fan Federation, 1920 Division St., Murphysboro, IL 62966; Series Book Collector Society, c/o J. Brahce, 5270 Moceri Ln., Grand Blanc, MI 48439; Stowe-Day Foundation (Harriet Beecher Stowe), 77 Forest St., Hartford, CT 06105; American Hobbit Association (J.R.R. Tolkien), Rivendell-EA, 730-F Northland Rd., Forest Park, OH 45240; American Tolkien Society, P.O. Box 373, Highland, MI 48031; Tolkien Fellowships, c/o Bill Spicer, 329 N. Ave. 66, Los Angeles, CA 90042;

Mark Twain Boyhood Home Association, 208 Hill St., Hannibal, MO 63401; Mark Twain Memorial, 351 Farmington Ave., Hartford, CT 06105; Mark Twain Research Foundation, Perry, MO 63462.

Libraries and Museums: Many of the clubs maintain museums. *Subject Collections* edited by Lee Ash contains a list of public and academic libraries which have children's book collections. Large collections can be found at Florida State University, Tallahassee, FL; Free Library of Philadelphia, Philadelphia, PA; Library of Congress, Washington, DC; Pierpont Morgan Library, New York, NY; Toronto Public Library, Toronto, Ontario, Canada; Uncle Remus Museum (Joel Chandler Harris), Eatonton, GA; University of Minnesota, Walter Library, Minneapolis, MN; University of South Florida, Tampa, FL.

Notes: Prices are based on good-condition first editions with a dust jacket (dj). The absence of a dust jacket, later printings and less-than-good condition are all factors that lower the value of a book. Other factors which increase value are autographs, presence of a special box for books issued with one and award-winning titles.

Reprints: A number of replicas are now appearing on the market, most having been published by Evergreen Press and Merrimack. A new Children's Classics series offers reprints

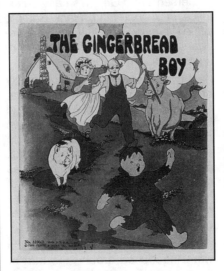

Gingerbread Boy, **No. 3100-O, Platt & Monk Co., Inc., 1932, $25.**

of books illustrated by Jessie Willcox Smith, Edmund Dulac, Frederick Richardson and others.

Alcott, Louisa May, *A Modern Cinderella*, Winfield S. Lukens, illus, Henry Altemus Co., 1904 ....50.00

Almond, Linda Stevens, *Peter Rabbit and Little Boy*, Platt and Munk Co., 1935 ....75.00

Appleton, Victor, II, *The New Tom Swift Jr. Adventures*, 35 vols, Grosset & Dunlop Publisher, 1954-67 ....250.00

Atwater, Richard and Florence, *Mr. Popper's Penguins*, Little-Brown, 1938, dj 12.00

Barrie, Sir James M., *Peter Pan in Kensington Gardens,* Arthur Rackham, illus, Scribner, 1919.................30.00

Barrows, Marjorie, *One Hundred Best Poems for Boys and Girls*, Whitman, 1930 ....12.00

Brandeis, Madeline, *Shaun O'Day of Ireland: The Children of All Lands Stories*, Grosset & Dunlop, 1929, sq 8vo, 191 pgs 25.00

Buck, Pearl, *The Chinese Children Next Door*, 1942 ....43.00

Calico Pup, McLoughlin, 1939 ......20.00

Carroll, Lewis, *Alice's Adventures in Wonderland*, Peter Newell, illus, Harper, 1902 ....45.00

Clyne, Geraldine, *Jolly Jump-Ups on the Farm*, a pop-up book, McLoughlin Brothers, 1948 .....42.00

Cooke, G.A., *Bossy the Calf Who Lost Her Tinkle Bell*, McLoughlin, 1939 ....20.00

Dahl, Roald, *James and the Giant Peach*, Nancy Ekholm Burkert, illus, Knopf, 1961 ....25.00

Disney, Walt, *The Cold Blooded Penguin*, Simon & Schuster, 1944, dj 110.00

Dixon, F.W.
Hardy Boys Secret of the Old Mill, G&D Publishers, 1927, red cover 25.00
Hardy Boys Secret of Wildcat Swamp, G&D, 1952, 212 pgs 7.00

Dore, Gustave, *Bible in Pictures*, William Wise, 1939, 4to, 217 plates, 444 pgs 20.00

Fairmont, Ethel, *Rhymes for Kindly Children*, Johnny Gruelle, illus, Wise-Parslow Publishing, 1937 ....45.00

Fairy Tales from Hans Christian Anderson, Tasha Tudor, illus, Oxford University Press, 1945, 273 pgs, dj 115.00

Field, Eugene, *Lullaby-Land*, drawings by Charles Robinson, Scribner, 1897 ....48.00

Gardner, Lucy and Eugene Rudzewicz, *Child's Bestiary*, Gardner family illus,

Knopf, 1946, dj 25.00
Garis, Howard
Uncle Wiggily's Holidays (Thanksgiving, Christmas and New Years Stories), Charles Graham, 1929....28.00
Uncle Wiggily's Squirt Gun, Charles Graham, 1929, 32 pgs 28.00
Gordon, Elizabeth, *Watermelon Pete and Other Stories*, Rand McNally & Co., 1937, Clara Powers Willson, illus 75.00
Gray, Arbuthnot
Dick & Jane--Fun Wherever We Are, The New Basic Reader, Scott, Foresman & Co., 1962, 77 pgs 45.00
Dick and Jane, Our New Friends, Keith Ward, illus, Scott, Foresman & Co., 1940 ....50.00
Gruelle, Johnny
Beloved Belindy, Volland, 1926, black mammy on cover 75.00
Orphan Annie Story Book, Bobbs-Merrill Co., 1921, 8vo, 86 pgs, 1st ed..........................30.00
Raggedy Ann's Magical Wishes, Donohue, 1928.....................38.00
Hillard & Campbell, *Franklin Second Reader*, Tainter Bros., 1873 ......7.50
Hope, Laura Lee, *The Bobbsey Twins*, 24 vols, Grosset & Dunlop, NY, 1920s, dj.........................150.00
Howard, Constance, *Amelia Anne and the Green Umbrella*, Macrae Smith Co., 1930s 25.00
Kipling, Rudyard, *How the Camel Got His Hump*, Just So Stories Series, Susan Beatrice Pearse, Rojankovsky, illus, Garden City, 1942, dj.............17.00
L'Hommedieu, D., *Nipper the Little Bull Pup*, Lippincott, 1943, 1st ed, dj........................45.00
Little Engine That Could, retold by Watty Piper, Lois Lenski, illus, Platt-Munk, 1930 ....16.00
Little Red Riding Hood, pop-up 35.00
Montgomery, F.T., *Zip, The Adventures of a Frisky Fox Terrier*, V.M. Higgins, illus, Saalfield Publishing Co., 1917 ....12.00
Mother Goose Nursery Rhymes & Fairy Tales, illus by Dore and others, 2 vols, 8vo, John J. Williams, NY, 1886.................................50.00
Peter Rabbit and Sammy Squirrel, Virginia Albert, illus, Saalfield Publishing Co., 1918, soft-cover 40.00
Piper, Watty, ed, *Fairy Tales That Never Grow Old*, Platt & Munk, 1932, dj.......................75.00
Price, Margaret E., *A Child's Book of Myths*, Rand McNally & Co., 1929, 112 pgs, dj....................18.00
Riley, James Whitcomb, *Joyful Poems*

for Children, Sally Tate, illus, Bobbs-Merrill, 1946 ....6.50
The Rooster, The Mouse and the Little Red Hen, Eulalie, illus, Platt & Munk, 3100-F, 1932 ....12.00
Scarry, Richard, *Richard Scarry's Best Mother Goose Ever*, Golden Press, 1964, 94 pgs............................15.00
Sidney, Margaret
Five Little Peppers Grown Up, Lothrop, Boston, 1892, 527 pgs...22.00
Five Little Peppers Midway, Lothrop, Boston, 1893, gilt cover, 512 pgs 22.00
Stevenson, R.L., *Child's Garden of Verses*, Florence Storer illus, Scribner, 1910, 9" x 6-1/2" 45.00
Three Little Pigs Pop-Up Book, V. Kubasta illus, Arita, 1977, small 4to 25.00
Tim Tyler in the Jungle, pop-up, copyright 1935 ....25.00
Travers, *Mary Poppins in the Park*, Harcourt, 1952, 1st ed, dj........20.00
Tudor, Tasha, *A Is for Anna Belle*, Rand McNally, 1954, soft-cover........15.00

Children's Dishes

Collecting Hints: Children's dishes were played with, so a bit of wear is to be expected. Avoid rusty metal dishes and broken glass dishes.

History: Dishes for children to play with have been popular from Victorian times to the present and have been made in aluminum, tin, china and glass. Many glass companies made small child-size sets in the same patterns as large table sets. This was especially true during the period when Depression glass was popular and manufacturers made child-size pieces to complement the full-size lines.

References: Doris Anderson Lechler, *Children's Glass Dishes, China and Furniture, Book I* (1983, 1991 value update), *Book II* (1986, 1993 value update), Collector Books; Lorraine Punchard, *Playtime Kitchen Items and Table Accessories*, published by author, 1993; —, *Playtime Pottery and Porcelain from the United Kingdom and the United States*, Schiffer Publishing, 1996; Noel Riley, *Gifts for Good Children*, Richard Dennis Publications, 1991; Ellen T. Schroy, *Warman's Glass*, 2nd Edition, Wallace-Homestead, 1995; Margaret and Kenn Whitmyer,

Collector's Encyclopedia of Children's Dishes, Collector Books, 1993, 1995 value update.

Collectors' Club: Toy Dish Collectors, Box 159, Bethlehem, CT 06751.

Additional Listings: Akro Agate.

Aluminum

Coffeepot, black wood
    handle and knob....................25.00
Silverware Set, 4 spoons,
    2 forks, knife, pie server 10.00
Teapot, black wood knob,
    swing handle 20.00

China

Blue Willow
  Creamer
    2" x 1-3/4" h 18.00
    2-1/4" x 1-3/4" h 19.00
    2-3/4" x 2" h 18.00
    3-1/4" x 2-3/4" h 18.00
  Cup
    1-3/4", Occupied Japan 15.00
    2" 12.00
    2-3/4" 10.00
  Cup and Saucer
    2-1/4" cup, 2-3/4" saucer 15.00
    2-3/4" cup, 3-3/4" saucer 15.00
  Plate
    3-3/4" d 9.00
    4-1/2" d 9.00
  Platter, 6-1/4" x 3-3/4", oval 25.00
  Saucer, 3-1/4" d,
    Occupied Japan 8.00
  Set, 26 pcs............................485.00
  Sugar, cov
    2-3/4" x 2-1/4" 24.00
    4-1/4" x 3-1/2" 25.00
  Teapot, cov, 4"..........................50.00
Geisha Girl, tea set,
    4 place settings, creamer,
    sugar, teapot, chips...............125.00
Moss Rose
  Cup and Saucer.........................7.50
  Platter, oval 10.00
  Tea Set 125.00
Occupied Japan, teapot, cov 85.00

Depression Era Glass

Bowl, Little Deb, ribbed 15.00
Creamer
  Cherry Blossom, pink...............45.00
  Laurel, jadeite 45.00
Creamer and Sugar,
    Moderntone, pink 30.00
Cup and Saucer
  Cherry Blossom 45.00
  Diana, pink..............................45.00
  Doric & Pansy, pink 43.00

Moderntone, beige 20.00
Cup
    Homespun, crystal 30.00
    Moderntone
        Blue.....................................14.00
        Pink.....................................14.00
        Yellow 14.00
Mixer, Glassbake, 3 ftd.................40.00
Plate
    Cherry Blossom,
    Delphite Blue...........................14.00
    Doric & Pansy, pink..................15.00
    Homespun, pink 15.00
    Laurel, red trim 15.00
    Moderntone
        Blue.....................................12.00
        Green...................................12.00
        Pink.....................................12.00
        Yellow 12.00
Saucer
    Doric & Pansy, teal..................15.00
    Moderntone
        Blue.....................................10.00
        Green...................................10.00
        Pink.....................................10.00
Set, Diana, crystal, gold trim, rack,
    price for 12-pc set..................125.00

Pattern Glass

Berry Bowl, Fine Cut X 20.00
Butter, cov, Doyle's 500, amber ..100.00
Creamer
    Fernland.................................18.00
    Hawaiian Lei...........................15.00
Cup and Saucer, Lion....................45.00
Mug, Fighting Cats 35.00
Pitcher, Nursery Rhyme 100.00
Punch Bowl Set, punch bowl and 6 cups
    Flattened Diamond
    and Sunburst..........................75.00
    Tulip and Honeycomb 90.00

Akro Agate, tea set, The Little American Maid, No. 3000, topaz, $295.

Spooner, Menagerie Fish, amber 150.00
Sugar, cov
    Hawaiian Lei 35.00
    Nursery Rhyme 48.00
Table Set, 4 pcs
    Arrowhead in Oval 95.00
    Beaded Swirl.........................125.00
Tumbler
    Nursery Rhyme 20.00
    Sandwich Ten Panel,
    sapphire blue 145.00

Plastic

Chocolate Set, Banner, service for four,
    napkin holder, silverware.........95.00
Dinnerware Set
    9 pcs, Tinkerbelle, Walt Disney,
    service for two 25.00
    17 pcs
        Alice in Wonderland, Plasco,
        service for four, beige 45.00
        Tupperware, service for four,
        multicolored 65.00
Silverware Set
    6 pcs, 2 knives, forks and spoons,
    Plasco, pink, orig cardboard 9.00
    8 pcs, serving set, 2 knives, forks
    and spoons, Bestmade, red,
    orig cardboard...........................7.50

Chintz China

Collecting Hints: Crown Ducal patterns called Blue Chintz and Florida both contained rich colors and mythical birds. They were quite popular on the East Coast in the 1920s and 1930s and are now quite popular in the same geographical areas. Grimwade's Marguerite was very successful when initially offered, but does not enjoy much interest with today's collectors, nor do Grimwade's 1950s patterns, known as Peony, Morning Glory and June Festival. Collectors now seek out the tightly grouped florals of the 1930s. However, some of the 1950s patterns, like Evesham, Florence and Stratford, enjoy as much popularity today as they did originally.

Care should be taken to assemble the proper components to the many sets available in Chintz China. Remember that terms and usage may be different from our modern terminology. Sauce boats should have underplates and jam pots also have underplates and either silverplated or ceramic lids. Salt and pep-

per shakers may have a tray, but many were sold without one.

Remembering that this china was made inexpensively for the masses, be aware that some fading may occur with the darker colors. Blue is especially delicate and it is not uncommon to find relish dishes whose base has some loss to color. Only the individual collector can determine if this color variation appeals to him or her.

History: Chintz China has been produced since the 17th century. It was created in response to the brightly colored exotic fabric being imported from India to England at that time. Early chintz patterns featured large flowers, loose arrangements and often exotic birds. The advent of transfer printing developed patterns which were cheap enough to appeal to the masses. A number of Staffordshire potteries were producing chintzware for everyday use by the 1820s. Gradual changes occurred in the chintz patterns over the years.

In 1920, A.G. Richardson and Leonard Grimwade began production of more-tightly designed chintz patterns. A.G. Richardson used the trademark Crown Ducal and his 1920s production of patterns such as Festival, Blue Chintz and Florida were exported in large quantities to the United States. Originally introduced in tea sets, these patterns soon expanded to dinnerware services. Grimwade's Royal Winton created their first chintz patterns in 1928 and named it Marguerite. Factories introduced new chintz patterns every year at the British Industries Fair, creating more than 65 patterns over the last 50 years. Grimwade came up with 15 new patterns in 1952, including Anemone, Floral Feast, Victorian Rose, Delphinium Chintz and Sweet Pea. To create these pattern variations, sometimes colors were reversed or the border color was changed. To capture the 1950s market, Grimwade designed a series of patterns with a modern look—large flowers, spaced further apart, rich dark blue, burgundy and black backgrounds.

By the 1930s, many of the Staffordshire potteries were trying to survive and began to copy whatever pattern seemed to be selling well. James Kent, Ltd., produced a whole series of chintzes. Named Dubarry, Rosalynde and Apple Blossom, they were sold widely in America. The most popular pattern is currently Hydrangea with a white background. The quality was not as good as Grimwade's.

Elijah Cotton's Lord Nelson Ware was another line of chintz patterns. Cotton's former earthenwares were more utilitarian and the company was a big producer of institutional wares with chunky forms. The patterns were not applied as skillfully; difficult areas, such as handles and spouts, were often left plain. The most popular patterns in this series are Black Beauty and Green Tulip.

Some bone china was used for chintz patterns, primarily by Shelley. The Japanese created copies of the Royal Winton patterns. Unfortunately for the chintz pattern companies, the American war brides of the early 1950s did not desire the old-fashioned-looking china patterns which had delighted their mothers and grandmothers. Chintz patterns soon lost out to the new bold dinnerware patterns.

References: Linda Eberle and Susan Scott, *Charlton Standard Catalogue of Chintz*, 2nd Edition, Charlton Press, 1997; Muriel M. Miller, *Collecting Royal Winton Chintz*, Francis Joseph Publications, 1996; Jo Anne P. Welch, *Chintz Ceramics*, Schiffer Publishing, 1996.

Periodical: *Chintz Connection*, P.O. Box 222, Riverdale, MD 20738.

Collectors' Clubs: Chintz Collectors Club, P.O. Box 50888, Pasadena, CA 91115; Royal Winton Collectors' Club, 2 Kareela Rd., Baulkham Hills, Australia 2153; Royal Winton International Collectors' Club at Dancer's End, Northall, Bedfordshire, England LU6 2EU.

Advisor: Susan Scott.

Ascot Plate
　6" d, Hazel, Royal Winton 75.00
　8" d, Nantwich, Royal Winton.195.00
　10" d, Summertime,
　　Royal Winton..........................175.00
Bowl, 8" d, Purple Chintz,
　Crown Ducal, octagonal 450.00

Breakfast Set, Rosebud
　Iridescent, green....................250.00
Butter Dish, cov, Spring Glory,
　Royal Winton 325.00
Cake Plate
　Dubarry, Kent, 2 handles 145.00
　Old Cottage Chintz,
　　Royal Winton........................175.00
Creamer, 2-1/2" h, Melody,
　Pasadena, Royal Crown..........65.00
Creamer and Sugar, Nantwich,
　Royal Winton 235.00
Creamer and Sugar on Tray
　Black Beauty, Lord Nelson.....300.00
　Welbeck, Royal Winton..........350.00
Cup and Saucer
　Ivory Chintz, Crown Ducal 105.00
　Nantwich, Royal Winton.........160.00
　Royal Brocade, Lord Nelson....85.00
Demitasse Cup and Saucer,
　Rosalynde, Kent 75.00
Dessert Set, cup, saucer and scalloped-
　edge dessert plate, Rose du Barry,
　Royal Winton 120.00
Dish, 4-1/2" sq, Dubarry, Kent.....125.00
Jam Pot, cov, liner, Sweet Pea,
　Royal Winton 300.00
Jug
　Apple Blossom, Kent..............325.00
　Rosetime, Lord Nelson, 5" h ..450.00
Lamp, Ivory, Chintz,
　Crown Ducal, 22" h................895.00
Mustard, cov, Summertime,
　Royal Winton 175.00
Plate
　5" sq, Sweet Pea,
　　Royal Winton........................100.00
　8-1/2" d, Dubarry, Kent 165.00
　9" d, Blue Chintz,
　　Crown Ducal, octagonal.........175.00
　10" d, Estelle, Royal Winton.....95.00
Sandwich Tray, Pekin,
　Royal Winton 150.00
Set, Floral Feast, Royal Winton,
　eight 6-pc place settings, teapot,
　coffeepot, serving pieces, cov jugs,
　price for 80-pc set...............8,500.00
Sugar, open, 2" d, Melody,
　Royal Crown 45.00
Sugar Shaker, Bird Chintz/Lorna Doone,
　Midwinter 275.00
Teapot, cov
　Marina, Lord Nelson...............325.00
　Stacking
　　Rosebud Iridescent,
　　　pink or green......................250.00
　　Royal Brocade,
　　　Lord Nelson 450.00
　　Sweet Pea,
　　　Royal Winton 1,200.00
Tea Set, Apple Blossom, Kent, teapot,
　creamer, sugar 595.00

Toast Rack, Evesham, Royal Winton,
　two-slice type 250.00
Tray, 7" x 10", Sweet Pea,
　Royal Winton.........................225.00
Trivet, Clyde, Royal Winton 65.00
Vase, bud, Rosetime,
　Lord Nelson 145.00

Christmas Items

Collecting Hints: Beware of reproduction ornaments. They are usually brighter in color and have shinier paint than the originals. Older ornaments should show some signs of handling. It is common to find tops replaced on ornaments.

History: Early Christmas decorations and ornaments were handmade. In 1865, the Pennsylvania Dutch brought the first glass ornaments to America. By 1870, glass ornaments were being sold in major cities. By the turn of the century, the demand created a cottage industry in European countries. Several towns in Germany and Czechoslovakia produced lovely ornaments that were imported by companies such as F.W. Woolworth and Sears Roebuck & Co., which found a ready market.

References: Ann Bahar, *Santa Dolls*, Hobby House Press, 1992; Robert Brenner, *Christmas through the Decades*, Schiffer Publishing, 1993; Jill Gallina, *Christmas Pins Past and Present*, Collector Books, 1996; George Johnson, *Christmas Ornaments, Lights & Decorations* (1987, 1995 value update), *Vol. II* (1996), *Vol. III* (1996), Collector Books; Polly and Pam Judd, *Santa Dolls & Figurines Price Guide*, Revised Edition, Hobby House Press, 1994; Chris Kirk, *Joy of Christmas*

Beads, glass, multicolored, various shapes and sizes, 100" l strand, $60.

Collecting, L-W Book Sales, 1994; Robert M. Merck, *Deck the Halls*, Abbeville Press, 1992; James S. Morrison, *Vintage View of Christmas Past*, Shuman Heritage Press, 1995; Mary Morrison, *Snow Babies, Santas and Elves*, Schiffer Publishing, 1993; Margaret Schiffer, *Christmas Ornaments*, Schiffer Publisher, 1984, 1995 value update; Lissa and Dick Smith, *Christmas Collectibles*, Chartwell Books, 1993; Margaret and Kenn Whitmyer, *Christmas Collectibles*, 2nd Edition, Collector Books, 1994.

Periodicals: *Golden Glow of Christmas Past*, 6401 Winsdale St., Golden Valley, MN 55427; *I Love Christmas*, P.O. Box 5708, Coralville, IA 52241; *Ornament Collector*, RR #1, Canton, IL 61520.

Collectors' Club: Golden Glow of Christmas Past, 6401 Winsdale St., Golden Valley, MN 55427.

Museums: Many museums prepare special Christmas exhibits.

Reproduction Alert.

Additional Listing: Santa Claus.

Advisor: Lissa Smith.

Christmas Village/Garden

Animals

    Camel, 6" h, composition, wood legs, mkd "Germany," flocked...........45.00

    Chicken, 1-1/2" h, composition, metal feet 10.00

    Cow, 3-1/2" h, celluloid 12.00

    Duck, 1-1/2" h, celluloid, metal feet 10.00

    Elephant, 5" h, composition, bone tusks, mkd "Germany".............75.00

    Goat, 4" h, composition, wood legs, wool covering, metal horns 28.00

    Horse, 5" h, composition, wood legs, mkd "Germany" 35.00

    Lamb, 1-1/2" h, standing in grass, plaster, mkd "Germany" 6.00

    Ram, 3-1/2" h, celluloid 8.00

    Sheep, 5" h, composition, wool covering, wood legs, paper collar mkd "Germany" with bell 45.00

    Stork, 3" h, celluloid body and legs............................10.00

Buildings

    Bank Office, 4" h, plaster, multicolored............................12.00

    Barn, 6" h, cardboard, litho, "Built-Rite" 30.00

    Church

        4" h, cardboard, white with mica, mkd "Japan".........................10.00

        8" h, wood, white with mica, metal bell in steeple, windup music box plays "Silent Night".............40.00

    House, 4" h, cardboard, cellophane windows, mkd "Japan"...................8.00

Fence

    Plastic, 2" h, white, "Plasticville," 6 sections.............................20.00

    Wood, 3" h, red, folding, 8 connected sections 38.00

    Wood, 5" h, picket, white, wired for Christmas lights on each post, 4 sections 24" long..................55.00

People

    Couple sitting on a park bench, 2" h, metal, USA......................20.00

    Skater, 2-1/2" h, metal, USA....12.00

    Sled Rider, removable figure sitting on sled, 2" h, mkd "France"......18.00

Non-Tree-Related Items

Bank, 5" h, snowman, white with black bowler hat and red scarf, original box 15.00

Book

    Christmas Carols Illustrated and Done into Simple Music, Hendrik Van Loon and Grace Castagnetta, 1937, 64 pgs 20.00

    Santa's Surprise Paint Book, Merrill Co., 1949, flocked Santa with pack on cover 12.00

    The Littlest Snowman, Wonder Books, Division of Grosset & Dunlap Inc., 1958......................6.00

    The Night Before Christmas, Clement C. Moore, J.B. Lippincott, c1930, Arthur Rackham illus................85.00

Candleholder, 5" l, metal, holly leaves and berries 18.00

Candy Box

    4-1/2" l, cardboard, string handle

        "Merry Christmas, Happy New Year," carolers in village, 1920s 8.00

        Three Wise Men, USA, 1970s......................3.00

    10-1/2" l, cardboard, paper label "Charms," red background, coach driving through village scene ...18.00

Candy Container, 7-1/2" h, snowman, pressed cardboard, black hat, opening in base, USA..............40.00

Figure

    Choir Boy, 3-1/2" h, hard plastic, red and white...................................4.00

    Reindeer

        2" h, glass, white, Germany 20.00

        3" h

            Celluloid, brown 8.00

Ornament, house, blown glass, painted red roof, door, and windows, 2-1/2", $22.

        Hard pressed cotton, brown, Japan.....................20.00

        4" h, hard plastic, white..........4.00

        5" h, composition, brown, glass eyes, wood legs, mkd "Germany"...................60.00

    Snowman, 8" h, hard plastic, electric-light insert, white holding black lantern, original box 22.00

Nativity

    Boxed set, 14" h, 20" l, cardboard, foldout, USA, 1950s.................22.00

    Shepherd, 6", composition, standing, lamb on shoulders, German 14.00

Paper

    Calling card, 3-1/4" l, emb with holly and "Season's Greetings" 5.00

    Greeting Card, 7" h, "A Christmas Message," Victorian, foldout, angels, Raphael Tuck & Sons, London 25.00

    Stickers, pkg, cellophane envelope, "Made in USA," assortment, 1960s 7.00

    Tag, 2-3/4" l, "Christmas Greetings," dog in wrapped box, made in USA............................2.00

Pinback Button

    7/8" d, metal, "Health To All," National Tuberculosis Association 7.00

    1-1/4" d, celluloid, "Shop in Danville," Santa head 14.00

Postcard, 3" x 5"

    "A Hearty Christmas Greeting," Victorian children sledding.....3.00

    Wishing You a Very Happy Christmas," dog with riding crop in mouth and toy horse..............4.00

Stocking

    10" d, red cellophane with silver-foil trim, electric candle inside 18.00

    12" l, red flannel, stenciled Santa and sleigh 14.00

Tree-Related Items

Beads

48" l, glass, blue,
paper tag, German 18.00
Candy Cane, 6"
Chenille, red and white..............4.00
Glass, blue and silver..............18.00
Icicles, 4"
Plastic, clear, set of 12 ....5.00
Metal, twisted,
color and silver 1.00
Light Bulb
Bubble, Noma 3.00
Figural, milk glass
2" h, Santa head 22.00
3" h, snowman 18.00
4" h, Japanese lantern 14.00
Ornament
Beaded, 3" h, cross, double-sided,
Czechoslovakian 24.00
Chromolithograph
4" h, bell with girl's face, tinsel trim,
German...............................15.00
7" h, angels,
tinsel trim, German..............18.00
Glass
Clown bust, 2" h....................32.00
Heart, 2-1/2" , red 14.00
Pinecone, 3-1/2" , unsilvered
with tinsel inside...................14.00
Round, 3" d, striped, unsilvered
with paper cap........................5.00
Santa, 3" h 35.00
Plastic
Lion, red and white.................7.50
Rudolph, brown......................4.00
Reflector
Foil, 3" d, set of 6 ....5.00
Metal, 3" d, pierced tin 4.00
Tinsel, lead strips, original box......10.00
Tree
Brush
1-1/2" h, green,
red wood base 3.00
3" h, green, mica trim,
red wood base 4.00
5" h
Green dec with glass beads,
red wood base....................10.00
Red, red base 7.00
Feather
3" h, green, red wood base..15.00
12" h, white, square red base, mkd
"West Germany"....................70.00
36" h, green, candle clips,
round wood base, mkd
Germany 300.00
Tree Stand, tin, litho, lighted..........45.00
Tree Topper
Angel, 6" h, cardboard and
spun glass 24.00
Glass, 9" h, silvered,
multicolored..............................20.00

Tree topper, angel, papier-mâché, blue dress, silver cardboard wings and crown, angel kneeling on silver-sparkle-covered sphere, silver tube, $42.

Cigar Collectibles

Collecting Hints: Concentrate on one geographical region or company. Cigar box labels usually are found in large concentrations. Check on availability before paying high prices.

History: Tobacco was one of the first export products of the American colonies. By 1750, smoking began to become socially acceptable for males. Cigar smoking was most popular from 1880 to 1930 when it was the custom for men to withdraw from the boardroom or dining table and participate in male-only conversation or activities.

Cigar companies were quick to recognize national political, sports and popular heroes. They encouraged them to use cigars and placed their faces on promotional material. The lithograph printing press brought color and popularity to labels, seals and bands. Many people have memories of cigar-band rings given by a grandfather or family friend. Cigars took second place to cigarettes in the 1940s. Today, there is less cigar- than cigarette-related material because fewer companies made cigars.

References: Edwin Barnes and Wayne Dunn, *Cigar-Label Art Visual Encyclopedia with Index and Price Guide*, published by authors (P.O. Box 3, Lake Forest, CA 92630), 1995; Douglas Congdon-Martin, *Tobacco Tins*, Schiffer Publishing, 1992; Glyn V. Farber, *Hickey Brothers Cigar Store Tokens*, The Token and Medal Society, Inc., 1992; Gerald S. Petrone, *Tobacco Advertising*, Schiffer Publishing, 1996; Jerry Terranova and Douglas Congdon-Martin, *Antique Cigar Cutters & Lighters*, Schiffer Publishing, 1996; Neil Wood, *Smoking Collectibles*, L-W Book Sales, 1994.

Periodical: *Tobacco Antiques and Collectibles Market*, Box 11652, Houston, TX 77293.

Collectors' Clubs: Cigar Label Collectors International, P.O. Box 66, Sharon Center, OH 44274; International Lighter Collectors, P.O. Box 536, Quitman, TX 75783; International Seal, Label and Cigar Band Society, 8915 E. Bellevue St., Tucson, AZ 85715; Pocket Lighter Preservation Guild, P.O. Box 1054, Addison, IL 60101.

Museum: Arnet Collection, New York Public Library, New York, NY.

Box, oak, zinc liner 35.00
Cigar Cutter, figural, pelican,
cast iron..................................75.00
Cigar Holder
Amber, solid gold band 65.00
Tortoiseshell 10.00
Cigar Piercer, 3" l, silvered brass,
celluloid wrapper band inscribed
"Westchester County Bar
Association, Annual Dinner, 1995,"
sharp metal point....................60.00
Counter, 1-1/2" x 3", celluloid, Bloomer

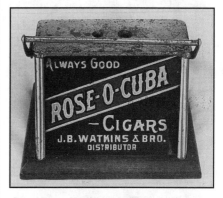

Cigar cutter, counter top, Rose-O-Cuba, 6" x 8" base, 4-1/2" h, $350.

Club Cigar adv, movable disk wheels, 2 ladies in bloomers sipping champagne, c1900 ....25.00

Display Cigar Box, 2-1/2" x 5-1/2" x 8-1/2", Certified Primo Cigar Box, wood, full-color litho paper designs, c1930 ....50.00

Dish, 7-1/8" d, multicolored cigar bands all-over, diecut beautiful woman in center, green felt back 35.00

Label
American Citizen 7.00
Canadian Club 7.00
Tampa Girl 20.00

Lighter, 4-1/2" h, counter type, cast iron, bulldog-shape 90.00

Matchbook Holder, blued metal, c1920 1-1/8" x 1-5/8", Muriel Cigars, celluloid insert, woman in multicolored portrait, small gold frame, dark red ground.......................65.00

1-1/2" x 2-1/4", celluloid oval, multicolored insert inscribed "For Gentlemen of Good Taste," well-dressed gentleman seated in wicker chair, smoking cigar 75.00

Match Safe, Union Made Cigars, bright silvered brass, celluloid cover with light blue Union Cigar label, black inscriptions and artwork, issued by Cigar Makers Union #97, Boston 95.00

Pinback Button
Bachelor Cigars, 100% Havana Filler, green and white, red serial number, c1930 ....20.00

Enjoy a Cigar, brown on yellow, slogan "Join the Cigar Enjoyment Parade," c1930........................30.00

Recruit Little Cigars, 1" d, military

Sign, Odin 5¢ Cigars, litho tin, emb, 19-1/8" x 27-1/4", $65.

cadet, red ground, white letters "Join the Army of Recruit Little Cigar Smokers," short product slogan on back paper, early 1900s...........40.00

Pocket Mirror, 2-1/8" d, Union Made Cigars, celluloid, detailed union label, light blue, black lettering, c1900......................................65.00

Notepad, 2" x 3", Hemmeter Cigar Co., floral and cigar design on cover, calendar, unused....................25.00

Sign
8" x 10", Fame & Fortune 3¢ Cigars, tin................................65.00

19-1/4" x 7", Napoleon Cigar 10¢, metal, emb letters, yellow, orange and black picture of Napoleon 60.00

Tin
Club House Cigars, 3" x 5" 35.00
Old Abe Cigars, round, paper label 65.00
Possum Cigars, full 175.00
Reichard's Cadet Cigar............85.00

Tobacco Humidor, Don Porto Cigar, tin 25.00

Watch Fob, 1-3/4" d, United Cigar Makers League, black and white, mirror back, metal strap loop, c1900 .65.00

Cigarette Items

Collecting Hints: Don't overlook the advertising which appeared in the national magazines from the 1940s to 1960s. Many star and public heroes endorsed cigarettes. Modern promotional material for brands such as Marlboro and Salem has been issued in large quantities and much has been put aside by collectors. Most collectors tend to concentrate on the pre-1950 period.

History: Although the cigarette industry dates back to the late 19th century, it was during the 1930s and 1940s that cigarettes became the primary tobacco product. The cigarette industry launched massive radio advertising and promotional campaigns. In the 1950s, television became the dominant advertising medium.

The Surgeon General's Report, which warned of the danger of cigarette smoking, led to restrictions on advertising and limited the places where cigarettes could be smoked. The industry reacted with a new advertising approach aimed at 20- to 40-year olds and at females. Recent government regulations and changes in public opinion towards smoking have altered the style and quantity of cigarette-related collectibles.

References: Art Anderson, *Casinos and Their Ashtrays*, published by author, 1994; *Cigarette Card Values*, Murray Cards International Ltd., 1992; Philip Collins, *Smokerama*, Chronicle Books, 1992; Douglas Congdon-Martin, *Camel Cigarette Collectibles*, Schiffer Publishing, 1996; Urban K. and Christine Cummings, *The World's Greatest Lighter*, Bird Dog Books (P.O. Box 1482, Palo Alto, CA 94302), 1996; ——, *Tobacco Tins*, Schiffer Publishing, 1992; James Flanagan, *Collector's Guide to Cigarette Lighters*, Collector Books, 1995; Gerald S. Petrone, *Tobacco Advertising*, Schiffer Publishing, 1996; Urban K. Cummings, *Ronson, World's Greatest Lighter*, Bird Dog Books, 1993; Nancy Wanvig, *Collector's Guide to Ashtrays*, Collector Books, 1997; A.M.W. van Weert, *Legend of the Lighter*, Electa, 1995; Neil Wood, *Collecting Cigarette Lighters* (1994), *Vol. II* (1995), L-W Book Sales; ——, *Smoking Collectibles*, L-W Book Sales, 1994.

Periodical: *Tobacco Antiques and Collectibles Market*, Box 11652, Houston, TX 77283.

Collectors' Clubs: Ashtray Collectors Club, P.O. Box 11652, Houston, TX 77293; Cigarette Pack Collectors Association, 61 Searle St., Georgetown, MA 01833; International Lighter Collectors, P.O. Box 536, Quitman, TX 75783; International Seal, Label & Cigar Band Society, 8915 E. Bellevue St., Tucson, AZ 85715; Pocket Lighter Preservation Guild, P.O. Box 1054, Addison, IL 60101.

Ashtray, unused, orig box
Chesterfield..............................20.00
Lucky Strike 20.00

Banner
Chesterfield, Jerry Lewis and Dean Martin 195.00

Old Gold Cigarettes, Not a Cough in the Car Load, 42" x 120".........95.00

Carton, Chesterfield, Christmas....12.00

Cigarette Card, American
Allen & Ginter, Pirates of the Spanish Main, 1888 ....15.00

Kinney Tobacco Co., military and naval uniforms, 1887 ....5.00

Lighter, Regens, AAA Club insignia, Pat No. 1896140, SP, 1-1/8" x 2-1/8" x 1/2", $18.

Wing Cigarettes,
first series of 50 ....50.00
Cigarette Card Album
Allen & Ginter, Napoleon 60.00
W. Duck & Sons,
Terrors of America 65.00
Cigarette Case
2-1/2" x 3", tan leather and
cardboard, Fatima, veiled lady
in gold, "Ninth Annual Conven-
tion/AAC of A/Baltimore,
June 1913" on reverse 35.00
3" x 4", enameled, woman's, black,
envelope style, red stone dec ..35.00
Clock, Vantage Cigarettes, battery
operated 40.00
Dexterity Puzzle, Camel Lights, clear
styrene plastic key-chain case,
miniature replica of cigarette pack,
small sq opening in top to capture
9 miniature filter-tip cigarettes in filter
ends up, c1980 ....25.00
Game, Camel,
The Game, MIB, 1992 ....10.00
Lighter
ASR, Ascot hidden watch,
swivels 82.00
Beatti Jet, pipe lighter,
chrome 35.00
Beny, England, lift arm, lift top,
c1930, worn SP over brass 65.00
Corona, gun shape,
chrome, black 33.00
Crestline, musical, Colonel Reb &
Confederate flags 50.00
Dupont
1950s, SP, slight wear 50.00
1960s, gold plated, butane .175.00
Flaminaire, Limoges, cobalt blue and
gold, table model, 3-1/2" h 30.00
Jet 200, torpedo shape, black plastic
and aluminum, MIB 15.00
MEB, Austrian, pull-apart,

pat April 2, 1912 ....22.00
Playboy, brass, engraved bunny,
MIB 30.00
Rexxy, chrome, 1930s, 4-hinge
mechanism, Swiss 37.00
Rite Point, pocket clip,
pen shape 9.50
Ronson, Standard, England,
mkd "Sterling Silver," picture
of Queen 85.00
Stankyo, musical,
brass, large 45.00
Zippo
1959, Boston, ME RR, MIB ..42.50
1966, pin-up girl in
collector's tin 30.00
1968, slim submarine,
Tullibee 35.00
Matchbook Holder, hanging,
Kool Cigarettes 10.00
Matches, Jokers for Smokers,
Bang Matches, risqué covers,
price for set of 12 ....20.00
Pack, Picayune 6.00
Pinback Button
High Admiral Cigarettes,
red, white and blue flag,
white ground, blue letters "A
National Favorite/High
Admiral," c1896 ....35.00
Perfection Cigarettes, multicolored
image of lady, back paper with list
of tobacco products 20.00
Philip Morris Cigarettes, black, white
and flesh tones, c1930 ....50.00
Playing Cards, Camel Cigarettes ..25.00
Radio
Chester Cheetah, MIB 35.00
Marlboro Pack, MIB 65.00
Server, chrome, smokestack shape,
Chase Chrome 66.00
Silk
1" l, Wm. Randolph Hearst for
Governor 10.00
3-3/4" l, Wm. McKinley 25.00
Sign, 24" x 3", Spud Cigarettes,

Tin Container, Lucky Strike flat-50s, American Tobacco Co., green ground, $10.

girl and puppy 45.00
Store Display, Chesterfield, Christmas,
1940s 10.00
Thermometer
Marlboro, Marlboro Man 40.00
Winston Tastes Good...
Like a Cigarette Should,
9" d, round, metal 60.00
Tin
Black Cat Cigarettes 15.00
Cavalier, 100, oval 12.00
Lucky Strike 100, round 20.00
Murad, 5-1/2" x 3" x 1-1/4",
Canadian, 1897 stamp 40.00
Pall Mall, 7" x 8",
Christmas dec 15.00
Phillip Morris, 50, round 12.00

Circus Items

Collecting Hints: Circus programs are one of the most popular items in this category. Individuals have collected them since the 1920s. Programs prior to the 1930s are hard to find; post-1930 material is readily available. Model building plays an active part in collecting. Some kits are available; however, most collectors like to build models from scratch. Great attention is placed on accurate details. There are many books published about the circus. These are sought by collectors for intrinsic, as well as research, value.

History: The 18th-century circus was a small traveling company of acrobats and jugglers and the first record of an American troupe is from that time. Washington is known to have attended a circus performance.

By the mid-19th century, the tent circus with accompanying side shows and menagerie became popular throughout America. P.T. Barnum was one of the early circus promoters. His American Museum in New York featured live animal acts in 1841. Other successful Barnum promotions included Jenny Lind in 1850, Tom Thumb from 1843 to 1883 and Jumbo, who was purchased from the London Zoo, in 1883. The Ringlings and Barnum and Bailey brought a magical quality to the circus. The golden age of the tent circus was the 1920s to the 1940s, when a large circus consisted of more than 100 railroad cars.

As television challenged live entertainment, the tent circus fell on hard times. Expenses for travel, food, staff, etc., mounted. A number of mergers took place and many smaller companies simply went out of business. There are a few tent circuses remaining. However, most modern circuses now perform inside large convention centers.

Periodical: *Circus Report*, 525 Oak St., El Cerrito, CA 94530.

Collectors' Clubs: Circus Fans Association of America, P.O. Box 59710, Potomac, MD 20859; Circus Historical Society, 743 Beverly Park Pl., Jackson, MI 49203; Circus Model Builders International, 347 Lonsdale Ave., Dayton, OH 45419.

Museums: Circus World Museum Library-Research Center, Baraboo, WI; P.T. Barnum Museum, Bridgeport, CT; Ringling Circus Museum, Sarasota, FL.

Book
  Barnum Presents General Tom Thumb, 1954, Alice Desmond..15.00
  The Biggest, The Smallest, The Longest, The Shortest: A History of Wisconsin Circuses, Dean Jensen, 230 pgs, 8-1/2" x 11" 15.00
  Circus Days, Jill Freedman, 100 pgs 8.00
  Jungle Performers, 1941, 1st ed, dj, autographed by author, Clyde Beatty............................90.00
  Little Old Show, Art "Doc" Miller, paperback 8.00
  Maestro of the Circus: The Story of Merle Evans, Genew Ploweden, 1971 ....12.50
  When the Circus Comes to Town, Dean August, contemporary 2.00
Calendar, Circus World Museum, 1974 ....5.00
Letterhead, Ringling Bros., multicolored, 5 brothers with crest, 1909 ......18.00
Lithograph
  Christiani Bros., Big Wild Animal Circus, 22" x 28", litho, polar bear, lion, giraffe, rhino, tiger and hippo drawing, yellow lettering, black trim, plastic cover, F.D. Freeland............26.00
  Dailey Bros., Big 5 Ring Railroad Wild Animal Circus, full color, blond woman riding pair of tigers, purple and green banner, white and green lettering, Central Show Printing Co., Inc........................25.00
Magazine, Ringling Brothers & Barnum

& Bailey, 1936 ....8.00
Menu, Greatest Show on Earth, Nov. 12, 1898, full color 100.00
Model, 1" scale
  Bareback riders, man and woman, 2 horses 800.00
  Clarke Bros. Circus, 2-wheel hitch...........................50.00
  Hay wagon and harness, blue and red 300.00
  Railroad flat car.....................200.00
  Sideshow paraphernalia, 14 set-ups 1,120.00
Pass, annual, 1953, cardboard, emb animals 2.00
Pinback Button
  Barnum '76 Festival, red, white and blue.....................10.00
  Cole Bros., Clyde Beatty, 1930s 25.00
  King Reid Shows, black and white clown, red, yellow and green accents, light blue ground, c1950.....................30.00
  Little Hip and His Owner Prof. Andre, trained elephant, c1910 45.00
  Setlin & Wilson Shows, 1-3/4" d, black and white clown, red, yellow and green accents, light blue ground, dark blue rim border, c1940.................50.00
Playing Cards
  Old Maid, circus edition.............5.00
  Ringling Bros. and Barnum & Bailey Circus, miniature size..............12.00
Poster
  Arthur Bros.
    1940, Big Railroad Show, arrival parade with showgirls on horses and elephants 90.00
    1943, Amusing Wire Display, navy, orange and red, tightrope walker in top hat................170.00
  Barnum & Bailey
    1894, The Grand Equestrian Tournament, rough riders, inset Civil and Military horsemanship illus, Strobridge Litho 725.00
    1913, Lion and Tiger, reclining jungle cats, circus logo, Strobridge Litho 275.00
  Clyde Beatty Circus, holds reign over field of wild jungle cats, date tag "July 4, Glendale Speedway"............50.00
  Cole Bros., All the Marvels, animal-sign cages, Erie Litho 210.00
  Hagenbeck-Wallace, 1925, Capt. Clyde Beatty, World's Most Daring Trainer, posing with lions, tigers and leopards pyramid 270.00
  King Bros., 1946, clown face, red and yellow, adv arrival 210.00
  Ringling Bros., and Barnum & Bailey

1935, Jolly clown portrait, blue ground, Erie Litho 270.00
  1938, The Greatest Wild Animal Display, presents Terrell Jacobs, World's Foremost Trainer, Strobridge Litho 625.00
  1940, The Great Alzanax, high-wire act, red ground...150.00
Program
  Barnum & Bailey, 1953 ....10.00
  Cole Bros. Clyde Beatty, 1969, 24 pgs, 40 photos 5.00
  Gentry Bros. & James Patterson, 1924.......................................15.00
  Hamid-Morgan, 1948 ....7.00
  Ringling Bros. Barnum & Bailey, 1962, 53 pgs, 10 articles, 90 photos 6.00
Record, Old Time Circus Calliola, Wurlitzer, Calliola, Paul Eakin's Gay 90s Village 5.00
Route Book
  Barnum & Bailey, 1906 ....225.00
  Cristiani Bros. Circus, 1958 .....25.00
  Adam Forepaugh, shows, 1891 ....225.00
Sign, 43" x 65", Aqua Circus, wood, painted, scalloped border, woman in 1890s garb with parachute 140.00
Souvenir Book, Ringling Bros. and Barnum & Bailey Circus, 1939 ......15.00
Ticket Stub Book, Hagenbeck-Wallace Circus, 1935 ....10.00
Toy, wood, Schoenhut
  Horse, painted eyes, brown saddle 130.00
  Ringmaster, 8-1/2" h, painted eyes 185.00
  Tiger, glass eyes...................200.00
Wagon Wheel, wood, metal rim, red, white and blue painted spokes 250.00

Pinback button, Canada Dry, sponsor of "Super Circus" TV show, 1950s, litho tin, Green Duck Co., Chicago, 1-1/2", $24.

Cleminson Clay

Collecting Hints: Each piece produced by this firm was hand decorated with colored slip, which accounts for the slight variations from piece to piece. The Distlefink dinnerware line is currently finding favor with many collectors.

History: In 1941, Betty Cleminson established Cleminson Clay in the garage of her home in El Monte, CA, with her husband, George, handling the business affairs. In 1943, the company expanded to a new plant constructed in El Monte and its name was changed to The California Cleminsons. In addition to a popular line of tableware called Distlefink, the pottery produced hand-decorated artware and kitchen accessories including pie birds, lazy Susans, spoon holders and pitchers.

Reference: Jack Chipman, *Collector's Encyclopedia of California Pottery*, Collector Books, 1992.

Periodical: *Pottery Collectors Express*, P.O. Box 221, Mayview, MO 64071.

Cookie Jar, cov
    Candy House 95.00
    Card King, gold
       trim on hearts 400.00
    Christmas House.....................150.00
Creamer and Sugar, Pop 20.00
Egg Separator 20.00
Hair Receiver, girl, 2 pcs 35.00
Lazy Susan, Distlefink...................85.00
Pie Bird, rooster............................30.00
Pitcher, Distlefink..........................40.00
Plate, hillbilly.................................24.00
Razor Bank, dome.........................20.00
Ring Holder, bulldog......................20.00
Spoon Rest, leaf............................15.00
Wall Plaque, spray of flowers........60.00
Wall Pocket, clock 20.00

Clickers

Collecting Hints: Clickers with pictures are more desirable than clickers that display only printed words. Value is reduced by scratches in the paint and rust. Some companies issued several variations of a single design—be alert for them when collecting.

History: Clickers were a popular medium for advertising products, services and people; and subjects ranged from plumbing supplies, political aspirants, soft drinks and hotels, to beer and whiskey. The most commonly found clickers are those which were given to children in shoe stores to advertise brands such as Buster Brown, Poll Parrot and Red Goose. Many shoe-store clickers have advertising-whistle mates.

Clickers were not confined to advertising. They were a popular holiday item, especially at Halloween. Impressed animal forms also provided a style for clickers. The vast majority of clickers were made of tin. The older and rarer clickers were made of celluloid.

Advertising

Allen's Parlor Furnace, heating stove,
    yellow ground, 2" l 35.00
Barton's Dynashine Shoe Polish, brown
    and white, 1-3/4" d....................50.00
Benzo Gas, "Does What Gasoline
    Can't," red, black, white and lime
    green, 2" l 15.00
Billiken Shoes, "The Billykid" illus,
    yellow, blue and white, light blue
    ground, 1930s, 2" l 32.00
Buster Brown Shoes, 5-star symbol
    with emb title and portrait,
    1930s, 2" l...............................35.00
Duo-Therm, "Snappy Weather Ahead,"
    yellow litho tin, red and black letters,
    home-heater products, c1940 .30.00
Endicott-Johnson Shoes, yellow and
    black litho tin, 2" l...................15.00
Gunther's Beer, "The Beer That Clicks,"
    white litho tin, red letters, made by
    Kirchof Co., c1930...................25.00
Hafner's 365 Brand Coffee, orange, blue

Frog, Life of the Party Products, Kirchof, Newark, NJ, 3", $10.

and white, c1930, 2" l 20.00
Hirshberg's Stag Paste Paint, litho tin,
    multicolored image of boy holding
    shoulder strap, yellow billboard sign
    inscribed with mane, 1930s.....60.00
Jolly Time Popcorn, blue and white
    popcorn box, yellow accents,
    1930s, 1-7/8" l 50.00
Mule-Hide Roofing and Shingles,
    yellow and black litho tin 20.00
Penn Maid Sour Cream, blue and white,
    1930s, 2-1/2" l 25.00
Pez, tin litho, Pez girl leans forward to
    offer candy to boy leaning against
    large peppermint Pez pkg, German
    text and "U.S. Zone Germany,"
    c1950, 2-1/4" x 3-1/4"............425.00
Poll-Parrot Shoes, emb litho tin, green,
    wash-tint parrot image, 1930s.50.00
Red Goose Shoes, 1930s, 1-7/8" l20.00
Sundial Shoes, litho tin, yellow and gray
    inscriptions, red ground, 1930s
    aircraft as skywriter 50.00
Twinkles Shoes for Boys and Girls,
    Twinkle character, blue ground30.00
Weston's Crackers, yellow litho tin, red
    letters "Crack-ettes" product line,
    made by Kirchof Co., c1930....35.00

Non-Advertising

Beetle, diecut metal 15.00
Bonzo, black,
    white and red, 1930s...............20.00
Cricket, yellow and
    black litho tin, 2" l 10.00
Halloween, orange,
    black and white litho tin,
    1930s 17.50
Ladybug, red and
    black litho tin, 1946 ....10.00
Santa, green, red, black and white,
    Grant's Toy Department,
    1930s, 1-1/2" l 40.00

Clocks

Collecting Hints: Many clocks of the 20th century were reproductions of earlier styles. Therefore, dates should be verified by checking patent dates on the mechanism, makers' labels and construction techniques.

The principal buyers for the advertising and figural clocks are not the clock collectors, but the specialists with whose area of interest the clock overlaps. For example, the Pluto alarm clock is of far greater importance to a Disneyana collector than to most clock collectors. Condition is critical. Rust and non-working parts have a major affect on prices.

History: The clock always has served a dual function: decorative and utilitarian. Beginning in the late 19th century the clock became an important advertising vehicle, a tradition which continues today. As character and personality recognition became part of the American scene, clocks, whether alarm or wall models, were a logical extension. Novelty clocks, especially figural ones, were common from 1930 to the 1960s. Since digital wristwatches and clocks became popular in the 1970s, clocks have been less commonly used as promotional items.

References: Robert W.D. Ball, *American Shelf and Wall Clocks*, Schiffer Publishing, 1992; Hy Brown, *Comic Character Timepieces*, Schiffer Publishing, 1992; Philip Collins, *Pastime*, Chronicle Books, 1993.

Periodical: *Clocks*, 4314 W. 238th St., Torrance, CA 90505; *Watch & Clock Review*, 2403 Champa St., Denver, CO 80205.

Collectors' Club: National Association of Watch and Clock Collectors, Inc., 514 Poplar St., Columbia, PA 17512.

Museums: American Clock & Watch Museum, Bristol, CT; Greensboro Clock Museum, Greensboro, NC; Museum of National Association of Watch and Clock Collectors, Columbia, PA; Old Clock Museum, Pharr, TX; Time Museum, Rockford, IL.

Additional Listings: See Warman's Antiques and Collectibles Price Guide.

Advertising

Breyer's Ice Cream, wood, sailboat,
   chrome sails 50.00
Budweiser, 5-1/2" x 4-1/2" x 14",
   revolving, duck in flight on reverse,
   marble base with emblem........85.00
Bulova, wall 48.00
Busch Beer, electric,
   horse-and-rider scene 35.00
Cincinnati Reds, logo, wood frame,
   electric, 1940s 60.00
Coca-Cola, "Drink Coca-Cola in Bottles,"
   sq wood case, electric, Selected
   Devices Co., NY 215.00
Frostie Root Beer, metal,
   fluorescent bulb 150.00
General Electric, peach,

mirror, electric...........................55.00
Jefferson "Golden Hour," electric ..85.00
John Deere, 14" d, round, electric.65.00
Kodak, "Pictures Are Priceless—
   Use Kodak Film," 15-1/2", sq,
   lights up 35.00
Paramount Pictures, 15" x 8",
   battery, 1994, MIB 25.00
Sauers Extract, New Haven
   Clock Co., wall.......................975.00
7-Up, oak frame, c1950...............100.00
Sprite, wood frame,
   quartz, c1980...........................30.00
St. Joseph's Aspirin, neon...........300.00
Tetley, Tea Time, 13", blue and gray,
   tin, Art Deco............................85.00
Warren Telephone Co., Ashland,
   MA, oak 80.00
Wise Potato Chip, owl, electric......75.00

Alarm

Bradley, brass, double bells,
   Germany..................................35.00
Peter's Shoes, New Haven Clock Co.,
   4" x 4", Art Deco, c1930 ....50.00
Purina Poultry Chows, electric,
   3 dials, red, white and blue
   checkered bag.........................40.00
Star Wars, talking..........................25.00

Animated

Fish swimming around dial,
   Art Deco style, Sessions 250.00
Haddon, rocking grandmother.....175.00
Mastercrafter's
   Fireplace 115.00
   Swinging playmates,
   onyx case, 1950s 225.00
United
   Ballerina, music box...............150.00
   Boy, gold fishing, 1950s.........175.00

Character

Refrigerator shape, white metal, GE label, electric, Warren Telechron Co., Ashland, MA, 8-1/2", $185.

Davy Crockett, wall, pendulum 75.00
Donald Duck, 9" h, wall, glazed china,
   2-1/4" d case inscribed "Blessings,"
   blue outfit, green glazed ground,
   orig gold sticker mkd "Waechters-
   bach," inscribed "Walt Disney Productions, J.A. Sural Hanua/Main—
   Made in Germany," c1950.....175.00
Howdy Doody, talking 65.00
Mickey Mouse,
   Bradley animated hands 45.00
Pluto, 4" x 5" x 9", electric, black, white
   and red plastic, bone hands, moving
   eyes and tongue, c1940........100.00
Sesame Street,
   schoolhouse shape 25.00
Trix the Rabbit, alarm, c1960........15.00

Figural

Artist's Palette, Bakelite 35.00
Chef, 10-1/2" h, electric,
   wall, white, Sessions
   Clock Co., Forestville 24.00
Doghouse, 11" h, iron,
   dog looking out, flowers 80.00
Donut, 8-3/4" h, dark herbal green glaze,
   Clifton Art Pottery 85.00
Refrigerator, 8-1/2" h, metal, painted
   white, G.E. label, Warren Telechron
   Co., Ashland, MA 185.00
Spinning Wheel, Lux, animated 80.00
Tape Measure, tan, Lux 45.00

Clothing and Clothing Accessories

Collecting Hints: Vintage clothing should be clean and in good repair. Designer labels and original boxes can add to the value. Collecting vintage clothing appears to have reached a plateau. Although there are still dedicated collectors, the category is no longer annually attracting a rash of new collectors.

History: Clothing is collected and studied as a reference for learning about fashion, construction and types of materials used.

References: Joanne Dubbs Ball and Dorothy Hehl Torem, *Art of Fashion Accessories*, Schiffer Publishing, 1993; Adele Campione, *Women's Hats*, Chronicle Books, 1994; C. Willett and Phillis Cunnington, *History of Underclothes*, Dover, 1992; Maryanne Dolan, *Vintage Clothing*, 3rd Edition, Books Americana, 1995; Kate Dooner, *Century of*

Handbags, Schiffer Publishing, 1993; ——, *Plastic Handbags*, Schiffer Publishing, 1993; Roseann Ettinger, *'50s Popular Fashions for Men, Women, Boys & Girls*, Schiffer Publishing, 1995; ——, *Handbags*, Schiffer Publishing, 1991; *Franklin Simon Fashion Catalog for 1923*, Dover, 1993; Roselyn Gerson, *Vintage Vanity Bags and Purses*, Collector Books, 1994; Sarah Gibbings, *The Tie*, Barrons, 1990; *Gimbel's Illustrated 1915 Fashion Catalog, Gimbel Brothers*, Dover, 1994; Kristina Harris, *Vintage Fashions for Women*, Schiffer Publishing, 1996; Richard Holiner, *Antique Purses*, 2nd Edition, Collector Books, 1987, 1994 value update; Ellie Laubner, *Fashions of the Roaring '20s*, Schiffer Publishing 1996; Jan Lindenberger, *Clothing & Accessories from the '40s, '50s, & '60s*, Schiffer Publishing, 1996; Phillip Livoni (ed.), *Russell's Standard Fashions 1915-1919*, Dover Publications, 1996; Hunter and Shelkie Montana, *Cowboy Ties*, Gibbs Smith, 1994; Jo Anne Olian (ed.), *Children's Fashions*, Dover, 1994; ——, *Everyday Fashions of the Forties as Pictured in Sears Catalogs*, Dover, 1992; Lynell K. Schwartz, *Vintage Purses at Their Best*, Schiffer Publishing, 1995; Joy Shih, *Fun Fabrics of the 50s*, Schiffer Publishing, 1996; ——, *Funky Fabrics of the 60s*, Schiffer Publishing, 1996; Desire Smith, *Hats*, Schiffer Publishing, 1996; Pamela Smith, *Instant Expert: Vintage Fashion and Fabrics*, Alliance Publishing, 1996; Diane Snyder-Haug, *Antique & Vintage Clothing*, Collector Books, 1996; Sheila Steinberg and Kate E. Dooner, *Fabulous Fifties*, Schiffer Publishing, 1993; Debra J. Wisniewski, *Antique & Collectible Buttons*, Collector Books, 1996; *Women's Fashions of the Early 1900s*, Dover, 1992; Merideth Wright, *Everyday Dress of Rural America*, Dover, 1992.

Periodicals: *Glass Slipper*, 653 S. Orange Ave., Sarasota, FL 34236; *Lady's Gallery*, P.O. Box 1761, Independence, MO 64055; *Lill's Vintage Clothing Newsletter*, 19 Jamestown Dr., Cincinnati, OH 45241; *Vintage Clothing Newsletter*, P.O. Box 1422, Corvallis, OR 97339; *Vintage Gazette*, 194 Amity St., Amherst, MA 01002.

Collectors' Clubs: Costume Society of America, 55 Edgewater Dr., P.O. Box 73, Earleville, MD 21919; Federation of Vintage Fashion, P.O. Box 412, Alamo, CA 94507; Living History Association, P.O. Box 578, Wilmington, VT 05363; Textile & Costume Guild, 301 N. Pomona Ave., Fullerton, CA 92632; Vintage Fashion and Costume Jewelry Club, P.O. Box 265, Glen Oaks, NY 11004.

Museums: The Arizona Costume Institute, Phoenix Art Museum, Phoenix, AZ; Boston Museum of Fine Arts, Boston, MA; Chicago Historical Society, Chicago, IL; Detroit Historical Museum, Detroit, MI; Fashion Institute of Technology, New York, NY; Indianapolis Museum of Art, Indianapolis, IN; Los Angeles County Museum of Art, Costume and Textile Dept, Los Angeles, CA; Metropolitan Museum of Art, New York, NY; Missouri Historical Society, St. Louis, MO; Museum at Stony Brook, Stony Brook, NY; Museum of Art, Rhode Island School of Design, Providence, RI; Museum of Vintage Fashion, Lafayette, CA; National Museum of American History, Washington, DC; Philadelphia College of Textiles & Science, Philadelphia, PA; Philadelphia Museum of Art, Philadelphia, PA; Valentine Museum, Richmond, VA; Wadsworth Atheneum, Hartford, CT; Western Reserve Historical Society, Cleveland, OH.

Apron, calico, red and white 25.00

Baby Bonnet, cotton, tatted,
   ribbon rosettes.........................15.00

Bathing Suit
  Adult
    Cotton, black and white, matching
    slippers and hat, c1890........50.00
    Stretchy fabric, back button, flared
    skirt, black, c1930 ....45.00
    Wool blend knit, black 35.00
  Girl's, cotton print,
    ruffles, 1950s 15.00

Bed Jacket, satin, pink, lavish
   ecru lace, labeled "B. Altman & Co.
   NY," 1930s 30.00

Bloomers
  Crepe Satin, peach, silk embroidery,
   lace trim, 1920s......................18.00

Wool, cream............................25.00

Blouse
  Beaded taffeta, black, black glass
   beads at yoke, hand sewn 85.00
  Chiffon, green, child's ,multiple rows
   of ruffles 15.00
  Cotton, white,
   cutwork, Victorian 20.00
  Lace, ecru, evening style, gathered
   waist, 1950s...........................18.00
  Poplin, white,
   middy style, c1910 ....15.00
  Silk, cream,
   embroidered, 1900s.................65.00

Bonnet
  Silk, hand-crocheted lace 36.00
  Straw, finely woven,
   worn silk lining 135.00

Boudoir Cap, crocheted,
   pink rosettes...........................12.00

Bustle, canvas and woven wire.....30.00

Cape
  Girl's, flannel wool, ivory, silk-cord
   embroidery..............................45.00
  Woman's
    Cotton, white, corded, wide emb
    ruffle trim...........................45.00
    Mohair, black, ankle length,
    c1930 ....75.00
    Velvet, red,
    white satin lining 70.00
    Wool, dark blue, quilted lining,
    18" l, c1920........................65.00

Capelet
  Beaded, all-over design, beaded
   fringe, c1850 ....100.00
  Feathers, ostrich,
   gray satin ribbon 50.00
  Fur, black beaver 25.00

Change Purse, cut steel beads, ecru
  crochet, push bottom clasp, fringe,
  leaf dec, 2-1/2" x 3-1/2", inscribed "B.
  Cottle, 1847"..........................65.00

Christening Gown, white
  Cotton, matching
   bonnet, 47" l..........................100.00
  Cutwork embroidery bodice, tuck
   pleats around ruffled skirt 65.00
  Machine sewn, lace, hand
   embroidery, 42" l.....................50.00
  Net, embroidered,
   silk slip, 44" l 150.00

Coat
  Baby's
    Cotton, gathered yoke and
    capelet, embroidery, flannel
    lining 25.00
    Silk, pink,
    label "Paris Best" 45.00
  Boy's, linen, hand stitched,
   dec cuffs 35.00
  Woman's

Blouse, white, turquoise sequins, $15.

Cashmere, red, silver fox collar,
full length, c1940 .... 50.00
Fur
  Alaskan Seal, black, mink trim,
  padded shoulders, c1940 . 100.00
  Muskrat, bell-shaped sleeves,
  c1940 .... 90.00
  Persian Lamb, black,
  matching hat 75.00
  Squirrel, gray, wide cuffs, padded
  shoulders, c1940 .... 80.00
  Plush, black, Flapper style,
  bat-wing sleeves 125.00
  Silk, black, evening, 3/4 length,
  c1915 .... 36.00
  Velvet, navy blue, beaded dec,
  black fox collar and cuffs, red satin
  lining, 1920s 250.00
  Wool, blue, beaver collar and
  cuffs, blouson, drop-waist style,
  c1920 .... 100.00
Collar
  Beaded, white, 1930s 12.00
  Cotton, white, embroidered, wide,
  scalloped 20.00
Corset, sateen, orig Sears
  Roebuck box 15.00
Cosmetic Case, gold mesh,
  Whiting Davis, 3" x 4" 15.00
Costume, matador, heavily embroi-
  dered, sequins and gold metallic
  thread, minor wear 120.00
Cowboy, child's
  Boots, Acme 85.00
  Chaps 90.00
  Outfit, 4 pcs, 1960s 200.00
  Vest and Chaps,
  hide rosettes 150.00
Dress
  Child's
    Cotton, day type, gold, net trim,
    c1900 .... 20.00
    Crepe, red, red beaded edge trim
    at collar and sleeves, minor holes
    and wear 25.00
    Georgette, pink, many

layers of georgette and
chiffon, c1920 .... 75.00
Gingham, blue and white, hand
and machine sewn, white
embroidery trim, 25" h 50.00
Knit, 2 pc, 1930 .... 25.00
Lawn, white, lace, drop waist,
c1910 .... 60.00
Linen, embroidered wisteria in-
serts, Irish lace trim 150.00
Net, silk lining, ruffles at neck,
sleeves, pink rosette trim ... 120.00
Rayon, raspberry, accordion
pleats, c1930 .... 15.00
Silk
  Black, chiffon sleeve,
  embroidery, 1923 .... 48.00
  Black, lace, ecru beaded bodice,
  c1920 .... 75.00
  Blue, floral print, lace trim,
  Victorian 150.00
  Brown, black accents,
  c1910 .... 50.00
  Peach, embroidered collar and
  skirt, short sleeves, c1920 .. 35.00
  Red, drop waist, black trim,
  bowed sash, c1910 .... 75.00
  Silk Faille, mourning, black,
  c1890 .... 100.00
  Silk Taffeta, purple, marcasite
  buttons, late 1800s 35.00
  Velvet, red, white nylon,
  Shirley Temple style,
  Cinderella tag 15.00
Wool
  Dark green,
  Amish, c1930 .... 45.00
  Pink, lace trim, c1890 ..... 125.00
Woman's
  Batiste, white, lace, high neck, full
  skirt, long sleeves, c1900 .. 150.00
  Calico, blue, 2 pcs, matching bon-
  net, c1900 .... 165.00
  Chiffon, blue, edges trimmed with
  braided fabric, 1925 .... 40.00
  Lawn, drop waist 60.00
  Satin, black, 1920s 85.00
  Taffeta, blue, emb dec, 1950s,
  dinner-type 10.00
Dressing Gown, satin, ruby red, fagoted
  ruffled edges, 1930 .... 28.00
Evening Gown
  Chiffon and velvet, black, Empire
  waist, shirred bodice, 1930 ... 45.00
  Crepe, brown, matching velvet cape-
  let with feather trim, c1930 ..... 40.00
  Net and Taffeta, black, lace flowers,
  c1940 .... 48.00
  Organza, white, shirred, rhinestones,
  c1940 .... 45.00
Evening Jacket, crepe, pink, floral-
  patterned sequins, lined, 1940 58.00
Gloves

Woman's
  Kid, white, long 20.00
  Nylon, short style, scalloped edge,
  yellow 4.00
Man's, driving, leather,
  black, c1910 .... 25.00
Handbag
  Alligator, suede lining 18.00
  Beaded, abstract design, white and
  gray, milk glass beads, beaded
  handle, zipper, 5", mkd
  "Czechoslovakia" 20.00
  Florals, pink and blue, shiny beads,
  gold frame 45.00
  Lucite, pearlized, round lid,
  lunch box clasp, twisted handle,
  seashell dec 17.50
  Mesh, enameled, white ground, black
  leaf spray, Mandalian 55.00
  Patchwork, Seminole, drawstring,
  grass bottom, blue, c1960 .... 25.00
  Pearl, envelope,
  Hong Kong label 15.00
  Plastic, child's, red, imitation leather,
  3 Scotties dec, silver frame and
  chain, int mirror 20.00
  Sequins, irid multicolored, silver and
  seed pearl dec, rhinestone clasp,
  fancy frame, Belgium 30.00
  Silk, clutch, black, cut steel beads,
  mkd "France," c1930 .... 42.00
  Wool, hand woven, New Mexico,
  Navajo rug design, white ground,
  Fred Harvey, c1940 .... 35.00
Handkerchief
  10-3/4" x 18", printed, white cotton,
  red design, "Old Mother Hubbard,"
  framed 50.00
  14-3/4" sq, printed, white cotton, red
  design, birds and wild beasts,
  framed, pr 130.00
  17-3/4" x 18-1/2", printed, white
  cotton, multicolored Indian heads,
  blue border 85.00
  Snow White and the Seven Dwarfs,
  1938, price for set 225.00
Hat, Woman's
  Felt, cloche, black 15.00
  Satin, pillbox, black, netting 18.00
  Straw, wide brim, multicolored chiffon
  flowers, c1940 .... 20.00
Hat and Purse Set, leopard skin pillbox,
  matching purse 100.00
Muff
  Marabou, white 45.00
  Rabbit fur, white, child's 25.00
  Sable, brown, tails 100.00
Necktie, men's, striped,
  rayon, 1930s 3.00
Pajamas, girl's, baby-doll style, cotton,
  pink hearts, 1960s 7.00
Petticoat, cotton, white
  Crocheted insert, wide

crocheted hem 45.00
   Three rows crochet trim 40.00
Prom Gown
   Georgette, yellow, embroidered
   bodice, strapless, c1960 ....25.00
   Net and taffeta, pink, layered skirt,
   bow trim, c1950......................35.00
Purse, Mexican, tooled leather, brown,
   white inserts............................45.00
Sash, purple, beaded, c1850 ......100.00
Scarf
   Cotton, dog print, mkd "Occupied
   Japan" 18.00
   Silk, man's, fringed...................15.00
Shawl
   Cotton, mint green, fully embroi-
   dered, fringed edges, 1925 ......35.00
   Paisley, printed design, 66" x 128",
   minor wear and stains..............60.00
   Woven Design
      59" x 118", black
      center medallion.................215.00
      68" x 69", minor damage....165.00
Shoes
   Boy's, leather, Oxford style, two-tone
   brown 35.00
   Children's
      Faux crocodile and suede, side
      buckle, rust, 1930s...............36.00
      Leather
       Mary Jane, 2-strap style, camel
       kid, side buttons, Buster Brown
       brand, 1930s 42.00
       Oxford, black kid, Buster Brown
       brand, 1930s 40.00
       Saddle, black and white,
       late 1950s..........................35.00
       T-strap style, brown leather,
       black, rust and tan suede,
       Red Goose brand, 1930s ...40.00
      Leather mesh, brown, boy's,
      late 1950s 15.00

Handbag, beaded, floral design, crocheted top, green, rose, yellow, white, $60.

Woman's
   Leather, boots, brown or black,
   lace up, pointed toes..........125.00
   Leather, brown,
   high-button top.....................40.00
   Low heels, black kid, black patent
   toes, Buster Brown brand ..145.00
   Suede, gray, c1920..............25.00
   White bucks, pointed toes..118.00
Man's
   Boots, work type, leather,
   early, 11" h, pr.....................25.00
   Tennis, high top, c1920 ....20.00
Skirt
   Cotton, white, Victorian,
   walking-type 40.00
   Linen, gore style,
   Edwardian type 40.00
   Polished cotton, floral print,
   full, c1950...............................24.00
   Wool, black, Victorian 40.00
Socks, men's, rayon and silk, cotton toe
   and heal, black, colored arrow,
   1950s.......................................5.00
Spats, wool, gray, c1900..............24.00
Suit
   Boy's, wool
      Blazer, short pants, navy, 26"
      chest, Tom Sawyer brand....42.00
      Herringbone, lined,
      Amish, c1920 ....40.00
   Woman's, wool, navy pin tucks,
   silk lining, 1921 ....55.00
Sweater
   Cashmere, white pearl trim 35.00
   Crew neck, Playboy, red, cream-
   colored Bunnies, small, wool,
   orig Playboy tag attached 100.00
Teddy, yellow, pink emb trim on bodice,
   1920s......................................25.00
Travel Kit, gentleman's, alligator,
   7 accessories, c1940...............18.00
Wedding Gown
   Net and lace, cream, high neck,
   2-pc style, c1900.....................165.00
   Satin, ivory, padded shoulders,
   sweetheart neckline, waist swag,
   self train, c1940.......................125.00
   Silk Faille, lace, ribbon and pearl trim,
   train 170.00
Yoke, crocheted, ribbon trim 15.00

Coca Cola Items

Collecting Hints: Most Coca-Cola items were produced in large quantity; the company was a leader in sales and promotional materials. Don't ignore the large amount of Coca-Cola material printed in languages other than English. Remember, Coke has a worldwide market.

History: The originator of Coca-Cola was John Pemberton, a pharmacist from Atlanta. In 1886, Dr. Pemberton introduced a patent medicine to relieve headaches, stomach disorders and other minor maladies. Unfortunately, his failing health and meager finances forced him to sell his interest. In 1888, Asa G. Candler became the sole owner of Coca-Cola. Candler improved the formula, increased the advertising budget and widened the distribution. Accidentally, a patient was given a dose of the syrup mixed with carbonated water instead of the usual still water. The result was a tastier, more refreshing drink.

As sales increased in the 1890s, Candler recognized that the product was more suitable for the soft drink market and began advertising it as such. From these beginnings a myriad of advertising items have been issued to invite all to "Drink Coca-Cola." Dates of interest: "Coke" was first used in advertising in 1941. The distinctively shaped bottle was registered as a trademark on April 12, 1960.

References: Gael de Courtivron, *Collectible Coca-Cola Toy Trucks*, Collector Books, 1995; Steve Ebner, *Vintage Coca-Cola Machines, Vol. II*, published by author (P.O. Box 448, Middletown, MD 21769), 1996; Deborah Goldstein Hill, *Wallace-Homestead Price Guide to Coca-Cola Collectibles*, Wallace-Homestead, 1984, 1991 value update; *Goldstein's Coca-Cola Collectibles*, Collector Books, 1991, 1993 value update; Bill McClintock, *Coca-Cola Trays*, Schiffer Publishing, 1996; Allan Petretti, *Petretti's Coca-Cola Collectibles Price Guide*, 10th Edition, Antique Trader Books, 1997; B.J. Summers, *B.J. Summers' Guide to*

Blotter, 1944, 3-1/2" x 7-3/4, $15.

Coca-Cola, Collector Books, 1997; Al Wilson, *Collectors Guide to Coca-Cola Items, Vol. I* (1985, 1996 value update), *Vol. II* (1987, 1994 value update), L-W Book Sales; Al and Helen Wilson, *Coca-Cola*, Schiffer Publishing, 1994.

Collectors' Clubs: Coca-Cola Collectors Club, 400 Monemar Ave., Baltimore, MD 21228; Coca-Cola Collectors Club International, P.O. Box 49166, Atlanta, GA 30359; Florida West Coast Chapter of the Coca-Cola Collectors Club International, 1007 Emerald Dr., Brandon, FL 33511.

Museums: Coca-Cola Memorabilia Museum of Elizabethtown, Inc., Elizabethtown, KY; The World of Coca-Cola Pavilion, Atlanta, GA.

Reproduction Alert: Coca-Cola trays, pocket mirrors.

Advertisement, hanging type, 3D, "Put your thirst on ice," 1990s..12.00
Apron, white, green strip, Lee tag and button................................45.00
Arcade Card, bathing beauty.........10.00
Ashtray, 4" d, bright red, white logo, 1980s......................................12.00
Bank, plastic, vending-machine shape, C&G Toys, 1960s 35.00
Banner, 11" x 22", printed paper, c1951................15.00
Billfold, pigskin, 1950s...................25.00
Blotter
  3-1/2" x 7-1/2", full color, unused "58 Million a Day, Sign of Good Taste," stacks Coke bottles up, 1957 ...18.00
  "Friendliest drink on earth, drink Coca-Cola," hand holding Coke bottle in front of planet, 1956........20.00
  3-1/2" x 7-3/4", full color, cardboard, 1937 publication date, unused 50.00
Booklet, "Classic Cooking with Coca-Cola" 5.00
Bottle, commemorative
  Astrodome 30th Anniversary 4.00
  Cal Ripken................................5.00
  Cincinnati Reds, World Champs, 1994 ....4.00
  Dallas Cowboy Super Bowl, commemorative 6-bottle set.....30.00
  Denver Broncos 1st Team logo..4.00
  Detroit Red Wings, 70th anniversary........................4.00
  Eskimo Joe's 3.00
  Florida Aquarium.......................4.00
  Ft. Worth Stock Show 4.00

Miniature bottles, 6 in carrier, cardboard, Bill's Novelties Premiums, Milwaukee, $22.50.

  Graceland, 1995 ....10.00
  Houston Rockets, Back-to-Back Champs, 1995...........................3.00
  Kentucky Derby 122...................4.00
  NBA All-Star Weekend 1995, desert scene, NBA logo, Feb. date, made and issued in Phoenix, limited to 300,000, 6-pack with orig bottles and contents..........35.00
  Oriole Park at Camden Yards 4.00
  Selena, Five Years with You....35.00
  Texas Tech Lady Red Raiders ..3.00
Bottle Carrier, shopping cart 50.00
Box, wood 65.00
Bridge Score Pad 12.00
Calendar, 1955............................52.50
Chalkboard, diner menu...............45.00
Check, used
  1946, May 3, bottle logo 14.00
  1960, July 28, bottle logo, small hole...................................8.00
  1961, April 14, bottle logo 12.00
Cigarette Lighter, miniature...........10.00
Clock, 15" sq, electric, metal.......115.00
Coaster, Santa Claus, set 15.00
Cookie Jar, jug shape, red label with Coca-Cola logo, McCoy 80.00
Cuff Links, pr, bottle shape 45.00
Dart Board, 1950s.........................40.00
Door Push, 11" x 4", porcelain, 1930s.....................85.00
Folder, 8-1/2" x 11", black, white and red, 4 pgs plus overleaf, "More Profit Per Patron," Coca-Cola refreshment counter in movie house lobbies or vending machines, back text describes average weekly gross profits from lobby sales, late 1930s....65.00
Glass
  Set, 8 glasses
    10-oz size, sealed in orig carton, Libbey, c1960 ....125.00
    16-oz size
      Georgia Green, Indiana Glass,

  1992, bell shape.................14.00
  Polar Bear, "Always Cool, Always Coca-Cola," Indiana Glass, 1992 ....12.00
Ice Chest, airline cooler 410.00
Ice Pick, with opener...................122.00
Kite, High Flyer, 6-oz bottle illus, 1930s 45.00
Magazine Ad
  The Housewife, 1910, matted and framed...................70.00
  Life, March 15, 1963 ....7.50
Menu Board, 1950s....................175.00
Necktie, c1950 ....35.00
Pencil Box, orig contents 35.00
Pencil Sharpener, figural bottle, cast metal.................................45.00
Pinback Button
  Hi Fi Club, red, green and yellow litho tin, brown bottle in center of red 45 RPM record, 1950s sponsorship of teen music TV show 30.00
  Insignia Series, 15-1/6" d, celluloid, Parisian Novelty Co., insert back paper with "Drink Coca-Cola" trademark along with designation of insignia and series number, 1940s
    No. 7, 26th Bombardment Squadron, orange and gray 75.00
    No. 8, Third Pursuit Squadron, black, white, red on gray triangle..............75.00
Ping Pong Paddle, set of four 35.00
Playing Cards, "It's the Real Thing," 1971 ....8.00
Pocket Knife, black, smooth handle, case in shape of Coca-Cola bottle, "Coke" engraved on each side..........200.00
Pocket Mirror, 2-3/4" oval, World War I Girl, 1917..........210.00
Postcard, 5-1/2" x 6-1/2" perforated cardboard sheets, lower half of back side for "Occupant," rest of address unused, red and dark green carton with white and flesh-tone hand, upper half of card front with full-color "Take home a carton" with young lady, lower half pictures full-color 6-bottle carton, coupon for 6 free bottles and deposit of 12¢, local sponsor Coca-Cola Bottling Works, Fort Wayne, IN, late 1930s, price for pr 40.00
Poster, girl preparing to ice skate, copyright 1940, well worn......105.00
Pretzel Dish, aluminum, c1938 .....45.00
Punchboard, 7" x 8", 1940s, unused........................8.00
Salt and Pepper Shakers, pr, red, white logo, tin-can shape, unpunched holes, 1970s, MIB 25.00
Sheet Music,

Tray, Spring Board Girl, 1939, Sunblom, artist, 13" x 10", $300.

The Coca-Cola Girl, 1927 ...... 145.00
Sign
    Double-Sided, 1952, large
    round logo and bottle, 16" d,
    22" h, minor wear 275.00
    Light-Up, waterfall 1,500.00
    Man standing at roadside,
    "Pause that Refreshes" 25.00
    Umbrella Girl, cardboard, 1942,
    framed 875.00
Straw Holder 25.00
Syrup Jug, gallon size, 1930 .... 30.00
Thimble, aluminum 25.00
Tip Tray, Exposition Girl 325.00
Toy
    Delivery Truck, Matchbox
    No. 38, 1958 .... 60.00
    Soda-fountain dispenser, plastic,
    4 miniature glasses 135.00
Tray
    Glass, square,
    International, 1967 .... 95.00
    Metal
        Boy eating sandwich,
        Rockwell, 1931 .... 700.00
        Girl preparing to ice
        skate, 1941 .... 350.00
        Hand pouring Coke
        into glass, "Coke Refreshes
        You Best," 1961 .... 25.00
        Menu Girl, 1950 .... 55.00
Uniform Patch, "Enjoy Coke" 3.00
Whistle, litho tin, red, yellow
    and black, "The Pause That
    Refreshes," 1930s 100.00
Yo-Yo, Edwards Bo-Lo 85.00

Cocktail Shakers

Collecting Hints: Concentrate on cocktail shakers that are style statements of their era. Make aesthetics, line, form and materials principal focus points. A collection numbering in the hundreds can be built around examples of the streamlined-modern style.

Run your fingers around the edge of glass shakers to check for chipping. A small chip reduces the price by a minimum of 30%. Shakers with brilliant sharp colors are more desirable than those made of clear glass. Be on the constant alert for cracks and fractures. Most individuals want shakers that are usable and are at least in fine condition. Figural shakers are in a class of their own. Among the more common forms are bowling pins, dumbbells, golf bags and penguins. Shakers based on the designs of Norman Bel Geddes often command in excess of $500.

History: The cocktail shaker traces its origins as far back as 7000 B.C. and the South American jar gourd, a closed container used to mix liquids. The ancient Egyptians of 3500 B.C. added spices to fermented grain— perhaps history's first cocktails. Alcoholic drinks have been a part of recorded history into the modern era.

By the late 1800s, bartenders used a shaker as a standard tool. Passing the liquid back and forth between two containers created a much appreciated show. The modern cocktail shaker arrived on the scene in the 1920s when martinis were in vogue. Shapes tended to be stylish; materials ranged from glass to sterling silver. Perhaps nothing symbolizes the Jazz Age more than the flapper dress and cocktail shaker. When Prohibition ended in 1933, the cocktail shaker enjoyed another surge of popularity.

Movies helped popularize the cocktail shaker. William Powell showed a bartender how to mix a proper martini in "The Thin Man," a tradition continued by James Bond in the 007 movies. Tom Cruise's portrayal of a bartender in "Cocktail" helped solidify the collecting interest in cocktail shakers during the 1980s.

Following World War II, a bar became a common fixture in many homes. Every home bar featured one or more cocktail shakers and/or cocktail shaker sets. Chrome-plated stainless-steel shakers replaced the sterling-silver shakers of the 1920s and 1930s. Major glass companies such as Cambridge, Heisey and Imperial offered cocktail shakers. Life in the fabulous 1950s was filled with novelties; cocktail shakers were no exception. Figural and other forms of novelty shakers appeared. The electric blender and ready-mix cocktail packets ended the reign of the cocktail shaker. Showmanship was replaced by button pushing.

Reference: Stephen Visakay, *Vintage Bar Ware*, Collector Books, 1997.

Note: In addition to prices for cocktail shakers, the following listing includes many types of related items.

Bar Set, animated, musical,
    Anri, 1930s 400.00
Beverage Set, Depression Glass,
    pitcher, decanter, orig stopper,
    seven 4" h tumblers, eight 3-1/2" h
    tumblers, Scottie dog dec on
    each, price for set 135.00
Bottle Stopper, figural
    Kissing Couple 25.00
    Man, tips hat 25.00
    Man, pop-up head 40.00
Cocktail Set, Art Deco style, glass shak
    er, 6 tall glasses, 5 shorter glasses,
    stippled frosted surface, gold and
    colored mid-bands, 1950s 65.00
Cocktail Shaker
    Aluminum, hand wrought, straight
    sides, grooved Modernistic top, clear
    plastic knob lid, Buenilum 25.00
    Glass
        Cambridge, Diane pattern, clear,
        matching glass top 145.00
        New Martinsville, Moondrops,
        green, handle, top missing .. 20.00
        Paden City, Utopia, clear ... 165.00
        Sportsman Series, cobalt blue,
        white image
            Ship dec 60.00
            Windmill dec 25.00
Cordial Set
    Central Glass Co., Balda Orchid
    pattern, decanter, 6 matching
    cordial glasses 375.00
    Cambridge, amber, 12-oz
    decanter 3400/119 and four
    1-oz 1341 cordials 50.00
    Rooster, martini pitcher,
    4 matching tumblers, clear,
    red and black dec 35.00
Cup, Chase Chrome,
    Blue Moon 100.00
Decanter, orig stopper, glass

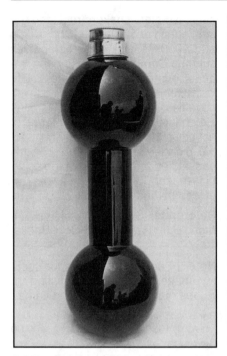

Art Deco, ruby red glass, chrome top, 12-/12" h, 3-1/2" d bowl, $55.

Duncan Miller, First Love,
32 oz 295.00
Farber Ware, Mandarin gold,
32 oz, 3400/92 ....60.00
Fostoria, American pattern,
24 oz, 9-1/2" h.......................100.00
Imperial, Cape Cod,
etched "Rye"...........................70.00
Hor D'ouevre Pick
Fruit, set of 12 ....20.00
Man, top hat 3.50
Ice Bucket
Aluminum, hand wrought
Buenilum, ridged band handles,
ring finial.............................20.00
Lehman, double twisted handles,
plastic knob 18.00
Glass
Cambridge, Apple Blossom,
amber...................................30.00
Duncan Miller,
Canterbury, clear 35.00
Fostoria
Baroque, yellow...............125.00
Bouquet, Century, clear 80.00
Chintz, clear
with etching 135.00
Imperial Glass,
Cape Cod, clear................125.00
Jewelry, pin and earrings set, large
martini glass with olive, silvertone,
open-work earrings, 1960s 35.00
Liqueur Set, Farber Ware,
Cubist nude woman surrounded
by 6 glasses...........................66.00

Martini Pitcher
Cambridge
Apple Blossom, clear 200.00
Diane, clear, etching 600.00
Tiffin, Twilight, 11-1/2" h.........450.00
Martini Set, 32-oz stainless steel martini
shaker, James Bond silhouette logo,
two 8-oz martini glasses with satin-
etched 007 gun logo, United Artist
exclusive set, MIB 70.00
Old Fashion Tumbler,
Catalonia, Consolidated,
yellow, 3-7/8" h........................20.00
Pilsner, Old Sandwich, Heisey,
10 oz, Moongleam green.........45.00
Punch Bowl Set
Cambridge, Tally Ho, emerald green,
mugs, price for 12-pc set 295.00
Hall China, Old Crow, bowl,
10 cups, ladle 200.00
Heisey, Lariat, crystal,
seven-qt punch bowl, 10 cups,
price for set 255.00
Westmoreland, Paneled Grape,
milk glass, 15 pcs...................795.00
Shot Glass, Russel Wright, Theme
Formal 300.00
Stemware, glass
Brandy, Cambridge, Nude,
Tahoe blue 295.00
Champagne
Duncan Miller,
Terrace, red 95.00
Fostoria, American,
amethyst 22.50
Claret
Cambridge
Nudes, forest green 150.00
Rosepoint pattern
Fostoria, Navarre, 6" h.........60.00
Cocktail
Cambridge
Moonlight Blue 10.00
Nude, amethyst...............110.00
Fostoria
American............................15.00
Buttercup............................24.00
Tiffin, June Night.................45.00
Cordial, McKee,
Rock Crystal...........................12.00
Swizzle Stick, glass
Advertising, colored 3.50
Amber 1.50
Black 2.00
Christmas, set of six.................25.00
Man, top hat 3.50
Souvenir, Hotel Lexington, amethyst,
1939 World's Fair....................20.00
Spatter knob, clear stirrer...........1.00
Toddy Mixer, crystal,
green, 12 oz 24.00
Tom and Jerry Set

Fostoria, American pattern,
bowl and 8 mugs....................340.00
Hall China
Black, ftd bowl,
eighteen 5-oz cups 240.00
Ivory, ftd bowl, 6 cups........100.00
Tray, 11" d, tin, red, black and white,
martini center, card border 55.00
Tumbler
Central Glass Co., Balda, light
amethyst, ftd, 3" h...................37.50
Duncan Miller, Terrace, red 37.50
Fostoria
June, yellow, ftd...................32.50
Versailles, blue, ftd 45.00
Heisey, New Era, ftd, 12 oz 25.00
Sportsman Series, cobalt blue,
white windmill dec, 12 oz.........27.50
Whiskey
Duncan and Miller,
amethyst, 1 oz.........................15.00
Farber Ware, 3400/92, amethyst,
2 oz, price for 6-pc set 55.00
Fostoria, June, ftd, yellow 75.00
New Martinsville, Moondrops,
cobalt blue 17.00

Comic Books

Collecting Hints: Remember, age does *not* determine value! Prices fluctuate according to supply and demand. Collectors should always buy comic books in the best possible condition. While archival restoration is available, it's frequently costly and may involve a certain amount of risk.

Comic books should be stored in an upright position away from sunlight, dampness and insect infestations. Avoid stacking comic books because the weight of the uppermost books may cause acid and oils to migrate. As a result, covers on books near the bottom of the stack may become stained with material that is difficult or impossible to remove. Golden Age (1939-1950s) Marvel and D.C. first issues and key later issues continue to gain in popularity as do current favorites such as Marvel's X-Men and D.C.'s New Teen Titans.

History: Who would ever believe that an inexpensive, disposable product sold in the 1890s would be responsible for a current multimillion dollar industry? That 2¢ item—none other than the Sunday newspaper—has its modern counterpart in flashy comic books and related spin-offs.

Improved printing techniques helped 1890s newspaper publishers change from a weekly format to a daily one that included a full page of comics. The rotary printing press allowed the use of color in the "funnies," and comics soon became the newest form of advertising.

It wasn't long before these promotional giveaways were reprinted into books and sold in candy and stationery stores for 10¢ each. They appeared in various formats and sizes, many with odd shapes and cardboard covers. Others were printed on newsprint and resembled the comic books sold today. Comics printed prior to 1938 have value today only as historical artifacts or intellectual curiosities.

From 1939 to 1950 comic book publishers regaled readers with humor, adventure, Western and mystery tales. Super heroes such as Batman, Superman and Captain America first appeared in books during this era. This was the "Golden Age" of comics—a time for expansion and growth. Unfortunately, the bubble burst in the spring of 1954 when Fredric Wertham published his book *Seduction of the Innocent* which pointed a guilt-laden finger at the comic industry for corrupting youth, causing juvenile delinquency and undermining American values. This book forced many publishers out of business, while others fought to establish a "comics code" to assure parents that comics complied with morality and decency mores. Thus, the "Silver Age" of comics is marked by a decline in the number of publishers, caused by the public uproar surrounding Wertham's book and the increased production costs of an inflationary economy.

The period starting with 1960 and continuing to the present has been marked by a resurgence of interest in comic books. Starting with Marvel's introduction of "The Fantastic Four" and "The Amazing Spiderman," the market has grown to the extent that many new publishers are now rubbing elbows with the giants and the competition is keen!

Part of the reason for this upswing must be credited to that same inflationary economy that spelled disaster for publishers in the 1950s. This time, however, people are buying valuable comics as a hedge against inflation. Even young people are aware of the market potential. Today's piggy-bank investors may well be tomorrow's Wall Street tycoons.

References: Mike Benton, *Comic Book in America*, Taylor Publishing, 1993; ——, *Crime Comics*, Taylor Publishing, 1993; ——, *Horror Comics*, Taylor Publishing, 1991; ——, *Science Fiction Comics*, Taylor Publishing, 1992; ——, *Superhero Comics of the Golden Age*, Taylor Publishing, 1992; ——, *Superhero Comics of the Silver Age*, Taylor Publishing, 1992; *Comic Buyer's Guide*, Krause Publications, 1996; Ernst and Mary Gerber (comps.), *Photo-Journal Guide to Comics, Vols. 1 and 2*, Gerber Publishing, 1990; John Hegenberger, *Collector's Guide to Comic Books*, Wallace-Homestead, 1990; Maurice Horn (ed.), *World Encyclopedia of Comics*, Chelsea House, out of print; Alex Malloy, *Comics Values Annual*, Antique Trader Books, 1996; Robert M. Overstreet, *Overstreet Comic Book Price Guide*, 26th Edition, Avon Books, 1996; Robert M. Overstreet and Gary M. Carter, *Overstreet Comic Book Grading Guide*, Avon Books, 1992; Don and Maggie Thompson (eds.), *Comic Book Superstars*, Krause Publications, 1993; ——, *Marvel Comics Checklist & Price Guide*, Krause Publications, 1993; Maggie Thompson and Brent Frankenhoff, *1997 Comic Book Checklist & Price Guide*, 3rd Edition, Krause Publications, 1996; Jerry Weist, *Original Comic Art*, Avon Books, 1993.

Periodicals: *Comic Book Market Place*, P.O. Box 180900, Coronado, CA 92178; *Comic Buyers Guide*, 700 E. State St., Iola, WI 54990; *Comic Scene*, 475 Park Ave., New York, NY 10016; *Duckburg Times*, 3010 Wilshire Blvd. #362, Los Angeles, CA 90010; *Overstreet Comic Book Marketplace*, 801 20th St. NW, Ste.3, Cleveland, TN 37311; *Overstreet's Advanced Collector*, 801 20th St. NW, Ste.3, Cleveland, TN 37311; *Western Comics Journal*, 143 Milton St., Brooklyn, NY 11222.

Collectors' Club: Fawcett Collectors of America & Magazine Enterprise, Too!, 301 E. Buena Vista Ave., North Augusta, SC 29841.

Videotape: *Overstreet World of Comic Books,* Overstreet Productions and Tom Barker Video, 1994.

Museum: Museum of Cartoon Art, Rye, NY.

Reproduction Alert: Publishers frequently reprint popular stories, even complete books, so the buyer must pay strict attention to the title, not just the portion printed in outsized letters on the front cover. If there's ever any doubt, look inside at the fine print on the bottom of the inside cover or first page. The correct title will be printed there in capital letters.

Buyers also should pay attention to the size of the comic they purchase. Many customers recently have been misled by unscrupulous dealers. The comics offered are exact replicas of Golden Age D.C. titles which normally sell for thousands of dollars. The seller offers the large, 10-by-13-inch copy of Superman #1 in mint condition for $10 to $100. The naive collector jumps at the chance since he knows this book sells for thousands on the open market. When the buyer gets his "find" home and checks further, he discovers that

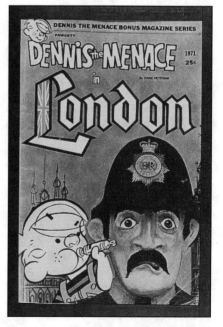

Dennis the Menace in London, Fawcett, $4.

he's paid way too much for the treasury-sized "Famous First Edition" comic printed in the mid-1970s by D.C. These comics originally sold for $1 each and are exact reprints except for the size. Several came with outer covers which announced the fact that they were reprints, but it didn't take long for dishonest dealers to remove these and sell the comic at greatly inflated prices.

Notes: Just like advertising, comic books affect and reflect the culture which nurtures them. Large letters, bright colors and pulse-pounding action hype this product. Since good almost always triumphs over evil, many would say comics are as American as mom's apple pie. Yet there's truly something for every taste in the vast array of comics available today. There are underground (adult situation) comics, foreign comics, educational comics and comics intended to promote the sale of products or services. The following listing concentrates on mainstream American comics published between 1938 and 1985. Prices may vary from region to region due to excessive demand in some areas. Prices given are for comic books in fine condition; that is, comics that are like-new in most respects, but may show a little wear. Comics should be complete; no pages or chunks missing.

Classics Comics

The Adventures of
   Marco Polo, #1 ....100.00
Benjamin Franklin, #1....................45.00
Black Beauty, #1 ....30.00
Dr. Jekyll and Mr. Hyde, #1 ....260.00
Frankenstein, #1...........................275.00
Gulliver's Travels, #1 ....75.00
Kidnapped, #1 ....45.00
The Pathfinder, #1.........................135.00
The Prince and the Pauper, #1 ...200.00
Rip Van Winkle and the
   Headless Horseman, #1 ....125.00
Twenty-Thousand Leagues
   Under the Sea, #1 ....65.00
Westward Ho!, #1 ....250.00

Crime

Authentic Police Cases, #15 ....20.00
Crime and Punishment, #40..........16.00
Crime Mysteries, #14 ....20.00
Famous Crimes, #3 ....25.00
Keen Detective Funnies, #5 ....75.00
Kerry Drake Detective Cases, #6..10.00

Tim Tyler Cowboy, red letters, King Features, $2.

Mr. District Attorney, #15...............15.00
Parole Breakers, #3 ....30.00
True Crime Comics, #5 ....65.00

Funny Animals

Animal Adventures, #3 ....5.00
Animal Comics, #6 ....40.00
Bugs Bunny, #300...........................5.00
Daffy, #50.......................................2.00
Huckleberry Hound
   Chuckleberry Tales, #19 50
Mighty Mouse, #10...........................8.00
Porky Pig, #180..............................10.00
Scooby Doo, #5...............................2.00
Tom and Jerry, #80 ....5.00
Woody Woodpecker, #200..............4.50

Horror

Amazing Detective Cases, #12 ....7.50
Chilling Tales of Horror, #4 ....1.25
Dark Mysteries, #20 ....15.00
Eerie, #14......................................15.00
House of Secrets, #48......................2.00
House of Terror, #226 ....11.00
Tales of Horror, #7 ....8.50
Vault of Horror, #14.....................125.00
Worlds of Fear, #7...........................9.00

Jungle

All Top, #18 ....35.00
Evangeline, #6 ....2.00
Jo Jo, 37..75.00
Jungle Action, #13...........................1.00
Jungle Jim, #5 ....2.00
Jungle Twins, #3 ....1.00
Nyoka, The Jungle Girl14...............30.00
Ramar of the Jungle, #5..................8.50
Tarzan, #25 ....35.00

Wambi Jungle Boy, #9 ....12.00
Zoot, #11.......................................50.00

Juvenile

Archie Comics, #65........................7.50
Casper, #3 ....5.00
Henry, 1946, #3 ....11.00
Hug A Bunch #3..............................1.00
Katy Keene, #11 ....30.00
Josie, #22..2.25
Little Lulu, #146.............................60.00
Nutty Comics, #6............................4.50
Patsy Walker, #20 ....15.00
Pebbles & Bam Bam, #10...............2.00
Richie Rich, #80..............................5.00
Wendy the Witch, #6......................24.00

Newspaper Reprints

Comics on Parade, #36 ....17.50
Dick Tracy, #25 ....35.00
Foxy Grandpa, #1900 ....60.00
Gasoline Alley, #1 ....24.00
Joe Palooka, #2 ....25.00
Mutt & Jeff, #10 ....25.00
Penny, #6..8.00
Sparkler, #53.................................20.00
Tip Top, #2.....................................75.00

Radio/TV/Movie Related

Augie Doogie, #1 ....7.50
Big Town, #35 ....4.50
Fury, #1218....................................10.00
Gang Busters, #15 ....50.00
Lucy Show, #2 ....20.00
McHale's Navy, #2 ....3.25
Space Ghost, #3 ....2.25
Star Wars, #4 ....5.00
Uncle Milty, #2 ....12.00

Romance

Boy Meets Girl, #8 ....4.00
Date with Debbi, #15.......................3.00
Dream of Love, #2 ....1.50
Exciting Romances, #30 ....12.00
Falling in Love, #20 ....3.00
Love Letters, #49 ....8.00
Love Mystery, #3............................17.50
Love Stories, #2 ....8.00
Romantic Secrets, #23....................4.00

Science Fiction

Amazing Adventures, #2 ....18.00
Mags, Robotfigher, #3....................12.00
Micronauts, #30 ....1.00
Planet Comics, #20......................120.00
Strange Adventures, #18 ....25.00
Strange Mysteries, #3 ....28.00
Weird Mysteries, #7 ....50.00
Weird Science Fantasy, #25 ....60.00

Sports

All Sports Comics, #4......................8.00
Babe Ruth Sports Comics, #5.........5.00
Football Thrills, #2...........................7.00

Joe Louis, #2 ....20.00
Sport Comics, #3 ....10.00
Sport Stars, #4 ....7.00
True Sport Picture Stories, #5 ....12.00

Star Trek

Gold Key, #1 ....150.00
Gold Key, #2 ....100.00
Gold Key, #3 ....75.00
Gold Key, #4 ....75.00
Gold Key, #5 ....75.00
Gold Key, #10 ....25.00
Gold Key, #15 ....25.00
Gold Key, #20 ....25.00
Gold Key, #25 ....20.00
Gold Key, #30 ....20.00
Gold Key, #51 ....10.00

Star Wars

Marvel, #1, 30-cent version 20.00
Marvel, #1, 35-cent version 75.00
Marvel, #2 ....7.50
Marvel, #3 ....7.50
Marvel, #4 ....5.00
Marvel, #5 ....3.50
Marvel, #10 ....3.50
Marvel, #25 ....2.50
Marvel, #60 ....2.00

Super Heroes

Amazing Spiderman, #30 ....15.00
Batman, #78 ....30.00
Captain America, #112 ....15.00
The Dazzler, #21 ....2.00
Detective, #80 ....50.00
The Eagle, #2 ....75.00
Human Torch, #12 ....95.00
Plastic Man, #64 ....20.00
Wonder Woman, #145 ....3.00

Walt Disney

Beagle Boy, #10 ....2.00
Chip 'n Dale, #17 ....2.25
Dynabrite, Donald Duck, #4 80
Huey, Dewey and Louie Junior
    Woodchucks, #23 ....5.00
Ludwig Von Drake, #4 ....3.50
Pinocchio Learns
    about Kites, 1954 ....60.00
Super Goof, #11 ....2.00
Walt Disney Presents, #6 ....5.00
Walt Disney's Comics & Stories, #3 5.00
Zorro, #3 ....21.00

War

All American Men of War, #30 ....51.00
Attack, #16 ....1.00
Attack At Sea, #5 50
Black Cat Mystery, #30 ....15.00
Black Diamond Western, #18 ....12.00
Boys' Ranch, #4 ....55.00
G.I. Joe, #14 ....4.50
How the Boys and Girls Can
    Help Win the War, #1 ....60.00

Jet Heroes, #1 ....10.00
Judy Joins the Waves, 1951 ....4.50
Navy War Heroes, #3 ....2.00
War Comics, #45 ....5.00
War Heroes, #8 ....2.00

Western

Annie Oakley and Tagg, #4 ....10.00
Bill Boyd Western, #7 ....20.00
Cheyenne Kid, #12 ....16.00
Dale Evans, #3 ....20.00
Gabby Hayes Western, #50 ....10.00
Gene Autry Comics, #25 ....5.00
Ken Maynard Western, #2 ....20.00
Luke Short's Western
    Stories, #848 ....18.00
Rawhide Kid, #60 ....2.00
Roy Rogers Comics, #12 ....18.00
Tom Mix Western, #35 ....12.00
Western Gunfighters, #12 ....35.00

X-Files

Topps, #1 ....25.00
Topps, #2 ....15.00
Topps, #3 ....8.00
Topps, #4 ....6.00

X-Men

#1, 1963 ....3,000.00
#2, 1963 ....800.00
#3, 1964 ....400.00
#4, 1964 ....400.00
#5, 1964 ....180.00
#6, 1964 ....90.00
#7, 1964 ....90.00
#8, 1964 ....90.00
#9, 1965 ....90.00
#10, 1965 ....90.00
#30, 1964 ....30.00
#50, 1968 ....20.00
#94, 1975 ....170.00
#110, 1978 ....14.00
#140, 1980 ....14.00

Compacts

Collecting Hints: Only mirrors that are broken should be removed and replaced in a vintage compact. Do not replace a mirror that is discolored, flawed or in need of resilvering. The original mirror enhances the value of the compact, as does the presence of the box or pouch in which the compact was originally sold. Never apply a sticker directly to the surface of a compact. The acids from the glue may discolor or irreparably damage the finish, especially an enamel finish.

History: In the first quarter of the 20th century, attitudes regarding cosmet-

ics changed drastically. The use of make-up during the day was no longer looked upon with disdain. As women became "liberated," and as more and more of them entered the business world, the use of cosmetics became a routine part of a woman's grooming. Portable containers for cosmetics became a necessity.

Compacts were made in myriad shapes, styles, combinations and motifs, all reflecting the mood of the times. Every conceivable natural or man-made material was used in their manufacture. Commemorative, premium, souvenir, patriotic, figural, Art Deco and enamel compacts are a few examples of the types of compacts that were made in the United States and abroad. Compacts combined with other forms, such as cigarette cases, music boxes, watches, hatpins, canes and lighters, also were very popular.

Compacts were made and used until the late 1950s when women opted for the *au naturel* look. The term "vintage" is used to distinguish the compacts made during the first half of the 20th century from contemporary examples. Some vintage compacts were exquisitely crafted, often enameled or encrusted with precious or synthetic jewels. These compacts were considered a form of jewelry or fashion accessory. The intricate and exacting workmanship of some vintage compacts would be virtually impossible to duplicate today.

References: Roselyn Gerson—Vintage Contemporary Purse Accessories, Collector Books, 1997; Roselyn Gerson, *Ladies' Compacts of the 19th and 20th Centuries*, Wallace-Homestead, 1989; ——, *Vintage Vanity Bags and Purses*, Collector Books, 1994; Frances Johnson—*Compacts, Powder and Paint*, Schiffer Publishing, 1996; Laura M. Mueller, *Collector's Encyclopedia of Compacts, Carryalls & Face Boxes*, Vol. I (1994, 1996 value update), *Vol. II* (1997), Collector Books.

Collectors' Club: Compact Collectors Club, P.O. Box 40, Lynbrook, NY 11563.

Arden, Elizabeth, light blue enamel,
    harlequin mask dec 85.00
Avon, oval, lid dec with blue and
    green checkerboard pattern 35.00

Bakelite vanity case, rect, black, rhinestone geometric design on lid, int mirror, powder and rouge compartments, coin pocket on back, black carrying cord, lipstick concealed in tassel, $250.

EAM, Art Deco, blue-enameled tango-chain compact, red and yellow abstract design, powder sifter and attached lipstick, finger-ring carrying chain 200.00

Evans, goldtone and mother-of-pearl, compact and lipstick combination 45.00

Hudnut, Richard, Deauville, blue, cloisonné tango-chain vanity, metal mirror, compartments for power and rouge, lipstick attached to finger-ring chain 200.00

K&K, brass, colored engine-tooled dec basket compact, multicolored silk flowers enclosed in plastic dome lid, emb swinging handle 125.00

Rowanta, brown enamel, oval petit-point compact 65.00

Unknown Maker
Enamel, ebony, 8-ball style 115.00
Enamel and goldtone, roll-top style, Germany 135.00
German Silver, fluted, vanity, chatelaine, orig compact, coin holder, memo book, locket, pin container and stamp holder 550.00
Goldtone, heart shape, brocade lid 50.00
Lucite, blue, SS repoussé medallion of two doves 135.00
Plastic, red, white and blue, Naval Officer's cap shape 85.00
Silver Plated, antique, triangular, hand-mirror shape, lipstick concealed in handle, int and ext mirrors, turquoise cabochon thumbpiece 155.00

Volupt, USA
Adam and Eve, under apple tree 50.00
Watch Case, picture locket on flower dec lid 65.00

Whiting and Davis, Piccadilly,

gilded mesh, vanity bag, compact incorporated in front lid, carrying chain 250.00

Woolworth, Karess, polished goldtone, corset shape, vanity case, powder and rouge compartments 45.00

Yardley, goldtone, vanity case, red, white and blue emb design no lid, powder and rouge compartments 75.00

Cookbooks

Collecting Hints: Look for books in good, clean condition. Watch for special interesting notes in margins.

History: Among the earliest American cookbooks are *Frugal Housewife or Complete Woman Cook* by Susanna Carter, published in Philadelphia in 1796 and *American Cookery* by Amelia Simmons, published in Hartford, Connecticut, in 1796. Cookbooks of this era were crudely written, for most cooks could not read well and measuring devices were not yet refined.

Collectible cookbooks include those used as premiums or advertisements. This type is much less expensive than the rare 18th-century books.

References: Bob Allen, *Guide to Collecting Cookbooks and Advertising Cookbooks*, Collector Books, 1990, 1995 value update; Mary Barile, *Cookbooks Worth Collecting*, Wallace-Homestead, 1994; *Boston Cooking School Cook Book: A Reprint of the 1884 Classic by Mrs. D.A. Lincoln*, Dover Publications, 1996; Linda J. Dickinson, *Price Guide to Cookbooks and Recipe Leaflets*, Collector Books, 1990, 1995 value update.

Periodical: *Cookbook Collectors' Exchange*, P.O. Box 32369, San Jose, CA 95152.

Collectors' Club: Cook Book Collectors Club of America, 231 E. James Blvd., P.O. Box 85, St. James, MO 65559.

America's Best Vegetable Recipes, food ed of *Farm Journal*, Doubleday, 1970, dj 7.50

American Woman's Cook Book, Ella Blackstone, Chicago, 1910, 384 pgs 35.00

Amy Vanderbilt's Complete Cookbook, 1961, 811 pgs 15.00

The Best from Midwest Kitchens, Ada B. Lothe, M.S. Mill Co., 1946, dj 6.50

Betty Crocker's Cookbook, Golden Press, 1969 .... 15.00

Betty Crocker's Cookbook for Boys and Girls, Golden Press, 1975, spiral bound, 1st ed, 160 pgs 16.00

Betty Crocker's Picture Cook Book, General Mills, Minneapolis, 1950, 1st ed 50.00

Betty Furness Westinghouse Cookbook, Julia Kiene, Simon & Schuster, 1954 .... 8.00

Calumet Cook Book, 27th ed, Kewpies illus, Calumet, 1922, 80 pgs, ... 25.00

Chemistry of Cookery, W. Mattieu Williams, Appleton, NY, 1885, 328 pgs, 1st ed 60.00

Elsie Lee's Party Cookbook, Elsie Lee Publishing, 1974, dj 15.00

Encyclopedia of Cooking, Mary Margaret McBride, 12 vols, Homemakers Research Institute, 1958 .... 50.00

Grandma's Cooking: Recollections of Yankee Life and Grandma's New England Dishes Intertwined, Allan Keller, Grammercy, NY, 1955, 8vo, 240 pgs, 1st ed 15.00

Helen Corbitt's Cookbook, Houghton Mifflin, 1957, dj, general wear 15.00

Italian-Kosher Cookbook, Ruth and Bob Grossman, 1964, 84 pgs ... 7.50

James Beard Cookbook, Dalton & Co., 1961 .... 7.00

Jewish Cookery Book, on Principles of Economy, adapted for Jewish Housekeepers, Esther Levy, Philadelphia, 1871, 8vo, publisher's blue cloth, 1st ed 1,265.00

Kitchen Directory and American Housewife Containing Valuable Receipts in All the Various Branches etc, Ivison, Phinney & Co., NY, 1862, 16 engravings, 195 pgs 37.40

Ladies' Home Journal of Holiday Cuisine, M. Hoppel, E. Harrington,

Late 1940s-early 1950s: *Kate Smith's 55 Favorite Ann Pillsbury Cake Recipes*, $9.50; *The Heinz Salad Book*, $7.50; *Chiquita Bananas Recipe Book*, $9; *Betty Crocker's Softasilk Special Occasion Cakes*, $9.50.

Downe Pub, NY, 1970 ....7.00

Lowney's Cook Book, Maria W. Howard, 1912, revised ed 17.50

Magic in Herbs, Leonie de Sounin, Gramercy, 1941 ....9.50

Mastering the Art of French Cooking, Julia Childs, NY, 1961, 14th printing...................15.00

Maxwell House, How to Make Cook Coffee, 1931, black and white illus 12.00

McCall's Cookbook, Random House, 1963, 786 pgs.........................20.00

Meal Planning & Table Service in the American Home, N.B. Bailey, Manual Arts Press, 1942, 4th ed, 149 pgs..............15.00

Mrs. Rorer's Philadelphia Cook Book, Mrs. S.T. Rorer, Arnold & Co., 1886, 8vo, 581 pgs, 1st ed 20.00

Mrs. Peterson's Simplified Cooking, Anna J. Peterson and Nena W. Badenoch, Peoples Gas Light and Coke, 1927, 4th ed 10.00

Mystery Chef's Own Cook Book: The Radio Chef's Famous Easy Recipes for Low Cost Dishes, Blakiston, Philadelphia, 1934, 8vo, 366 pgs ..15.00

Peter Hunt's Cape Cod Cookbook, Peter Hunt, Hawthorn Books, 1954, sgd by author, 1st ed..............................8.50

A Piece of Cake, A Lively Collection of More Than 300 (Cake) Recipes, Susan Purdy, Athenum, 1989, 9-1/2" x 8", 498 pgs, 1st ed 13.50

Plain Cooking: Low Cost Good-Tasting Amish Recipes, Bill Randle and Nancy Predina, ed, *New York Times*, 1974, sgd by authors, 270 pgs 22.00

Popcorn & Diet Book, Joel Herskowitz, Phar, 1987, dj 10.00

Practical Cooking and Dinner Giving, Mary Henderson, NY, 1877, 376 pgs.........................40.00

Stillmeadow Cook Book, Gladys Taber, J.B. Lippincott & Co., 1965, illus by Ann Grifa Grifalconi 25.00

Talsiman Italian Cook Book, Boni, Crown, NY, 1950, special ed for Ranzoni, 292 pgs, dj...............15.00

The Universal Receipt Book or Complete Family Directory...by a Society of Gentlemen in New York, New York, 1814, 8vo...............................430.00

Today, What Salad, What Dessert, Jell-O, 1928, 22 pgs 25.00

Treasury of Great Recipes: Famous Specialties of the World's Foremost Restaurants Adapted for the American Kitchen, Mary and Vincent Price, Ampersand Press, 1965, 1st ed, mylar jacket, 456 pgs...48.00

Twelve Days of Christmas Cookbook, S. Huntley, Atheneum Books, Club Ed, 1965, 143 pgs, dj 8.00

200 Years of New Orleans Cooking, Natalie Scott, Cape & Smith, 1931, 17 pen-and-ink illus by William Spratling, 1st ed 17.50

Vitality Demands Energy, 109 Smart New Ways to Serve Bread, Our Outstanding Energy Food, Betty Crocker, General Mills, 1934, 52 pgs 50.00

Watkins Salad Book, Elaine Allen, 1946, rubbed 15.50

White House Cook Book, Hugo Ziemann and Mrs. F.L. Gilette, Saalfield Publishing Co., 1913, 619 pgs.......25.00

Cookie Cutters, Plastic

Collecting Hints: Plastic cookie cutters have become quite popular with collectors in recent years, as have other kitchen plastics. Plastic cookie cutters were mass-produced in the thousands and older examples are still available at reasonable prices. Popularity of certain cutters has driven up prices, but wise collectors should be patient in their search for Peanuts, Walt Disney and other popular themes.

Many companies produced cookie cutter sets with anywhere from four to 12 pieces. Complete sets demand higher prices, but collectors can usually piece together the set at a reasonable cost. Collectors often specialize in various categories such as Hallmark or other manufacturers.

Cutters made by Educational Products, better known as HRM because of their mark, are quite prevalent and popular. The company continues to produce clear red plastic cutters in 150 different shapes. Some shapes have been discontinued and older cutters cannot be distinguished from newer ones in the same shape. HRM also bought molds from other

Mickey Mouse and Donald Duck, Disney mark, 1977, each, $6.

companies. The original cutters do not have the "HRM" mark and the handles differ. Current catalogs are available to help collectors identify objects (see References).

Collectors should concentrate on cutters with a manufacturer or copyright mark and beware of those marked only "China," as they are hard to identify.

History: Plastic cookie cutters are predominantly made from Polystyrene, Styron, Acrylic or Polypropylene, all of which were developed between the late 1920s and early 1930s but were not used for kitchen items until the 1930s. The majority of cutters found today were made after 1950 and collectors are scooping up those dated as late as the 1970s. Older cutters were molded from hard plastic and are thus prone to cracks or chipping on the cutting edge. Also, most types of plastic scratch easily.

References: Cookie Craft, Educational Products annual catalogs (P.O. Box 295, Hope, NJ 07844); Lee Stephenson and Byrna Fancher, *Guide to Hallmark Cookie Cutters*, published by authors (5909 Montebello, Haslett, MI 48840), n.d.; Phyllis S. Wetherill, *Cookie Cutters and Cookie Molds*, Schiffer Publishing, 1985 (out of print); Phyllis Whidden, *The HRM Book*, published by author (4286 Bond Ave., Holt, MI, 48842), n.d.

Periodical: *Cookies*, 9610 Greenview Ln., Manassas, VA 20109.

Collectors' Club: Cookie Cutter Collectors Club, 1167 Teal Rd. S.W., Dellroy, OH 44620.

Reproduction Alert: Discount and dollar stores sell cookie cutter sets marked "China" or "made in China" which may copy Hallmark or Wilton designs. One clue: the inside designs may not be as detailed. Some reproductions of HRM cutters have been made but the quality is not the same and colors may differ.

Advisor: Tina M. Carter.

Avon, boy and girl, price for set 10.00
Biscuit Cutters,
    2 sizes, Bonny Ware 6.00
Cabbage Patch Kids, Easy Bake, price for set of 3 ....6.00

Card Party Set, red-outlined cutters,
    boxed set 10.00
Circus Animals, Hutzler, c1960,
    orig pkg 12.00
Donald Duck, Hallmark, 1977 ....6.00
Donut and Cookie Cutter,
    2-pc red plastic 4.50
Doughboy, Pillsbury, white, dated 1989,
    still in production 1.00
Easter, HRM, set of 8, box 15.00
Football player, Hallmark, 1983 ....5.00
Gingerbread Boy
    Betty Crocker,
    Gingerbread mix, red 3.50
    Miller Co., 2 handles, on card 8.00
Grimace, McDonald's, 1980 ....5.00
Holly Hobbie,
    Hallmark, mid-1970s 4.00
Jell-O Jigglers,
    alphabet set, 1980s 4.50
Kittens, pink, Wilton, 1990,
    price for set of 4 ....6.00
Mickey Mouse, Hallmark, 1977 ....6.00
Mini Cutters, Hallmark,
    various designs 2.50
Mr. Peanut, Planters, red or blue,
    price for set of 2 ....18.00
Nested set, heart, flowers, biscuit,
    Tupperware 3.00
Ninja Turtles, Wilton, 1990, in pkg,
    price for set of 4 ....6.00
Old McDonald Farm Set, Chilton,
    12 pcs 18.00
Peanuts, Hallmark, mkd "United
    Features Syndicate," 1950s 10.00
Raggedy Ann and Andy, Hallmark,
    mkd "Bobbs-Merrill" 10.00
Robin Hood Flour, various colors,
    mkd, price for set of 7 ....75.00
Ronald McDonald,
    McDonald's, 1980 ....5.00
Snoopy, 4 poses, Hallmark, mkd "United
    Features Syndicate" 28.00
Tom and Jerry, Loew's, 1956,
    price for set of 6 ....30.00
Twelve Days of Christmas, Wilton,
    12 pcs 18.00

Cookie Jars

Collecting Hints: It is not unusual to find two cookie jars made by the same company which have been decorated differently. These variations add some interest to cookie jar collections.

History: The date the first cookie was made is unknown. However, early forms of cookie jars can be found in several mediums, including glass and pottery. Perhaps it was the Depression that caused people to bake more cookies at home, coupled with the pretty Depression-era glass jars that created the first real interest in cookie jars. A canister, complete with matching lid, was made in the popular Kolorkraft line by Brush Pottery Company in Roseville, OH, in the 1920s. By embossing the word "Cookies" on it, the piece became one of the first such documented cookie jars. By 1931, McKee Glass Company, Jeannette, PA, was advertising a cookie jar that consisted of a 5-1/2 inch jar with a lid; by 1932, Hocking Glass was advertising a large glass jar with a wide screw-on metal lid. These products were additions to canister sets.

The clever figural jars so often associated with cookie jars were introduced by several companies during the early 1940s. Soon, apples, animals and comic characters were added to more colorful kitchens. Production of American cookie jars flourished until the mid- or late 1970s, when foreign competition became too great for several companies. However, a resurgence in the cookie jar collecting market has helped spur new companies to develop interesting jars and production is starting to increase. As Americans fall in love with new characters, from Sesame Street to Star Wars, cookie jar manufacturers eagerly fill orders.

References: Mary Jane Giacomini, *American Bisque*, Schiffer Publishing, 1994; John W. Humphries, *Humphries Price Guide to Cookie Jars*, published by author, 1992, 1994-95 value update, distributed by L-W Book Sales; Harold Nichols, *McCoy Cookie Jars*, 2nd Edition, Nichols Publishing, 1991; *1995 Cookie Jar Express Pricing Guide to Cookie Jars*, Paradise Publications, 1995; Fred and Joyce Herndon Roerig, *Collector's Encyclopedia of Cookie Jars, Book I* (1990, 1995 value update), *Book II* (1994), Collector Books; Mike Schneider, *Complete Cookie Jar Book*, Schiffer Publishing, 1991; Diane Stoneback, *Kitchen Collectibles*, Wallace-Homestead, 1994; Mark and Ellen Supnick, *Wonderful World of Cookie Jars*, Revised Edition, L-W Book Sales, 1995; Ermagene Westfall, *Illustrated Value Guide to Cookie Jars* (1983, 1995 value update), *Book II* (1993, 1995 value update), Collector Books.

Periodicals: *Cookie Jar Express*, P.O. Box 221, Mayview, MO 64071; *Cookie Jarrin'*, RR #2, Box 504, Walterboro, SC 29488; *Crazed over Cookie Jars*, P.O. Box 254, Savanna, IL 61074.

Collectors' Club: Cookie Jar Collector's Club, 595 Cross River Rd., Katonah, NY 10536.

Reproduction Alert: Reproduction cookie jars are starting to plague the market. Oddly enough, it's not only the old cookie jars being reproduced. The cute blue Cookie Monster made by California Originals in 1970 has been copied. California Originals are clearly marked "copyright Muppets, Inc. 1970" along the base. Brayton Pottery's Mammy has been reproduced. Unmarked copies have been found in addition to well-made copies with a date on the bottom and new-looking decals on the apron. Other reproductions include American Bisque: Casper; Brush: elephant with an ice cream cone and Peter Pumpkin Eater; California Originals: Count and Cookie Monster; McCoy: Davy Crockett; Regal China: Davy Crockett; Robinson-Ransbottom: World War II soldier and Oscar.

Abingdon Pottery

Hobby Horse,
    mkd "Abingdon USA" 95.00
Jack-In-Box, ABC on front,
    incised mark "611" 125.00
Money Sack 95.00

Advertising

Cookie Bandit, Hallmark 190.00
Keebler Tree House,
    Brush-McCoy 100.00
Regency Insurance, Buick sedan, royal
    blue, Glenn Appleman 800.00
Sid's Taxi, Glenn Appleman 800.00
Ziggy, stack of cookies 325.00

American Bisque

Cowboy Boots 235.00
Churn Boy 225.00
Ernie 95.00
Ice Cream Freezer 460.00
Milk and Cookies 225.00
Mr. Rabbit 185.00
Poodle, gold trim 275.00

Avon

African Village 35.00
Spatter Bear 30.00
Townhouse, small, MIB 15.00

Brush

Bobby Baker...............................75.00
Clock 185.00
Clown Bust, crazing...................375.00
Elephant, ice cream cone, gray body,
	purple jacket 610.00
Happy Bunny, heavy crazing.......250.00
Humpty Dumpty, cowboy hat 275.00
Night Owl.....................................75.00
Panda, black and white 325.00

California Original

Koala on Stump.........................275.00
Superman in Phone Booth,
	c1970....................................495.00
Tigger 170.00
Winnie-the-Pooh...........................95.00

Certified International

Barney Rubble.............................65.00
Bugs Bunny.................................85.00
Christmas Bugs............................95.00
Christmas Tweety, in stocking.....125.00
Dino and Pebbles.........................65.00
Fred Flintstone 65.00
Talking Tax..................................95.00

Doranne

Dragon......................................275.00
Hound Dog, yellow 30.00

Fitz and Floyd

Autumn Woods Rabbit 70.00
Busy Bunnies Tree.....................145.00
Christmas Wreath Santa 150.00
Cotton Tailors Hat Box 95.00
English Garden Wheelbarrow 145.00
Father Christmas........................270.00
Herb Garden Rabbit 95.00
Hydrangea Bears 150.00
Rocking Horse............................265.00
Rose Terrace Rabbit 80.00
Santa in Airplane 195.00
Santa's Magic Workshop.............165.00
Sock Hoppers............................290.00
Unicorn.......................................85.00

Harley

Gas Tank.....................................65.00
Hog...425.00

James Pottery, Henry James

Boo Boo.....................................325.00
Mrs. Potato Head,
	Hasbro license......................250.00

Looney Tunes

Bugs Bunny.................................20.00
Daffy Duck...................................20.00

McCoy

Clyde Dog..................................165.00

Corn 90.00
Football Boy 220.00
Friendship Spaceship.................165.00
Lantern Stagecoach 40.00
Mammy 90.00
Santa, large...........................2,500.00

Metlox

Apple, yellow 150.00
Chef Pierre 65.00
Cookie Bandit.............................215.00
Fido 245.00
Francine 95.00
Frosty 65.00
Hippo, gray................................550.00
Miss Cutie Pie 240.00
Mona-Monocionius Rose 150.00
Panda Bear 95.00
Puddles, yellow coat 35.00
Raggedy Andy............................165.00
Squirrel, pine cone 95.00
Tulip 425.00

Miscellaneous

California Cleminsons, Card King,
	gold trim on hearts................400.00
Cardinal, French Chef 225.00
Clay Art, Humpty Dumpty...........125.00
Enesco, Sugar Town
	General Store 60.00
Fredericksburg Art Pottery,
	Dutch Windmill 75.00
Hallmark, Maxine 135.00
Hoan, Disney Chef Mickey..........110.00
Hull, Gingerbread Boy.................145.00
Kellogg's, Tony the Tiger 80.00
LA Pottery, Bernadine..................32.00
Lantz, Walter, Woody
	Woodpecker head, Home Shopping
	Channel, 1990 ....710.00
North America Ceramics,
	dinosaur, blue.........................85.00
Pfaltzgraff, cookie car, brown,

Morton Pottery, Clown $25.

mkd "CJ-1" 175.00
Pottery Guild, Dutch boy 125.00
Purinton, intaglio 75.00
Robinson Ransbottom,
	Hootie Owl.............................125.00
San Jose Potteries,
	Southern Belle......................145.00
Sears Roebuck,
	Baker Girl with Cat, 1975 ....75.00
Terrace Ceramics,
	Mugsey, orig paper label.......185.00
Vandor, Popeye 395.00
Weller, Pierre 85.00

Regal China

Churn Boy..................................245.00
Humpty Dumpty, #707 ....220.00
Jim Beam, cylinder......................90.00
Quaker Oats...............................145.00

Shawnee

Mugsey 475.00
Puss 'n' Boots 275.00
Smiley, blue collar
	and black hooves 270.00

Treasure Craft

Birdhouse....................................45.00
Cactus...45.00
Flop Ear Rabbit 50.00
Humpty Dumpty 45.00
Monk, Thou Shalt Not Steal 45.00
Noah's Ark 65.00
Peter Pumpkin Eater....................45.00
Pink Panther 175.00

Twin Winton

Elf, Collector Series 175.00
Gunfighter Rabbit,
	Collector Series....................250.00
Ranger Bear................................45.00

Warner Brothers

Hole Sweet Hole 85.00
Superman 95.00
Tweety on Flour Sack 85.00

Coors Pottery

Collecting Hints: Coors Pottery collectors concentrate on cookie jars and the bright, solid-colored dinnerware lines made by the company in the tradition of Bauer and Homer Laughlin's Fiesta. Kitchen collectors focus on the company's utilitarian products.

Coors products were meant to be used; and they were. Look for those pieces that still have bright and complete decorations. Add 10% if a period paper sales label is still attached.

History: J.J. Herold, a former designer and manager for companies such as J.B. Owens, Roseville Pottery and Weller Pottery, moved to Golden, CO, late in the first decade of the 20th century. His experiments in making pottery from local clay attracted the attention of Adolph Coors, a brewery owner in the area. In 1910, Coors offered Herold the use of his abandoned Colorado Glass Works plant. Shortly thereafter, Herold founded the Herold China and Pottery Company for the purpose of making ovenproof china cooking utensils.

Herold left in January 1912 to work for Western Pottery Company in Denver. Coors and other stockholders kept the plant open and expanded its product line to include spark plugs and scientific wares. Herold Pottery also was known as the Golden Pottery. By 1914, a line of chemical porcelain products was available. Herold returned for a one-year stint as manager in 1915 and left again to work for Guernsey Earthenware Company (Cambridge Art Pottery). An injunction prevented Guernsey from using formulas Herold had learned about while at Golden.

In 1920, the company's name legally became Coors Porcelain Co. The firm continued to concentrate on chemical, industrial and scientific porcelain products. The household cooking line was trademarked "Thermo-Porcelain." A Thermo-Porcelain white hotel-ware line was developed, one result of which was Coors involvement in the manufacturer of dinnerware and other kitchen accessories.

In the 1930s, Coors introduced six colored, decorated dinnerware lines: Coorado, Golden Ivory, Golden Rainbow, Mello-Tone, Rock-Mount and Rosebud Cook-N-Serve. The dinnerware had a high-gloss, colored glaze; vases tended to be matte glazed. When Prohibition ended in 1933, Coors also began making accessories for the tavern trade.

Dinnerware production stopped when the company switched to wartime production in 1941. When the war was over, the company manufactured some ovenware, teapots, coffeemakers, beer mugs, ashtrays and novelty items, but no dinnerware. Coffeemakers, ovenware, teapots and vases were discontinued in

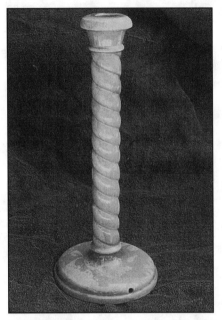

Lamp base, yellow lustre, 17", 1920s, $65.

the 1950s, mugs in the early 1960s and ashtrays by the late 1970s. Herman Coors, third son of Adolph Coors, founded the H.F. Coors Co., at Englewood, CA, in 1925. It was an entirely separate company from Coors Porcelain Co. H.F. Coors made hotel and institutional commercial pottery, dolls' heads, plumbing fixtures and wall tiles.

References: Carol and Jim Carlton, *Colorado Pottery*, Collector Books, 1994; Robert H. Schneider, *Coors Rosebud Pottery*, published by author, 1984.

Periodical: *Coors Pottery Newsletter*, 3808 Carr Pl. N., Seattle, WA 98103.

Mello-Tone: Produced in the late 1930s and early 1940s. Pastel colors of azure blue, canary yellow, coral pink and spring green. Pieces were marked with the "Rising Sun" backstamp.

Cereal Bowl, 6-1/2" d, coral pink ...12.00
Cup and Saucer, spring green 20.00
Gravy, attached underplate,
   azure blue..............................25.00
Pitcher, 2 qt, coral pink..................30.00
Plate
   4" d, bread and butter,
     canary yellow 9.00
   7" d, dinner, azure blue...........15.00
Platter, 15" l, oval, canary yellow ..20.00
Vegetable Bowl, 9" d,
   spring green 24.00

Rosebud: Introduced in 1934. Embossed and hand-painted rosebud and leaves on solid-colored dinnerware. Original four colors were blue, green, rose and yellow. Ivory and orange colors were added later.

Baking Pan, 12-1/4" x
   8-1/4" x 2-1/4".........................35.00
Bean Pot, cov, yellow...................25.00
Cake Knife, 10" l, maroon, yellow
   rosebud, 3 green leaves..........35.00
Cake Plate, blue...........................35.00
Casserole, cov, 3-1/2 pt, green.....45.00
Cereal Bowl, 6" d, yellow 15.00
Cookie Jar, cov, yellow 50.00
Custard Cup, blue 15.00
Fruit Bowl, 5" d............................15.00
Honey Pot, cov.............................35.00
Mixing Bowl, handle 40.00
Pie Baker 20.00
Plate
   6" d, bread and butter 12.00
   7" d, salad 15.00
   9" d, dinner.............................20.00
Saucer...10.00
Soup Plate, 8" d 20.00
Sugar, cov...................................30.00
Teapot, large, rose.......................65.00
Utility Jar, cov, yellow...................30.00

Cowan Pottery

Collecting Hints: Cowan was primarily a designer of modernistic products. In addition to focusing on design, he also worked on developing glaze formulas that complemented his work. Several pieces were made in limited numbers.

Focus on pieces that have delicate decorative elements. Aesthetics is a major pricing factor. A slight difference in glaze or assembly can affect price. In 1931, Cowan brought together a group of distinguished potters including Alexander Blazys, Paul Bogatay, Thelma Frazier, Waylande Gregory, A.D. Jacobson and Margaret Postgate. Pieces made by these artists while at Cowan often command premium prices.

History: R. Guy Cowan operated a pottery on Nicholson Avenue in Lakewood, OH, a suburb of Cleveland, between 1912 and 1917. After a period of service during World War I, Cowan returned to Lakewood and reopened the pottery. Within a short period, Cowan's gas-well ran dry, necessitating a move to Rocky River.

While working in Lakewood, Cowan used red clay for his pieces. But upon arriving in Rocky River he switched to high-fired porcelain. By 1921, he had developed more than 1,000 outlets for his wares. A commercial line was launched in the early 1920s. By 1925, Cowan was involved in the manufacture of dinnerware, console sets and figures. One of his clients was Wahl Pen Company for whom he made ceramic desk sets. The 1930 product line included planters and ivy jars.

In addition to utilitarian products, Cowan also made art pottery. He exhibited regularly at the Cleveland Museum of Art, the Pennsylvania Academy of Art and the Metropolitan Museum of Art, winning numerous awards for his work. In 1930, Cowan Potters, Inc., was organized as an artists' colony. The project lasted only one year, a period during which many of the most desirable Cowan pieces were produced. Cowan ceased operations in December 1931.

Initially, the name "Cowan Pottery" was incised on pieces. Later a black stamp with "Cowan" or "Cowan Potteries" or a mark with the initials "R.G." and "Cowan" in a circle were used.

References: Susan and Al Bagdade, *Warman's American Pottery and Porcelain*, Wallace-Homestead, 1994; Ralph and Terry Kovel, *Kovels' American Art Pottery*, Crown Publishers, 1993; Leslie Pina, *Pottery*, Schiffer Publishing, 1994; Tim and Jamie Saloff, *Collector's Encyclopedia of Cowan Pottery*, Collector Books, 1994.

Videotape: Ralph and Terry Kovel, *Collecting with the Kovels: American Art Pottery*, available from producers (P.O. Box 22990, Beachwood, OH 44122).

Museums: Cowan Pottery Museum, Rocky River Public Library, Rocky River, OH; Everson Museum of Art, Syracuse, NY.

Bookends, pr, Sunbonnet Girl
   Green, gold, fine
     crystalline streaking................450.00
     Yellow glaze 225.00
Candlesticks, pr
   Gazelles, tan 150.00

Sea Horses, green 65.00
Cigarette Holder, sea horse, aqua 35.00
Compote, 2" h, diamond shape,
   tan, green lining......................35.00
Console Bowl, 17" d, 3" h, cream,
   pink lining, minor base chips ...35.00
Cup and Saucer, melon dec,
   tan glaze 40.00
Figure, Elephant.........................225.00
Flower Frog, 11" h, flamingo,
   perforated base, white glaze,
   die-stamped mark..................350.00
Plaque, hanging, 11-1/2" d, plain,
   turquoise glaze 200.00
Soap Dish, 4" d, sea horse, blue...65.00
Trivet, 6-1/2" d, scalloped rim,
   bust of young girl framed by
   flowers, sgd 295.00
Vase
   5" h, fan, apple green,
     gold specks 85.00
   5-1/2" h, ftd, fluted, blue luster .95.00
   6-1/4" h, bulbous, yellow 50.00

Cow Collectibles

Collecting Hints: Image is everything. It makes no difference if the object was made yesterday or 100 years ago, just so long as it pictures the collector's favorite bovine.

Cow collectors collect in quantity. Advertising and folk art collectors also vie for pieces displaying cow images. Cow creamers, some dating as early as the 18th century, are a favorite specialized collecting category. Antiques devotees focus on early examples; most cow collectors are perfectly willing to settle for 20th-century examples.

For an object to be considered a true cow collectible, it must either be in the shape of a cow or have a picture of a cow on its surface. Milk- and dairy-related items without a cow image are not cow collectibles. T-shirts with cow sayings fall into a gray area.

History: The domesticated cow has been around for more than 8,000 years: cows are part of Greek mythology, the Egyptians worshipped Hathor the cow-goddess, and the Hindus still venerate the cow as a sacred being. Cows have long been a focal point for artists and sculptors.

Some of the more famous nursery rhymes feature a cow, e.g. "Hey, Diddle, Diddle" and "The House That Jack Built." Poetry and literature are rich with cow references. It is impos-

sible to divorce the cow from the dairy industry. Cow motifs appear throughout a wide range of dairy-product advertising, the three most popular images being the Guernsey, Holstein and Jersey.

There are a number of famous 20th-century cows: early Disney cartoons featured Clarabelle; the dairy industry created Brooksie, Bossie and *La Vache Qui Ri*; and, of course, there is Elsie. When she was at her peak of popularity, only the president of the United States had more public recognition than Elsie the Borden Cow. In the late 1930s, Elsie made her initial appearances in a series of medical journal advertisements for Borden's Eagle Brand condensed milk. Her popularity grew as a result of Borden's 1939-1940 World's Fair exhibition. A 1940 Hollywood appearance further enhanced her national reputation. In 1957, a name-Elsie's-calf contest produced 3 million entries. Borden briefly retired Elsie in the late 1960s, but the public demanded her return. Today, she is once again found on labels, in animated commercials and at live appearances across the country.

Alas, in this age of equality, the fabled bull receives short shrift. With the exception of Walt Disney's Ferdinand and the Schlitz Malt Liquor Bull, the male of the species is relegated to a conspicuous second place.

Reference: Emily Margolin Gwathmey, *Wholly Cow!*, Abbeville Press, 1988.

Periodical: *Moosletter*, 240 Wahl Ave., Evans City, PA 16033.

Bank, cast iron, orig gold paint....225.00
Blotter, 4" x 9-1/4", Cow Brand Baking
   Soda, cow illus, c1920 ....12.00
Booklet, Milk, An All-Round Food,
   Metropolitan Life Insurance, silhouettes on cov, c1930, 8 pgs 3.00
Butter Print, wood, round
   4-1/2" d, standing cow, 1-pc
     turned handle, dark finish 350.00
   5-1/4" d, cow with tree
     and flower, scrubbed white,
     1-pc turned handle.................175.00
Charm, 1" d, Swift's Brookfield, brass,
   emb cow on award base,
   inscribed "June Dairy Month
   Award," early 1900s 17.50
Cookie Jar, cov

Cow Jumped over the Moon,
Doranne 250.00
Elsie the Cow, Pottery Guild,
late 1940s..............................250.00
Purple Cow, Metlox................550.00
Figure, 3" x 5-1/2" x 4", Ferdinand,
rubber, Seiberling, Walt Disney
Enterprises copyright, c1930 ...85.00
Mug, 2-1/2" h, china, white,
full-color illus of Elsie, blue
accent stripe, Juvenile Ware
and Borden copyright, c1940 ...75.00
Pinback Button
Dairy Class '01, black and white
cow and initials "KSAC"............18.00
Borden's Golden Crest Milk,
red, white and blue, gold
lettering, 1930s........................30.00
Farm Maid Milk, red, white
and blue, Junior Member, serial
number, 1930s 20.00
Guernsey's Rich Inheritance,
cow illus, yellow, brown and white,
1930-40 ....20.00
Jerseys for Mine, tan, blue rim,
white lettering, "Compliments of
AJCC" on back paper, c1920 ...25.00
Livestock Steer, blue and white,
blue illus, 1901-12 ....15.00
Sharples Cream Separators,
multicolored, 2 young farm girls
using product in pasture...........50.00
Whitings Milk, red, white,
blue, gold circle accents
around logo, 1930s 20.00
Pitcher
Black, glazed, orig sticker reads
"Ellsworth" 35.00
Stoneware, 8" h......................240.00
Poster
Bull Durham, 19-1/2" x 13-1/2",
includes cow figure.................375.00
Evaporated Milk-Pure Cow's Milk,
black and white illus of cows,

Sugar, open, Purple Cow, Pick-Ohio Hotel, Youngstown, OH, Shenango China $10.

green ground, c1940................25.00
Swift's Annual Fertilizers,
linen, dark blue steer illus
and print, 1920s 75.00
Salt and Pepper shakers, pr, Elsie the
Cow, head and shoulders........85.00
Sugar, cov, figural, Elmer, c1940 ..40.00
Toy
3-1/2" l, ramp walker, plastic,
brown and white, orig sealed
cellophane bag, mkd "Made in Hong
Kong," 1950s...........................15.00
5-1/4" h, Elsie, hard rubber,
jointed wood legs, dark green base
with white name decal, Mespo
Products Co., late 1940s..........85.00

Cowboy Heroes

Collecting Hints: Cowboy hero material was collected and saved in great numbers. Don't get fooled into thinking an object is rare—check carefully. Tom Mix material remains the most desirable, followed closely by Hopalong Cassidy, Roy Rogers and Gene Autry memorabilia. Material associated with the Western stars of the silent era and early talking films still has not achieved its full potential as a collectible.

History: The era when the cowboy and longhorn cattle dominated the Great Western Plains was short, lasting only from the end of the Civil War to the late 1880s. Dime novelists romanticized this period and created a love affair in America's heart for the Golden West.

The cowboy was a prime entertainment subject in motion pictures. William S. Hart developed the character of the cowboy hero—often in love with his horse more than the girl. He was followed by Tom Mix, Ken Maynard, Tim McCoy and Buck Jones. The "B" movie, the second feature of a double bill, was often of the cowboy genre.

In 1935, William Boyd starred in the first of the Hopalong Cassidy films. Gene Autry, "a singing cowboy," gained popularity over the airwaves; by the late 1930s, Autry's Melody Ranch was a national institution on the air as well as on the screen. Roy Rogers replaced Autry as the featured cowboy at Republic Pictures in the mid-1940s. Although the Lone Ranger first starred in radio

shows in 1933, he did not appear in movies until 1938.

The early years of television enhanced the careers of the big three—Autry, Boyd and Rogers. The appearance of the Lone Ranger in shows made specifically for television strengthened the popularity of the cowboy hero. "Gunsmoke," "Wagon Train," "Rawhide," "The Rifleman," "Paladin." "Maverick" and "Bonanza" were just a few of the shows that followed.

By the early 1970s, the cowboy hero had fallen from grace, relegated to reruns or specials. In early 1983, the Library of Congress in Washington, DC, conducted a major show on the cowboy heroes, perhaps a true indication that they are now a part of history.

References: Joseph J. Caro, *Collector's Guide Hopalong Cassidy Memorabilia*, L-W Book Sales, 1992; Bernard A. Drew, *Hopalong Cassidy*, The Scarecrow Press, 1991; Ted Hake, *Hake's Guide to Cowboy Character Collectibles*, Wallace-Homestead, 1994; Jerrell Little, *Cowboy Cap Guns and Guitars*, L-W Book Sales, 1996; Harry L. Rinker, *Hopalong Cassidy*, Schiffer Publishing, 1995; Jim Schleyer, *Collecting Toy Western Guns*, Krause Publications, 1996; Neil Summers, *Official TV Western Book*, *Vol. 1* (1987), *Vol. 2* (1989), *Vol. 3* (1991), *Vol. 4* (1992), The Old West Shop Publishing.

Periodicals: *Collecting Hollywood*, American Collectors Exchange, 2401 Broad St., Chattanooga, TN 37408; *Cowboy Collector Newsletter*, P.O. Box 7486, Long Beach, CA 90807; *Favorite Westerns & Serial World*, Rte. 1, Box 103, Vernon Center, MN 56090; *Westerner*, Box 5232-32, Vienna, WV 26105.

Collectors' Club: Friends of Hopalong Cassidy Fan Club, 6310 Friendship Dr., New Concord, OH 43762.

Museums: Gene Autry Western Heritage Museum, Los Angeles, CA; National Cowboy Hall of Fame and Western Heroes, Oklahoma City, OK; Roy Rogers Museum, Victorville, CA.

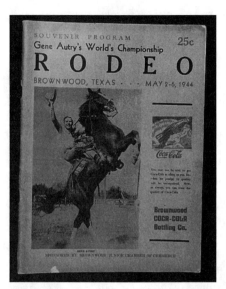

Gene Autry program, *Gene Autry's World's Championship Rodeo*, May 2-6, 1944, Brownwood, TX, Coca-Cola ad and black-and-white photo on cover, 36 pgs, 8-1/2" x 11", $35.

Additional Listings: Western Americana.

Gene Autry

Arcade Card, c1950 ....2.00

Belt, size 28, leather, brown, tooled, floral design, silvered metal buckle, diecut circular silvered metal belt loop, engraved red depiction of Autry and signature, name inscribed inner side, c1940 ....100.00

Belt Buckle, brass, name and figure outlined in red, c1950 ....35.00

Better Little Book, *Gene Autry and the Bandits of Silver Tip*, Whitman, 1940 ....15.00

Big Little Book, Whitman

Gene Autry/Cowboy Detective, 1940, full-color illus 25.00

Gene Autry Makes a New Friend, Tell-A-Tale Book, 28 pgs, 1952 ....20.00

Cap Pistol, 8" l, silvered metal, simulated-pearl handle, c1950 35.00

Comic Book, Vol. 1, No. 12, Feb. 1948, Gene Autry Comics 8.00

Decal, 5" x 7", iron-on, Autry and Champ Junior, black, white and red, c1950 ....8.00

Galoshes, rubber, Cowboy-boot shape, red and white 45.00

Guitar, orig box, Emenee 55.00

Holster, 11", "Gene Autry Flying A Ranch," leather, black, rigid silvered metal with floral pattern and oval blank center, white inscription on belt strip, c1950 ....75.00

Lobby Card, 11" x 14"

"Gene Autry and the Mounties," Columbia, 1950 ....10.00

Silver Canyon, Columbia," 1951 ....8.00

"Sioux City Sue," multicolored, 1950 ....15.00

"Whirlwind," set of eight, red, white, blue and yellow design...........100.00

Lunch Box, 1954, steel with glass bottle, for both 550.00

Magazine

Look, Aug. 1, 1950, "Gene Autry Millionaire Cowboy".................10.00

Screen Stories, May 1948, "The Strawberry Roan," story and photos 5.00

Magic Slate, Lowe.......................65.00

Movie Serial, VHS, "Phantom Empire" 35.00

Paper Dolls, 10-1/2" x 13", Whitman, 4 punch-out figures, 6 uncut clothing pgs, 1950 ....150.00

Pinback Button, 1-1/4" d, celluloid, blue and white photo of Gene, red ground, ribbon with silvered metal horseshoe with horse inside....45.00

Plaque, 4-1/2" x 5-1/2", masonite, full-color photo, beveled edges, metal hanging loop on back, c1950 ..40.00

Plate, 9-1/2" d, china, white, Gene with Champion center, brands border 25.00

Postcard, 2-1/2" x 5", Home of Gene Autry, full color, c1940 ....10.00

Poster, 27" x 41", Rim of the Canyon, Columbia Pictures, Morgan Litho, 1949 ....35.00

Program, *Gene Autry Championship Rodeo*, April 11-16, 1941, 18 pgs, 8-1/2" x 10-1/2", blue photo of Autry and Champion on front cover ..50.00

Puzzle, frame tray, Autry and Champion, Whitman, #2891, c1950 ....8.50

Record

"Gene Autry's Western Classics," 78 RPM, Columbia, 4-record set...45.00

"My Alabama Home," Banner ..14.00

"The Yellow Rose of Texas," Oriole 10.00

Scarf, 18" x 21", silk, purple, green, dark blue and white illus and design, Gene with guitar in horseshoe in corner and Western motifs, 1940s......75.00

School Bag, 10" x 14", vinyl, dark tan pebble-grained design, fabric int, carrying strap, Autry on Champion on front, 1940-50 ....100.00

Sheet Music

"Goodbye, Little Darlin', Goodbye," 9" x 12", 6 pgs, blue tone photo, 1940 copyright 20.00

"You're the Only Star in My Blue Heaven," 9" x 12", small picture

of Gene, large picture of Enoch Light, 1938 ....8.00

Shirt, custom, c1940 ....2,000.00

Songbook, #2, 1934, cover illus....25.00

Thermos.......................................25.00

Tie Bar, brass, portrait of Gene, small Western symbols, 2-3/4 l, c 1950 ....35.00

View-Master Reel, "Gene Autry and His Wonder Horse "Champion," #950, 1950 ....10.00

Wall Plaque.................................25.00

Waste Can, 6" x 7" x 12", oval, white ground, decal inscribed "Gene Autry, America's No. 1 Cowboy and Champion, His Wonder Horse"40.00

Wristwatch 125.00

Writing Pad, 9" x 5-1/2", full color, 1950s 32.00

Hopalong Cassidy

Bedspread, green, chenille 275.00

Book, *Hopalong Cassidy and His Young Friend, Danny*, c1950 ....95.00

Bread Label, Bond Bread............105.00

Birthday Card 35.00

Canasta Set, rotating saddle tray, 2 decks of cards, orig box 275.00

Clothing, child's sweater, button down..........................275.00

Coloring Set, watercolor prints, pictures, stencils, orig box 195.00

Cup, milk glass.............................25.00

Diecut, store display, Hoppy leaning on rock.......................75.00

Knife, 3 blades, black, Hoppy on Topper decal 75.00

Plate, porcelain 155.00

Radio, Arvin, red metal case, embossed image of Hoppy and Topper on front, 1950s..........675.00

Rocking Chair, child's 650.00

Soap, Topper, orig box 125.00

Spurs, Hoppy bust and raised figure on each, price for pr 195.00

Straws, full box.............................40.00

Target Game, tin, orig back holders, 27" h, 16" w 175.00

Watch, black, orig leather band 95.00

Writing Pad, 8" x 10", hard cover, multicolored graphics 65.00

Cisco Kid

Bowl 40.00

Label Sheet, 8" x 8-1/4" folded, holds 16 adventure pictures from Ward's Tip-Top Bread end labels, titled "Bolder & Bullets Story," b&w photo front panel 75.00

Premium, gun, red, white and blue cardboard, Cisco' s picture on handle, clicker mounted inside, advertises TV show and Tip-Top Bread ...40.00

Snack Set, plate and mug.............50.00

Tablet, 8" x 10", color picture on
pink ground, inscribed "From
Your Good Amigo, Duncan
Renaldo—Cisco Kid" 20.00
Tie clasp 15.00
View-Master Reel, Cisco Kid,
Duncan Renaldo, 1950............15.00

Davy Crockett

Badge, orig card 15.00
Bank, 2-1/2" x 2-1/2" x 5/8", dime-
register type, litho metal, full-color
scenes, mid 1950s..................75.00
Bedspread, poplin,
Alamo scenes 225.00
Belt, size 24, leather, diecut brass buckle
with red accents, "Davy Crockett,"
3 repeated long rifles and tooled
designs, mid 1950s..................40.00
Bow Tie 15.00
Cookie Jar, 7" x 8" x 10", china,
raised gold letter name on front,
C. Miller copyright and "55" on
bottom, no lid 75.00
Game, Davy Crockett's Alamo Game,
16 playing cards, 94 paper marker
playing pieces, 8-pg instruction leaflet, 13-1/4" x 17" x 1-1/2" box, Lowell
Toy Corp., mid 1950s 50.00
Glass, 3" h, Crockett on horseback in
brown and yellow, mid 1950s ..15.00
Hat, rabbit fur tail and sides,
plastic top with imprinted Davy
image, 1950s 50.00
Horseshoe Set, 4 rubber horseshoes
with name and Western symbols,
2 rubber bases with wood pegs,
Auburn Toys, mid 1950s..........40.00
Lamp, 7-1/2" h, china, glazed,
4-1/2" x 6-1/2" green base,
felt bottom, 1950s 75.00
Record, "Ballad of Davy Crockett,"
orig envelope, Derby Foods 40.00
Ring, plastic, figural, silvertone, emb
lettering across back................35.00
Ruler, 6", paper, adv Atlas Soap 5.00
School Bag, 11" x 12", fabric, brown, tan
vinyl fringe, vinyl cover with Crockett
scene, brown shoulder strap, brass
buckle, unused, 1950s............75.00
Teepee, full size 65.00
Wallet, 3" x 3-1/2", vinyl, brown,
gold foil-like picture sticker, molded
clear plastic cover, blue accents,
name in red..............................25.00
Wastebasket, litho tin, Indian
fighter pose, 9-1/4" h, 10" oval
opening..................................155.00

Wyatt Earp

Badge, Marshall, metal, orig card..10.00
Gun and Holster set, 8-1/2" l, silvered
white-metal gun with grained white
plastic grips, uses roll caps, leather
holster brown and tan design and

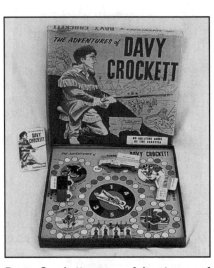

Davy Crockett game, Adventures of
Davy Crockett, Harett-Gilmar, Inc., Far
Rockaway, NY, 1955, $15.

Wyatt Earp name, emb floral design
around belt slots 75.00
Puzzle, frame tray, 11-1/2" x 14-1/2",
full-color photo portrait, Whitman,
1958 copyright..........................25.00
Statue, Hartland 150.00
Sunglasses, 12-1/2" x 19" display
card holding 12 plastic sunglasses
with green lenses, 1" flasher picture
in center of each, Merit Mfg.
Co., 1950-60................................75.00

Wild Bill Hickok

Game
Cavalry and Indians, 14" x 14" board,
punched cardboard disks,
7-1/2" x 14" x 1-1/2" box with
Hickok on horse talking to
Indian Chief..............................40.00
Wild Bill Hickok, Bilt-Rite, 1956 75.00
Map, 24" x 35", paper, "Wild
Bill Hickok Treasure Map," Hickok
drawing and jingles in lower left
corner, Western illus throughout,
shows over 300 treasure sites,
Rand McNally, 1950s 60.00

Hopalong Cassidy Game, Milton Bradley, No. 4047, Wm. Boyd, 1950, $35.

Poster, 27" x 41", full color, red sky
background, "The Ghost Of Cross-
bone Canyon" in red and blue on
yellow background 50.00

Lone Ranger

Adventure Set, The Carson
City Bank Robbery, orig box,
Hubley, 1972 ....22.00
Badge, secret compartment..........45.00
Better Little Book, Whitman
*The Lone Ranger and Dead
Men's Mine*, 1939 ....50.00
*The Lone Ranger and the Black
Shirt Highwayman*, 1939..........40.00
Big Little Book, Whitman
*The Lone Ranger and His Horse
Silver*, 1935 ....50.00
*.. The Lone Ranger and The Menace
of Murder Valley*, 1938.............40.00
Binoculars, orig decals 75.00
Book Bag, 10" x 12", Lone
Ranger and Tonto riding across
desert, 1940s 40.00
Calendar, 1939 ....75.00
Cereal Box Cheerios,
Frontiertown 75.00
Clothing, Cowboy Outfit, 5 pcs,
Yankiboy, orig box, 1947.......150.00
Coloring Book, "Lone Ranger Ranch Fun
Book," 8-1/2" x 11", Whitman, 1956,
64 pgs, Cheerios premium 75.00
Comic Book, 2-1/2" x 7", *The Lone
Ranger and the Story of Silver*,
Cheerios premium, 1954 ....8.00
Diecut, store display, Clayton
Moore as Lone Ranger on top
of rearing Silver 75.00
Flashlight, 7" l, red plastic head,
litho scene around side, diecut bullet
shape, 4-pg instruction sheet,
boxed, early 1950s..................75.00
Game
Board, The Lone Ranger &
Tonto Board Game, unopened,
Warren, 1978 ....15.00
Card, Parker Bros., Lone Ranger,
Tonto and Western motifs pictured
on cards, 3-1/2" x 5", 1938.......65.00
Target, Marx, 1946, orig box..250.00
Guitar, orig box 120.00
Gun and Holster set, unknown
maker, MIB 130.00
Hairbrush, late 1930s....................45.00
Harmonica, orig pkg......................45.00
Hat, 11-1/2" x 13" x 3", felt, brown,
molded and starched, red label
attachment, adjustable drawstring,
orig label stitched on brim, Arlington
Co., 1966 copyright 50.00
Manual, Cramer's Lone Ranger
Safety Club, 5-1/4" x 8-1/4",
32 pgs, issued by Cramer's
Butter-Cream Sliced Bread,

1939 copyright 150.00

Mask, 3-1/4" x 14", diecut paper, black, inscribed "Hi Yo Silver," 1938 Lone Ranger copyright, Schultz Butter-Nut Bread and Dolly Madison Cakes on back 60.00

Model, Aurora, 1967, MIB 175.00

Movie and Lobby Card Set, 1956 ....400.00

Noisemaker, horn, 5" l, litho metal, white plastic mouthpiece, "Ichi," Japan, 1960s 15.00

Paint Set, Bradley, c1940, MIB 55.00

Pedometer, boxed 60.00

Pencil, silver, bullet shape 14.00

Pencil Box, 4" x 8-1/2", cardboard, dark brown, Lone Ranger on Silver image, silver signature, late 1930s 35.00

Photo, Silver Cup premium, 1936 ....25.00

Pinback Button, 1", Lone Ranger Safety Scout, silver, blue enamel, c1930 ....20.00

Record, "He Saves Booneville Gold," 78 RPM, 10" x 10" jacket, Decca No. 6, 1952 ....15.00

Record Player, wood 185.00

Ring, filmstrip, orig box and instructions 175.00

Snow Dome, Lone Ranger roping calf 65.00

Spoon, 6", silvered brass, "The Lone Ranger Hi-Yo Silver" on handle, 1938 copyright 35.00

Suspenders, child's, Lone Ranger, Tonto, silver guns and other illus, 1938 patent date 450.00

Target, tin 95.00

Toothbrush Holder, 4" h, plaster, painted, 1938 ....75.00

Toy, Marx, Lone Ranger on rearing Silver, rotating lasso, moving arm holds gun, silver color on tin, 1939 ..395.00

Wristwatch, metal case, clear Plexiglas crystal, Lone Ranger on galloping Silver, black numerals, orig tan leather straps, c1940 ....150.00

Tom Mix

Bandanna, multicolored, Tom on horseback, "Best Wishes-Tom Mix" ..50.00

Banner, 36" x 120", adv Hoot Gibson's "The Silent Rider" 1,430.00

Belt, 26" l, glow-in-the-dark, secret compartment, brass buckle, 1945 ..90.00

Big Little Book, Whitman
Tom Mix and the Hoard of Montezuma, 1937, 424 pgs 30.00
Tom Mix and the Stranger from the South, 1936, 424 pgs 25.00

Coloring Book, 11" x 14", 96 pgs, full-color portrait on cover, Whitman, 1935 ....50.00

Decoder Button, set of five, 3-1/2" x 5"

folder explaining use 50.00

Film, *Fights Redskins,* 1930s, 2-1/4" sq orig box 25.00

Glass Lantern Slide, tinted glass, Tom Mix, Hoot Gibson and Buck Jones, price for set of three ...465.00

Hat, white Stetson, orig box, accompanied by photo 7,700.00

Lariat, orig mailing envelope 40.00

Letterhead, 8" x 11", b&w photo, red with blue outline "Tom Mix Circus" title, bamboo frame under glass, late 1930s 75.00

Magazine, *Motion Picture Classic,* Just Him and Tony story, 1929 ....20.00

Makeup Kit, black diecut cardboard eyeglasses and patch, pink fabric nose, 2 mustaches, 2 tin containers, instruction sheet with 10 example disguises, orig mailing envelope, 1940 Ralston premium 125.00

Paint Book, 8-1/2" x 11-1/2", Whitman, 1940 copyright, unused 40.00

Pennant, 22-1/2" l, felt, Tom Mix Circus and Wild West, Tom on horseback, burnt orange background, streamers on end 120.00

Periscope, 9" l, cardboard, blue, inscribed "Ralston Straight Shooters" 65.00

Premium Catalog, 2-1/2" x 3-1/2", opens to 9" x 14", brown, dark green and white, 1938 ....35.00

Puppet, 9", hand, fabric body, molded vinyl head, 1950-60 ....60.00

Rocking Horse 200.00

Sign, 6" x 24", paper, "Round Up the Boys and Bring 'Em In," orange, yellow, black and white print, Imperial Knife Co., Providence, RI, 1930s 150.00

Spurs, pr, aluminum, stamped "TM Bar Brand," orig mailing box, Ralston premium, c1949 ....50.00

Target, 12" x 15", Indian Blow Gun Target, paper mounted on cardboard, red, white and blue, Ralston Cereal premium, 1940 ....60.00

Telegraph Set, metal telegraph key, blue and white cardboard box with Tom and Ralston photo, 5" x 7-1/2" 40.00

Telescope Set, 3-1/2" l, gold plastic bullet-shaped telescope, magnifying glass, secret-code signaler and birdcall, 9" x 12" instruction sheet, orig mailing box, Ralston premium, 1950 ....150.00

Watch Fob, 1-1/2" x 2", metal, gold finish, shovel and pick design, clear plastic dome inset holds gold ore sample, "Ralston Straight Shooters, Genuine Gold Ore from America's Richest Gold District" and Tom Mix bar brand on reverse,

Ralston premium, c1940 ....75.00

Annie Oakley

Book, *Annie Oakley*, Shannon Garst, Julian Messner, 1968, 186 pgs 10.00

Cabinet Photo, 4" x 6-1/2", holding rifle 250.00

Craft Set, 2 full-color cloth pictures, diecut cardboard frames, unopened sequins and beads, Gabriel, 1955 copyright, 12" x 17" x 1-1/2" box, unused 75.00

Game, 16" x 16" board of adventure map, Annie on horseback center, includes markers, disks, spinner and play money, 8-1/2" x 16-1/2" x 1-1/2" box, Milton Bradley 20.00

Lunch Box, Aladdin, with thermos, 1955 ....400.00

Pinback Button, 7/8" w, b&w portrait surrounded by gray horseshoe, green 4-leaf clover, red slogan "I Use U.M.C. Ammunition to Obtain the Best Results," back paper text "Compliments Of Annie Oakley," brass pin 90.00

Paladin

Business Card, 2" x 3-1/2", black and white 5.00

Game, checkers, 12" sq board with pictures of Paladin on side, plastic playing pieces, plastic bag with label, 1960 ....18.00

Lunch box, Aladdin, with thermos, 1960 ....400.00

Ranger Joe

Gun, 6-1/2" l, wood, painted black, white cardboard grips, yellow lettering, red insignia, fires rubber bands, c1950 ....75.00

Mug, 3" h, glass, white, blue portrait illus, c1950 ....15.00

Red Ryder

Better Little Book, Whitman
Red Ryder and the Secret Canyon, 1948, standard size, 288 pgs, hard cover 18.00
Red Ryder in War on the Range, #1473, 1945, standard size, 352 pgs, hard cover 15.00
Red Ryder, The Fighting Westerner, 1940 ....20.00

Coin, metal, gold, J.C. Penney premium, 1942-45 ....5.00

Gloves, pr, leather, black, white suede fringe, silver Red Ryder depiction, tag with premium offer on reverse, Wells Lamont Corp., sized for 8-10 years old child 50.00

Handkerchief, 11" x 13", white, red, green and tan print design, c1940 ....15.00

Pocket Knife, 3-1/2" l, steel, light yellow marbled plastic inserts, portrait and

name in red on one side, 2 blades,
Camco USA, c1940 ....75.00

Rifleman

Game, Rifleman,
Milton Bradley, 1959 ....20.00

Hat, 11" x 13" x 3", red felt, diecut fabric
label on front with silvery b&w photo
on yellow and red background,
gold dec crown cord with adjustable
chin strap, orig label "Official
Western Hat as seen on TV,"
Tex-Felt, 1958 copyright 75.00

Lunch Box, Aladdin,
with thermos, 1961 ....450.00

Rifle, 36" l, metal and plastic,
Hubley New Flip Special,
orig box, 1958 ....225.00

Rin-Tin-Tin

Book, *Rin-Tin-Tin Book
of Dog Care*, 7" x 10", 182 pgs,
Lee Duncan 40.00

Game, Adventures of Rin-Tin-Tin,
17" x 17" board, playing pieces,
cards and unopened plastic coins,
Transogram, 1955 ....25.00

Little Golden Book, *Rin-Tin-Tin
and Rusty*, 1955 ....8.00

Puzzle, 14" x 18-1/2" assembled,
full-color photo, 7-1/2" x 10" x 2-1/2"
box, Jaymar, 1957 copyright ...40.00

Record, Rinty Breaks Through, 78 RPM,
10" x 10", cardboard cover, Columbia label, 1955 copyright 35.00

Statue, Hartland, 1950s 35.00

View-Master Reel, set of 3 reels with orig
envelopes, 1955 copyright 25.00

Roy Rogers

Advertising Display, 9" x 12-1/2", "Roy
Rogers Cub Hunter Pocket Knives,"
cardboard, c1950 ....90.00

Bank, still
Metal, boot and spur 30.00
Tin litho, Trigger 55.00

Bedspread, 66" x 92", woven, tan,
repeated band design, rope inscription "Roy Rogers and Trigger,"
1940-50 ....125.00

Belt and Holster Set, leather, dark
brown, white accent trims, 7-1/2"
l holster with silvered tin decorative
piece with red glass stone in center,
4 metal bullets, 1940-50 ....60.00

Binoculars, 5" x 6", plastic, black,
2 color decals 30.00

Book
Gopher Creek Gunman 15.00
*Roy Rogers and the Sure
'nough Cowpoke*, Tell-A-Tale,
Whitman, 1950 ....5.00

Camera, box, MIB 45.00

Clock
Alarm, color dial, c1970 ....25.00

Motion, 4" square, Roy and Trigger,
mkd "Ingraham," 1950s 400.00

Clothing
Chaps, vinyl 30.00
Gloves, 9" l, leather, yellow silhouette
of Roy on Trigger, Western motifs,
fringe sides 40.00
Outfit, girl's,
Dale Evans, 2 pcs 80.00
Shirt, boy's size small, cotton,
light blue, dark blue collar and
shoulder, red, green and blue plaid
collar, raised stitched design on front,
green stitched lettering, slash pocket,
mid 1950s 50.00
Vest and Chaps,
boy's, cowhide 60.00

Coin, copper, emb Roy Rogers on front,
Trigger on back, c1950 ....7.50

Coloring Book, 15" x 11",
Roy Rogers and Dale Evans,
color cover, 1952 ....20.00

Curtains, 78" l, 30" w,
beige, 2-panel set 250.00

Diecut, store display,
Roy standing next to Trigger ...75.00

Flashlight 110.00

Game, Roy Rogers
Rodeo Game, 1949 ....125.00

Guitar, wood, full size,
orig case, instruction book 250.00

Gun and Holster Set, Classy, diecast,
8-1/2", nickel-finish pistols with copper figural grips, holster is brown and
black leather with raised detail,
plastic play bullets, leather
tie-downs, 1950s, MIP 800.00

Handkerchief, green and red illus of Roy
and Trigger, white linen 15.00

Harmonica, 1-1/4" x 4-1/4", white plastic

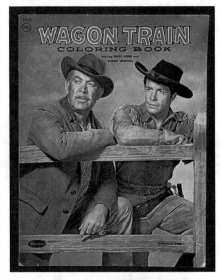

**Wagon Train Coloring Book, Whitman,
#1122, 1959, 18-1/2" x 11", unused, $25.**

and silvered metal, engraved "Good
Luck" and "King of the Cowboys" on
top, orig unopened plastic blister
retail card 50.00

Horseshoe Set, 4 rubber horseshoes,
wood stakes with rubber bases,
2 black, 2 brown, Roy and Trigger
signatures, boxed, unused,
Knox-Rees, 1940-50 ....200.00

Lantern, missing insert 30.00

Lobby Card, 11" x 14"
"In Old Amarillo," 1951 ....10.00
"North of the Great
Divide," 1950 ....8.00
Lunch Pail, Chow Wagon Dome,
1958, King Seeley Thermos, steel
with glass bottle, for both 300.00

Magazine
Movie Life Magazine,
"Life Story in Pix of Roy's
Bride-Dale Evans," story and
b&w photos, March, 1948 ....25.00
Saturday Evening Post, Roy and
Dale on cover, full-page photo inside,
April, 1980 ....8.50

Magazine Ad, *Life,* July 12, 1943 ..10.00

Mug, plastic, Quaker
Oats premium, c1940 ....10.00

Nodder, 6-1/2" h, square green
base, Japan marking, 1962
copyright 165.00

Notebook, 10-1/2" x 13", 2 ring, brown,
tan and maroon picture on white
background, dark brown vinyl trim,
zippered, late 1940s 150.00

Paint Book, 1944 ....12.00

Paper Dolls
1953, Roy and Dale, cut out,
orig folder 65.00
1954, Whitman 55.00

Pen, 5" l, retractable ball-point, silvered
metal top with "RR" initials, light blue
plastic bottom with black Roy and
Trigger and inscription, 1950s .30.00

Pinback Button, celluloid,
real photo of Roy, yellow
background, large size 55.00

Playset, Rodeo Ranch, Marx, orig box,
#3979, 1952 ....275.00

Playset, Rodeo Ranch, Marx, orig box,
#3986R, 1958 ....1,250.00

Pocket Knife, horseshoe, 2 blades,
pearl insert 10.00

Pocket Watch 260.00

Program, *World Championship
Rodeo,* featuring Roy Rogers
and Trigger, 25th year, stories
and photos, 1955 ....15.00

Puzzle, Trigger and Bullet 10.00

Spurs 100.00

Statue, 5", Hartland,
with Trigger, MIB, 1960s 60.00

Statue, 9", Hartland,
with Trigger, MIB, 1950s 175.00

Tent, canvas................................125.00
Thermos, Double
    R bar Ranch, c1950.................75.00
Toy
    Pull, 7" x 9" x 12", covered wagon
      with canvas top and blue metal
      wheels, horse, paper labels,
      N.H. Hill Brass Co. 45.00
    Roy Rogers Mineral city, litho tin,
      post office, bank, hotel,
      Bar-M house, Marx................350.00
Wristwatch, Dale Evans with Buttermilk,
    orig straps, 1950s....................50.00
Yo-Yo, promotion, Roy and Trigger, orig
    wrapper....................................40.00

Straight Arrow

Bandanna, 16-1/2" x 18", red, white and
    blue portrait, Straight Arrow on
    racing horse and Indian motifs,
    red background, inscribed "Kanee-
    wah Fury," 1949 copyright,
    Nabisco premium.....................60.00
Bracelet, "Mystic Wrist Kit," plastic,
    gold, Straight Arrow profile on lid,
    gold-colored metal arrowhead in-
    scribed "Straight Arrow," removable
    secret compartment, key chain and
    gold plastic cowry-shell charm,
    Nabisco premium, 1950........150.00
Game, Target Game, 10-1/2" x 14"
    litho tin board, 3 magnetic feather-
    tipped arrows, spring steel crossbow,
    orig box, National Biscuit Co.,
    c1950.....................................70.00

Wagon Train

Coloring Book, full-color photo
    of Ward Bond and Robert
    Horton front and back, 8 colored pgs,
    Whitman, 1959 ....25.00
Cowboy Outfit, leather gun and holster,
    repeater rifle, metal spurs, 27" x 8" x
    12" box with Ward Bond and Robert
    Horton picture, Leslie Henry 60.00

Western Personalities

Bobby Benson

Big Little Book, *Bobby Benson on the H-
    Bar-O Ranch*, Whitman, 1934 .40.00
Hobby Kit, diecut leather parts, assem-
    bles to gun belt and double holster,
    grained Western motifs, plastic
    stitching cords and rivets, orig pack-
    aging and box, 1954 copyright,
    Street & Smith Publications 50.00

Johnny Mack Brown

Lobby Card, 11" x 14","Rustlers of Red
    Dog,"blue and white, Universal..8.00
Photograph, 8" x 10", full color, yellow
    margin band on top, 1950s movie
    titled "Border Renegades" 15.00

Buffalo Bill

Cabinet Photo, 4-1/4" x 6-1/2", b&w
    close-up portrait, c1890...........75.00

Figurine, 2-1/8", metal, Blenheim..20.00
Show poster 700.00
Daniel Boone, whistle, 6" l, Fess Parker,
    Autolite, instructions on one side of
    box, late 1950s 15.00

William S. Hart

Exhibit Card, 3-1/2" x 5-1/2", yellow-tone
    photo, 1931 ....15.00
Tablet, 6" x 9", brown and white
    portrait, Picture Land Stars
    series, c1920 ....40.00

Gabby Hayes

Coloring Book, 8" x 10-1/2",
    Magic Dial Funny Coloring
    Book, diecut TV screen opening in
    front with disk wheel, Samuel Lowe
    Co., c1950 ....50.00
Dixie Lid, 2-1/4", brown photo,
    rim inscription titled "Wyoming,"
    1947 ....25.00
Puzzle, 10-1/4" x 14-1/2", frame tray,
    full-color illus, Hayes and Kagran
    copyrights, early 1950s 25.00
Rocking horse 200.00

Buck Jones

BB Gun, 36", wood stock with printed
    sundial, metal side with name,
    metal compass insert, Daisy ...90.00
Book
    Better Little Book, *Buck Jones
    and the Two-Gun Kid*, Whitman,
    #1404, 1937 ....30.00
    Big Little Book, *The Fighting Code*,
    #1104, Columbia Pictures, artists,
    Pat Patterson,author, 1934, 160 pgs,
    hardcover, soft spine................35.00
    Rocky Rhodes, Five Star Library
    Series, #15, Engel-Van Wiseman,
    Universal Pictures, artist, adapted by
    Harry Ormiston, 1935, 160 pgs,
    hardcover 35.00
    Songs of the Western Trails,
    60 pgs, words and music, 9" x 12",
    1940 copyright 40.00
Magazine, *Remember When Magazine*,
    8-1/2" x 11", Jones on cover, story
    and b&w photos inside, 1974 ....7.50
Pinback Button, Bucks Jones Club,
    enamel on brass, horseshoe,
    picture in center, 1930s 15.00

Bat Masterson

Arcade Card, c1950 ....2.00
Costume, orig box 125.00
Game, Bat Masterson Board Game,
    Lowell Toy Mfg. Co., 1958.......75.00

Ken Maynard

Autograph, 8" x 10" b&w glossy photo,
    black-inked signature "Ken
    Maynard 1941" 125.00
Big Little Book
    Ken Maynard in Western Justice,

Whitman, #1430, Irwin Myers, artist,
    Rex Loomis, author, 1938, standard
    size, 432 pgs, hardcover.........22.00
    Strawberry Roan, Saalfield,
    Universal Pictures, artist, Grace
    Mack, author, 1934, 4-3/4" x 5-1/4",
    160 pgs, hardcover 22.00
Premium, photo, 9" x 11", color, black
    and white "In Old Santa Fe" scenes
    on back, Dixie.........................30.00

Tim McCoy

Autograph, 8" x 10" b&w glossy photo,
    purple-inked signature "Best Wishes
    Tim McCoy," c1940 ....75.00
Better Little Book, *Tim McCoy and the
    Sandy Gulch Stampede*, Whitman,
    #1490, 1939 ....40.00
Big Little book, *The Prescott Kid*,
    Whitman, #1152, Columbia Pictures,
    artist, adapted by Eleanor Packer,
    1935, 4-5/8" x 5-1/4", 160 pgs,
    hardcover, soft spine...............25.00
Lobby Poster, 11" x 14", set of 8, 1930s
    "Fighting Renegade" 100.00
    "Straight Shooter" 125.00
Premium, photo, 9" x 11", color, b&w
    movie scenes on back, Dixie...15.00
Dale Robertson, platter, 12-1/2" oval,
    china, Western scene includes
    "Star Hotel, Dale Robertson" on top,
    Wellsville China Co., signature
    on bottom 75.00
Will Rogers, figure, 5-7/8" h, wood,
    wearing brown suit, name on front,
    1940s copyright 50.00

Clint Walker

Autograph, 8" x 10" glossy photo,
    blue-inked signature 100.00
Tablet, 8" x 10", "Cheyenne"...........8.00

John Wayne

Arcade Card, c1950 ....2.00
Coin, metal, gold, c1979 ....7.50
Coloring Book, 11" x 15", 32 pgs,
    10 colored pages, Saalfield,
    #2354-15, 1951 copyright 50.00
Holster Set, leather belt,
    2 holsters with name on side,
    orig box, early 1950s 45.00
Knife, memorial, metal and plastic,
    "The Duke—John Wayne
    (1907-1979)" 10.00
Movie Still, 8" x 10",
    black and white 4.00
Pinback Button, 2-1/2" d,
    In Memory of a Great American 5.00
Sheet Music, "Put Your Arms Around
    Me, Honey," 9" x 12", 4 pgs, b&w
    photo of Wayne, Martha Scott and
    Dale Evans, 1937 copyright 15.00
Stationery, b&w drawing,
    includes envelope 2.50

Top, litho tin, 1930s, $18.

Cracker Jack

Collecting Hints: Most collectors concentrate on the pre-plastic era. Toys in the original packaging are very rare. One possibility for specializing is collecting toys from a given decade, for example World War II soldiers, tanks, artillery pieces and other war-related items.

Many prizes are marked "Cracker Jack" or carry a picture of the Sailor Boy and Bingo, his dog. Unmarked prizes can be confused with gumball machine novelties or prizes from Checkers, a rival firm.

History: F.W. Rueckheim, a popcorn store owner in Chicago, introduced a mixture of popcorn, peanuts and molasses at the World's Columbian Exposition in 1893. Three years later, the name Cracker Jack was applied to it. It gained popularity quickly and by 1908 appeared in the lyrics of "Take Me out to the Ball Game." In 1910, Rueckheim included on each box coupons which could be redeemed for prizes. In 1912, prizes were packaged directly in the boxes. The early prizes were made of paper, tin, lead, wood and porcelain. Plastic prizes were introduced in 1948.

The Borden Company's Cracker Jack prize collection includes more than 10,000 examples; but this is not all of them. More examples are still to be found in drawer bottoms, old jewelry boxes and attics. Items currently included in the product boxes are largely paper, the plastic magnifying glass being one exception. The company buys toys in lots of 25 million and keeps hundreds of prizes in circulation

at one time. Borden's annual production is about 400 million boxes.

Reference: Alex Jaramillo, *Cracker Jack Prizes*, Abbeville Press, 1989.

Collectors' Club: Cracker Jack Collectors Association, 108 Central St., Rowley, MA 01969.

Museum: Columbus Science Museum, Columbus, OH.

Baseball Score Counter, 3-1/2" ...150.00
Book, *Cracker Jack Painting & Drawing Book,* Saalfield, 1917, 24 pgs..40.00
Booklet
  Cracker Jack In Switzerland,
  4 pgs, 1926 copyright...............50.00
  Cracker Jack Riddles, red, white and blue cover, 42 pgs, 1920s........60.00
Bookmark, Spaniel,
  brown and white diecut litho tin, mkd "Cracker Jack" 35.00
Box, 7" h, red, white and blue cardboard, 1930s 40.00
Cereal Cup, Ralston.........................5.00
Clicker, aluminum,
  pear shape, 1949 ....35.00
Coin, 1" d, Mystery Club, emb aluminum, presidential profile, back emb "Join Cracker Jack Mystery Club/Save This Coin," 1930s 20.00
Doll, 12" h, vinyl, Vogue Dolls,
  orig unopened display card, 1980 copyright........................35.00
Game, Cracker Jack Toy
  Surprise Game, Milton Bradley, orig box, 1976..........................35.00
Lapel Stud, 1" l, oval, metal, emb Sailor Boy Jack and dog, dark finish, early 1920s 30.00
Lunch Box, metal, Aladdin Industries, with thermos, 1969 ....70.00
Pencil, 3-1/2" l, red name 15.00
Pinback Button, 1-1/4" d, multicolored portrait illus of young lady, back inscribed "Cracker Jack 5¢ Candied Popcorn and Roasted Peanuts," early 1900s..............................60.00
Postcard, 3" x 5-1/2" d, Cracker Jack Bears #7, bears greeting President Roosevelt, 1907 postmark.......25.00
Prize
  Battleship, red enameled white metal, portholes on both sides .17.50
  Binoculars,
  dark finish white metal 12.00
  Carnival Barker, black,
  white and red litho, stand-up turning chance wheel...............50.00
  Gun, Smith & Wesson .38 replica, black finish white metal 20.00
  Magnet, silvered-wire horseshoe magnet, orig red and white paper

Prize whistle, tin, round, $15.

  wrapper mkd "Made in Japan" .15.00
  Man's Shoe, dark finish white metal, hobnail sole design 30.00
  Model T Touring Car, dark-finish white metal..............................35.00
  Owl, red, blue and yellow
  emb stiff paper stand-up, mkd "Cracker Jack".................40.00
  Pocket Watch, dark silver luster white metal
    Ornate back, 9:27 time 30.00
    Plain back, 4:00 time 35.00
  Rocking Chair, yellow enameled litho tin doll furniture chair, curved slat back.......................20.00
  Rocking Horse,
  dark blue wash tint...................20.00
  Scottie, bright silver luster white metal..............................25.00
  Spinner Top, red, white and blue litho, Cracker Jack mystery toy box 35.00
  Train Engine, dark white metal, engine and joined coal car.......20.00
  Washboard,
  yellow enameled tin 15.00
Watch, litho, 1940s, near mint 75.00

Credit Coins and Tokens

Collecting Hints: Specialization is the key to successful collecting. Plan a collection that can eventually be completed. Complete collections are more valuable. Do not buy rusted or damaged charge coins. Unless rare, an inferior piece attracts little interest. Metal charge plates have little collector interest. They should remain affordable for years, which means they'll probably not increase in value.

Most collectors favor credit cards. Scarce and rare cards, when they can be located, are still affordable. National credit cards are eagerly sought—American Express being the most popular. Paper and laminated paper credit cards are very desirable. When it comes to collecting these, don't concern yourself with condition. Go ahead and acquire any you find. They're so difficult to locate that it could take years to find another specimen. Plastic credit cards issued before 1970 are scarce. Occasionally, you'll find a mint condition card. Generally, you'll have to settle for "used." Plastic cards issued after 1980 are of interest to collectors only if in mint condition.

The best collecting hint is collect what you like. You'll provide yourself with years of enjoyment and that's the best investment you'll ever make!

History: Charge coins, the first credit pieces, were first issued in the 1890s. Charge coins are approximately the size of a quarter or half dollar. Because of their size, they were often carried with change. This is why they were commonly referred to as coins.

Charge coins come in various shapes, sizes and materials. Most are square, round or oval, but some are shaped like shirts, socks or hats. They're made from many different materials, including fiber, German silver, celluloid, steel or copper. The issuing stores has its name, monogram or initials on the coin and each coin has a customer identification number. Charge coins were still used as late as 1959.

Metal charge plates were used from the 1930s to the 1950s. These plates look like military dog tags. The front of the plate contains the customer's name, address and account number. The back has a piece of cardboard that carries the store's name and a space for the customer's signature.

Paper credit cards were used in the early 1930s. They were easily damaged, so some companies began laminating them with clear plastic in the 1940s. Laminated cards were issued until the 1950s. Plastic cards, like those we use today, replaced the laminated cards in the late 1950s.

References: Stephen P. Albert and Lawrence E. Elman, *Tokens and Medals*, published by authors, 1991; Glyn V. Farber, *Hickey Brothers Ci-gar Store Tokens*, Token and Medal Society, Inc., 1992; Gerald E. Johnson, *Trade Tokens of Wisconsin*, Krause Publications, 1993; Russell Rulau, *Early American Tokens*, 3rd Edition, Krause Publications, 1991; ——, *Hard Times Tokens*, 4th Edition, Krause Publications, 1992; ——, *Standard Catalog of U.S. Tokens*, Krause Publications, 1994; ——, *U.S. Merchant Tokens*, Krause Publications, 1990.

Periodical: *Credit Card Collector*, 150 Hohldale, Houston, TX 77022.

Collectors' Clubs: Active Token Collectors Organization, P.O. Box 1573, Stone Falls, SD 57101; American Numismatic Association, 818 N. Cascade Ave., Colorado Springs, CO 80903; American Tax Token Society, P.O. Box 260170, Lakewood, CO 80226; American Vecturist Association, P.O. Box 1204, Boston, MA 02104; Indiana, Kentucky & Ohio Token & Medal Collectors, 1725 N. 650 West, Columbia City, IN 46725; New Jersey Exonumia Society, 112 Carlton Ave., Westmont, NJ 08108; Token & Medal Society, Inc., P.O. Box 366, Bryantown, MD 20617.

Museum: Museum of the American Numismatic Association, Colorado Springs, CO.

Cards

Abraham & Straus, A & S, hat shape 20.00
American Express
1959, paperboard, April 30 .... 425.00
1971, green, large centurion profile 22.00
1974, green, The Money Card in center 20.00
1975, gold, Executive Card 30.00
Arco, Lifetime Credit Card, gold top 22.00
Bloomingdale's, white, tan border ... 6.00
Boggs & Buhl, B & B, oval, white metal 20.00
Carte Blanche, 1968, First National City Bank 25.00
Chevron, 2 attendants servicing car, 1967 .... 13.00
Conrad's, picture of store, round ... 20.00
Diners Club
1962, red top 50.00
1966, colored blocks, blue top 48.00
General Tire, 1953, paperboard, calendar on back 25.00
Gimbels, gold card 5.00
Horace Partridge, round, copper ... 15.00

Credit Card Token, E. Keller & Sons, Allentown, PA, brass, $8.

John Wanamaker, metal charge plate, carrying case 22.00
Lit Brothers
Blue and white stripes 8.00
Metal charge plate, leather carrying case 20.00
Scalloped, oval, 1921 .... 20.00
Macy's, red star 5.00
Midwest Bank Card, late 1960s 10.00
Mobilgas, 1951, paperboard 62.00
Montgomery Ward, punched data char-all card 10.00
Playboy Club International, 1979, gold 8.00
R.A. McWhirr, oval, white metal, 3 digit account number 17.50
R.H. White Co, RWWCo, irregular pear shape 25.00
Saks Fifth Avenue, paperboard 22.00
Sinclair, 1970, waving dinosaur, red top 10.00
Standard Oil, 1965, emb customer's address 15.00
Tresler Comet, photo of Cincinnati 10.00
TWA, 1974, getaway card, couple in swim suits holding hands 12.00
Uni-Card, 1969, emb 23.00
Visa, hologram 3.50

Tokens

C.F. Massey, Rochester, MN, interlocking CFM logo, white metal, octagonal 14.00
L. Bamberger & Co., celluloid 225.00
Gimbel Bros., rect, lion and shield 10.00
Jordan March Co., J.M. Co., logo, irregular oval 17.00
Nathan Snellenberg, N.S. & Co., logo, irregular circle, white metal 10.00
Plotkin Bros., Boston, white metal, lion's head over shield with PB logo, rect 16.00
Strawbridge & Clothier, arrowhead shape 25.00

D

Degenhart Glass

Collecting Hints: Degenhart pressed glass novelties are collected by mold (Forget-Me-Not toothpick holders or all Degenhart toothpick holders), by individual colors (Rubina or Bloody Mary) or by group colors (opaque, iridescent, crystal or slag).

Correct color identification is a key factor when collecting Degenhart glass. Because of the slight variations in the hundreds of colors produced at the Degenhart Crystal Art Glass factory from 1947 to 1978, it is important for beginning collectors to learn to distinguish Degenhart colors, particularly the green and blue variations. Seek guidance from knowledgeable collectors or dealers. Side-by-side color comparison is extremely helpful.

Later glass produced by the factory can be distinguished by the "D" in a heart trademark or a "D" by itself on molds where there was insufficient space for the full mark. Use of the "D" mark began around 1972; by late 1977, most of the molds had been marked. From c1947 to 1972, pieces were not marked except for owls and the occasional piece hand stamped with a block letter "D" as it came out of the mold. This hand stamping was used from 1967 to 1972.

Collecting unmarked Degenhart glass made from 1947 to c1970 poses no problem once a collector becomes familiar with the molds and colors which were used during that period. Some of the most desirable colors, such as Amethyst & White Slag, Amethyst Carnival and Custard Slag, are unmarked. Keep in mind that some colors, e.g., Custard (opaque yellow), Heliotrope (opaque purple) and Tomato (opaque orange red), were used repeatedly and both marked and unmarked pieces can be found, depending on production date.

History: John (1884-1964) and Elizabeth (1889-1978) Degenhart operated the Crystal Art Glass factory of Cambridge, OH, from 1947 to 1978. The factory specialized in reproduction pressed glass novelties and paperweights. More than 50 molds were worked by this factory including 10 toothpick holders, five salts and six animal-covered dishes of various sizes. When the factory ceased operation, many of the molds were purchased by Boyd Crystal Art Glass in Cambridge. Boyd has issued pieces in many new colors and has marked them all with a "B" in a diamond.

References: Gene Florence, *Degenhart Glass and Paperweights*, Degenhart Paperweight and Glass Museum, 1982; Ellen T. Schroy, *Warman's Glass*, 2nd Edition, Wallace-Homestead, 1995.

Collectors' Club: The Friends of Degenhart, Degenhart Paperweight and Glass Museum, Inc., 65323 Highland Hills Rd., P.O. Box 186, Cambridge, OH 43725.

Museum: The Degenhart Paperweight and Glass Museum, Inc., Cambridge, OH. The museum displays all types of Ohio valley glass.

Reproduction Alert: Although most of the Degenhart molds were reproductions themselves, there are contemporary pieces that can be confusing, such as Kanawha's bird salt and bow slipper; L.G. Wright's mini-slipper, Daisy & Button salt and 5-inch robin-covered dish; and many other contemporary American pieces. The 3-inch bird salt and mini-pitcher also are made by an unknown glassmaker in Taiwan.

Owl, Crown Tuscan, 3-1/2", $35.

Animal-Covered Dish
 Hen, 3", intro 1968, mkd 1973
  Dark green 27.00
  Mint Green 20.00
  Sapphire Blue 21.00
 Robin, intro 1960,
  mkd 1972, Taffeta 50.00
 Turkey, intro 1971, mkd 1972
  Crown Tuscan 50.00
  Custard 62.00
Bell, Bicentennial, intro 1974, mkd 1974
 Amethyst 5.00
 Heatherbloom 5.00
 Ivorine 12.00
Candy Dish, cov, Wildflower
  pattern, intro 1971, mkd
  1972, Twilight Blue 30.00
Coaster, intro 1974,
  mkd 1975, crystal 8.00
Creamer and Sugar,
  Texas, intro 1962, mkd 1972
 Pine Green 45.00
 Pink 50.00
Cup Plate
 Heart and Lyre, intro 1965,
  mkd c1977
  Cobalt blue 10.00
  Mulberry 15.00
 Seal of Ohio, intro 1971, mkd c1977
  Amethyst 14.00
  Opalescent 15.00
  Sunset 12.00
Hand, intro 1949, mkd c1975
 Blue and White 20.00
 Crown Tuscan 20.00
 Tomato 32.00
Hat, Daisy and Button, intro 1974,
  mkd 1972
 Milk Blue 12.00
 Opalescent 15.00
 Vaseline 14.00
Jewelry Box, heart shape, intro 1964,
  mkd 1972
 Crown Tuscan 50.00
 Light Chocolate Creme 35.00
 Old Lavender 24.00
Owl, intro 1967, mkd 1967
 Bluebell 28.00
 Charcoal 38.00
 Ivorne 32.00
 Midnight Sun 30.00
 Nile Green Opal 45.00
Paperweight, by John or Charles
  Degenhart
 Cartoon Characters 175.00
 Flowerpot 80.00
 Morning Glories 80.00
 Name Weight 35.00
 Rose, red and white 300.00

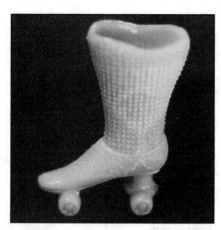

Skate Boot, 1961, mkd 1974, reproduction of 1885 skate by Central Glass Works, $30.

Window Weight, overlay.........390.00
Portrait Plate, intro and mkd 1974,
   crystal 34.00
Salt
   Bird, 1-1/2" h, intro 1966,
   mkd 1972, Orchid......................15.00
   Daisy and Button, intro 1970, mkd
   1972
      Amethyst..............................13.00
      Lime Ice 15.00
   Star and Dewdrop, intro 1952,
   mkd 1972
      Henry's Blue.........................15.00
      Lemon Opal 20.00
      Sapphire Blue 16.00
Tomahawk, intro 1947, mkd c1975,
   Custard Maverick.....................58.00
Tiger, lavender blue........................33.00
Toothpick Holder
   Basket, intro 1963, mkd c1974,
   milk white 18.00
   Beaded Oval, intro 1967, mkd 1972
      Fog.......................................12.00
      Old Lavender 22.00
   Colonial Drape and Heart, intro 1961,
   mkd 1974
      Amber 13.00
      Clear 13.00
      Custard 18.00
      Ruby.....................................20.00
   Elephant's Head, intro c1957,
   mkd 1972, Jade........................50.00
   Forget-Me-Not, intro 1965, mkd 1972
      April Green #1 ....17.00
      Caramel 10.00
      Heatherbloom 20.00
      Misty Green..........................10.00
      Toffee...................................22.00
   Heart, crystal 12.00
Wine, Buzz Saw, intro 1967, mkd 1973,
   Pistachio 20.00

Depression Glass

Collecting Hint: Many collectors specialize in one pattern; others collect by a particular color.

History: Depression glass was made from 1920 to 1940. It was an inexpensive machine-made glass and was produced by several companies in various patterns and colors. The number of forms made in different patterns also varied.

The colors varied from company to company. The number of items made in each pattern also varied. Knowing the proper name of a pattern is the key to collecting. Collectors should be prepared to do research.

References: Gene Florence, *Collectible Glassware from the 40's, 50's & 60's, 4th Edition*, Collector Books, 1997; ——, *Collector's Encyclopedia of Depression Glass, 13th Edition*, Collector Books, 1997; ——, *Elegant Glassware of the Depression Era, 7th Edition*, Collector Books, 1996; ——, *Kitchen Glassware of the Depression Years, 5th Edition*, Collector Books, 1995; ——, *Pocket Guide to Depression Glass & More, 10th Edition*, Collector Books, 1996; ——, *Stemware Identification*, Collector Books, 1996; ——, *Very Rare Glassware of the Depression Years, 1st Series* (1988, 1990 value update), *2nd Series* (1990), *3rd Series* (1993, 1995 value update), *4th Series* (1995), *5th Series* (1996), Collector Books; Ralph and Terry Kovel, *Kovels' Depression Glass & American Dinnerware Price List, 5th Edition*, Crown, 1995; Carl F. Luckey and Mary Burris, *Identification & Value Guide to Depression Era Glassware, 3rd Edition*, Books Americana, 1994; Naomi L. Over, *Ruby Glass of the 20th Century*, Antique Publications, 1990, 1993-94 value update; Ellen T. Schroy, *Warman's Glass, 2nd Edition*, Wallace-Homestead, 1995; ——, *Warman's Depression Glass*, Krause Publications, 1997; Kent G. Washburn, *Price Survey, 4th Edition*, published by author, 1994; Hazel Marie Weatherman, *Colored Glassware of the Depression Era, Book 2*, published by author, 1974, available in reprint; ——, *1984 Supplement & Price Trends for Colored Glassware of the Depression Era, Book 1*, published by author, 1984.

Periodical: *The Daze*, Box 57, Otisville, MI 48463.

Collectors' Clubs: Canadian Depression Glass Club, P.O. Box 104, Mississaugua, Ontario L53 2K1 Canada; National Depression Glass Association, P.O. Box 8264, Wichita, KS 67208; 20-30-40 Society Inc., P.O. Box 856, La Grange, IL 60525; Western Reserve Depression Glass Club, 8669 Courtland Dr., Strongsville OH 44136.

Videotape: *Living Glass, Popular Patterns of the Depression Era, Vols. I* and *II*, Ro Cliff Communications, 1993.

Reproduction Alert: Because of renewed interest in collecting Depression glass, many reproductions are surfacing. Most reproductions are made in colors not used for original pieces. However, the reproductions are sometimes made in the original molds and often are marked. Several patterns have been reproduced in original colors but in slightly different molds. Knowledge of patterns, colors and markings is very important.

Send a self-addressed stamped business envelope to *The Daze* and request a copy of their glass reproduction list. It is one of the best bargains in the collectibles field.

Note: Prices listed are for pieces in mint condition—no chips, scratches, etc.

Adam: Jeannette Glass Co., Jeannette, PA, 1932 to 1934. Made in crystal, Delphite blue, green, pink, some topaz and

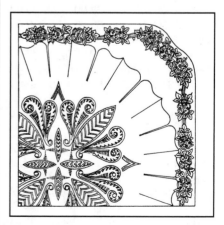

Adam

yellow. Reproductions: † Butter Dish in pink and green.

Item	Green	Pink
Ashtray, 4-1/2" d	25.00	32.00
Berry Bowl, small	18.00	16.00
Bowl, 9" d, cov	85.00	75.00
Bowl, 9" d, open	45.00	30.00
Bowl, 10" l, oval	40.00	40.00
Butter Dish, cov †	325.00	95.00
Cake Plate, 10" d, ftd	32.00	30.00
Candlesticks, pr, 4" h	125.00	100.00
Candy Jar, cov, 2-1/2" h	100.00	95.00
Casserole, cov	90.00	75.00
Cereal Bowl, 5-3/4" d	46.00	46.00
Coaster, 3-1/4" d	22.00	32.00
Creamer	22.00	20.00
Cup	22.00	24.00
Dessert Bowl, 4-3/4" d	18.00	16.00
Iced Tea Tumbler, 5-1/2" h	60.00	65.00
Lamp	285.00	265.00
Pitcher, 32 oz, round base	-	125.00
Pitcher, 32 oz, 8" h	48.00	45.00
Plate, 6" d, sherbet	9.50	9.00
Plate, 7-3/4" d, salad, sq	17.00	17.00
Plate, 9" d, dinner, sq	30.00	32.00
Plate, 9" d, grill	20.00	20.00
Platter, 11-3/4" l, rect	32.00	30.00
Relish Dish, 8" l, divided	27.00	20.00
Salt and Pepper Shakers, pr, 4" h	100.00	80.00
Saucer, 6" sq	7.00	7.00
Sherbet, 3"	40.00	35.00
Sugar, cov	48.00	42.00
Tumbler, 4-1/2" h	28.00	30.00
Vase, 7-1/2" h	60.00	250.00
Vegetable Bowl, 7-3/4" d	30.00	30.00

Fortune: Hocking Glass Co., Lancaster, OH, 1937 to 1938. Made in crystal and pink.

Item	Crystal	Pink
Berry Bowl, 4" d	5.00	6.00
Berry Bowl, 7-3/4" d	15.00	15.00
Bowl, 4-1/2" d, handle	4.50	4.50
Bowl, 5-1/4" d, rolled edge	6.00	6.50
Candy Dish, cov, flat	22.50	25.00
Cup	7.50	10.00
Dessert Bowl, 4-1/2" d	4.50	4.50

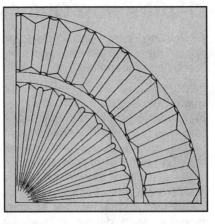

Fortune

Item	Crystal	Pink
Juice Tumbler, 5 oz, 3-1/2" h	8.00	10.00
Plate, 6" d, salad	5.00	12.50
Plate, 8" d, luncheon	17.50	17.50
Salad Bowl, 7-3/4" d	15.00	15.00
Saucer	4.00	6.50
Tumbler, 9 oz, 4" h	10.00	10.00

Harp: Jeannette Glass Co., Jeannette, PA, 1954 to 1957. Made in crystal, crystal with gold trim, limited pieces made in ice blue, iridescent white, pink and shell pink.

Item	Crystal	Other Colors
Ashtray	4.50	-
Cake Stand, 9" d	25.00	35.00
Coaster	4.50	-
Cup	26.00	-
Parfait	18.00	-
Plate, 7" d	14.00	12.00
Saucer	10.00	-
Snack Set, cup, saucer, 7" plate	47.00	-
Tray, 2 handles, rectangular	35.00	30.00
Vase, 7-1/2" h	25.00	-

Lake Como: Hocking Glass Co., Lancaster, OH, 1934 to 1937. Made in opaque white with a blue scene.

Harp

Lake Como

Item	White
Cereal Bowl, 6" d	14.00
Creamer, ftd	31.00
Cup, regular	30.00
Cup, St. Denis	30.00
Plate, 7-1/4" d, salad	20.00
Plate, 9-1/4" d, dinner	30.00
Platter, 11" d	65.00
Salt and Pepper Shakers, pr	45.00
Saucer	12.00
Saucer, St. Denis	12.00
Soup Bowl, flat	90.00
Sugar, ftd	32.00
Vegetable Bowl, 9-3/4" l	60.00

Moroccan Amethyst: Hazel Ware, division of Continental Can, 1960s. Made in amethyst.

Item	Amethyst
Ashtray, 3-1/4" d, round	5.75
Ashtray, 3-1/4" w, triangular	5.75
Ashtray, 6-7/8" w, triangular	10.00
Ashtray, 8" w, square	14.00
Bowl, 5-3/4" w, deep, square	10.00
Bowl, 6" d, round	8.50
Bowl, 7-3/4" l, oval	17.50
Bowl, 7-3/4" l, rectangular	14.00
Bowl, 7-3/4" l, rectangular, metal handle	17.50
Bowls, 10-3/4" d	30.00
Candy, cov, short	35.00
Candy, cov, tall	32.00
Chip and Dip, 10-3/4" and 5-3/4" bowls in metal frame	40.00
Cocktail Shaker, chrome lid	30.00
Cocktail, stirrer, 16 oz, 6-1/4" h, lip	30.00
Cup	5.00
Fruit Bowl, 4-3/4" d, octagonal	9.00
Goblet, 9 oz, 5-1/2" h	10.00
Ice Bucket, 6" h	35.00
Iced Tea Tumbler, 16 oz, 6-1/2" h	16.00
Juice Goblet, 5-1/2 oz, 4-3/8" h	9.00
Juice Tumbler, 4 oz, 2-1/2" h	10.00

Old Fashioned Tumbler,
8 oz, 3-1/4" h 14.00
Plate, 5-3/4" d, sherbet.............4.50
Plate, 7-1/4" d, salad.................4.75
Plate, 9-3/4" d, dinner................7.00
Punch Bowl 85.00
Relish, 7-3/4" l 14.00
Salad Fork and Spoon..................12.00
Sandwich Plate, 12" d,
metal handle 15.00
Saucer...1.00
Sherbet, 7-1/2 oz, 4-1/4" h 8.00
Snack Plate, 10" l, fan shaped,
cup rest......................................8.00
Snack Set, square plate, cup 12.00
Tumbler, 9 oz 10.00
Tumbler, 11 oz, 4-1/4" h,
crinkled bottom 12.00
Tumbler, 11 oz, 4-5/8" h................12.00
Vase, 8-1/2" h, ruffled...................40.00
Wine, 4-1/2 oz, 4" h 10.00

Pretzel: "No. 622." Indiana Glass Co., Dunkirk, IN, late 1930s to 1960s. Made in avocado, crystal and teal. Some crystal pieces have a fruit decoration. Recent amber, blue and opaque white issues.

Item	Crystal/Plain
Berry Bowl, 9-3/8" d	18.00
Bowl, 8" d	7.00
Celery Tray, 10-1/4" l	7.50
Creamer	6.00
Cup	8.00
Cup and Saucer	9.50
Fruit Cup, 4-1/2" d	8.00
Iced Tea Tumbler, 12 oz, 5-1/2" h	77.50
Juice Tumbler	35.00
Olive, 7" l, leaf-shape	7.00
Pickle, 8-1/2" d, two handles	4.00
Pitcher, 39 oz	200.00
Plate, 6" d	2.50
Plate, 6" d, tab handle	7.00
Plate, 7" sq, wings	9.00
Plate, 7-1/4" w, sq, indent	9.00

Plate, 7-1/4" w, sq, indent, 3 part 9.00
Plate, 8-3/8" d, salad......................6.00
Plate, 9-3/8" d, dinner...................10.00
Plate, 10" d, dinner.......................10.00
Relish, 7", 3 part............................9.00
Sandwich Plate, 11-1/2" d............11.00
Saucer...1.50
Soup Bowl, 7-1/2" d 15.00
Sugar...6.00
Tumbler, 5 oz, 3-1/2" h..................50.00
Tumbler, 9 oz, 4-1/2" h..................55.00

Ribbon: Hazel Atlas Glass Co., Clarksburg, WV, and Zanesville, OH, early 1930s. Made in black, crystal, green and pink.

Item	Crystal	Green
Berry Bowl, 4" d	20.00	22.00
Berry Bowl, 8" d	27.50	30.00
Candy Dish, cov	30.00	32.00
Cereal Bowl, 5" d	20.00	25.00
Creamer, ftd	10.00	15.00
Cup	3.50	5.50
Plate, 6-1/4" d, sherbet	2.50	3.50
Plate, 8" d, luncheon	4.00	5.50
Salt and Pepper Shakers, pr	22.00	32.00
Saucer	1.00	2.50
Sherbet	4.00	6.00
Sugar, ftd	10.00	12.00
Tumbler, 10 oz, 6" h	27.00	30.00

Royal Ruby: Anchor Hocking Glass Corp., Lancaster, PA, 1938 to 1967. Made only in Royal Ruby.

Item	Royal Ruby
Ashtray, 4-1/2", leaf	5.00
Beer Bottle, 7 oz	30.00
Beer Bottle, 12 oz	32.00
Beer Bottle, 16 oz	35.00
Beer Bottle, 32 oz	40.00
Berry, 4-5/8" d, small, square	7.50
Berry, 8-1/2" d, round	17.50
Bonbon, 6-1/2" d	18.00
Bowl, 7-3/8" w, sq	17.50

	Royal Ruby
Bowl, 11" d, Rachael	50.00
Bowl, 12" l, oval, Rachael	50.00
Cereal Bowl, 5-1/4" d	12.00
Cigarette Box, card holder, 6-1/8" x 4"	90.00
Cocktail, 3-1/2 oz, Boopie	8.50
Cocktail, 3-1/2 oz, tumbler	10.00
Creamer, flat	8.00
Creamer, ftd	8.00
Cup, round	5.00
Cup, square	6.00
Cup and Saucer, round	12.00
Cup and Saucer, square	8.50
Dessert Bowl, 4-3/4" w, sq	5.25
Fruit Bowl, 4-1/4" d	6.00
Goblet, 9 oz	9.00
Goblet, 9-1/2 oz	14.00
Goblet, ball stem	12.00
Ice Bucket	55.00
Iced Tea Goblet, 14 oz, Boopie	20.00
Iced Tea Tumbler, 13 oz, 6" h, ftd	10.00
Ivy Ball, 4" h, Wilson	4.00
Juice Tumbler, 4 oz	5.00
Juice Tumbler, 5-1/2 oz	7.00
Juice Tumbler, 5 oz, flat or ftd	9.00
Juice Pitcher	39.00
Lamp	35.00
Pitcher, 3 qt, tilted	45.00
Pitcher, 3 qt, upright	35.00
Pitcher, 42 oz, tilted	32.00
Pitcher, 42 oz, upright	35.00
Plate, 6-1/4" d, sherbet	4.00
Plate, 7" d, salad	3.00
Plate, 7-3/4" w, sq, salad	2.00
Plate, 8-3/8" w, sq, luncheon	11.00
Plate, 9-1/8" d, dinner	14.00
Plate, 13-3/4" d	35.00
Popcorn Bowl, 5-1/4" d	12.50
Popcorn Bowl, 10" d, deep	40.00
Punch Bowl and Stand	75.00
Punch Set, 14 pieces	110.00
Punch Cup	3.00
Salad Bowl, 8-1/2" d	19.00
Salad Bowl, 11-1/2" d	40.00
Saucer, 5-3/8" w, sq	4.00
Saucer, round	4.00
Set, 50 pcs, orig labels, orig box	325.00
Sherbet, 6-1/2 oz, stemmed	7.50
Sherbet, 6 oz, Boopie	8.00
Soup Bowl, 7-1/2" d	14.00
Sugar, flat	8.00
Sugar, footed	8.00
Sugar Lid, notched	11.00
Tray, center handle, ruffled	16.00
Tumbler, 5 oz, 3-1/2" h	5.00
Tumbler, 9 oz	5.00
Tumbler, 10 oz, 5" h, ftd	5.00
Tumbler, 14 oz, 5" h	9.00
Tumbler, 15 oz, long boy	15.00
Vase, 3-3/4" h, Roosevelt	7.50
Vase, 6-3/8" h, Harding	10.00

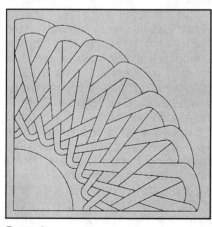

Pretzel

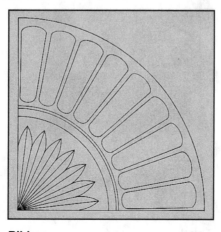

Ribbon

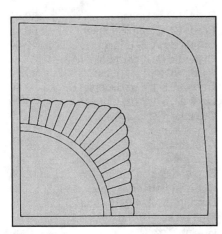

Royal Ruby

Vase, 6-5/8" h, Coolidge 12.00

Vase, 9" h, Hoover 16.00

Vase, 10" h, fluted, star base 35.00

Vase, 10" h, ftd, Rachael...............50.00

Vegetable Bowl, 8" l, oval.............45.00

Wine, 2-1/2 oz, ftd 12.50

Ships: "Sailboat, Sportsman Series" Hazel Atlas Glass Co., Clarksburg, WV, and Zanesville, OH, late 1930s. Made in cobalt blue with white, yellow and red decoration. Pieces with yellow or red decoration are worth slightly more than the traditional white decoration.

Item	Cobalt Blue with white dec
Cocktail Mixer, stirrer....................25.00
Cocktail Shaker 35.00
Cup...12.00
Ice Bowl..45.00
Iced Tea Tumbler, 10-1/2 oz, 4-7/8" h 18.00
Iced Tea Tumbler, 12 oz 24.00
Juice Tumbler, 5 oz, 3-3/4" h 12.50
Old-Fashioned Tumbler, 8 oz, 3-3/8" h 18.00
Pitcher, 82 oz, no ice lip 50.00
Pitcher, 86 oz, ice lip 50.00
Plate, 5-7/8" d, bread & butter......24.00
Plate, 8" d, salad 27.50
Plate, 9" d, dinner.........................32.00
Roly Poly, 6 oz 10.00
Saucer..18.00
Shot Glass, 2 oz, 2-1/4" h 165.00
Tumbler, 4 oz, 3-1/4" h, heavy bottom 27.50
Tumbler, 4 oz, heavy bottom........11.00
Tumbler, 9 oz, 3-3/4" h 11.00

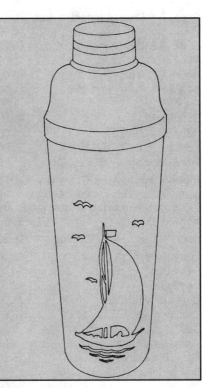

Ships

Tumbler, 9 oz, 4-5/8" h.................. 14.00

Whiskey, 3-1/2" h 30.00

Thistle: MacBeth-Evans, Charleroi, PA, 1929-1930. Made in crystal, green, pink and yellow.

Item	Green	Pink
Cake Plate, 13" d, heavy...................150.00 ......125.00
Cereal Bowl, 5-1/2" d ..27.50 ....80.00
Cup, thin......................32.00 ....24.00
Fruit Bowl, 10-1/4" d...295.00 ......195.00
Plate, 8" d, luncheon ...22.00 ....18.00
Plate, 10-1/4" d, grill....32.00 ....28.00
Saucer..........................12.00 ....12.00

Vernon: "No. 616." Indiana Glass Co.,

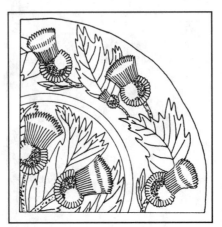

Thistle

Vernon

Dunkirk, IN, 1930 to 1932. Made in crystal, green and yellow.

Item	Crystal	Green	Yellow
Creamer, ftd	12.00	25.00	25.00
Cup	10.00	15.00	15.00
Plate, 8" d, luncheon.........	7.00	10.00	10.00
Sandwich Plate, 11-1/2" d	14.00	25.00	25.00
Saucer.................	4.00	6.00	6.00
Sugar, ftd	12.00	25.00	25.00
Tumbler, 5" h, ftd	15.00	35.00	35.00

Dirigibles

Collecting Hints: All types of dirigible material remain stable. Specialize in one specific topic, e.g., material about one airship, models and toys or postcards. The field is very broad and a collector might exhaust his funds trying to be comprehensive. The most common collecting trend focuses on material relating to specific flights.

History: The terms "airship" and "dirigible" are synonymous. Dirigible (from Latin) means steerable and the term originally applied to bicycles although it evolved into a synonym for airship. There are three types of dirigibles: 1) Rigid—a zeppelin, e.g., *Hindenburg*, *Graf*, *Shenandoah*; 2) Non-Rigid—a blimp, e.g., those flown by the Navy or bearing Goodyear advertising; and 3) Semi-Rigid—non-rigid with a keel, e.g., *Norge* and *Italia*. Only non-rigid and semi-rigid dirigibles were made prior to 1900. Hot-air balloons, barrage balloons, hydrogen balloons and similar types are not dirigibles because they

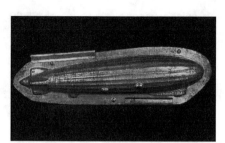

Chocolate Mold, Anton Reiche, Dresden, #25647, 2 pcs, clamp style, 11-3/4" w, 2-3/4" h, $125.

are not directable. They go where the wind takes them.

Zeppelins were made from 1900 to 1940, the last being the *LZ130*, sister ship to the *Hindenburg*. The *Graf* zeppelin was the most successful one, flying between 1928 and 1940. The *Hindenburg*, which flew in 1936 and 1937, was the most famous due to the spectacular fire that destroyed it in 1937. America never used its four zeppelins for passenger travel; they were strictly for military use. The Naval Air Station at Lakehurst, NJ, where the well-known zeppelins docked, is still open, although its name has been changed to the Naval Air Engineering Center. The last Navy blimp flew from Lakehurst in 1962.

References: Walter Curley, *Graf Zeppelin's Flights to South America*, Spellman Museum, 1970; Arthur Falk, *Hindenburg Crash Mail*, Clear Color Litho, 1976; Sieger, *Zeppelin Post Katalog* (in German), Wurttemberg, 1981.

Collectors' Club: Zeppelin Collectors Club, c/o Aerophilatelic Federation, P.O. Box 1239, Elgin, IL 60121.

Museum: Navy Lakehurst Historical Society, Cinnaminson, NJ.

Reproduction Alert.

Bank, 6-1/2" l, *Graf Zeppelin,* silver-painted cast iron, c1920......................................50.00
Big Little Book, Russell R. Winterbotham, *Captain Robb of Dirigible ZR-90 and the Disappearing Zeppelin*, Whitman Better Little Book, 1941, Al Lewin, artist, 3-5/8" x 4-1/2" x 1-1/2".............35.00
Book, Hugh Allen, *The Story of the Airship, Goodyear*, Goodyear, Tire and Rubber Co., 1932, hardcover, 96 pgs....................20.00

Bookmark, heart shape, mkd "Duralumin Used in the Airship *Akron*, Made by Goodyear Zeppelin Corp., Akron OH," illus of zeppelin.....35.00
Brochure, 5-1/2" x 8", "Al-Cariod, the Ideal Antacid," illus of *Los Angeles*............................25.00
Candy Mold, 10" l, 3-1/2" h, tin, *Los Angeles*..........................125.00
Comb, 4" l, mkd "Duralumin Used in the Airship *Akron*, Made by Goodyear Zeppelin Corp., Akron OH," illus of zeppelin...............35.00
Employee Badge, 2-1/8", black and white, Lakehurst, NJ, 1939......24.00
Game
   Graf Zeppelin, 3-1/2" x 5" x 1-1/2", 48 cards, instruction booklet, printed in German, 1928, orig box 125.00
   Graf Zeppelin World Flight Game, 14" x 21-1/2" board, 11" x 15" x 1-1/2" orig box, German instructions, 1928 flight 225.00
Nail File, 3" l, stamped metal, zeppelin shape......................................65.00
Needle Book,
   China Clipper brand 12.00
Patch, Zeppelin *Eckener Spende*, cloth, brass rim, Germany, 1930s 55.00
Pencil Sharpener, figural.............125.00
Pennant, 29" l, *Graf Zeppelin*, brown felt, white airship and inscription ..120.00
Pin
   1/2" x 1-7/8", diecut aluminum, detailed airship inset, b&w glossy photo of Count Ferdinand Von Zeppelin, c1920 ....175.00
   1-5/8" diecut, rolled silvered brass, swastika on each tail fin, c1936....................75.00
Pinback Button
   1-1/4" d, red, white and blue, zeppelin in hanger at Lakehurst

Diecut, *Graf Zeppelin* over New York skyline, Statue of Liberty, G. Schwarz, artist, shipped by first air freight from Germany to USA on *Graf Zeppelin*, 1929, 8-5/16" x 6-1/16", $125.

Naval Air Station, 1930s 75.00
   1-3/4" d, celluloid, Honorary Pilot, Tydol Flying A Airship 20.00
Pocket Mirror, 2-1/2"d, *Graf Zeppelin*, celluloid, photo and illus of aerial view of North and South America......125.00
Postcard, eagle over zeppelin and bust of Count Zeppelin, Imperial German colors, 1918............................50.00
Schedule, 4" x 9" glossy paper folds to 9" x 24" sheet, *Hindenburg, Graf Zeppelin*, int b&w photos, plans, menus, text on flights, published March 1937, by German Zeppelin Transport Co., and American Zeppelin Transport Inc. 75.00
Toy
   4-1/4", cast iron, painted green, mkd "Navy" 85.00
   10-1/2", litho tin windup, Trans-Atlantic, silver ground, red and blue lettering, U.S. flag and stars ..165.00
Whistle, multicolored litho tin, figural 25.00

Disneyana

Collecting Hints: The products from the 1930s command the most attention. Disneyana is a popular subject and items tend to be priced on the high side. Condition should be a prime consideration before making purchasing any item. An incomplete toy or game should sell for 40% to 50% less than one in mint condition.

History: Walt Disney and the creations of the famous Disney Studios hold a place of fondness and enchantment in the hearts of people throughout the world. The 1928 release of "Steamboat Willie," featuring Mickey Mouse, heralded an entertainment empire. Walt and his brother, Roy, were shrewd businessmen. From the beginning, they licensed the reproduction of Disney characters on products ranging from wristwatches to clothing.

The market in Disneyana has been established by a few determined dealers and auction houses. Hake's Americana and Collectibles has specialized in Disney material for more than a decade. Sotheby's Collector Carousel auctions and Christie's auctions have continued the trend.

Walt Disney characters are popular throughout the world. Belgium is a leading producer of Disneyana along with England, France and Japan. The Disney characters often take on the regional characteristics of the host country; don't be surprised to find a strange-looking Mickey Mouse or Donald Duck. Disney has opened a theme park in Japan and a wealth of new Disney collectibles will result.

References: Ted Hake, *Hake's Guide to Character Toy Premiums*, Gemstone Publishing (1966 Greenspring, Ste. 405, Timonium, MD 21093), 1996; Robert Heide and John Gilman, *Disneyana: Classic Collectibles 1928-1958*, Hyperion, 1994; David Longest and Michael Stern, *Collector's Encyclopedia of Disneyana*, Collector Books, 1992; Maxine A. Pinksy, *Marx Toys: Robots, Space, Comic, Disney & TV Characters*, Schiffer Publishing, 1996; Walton Rawls, *Disney Dons Dogtags*, Abbeville Press, 1992; Michael Stern, *Stern's Guide to Disney Collectibles, 1st Series* (1989, 1992 value update), *2nd Series* (1990, 1993 value update), *3rd Series* (1995), Collector Books; Tom Tumbusch, *Tomart's Illustrated Disneyana Catalog and Price Guide, Vols. 1, 2, 3 and 4*, Tomart Publications, 1985.

Periodicals: *Mouse Rap Monthly*, P.O. Box 1064, Ojai, CA 93024; *Storyboard Magazine for Disneyana Collectors*, 2512 Artesia Blvd., Redondo Beach, CA 90278; *Tomart's Disneyana Digest*, 3300 Encrete Ln., Dayton, OH 45439; *Tomart's Disneyana Update*, 3300 Encrete Ln., Dayton, OH 45439.

Collectors' Clubs: Imagination Guild, P.O. Box 907, Boulder Creek, CA 95006; Mouse Club, 2056 Cirone Way, San Jose, CA 95124; Mouse Club East, P.O. Box 3195, Wakefield, MA 01880; National Fantasy Club for Disneyana Collector & Enthusiasts, P.O. Box 19212, Irvine, CA 92713.

Archives: Walt Disney Archives, Burbank, CA.

Additional Listings: Animation Art.

Advisor: Ted Hake.

Alice in Wonderland

Hat Display, 10" x 12" diecut stiff cardboard, cardboard easel back, "Walt Disney's Mad Hatter Says: She'll Be Mad About You in a Cream Hat/See Walt Disney's Alice in Wonderland at Your Local Theater," c1951.....90.00
Shaker, 2-1/2" x 3" x 5" h, china, cork stopper, Regal China, 1951...225.00
Stationery, 8" x 9-1/4" cardboard folder, diecut storage pockets, 5" x 8" sheets of note paper, envelopes, Whitman, 1951 copyright, missing one sheet of paper and one envelope..........30.00

Bambi

Book, *Thumper,* Grosset & Dunlap, 1942 copyright, 7" x 8-1/4", 32 pgs, b&w and color art, dj...............30.00
Comic Book, *Walt Disney's Bambi,* 7-3/4" x 10-1/4", KK Publications, Inc., 1941 copyright, 32 pgs, glossy cover, large story art and text, used as premium by various stores, room for advertising on back ...75.00
Figure, Thumper, 1-1/4", painted and glazed ceramic, tan, brown and pink, Hagen-Renaker, 1940s 50.00
Poster, 14-1/4" x 20", Prevent Forest Fires, issued by U.S. Dept of Agricultural Forest Service, 1943, reads "Please Mister, Don't Be Careless. Prevent Forest Fires/Greater Danger Than Ever!"...............325.00
Studio Fan Card, 7-1/8" x 9-1/4", stiff tan paper, brown design, facsimile Walt Disney signature, 1942............50.00

Cinderella

Figure, 2-1/2" x 3" x 5-1/4", painted and glazed ceramic, blue and white dress, 1970s 25.00
Magazine, 8-1/4" x 11", *Newsweek*, Feb. 13, 1950, 3-pg article,

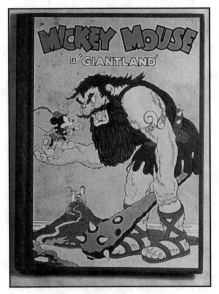

Book, *Mickey Mouse in 'Giantland,'* Staff of Walt Disney Studio, David McKay Co., Philadelphia, 1934, hardcover, 45 pgs, $125.

color cover................................25.00

Disneyland

Charm, enameled front shows castle and red, white, blue and yellow Tinkerbell, Disney Productions copyright, SS 925, mkd "Made in Germany," 1955 ....35.00
Coloring Book, 8-1/4" x 10-3/4", Whitman, 1955 copyright, 128 pgs, three pgs colored 45.00
Guide Book, 6" x 8-3/4", 20 pgs, stiff glossy covers, artwork, two photos of Walt Disney, c1955 125.00
Magazine, *Disneyland Magazine*, No. 1, 10-1/4" x 12-1/2", Fawcett Publication, 1972 copyright, 16 pgs, color art 30.00
Pamphlet, "Your Guide to Disneyland," 3-1/2" x 8", issued by Bank of America, 1955 copyright, opens to 13-1/2" x 16" with map on one side, other side with text and Bank of America CA locations 30.00
Pinback Button, 4" d, Main Street Commemorative, blue text, 3000th Performance Sept. 4, 1991, color photo of Main Street Electrical Parade, castle in background..35.00
Plate, 9-1/2" d, white china, gold trim, six large color illus, pierced for hanging, c1950.........................60.00
Tray, 11" d, metal, bright gold luster, white designs around rim and recessed areas, 1960s............15.00

Donald Duck

Bank, 3" x 6" x 5" h, TV shape, blue paint under glaze, brown over-glaze paint around screen, full-color decal of Donald and nephews having a picnic, copyright WD-23, foil "Dan Brechner" sticker, 1960s, rubber trap missing 40.00
Birthday Card, 4-3/4" x 4-3/4", lightly textured paper, Hallmark, 1943 copyright, front with Donald in sailboat, attached fabric U.S. flag..........30.00
Book, *Donald Duck and Chip 'n' Dale*, Whitman Tell-a-Tale, 1954 copyright, 5-1/2" x 6-1/2", 28 pgs, color art 10.00
Pencil, 5-1/2" l, red, white and blue, Donald Duck Bread, loaf of bread, imprint of Ungles Baking Co., 1950s...................25.00
Pencil Sharpener, 1" d, dark green plastic, octagonal, full-color decal of Donald waving, c1940.........60.00
Puzzle, The 3-Dimensional Jigsaw Puzzle, 9-3/4" x 11-1/4" x 2" deep colorful box, Jaymar, 1950s, 18" x 18" assembled, title "Donald Duck and Pluto".....................35.00
Sand Pail, tin litho, attached carrying handle, Ohio Art, c1940, angry

Sand pail, Mickey Mouse, multicolored, J. Chein & Co., Made in USA, 4-3/8" h, 8" h with handle, 5" d, $75.

Donald on inner tube being attacked by sea gulls as nephews swim and play on raft, only slight wear..150.00

Snowdome, 3" x 4-1/2" x 5" h, plastic figure holding round snow globe in his hands, inside diecut plastic figure of Pluto moving in front of doghouse, 1960s 50.00

Watch, Ingersoll, 1950, case mkd "Timex," full-color image of Donald, diecut arms and hands 65.00

Water Gun, 4-1/2" l, hard plastic, 3D shape of Donald's body, white plastic, blue and white sailor suit, red bow, yellow beak, 1970s ...15.00

Dumbo

Card Game, 2-1/2" x 3-1/2" x 3/4" deep blue and white box, 45 cards and instructions, English, mkd "Pepy Series," c1941 ....125.00

Cookie Jar, 7" x 9" x 13" h, glazed white china, over glaze green, orange, blue and dark brown paint, turnabout type, Leeds China, late 1940s........100.00

Goofy

Lunch Box and Thermos, 7" x 8" x 4" deep, emb metal, 6-1/2" h plastic thermos with yellow cap, Sport Goofy, Aladdin, c1983, unused, orig cardboard tag 25.00

Pinback Button, I'm Goofy about Disneyland, colorful image, blue background changes to light yellow slogan against red background, Disney copyright, c1960 ....25.00

Toy, 2" x 4" x 3-1/4" h hard-plastic friction toy, 3D figure of Goofy as driver of Stanley Steamer car, Marx sticker, 1960s 55.00

Lady and the Tramp

Book, *Lady,* Whitman Tell-a-Tale, 1954 copyright, 5-1/2" x 6-1/2", 28 pgs, color art.......................20.00

Dog Premium, 2-1/2" x 3-1/2" stiff plastic sheet, punch-out figure of Jock, issued by Scotch Brand tape, c1955 ....25.00

Mary Poppins

Figure, 2-1/2" x 3-1/4" x 8" h, painted and glazed ceramic, detachable umbrella, cardboard tag, 1964 copyright.......................100.00

Paper Dolls, Jane and Michael from Mary Poppins Cut-Out Doll Book, Watkins-Strathmore Co., 1964 copyright, 8-1/4" x 11", stiff-cardboard cover with punch-outs of Jane and Michael on front, Mary Poppins on back, 8 pgs of uncut outfits......40.00

Mickey Mouse

Ashtray, 3-1/4" x 5" x 2-7/8" h, 3D Mickey figure playing saxophone, glazed china, small paper sticker "Mickey Mouse Copr 1928 1930 by Walter E. Disney".....300.00

Better Little Book, *Mickey Mouse in the World of Tomorrow,* Whitman Better Little Book, #1444, 1948 copyright, black, white and red cover art, 96 pgs.......................60.00

Birthday Card, 4" x 5", Hall Brothers Inc., glossy textured paper, black, white, yellow, pink, silver front with diecut Mickey, black plastic button nose, front reads "S'cuse Me for Button In!", int reads "But Goodness Nose I Just Had to Wish You a Happy Birthday," two images of Mickey inside, small inked name on lower right 35.00

Book

Mickey Mouse in 'Giant Land,' 6-1/4" x 8-1/4", David McCay Co., copyright 1934, hardcover, 48 pgs, color story art on each pg, extensive wear.......................125.00

Mickey Mouse's Friends Wait for the County Fair, Walt Disney Picture Storybook, #883, Whitman, copyright 1937, 8-1/2" x 9-1/2", 24 pgs, color throughout, some wear 90.00

Booklet, Sunoco Oil, 4-3/4" x 7-1/4", 8 pgs, copyright 1938, Sun Oil Co., *What Causes Motor Knocks,* black, white and yellow illus on every pg, Mickey, nephews, Goofy and Donald 125.00

Card Game, 2-1/2" x 3-1/2" x 3/4", Shuffled Symphonies, red and white box, deck of 45 cards, rule booklet, c1938, English 75.00

Cereal Spoon, 1933, SS, mkd "Walt Disney"..........................15.00

Gumball Bank, 7-1/4" x 9-1/2" x 6" deep colorful box, sealed in orig shrink wrap, Hasbro, 1970s, hard-plastic bank, 3D head.........................40.00

Magic Trick, 3" x 4-1/2" brown paper envelope, The Wonder Mouse, red printing, small image on front, instructions on back of envelope, wear, thin wire missing...........30.00

Pencil Tablet, 8" x 9-3/4", black, white and red cover, Mickey with bow and arrow, small dog in front of him, apple on his head, pg or two missing, c1929 ....85.00

Pinback Button

Eat More Sherlocks Bread.......75.00

Mickey Mouse, black, white and red, classic pose, Enterprises back paper...........95.00

Puzzle, The 3-Dimensional Jigsaw Puzzle, 9-3/4" x 11-1/4" x 2" deep colorful box, Jaymar, 1950s, 18" x 18" assembled, brown, orange and green litho titled "Mickey Mouse-High Diver," 3D glasses missing......35.00

Ring, SS, leaf-like accents on left and right, oval top with diecut Mickey, authorized and distributed by Cohn & Rosenberger, c1932 ....85.00

Sand Pail, tin litho pail, attached carrying handle, matching shovel with wooden handle, Ohio Art, 1930s, color graphics of Mickey performing magic tricks for Minnie, Mickey on roller skates being pulled by Pluto, extensive interior wear, slight wear and paint loss to ext. 150.00

Wristwatch, silvered metal case, white dial, Mickey with red-gloved hands, running, c1970 ....50.00

Mickey Mouse Club

Membership Certificate, 8-1/2" x 11", tan parchment-like paper, black text, repeated gold Mickey portrait, facsimile Mickey signature and seal design, unused 30.00

Record, "Mickey Mouse Club March," 7" x 7" colorful stiff-paper sleeve, 45 RPM record, Disneyland label, 1962 copyright.........................20.00

Stick-Ons Set, 8-1/2" x 13" x 1" deep colorful box, Standard Toykraft, 1961 copyright, colorful fabric pieces, 8" x 9" stiff-cardboard section with felt covering 30.00

Thermos, 6-1/2" h, metal, color illus, white cup, Mickey as band leader, other characters playing instruments, Aladdin Industries, 1960s.....................50.00

Minnie Mouse

Ashtray, green dress, white polka dots, red hat, yellow flower 150.00

Cigarette Holder, 1-1/2" x 3-1/4" x 2-1/2"

h, white china, gold trim, Minnie images on both sides, one side brushing hair, other side with finger pointing in the air 225.00

Figure, bisque

3-1/4" h, nurse, yellow dress, dark orange polka dots, gold hat, orange shoes, silver case with orange cross, 1930s.................80.00

3-1/2" h, light blue dress, green hat, yellow shoes, holding tan and gold mandolin, 1930s, incised "C69" on back...........................75.00

Pinocchio

Book, *Pinocchio,* Walt Disney Story-books series, #2467, DC Heath and Co., 1940 copyright, 6-1/4" x 8", red, blue and cream hardcover, 96 pgs, color art.......................45.00

Coloring Book, 8-14" x 10-3/4", 128 pgs, Whitman, 1954 copyright, one pg neatly colored 15.00

Figure, 3" h, bisque, blue, red, yellow, brown shoes, c1940 ....30.00

Sheet Music, *Pinocchio Song Hit Folio,* 9" x 12", 16 pgs of words and music, 1940 copyright, Allan & Co., Pty Ltd. Australian issue 20.00

Toy, Pinocchio Pop Pal, 2-1/2" x 3" x 3" h, hard-plastic push-button, Kohner, c1970, dark brown, tree stump opens to view 3D Pinocchio, squeaks 15.00

Whistle, 1-1/2" h, Jiminy Cricket, aluminum, name, image and Disney copyright stamped on stem, c1960 ....10.00

Pluto

Bobbing Head, 5-1/4" h, composition, blue collar, green base, black-felt ears, 1960s gold-foil sticker, "Made in Japan" 70.00

Card Game, 5" x 6-1/2" x 1" deep box, 35 playing cards, Whitman, 1939 copy-right, black, white and red illus 50.00

Figure, 1-1/2" x 2-1/4" x 1-3/4" h, painted and glazed ceramic, brown, black and white accents, red collar, Shaw sticker missing, 1950s 125.00

Salt and Pepper Shakers, pr, 3-1/4" h, glazed white china, over-glaze black and red paint dec, Leeds China, unmkd, 1947 ....30.00

Toy, Marx Wiz Walker, 5" x 9" diecut card, 1-1/2" l hard-plastic ramp walker, metal legs, yellow, black and red, small Disney copyright, c1960 ....25.00

Sleeping Beauty

Book, *Sleeping Beauty,* Whitman Tell-a-Tale, 1959 copyright, 5-1/2" x 6-1/2", 28 pgs, color story art 18.00

View-Master, 4-1/2" x 4-1/2", color enve-lope with individual sleeve and story booklet, 1959 copyright 30.00

Snow White

Blowing Bubbles Boxed Set, 9" x 14" x 1-1/2" illus box, orig con-tents, pr of washcloths, cardboard storage tray with red illus, Milton Bra-dley, 1938, contents good 50.00

Book, *Snow White and the Seven Dwarfs Storybook,* Whitman, #714, 1938 copyright, 8-1/2" x 11-1/4", stiff color cover, 96 pgs, 36 pgs crayoned or watercolored........30.00

Cake Decoration Figure, 1-5/8" h, Dopey, bisque, dark pink hat, yellow coat, green pants, tan shoes, c1938 ....35.00

Cereal BoxBack, Post Toasties, 7-1/2" x 10-1/2" cardboard panel, three black, yellow, red cutouts of Snow White and Prince, Bashful and Dopey, 1937 copyright 25.00

Figure

3" x 4" x 6-1/2" h, Snow White, painted and glazed china, blue and yellow dress, dark pink bow and facial features, black hair, Leeds China, c1949 ....65.00

3-1/2" h, Happy, hard celluloid head, pipe cleaner beard, arms and legs, red fabric hat, red felt jacket, black belt, brown pants, green shoes, 1938 ....40.00

Mask, diecut stiff paper, premium from Stroehmann's Bread, ad for Snow White Cake, mkd "Part-T-Mask/Ei-son-Freeman Co., Inc., poem on back, 1937 copyright

Doc, 9-1/4" x 11" 25.00

Grumpy, 9-1/4" x 13"................25.00

Snow White, 7-3/4" x 8-1/4" 30.00

Witch, 8" x 10-1/4" 45.00

Paint Book, 10-3/4" x 15", Whitman #696, 1938 copyright, 40 pgs, one pg crayoned, four painted.75.00

Paper Dolls, 10" x 12-3/4", Whitman, 1972 copyright, stiff-paper full-color covers, six glossy pgs of outfits, unused....................................30.00

Winnie the Pooh

Game, 9" x 17" x 1-1/2" deep colorful box, Parker Brothers, 1964 copy-right, 16-1/2" x 16-1/2" board, fabric "grab-bag," plastic disks, four figural playing pieces........................30.00

Glass, 4-3/4" h, black design, Canadian, text on back reads "Inspired by Walt Disney's Winnie the Pooh and the Honey Tree," 1965 copyright...40.00

Zorro

Book, *Zorro Golden Book,* Golden Press, 1958 copyright, 9-1/4" x 12-1/4", stiff cover, 32 pgs, color and

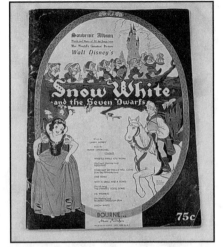

Songbook, *Snow White,* Bourne Inc., Souvenir Album, black, white, and orange, $45.

black, white and red story art ..20.00

Gloves, 4-1/2" x 7-1/2", vinyl cuff section, black fabric fingers, black, white and red, Zorro image and name, orig sta-ple, red and blue Disneyland Gloves tag, late 1950s, unused...........25.00

Hat, 12" x 12-1/2" x 3", black starched straw, thin felt trim, orig black and white fabric chin strap, black and white patch, c1940 ....60.00

Puzzle, 11-1/4" x 14-1/2", Whitman, frame tray, 1965 copyright, Zorro on rearing horse 15.00

Wallet, 3-1/4" x 4-1/4" brown vinyl, red name on front, black and blue image of Zorro on rearing horse on one side, black, gray and flesh-tone portrait on reverse, 1957 copyright.........................55.00

Other

Babes In Toyland, punch-out book, Whitman, 1961 copyright, 11" x 22-1/4", four stiff-cardboard punch-out pgs, plus punch-outs on front and back cover...........50.00

Three Little Pigs, book, 9-1/2" x 13", Whitman #895, 1937 copyright, 16 pgs, linen-like, large story art on every pg 100.00

Toby Tyler, movie press book, 11-1/2" x 15", glossy paper book, color cover, b&w int, film released in 1960, missing a few pgs, 2" spine edge split 12.00

Walt Disney Studio, restaurant menu, 6-1/4" x 9", stiff cardboard, front with title "Good Morning," sleepy Donald holding cup of coffee with text "What's Good About It?" black and red small character illus of Mick-ey, Pluto, Donald, Goofy, Jiminy Cricket, Chip and Dale, Lady and the Tramp, mid 1950s 150.00

Dog Collectibles

Collecting Hints: A collection of dog-related items may be based on one particular breed or may be composed of items picturing a dog or even dog-shaped objects. With millions of dog owners in the United States, dog collectibles are very popular.

History: Dogs, long recognized as "Man's Best Friend," have been associated with humans since the early cavemen. The first dogs probably were used for hunting and protection against the wilder animals. After man learned that dogs could be taught to provide useful services, many types of dogs were bred and trained for specific purposes. More than 100 breeds of dogs have evolved from the first dog which roamed the earth over 15 million years ago. Today, dogs are still hunters, protectors and herders and are trained to see, hear and perform routine tasks for handicapped people.

Man has continued to domesticate the dog, developing today's popular breeds. The American Kennel Club has divided the breeds into seven classifications: herding, hounds, sporting, non-sporting, terriers, toy breeds and working dogs. The first modern dog show was held in Newcastle, England, in 1859. Its success spawned many other shows. The breeding of prize dogs became popular and the bloodlines of important dogs were established and recorded. Today, the dogs with the most impressive pedigrees command the highest prices. As dogs' popularity grew, so did the frequency of their appearance on objects. They became popular in literature, paintings and other art forms.

References: Elaine Butler, *Poodle Collectibles of the 50s & 60s*, L-W Book Sales, 1996; Alice L. Muncaster and Ellen Sawyer, *The Dog Made Me Buy It!*, Crown Publishers, 1990; William Secord, *Dog Painting*, Antique Collectors' Club, 1992.

Collectors' Clubs: Canine Collectibles Club of America, 736 N. Western Ave., Ste. 314, Lake Forest, IL 60045; Collieactively Speaking, 428 Philadelphia Rd., Joppa, MD 21085; Wee Scots, Inc., P.O. Box 1512, Columbus, IN 47202.

Museum: The Dog Museum of America, Jarville House, St. Louis.

Advisor: Jocelyn C. Mousley.

Ashtray
    Cast Metal, 5" x 6", setter-type head in center, sgd "Bruce Cox" 25.00
    Pottery, Stangl, Scottie 85.00
Bank
    Mack Bulldog 175.00
    Scottie, Hubley 115.00
    Snoopy, on top of doghouse 20.00
    St. Bernard, cast iron, black and gold, 7-3/4" l 130.00
Belt Buckle, Winchester, brass, dog's heads 375.00
Book, *Orphan Annie Book of Dogs*, c1930 ....35.00
Bookends, pr
    German Shepherds, figural 50.00
    Golden Retriever, profile, Bruce Cox 60.00
    Great Dane, cast iron, bronze finish 60.00
    Scottie, 6-1/4" h, black satin glass.....................210.00
Booklet
    Dog Owners Digest, Pulvex, 32 pgs, 1943, photographs 12.50
    Rival Dog Food, Dogs of the World, 32 pgs, multicolored illus, 1940..8.00
    Sergeants Dog Book, 36 pgs, 1949 ....6.00
Bottle, lusterware, Scottie 75.00
Calendar, 1959, Texaco, girl on phone with Scottie 20.00
Candy Container, 8-1/2" h, American Eskimo dog, white rabbit fur, glass eyes, composition nose, head lifts off, early 20th C...............225.00
Cane, dog's head, with hidden dagger 675.00
Cigarette Box, large emb Borzoi heads 30.00
Cigarette Lighter, English Setter, Zippo, painted, 1950..............125.00
Cigar Lighter, Egyptian dog, brass...............395.00
Cookie Jar
    Alpo Dog 80.00
    French Poodle, blue, American Bisque 75.00
    Liva-Snap Dog, figural 65.00
    Scottie, Metlox 145.00
    Snoopy, on doghouse, McCoy...................................185.00
Cup and Saucer, handleless, three children around hooded basket holding dog, Clews Ware square mark.................235.00
Doorstop
    Bulldog, composition................50.00
    Cocker Spaniel, metal, Hubley 495.00
    Setter, on point, side view, black and white, Hubley.........295.00
    Spaniel, seated, free-standing legs, oval base, cast iron, traces of old red paint 110.00
    Terrier, painted cast iron........150.00
Dresser Tray, 9-1/2" x 6", porcelain, off-white ground, green and beige ground, portrait of smooth-haired terrier, mkd "Germany" 140.00
Figure
    Airedale, studio pottery, unsgd, large 170.00
    Basset Hound, Napco.............40.00
    Beagle, #1072, Lladro............135.00
    Borzoi, Mortens Studio, #749 125.00
    Boxer, chalkware 100.00
    Bulldog
        Chained, bronze, golden brown patina, sgd "A. Lenard," c1850 ....350.00
        Doghouse, black dog, white doghouse, mkd "The Black Watch" 50.00
        Glass, amber satin, Tiffin.....30.00
        Puppy, Hagen-Renaker 55.00
    Bull Terrier, white, Beswick, #970......................125.00
    Collie, large basket, bisque......25.00
    Dalmatian, Sparky, Hagen-Renaker 75.00
    Dachshund
        Beswick, #1469 ....50.00
        Sterling Silver, 2-1/2" x 3-1/2"...................225.00
    Doberman, Mortens Studios, #785.............95.00
    Dog, in basket, Royal Copley ..65.00
    German Shepherd
        Bronze, reclining, dark patina, Austria...................250.00
        Porcelain, Royal Dux 60.00
    Great Dane, porcelain
        Bing and Grondahl, large, recumbent................500.00
        Royal Copenhagen............175.00
    Irish Setter, Mortens Studios, #856.............95.00
    Jack Russell Terrier, puppy, bisque 25.00
    Pointer, Mortens Studios, #851 95.00
    Poodle, sitting, matte finish, Goebel.................90.00
    Pug, Mortens Studios, #738 ..125.00
    Rin-Tin-Tin, standing on rock, emb name, chalkware, 21" h .150.00
    Scottie
        Bronze, 2-1/2" h...................95.00
        Porcelain, underglaze black and white mottled, mkd "Made in

Japan," c1940 ....20.00
Siberian Husky, 10" h,
Vernon Kilns.............................45.00
Sky Terrier, #4643,
Lladro, c1970 ....450.00
Spaniel
Ceramic Arts Studios,
standing 55.00
Staffordshire, white, rust-colored
spots, gold collar, glass eyes,
11" h, price for pr 300.00
St. Bernard, Friar,
Hagen-Renaker.......................60.00
Westie, Beswick, #2038.........125.00
Flask, Scottie.............................35.00
Food Holder,
Scottie, wrought iron..............145.00
Hatpin Holder, Beagle, ceramic,
sitting, Royal Bayreuth...........950.00
Inkwell, Derby, figural,
glass inkwell 15.00
Jewelry, pin
Cocker Spaniel, SS,
emb detail, mkd "Cini" 85.00
Dachshund, Bakelite, 4" l.......225.00
Scottie, finely carved
wood, glass eye 35.00
Jug, Spaniel-form, Staffordshire Pottery,
bluish-black mottled body,
black-ringed eyes, foliated dec
tricorn hat, 10-1/4" h 250.00
Match Box, English Setter, reclining
on sea chest, brown, terra-cotta,
Sciller mark............................125.00
Nodder
Bulldog, large 40.00
Dalmatian..................................80.00
German Shepherd.....................75.00
Paperweight, figural, Beagle,
marble base...........................80.00
Pen-and-Ink Sketch, Bulldog, watercolor
tint, framed, sgd "Luckett"........90.00
Pen Tray, Labrador, head, bronze 45.00
Pipe Rack, Terrier, Bulldog peeking

Calendar Plate, white china, gold trim, 1910, 8-5/8" d, $45.

Figure, bulldog, china, white with black highlights, "Made in Japan," 3" h, 6" l, $10.

over fence................................35.00
Place Mats, poodle illus,
unopened set...........................65.00
Planter
Bird Dog, large, McCoy..........185.00
Cocker Spaniel, white pebble, Royal
Copley....................................40.00
Poodle
Lane, two poodles................80.00
Royal Copley 75.00
Scottie, pottery, Illinois
Pottery Co., c1950 ....600.00
Spotted Dog, McCoy..............145.00
Plaque, Dalmatian,
Mortens Studios, #636 ....165.00
Platter, running stag and dog,
turquoise ground, 11" d, round,
Majolica 225.00
Play Set, Rin-Tin-Tin at
Fort Apache, #3628, orig box,
figures in bags 275.00
Puppet, Huckleberry Hound,
push-up 30.00
Radio, Poodle, pink......................30.00
Rug, puppies and
black cat, c1900 ....110.00
Salt and Pepper Shakers, pr
Poodle, heads, Rosemeade...165.00
RCA Dogs, Lenox 75.00
Sign
Schaefer Real Beer, dogs playing
and watching baseball game,
orig litho, framed 95.00
Spratts Ovals for Doggies Fitness,
porcelain 250.00
Vitality Dog Food, tin,
shows pointer.........................395.00
String Holder
Our Gang dog 125.00
Scottie, figural 95.00
Tape Measure, bulldog,
brass, glass eyes....................80.00
Towel, Retriever, woven image.....20.00
Toy
Chow Dog, standing, early,
underscored button 375.00
Scottie
Fisher-Price, 1942 ....70.00
Marx, windup 275.00

Spuds MacKenzie, light-up,
new in box.............................385.00
Umbrella Handle, dog's head, Bakelite,
rhinestone eyes.......................65.00
Vase
Figural, dog barking at owl in tree,
blue luster, 7" h 130.00
Poodle, Sascha Brastoff 75.00
Wall Plaque
Collie, Mortens Studio..............20.00
Dog with Flowers, metal, high relief,
price for pr............................185.00
Pekinese, Kay Finch 125.00
Scottie, metal 20.00
Walking Stick, Dachshund, 10K gold
head, 30" hickory shaft..........225.00

Dollhouse Furnishings

Collecting Hints: Dollhouse furnishings are children's toys, so some wear is to be expected. It is possible to find entire room sets in original boxes and these sets command high prices.

History: Dollhouse furnishings are the tiny articles used to furnish and accessorize a dollhouse. Materials and methods of production range from fine handmade wooden pieces to molded plastic items. Several toy manufacturers, such as Tootsietoy, Petite Princess and Renwal, made dollhouse furnishings.

There is renewed interest in collecting dollhouses and dollhouse furnishings. Many artists and craftsmen devote hours to making furniture and accessories to scale. These types of handmade dollhouse furnishings are not included in this listing. They do, however, affect the market by offering buyers a choice between old pieces and modern handcrafted ones.

References: Flora Gill Jacobs, *Dolls Houses in America*, Charles Scribner's Sons, 1974; Constance Eileen King, *Dolls and Dolls Houses*, Hamlyn, 1989; Margaret Towner, *Dollhouse Furniture*, Running Press, 1993; Dian Zillner, *American Dollhouses and Furniture from the 20th Century*, Schiffer Publishing, 1995.

Periodicals: *Doll Castle News*, P.O. Box 247, Washington, NJ 07882; *Miniature Collector*, P.O. Box 631, Boiling Springs, PA 17007; *Nutshell*

News, 21027 Crossroads Circle, P.O. Box 986, Waukesha, WI 53187.

Collectors' Clubs: Dollhouse & Miniature Collectors, 9451 Lee Hwy. #515, Fairfax, VA 22302; International Guild Miniature Artisans, P.O. Box 71, Bridgeport, NY 13030; National Association of Miniature Enthusiasts, P.O. Box 69, Carmel, IN 46032.

Museums: Margaret Woodbury Strong Museum, Rochester, NY; Mildred Mahoney Jubilee Doll House Museum, Fort Erie, Canada; Toy and Miniature Museum of Kansas City, Kansas City, MO; Toy Museum of Atlanta, Atlanta, GA; Washington Dolls' House and Toy Museum, Washington, DC.

Bathinette, Renwal 15.00
Bathroom Set, Tootsietoy,
    10 pcs, orig box 80.00
Bath Tub, metal, Tootsietoy 15.00
Bed, Renwal, twin size 8.50
Bedroom Suite
    Biedermeier, bed, marble-topped
    stand, armoire 375.00
    Tootsietoy, 6 pcs, orig box 60.00
Buffet, Petite Princess, MIB..........18.00
Chair
    Arm, Petite Princess,
    matching ottoman.....................24.00
    Wing Back,
    Petite Princess, MIB.................14.00
Chaise Lounge, Petite Princess,
    c1964, MIB 24.00
Chest of Drawers, handmade,
    walnut, 4" x 6" x 7"...................55.00
Cradle, wood 25.00
Desk, maple, hinged front, royal blue
    and black int, 3-1/2" x 6"........110.00
Dining Room
    Suite, Arcade, Curtis, cast iron,
    white lacquer finish, two high-backed
    benches, 4-1/4" l table,
    openwork legs, 1936................54.00
    Table, Petite Princess, MIB......24.00
    Table and Chairs, Renwal,
    four chairs 30.00
Doll, bisque, shoulder head, molded
    hair, painted facial features, muslin
    body
    5", Maid, bobbed hair, short blue
    dress, lace-trimmed apron 64.00
    7", father, brown hair and
    mustache, orig wool tweed suit,
    white shirt, tie 65.00
Fireplace, Renwal, brown..............33.00
Foot Warmer, brass,
    working drawer, 3/4" 34.00
High Chair, cast iron......................25.00

Ironing Board, Kilgore, folding,
    cast iron, c1930 ....21.00
Kitchen
    Refrigerator, Arcade, cast iron,
    white lacquer, gray trim, 5-3/4" h,
    mkd "Leonard"..........................38.00
    Sink, Petite Princess,
    accessories, MIB......................55.00
    Suite, Ideal, plastic, c1940,
    MIB, 7 pcs 33.00
Lamp, table, 3", blue painted base,
    bulbous milk glass shade 44.00
Living Room Suite
    Arcade, cast iron, sofa, chair,
    deep pink, maroon trim, removable
    cushion, 2 pcs 175.00
    Tootsietoy, Daisy Doll House
    Furniture, gold, sofa, two chairs,
    library table, floor lamp,
    table lamp, phonograph stand,
    price for 7 pcs 68.00
Piano
    Ideal plastic, litho, mirror..........24.00
    Petite Princess, grand, MIB 22.00
    Renwal, matching bench..........13.50
Radio, Renwal................................32.00
Rocking Chair, carved arms,
    fabric seat and back 24.00
Rug
    Braided, oval, rose,
    red and white 18.00
    Polar bear, white, purple velvet lining,
    glass-bead eyes.......................27.00
Settee, Arcade, cast iron...............82.00
Sofa, Tootsietoy, metal 37.50
Tea Set, porcelain, teapot,
    creamer, sugar and tray,
    price for 6 pcs..........................55.00

Jaydon, 9-pc set, piano, table and chairs, corner cupboard and desk, maroon plastic, orig box, $35.

Television, Petite Princess, MIB ...64.00
Toilet, Tootsietoy, metal, c1920 ....24.00
Washing Machine, Sally Ann,
    cast iron, working rubber
    wringers, c1920 ....50.00

Dolls

Collecting Hints: The most important criteria in buying dolls are sentiment and condition. The value of a particular doll increases if it is a childhood favorite or family heirloom.

When pricing a doll, condition is the most important aspect. Excellent condition means that the doll has all original parts, a wig that is not soiled or restyled, skin surface free of marks and blemishes, the original free-moving sleep eyes and mechanical parts that are all operational. Original clothing means original dress, underclothes, shoes and socks—all in excellent and clean condition and preferably with original tags and labels.

A doll that is mint in the original box is listed as "MIB." Many modern collectible doll prices depend on the inclusion of the original box. Mattel's original Barbie doll, for example, is valued at more than $1,000 MIB. However, without the original box, the doll is worth much less. Another pricing consideration is appeal. How important and valuable a particular doll is depends on the individual's collection.

Modern and 20th-century dolls are highly collectible. They offer many appealing features to collectors, one of which is an affordable price tag. Modern dolls are readily available at flea markets, garage sales, swap meets, etc. Other determinants for collectors is whether the size of a doll is such that it can be artfully displayed and whether it is made of materials that can be easily cleaned and maintained.

History: The history of modern doll manufacturers is long and varied. Competition between companies often resulted in similar doll-making procedures, molds and ideas. When Effanbee was successful with the Patsy dolls, Horsman soon followed with a Patsy look-alike named Dorothy. Vogue's Ginny doll was imitated by Cosmopolitan's Ginger. Some manufacturers reused molds and changed sizes and names to produce similar dolls for many years.

Dolls have always been popular with Americans. The early Patsy dolls with their own wardrobes were a success in the 1930s and 1940s. During the 1950s the popularity of Vogue's Ginny Doll generated the sales of dolls, clothes and accessories. The next decade of children enjoyed Mattel's Barbie. Doll collecting has become a major hobby and collectors will determine what the next hot collectible will be.

References: Kim Avery, *The World of Raggedy Ann Collectibles*, Collector Books, 1997; John Axe, *Tammy and Her Family of Dolls*, Hobby House Press, 1995; Joseph Bourgeois, *Collector's Guide to Dolls in Uniform*, Collector Books, 1995; Debra Clark, *Troll*, Hobby House Press, 1993; Carla Marie Cross, *Modern Doll Rarities*, Antique Trader Books, 1997; Linda Crowsey, *Madame Alexander Collector's Dolls Price Guide, #22*, Collector Books, 1997; Jan Foulke, *12th Blue Book Dolls & Values*, Hobby House Press, 1995; Dee Hackenberry, *Enchanting Friends*, Schiffer Publishing, 1995; Patricia Hall, *Johnny Gruelle*, Pelican Publishing, 1993; Dawn Herlocher, *200 Years of Dolls*, Antique Trader Books, 1996; Judith Izen, *Collector's Guide to Ideal Dolls*, Collector Books, 1994; Judith Izen and Carol Stover, *Collector's Guide to Vogue Dolls*, Collector Books, 1997; Polly Judd, *Cloth Dolls of the 1920s and 1930s*, Hobby House Press, 1990; Polly and Pam Judd, *Composition Dolls*, Vol. I (1991), Vol. II (1994), Hobby House Press; ——, *European Costumed Dolls*, Hobby House Press, 1994; ——, *Glamour Dolls of the 1950s & 1960s*, Revised Edition, Hobby House Press, 1993; ——, *Hard Plastic Dolls*, Book I (3rd Edition, 1993), Book II (Revised, 1994), Hobby House Press; Kathy and Don Lewis, *Chatty Cathy Dolls*, Collector Books, 1994; A. Glenn Mandeville, *Alexander Dolls Collector's Price Guide*, 2nd Edition, Hobby House Press, 1995; ——, *Contemporary Doll Stars*, Hobby House Press, 1992; ——, *Doll Fashion Anthology & Price Guide*, 4th Edition, Hobby House Press, 1993; ——, *Ginny*, 2nd Edition, Hobby House Press, 1994; ——, *Madame Alexander Dolls Value Guide*, Hobby House Press, 1994; Patsy Moyer, *Modern Collectible Dolls*, Collector Books, 1997; Edward R. Pardella, *Shirley Temple Dolls and Fashion*, Schiffer Publishing, 1992; Myla Perkins, *Black Dolls, Book I* (1993, 1995 value update), *Book II* (1995), Collector Books; Pat Peterson, *Collector's Guide to Trolls*, Collector Books, 1995; Joleen Ashman Robison and Kay Sellers, *Advertising Dolls*, Collector Books, 1980, 1994 value update; Cindy Sabulis and Susan Weglewski, *Collector's Guide to Tammy, "The Ideal Teen,"* Collector Books, 1997; Patricia N. Schoonmaker, *Patsy Doll Family*, Hobby House Press, 1992; Patricia R. Smith, *Collector's Encyclopedia of Madame Alexander Dolls*, Collector Books, 1991, 1994 value update; ——, *Modern Collector's Dolls*, Series 1-7 (1973-1995), 1995 value update, Collector Books; ——, *Patricia Smith's Doll Values*, 11th Edition, Collector Books, 1995; Evelyn Robson Stahlendorf, *Charlton Standard Catalogue of Canadian Dolls*, 3rd Edition, Charlton Press, 1996; Andrew Tabbat, *Collector's World of Raggedy Ann and Andy*, Dollmasters, 1996; Florence Theriault, *More Dolls*, Gold Horse Publishing, 1992.

Periodicals: *Celebrity Doll Journal*, 5 Court Pl., Puyallup, WA 98372; *Cloth Doll Magazine*, P.O. Box 1089, Mt. Shasta, CA 96067; *Costume Quarterly for Doll Collectors*, 118-01 Sutter Ave., Jamaica, NY 11420; *Doll Collector's Price Guide*, 306 E. Parr Rd., Berne IN 46711; *Doll Life*, 243 Newton-Sparta Rd., Newton, NJ 07860; *Doll Reader*, 6405 Flank Dr., Harrisburg, PA 17112; *Doll Times*, 218 West Woodin Blvd., Dallas, TX 75224; *Doll World*, P.O. Box 9001, Big Sandy, TX 75755; *Dolls-The Collector's Magazine*, P.O. Box 1972, Marion, OH 43305; *Rags*, P.O. Box 823, Atlanta, GA 30301.

Collectors' Clubs: Cabbage Patch Kids Collectors Club, P.O. Box 714, Cleveland, GA 30528; Chatty Cathy Collectors Club, 2610 Dover St., Piscataway, NJ 08854; Ginny Doll Club, 9628 Hidden Oaks Cir., Tampa, FL 33612; Ideal Doll Collector's Club, P.O. Box 623, Lexington, MA 02173; Madame Alexander Fan Club, P.O. Box 330, Mundeline, IL 60060; United Federation of Doll Clubs, 8B East St., P.O. Box 14146, Parkville, MO 64152.

Videotapes: *The Coronation Story*, Sirocco Productions, 1993; *Doll Art*, Sirocco Productions; *Extraordinary World of Doll Collecting*, Cinebar Productions, 1994; *Scarlett Dolls*, Sirocco Productions, 1991 (Sirocco Productions, 5660 E. Virginia Beach Blvd., #103, Norfolk, VA 23502).

Museums: Doll Museum, Newport, RI; Margaret Woodbury Strong Museum, Rochester, NY; Museum of Collectible Dolls, Lakeland, FL; Yesteryears Museum, Sandwich, MA.

Additional Listings: Barbie, GI Joe.

Note: All dolls listed here are in excellent condition and have their original clothes, unless otherwise noted.

Advertising: Advertising dolls come in many shapes and sizes. They range from composition, vinyl and plastic to stuffed cloth. Value is enhanced when the original mailing envelope, packaging or box is included.

Allied Van Lines,
18" h, 7" w, soiled....................10.00
Blue Bonnet, 12" h,
5" w, 1986 mail-in premium.....25.00
Buddy Lee, 12" h, hard-plastic head, large painted eyes, hard-plastic body, jointed at shoulders, molded and painted black boots, orig Lee denim shirt, bib overalls, hat and red bandanna, marks: "Buddy Lee" on back, "Lee" on hat, "Union Made" on label on back of pants 350.00
Campbell Kid, 12" h, composition character head, large painted eyes, molded and painted hair, 5-pc chubby composition body, molded and painted socks and shoes, orig blue romper, white apron, white chef's hat, marks: "Campbell's Kid, A Horsman Doll, Permission of Campbell Soup Company" on paper tag 475.00
Chlorox, Lots of Legs,
12" l, 4" w, 1985 ....25.00
Johnson Wax, Minnie Mouse, 11-1/2" h, 6" w, Applause, 1988 mail-in premium, mint in orig envelope 20.00
Jolly Green Giant, 16" l, 6" w, 1969 mail-in premium, mint in orig envelope...........................50.00
Little Debbie, 12" h, 4" w, 1985 mail-in

premium, mint in orig envelope50.00
Lysol 1988 mail-in premium, mint in orig
envelope
　Fancy Fresh, 7" h, 5" w 20.00
　Squeaky Clean, 7" h, 5" w........20.00
Northern Tissue, 16" h, 6-1/2" w,
　1987 mail-in premium, mint in
　orig envelope 60.00
Planters Peanut, Mr. Peanut, 17" h,
　6" w, monocle on left eye, 1960s,
　slightly soiled 20.00
Scrubbing Bubbles, Mr. Bubble,
　10" h, 7" w, plush 20.00

American Character: The American
Character Doll Co., was founded in 1918
and made high-quality dolls. When the
company was liquidated in 1968, many
molds were purchased by the Ideal Toy
Co. American Character Dolls are
marked with the full company name,
"Amer. Char." or "Amer. Char" in a circle.
Early composition dolls were marked
"Petite."

8" h

Betsy McCall, hard plastic,
jointed knees, brunette rooted hair,
sleep eyes, orig red and white
striped skirt, white organdy top,
red shoes, c1960 ....45.00
Michael Landon, Little Joe,
Bonanza, vinyl, fully jointed body,
painted brown hair and eyes,
molded clothing, c1965 ....65.00
10" h, Toni, collegiate outfit,
orig booklet 70.00
10-1/2" h, Tiny Toodles, vinyl,
molded, painted hair, 1958 ......25.00
12" h, Tiny Tears, hard-plastic head,
vinyl body, curly rooted hair,
sunsuit, wood and plastic bathinette,
c1955, MIB 2,500.00
13" h, Bottle Tot, composition
head, body mark, orig
tagged clothes 175.00
16" h, Baby, composition head,
stuffed cloth body and limbs,
molded painted brown hair,
brown sleep eyes, c1925 ....125.00
18" h, Sally, composition head,
cloth body, orig clothes..........200.00
19" h, Sweet Sue Sophisticate, vinyl
head, rooted saran hair in orig set,
jointed vinyl adult body, orig red and
white dress, white netting over shoulders, pearl circle pin, orig nylon
stockings, high-heeled shoes,
marks: "Sweet Sue Sophisticate,
Your Grown Up Doll" on paper tag on
cord around neck, MIB 325.00
20" h, Toni, MIB..........................365.00
30" h, Betsy McCall, vinyl socket head,
blue sleep eyes, closed smiling
mouth, vinyl body jointed at
shoulders, wrists, hips and ankles,

Betsy McCall, orig blue and white
dress, black velvet ribbon trim,
silver sandals, necklace, black hair
ribbon, marks: "McCall 19copyright
61 Corp" on head 275.00
35" h, Sandy McCall, vinyl socket head,
blue sleep eyes, freckles on bridge
of nose, closed smiling mouth,
vinyl body jointed at shoulders and
hips, orig white shirt, black bow tie,
red corduroy jacket with black trim
and coat-of-arms patch, black
corduroy shorts, red knit underwear,
white cotton socks, black and white
shoes, marks: "McCall copyright
1959" on back of head...........530.00

Arranbee: This company was founded
in 1922. Arranbee's finest dolls were
made of hard plastic. Two of Arranbee's
most popular dolls were Nancy and, later, Nanette. The company was sold to
Vogue Dolls, Inc., in 1959. Marks used
by this company include "Arranbee,"
"R&B," and "Made in USA"

8" h, Little Dear, stuffed vinyl body,
rooted hair, blue sleep eyes,
c1956......................................80.00
11" h, Littlest Angel, vinyl head,
hard-plastic body, jointed,
rooted dark brown hair; mark: "R&B"
on head, 1959 ....40.00
13" h, Angel Skin, stuffed
soft-vinyl head, stuffed
magic-skin body and limbs,
molded, painted hair, inset stationary
blue eyes, closed mouth; mark:
"R&B" on head, orig tag: "The
R&B Family/Rock Me/Nanette/Little
Angel, Dream Baby/Baby

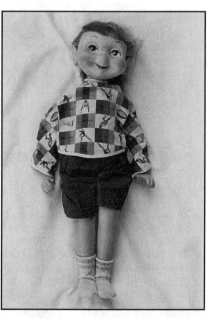

**American Character Doll Co., Whimsie,
21", $80.**

**Arranbee, Nancy Lee, vinyl head, hard
plastic body, arms, and legs, rooted
dark blond hair, high-heeled shoes, orig
dress, 19", $85.**

Bunting, Angel Skin/Taffy,
c1954," MIB 80.00
14" h, Nancy Lee, vinyl, blond wig,
blue sleep eyes, closed mouth,
orig red and white taffeta dress;
mark: "R&B/Quality/Doll/Nancy
Lee," c 1947 ....115.00
15" h

Baby Bunting, vinylite plastic head,
stuffed magic-skin body, molded,
painted hair, pink fleece bunting;
mark: "17BBS/R&B/D6" on head,
orig tag: "Head is of Vinylite Plastic
by Bakelite Company"..............60.00
Nanette, all hard plastic, glued-on
wig, sleep eyes, walker, cotton pinafore, straw hat, 1952, MIB....250.00
17-1/2" h, child, all composition,
jointed body, blue sleep eyes,
brown wig, closed mouth, c1940;
mark: "R&B" 70.00
19" h

Judy, hard plastic, nylon blond wig,
braids, metal knob to wind hair back
into head, open mouth; mark: "210"
on head and body, c1951 ....75.00
Rosie, composition, swivel head,
cloth body, molded hair, 1935..85.00
20" h, Dream Baby, composition
shoulder head, cloth body, painted
hair, redressed, c1925 ....110.00
21" h

Nancy, composition, blue glass eyes,
orig dress and cutout shoes...395.00

Nanette, hard-plastic fully jointed body, saran braided wig, blue sleep eyes, closed mouth, orig clothes, 1953..........................155.00

23" h, Taffy, plastic, socket head, blue eyes, brunette saran wig, straight walker legs, blue striped satin skirt, white organdy blouse, ruffled sleeves, straw hat, 1954........175.00

Cosmopolitan Doll Co.: Little recorded history about this company is available. Dolls dating from the late 1940s through the 1960s are found with the mark of CDC. It is believed that the company made many unmarked dolls. One of its most popular dolls was Ginger, which made in 1955—1956 and was a take-off of Vogue Doll's Ginny. Many of these Ginger dolls are found with original clothes made by the Terri Lee Doll Co.

7-1/2" h, Ginger
  Hard plastic, glued-on wig, walker, head turns, 1955
  Bedtime Outfit 35.00
  Bride's Outfit.............................40.00
  Ice Skating Outfit......................40.00
  Mousketeer Outfit.....................45.00
  Vinyl head, hard-plastic body, arms and legs, rooted medium-blond hair, closed mouth; mark: "Ginger" on head, 1956 ....35.00

8-1/2" h, Little Miss Ginger, vinyl head, hard-plastic body, rooted ash-blond hair, closed mouth, high-heeled shoes; mark: "Little Miss Ginger," 1956...........................20.00

14" h, Merri, plastic, rooted blond hair, high-heeled shoes, red gown, white fur trim; mark: "AE1406/41," backward "AE" on lower back, 1960 ....20.00

25" h, Emily, hard-plastic swivel head shoulder plate, cloth body, composition arms and legs, glued-on blond wig, open mouth, two teeth, 1949 ....60.00

Deluxe Reading, Deluxe Topper, Topper Corp., Topper Toys: These are all names used by Deluxe Toys. This company, which specialized in dolls that move or perform various actions, went out of business in 1972.

6" h, Dawn and Friends, series, vinyl, jointed at neck, shoulders, waist, hips, posable legs, rooted hair; mark: "copyright 1970/Topper Corp/Hong Kong" on lower back, additional mark on head
  Angie, black hair, brown eyes; mark: "51/D10" 10.00
  Dale, Negro, black hair, brown eyes; mark: "4/H86" 12.00

Dawn, blond hair, blue eyes; mark: "343/S11A"................................15.00

7" h, Susie Cutie, vinyl, rooted blond hair, stationary blue eyes, battery operated; mark: "Deluxe Reading/1967/GX" on head, "Pat. Pending/1" on back 20.00

10" h, Baby Party, vinyl head and arms, hard-plastic body and legs, rooted blond hair, painted eyes, blows whistle and balloon, redressed.........................35.00

18" h, Luv-N-Care, vinyl head, hard-plastic body, rooted blond hair, blue sleep eyes, open mouth, battery operated; mark: "Deluxe Topper," 1969 ....48.00

23" h, Sweet Amy School Girl, vinyl head, 1-pc latex body; mark: "A-1" on head, MIB 50.00

Eegee Doll Mfg., Co.: E.G. Goldberger, the owner and founder, started the company in 1917, marking his dolls "E.G." Other marks used by the firm include "E. Goldberger" and "Eegee Co." This American doll company is one of the longest-lasting doll manufacturers.

11" h, Dimples, vinyl head, cloth bean-bag-type body, rooted blond hair, painted eyes, dimples, music box, key-wind on back; mark: "148D/Eegee Co." 24.00

12" h, Andy, vinyl head and arms, plastic body and legs, molded blond hair, painted side-glancing eyes, dressed as airline pilot; mark: "EG-1961" on head and lower back 18.00

14" h
  Granny, vinyl head, plastic body, long white hair in bun, hair grows, mature face; mark: "Eegee/3" ..65.00
  Layette Baby, hard-plastic head, latex body, molded, painted hair, glassine sleep eyes, orig layette, c1948, MIB 65.00

19" h
  Bundle of Joy, vinyl head, arms, plastic legs, stuffed cloth body, light brown rooted hair, open mouth, two curled fingers; mark: "19-4 Eegee Co." 1964.....................18.00
  My Fair Lady, vinyl head and body, blond hair, black net, orig costume, c1958 ....55.00

21" h, Karne Ballerina, hard plastic and vinyl, rooted hair, sleep eyes, jointed at knees, ankles, neck, shoulders and hips, ballet shoes, satin-and-net ballet dress, c1958, MIB..........45.00

23" h, Susan Strolled, vinyl head, hard-plastic walker, cries, c1958 .....50.00

Effanbee Doll Corp.: The Effanbee Doll Corp. was founded in 1912 by Bernard E. Fleischaker and Hugo Baum. Its most successful line was the Patsy Doll and its many variations. Patsy was so popular that a whole wardrobe was designed and it also sold well. This was the first time a doll and her mass-produced wardrobe were profitably marketed. Effanbee experimented with materials, as well as molds. Rubber was first used in 1930; the use of hard-plastic began in 1949. Today vinyl has replaced composition. Effanbee is still making dolls and has become one of the major manufacturers of limited edition collector dolls.

8" h
  Baby Tinyette, 1932..............165.00
  Button Nose, Betty, 1943.......165.00
  Fluffy, 1954 ....40.00

9" h, Fairy Princess, 1935 ....185.00

10" h, Wolf, 1934.......................185.00

11" h, Patsy Baby, composition head, blue set eyes, closed mouth, molded and painted curly hair, composition bent-limb baby body, magnets in hands to hold small red ball and bottle, orig yellow baby dress, ribbon trim, matching bonnet, slip and diaper, mark: "Effanbee, Patsy Baby" on back of head and on back 275.00

11-1/2" h, Babette, composition head and hands, stuffed pink cloth body, molded painted brown hair, closed eyes and mouth, orig tags and box, c1945 ....100.00

12" h
  Butterball, all vinyl, molded blond hair, orig box, 1969 ....60.00
  Cupcake, 1963.........................40.00
  Dy Dee Baby, caracal wig, orig wardrobe and trunk.........185.00
  Miss Coquette, 1916..............125.00
  Newborn Baby, 1925..............125.00
  Red Cross Nurse, 1918 ....125.00

14" h, Patricia Walker, 1952........125.00

15" h, Alice, 1958 ....145.00

Cameo Doll Products Co., Scootles, orig outfit, 12-1/2", $385.

16" h, American Child, Barbara Ann,
composition head, green sleep eyes,
orig human hair wig, 5-pc composition child's body, pink dress,
orig socks and tie shoes 450.00

18" h

Anne Shirley, composition,
orig clothes............................175.00
Cinderella, 1952 ....200.00
Prince Charming, 1952 ....225.00
Schoolgirl Writing, 1963 ....80.00
Snowsuit Susan, 1967 ....85.00
Today's Girl, 1943 ....140.00

20" h, Sugar Plum, 1980 ....65.00

21" h, Sweetie Pie,
composition head, blue flirty
eyes, closed mouth, orig skin wig,
5-pc composition bent limb baby
body, contemporary dress 225.00

24" h, Boudoir Doll, 1938 ....125.00

29" h, Elizabeth, 1938 ....175.00

Hasbro: Hasbro, which was founded by
Henry and Hillel Hassenfeld in Pawtuck-
et, Rhode Island, in 1923, is primarily a
toy manufacturer. Among their most
popular dolls were GI Joe and his
friends. Hasbro is also noted for its advertising and personality dolls.

7-1/2" h, Junior Miss Sewing Kit,
jointed arms, orig box contains
doll patterns, material, dresses to
sew, sewing implements, orig
11-1/2" x 15-1/2" box, c1948 ...25.00

9" h, Choo Choo Charlie, soft vinyl head,
stuffed cotton bean-bag body,
rooted hair, painted eyes; mark:
"copyright 1973 Quaker City
Chocolate & Conf'y Co., Inc" ...20.00

17" h, Amanda, Sweet Dreams,
stuffed gingham head and body,
yarn hair, black felt eyes, button
nose, embroidered smile,
eyelet-lace-trimmed night cap,
orchid print dress, 1974 ....12.00

Horsman Dolls Co., Inc.: The Horsman
Dolls Co., Inc. was founded in 1865 by
E.I. Horsman, who began importing
dolls. Soon after the founding, Horsman
produced bisque dolls. This was the first
company to produce the Campbell Kids.
Horsman invented Fairy Skin in 1946,
Miracle Hair in 1952 and Super Flex in
1954. The Horsman processes used for
synthetic rubber and early vinyl have always resulted in high-quality products.

11" h, Peterkin, composition,
character face, molded hair,
painted side-glancing eyes,
watermelon smile, c1915.......215.00

12" h

Baby Bumps, Negro, cloth body,
arms, legs, painted hair, eyes,
large well-molded ears, orig romper,

c1912 ....250.00
Mary Poppins, all vinyl, 5-pc body,
black rooted hair, painted blue eyes,
extra clothes, c1965.................55.00

12-1/2" h, Ruthie, all vinyl,
rooted black hair, Oriental hair style,
long straight legs, dimpled
knees; mark: "12-6aa" on upper legs,
"B-1" on upper arms 30.00

14" h, Bye-Lo, vinyl head, arms
and legs, cloth body, molded straight
hair, painted eyes, christening outfit;
mark: "Horsman Doll/1972" on
head, MIB 50.00

15" h

Dimples Toddler, redressed...150.00
Tynie Baby, composition head,
cloth body, composition arms,
sleep eyes, closed mouth 250.00

16" h, Baby Dimples, composition,
orig clothes 185.00

18" h

Ella Cinders, composition head, cloth
body, composition arms and lower
legs, molded black hair, painted facial
features, orig dress, c1925 ....225.00
Joyce, composition shoulder, head,
arms and legs, cloth body, glued-on
bright red mohair hair...............50.00

19" h, Pram Baby, vinyl, jointed head,
glass sleep eyes, closed mouth,
coos...65.00

20" h, Rosebud, composition head, arms
and legs, cloth body, painted eyes,
human hair wig 100.00

Ideal Toy Corp.: The Ideal Toy Co., was
formed in 1902 by Morris Michtom to
produce his Teddy Bear. By 1915, the
company had become a leader in the
doll industry by introducing the first sleep
eyes. In 1939, Ideal developed Magic
Skin. It was the first company to use
plastic. Some of their most popular lines
include Shirley Temple, Betsy Wetsy
and Toni dolls.

10" h, Little Miss Revlon, vinyl,
rooted saran hair, sleep eyes, orig
clothes, c1957 ....95.00

12"

Baby Snooks, composition head
and hands, wood torso, wire limbs,
redressed 200.00
Betsy Wetsy, composition head,
rubber body, jointed at neck,
shoulders and hips, drinks, wets and
cries; mark: "Ideal" 50.00
Fanny Brice, composition head,
flexible wire body, composition
hands, wood feet, molded brown
hair, painted features, orig
clothes, c1938 ....185.00
Liberty Boy, World War I soldier,
composition head,jointed at neck,
shoulders and hips, molded khaki

uniform, c1917 ....200.00

13" h, Marama, brown composition
head, painted brown eyes, open-
close mouth, orig yarn hair, 5-pc
brown composition body, grass skirt,
orange lei, matching hair dec and
bracelets, black shoes, marks: "Ideal
Doll, Made in U.S.A." on back of
head, "U.S.A. 13" on back.....590.00

14" h, Betsy McCall, vinyl head,
hard-plastic body, dark brown
curly saran wig, round brown
sleep eyes; mark: "P-90 on head,"
orig clothes, c1953 ....100.00

16" h, Mary Hartline, hard plastic,
jointed neck, shoulders and hips,
nylon wig, sleep eyes, closed
mouth, MIB 700.00

17" h, Bonnie Walker, hard plastic, walker, blue sleep eyes, open mouth, two
upper teeth, crier, redressed ...85.00

18" h

Baby, composition head, lower
arms and legs, cloth body, molded
hair, flirty eyes, closed mouth;
mark: "Ideal Doll," c1938........175.00
Betty Jane, composition, jointed
neck, shoulders and hips,
lashed sleep eyes, open mouth,
teeth, orig clothes; mark: "Ideal 18,"
1943.....................................200.00
Judy Garland, composition, 5-pc
body, red-brown mohair braids,
brown sleep eyes, orig Wizard of Oz
blue checkered dress, c1939.650.00

20" h, Thumbelina, vinyl head, arms and
legs, cloth body, rooted dark-blond
hair, painted blue eyes, music box;

**Horsman, Mary Poppins, vinyl head and
arms, plastic body and legs, 11-1/2",
1964, $55.**

Knickerbocker, Heather, cloth, painted features, calico hat and dress, polka dot pantaloons, long apron, "Holly Hobbie's Friend/Heather/American Greetings Corp." on tag, 16", MIB, $10.

mark: "Ideal Toy Corp., 1962"..45.00

21" h, Princess Mary, vinyl head, plastic body, orig ball gown and wrist tags, 1952 ....150.00

22" h

Kissy, soft vinyl head, rigid vinyl body, rooted hair, MIB, c1962 ..48.00

Saucy Walker, vinyl head, hard-plastic body, orig wig, flirty eyes, orig dress, c1955.....................75.00

27" h, Sister-Coos, composition head and shoulder plate, stuffed cloth body, composition arms and legs, brown mohair wig, brown sleep eyes, redressed, c1935...................175.00

36" h, Patty Playpal, vinyl head and arms, plastic body, rooted brown hair, blue sleep eyes, closed mouth, orig clothes, 1960 ....125.00

Madame Alexander: The Madame Alexander Doll Co., was started in 1923 by Bertha Alexander. The dolls made by this company are beautifully designed with exquisite costumes. The firm has made hundreds of dolls, including several series, such as the International Dolls and the Americana Dolls. Marks used by this company include "Madame Alexander," "Alexander," and "Alex." Many dolls which are unmarked on the body can be identified by clothing tags. Madame Alexander continues to make dolls which are very collectible. Many are made for only one year; others are offered for several years

before being discontinued.

7" h, Emelie, composition head, painted brown eyes, closed mouth, molded and painted brown hair, 5-pc composition toddler body, orig tagged lavender dress, matching bonnet, socks, center snap leatherette shoes, marks: "Alexander" on back of head, "Dionne Quintuplets, Madame Alexander, New York," on dress tag, name on pin..........200.00

7-1/2" h, Quiz-Kid, hard-plastic head, blue sleep eyes, closed mouth, molded and painted hair, hard-plastic walker body, two buttons on back make doll nod head yes or no, orig tagged romper, socks, white side-snap shoes, marks: "Alex" on back, "Alexander-Kins, by Madame Alexander, Reg. U.S. Pat. Off, N.Y., U.S.A." on clothing tag, c1953..............................225.00

8" h, Americana Series

Amish Boy, orig clothes, c1965.................450.00

Colonial Girl, orig clothes, c1962.................350.00

8" h, International Series

China, 1973............................235.00

Greek Boy, jointed knees, 1968................275.00

Spanish Boy, 1964.................375.00

Thailand, 1970 ....135.00

9" h, Wendy-Ann, composition, jointed at neck, shoulders and hips, human hair, wig, painted eyes, orig clothes; mark: "Wendy-Ann Mme Alexander"....................265.00

Madame Alexander Doll Company, International Series, Scottish, bent knee, $125.

9-1/2" h, Cissette Renoir, hard plastic, jointed knees, high-heeled shoes, brown hair, blue sleep eyes, red taffeta hat, navy blue dress, orig dress tag 100.00

12" h

Brenda Starr, vinyl head and arms, hard-plastic body and legs, jointed hips and knees, rooted red hair, orig clothes, 1964 ....800.00

Lissy Ballerina, hard plastic ...250.00

14" h

Alice in Wonderland, hard plastic, blond hair, blue eyes, blue taffeta dress, 1950 ....700.00

Binnie Walker, hard plastic, blond hair, black striped dress, yellow pinafore and straw hat, MIB, c1950............................500.00

Goldilocks, vinyl head and arms, hard-plastic torso and legs, blond synthetic wig, sleep eyes, orig clothes; mark: "Alexander," copyright 1978 ....100.00

Jenny Lind and Cat, vinyl head and arms, hard-plastic torso and legs, synthetic wig, sleep eyes, orig clothes; mark: "Alexander," copyright 1969 ....300.00

Madelaine, composition, jointed at neck, arms and legs, blond wig, brown sleep eyes, orig clothes, orig dress tag, gold octagonal wrist tag 200.00

Maggie, hard plastic, walker, blond mohair wig, brown sleep eyes, peach-colored taffeta dress, rhinestone buttons, name on dress tag 125.00

Nina Ballerina, hard plastic, jointed at neck, shoulders and hips, brown wig, sleep eyes, closed mouth, orig pink-satin tutu with tulle skirt, matching hat; mark: "Alexander" 300.00

15" h, Caroline, vinyl head, blue sleep eyes, rooted hair in orig set, 5-pc vinyl child's body, orig tagged red and white dress, orig socks, blue strap shoes, marks: "Alexander 19copyright 61" on back of head, Caroline on wrist tag and end label of box, "Madame Alexander, New York, All Rights Reserved" on dress tag, unplayed-with condition, orig box 300.00

16" h

Amy, cloth doll, dressed mask face, blond hair, painted blue eyes, flowered print dress, replaced shoes and socks, cloth dress tag 80.00

Marybel, vinyl head, rigid vinyl body and limbs, jointed waist, blond rooted hair, brown sleep eyes, open-closed mouth, orig clothes

and case, c1959....................160.00
17" h
Elise Bridesmaid,
vinyl, 1966..............................250.00
Polly, vinyl, 1965, ball gown...195.00
Sonja Henie, composition,
brown eyes, orig mohair wig,
gold-satin skating dress, marabou
trim, white skates 400.00
18" h
Baby, hard-plastic head, vinyl arms
and legs, cloth body, orig pink
organdy dress, smocked coat,
matching bonnet, orig Madame
Alexander dress tag 85.00
Wendy Bride, composition head,
closed mouth, orig mohair wig,
5-pc composition body, orig
white-satin wedding dress, orig
side-snap shoes, tulle veil, mark:
"Madame Alexander, New York,
U.S.A." on dress tag...............125.00
19" h, Princess Elizabeth, composition,
jointed at neck, shoulders and hips,
mohair wig, Betty face, sleep eyes;
mark: "Princess Elizabeth, Alexander Doll Co" 225.00
20" h
Cissy, brown hair, blue sleep eyes,
orig bridal gown and accessories,
cloth dress tag.......................150.00
Flora McFlimsey,
composition............................500.00
Princess Margarite Ann Rose,
composition............................650.00
21" h
Goya, vinyl 250.00
Madame, vinyl.......................325.00
Melanie, vinyl 275.00
31" h, Mary Ellen, hard-plastic
head, blue sleep eyes, closed
mouth, orig saran wig,
hard-plastic walker body,
orig white blouse with lace trim,
red jumper, orig socks and shoes,
marks: "Mme Alexander"
on back of head and
on back 215.00

Mary Hoyer: The Mary Hoyer Doll Manufacturing Co., was named for its
founder in 1925. Mary Hoyer operated a
yarn shop and soon began designing
doll clothes. She wanted to find a perfect
doll and approached well-known sculptor Bernard Lipfert, who designed what
became the popular style associated
with this company. The Fiberoid Doll
Co., New York, produced composition
Mary Hoyer dolls until 1946, when hard-
plastic production began. Mary Hoyer
continued until the 1970s, when all production of these popular dolls ceased.
Mary Hoyer's family has recently released a vinyl version of the vintage

Mary Hoyer doll.
14" h, composition head, blue sleep
eyes, mohair wig, 5-pc composition
body, tagged blue and yellow silk
dress, gold sandals, orig marked
box, marks: "The Mary Hoyer Doll"
on back, "Another exclusive Mary
Hoyer creation, 1007 Penn St.,
Reading, Pa," on lid of box, "Mary
Hoyer, Reading Pa, Ocean City, NJ"
on dress tag, MIB 450.00
14" h, 5-pc hard-plastic body
Cowgirl, blue sleep eyes, orig set
brunette wig, cowgirl outfit, one
orig felt boot, mark: "Original Mary
Hoyer Doll" 360.00
Walker, blue sleep eyes,
closed mouth, orig saran wig in
braids, peach 2-pc knitted outfit,
matching cap and panties, gold
sandals, trunk with 5 complete
Mary Hoyer outfits, marks: "Made in
U.S.A., Mary Hoyer" in black ink
on back, circular mark............240.00

Mattel, Inc.: Mattel, Inc. was started in
1945. The company first produced items
in the dollhouse furniture line. The toy
line was expanded to include music boxes, guns and several character-type
dolls. The most celebrated doll they
make is Barbie, which was designed by
one of the company's founders, Ruth
Handler, in 1958. (See Barbie category.)
10-1/2" h
Buffy and Mrs. Beasley, vinyl head,
plastic body, blond ponytails,
painted blue eyes, painted upper
teeth, pull talk string, holding
Mrs. Beasley, MIB, c1969......125.00
Donny and Marie Osmond,
vinyl heads, plastic bodies,
painted eyes, orig clothes,
sold as pr, MIB, c1977 ....40.00
11-1/2" h, Truly Scrumptious, Chitty
Chitty Bang Bang, vinyl, straight
legs, blond hair, pink and white
gown, matching hat; mark: "Mattel,
#1108," c1969 ....90.00
12" h, Cheerful Tearful, vinyl head and
body, orig clothes, 1966 ....35.00
16" h, Bozo the Clown, vinyl head, cloth
body, pull talk string, c1962.....65.00
18" h, Chatty Cathy, soft vinyl head,
hard-plastic body, rooted blond
Dynel hair, blue sleep eyes, open
mouth, two teeth, voice box, MIB,
c1965......................................60.00
25" h, Charmin Cathy, vinyl head and
arms, plastic body and legs, rooted
blond hair, blue side-glancing sleep
eyes, closed mouth, orig clothes and
metal trunk, 1961..................100.00

Nancy Ann Storybook Dolls: Nancy Ann
Storybook Dolls were first made by Nancy

Ann Abbott in 1941. Originally, dolls were
purchased overseas, repainted and then
dressed in Nancy Ann Storybook Doll Costumes. However, the bodies were not suitable and production soon began in
California using imported English clays to
make bisque bodies. The company used
hard plastic and vinyl from 1952 through
1959. Nancy Ann Storybook Dolls have
been reintroduced and are being packed
in polka-dot boxes by Nancy Ann Storybook Dolls, Division of Giant Consolidated
Industries of Salt Lake City, UT.
3-1/2" h, Christening Baby, all hard
plastic, molded painted yellow hair,
closed mouth, straight baby legs,
jointed shoulders, hips; mark:
"Storybook Dolls/USA/Trade-
mark/Reg 1952" 25.00
5" h, all bisque, 1-pc body, head, painted
eyes; mark: "Story/Book/Doll/USA"
on back, wrist tag with name, 1941-
47
Autumn 28.00
Little Joan 25.00
Lucy Locket, blue hat...............25.00
5-1/2" h, all bisque, one pc, painted features
Bridesmaid Teen.....................30.00
Southern Belle 28.00
Valentine.................................20.00
5-1/2" h, all hard plastic, fully jointed,
painted features, black sleep eyes
Daffidown Dilly 30.00
First Communion 25.00
School Days............................20.00
6" h, Jeannie, Moonlight and Roses,
hard plastic, black sleep eyes; mark:
"Storybook Dolls/USA/Trademark,
Reg 1952" 25.00
10" h, Lori Ann Walker, all hard plastic,
head turns, glued-on brown wig;
mark: "Nancy Ann" on head, "Styled
by Nancy Ann Storybook Dolls,
Inc/San Francisco/Calif, 1953" on
dress tag 35.00
11" h, Debbie, all hard plastic, orig
clothes....................................60.00

Sun Rubber Co.: The Sun Rubber Co.,
produced all-rubber or Lasiloid vinyl
dolls. Many have molded features and
clothes.
7" h, Happy Kappy, 1-pc rubber body,
molded painted hair, painted blue
eyes, open-close mouth, yellow hat;
mark: "The Sun Rubber Co./Barber-
ton, OH/Made in USA/Ruth E. New-
ton/New York/NY" 25.00
10" h, SoWee, bottle, booties, jacket,
towel, soap, MIB.....................35.00
10-1/2" h, Tod-L-Dee, 1-pc rubber body,
molded painted hair, open
nurser mouth, molded diaper,
shoes and socks 25.00

11" h

Betty Bows, rubber, fully jointed, molded hair, blue sleep eyes, drinks and wets; mark: "Betty Bows/copyright The Sun Rubber Co/Barberton, OH USA/34A, c1953" 35.00

Gerber Baby, all rubber, molded, painted hair, open mouth, nurser, dimples, crossed baby legs; mark: Gerber Baby/Gerber Products Co., on head 45.00

Terri Lee Dolls: The founder and designer of the Terri Lee family was Violet Lee Gradwohl of Lincoln, NE. She made the first Terri Lee doll in 1948; Jerri Lee, a brother, was trademarked in 1948. Connie Lee joined the family in 1955. Mrs. Gradwohl issued lifetime guarantees for each doll, which were honored until the demise of the company in 1958.

8" h, Ginger Girl Scout, orig clothes 100.00

9" h, Baby Linda, all vinyl, molded painted hair, black eyes, c1951.......90.00

10" h

Tiny Jerri Lee, hard plastic, fully jointed, blond curly wig, brown sleep eyes, closed mouth 175.00

Tiny Terri Lee, hard plastic, fully jointed, blond wig, inset eyes, closed mouth, trunk with six tagged outfits..........................425.00

16" h

Benji, hard-plastic swivel head, jointed hard-plastic body, black wig, painted features; mark: "Terri Lee/Pat Pending," c1946........450.00

Jerri Lee, hard plastic, jointed at neck, shoulders and hips, orig curly wig, painted eyes, orig clothing and accessories; mark: "Jerri Lee"225.00

Terri Lee, hard plastic, jointed at neck, shoulders and hips, orig curly wig, painted eyes, orig clothing and accessories; mark: "Terri Lee" 200.00

17" h, Patty Jo, hard plastic, swivel head, jointed hard-plastic body, black wig, painted brown eyes, closed mouth, orig dress, c1946 ....450.00

Vogue: Vogue Dolls, Inc., was founded by Jennie H. Graves. She began with a small doll shop which specialized in well-made costumes. The original business of doll clothing lead to a cottage industry that employed more than 500 home sewers in 1950. This branch of the industry peaked in the late 1950s with more than 800 home workers plus several hundred more at the factory. During World War II, the shortages created a market for an American doll source. Mrs. Graves created the Ginny doll and promoted her heavily. The Ginny Doll was the first doll created with a

separate wardrobe and accessories that were produced by home sewers. For many years, Vogue issued 100 new outfits for Ginny alone. The company continued to produce its own dolls and clothing for those dolls, as well as costumes for other doll manufacturers. Ginny Dolls, which reached their heyday in the 1950s, are still being made today.

7" h Hansel and Gretel, hard plastic, jointed at neck, shoulders and hips, blond mohair wigs, blue sleep eyes, orig clothes and booklet "The Vogue Doll Family," copyright 1958; mark: "Ginny/Vogue Dolls and Hansel/Vogue Dolls," price for pr 325.00

Toddles, composition, jointed neck, shoulders and hips, molded hair, painted side-glancing eyes, orig clothes; mark: "Vogue" on head, "Doll Co" on back, "Toddles" stamped on sole of shoe, MIB 265.00

7-1/2" h, Crib Crow Baby, all hard plastic, curved baby legs, painted eyes, blond synthetic ringlets wig, orig tagged dress, rubber pants, c1949 ....425.00

8" h

Ginny

1948-1950, all hard plastic, painted eyes, molded hair, mohair wig; mark: "Vogue" on head, "Vogue Doll" on back

Cinderella..........................150.00

Clown 225.00

Coronation Queen, MIB...............................1,100.00

Springtime.......................115.00

Valentine 125.00

1950-1953, moving eyes; mark: "Vogue" on head, "Vogue Doll" on back

Catholic Nun 165.00

Christmas..........................125.00

Mistress Mary...................135.00

Roller Skating...................200.00

1954, walking mechanism; mark: "Ginny" on back, "Vogue Dolls, Inc., Pat. Pend., Made in USA"

Ballerina, poodle cut wig..100.00

Rainy Day 75.00

School Dress......................75.00

Springtime.........................70.00

1957, bending knees

Beach outfit.......................75.00

Davy Crockett 80.00

Southern Belle 90.00

Wee Imp.............................155.00

10" h

Jeff, orig clothes.....................35.00

Jill, hp, bride's dress 50.00

12" h

Baby Dear, all composition, bent baby limbs, 1961......................40.00

Betty Jane, all composition, bent right arm, braided pigtails, red plaid woven cotton dress, white eyelet trim; tag: "Vogue Dolls Inc., 1947" 85.00

20" h, Welcome Home Baby.........50.00

22" h, Hug-a-Bye Baby, pink pajamas, MIB..................40.00

Drugstore Collectibles

Collecting Hints: There are several considerations when starting a drugstore collection:

- Buy the best that you can afford. (It is wise to pay a bit more for mint/near-mint items if available.)
- Look for excellent graphics onthe packaging of items.
- Do not buy anything that is rusty or damp.
- Before purchasing an item, ask the dealer to remove price tags or prices written on the piece. (If this isn't possible, determine how badly you want the item.)
- Buy a variety of items. (Consider placing several similar items together on a shelf for increased visual effect.)
- Purchase examples from a variety of time periods.

History: The increasing diversity of health-related occupations has encouraged an awareness of pharmaceutical materials, items that appeared in drugstores from the turn of the century through the 1950s. Products manufactured before the Pure Food and Drug Act of 1906 are eagerly sought by collectors. Patent medicines, medicinal tins, items from a specific pharmaceutical com-

WHAT EVERY PARENT SHOULD KNOW ABOUT NEW IODENT Junior WITH STANNOUS FLUORIDE

Iodent Junior Toothpaste, Iodent Co., Detroit, MI, full 2-3/4 oz bottle, 6" x 1-1/2" x 1-1/4", red, white, and blue box, cartoon drawings of children holding tube of Iodent, instruction sheet, $10.

pany, dental items and shaving supplies are a key collecting specialties.

The copyright date on a package, graphics, style of lettering or the popularity of a specific item at a particular period in history are clues to dating a product. Pharmacists who have been in the business for a number of years are good sources for information, as are old manufacturing directories which are available at regional libraries.

References: Al Bergevin, *Drugstore Tins & Their Prices*, Wallace-Homestead, 1990; A. Walker Bingham, *Snake-Oil Syndrome*, Christopher Publishing House, 1994; Douglas Congdon-Martin, *Drugstore & Soda Fountain Antiques*, Schiffer Publishing, 1991; Martin R. Lipp, *Medical Museums USA*, McGraw Hill Publishing, 1991; Patricia McDaniel, *Drugstore Collectibles*, Wallace-Homestead, 1994.

Periodical: *Siren Soundings*, 1439 Main St., Brewster, MA 02631.

Museums: National Museum of Health & Medicine, Walter Reed Medical Center, Washington, DC; New England Fire & History Museum, Brewster, MA.

Advisor: Patricia McDaniel.

Cold, Allergy, Hay Fever Remedies

Citrisun, hot lemonade drink for colds, Bristol-Myers Co., NY, 1965, 3-1/4" x 3" x 1-1/4", green-yellow box with picture of product in a glass, eight packets 8.00

Drew's Vaporizing Croup and Pneumonia Salve, The B.H. Drew Chemical Co., Macon, GA, 2-3/4" x 2-1/2" x 2-1/2", tan box, red and blue trim and lettering, 1-1/2 oz jar of salve, "price 30 cents" 15.00

Dr. Hands Cough Medicine for Coughs Due to Colds, Hand Medicine Co., Philadelphia, PA, for children, 6" x 2" x 1" green box, black letters, pictures two hands with a child's face on each, 6" x 1-3/4" x 3/4" full 2 oz bottle, tan label with black lettering 15.00

Pineoleum, Baybank Drug Co., New York, NY, for symptomatic relief of simple head cold, 3-1/2" x 2" x 2" green and white box, pictures pine branch, green glass bottle, dropper and instruction leaflet..............10.00

Dental

Green Mint Mouthwash with Chlo-

rawuett, Hudson, division of Block Drug Co., Jersey City, NJ, 6" x 2-1/4" full 7 oz green glass bottle, gold, green and white label 8.00

Iodent Junior Toothpaste, Iodent Co., Detroit, MI, full 2-3/4 oz bottle, 6" x 1-1/2" x 1-1/4" red, white and blue box, cartoon drawings of children holding tube of Iodent, instruction sheet 10.00

Polident Mouthwash for Denture Wearers, 7" x 2-1/2" x 1" full bottle, picture of dentist and patient on blue and white label...................8.00

Feminine Hygiene

Birth Control Pill, plastic container, Lederle, blue, instruction sheet 5.75

Female Prescription, The Baltzly Co., Massillion, OH, "anti-spasmodic & sedative for functional utero-ovarian disturbances," 9" x 3" x 2-1/2" full 14 oz bottle 23.00

Koromex Jelly, vaginal jelly, Holland-Rantos Co., NY, 6-3/4" x 2-1/2" x 1-1/2" pink and white box, black lettering, 3 oz pink tube and applicator 9.00

Ramses, coil-spring diaphragm, Julius Schmid, NY, 4-1/4" x 4-1/4" x 3/4" turquoise box, black letters, cellophane wrapper.........................8.50

First Aid

Benetol, internal and external germicide, Carel Laboratories, Redondo Beach, CA, 3-3/4" x 1-1/2" x 1-1/2" red and white box, 3-1/2" x 1-1/2" full glass bottle, blue, red and gold label, in-

Gay Top Hairdressing Conditioner, Helene Curtis Industries, Chicago, IL, 6-1/2" x 1-1/2" x 1", pink, yellow, and black box, pictures smiling woman brushing her hair, full 1.5 oz tube, instruction sheet, $10.

Garfield's Seidlitz Powders, Garfield &Co., New York, NY, Sparkling Laxative Antacid, 9 individually sealed doses,green, gold, and blue, 4-3/4" x 3-1/8" x 1-1/4", $60.

struction sheet 12.00

Burn-a-Lay, medicated cream for burns, Kendall Co., Health Care Division, Chicago, IL, 1 oz, 4-3/4" x 1-1/4" tan tube, brown lettering.................7.50

Gauztex, self-adhering gauze for sportsmen, light blue, navy and white tin, sliding cover, pictures sports figures, 3-1/4" x 7-1/2 yd gauze 12.00

Hygienic Gloves, Lindfelt Glove Mfg. Co., Des Moines, IA, lady's small, pure virgin cotton, light brown 10" x 4-1/2" clear paper sack, blue lettering..............................8.50

Swan, boric acid powder, Cumberland Mfg. Co., Nashville, TN, 3-1/4" x 2" full 3 oz blue and white cylinder, cardboard, pictures swan 4.50

Foot

Dr Scholl's Ball-O-Foot, right foot, cellophane wrapper...................4.00

Meritt medicated powder, Meritt Chemical Co., Greensboro, NC, 5" x 3" full blue and white tin, shaker top . 16.00

Fut-pax, Formalax Mfg. Co., Chicago, IL, yellow and red, 1-3/4" x 2-1/2" x 3/4" box, 12 pads "for quickly removing corns," pictures foot...................5.50

Pine Needle Corn Remover, analgesic, Lenwells, Chicago, IL, 1-1/2" x 2" x 1-1/2" green and white box, pictures pine branch and pinecones, 1-1/2" x 1-1/2" 1/2 oz jar, 6 pads 10.00

Herbs

Chestnut Leaves, S.B Penick & Co., Crude Drugs, NY, loose pressed leaves, 2-1/2" x 2-1/2" x 1-1/2", sealed tan box, blue and black "The Initial Source of Supply" 6.00

Dandelion Root, "put up by" Allaire Woodward & Co., Peoria, IL, 2-1/2" x 2-1/4" x 3/4" sealed box, black letters, pictures dandelion and root 10.00

Herbaline......................................65.00

Mullein Leaves, Murray & Nickell Mfg. Co., Chicago, IL, "Guaranteed under the Food & Drugs Act, June 30, 1906," 2-1/2" x 2-1/4" x 3/4" sealed brown box, black letters, pictures herbs...10.00

Sassafras Bark, Purepac Corp., NY, 3" x 3-1/2" x 1-3/4" blue and tan tin ..8.00

Infants and Children

Baby Breck, diaper-rash ointment, John H. Breck, Springfield, MA, 2-1/4" x 2-1/2" x 2-1/2" gold box, black and red lettering, full 2-1/4 oz white jar.12.00

Baby Trainer, styled by Sanitoy, blue plastic portable potty, "It's a honey...so handy in a car...so handy at home," 8" x 8" x 3" pink and white box, blue letters, pictures family in car and child on seat 10.00

Binky Teething Toy Rattle, Binky Baby Products, Co., NY, lightweight pink rattle with center squirrel, 5-1/2" x 3-1/4" x 1/2" blue and white box, black lettering, pictures infant holding rattle..8.00

Davol Breast Shield, Davol Rubber Co., Providence, RI, 2-3/8" x 2-3/8" x 3/4" blue, white and orange box, pictures shield 5.00

Laxatives

Dr. Lemke's Bitter Drops, Dr. H.C. Lemke Medicine Co., Chicago, IL, 5-1/2" x 1-1/2" x 1-1/2" tan box, black letters, 4-3/4" x 1-1/2" brown bottle, b&w label, country scene of man entering a mine.........................16.00

Floramalt Borcherdt, dietary treatment of constipation, Borcherdt Co., Chicago, IL, 12-1/2 oz full brown jar, white cover, tan, blue and white label............8.00

Hope Mineral Tablets, The Hope Co., E. St. Louis, IL, 3-3/4" x 1-1/2" x 3/4" full brown bottle, white, green and red label.....................................6.50

Looz by Kay Kavanaugh, Chicago, IL, 3-1/2" x 1-1/2" x 3/4" full brown bottle, red label, blue and white picture of woman, 30 tablets 15.00

Metamucil, GD Searle & Co., Chicago, IL, 3-1/2" x 2-1/2" x 1" green and white box, 5 packets 8.50

Triena Laxative for Children, Allied Drug Products Co., Chattanooga, TN, 4-1/2" x 2" x 1" orange, brown and white box, pictures child's head, 2 oz bottle, b&w label 15.00

Miscellaneous

Burma Bey After-Shave Lotion, Minneapolis, MN, 4" x 2" full 2 oz red and black glass bottle,

background map......................12.00

Carlsbad Salt, McKesson's, Bridgeport, NY, artificial crystals, 4-1/2" x 4" cylinder, brown cardboard container, maroon and white label, sealed...........20.00

Fluid Red Clover Syrup, Sharp & Dohme, Baltimore, MD, 4-1/2" x 2-1/2" empty brown bottle, cork, brown label, black letters.........18.00

Gay Top Hairdressing Conditioner, Helene Curtis Industries, Chicago, IL, 6-1/2" x 1-1/2" x 1" pink, yellow and black box, pictures smiling woman brushing her hair, full 1.5 oz tube, instruction sheet ..10.00

Glutamic Acid, Parke, Davis & Co., Detroit, MI, 4" x 1-1/2" x 1" full brown glass bottle, white and maroon label...........................12.00

Itch-Me-Not, Sorbol Co., Mechanicsburg, OH, 3" x 1-1/2" brown glass bottle, red, green and white label 70.00

Matey Easy-Rinse Shampoo, Nelson Prewitt, Rochester, NY, 7" x 2-1/2" 7 oz green plastic bottle, red, yellow, brown and black label, cartoon children dressed as pirates 10.00

W.H. Bull's Worm Syrup, cardboard box, 1920s boy on front, 12% alcohol, bull bottle, $20.

Nelson's Hair Dressing, MIB 12.00

Okra, Vege Mucene, Chicago, IL, 3-1/4" x 1-1/2" full 25-tablet brown glass jar, Lred, blue and yellow label......10.00

Sodii Salicylas, Mallinkrodt, 5" x 2" x 2-1/2" brown bottle, b&w label, empty 17.00

Sodium Succinate, Eli Lily & Co., Indianapolis, IN, 100 tablets in 4" x 1-1/2" x 1" brown glass bottle, green label, black and red lettering.............23.00

Steamex Mask, 6" x 5-1/2", cardboard, "Confines Vapors to Nose & Mouth, use with Steamex," blue and white wax-paper envelope..................8.50

Tirend, Norcliff Laboratories, Fairfield, CT, 4-1/4" x 2-1/2" x 3/8" cardboard, red, yellow and blue, "Tired? Take the Activity Booster," 12 tablets, unopened.................6.00

United Drug Co., Diuretic Pills, Boston-St. Louis, packed for Rexall, 3-1/2" x 1-1/2" x 1" box, blue Vacutex Blackhead Extractor, 8" x 5" x 1-3/4" store display box, one extractor 10.00

Prophylactic

Automatic-Kling-Tite, Young Rubber Co., NY, elastic top, 2-1/2" x 2" green and white envelope, picture of lamb 8.50

Esquire, Julius Schmid, NY, 2-1/2" x 2-1/2" x 1/2" gray box, red and white letters, three prophylactics 6.00

Guardian Lubricated, sealed in foil, professional sample, 2-1/2" sq white and gray envelope, pictures knight 4.00

Wet Skin, Trojan Natural Lamb Rolled, sample, 2-1/2" sq white and turquoise envelope....................4.00

E

Electric Appliances

Collecting Hints: Small electric appliances are still readily available and can be found at estate and garage sales, flea markets, auctions, antiques malls and, best of all, in the back of your mom's upper cabinets or even in Grandma's attic.

Popularity, especially of toasters and some high-styled Art Deco appliances, has caused prices to jump dramatically in the past few years, particularly in coastal and metropolitan areas. Appliances are also now being used by decorators and even reproductions of old toasters are showing up in catalogs at tremendous prices (one was spotted priced at more than $300). Appliance clubs have also contributed to the drastic increase in values. Don't despair! Everyone out there doesn't know how hot this area of collecting has become and so there are still bargains to be found by the diligent or lucky collectors in this and other categories. Keep on looking.

Most old toasters, waffle irons and other appliances still work. Construction was simple with basic, two-wire connections. If repairs are necessary, it usually is easy to return an appliance to good working order. Whenever possible, ask to plug in the appliance to see if it heats. Use extreme caution—there could be a short as a result of any number of factors (dirt, bare wires, etc.). On "flip-flop" type toasters (the most numerous kind), check to see if elements are intact around mica.

Most appliances used a standard-size cord, still available at hardware stores. Some early companies did have strange plugs and their appliances will only accept cords made for that company. In such an instance, buy the appliance only if the cord accompanies it.

Do not buy an appliance that does not work, is in poor condition, is rusted or has missing parts (unless you plan to strip it for parts). Dirt does not count. With a little effort, most of the old appliances can be cleaned to a sparkling appearance. Use aluminum mag-wheel polish, available at auto parts stores; apply it with a soft rag for wonderful results. Also, a non-abrasive kitchen cleanser can be a great help, but do not use steel wool.

As with most collectibles, the original box or instructions will enhance the value, adding up to 25% more. Beware of chrome, silver and other plated articles stripped to their base metal, usually brass or copper. Devalue these by 50%.

History: The first all electric-kitchen appeared at the 1893 Chicago World's Fair and included a dishwasher (it looked like a torture device) and a range. Electric appliances for the home began gaining popularity just after 1900 in the major Eastern and Western cities. Appliances were sold door-to-door by their inventors. Small appliances did not gain favor in the rural areas until the late 1910s and early 1920s. However, most people did not trust electricity.

By the 1920s, competition among electrical companies was keen and there were many innovations. Changes occurred frequently, but the electric servants were here to stay. Most small appliance companies were bought by bigger firms. These, in turn, have been swallowed up by the huge conglomerates of today. By the 1930s, it was evident that our new electric servants were making life a lot easier and were here to stay. The American housewife, even in rural areas, was beginning to depend on the electric age, enthusiastically accepting each new invention.

Some firsts in electrical appliances are:

1882	Patent for electric iron (H.W. Seeley [Hotpoint])
1903	Detachable cord (G.E. Iron)
1905	G.E. Toaster (Model X-2)
1905	Westinghouse toaster (Toaster Stove)
1909	Travel iron (G.E.)
1911	Electric frying pan (Westinghouse)
1912	Electric waffle iron (Westinghouse)
1917	Table Stove (Armstrong)

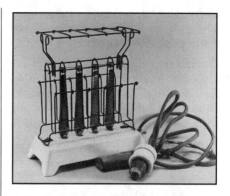

G.E. Model D-12 Toaster, removable warming rack, patent 1908, $135.

1918	Toaster/Percolator (Armstrong "Perc-O-Toaster")
1920	Heat indicator on waffle iron (Armstrong)
1920	Flip-flop toasters (many companies)
1920	Mixer on permanent base (Hobart Kitchen Aid)
1923	Portable mixer (Air-O-Mix "Whip-All")
1924	Automatic iron (Westinghouse)
1924	Home malt mixer (Hamilton Beach #1)
1926	Automatic pop-up toaster (Toastmaster Model 1-A-1)
1926	Steam iron (Eldec)
1937	Home coffee mill (Hobart Kitchen Aid)
1937	Automatic coffee maker (Farberware "Coffee Robot")
1937	Conveyance toaster ("Toast-O-Lator")

References: E. Townsend Artman, *Toasters*, Schiffer Publishing, 1996; Linda Campbell Franklin, *300 Years of Kitchen Collectibles*, 3rd Edition, Books Americana, 1991; Michael J. Goldberg, *Groovy Kitchen Designs for Collectors*, Schiffer Publishing, 1996; Helen Greguire, *Collector's Guide to Toasters & Accessories*, Collector Books, 1997; Gary Miller and K.M. Scotty Mitchell, *Price Guide to Collectible Kitchen Appliances*, Wallace-Homestead, 1991; Ellen M. Plante, *Kitchen Collectibles*, Wallace-Homestead, 1991; Diane Stoneback, *Kitchen Collectibles*, Wallace-Homestead, 1994; *Toasters and Small Kitchen Appliances*, L-W Book Sales, 1995; John M. Witt, *Collector's Guide to Electric*

Fans, Collector Books, 1996; ——, *Witt's Field Guide to Electric Desk Fans*, published by author, 1993.

Collectors' Clubs: American Fan Collector Association, P.O. Box 804, South Bend, IN 46624; Electric Breakfast Club, P.O. Box 306, White Mills, PA 18473.

Advisors: Gary L. Miller and K.M. Scotty Mitchell.

Blenders

Berstead Drink Mixer, 1930s, Eskimo Kitchen Mechanic, Berstead Mfg. Co., domed chrome motor, single shaft, lift-off metal base with receptacle for tapered ribbed glass, 12" 60.00

Chronmaster Mixall, 1930s, Chronmaster Electric Corp., NY & Chicago, chrome and black motor, single shaft on hinged black base, orig silver-striped glass 45.00

Dorby Whipper, 1940s, Model E, chrome motor with black Bakelite handle, off/on toggle, clear, measured Vidrio glass 45.00

Electromix Whipper, 1930s, Chicago, ivory colored, offset metal motor housing with push-down break, filler hole in lid, measured glass base, 7-1/2" 40.00

Gilbert Mixer, Polar Cub, 1929, A.C. Gilbert Co., New Haven, CT, 10" h, lift-off gray painted metal, rear switch, blue wood handle, premium for Wesson-Snowdrift, orig box ... 125.00

Hamilton Beach Malt Machine, mid 1920s, forerunner to home malt maker, Cyclone #1, 19" h, heavy nickel housing, sq stand on marble base, int push-down switch ... 295.00

Kenmore Hand Mixer, 1940s, Sears, Roebuck & Co., Chicago, small, cream-colored plastic, single 4-1/2" beater, orig box, booklet, warranty and hanger plate 35.00

Kenmore Whipper, 1940s, Sears, Roebuck & Co., Chicago, cream-colored metal domed top, large blue Bakelite knob, clear glass bottom, 8-1/2" 25.00

Knapp Monarch Whipper, mid 1930s, St. Louis, 9-1/2" h, white metal motor, red plastic top handle, round mild glass base with reeded, fin feet, white plastic beater 65.00

Kwick Way, St. Louis, 7-1/2" h, white metal motor top over angular clear glass base, no switch, decal label 30.00

Made-Rite Drink Mixer, 1930s, Weinig Made Rite Co., Cleveland, lightweight metal, cream and green mo-

Malt Mixer, Model B, Machine Craft Mixer, Los Angeles, CA, 18-3/4" h, $65.

tor, single shaft, no switch, stamped, permanent support, no glass ... 25.00

Silex Blender, 1940s, NY, sq, white cast base, push-button switch, silver foil, Art Deco label, clear glass 4-cup top with vertical "Silex" on black stripe, plastic lid 35.00

Chafing dishes

American Beauty, c1910, American Electrical Heater Co., Detroit, MI, 3-part, nickel on cooper, base serves as hot-water container and has sealed element, separate plugs mkd "fast" and "slow," black painted wood handles and knob 50.00

Manning Bowman, 1930s, Meriden, CT, bright chrome Art Deco design, reeded edges, 2-part top on hot-plate base, black Bakelite knob and handles 75.00

Universal, c1910, Landers, Frary & Clark, New Britain, CT, nickel on copper faceted 3-part body, sealed element in base hot-water pan, 3-prong heat adjuster in base, large black wood handle and knob ... 50.00

Coffee Makers and Sets

Farberware Coffee Robot, coffee set, 1937, S.W. Farber, Brooklyn, NY, coffee maker #500, set #501, 2-part coffee dripolator, creamer, open sugar and tray, nickel chrome, walnut handles, orig booklet, price for set 95.00

Manning Bowman

Percolator, mid 1930s, Meriden, CT, ser #636, tall graceful Art Deco design, reeded decoration around neck and base, bright chrome, 12" h 60.00

Percolator Urn, late 1920s, Meriden, CT, article #250, 3-part aluminum body, unique design prevents re-perking, front spigot, out-turned handles, clear glass insert in domed lid, 12-1/2" h 50.00

Meriden Homelectrics Percolator Set, 1920s, Manning Bowman Co., Meriden, CT, catalog #32, ser. #4-30, 15" h percolator/urn, creamer, open sugar, nickel chrome vertically faceted bodies, urn on short cabriole legs, up-turned black wood handles, glass knob insert on top, set ... 95.00

Porcelier

Porcelier, Breakfast Set, 1930s, Greensburg, PA, all-porcelain bodies accented by basketweave design, floral transfers, silver line dec

Coffee Urn 125.00

Cream and Sugar, cov 40.00

Percolator #5007 .... 95.00

Sandwich Grill #5004 .... 85.00

Set 695.00

Toaster #5002 .... 250.00

Royal Rochester Percolator, 1930s, Robeson Rochester Corp., Rochester, NY, #D-30, almost-white porcelain, slight greenish luster around shoulder and spout, spring bouquet floral transfer, chrome lid and base, clear glass insert 80.00

Universal

Breakfast Set, 1930s, Landers, Frary & Clark, New Britain, CT, cream-colored porcelain, blue and orange floral transfers, waffle iron on pierced chrome base has porcelain insert, front drop handle

Creamer and sugar, cov 45.00

Percolator #E6927 .... 95.00

Set, 5-pc 450.00

Syrup, chrome cov 60.00

Waffle Iron E6324 .... 125.00

Coffee Set

c1915, Landers, Frary & Clark, New Britain, CT, coffee urn #E9219, 14" h, squat cabriole legs, large wood ear-shaped handles; nickel bodies, oval tray, price for 4-pc set 85.00

1920s, Landers, Frary & Clark, New Britain, CT, urn #E9119-1, 16-1/2" h, chrome, chrome handles, swirl glass insert, octagonal body, handled tray, price for 4-pc set 150.00

Egg cookers

Hankscraft Co., 1920s, Madison,

WI, model #599, yellow china base, large dish on top of domed chrome serves as knob and filler with hole in bottom, instructions on metal plate on bottom 35.00

Rochester Stamping Co., c1910, Rochester, NY, egg-shaped, 4-part chrome on small base, interior fitted with skillet with turned black wood handle, 6-egg holder with lift-out handle, enclosed heating element.65.00

Food Cookers

Eureka Portable Oven, 1930s, Eureka Vacuum Cleaner Co., Detroit, MI, 15" x 13" x 19", Art Deco style, cream-colored painted body, black edges, sides fold down and contain hot plates on chrome surfaces, int fitted with wire racks, controls across bottom front................195.00

Everhot, 1920s, Swartz Baugh Mfg. Co., Toledo, OH, EC Junior 10, 13" h, large chrome and black cylindrical body, aluminum cov, Art Deco design, "Everhot" embossed on front, int fitted with rack, 2 open semicircular pans, 1 round cov pan, 3-prong heat control 50.00

Hankscraft, 1920s, Madison, WI, green enamel pan, detachable hinge-pin chrome cov, green ceramic lusterware knob, chrome base, black wood handles flare from sides of body 95.00

Nesco Electric Casserole, early 1930s, National Enamel & Stamping Co., Inc., Milwaukee, WI, 9" d, forerunner of crock pot, cream-colored body with green enamel cov, high/low control, 3-prong plug................35.00

Quality Brand, 1920s, Great Northern Mfg. Co., Chicago, IL, model #950, 14" h, cylindrical body, insulated sides and cov, fitted int with cov aluminum pans, brown with red stripe body, lift-out rods 40.00

Hot plates

Edison-Hotpoint, c1910, Edison Electric, NY, Chicago and Ontario, CA, solid iron surface, clay-filled int, very heavy pierced legs, ceramic feet, copper control with ceramic knob....................35.00

El Stovo, c1910, Pacific Electric Heating Co., sometimes mkd "G.E. Hotpoint," solid iron surface, clay-filled int, very heavy pierced legs, pad feet, no control 25.00

Volcano, 1930s, Hilco Engineering Co., Chicago, IL, slightly conical nickel body, black wood handle, slide lever as control on side that lifts grate 40.00

Westinghouse, 1920s, Mansfield, OH, 7-1/2" d top with green porce-

lain-metal top surrounding element, hollow legs, no control 25.00

Miscellaneous

Angelus-Campfire Bar-B-Q Marshmallow Toaster, 1920s, Milwaukee, WI, 3" sq, flat top, pierced pyramid top piece, base on loop, wire legs with rubber-encased feet, flat wire forks.....75.00

Buffet warming oven, Chase Chrome and Brass 130.00

Clock/Timer, late 1930s, made for Montgomery Ward & Co., cream body, silver and red face, curved glass, body swivels on weighted base, clock mechanism winds up manually, cord at back with appliance receptacle 40.00

Coffee Grinder, Kitchen Aid, Hobart, Troy, OH, model #A-9, heavy cream-colored cast base with motor, course/fine adjustment on neck, clear glass jar container with screw-off top serves as storage for beans 75.00

Miracle Flour Sifter, c1934, Chicago, IL, electric, cream body, blue wood hold-down button handle at base, vibrates flour through wire strainer............................35.00

Sunkist Juicer, 1930s, 9" h, opaque green Depression glass top, int metal strainer, chrome body/motor housing with dark green painted center, metal "Sunkist" plate on front 75.00

Universal Tea Kettle, c1910, Landers, Frary & Clark, New Britain, CT, model #E973, bright nickel 1-pc squat body and base, long spout, black painted wood high curved handle on pierced vertically curved mounts 45.00

Vita-Juicer, 1930s, Kold King Distributing Corp., Los Angeles, Hoek Rotor Mfg. Co., Reseda, CA, 10" h, heavy, cream-painted cast metal, base motor, container and lid fitted with lock groove and lock-down wire handle, aluminum pusher fits in top holder ...35.00

Mixers

Dominion Modern Mode, 1923-33, Dominion Electrical Mfg. Co., Minneapolis, MN, faceted, angular Art Deco body and base, 3-speed rear lever control, runs on A.C. or D.C., 2 custard glass bowls and juicer, mechanism to control beater height ...75.00

General Electric, 1938, G.E. Corp.,

upright housed motor, no speed control, 3 synchronized beaters in a row, work light shines in handle, 2 white glass bowls, black Bakelite handle, ser. #10-A 50.00

Hamilton Beach, 1930s, Racine, WI, model G, cream-colored metal, black Bakelite handle, on/off lever control, "Mix Guide" in window below handle, mixer lifts off base to become portable, 2 white glass bowls ..35.00

Sunbeam Mixmaster

    Attachments, fit most models

        Bean slicer 20.00

        Can opener 15.00

        Coffee grinder 45.00

        Drink mixer 15.00

        Grater, slicer, shredder, price for 3 blades 35.00

        Grinder/chopper...................25.00

        Juicer, mayonnaise maker...20.00

        Knife sharpener 15.00

        Potato peeler 35.00

        Power unit...........................10.00

        Silver polisher and buffer.....10.00

    Cabinet, 60-1/2" x 24" 295.00

Mixmaster, early 1930s, Chicago Flexible Shaft Co., model K, cream-colored body, fold-over black wood handle, rear speed control, light green opaque Depression glass bowls, juicer and strainer, orig booklet 65.00

Popcorn Poppers

Berstead, 1930s, model #302, sq, chrome, body with circular int, Fry Glass lid, large black knob on top, rod through lid for stirring 45.00

Excel, 1920s, Excel Electric Co., Muncie, IN, 1-pc cylindrical nickel body, metal handles form legs, lock-down levers, hand crank, black wood knob, top vent holes 25.00

Manning Bowman, early 1940s, Meriden, CT, model #500, detachable large aluminum container, fits

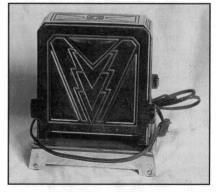

Toaster, Challenge, E10552, cat. S-76, Art Deco design, 2 slice, chrome plated, $18.

chrome hot plate, glass lid emb with floral motif, black Bakelite knob, unused 15.00

Rapaport, 1920s, Rapaport Bros., Inc., Chicago, 5-1/2" sq black base, metal legs, round aluminum upper part with attached lid and red knob, chrome handle squeezes through slot in side to agitate corn........25.00

U.S. Mfg. Corp., 1930s, Decatur, IL, #10, body and lid separate from hot plate base, top crank handle 15.00

White Cross, c1918, National Stamping & Electrical Co., Chicago, IL, tin can base with heater and cord, wire basket fits onto can, metal top with stirrer mounted through handle, woo handle to side, primitive ...30.00

Toasters

Edison Appliance Co., c1918, NY, cat. #214-T-5, open nickel body with free-swinging tab closures at top, single side knob, removable toast warming rack 95.00

General Mills, early 1940s, Minneapolis, MN, cat. #GM5A, 2-slice pop-up chrome body, wheat dec on side, black Bakelite base, A.C. or D.C., red knob, light/dark control 35.00

Heat Master, 1923-35, sq chrome body, rounded corners, end opening, 2-slice, manual operation, black Bakelite handle and feet 50.00

Kenmore, early 1940s, Sears, Roebuck & Co., Chicago, mechanical, 2-slice pop-up, chrome body, rounded edges and sides, black Bakelite handles, mechanical clock mechanism, light/dark control 25.00

Knapp Monarch Reverso, 1930, cat. #505, light-weight rect nickel body, rounded corners, black painted base, flip-flop doors with tab handles, no mica, wires stretched across ...30.00

Montgomery Ward & Co., mid-1930s, Chicago, IL, model #94-KW2298-B, flip-flop type, solid nickel-chrome body, Bakelite handle on end opens both doors simultaneously.......50.00

Steel Craft, late 1920s, open, painted green wire construction, flip-flop type, red painted wood knobs and feet 45.00

Sunbeam, early 1920s, Chicago Flexible Shaft Co., model B, 5" x 9", flat, rect dec chrome body, round, reeded legs, hexagonal Bakelite feet, double wire cages flip over horizontally, small drop bail handles for carrying 125.00

Toastmaster, 1927, Waters-Genter Co., Minneapolis, MN, model 1-A-1, recognized as first automatic pop-up, chrome Art Deco body, louvered sides, rounded end, manual clock

timer mechanism, light/dark control from A to G, panic button 195.00

Toastolater 145.00

Universal, 1913-15, Landers, Frary & Clark, nickel body, flat base, tab feet, pierced concave spring-loaded doors, permanent warming rack 60.00

Westinghouse
Toaster Stove, 1909, Mansfield, OH, flat rect body, 4 flat strip plates, removable cabriole legs, tray and wire rack, orig box and paper guarantee, unused 175.00
Turnover Toaster, 1920s, Mansfield, OH, cat. #TT3, nickel body, pierced doors and top, flat tab handles, pierced, flat warming rack top ..35.00

Waffle Irons and Sandwich Grills

Armstrong Waffle Iron, 1920, model W, first example with heat read/thermometer light on top, 7" round nickel body, black wood handles, distinctive prongs, with cord 45.00

Coleman Waffle Iron, early 1930s, Coleman Lamp & Stove Co., Wichita, KS, high Art Deco style, chrome, low profile, small b&w porcelain top impala insert, black Bakelite handles..65.00

Electrahot Double Waffle Iron, 1940s, Mansfield, OH, two 6" sets of plates mounted on oval base, heat indicators with surrounding dec on top................................30.00

Excelsior Waffle Iron, 1930s, Perfection Electric Co., New Washington, OH, 6" round white porcelainized iron body, 4 little stamped legs, plug in front, turned painted wood handle 25.00

Fitzgerald Star Waffle Iron, 1920s, Torrington, CT, 7", solid flared base, unique handle design locks in position for raising or carrying 35.00

Hostess Sandwich Grill, 1930s, All Rite Co., Rushville, IN, 5" sq cast-aluminum body, angled at bottom to form feet, screw-off wood handle, orig box and booklet of suggestions......65.00

Hotpoint Waffle Iron, 1920s, Edison, General Electric, Chicago, IL and Ontario, CA, "Automatic" below front handle, rotating cold/hot in small front window, round chrome body, top dec, ivory Bakelite handles, scalloped base dec 35.00

Lady Hibbard Sandwich Grill, 1930s, Hibbard, Spencer, Bartlet & Co., Chicago, IL, nickel rect body, cast cabriole legs, black wood side handles, front handle swivels to form foot for top plate enabling use of both plates as grills, drip spout........25.00

Manning Bowman Twin-O-Matic Waffle

Iron, late 1930s, Meriden, CT, Art Deco design, top heat indicator with rotating knob, chrome body flips over in brown Bakelite stand mounted on chrome base 90.00

Montgomery Ward Waffle Iron, chrome, white Bakelite trim 45.00

Sampson Waffle Iron1930s, Sampson United Corp., Rochester, NY, Art Deco design, chrome boy with winglike flared Bakelite side handles set asymmetrically, stationary front handle.............40.00

Torrid Waffle Iron, 1920s, Beardsley & Wolcott Mfg. Co., Waterbury, CT, flared base, 7-1/2" round plated-chrome body, green up-turned handles and front knob, front window indicates "too cold," "too hot," and "bake"................35.00

Westinghouse Waffle Iron, 1905-21 pat date, rect chrome body, mechanical front handle with wood handhold, removable cabriole legs slip into body slots, off/on switch ...90.00

Elephant Collectibles

Collecting Hints: There are vast quantities of elephant-shaped and elephant-related items. Concentrate on one type of object (toys, vases, bookends, etc.), one substance (china, wood, paper), one chronological period or one type of elephant (African or Indian). The elephants of Africa and India do differ, a fact not widely recognized.

Perhaps the most popular elephant collectibles are those related to Jumbo and Dumbo, the Disney character who was a circus outcast and the first flying elephant. GOP material associated with the Republican party is usually left to the political collector. Because of the large number of items available, stress quality. Study the market carefully before buying. Interest in elephant collecting is subject to phases, is and is currently at a modest level.

History: Elephants were unique and fascinating when they first reached America. Early specimens were shown in barns and moved at night to avoid anyone getting a free look. The arrival of Jumbo in England, his subsequent purchase by P.T. Barnum and his removal to America brought elephant mania to new heights. Elephants have always been a main attraction at American zoological parks. The popularity of the circus in the early 20th century kept attention focused on elephants.

Hunting elephants was considered "big game" sport and President Theodore Roosevelt was one well-known participant. The hunt always focused on finding the largest known example. It is not a surprise that an elephant dominates the entrance to the Museum of Natural History of the Smithsonian Institution in Washington, D.C. Television, through shows such as "Wild Kingdom," has contributed to knowledge about all wild animals, including the now quite-commonplace elephant.

Periodical: *Jumbo Jargon*, 1002 W. 25th St., Erie, PA 16502.

Animation Art, 6" x 7", Dumbo portrait, 1941, label on back reads "prepared by Courvoisier" 2,750.00

Automata, 3-1/4" x 4" x 6", playing cymbal and drum, made by M&M, Japan, c1960.................45.00

Bank, mechanical, cast iron
Elephant with Clown, 5-3/4" l .900.00
Jumbo the Elephant 750.00

Bank, still
3" x 3-1/2" x 5", Elmer the Elephant, movable trunk, gray, yellow and red, bisque 295.00
5" x 6" x 6", Dumbo, red, gray and pink, mkd "Hagen-Renaker Potteries"................................250.00

Advertising trade card, Clark's Spool Cotton, Jumbo's Arrival, sepia, white, adv on back, 4-7/8" x 3", $5.

Book, Edward Allen,
Fun by the Ton 20.00
Bookends, pr, 6-1/2" h, Syrocowood, metal base, white elephant standing under palm tree, mkd "Made in USA"..........................35.00
Bottle Opener, cast iron, elephant standing on rear legs, curl up trunk..35.00
Christmas Ornament
3" h, silver emb cardboard, Dresden, Germany.................140.00
3-1/2" l, blown glass, gray body, red blanket 95.00
Figure, ceramic
2" l, 1-1/2" h, shaded gray glaze......................7.00
3" x 3-1/2" x 4", Dumbo, gray, pink ears, yellow hat, Shaw, c1949 ....150.00
4" x 6" x 4", seated Dumbo, mkd "Ceramic Kiln," made by Vernon Kilns.......................150.00
Jar, 2" d, 3-1/2" h, Jumbo Peanuts, litho tin lid, illus of elephant on top and side, Frank Tea & Spice Co., c1930 ....45.00
Letter Opener, 7-1/2" l, celluloid, mkd "Depose-Germany," c1900......40.00
MatchSafe, 2-1/4" h, silver plated brass, ivory tusks, English.................195.00
Mug, Frankoma, 1970s 20.00
Nodder, 3-1/2" l, 1-3/4" h, celluloid, gray back and head, pink ears, white belly, silver-painted tusks 35.00
Paperweight, 3-1/2" d, glass, limited ed of 100, Max Erlacher, sgd 295.00
Pie Bird, figural, c1930.................40.00

Children's Book, Kellogg's Fun-gleland Moving Pitures, fold-out, three sections, movable flaps, copyright 1909, patented Jan. 15, 1907, published by W.K. Kellogg, $20.

Toy, Jumbo, windup, litho tin, "Made in U.S. Zone/Germany, 4-1/4" l, 3-1/2" h, $85.

Pitcher
4" x 5" x 6", Dumbo, blue and white, Disney copyright, c1940 ....65.00
4-1/2" h, Blue Ridge.................30.00
6-1/2" x 8" x 8", Dumbo, mkd "Leeds China," 1947, pink and white base mkd "Disney/Dumbo" 95.00
Plate, 4" d, elephant and baby elephant, Dedham pottery.....................365.00
Poster, 47" x 58", Lil Nil Cigarette Papers, litho, trumpeting elephant, linen backing 250.00
Puppet, 39" h, marionette, plastic and fur, Bill Baird, used for *Carnival of the Animals* and *Ed Sullivan Show* 3,600.00
Salt and Pepper Shakers, pr, Noah's Ark, porcelain, hp, gray, pink ears, elephants cuddle, issued by Franklin Mint, Jonathan Goode design 25.00
Sign, 15" x 13", Brown's Jumbo Bread, diecut tin, elephant with trunk curled down, blanket on back, c1930..........................150.00
Stuffed Animal, 21" x 23", Steiff, white, red blanket, wood handle, wheels, button in ear 650.00
Tobacco Tag, tin, diecut, Red Elephant Tobacco..............7.50
Toy
5" h, rubber, Elmer Elephant, gray, bow tie and hat, Sieberling 150.00
11" h, pull-type, elephant on wheels, tan mohair, red felt trappings, head moves from side to side when tail is turned, Schuco, Germany......250.00
Umbrella Stand, foot 350.00
Vase, figural handle, ivory matte finish 125.00
Watch, Republican Campaign type, Bush '88 ....30.00

F

Farm Collectibles

Collecting Hints: The country look makes farm implements and other items very popular with interior decorators. Often, items are varnished or refinished to make them more appealing; this, in fact, lowers their value, as far as the serious collector is concerned. Farm items were used heavily; collectors should look for signs of use to add individuality and authenticity to the pieces.

When collecting farm toys, it is best to specialize in a single type, e.g., cast iron, models by one specific company, models of one type of farm machinery or models in one size (1/16 scale being the most popular). Farm collectibles made after 1940 have not yet achieved great popularity.

History: Initially, farm products were made by local craftsmen—the blacksmith, wheelwright or the farmer himself. Product designs varied greatly.

The Industrial Age and the golden age of American agriculture go hand in hand. The farm market was important to manufacturers between 1880 and 1900. Farmers demanded quality products, capable of withstanding hard use. In the 1940s, urban growth began to draw attention away from the rural areas and the consolidation of farms began. Larger machinery was developed.

The vast majority of farm models date between the early 1920s and the present. Manufacturers of farm equipment, such as John Deere, International Harvester, Massey-Ferguson, Ford and White Motors, issued models to correspond to their full-sized products. These firms contracted with America's leading toy manufacturers, such as Arcade Company, Dent, Ertl, Hubley, Killgore and Vindex, to make the models.

References: *Bristol Wagon & Carriage Illustrated Catalog 1900*, Dover, 1994; Terri Clemens, *American Family Farm Antiques*, Wallace-Homestead, 1994; David Erb and Eldon Brumbaugh, *Full Steam Ahead: J.I. Case Tractors & Equipment*, American Society of Agricultural Engineers, 1993; Carol Belanger Grafton (ed.), *Horses and Horse-Drawn Vehicles*, Dover, 1994; Jim Moffet, *American Corn Huskers*, Off Beat Books, 1994; Robert Rauhauser, *Hog Oilers Plus*, published by author (Box 766, RR #2, Thomasville, PA 17364), 1996; C.H. Wendel, *Unusual Vintage Tractors*, Krause Publications, 1996; ——, *Encyclopedia of American Farm Implements & Antiques*, Krause Publications, 1997.

Periodicals: *Antique Power*, P.O. Box 1000, Westerville, OH 43081; *Belt Pulley*, P.O. Box 83, Nokomis, IL 62075; *Country Wagon Journal*, P.O. Box 331, W. Milford, NJ 07480; *Farm & Horticultural Equipment Collector*, Kelsey House, 77 High St., Beckenham Kent BR3 1AN England, *Farm Antiques News*, 812 N. Third St., Tarkio, MO 64491; *Iron-Men Album*, P.O. Box 328, Lancaster, PA 17603; *Rusty Iron Monthly*, P.O. Box 342, Sandwich, IL 60548; *Spec-Tuclar News*, P.O. Box 324, Dyersville, IA 52040; *Toy Farmer*, HC 2, Box 5, LaMoure, ND 58458; *Toy Tractor Times*, P.O. Box 156, Osage, IA 50461; *Tractor Classics*, P.O. Box 191, Listowel, Ontario N4H 3HE Canada; *Turtle River Toy News & Oliver Collector's News*, RR1, Box 44, Manvel, ND 58256.

Collectors' Clubs: Antique Engine, Tractor & Toy Club, 5731 Paradise Rd., Slatington, PA 18080; Cast Iron Seat Collectors Association, P.O. Box 14, Ionia, MO 65335; CTM Farm Toy & Collectors Club, P.O. Box 489, Rocanville, Saskatchewan S0A 3L0 Canada; Early American Steam Engine & Old Equipment Society, P.O. Box 652, Red Lion, PA 17356; Ertl Replicas Collectors' Club, Hwys. 136 and 20, Dyersville, IA 52040; Farm Toy Collectors Club, P.O. Box 38, Boxholm, IA 50040; International Harvester Collectors, RR2 Box 286, Winamac, IN 46996.

Museums: Billings Farm & Museum, Woodstock, VT; Bucks County Historical Society, Doylestown, PA; Carroll County Farm Museum, Westminster, MD; Living History Farms, Urbandale, IA; Makoti Threshers Museum, Makoti, ND; National Agricultural Center & Hall of

Egg Scale, Farm Master, red ground, black, yellow and red, $28.

Fame, Bonner Springs, KS; Never Rest Museum, Mason, MI; New York State Historical Association and The Farmers' Museum, Cooperstown, NY; Pennsylvania Farm Museum, Landis Valley, PA.

Badge, Buckeye T.D. Co., silvered red-enameled brass, serial number, c1940 .... 30.00
Barn Hinge, 27" l, wrought iron, strap type 75.00
Book
   Caterpillar, Great American Legend Photo Book, orig dj, 128 pgs, 1986 .... 15.00
   John Deere, Care & Repair, Farm Machinery, 12th ed, 250 pgs ... 25.00
   Wanamaker Dairy, 446 pgs, foldout map of Philadelphia, 1933 .... 25.00
Booklet
   Allis Chalmers Gleaner Combine, 34 pgs, 1950s 4.00
   Beacon Feeds
      Chick Battery & Laying, 84 pgs, 1941 .... 5.00
      Dairy Management, 3rd ed, 86 pgs, 1939 .... 6.00
   Eshelman Broiler Feed, chicken photos, 54 pgs, 1941 .... 7.50
   International Harvester, Make Soil Productive, 64 pgs, 1931 .... 8.00
   Kresco Insecticides, 8 pgs, 1922 .... 3.00
   Massey-Ferguson, Elf Tractor, foldout, German text, 1964 .... 4.00
   National Lime Association, Lime in Agriculture, 54 pgs, 1936 .... 6.00
   Purina Broiler Book, 32 pgs, 1941 .... 7.50
Branding Iron, Lazy B, wrought iron 40.00
Chick Feeder, tin 20.00
Clock, Prairie Farms Dairy Products, lighted 20.00
Corn Dryer, wrought iron 25.00
Egg Candler, 8" h, tin, kerosene burner, mica window 30.00

Egg Crate
  Tin 10.00
  Wood.......................................25.00
Feed Bag, cotton,
  black illus of sheep 10.00
Flax Comb, 17-1/2" l, wrought iron,
  ram's horn finials 130.00
Grain Shovel, wood,
  carved dec.............................295.00
Handbook, Griffith & Boyd Fertilizer,
  72 pgs, 1909.............................7.00
Hay Rake, 48-1/2" l, varnished......60.00
Implement Seat, cast iron
  Bradley's Mower.....................115.00
  Hoover & Co............................95.00
Key-Chain Fob, McCormick Line,
  bright gold luster metal, figural
  world globe, inscribed "The OK
  Line/McCormick Line/OK, All
  Over the World," 1920s 20.00
Magazine, John Deere, *The Furrow*,
  32 pgs, March 1977...................5.00
Match Safe, Hudson & Thurber Co.,
  Minneapolis, celluloid cov silvered
  brass, multicolored illus of nude
  woman, titled "Love's Repose,"
  products listed, 1905 ....115.00
Memo Book, Agrico Fertilizer,
  1947 calendar............................3.00
Parts List, Co-Op Universal,
  Milkers, 8 pgs, June 1945..........5.00
Pinback Button, celluloid
  Avery Mfg. Co., Bulldog,
  multicolored, stern-looking
  bulldog, cog-like teeth, spiked
  "Avery" collar, early 1900s 125.00
  Boys Agricultural Club,
  Berks County, multicolored,
  farm symbols rimmed in white,
  blue letters, c1920....................30.00
  Dr. LeGear, King of Horses,
  issued by Dr. LeGear's Stock
  Remedies of St. Louis, man
  holding very large horse...........85.00
  Globe Poultry Feed, Makes 'em Lay,
  rooster standing on globe, hen
  sitting on eggs below................65.00
  Harrisburg Farm Show, multicolored,
  black letters, c1950 ....12.00
  International Harvester Co., Union,
  lavender, black and white, May 1938,
  Employees Association of East
  Moline Works 12.00
  Ohio Cultivator Co., multicolored,
  detailed horse-drawn "Famous
  Ohio/Over 100,000 in Use"
  cultivator, Bellevue, OH, maker,
  late 1890s.................................35.00
  Old Trusty Incubator, M.M. Johnson,
  Clay Center, NE, St. Bernard's
  head center 45.00
  Omaha Merchant, Lininger & Metcalf
  Co., gold letters, black rim, red
  entwined company initials, soft

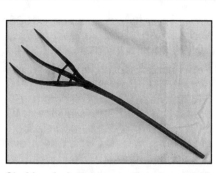

Shaking fork, 3 prongs, wood and metal, salesman's sample, 18-1/2" l, $225.

  green ground, early 1900s 20.00
  Vitality Feeds, red, white and blue,
  red-combed rooster, coop-like
  window, c1920 ....20.00
Ring, FFA, SS, mkd "Balfour Sterling,"
  small detailed symbol for Future
  Farmers of America Vocational
  Agriculture, 1930s 20.00
Ruler, 1/2" x 4-1/2", folding, celluloid,
  International Harvester Co.,
  printed monthly calendars for
  1909 and 1910, lists of farm
  products, black inscriptions on 1
  side, red on reverse.................25.00
Seed Dryer, chestnut frame, pine
  spindles, 21" x 43"...................85.00
Shovel, cast iron, wood handle 30.00
Toy
  Baler, International Harvester,
  die cast, 1/16 scale, 4 bales,
  Ertl, 1967.................................24.00
  Combine
    Case, die cast, 1/16 scale,
    plastic reel, Ertl, 1974 ....85.00
    Marx, tin, friction, MIB..........35.00
  Corn Picker, pressed steel, 1/16
  scale, Carter
    John Deere, 1952 ....125.00
    Tru-Scale 85.00
  Corn Sheller, Minneapolis Moline,
  pull type, decaled, rubber tires,
  1/16 scale................................125.00
  Cream Separator, International
  Harvester, cast iron, black
  plated bowl and pail, 1/12 scale,
  Arcade, 1930..........................295.00
  Disc, International Harvester,
  die cast, 1/16 scale, Ertl, 1965.60.00
  Grain Drill, John Deere,
  pressed steel, 1/16 scale,
  Carter, 1965 ....145.00
  Harrow, tandem disc, Corgi,
  1967, MIB.................................20.00
  Manure Spreader, New Holland,
  high sides, Ertl 65.00
  Pedal Car
    International
      400, needs restoration 400.00
      860, pedals missing 250.00

John Deere
  20, needs restoration 150.00
  720, orig parts,
  needs paint 475.00
  Lawn and Garden
  Pedal Tractor...................500.00
Plow, McCormick-Deering,
cast iron, red, yellow wheels,
Arcade, 1932 ....95.00
Threshing Machine, John Deere,
cast iron, Arcade, 1930..........150.00
Tractor
  Arcade, cast iron
    Allis Chalmers, 6-1/4" l,
    emb name on rear wheels,
    1940 ....195.00
    International Harvester,
    nickel-plated man, rubber
    wheels, 1940....................325.00
  Ertl, die cast, 1/16 scale,
  Agri King, Case,
  white, 1974......................185.00
  Minneapolis Moline, yellow 95.00
  Marx, litho tin windup,
  driver, 8" l............................45.00
  Tootsietoy, Ford,
  red, rubber tires 40.00
  Tru-Scale, Carter,
  die cast, 1/16 scale, 1975....75.00
Wagon, John Deere,
die cast, 1/16 scale, metal
wheels, 1960, Ertl 95.00
Wagon Seat, wood, wrought-iron trim,
  hinged compartment, 42" l 250.00
Yearbook, De Laval,
  1947, 48 pages 30.00

Fast Food Memorabilia

Collecting Hints: Premiums, made primarily of cardboard or plastic and of recent vintage, are the mainstay of today's fast food collector. Other collectible items are advertising signs and posters, character dolls, promotional glasses and tray liners. In fact, anything associated with a restaurant chain is collectible, although McDonald's items are the most popular.

Collectors should concentrate only on items in mint condition. Premiums should be unassembled or sealed in an unopened plastic bag. Collecting fast food memorabilia has grown rapidly, and, more than ever before, the fast food chains continue to churn out an amazing array of collectibles.

History: During the period just after World War II, the only convenience restaurants were the coffee shops and diners located along America's highways or in the towns and cities. As suburbia grew, young families created a demand for a faster and less-expensive type of food service. Ray A. Kroc responded by opening his first McDonald's drive-in restaurant in Des Plaines, IL, in 1955. By offering a limited menu of hamburgers, french fries and drinks, Kroc kept his costs and prices down. This successful concept of assembly-line food preparation soon was imitated, but never surpassed, by a myriad of competitors.

By the mid-1960s the race was on and franchising was seen as the new economic frontier. As the competition increased, the need to develop advertising promotions became imperative. A plethora of promotional give-aways entered the scene.

References: Ron Abler, *Happy Meal Pocket Checklist*, published by author, 1993; Ken Clee and Susan Huffard, *Tomart's Price Guide to Kid's Meal Collectibles (Non-McDonald's)*, Tomart Publications, 1993; Gary Henriques and Audre DuVall, *McDonald's Collectibles*, Collector Books, 1997; Terry and Joyce Losonsky, *McDonald's Happy Meal Toys around the World*, Schiffer Publishing, 1995; Jeffrey Tennyson, *Hamburger Heaven*, Hyperion, 1993; Meredith Williams, *Tomart's Price Guide to McDonald's Happy Meal Collectibles*, 2nd Edition, Tomart Publications, 1995; Michael Karl Witzel, *American Drive-In*, Motorbooks International, 1994.

Periodicals: *Collecting Tips Newsletter*, P.O. Box 633, Joplin, MO 64802; *Fast Food Collectors Express*, P.O. Box 221, Mayview, MO 64071; *World of Fast Food Collectibles Newsletter*, P.O. Box 64, Powder Springs, GA 30073.

Collectors' Clubs: McD International Pin Club, 3587 Oak Ridge, Slatington, PA 18080; McDonald's Collectors Club, 424 White Rd., Fremont, OH 43420.

Note: Prices are for mint condition items sealed in their original wrappers or packages and unassembled.

A&W

Decals, iron-on, Root Beer Bear and A&W, logo, 1977, unused sheet 7.50
Doll, Root Beer Bear, plush...........30.00
Meal Box, A&W, Playtown, folds into A&W Root Beer stand, 1984 ...10.00
Pitcher with six glasses, Root Beer Bear and A&W, logo, 1970s 50.00
Puppet, hand, Root Beer Bear, cloth 10.00
Record, "Vic Damone Swings With A&W," 45 RPM, 1960s 20.00

Big Boy

Bank, 8-3/4" h, vinyl, Marriott Corp., 1976 ....10.00
Doll Set, 3 stuffed cloth dolls, unopened clear plastic bags, printed outfits, Big Boy, Dolly and Nugget the dog, c1978......................75.00
Figure, PVC, plastic car 6.00
Pinback Button, Big Boy Club, red, white, blue and brown hair, c1950...............................60.00
Salt and Pepper Shakers, pr, china, 1960s.....................125.00

Burger King

Airplane, Yumbo Yet, Styrofoam, 1976 ....7.50
Bicycle Clip, colorful wheel spokes, 1981 ....5.00
Bookmark, strip of five, cardboard, characters, 1979........................5.00
Calendar, 1980, The Year of the Olympic Games.......................15.00
Card Game, Burger King Rummy, orig box, 1978...........................10.00
Chess Game, King Checker Chess, 1978 ....9.00
Crown, paper, jewel-like design, "Have It Your Way"...................4.00
Frisbee, 9-1/2" d, R2D2, C3P0

and Darth Vader from "Empire Strikes Back," 1981 ....12.00
Meal Box
  Burger King Magic Meal, magic tricks printed on side, 1981 ....5.00
  Burger King Restaurant, 1986 ...4.00
  Thundercats, 1986....................5.00
Pinback Button, 3/4" d, Happy Face, eyes are Burger King logo.........5.00
Puppet, hand, plastic, King, older version...................................10.00
Trading Cards, The Empire Strikes Back, complete set of 36, 1981 ....35.00
Valentine, King illus, sheet of six, 1977, unused 8.00
Whistle, plastic, pickle, green..........7.50

Carl's Jr.

Bookmark, plastic, Happy Star character, 1985 ....4.00
Pencil Top, plastic, standing Happy Star character............................4.00
Meal Box, Magnet School, 1988 .....3.00
Puppet, hand, plastic, Count on Carl's Jr., 1983 ....7.00
Sticker, puffy, Happy Star, wiggly eyes, 1984 ....3.00
Sticker Puzzle, Carl's Jr., 1984 ....4.00

Dairy Queen

Meal Box, Hot Doggity, Dennis the Menace 3.00
Puppet, hand, plastic, Dennis the Menace 5.00
Salt and Pepper Shakers, pr, ceramic, ice cream cone shape 10.00
Spoon, plastic, red, long handle, ice cream cone top....................1.00
Whistle, plastic, ice cream cone shape 20.00

Denny's

Menu, plastic coated, c1990 ....2.00
Ring, brass, expansion bands, traces of orig yellow paint, 1-3/4" l flat piece of brass on top, with brown "D" in center, 1970s.................60.00

Domino's

Car Stick-Up, 14" h, Noid, plush ...15.00
Doll, 20" l, stuffed cloth, big "N" on chest, red outfit, Acme, 1988 Dominos Pizza Inc. 20.00
Figure, boxer, Noid 5.00
Dunkin' Donuts, toy, die-cast tractor trailer, orig box, 1995, MIB 15.00
Howard Johnson, sign, pancake man with pancake stack, boy with dog at top, back reads "Turner Turnpike, Okla," mkd "Holland" 45.00
International House of Pancakes, dish, ceramic, chicken shape, IHOP logo, 1960s..............................32.00
Jack in the Box, figure, registered to

Doll, Burger King, cloth, printed, red, yellow, flesh, black, and white, 16" h, $5.

Jack-in-the-Box, "Made by Imperial, Hong Kong," 1970s

    Jack Bendy...............................15.00
    Jack Boy...................................15.00
    Old Man Jack 15.00
    Onion Ring Man 12.00
    Secret Sauce Man....................12.00
Jerry's Restaurant, flicker ring, cartoon chef, red plastic, 1960s............25.00
Kentucky Fried Chicken, bank, 12-1/2" h, Colonel Sanders, plastic, figural..........................25.00
Little Caesar's, finger puppet, Pizza Pizza, 6" h, 3-1/2" w, 1990s.......5.00

McDonald's
Bank
    7" h, 4" d, Ronald McDonald, painted hard vinyl, white base, seated figure, late 1970s..........35.00
    12" h, hard vinyl smiling waste dumpster, removable yellow lid, coin slot in top, McDonald's symbol on reverse, 1975 ....25.00
Car Door Tray, 4" x 8", pale turquoise blue plastic tray, 1" molded flange to be inserted in car window, yellow, black and white illus of drive-in with arches, Art Combed Plastics by Demaraee, Kokomo, IN, mid 1950s 100.00
Coloring Book, Ronald McDonald Goes to the Moon, 9" x 12-1/4", 1967, 12 pgs, full-color front and back covers, b&w story about race to moon, unused............125.00
Doll, 26" h, 22" arm span, 9" l feet, vinyl, inflatable, multicolored, 1978...75.00
Figure
    Grimace, Remco Toys, Inc., 1976, MOC..............................45.00
    Ronald McDonald, PVC 9.00
Meal Box, Happy Meal
    Giggles & Games, 1982.............6.00
    Lego Building Set, 1984.............5.00
    Mac Tonight, 1988 ....4.00
Mug, Garfield characters, slogans "It's not a pretty life but someone has to live it," "Use your friends wisely," and "I'm not one who rises to the occasion," United Features, Inc., 1978, price for 3-pc set............18.00
Plate, set of 4, Melmac, colorful, 1 plate for each season of the year, 1977...............................30.00
Punching Bag, 13" h, Ronald McDonald, mkd "Taiwan," c1980...............10.00
Ring
    Hamburglar, 1-3/8" h, diecut bright yellow, black details, late 1970s...........25.00
    Ronald McDonald, flexible, orange vinyl base, hard-vinyl bright yellow figural head, orange eyes, mkd "Spe-

cialty Premiums Inc.," 1974......55.00
Ruler, Ronald McDonald Ruler, cardboard, early 1970s............10.00
Teenie Beanie Babies, 1997, set of 10, MIP, for set 45.00
Sambos, coaster, 3" d, "Sambos has it 10¢," red and blue coffee cup, 1970s....................................10.00
South of the Border, bobbing head, 6-1/4" h, 2" x 2" base, painted wood, Pedro, yellow sombrero, decal inscription in red letters, white serape, 5-color shawl, c1960 ....75.00
Taco Bell, doll, orig tag, Hallmark Cards, Inc.
    Happy Talk Sprite, Champ, "Sprite Talk by Champ" booklet 1983..10.00
    Hugga Bunch, Tuggins, "Tiny Book of Hugga Jokes" booklet, 1984, MIP 10.00

Wendy's
Fun Flyer, 3-1/2" d, round, plastic ...2.00
Meal Box, The Good Stuff Gang, 1988 ......3.00
Mug, Wendy's Old-Fashioned Hamburgers, ceramic, red, white and black trademark, 1970s......5.00
Premium, Mighty Mouse, Pearl Pureheart, the Cow, Bat-Bat, Scrappy and Tey Pate, all sealed in orig pkgs, 1989, price for set of 6.............25.00
Puppet, hand, Wendy.....................5.00

Fiesta Ware

Collecting Hints: Whenever possible, buy pieces without cracks, chips or scratches. Fiestaware can be identified by bands of concentric circles.

History: The Homer Laughlin China Company introduced Fiesta dinnerware in January 1936 at the Pottery and Glass Show in Pittsburgh. Frederick Rhead designed the pattern; Arthur Kraft and Bill Bensford molded it. Dr. AV. Bleininger and H.W. Thiemecke developed the glazes. A vigorous marketing campaign took place between 1939 and 1943.

The original five colors were red, dark blue, light green (with a trace of blue), brilliant yellow and ivory. In mid-1937, turquoise was added. Red was removed in 1943 because some of the chemicals used to produce it were essential to the war effort; it did not reappear until 1959. In 1951, light green, dark blue and ivory were retired and forest green, rose, chartreuse and gray were added to the line. Other color

changes took place in the late 1950s, including the addition of a medium green.

Fiesta ware was redesigned in 1969 and discontinued about 1972. In 1986, Fiesta was reintroduced by Homer Laughlin China Company. The new china body shrinks more than the old semi-vitreous and ironstone pieces, thus making the new pieces slightly smaller than the earlier pieces. The modern colors are also different in tone or hue, e.g., the cobalt blue is darker than the old blue. Other modern colors are black, white, apricot and rose.

References: Susan and Al Bagdade, *Warman's American Pottery and Porcelain*, Wallace-Homestead, 1994; Sharon and Bob Huxford, *Collectors Encyclopedia of Fiesta with Harlequin and Riviera*, 7th Edition, Collector Books, 1992 value update; Leslie Pina, *Pottery, Modern Wares 1920-1960*, Schiffer Publishing, 1994.

Periodical: *Fiesta Collectors Quarterly*, 19238 Dorchester Cir., Strongsville, OH 44136.

Collectors' Clubs: Fiesta Club of America, P.O. Box 15383, Loves Park, IL 61115; Fiesta Collectors Club, 19238 Dorchester Cir., Strongsville, OH 44136.

Advertising, mug, Kappa Delta, 1965, green int 45.00
Ashtray
    Cobalt Blue 40.00
    Red 50.00
Cake Server, red, Kitchen Kraft ..150.00
Calendar Plate, ivory, 1954, 10" d 45.00
Candlestick
    Bulb, price for pr
        Cobalt Blue 125.00
        Ivory...................................125.00
        Turquoise...........................110.00
        Yellow 100.00
    Tripod, price for pr
        Cobalt Blue 795.00
        Ivory...................................795.00
        Light Green 695.00
        Red 795.00
        Turquoise...........................795.00
        Yellow 695.00
Casserole, cov
    Cobalt Blue 295.00
    Dark Green 295.00

Gray 295.00
Ivory 275.00
Light Green 175.00
Red...295.00
Rose..275.00
Turquoise 135.00
Yellow......................................125.00
Casserole, French, yellow..........190.00
Carafe
    Cobalt Blue, spout repaired....120.00
    Ivory 230.00
    Light Green 145.00
    Red...375.00
    Turquoise 380.00
Chop Plate
    Ivory, 13" d 25.00
    Light Green 38.00
    Red, 15" d.................................50.00
Coffeepot
    Light Green 195.00
    Turquoise 155.00
Compote
    Ivory, 12" d 225.00
    Red, 12" d 140.00
    Yellow..42.00
Creamer
    Individual, red.........................200.00
    Stick handle
        Cobalt Blue 65.00
        Ivory 75.00
        Light Green 45.00
        Red 75.00
        Turquoise............................115.00
        Yellow 45.00
Cream Soup
    Ivory 60.00
    Red..75.00
    Rose..95.00
Cup and Saucer
    Chartreuse 25.00
    Cobalt Blue................................27.00
    Gray 24.00
    Ivory 20.00
    Light Green 16.00
    Medium Green 55.00
    Red..27.00

Candleholder, round, orange, $50.

Turquoise 22.00
Yellow 22.00
Deep Dish Plate
    Cobalt Blue 35.00
    Ivory 27.50
    Light Green 33.00
    Medium Green 100.00
    Red 35.00
    Turquoise 20.00
    Yellow 25.00
Demitasse Cup and Saucer
    Chartreuse 495.00
    Cobalt Blue 95.00
    Dark Green 695.00
    Gray 695.00
    Ivory 55.00
    Light Green 65.00
    Red 95.00
    Rose..695.00
    Turquoise 70.00
    Yellow 115.00
Demitasse Pot, cov
    Cobalt Blue 495.00
    Green..475.00
    Ivory 750.00
Dessert Bowl, 6" d
    Chartreuse 50.00
    Cobalt Blue 38.00
    Green..29.00
    Ivory 38.00
    Red 38.00
    Turquoise 29.00
Eggcup
    Chartreuse 115.00
    Green..36.00
    Ivory 45.00
    Yellow 40.00
Fruit Bowl, 4-3/4" d
    Cobalt Blue 25.00
    Red 35.00
    Turquoise 20.00
    Yellow 20.00
Fruit Bowl, 11-3/4" d
    Cobalt Blue 485.00
    Yellow 350.00
Gravy, turquoise...........................30.00
Juice Pitcher
    Cobalt Blue 45.00
    Ivory 45.00
    Rose..45.00
Juice Tumbler
    Cobalt Blue 45.00
    Ivory 29.00
    Light Green 27.50
    Red 50.00
Marmalade, cobalt blue...............300.00
Mixing Bowl
    #1
        Green................................230.00
        Red 170.00

#2
    Cobalt Blue 195.00
    Ivory...................................230.00
    Light Green.........................44.00
#3
    Cobalt Blue, chipped 420.00
    Ivory....................................77.00
#4
    Cobalt Blue 225.00
    Ivory....................................77.00
#5
    Light Green.........................100.00
    Red 82.00
    Turquoise............................93.00
#6
    Light Green.........................110.00
    Red 135.00
    Yellow 105.00
#7, cobalt blue, rim repaired ..137.00
Mug
    Chartreuse 90.00
    Cobalt Blue 55.00
    Ivory, gold letters 45.00
    Light Green 40.00
    Medium Green, chips...........22.00
    Yellow 40.00
Mustard
    Cobalt Blue 325.00
    Green...................................250.00
    Red, chip...............................90.00
Nappy
    8-1/2" d
        Chartreuse...........................27.50
        Dark Green 35.00
        Medium Green 95.00
        Gray.....................................40.00
        Red 30.00
        Rose 40.00
        Turquoise.............................19.00
        Yellow 77.00
    9-1/2" d, ivory.........................45.00
Onion Soup, cov
    Ivory 360.00
    Yellow 415.00
Plate, 6" d
    Cobalt Blue 5.00
    Ivory......................................5.00
    Turquoise 3.00
    Yellow 3.00
Plate, 7" d
    Green....................................6.00
    Ivory......................................8.00
    Turquoise 6.00
    Yellow 6.00
Plate, 9" d
    Chartreuse 15.00
    Cobalt Blue 15.00
    Ivory.....................................14.00
    Medium Green 37.50
    Red 15.00

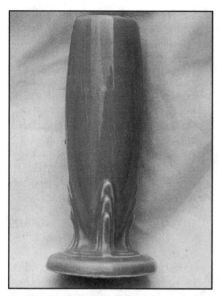

Vase, light blue, 6-1/4" h, $35.

Rose	15.00
Yellow	8.00
Plate, 10" d	
Ivory	40.00
Yellow	22.00
Plate, 10-1/2" d, grill, green	22.00
Platter, oval	
Cobalt Blue	30.00
Gray	35.00
Ivory	25.00
Red	32.00
Rose	45.00
Turquoise	27.50
Yellow	22.00
Relish	
Green	175.00
Ivory, cobalt blue center, turquoise and yellow side dishes	165.00
Red	425.00
Salad Bowl, individual	
Medium Green	80.00
Red	55.00
Turquoise	72.00
Salt and Pepper Shakers, pr	
Cobalt Blue	21.00
Red	24.00
Yellow	35.00
Sauce Boat	
Gray	50.00
Ivory	43.00
Light Green	33.00
Red	55.00
Soup Plate	
Ivory	36.00
Turquoise	29.00
Sugar, cov	
Chartreuse	65.00
Gray	75.00

Rose	75.00
Syrup	
Red	385.00
Turquoise, green top	145.00
Teapot	
Medium Green, medium size	770.00
Red, medium	285.00
Turquoise, large	150.00
Yellow, medium	90.00
Tom and Jerry Jug	
Green	45.00
Ivory	45.00
Turquoise	45.00
Utility Tray	
Cobalt Blue	25.00
Red	55.00
Vase	
Bud	
Ivory	67.00
Light Green	42.00
Red	100.00
10" h, ivory	770.00
12" h, ivory	825.00
Water Pitcher, disc	
Chartreuse	180.00
Cobalt Blue	185.00
Dark Green	185.00
Gray	265.00
Ivory	130.00
Light Green	115.00
Medium Green	1,495.00
Red	185.00
Rose	265.00
Turquoise	125.00
Yellow	115.00
Water Tumbler, cobalt blue	75.00

Firehouse Collectibles

Collecting Hints: For a period of time, it was fashionable to put a date on the back of firemen's helmets. This date is usually the date the fire company was organized, not the date the helmet was made. Firehouse collectibles cover a very broad area. The older, scarcer collectibles, such as helmets and fire marks, command high prices. The newer collectibles, e.g., cards and badges, are more reasonably priced.

History: The volunteer fire company has played a vital role in the protection and social growth of many towns and rural areas. Paid professional firemen are usually found in large metropolitan areas. Each fire compa-

ny prided itself on its equipment and uniforms. Annual conventions and parades, which gave the individual fire companies a chance to show off their equipment, produced a wealth of firehouse-related collectibles.

References: Andrew G. Gurka, *Hot Stuff! Firefighting Collectibles*, L-W Book Sales, 1994, 1996 value update; Charles V. Hansen, *History of American Firefighting Toys*, Greenberg Publishing, 1990; James Piatti, *Firehouse Memorabilia*, Avon Books, 1994; Donald F. Wood and Wayne Sorenson, *American Volunteer Fire Trucks*, Krause Publications, 1993; ——, *Big City Fire Trucks, 1900-1950*, Krause Publications, 1996.

Periodical: *Fire Apparatus Journal*, P.O. Box 121205, Staten Island, NY 10314.

Collectors' Clubs: Antique Fire Apparatus Club of America, 5420 S. Kedvale Ave., Chicago, IL 60632; Fire Collectors Club, P.O. Box 992, Milwaukee, WI 53201; Fire Mark Circle of the Americas, 2859 Marlin Dr., Chamblee, GA 30341; Great Lakes International Antique Fire Apparatus Association, 4457 285th St., Toledo, OH 43611; The International Fire Buff Associates, Inc., 7509 Chesapeake Ave., Baltimore, MD 21219; International Fire Photographers Association, P.O. Box 8337, Rolling Meadows, IL 60008; Society for the Preservation & Appreciation of Motor Fire Apparatus in America, P.O. Box 2005, Syracuse, NY 13320.

Museums: There are many museums devoted to firehouse collectibles. Large collections are housed at the following: American Museum of Fire Fighting, Corton Falls, NY; Fire Museum of Maryland, Lutherville, MD; Hall of Flame, Scottsdale, AZ; Insurance Company of North America (I.N.A.) Museum, Philadelphia, PA; New England Fire & History Museum, Brewster, MA; New York City Fire Museum, New York, NY; Oklahoma State Fireman's Association Museum, Inc., Oklahoma City, OK; San Francisco Fire Dept. Pioneer Memorial Museum, San Francisco, CA.

Advertising
    Booklet, American Fire Extinguisher Co., Boston, 60 pgs, 1967 .... 45.00

Poster, Hydropult-Most Efficient Fire Engine in the World, scene of fire at Palace Garden, Oct. 1860, 11" x 14", framed....................175.00

Sign, 13" x 28", Lux Fire Extinguishing Equipment, porcelain, double-sided, multicolored illus of motorboat.....................75.00

Trade Card, Buckeye Force Pumps, Negro pumping water to put out house fire, Springfield, OH.......24.00

Alarm box, cast iron, pedestal, emb "City of Chicago," restored.............275.00

Badge

  1-1/2", diecut, SP, "Vigilance," spear on shield..........................40.00

  2-3/4", celluloid, red helmet, Kearny & Trecker District 7......20.00

Bell, 12", brass 75.00

Belt, black leather, white lettering "Rescue No. 1" 65.00

Book

  Adult

    Ahrens-Fox: The Rolls-Royce of Fire Engines, Haas, 1982, paperback, 159 pgs 25.00

    Brief History of the Massachusetts Charitable Fire Society, Sprague, 1893 ....36.00

    1917 New York Fire Dept History, hardcover, 218 pgs, 8" x 10"..5.00

  Children's, *The Mickey Mouse Fire Brigade*, Whitman, 1936, hardcover 7" x 10", color cover, b&w illus 80.00

Bucket, galvanized tin, red lettering, "Fire Only"................................35.00

Catalog, Darling Valves & Fire Hydrants, 302 pgs, black-and white-photos, hardcover, 1944.......................30.00

Daguerreotype, fireman, hat, horn and uniform, tinted........................500.00

Engine House Gong, Gamewell

  6", key wind, chrome..............100.00

  10", pull chain, aluminum 125.00

Engine Name Plate

  Ahrens-Fox...............................10.00

  LaFrance 15.00

  Mack Trucks, bulldog 20.00

Postcard, photographic, Chemical and Hose Co. No. 2, Johnstown, PA, $12

Extinguisher

  Bottle type, glass, orig label, holder and box, Larkin 75.00

  Hand-grenade type, Harden, blue glass, patent Aug. 8, 1871 ....90.00

Fire Engine, pumper

  Dodge, 1932 ....3,500.00

  Mack Truck, 1936, Hale pump...........................4,000.00

Hose Nozzle, brass 50.00

Lantern, Goodwill Fire Co., brass, etched globe, King.................450.00

Lapel Stud, 7/8", red, white and blue, celluloid, "Woolf's Best Made Clothing," 1890 ....15.00

Paperweight, 4", cast iron, hat shape, insurance company adv 37.50

Photograph, negative, glass, Chicago Fire Dept #6 pumper 40.00

Pinback Button

  7/8"

    Fire Department Ambulance, white, red lettering, red cross, c1920 ....15.00

    Fire Prevention Week, red and white, paper back with funeral home text, c1940 ....12.00

    Junior Fire Prevention League, red and white, c1940 ....15.00

  1"

    Firemen's Booster, black and white pumper, red inscription, c1900 ....20.00

    Grinnel Automatic Sprinkler, celluloid, brass frame, early 1900s 18.00

    Harrisburg Firemen's Soldiers' Monument, dedication June 21, 1924 ....10.00

  1-1/4", celluloid

    Eastern Association of Fire Chiefs, gold and brown, crossed hose nozzles, c1940 ....12.00

    Fire Dept. Day, multicolored portrait, blue and white rim, 1915....................................24.00

    Fire Scene, silver horse-drawn pumper, black ground, early 1900s 24.00

    Good Will Ambulance, black and white, 1900s horse-drawn ambulance 15.00

    Greensburg, VFD, black picture, bright gold ground, 1940s PA celebration...........10.00

    Hose Co., #2, white, red, blue and flesh tones, black lettering, 1904 ....20.00

    Iowa Firemen's Association, red, white and blue, c1940..........10.00

    Park Extension, black-and white-photo of 1938 ambulance 7.50

    Portrait, fireman, multicolored, white ground 18.00

    Rainbow Fire Company, multicolored, white ground, 1928 department outing...............10.00

    Rescue Scene, multicolored, firemen rescuing baby, early 1900s 28.00

Postcard, Chemical and Hose Co., No. 2, Johnstown, PA, photograph of horse-drawn wagon in front of fire house 12.00

Puzzle, slice type, Milton Bradley Co., orig 8" x 9" box, c 1913-35 ......75.00

Stevengraph, titled "For Life or Death," fire engine rushing to burning house, orig mat and frame 325.00

Toy

  10-1/2", metal, emb "Fire Engine No. 526," Hubley, c1936.................65.00

  13-1/2", rubber tires, removable hose reel, bell, 6 firemen, steam boiler, 1936, Arcade 110.00

  17-1/2", red and yellow, sharply streamlined skirted fenders, white ladders, open cargo back, Buddy L, 1940..........................38.00

  35", extension ladder, red body, silver-painted ladders, yellow removable saddle, leatherette seat, crank, orig decals, Buddy L, 1945 ......65.00

Fire King

Collecting Hints: Anchor Hocking's Fire-King is a contemporary of Pyrex and other "oven-proof" glassware of the 1940s and 1950s. It is only within the past decade that collectors have begun to focus on this material. As a result, prices fluctuate and a stable market is several years in the future.

In 1938, Anchor Hocking introduced a line of children's dishes which became part of the Fire-King line. A popular pattern is Little Bo Peep. Like all children's dishes, these objects command strong prices. Some Fire-King collectors focus on a single color. Jane Ray, a jadite-colored pattern, was introduced in 1945. In 1948, the color was first used in a series of restaurant wares and it was discontinued in 1963.

Fire-King was sold in sets. Add an additional 25% to 35% to the price of the individual pieces for an intact set in its original box. Fire-King pieces are found with two types of marks. The first is a mold mark directly on the piece; the second, an oval foil paper label.

History: Fire-King was a product of the Anchor Hocking Glass Co. In 1905, Isaac J. Collins founded the Hocking Glass Co., along the banks of the Hocking River near Lancaster, OH. On March 6, 1924, fire completely destroyed the plant, but it was rebuilt in six months. Hocking produced pressed glass dinnerware, many patterns of which are considered Depression glass. In 1937, Hocking Glass Company merged with the Anchor Cap Co., and became Anchor Hocking Glass Corp. Shortly thereafter, the new company began to manufacture glass ovenware that could withstand high temperatures in a kitchen oven.

Production of oven-proof glass marked "FIRE-KING" began in 1942 and lasted until 1976. Dinnerware patterns include Alice, Charm, Fleurette, Game Bird, Honeysuckle, Jane Ray, Laurel, Primrose, Turquoise Blue, Swirl and Wheat. Utilitarian kitchen items and ovenware patterns also were produced. Housewives eagerly purchased Fire-King sets and could also assemble sets of matching dinnerware and ovenware patterns. Advertising encouraged consumers to purchase prepackaged starter, luncheon, baking and snack sets, as well as casseroles. Oven glassware items included almost everything needed to completely stock the kitchen.

Fire-King patterns are found in azurite, forest green, gray, ivory, jadite, peach luster, pink, plain white, ruby red, sapphire blue, opaque turquoise and white, with an assortment of rim colors. To increase sales, decals were applied.

References: Gene Florence, *Collectible Glassware from the 40's, 50's, 60's*, 3rd Edition, Collector Books, 1997; ——, *Kitchen Glassware of the Depression Years*, 5th Edition, Collector Books, 1995; Gary and Dale Kilgo and Jerry and Gail Wilkins, *Collectors Guide to Anchor Hocking's Fire-King Glassware*, K&W Collectibles Publisher, 1991; April M. Tvorak, *Fire-King*, 5th Edition, published by author (P.O. Box 126, Canon City, CO 81215), 1997.

Periodicals: *Fire-King Monthly*, P.O. Box 70594, Tuscaloosa, AL 35407; *Fire-King News*, K&W Collectibles, Inc., P.O. Box 374, Addison, AL 35540.

Collectors' Club: The Fire-King Collectors Club, 1161 Woodrow St., #3, Redwood City, CA 94061.

Dinnerware

Bowl
    4-1/2" d, Meadow Green 4.00
    4-5/8" d, Wheat 3.00
    4-3/4" d, Charm, Azurite 5.00
    4-7/8" d
        Jane Ray, jadeite 6.00
        Swirl, Sunrise 8.00
    8" d, Turquoise Blue 15.00
    8-3/8" d, Bubble, Peach Luster .. 8.00
Cake Plate, 9" d,
    Country Kitchens 5.00
Cereal Bowl
    Charm, Azurite, 6" d 18.00
    Sapphire Blue, 6" d 22.00
    Turquoise Blue, 5" d 12.00
Children's Ware, alphabet mug 12.00
Chili Bowl, Peach Luster,
    copper tint 5.00
Creamer
    Game Bird Pattern,
    Pheasant dec 10.00
    Laurel, Peach Luster 2.50
    Swirl, azurite 6.00
    Vienna Lace 2.50
Creamer and Sugar,
    Jane Ray, jadeite 10.00
Custard Cup
    Candleglow 2.00
    Peach Luster, ruffled 1.00
Cup and Saucer
    Alice
        Blue and white 15.00
        Jadeite 6.00
    Charm
        Azurite 4.00
        Jadeite 12.00
    Honeysuckle 6.00
    Turquoise Blue 5.00
Demitasse Cup and Saucer
    Fishscale Luster 35.00
    Luster Shell 6.00
Dessert Bowl
    Game Bird Pattern
        Canada Goose dec 5.00
        Mallard Duck dec 5.00
        Pheasant dec 5.00
    Royal Ruby 6.00
    Vienna Lace 2.00
Mug
    Bubble, Peach Luster 3.00
    Game Bird Pattern
        Canada Goose dec 10.00

        Mallard Duck dec 10.00
        Ruffled Grouse dec 12.00
    Red Rose 3.00
    Sapphire Blue 25.00
    Turquoise Blue 10.00
Pitcher, Milano, aqua, ice lip 35.00
Plate, 7-1/4" to 7-3/8" d, salad
    Blue Mosaic 6.00
    Charm, Azurite 15.00
    Meadow Green 4.00
    Swirl, Sunrise 8.00
Plate, 8-3/8" d, luncheon,
    Charm, Azurite 5.00
Plate, 10" d, dinner
    Blue Mosaic 8.00
    Game Bird Pattern
        Canada Goose dec 9.00
        Mallard Duck dec 9.00
        Pheasant dec 9.00
        Ruffled Grouse dec 9.00
    Leaf and Blossom,
    green and pink 8.00
    Meadow Green 5.00
    Swirl, ivory 4.50
    Vienna Lace 3.00
Platter
    Swirl, Sunrise 20.00
    Vienna Lace, oval 8.00
    Wheat 10.00
Relish, Turquoise Blue,
    3 part, gold trim 12.00
Saucer, Charm, Azurite 1.50
Snack Set
    Colonial Lady,
    ruby and crystal 10.00
    Ivory, gold trim 5.00
Souvenir Plate, 10" d, World's Fair,
    1964, Golden Shell 45.00
Soup Bowl
    Jane Ray, jadeite 16.00
    Meadow Green 6.00
    Swirl, ivory 8.00
Sugar
    Game Bird pattern,
    Pheasant dec 10.00
    Laurel, Peach Luster 2.50
    Primrose, open 4.00
    Shell, Peach Luster, cov 8.00
    Vienna Lace, cov 5.00
Tumbler, Game Bird pattern
    Canada Goose dec 22.00
    Mallard Duck dec 12.00
    Pheasant dec 12.00
    Ruffled Grouse dec 12.00
Vegetable Bowl
    Luster Shell 6.00
    Vienna Lace, 8-1/4" 8.00

Kitchenware

Batter Bowl, 7-1/2" d,
    1 handle, jadeite 24.00

Coffee Maker, Silex, 2 cup, 2 pc ...20.00
Hot Plate, Sapphire Blue 16.00
Measuring Cup,
    Sapphire Blue, 1 spout 18.00
Mixing Bowl
    Beaded Rim, 4-7/8" d, white 6.00
    Sapphire Blue, turned rim 23.00
    Swirl
        6" d, jadeite 12.00
        9" d, white 10.00
Mixing Bowl Set, 6",
    7", 8", ivory swirl 30.00
Mug
    Jadeite......................................8.00
    Sapphire Blue, thick 25.00
Nurser, Sapphire Blue, 4 oz 8.50
Refrigerator Dish
    4-1/2" x 5-1/2", open, jadeite....16.00
    5" x 9", cov, emb lid, jadeite 40.00
Utility Bowl, Sapphire Blue
    6-7/8" d..................................15.00
    8-1/4" d..................................18.00

Ovenware

Baker, Sapphire Blue,
6 oz, individual................................3.25
Casserole, cov
    Ivory, knob,
    1-1/2" qt, knob lid 15.00
    Peach Luster, copper tint,
    French-style, tab lids,
    orig label.....................................5.00
    Sapphire Blue, 1 pint...............14.00
Custard Cup, 6 oz
    Crystal, orig label 2.00
    Sapphire Blue............................3.00
Loaf Pan, Sapphire Blue 16.00
Pie Plate
    Crystal, 10 oz, deep, orig label...3.00
    Ivory, 15 oz..............................16.00
    Sapphire Blue, 9-1/2" d 7.00
Pie Plate Cover,
Sapphire Blue, 9" d 15.00
Roaster, Sapphire Blue, 2 pcs.......90.00
Set, Peach Luster, copper tint,
    1-1/2" qt casserole, 5" x 9" deep loaf,
    9" d pie plate, 6" x 10" utility pan,
    8" round cake plan, 6-oz custard cup,
    orig box and labels 45.00
Table Server, Sapphire Blue 19.00
Utility Bowl, Sapphire Blue, 7" d....12.00

Fishing Collectibles

Collecting Hints: The types of fishing items collected are rapidly expanding as the rare specimens become more expensive and harder to locate. New categories include landing nets, minnow traps, bait boxes, advertising signs, catalogs and fish decoys used in ice spearing.

Items in original containers and in mint condition command top prices. There is little collector value if paint has been spread over the original decoration or if rods have been refinished or are broken. Early wooden plugs (before 1920), split bamboo fly rods made by the master craftsmen of that era and reels constructed of German silver with special detail or unique mechanical features are the items most sought by advanced collectors.

The number of serious collectors is steadily increasing as indicated by the membership in the National Fishing Lure Collectors Club which has approximately 2,000 active members.

History: Early man caught fish with crude spears and hooks made of bone, horn or flint. By the mid-1800s, metal lures with attached hooks were produced in New York State. Later, the metal was curved and glass beads added to make them more attractive. Spinners with painted-wood bodies and glass eyes appeared around 1890. Soon after, wood plugs with glass eyes were being produced by many different makers. Patents, which were issued in large numbers around this time, covered the development of hook hangers, body styles and devices to add movement to the plug as it was drawn through the water. The wood plug era lasted up to the mid-1930s when plugs constructed of plastic were introduced.

With the development of casting plugs, it became necessary to

Creel, wicker, ribbed bow front, straight back, 12" l, 8" h, 6" w, $25.

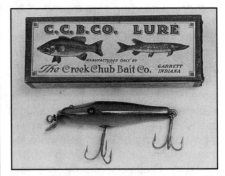

Lure, Creek Chub Bait Co., Garrett, IN, "Baby Pike Minnow" trademark, Rainbow, series 908, 2 treble hooks, glass eyes, white, yellow, red, and silver blue body, 3-1/4", with box, $20.

produce fishing reels capable of accomplishing the task with ease. Reels first appeared as a simple device to hold a fishing line. Improvements included multiplying gears, retrieving line levelers, drags, clicks and a variety of construction materials. The range of quality in reel manufacture varied considerably. Collectors are mainly interested in reels made with high-quality materials and workmanship or those exhibiting unusual features.

Early fishing rods, which were made of solid wood, were heavy and prone to breakage. By gluing together tapered strips of split bamboo, a rod was fashioned which was light in weight and had greatly improved strength. The early split-bamboo rods were round and were wrapped with silk to hold them together. As glue improved, fewer wrappings were needed and rods became slim and lightweight. Rods were built in various lengths and thicknesses, depending upon the type of fishing and bait used. Rod-makers' names and models can usually be found on the metal parts of the handle or on the rod near the handle.

References: Jim Bourdon, *South Bend: Their Artificial Bates and Reels*, John Shoffner (P.O. Box 250, Fife Lake, MI 49633), 1996; Bruce Boyden, *Fishing Collectibles*, Avon Books, 1995; Ralf Coykendall Jr., *Coykendall's Complete Guide to Sporting Collectibles*, Wallace-Homestead, 1996: Art, Brad and Scott Kimball, *The Fish Decoy, Vol. II* (1987), *Vol. III* (1993), Aardvark Publications; Carl F. Luckey, *Old Fishing Lures and Tackle*, 4th Edition, Books Americana, 1996; Dudley Murphy and Rick Edmisten, *Fishing Lure Collectibles*, Collector Books, 1995; Donald J. Peterson, *Folk Art Fish Decoys*, Schiffer Publishing, 1996; Harold E. Smith, *Collector's Guide to Creek Chub Lures &* Collectibles, Collector Books, 1997; Bob and Beverly Strauss, *American Sporting Advertising*, *Vol. 2*, L-W Book Sales, 1990, 1992 value update.

Periodicals: *American Fly Fisher*, P.O. Box 42, Manchester, VT 05254; *Antique Angler Newsletter*, P.O. Box K, Stockton, NJ 08559; *Fishing Collectibles Magazine*, 2005 Tree House Ln., Plano, TX 75023.

Collectors' Clubs: National Fishing Lure Collectors Club, P.O. Box 0184, Chicago, IL 60690; Old Reel Collectors Association, Inc., 3501 Riverview Dr., P.O. Box 2540, Weirton, WV 26062.

Museums: American Fishing Tackle Manufacturing Association Museum, Arlington Heights, IL; American Museum of Fly Fishing, Manchester, VT; Sayner Museum, Sayner, WI.

Reproduction Alert: Lures and fish decoys.

Equipment

Bobber
>5" l, panfish float, 5" l, hp, black, red and white stripes 10.00
>8" l, hand carved and painted float, tapered ends, orange, green, white and red stripes 65.00
>12" l, pike float, hp, yellow, green and red stripes 24.00

Creel
>Crushed willow, 14" x 9" x 7", leather bound, form fit 24.00
>Turtle, leather bound 935.00
>Wicker, center lid hole, early 1900 ....55.00

Decoy
>6" l, Randall, cast aluminum, green painted scale 20.00
>6-1/2" l, Leroy Howell, fish, gray body, black metal fins.............110.00
>7" l, Ice King, perch, wood, painted, Bear Creek Co............65.00

Flies
>Jorgensen, Poul, salmon........440.00
>Stone Flies Book, 1982, framed set 1,650.00

Minnow Trap

Checotach Okla Pat, glass, camp type, tinted blue and green 45.00
Handmade, 12" x 10" x 10", metal and mesh, hinged door 32.00
Shakespeare, glass, pale green, metal lid, emb name, l gal 85.00
Tackle Box, leather 440.00

Lure

Al Foss Oriental Wiggler, white, glass eyes, molded hook, #3 ....25.00
Calkin, 2-5/8" l, insect, glass, sgd "L.B.C.," bulbous midsection, raised rings at front and back to retain wire line tie and rear hook hangers, holes for corks at each end..............300.00
Carters Bestever, 3" l, white and red, pressed eyes 8.00
Creek Chub Co.
>Baby Beetle, yellow and green wings............35.00
>Fin Tail Shiner, box 1,350.00
>Jointed Pikie, perch finish, glass eyes, orig box, #700.................18.00
>Mouse, black, short fat body, pressed eyes............................12.00
Hastings, 3-1/2" l, frog, hollow rubber, hp, thick line tie wire follows the body into external bellow weight, 2 tail hooks, weed guard, c1895 ....175.00
Heddon
>Bubbling Bug, fly rod lure.......880.00
>Minnow, rainbow color, fat body, glass eyes L-rig, #150..............25.00
>Musky Crazy Crawler, yellow and red, pressed eyes 38.00
>King Bassor, red, gold spot, glass eyes 30.00
>SOS Wounded Minnow, L-Rigs, 4-1/2" l, #170, early shiner finish, glass eyes, age lines, minor chips.....90.00
>Spin diver, white, red head and tail, glass eyes, L-Rig 120.00
>Zig Wag, shiner scale finish, glass eyes, L-Rig, 2 hooks 15.00
Michigan, Life-Like 880.00
Musky Minnow 550.00
Musky Rush Tango 1,265.00
Paw Paw
>Sucker, perch finish, tack eyes..................................27.00
>Underwater minnow, green and black, tack eyes, 3 hook...........15.00
Pfleuger
>5-hook, 3-5/8" l, polished nickel minnow, glass eyes, never-fail hangers, front prop mkd "Pfleuger".......225.00
>3-hook, 2-3/4" l, Never Fail Minnow, early perch finish, hp gill marks, large glass eyes, unmkd props, never-fail hook hangers 285.00
>Tree Root Spinner, c1890......770.00
Rhead, Lou, American Nature Lure,

handmade, c1925
>Crayfish.................................770.00
>Frog 1,430.00
>Grasshopper, 1-1/4" l.............990.00
Shakespeare
>Baby Frog, pop eye 15.00
>Mouse, 3-5/8" l, white and red, thin body, glass eyes 27.00
>Revolution, hollow aluminum, prop mkd "Pat. Appl'd For," trailing feathered double hook 90.00
>Submerged Minnow, box 1,650.00
South Bend, Bass-Oreno, red, white and blue 1,375.00
>Welch & Graves, box 910.00
>Wiggle-King 660.00
>Wilson, Winged Wobbler 770.00
Strike-It Lure, green, yellow and red spots, glass eyes....................40.00
South Bend
>Bass Oreno, 3-1/2" l, frog spot color 15.00
>Panatella, green crackleback finish, glass eyes, boxed 45.00
>Truck-Oreno, 5" l, red and white wooden body, wooden prop, large feathered treble hook.............450.00
Weller, 3-1/8" l, Simplex Wiggler, No. 3, chub finish, glass eyes, hp gill marks, early 1 piece lip and line tie, orig box 160.00

Reel

Bate, T.H., NY, trout, Peerless, c1860 ....2,200.00
Bogdan, salmon
>#0..880.00
>#2...1,375.00
Chubb, Henshall-Van Antwerp, black bass 4,070.00
H.L. Leonard, Pat #191813, 4" d, salmon, German silver and hard rubber, mkd..................475.00
Hardy, Perfect Fly Reel, 3-3/8" x 1-1/4", English 145.00
Haskell, Robert, Naples, ME, trout, titanium 1,320.00
Hendryx Safety Reel, trout.........990.00

Reel, bait casting, Takapart No. 480, Pat. 1904-09, A.F. Meissel Mfg, $50.

Horton Mfg. Co., #25, blue Grass
Simplex...................................165.00
Meek, B.F. & Sons, Louisville,
KY, No. 3 ....300.00
Meek, Horton, No. 2 ....605.00
Meisselbach Co., tripart #580, casting,
nickel-plated brass.................25.00
Milam, B.C., Frankfort,
KY, No. 3 ....990.00
Pfleuger Summit, Model 1993,
level-wind casting, boxed 20.00
St. George
3-3/4", trout,
British Hardy, 1912.................825.00
3-3/8", trout,
British Hardy, 1912.................580.00
South Bend, #1131A, casting,
shiny finish, orig box 15.00
Union Hardware Co., raised pillar type,
nickel and brass.......................20.00
Vom Hofe, Edward
Salmon
2/0...................................1,375.00
3/0...................................1,200.00
Trout, Perfection
Size 1/0...........................2,750.00
Size 3, trout reel..............6,050.00
Vom Hofe, Julius, trout,
narrow spool 990.00
Winchester, Model #1135,
fly, black finish 60.00
Zwarg, salmon, 3/0.....................660.00

Related Items

Advertising
Brochure, New York Toy, Fishing for
Fun, 6 pgs, foldout, 1937 ....4.00
Calendar, 14" x 18", Bristol Steel Rod
Co., color, 1935.......................55.00
Catalog, Heddon Co.,
color illus, 1934 ....45.00
Sign, 30" x 50", from old store,
wood, carved fish, handmade,
painted, black and white.........235.00
Book
Atlantic Salmon Flies & Fishing, Jo-
seph D. Bates Jr., Stackpole Books,
1970, 362 pgs, 1st ed, dj..........37.00
The Complete Angler, Izaac Walton
and C. Cotton, Cassell Co.,
1909, 344 pgs 10.00
*Familiar Freshwater Fishes of
America*, Howard J. Walden, Harper,
1964, 8vo, drawings by Carl Burger,
1st ed, dj...................................17.50
Fish by Schaldach, William J.
Schaldach, J.B. Lippincott, Philadelphia, 1937, collected etchings,
drawings and watercolors 100.00
*Izaak Walton The Complete Angler
and His Turbulent Times*, J.
Lawrence Pool, Stinehour Press,
1976, ed of 2,000, 134 pgs, dj..21.00

*Professional Fly Tying and
Spinning Lure Making Manual*,
George Leonard Herter, 1969,
illus, 192 pgs 19.50
*Professional Fly Tying and Tackle
Making*, George Leonard Herter,
Herters, Waseca, MN, 1950.....40.00
The Treasure of Angling, Ridge
Press, 1963, b&w illus..............16.00
Catalog
Abercrombie & Fitch,
The Big Little Book of Fishing,
1968, 132 pgs 20.00
Heddon
#19....................................880.00
1911.................................1,650.00
Shakespeare, 1928................315.00
Vom Hofe, Edward, 1928.......275.00
Poster
Pfleuger, 1926........................550.00
Simmons, tackle, c1915.........250.00
Winchester, tackle, 1920s......385.00

Rod

Carlson, Sam, 7-1/2 ft,
Housatonic model..............4,400.00
Garrison, 7 ft,
model 104 trout rod 9,350.00
Gillum
7 ft, 2-3/4 oz 8,660.00
8 ft, refurbished 3,025.00
Hardy, 7 ft, 2 pc, 1 tip,
split-bamboo fly, English 200.00
Heddon Co., 5-1/2 ft, casting,
nickel silver fittings, split-bamboo fly,
fish decal brown wraps,
bag and tube 35.00
Horrocks & Ibbotson, 9 ft, 3 pc,
2 tips, split-bamboo fly,
maroon wraps...........................40.00
Kusse, Ron, 7 ft........................1,375.00
H.L. Leonard
6 ft #37 ....2,200.00
6-1/2 ft.................................1,350.00
Orvis Impregnated Battenkill,
8-1/2 ft, 2 tips, split-bamboo fly,
cloth bag, aluminum tube 235.00
Jim Payne, 8 ft
#102-L.................................2,200.00
#202.....................................1,870.00
Shakespeare Co., 9 ft, Premier Model,
3 pcs, 2 tips, split-bamboo fly,
red silk wrappings, cloth bag,
metal tube.................................55.00
Union Hardware, 7-1/2 ft, Kingfisher,
saltwater boat rod, split-bamboo fly,
dark brown wraps 25.00
Paul H. Young, 7-1/2 ft
Martha Marie.......................2,420.00
Perfectionist 3,300.00

Flag Collectibles

Collecting Hints: Public Law 829,
77th Congress, approved Dec. 22,
1942, outlines a detailed set of rules
for flag etiquette. Collectors should
become familiar with this law. The
amount of material on which the
American flag is portrayed is limit-
less. Collectors tend to focus on
those items on which the flag enjoys
a prominent position.

History: The Continental or Grand
Union flag, consisting of 13 alternate
red and white stripes with a British
Union Jack in the upper left corner,
was first used on Jan. 1, 1776, on
Prospect Hill near Boston. On June
14, 1777, the Continental Congress
adopted a flag design similar to the
Continental flag, but with the Union
Jack replaced by a blue field with 13
stars. The stars could be arranged in
any fashion. The claim that Betsy
Ross made the first Stars and Stripes
lacks historical documentation.

On Jan. 13, 1794, Congress voted to add two stars and two stripes to
the flag in recognition of Vermont and
Kentucky joining the Union. On April
18, 1818, when there were 20 states,
Congress adopted a law returning to
the original 13 stripes and adding a
new star for each state admitted. The
stars were to be added on the July
4th following admission. The 49th
star, for Alaska, was added July 4,
1959; the 50th star, for Hawaii, was
added July 4, 1960.

Reference: Boleslow and Marie-
Louis D'Otrange Mastai, *Stars and
Stripes*, Alfred Knopf, 1973.

**Auto attachment, flag, litho tin, red,
white, and blue, 6" x 4", $15.**

Collectors' Club: North American Vexillological Association, Ste. 225, 1977 N. Olden Ave., Trenton, NJ 08618.

Museums: State capitals in northern states; Hardisty Flag Museum, Hardisty, Alberta, Canada; Prattaugan Museum, Prattville, AL.

Advertising
  Ribbon, Leonards Spool Silk, Northampton, MA, silk.............20.00
  Trade Card
    Hub Gore, 3-1/2" x 6-1/4", Uncle Sam holding shoe, saying "Hub Gore Makers of Elastic for Shoes, It Was Honored at the World's Fair of 1893" 9.00
    Major's Cement, 3" x 4-1/4", 2 American flags decorating display of 125-lb weights holding suspended object, full color, adv "Major's Leather Cement-For-Sale by Druggists and Crockery Dealers" 9.00
    Merrick's Thread, 2-3/4" x 4-1/2", 2 infant children, 1 beating Civil War-type drum, other waving flag, titled "Young America" 4.00
Armband, World War II, 48 star flag, worn by paratrooper at D-Day invasion, 2 safety pins 45.00
Badge, Foresters of America, with red, white and blue ribbon 14.00
Bandanna, 22" x 25", silk, flag inside wreath of 36 stars 140.00
Booklet, Marine Corps, Our Flag, Display and Respect, 28 pgs, 1942..............5.00
Button
  1/2" d, glass dome, flag printed inside, 6 mounted on card........20.00
  1-3/4" d, horse, glass dome with eagle and flag..........................24.00
Catalog, Detra Flag Company, Catalog #24, 6-1/2" x 9", 1941, NY and Los Angeles................40.00
Certificate, Betsy Ross Flag Association, 1917, serial #38181, Series N, 12" x 16", C.H. Weisgerber painting 55.00
Clock, God Bless America, mantel, World War II vintage, small American flag waves back and forth as second hand moves, Howard Miller Mfg..................150.00
Envelope
  Civil War, angry eagle with shield hanging from its mouth and ribbon that reads "Liberty of Death," 34 large stars going around all 4 edges, each state has its name within its own star 48.00
  Printed semblance of Stars

Sheet music, *Star Spangled Banner*, Calumet Music Co., $5.

and Stripes with 45 stars covering address side...........................220.00
Flag
  29-star, 7" x 10", parade flag, coarse cotton material, Great Star pattern, used during Mexican-American War, discolored......135.00
  36-star, 21-1/2" x 36", parade flag, mounted on stick, 5-pointed star design, star pattern of 6-6-6-6-6-6..95.00
  36-star, 25" x 22", parade flag, printed muslin..........................95.00
  37-star, 16" x 24", parade flag, 1867-1877, muslin, all printed..50.00
  38-star, 12-1/2" x 22", coarse muslin, mounted on stick, star pattern of 6-7-6-6-7-6 ....12.00
  45-star, 3-1/2" x 2-1/4", child's parade type, pattern of 8-7-7-7-7-8 and 5-pointed star 25.00
  45-star, 32" x 47", 1896-1908, printed on silk, bright colors, black heading and no grommets 95.00
  46-star, 4" x 5", 1908-1912, stars sewn on, Oklahoma 65.00
  48-star, 5-3/4" x 4-1/2", 1912-1959, printed on heavy canvas-type material, used at D-Day in Infantry invasion, men wore them under the camouflage net on their helmets.........75.00
  49-star, 4" x 5-1/4", 1959-1960, child's parade flag, silk, wood stick, Alaska 45.00
Handkerchief, World War I, flags of U.S. and France, embroidered
  A Kiss from France 15.00
  Souvenir France 1919.............15.00
  To My Dear Sweetheart 15.00
Lapel Stud, red, white and blue enamel

flag, white ground, Harrison/Morton 1888, enameled brass.............35.00
Magic Lantern Slide, 42-star flag, c1889, hand tinted, mounted in wood .30.00
Magnifying Glass, pocket, 3/4" x 1-1/4", oval, Voorhees Rubber Mfg. Co., adv, American flag artwork......37.00
Match Box, 1-1/2" x 2-3/4", Civil War period, emb, picture of Stars and Stripes on 1 side, Miss Columbia on reverse 65.00
Plate
  St. Louis World's Fair, Washington, Jefferson, Lafayette and Napoleon's faces, very colorful, 1904.......120.00
  Washington's Headquarters, Newburg, NY, 1783-1883, crossed flags under house, 10" d 95.00
Postcard, printed semblance of Stars and Stripes covering address side, picture of Wm. H. Taft for President, July 4, 1908, 46 stars, used 18.00
Poster, 14" x 29", lithograph, "History of Old Glory," Babbitt soap giveaway 145.00
Print, Currier and Ives, "The Star Spangled Banner," #481, 11-1/4" x 15-1/2"....................165.00
Scarf, 17" x 15", silk, Chicago 1893, Expo, panorama of Expos overlaying American flag.........45.00
Sheet Music
  America Forever March, E.T. Paull Music Co., Columbia draped in flag, shield and eagle......................30.00
  The Female Auctioneer, lady dressed in costume, waving flag...............................30.00
  The Flag with the 34 Stars, 6 verses and chorus, illus of soldiers marching with hand-colored flag..............35.00
  Miss America, 2-step by J. Edmund Barnum, lady with stars, red and white striped dress, large flowing flag.....................20.00
  Stars and Stripes Forever March, John Phillip Sousa portrait in upper left hand corner, Old Glory in center, published by John Church Co..20.00
  The Triumphant Banner, E.T. Paull 25.00
Song Sheet, published by Chas Magnus, NY, 5" x 8"
Stickpin
  Celluloid, American flag, 48 stars, advertising, S.A. Cook for U.S. Senator.............20.00
  Metal
    3/8" x 5/8", 13 stars, c1925, 2" long pin............................15.00
    1-3/4" h, red, white and blue painted furling flag at half staff, sign at left "Vietnam 1961," orig cardboard box with clear-plastic

window inscribed "Wear This Pin for Peace," Pace Emblem Co., New York, NY, c1970...........35.00

Token, 3-3/4" d, "The Dix Token Coin," Civil War, commemorates the order of General John Adams Dix, Jan. 29, 1861, "If anyone attempts to haul down the American flag, shoot him on the spot," copper-colored coin, picture of "The Flag of Our Union" on 1 side, quote on the other........10.00

Flashlights

Collecting Hints: Flashlight collecting is like many other categories: name brands count and if the manufacturer is not known, the value is much lower. Check for brand name and/or trademark, patent date or patent number and any other information that will help identify the manufacturer and the date the item was made. Also, check the overall outside appearance and look for signs of wear, dents, splits, scratches, discoloration, rust, corrosion, deformities, etc. Carefully look for any cracks in the metal on both ends of tubular flashlights and determine if both ends can be unscrewed easily. End caps and switches are the most reliable way to identify the date and make since these parts cannot be easily changed. The finish, as well as the design, should be the same on both ends. Check all rivets and make sure they are intact. Brass becomes brittle with age and it is not uncommon to find splits on both the lens ring and end caps.

The lens cap should be checked for any visible chips and paint chips. The reflector may be silvered and should be checked for tarnish and scratches. A rusty spring or corrosion damage is a clear sign that the batteries have leaked, which may affect the switch mechanism. Make sure the bulb is original, threaded, flanged or an unusual shape. The entire flashlight should be checked for completeness, making sure the lens caps and rings all match and all switches work.

Flashlight collectors rely on old catalogs and magazine advertisements to help date and identify their flashlights. They are especially drawn to material with detailed illustrations of switches, finishes and

Pennsylvania RR, Bright Star, domed glass, 7-1/2", $50.

proper end caps. Many collectors specialize in one type of flashlight, such as pocket watch, vest pocket, pistol or character flashlights.

History: The flashlight evolved from early bicycle lights. The first bicycle light was invented by Acme Electric Lamp Co., of New York City in 1896. A year later, the Ohio Electric Works Co., advertised bicycle lights. In 1898, Conrad Hubert, who had been selling electric scarf pins, bought a wood bicycle-light patent and began manufacturing them under the name American Electrical Novelty and Mfg. Co. This company later became the American Eveready Co. Owen T. Bugg patented a tubular bicycle light in 1898. The next year, Conrad Hubert worked with an inventor who patented the first tubular hand-held flashlight, which became the basis for the flashlight industry.

Conrad Hubert moved swiftly to take advantage of this unique tubular electrical "novelty." He displayed his products at the first electrical show at Madison Square Garden and again at the Paris Exposition in 1900. He won the only award at the exposition for "Portable Electric Lamps." He had opened offices in London, Berlin, Paris, Chicago, Montreal and Sydney by 1901. After the death of Hubert, Joshua Lionel Cowan, founder of Lionel trains, began taking credit for inventing the flashlight. He often gave detailed accounts of his invention, changing specifics from one account to another. However, his timetable, which coincided with that of Conrad Hubert, clouds the facts of flashlight history.

American Eveready has dominated the flashlight and battery industry since the beginning. In 1906, National Carbon bought one-half interest in American Eveready for

$200,000. American Eveready purchased the remaining interest in 1914 for an additional $2 million. Companies such as Ray-O-Vac, Yale, Franco, Bond, Beacon, Delta, Uneedit, Saunders, Winchester, Sharpleigh and Underwood also made many interesting flashlights.

References: *Collector's Digest Flashlights*, L-W Book Sales, 1995; Stuart Schneider, *Collecting Flashlights*, Schiffer Publishing, 1996.

Collectors' Club: Flashlight Collectors of America, P.O. Box 4095, Tustin, CA 92681.

Aurora, tubular, 2 C batteries, all-nickel case..18.00
Beacon, tubular, 1919, 2 C batteries, vulcanite case, nickel ends 14.00
Bond, tubular, 1930, 2 D batteries, nickel-plated brass 15.00
British Ever Ready, wood flashlight lantern, all orig........................60.00
Burgess Sub, tubular, 2 D batteries, colorful adv.............................22.00
Chase, Bomb Light, 2 C batteries, nickel, bail handle, donut shape and size...................................28.00
Delta Lantern, Buddy Flashlight Lantern, 1919, 2 D batteries..................10.00
Eveready
    Tubular
        #2604, 1924, 2 C batteries, black painted case nickel ends, small bulls-eye lens 24.00
        #2630, 1915, 2 C batteries, nickel-plated case and ends, small bulls-eye lens 14.00
        #2632, 1915, 3 D batteries, nickel-plated case and ends, small bulls-eye lens 22.00
    Candle, #1643, 1932, 2 C batteries, cast metal base, cream-colored painted candle 35.00
    Daylo
        Cartridge, #2690, rare 38.00
        Tubular
        #2602, 1917, 2 C batteries, vulcanite case, nickel-plated ends, small bulls-eye lens 20.00
        #2616, 1917, 2 D batteries, vulcanite case, nickel ends, large bulls-eye lens..............17.00
        #2631, 1917, 2 D batteries, all nickel plated, small bulls-eye lens........................15.00
    Lantern
        #4707, 1912, nickel-plated case, large bulls-eye lens..............22.00
        #4709, 1915, railroad, resembles kerosene lantern..................28.00

#4708, 1915, round, nickel case,
large bulls-eye lens 42.00

Liberty Daylo, #3661, 1919, box
lantern, gun-metal finish 25.00

Masterlite

#2238, 1935, table model,
2 C batteries, nickel plated,
opaque milk glass globe 32.00

#2253, 1935, tubular,
2 D batteries 24.00

Pistol Light, #2675, resembles
automatic pistol 26.00

Vest Pocket

#6661, 1904, 2 AA batteries,
nickel plated, ruby push-button
switch, smaller size 18.00

#6662, 1904, 3 AA batteries,
nickel plated, ruby push-button
switch, larger size 20.00

#6961, Dec. 1912, 2 AA batteries,
nickel plated, hinged bottom 14.00

#6982, 1912, 3 AA batteries,
silver plated 32.00

#6992, 1914, 3 AA batteries, nickel
plated, cigarette-case type ... 16.00

Wallite, 1931, wall hanging, black
hammer tone, oval shape 28.00

Wood Light, 1911, oak flashlight-
lantern, black 55.00

Franco, vest pocket,
glass button switch 20.00

Fumalux, #400, combination
flashlight-cigarette lighter 15.00

Jenks, railroad, brass,
pat July 25, 1911 .... 75.00

Kwik-Lite, tubular, 2 C batteries,
all nickel, case unscrews in
middle of tube 12.00

Peerless, vest pocket,
push-rod switch 14.00

Ray-O-Vac, tubular

Captain Ray-O-Vac,
2 D batteries 28.00

Miniature, 2 B batteries, all nickel,
flush bulls-eye lens 32.00

Space Patrol, 2 D batteries 32.00

Sportsman, 1960, 2 D batteries,
ribbed 7.00

Seiss, bicycle, 1 D battery,
all nickel 25.00

Stewart Browne, 2 D batteries, Bakelite,
mine approved 24.00

USALite, Redhead, 2 D batteries, stand,
red glass reflector behind lens. 14.00

W.B. Mfg., candle, 2 C batteries,
bronze, ornate 32.00

Yale

3-Way, 3 D batteries, 3-way signal,
3 bulbs 24.00

Tubular, #3302, 3 D batteries,
double ended, flood lens 1 end, spot
lens other end 24.00

Florence Ceramics

Collecting Hints: Pieces of Florence Ceramics are well marked. Most figures have their names marked on the bottom. Six different backstamps were used, all containing a variation of the name of the company, location, and/or copyright.

Florence Ceramics is a relatively new collectible. As a result, stable national pricing has not yet been achieved. It pays to shop around. Several figures have articulated fingers; some figures were issued with both articulated and closed fingers. The former type command a slight premium. Look for figures with especially rich colors, elaborate decorations—such as bows, flowers, lace, ringlets and tresses—and gold trim. Aqua, beige, maroon and gray, occasionally highlighted with green or maroon, are most commonly found on economy-line figures. Yellow is hard to find.

History: In 1939, following the death of a young son, Florence Ward began working with clay as a way of dealing with her grief. Her first pieces were figures of children, individually shaped, decorated and fired in a workshop in her Pasadena, CA, garage. Untrained at first, she attended a ceramics class in 1942. She continued to sell her pottery as a means of supplementing her income during World War II. Her business grew. In 1946, the Florence Ceramics Co., moved to a plant located on the east side of Pasadena. Clifford, Ward's husband, and Clifford Jr., another son, joined the firm. With the acquisition of increased production facilities, Florence Ceramics began exhibiting its wares at major Los Angeles gift shows. A worldwide business quickly developed. In 1949, a modern factory featuring a continuous tunnel kiln was opened at 74 S. San Gabriel Boulevard in Pasadena. More than 100 employees worked at the new plant.

Florence Ceramics produced semi-porcelain figurines that featured historic couples in period costumes and ladies and gentlemen outfitted in costumes copied from late 19th-century Godey fashions. Fictional characters, including movie-related ones such as Rhett and Scarlet from "Gone with the Wind," were made. Inexpensive small figurines of children and figural vases also were manufactured. Florence Ceramics offered a full line of period decorative accessories that included birds, busts, candleholders, clock frames, smoking sets, wall plaques and wall pockets. Lamp bases, which were made using some of the figural pieces, were offered for sale with custom shades.

In 1956, the company employed Betty Davenport Ford, a modeler, to develop a line of bisque-finished animal figures. The series included cats, dogs, doves, rabbits and squirrels. A minimal airbrush decoration was added. Production lasted only two years. Florence Ceramics was sold to Scripto Corp., following the death of Clifford Ward in 1964. Scripto retained the Florence Ceramics name but produced primarily advertising specialty wares. The plant closed in 1977.

References: Susan and Al Bagdade, *Warman's American Pottery and Porcelain*, Wallace-Homestead, 1994; Jack Chipman, *Collector's Encyclopedia of California Pottery*, Collector Books, 1992, 1995 value update; Harvey Duke, *Official Identification and Price Guide to Pottery and Porcelain*, 8th Edition, House of Collectibles, 1995; Lois Lehner, *Lehner's Encyclopedia of U.S. Marks on Pottery, Porcelain & Clay*, Collector Books, 1988.

Periodical: Florence Collector's Club Newsletter, P.O. Box 122, Richland, WA 99352.

Dealer Sign 395.00

Figure

Abigail, green and gold, 8" h .. 175.00

Ava, yellow 300.00

Bea, teal and rose, 7-1/4" h ... 150.00

Blue Boy and Pinky,
price for pr 700.00

Charmaine, green 460.00

Della, green and sand,
7-1/4" h 175.00

Douglas 240.00

Edward 430.00

Elaine, white and gold, 6" h 85.00

Elizabeth 600.00

Irene, 6" h

Beige and green 55.00

Pink and gold 55.00

Jim
 Beige and green, 6-1/4" h 75.00
 Gray and aqua 75.00
 White and gold 75.00
Lady Diana, 9-1/2" h, separated
fingers, lace collar and bodice,
applied flowers 175.00
Laura
 Burgundy............................165.00
 Green and gold 130.00
Lillian, green, white and gold,
7-1/4" h...............................110.00
Louise, green, white and gold,
7-1/4" h...............................110.00
Mary 550.00
Melanie, green and brown,
7-1/2" h...............................100.00
Musette 400.00
Rhett, 9" h, rose and green 200.00
Rosemarie............................190.00
Sarah....................................140.00
Scarlett..................................250.00
Sue, green and maroon, 6" h ...75.00
Sue Ellen...............................225.00
Tess, light green.....................430.00
Victoria, pink, hat...................530.00
Flower Holder
 Lea, green and rose, 6" h.........60.00
 Peg, beige and green,
 7-1/2" h...............................60.00
Lamp, David and Betsy,
 price for pr 500.00
Wall Plaque, full-figured ladies, maroon
 and green, price for pr 200.00

Flow Blue China, American

Collecting Hints: As with any Flow Blue china, value for American-made pieces depends upon condition, quality, pattern and type. Avoid those pieces with flaws which cannot be repaired, unless you plan to use them only for decorative purposes.

History: When imported, Flow Blue china, i.e., English, German, etc., became popular, American manufacturers soon followed suit. There is great variation in quality. Compared to European makers, the number of U.S. manufacturers is small. The most well-known are the French China Co., Homer Laughlin China Co., Mercer Pottery Co., Sebring Pottery Co., Warwick China and Wheeling Pottery Co.

References: Mary Frank Gaston, *Collectors Encyclopedia of Flow Blue*, Collector Books, Paducah, KY,

Colonial, cup and saucer, $85.

1983; Norma Jean Hoener, *Flow Blue China: Additional Patterns and New Information*, Flow Blue International Collectors Club (11560 W. 95th #297, Overland Park, KS 66214); Jeffrey B. Snyder, *Historic Flow Blue*, Schiffer Publications, 1994; —, *Pocket Guide to Flow Blue*, Schiffer Publications, 1995; Petra Williams, *Flow Blue China: An Aid to Identification*, Vols. I, II and III, Fountain House East (P.O. Box 99298, Jeffersontown, KY 40299), 1971-1991.

Collectors' Club: Flow Blue International Collectors Club, 11560 W. 95th #297, Overland Park, KS 66214.

Museum: Margaret Woodbury Strong Museum, Rochester, NY.

Additional Listings: See *Warman's Antiques and Collectibles Price Guide*.

Advisor: Ellen G. King

Argyle, J&E Mayer,
 milk pitcher, 7" 145.00
Autumn Leaves, Warwick
 Jardiniere, 8" x 7-1/2".............500.00
 Plate, 10-1/2" 125.00
Colonial, Homer Laughlin Co.
 Plate, 10"...................................65.00
 Teacup and saucer 85.00
Cracked Ice, International Pottery
 Bowl, open, round, 10"...........150.00
 Cake plate, open handle,
 10-1/4"...................................120.00
 Demitasse cup and saucer 65.00
Delph, Sebring Pottery
 Bowl to wash set, 17".............250.00
 Butter pat, 3" 35.00
La Belle/Blue Diamond, La Belle or
 Wheeling Pottery

La Francais, vegetable tureen, cov, ivy design, $295.

Biscuit jar, cov, 7" 250.00
Bone dish, individual...............65.00
Bowl
 Dessert or individual vegetable,
 5-1/2" 45.00
 Fruit, ftd, 12" 225.00
 Serving
 Oval, 10-1/4" x 9".............250.00
 Round, 9-1/2"...................295.00
Butter pat, 3" 45.00
Charger, round, 11-1/4" 350.00
Creamer and sugar...............335.00
Ice cream tray, 13-5/8"...........375.00
Plate
 7-1/2" 45.00
 10" 75.00
Platter, 15" 185.00
Punch cup, ftd.......................450.00
Relish, long oval, 8" 275.00
Syrup pitcher, pewter lid 295.00
La Francaise, The French China Co
 Butter dish, cov, with insert......95.00
 Butter pat 28.00
 Creamer, 5"..............................85.00
 Plate, 9-1/2" 60.00
 Platter, 13-1/2" 75.00
 Vegetable tureen, cov,
 ivy design...............................295.00

Cracked Ice, demitasse cup and saucer, $65.

Pansy, milk pitcher, 6-1/2, $275.

Paisley, Mercer Pottery
   Plate, 8"......................................75.00
   Soup tureen, cov, no ladle 425.00
Pansy, Warwick China
   Cake plate, handle, 10"..........175.00
   Milk pitcher, 6-1/2" 275.00
   Relish/celery dish,
   12-1/2" x 5-1/2" 100.00
   Tray, 10-1/2" x 6" 85.00
   Vegetable bowl, open,
   round, 10"...............................125.00
Poppy, Warwick China
   Dessert bowl, 6" 30.00
   Syrup pitcher, pewter lid.........250.00
   Vegetable bowl, round, 10" 200.00
Royal Blue, Burgess & Campbell
   Plate, 9-7/8" 75.00
   Soup bowl, rimmed, 9" 55.00
Wild Rose, Warwick China,
   chocolate pot, 5 cups and saucers,
   price for set.........................1,500.00
Windmill, The French China Co.
   Butter pat, 3" 38.00
   Platter, 13" 125.00
Winona, The French China Co.
   Pitcher, 5"...............................120.00
   Plate
     5"..120.00
     6"..35.00
   Teacup and saucer 65.00

Football Cards

Collecting Hints: Condition is critical—buy cards that are in very good condition, i.e., free from creases and damaged corners. When possible, strive to acquire cards in excellent to mint condition. The introduction to Rob Erbe's *American Premium Guide to Baseball Cards* (Books Americana, 1982) includes photographs which illustrate how to determine the condition of a card. What applies to baseball cards is equally true for football cards.

Devise a collecting strategy, such as cards related to one year, one player, Heisman trophy winners or one team. A large quantity of cards is available; a novice collector can be easily overwhelmed.

History: Football cards have been printed since the 1890s. However, it was not until 1933 that the first bubblegum football card appeared in the Goudey Sport Kings set. In 1935 National Chickle of Cambridge, MA, produced the first full set of gum cards devoted exclusively to football. Both Leaf Gum of Chicago and Bowman Gum of Philadelphia produced sets of football cards in 1948. Leaf discontinued production after their 1949 issue; Bowman continued until 1955.

Topps Chewing Gum entered the market in 1950 with its college-stars set. Topps became a fixture in the football card market with its 1955 All-American set. From 1956 thorough 1963 Topps printed card sets of National Football League players, combining them with the American Football League players in 1961. Topps produced sets with only American Football League players from 1964 to 1967. The Philadelphia Gum Company made National Football League card sets during this period. Beginning in 1968 and continuing to the present, Topps has produced sets of National Football League cards, the name adopted after the merger of the two leagues.

References: *All Sport Alphabetical Price Guide*, Krause Publications, 1995; James Beckett, *Official 1995 Price Guide to Football Cards*, 14th Edition, House of Collectibles, 1994; *Charlton Standard Catalogue of Canadian Baseball & Football Cards*, 4th Edition, Charlton Press, 1995; *Football, Basketball & Hockey Price Guide*, Krause Publications, 1991; Allan Kaye and Michael McKeever, *Football Card Price Guide*, 1995, Avon Books, 1994; Roderick A. Malloy, *Malloy's Guide to Sports Cards Values*, Wallace-Homestead, 1995; *Standard Catalog of Football, Basketball & Hockey Cards*, 2nd Edition, Krause Publications, 1996.

Periodicals: *Beckett Football Card Magazine*, 4887 Alpha Rd., Ste 200, Dallas, TX 75244; *Card Trade*, *Sports Cards*, and *Sports Collectors Digest*, all located at 700 E. State St., Iola, WI 54990.

Note: See Baseball Cards category for special terms and abbreviations.

Bowman Card Company
1948
   Complete Set (108).............6,000.00
   Common Player (1-108) 15.00
1951
   Complete Set (144).............3,500.00
   Common Player (1-144) 18.00
1952, Large
   Complete Set (144)...........12,000.00
   Common Player (1-72) 25.00
   Common Player (73-144) 35.00
1952, Small
   Complete Set (144).............5,000.00
   Common Player (1-72) 20.00
   Common Player (73-144) 25.00
1954 ....
   Complete Set (128).............1,600.00
   Common Player (1-64) 6.00
   Common Player (65-96) 14.00
   Common Player (97-128) 6.00
1955
   Complete Set (160).............1,500.00
   Common Player (1-64) 4.50
   Common Player (65-160) 6.00

Fleer
1960
   Complete Set (132)................750.00
   Common Player (1-132) 3.00
1961
   Complete Set (220).............1,600.00
   Common Player (1-132) 3.50
   Common Player (133-220) 5.00

Marion Campbell, #19, 2-1/16" x 2-15/16", $2.50.

1963
Complete Set (88) 1,900.00
Common Player (1-88) 8.00
1990
Complete Set (400) 7.00
Common Player (1-400) 03
1991
Complete Set (432) 6.00
Common Player (1-432) 03

Leaf
1948
Complete Set (98) 5,800.00
Common Player (1-49) 20.00
Common Player (50-98) 100.00
1949
Complete Set (49) 2,000.00
Common Player (1-49) 25.00

Philadelphia
1964
Complete Set (198) 875.00
Common Player (1-198) 1.75
1966
Complete Set (198) 875.00
Common Player (1-198) 1.75

Score
1989
Complete Set (330) 150.00
Common Player (1-330) 10
1990
Complete Set (660) 8.00
Common Player (1-660) 03

Topps
1956
Complete Set (120) 1,000.00
Common Player (1-120) 3.75
1958
Complete Set (132) 1,300.00
Common Player (1-132) 3.75
1960
Complete Set (132) 625.00
Common Player (1-132) 2.50
1962
Complete Set (176) 1,700.00

Topps, 1979, 1978 NFL Leaders, Frank Corral and Pat Leahy, 50 cents.

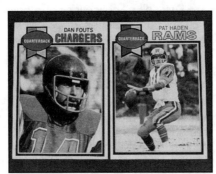

Left: Topps, 1979, Dan Fouts; right: Topps, 1979, Pat Haden, 25 cents each.

Common Player (1-176) 3.50
1964
Complete Set (176) 1,350.00
Common Player (1-176) 3.00
Common Player SP 3.00
1966
Complete Set (132) 1,300.00
Common Player (1-132) 4.00
1968
Complete Set (219) 575.00
Common Player (1-131) 1.50
Common Player (132-219) 1.25
1970
Complete Set (263) 450.00
Common Player (1-132) 50
Common Player (133-263) 75
1972
Complete Set (351) 2,300.00
Common Player (1-132) 50
Common Player (133-263) 75
Common Player (264-351) 20.00
1975
Complete Set (528) 325.00
Common Player (1-528) 20
1977
Complete Set (528) 230.00
Common Player (1-528) 20
1979
Complete Set (528) 120.00
Common Player (1-528) 15
1981
Complete Set (528) 250.00
Common Player (1-528) 08
1983
Complete Set (396) 50.00
Common Player (1-396) 05
Common Player DP 05
1985
Complete Set (396) 80.00
Common Player (1-396) 05
1987
Complete Set (396) 40.00
Common Player (1-396) 05
1990
Complete Set (528) 10.00
Common Player (1-528) 03

Football Collectibles

Collecting Hints: Collectors of football items may decide to specialize in one team, one conference or one type of collectible, i.e., helmets or pennants. Collectors should not overlook the wealth of items generated by colleges, high schools and even younger participants.

History: The first American college football match was held between Princeton and Rutgers in New Brunswick, NJ, in 1869. Harvard documents a more rugby-type game in the 1870s. A professional football association was founded in 1920 and renamed the National Football League (NFL) in 1922. Football really took off after World War II and grew to 28 teams in two conferences by the 1980s. Expansion continued until 30 teams were playing by 1995. The Super Bowl was created in 1967 and has become the exciting termination of the season for many fans. The Canadian Football League (CFL) was created in 1959 and oversees a professional circuit.

References: Mark Allen Baker, *All Sport Autograph Guide*, Krause Publications, 1994; David Bushing, *Sports Equipment Price Guide*, Krause Publications, 1995; Roderick A. Malloy, *Malloy's Sports Collectibles Value Guide*, Wallace-Homestead, 1994; Michael McKeever, *Collecting Sports Memorabilia*, Alliance Publishing, 1966.

Periodicals: *Olympic Collectors Newsletter*, P.O. Box 41630, Tucson, AZ 85717; *Sports Collectors Digest*, 700 E. State St., Iola, WI 54990.

Autograph
Troy Aikman, photograph 40.00
Jerome Bettis,
Helmet, mini, Pitt, Riddell 60.00
Photograph 25.00
James Brown, mini helmet,
Browns, Sharco 85.00
Kerry Collins, photograph 25.00
Joe Greene, mini helmet,
Pitt, Riddell.............................50.00
Rodney Hampton, photograph.25.00
Paul Hornung, mini helmet,
Sharco, ND 80.00

Michael Irvin, photograph.........30.00
Ed Jovanovski, mini helmet,
Riddell.....................................45.00
Greg Lloyd, photograph...........25.00
Joe Montana, photograph........50.00
Joe Namath, photograph..........50.00
Orlando Pace, mini helmet,
Riddell, Ohio St. 75.00
Walter Payton, photograph......40.00
Ricky Walters, photograph.......25.00
Bobbing Head, 3-1/2" x 3-1/2" x 7-1/2"
box, 7" h painted composition figure,
spring-mounted head, gold round
base, gold helmet striped in green,
green jersey and stockings, gold
trousers, foil sticker reads "Sports
Specialties, Japan, 67," box label
with 1968 copyright..................50.00
Figure, 5" h, cast iron,
player, c1900...........................85.00
Football, autographed, Cleveland
Browns, white Wilson ball, 25 signa-
tures, including Jim Brown.....245.00
Jersey, game used
J. Collins, L.A. Rams,
white mesh, 1980s.................225.00
Tim Johnson, Redskins, 1990s, red
mesh, autographed 250.00
Dan Marino, Dolphins, aqua,
autographed..........................350.00
Reeves, Eagles,
white mesh, 1990s.................110.00
Dewey Selman, Tampa Bay,
white mesh, 1970s.................325.00
Warren, Univ. of Miami, white mesh,
Fiesta Bowl, 1990s.................245.00
T. Williams, Dallas Cowboys,
white mesh, nameplate
restored, 1980s 145.00
Mug, Super Bowl IV, thermos type,
Dallas vs. Miami, Lombardi trophy
illus, 1972 ....35.00
Nodder, Cleveland Browns,
sq brown wood base................75.00
Patch, Super Bowl V, 1970,
Baltimore and Dallas 60.00
Pendant, Notre Dame, 1957 Conference
Champions, gold filled, football
shape, chain 75.00
Pennant, Chicago Bears, 11-1/2" x 28-1/2"
black felt, "Bears" in orange, orange,
green and red football art, orange felt
trim strip, late 1940s 25.00
Pin, Navy, miniature diecut stiff paper,
figural, football overprinted with
"Navy" in blue lettering, blank back,
short stickpin back, c1920 ....35.00
Pinback Button
NFL Teams Official Booster Series,
mail premium from H.J. Heinz,
c1967, 1-5/8" d, litho
Atlanta Falcons, red-and-
black helmet, white ground,
black letters...........................18.00

Baltimore Colts, blue and white,
light surface wear................15.00
Detroit Lions, blue and silver,
white letters.........................20.00
New York Giants, black-and-white
helmet, orange ground, white
letters 20.00
Philadelphia Eagles,
green and silver 18.00
Super Bowl XV/ABC Sports, 1981,
black and white, gray rim, black
letters, Superdome, New Orleans,
Oakland Raiders and Philadelphia
Eagles 30.00
Press Badge, U.S.C., blue lettering,
taupe-gray cello, "Camera"
operator at Nov. 1, 1924 game, Los
Angeles Coliseum, freshmen
teams from Univ. of Southern CA
and Univ. of CA 80.00
Program
New York Giants-Chicago Bears
Playoff, 7-3/4" x 10-1/2", official pro-
gram for Dec. 30, 1956, National
Football league championship game,
Yankee Stadium, red, white and blue
art on cov, 20 pages, b&w photos and
profiles of players....................30.00
Penn State-Navy Homecoming
Game, 8" x 10-1/2", official program
for Oct. 15, 1955, game, Beaver
Field, Penn State Centennial cele-
bration, 64 pgs, player photos, blue,
white and gold cov design........35.00
Soda Bottle, Dr Pepper, 1972
Commemorative, Miami
Dolphins, unopened 95.00
Ticket Stub
American Football League
Championship, 1967,
Oakland and Houston 25.00
NFC Division, 1977,
Minnesota and LA Rams..........12.00
Super Bowl I, 1966, Green Bay
and Kansas City.....................125.00
Yearbook, Green Bay Packers,
1974, autographed by coaches
and players..............................35.00

Franciscan Dinnerware

Collecting Hints: The emphasis on
Franciscan art ware and dinnerware
has overshadowed the many other
collectible lines from Gladding, Mc-
Bean and Co. Keep your eye open
for Tropico Art Ware, made between
1934 and 1937. This company also
made some high-style birdbaths, florists' vases, flowerpots, garden urns
and hotel cigarette snuffers. Catali-

na Art Ware (1937-1941) also is attracting collector attention.

Most buyers of Franciscan's big
three patterns (Apple, Desert Rose
and Ivy) are seeking replacement
pieces for sets currently in use. As a
result, prices tend to be somewhat in-
flated, especially for hollow pieces.
Keep in mind that these patterns were
popular throughout the country. Early
Franciscan lines, which are similar to
Bauer designs and Homer Laughlin's
Fiesta, can be distinguished from their
more popular counterparts by differences in shape and color. These pieces are more commonly found on the
West Coast than the East.

History: Gladding, McBean and Co.,
Los Angeles, produced the Franciscan dinnerware patterns at their
Glendale, CA, pottery. The company
began in 1875 as a manufacturer of
sewer pipe and terra-cotta tile. In
1922, Gladding, McBean and Co.,
acquired Tropico Pottery in Glendale
and the West Coast properties of
American Encaustic Tile in 1933. In
1934, the company began producing
and marketing dinnerware and art
pottery under the name Franciscan
Ware. Franciscan dinnerware had
talc (magnesium silicate) rather than
clay as a base. Early lines, which
used bright primary colors on plain
shapes, include Coronado, El Patio,
Metropolitan, Montecito, Padua and
Rancho. As the line developed, more
graceful shapes and pastel colors
were introduced.

Three patterns are considered
Franciscan classics. The Apple pattern with its embossed body, hand
decoration and underglaze staining
was introduced in 1940. The Desert
Rose pattern (1941) is the most popular dinnerware pattern ever manufactured in the United States. Ivy, the last
of the big three, was first made in
1948. There are three distinct types of
Franciscan products: 1) masterpiece
china, a high-quality translucent ceramic; 2) earthenware, a cream-colored ware found in a variety of decal-
and hand-decorated patterns; and 3)
whitestone or white earthenware.

Gladding, McBean and Co., became Interpace Corp., in 1963. In
1979, Josiah Wedgwood and Sons,
Ltd., acquired the company. In 1986,

the Glendale plant was closed, marking the end of American production.

References: Susan and Al Bagdade, *Warman's American Pottery and Porcelain*, Wallace-Homestead, 1994; Jack Chipman, *Collector's Encyclopedia of California Pottery*, Collector Books, 1992, 1995 value update; Delleen Enge, *Franciscan*, published by author, 1992; Lois Lehner, *Lehner's Encyclopedia of U.S. Marks on Pottery, Porcelain & Clay*, Collector Books, 1988; Jeffrey B. Snyder, *Franciscan Dining Services*, Schiffer Publishing, 1996.

Collectors' Club: Franciscan Collectors Club USA, 8412 5th Ave. NE, Seattle, WA 98115.

Apple: Introduced in 1940. Embossed earthenware body, hand decorated and under-the-glaze stain.

Ashtray, individual 22.00
Bowl
    6" d..12.00
    7-1/2" d......................................25.00
Butter, cov 35.00
Casserole, cov, individual.............50.00
Cereal Bowl......................................12.00
Coaster..65.00
Cocoa Mug......................................125.00
Compote, large 125.00
Creamer and Sugar, cov 40.00
Cup and Saucer
    Oversized...................................65.00
    Table size...................................11.00
Gravy and Underplate 40.00
Jam Jar..125.00
Juice Tumbler...................................35.00
Mixing Bowl
    9" d...85.00
    Medium, light use 165.00
    Small, light use 115.00
Pickle, 10-1/4" l 35.00
Plate
    6-1/4" d......................................10.00
    8" d...7.50
    8-1/2" d......................................14.00
    9-1/2" d......................................16.00
    10-1/2" d....................................18.00
    12" d...75.00
    Grill...125.00
Platter, 12-3/4" d 48.00
Relish, 3 part 75.00
Salad Bowl 100.00
Salt and Pepper Shakers,
    pr, small 25.00
Saucer...2.00
Soup Plate, flange 26.00
Sugar, cov 28.00

Syrup Pitcher....................................75.00
Teapot, open 25.00
Turkey Platter.................................295.00
Tureen
    Footed......................................495.00
    Small feet 850.00
Vegetable Bowl, 7-1/2" l................60.00

Coronado: Dinnerware line produced from 1936 until 1956. Made in 15 different colors with both satin and glossy glazes.

Bowl, 7-1/2" d, turquoise 15.00
Butter, cov, satin turquoise............30.00
Candlesticks, pr, ivory satin 45.00
Chop Plate, 12" d, yellow 17.50
Creamer and Sugar,
    jumbo, coral.............................40.00
Cup and Saucer
    Coral...9.00
    Maroon......................................18.00
Demitasse Cup and Saucer,
    white..35.00
Gravy, attached
    underplate, yellow 20.00
Pitcher, water, coral 45.00
Plate
    6" d, turquoise 4.00
    7-1/2" d, coral............................8.00
    9-3/4" d, yellow..........................9.00
    10-1/2" d, turquoise.................10.00
Platter, 15" l, oval, yellow 15.00
Vegetable, oval, yellow 27.50

Desert Rose: Introduced in 1941. Embossed earthenware with hand painted under-the-glaze decoration. Known for it's rosebud shaped finials.

Ashtray, oval 85.00
Bank, open base 180.00
Bowl, 9" d...40.00
Box, heart shape 125.00
Butter Dish, cov...............................50.00
Candleholders, pr, 3" h.................75.00
Casserole, cov, 1-1/2" qt...............90.00
Celery Tray, 4-1/2" x 10-1/2".........35.00
Cereal Bowl, 6" d, 1-5/8" h............15.00
Chop Plate
    12" d...60.00
    14" d...95.00
Cigarette Box 125.00
Coffeepot, cov 110.00
Compote, 8" 95.00
Cookie Jar, cov 300.00
Creamer and Sugar, cov 35.00
Cup, 4" x 3-3/4", 10 oz 40.00
Cup and Saucer
    Oversize....................................65.00
    Table..12.00
Dessert, coupe, 7-1/4"....................70.00
Demitasse Cup and Saucer 48.00
Eggcup..35.00

Fruit Bowl, 5-1/4" d..........................8.00
Gravy, 2 spouts...............................50.00
Jam Jar, cov.....................................90.00
Mixing Bowl, large.......................175.00
Mug
    7 oz..25.00
    12 oz..45.00
Pitcher
    Milk, 1 qt 90.00
    Water 125.00
Plate
    6-1/2" d, bread and butter 6.00
    8-1/2" d, salad.........................12.00
    9-1/4" d, luncheon...................12.00
    10-1/4" d, dinner 14.00
    Grill...90.00
Platter
    11-1/2" d, round 75.00
    12-1/2" l, 8-1/2" w, oval...........45.00
    14-1/2" l, 10-1/4" w, oval.........65.00
Relish
    11" d...40.00
    12" d, 3 part 70.00
Salt and Pepper Shakers,
    pr, 6-1/2" h...............................55.00
Saltshaker, Pepper Mill 250.00
Saucer...2.00
Sherbet 25.00
Side Salad, 8", crescent shape 45.00
Soup Bowl
    Flat...28.00
    Footed.......................................27.00
Soup Tureen, large 500.00
Sugar, cov, small 20.00
Syrup Pitcher, 1 pt, 6-1/4" h..........65.00
Tea Cup and Saucer........................8.50
Teapot...125.00
Toast Cover 125.00
Turkey Platter, 19" l.....................300.00
Vegetable Bowl
    8" d...45.00
    8" x 4-1/2", cov, #45................125.00
    10" l, divided 55.00
    11" x 7", divided......................50.00

El Patio

Dinnerware Set, Satin Coral,
    eight 5-pc place settings,
    plus creamer 125.00
Luncheon Set, Glossy Coral,
    luncheon plate and 5" tumbler,
    eight 2-pc place settings 165.00

Fine China

Renaissance Gray, 51 pc set......495.00

Ivy: Introduced in 1948. Embossed earthenware with hand painted under-the-glaze decoration.

Ashtray...20.00
Bowl, 7-1/4" d..................................50.00
Cereal Bowl, 6" d 19.00
Creamer and Sugar 100.00

Cup and Saucer 20.00
Fruit Bowl, 5-1/4" d......................15.00
Gravy and Underplate 75.00
Plate, 6" d.....................................9.00
Platter
    12" l 100.00
    13-3/4" l 55.00
Relish, 11" l 55.00
Salad Bowl, 11" d, ftd 150.00
Saucer
    Jumbo 10.00
    Table size.................................4.00
Soup, flat 30.00
Tumbler, water 30.00
Turkey Platter..............................325.00
Vegetable Bowl
    8-1/4" d...................................60.00
    Divided 60.00

Meadow Rose

Butter, cov 65.00
Cereal Bowl 18.00
Goblet..175.00
Saucer...5.00
Side Salad.....................................45.00
Snack Plate 165.00
Teapot 195.00

Metropolitan

Cup and saucer, satin, turquoise
    and white, line designed by
    Morris Sanders 15.00

Poppy

Ashtray 15.00
Chop Plate...................................150.00
Cup and Saucer 30.00
Fruit Bowl 30.00
Plate
    8" d, salad...............................35.00
    10" d, dinner............................35.00
    Bread and butter 12.00
Tumbler 145.00

Starburst: Introduced in 1954. Designed by George James, utilizing the eclipse shape.

Ashtray 60.00
Bonbon Dish..................................45.00
Butter Dish, cov 45.00
Casserole, cov, large...................250.00
Chop Plate.....................................60.00
Cup and Saucer 25.00
Fruit Bowl 10.00
Gravy Boat 45.00
Jelly Dish 45.00
Nappy..35.00
Pitcher, water 100.00
Plate, 10" d...................................17.50
Side Salad, crescent shape...........25.00
Soup Bowl 20.00

Fraternal Organizations

Collecting Hints: Fraternal items are broken down into three groups. The first focuses on the literature, pins, badges and costume paraphernalia which belonged to individual members of each organization. This material can be found easily. The second group consists of the ornaments and furniture used in lodge halls for ceremonial purposes. Many of these items were made locally and are highly symbolic. Folk art collectors have latched on to them and have driven prices artificially high.

The third group relates to the regional and national conventions of the fraternal organizations. Each meeting generally produces a number of specialized souvenir items. During conventions public visibility is heightened; hence, convention souvenirs are the most commonly found items. Concentrate on one fraternal group. Since Masons and Shriners are best known, new collectors are urged to focus on one of the other organizations.

History: Benevolent and secret societies played an important part in American life from the late 18th century to the mid-20th century. Groups ranged from Eagles, Elks, Moose and Orioles to Odd Fellows, Redmen and Woodmen. These societies had their own lodges or meeting halls, held secret ceremonies, practiced clearly defined rituals and held conventions and regional meetings. All these factors led to the availability of collectible material.

Initially, the societies were organized to aid members or their families in times of distress. By the late 19th century, they evolved into important social clubs and women's auxiliaries were organized. In the 1950s, increased interest in civil rights led to attacks on the covert and often discriminatory practices of these societies. Americans had more outlets for leisure and social life and less need for the benevolent aspects of the groups. Membership in fraternal organizations, with the exception of the Masons, dropped significantly. Many local chapters closed and sold their lodge halls, resulting in the appearance of many fraternal items in the antiques market.

Museums: Iowa Masonic Library & Museum, Cedar Rapids, IA; Knights of Columbus Headquarters Museum, New Haven, CT; Masonic Grand Lodge Library & Museum of Texas, Waco, TX; Museum of Our National Heritage, Lexington, MA; Odd Fellows Historical Society, Payepte, ID.

Notes: This category does not include souvenir and other items related to the many service clubs of the 20th century, such as the Lions, Rotary, etc., whose focus was a substitute for many who had previously belonged to fraternal organizations. Items from the service groups have not yet become widely collected.

Benevolent & Protective Order of Elks, B.P.O.E.

Ashtray, bronze 30.00
Book, Charles Ellis, *Authentic*
    History of Elk's, 1910,
    purple cover, 700 pgs..............35.00
Bookmark, emb, elk's head, SS ..120.00
Calendar Plate, 1907, 9-1/2",
    Order of Elks center 50.00
Collar Box, leather, drawer,
    Elk emblem 40.00
Container, 2" x 1-1/2", brass, presented
    to Bert Cook, Norwalk, OH......25.00
Fountain Pen, 10K gold 20.00
Mug, pottery, Roseville 70.00
Paperweight, round, glass, elk......20.00
Pinback Button, BPOE, 1910........22.00
Plate, Grand Lodge Reunion, Philadelphia, July 15-20, 1907, tin 50.00
Shaving Mug, full-color elk,
    gold letters..............................70.00
Stein, stoneware, green and brown glaze, Elks slogan and "Detroit Michigan" on front, pewter lid,

Knights Templer, plate, 9" d, $25.

mkd "Germany".....................75.00
Tie Rack, 7" x 8", wall type, plated
    brass.....................15.00
Watch Fob, elk's head, 2 teeth....150.00

Fraternal Order of Eagles, F.O.E.

Ashtray..........................17.50
Pinback Button, 1-3/4", celluloid, multi-
    colored, Great Lakes excursion
    steamship, "Cleveland 1912" in blue
    border with multi-floral design, red,
    white and blue fabric flag ribbon, 1-
    1/4" x 1-1/2" red, white and blue
    enameled brass pendant with en-
    twined initials "FOE"................75.00
Watch Fob, bronze, F.O.E., Liberty,
    Truth, Justice, Equality, 1918 ..20.00

Foresters of America, ax,
    34" l, wood, painted folk art dec,
    red, white and blue, gilt flags,
    elk, curved handles, Medford,
    MA, 1911 ....265.00

Improved Order of Red Man

Grave Marker, brass,
    Indian on top.....................50.00
Pinback Button, gold and
    red ribbon, 1904 ....45.00

Independent Order of Odd Fellows, I.O.O.F

Automobile Tail-Light Lens,
    glass, red, emb IOOF,
    3-link chain, c1910................120.00
Badge, hanging, 1893 World's Colombi-
    an Exposition, Chicago souvenir,
    brass, inlaid black enamel 60.00
Coin, nickel silver,
    detailed graphics 40.00
Letterhead, 7-1/2" x 9-3/4",
    Canal Lodge No. 48,
    Searsmont, ME, 1840s............20.00
Plate, 8", Royal Copenhagen,
    Frigate, 1905 ....100.00
Shaving Mug, multi-shaded, green
    transfer, F.L.T. in chain link, mkd
    "CT Altwasser Silesia" 65.00
Teaspoon, IOOF, SS, 1915..........25.00
Trivet, 8-1/4" l, insignia and heart-in-
    hand in laurel wreath 30.00

Knights of Columbus

Paperweight, glass, clear, milk glass in-
    sert, black logo, floral border ...30.00
Plate, Vienna Art, 1905 ....320.00
Shaving Mug, name and emblem100.00
Sword and Scabbard, brass hilt,
    black grips, raised eagle dec,
    metal scabbard.......................55.00

Knights of Pythias

Goblet, green, 1900.....................220.00
Medal, metal.................................15.00
Ribbon, 1903..............................20.00
Shaving Mug, armor center, gold letter-
    ing and trim, mkd "T&V France" and

Shrine Circus, fan, hat shape, Wabash Railroad adv on back, $12.

artist's initials 125.00
Sword...650.00

Knights Templar

Letter Opener, bronze 15.00
Mug, blue, symbols, 1910 ....35.00
Plate, 10", Grand Knights Templar Com-
    mandery, 54th Annual Conclave,
    Harrisburg, PA, 1909 ....90.00

Loyal Order of Moose

Shaving Mug, black, gold trim,
    brown moose, "Vic Chamar," mkd
    "T&V Limoges" 620.00
Watch Fob, double tooth 75.00

Masonic

Belt Buckle, SP 22.00
Bible, 1,200 pgs, 9-1/2" x 11-1/2" x
    2-1/2", leather binding, 22K gold
    stamping, illus, c1931 ....65.00
Book, *Encyclopedia of Free
    Masonry*, published by Masonic
    History Co., 1919, 2 vols, 943 pgs,
    black cov, gold trim..................50.00
Bookends, bronzed,
    relief symbols, pr 20.00
Catalog, Henderson-Ames Co.,
    Masonic Lodge Supplies,
    1924, 104 pgs........................50.00
Chart, 19" x 24", Masonic motif
    scenes and symbols, Hatch &
    Co., Trinity Bldg., Broadway,
    NY, 1865 ....40.00
Coin, SS......................................22.00
Creamer, 4-3/4",
    Gloversville, German..............20.00
Cup Plate, 3-1/4", Beth Horon Lodge,
    Brookline, MA, Sept. 1870,
    light blue transfer, gilt trim 80.00
Jug, 5-1/4", pink transfer symbols,
    Liverpool..................................90.00
Magazine, *Masonic World*, War Unity is-

sue, Sept. 1942 ....22.00
Match Safe, symbols, SP, 1905....60.00
Mirror, hand..................................35.00
Nodder, 7", papier-mâché,
    Mystic Shrine decal on fez,
    string tassel, orig paint 30.00
Penny, 1916, Norfolk, VA............120.00
Pitcher, custard glass,
    Chicago, IL 75.00
Plate
    8" d, Pittsburgh,
        PA, Oct. 1912 ....20.00
    10-1/4" d, portrait, Benton,
        cobalt border, Rosenthal.........50.00
Ring, man's gold, 19th C.............145.00
Shaving Mug, Masonic symbol and flow-
    ers, gold and blue details, "JM Abell,"
    mkd "Vienna Austria"...............25.00
Sign, convex, reverse painted,
    MOP and silver-foil dec, red, white
    and blue shield, yellow stars, gold
    and black trim, framed............85.00
Spoon, Klitzner, Providence, RI 22.00
Tape Measure, round, celluloid,
    symbols, c1920 ....15.00
Trivet..22.00

Order of Eastern Star, O.E.S.

Cup and Saucer, emblem 15.00
Hatpin, long shank 30.00
Pin, star shape, 14k gold,
    3 diamond chips 60.00
Ring, white gold, jeweled star,
    diamond center 90.00

Order of Red Men, certificate,late 19th
    C, framed 400.00

Shrine

Candlesticks, pr,
    cut glass, 1900 ....100.00
Cup, glass, Cleveland, 1896".........45.00
Glass, Detroit, 1897 ....45.00
Hat, fez, brass scarab 22.00
Loving Cup, 3 handles,
    Niagara Falls, 1905................40.00
Mug, Saratoga, Indian, 1903.........35.00
Nodder, 7", composition,
    man wearing tuxedo and
    maroon shrine hat, c1960 ....45.00
Pin, lapel, 32nd emblem, SS.........17.50
Tumbler, 4-1/2", milk glass,
    gold emblems, c1910 ....60.00
Wine Glass, commemorative,
    Washington, DC, 1900 ....30.00

Syria Shrine, tumbler

Buffalo, milk glass, 1916 ....40.00
Louisville, KY, 1909 ....35.00
New Orleans, LA, 1910................35.00
Pittsburgh, PA, Charters
    Commandery, 1912................35.00
Rochester, NY, 1910....................35.00
St. Paul, ruby stained, 1908.........45.00

Frog Collectibles

Collecting Hints: The frog is a popular theme in art work, often in a secondary position. As with other animals, the frog collector competes with those from other subject areas. The frog has lent its name to several items from flower frog to railroad frog switches to the device which attaches a scabbard to a belt. True frog collectors usually include examples of these in their collections.

History: A frog is small, with bulging eyes, long back legs and no tail. The first frogs appeared about 180 million years ago; today there are more than 2,000 species. Throughout history, frogs have been a source of superstition.

Collectors' Club: The Frog Pond, P.O. Box 193, Beech Grove, IN 46107.

Museum: Frog Fantasies Museum, Eureka Springs, AR.

Advertising Trade Card, Pond's Extract, black, light green and buff 6.00
Bank, 6" h, pottery, seated,
    green glaze.............................30.00
Basket, figural................................30.00
Candleholder, 5", glass, black,
    R Tiffin, OH.............................75.00
Candy Mold, 5", tin, chocolate.......45.00
Canister Set, 3 covered jars and 11" h
    cookie jar, Sears, 1979.........125.00
Christmas Ornament, blown glass,
    crouching position, c1930........25.00
Clicker, 3" l, Life of Party Products,
    Kirchhof, Newark, NJ...............16.00
Condiment Set, "A Frog He Would
    A Wooing Go"..........................45.00
Cookie Jar, cov

Food mold, ice cream, frog on mushroom, pewter, $55.

Figural frog holding flower bouquet, wearing dark green jacket, red bow tie, black top hat, c1950 ....90.00
Kermit the Frog
    on TV, Sigma 475.00
Doorstop, 7-1/4" l, cast iron, orig green
    and yellow paint.....................135.00
Figure
    Bisque, 2-3/4" x 3-1/4", 2 frogs
        sitting in front of 2 eggs............75.00
    Ceramic, brown frog beating blue
        drum, Occupied Japan.............12.00
    Pewter, 1", cast........................10.00
    Redware, 4-3/4" l,
        green glaze.............................85.00
    Soapstone...............................35.00
Flower Frog, figural,
    Van Briggle, 1915..................160.00
Garden Ornament,
    5" x 6", bronze.........................45.00
Key Chain
    Kermit the Frog.........................3.00
    Metal Disc, frog riding bicycle,
        1" d, c1940................................8.00
Paperweight, celluloid and iron,
    advertising...............................35.00
Planter
    2-1/2" x 3-1/2" x 4", china, glazed,
        Flip the Frog playing leap frog
        with a horse, c1930..................35.00
    7-1/2", frog and lily pad,
        McCoy.....................................32.00
Salt and Pepper Set, figural, on tray,
    3 pcs, Occupied Japan............12.50
Sparkler, frog with tie, Roselane ...25.00
Toothpick Holder, frog pulling
    snail shell, SP..........................55.00
Toy
    3" h, Flip the Frog, wood, jointed,
        green, beige hands and feet,
        raised eyeballs, c1930 ....75.00
    5" l, Froggy, felt.......................45.00
    10-1/2" h, Croaker the Frog,
        rubber, Rempel Man, boxed 45.00
Vase, 6", figural, seated, floral top,
    Occupied Japan 12.00

Fruit Jars

Collecting Hints: Old canning jars can be found at flea markets, household sales and antiques shows. Interest in fruit jars is stable. Some collectors base their collections on a specific geographical area, others on one manufacturer or one color. Another possible way to collect fruit jars is by patent date. More than 50 different types bear a patent date of 1858. It is important to remember that the patent date does not necessarily indicate the year in which the jar was made.

History: An innovative Philadelphia glassmaker, Thomas W. Dyott, began promoting his glass canning jars in 1829. John Landis Mason patented the screw-type canning jar on Nov. 30, 1858. The progress of the American glass industry and manufacturing processes can be studied through the development of fruit jars. Early handmade jars record bits of local history.

References: Douglas M. Leybourne Jr., *Red Book No. 7*, published by author, 1993; Dick Roller (comp.), *Indiana Glass Factories Notes*, Acorn Press, 1994; Bill Schroeder, *1000 Fruit Jars*, 5th Edition, Collector Books, 1987, 1995 value update.

Periodical: *Fruit Jar Newsletter*, 364 Gregory Ave., West Orange, NJ 07052.

Collectors' Clubs: Ball Collectors Club, 22203 Doncaster, Riverview, MI 48192; Federation of Historical Bottle Collectors, Inc., 88 Sweetbriar Branch, Longwood, FL 32750; Midwest Antique Fruit Jar & Bottle Club, P.O. Box 38, Flat Rock, IN 47234.

Note: Fruit Jars listed below are machine-made, unless otherwise noted.

All Right, aqua, qt, metal disc,
    wire clamp...............................76.00
Amazon Swift Seal, clear, qt,
    glass lid, wire bail.....................5.50
Atlas, qt, #109
    Apple Green............................15.00
    Cornflower 35.00
Automatic, aqua, qt, #177..........225.00
Ball
    Ideal, aqua, pt, glass lid,
        wire bail.................................2.50
    Mason, aqua, qt,
        emb backwards "s," zinc lid 3.50
    Perfection, aqua, qt, glass lid,
        zinc band, handmade 19.00
Bamberger's Mason Jar, blue, qt,
    glass lid, wire bail...................10.00
BBGM Co., aqua, qt, #197............35.00
Beaver, aqua, qt,
    circular, #424-1 ....30.00
Brighton, aqua, qt,
    circular, #512...........................85.00
Dandy, #751
    Qt, amber................................225.00
    1/2 gal, aqua 70.00
Dexter, aqua, qt, glass lid,
    screw band...............................30.00
Dunkley, clear, qt,
    hinged glass lid 6.00

Easy Vacuum Jar, clear,
qt, glass lid, wire clamp 25.00
Eclipse, aqua, qt, no lid, #885 .....500.00
Everlasting, #952
Pt, aqua....................................45.00
Qt, aqua 35.00
Globe, #1123
Qt
Amber 100.00
Aqua....................................25.00
1/2 gal, aqua 40.00
Jewell Jar, clear, 1/2 gal, glass lid,
screw band 8.50
Johnson & Johnson, NJ, amber,
qt, glass lid............................22.00
Kerr, aqua, qt, #1371....................65.00
Mason
#1664-1, qt, aqua 25.00
#1787
1/2 gal, dark amber 250.00
Qt, apple green, whittled 25.00
Mid West, Canadian Made, clear, qt,
glass lid, screw band 5.50
Millville, aqua
#2181
1/2 gal 50.00
Qt 45.00
#2182, pt, error........................75.00
#2185, 1/2 pt 300.00
Moore's, aqua, qt, clip-on back,
no closure, #2204 ....75.00
Phoenix, amber, qt, #2364 ....450.00
Presto Wide Mouth, clear,
1/2 pt, glass lid, wire bail 3.00
Rhodes, Kalamazoo, MI, aqua,
pt, zinc lid................................5.50
Safety, amber, qt, #2534 ....175.00
Standard, aqua, qt, wax seal.........21.00

Atlas, E-Z Seal, blue glass, raised letters, glass lid, wire bail, qt, $10.

Star Glass Co., aqua, qt, wax seal,
emb "The Star Glass Co.,
Albany, Ind." 31.00
Stark, aqua, qt, circular, #2730 ...200.00
Sun, aqua, qt, #2761...................125.00
Tropical Canners,
clear, pt, zinc lid.........................4.50
Vaccum Seal, aqua,
qt, circular, #2870..................200.00
Victory, clear, pt, glass lid, top
emb "Victory Reg'd 1925"..........6.00
Wilcox, aqua, qt, #3000...............100.00
Young's, stoneware, brown neck, metal
clamp lid, Pat May 27, 1902 ....19.00

Funeral Memorabilia

Collecting Hints: Funeral memorabilia should be collected because of love of the items, not strong financial incentives. Advertising hand fans and calendars were produced in abundance and, therefore, are easy to find. Items which predate the decline of the in-home wake will be much rarer and worth a great deal more than later items.

Museum: The American Funeral Home Museum, Houston, TX.

Advisor: Shad John Kvetko.

Bottle, embalming fluid
7-1/2" h, Frigid Fluid, paper label,
screw top, 1940s.....................10.00
9-1/2" h, emb "Undertakers Supply
Company," c1920.....................65.00
Bracelet, woven hair, gold fittings,
engraved "In Remembrance,"
1870s...................................250.00
Brooch, 2" x 2-1/2", celluloid, black,
emb "In Memoriam," 1870s ...100.00
Brush, wood, Wunderlich & Harris,
Funeral Directors, 1930s 25.00
Bumper Flags, blue,
white cross, 1940s...................35.00
Burial Suit, child's, tuxedo,
black, white shirt, 1940s 35.00
Calendar
Crowell Funeral Home, 1947 ...25.00
Hubbard Casket Co.,
automatic, plastic, brown and
cream, 1950s 15.00
Casket Plate, silver finish
Allice Sheham, Died Sept. 3, 1854,
aged 26 years, emb cross........20.00
Our Darling...............................15.00
Rest in Peace IHS,
cross shape...............................25.00
Catafalque, child's, portable, pink
crushed velvet, 5' h, 4' w, folds into
carrying case, 1900s 275.00

Clock, wall, lights up, Barre Guild
Monuments, 1950s................145.00
Coffee Mug, Ruzich Funeral Home,
"The last word in fine service,"
1950s 12.00
Coffin
Child's, 36-1/2" x 12-1/2", white
velour ext, white satin int, Bakelite
handles, 1940s 350.00
Shoulder Casket Style, 60-1/2" l,
ornate, pin striping, viewing window,
pewter handles, 1880s...........600.00
Cooling Board, portable, wood, brass
hardware, B.F. Gleason, Rochester,
NY, late 19th C 200.00
Cup, collapsible, plastic, green,
emb "Becks Casket Company,"
1950s 10.00
Embalmers Cosmetic Kit, ESCO, The
Embalmers Supply, 8 large bottles,
5 small bottles, 1930s 50.00
Embalming Kit, 9-1/2" h embalming
bottle, 9-1/2" h waste bottle, hand
pump, trocars, scissors, tubes,
scalpels and suture, 1930s ...150.00
Embalming Table, cast-iron base,
porcelain top, ornate, early
20th C...................................375.00
Head Elevator,
stainless steel, 1930s..............45.00
Memorial Sacred Heart, The Crane
and Breed Casket Co., brass,
box, 1930s...............................45.00
Mirror, silhouette illus, Wheeler Mortuary, Portales, NM, 1950s.........35.00
Mourning Card, 6" x 4", black, gold
inscription "In loving remembrance,
Fred E. Yoder, Died June 27,
1893, Aged 16 years 2 days" 3.00
Photograph, post mortem, 8" x 10", man
lying in coffin, late 19th C 15.00
Pin
Celluloid, black,
hair in locket, 1870s................75.00
Jet, carved weeping willow
mourning scene, 1860s 145.00
Plate, "Made expressly for F.D.
Gardner St. Louis Coffin Company,"
Vienna Art, 1905 ....95.00
Playing Cards, Oehler Funeral Home,
1970s 7.00
Railroad Sign, "Funeral Coach,"
emb, early 20th C 125.00
Salesman's Samples
Burial Vault, 12" x 3"
Ceramic, Christie Vaults,
1950s...................................35.00
Hammered Metal,
felt int, unmkd 30.00
Sign
D. Brown Joiner and Funeral Director, oak, brass plate, 1880s ...200.00
Funeral No Parking, double sided,
emb, 1930s 95.00

G

Gambling Collectibles

Collecting Hints: All the equipment used in the various banking games, such as Chuck-A-Luck, Faro, Hazard, Keno and Roulette, are collected today. Cheating devices used by professional sharpers are highly sought.

Almost all the different types of casino "money" are collected. In the gaming industry, "checks" refers to chips with a stated value; "chips" do not have a stated value. Their value is determined at the time of play. The methods used by coin collectors are also the best way to store chips, checks and tokens. A well-rounded gambling-collectibles display also includes old books, prints, postcards, photographs and articles relating to the field.

History: History reveals that gambling in America always has been a popular pastime for the general public, as well as a sure way for sharpers to make a "quick buck."

Government agencies and other entities use lotteries to supplement taxes and raise funds for schools, libraries and other civic projects. Many of the state and city lotteries of the late 18th and early 19th centuries proved to be dishonest, a fact which adds to the collecting appeal. Lottery tickets, broadsides, ads and brochures are very ornate and make excellent displays when mounted and framed.

Most of the gambling paraphernalia was manufactured by gambling supply houses that were located throughout the country. They sold their equipment through catalogs. As the majority of the equipment offered was "gaffed," the catalogs never were meant to be viewed by the general public. These catalogs, which provide excellent information for collectors, are difficult to find.

References: Art Anderson, *Casinos and Their Ashtrays*, published by author (P.O. Box 1403, Flint, MI 48504), 1994; Leonard Schneir, *Gambling Collectibles*, Schiffer Publishing, 1994.

Collectors' Club: Casino Chips & Gaming Tokens Collector Club, 5410 Banbury Dr., Worthington, OH 43235.

Bingo Cage, 9" h, metal, red celluloid handle, 11 wood balls, 9 cards, 1941............................20.00

Book

   Card Games and How to Play Them, 123 pgs, soft-cover, 1900 ....20.00

   Gamblers Don't Gamble, Michael MacDougall and J.C. Gurnas, 167 pgs, illus, 1939 ....30.00

   Game of Draw Poker, John Keller, NY, 84 pgs, 1887, 4-1/2" x 4-1/4" 27.00

   Playing Cards: History & Secrets, Benham, Spring Books, London, illus, dj 25.00

   Tricks with Cards, Complete Manual of Card Conjuring, Professor Hoffman, 250 pgs, hardcover, gold lettering, 1st ed, 1889.......18.00

Card Box, SS, rect, single deck, emb, 4 enameled aces on tortoiseshell lid, silver and blue enameled border, c1900, 3" x 6" x 1-1/2" 475.00

Card Counter, plated, imitation ivory face, black lettering 20.00

Card Press, 9-1/2" x 4-1/2" x 3", dovetailed, holds 10 decks, handle.....................................138.00

Cards

   Faro, sq corners, Samuel Hart & Co., NY, complete.................125.00

   Keno, 136, wood, paper and material covered, H.C. Evans & Co., Chicago.......................230.00

Catalog

   Bookmaker's Supplies, 19 pgs, 1895, illus...............................29.00

   H.C. Evans & Co., Secret Blue Book, Gambling Supply, 1936, 72 pgs 52.00

Chip Holder, poker, Bakelite, pink and black, Art Deco, pressed red, white and blue composition chips, holds 4 sets of 50 chips, card rack.......77.00

Chip Rack

   Faro, 18" l, 10" w, blue-green billiard-cloth lining bottom 78.00

   Roulette, walnut, holds 1,500 chips............................100.00

Chips, Poker

   Bone, round, sq and rect, red, purple, yellow and green, incised designs, fitted handmade mahogany box, c1870, price for set of 160 .....660.00

   Ivory, scrimshawed florals, 11 white, 4 white with red border, price for 15 ....475.00

Chromolithograph, 16" x 24", "Respecters of Limits," men playing poker in

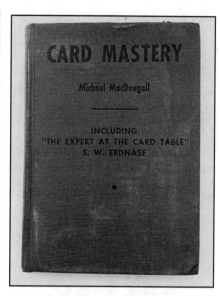

Book, *Card Mastery*, Michael MacDougall, Circle Magic Shop, NY, 1944, 205 pgs, 5-1/4" x 7", $15.

   hunting lodge, framed, sgd "William Eaton".....................110.00

Cigarette Lighter, gun shape, enameled suit signs on grips 50.00

Dealing Box, faro, German silver, straight, unmkd......................180.00

Dice

   Celluloid, 5/8", used in chuck-a-luck cage, set of three 12.00

   Weighted, black with white, always total 12, set of three 36.00

Dice Cage, 18-1/2" h, 13" w, nickel-plated brass, calfskin ends, 16 lbs, Mason & Co., Newark, NJ.....400.00

Hopper, Keno, walnut, blue-green billiard-cloth lining bowl, plated metal mouth, acorn finial, 3 carved feet 450.00

Layout

   Chuck-a-Luck, 30-1/2" x 9-1/2" x 3/4", vinyl, black, yellow painted numbers, pr...58.00

   Faro, felt, walnut trim, George Mason & Co., Denver 575.00

Pocket Watch, playing card, pointer lands on number, card or color on metal dial, beveled glass, c1890 ....550.00

Shot Glass, ribbed dec, porcelain dice in bottom 25.00

Sign, 11" x 30", Carlisle Whiskey adv, "A Bold Bluff," dogs gambling, silver and black ground, orig frame imp "Carlisle Rye" 72.50

Tray, 11" d, tin, red, black and white, martini center, card border 50.00

Wheel

   Roulette

      8" d, wood and metal, single and

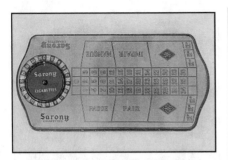

Roulette table card, Sarony Cigarettes adv, green ground, yellow, black, and red letters, English, 12-3/8" x 6" x 1-1/2", $65.

double zero decals, 4 prong
spinner, cloth layout 38.00
14", double Roulette Type,
fixed, carved cherrywood upper
wheel with 6 holes, 20" wood
lower wheel, controlled
underneath, 1870 ....975.00
Wheel of Fortune
20", 30 numbers, hp, cutout
painted center, yellow and white,
red ground, unmkd 150.00
60", complete wheel, "Dice" on
glass face, mounting hardware,
G. Mason, Chicago 1,100.00
Whiskey Bottle, figural, slot-machine
shape
8" x 5", Liberty Bell, gray, gold trim,
Ezra Brooks 25.00
9" x 9", Barney's, red 17.50

Games

Collecting Hints: Make certain a game has all its parts. The box lid or instruction booklet usually contains a list of all pieces. Collectors tend to specialize by theme, e.g., Western, science fiction, Disney, etc. The price of most television games falls into the $10 to $25 range, offering the beginning collector a chance to acquire a large number of games without spending huge sums.

Don't stack game boxes more than five deep or mix sizes. Place a piece of acid-free paper between each game to prevent bleeding from inks and to minimize wear. Keep the games stored in a dry location; remember, extremes of dryness or moisture are both undesirable.

History: A board game dating from 4000 B.C. was discovered in ruins in upper Egypt. Board games were used throughout recorded history but reached their greatest popularity during the Victorian era. Most board games combine skill (e.g., chess), luck and ability (e.g., cards) and pure chance (dice). By 1900, Milton Bradley, Parker Brothers, C.H. Joslin and McLoughlin were the leading manufacturers.

Monopoly was invented in 1933 and first issued by Parker Brothers in 1935. Before the advent of television, the board game was a staple of evening entertainment. Many board games from the 1930s and 1940s focused on radio personalities, e.g., Fibber McGee or The Quiz Kids. In the late 1940s, the game industry responded to the popularity of television and TV board games were at their zenith from 1955 to 1968. Movies, e.g., James Bond features, also led to the creation of games but never to the extent of television programs.

References: *Board Games of the 50's, 60's and 70's with Prices*, L-W Book Sales, 1994; Mark Cooper, *Baseball Games*, Schiffer Publishing, 1995; Lee Dennis, *Warman's Antique American Games, 1840-1940*, 2nd Edition, Wallace-Homestead, 1991; *Dexterity Games and Other Hand-Held Puzzles* L-W Book Sales, 1995; Caroline Goodfellow, *Collector's Guide to Games and Puzzles*, The Apple Press, 1991; Jack Matthews, *Toys Go to War*, Pictorial Histories Publishing, 1994; Rick Polizzi, *Baby Boomer Games*, Collector Books, 1995; Rick Polizzi and Fred Schaefer, *Spin Again*, Chronicle Books, 1991; Harry L. Rinker, *Guide to Games and Puzzles*, Antique Trader Books, 1996; Desi Scarpone, *Board Games*, Schiffer Publishing, 1995; Bruce Whitehill, *Games*, Wallace-Homestead, 1992.

Beat the Clock, Lowell Toy Corp., c1950, 18-3/8" x 13-1/2" x 2" box, $25.

Periodicals: *Toy Shop*, 700 E. State St., Iola, WI 54990; *Toy Trader*, P.O. Box 1050, Dubuque, IA 52004.

Collectors' Clubs: American Game Collectors Association, 49 Brooks Ave., Lewiston, ME 04240; American Play Money Society, 2044 Pine Lake Trail NW, Arab, AL 35016; Gamers Alliance, P.O. Box 197, East Meadow, NY 11554.

Note: Prices listed below are for boxed games in mint condition.

Air Race Around the World, Lido Toy
Co., 1950s 45.00
Air Traffic Controller 35.00
Alfred Hitchcock Presents Why, Milton
Bradley, 1958 ....25.00
Annie Oakley,
Milton Bradley, 1955 ....35.00
Apple's Way,
Milton Bradley, 1974 ....25.00
Aquanauts, Transogram 20.00
As the World Turns,
Parker Brothers, 1966 ....40.00
Autographs,
Leister Game Co., 1945 ....30.00
Barney Miller,
Parker Brothers, 1977 ....15.00
Baretta, Milton Bradley, 1975 ....25.00
Baseball Game,
Parker Brothers, 1946 ....70.00
Batman, Milton Bradley, 1966 ....75.00
Bat Masterson, Lowell, 1958 ....75.00
Beat the Clock, Lowell,
1954, first edition 60.00
Bewitched, T. Cohn, 1965 ....80.00
The Blondie Game,
Parker Brothers, 1969 ....10.00
Boots and Saddles,
Gardner, 1958 ....45.00
Bozo the Clown
Circus Game, Transogram 10.00
Branded, Milton Bradley, 1966 ......60.00
Break the Bank, Betty-B, 1955 ......50.00
Bugs Bunny, Ideal, 1974 ....50.00
Bullwinkle Hide and Seek, 1961 ...35.00
Camelot, Parker Brothers, 1940s ..20.00
Candid Camera, Lowell, 1963 ....25.00
Candy Land, Milton Bradley,
first edition, 1949 ....40.00
Captain America,
Milton Bradley, 1967 ....65.00
Captain Gallant Adventure Board Game,
Transogram, 1950s 45.00
Captain Video,
Milton Bradley, 1950 ....125.00
Car 54, Allison, 1961 ....50.00
Casey Jr. Game, Disney 60.00
Casper the Friendly Ghost, 1959 ..15.00
Charge Account, Lowell, 1961 ......10.00
Charlie's Angels,

Milton Bradley, 1977 ....15.00

Cheyene, Milton Bradley, 1958 .....50.00

Children's Hour,
Parker Brothers, 1946 ....30.00

Chutes and Ladders,
first edition, 1956 ....15.00

Circus Boy, H-G, 1956 ....45.00

Clash of the Titans, Whitman Publishing
Co., 1981 ....20.00

Clue, Parker Brothers, first edition,
1949...35.00

Conflict, 1960s 35.00

Dark Shadows, Whitman
Publishing Co., 1968 ....65.00

Dating Game, Hasbro, first edition,
1968...20.00

Davy Crockett, Ewing, 1955 ....85.00

Dennis the Menace, Standard Toycraft,
1960...30.00

Deputy, Milton Bradley, 1960 ....50.00

Disney's Swamp Fox.....................35.00

Dragnet, Transogram, 1955 ....60.00

Dr. Kildare, Ideal, 1962.................35.00

Dukes of Hazzard, card game,
English and French, Gaye
Distributing Co., 1980s 16.00

Easy Money, Milton Bradley............5.00

Ella Cinders,
Milton Bradley, 1944 ....30.00

Emergency,
Milton Bradley, 1974 ....10.00

Family Affair, Remco, 1968 ....50.00

Flintstone Kids, 1967 ....25.00

Flying Nun,
Milton Bradley, 1968 ....35.00

Fox Hunt, E.S. Lowe Co., 1940s ...18.00

F Troop, Ideal, 1965 ....90.00

Fugitive, Ideal, 1964 ....150.00

Game of the Kennedys, Transogram,
1962..100.00

Gas Crisis, 1979, sealed, MIB.......10.00

General Hospital,
Cardinal, 1982 ....15.00

Gentle Ben, Mattel, 1967...............20.00

Get Smart, Ideal, 1965 ....100.00

Gidget, Standard Toycraft, 1966 ...30.00

Gilligan's Island, Gem, 1965 ....200.00

Gong Show, American

Flying Nun, Milton Bradley, Springfield, MA, No. 4859, 1968, $35.

Publishing, 1977 ....15.00

Goodbye Mr. Chips, Parker Brothers,
1969 ....15.00

Go to the Head of the Class,
Milton Bradley...........................5.00

Green Hornet,
Milton Bradley, 1966.................90.00

Gunsmoke, Lowell, 1958...............65.00

Happy Days,
Parker Brothers, 1975 ....15.00

Have Gun Will Travel,
Parker Brothers, 1959 ....75.00

Hawaiian Eye, Lowell, 1963..........45.00

Hopalong Cassidy,
Milton Bradley, 1950.............100.00

Howdy Doody's TV Game,
Milton Bradley, 1950.................45.00

Huckleberry Hound Bumps,
Transogram, 1961 ....50.00

Huggin' the Rail, Selchow & Righter,
1948 ....60.00

I Dream of Jeannie, Milton Bradley,
1965 ....75.00

Indiana Jones Temple of Doom Action
Game, LIN, 1984 ....72.00

Intrigue, Milton Bradley 25.00

Jack-Be-Nimble,
Embossing Co., 1940s 10.00

Jackie Gleason, Away We Go,
Transogram, 1956 ....125.00

Knight Rider, 1983 ....20.00

Kojak, 1975, 3-D 25.00

Land of the Lost, 1975 ....40.00

Laramie, Lowell, 1958 ....85.00

Lassie, Whiting, 1955 ....20.00

Leave It to Beaver Ambush Game,
Hasbro, 1959 ....35.00

Li'l Abner: His Game, Milton Bradley,
1946 ....30.00

Looney Tunes, 1968 ....45.00

Magic Miles, Hasbro, 1950s..........30.00

Manchu's Hidden Hoard................50.00

Mandrake the Magician, some parts
missing 20.00

Man from U.N.C.L.E.,
Ideal, 1965...............................30.00

Margie, Milton Bradley, 1961 ....35.00

Marlin Perkins Zoo Parade,
Cadaco-Ellis, 1965 ....40.00

Marlin Perkins Wild Kingdom 10.00

Matchbox Traffic Game, 1967.......50.00

Men into Space,
Milton Bradley, 1960.................55.00

Mighty Comics, Super Heroes,
Transogram, 1966 ....60.00

Mission Impossible, Ideal, 1966....85.00

Mod Squad, Remco, 1968 ....40.00

Monopoly,
Parker Brothers, modern 5.00

Monster Squad,
Milton Bradley, 1977.................55.00

Mystic Skull, Game of Voodoo, Ideal,
1964, 18-3/4" x 13" 75.00

Name That Tune,
Milton Bradley, 1959 ....20.00

Nancy and Sluggo, Milton Bradley,
1944 ....35.00

Nancy Drew
Mystery Game, 1950s 60.00

Number Please,
Parker Brothers, 1961 ....25.00

Nurses, Ideal, 1963.......................25.00

Outer Limits,
Milton Bradley, 1964 ....175.00

Parcheesi, Selchow & Righter 5.00

Patty Duke,
Milton Bradley, 1963 ....25.00

Perry Mason, Transogram, 1959 ..25.00

Petticoat Junction,
Standard Toycraft, 1963..........40.00

Pirate and Traveler, Milton Bradley,
1953 ....25.00

Pit, Parker Brothers.........................5.00

Planet of the Apes, Milton Bradley,
1974 ....45.00

Prisoner of Zenda, Milton Bradley,
1930s 20.00

Rack-O, Milton Bradley 10.00

Raiders of the Lost Ark,
Kenner, 1981.......................... 45.00

Rifleman, Milton Bradley,
Milton Bradley, 1959 ....45.00

Rin-Tin-Tin, Transogram, 1950s ...50.00

Road Runner, Warner Bros. copyright,
Milton Bradley, 1968 ....65.00

Robin Hood, Betty-B, 1955 ....65.00

Rook, Parker Brothers 5.00

Scrabble, Selchow & Righter 5.00

Screwball Mad Mad Mad, Transogram,
1960 ....60.00

Sea Hunt, Lowell, 1961 ....35.00

Sgt. Preston,
Milton Bradley, 1956 ....30.00

Sigmund and the
Sea Monsters, 1975 ....20.00

Snake Eyes,
Selchow & Righter, 1940s........45.00

Sorry, Parker Brothers 5.00

Spot a Car Bingo...........................10.00

Star Trek, Ideal, 1967 ....95.00

Straightaway,
Selchow & Righter, 1961........60.00

Superboy, Hasbro, 1960s 60.00

Surfside Six, Lowell, 1959.............65.00

Syncron 8, Transogram, 1963 ......15.00

Take It and Double, second series,
Frederich H. Beach, 1941 ....20.00

Tarzan to the Rescue, Milton Bradley,
1977 ....27.00

Terry Toons, TV lotto, Ideal 45.00

That Girl, Remco, 1968.................30.00

T.H.E. Cat, Ideal, 1966, sealed.....65.00

Thunderbirds,
Parker Brothers, 1968 ....50.00

Tic Tac Dough, Transogram,
1957, first edition.....................20.00

Happy Days, Parker Brothers, $15.

Today with Dave Garroway, Athletic
    Products Co., Inc., 1950s 25.00
Treasure Hunt, Milton Bradley.........5.00
Uncle Wiggly, Milton Bradley...........8.00
Undersea World of Jacques Cousteau,
    Parker Brothers, 1968 ....35.00
Virginian, Transogram, 1962.........40.00
The Waltons,
    Milton Bradley, 1974, MIB 24.00
Watergate Scandal,
    American Symbolic, 1973........15.00
Wicket the Ewok,
    Parker Brothers, 1983 ....5.00
Wild Bill Hickok, Bilt-Rite, 1956 .....60.00
Woody Woodpecker,
    some missing parts..................15.00
You're Out, baseball game,
    Corey Game Co., 1941............35.00
Zorro, Whitman
    Publishing Co., 1958 ....25.00

Gasoline Collectibles

Collecting Hints: There still is plenty of material stored in old garages; try to find cooperative owners. If your budget is modest, concentrate on paper ephemera, such as maps. Regional items will bring slightly more in their area of origin.

History: The selling of gasoline has come full circle. The general store, livery stable and blacksmith were the first to sell gasoline. Gas stations, so prevalent from the 1930s to the 1960s, have almost disappeared, partially due to the 1973 gas crises. The loss of independently owned stations is doubly felt because they also were centers for automobile repair. Today gas sales at mini-markets are common.

    The abolition of credit cards by ARCO marked another shift, as did price reduction for cash sales by other brands. The growing numbers of "pay-at-the-pump" stations will also influence the marketplace. Elimination of free maps, promotional trinkets and other advertising material already is a factor. As more and more stores in shopping centers sell oil, parts and other related automobile products, it is doubtful if the gasoline station will ever recover its past position.

References: Mark Anderton and Sherry Mullen, *Gas Station Collectibles*, Wallace-Homestead, 1994; Robert W.D. Ball, *Texaco Collectibles*, Schiffer Publishing, 1994; Michael Bruner, *Gasoline Treasures*, Schiffer Publishing, 1996; Todd P. Helms, *Conoco Collector's Bible*, Schiffer Publishing, 1995; Scott Benjamin and Wayne Henderson, *Gas Pump Globes*, Motorbooks International (P.O. Box 1, Osceola, WI 54020), 1993; Bob Crisler, *License Plate Values*, King Publishing, 1994; *Gasoline*, Abbeville, 1995; John A. Gunnell (ed.), *Collector's Guide to Automobilia*, Krause Publications, 1994; Rick Pease, *Service Station Collectibles*, Schiffer Publishing, 1996; Jim and Nancy Schaut, *American Automobilia*, Wallace-Homestead, 1994; B.J. Sommers and Wayne Priddy, *Value Guide to Gas Station Memorabilia*, Collector Books, 1995; Mitch Stenzler and Rick Pease, *Gas Station Collectibles*, Schiffer Publishing, 1993; Michael Karl Witzel, *Gas Station Memories*, Motorbooks International (P.O. Box 1, Osceola, WI 54020), 1994.

Periodical: *Gameroom*, P.O. Box 41, Keyport, NJ 07735; *Hemmings Motor News*, Box 100, Bennington, VT 05201.

Collectors' Clubs: American Petroleum Collectors/Iowa Gas, 6555 Colby Ave., Des Moines, IA 50311; International Petroliana Collectors Association, P.O. Box 1000, Westerville, OH 43081; Spark Plug Collectors of America, 14018 NE 85th St., Elk River, MN 55330; World Oil Can Collector's Organization, 20 Worley Rd., Marshall, NC 28753.

Reproduction Alert: Small advertising signs and pump globes have been extensively reproduced.

Architectural Element, building star,
    Texaco, red plastic 30.00
Ashtray, Goodyear, tire shape,
    amber glass center..................35.00

Booklet, dirigible shape, Flying A Gasoline, cardboard, c1935, 9-3/8", $20.

Badge, Texaco Refinery, metal, photo,
    1920s 16.00
Bank, Texaco, 1905 ....50.00
Booklet
    Chevrolet, See the U.S.A., 64 pgs,
        1962.................................8.00
    Esso, 1920s 10.00
    Mobiloil, 1920s 10.00
Brochure, Pontiac Parts, Doll's
    Garage, Feb. 1966 ....4.00
Calendar, 1968, Crown Gasoline,
    tin over cardboard, dial
    thermometer, gold, orange letters,
    19-1/2" x 8-1/2"........................48.00
Can
    Eveready Prestone Anti-Freeze,
        1 gal, 1929 ....24.00
    Gargoyle Mobiloil B Vacuum
        Oil Co., Ltd, London, sq, handle
        and spout 65.00
    Texaco Home Lubricant Oil 20.00
Catalog
    Autolite Spark Plugs,
        128 pgs, 1983 ....5.00
    Champion Dealer, No. 5D,
        85 pgs, 1976 ....4.00
    Essex Auto Parts, Wire & Cable
        Catalog, 60 pgs, 1971...............5.00
Clock, wall, Texaco, 8" d, round, wood
    casing......................................60.00
Dealer display, Shell Oil..............300.00
Figure, Stopper Dog, American Brakelok
    Brake Shoes, MIB 140.00
Game, Touring Auto, 1930s..........25.00
Gas Pump Globe, Pemco 150.00
Magnet Set, Texaco, set of
    4 different round magnets
    with Texaco logos 15.00
Manual
    Bendix Brake Service,
        136 pgs, 1973 ....5.00
    Emission Control Bypass, 32 pgs,
        1974.................................4.00
    General Motors, Air Conditioning,
        46 pgs, 1970 ....4.00
Money Clip, Exxon Shute Creek Gas
    Plant, includes pocket knife.....15.00
Oil Can

Globe, Hall Bros. Super 67, 16", $250.

Macmillan, 1 gal 35.00
Sinclair, Opaline Motor
   Oil, empty 20.00
Universal, qt, full........................30.00
Wolf's Head Motor Oil,
   glass jar 40.00
Oil Change Reminder,
   miniature car, 1920s 25.00
Paperweight,
   Exide Battery, figural 35.00
Pump Sign, Gulf-tane, porcelain,
   slight edge chipping.................50.00
Radio, transistor, Atlas Battery......50.00
Sewing Kit, Rio Grande Gasoline, 2" l,
   brass cylinder, celluloid cov, red,

**Oil can, Texaco Home Lubricant, 6-1/4",
$3.**

white and blue logos, removable
   brass thimble, 1930 ....30.00
Sign
   Atlantic Pipeline Co., 18" sq,
   porcelain, "Warning High Pressure
   Oil Line," red and white 65.00
   Castrol Oil, double, swinging bracket,
   white, red, green and black painted
   metal, 24" x 30" 40.00
   Cooper Tires, metal, red, white
   and blue, 22" x 8" 40.00
   Fram Oil Filter, metal, double, Fram
   Man holding dip stick, white,
   black and orange, 18 x10" 65.00
   Goodrich Silvertowns, tin,
   48" x 18" 70.00
   Indian Gasoline, Lawrenceville, IL,
   gas pump illus, tin, 12" x 18"..200.00
   Mobilgas, metal sign, red flying
   horse, white ground, 1941 .....245.00
   RPM Oil, round, tin.................190.00
   Sunoco Motor Oil, tin 90.00
   Texaco Fire Chief, porcelain, pump
   type, 12" x 18" 85.00
   Zerolene Motor Oil, porcelain,
   20" x 20", diamond shape,
   double-sided 600.00
Stickpin, 5/8", Texaco,
   silvered brass, red star,
   green enameled "T," c1940 .....20.00
Tire Pressure Gauge, Firestone Tires,
   Schrader, patent 1909.............20.00
Toy, Hess Truck, 1988, no box ...350.00
Uniform Patch, Service Station, logo
   Gulf Oil 10.00
   Shell Oil...................................10.00
   Texaco 10.00

G.I. Joe Collectibles

Collecting Hints: It is extremely important to determine the manufacturing date of any G.I. Joe doll or related figure. The ideal method takes discipline—do a point-by-point comparison with the dolls described and dated in the existing reference books. Be alert to subtle variations; you do not have a match unless all details are exactly the same. It also is helpful to learn the proper period costume for each doll variation.

Accessory pieces can be every bit as valuable as the dolls themselves. Whenever possible, accessory pieces should be accompanied by their original packaging and paper inserts. G.I. Joe dolls and accessories were produced in the millions. Rarity is not a factor; condition is.

When buying dolls or accessories as collectibles, as opposed to acquiring them for play, do not purchase any items in less than fine condition.

History: Hasbro Manufacturing Co., produced the first G.I. Joe 12-inch posable action figures in 1964. The original line consisted of one male action figure for each branch of the military service. Their outfits were styled after uniforms from World War II, the Korean Conflict and the Vietnam Conflict.

In 1965, the first Black figure was introduced. The year 1967 saw two additions to the line—a female nurse and Talking G.I. Joe. To keep abreast of changing times, Joe received flocked hair and a beard in 1970. The creation of the G.I. Joe Adventure Team made Joe a prodigious explorer, hunter, deep sea diver and astronaut, rather than just an American serviceman. Due to the Arab oil embargo in 1976 and its impact on the plastics industry, the figure was renamed Super Joe and reduced in height to 8 inches. Production was halted in 1977.

In 1982, G.I. Joe staged his comeback. A few changes were made to the character line and to the way in which the figures were presented. The Great American Hero line consisted of 3-3/4 inch posable plastic figures with code names that corresponded to the various costumes. These new Joes, which dealt with contemporary and science fiction villains and issues, had about a 10-year run on store shelves. In 1994, the G.I. Joe line was changed to Sgt. Savage, a 4-1/2 inch line of figures with a World War II theme. The Savage line was a commercial flop. G.I. Joe X-treme was next introduced; it seems to have similar sales to that of Savage. In 1997, Hasbro brought back the 3-3/4 inch line for another try. Currently, the 12-inch line of Joes appears to be most popular.

References: Jeff Killian and Charles Griffith, *Tomart's Price Guide to G.I. Joe Collectibles*, Tomart Publications, 1992; Paris and Susan Mano, *Collectible Male Action Figures*, Collector Books, 1990, 1992 value update; Carol Markowski and Bill Sikora, *Tomart's Price Guide to Ac-*

tion Figure Collectibles, Tomart Publications, 1991; Vincent Santelmo, *Complete Encyclopedia to GI Joe*, 2nd Edition, Krause Publications, 1996; ——, *Official 30th Anniversary Salute to G.I. Joe*, Krause Publications, 1994.

Periodical: *The Barracks: The GI Joe Collectors Magazine*, 14 Bostwick Pl., New Milford, CT 06776.

Collectors' Club: GI Joe Collectors Club, 150 S. Glenoaks Blvd, Burbank, CA 91510.

Action Figure

Action GI Nurse, green medic bag, #8060, 1967, NRFB............3,200.00
Action Marine, #7700,
   1964, NRFB..........................415.00
Action Pilot, #7800,
   1964, NRFB..........................500.00
Action Soldier,
   #7500, 1964, NRFB...............350.00
Aquanaut, #7910,
   1969, NRFB........................2,200.00
Australian Jungle Fighter, #8105, complete, all accessories, mint 350.00
British Commando, #8104, complete, all accessories, mint...................395.00
Construction, jackhammer, complete, all accessories, mint...................495.00
Canadian Mountie, with dog, complete, all accessories, mint 375.00
French Resistance Fighter, #8103, complete, all accessories, mint 350.00
German Camp Kumandant, complete, all accessories, mint 350.00
German Soldier, #8100, complete, all accessories, mint...................385.00
Japanese Imperial Soldier, #8101, complete, all accessories, mint 425.00
Land Adventurer,
   #7401, 1970, NRFB...............175.00
Machine Gun Emplacement Set, #7531, 1964, Sears, NRFB 825.00
Marine Jungle Fighter, complete, all accessories, mint 850.00
Marine Medic, painted hair, complete, all accessories, mint...................385.00
Rescue Diver, complete,
   all accessories, mint 495.00
Russian Infantry Man, #8102, complete, all accessories, mint 395.00
Space Walk Astronaut, complete, all accessories, mint 325.00
Super Joe, #7503, 1977, NRFB 75.00
Talking, NRFB
   Action Marine, #7790, 1967 ...715.00
   Action Pilot, #7800, 1967 ....1,650.00
   Action Soldier, Mountain Troops
      Series, #7557.83, 1968 ....2,200.00

Astronaut, #7915, 1969..........895.00
Man of Action, #7590, 1970 ...325.00
Target Exclusive, masterpiece edition, figure and all accessories, MIB
   Marine, black....................125.00
   Marine, white....................95.00
   Sailor, black 125.00
   Sailor, white 110.00
Wal-Mart Exclusive, Home for the Holidays, soldier
   Black 95.00
   White..................................75.00

Equipment Set, NRFB

Air Force Basics Set,
   #7814, 1966 ....185.00
Combat Field Jacket Set,
   #7501, 1964 ....450.00
Escape Car Set, #7360, 1971 ....45.00
Footlocker, Adventurer Locker,
   #7940, 1969 ....400.00
Helipack, #7538-2, 1977 ....40.00
Marine Beachhead Field Pack Set,
   #7712, 1964 ....415.00
Marine Communications Poncho Set,
   #7701, 1964 ....350.00
Marine Weapons Rack Set, #7727,
   1967 ....500.00
MP Duffel Bag Set,
   #7523, 1964 ....110.00
Rescue Raft Set, #7350, 1971 ......45.00
Sabotage Set, #7516, 1967 ....500.00
Secret Agent Set, #7375, 1971 .....50.00
Solar Communicator Set,
   #7314, 1972 ....35.00
Special Forces Bazooka Set, #7528,
   1966 ....175.00
Survival Life Raft, #7802, 1964 ...300.00
Underwater Demolition Set, #7310,
   1972 ....35.00
Wind Boat Set, #7353, 1971 ....45.00

Miscellaneous

Pencil Case 195.00
Postcard, 3D, 2 GI Joe's
   performing a space walk,
   postmarked Cape Canaveral,
   FL, July 20, 1969 ....250.00
Water Pistol, GI Joe performing space
   walk on hand grip 250.00

Play Wear, child size

Ammo Box, first issue,
   Hasbro, Japan 25.00
Canteen, first issue,
   Hasbro, Japan 35.00
Combat Helmet, first issue,
   Hasbro, Japan 95.00
Laser Communicator, 1977...........35.00
Mess Kit, first issue,
   Hasbro, Japan 35.00
Shaving Kit 195.00
Swim Fins, 1983............................15.00
Wire Spool, first issue,

Hasbro, Japan 35.00

Uniform Set, NRFB

Annapolis Cadet Set,
   #7624, 1967 ....900.00
Astronaut Set, #7824, 1967 .....1,250.00
Marine Dress Parade Set,
   #7710, 1964 ....415.00
Military Police Set,
   #7521, 1964 ....550.00
Pilot Scramble Set,
   #7807, 1964 ....440.00
Super Joe, Invisible Danger,
   #7518-1, 1977 ....40.00

Vehicle, NRFB

Adventure team Vehicle Set,
   #7005, 1970 ....325.00
Crash Crew Fire Truck Set, silver fire-fighter suit, #8040, 1967.....3,250.00
Desert Patrol Attack Jeep Set,
   GI Joe Desert Fighter,
   #8030, 1967 ....3,300.00
Fight for Survival Set, Polar Explorer,
   #7982, 1969 ....625.00
Helicopter Set, #7380, 1973 ....135.00
Official Sea Sled and Frogman Set,
   #8050, 1966 ....600.00
Shark's Surprise Set, Frogman,
   #7980, 1969 ....550.00

Golf Collectibles

Collecting Hints: Condition is becoming more important as collectors' sophistication and knowledge grow. The newer the item, the better the condition should be.

It is extremely rare to find a club or ball made before 1800; in fact, any equipment made before 1850 is scarce. Few books on the subject were published before 1857. Most equipment made after 1895 is quite readily available. Common items, such as scorecards, ball markers, golf pencils and bag tags, have negligible value. Some modern equipment, particularly from 1950 and 1965, is in demand, but primarily to use for actual play rather than to collect or display.

The very old material is generally found in Scotland and England, unless items were brought to America early in this century. Christie's, Sotheby's and Phillips' each hold several major auctions of golf collectibles every year in London, Edinburgh and Chester. Golf collectible sales often coincide with the British Open Championship each July. Although the English market is more established, the

American market is growing rapidly and auctions of golf items and memorabilia now are held in the United States, as well as overseas.

The price of golf clubs escalated tremendously in the 1970s but stabilized in more recent years. For many years, golf book prices remained static, but they rose dramatically in the 1980s. Art prints, drawings, etchings, etc., have not seen dramatic changes in value, but pottery, china, glass and other secondary items, especially those by Royal Doulton, have attracted premium prices.

History: Golf has been played in Scotland since the 15th century and existing documents indicate golf was played in America before the Revolution. However, it was played primarily by "gentry" until the less expensive and more durable "guttie" ball was introduced in 1848. This development led to increased participation and play spread to England and other countries, especially where Scottish immigrants settled. The great popularity of golf began about 1890 in both England and the United States.

References: Sarah Fabian Baddiel, *World of Golf Collectables*, Wellfleet Press, 1992; John F. Hotchkiss, *Collectible Golf Balls*, Antique Trader Books, 1997; John M. Olman and Morton W. Olman, *Golf Antiques & Other Treasures of the Game*, Expanded Edition, Market Street Press, 1993; Beverly Robb, *Collectible Golfing Novelties*, Schiffer Publishing, 1992; Shirley and Jerry Sprung, *Decorative Golf Collectibles: Collector's Information, Current Prices*, Glentiques, 1991; Mark Wilson (ed.), *Golf Club Identification & Price Guide III*, Ralph Maltby Enterprises, 1993.

Periodicals: *Golfiana Magazine*, P.O. Box 688, Edwardsville, IL 62025; *U.S. Golf Classics & Heritage Hickories*, 5407 Pennock Point Rd., Jupiter, FL 33458.

Collectors' Clubs: Golf Club Collectors Association, 640 E. Liberty St., Girard, OH 44420; Golf Collectors' Society, P.O. Box 20546, Dayton, OH 45420; Logo Golf Ball Collector's Association, 4552 Barclay Fairway, Lake Worth, FL 33467.

Ashtray, caddy, white metal, pewter finish, 4" h, $85.

Museums: PGA World Golf Hall of Fame, Pinehurst, NC; Ralph Miller Memorial Library, City of Industry, CA; United States Golf Association, "Golf House," Far Hills, NJ.

Books

R.U. Adams, *John Henry Smith, A Humorous Romance of Outdoor Life*, 1905 .... 75.00
John Anderson, *The American Annual Golf Guide*, 1924 .... 42.00
Raymond Baeert, *The Adventures of Monsieur Depont: Golf Champion* 228.00
Gerald Batchelor, *Golf Stories*, 1914 .... 38.00
Peter Baxter, *Golf in Perth and Perthshire: Traditional, Historical and Modern*, 1899 .... 425.00
George W. Bedlam, *World's Champion Golfers: Their Art Disclosed by the Ultra-Rapid Camera*, 1924 ...... 45.00
Percy Boomer, *On Learning Golf*, 1942 .... 15.00
Robert H.K. Browning, *Golf in the Sun All Year Round*, 1931 .... 35.00
Patrick Campbell, *How to Become a Scratch Golfer*, 1963 .... 15.00
Robert Clark, *Royal and Ancient Game*, 3rd ed, 1899 .... 225.00
Joe Chronicles, *Uncle Jed, Caddie Master*, 1934 .... 90.00
Robert Clark, *Royal and Ancient Game*, 3rd ed, 1899 .... 200.00
B. Darwin, *Green Memories*, 1928 .... 300.00
EMB and GRT, *Humours and Emotions of Golf*, 1905 .... 50.00
John Gordon, *Understanding Golf*, 1926 .... 35.00
Haultain, *The Mystery of Golf*, 2nd ed, 1912 .... 75.00
Eleanor E. Helme, *Lady Golfer's Tip Book*, 1923 .... 30.00
Harold H. Hilton, *My Golfing Remembrances*, 1891 .... 325.00

Robert Hunter, *The Links*, NY, 1926 .... 272.00
H.G. Hutchinson, *The Badminton Library: Golf*, 1st ed, 1890 ..... 100.00
J.F. Irwin, *Golf Sketches*, 1892 ... 140.00
Bobby Jones, *How to Play Golf and How I Play Golf*, Spalding's Athletic Library, 1935 .... 35.00
Charles G. Mortimer and Fred Pignon, *The Story of the Open Championship 1860-1950*, 1952 .... 50.00
Byron Nelson, *Winning Golf*, 1947 .... 15.00
Jack Nicklaus, *Golf My Way*, with Ken Bowden, Simon Schuster, NY, 1974, sgd by author, 265 pgs 27.50
Willie Park, *The Game of Golf*, 1896 .... 135.00
Edward Ray, *Driving, Approaching and Putting*, 1922 .... 40.00
Sapper, *Uncle James' Golf Match*, 1950 .... 50.00
Robert Howie Smith, *The Golfer's Year Book for 1866* 450.00
Sam Snead, *Sam Snead Teaches You His Simple "Key" Approach to Golf*, Atheneum, NY, 1975, 78 pgs 12.00
W.J. Travis, *Practical Golf*, NY, 1902 .... 50.00
USGA Yearbook, 1931 .... 50.00

Equipment

Bag

Busey Patent Caddy, mahogany and ash, birch handle, canvas and leather ball picket, club tube 325.00
Leather, Tony Lema, 1964 British Open Champion 100.00
Osmond Patent Caddy, ashwood, leather handles, straps, canvas club tube, ball pocket 255.00

Ball

Bramble
    Crown 25.00
    Haskell, pat. 1899 .... 46.00
    Pneumatic 75.00
    Spring Vale Hawk 30.00
Feather
    J. Gourlay, early 19th C, maker's name 1,250.00
    Tom Morris 2,750.00
Glexite, Phantom, orig wrappers, price for 6 .... 48.00
Gutty
    Hand hammered 200.00
    Mitchell, Manchester 50.00
    Ocobo 150.00
Lynx, rubber core 15.00
Sq Dimple, North British, practice, box of 12 .... 125.00

Club

Doorstop, green grass, red coat, gray pants, black highlights, 10" h, $450.

(**Note**: w/s = wood shaft; s/s = steel shaft)

Iron

Burke juvenile mashie, w/s............25.00
George Nicol niblic,
    anti-shank, w/s......................55.00
Hagen iron-man
    sand wedge, w/s....................150.00
Spalding F-4, c1922, w/s..............12.00
Tom Stewart lofter,
    smooth face, w/s....................55.00
Urquehart pat
    adjustable club, w/s..............275.00
Wilson wedge,
    Staff model, c1959, s/s............50.00

Putter

A. Patrick, long nose,
    care head, w/s.....................160.00
R.T. Jones, Calamity Jane, s/s......75.00
Mills, L model, aluminum head......45.00
R. Simpson,
    socket head, c1900, w/s........100.00
Schenectady, w/s.......................60.00
Spalding Cash-in, s/s..................50.00
Tommy Armour IMG
    Ironmaster, s/s.....................95.00

Wood

Auchterlonie,
    scare-head brassie, w/s...........45.00
Ben Sayers, spoon,
    scare head, w/s.....................45.00
C.S. Butchart, scare-head driver,
    stamped shaft.......................45.00
Davie Anderson,
    scare-head driver, w/s.............75.00
Dunn's pat 1-pc driver.............1,150.00
McGregor, Tourney 693W driver,
    c1953, s/s..........................125.00

Tom Morris, scare head, bulger and
    brassie, horn insert, stamped "T.
    Morris, St. Andrews".............140.00
Willie Dunn, long nose, stained beech
    head, inset horn.................1,700.00

Miscellaneous

Advertising Trade Card,
    Humphries Witch Hazel Oil,
    woman golfer in full color.........24.00
Autograph, ALS, sgd by Harry Vardon,
    1931, framed and glazed.......127.00
Bookends, 4" x 6", golfer in relief ..60.00
Cigarette Box, hammered pewter, mesh
    gutty ball and 2 clubs on cov ...40.00
Cigarette Card
    Player Cigarettes, set of 25......44.00
    Wills, Famous Golfers.............52.00
Cigarette Case, cov, silver, enameled
    Edwardian golf scene...........290.00
Decanter
    Jim Beam, 53rd PGA Championship,
    1971.................................38.00
    Limited Edition Whiskey, Hawaiian
    Open, 1972.........................19.00
Doorstop, golfer putting,
    green cap, red shoes, coat
    and knickers, 6-1/2" x 8"..........85.00
Figurine, Harry Vardon, bronze, by
    Henry Pegram, 1908..........1,500.00
Game
    Golf-o-Matics,
    Royal London.......................20.00
    Spin-Golf, Chad Valley, box.....47.00
Hatpin, golf club-shape.................25.00
Magazine,
    Golf Digest, 1963, 12 issues ...22.00
Medal
    Amateur Championship,
    British.............................940.00
    Royal Aberdeen,
    weekly handicap, 1937..........140.00
Paperweight,
    glass, U.S. Open, 1980...........29.00
Plate
    Golfing rabbits, Royal Doulton
    Bunnykins...........................43.00
    Transfer after Reynolds,
    pottery..............................84.00
Postcard
    Gibson, c1905,
    price for set of 5...................25.00
    Rules of Golf, Crombie,
    price for set of 9...................36.00
    St. Andrews, sepia views,
    c1900, price for 24..............157.00
Program, Bob Hope Desert Classic,
    1967.................................17.00
Scorecard, 5,300, all different.....450.00
Toast Rack, electroplated, crossed clubs
    create 4 sections..................85.00
Towel, bag, U.S. Open, 1980..........7.50
Vase, blue and white pottery,

printed golf scenes, Mitchell,
    1910, price for pr.................220.00
Watch, mesh,
    golf-ball shape, Swiss...........115.00

Prints, Drawings, Etc.

Cartoon
    "Fore" and "After," John Hassall,
    price for pr.........................180.00
    "Golf Amenities," A.T. Smith,
    orig Punch, India ink.............250.00
    "Spy," H.H. Hilton,
    Vanity Fair...........................60.00
Painting
    "Golfer Playing Long
    Shot from Bunker," Tom Peddie,
    oil on board, sgd.................415.00
    The Golfing Lassie," unknown,
    oil on board........................175.00
    Winter Scene, golfers playing to
    the mark, 17th C Dutch school,
    oil on relaid canvas............2,900.00
Photograph, Harry Vardon,
    sgd, 1929...........................215.00
Print
    "The First Tee," Dendy Sadler,
    etching, colored.....................32.00
    "In the Sand, St. Andrews," after
    Michael Brown.......................40.00
    "North Berwick: Perfection
    and the Redan," Cecil Aldin,
    artist sgd..........................1,250.00
    "Royal and Ancient, St. Andrews,
    1798," Frank Paton, etching, vi-
    gnettes in margin, artist sgd...250.00
Sketch, Gene Sarazen, black chalk,
    Ridgewell.............................38.00

Graniteware

Collecting Hints: Old graniteware is heavier than new graniteware. Pieces with cast iron handles date from 1870 to 1890; wood handles date from 1900 to 1910. Other dating clues are seams, wood knobs and tin lids.

History: Graniteware is the name commonly given to enamel-coated iron or steel kitchenware. The first graniteware was made in Germany in the 1830s. Graniteware was not produced in the United States until the 1860s. At the start of World War I, when European companies turned to manufacturing war weapons, American producers took over the market. Gray and white were the most common graniteware colors, although each company made its own special shades of blue, green, brown, violet, cream or red.

References: Helen Greguire, *Collector's Encyclopedia of Graniteware, Book 1* (1990, 1994 value update), *Book 2* (1993), Collector Books; Dana Gehman Morykan and Harry L. Rinker, *Warman's Country Antiques & Collectibles*, 3rd Edition, Wallace-Homestead, 1996.

Collectors' Club: National Graniteware Society, P.O. Box 10013, Cedar Rapids, IA 52410.

Bacon Platter,
    brown and white swirl 215.00
Baking Pan
    9" x 12", blue and white swirl ...70.00
    11" x 15", blue and white swirl,
    applied wire handles 100.00
Berry Bucket
    4" h, small blue and white
    swirl, tin lid................................90.00
    4-1/2" h, blue and white swirl, riveted
    handle, tin lid 150.00
Bowl, 2" d, blue and white, U.S.
    Stamping paper label...............70.00
Bread Riser, 16" d, ftd, large blue and
    white swirl, white int, tin lid 160.00
Butter dish, cobalt blue and white,
    mottled....................................215.00
Cake Pan, robin's-egg blue 30.00
Candlestick, 2-1/4" h,
    blue and white swirl, thumb
    rest on finger ring...................290.00
Chamber Pot, medium blue and white
    swirl, black trim 75.00
Coffee Boiler, gray..........................35.00
Coffee Mug, blue and white swirl, white
    int, black trim and handle.........40.00
Coffeepot, cov
    Blue and white, large swirl 115.00
    Gray, Columbian label..............95.00
Colander
    Blue and gray swirl...................85.00
    Emerald and white swirl 165.00
Cream Can, medium blue
    and white swirl, white int,
    black handle, tin lid................275.00

Basin, green and white swirl ext, white int, cobalt rim, riveted handles, 20" w handle to handle, 17-1/2" d, 5-1/2" h, $85.

Creamer, 7" h, Iris Swirl 400.00
Cuspidor, seamed, large
    blue and white swirl 190.00
Dinner Bucket, 3 pcs, oval, blue
    and white, white int, black trim,
    wood handle 500.00
Dipper, Windsor, eyelet for hanging
    Medium blue and white swirl,
    cobalt blue trim and handle......60.00
    Large blue and white swirl,
    black trim and handle...............57.00
    Double Boiler, blue and white swirl
    Bell shape, black trim,
    black handle...........................115.00
    Black handles...........................70.00
Dust Pan, speckled gray 100.00
Eggcup, cobalt blue and white, checker-
    board trim, price for pr 120.00
Funnel
    Blue Diamond Ware, 9" d.........95.00
    Gray, Acme 45.00
Grater, cream-colored
    and green, flat 95.00
Ladle, perforated,
    blue and white swirl 30.00
Measure, 8" h, blue and white swirl,
    seamed lip 250.00
Melon mold, gray, ribbed, tin
    bottom with ring, mkd "Extra
    Agate," #50 ....75.00
Milk Bowl, small............................10.00
Milk Pitcher, 7" h, medium blue and
    white swirl 185.00
Mixing Spoon, large blue and white swirl,
    black handles, white int 37.50
Mold, fluted, gray speckled 135.00
Muffin Pan, 6 cup, blue and white,
    white int 425.00
Pie Pan, blue and white swirl 35.00
Platter, mottled blue
    and white, large 75.00
Preserving Kettle, blue and white swirl
    American Stamping and Enameling
    Co., brown wood bail handle, tipping
    handle, orig label....................105.00
    Belmont Stamping and Enameling
    Co Azure Ware, orig label......115.00
Pudding Pan, medium blue and white
    swirl, Cream City Tulip Ware,
    orig paper label........................70.00
Rice Steamer, medium blue and white
    swirl, bail handle....................110.00
Roaster, cov
    Cobalt blue and white swirl, lifting
    rack 95.00
    Gray 20.00
Sauce, 6", blue and white swirl,
    Geuder, Pacshke and Frey Co.
    Tulip Brand paper label 50.00
Scoop, white, small 75.00
Skillet, red 50.00
Stewing Pan, blue and white swirl,

Chamberstick, marbleized pink and green, round base, 6", $67.50.

    long black handle 110.00
Sugar Bowl, gray, tin lid, L&G 315.00
Tea Kettle, gooseneck,
    blue and white swirl,
    Columbian, black trimmed ears,
    black wood bail handle 900.00
Teapot, 9" h, gooseneck, blue and white
    swirl 100.00
Tea Steeper, blue and white swirl, black
    handle 70.00
Tea Strainer,
    blue and white swirl...............190.00
Tube Pan, gray 24.00
Tumbler,
    mottled blue and white, 5" d 70.00
Wash Basin, 11-1/2" d, blue and white,
    eyelet for hanging....................75.00
Water Pail, blue and white, Coonley Mfg.
    Co., Clyde, IL, blue and white swirl,
    orig label................................170.00
Water Pitcher
    8" h, large blue and white swirl,
    black handle and trim.............280.00
    9" h, medium blue and white swirl,
    granite handle 280.00

H

Hall China

Collecting Hints: Hall China Co., identified many of its patterns by name, but some of these are being gradually changed by dealers. A good example is the Silhouette pattern, which is also known as Taverne. Many shapes are also referred to by more than one name, i.e., Radiance is also known as Sunshine, Terrace as Stepdown and Pert as Sani-Grid. Because of their high quality, most Hall China pieces are still in wonderful condition. There is no reason to pay full price for imperfect pieces.

History: Hall China was formed as a result of the dissolution of the East Liverpool Potteries Co. Robert Hall, a partner in the merger, died within months of establishing the new company. Robert T. Hall, his son, took over. At first, the company produced the same semi-porcelain dinnerware and toiletware that was being made at the other potteries in East Liverpool, OH. Robert T. Hall began experiments to duplicate an ancient Chinese one-fire process that would produce a non-crazing vitrified china, with body and glaze fired at the same time. He succeeded in 1911 and Hall products have been made that way ever since.

Hall's basic products—hotel and restaurant institutional ware—are sold to the trade only. However, the firm also has produced many retail and premium lines, e.g. Autumn Leaf for Jewel Tea and Blue Bouquet for the Standard Coffee Co., of New Orleans. A popular line is the gold-decorated teapots that were introduced for retail sale in 1920. In 1931, kitchenware was introduced, soon followed by dinnerware. These lines were made in both solid colors and with decals for retail and premium sales. Hall is still producing china at its plant in East Liverpool, OH.

References: Susan and Al Bagdade, *Warman's American Pottery and Porcelain*, Wallace-Homestead, 1994; Harvey Duke, *Hall: Price Guide Update*, ELO Books, 1992; ——, *Official Price Guide to Pottery and Porcelain*, 8th Edition, House of Collectibles, 1995; C.L. Miller, *Jewel Tea Company*, Schiffer Publishing, 1994; Jim and Lynn Salko, *Halls Autumn Leaf China and Jewel Tea Collectibles*, published by authors (143 Topeg Dr., Severna Park, MD 21146), 1996; Margaret and Kenn Whitmyer, *Collector's Encyclopedia of Hall China*, 2nd Edition, Collector Books, 1994.

Periodical: *Hall China Encore*, 317 N. Pleasant St., Oberlin, OH 44074.

Collectors' Clubs: Autumn Leaf Reissues Association, 19238 Dorchester Cr., Strongsville, OH 44136; National Autumn Leaf Collectors Club, 7346 Shamrock Dr., Indianapolis, IN 46217.

Notes: For several years, Hall has been reissuing many of its products as part of its new solid-color Americana retail line. If you are a new collector and are unsure if an item is new or old, you may want to buy only the items with decals or gold decorations, as these pieces have not been reissued and there is apparently no intention of doing so. Prices have dropped slightly on some of the original solid-colored items because of the reissues.

Dinnerware Patterns

Autumn Leaf: Premium for the Jewel Tea Co. Produced 1933 until 1978. Other companies made matching fabric, metal, glass and plastic accessories.

Bean Pot, 2 handles	150.00
Berry Bowl, 5-1/2" d	5.00
Butter Dish, cov, 1 lb	190.00
Clock	725.00
Coasters, set of 8	45.00
Coffeepot, cov, mkd "Jewel"	100.00
Cookie Jar, cov, big-ear version	275.00
Creamer and Sugar, cov, ruffled D	35.00
Cream Soup	20.00
Cup and Saucer, St. Denis	50.00
French Baker, 4-1/2" l	70.00
Gravy Boat	20.00
Hot Pad, tin back, 7-1/4"	35.00
Jug, ball	50.00
Plate, 9" d	6.50
Range Salt and Pepper Shakers, pr	35.00
Salt and Pepper Shakers, pr	15.00
Stack Set	75.00
Teapot, cov, mkd "Jewel"	90.00

Autumn Leaf, pitcher, Jewel Tea, Hall's Superior, 5-1/2" h, $35.

Tumbler, glass, frosted	
3-3/4" h	40.00
5-1/2" h	22.00
Vegetable Bowl, oval, divided	175.00

Crocus: Dinnerware pattern produced during the 1930s. This decal has multi-colored stylized crocuses and green and black leaves. It is also found on a wide array of kitchenware shapes.

Bowl, Radiance	
7" d	30.00
9" d	45.00
Butter Dish, cov, 1 lb	550.00
Cake Plate	25.00
Casserole, cov	60.00
Cereal Bowl, 6" d	15.00
Coffeepot, Terrace	100.00
Coffee Server, metal	25.00
Gravy Boat	32.00
Jug, ball	195.00
Plate	
7-1/4" d, bread and butter	8.00
8-1/4" d, salad	10.00
9" d, luncheon	15.00
10" d, diner	35.00
Platter, 13-1/4" l	35.00
Salt and Pepper Shakers, pr, teardrop shape	45.00
Soup Tureen	395.00
Teapot, banded	175.00
Tidbit, 3 tier	50.00

Orange Poppy: Premium for the Great American Tea Co. Introduced in 1933 and discontinued in the 1950s. Dinnerware was made in the C-style shape. Metal accessories are available, though scarce.

Bean Pot	105.00
Cake Plate	18.00
Casserole, 8" l, oval	65.00
Coffee Canister	325.00
Coffeepot	80.00
Custard	6.00
Platter, 13" l	18.00

Salad Bowl 12.00
Salt and Pepper Shakers,
    pr, handled.............................35.00
Sugar, Great American mark.........30.00
Teapot, Boston............................350.00
Vegetable Bowl, round 25.00

Pastel Morning Glory: Dinnerware line produced in the late 1930s and readily found in northern Michigan, Wisconsin and Minnesota. Design consists of large pink morning glories surrounded by green leaves and small blue flowers on white ground. The pattern was also used on kitchenware items.

Casserole, cov.............................45.00
Cereal Bowl, 6" d..........................17.50
Cup and Saucer 15.00
Custard...17.50
Drip Jar, pink, #1166 ....60.00
Fruit Bowl, 5-1/2" d.........................7.50
Gravy Boat 25.00
Jug, ball, pink 165.00
Pie Baker......................................30.00
Plate
    6" d, bread and butter 5.00
    8-1/4" d, salad 7.50
    9" d, luncheon 10.00
    10" d, dinner..............................25.00
Platter, oval
    11-1/4" l....................................25.00
    13-1/4" l....................................30.00
Sugar, cov, pink, deco-style 40.00
Vegetable Bowl, oval....................22.50

Red Dot (a.k.a. Eggshell Polka Dot): This pattern is found on the Eggshell Buffet Service. Red is the most commonly found Dot color, but the pattern was also produced in blue, green and orange.

Baker, 13-1/2" l, fish shape 45.00
Bean Pot, small, #1 ....95.00
Bowl, 8-1/2" d..............................25.00
Casserole, cov
    Oval..38.00
    Round..38.00
Cocotte, 4" d, handle....................25.00
Drip Jar, tab handle, #1188 ....45.00
Jug, cov
    #2 ....125.00
    #4 ....125.00
Jug, room service-type, 6" h.........95.00
Mustard, cov, slotted cov..............95.00
Onion Soup, cov...........................45.00
Pitcher, Baron...............................95.00
Range Shakers, salt, pepper,
    flour, sugar.............................150.00
Shirred-Egg Dish, 6-1/2" d 25.00
Tom and Jerry Punch Bowl Set,
    bowl and 12 mugs 250.00

Red Poppy: Premium for Grand Union Tea Co. Produced from mid 1930s until mid 1950s. Complete line of D-style din-

nerware and kitchenware in various forms. The design features red poppies and black leaves on a white background. Glass, metal, wood and cloth accessories were also marketed.

Cereal Bowl, 6" d..........................17.50
Coffeepot, Daniel, metal dropper ..40.00
Cup and Saucer 15.00
Custard Cup, Radiance.................17.50
Drip Jar..30.00
Plate, 10" d, dinner.......................15.00
Salt and Pepper Shakers, pr, egg
    shape.......................................45.00
Soup Plate, flat............................20.00
Stack Set......................................75.00

Taverne: This popular pattern was used as a premium for Hellick's Coffee in Pennsylvania. Other mediums are found with this pattern.

Bowl, Medallion
    6" d...20.00
    7" d...25.00
Casserole, medallion....................75.00
Coffeepot, 5-band 125.00
Coffee Server, medallion.............150.00
Drip Jar, cov 40.00
French Baker, 8" d 30.00
Iced Tea Glass 50.00
Jug, #3 ....45.00
Leftover, cov
    4" x 8".....................................70.00
    8" x 8".....................................85.00
Pretzel Jar, cov 165.00
Salad Bowl, 9" d 25.00
Salt and Pepper Shakers,
    pr, Five Band 75.00
Saucer...10.00
Teapot
    Medallion................................125.00
    Streamline, no cov 100.00

Kitchenware Patterns

Blue Garden/Blue Blossom: This 1939

Orange Poppy pitcher, 6-3/8" h, $65.

pattern is a silk-screen decal on a cobalt blue glaze. Hall claims that this was the first time that cobalt blue had been used successfully for vitrified kitchen cooking items.

Batter Jar 250.00
Butter, cov, Radiance..................475.00
Casserole, #4, Sundial.................75.00
Cookie Jar, cov 375.00
Jug, loop handle.........................245.00
Leftover, loop handle 195.00
Mixing Bowl, 6" d..........................85.00
Range Shakers, handle 90.00
Refrigerator Bowl,
    cov, loop handle 155.00
Syrup Pitcher, banded 395.00

Chinese Red: This pattern name refers to the bright red color found on various shapes of solid-colored kitchenware. Chinese red is the most commonly found color.

Ashtray, triangular.......................30.00
Batter Bowl, Five Band 75.00
Bean Pot, #5 ....155.00
Casserole, tab handle 28.00
Creamer and Sugar,
    cov, Morning...........................95.00
Drip Jar, open, #1188 ....35.00
Jug, ball, #3.................................45.00
Leftover, Zephyr.........................165.00
Pretzel Jar, cov 125.00
Ramekin.......................................50.00
Water Bottle, Zephyr 90.00

#488: Accessory pattern produced in the early 1930s until 1940.

Berry Bowl...................................12.00
Bowl, 8" d....................................35.00
Custard..24.00
Jug, #5, Radiance 65.00
Refrigerator Jar, cov, square 65.00

Refrigerator Ware

General Electric Adonis, water server
    Blue and yellow.......................55.00
    Gray and yellow 55.00
Hotpoint, Dresden, water server ...90.00
Norris, Turk, water server 20.00
Westinghouse
    Butter Dish, cov,
        yellow, Hercules.....................30.00
    Leftover
        Delphite 16.00
        Yellow, Hercules.................30.00
    Water Server, green, General..95.00

Rose White: Kitchenware pattern with Hi-White body and pink rose decal.

Bean Pot, cov............................115.00
Bowl, 9" d, straight sides.............25.00
Casserole, cov, tab handles.........27.50
Jug, 7-1/2" h, Perk 40.00
Pitcher, small 30.00

Salt and Pepper Shakers, pr 35.00

Wild Poppy (a.k.a. Poppy and Wheat): Kitchenware line introduced in late 1930s and sold by Macy's.

Bean Pot......................................225.00
Casserole, cov, Sundial, #1.........125.00
Cookie Jar, cov, Five Band 300.00
Custard, Radiance..........................20.00
Salt and Pepper Shakers,
    pr, handles.............................100.00
Shirred-Egg Dish
    5-1/4" d...................................40.00
    6" d...40.00
Stack Set, Radiance....................175.00
Sugar, handle................................75.00
Teapot, cov, 6 cup, Manhattan....400.00
Tea Tile, 6" sq 85.00

Hall Teapots

Airflow, orange, 6 cup..................100.00
Aladdin
    Cobalt Blue, gold trim...............45.00
    Yellow, gold trim, infuser..........45.00
Albany
    Brown, gold trim 70.00
    Yellow, gold trim......................85.00
Autumn Leaf, rayed, long spout 85.00
Baltimore, yellow 50.00
Basket, canary yellow, gold trim..110.00
Birdcage,
    emerald green, gold trim........600.00
Boston, gray, 4 cup 60.00
Coverlet, canary yellow 50.00
Cube, 1 cup
    Bright Yellow 250.00
    Turquoise 125.00
Doughnut, cobalt blue 160.00
Flareware 60.00
French Flower
    Black 50.00
    Brown, gold daisies, 1 cup 50.00
Globe
    Canary Yellow 80.00
    Cobalt Blue, gold trim.............225.00
    Emerald Green, gold trim.........95.00
    Gray, no drip 85.00
    Light Green, gold trim...............80.00
Manhattan, blue.............................65.00
McCormick, turquoise,
    2 cup, emb............................110.00
Murphy, light blue 85.00
Newport, pink,
    floral decal, 5 cup 50.00
Philadelphia
    Green, gold trim, c1920............75.00
    Pink, gold trim 45.00
Plume, pink....................................20.00
Royal, ivory..................................150.00
Starlight, canary yellow 25.00
Sundial, yellow, safety handle.......75.00
Teamster, double spout, yellow

and gold...............................110.00
Twin Spout, emerald green 80.00
Windshield,
    gold dot dec, gold label 65.00

Harker Pottery

Collecting Hints: In 1965, Harker China had the capacity to annually produce 25 million pieces of dinnerware. Hence, there is a great deal of Harker material available at garage sales and flea markets. Shapes and forms changed through the decades of production. Many patterns were kept in production for decades and the same pattern was often made using different colors for the background. Patterns designed to have mass appeals include those like Colonial Lady, which was popular at "dish nites" at the movies or other businesses.

Between 1935 and 1955, Columbia Chinaware, which was organized to market Harker products in small towns across the country, promoted enamel ware, glass and aluminum products. One of Columbia Chinaware's patterns was Autumn Leaf, which is eagerly sought by collectors. Harker used a large variety of backstamps and names. Hotoven cookware featured a scroll, draped over pots, with a kiln design at top. Columbia Chinaware had a circular stamp showing the Statue of Liberty.

Collectors should consider buying only Harker patterns by famous designers. Among these are Russel Wright's White Clover and George Bauer's Cameoware. Or an interesting collection could focus on one object, e.g., a sugar or creamer, collected in a variety of patterns from different historical periods. Watch for unusual pieces. The Countryside pattern features a rolling pin, scoop and cake server.

History: The Harker Co., began in 1840 when Benjamin Harker, an English slater turned farmer in East Liverpool, OH, built a kiln and began making yellowware products from clay deposits on his land. The business was managed by members of the Harker family until the Civil War, at which time David Boyce, a brother-in-law, took over the operation. Although a Harker resumed management after the war, members of the Boyce family

Cameo, creamer, blue and white, 5-1/4" w, 3" h, $5.

also assumed key roles within the firm; David G. Boyce, a grandson of David, served as president.

In 1879, the first whiteware products were introduced. The company was able to overcome severe financial problems caused by a disastrous flood in 1884. In 1931, the company moved to Chester, WV, to escape repeated flooding. In 1945, Harker introduced Cameoware made by the engobe process in which a layered effect was achieved by placing a copper mask over the bisque and then sand blasting to leave the design imprint. The white rose pattern on blue ground was marketed as White Rose Carv-Kraft in Montgomery Ward stores.

In the 1960s, Harker made a Rockingham ware line which included the hound-handled pitcher and mugs. The Jeannette Glass Co., purchased the Harker and the plant was closed in March 1972. Ohio Stoneware, Inc., utilized the plant building until it was destroyed by fire in 1975.

References: Susan and Al Bagdade, Warman's American Pottery and Porcelain, Wallace-Homestead, 1994; Neva W. Colbert, Collector's Guide to Harker Pottery, U.S.A., Collector Books, 1993; Jo Cunningham, *Collector's Encyclopedia of American Dinnerware*, Collector Books, 1982, 1995 value update.

Additional Listings: Russel Wright.

Advertising

Hot Oven Hearth, teapot 48.00
Kriebel's Dairy, Hereford,
    PA, creamer 45.00

Cameo: Production of Cameo line at Harker began in 1940. The process was perfected by George Bauer. After the Bauer pottery closed, production began at the Harker Pottery Co. Dinnerware was added in 1941. Bauer continued to own the rights to the process and received a royalty. It was made in blue and pink. Several distinct patterns exist in this line, including Dainty Flower, Shell Ware, Virginia and Zephyr.

Bowl, 8" d, Zephyr, blue 15.00
Casserole, cov, square, blue.........50.00
Cheese Box, cov, Zephyr, blue 40.00
Cup and Saucer,
    Shell Ware, blue 15.00
Dish, lug handle,
    Shell Ware, blue 10.00
Pie Baker, Dainty Flower,
    blue, 10" d 75.00
Plate
    7-1/2" d, Shell Ware, blue 10.00
    9-3/4" d, Virginia, pink 12.00
Platter, Shell Ware, blue................20.00
Range Shaker,
    Dainty Flower, blue..................20.00
Rolling Pin, blue 85.00
Salad Bowl, 6-1/2" w,
    square, blue............................15.00
Sugar, Virginia, blue 20.00

Petit Point Rose: Decal decoration of multicolored petit-point roses on white background, with silver trim. There are two variations of this design. Most items can be found in both styles and prices are comparable.

Batter Bowl.....................................60.00
Bowl, 8-1/2" d 15.00
Cake Plate......................................15.00
Cake Server 15.00
Casserole, cov, 8-1/2" d 15.00
Coffeepot..42.00
Cup and Saucer 18.00
Pie Baker..15.00
Plate, 8-1/2" d................................10.00
Spoon..20.00
Sugar, cov 15.00

Red Apple: Decal of large red apple and yellow pear on white background. Red band trim.

Casserole Lid, 7-7/8", heavy 17.00
Cheese Plate, 10" d 22.00
Custard...7.50
Fork...25.00
Mixing Bowl, 9" d...........................30.00
Pie Baker, 9" d 24.00
Plate, 10" d.....................................12.00
Rolling Pin, #2 ....150.00
Salad Bowl, 9" d, swirl...................24.00
Spoon..27.00
Utility Tray, 11" l 22.00
Vegetable Bowl, 9" d 30.00

Holiday Collectibles

Collecting Hints: Collectors often start with one holiday and eventually branch out and collect all the holidays. Reasonably priced items can still be found—especially items from the 1950s and 1960s.

History: Holidays are an important part of American life. Many have both secular and religious overtones such as Christmas, St. Patrick's Day, Easter, Valentine's Day and Halloween. National holidays such as the Fourth of July and Thanksgiving are part of one's yearly planning. Collectors usually consider President's Day, Memorial Day, Flag Day and the Fourth of July as part of the general category of patriotic collectibles.

Each holiday has its own origins and background and owes its current face to a variety of legends, lore and customs. Holiday decorations were popularized by German cottage industries at the turn of the century. Germany dominated the holiday market until the 1920s when Japan began producing holiday items. Both countries lost their place during World War II and U.S. manufacturers filled the American appetite for holiday decorations.

References: Juanita Burnett, *Guide to Easter Collectibles*, Collector Books, 1992; Dan and Pauline Campanelli, *Halloween Collectables*, L-W Books, 1995; Helaine Fendelman and Jeri Schwartz, *Official Pride Guide Holiday Collectibles*, House of Collectibles, 1991; Jeanette Lasansky, *Collecting Guide: Holiday Paper Honeycomb, Cards, Garlands, Centerpieces and Other Tissue-Paper Fantasies of the 20th Century*, published by author, 1993; *Favors and Novelties: Wholesale Trade List No. 26, 1924-1925*, L-W Book Sales, 1985, 1994-95 value update; Herbert N. Schiffer, *Collectible Rabbits*, Schiffer Publishing, Ltd., 1990; Stuart Schneider, *Halloween in America*, Schiffer Publishing, 1995.

Periodicals: *BooNews*, P.O. Box 143, Brookfield, IL 60513; *Trick or Treat Trader*, P.O. Box 499, Winchester, NH 03470.

Reproduction Alert.

Additional Listings: Christmas Items, Flag Collectibles, Patriotic Collectibles, Santa Claus, Valentines.

Advisor: Lissa Bryan-Smith and Richard Smith.

Easter

Bank, 6-1/2" h, hard plastic, yellow
    and black rabbit head, Round Tubes
    & Cors, Chicago 12.00
Basket, reed
    6" h, pink, handle, Germany 20.00
    12" h, red, green and natural,
    handle, Mexican......................12.00
Candy Container
    Chicken, 7" h, cardboard, flocked,
    yellow, head on spring, 1960s,
    West Germany.......................32.00
    Egg, 6-1/2" l, tin, litho, multicolored,
    USA 17.00
    Rabbit
        4" h, hard plastic, yellow,
        rabbit holding egg, egg holds
        lollipops, USA 6.00
        9" h, papier-mâché, flocked,
        brown, glass eyes, removable
        head....................................80.00
Chicken
    1-3/4" h, chick, celluloid, yellow
    and orange, Japanese 14.00
    2-3/4" h, cotton batting chick in purple
    cardboard eggshell, wire feet, Japanese 10.00
    4-1/2" h, cotton batting, yellow, glass
    eyes, wire feet, Germany.........28.00

Easter, candy container, bag-type opening, Spanish costume, teal hood, white cape, blue gown, pink bag, c1950, 10" h, orig paper label, $28.

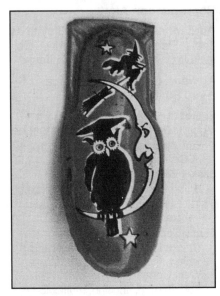

Halloween, clicker, $7.

Egg
    3" l, cardboard, open in middle,
    black with violets, gold Dresden trim,
    Germany 22.00
    4-1/2" l, milk glass, hp flowers..25.00
Magazine Cover, *Life*, Easter 1904,
    woman holding rabbit, Allan
    Gilbert illus...............................16.00
Postcard
    A Happy Easter To You, hen and
    chicks, clutch of rose eggs in violets,
    Raphael Tuck.............................5.00
    A Peaceful Easter, girl and rabbit
    looking at Easter eggs, 1911......4.00
    Easter Greetings, 4 chicks
    looking at eggs hanging on
    apple tree, Germany 3.50
Rabbit
    2-1/2" h, cotton batting, cardboard
    ears, holding carrot, Germany..12.00
    3-1/2" h and 1-1/2" h, set of pot-metal
    mother rabbit and 3 baby rabbits,
    white, German, price for set.....65.00
    6", hard plastic, mother rabbit, yellow,
    blue apron, pink hat..................10.00
    11" h, egg-crate cardboard, brown,
    glass eyes 85.00
Toy, windup
    4" h, celluloid rabbit riding litho tin
    tricycle with bell, Japan 30.00
    8-1/2" l, green metal-wheeled sled
    with bell, pulled by white celluloid
    rabbit, Occupied Japan 125.00

Halloween

Candy Container
    Black Cat, head, 3" h, pressed
    cardboard, cutout eyes and mouth,
    wire handle, Germany..............60.00
    Pumpkin

        Glass, painted, 4" h,
        scary face, wire handle,
        metal screw-on lid.............120.00
        Papier-mâché, cutout eyes and
        mouth, tissue-paper eyes and
        mouth, wire handle, candleholder
        in base, German
            5" h....................................50.00
            7" h....................................75.00
            10" h..................................95.00
Clicker, litho tin, orange and black, frog
    shape, mkd "T. Cohn, USA" 7.00
Fan, foldout, wooden stick, tissue paper,
    witch riding broom, black and
    orange, 1920s, Germany.........25.00
Figure
    Black cat, 9" h, cardboard, flat,
    movable legs and tail, Beistle
    Co., USA 18.00
    Ghost, 9-1/2" h, cardboard standup,
    USA..15.00
    Scarecrow with pumpkin head, 5" h,
    hard plastic...............................12.00
    Skull on book, 4" h,
    bisque, Japan...........................20.00
    Witch
        Roly poly, 3" h, celluloid, orange
        and black, Japanese..........180.00
        Sitting on pumpkin, 6" h, papier-
        mâché, orange and black 70.00
Hat
    4" h, cardboard and crepe paper,
    black and orange, Germany.....15.00
    10" h, crepe paper, orange and black,
    gold and black cardboard band,
    Germany 25.00
Horn
    4" h, wood, black and orange,
    painted cat face, mkd "Czecho-
    Slavakia" 24.00
    8" h, paper, orange and black, wood
    mouthpiece, Germany..............10.00
    9" h, cardboard, black and orange,
    cat, witch and moon litho figures,
    USA..12.00
Lantern, pumpkin
    4" h, papier-mâché, paper eyes
    and mouth, wire handle, candlehold-
    er in base, Germany 60.00
    6" h, glass and metal,
    battery operated, Hong Kong,
    1960s, orig box 35.00
Magazine Cover, *The
    Farmer's Wife*, October 1925,
    costumed boy, holding pumpkin
    on pole, black cat 16.00
Mask
    Boy, papier-mâché,
    painted face, cloth ties,
    stamped "Germany" 35.00
    Devil, rubber, red, black
    and white, rubber ties..............15.00
    Duck, buckram, molded bill, cloth

    ties 28.00
    Man, wire mesh, painted feature,
    cloth ties...................................75.00
Noisemaker, clicker
    Tin, frying pan shape, litho, orange
    and black, mkd "J. Chein" 25.00
    Wood, with papier-mâché witch,
    Germany 250.00
Postcard
    Girl scared by pumpkin in mirror,
    Raphael Tuck...........................18.00
    Witch riding broom
    through sky 10.00
Tambourine, litho tin,
    cat face, orange and
    black, mkd "T. Cohn, Inc." 20.00

St. Patrick's Day

Candy Box, shamrock, 8-1/2" h, card-
    board, green, shamrock shape, litho
    print shamrocks on top............14.00
Candy Container
    Hat, 3" h, cardboard,
    green and gold, label on base,
    Loft Candy Corp......................25.00
    Potato, 4" l, pressed cardboard,
    brown, velvet green and gold s
    hamrock, Germany 45.00
    Irish Girl, 4-1/2" h, composition,
    holding harp, standing on box,
    mkd "Germany" 75.00
Figure
    Leprechaun, 7" h, celluloid, holding
    pig, weighted, Japanese 35.00
    Man, 6" h, composition, green felt
    coat, spring legs when pushed
    squeaks and beer stein goes to
    mouth.......................................65.00

**New Year, postcard, Prosit Nev Jahr!,
Raphael Kirchner, Paris, artist, $60.**

Pig

4" l, composition, green flocked,
Germany 50.00

6" l, composition, pink,
Germany 50.00

Magazine Cover, *Life*, March 15,
1923, cherub wearing Irish hat
and playing harp 15.00

Nodder, 3" h, Irish boy, bisque,
Germany 45.00

Nut Cup, 4" h, green and white crepe
paper, foil Irish symbols, twisted
paper handle, Kupper Favor Co.,
Peru, IN, set of 4 ....20.00

Postcard

Ireland Forever, scenes of Ireland
pictured in shamrock, green
and gold 3.00

On March 17 May You Be Seen A'
Wearing of The Green, Irish man
standing on "17," Quality Cards-The
A.M. Davis Co., Boston, 1912 ....3.50

Shamrock, 2-1/2" l, green silk-floss-
wrapped wire, small bisque hat
attached to center 5.00

Stand-Up

8" h, cardboard, shamrock, green,
"Made in USA" 4.00

15" h, cardboard, Irish man riding
goat, "Made in USA" 7.00

Thanksgiving

Candy Container, turkey

5" h, composition, metal legs, horsehair beard, removable head 60.00

7-1/2", composition, metal legs,
removable head, Germany.....250.00

8" h, egg-crate cardboard, pale orange, mkd "Atco Co.," USA......65.00

Candle, wax

3" h, pilgrim couple......................5.00

4" h, gobbler, USA 5.00

Thanksgiving, candy container, turkey, painted papier-mâché body, lead feet, 3-3/4" h, $10.

Figure

Gobbler, 2-1/2",
hard plastic, USA 10.00

Turkey

2-1/2" h, composition, metal legs
and feet, Germany 15.00

4" h, celluloid, red,
white and blue......................15.00

Greeting Card, The Mayflower-
With Joyful Thanksgiving Wishes,
Mayflower off the coast 8.00

Magazine Cover, *Farmer's Wife*,
November 1936........................14.00

Place Card Holder, 2-1/2" h, celluloid,
standing turkey with holder at base
of metal spring legs 18.00

Postcard, A Joyous Thanksgiving,
boy carving pumpkin, 1913 ....4.00

Home Front Collectibles

Collecting Hints: Some of the most recognizable home front collectibles are posters and these are still quite affordable. A general rule is that the smaller the size, the lower the price. An identifiable illustrator adds value. Graphics and image are everything.

Propaganda played a major role in home front material. One of the key propaganda ploys was to depersonalize the enemy and enemy leaders by viewing them as ethnic stereotypes, a throwback to the image of the Hun in World War I. The effort was most successful in respect to the Axis leaders—Hitler, Tojo and Mussolini—and the "Jap." Home front collectibles with stereotypical images command high prices. They are frequently among the most expensive of the home front collectibles, a result of their great graphics and the fact that many are three dimensional.

History: World War II was fought on three fronts: European, Pacific/Asian and Home. The recognition and honor given the battle waged on the home front was one of the most surprising aspects of the celebrations for the 50th anniversary of World War II. Museums across America mounted exhibits focusing on the war effort made by industry and individuals in their localities. Home front and battlefront articles shared equal billing in the media, from magazines to television, in recognition of the fact that the war

abroad would have been lost if the war at home had not been won.

The home front war was a total effort. The civilian population was mobilized, as was the military. All aspects of civilian life were the focus of propaganda and voluntary and sometimes involuntary, control. Each individual had to be convinced that he or she was essential to the war effort—as a worker, volunteer, war bond purchaser or young woman willing to use a stocking stick in lieu of nylons. Civil Defense provided opportunities for active participation.

A home front collectible is an object that was made between 1939 and 1946 and that was designed to evoke in civilians a spirit of patriotism or sense of commitment to the war effort. The year 1939 is used as the starting point rather than 1941 because of America's support for England and France prior to U.S. entry into the war. This also takes into account the anti-war material considered part of this collecting category. The year 1946 serves as the concluding date because war efforts did not simply end on V-J Day, Aug. 14, 1945. The troops still had to come home and the occupation forces be put into place.

Virtually every collecting category that encompasses this time period has some form of home front collectible associated with it. The war effort also produced new types of collectibles including Civilian Defense material, ration stamps, substitutes, victory garden memorabilia and enemy stereotype material.

References: Stan Cohen, *V for Victory: America's Home Front During World War II*, Motorbooks International, 1991; Robert Heide and John Gilman, *Home Front America: Popular Culture of the World War II Era*, Chronicle Books, 1995; Jack Matthews, *Toys Go to War*, published by author, 1995.

Ashtray, 3-1/4" x 4-1/2", Keep 'Em
Flying, white glass, red art and inscriptions, toothed edge 50.00

Badge, American Boy Junior Pilot, gold-
luster finish metal, wings, red, white
and blue paper insert center, metal
lettering Keep 'Em Flying 25.00

Bank, 3-1/4" d, 2-1/4" h, drum shape,

Remember Pearl Harbor, red, white and blue litho tin, slot in top, Ohio Art Co. 125.00

Bank Counter Sign, 9-1/2" x 13-3/4", War Bonds and Stamps, cardboard, easel back, green bronze Minuteman-type symbol, pale olive green ground, red and dark olive green letters, 1941 government printing date 60.00

Banner, 35" x 36", Welcome Home, red and white inscription, blue background, white fabric horiz band with grommets 70.00

Bar Pin, diecut metal, Husband in Service, cardboard slogan insert, blue letters, white cardboard, tiny red stars, lower diecut with open-lettered USA, red, white and blue accents, gold-luster finish 195.00

Booklet
Gardening, Ford Motor Co., 1945, 36 pgs 15.00
Thought for Food, What You Can Do for Victory, Kroeger Grocery & Baking Co., red white and blue weekly folder, Feb. 9, 1942 .... 20.00
Victory Cake Recipes, Standard Brands Inc., 1942 .... 20.00
War Birds of the U.S.A., Hart Schaffner & Marx Clothes premium, multicolored artwork, 24 pgs, "The Boy Upstairs" dedication on inner front, 34 U.S. bombers identification illus, 7-1/4" x 7-1/4" 50.00

Box, 4" x 4-1/2" x 8-1/2", Victory Chicken from Dee-Jay Farms/Rural Route No. 1 Loveland, Ohio," red, white and blue cartoon art on 3 panels 30.00

Clock, Howard Miller Mfg., mantel, God Bless America, small American flag waves back and forth as second hand 150.00

Dexterity Puzzle, 1" x 3-1/4" x 5", V for Victory, cardboard box frame holding clear plastic over recessed colorful

Document, photograph, and reverse painting, discharge, U.S. Army, Warren Bennethum, 1919, 16-1/8" x 20-1/8", framed, $55.

Armband, Civil Defense Air Raid Warden, World War II, white, blue circle, red and white diagonal stripes within triangle, 4" w, $3.

cardboard playing surface, 3 tiny circular traps and 1 slot trap, 3 metal balls, wooden dowel, floral design thin paper, lightly worn edges .. 75.00

Fan, 8" x 8" diecut, cardboard, 3-1/2" thin balsa-wood handle, full-color image of young blond lady in white military uniform, soft blue ground, red, white and blue border, caption text of Patrick Henry's "Give Me Liberty...," back inscribed "The Starlight Roof/Waldorf-Astoria" 40.00

Game, 9-1/2" x 19" x 2", Get in the Scrap, Milton Bradley, 1944, 18-1/2" sq playing board, 16 wood pawns 60.00

Glass, 4-3/4" h, Remember Pearl Harbor, inscription in red shading to white and light blue, graphics include islands, Pearl Harbor, warships, red aircraft 60.00

Map, 13" x 20-1/2" cardboard folder opens to 26" x 41", Rand McNally & Co., 1943, War Planning Map of the World, full-color maps on both sides, loose supplement sheet of full-color Allied and Axis flags plus symbols indicating bomb grades, U-boats, bombed and active warships, gummed on reverse, unused ... 70.00

Newspaper Supplement, Home Defense Guide, March 23, 1942, *Philadelphia Inquirer*, 20 pgs of pictorial and text instructions on home-defense procedures, full-color insignias, full-page portrait of Gen. MacArthur, 11" x 14", small tape repair 35.00

Patch, 4" d, American War Mothers, red, white and blue stiff felt, graying to colors 25.00

Pinback Button
3/4" d, Welcome Home Our Heroes!, red,ower, red, white and blue litho, holding purple fabric ribbon, lightly worn ribbon 40.00
2-1/4" d, Remember Pearl Harbor, red, white and blue, tinted full-color portrait of young man in civilian clothes 85.00

3-1/2" d, Save Your Bull...For Your Victory Garden, celluloid, red and white cartoon bull, white background, blue lettering 115.00

Poster
16-1/4" x 22-1/2", Uncle Sam, anti-runaway prices, James Montgomery Flagg image, Office of War Information for Office of Economic Stabilization, fold marks 150.00
28-1/2" x 40", War Ration Book Two, instructions type, published Feb. 1943 by Office of Price Administration, 6 full-color illus blocks showing rationed and non-rationed foods, fold marks 85.00

Punch Kit, 3 Flying Models, 9" x 12" stiff-paper folder, 4 panels, introductory panel by Judd Reed, punch-out parts for assembly of 3D models of American Hellcat, British Spitfire and Russian Stormovik, part of front cover designed as mechanical "America Ace Spotter" identification wheel, 48 silhouettes of 16 famous American planes, Reed & Associates, 1944 .... 60.00

Ruler, 12" l, wood, striping and inscription on measurements side in red and blue, inscriptions include 2 V's plus slogan "All Out for Victory," bank-sponsor's name on back 30.00

Window Banner, 7-3/4" x 11", U.S. Marine in Service, silver fabric, red and blue flocking, red, white and blue hanging cord 60.00

Homer Laughlin

Collecting Hints: The original 1871 to 1890 trademark used the term "Laughlin Brothers." The next trademark featured the American eagle astride the prostrate British lion. The third mark, which featured the "HLC" monogram, has appeared, with slight variations, on all dinnerware since about 1900. The 1900 version included a number that identified month, year and plant at which the product was made. Letter codes were used in later periods.

So much attention has been given to Fiesta that other interesting Homer Laughlin patterns have not achieved the popularity which they deserve and prices for these less-recognized patterns are still moderate. Some of the patterns made during the 1930s and 1940s have highly artistic contemporary designs. Virginia Rose is not a pattern name but a shape on which several different decals were used. Delicate pink flowers are the most common.

History: Homer Laughlin and his brother, Shakespeare, built two pottery kilns in East Liverpool, OH, in 1871. Shakespeare resigned in 1879, leaving Homer to operate the business alone. Laughlin became one of the first firms to produce American-made whiteware. In 1896, William Wills and a Pittsburgh group led by Marcus Aaron bought the Laughlin firm.

Expansion followed. Two new plants were built in Laughlin Station, OH. In 1906, the first Newall, WV, plant (#4) was built in. Plant #6, which was built at Newall in 1923, featured a continuous-tunnel kiln. Similar kilns were added at the other plants. Other advances instituted by the company include spray glazing and mechanical jiggering.

Between 1930 and 1960, several new dinnerware lines were added, including the Wells Art Glaze line. Ovenserve and Kitchen Kraft were cookware products. The colored-glaze lines of Fiesta, Harlequin and Rhythm captured major market shares. In 1959, a translucent table china line was introduced. Today, the annual manufacturing capacity is more than 45 million pieces.

References: Susan and Al Bagdade, *Warman's American Pottery and Porcelain*, Wallace-Homestead, 1994; Jo Cunningham, *Collector's Encyclopedia of American Dinnerware*, Collector Books, 1982, 1995 value update; Bob and Sharon Huxford, *Collector's Encyclopedia of Fiesta with Harlequin and Riviera*, 7th Edition, Collector Books, 1992; Joanne Jasper, *Collector's Encyclopedia of Homer Laughlin China*, Collector Books, 1993, 1995 value update; Richard G. Racheter, *Collector's Guide to Homer Laughlin's Virginia Rose*, Collector Books, 1997.

Periodicals: *Fiesta Collectors Quarterly*, 19238 Dorchester Cr., Strongsville, OH 44136; *Laughlin Eagle*, 1270 63rd Ter. South, St. Petersburg, FL 33705.

Rhythm, gravy boat, red, gold, green black dec, 9" l, $15.

Reproduction Alert: Harlequin and Fiesta lines were reissued in 1978 and marked accordingly.

Additional Listings: Fiesta.

Harlequin: Sold by F.W. Woolworth Co. Introduced in the late 1930s in four colors: bright yellow, spruce green, maroon and mauve blue. Harlequin was eventually produced in all the Fiesta colors except ivory and cobalt blue. The line was discontinued in 1964. It was reissued in 1979 in turquoise, yellow, medium green and coral. The reissued plates have a Homer Laughlin backstamp.

Baker, oval, spruce	22.00
Berry Bowl	
Maroon	6.50
Spruce	6.00
Turquoise	6.00
Yellow	6.50
Candlestick, red	195.00
Creamer, individual size	
Mauve	23.00
Orange	20.00
Spruce	25.00
Cream Soup	
Mauve	22.00
Orange	22.00
Cup, rose	6.50
Cup and Saucer	
Spruce	10.00
Yellow	10.00
Deep Plate	
Gray	45.00
Mauve	28.00
Medium Green	95.00
Turquoise	22.00
Eggcup	
Double	
Chartreuse	20.00
Gray	24.00
Maroon	22.00
Rose	24.00
Single	
Maroon	30.00
Mauve	25.00
Orange	25.00
Nappy, 9" d	

Turquoise	18.00
Yellow	18.00
Nut Dish	
Mauve	15.00
Orange	15.00
Rose	20.00
Spruce	15.00
Plate, 10" d, mauve	15.00
Platter	
11" l, maroon	18.00
13" l, oval, rose	13.00
Relish Insert	
Maroon	50.00
Mauve	75.00
Red	35.00
Rose	90.00
Yellow	75.00
Relish Tray, turquoise base, yellow, red, mauve and turquoise inserts	495.00
Salad Bowl, individual	
Chartreuse	45.00
Light Green	45.00
Mauve	45.00
Medium Green	175.00
Yellow	25.00
Salt and Pepper Shakers, pr	
Gray	10.00
Maroon	10.00
Mauve	8.00
Yellow	12.00
Sauceboat, rose	15.00

Kitchen Kraft: Kitchenware line with floral decals produced from the early 1930s. Pieces are marked "Kitchen Kraft" and/or "Oven-Serve."

Cake Server, cobalt blue	135.00
Casserole, cov	
Individual	
Cobalt Blue	200.00
Light Green	150.00
Red	255.00
Yellow	110.00
7-1/2" d	
Cobalt Blue	66.00
Light Green	44.00
8-1/2" h	
Red	60.00
Yellow	63.00
Cream Soup Bowl, double handle, pink	6.00
Fork	
Cobalt Blue	150.00
Light Green	82.00
Mixing Bowl	
6" d, red	100.00
8" d, green	100.00
Pie Plate, cobalt blue, 10" d	30.00
Platter, green	38.00
Refrigerator Unit, yellow and light green,	

stacking, each.........................44.00
Salt and Pepper Shakers, pr, red..90.00
Spoon, red.....................................90.00

Mexicana: Introduced in 1937. Cactus and pottery decal. Produced in the Century shape, although it is occasionally found on other shapes. Trimmed in red, blue, green or yellow bands with red being the most common.

Baker, oval 25.00
Batter Jug, cov 77.00
Bowl, 5" d...................................20.00
Butter Dish, cov, 1/4 lb, nicks.......27.50
Cake Server 30.00
Creamer 20.00
Cup and Saucer 15.00
Jar, cov, orig paper label.............88.00
Nappy...25.00
Pie Baker....................................35.00
Pitcher, cov...............................335.00
Plate, 9" d...................................15.00
Soup, flat....................................24.00

Riviera: Introduced in 1938, this dinnerware line was sold by the Murphy Co. Though usually unmarked, it is occasionally found with a gold backstamp. Produced in the Century shape in dark blue (rare), light green, ivory, mauve blue, red and yellow.

Baker, oval, ivory.........................12.00
Bowl, 5-1/2" d, ivory 7.00
Butter Dish, cov, 1/4 lb, Century
   Green 185.00
   Red.....................................185.00
   Turquoise 295.00
Casserole, cov
   Green 125.00
   Ivory 125.00
   Mauve 110.00
   Red.....................................125.00
Creamer
   Blue 7.00
   Ivory 7.00
Cup
   Blue 7.00
   Green 7.00
   Ivory 7.00
   Light Green 11.00
   Red..7.00
   Yellow......................................7.00
Demitasse Cup and Saucer, Century,
   ivory......................................95.00
Juice Pitcher, yellow....................185.00
Juice Tumbler
   Green 85.00
   Ivory 95.00
   Mauve 95.00
   Red...95.00
   Turquoise 95.00
   Yellow.....................................85.00

Nappy
   Green 20.00
   Mauve 25.00
   Red...25.00
   Yellow.....................................20.00
Oatmeal Bowl, Century
   Green 65.00
   Ivory 65.00
   Yellow.....................................65.00
Plate, 6" d
   Ivory 5.00
   Light green 9.50
   Red..9.50
Plate, 9" d
   Blue 12.00
   Green 12.00
   Ivory 12.00
   Red..12.00
   Yellow.....................................12.00
Platter
   Ivory 12.00
   Yellow.....................................22.00
Soup Plate, flat, red.....................32.00
Saucer
   Green 3.00
   Ivory 3.00
Sugar, cov
   Green 10.00
   Ivory 10.00
Tumbler, handle, Century
   Green 55.00
   Mauve 75.00
   Red...95.00

Virginia Rose: This is the name of a shape rather than a decal pattern as the name might imply. It was produced from 1929 until the early 1970s and was decorated with numerous floral decals. Pieces were trimmed with either silver or gold bands.

Baker, oval, 8" l 20.00
Butter, cov, jade 75.00
Creamer and Sugar, cov 35.00
Cup and Saucer 4.00
Fruit Bowl, 5-1/2" d.......................5.00
Mixing Bowl, large 47.00
Nappy, 10" d 20.00
Pie Plate.....................................24.00
Plate, 9" d, dinner.........................6.50
Platter, 11-1/2" l, platinum edge 21.00
Soup...7.50
Tray, handles 25.00
Vegetable, cov 42.00

Horse Collectibles

Collecting Hints: The hottest area in equine collecting continues to be figures. Early Breyer horses with a glossy finish or better yet, the rare

Budweiser Clydesdale adv light, $50.

wood-grain and blue or gold Decorator finish, remain the most popular with enthusiasts. Hartlands are becoming more popular, especially those horse-and-rider combinations depicting television cowboy figures of the 1950s—Roy Rogers on Trigger and Dale Evans on Buttermilk remain the most sought after.

Ceramic figurines, whether English (such as Wade and Beswick), German Goebels or American Hagen-Renakers from California continue to grow in popularity. Prices are going up quickly, with even recent Wade miniatures selling for $15 to $25. Western-themed blankets, lamps and china like Wallace's Rodeo have many enthusiastic fans and prices have remained high.

There are few categories of collecting that do not include some sort of equine image. Advertising featuring the horse abounds, from the earliest saddle and tack catalogs to elaborately designed Wild West show posters. Current advertising promotions featuring the Budweiser Clydesdales are popular with horse lovers, as are the older advertising for A-C Spark Plugs featuring Sparky, their "spokeshorse."

Papercollectors enthusiastically seek old rodeo programs, posters, horse show memorabilia and horse racing collectibles, especially those from the Kentucky Derby. Commemorative glass prices have leveled off except for Derby glassware from the 1964 race and earlier. Carousel horses remain a high-ticket item. On the whole, prices have been influenced by the hand-carved horses imported from Mexico, but the market for authentic carousel animals from craftsmen like Mueller, Loof and Dentzel has stayed strong.

Cast-iron toys are enjoying the interest of a new generation of collectors, possibly because prices have come down somewhat in recent years. Horse-drawn vehicles are the most popular, with elaborate circus wagons being a top draw. Do buy cast iron from a dealer you trust; there are many recent reproductions.

History: Horses have been a strong influence on many aspects of the American lifestyle and have played a vital role in America's growth since the earliest days of our nation's history. Even our language reflects our love and respect for the horse. If we make an especially intelligent decision, we are credited with having "horse sense." The English colonist brought the horse to the New World to use for transportation, farming and even as a food source. A person's social status was determined by the quality and quantity of his horses. Remember the condescending phrase "one-horse town"?

As the country became more civilized, people could afford an occasional day of rest. It quickly became a day of organized picnics with competitions to see who had the fastest or strongest horse. As the motorcar became more affordable, the need for the horse died out. Today's horses are likely to be pampered family pets, living a sheltered life totally unlike that of a hard-working draft animal of the 1800s.

References: Jan Lindenberger, *501 Collectible Horses*, Schiffer Publishing, 1995; Jim and Nancy Schaut, *Horsin' Around*, L-W Books, 1990.

Periodicals: *The Beswick Quarterly*, 7525 W. Bernill Rd., Spokane, WA 99208; *The Equine Image*, P.O. Box 916, Ft. Dodge, IA 50501.

Museums: Aiken Thoroughbred Racing Hall of Fame & Museum, Aiken, SC; American Quarter Horse Heritage Center, Amarillo, TX; Gene Autry Western Heritage Museum, Los Angeles, CA; Harness Racing Hall of Fame, Goshen, NY; Kentucky Derby Museum, Louisville, KY; Pony Express Museum, Joplin, MO; Roy Rogers Museum, Victorville, CA.

Additional Listings: Racing Collectibles.

Advisors: Jim and Nancy Schaut.

Horse Equipment and Related Items

Bells
    8" l metal strap, 4 graduated cast bells from wagon shaft 125.00
    84" l, more than 40 nickel bells, worn leather strap, tug hook 200.00
Bit
    Eagle, mkd "G.S. Garcia" 700.00
    Emblem, cavalry, brass, mkd "U.S.," price for pr 50.00
Blanket, saddle,
    early 1900s, Navajo 950.00
Bridle
    Heiser 235.00
    Horsehair 450.00
    Walla Walla Prison made 950.00
Brush, cavalry, stamped "U.S.," pat 1850, Herbert Brush Mfg. Co., unused 95.00
Catalog, Chicago, 1929, polo saddles, equipment 75.00
Collar, draft horse, leather-covered wood, brass trim 125.00
Curry Comb, tin back, leather handle, early 1900s 40.00
Harness Decoration, brass, rearing horse in center, mkd "England" 35.00
Hobbles, chain and leather, sideline type 150.00
Hoof Pick, bone handle, Wastenholm, Germany, pat 1885 ....50.00
Horse-Drawn Wagon
    Ice delivery, 2-horse hitch, orig lettering on side, wood needs restoring 1,800.00
    Popcorn, Creators, unrestored, needs minor cosmetic work 7,500.00
Horsehide Rug, 48" x 72" 250.00
Lasso
    Braided rawhide Mexican "reata" 175.00
    Horsehair 125.00
    Rawhide-covered tips, 1890s 250.00
Mane and Tail Comb, stamped "Oliver Slant Tooth," 1940s 35.00
Newspaper, *Horse & Stable Weekly*, Boston, Jan. 2, 1891, 16 pgs ...30.00
Saddle
    F.M. Sterns, CA, tooled leather 1,200.00
    McClelland type, large fenders for leg protection, early 1900s 800.00
    Shippley, 16" slick fork, half seat 2,500.00
Sidesaddle, tapestry seat, fair condition, pre-1920 ....850.00

Celluloid button, Tennessee Walker, winner's ribbon from Kansas Horse Show, 1933, $25.

Spurs
    Crockett, arrow shank 650.00
    CSA, brass, very rare 900.00
Wagon Seat, springs, padded seat, replaced leather upholstery ...150.00
Watering Trough, hollowed-out log, tin liner, 2" x 72" 125.00

Horse-Theme Items

Bank
    Arcade, still, cast-iron horse and horseshoe, Buster Brown and Tige, shoe adv, 4-1/2" 450.00
    Ertl, horse and tank wagon, Texaco, #8 ....45.00
Blanket, brown wool, western theme, cowboys and horses, 1950s, twin size 150.00
Board Game, Pony Express, cast-metal horses, 1940s 75.00
Book
    American Trotting and Pacing Horses, Henry T. Coates, Philadelphia, 1902, 8vo, 1st ed 25.00
    The Black Stallion, Walter Farley, first ed, dj 15.00
    The Horse, William Youatt, Philadelphia, 1844, 448 pgs 45.00
    The Horse in Art, John Baskett, NY Graphic Society, Boston, 1980,

160 pgs, slipcase 40.00
Calendar, 1907, cardboard,
    Dousman Milling, cowgirl
    and horse, 10" x 20" 75.00
Carousel Horse, jumper,
    flag on side, C.W. Parker,
    American, c1918.................6,500.00
Catalog, D.F. Mangels Co.,
    Carousel Works, Coney Island,
    NY, 1928, 28 pgs...................250.00
Clock, United, brass horse next to
    western saddle, wood base ...150.00
Cookie Cutter, prancing horse, bobtail,
    flat back, 6-1/2" x 7-1/2" 75.00
Cookie Jar, McCoy,
    circus horse 200.00
Decanter, Man O' War,
    Ezra Brooks 35.00
Doorstop, racehorse, stamped "Virginia
    Metalcrafters," 1949...............150.00
Fan, Moxie adv, rocking horse on front,
    1920s.....................................35.00
Figure
    Beswick, reclining foal, 3" l.......65.00
    Breyer, Arabian mare, alabaster,
        plastic 45.00
    Hagen-Renaker, Pegasus, mini,
        1985 ....25.00
    Hartland, polo pony,
        gray plastic...............................25.00
    Heisey, Clydesdale,
        amber glass..............................45.00
    Rookwood, horse,
        #6140, 1939 ....300.00
    Summit Art Glass, horse, blue, very
        short legs...................................25.00
    Vernon Kilns, unicorn, #16, black,
        from Disney's "Fantasia" 450.00
    Wade, pony, miniature, Tom Smith
        artist 50.00
Fruit Crate Label, Loop Loop Washing-
    ton State Apples, Indian chief on
    palomino 10.00
Hobby Horse, Tom Mix's Tony, wood
    on wheeled platform 750.00
Lithograph, Buffalo
    Bill on horse, 1922.................450.00
Magazine, *Western Horseman*,
    Vol. 1, #1, 1935 ....25.00
Mug
    Clydesdales, Budweiser, Christmas,
        Ceramarte, 1985 ....45.00
    Donkey, figural, Democratic
        Convention souvenir,
        Frankoma, dated 1976 ....50.00
Nodder, donkey in navy
    blue suit, carrying flag,
    papier-mâché, Japanese 45.00
Plate
    7", cowboy on
        bucking horse, unmkd 35.00
    13", Wallace, Rodeo pattern ..175.00
Postcard

Bucking bronco, cowboy flying off,
    Prescott, AZ, rodeo, 1920s 12.00
3 draft horses, heads only, German,
    pre-1920..................................15.00
White stallion in moonlight,
    artist sgd 10.00
Poster, Berry Exhibitions, Dayton, OH,
    fairgrounds, Saddle Horse Contest,
    1913, framed, under glass.....350.00
Program, pencil sgd "Shoofly" program,
    Kentucky Derby, 1964 ....45.00
Rocking Horse, white,
    black spots, horsehair mane
    and tail, 75% orig paint, handmade,
    1 rocker split 275.00
Salt and Pepper Shakers, pr, mules,
    figural, Japanese 25.00
Sheet Music, *Dan Patch March*, famous
    racehorse photo on cover........75.00
Sign
    Hunter Cigars, tin, 19" x 27", fox
        hunter and horse, 1915..........250.00
    Mobil Oil, porcelain on steel, 72" l,
        red Pegasus 1,200.00
Snowdome, Budweiser Clydesdale,
    1988 limited ed 55.00
Toy
    Circus wagon, 14" l,
        cast iron, 2 horses, cloth
        bear in cage, Kenton...........1,200.00
    Fire pumper, 21" l, cast iron,
        3 horses, Hubley 1,750.00
    Hay cart, 19" l, paper litho and paint-
        ed wood, Gibbs, 1910 ....450.00
    Mr. Ed, plush hand puppet, TV talking
        horse 45.00
Tray, 12" d, Genessee Twelve Horse
    Ale, horse team illus 95.00
Trophy, metal horse figure,
    wood base, 1964 Oklahoma
    horse of the year 15.00
Watch Fob, running horse, ruby eyes,
    watch chain 575.00
Windmill Weight, 17" l, bobtail horse,
    Dempster, Beatrice, NE.........950.00

Hull Pottery

Collecting Hints: Distinctive markings on the bottom of Hull Pottery
vases help the collector to identify
them immediately. Early stoneware
pottery has an "H." The famous
matte pieces, a favorite of most collectors, contain pattern numbers.
For example, Camelia pieces are
marked with numbers in the 100s,
Iris pieces have 400 numbers and
Wildflower a "W" preceding their
number. Most of Hull's vases are
also marked with their height in inches, making it easy to determine their
value. Items made after 1950 are

Vase, ftd, pink birds, white int, mkd "Hull, USA, 1957," $35.

usually glossy and are marked "hull"
or "Hull" in large script letters. Hull
collectors are beginning to seriously
collect the glossy ware and kitchen
items.

History: In 1905, Addis E. Hull purchased the Acme Pottery Co., in
Crooksville, OH. In 1917, A.E. Hull
Pottery Co., began to make a line of
art pottery for florists and gift shops.
The company also made novelties,
kitchenware and stoneware. During
the Depression, the company primarily produced tiles. Hull's Little Red
Riding Hood kitchenware was manufactured between 1943 and 1957
and is a favorite of collectors, including many who do not collect other
Hull items.

In 1950, the factory was destroyed by a flood and fire; by 1952,
it was back in production, operating
under the Hull Pottery Co., name. At
this time, Hull added its newer
glossy finish pottery, plus the firm
developed pieces sold in flower
shops under the Regal and Floraline
trade names. Hull's brown House 'n'
Garden line of kitchen and dinnerware achieved great popularity and
was the main line being produced
prior to the plant's closing in 1986.

References: Susan and Al Bagdade,
*Warman's American Pottery and Por-
celain*, Wallace-Homestead, 1994;
Joan Gray Hull, *Hull: The Heavenly*

Pottery, 4th Edition, published by author, 1995; ——, *Hull: The Heavenly Pottery Shirt Pocket Price Guide*, published by author, 1994; Barbara Loveless Gick-Burke, *Collector's Guide to Hull Pottery*, Collector Books, 1993; Brenda Roberts, *Roberts Ultimate Encyclopedia of Hull Pottery*, Walsworth Publishing, 1992; ——, *Collectors Encyclopedia of Hull Pottery*, Collector Books, 1980, 1995 value update; ——, *Companion Guide to Roberts' Ultimate Encyclopedia of Hull Pottery*, Walsworth Publishing Co., 1992; Mark E. Supnick, *Collecting Hull Pottery's Little Red Riding Hood*, L-W Book Sales, 1989, 1992 value update.

Periodicals: *Hull Pottery News*, 466 Foreston Pl., St. Louis, MO 63119; *Hull Pottery Newsletter*, 11023 Tunnel Hill NE, New Lexington, OH 43764.

Collectors' Club: Hull Pottery Association, 4 Hilltop Rd., Council Bluff, IA 51503.

Advisor: Joan Hull.

Pre-1950 Patterns

Bow Knot
 B 3, 6" vase 200.00
 B 7, 8-1/2" vase.....................275.00
 B 13, double cornucopia 295.00
 B 28, 10" d, plate................1,200.00
Dogwood (Wildflower)
 504, 8-1/2" vase 150.00
 507, 5-1/2" teapot..................350.00
 514, 4" jardiniere 110.00
Iris
 405, 4-3/4" vase 80.00
 406, 7" vase 125.00
 412, 7" hanging planter 175.00
Jack-in-the-Pulpit/Calla Lily
 500/32, 10" bowl 185.00
 505, 6" vase 125.00
 550, 7" vase 140.00
Magnolia
 4, 6-1/4" vase 55.00
 8, 10-1/2" vase 150.00
 14, 4-3/4" pitcher.....................55.00
 22, 12-1/2" vase 250.00
Magnolia (Pink Gloss)
 H 5, 6-1/2" vase 30.00
 H 17, 12-1/2" vase 200.00
Open Rose (Camelia)
 105, 7" pitcher 225.00
 114, 8-1/2" jardiniere..............375.00
 120, 6-1/2" vase 110.00
 140, 10-1/2" basket 1,300.00

Orchid
 301, 10" vase 325.00
 306, 6-3/4" bud vase 145.00
 311, 13" pitcher 650.00
Pinecone, 55, 6" vase 150.00
Poppy
 606, 6-1/2" vase 200.00
 607, 8-1/2" vase 250.00
 609, 9" wall planter.................450.00
Rosella
 R 1, 5" vase..............................35.00
 R 8, 6-1/2" vase 75.00
 R 15, 8-1/2" vase 85.00
Stoneware
 26 H, vase.................................80.00
 536 H, 9" jardiniere 110.00
Thistle, #53, 6" 150.00
Tulip
 101-33, 9" vase 245.00
 109-33, 8" pitcher...................235.00
 110-33, 6" vase 150.00
Waterlily
 L-8, 8-1/4" vase 145.00
 L-18, 6" teapot........................225.00
 L-19, 5" creamer 75.00
 L-20, 5" sugar...........................75.00
Wildflower
 54, 6-1/2" vase 145.00
 66, 10-1/2" basket 2,000.00
 76, 8-1/2" vase 325.00
 W-3, 5-1/2" vase 55.00
 W-8, 7-1/2" vase 85.00
 W-18, 12-1/2" vase 250.00
Woodland (matte)
 W1, 5-1/2" vase........................95.00
 W10, 11" cornucopia..............195.00
 W25, 12-1/2" vase..................395.00

Post-1950 Patterns (Glossy)

Blossom Flite
 T8, basket 125.00
 T10, 16-1/2" console bowl......125.00
 T11, candleholders,
 price for pr...............................75.00
Butterfly
 B4, 6" bonbon dish...................45.00
 B13, 8" basket........................150.00
 B15, 13-1/2" pitcher 185.00

Console, Ebbtide, E-12, 15-3/4", $140.

Ebbtide
 E3, 7-1/2"
 mermaid cornucopia 195.00
 E7, 11" fish vase 167.00
Figural Planters
 27, Madonna, standing 30.00
 82, clown..................................50.00
 95, twin geese..........................50.00
Parchment & Pine
 S-5, 10-1/2" scroll planter 85.00
 S-15, 8" coffeepot 125.00
Serenade (Birds)
 S7, 8-1/2" vase 55.00
 S15, 11-1/2" ftd fruit bowl.......110.00
Sunglow
 51, 7-1/2" cov casserole 50.00
 80, cup and
 saucer wall pocket 65.00
 95, 8-1/4" vase.........................45.00
Tokay (Grapes)
 4, 8-1/4" vase...........................95.00
 12, 12" vase 125.00
 19, large leaf dish 95.00
Tropicana, T53, 8-1/2" vase........500.00
Woodland
 W-6, 6-1/2" pitcher 65.00
 W-9, 8-3/4" basket 110.00
 W-13, 7-1/2" shell wall pocket..75.00

Hummel Items

Collecting Hints: A key to pricing Hummel figures is the mark. All authentic Hummel pieces bear both the signature "M.I. Hummel" and a Goebel trademark. Various trademarks were used to identify the year of production:

Crown Mark (trademark 1):
    1935-1949
Full Bee (trademark 2):
    1950-1959
Stylized Bee (trademark 3):
    1957-1972
3 Line Mark (trademark 4):
    1964-1972
Last Bee Mark (trademark 5):
    1972-1979
Missing Bee Mark (trademark 6):
    1979-1990
Current Mark or New Crown Mark (trademark 7): 1991-present

Collectors are advised to buy pieces with the early marks whenever possible. Since production runs were large, almost all figurines, no matter what the mark, exist in large numbers. Prices fluctuate a great deal. Antiques newspapers, such as *The Antique Trader Weekly* often carry ads by dealers offering discounts on the modern pieces. The slightest damage to a piece lowers the value significantly.

Before World War II and for a few years after, the Goebel Co., made objects, such as vases, for export. These often had the early mark. Prices are modest for these items because few collectors are interested in them; the Hummel books do not even list them. This aspect of Goebel production would be an excellent subject for a research project.

History: Hummel items are the original creations of Berta Hummel, who was born in 1909 in Massing, Bavaria, Germany. At 18, she was enrolled in the Academy of Fine Arts in Munich to further her mastery of drawing and the palette. Berta entered the Convent of Siessen and became Sister Maria Innocentia in 1934. While in this Franciscan cloister she continued drawing and painting images of her childhood friends. In 1935, W. Goebel Co., in Rodental, Germany, began producing Sister Maria Innocentia's sketches as three-dimensional bisque figurines. The Schmid Brothers of Randolph, MA, introduced the figurines to America and became Goebel's U.S. distributor.

In 1967, Goebel began distributing Hummel items in the United States. A controversy developed between the two companies, the Hummel family and the convent. Law suits and countersuits ensued. The German courts finally effected a compromise: the convent held legal

Figurine, Chicken Licken, 385, trademark 4, $100.

rights to all works produced by Sister Maria Innocentia from 1934 until her death in 1946 and licensed Goebel to reproduce these works; Schmid was to deal directly with the Hummel family for permission to reproduce any pre-convent art.

References: Ken Armke, *Hummel: An Illustrated Handbook and Price Guide*, Wallace-Homestead, 1995; Carl F. Luckey, *Luckey's Hummel Figurines & Plates*, 10th Edition, Books Americana, 1994; Robert L. Miller, *No. 1 Price Guide to M.I. Hummel: Figurines, Plates, More...*, 6th Edition, Portfolio Press, 1995; Wolfgang Schwalto, *M.I. Hummel Collector's Handbook, Part I: Rarities and Collector Pieces*, Schwalto GMBH, 1994; Lawrence L. Wonsch, *Hummel Copycats with Values*, Wallace-Homestead, 1987.

Collectors' Clubs: Hummel Collector's Club, 1261 University Dr., Yardley, PA 19067; M.I. Hummel Club, Goebel Plaza, Rte. 31, P.O. Box 11, Pennington, NJ 08534.

Museum: Hummel Museum, New Braunfels, TX.

Anniversary Plate
    1975, Stormy Weather,
    #280, FE 165.00
    1980, Spring Dance, #281 .....135.00
    1985, Auf Wiedersehen 160.00
Ashtray
    Boy with Bird, #166 ....80.00
    Joyful, #33................................75.00
    Let's Sing, #114 ....75.00
Bank, Little Thrifty, c1972..............50.00
Bell
    Knit One 85.00
    Let's Sing 140.00
    Mountaineer 85.00
    Sing Along................................80.00
    Thoughtful 80.00
Calendar, 1955, 12 illus 15.00
Candlestick,
    Girl with Fir Tree, 1956............35.00
Christmas Plate
    1971, Heavenly Angel, #264..725.00
    1972, Hear Ye,
    Hear Ye, #265.........................125.00
    1973, Globetrotter, #266 ....70.00
    1974, Goose Girl, #267 ....100.00
    1975, Ride into
    Christmas, #268.......................90.00
    1976, Apple Tree Girl, #269...880.00
    1977, Apple Tree Boy, #270 ....95.00
    1978, Happy Pastime, #271.....75.00

    1979, Singing Lesson, #272 ....85.00
    1980, School Girl, #273 ....100.00
    1981, Umbrella Boy, #274 .....100.00
    1983, Postman, #276.............110.00
    1984, A Gift from
    Heaven, #277 ....105.00
    1985, Chick Girl, #278 ....110.00
    1986, Playmates, #279 ....135.00
    1987, Feeding Time, #283.....135.00
    1988, Little Goat
    Herder, #284..........................135.00
    1989, Farm Boy 115.00
Doll
    Carnival, porcelain 190.00
    Chimney Sweep........................80.00
    Easter Greetings, porcelain ...200.00
    Gretel 60.00
    Hansel......................................60.00
    Little Knitter 65.00
    Postman, porcelain 200.00
    Rose, pink 50.00
Figure
    Adoration, #23/111,
    7-1/8", TM 5 ....375.00
    Angelic Song, #144, TM 6 ....65.00
    Apple Tree Girl,
    #141/1, TM 5...........................145.00
    Artist, #304, TM 6 ....90.00
    Barnyard Hero,
    #195/2/0, TM 2.......................115.00
    Be Patient, 6", TM 3 ....145.00
    Bookworm, #8, TM 5................75.00
    Boots, #143/1, TM 3 ....175.00
    Builder, #305, TM 4 ....82.00
    Carnival, #328, TM 6 ....80.00
    Cinderella, #337, TM 6 ....110.00
    Culprits, #56, TM 3 ....200.00
    Doll Bath, #319, TM 5 ....75.00
    Duet, #130, TM 1 ....300.00
    Eventide, TM 3........................135.00
    Farewell, TM 2 ....275.00
    Feeding Time, #199/I, TM 2...215.00
    Follow The Leader, TM 5........425.00
    Gay Adventure, #356, TM 6.....75.00
    Girl with Doll, #239, TM 6 ....25.00
    Good Hunting, #307, TM 4 ....130.00
    Goose Girl, #47/0,
    TM 2, 4-1/4" 200.00
    Hear Ye, #15/0, TM 1 ....300.00
    Herald Angels, #37, TM 2........80.00
    Just Resting, #112/I, TM 1.....300.00
    Kiss Me, #311, TM 4..............145.00
    Little Fiddler, #4, TM 1 ....250.00
    Little Gardener, #72, TM 2.......60.00
    Little Scholar, #80, TM 3..........55.00
    Lost Sheep, #68/0, TM 3 ....72.00
    Merry Wanderer,
    #7/II, TM 1..............................500.00
    Mountaineer, #315, TM 4.......145.00
    Out of Danger, #56/B, TM 3...110.00

Plate, Christmas, 1973, Globe Trotter, orig box, $70.

Photographer, TM 2 ....225.00
Puppy Love, #1, TM 3 ....75.00
Retreat to Safety,
#201/2/0, TM 4 ....90.00
School Girl, #81/2/0, TM 3 ....60.00
Sensitive Hunter,
#6/0, TM 1 ....275.00
Sister, #98/0, TM 6 ....65.00
Soloist, #135, TM 2 ....80.00
Spring Cheer, #72, TM 3..........80.00
Sweet Music, #186, TM 1.......125.00
Telling Her Secret,
#196/0, TM 2 ....235.00
Tuneful Angel, #359, TM 6.......45.00
Village Boy, #51/2/0, TM 1 .....115.00
Waiter, #154/0, TM 2............1309.00
Wash Day, #321, TM 4 ....80.00
Weary Wanderer, #204, TM 6..80.00
Worship, #84/0, TM 1.............250.00
Font
  Angel Cloud, #206, TM 4 ....25.00
  Angel Sitting, #167, TM 4.........40.00
  Angel with Birds, #22/0, TM 6 ..18.00
  Angels at Prayer, #91B, TM 3..70.00
  Child with Flowers,
  #36/0, TM 2 ....48.00
  Good Shepherd, #35/0, TM 6...25.00
  Madonna and Child,
  #243, TM 6 ....25.00
  Worship, #164, TM 2..............120.00
  Inkwell, With Loving
  Greetings, blue.......................135.00
Lamp
  Apple Tree Boy,
  #M/230, TM 5 ....165.00
  Birthday Serenade, #M/231/I, TM 2,
  reverse mold 900.00
  Good Friends,
  #M/228, TM 5 ....165.00

Just Resting,
#M/225/II, TM 5 ....175.00
Loves Me, Loves Me Not, #M/227,
TM 2 ....180.00
Out of Danger, TM 2 ....275.00
Music Box
  Chick Girl 235.00
  Ride Into Christmas 240.00
Nativity Figures
  Angel Serenade, #214/D/II.......40.00
  Donkey, #214/J/II 35.00
  Infant Jesus, #260....................80.00
  King, kneeling on 1 knee,
  #214/M/II 100.00
  Lamb, #214/0/II 15.00
  Little Tooter, #214/H/II 65.00
  Madonna, #214/A/M/II............110.00
  Stable, 3 pc, #214/S/II..............35.00
  Print, Moonlight Return,
  litho, FE................................500.00

Hunting Collectibles

Collecting Hints: Sporting-minded collectors can easily find more and more items to add to their collections. Most flea markets yield everything from big-game trophy heads to canoes to hunting licenses.

History: Hunting became a necessity as soon as man discovered it could end hunger pains. Hunting collectibles, also known as sporting collectibles, encompass those items used for hunting, whether fox or big game. Today's hunters often choose to use binoculars and cameras in lieu of rifles, arrows or caveman's clubs.

Reference: Ralf Coykendall Jr., *Coykendall's Complete Guide to Sporting Collectibles*, Wallace-Homestead, 1996.

Periodicals: *Sports Collectors Digest*, 700 E. State St., Iola, WI 54990.

Book
  Edward A. Freeman, *How To Hunt Deer*, 1960, 2nd ed, Stackpole Co., Harrisburg, PA, dj....................8.50
  O'Connor, *The Art of Hunting Big Game in North America*, Outdoor Life, 1967, 404 pgs, dj.............23.00
  Olin Industries, *Ammunition Handboo*k, 1944, profusely illus, soft-cover 8.00
  F. Philip Rice, *Gun Data Book*, Harper and Row, Outdoor Life, 1975, 570 pgs, dj 7.50

W.H.B. Smith and Joseph, *Book of Rifles*, spine poor 7.50
Call
  Crow, Charles Perdew, Henry, IL, fair condition 175.00
  Duck, Herter's, orig box 35.00
  Turkey Hooter Owl,
  Olt, orig box 35.00
Catalog
  Dave Cook Sporting Goods, 48 pgs, 1968...5.00
  Edw. Tryon Sporting Goods, 72 pgs, 1923......................................27.50
  Kirtland Bros. Sporting Goods, 16 pgs, 1924 ....15.00
  Winchester Rifle, John Wayne cover, 16 pgs, 1982 ....8.50
Counter Felt
  Dead Shot Powder, "Kill Your Bird Not Your Shoulder," multicolored on black, trimmed 90.00
  Winchester, "Shoot Where You Aim" 175.00
Decoy Basket, clam-style............200.00
Flask, copper, emb setter and game birds 60.00
Handbook, Winchester Ammunition, 112 pgs, 1951 ....13.50
Head, mounted, fine condition
  Alaskan Wolf 350.00
  Deer 75.00
  Elk...400.00
  Moose 450.00
License, pinback-button style
  1-1/2" d
    1936 New York State Deer License, buff, black and white, resident use 35.00
    1950 PA Fishing License, red and white, black serial number, resident use 25.00
  1-3/4" d, 1936 Delaware Fishing License, black and white, resident use...................55.00
  2-1/2" d, 1940 Delaware Fishing License, tin, clear-plastic-over-paper license, resident use, ink name and identification number................60.00
Shooter's Box,
fired brass shells, 24 ....280.00
Skiff, gunning, canvas covered, Havre de Grace, MD, tidewaters, c1910 ....500.00
Stickpin, Ask for Winchester Nublack, brass, shotgun-shell shape, firing cap emb "Winchester Nublack No. 12," green enamel shell casing with inscription, early 1900s 125.00
Target Ball, glass
  Amber, Bogardus...................255.00
  Green, basketweave, shooting figure 185.00
  Purple, dark 225.00

I

Ice Cream Collectibles

Collecting Hints: The ice cream collector has many competitors. Those who do not have a specialty collection are sometimes hampered by the regional collector, i.e., an individual who exclusively collects ice cream memorabilia related to a specific manufacturer or area. Many ice cream collectibles are associated with a specific dairy, thus adding dairy collectors to the equation. Since most ice cream was made of milk, milk and milk bottle collectors also hover around the edge of the ice cream collecting scene and do not forget to factor in the cow collector (ice cream advertising often features cows). Advertising, food mold, kitchen and premium collectors are secondary considerations. The result is fierce competition for ice cream material, often resulting in higher prices.

When buying an ice cream tray, the scene is the most important element. Most trays were stock items with the store or firm's name added later. Condition is critical. Beware of reproductions. They became part of the ice cream collectibles world in the 1980s. Many reproductions are introduced into the market as "warehouse" finds. Although these items look old, many are poor copies or fantasy pieces.

History: During the 1st century A.D. in ancient Rome, nearby mountains provided the Emperor Nero with snow and ice which he flavored with fruit pulp and honey. This fruit ice was the forerunner of ice cream. The next development occurred in the 13th century. Among the many treasures that Marco Polo brought back from the Orient was a recipe for a frozen milk dessert resembling sherbet. In the 1530s Catherine de Medici, bride of King Henry II of France, introduced Italian ices to the French court. By the end of the 16th century, ices had evolved into a product similar to today's modern ice cream. By the middle of the 17th century, ice cream became fashionable at the English court.

Ice cream changed from being a luxury food for kings and their courts to a popular commodity in 1670 when the Cafe Procope (rue de l'Ancienne) in Paris introduced ice cream to the general populace and by 1700 the first ice cream recipe book appeared. Ice cream was the rage of 18th-century Europe. Ice cream appeared in America by the early 18th century. In 1777, an advertisement by Philip Lenzi, confectioner, appeared in the New York *Gazette*, noting that ice cream was available on a daily basis. George Washington was an ice cream enthusiast, spending more than $200 with a New York ice cream merchant in 1790. Thomas Jefferson developed an 18-step process to make ice cream and is credited with the invention of baked Alaska.

By the mid-19th century, ice cream "gardens" sprang up in major urban areas; by the late 1820s, the ice cream street vendor arrived on the scene. However, because ice cream was still difficult to prepare, production remained largely in commercial hands. In 1846, Nancy Johnson invented the hand-cranked ice cream freezer, allowing ice cream to enter the average American household. As the century progressed, the ice cream parlor arrived on the scene and homemade ice cream competed with commercial products from local, regional and national dairies.

The arrival of the home refrigerator/freezer and large commercial freezers in grocery stores marked the beginning of the end for the ice cream parlor. A few survived into the post-World War II era. The drugstore soda fountain, which replaced many of them, became, in turn, a thing of the past in the 1970s when drugstore chains arrived on the scene.

America manufacturers and consumes more ice cream than any other nation in the world. But Americans do not hold a monopoly. Ice cream reigns worldwide as one of the most popular foods known. In France it is called *glace*; in Germany, *eis*; and

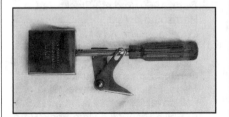

Scoop, Icypi Automatic Cone Co., Cambridge, MA, amber plastic handle, $125.

in Russia, *marozhnye*. No matter what it is called, ice cream is eaten and enjoyed around the globe.

References: Paul Dickson, *Great American Ice Cream Book*, Galahad Books, out of print; Ralph Pomeroy, *Ice Cream Connection*, Paddington Press, out of print; Wayne Smith, *Ice Cream Dippers*, published by author, 1986. Also check general price guides to advertising and advertising character collectibles for ice cream-related material.

Collector's Club: Ice Screamers, P.O. Box 5387, Lancaster, PA 17601.

Museums: Greenfield Village, Dearborn, MI; Museum of Science and Industry, Finigran's Ice Cream Parlor, Chicago, IL; Smithsonian Institution, Washington, DC.

Advertising Trade Card, Lightning Blizzard Freezers, diecut, girl giving dish of ice cream out window, mother hand-cranking ice cream freezer on reverse 15.00

Book, *Snow Ice Cream Makers Guide*, B. Heller & Co., 1911 .... 15.00

Carton, Hershey's Ice Cream, 1 pt, orange and blue 18.00

Catalog, Ice Cream Maker's Formulary & Price List, Frank A. Beeler, 1910-15....................... 30.00

Christmas Decoration, 6-1/2" x 10", diecut stiff-paper string hanger, front illus of Santa making deliveries on foot, holding Christmas wreath under 1 arm, Merry Christmas placard in other hand, Bartholomay Ice Cream inscription in black on white snow, 1930s................. 125.00

Cone Dispenser, glass, copper insert 350.00

Doll, Eskimo Pie 12.00

Ice Cream Scoop Rest, Hendler's Ice Cream, molded brass, inscription "Friendship of Hendler's The Velvet Kind," 1930-40........................ 45.00

Menu Clip, Fairmont Ice Cream, 1930-40 .... 18.00

Mold, pewter
Grape Cluster 30.00
Indian 45.00
Star in Circle 40.00
Turkey..................................... 45.00

Movie, "Ice Cream Face," Our Gang Comedy, 1930s, 16 mm, 2-1/4" orig sq box 25.00

Pennant, Tellings Ice Cream, felt, children making ice cream 90.00

Pinback Button
3/4" d, Good Humor Deerslayer Scout, orange, blue and white litho, c1930 .... 25.00

7/8" d, Arctic Rainbow
Ice Cream Cones, multicolored,
celluloid, c1912 ....25.00
1" d, National Ice Cream Week,
blue and white, Ice Cream Review,
rim copyright, 1930s.................20.00
1-1/4" d, Frosty Treat, red, white
and blue, female ice skater, red
outfit, c1930..............................25.00
Pocket Mirror, Better
Made Ice Cream 35.00
Scoop
Gilchrest #31 ....95.00
Gilchrest #33 ....125.00
No-Pak, #31, hole in scoop......85.00
Sign
Chippewa Pride Ice Cream, tin and
wood, hinged, Indian head.....425.00
Golden Rod Ice Cream, diecut,
schoolgirl riding cone 155.00
Rich Valley Ice Cream, yellow and
red, 9" d, 1940s.........................65.00
Song Brochure, Hendler's Ice Cream,
1950s...2.00
Tape Measure, Abbotts Ice Cream,
black, white and red illus 20.00
Thermometer, Abbottmaid Ice Cream,
2" x 6-1/4", 1920s 45.00
Toy
2" x 4-1/4" x 2", litho tin, Mister Softee
Truck, red, white and blue, silver and
black accents, Mister Softee image
on 3 sides, friction, marked "Made in
Japan," 1960s 40.00
2-1/2" l, die-cast metal truck,
Commer Ice Cream Canteen,
Lyons Maid decals in black, white,
red and yellow, white 3D figure,
Matchbox, c1963......................35.00
4" h, ice cream vendor, litho tin
windup, Deposé
France, 1930s 795.00
Tray
Brownies 180.00
Douglas Ice Cream,
girl eating ice cream,
wearing yellow dress, 1913....150.00
Folmers Ice Cream....................85.00
Herron's Ice Cream,
rect, monogram 75.00
Pure Milk Co., ice cream
and milk, 1900.........................115.00
Purity Ice Cream 20.00
Schuller's Ice Cream,
girl, ice cream cone,
woman and ice cream soda, woman
eating vanilla ice cream..........225.00
Whistle, Puritan Dairy Ice Cream, yellow
tin litho, black letters, c1930 ....35.00

Insulators

Collecting Hints: Learn the shapes
of the insulators and the abbreviations which appear on them. Some
commonly found abbreviations are:

Ice cream cone, pressed paper, 14" h, $180.

"B" (Brookfield), "B&O" (Baltimore
and Ohio), "EC&M Co. SF" (Electrical Construction and Maintenance
Company of San Francisco), "ER"
(Erie Railroad), "WGM Co." (Western Glass Manufacturing Company)
and "WUT Co," (Western Union
Telegraph Company).

Most insulators are priced below $50. However, there are exam-
ples of threaded and threadless
insulators which have exceeded
$2,000. There has been little move-
ment in the price of glass insulators
for the past several years. The top
insulators in each category are:

Threaded

CD 139, Combination Safety/Pat.
Applied for, aqua.................2,500.00
CD 180, Liquid Insulator/blank, ice
aqua 2,500.00
CD 138-9, Patent Applied for/blank,
aqua 2,400.00
CD 176, Lower wire ridge, Whitall
Tatum Co., No. 12 made in
U.S.A./lower wire ridge, Patent No.
1708038, straw 2,300.00
CD 181, no name
and no embossing...............2,200.00

Threadless

CD 731, no name and no embossing,
white milk glass...................3,000.00
CD 739, no name and
no embossing, similar to
jade green milk glass 3,000.00
CD 737, Leffert's/blank,
green...................................2,500.00
CD 790, no name and no embossing,
known as Tea Pot, aqua 2,200.00
CD 788, no name and no embossing,
known as slash top 2,200.00

The six Fry Glass insulators are
not counted in this survey. They are
not common threadless insulators

because they were made only between 1844 and 1865.

History: The invention of the telegraph in 1832 created the need for a
glass or ceramic insulator. The first
patent was given to Ezra Cornell in
1844. The principal manufacturing
era lasted from 1850 to the mid-
1900s. Leading companies included
Armstrong (1938-1969), Brookfield
(1865-1922), California (1912-
1916), Gayner (1920-1922), Hemingray (1871-1919), Lynchburg
(1923-1925), Maydwell (1935-
1940), McLaughlin (1923-1925) and
Whitall Tatum (1920-1938).

Initially, insulators were threadless. Shortly after the Civil War, L. A.
Cauvet received a patent for a threaded insulator. Drip points prevented
water from laying on the insulator and
causing a short. The double skirt kept
moisture from the peg or pin.

There are about 500 different
styles of glass insulators, each of
which has been given a "CD" (consolidated design) number as found
in N.R. Woodward's *Glass Insulator
in America*. The style of the insulator
is the only key to the numbering.
Colors and names of the makers and
all lettering found on the same style
insulator have nothing to do with the
CD number.

References: Marilyn Albers and N.R.
Woodward, *Glass Insulators from
Outside North America*, 2nd Revision
and companion price guide, available
from authors (14715 Oak Bend Dr.,
Houston, TX 77079), 1993; Michael
G. Guthrie, *Fake, Altered and Repaired Insulators*, available from author (1209 W. Menlo, Fresno, CA
93711), 1988; Mark Lauckner, *Canadian Railway Communications Insulators 1880-1920*, available from
author (Mayne Island, B.C. Canada
V0N-2J0), 1995; John and Carol Mc-
Dougald, *Insulators*, 2 vols, available
from authors (P.O. Box 1003, St.
Charles, IL 60174) 1990; ——, *1995
Price Guide for Insulators*, available
from authors (P.O. Box 1003, St.
Charles, IL 60174), 1995; N.R.
Woodward, *Glass Insulator in America*, published by author, 1973; Fred
Padgett, *Dreams of Glass: The Story
of William McLaughlin and His Glass
Company*, available from author

(P.O. Box 1122, Livermore, CA 94551), 1996

Periodicals: *Crown Jewels of the Wire*, P.O. Box 1003, St. Charles, IL 60174; *Rainbow Riders' Trading Post*, P.O. Box 1423, Port Heuneme, CA 93044.

Collectors' Clubs: Capital District Insulator Club, 41 Crestwood Dr., Schenectady, NY 12306; Central Florida Insulator Collectors Club, 707 NE 113th St., North Miami, FL 33161; Chesapeake Bay Insulator Club, 10 Ridge Rd., Catonsville, MD 21228; Lone Star Insulator Club, P.O. Box 1317, Buna, TX 77612; National Insulator Association, 1315 Old Mill Path, Broadview Heights, OH 44147; Yankee Polecat Insulator Club, 79 New Boltom Rd., Manchester, CT 06040.

Museums: Big Thicket Museum, Saratoga, TX; Edison Plaza Museum, Beaumont, TX.

Threaded Insulators

CD 104, N.E. Telephone & Telegraph
Co., aqua 4.00
CD 121, F.R. Good Jr., Denver, CO,
aqua...5.00
CD 125, Hemingray, Blue..............20.00
CD 127, WUT Co., aqua 8.00
CD 131, W. Brookfield, light blue ..30.00
CD 133, W. Brookfield,
light aqua 20.00
CD 134
G.E. Co., light aqua....................5.00
THE Co., aqua 9.00
CD 138
Postal Tel Co., light aqua.........22.00
W. Brookfield, aqua..................24.00
CD 145
GTP, dark aqua and olive 10.00
KCG W, light green 15.00
H.G. Co., light green 3.00
Star, yellow-green 5.00

Ceramic, white glazed, unmkd, 3-1/2"h, 3-1/4" d, $2.

Glass, Hemingray, No. 40, aqua, 4-1/4" h, 3-3/4" d, $4.50.

CD 152, Hemingray, 2-tone aqua ...6.00
CD 154, Hemingray, blue..............20.00
CD 160, H.G. Co.,
May 2nd date, aqua.................40.00
CD 161
California, rose color 28.00
McLaughlin, No. 20
Emerald green 22.00
Lime green 14.00
CD 162, Star, yellow-green 5.00
CD 164, Lynchburg,
yellow-green 19.00
CD 165, Hemingray, clear...............5.00
CD 214, Hemingray, pale green....22.00
CD 287, Locke, light aqua.............13.00

Threadless Insulators

CD 718, no name, no emb
Aqua.......................................220.00
Emerald Green.......................325.00
Olive Green............................325.00
CD 728, Boston Bottle Works, smooth
base, light aqua 72.00

Irons

Collecting Hints: Heavy rusting, pitting and missing parts detract from an iron's value. More advanced collectors may accept some of these defects on a rare or unusual iron. However, the beginning collector is urged to concentrate on irons in very good to excellent condition.

Many unusual types of irons came from Europe and the Orient. These foreign examples are desirable, especially since some models were prototypes for later American-made irons. Irons made between 1850 to 1910 are plentiful and varied. Many models and novelty irons still have not been documented by collectors. Electric irons are just beginning to find favor among collectors but are not being added to older collections. Those with special features (temperature indicators, self-contained stands, sets) and those with Deco styling are the most desirable.

History: Ironing devices have been used for many centuries, with the earliest references dating from 1100. Irons from medieval times, the Renaissance and the early industrial eras can be found in Europe but are rare. Fine engraved brass irons and hand-wrought irons predominated prior to 1850. After 1850, the iron underwent a series of rapid evolutionary changes.

Between 1850 and 1910, irons were heated in four ways: 1) a hot metal slug was inserted into the body, 2) a burning solid, e.g., coal or charcoal, was placed in the body, 3) a liquid or gas, e.g., alcohol, gasoline or natural gas, was fed from an external tank and burned in the body or 4) conduction heat was used, usually by drawing heat from a stove top.

References: Dave Irons, *Irons by Irons*, published by author, 1994; ——, *More Irons by Irons*, published by author, 1996; ——, *Pressing Iron Patents*, published by author, 1994. Note: The books by Dave Irons are available from the author at 223 Covered Bridge Rd., Northampton, PA 18067.

Periodical: *Iron Talk*, P.O. Box 68, Waelder, TX 78959.

Collectors' Clubs: Club of the Friends of Ancient Smoothing Irons, P.O. Box 215, Carlsbad, CA 92008; Midwest Sad Iron Collectors Club, 24 Nob Hill Dr., St. Louis, MO 63138.

Museums: Henry Ford Museum, Dearborn, MI; Shelburne Museum, Shelburne, VT; Sturbridge Village, Sturbridge, MA.

Reproduction Alert: The most frequently reproduced irons are the miniatures, especially the swan's neck and flat irons. Reproductions of some large European varieties have been made, but poor construction, use of thin metals and the unusually fine condition easily identifies them as new. More and more European styles are being reproduced each year. Construction techniques are better than before and aging processes can fool many knowledgeable collectors. Look for heavy pitting on the reproductions and two or more irons that are exactly alike. Few American irons have been reproduced at this time, other than the miniatures.

Advisors: David and Sue Irons.

Charcoal
  Box
    European, rooster, latch.......50.00
    German, multiple vent holes near
    bottom.................................65.00
    The Marvel, liftoff top 120.00
  Pan, Chinese, bronze,
  carved handle.......................120.00
  Turned chimney, European, brass
  heat shield.............................115.00
Children's
  Cylinder grip, double-pointed, all
  cast, 3-3/8"...............................30.00
  Enterprise
    Holes part way through handle,
    2-1/2" 100.00
    Holes through handle,
    2-1/2" 120.00
  The Gem, No. 2, wood
  handle, 4-5/8"......................150.00
  Hollow grip, handle folded under,
  Kenrick, 3"..............................85.00
  Oval cap, English,
  "Carron, O," 4"........................80.00
  The Pearl, wood rainbow handle,
  2-3/4".....................................120.00
  Rope handle, all cast,
  double-pointed, 2-7/8".............25.00
  Sensible, 2 pc,
  No. 4, 5-1/4" 90.00
  Sleeve with rope handle, chromed,
  4-1/4".....................................60.00
  Two-pc, lift-off handle, 3-5/8" ...55.00
  Tribump, 3 bulbous parts on handle,
  1-3/4" to 3-1/2" 50.00
  Wire Handle
    Mexican, mkd "1," 2-5/8"......40.00
    "Star" on top, 2-7/8" 70.00
  Wood handle,
  star with No. 14 ....120.00
Flat Iron
  Agate, European,
  gray-black...............................130.00
  Anchor symbol, 6-1/8".............30.00
  Double-pointed, keystone symbol,
  No. 7, 8-1/2"...........................150.00
  Enterprise, 3 cold-handle irons,
  1 handle, 1 trivet, with box 250.00
  French, sq back,
  Le Gaulois, No. 5 ....90.00
  IXL, No. 6, 5-3/4"......................20.00
  Sensible, No. 8,
  pat. June 18, 1888 ....110.00
  Wapak, No. 4, 4-1/8"................20.00
Fluter
  Combination-Type
    Charcoal, Acme, side fluter plate
    and rocker..........................165.00
    Flutes inside, held together by wire
    cup 110.00
  Machine-Type
    American, American Machine Co.,
    Philadelphia, good paint.....150.00
    Banner, belt-driven or
    hand-cranked.....................170.00

    Eagle, American Machine Co.,
    Philadelphia, 5-1/8" roll......170.00
  Rocker-Type
    The Erie Fluter, 2 pc, rare..400.00
    Geneva Hand Fluter, Improved,
    brass plates 300.00
    The Globe, 2 pc 170.00
  Roller-Type
    CW Whitfield, 2 pc 150.00
    Shepard Hardware, heater placed
    in base 120.00
Goffering
  Clamp-on,
  5" single barrel, rare..............500.00
  Single barrel, round base
    All brass, English 200.00
    All iron, S wire....................200.00
Liquid Fuel
  Gasoline
    Coleman, model 4A,
    blue enamel 70.00
    Comfort Iron,
    rear ball tank......................60.00
    The Diamond Iron,
    ball tank 75.00
    Jubilee Iron, cylinder tank,
    rainbow handle 150.00
    Tilley, English, tan body.....130.00
  Natural Gas
    GME, 1901, 6" 85.00
    Humphrey,
    odd heat shield 95.00
    The Perfect Gas Iron,
    hinged top 120.00
    The Swing,
    slotted vent holes...............120.00
Special Purpose
  Hat
    Rotary, nickeled, heated on gas
    jet......................................125.00
    Slug, large
    round nose, 15"..................110.00
    Tolliker
      2 grooves in bottom, wood
      handle 130.00
      Wavy bottom, cast 125.00
  Miscellaneous
    Billiard table, English 90.00
    Egg
      Standing,
      round cast base................160.00

Soapstone, mkd "Hood's Patent/Pat'd Jan. 15, 1867," $175.

    Wood handle, 2" egg 90.00
  Flower, brass
  top and bottom...................110.00
  Glove form, brass,
  4 fingers.............................140.00
  Long sleeve, French,
  oval head, 14"....................140.00
  Seam, thin width,
  tailor's iron 50.00
  Polisher
    Cap Iron, English, oval, cast,
    4-1/2" 70.00
    French, dimpled bottom.....140.00
    Kenrick, round bottom 70.00
    MAB Cooks, egg shape.....125.00
    M. Mahony, Troy, flat-iron style,
    leather-textured bottom 50.00
    Mrs. Streeters Gem Polisher, 2-pc
    slant front nose 160.00
    N.E. Butt Co., rope edge ...110.00
    Star Polisher, oval shape...130.00
Slug
  Box, English
    All brass, turned posts 170.00
    High-box body,
    lift-up gate...........................90.00
  Empire Co., lift-off top 180.00
  NRS Magic, lift-off top............180.00
  Ox tongue, European, bullet shape,
  lift-up gate 70.00
  Salamander box iron,
  lift-off top 350.00

J

Jewelry, Costume

Collecting Hints: Scarcity and demand drive the market for costume jewelry. Demand is greatest for pieces marked with a recognizable and sought-after designer's or manufacturer's name. Name alone, however, does not guarantee high value. Collectors should also consider quality of design and manufacture, size and color. Condition is of primary importance because costume jewelry is easily damaged and difficult to repair well. Certain types of unsigned pieces, particularly those made of Bakelite and other plastics, generate collector interest. Because costume jewelry is wearable, pieces should be chosen with personal style and wardrobe in mind.

History: The term "costume jewelry" was not used until the 1920s, when Coco Chanel made the wearing of frankly faux jewels an acceptable part of *haute couture*. Prior to the Jazz Age, manufacturers mass-produced imitation jewelry—exact copies of the real thing. Fine jewelry continued to exert its influence on costume jewelry in the 20th century but, because they were liberated from the costly constraints of valuable gemstones and metals, designers could be more extravagant in producing pieces made of non-precious materials.

By the 1930s, when more cost-effective methods were developed, casting superseded die-stamping in mass-production. The Great Depression instigated the use of the first entirely synthesized plastic, trade-named "Bakelite," for colorful and inexpensive jewelry. During World War II, restrictions and shortages forced manufacturers to turn to sterling silver as a replacement for base white metals and to experiment with new materials such as Lucite (DuPont's trade name for acrylic). Today, Lucite and sterling vermeil (gold-plated) animals and other figurals of the period, known as jelly bellies, are highly collectible. Other World War II novelty items were made of make-do materials such as wood, ceramic, textiles and natural pods and seeds.

In the prosperous 1950s, high-fashion rhinestone, faux pearl and colored-glass jewelry signed with the names of well-known couturiers and other designers was sold in elegant department stores. A matching suite—necklace, bracelet, earrings, brooch—was the proper complement to the ensemble of a well-groomed 1950s woman.

References: Lillian Baker, *Fifty Years of Collectible Fashion Jewelry*, Collector Books, 1986, 1992 value update; ——, *100 Years of Collectible Jewelry*, Collector Books, 1978, 1993 value update; ——, *Twentieth Century Fashionable Plastic Jewelry*, Collector Books, 1992; Joanne Dubbs Ball, *Costume Jewelers*, Schiffer Publishing, 1990; Dee Battle and Alayne Lesser, *Best of Bakelite and Other Plastic Jewelry*, Schiffer Publishing, 1995; Vivienne Becker, *Fabulous Costume Jewelry*, Schiffer Publishing, 1993; Howard L. Bell Jr., *Cuff Jewelry*, published by author, 1994; Jeanenne Bell, *Answers to Questions about Old Jewelry*, 4th Edition, Books Americana, 1995; Matthew L. Burkholz and Linda Lictenberg Kaplan, *Copper Art Jewelry*, Schiffer Publishing, 1992; Deanna Farneti

Cera (ed.), *Jewels of Fantasy*, Harry N. Abrams, 1992; Maryanne Dolan, *Collecting Rhinestone Jewelry*, 3rd Edition, Books Americana, 1993; Roseann Ettinger, *Forties & Fifties Popular Jewelry*, Schiffer Publishing, 1994; ——, *Popular Jewelry*, Schiffer Publishing, 1990; Tony Grasso, *Bakelite Jewelry*, Chartwell, 1996; Gabrielle Greindl, *Gems of Costume Jewelry*, Abbeville Press, 1990; S. Sylvia Henzel, *Collectible Costume Jewelry*, Revised Edition, Wallace-Homestead, 1987, 1990 value update; Sibylle Jargstorf, *Baubles, Buttons and Beads*, Schiffer Publishing, 1991; ——, *Glass in Jewelry*, Schiffer Publishing, 1991; Susan Jonas and Marilyn Nissenson, *Cuff Links*, Harry N. Abrams, 1991; Lyngerde Kelley and Nancy Schiffer, *Plastic Jewelry*, Schiffer Publishing, 1987, 1995 value update; J.J. Kellner, *First Complete Reference Guide Siam Sterling Nielloware*, published by author, 1993; Jack and Elynore "Pet" Kerins, *Collecting Antique Stickpins*, Collector Books, 1995; Jan Lindenberger, *Collecting Plastic Jewelry*, Schiffer Publishing, 1996; J.L. Lynnlee, *All That Glitters*, Schiffer Publishing, Ltd., 1986, 1993 value update; Harrice Simons Miller, *Costume Jewelry*, 2nd Edition, Avon Books, 1994; Christie Romero, *Warman's Jewelry*, Wallace-Homestead, 1995; Nancy N. Schiffer, *Costume Jewelry*, Schiffer Publishing, 1988, 1992 value update; ——, *Fun Jewelry*, Revised and Updated, Schiffer Publishing, 1996; ——, *Rhinestones!*, Schiffer Publishing, 1993; ——, *Silver Jewelry Designs*, Schiffer Publishing, 1997; Sheryl Gross Shatz, *What's It Made of?*, 3rd Edition, published by author (10931 Hunting Horn Dr., Santa Ana, CA 92705), 1996; Cherri Simonds, *Collectible Costume Jewelry*, Collector Books, 1997; Nicholas D. Snider, *Antique Sweetheart Jewelry*, Schiffer Publishing, 1996.

Videotapes: C. Jeanenne Bell, *Antique and Collectible Jewelry Video Series, Vol. I* (1994), *Vol. II* (1994), Antique Images; Christie Romero, *Hidden Treasures*, Venture Entertainment Group (P.O. Box 55113, Sherman Oaks, CA 91413), 1992, 1995 value update.

Collectors' Clubs: Leaping Frog Antique Jewelry and Collectable Club, 4841 Martin Luther Blvd, Sacramento, CA 95820; National Cuff Link Society, P.O. Box 346, Pros-

Pin and earrings, plastic, wood-grain pattern, 3-1/2" d pin, $5.

pect Heights, IL 60070; Vintage Fashion & Costume Jewelry Club, P.O. Box 265, Glen Oaks, NY 11004.

Reproduction Alert: Recasts and knockoffs are widespread. Copies of high-end signed pieces—e.g., Trifari jelly bellies, Eisenberg Originals and Boucher—are common. New Bakelite (sometimes called "fakelite") and marriages of old Bakelite parts are also cropping up in many areas.

Beads, unknown maker,
   3/4" l translucent emerald green oblong beads accented with 2 gold bands, alternating with 9mm filigree gold-tone metal beads, smaller round green and citrine color glass beads, gold-tone caps, oval 1" l push-in clasp, cabochon green matching stone, 22" l 35.00
Bracelet
   Buch Deichmann, Danish Art Deco style, plastic, 1 deep amber brown, other deep forest green, mkd in mold "Buch+Deichmann Denmark 1981," price for pr...............................30.00
   Ciner, cuff, black enamel, rhinestones panther, sgd 200.00
   Coro
      Charm, 8 charms, 4-leaf clover, acorn, snake head, lucky 13 and others, gold-tone links, 8" l ..15.00
      Floral links of clear rhinestones between gold-tone leaves, 1-1/8" w, 6-3/4" l, late 1940s 30.00
      Heart-shaped links edge silver-tone, pearl and blue irid stones, 7" l 20.00
      Plastic moonstone beads, baroques and rounds in greens, purples and pinks, matching rhinestones on leaf-like gold-tone cast lines, 1" w, 6-1/2" l, script sgd,

1950s 25.00
Danecraft, link, SS, lily-pad design, sgd 65.00
Eisenberg, rhinestone, 3 rows of clear stones, sgd 125.00
Theodore Fahrner, amazonite, lapis, marcasite, SS, Art Deco style, sgd, minor crazing......................1,380.00
Francois, Coro designer mark, pavé rhinestones on airy cross-links, aurora borealis center-row accents, light gold-tone cast, 1-1/4" w, 7" l 60.00
Harper, openwork scrolls, center golden-red petaled rose surrounded by etched silver leaves, open-back cuff, 3/4" w, gold-filled and SS appliqué, 1940s, mkd "Harper 1/20 12K G.F."......................60.00
Kramer, amethyst and clear oval rhinestones, 8 silver-tone cast S-links, 1" w, 7-1/2" l, safety chain, 1950s 35.00
Lobel, bangle, SS, scrolling abstract design, sgd, 1960s.................320.00
Lustern, 6 open-work lines, 1 aqua center rhinestone, 6 smaller center rhinestones on each, fine silver-tone sterling-like cast, 5/8" w, 7" l, mkd "Lustern" in triangle 20.00
Navajo, slave style with attached ring, SS, 3 light pink MOP stones in teethed gypsy-set mountings, feather and boule motifs, open bangle, medium size, ring size 7, sgd with initials 75.00
Siam-type, 7 golden faces in relief on black ground under plastic domes, filigree and scrolled gold-tone open links, 7-1/4" l, 3/4" w, 1950s 30.00
Tara, 6 curved semi-open links holding each other with tulip-set clear sparking rhinestones, shiny gold tone, 1" w, 7-1/4" l, script sgd, 1950s...............................30.00
Trifari
    Clear rhinestones in basketweave links, 1-1/8" w, 7" l, 1940s, back finish worn.............................50.00
    Turquoise and white enamel, textured gold tone, 3/4" w, medium size, 1970s...........................25.00
Unknown Maker
    Charm, locket opens to reveal 2 movie favorites, brass with gold wash, 1" d, 7-1/4" l, fancy scrolls 25.00
    Stretch, green plastic dominoes with white spots, separated by amber-colored beads...........40.00
Brooch/Pin
Art, poinsettia, large red and green enameled flower, clear rhinestones center, 2" d, mkd "Art" 25.00
Austrian, elongated marquis-bar shape, pronged aurora borealis smoked gray rhinestones along edges, assembled gold-tone open-

work, 2 deep rose and 1 large black aurora borealis rhinestones at center, mkd "Made Austria," 1-1/2" w, 1/2" h, late 1950s 20.00
Bakelite, orange triangles, brass studs, butterscotch circles, 2" l, price for pr....................35.00
Bauring, eagle with spread wings, heavy cast SS in high relief, 2-3/4" w, 2" h..........................90.00
Cathé, black faceted glass petals on flower, green and aurora borealis rhinestones 35.00
Coro
    Cameo, faux carnelian surrounded by clear rhinestones, scrolled mounting, 1-1/2" x 1-1/4" 30.00
    Eagle, 2" l, mkd "Sterlingcraft by Coro"......................................55.00
    Iris, enamel and pavé, gold filled, sgd 220.00
    Leaves, carved glass, 2-tone green and shimmery clear, silver-tone cast, 2-3/8" h, 1-1/8" w 35.00
Coventry, Sarah
    Flower, amber faceted flower, clear rhinestones, graceful 4" stem, gold tone 55.00
    3 ribbed petals, 2" d, gold tone......................15.00
DeNicola, Maltese cross, white and marbleized coral glass stones, gold tone, some wear to plating, 2-3/4" h, 2-1/4" w 25.00
Florenza, starfish, green, brown and gold rhinestones, gold tone, 3" w, mkd 65.00
German, multicolored and gold flecks embedded in center 1" oval glass cabochon, antique gold-tone filigree mounting with 3D raised filigree embellishments, golden aurora borealis rhinestone accents, mkd "Made in Western Germany," 2" h, 1-1/2" w..........35.00
Haskell, Miriam
    Circle, white flower-shaped beads, silver-filigree setting, 2" d.....40.00
    Daisy, 6 flowers formed by white stones wired to silver-filigree setting, 2-1/2" d....................40.00
    Fan, Oriental design, bamboo handle, gold tone, sgd "Haskell".......................45.00
Hobé, SS, tulip 295.00
KJL, lizard, reversible body, faux turquoise and rhinestone............200.00
Kramer, 3-drop mourning style, aurora borealis rhinestones, faceted crystals on top, sgd "Kramer" and "C" in circle, 2-3/4" h, 1-1/4" w, 1950s 60.00
Lisner, stylized spray, pink, green and blue rhinestones, gold tone, 2-1/2" w, 1950s 25.00
Macchiarini, SS and bronze, rect

bronze element on knife-edge mount, c1960 ....260.00
Mexican
    Bird in flight, Matisse style, high relief SS, mkd "P.J. 21 Mexico, 925, Nestor," 1-7/8" l body, 2-1/4" wing spread...............60.00
    Cermeno, SS, green plastic, carved Aztec deity face, ornate frame, 3 long solid SS hanging bangles, 3-1/2" l, sgd "Mexico Cermeno"............................95.00
    Taxco, swirling pinwheel design, inlaid black enamel and abalone, SS, mkd "Taxco Mexico 925," 1-3/4" d 35.00
    TBR, turtle, inlaid abalone shell, Mexican silver, mkd "TBR 25," 1-1/2" l, 1" w, 1/2" h 35.00
    Toltec Deity motif, SS, inlaid abalone, mkd "Mexico," 11/2" d.................30.00
Nye, classic feather, SS, 3-3/8" l, 7/8" w 45.00
Razza, bull, brassy horns, gold eyes...........95.00
W. Reinbold, hand-carved painted mallard in flight, wood, sgd 20.00
Trifari
    Bee, jelly belly, 1/2" l..........150.00
    Mourning Style, 7mm round faux turquoises at center and on 3 pendant drops, florentine gold-tone cast, sgd, 1-3/4" w, 3" h, 1950s 25.00
Ultra Craft, shoulder-type, domed, jungle animals, openwork, varying textures, gold tone, 4" x 4".......35.00
Unknown Maker
    Butterfly, multi-colored pastel rhinestones, center body on spring trembles, gold tone, 2" w, 1950s.................40.00
    Cameo, Bakelite and Lucite, clear, black ground 25.00
    Floral, black narrow marquis faceted glass stones form petals on 2 daisy-type flowers, clear aurora borealis round rhinestone centers and accents, set above each other, black leaves elongated in rhomboid shape, silver-tone backing, pronged stones, 2-7/8" w, 2" h, 1950s.........................20.00
    V-shape, free-hanging pendant, gold-tone chain bib and 7 tassels, baroque teardrop faux pearls, 3" w, 3-1/4" l.............................20.00
Weiss, Marguerite daisy, stem, leaf, white enamel, yellow center, little red ladybug, 2-3/4" h, 101/2" w, sgd, 1960s......................................20.00
Ed Wiener, pierced SS, abstract, sgd, c1950 ....750.00
Joseph Wiesner, branch, aqua marquis faceted rhinestones, pavé bow and streamers, silver-tone cast,

Suite, brooch/pin and earrings, rhinestones, sunburst pin, crescent-shaped earrings, silver-tone cast, 3-1/4" d pin, unknown maker, $18.

sgd "Joseph Wiesner, NY," 2-1/4" h, 7/8" w 35.00

Choker

Kramer

Pavé faux turquoise flower links, center aurora borealis rhinestone, gold-tone cast, sgd, late 1950s, adjustable to 15-3/4" 40.00

Teardrop faceted amethyst color crystal center stone, emerald color crystal accents, clear rhinestones on intricately swirled and turned silver-tone cast, snake chain, 14" l 35.00

Unknown Maker

Crackle and vaseline-style glass cabochons surrounded by rhinestones, adjustable to 15" l....50.00

Pink glass cabochons, large aurora borealis pink-hued rhinestone accents, gold tone, 5/8" w x 3/4" l stones, adjustable to 16" l....50.00

Clip, Victor Silson, happy tiger, holding ftd glass in 1 paw, tail with other, heavy gold-tone cast, black enamel stripes, tiny pavé rhinestones on face, chest and part of leg, double prongs on back, mkd "Silson Patented," 2-1/2" x 2-1/4", 1940s.....225.00

Collar, Lucien Piccard, raised 1/4" h, punched-out sides and tops, 1/2" l stainless steel SP rect links, 15" l, c1950, stamped-in cast 50.00

Cuff Links, pr

Hickok, fish..............................10.00

Unknown Maker

Crystal, ruby and yellow gold, Art Deco-style, bead set, collet-set cabochon ruby 375.00

Gold and diamond, Art Deco style, round diamond within openwork sq mount 520.00

Duettes, Coro, sgd

Birds on branch, enamel and rhinestone 200.00

Flowers

Blue, red and clear rhinestones, pin and matching necklace 425.00

Enamel and rhinestones, white enamel flowers, reen enamel leaves, clear

and red rhinestones 225.00

Earrings, pr

Alice Caviness, black irid 30.00

Corocraft, black enameled floral petals, rhinestone cluster center, c1940................40.00

Eisenberg, clear rhinestones, drop 45.00

Florenza, large red oval rhinestone faceted stones surrounded by small turquoise and red faceted stones, gold-tone mounting, 1-1/4" x 1", clip 65.00

Haskell, Miriam

Leaf shape, gold-filled, 7 marquise-shaped crystals, sgd.........................45.00

Modified door-knocker, 2 rope styles twisted around each other, gold-tone finish, polished top, 3/4" w, 1-1/8" l, clip 25.00

Hobé, light blue glass beads....30.00

Hollycraft, leaves, multicolored, screw back, 1" l, mkd 45.00

Trifari, 1-1/4" d buttons, baroque leaf and rope florentine gold-tone rim, 1" d rose-pink moonstone domed glass stones, clip, 1950s 20.00

Unknown Maker, mosaic, 1" d heart shape, multicolored, mkd "Italy," 1950s 20.00

Weiss, aurora borealis, blue, clip...................................25.00

Necklace

Coro, silver tone, teardrop motif, mkd "Coro"...............................15.00

Francois, Coro, wheat-style links with small spacers, gold tone, 15" l, 1937 ....25.00

Miriam Haskell, 1 strand detailed chain, 1 strand baroque pearls, gold tone, 18" l...............................115.00

Unknown Maker

Amethyst, faceted peridot and mixed metals, textured branch design, caged amethyst crystals, 24" l, c1950 ....865.00

Bakelite, ivory, graduated smooth egg-shaped beads from 5/8 to 1-1/8" l, 28" l, 1940s.............40.00

Copper, cast, eight 7/8" l figure-8-shaped links, high relief, adjustable to 16-1/2" l, 5-pointed star within diamond mark............40.00

Vendome, faux pearl, double strand of knotted faux pearls, 16" l, aurora borealis stone clasp 45.00

Pendant

Sarah Coventry, polished faux coral plastic, huge teardrop, gold-rimmed open center, 28" l lightweight gold-tone chain, 3" l pendant, mkd "SARAH COV" 20.00

Georg Jensen, SS, c1950

No. 334, arc-shaped top suspending bird in flight...................260.00

No. 143, concentric circles, center cabochon amethyst on silver tongue................................520.00

C.L. Razza, black Bakelite see-through cross, light green topaz color pronged rhinestones at center, 2-7/8" h, 1-1/2" w, 18" l pewter-finish snake chain..............................30.00

Shoe Clip, Musi, fancy drops, all pronged rhinestones, silver tone, mkd, 2" h 35.00

Suite

Art, pin and earrings, glass banded agate, 2" d round pin, ornate gold mounting, matching clip earrings, sgd 45.00

Beaujewels, Retro style, sapphire blue rhinestones combined with round blue aurora borealis and clear medium and light blue rhinestones, 2-1/2" d pin, 1-1/2" clip earrings 45.00

Danecraft, pin and earrings, roses, buds and leaves, 2-1/2" x 1-1/4" w 3D pink, 5/8" d screw-back earrings, mkd "Sterling Silver," 1950s 30.00

Eisenberg, pendant and earrings, enameled owl, 20" l gold-tone snake chain, matching clip earrings, c1973 ....125.00

Florenza, bracelet and earrings, silver casting, molded aurora borealis teardrops, faceted rhinestones in blue, pink, purples, accented by light amethyst and light yellow rhinestones, 7" l bracelet, 1" d, clip earrings 115.00

HAR, pin and earrings, white stones, gold filigree setting, oval-shaped 2" pin, intricate 2" drop-hinged earrings, mkd "HAR" on each pc...85.00

Lisner

Necklace and earrings, red and clear rhinestone flowers accent gold-plated link choker, adjustable to 16" l, 3/4" d clip earrings, 1950s....................35.00

Pin and earrings, tulip, emerald green accents, green irid stones, gold tone, clip-back earrings 25.00

M&SGF, pin and earrings, Gone With the Wind-style, assembled soldered openwork, deep amethyst and clear rhinestones, 2-pc pendant construction, loop for chain, matching screw-back earrings, 1940s 55.00

Schiaperelli, necklace, bracelet and earrings, pewter-type mounting, multicolored rhinestones........350.00

Trifari

Bracelet, choker, earrings, white plastic half-moon shapes, rich pink aurora borealis rhinestones, gold-tone cast, mkd, 1" w x 14-3/4" choker, 5/8" x 7-1/2" l pr of bracelets, 1" d clip earrings, 1960s....................85.00

Clip and earrings,
heart shape, aqua center,
clear rhinestones................200.00
Pin and earrings, 3D flowers
surround center flower, openwork
baguette studded background,
silver-tone cast, clear rhinestones,
1-3/4" d pin, mkd "Trifari"
with crowned T...................650.00
Unknown Maker, pin, earrings
and ring, Oriental Boy, faux ivory
face, c1950...........................250.00
Joseph Wiesner, necklace and earrings, large smoky gray marquis and
teardrop rhinestones, richly worked
clear rhinestone triple-bib choker
adjustable to 15-1/2" l, matching
marquis-shaped clip earrings, all
pronged stones, silver tone,
orig satin-lined box mkd "Joseph
Wiesner Orig, Fifth Avenue,
New York" 95.00

Jukeboxes

Collecting Hints: Jukebox chronology falls into four distinct periods:

Pre-1938 period: Jukeboxes
were constructed mainly of wood and
resembled a radio or phonograph
cabinet. Wurlitzer jukeboxes from this
era are the most collectible, but their
value usually is less than $600.

1938 to 1948: The addition of
plastics and animation units gave the
jukebox a gaudier appearance.
These jukeboxes played 78-RPM
records. Wurlitzer jukeboxes are
king, with Rock-Ola the second most
popular. This era contains the most
valuable models, e.g., Wurlitzer models 750, 850, 950, 1015 and 1080.

1940 to 1960: Referred to as
the Seeburg era. Jukeboxes of this
vintage are collected for the "Happy
Days" feeling (named for the TV
show): drive-in food, long skirts,
sweater girls and good times. The
jukeboxes, which play 45-RPM
records, rate second in value to
those of the 1938-1948 period, with
prices usually are below $1,500.

1961 and newer: These jukeboxes often are not considered collectible because the record
mechanism is not visible, thus removing an alluring quality.

There are exceptions to these
generalizations. Collectors should
have a price and identification guide
to help make choices. Many original
and reproduction parts are available
for Seeburg and Wurlitzer jukeboxes. In many cases, incomplete jukeboxes can be restored. Jukeboxes
that are in working order and can be
maintained in that condition are the

best machines to own. Do not buy
any jukebox without taking time to
thoroughly educate yourself, making
sure you know how collectible the
particular machine is and how missing components will affect its value.

History: First came the phonograph.
When electrical amplification became possible, the coin-operated
phonograph, known as the jukebox,
evolved. The heyday of the jukebox
was the 1940s. Between 1946 and
1947 Wurlitzer produced 56,000
model-1015 jukeboxes, the largest
production run of all time. The jukebox was the center of every teenage
hangout, from drugstores and restaurants to pool halls and dance par-
lors. They even invaded some
private homes. Jukeboxes were
cheaper than a live band, and, unlike
radio, allowed listeners to hear their
favorite songs whenever and as often as wished.

Styles changed in the 1960s.
Portable radios, coupled with "Top
40" radio stations, fulfilled the desire
for daily repetition of songs. Television changed evening entertainment
patterns and the jukebox vanished.

References: Michael Adams, Jür-
gen Lukas and Thomas Maschke,
Jukeboxes, Schiffer Publishing,
1995; Jerry Ayliffe, *American Premium Guide to Jukeboxes and Slot
Machines*, 3rd Edition, Books Americana, 1991; Rick Botts, *Complete
Identification Guide to the Wurlitzer
Jukebox*, published by author, 1984;
——, *Jukebox Restoration Guide*,
published by author, 1985; Stephan

Wurlitzer, Model 1100, $2,000.

K. Loots, *Official Victory Glass Price
Guide to Antique Jukeboxes*, pub-
lished by author, 1997; Vincent
Lynch, *American Jukebox*, Chroni-
cle Books, 1990; Scott Wood (ed.),
Blast from the Past, Jukeboxes, L-W
Book Sales, 1992.

Periodicals: *Always Jukin'*, 221
Yesler Way, Seattle, WA 98104; *An-
tique Amusements, Slot Machine &
Jukebox Gazette*, 909 26th St. NW,
Washington, DC 20037; *Chicago-
land Program*, 414 N. Prospect Man-
or Ave., Mt. Prospect, IL 60056;
Coin-Op Classics, 17844 Toiyabe
St., Fountain Valley, CA 92708;
Gameroom, P.O. Box 41, Keyport,
NJ 07735; *Jukebox Collector*, 2534
SE 60th Ct. #216, Des Moines, IA
50317; *Loose Change*, 1515 S.
Commerce St., Las Vegas, NV
89102-2703.

Museums: Jukeboxes have not
reached the status of museum pieces. The best way to see 100 or more
jukeboxes in one place is to visit a
coin-op show.

Advisor: Rick Botts.

AMI, model
A	1,200.00
B	800.00
C	500.00
D	400.00
E	500.00

Mills, model
Empress	1,400.00
Throne of Music	800.00

Packard, Manhattan.................2,500.00

Rock-Ola, model
1422	2,000.00
1426	2,000.00
1428	2,000.00
1432	800.00
1434	900.00
1436	900.00
1438	950.00

Seeburg, model
147	600.00
HF100G	950.00
HF100R	950.00
M100B	850.00
M100C	950.00
V-200	1,300.00

Wurlitzer, model
412	800.00
600	1,000.00
616	600.00
700	3,000.00
750	5,000.00
780	2,500.00
800	4,500.00
850	12,500.00
950	20,000.00
1015	4,500.00

K

Keys

Collecting Hints: The modern hobby of key collecting began with the publication of *Standard Guide to Key Collecting* which illustrates keys by function and describes keys by style and metal content. Most key collectors focus on a special type of key, e.g., folding keys, railroad keys or car keys.

Very few, if any, American-made keys can be called truly rare, although currently some may be very difficult to find. Little is known as to quantity that was manufactured, how popular they were when first produced and marketed or how many survived.

Some keys are abundant in certain areas of the country and scarce in others. Do not pay high prices just because you have never heard of or seen an example before. The best advice is to seek out other collectors and join a national organization.

History: The key has been a symbol of mystical charm since Biblical times. The Catholic Church has keys in its coat of arms and during the Middle Ages noblemen and women carried large collections of keys hanging from their girdles to denote status—the more keys the higher the status. Many kings and other members of the royalty practiced the art of key-making. The custom of granting presentation keys began during the earliest years when cities were walled enclaves. When a visitor was held in high esteem by the townspeople, he would be presented with a key to the city gate. Thus, we now have the honorary "Key to the City."

When it was popular to go on a Grand Tour of Europe, keys were among the most acquired souvenir objects. Unfortunately, many of these keys were fantasies created by the inventive local hustlers. Examples are King Tut's Tomb key, the key to the house where Mary stayed in Egypt, Bastille keys, Newgate Prison keys and Tower of London keys.

References (The following are all published by Key Collectors International): Don Stewart, *Antique Classic Marque Car Keys*, 2nd Edition, 1993; ——, *Paracentric Guide to Key Collecting*, 2nd Edition, 1993; ——, *Standard Guide to Key Collecting*, 3rd Edition, 1990; ——, *Railroad Switch Keys & Padlocks*, 2nd Edition, 1994.

Collectors' Club: Key Collectors International, P.O. Box 9397, Phoenix, AZ 85068.

Museums: Lock Museum of America, Terryville, CT; Mechanics Institute, New York, NY.

Cabinet, barrel type
  Brass
    Decorative bow, 3" 10.00
    Standard bow and bit
      1-1/2" 2.00
      2" 2.00
    Bronze, gold-plated bow, 2" d, Art Deco design 14.00
    Iron, painted, 3", plastic bow, Art Deco design 10.00
    Nickel plated, 2-1/4", lyre design bow 6.00
    Steel, 1-1/2", standard bow and bit 1.00
Casting Plate, bronze
    2-1/2" 17.50
    4" 24.00
Car
    Auburn, logo, Yale Jr. 2.50
    Chrysler Omega keys, brass, 5-pc set, 1934, Yale 15.00
    Dodge, brass, reverse Caskey-Dupree 1.50
    Ford, Model T, diamond mark 2.50
    Nash, logo key, Ilco, #132 .... 6.00
    Packard, logo key, gold plated, 50th anniversary 10.00
    Studebaker, logo key, Eagle Lock Co. 2.00
Door
    Brass, standard bow and bit, 4" 3.50
    Bronze, 4", Keen Kutter bow 7.00
    Steel, 5", standard bow and bit 4.00

Bureau, brass, double-dolphin top, 2-3/4" l, $5.

Folding, jackknife
    Bronze and Steel, bit cuts, 5", no maker's name 15.00
    Steel bit cuts, 5-1/2", maker's name, Ilco, Graham, etc. 7.00
Gate
    Bronze, bit type, 4" 7.50
    Iron, bit type, 8" 10.00
Hotel
    Bit type, bronze, 4", tag silhouette of hotel, white metal 12.00
    Bit type, steel, 3"
      Bronze tag 4.00
        Fiber tag, room number and tag 3.00
        Large tag, oval, silhouette, bronze 10.00
        Standard tag, room number, bronze 4.50
    Bit type, steel, 4", bronze tag 4.00
    Pin Tumbler, plastic or fiber tag 2.00
Jail
    Bronze, bit-type with cuts, 4-1/4", open oval bow, Newell 30.00
    Nickel-Silver, pin tumbler, Yale Mogul, uncut blank 15.00
    Spike Key, 5-1/2", steel-plated bow, serial number, Yale 40.00
Jewelers Key
    Brass, 6 point 20.00
    Steel and brass, 5 point 15.00
Pocket Door
    Bronze, Art Deco, bow folds sideways, triangular box 15.00
    Nickel Plated, bow folds sideways, Art Nouveau, oval bow 15.00
    Steel, T Box, screw 12.00
Presentation Keys
    1-1/2", gold plated, small jewel, city and/or recipient's name 10.00
    6", antique bronze 15.00
    7" l, gold plated, presentation leatherette-type folder 40.00
Railroad
    A&S Abilene & Southern 25.00
    AT&SF Atchison Topeka & Sante Fe 18.00
    C&O Chesapeake & Ohio 15.00
    DT RR Detroit Terminal 20.00
    FRISCO St. Louis-San Francisco 20.00
    IC RR Illinois Central 12.00
    MN RY Milwaukee Northern 45.00
    O&W RR Oregon & Washington 35.00
    TT RR Toledo Terminal Railroad 20.00

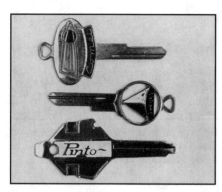

Car, enamel dec, top to bottom: $12, $10, $15.

UP RR Union Pacific	15.00
VGN Virginia	30.00

Ship, bit type

Bronze, ship name on bow	12.00
Iron/steel, bronze tag	3.00
Pin Tumbler Tag, U.S. Army ship tag	9.00

Watch

Brass, 1", advertising type, shield	12.00
Brass and steel, loop bow, folds	5.00
Gold-plated brass, 1"	4.00
Gold plated and silver, cigar cutter accessory	25.00

Kitchen Collectibles

Collecting Hints: Bargains still can be found, especially at flea markets and garage sales. An appliance's design can help determine its age, e.g., an Art Deco toaster or coffeepot was made around 1910 to 1920. The country decorating craze has caused most collectors to concentrate on the 1860 to 1900 period. Kitchen products of the 1900 to 1940s, with their enamel glazes and dependability, are just coming into vogue.

History: The kitchen was a focal point in a family's environment until frozen food, TV dinners and microwaves changed both meal preparation and dining habits. Many early kitchen utensils were handmade and prized by their owners. Next came a period of utilitarian products made of tin and other metals. When the housewife no longer wished to work in a sterile environment, enamel and plastic products added color and their unique design served both aesthetic and functional purposes.

The advent of home electricity changed the type and style of kitchen products. Fads affected many items. High technology already has made inroads into the kitchen and another revolution seems at hand.

References: Michael Breza and Craig R. Olson (eds.), *Identification and Dating of Round Oak Heating Stoves*, Southwestern College Museum (58900 Cherry Grove Rd., Dowagiac, MI 49047), 1995; *Collectors Guide to Wagner Ware and Other Companies*, L-W Book Sales, 1994; Linda Campbell Franklin, *300 Years of Housekeeping Collectibles*, Books Americana, 1992; ——, *300 Years of Kitchen Collectibles*, 3rd Edition, Books Americana, 1991; Ambrogio Fumagalli, *Coffee Makers*, Chronicle Books, 1995; Michael J. Goldberg, *Groovy Kitchen Designs for Collectors*, Schiffer Publishing, 1996; *Griswold Cast Iron*, Vol. 1 (1993), Vol. 2 (1995), L-W Book Sales; *Griswold Manufacturing Co. 1918 Catalog Reprint*, L-W Book Sales, 1996; Sharon Jacobs, *Stringholders Collectors Guide*, L-W Book Sales, 1996; Frances Johnson, *Kitchen Antiques with Values*, Schiffer Publishing, 1996; Jan Lindenberger, *Black Memorabilia for the Kitchen*, Schiffer Publishing, 1992; ——, *The 50s and 60s Kitchen*, Schiffer Publishing, 1994; ——, *Fun Kitchen Collectibles*, Schiffer Publishing, 1996; Kathryn McNerney, *Kitchen Antiques*, Collector Books, 1991, 1993 value update; Jim Moffet, *American Corn Huskers*, Off Beat Books (1345 Poplar Ave., Sunnyvale, CA 94087), 1994; Dana Gehman Morykan and Harry L. Rinker, *Warman's Country Antiques & Collectibles*, 3rd Edition, Wallace-Homestead, 1996; Ellen M. Plante, *Kitchen Collectibles: An Illustrated Price Guide*, Wallace-Homestead, 1991; David G. Smith and Charles Wafford, *Book of Griswold & Wagner*, Schiffer Publishing, 1995; Diane W. Stoneback, *Kitchen Collectibles: The Essential Buyer's Guide*, Wallace-Homestead, 1994; Pat Stott, *Collectors Book of Eggcups*, published by author, 1993; Don Thornton, *Beat This: The Eggbeater Chronicles*, Off Beat Books (1345 Poplar Ave., Sunnyvale, CA 94087), 1994; Jean Williams Turner, *Collectible Aunt Jemima*, Schiffer Publishing, 1994; April M. Tvorak, *History and Price Guide to Mothers-in-the-Kitchen*, published by author, 1994; *Wagner Ware and Other Companies*, L-W Book Sales, 1995.

Periodicals: *Cast Iron Cookware News*, 28 Angela Ave., San Anselmo, CA 94960; *Griswold Cast Iron Collectors' News & Marketplace*, P.O. Box 521, North East, PA 16428; *Kettles 'n Cookware*, P.O. Box B, Perrysville, NY 14129; *Kitchen Antiques & Collectibles News*, 4645 Laurel Ridge Dr., Harrisburg, PA 17110.

Collectors' Clubs: Association of Coffee Mill Enthusiasts, 5941 Wilkerson Rd., Rex, GA 30273; Cookie Cutter Collectors Club, 1167 Teal Rd., SW, Dellroy, OH 44620; Corn Items Collectors Association, Inc., 613 N. Long St., Shelbyville, IL 62565; Eggcup Collectors' Corner, 67 Stevens Ave., Old Bridge, NJ 08857; Griswold & Cast Iron Cookware Association, 54 Macon Ave., Asheville, NC 28801; International Society for Apple Parer Enthusiasts, 3911 Morgan Center Rd., Utica, OH 43080; Jelly Jammers Club, 110 White Oak Dr., Butler, PA 16001.

Museums and Libraries: Culinary Archives and Museum, Johnson & Wales University, Providence, RI; Culinary Institute of America; H.B. Meek Library, Cornell University; Judith Basin Museum, Stanford, MT; Kern County Museum, Bakersfield, CA; Mandeville Library, University of CA, San Diego, CA; Schlesinger Library, Radcliff College; Strong Museum, Rochester, NY; Wilbur Chocolate Co., Lititz, PA.

Additional Listings: Advertising, Cookbooks, Kitchen Glassware, Reamers.

Apple Corer, White Mountain, orig box	30.00
Apple Peeler, Turntable No. 98	85.00
Basket, 4-1/2" d, 5-1/2" h, wire, folding, tulip form	45.00
Basting Spoon, granite, cobalt blue handle	15.00

Biscuit Cutter, 1-12" d, tin, bail 10.00
Bowl
Treasure Craft, green, large, fruit-edged handles...........................10.00
Walnut, 10" w, 11" l, 3" h..........65.00
Box, Campfire Marshmallows,
1-1/2" x 3-1/2" x 6-3/4", red, white and blue lid, Campfire Co., Milwaukee, c1920, lid with Boy Scouts toasting marshmallows over campfire, other panel with housewife frosting cake with marshmallow topping, recipes on side panel, offer for Campfire Recipe Book.............60.00
Breadboard, 12" d,
7-1/2" l, pine handle.................90.00
Bread Box, tin, 12" l,
white, red top 20.00
Breadstick Pan, nickeled cast iron,
Wagner Ware 35.00
Bundt Pan, iron, scalloped,
4-1/2" x 10-1/2" 45.00
Butter Churn, Dazy, No. 40,
wood paddles 125.00
Butter Fork, 7" x 2-1/2",
hand-carved maple.................25.00
Butter Mold, 1-3/4" x 3-1/2", turned maple, carved floral design......45.00
Butter Paddle, 10" x 5", hand-carved maple.......................................75.00
Butter Hook, 7/8", Miller's Coca, multicolored celluloid oval, meal hook, c1896 ....40.00
Cake Pan, tin
8" d, Swans Down Cake Flour .15.00
12", black, wire loop
handle, Fries 12.00
Can Opener
Cast Iron, fish figure, c1865 ...140.00
Metal, red wood handle............15.00
Catalog
A.J. Lindemann & Hoverson, Milwaukee, WI, c1932, 34 pgs, 8" x 11", electric kitchen ranges, combination range with built-in heater, hot plates, etc................................21.00
New England Grocer, Boston, MA,

Cake pan, tin, lever to loosen cake, 8-7/8" d at top, $10.

1897, 68 pgs, 10-1/2" x 15", Vol XL, No. 24, Trade Journal, published every Friday by retail grocers, industry articles, products, prices, ads, minor wear 26.00
Shields & Brothery Co., Philadelphia, PA, c1901, 10, pgs, 3-1/4" x 6", "Never Break" wrought-steel hollow ware, kettles, steel cake griddles, illus, minor wear 15.00
Union Manufacturing Co., Toledo, OH, 1876, 24 pgs, 4-3/4" x 7-1/2, illus of product line, washboards, churns, clothes racks, food graters, etc. 145.00
Weir Stove Co., Taunton, MA, 8 pgs, 5-3/4" x 9-1/4", modern ranges 15.00
Cheese Grater, hanging, white china, gold trim, enameled blue forget-me-not dec 70.00
Cheese Slicer, enameled wood handle, mkd "Unsco-Germany" 10.00
Cherry Seeder, Dandy 50A, damaged orig box....................................12.50
Chopping Knife, 61/2" l, Henry Disston & Sons, curved steel blade, wood handle.....................................20.00
Cleanser, Guardian Service, unopened, black and silver Art Deco design.......................35.00
Clothes Sprinkler, ceramic, figural Chinese Man,
Shawnee Pottery....................110.00
Elephant...................................75.00
Coffee Grinder
Lap type, drawer with porcelain knob, crank handle, brass cup, sgd "D.D. Post, Lahaska, PA, Maker" 225.00
Table-top type, Enterprise Model 10, clamp-on, orig stenciling 65.00
Wall, Arcade, crystal 65.00
Cornbread Pan,
cast iron, Griswold...................45.00
Corn-Stick Pan, Junior Krusty Korn Kobs, italic "Wagner Ware" trademark 85.00
Dipper, 7" l, copper, tin lined, forged-brass handle, imp "MM" on side 75.00
Dish Pan, enamel, gray.................15.00
Dough Bowl, 12-1/2" d, wood........45.00
Dust Pan and Broom, Kitchen Prayer Lady.......................................265.00
Dutch Oven,
cov, cast iron, unmkd 25.00
Eggcup
Baby Bird 45.00
Bonzo, figural,
Germany, 1920s 125.00
Charlie McCarthy, lusterware, Canadian, 1930s......................60.00
Pluto, 1930s 125.00

Rolling pins; top: turned handle, incised design, 18", $20; bottom: turned handle, 18-1/2", $18.

Popeye, 1930s,
multicolored 110.00
Egg Timer
Chef 50.00
Girl on phone 50.00
Winking Chef, timer on back..195.00
Egg Whip, spring type, enameled wood handle...........................10.00
Fan, Ward's Bread, 7" x 7" diecut cardboard, 4-1/2" l wood handle, full-color fairy tale flour mill scene, inspirational verse and name of Ward Bread, reverse with 2 elf-like youngsters advertising "Dainty Maid" and "Tip-Top" bread, 1930s 50.00
Flour Sifter, Bromweld's, side crank, red wood knob 15.00
Folder
2-1/2" x 3", opens to 2-1/2" x 8-3/4", Jell-O recipes, full color strawberry Jell-O dessert, 1920s...............20.00
3-1/2" x 6", opens to 7" x 12" sheet, full color, Jell-O, America's Most Famous Dessert/Of What and How Made, 1920s 20.00
Food Chopper, Universal 8.00
Food Mill, Foley, 2 pcs 20.00
Fruit Press, Griswold, #2...............65.00
Funnel, Elliptical,
gray graniteware 30.00
Jelly Mold, 3-1/2" d, 3-1/2" h, tin, Madeline, stamped "Of 539"....25.00
Lemon Squeezer
6-1/2" l, tin-plated iron..............20.00
11" l, hinged maple 65.00
Meat Grinder, Sargent & Co., Patent March 8, 1892 ....40.00
Meat Tenderizer, 2" x 2-1/2" x 3", rect, iron, heavy handle 40.00
Meat Thermometer, 6" l, hanging, Taylor 10.00
Mixing Spoon, wood handle, slotted bowl, Androck, Made in USA ..18.00
Napkin Holder, figural, lady, ceramic, Kreiss 60.00
Oven Broom, 10-1/2" l, birch, splint, hewn handle, New York State, c1830 ....45.00
Oyster Ladle, tin...........................30.00
Pantry Box, 6-1/2" x 12-1/2" d, red paint, 4 overlapping fingers.............365.00

Patty Mold,
    Griswold, 1937, orig box..........40.00
Pea Sheller, 12" h, screw clamp, black
    wood handle, Vaughns............40.00
Pie Bird
    Blue and gray, long neck..........90.00
    Yellow and brown, long neck ...90.00
Pitcher, 8" h, pink and yellow, mkd
    "Royal Copley".........................35.00
Popover Pan, Griswold, mkd "Erie PA,
    USA 6141, No. 18" 55.00
Potato Masher, 9" h, zigzag wire end,
    red catalin handle 10.00
Rolling Pin
    Stainless steel...........................9.00
    Wooden, 17" l, red handles......35.00
Salt and Pepper shakers, pr, Kitchen
    Prayer Lady, pink......................8.00
Salt Box, 8" x 17-1/2", rect, pine,
    hinged lid 120.00
Sifter, 3 screens, colorful litho tin ..20.00
Skillet, cast iron
    Griswold No. 3..........................35.00
    Wagner Ware No. 3, italic trademark
    "Wagner Ware, Sidney-O"........15.00
Strainer, wire-mesh bowl, twisted wire
    and wood handle 10.00
String Holder,
    Prayer Lady, pink...................375.00
Tea Caddy, 8-1/2" h, tin, painted, red
    fruit, yellow leaves, orig cap ..265.00
Tea Kettle, copper, gooseneck,
    dovetailed, sgd "JMWE"
    and hallmark.........................175.00
Tin, rect, Krispy Crackers 35.00
Tomato Slicer, enameled wood handle,
    orig litho sleeve.......................18.00
Toothpick Holder, Kitchen Prayer Lady,
    white 15.00
Vegetable Basket, 7" d, 5" h, wire,
    tapered, bale handle, 1870......55.00
Waffle Iron
    Griswold #8 ....50.00
    Wagner, 3" d 65.00
Wall Pocket, bonnet, red

Tea strainer and base, porcelain, mkd "Germany," 4" h, $125.

"Royal Copley" mark................15.00
Whisk, 10" l, snow-shoe shape,
    twisted-wire handle.................15.00

Kitchen Glassware

Collecting Hints: Glassware for the kitchen was made in quantity. Although collectors tolerate signs of use, they will not accept pieces with heavy damage. Many of the products contain applied decals; these should be in good condition. A collection can be built inexpensively by concentrating on one form, such as canister sets, measuring cups or reamers.

History: The Depression era brought inexpensive kitchen and table products to center stage. The companies in the forefront of production included Hocking, Hazel Atlas, McKee, U.S. Glass and Westmoreland.

Kitchen glassware complemented Depression glass. Many items were produced in the same color and style. Because the glass was molded, added decorative elements included ribs, fluting, arches and thumbprint patterns. To be durable, the glassware had to be thick. This resulted in forms which were difficult to handle at times and often awkward aesthetically. After World War II, aluminum products began to replace kitchen glassware.

References: Gene Florence, *Kitchen Glassware of the Depression Years*, 5th Edition, Collector Books, 1995; Garry Kilgo and Dale, Jerry and Gail Wilkins, *Collectors Guide to Anchor Hocking's Fire-King Glassware*, K&W Collectibles Publisher, 1991; Susan Tobier Rogove and Marcia Buan Steinhauer, *Pyrex by Corning*, The Glass Press, 1993; Diane W. Stoneback, *Kitchen Collectibles: The Essential Buyer's Guide*, Wallace-Homestead, 1994; April M. Tvorak, *Fire-King '95*, published by author, 1995; ——, *Fire-King II*, published by author, 1993; ——, *History And Price Guide to Fire-King*, VAL Enterprises, 1992; ——, *Pyrex Price Guide*, published by author, 1992.

Periodical: *Kitchen Antiques & Collectibles News*, 4645 Laurel Ridge Dr., Harrisburg, PA 17110.

Collectors' Club: Glass Knife Collectors Club, P.O. Box 342, Los Alamitos, CA 90720.

Batter Bowl
    Anchor Hocking, set of 7",
    8", 9" and 10" d, rimmed,
    transparent green 95.00
    Tufglass, 2 handles, 2 spouts ..45.00
Batter Pitcher, 2 cup
    Milk Glass, Federal 15.00
    Pink, U.S. Glass......................55.00
Beer Mug, yellow 40.00
Bowl
    5-1/2" d, red, Platonite,
    Criss Cross 12.50
    6" d, jadeite, Jeannette 16.00
    7-1/2" d, cobalt blue,
    Hazel Atlas..............................45.00
    8" d, green, Hocking 15.00
    8-1/2" l, oval, Pyrex, beige, 2 handles, blue dec, 1-1/2" qt 15.00
    10" d, Emerald Glo...................50.00
Butter Box, cov,
    2-lb size, green......................145.00
Butter Dish, cov, 1-lb size
    Criss Cross
      Cobalt Blue 120.00
      Crystal 20.00
    Hocking, crystal 25.00
    Jadeite 95.00
Canister
    3" h, jadeite, Jeannette
      Allspice 65.00
      Ginger.................................65.00
      Nutmeg...............................65.00
      Pepper................................65.00
    5-1/2" h, sq, coffee, jadeite,
    Jeannette.................................55.00
    6" h, green, screw-on lid,
    smooth 38.00
    20 oz, tea, screw-on lid,
    Vitrock.....................................27.00
Casserole, cov, white, Pyrex.........25.00
Coffeepot, 4 cup, Pyrex 15.00
Cruet, stopper, Crystolite, amber ..30.00
Curtain Tiebacks, pr
    2-1/2" d, knob type, pink 35.00
    3-1/2" d, flat, floral,
    green and pink 20.00
    4-1/2" d, flat, floral, amber........25.00
Custard, green, Tufglass................6.00
Drawer Pull, crystal
    Double type.............................10.00
    Knob 3.00
Drippings Jar, cov, jadeite,
    Jeannette 32.00
Eggcup, double, black...................12.00
Fork and Spoon, amber handle 45.00
Funnel, green...............................35.00
Furniture Caster, 3" d, transparent
    green, Hazel-Atlas...................40.00
Grease Jar, Tulips,

cov, Hocking 15.00
Hand Beater, 32-oz measuring-cup base
    Green 45.00
    Green, stippled texture.............45.00
Iced Tea Spoons, colored handles,
    set of 12 ....60.00
Knife
    Block, 8-1/4" l
        Crystal, orig box 28.00
        Green.....................................45.00
    Plain, 9-1/8" l, green................40.00
    3 Leaf
        Crystal..................................15.00
        Green.....................................35.00
    3 Star
        Blue.......................................38.00
        Crystal, orig box 38.00
        Pink 25.00
Lemon Reamer
    Delphite, Jeannette 80.00
    Jadeite, Jeannette 35.00
    Pink, Hazel-Atlas 35.00
Loaf Pan, cov, 5" x 8", Glassbake, clear,
    knob finial 35.00
Mayonnaise Ladle
    Amber, flat.................................9.75
    Pink, transparent 20.00
Measuring Cup
    2 oz, 1/4 cup,
        jadeite, Jeannette 40.00
    8 oz
        Fire-King, 1 spout................18.00
        Green, transparent..............18.00
    16 oz
        Cobalt Blue, Hazel-Atlas 175.00
        Fired-on Green.....................20.00
        Green, stick handle,
        U.S. Glass.............................28.00
        Milk glass, white...................22.00
Mixing Bowl
    5-3/4" d, yellow
        banded dot, Pyrex.....................8.00
    6-1/2" d
        Amber, Federal 10.00
        Cobalt Blue, Hazel-Atlas 35.00
        Green, Restwell 10.00
    7-1/4" d, yellow
        banded dot, Pyrex 10.00
    7-1/2" d, cobalt blue,
        Hazel-Atlas.............................42.00
    8-1/2" d, cobalt blue,
        Hazel-Atlas.............................50.00
    9-1/2" d, amber, Federal 18.00
    11" d, Vitrock, white 15.00
    Nested Set, white, ivy dec,
        Hazel Atlas 50.00
Mug, Ranger Joe, Hazel Atlas
    Blue 9.50
    Red..9.50
Pitcher, jadeite,
    sunflower in base....................40.00

Range Shaker, sq, flour, jadeite,
    Jeannette..................................30.00
Refrigerator Dish, cov
    4" x 8", floral carved, transparent
        green, U.S. Glass....................30.00
    4-1/2" x 4-1/2" sq
        Jadeite, Jeannette 15.00
        Pink, Jennyware 35.00
    6" x 3", transparent green,
        Tufglass 45.00
    6-1/2" sq, Poppy Cocklebur, trans-
        parent green, U.S. Glass 55.00
    8" x 8", sq, amber, Federal 25.00
    8-1/2" x 4-1/2",
        jadeite, Jeannette.....................32.00
    32 oz, round, jadeite,
        Jeannette 35.00
Relish, 8-1/2" x 13" oval, delphite,
    divided, Pyrex...........................20.00
Rolling Pin, clambroth,
    metal handles 125.00
Salad Fork and Spoon, blue..........55.00
Salt and Pepper Shakers, pr
    Cobalt Blue, red lids,
        Hazel-Atlas.............................30.00
    Ribbed, jadeite, Jeannette 22.00
    Roman Arches, black, minor
        damage to lids.........................45.00
Salt Box, 4" x 5-1/2" d, round, yellow,
    no writing on lid 100.00
Spoon, clear, Higbee....................25.00
Straw Holder,
    crystal, lid missing 100.00
Sugar, cov, Criss Cross, transparent
    green, Hazel-Atlas 35.00
Sugar Shaker
    Green 145.00
    Jadeite 175.00
Syrup Pitcher
    Crystal, gold catalin handle......12.00
    Crystal, flower etch 35.00
    Green, Hazel-Atlas..................45.00
Towel Bar, 24" l,
    crystal, orig hardware 15.00
Tumbler, Hazel Atlas, white
    3-1/2" h, 9 oz...........................5.00
    4-1/2" h, 16 oz..........................7.00
Vase, bud, jadeite, Jeannette........14.00
Water Bottle, clear,
    glass lid, Hocking 24.00
Water Dispenser, 17" h, black base,
    crystal bowl, silver trim 95.00

Edwin M. Knowles China

Collecting Hints: Do not confuse Edwin M. Knowles China Co., with Knowles, Taylor and Knowles, also a manufacturer of fine dinnerware. They are two separate companies.

The only Edwin M. Knowles China Co., mark that might be confusing is "Knowles" spelled with a large "K."

Deanna: Introduced in 1938. This shape was available in pastel shades and in bright solid colors or designs using stripes, plains or decal decoration on white ground. Solid colors included green, light and dark blue, orange-red, bright and pastel yellow, turquoise, peach, burgundy, russet and pink.

Butter Dish, open, dark blue 15.00
Coffeepot, cov,
    red and blue stripes.................42.00
Creamer and Sugar,
    cov, light blue 25.00
Plate, 10" d, dinner, dark blue.......12.00
Platter, 12" d, green 17.50
Vegetable Bowl,
    8" d, orange-red 20.00

Esquire Dinnerware: Line designed by Russel Wright. Made from 1956 until 1962. It was available in five colors and six designs. Each pattern was produced on a single colored ground: Botanica on beige, Grass on blue, Queen Anne's Lace on white, Seeds on yellow, Snowflower on pink and Solar on white.

Cereal Bowl, 6-1/4" d,
    Queen Anne's Lace.................10.00
Cup and Saucer, Grass 15.00
Fruit Bowl, 5-1/2" d,
    Snowflower..............................10.00
Plate
    6-1/4" d, bread and butter,
        Botanica...................................7.50
    10-3/4" d, dinner, Seeds 15.00
Platter, 16" l, oval, Solar...............35.00
Teapot, Botanica...........................95.00
Vegetable Bowl, divided, Grass 60.00

Yorktown Dinnerware: Line introduced in 1936. Original four colors were burgundy, cadet blue, russet and yellow. Later produced in Chinese red, green, orange-red and pink. Also available with decal decoration on white ground.

Cereal Bowl, 6" d, russet.................7.50
Casserole, cadet blue 35.00
Chop Plate, 10-3/4" d, yellow........18.00
Cup and Saucer, orange-red 120.00
Gravy Boat, pink 20.00
Plate
    6" d, bread and butter,
        cadet blue 6.00
    10" d, dinner, Chinese red 15.00
Platter, 12" d, russet.....................22.00
Teapot, green...............................50.00

L

Labels

Collecting Hints: Damaged, trimmed or torn labels are less valuable than labels in mint condition. Collectors prefer labels that can be removed from the product and stored flat in drawers or albums.

History: The first fruit-crate art was created by California fruit growers about 1880. The labels became very colorful and covered many subjects. Most depict the type of fruit held in the box. Cardboard boxes replaced fruit crates in the 1940s, making the labels collectible. Over the last decade, label collectors have begun to widen their collecting range. Today, can, luggage and wine labels are sought as well as cigar, fruit crate and other household-type labels.

References: Joe Davidson, *Fruit Crate Art*, Wellfleet Press, 1990; Lynn Johnson and Michael O'Leary, *En Route: Label Art from the Golden Age of Air Travel*, Chronicle Books, 1993; Norman E. Martinus and Harry L. Rinker, *Warman's Paper*, Wallace-Homestead, 1994; Gorden T. McClelland and Jay T. Last, *Fruit Box Labels*, Hillcrest Press (3412-G MacArthur Blvd., Santa Ana, CA 92704), 1995.

Collectors' Clubs: Citrus Label Society, 131 Miramonte Dr., Fullerton, CA 92365; Florida Citrus Labels Collectors Association, P.O. Box 547636, Orlando, FL 32854; International Seal, Label & Cigar Band Society, 8915 E. Bellevue St., Tucson, AZ 85715; Society of Antique Label Collectors, P.O. Box 24811, Tampa FL 33623.

Advisor: Lorie Cairns.

Fruit Crate

Apple
  Blue Larkspur, racehorse with blue winner's wreath around neck 5.00
  Duckwall, wood duck by stone wall 10.00
  Hula, topless hula girl sitting beneath palm tree 4.00
  Jackie Boy, boy in sailor suit holding apple 6.00
  Morjon, yellow apple, blue triangle, Oriental writing 1.00

Grape, Emblem, Almeria grapes, Rocky Hill, Inc., Exeter, CA, orange poppies, blue ground, 25 cents.

  Paradise, bird of paradise 6.00
  State Seal, George Washington portrait 50
  Triton, Neptune holding trident, apple and pear, dehydrated apples, 6-1/4" x 10" 1.00
  Wilko, red apple, red border.......1.00
Apricot
  Brentwood Aces, 3 apricots on branch 25
  Silver Spruce, pine tree, snowy mountain 50
Artichoke, Glamour Girl, Donna Reed look-alike, 6-3/4" x 10-3/4" 1.00
Asparagus
  Air King, jet plane......................2.00
  Caligras, men harvesting asparagus, horse-drawn wagon 2.00
  Mo-Chief, large bundle of asparagus, scenic, Fresno, CA......................1.00
  Pride of the River, paddle-wheel boat, bunch of asparagus 4.00
Avocado, Keystone, red keystone.....25
Cantaloupe, Ekco, boy shouting at red mountains, 4" x 9-1/2" 75
Celery
  Ligo, large bunch of celery, 5" x 7" 50
  Moon Lake, moon rising over palm-tree-lined lake 75
Cherries
  Beaver, beaver at edge of water...50
  G. Saporito, maroon cherries........15
Citrus
  Better'n Ever, half sliced grapefruit, Texas 50
  Cordial, whole grapefruit and half orange, orange juice in glass, leaves, blossoms, 9" x 9", Florida 2.00
  Dixie Boy, black child eating half grapefruit, 9" sq, Florida............3.00
  Golden Hill, packing house, old truck, 9" sq 1.00
  Mountain's Pride, 3 different citrus leaves, blossoms, Florida 50
  Orkideer, 2 men in dugout filled with oranges, deer on shore, 9" sq, Florida 3.00
  Wren, bird on flowered branch, swamp scene, 9" sq...................4.00
Corn

Hi Up, large ear of corn, 7-1/2" x 4-1/2" 75
  Topit, large ear of corn, 7-1/2" x 4-1/2" 75
Grapes
  Angelina, woman with brunette hair, green and red scarf, holding basket of yellow and black grapes, 13" x 5-1/2" 50
  Carousel, girl on carousel pony . 1.00
  Fremont, silhouette of soldier, "Fremont" in orange circle............25
  La Campana, ranch scene, red-tile-roofed house, snow mountains, palm trees 1.00
  Luscious, bunch of green grapes.................................25
  Mission Vineyards, monk looking over vineyard near mission 4.00
  Race Track, rack track scene with horses and cars, tokay in center of horseshoe 75
  Sure Winner, hearts royal flush poker hand..25
  Wow, bug-eyed cartoon bear cub swinging from tree branch 1.00
  Kiwi, Rose, cerise rose, 1-3/4" x 10" 25
Lemon
  Anacapa, gull flying over ocean and islands, Saticoy 3.00
  Bridal Veil, Bridal Veil Falls, Yosemite Park, lemon, Santa Paula 6.00
  Estero, estuary scene, clipper ships near sheer rocky coastline, palm trees, Goleta 2.00
  Evening Star, star shining over Spanish mission, palm trees, groves, mountain, city lights, San Fernando 2.00
  Galleon, galleon sailing on high seas, sky, c1937, Oxnard...................6.00
  Kaweah Maid, Indian girl in turquoise beads, Lemon Cove..................5.00
  Morning Sun, Spanish mission, palm trees, groves, sunrise over mountain, San Fernando 2.00
  Sea Bird, large white flying seagull, Carpinteria 4.00
  Vesper, people going to church in evening, Porterville 1.00
Melon
  Cal Heart, map of CA, arrow pointing to Turlock 2.00
  Foothigh, sexy girl, 9" x 4" 1.00
  Hillview, farm scene, 4-1/4" x 9-3/4" 75
  Levon, snarling green-eyed lion, 9" x 11-1/4", Los Banos, Blythe, CA..................................3.00
  Vaughn's Melons, map of CA, yellow sun 75
Nectarine, Camera, pictures nectarines

Lemons, All Year, Ventura County Lemons, Fillmore Lemon Association, desert scene, blue border, $2.

and cherries 50
Orange
  Ak-Sar-Ben, oranges, bright colors, Lemon Cove 1.00
  Blue Goose, blue goose, Los Angeles 2.00
  Carro Amano Aranci, Italian fruit peddler with cart full of oranges, woman customer, E. Highlands 2.00
  Collegiate, 1/2 sliced grapefruit on plate, spoon, inset of male golfer and female tennis player, Claremont 3.00
  Eat One, blue arrow pointing to large orange, Lindsay..........................4.00
  Full O'Juice, partially peeled orange, glass of juice, Redlands 2.00
  Goodyear, large orange, blossoms, Rayo...1.00
  Kaweah River Belle, country scene, Spanish mission, snow-capped mountain peaks, bunch of oranges, Lemon Cove..............................5.00
  Loch Lomond, Scottish scene, Loch Lomond, houses, heather, Strathmore...2.00
  Memory, silhouette of girl in picture frame, pink roses in glass bud vase, Porterville 8.00
  Polo, polo player and bay pony, E. Highlands..............................5.00
  Stalwart, large polar bear, Northern Lights, Santa Paula 35.00
  Star of California, red star with Exeter on map of CA 1.00
  Valley View, red-tile-roofed house, orchards, snowy mountains, Claremont...................................2.00
  Yokohl, Indian fishing in stream, Exeter 4.00
Peach
  Federal, Uncle Sam hat 75
  Silver Spruce, pine tree, snowy mountain 50
  Vincennes, 2 peaches, soft colors, Indiana 35
Pear

Blue Parrot, large parrot on flowering branch 1.50
Covered Wagon, pioneers in covered wagons, team of oxen 3.00
El Rio Orchards, 2 yellow pears....50
Golden Bosc, yellow train 2.00
Mad River, rushing mountain stream, green pear...............................1.00
Quail, California quail walking through grass 5.00
Top Card, ace of spades............1.00
Violet, large punch of purple violets.........................4.00
Peas, Elkhorn, elk's head, peas in pods, 7" x 4-1/2"..............................50
Persimmon, Oh Yes, We Grow the Best, 2 large persimmons 25
Plum
  Saunders Boys, fisherman, hunter, flying geese.................................2.00
  Valley Home, purple plums on aqua ground, 7" x 9" 1.00
Sweet Potato, White House, large white-columned house, 4-1/2" x 7" 50
Tomato
  Ekco, boy, red mountains, tomatoes 1.00
  Green Feather, large green feather........................25
  Ivanhoe, tomatoes, green leaves, yellow tag 25
  Le Grande, harvest scene, farmer with basket 50
  White House, large white-columned house, 5" x 13" 50
Yam, White House, large white-columned house, 4-1/2" x 7" 50

Miscellaneous

Ammonia, Violet, 15 purple flowers on white ground, 3-1/2" sq, York, PA 75
Broom
  Auto No. 6, speeding race car 50
  Winner, woman holding torch 50
Egg Crate, Sleepy Eye, portrait of Chief Sleepy Eye, 9-1/4" x 11"............2.00
Hair Tonic, Crown, oval, florals, gilt, Art

Pears, Repetition, 3 identical boys in knitted caps and striped shirts standing behind crates of pears, 10-3/4" x 7-1/4", $2.

Nouveau, 3-1/4" x 2-1/4" 50
Toilet Water, San Remo, Art Nouveau designs, roses, arch shape, 3-3/4" x 1-1/2"...............................50
Tooth Wash, Imperial, oval, florals, gilt, Art Nouveau..........................50

Tin Can

Apple Butter
  Mt. Vernon, white mansion, 7 lb, 6-1/2" x 8-1/2", Virginia 1.00
  Premier, apple, slices of bread, gilt emb, New York 1.00
Applesauce, Orchard Fresh, whole and half apples, Indiana 75
Baking Powder
  Capitol, capitol dome and building, 2 lb, Charleston, WV 1.00
  Popover, plate of biscuits, 10 oz 1.00
Beets, Peter Piper, Peter Piper with basket of produce, Rhode Island 3.00
Black-Eyed Peas, Old Black Joe, elderly black man, cabin 1.00
Blueberry, Gaddis, blueberries in cut glass bowl, 6-1/2" x 10" 2.00
Evaporated Milk
  Bess, tan cow's head, Ohio 2.00
  Clover Farm, cow and clover blossom, 2-1/4" x 8", Ohio 1.50
Finnan Haddie, Alfred Jones Sons, ocean, ships, lighthouse, 3" d, Maine 50
Grape Juice, Jo Sole, "So soul tasty, " black boy, 13-1/2" x 6-1/2", 1969...............2.00
Jam, Bendigo, 4 small colorful cornucopias, Art Deco, Australia............4.00
Lima Beans
  Dubon, 2 bowls of beans, New Orleans, LA...................................50
  Preston, beans and pods, leaves, Maryland 1.00
Olives, La Perla, old-fashioned boy, California 25
Peas, Squaw, Indian mother and papoose 2.00
Prunes, Kingwood Orchards, bowl of prunes, fresh plums on branch, 5-1/2" x 10"................................2.00
Pumpkin, Cloth of Gold, red bird.....2.00
Raspberries, Kingwood Orchards, berry clusters and bowl of berries, Salem, OR...................................2.00
Sauerkraut, Norwish, 2 heads of cabbage, 1920s, Norwich, NY 1.50
Succotash, Butterfly, butterfly, bowl of beans, 2 ears of corn 1.00
Syrup, Crossroads, old cabin, man making syrup in big kettle, Georgia 2.00
Whole Wax Beans, Arcadia Beauty, 2 bunches of yellow beans, leaves, gilt, emb, Newark, NY 5.00

Lamps

Collecting Hints: Be aware that every lamp has two values—a collectible value and a decorative value. Often the decorative value exceeds the collectible value, in part because most lamps are purchased as decorative accessories, often as accent pieces in a period room setting.

In the 1980s, the hot lamp collectibles were the odd-shaped examples from the 1950s. Some of these were abstract; some were figural. This craze is documented in Leland & Crystal Payton's *Turned On: Decorative Lamps of the 'Fifties*. While 1950s lamps continue to sell well as part of the 1950s/1960s revival, prices have stabilized primarily because of the market saturation resulting from the large quantity of lamps of this era that survived in attics and basements.

Lamp collectors specialize. In the 1970s and 1980s, Aladdin was the magic name, due in large part to the promotional efforts of J.W. Courter. One man can make a market. Within the past five years, collector interest is spreading to other manufacturers and into electric lamps. One of biggest drawbacks is the lack of a definitive lamp-collecting manual and price guide that shows the full range of the lamp market. Far too many of the lamp books are nothing more than catalog reprints.

Just as post-World War II collectors discovered figural transistor and character radios, so also are they discovering motion lamps, many of which are character related. Look for a growing interest in character lamps and a corresponding rise in prices.

The 1990s marks a major transitional period in lamp collecting. The kerosene lamp which dominated lamp collecting through virtually the entire 20th century is slowly being upstaged by the electric lamp. By the 21st century, the electric, not the kerosene lamp, will dominate.

History: The kerosene lamp was the predominant lighting device during the 19th century and the first quarter of the 20th century. However, its death knell was sounded in 1879 when Thomas A. Edison developed a viable electric light bulb. The success of the electric lamp depended on the availability of electricity. However, what we take for granted today did not arrive in many rural areas until the 1930s.

Most electric lamps were designed to serve as silent compliments to period design styles. They were meant to blend, rather than stand out. Pairs were quite common. Famous industrial designers did lend their talents to lamp design and their products are eagerly sought by collectors. Bradley and Hubbard and Handel are two companies whose products have attracted strong collector interest.

References: *Better Electric Lamps of the 20's and 30's*, L-W Book Sales, 1996; J.W. Courter, *Aladdin Collectors Manual & Price Guide #15, Kerosene Mantle Lamps*, published by author (note: all the Courter books are available from the author, 3935 Kelley Rd., Kevil, KY 42053), 1994; ——, *Aladdin Electric Lamps Price Guide #2*, published by author, 1993; ——, *Angle Lamps: Collectors Manual & Price Guide*, published by author, 1992; *Electric Lighting of the 20s & 30s*, *Vol. 1* (1988, 1994 value update), *Vol. 2* (1994), L-W Book Sales; Nadja Maril, *American Lighting*, Schiffer Publishing, 1995; Richard C. Miller and John F. Solverson, *Student Lamps of the Victorian Era*, The Glass Press, 1992, 1992-93 Value Guide; Bill and Linda Montgomery, *Animation Motion Lamps*, L-W Book Sales, 1991; Leland and Crystal Payton, *Turned On: Decorative Lamps of the Fifties*, Abbeville Press, 1989; *Quality Electric Lamps*, L-W Book Sales, 1992, 1996 value update; Bob and Pat Ruf, *Fairy Lamps with Values*, Schiffer Publishing, 1996.

Collectors' Clubs: Aladdin Knights of the Mystic Light, 3935 Kelley Rd., Kevil, KY 42053; Coleman Collector Network, 1822 E. Fernwood, Wichita, KS 67216; Historical Lighting Society of Canada, 9013 Oxbox Rd., North East, PA 16428.

Boudoir, custard glass shade, metal base, beige with multi-floral dec, 16" h, price for pr, $165.

Aladdin, Alacite, electric

#25	45.00
#185	45.00
#185A	25.00
#236	55.00
#266	50.00
#328, glass base	37.50
#351, round wall	65.00
#354, rect wall	65.00
#411, price for pr	75.00

Bedroom, Southern Belle, blue, orig shade ... 80.00

Character

Davy Crockett, 16" h, Davy, tree and bear, ceramic base, Davy, Indians and fort on shade, 1950s ... 190.00

Fred Flintstone, 13-1/4" h, painted vinyl, black metal base, missing shade ... 45.00

Mickey Mouse, 4" d, 6-1/2" h, globular metal base, beige ground, 3 Mickey decals around sides, Soreng-Manegold Co ... 85.00

Children's

ABC Blocks, wood and plastic, linen-over-cardboard shade ... 20.00

Cookie Monster, figural, Sesame Street characters on shade ... 45.00

Elephant, figural, ceramic, carousel beaded shade ... 195.00

Football Player, 14-1/2" h, hollow plaster, football player standing next to figural football standard, linen over cardboard shade, WK, Japan, Sears, Roebuck, 1978 ... 25.00

Headboard, pink, chrome ... 65.00

Lava, Lava

Simplex Corp., c1968 ... 80.00

Motion

Antique Cars, Econolite, 1957, 11" h ... 110.00

Cheers Bar, sexy girls, MIB....125.00

Fireside Peanut Vendor, dancing
devil graphics, 1930s 400.00

Forest Fire, Econolite, 1955.....85.00

Fountain of Youth....................118.00

Goldfish,
green satin glass, 1931 ....325.00

Niagara Falls, Goodman, extra-wide
style...140.00

Snow Scene,
bridge, Econolite 165.00

Organ Grinder, monkey, pink 95.00

Radio, Michael Lumitone.............200.00

Stenographer's, Emeralite, clamps onto
desk...395.00

Television

Gondola, ceramic, brown with gold
trim, mkd "Premco Mfg. Co., Chicago, IL, 1954," 16" w, 7" h..........45.00

Horse's Head, ceramic,
12" x 10-3/4".............................25.00

Panther, black,
8-1/2" x 6-1/2" 35.00

Ship, 11" x 10-1/2", gold trim....30.00

Limited Edition Collectibles

Collecting Hints: The first item issued in a series usually commands a
higher price. When buying a limited
edition collectible, be aware that the
original box and/or certificates increase the value of the piece. Be
alert to special discounts and sales.

History: Limited edition plate collecting began with the advent of Christmas plates issued by Bing and
Grondahl in 1895. Royal Copenhagen soon followed. During the late
1960s and early 1970s, several potteries, glass factories and mints began to issue plates, bells, eggs,

**Edwin M. Knowles, plate, Gone with the
Wind series, 1978, Scarlett, Raymond
Kurshar, artist, $300.**

mugs, etc., which commemorated
special events, people, places or holidays. For a period of time, these
items increased in popularity and value. In the late 1970s, however, the
market became flooded with many
collectibles and prices declined.

There are many new issues of
collector items annually. Some of
these collectibles can be found listed
under specific headings, such as
Hummel, Norman Rockwell, etc.

References: *Collectors' Information
Bureau's Collectibles Market Guide &
Price Index*, 14th Edition, Wallace-
Homestead (available from Collec-
tors' Information Bureau, 5065 Shore-
line Rd., Ste. 200, Barrington, IL
60010), 1996; Susan K. Elliott and J.
Kevin Samara, *Official Club Directory
and Price Guide to Limited Edition
Collectibles*, House of Collectibles,
1993; Pat Owen, *Bing & Grondahl
Christmas Plates*, Landfall Press,
1995; Mary Sieber (ed.), *1997 Price
Guide to Limited Edition Collectibles*,
Krause Publications, 1996; Rosie
Wells (ed.), *Official 1993 Secondary
Market Price Guide for Precious Moments Collectibles*, 11th Edition, Rosie Wells Enterprises, 1993.

Periodicals: *Collector Editions*, 170
Fifth Ave., 12th Floor, New York, NY
10010; *Collectors Mart Magazine*,
700 E. State St., Iola, WI 54990; *Collector News & Antique Reporter*,
P.O. Box 156, Grundy Center, IA
50638; *Collectors' Bulletin*, RR#1,
Canton, IL 61520; *Collectors Mart
Magazine*, P.O. Box 12830, Wichita,
KS 67277; *Contemporary Doll Mag-
azine*, 30595 Eight Mile, Livonia, MI
48152; *Hallmarkers Holiday Hap-
pening Collectors Club*, 6151 Main
St., Springfield, OR 97478; *Insight
on Collectibles*, 103 Lakeshore Rd.,
Ste. 202, St. Catharines, Ontario
L2N 2T6 Canada; *International Col-
lectible Showcase*, One Westmin-
ster Pl., Lake Forest, IL 60045;
Ornament Trader Magazine, P.O.
Box 7908, Clearwater, FL 34618;
Plate World, 9200 N. Maryland Ave.,
Niles, IL 60648; *Toybox Magazine*,
8393 E. Holly Rd., Holly MI 48442.

Collectors' Clubs: Club Anri, 55
Parcella Park Dr., Randolph, MA
02368; Del-Mar-Pa Ornament Kol-
lector's Club, 131 S. Tartan Dr., Elk-

ton, MD 21921; Donald Zolan
Collectors Society, 133 E. Carillo St.,
Santa Barbara, CA 93101; Franklin
Mint Collectors Society, U.S. Rte. 1,
Franklin Center, PA 19091; Gorham
Collectors Club, P.O. Box 6472,
Providence, RI 02940; International
Plate Collectors Guild, P.O. Box
487, Artesia, CA 90702; Lladro Col-
lectors Society, 43 W. 57th St., New
York, NY 10019; Lowell Davis Farm
Club, 55 Pacella Park Dr., Randolph,
MA 02368; Modern Doll Club, 9628
Hidden Oaks Cr., Tampa, FL 33612;
Precious Moments Collectors' Club,
One Enesco Plaza, P.O. Box 1466,
Elk Grove Village, IL 60009.

Museum: Bradford Museum, Niles,
IL.

Abbreviation: FE = First Edition.

Christmas Ornaments

Anri

Disney Four Star Collection, Disney
Studios

1989, Maestro Mickey 75.00

1990, Minnie Mouse 50.00

Ferrandiz Woodcarvings, J.
Ferrandiz, artist

1988, Heavenly Drummer..250.00

1989, Heavenly Strings 175.00

Bing & Grondahl, Santa Claus

1989, Santa's Workshop..........55.00

1990, Santa's Sleigh................55.00

1991, The Journey...................40.00

1994, Christmas Stories 25.00

Danbury Mint, angel, 4"................45.00

Dave Grossman Creations

Gone with the Wind

1987, Ashley........................40.00

1989, Mammy.....................15.00

1990, Scarlett, red dress 18.00

Rockwell Collection, annual figurine
ornament

1978, Caroler.......................44.00

1979, Drum for Tommy........28.00

1983, Fiddler........................27.00

1987, Skating Lesson 30.00

1992, On the Ice 30.00

Enesco, Precious Moments, S. Butcher,
artist

1982, Dropping
in for Christmas.......................40.00

1983, O Come All Ye Faithful ..55.00

1985, God Sent His Love.........35.00

1986, Rocking Horse 25.00

1988, Cheers to the Leader 35.00

1992, I'm Nuts About You........15.00

1994, You Are
Always in My Heart 20.00

Gorham. Annual Snowflake, SS
  1972 ....100.00
  1973 ....90.00
  1976 ....60.00
  1981 ....300.00
  1987 ....80.00
  1990 ....65.00
  1994 ....45.00
Hallmark
  1974, Mary Hamilton, orig, Charmer
  Design 7.50
  1975, Betsy Clark 7.50
  1979, Special Teacher, satin 4.50
  1980, Baby's First Christmas ...15.00
  1981
    Candyville Express 25.00
    Friendly Fiddler 15.00
    St. Nicholas, tin 10.00
  1982
    Cookie Mouse 17.50
    Cowboy Snowman 10.00
    Jingling Teddy 12.00
    Peeking Elf 6.50
    Soldier, clothespin, FE 25.00
Haviland
  1972 ....8.00
  1973 ....8.00
  1974 ....12.00
  1975 ....6.00
  1976 ....6.00
  1977 ....8.00
  1978 ....7.50
  1979 ....7.50
  1980 ....18.00
  1981 ....20.00
  1982 ....22.00
International Silver, Twelve Days of
  Christmas, SS, each 25.00
Lenox, 1982, FE, snowflake
  emb porcelain, 24K gold finials,
  date, 6" h 40.00
Lladro, Christmas Ball
  1989 ....60.00
  1990 ....70.00
  1993 ....50.00
  1994 ....50.00
  1995 ....50.00
Lunt
  1974, Trefoil 20.00
  1980, Medallion 18.00
Reed & Barton
  Carousel Horse, SP
    1988 ....20.00
    1990 ....15.00
    1994 ....15.00
  Christmas Cross
    SS
      1971 ....350.00
      1973 ....87.00
      1976 ....80.00
      1982 ....140.00

Reco, plate, Mother Goose series, 1980, Little Boy Blue, John McClelland, artist, 8-1/2" d, $100.

  1985 ....80.00
  1991 ....75.00
  1994 ....35.00
  24K gold over SS
    1971 ....300.00
    1974 ....55.00
    1978 ....50.00
    1982 ....43.00
    1989 ....38.00
    1992 ....40.00
    1994 ....45.00
    1995 ....45.00
Schmid
  Paddington Bear, 1982
    Ball 5.00
    Figural 10.00
  Raggedy Ann
    1976, FE 6.00
    1977 ....3.50
    1978 ....3.00
    1979 ....3.25
    1980 ....3.00
    1982, figural 10.00
  Walt Disney
    1974, FE 15.00
    1975 ....5.00
    1976 ....10.00
    1977 ....4.50
    1978 ....4.00
    1979 ....4.00
    1980 ....3.50
    1981 ....3.00
    1982, figural 10.00
Towle
  Twelve Days of
  Christmas medallion, SS
    1971, Partridge
    in a Pear Tree 550.00
    1972, Two Turtle Doves.....275.00
    1973, Three French Hens..100.00
    1974, Four Calling Birds 150.00
    1975, Five Golden Rings ...100.00
    1976, Six Geese a Laying..125.00
    1977, Seven

    Swans a Swimming 200.00
    1978, Eight
    Maids a Milking.................100.00
    1979, Nine
    Ladies Dancing.................100.00
    1980, Ten
    Lords a Leaping................100.00
    1981, Eleven
    Pipers Piping 100.00
    1982, Twelve
    Drummers Drumming 100.00
  Songs of Christmas Medallions
    1978, Silent Night 70.00
    1979, Deck the Halls 70.00
    1980, Jingle Bells 80.00
    1981, Hark the
    Herald Angels Sing...........130.00
    1983, Silver Bells...............75.00
    1984, Let It Snow................75.00
    1987, White Christmas 70.00
Wallace Silversmiths
  Sleigh Bells, SP
    1971...............................900.00
    1972...............................450.00
    1977...............................200.00
    1978 ....100.00
    1983 ....90.00
    1988 ....50.00
    1990 ....50.00
    1994 ....30.00
  Candy Canes
    1981, Peppermint 200.00
    1982, Wintergreen.............100.00
    1983, Cinnamon 60.00
    1986, Christmas Candle 40.00
    1991, Christmas Goose.......30.00
    1994, Canes 20.00

Dolls

Annalee Mobilitee Dolls, Inc.
  Doll Society, Folk Heroes, A.
  Thorndike, artist, 10" h
    1984, Johnny Appleseed ...950.00
    1985, Annie Oakley 700.00
    1988, Sherlock Holmes 450.00
    1991, Christopher
    Columbus 300.00
    1995, Pocahontas...............80.00
  Doll Society, Logo Kids, A.Thorndike,
  artist
    1985, Christmas
    Logo with Cookie 650.00
    1987, Naughty Logo 400.00
    1989, Christmas
    Morning Logo....................150.00
    1992, Back to
    School Logo........................80.00
Enesco Imports, Precious Moments
  1981, Mikey, 18" h 225.00
  1982, Tammy, 18" h..............650.00
  1983, Katie Lynne, 16" h........185.00

1984, Kristy, 12" h 160.00
1985, Bethany, 12" h 145.00
1986, Bong Bong, 13" h 165.00
1987, Angie,
The Angel of Mercy 160.00
1989, Wishing You
Cloudless Skies.....................115.00
1990, The Voice of Spring......150.00
1991, You Have
Touched So Many Hearts 90.00
Gorham
Gorham Dolls, S. Stone Aiken, artist
1981
Cecile, 16" 750.00
Christopher, 19" 500.00
1982
Baby in apricot dress,
16" 350.00
Baby in blue dress,
12" 300.00
1983, Jennifer, bride, 19" ...700.00
1985
Alexander, 19" 400.00
Odette, 19" 450.00
1986
Alissa 300.00
Emily, 14" 375.00
1987, Juliet.........................375.00
Holly Hobbie, 1983
Blue girl
14"....................................225.00
18"....................................280.00
Little Amy, 14" 235.00
Yesterday's
Memories, 18" 360.00
Limited Edition, S. Stone Aiken, artist
1982, Allison, 19" 4,300.00
1983, Ashley, 19" 950.00
1984, Nicole,19"................850.00
1985, Lydia, 19" 1,650.00
1986, Noel,
Christmas, 19" 750.00
1988, Andrew, 19" 720.00
Valentine Ladies, P. Valentine, artist
1987
Elizabeth 450.00
Marianna 400.00
1988, Felicia......................300.00
1989
Julianna...........................275.00
Rose.................................275.00
Hamilton Collection
1981, Hakata,
Peony Maiden 150.00
1985, Heather 125.00
1986, Nicole 50.00
1987, Priscilla........................50.00
1988, Mr. Spock 75.00
1989, Scotty 75.00
Royal Doulton by Nisbet
Little Model..........................185.00
Pink Sash 145.00

Royal Baby...........................350.00
The Muffs 175.00
Winter...................................180.00
Seymour Mann, Connoisseur Collection
1984, Miss Debutante 180.00
1985, Wendy........................150.00
1986, Camelot Fairy..............225.00
1987, Dawn..........................175.00
1988, Jolie............................150.00
1989, Elizabeth 200.00
1990, Baby Sunshine 90.00
1991, Dephine.......................125.00

Figurines

Anri, Sarah Kay, artist
1983, Morning Chores,
6", FE 475.00
1984, Flowers for You, 6".......400.00
1985, Afternoon Tea, 6".........325.00
1986, Our Puppy, 1-1/2" 90.00
1987, Little Nanny, 4".............180.00
1988, Purrfect Day, 6"...........400.00
1989, Garden Party, 4" 195.00
1990, Season's
Greetings, 4" 225.00
1991, Season's Joy, 4" 250.00
Cybis
1963, Magnolia 400.00
1964, Rebecca......................345.00
1965, Christmas Rose 750.00
1967, Kitten, blue ribbon 500.00
1968, Narcissus 500.00
1969, Clematis
with house wren 315.00
1970, Dutch Crocus 750.00
1971, Appaloosa Colt.............285.00
1972, Pansies 350.00
1973, Goldilocks 325.00
1974, Mary, Mary 750.00
1975, George
Washington Bust...................300.00
1976, Bunny 125.00
1977, Tiffin 400.00
1978, Edith............................300.00
1982, Spring Bouquet 750.00
1985, Nativity Lamb 125.00
1986, Dapple Gray Foal.........185.00
Dave Grossman Designs, Norman
Rockwell Collection
1973
Back to School....................40.00
Redhead 200.00
1975, Discovery 160.00
1978, At the Doctor 175.00
1980, Handkerchief.................95.00
1981, Spirit of Education........100.00
1982, American Mother..........110.00
1987, Young Love..................100.00
Department 56, Snowbabies
1986, Hold on Tight.................12.00
1987, Down the Hill We Go......20.00

Royal Copenhagen, plate, Christmas, 1920, Mary and Child Jesus, $75.

1988, Tiny Trio........................60.00
1989, Icy Igloo 35.00
1990, A Special Delivery..........12.00
1991, Just for You...................20.00
Enesco Corp., Precious Moments
1979, Jesus Loves Me.............30.00
1980, Come Let
Us Adore Him 90.00
1981, But Love
Goes on Forever....................165.00
1982, I Believe in Miracles.......90.00
1983, Sharing Our Season 110.00
1984, Joy to the World............40.00
1985, Baby's First Christmas...35.00
1986, God Bless America 50.00
1987, This Is the
Day the Lord Hath Made..........35.00
1988, Faith Takes the Plunge ..30.00
1989, Wishing You Roads
of Happiness...........................50.00
1990, To My Favorite Fan........15.00
(Hummel, see HUMMEL)
Lladro
1970, Girl with Guitar 1,800.00
1971
Hamlet 3,000.00
Oriental Man 1,800.00
1972, Turkey Group............1,500.00
1973
Buck Hunters 2,700.00
Passionate Dance 4,250.00
Turtle Doves 2,375.00
1974
Ducks at Pond 5,500.00
Partridge 1,800.00
1978
Car in Trouble....................6,000
Flight of Gazelles............3,000.00
Henry VII........................1,100.00
1981
Nest of Eagles,
with base 10,000.00

Philippine Folklore...........2,000.00
The Rescue.....................5,000.00
1983
   Bather 950.00
   In the Distance 1,100.00
   Reclining Nude..................650.00
   Tranquillity.....................1,300.00
   Youth............................1,000.00
1985, Thoroughbred Horse, with
base 600.00
1986, Oriental Music,
with base 2,400.00
1989
   Southern Tea 2,200.00
1991, Champion.................1,900.00
1992, Tea in the Garden 9,500.00
1993
   Autumn Glow, with base 770.00
   Indian Brave....................2,200.00
River Shore
1978, Akiku, Baby Seal, FE ...145.00
1979, Rosecoe, red fox kit 50.00
1980, Lamb 48.00
1981, Zuela, elephant 60.00
1982, Kay's Doll 90.00
*(Rockwell, Norman, see NORMAN
ROCKWELL)*
Royal Doulton
   Beatrix Potter
      Benjamin Bunny..................25.00
      Lady Mouse 20.00
      Mrs. Rabbit & Bunnies 25.00
      Old Mr. Brown.....................20.00
      Peter Rabbit.......................25.00
      Rebecca Puddle-Duck 20.00
   Bunnykins
      Autumn Days 17.00
      Clean Sweep.......................14.00
      Family Photograph...............24.00
      Grandpa's Story...................17.00
      Sleepy Time 12.00
      Springtime...........................18.00
      Tally Ho.............................15.00
   Dickens
      Mrs. Bardell........................24.00
      Scrooge..............................25.00
   Lord of Rings, Tolkien
      Aragorn 45.00
      Bilbo.................................35.00
      Gandalf 50.00
      Gimli.................................45.00
      Gollum...............................35.00
      Legolas 45.00
   Myths and Maidens
      1982, Lady and the Unicorn,
      HN2825..........................2,400.00
      1983, Leda and the Swan,
      HN2826..........................2,800.00
      1984, Juno and the Peacock,
      HN2827..........................3,000.00

1985, Europa and the Bull,
HN2828..........................3,000.00
1986, Diana the Huntress,
HN2829..........................3,000.00
Prestige Figure, 1964, Indian Brave,
HN2376..........................5,250.00
Royalty
   1973, Queen Elizabeth II,
   HN2502..........................1,775.00
   1981
      Duke of Edinburgh,
      HN2386..........................440.00
      Prince of Wales,
      HN2884..........................1,000.00
   1982
      Princess of Wales,
      HN2887 ....1,450.00
      Lady Diana Spencer,
      HN2885..........................500.00
   1986, Duchess of York,
   HN3086..........................600.00
   1990, Queen Elizabeth, the Queen
   Mother, HN3189 ....450.00
Royal Orleans Porcelain, Marilyn
Monroe 80.00
Schmid
1979, Country Road................275.00
1980, Two's Company 45.00
1981, Plum Tuckered Out......225.00
1982, Right Church,
Wrong Pew 80.00
1983, Stirring Up Trouble.......165.00
1984, Catnapping Too 72.00
1985, Out of Step...................45.00

Plates

Bareuther (Germany), Christmas, Hans
   Mueller artist, 8" d
1967, Stiftskirche, FE..............90.00
1968, Kapplkirche 25.00
1969, Christkindlmarkt 20.00
1970, Chapel in Oberndorf.......18.00
1971, Toys for Sale.................20.00
1972, Christmas in Munich 35.00
1973, Christmas Sleigh Ride ...20.00
1974, Church in
the Black Forest 20.00
1975, Snowman.......................25.00
1976, Chapel in the Hills 25.00
1977, Story Time.....................30.00
1978, Mittenwald.....................30.00
1979, Winter Day 40.00
1980, Miltenberg 38.00
1981, Walk in the Forest 40.00
1982, Bad Wimpfen 40.00
1983, The Night
Before Christmas 45.00
1984, Zeil on the River Main 42.50
1985, Winter Wonderland 42.50
1986, Christmas in Forchhe.....42.50
1987, Decorating the Tree 46.50
1988, St. Coloman Church.......80.00

1989, Sleigh Ride 50.00
1990, The Old
Forge in Rothenburg...............50.00
1991, Christmas Joy 55.00
1992, Marketplace
in Heppenheim.......................55.00
Berlin (Germany), Christmas, various
   artists, 7-3/4" d
   1970, Christmas
   in Bernkastel 130.00
   1971, Christmas in Rothenburg on
   Tauber 30.00
   1972, Christmas
   in Michelstadt......................50.00
   1973, Christmas
   in Wendelstein 42.00
   1974, Christmas in Bremen 25.00
   1975, Christmas in Dortland 60.00
   1976, Christmas
   Eve in Augsburg 30.00
   1977, Christmas
   Eve in Hamburg.....................32.00
   1978, Christmas Market at the Berlin
   Cathedral 55.00
   1979, Christmas
   Eve in Greetsiel 55.00
   1980, Christmas
   Eve in Miltenberg 55.00
   1981, Christmas
   Eve in Hahnenklee.................50.00
   1982, Christmas
   Eve in Wasserburg 55.00
   1983, Chapel in Oberndorf 55.00
   1984, Christmas in Ramsau 50.00
   1985, Christmas
   Eve in Bad Wimpfen 55.00
   1986, Christmas
   Eve in Gelnhaus 65.00
   1987, Christmas
   Eve in Goslar 70.00
   1988, Christmas
   Eve in Ruhpolding.................100.00
   1989, Christmas
   Eve in Freidechsdadt 100.00
   1990, Christmas Eve in
   Partenkirchen.......................80.00
   1991, Christmas
   Eve in Allendorf.....................80.00
Bing and Grondahl (Denmark)
   Christmas, various artists, 7" d
      1895, Behind the
      Frozen Window..............3,400.00
      1896, New Moon Over
      Snow-Covered Trees......1,975.00
      1897, Christmas Meal of the
      Sparrows 725.00
      1898, Christmas Roses and
      Christmas Star...............700.00
      1899, The Crows Enjoying
      Christmas 900.00
      1900, Church Bells Chiming in
      Christmas 800.00

1901, The Three Wise Men from the East............................450.00

1902, Interior of a Gothic Church....................285.00

1903, Happy Expectation of Children............................150.00

1904, View of Copenhagen from Frederiksberg Hill...............125.00

1905, Anxiety of the Coming Christmas Night 130.00

1906, Sleighing to Church on Christmas Eve.....................95.00

1907, The Little Match Girl..........................125.00

1908, St. Petri Church of Copenhagen 85.00

1909, Happiness Over the Yule Tree..............................100.00

1910, The Old Organist........90.00

1911, First It Was Sung by Angels to Shepherds in the Fields ...80.00

1912, Going to Church on Christmas Eve 80.00

1913, Bringing Home the Yule Tree................................85.00

1914, Royal Castle of Amalienborg, Copenhagen 75.00

1915, Chained Dog Getting Double Meal on Christmas Eve..............120.00

1916, Christmas Prayer of the Sparrows............................85.00

1917, Arrival of the Christmas Boat 75.00

1918, Fishing Boat Returning Home for Christmas.............85.00

1919, Outside the Lighted Window 80.00

1920, Hare in the Snow 70.00

1921, Pigeons in the Castle Court..........................55.00

1922, Star of Bethlehem 75.00

1923, Royal Hunting Castle, The Hermitage 55.00

1924, Lighthouse in Danish Waters.................................65.00

1925, The Child's Christmas...........................70.00

1926, Churchgoers on Christmas Day.......................................65.00

1927, Skating Couple...........80.00

1928, Eskimo Looking at Village Church in Greenland............60.00

1929, Fox Outside Farm 80.00

1930, Yule Tree in Town Hall Square of Copenhagen........85.00

1931, Arrival of the Christmas Train..................................75.00

1932, Lifeboat at Work.........90.00

1933, The Korsor-Nyborg Ferry....................................70.00

1934, Church

Bell in Tower 70.00

1935, Lillebelt Bridge Connecting Funen with Jutland..............65.00

1936, Royal Guard...............70.00

1937, Arrival of Christmas Guests 75.00

1938, Lighting the Candles 110.00

1939, Ole Lock-Eye, The Sandman 150.00

1940, Delivering Christmas Letters................................170.00

1941, Horses Enjoying Christmas Meal in Stable 345.00

1942, Danish Farm on Christmas Night 150.00

1943, The Ribe Cathedral..155.00

1944, Sorgenfri Castle 120.00

1945, The Old Water Mill ...135.00

1946, Commemoration Cross in Honor of Danish Sailors Who Lost Their Lives in World War II ..85.00

1947, Dybbol Mill 70.00

1948, Watchman, Sculpture of Town Hall, Copenhagen 80.00

1949, Landsoldaten, 19th Century Danish Soldier 70.00

1950, Kronborg Castle at Elsinore...............150.00

1951, Jens Bang, New Passenger Boat Running Between Copenhagen and Aalborg..115.00

1952, Old Copenhagen Canals at Wintertime with Thorvaldsen Museum in Background 85.00

1953, Royal Boat in Greenland Waters 95.00

1954, Birthplace of Hans Christian Andersen, with Snowman..100.00

1955, Kalundborg Church............115.00

1956, Christmas in Copenhagen 140.00

1957, Christmas Candles ..155.00

1958, Santa Claus 100.00

1959, Christmas Eve 120.00

1960, Danish Village Church 180.00

1961, Winter Harmony.......115.00

1962, Winter Night 80.00

1963, The Christmas Elf 120.00

1964, The Fir Tree and Hare.....................50.00

1965, Bringing Home the Christmas Tree 65.00

1966, Home for Christmas...50.00

1967, Sharing the Joy of Christmas...........................48.00

1968, Christmas in Church ..45.00

1969, Arrival of Christmas Guests 30.00

1970, Pheasants in the Snow at Christmas.........................20.00

1971, Christmas at Home....20.00

1972, Christmas in Greenland 20.00

1973, Country Christmas.....25.00

1974, Christmas in the Village 20.00

1975, The Old Water Mill.....24.00

1976, Christmas Welcome ..25.00

1977, Copenhagen Christmas 25.00

1978, A Christmas Tale 30.00

1979, White Christmas 30.00

1980, Christmasi in the Woods......................42.50

1981, Christmas Peace 50.00

1982, The Christmas Tree...55.00

1983, Christmas in Old Town 55.00

1984, Christmas Letter 55.00

1985, Christmas Eve at the Farmhouse 55.00

1986, Silent Night, Holy Night 55.00

1987, The Snowman's Christmas Eve 60.00

1988, In the Kings Garden...72.00

1989, Christmas Anchorage 65.00

1990, Changing of the Guards 60.00

1991, Copenhagen Stock Exchange............................70.00

1992, Christmas at the Rectory 65.00

1993, Father Christmas in Copenhagen 65.00

1994, A Day at the Deer Park 80.00

1995, The Towers of Copenhagen 85.00

1996, Winter at the Old Mill......................70.00

Franklin Mint (United States)
Audubon Society Birds

1972, Goldfinch 115.00

1972, Wood Duck 110.00

1973, Cardinal 110.00

1973, Ruffled Grouse 120.00

Christmas, Norman Rockwell, artist, etched SS, 8" d

1970, Bringing Home the Tree...................275.00

1971, Under the Mistletoe 125.00

1972, The Carolers...........125.00

1973, Trimming the Tree ...100.00

1974, Hanging the Wreath 100.00

1975, Home for Christmas 125.00

(Goebel, Germany, see Hummel)
Haviland (France)

Mother's Day (The French Collection)

1973, Breakfast....................25.00
1974, The Wash.................30.00
1975, In the Park...............25.00
1976, Market.......................40.00
1977, Wash Before Dinner...35.00
1978, Evening at Home 40.00
1979, Happy Mother's Day ..30.00
1980, Child & His Animals ...55.00

1,001 Arabian Nights, Lillian Tellier, artist

1979, Cheval Magique, Magic
Horse 60.00
1980, Aladdin et Lampe.......60.00
1981, Sheherazade..............55.00
1982, Sinbad the Sailor........55.00

The Twelve Days of Christmas Series, Remy Hetreau, artist, 8-3/8" d

1970, A Partridge in a Pear Tree,
FE 115.00
1971, Two Turtle Doves.......40.00
1972, Three French Hens 35.00
1973, Four Calling Birds 35.00
1974, Five Golden Rings 30.00
1975, Six Geese A' Laying...30.00
1976, Seven Swans
A' Swimming 30.00
1977, Eight Maids
A' Milking..............................45.00
1978, Nine Ladies
Dancing................................35.00
1979, Ten Lords
A' Leaping 40.00
1980, Eleven Pipers Piping..50.00
1981, Twelve Drummers
Drumming 55.00

Haviland & Parlon (France)

Christmas Series, various artists, 10" d

1972, Madonna and Child,
Raphael, FE 80.00
1973, Madonna, Feruzzi 95.00
1974, Cowper Madonna and
Child, Raphael 40.00
1975, Madonna and Child,
Murillo 45.00
1976, Madonna and Child,
Botticelli................................50.00
1977, Madonna and Child,
Bellini 40.00
1978, Madonna and Child, Fra
Filippo, Lippi.........................65.00
1979, Madonna of the Eucharist,
Botticelli..............................150.00

Lady and the Unicorn Series, artist unknown, 10" d

1977, To My Only
Desire, FE 60.00
1978, Sight...........................40.00
1979, Sound.........................50.00
1980, Touch 110.00

1981, Scent..........................60.00
1982, Taste...........................80.00

Tapestry Series, artists unknown, 10" d

1971, The Unicorn
in Captivity 145.00
1972, Start of the Hunt.........70.00
1973, Chase
of the Unicorn 120.00
1974, End of the Hunt........120.00
1975, The
Unicorn Surrounded.............75.00
1976, The Unicorn is Brought
to the Castle.........................55.00

Edwin M. Knowles (United States)

American Holidays Series, Don Spaulding, artist, 8-1/2" d

1978, Fourth of July, FE 35.00
1979, Thanksgiving..............35.00
1980, Easter 30.00
1981, Valentine's Day..........25.00
1982, Father's Day 35.00
1983, Christmas...................35.00
1984, Mother's Day..............20.00

Annie Series
1983

Annie and Sandy, FE 25.00
Daddy Warbucks...............20.00
Annie & Grace...................19.00
1984, Annie
and the Orphans 20.00
1985, Tomorrow..................21.00
1986

Annie, Lily and Rooster......24.00
Grand Finale 24.00

Gone with the Wind Series, Raymond Kursar, artist, 8-1/2" d

1978, Scarlett, FE 300.00
1979, Ashley 225.00
1980, Melanie 75.00
1981, Rhett 50.00
1982, Mammy
Lacing Scarlett.....................60.00
1983, Melanie Gives Birth....85.00
1984, Scarlett's
Green Dress 50.00
1985

Rhett and Bonnie 35.00
Scarlett and Rhett:
The Finale 30.00

Wizard of Oz Series, James Auckland, artist, 8-1/2" d

1977, Over the
Rainbow, FE 65.00
1978

If I Only Had a Brain..........30.00
If I Only Had a
of the Forest......................30.00
1979

Wicked Witch of the West..35.00
Follow the Yellow
Brick Road.........................35.00

Wonderful Wizard of Oz.....50.00
1980, The Grand Finale (We're
Off to See The Wizard) 60.00

Lalique (France), Annual Series, lead crystal, Marie-Claude Lalique, artist, 8-1/2" d

1965, Deux Oiseaux
(Two Birds), FE 800.00
1966, Rose de Songerie
(Dream Rose) 215.00
1967, Ballet de Poisson
(Fish Ballet)..........................200.00
1968, Gazelle Fantaisie
(Gazelle Fantasy) 70.00
1969, Papillon (Butterfly) 80.00
1970, Paon (Peacock) 50.00
1971, Hibou (Owl)....................60.00
1972, Coquillage (Shell) 55.00
1973, Petit Geai (Jayling) 60.00
1974, Sous d'Argent (Silver
Pennies)..................................65.00
1975, Due de Poisson
(Fish Duet).............................75.00
1976, Aigle (Eagle) 100.00

Lenox (United States)

Boehm Bird Series, Edward Marshall Boehm, artist, 10-1/2" d

1970, Wood Thrush, FE 135.00
1971, Goldfinch 60.00
1972, Mountain Bluebird......40.00
1973, Meadowlark 50.00
1974, Rufous
Hummingbird 45.00
1975, American Redstart.....50.00
1976, Cardinal 58.00
1977, Robins 55.00
1978, Mockingbirds 60.00
1979, Golden-
Crowned Kinglets 65.00
1980, Black-Throated Blue
Warblers 75.00
1981, Eastern Phoebes 90.00

Boehm Woodland Wildlife Series, Edward Marshall Boehm, artist, 10-1/2"

1973, Raccoons, FE 80.00
1974, Red Foxes 50.00
1975, Cottontail Rabbits 60.00
1976, Eastern Chipmunks ...60.00
1977, Beaver 60.00
1978, Whitetail Deer...........60.00
1979, Squirrels 75.00
1980, Bobcats....................90.00
1981, Martens...................100.00
1982, River Otters 100.00

Reco International Corp. (United States)

Days Gone By, Sandra Kuck, artist
1983

Sunday Best 55.00
Amy's Magic Horse...........30.00
1984

Little Anglers 30.00

Little Tutor 30.00

Easter at Grandma's 30.00

McClelland's Children's Circus Series, John McClelland, artist, 9"d

1981, Tommy the
Clown, FE 45.00

1982, Katie the
Tightrope Walker................35.00

1983, Johnny the
Strongman 35.00

1984, Maggie the
Animal Trainer...................30.00

McClelland's Mother Goose Series, John McClelland, artist, 8-1/2" d

1979, Mary, Mary, FE 250.00

1980, Little Boy Blue..........100.00

1981, Little Miss Muffet........30.00

1982, Little Jack Horner.......30.00

1983, Little Bo Peep............40.00

1984, Diddle, Diddle
Dumpling............................30.00

1985, Mary Had a
Little Lamb 42.00

1986, Jack and Jill 25.00

(Rockwell, see Norman Rockwell)

Rosenthal (Germany)

Christmas, Bjorn Wiinblad, artist

1971, Maria & Child 700.00

1972, Caspar 550.00

1973, Melchior 375.00

1974, Balthazar..................500.00

1975, The Annunciation 190.00

1976, Angel with Trumpet..200.00

1977, Adoration of
Shepherds..........................225.00

1978, Angel with Harp........275.00

1979, Exodus
From Egypt 310.00

1980, Angel with
a Glockenspiel 360.00

1981, Christ Child
Visits Temple 365.00

1982, Christening
of Christ..............................375.00

Christmas, various artists, 8-1/2" d

1910, Winter Peace 550.00

1911, The Three
Wise Men...........................325.00

1912, Shooting Stars 250.00

1913, Christmas Lights 235.00

1914, Christmas Song 350.00

1915, Walking to Church....180.00

1916, Christmas
During War..........................235.00

1917, Angel of Peace.........210.00

1918, Peace on Earth 210.00

1919, St. Christopher with the
Christ Child 225.00

1920, The Manger
in Bethlehem 325.00

1921, Christmas in
the Mountains 200.00

1922, Advent Branch 200.00

1923, Children in
the Winter Wood 200.00

1924, Deer in the Woods ...200.00

1925, The Three
Wise Men...........................200.00

1926, Christmas
in the Mountains 175.00

1927, Station on the Way ..200.00

1928, Chalet Christmas 175.00

1929, Christmas
in the Alps 225.00

1930, Group of Deer Under
the Pines.............................225.00

1931, Path of the Magi.......225.00

1932, Christ Child 195.00

1933, Through the
Night to Light.....................190.00

1934, Christmas Peace 200.00

1935, Christmas
By the Sea 185.00

1936, Nürnberg Angel........185.00

1937, Berchtesgaden.........195.00

1938, Christmas
in the Alps 190.00

1939, Schneekoppe
Mountain 195.00

1940, Marien Church
in Danzig............................250.00

1941, Strassburg
Cathedral 250.00

1942, Marianburg Castle ...300.00

1943, Winter Idyll 300.00

1944, Wood Scape 275.00

1945, Christmas Peace 370.00

1946, Christmas in an
Alpine Valley 250.00

1947, The
Dillingen Madonna 975.00

1948, Message
to the Shepherds 850.00

1949, The Holy Family.......185.00

1950, Christmas
in the Forest......................175.00

1951, Star of Bethlehem 450.00

1952, Christmas
in the Alps 190.00

1953, The Holy Light..........185.00

1954, Christmas Eve 180.00

1955, Christmas
in a Village 190.00

1956, Christmas
in the Alps 185.00

1957, Christmas
by the Sea..........................195.00

1958, Christmas Eve 185.00

1959, Midnight Mass..........195.00

1960, Christmas
Eve in a Small Village........190.00

1961, Solitary Christmas....225.00

1962, Christmas Eve 185.00

1963, Silent Night 185.00

1964, Christmas Market in
Nürnberg.............................225.00

1965, Christmas
in Munich 185.00

1966, Christmas in Ulm 250.00

1967, Christmas in
Regensburg 185.00

1968, Christmas
in Bremen 190.00

1969, Christmas in
Rothenburg.........................220.00

1970, Christmas
in Cologne 165.00

1971, Christmas in
Garmisch 100.00

1972, Christmas in
Franconia...........................90.00

1973, Christmas in
Lubeck-Holstein.................110.00

1974, Christmas
in Wurzburg 95.00

Royal Copenhagen (Denmark)

Christmas, various artists, 6" d 1908, 1909, 1910; 7" d 1911 to present

1909, Danish Landscape...150.00

1910, The Magi.................120.00

1911, Danish Landscape...135.00

1912, Elderly Couple by Christmas
Tree 120.00

1913, Spire of Frederik's Church,
Copenhagen 125.00

1914, Sparrows in
Tree at Church of the Holy
Spirit, Copenhagen............100.00

1915, Danish Landscape...150.00

1916, Shepherd in the Field on
Christmas Night 85.00

1917, Tower of Our Savior's
Church, Copenhagen 90.00

1918, Sheep and
Shepherds 80.00

1919, In the Park 80.00

1920, Mary with the
Child Jesus 75.00

1921, Aabenraa
Marketplace 75.00

1922, Three
Singing Angels....................70.00

1923, Danish Landscape.....70.00

1924, Christmas Star Over the
Sea and Sailing Ship 100.00

1925, Street Scene from Christian-
shavn, Copenhagen 85.00

1926, View of Christmas Canal,
Copenhagen 75.00

1927, Ship's Boy at the Tiller on
Christmas Night 140.00

1928, Vicar's Family on Way to
Church 75.00

1929, Grundtvig Church,
Copenhagen 100.00

1930, Fishing Boats on the

Way to the Harbor...............80.00
1931, Mother and Child........90.00
1932, Frederiksberg Gardens with Statue of Frederik VI............90.00
1933, The Great Belt Ferry 110.00
1934, The Hermitage Castle..................................115.00
1935, Fishing Boat off Kronborg Castle 145.00
1936, Roskilde Cathedral...130.00
1937, Christmas Scene in Main Street, Copenhagen............135.00
1938, Round Church in Osterlars on Bornholm.......................200.00
1939, Expeditionary Ship in Pack-Ice of Greenland 180.00
1940, The Good Shepherd 300.00
1941, Danish Village Church....................250.00
1942, Bell Tower of Old Church in Jutland 300.00
1943, Flight of Holy Family to Egypt.......................................425.00
1944, Typical Danish Winter Scene....................................160.00
1945, A Peaceful Motif.......325.00
1946, Zealand Village Church....................150.00
1947, The Good Shepherd 210.00
1948, Nodebo Church at Christmastime....................150.00
1949, Our Lady's Cathedral, Copenhagen 165.00
1950, Boeslunde Church, Zealand...............................175.00
1951, Christmas Angel.......300.00
1952, Christmas in the Forest......................120.00
1953, Frederiksborg Castle 120.00
1954, Amalienborg Palace, Copenhagen 150.00
1955, Fano Girl 185.00
1956, Rosenborg Castle, Copenhagen 160.00
1957, The Good Shepherd 115.00
1958, Sunshine over Greenland 140.00
1959, Christmas Night 120.00
1960, The Stag 125.00
1961, Training Ship Danmark 155.00
1962, The Little Mermaid at Wintertime..........................200.00
1963, Hojsager Mill 80.00
1964, Fetching the Tree.......75.00
1965, Little Skaters 60.00
1966, Blackbird 55.00
1967, The Royal Oak...........45.00
1968, The Last Umiak..........40.00
1969, The Old Farmyard......35.00

1970, Christmas Rose and Cat.....................40.00
1971, Hare in Winter...........80.00
1972, In the Desert 30.00
1973, Train Homeward Bound for Christmas 22.00
1974, Winter Twilight 20.00
1975, Queen's Palace 20.00
1976, Danish Watermill........35.00
1977, Immervad Bridge 25.00
1978, Greenland Scenery....33.00
1979, Choosing the Christmas Tree 50.00
1980, Bringing Home the Tree.....................45.00
1981, Admiring the Christmas Tree 55.00
1982, Waiting for Christmas 60.00
1983, Merry Christmas 50.00
1984, Jingle Bells.................55.00
1985, Snowman 65.00
1986, Christmas Vacation....55.00
1987, Winter Birds 58.00
1988, Christmas Eve in Copenhagen 60.00
1989, The Old Skating Pond 70.00
1990, Christmas at Tivoli ...130.00
1991, The Festival of Santa Lucia....................100.00
1992, The Queen's Carriage 85.00
1993, Christmas Guests 95.00
1994, Christmas Shopping ..70.00
Mother's Day, various artists, 6-1/4" d
1971, American Mother 125.00
1972, Oriental Mother 60.00
1973, Danish Mother 60.00
1974, Greenland Mother......55.00
1975, Bird in Nest 50.00
1976, Mermaids 50.00
1977, The Twins 50.00
1978, Mother and Child 25.00
1979, A Loving Mother.........30.00
1980, An Outing with Mother 35.00
1981, Reunion 40.00
1982, The Children's Hour...45.00
Royal Doulton (Great Britain)
Beswick Christmas Series, various artists, earthenware in hand-cast bas-relief, 8" sq
1972, Christmas in England, FE 40.00
1973, Christmas in Mexico............................25.00
1974, Christmas in Bulgaria..........................40.00
1975, Christmas in Norway...........................54.00
1976, Christmas in Holland...........................45.00

1977, Christmas in Poland...........................100.00
1978, Christmas in America...........................45.00
Mother and Child Series, Edna Hibel, artist, 8" d
1973, Colette and Child, FE.............................450.00
1974, Sayuri and Child 150.00
1975, Kristina and Child 125.00
1976, Marilyn and Child.....100.00
1977, Lucia and Child........100.00
1978, Kathleen and Child 95.00
Valentine's Day Series, artists unknown, 8-1/4" d
1976, Victorian Boy and Girl 60.00
1977, My Sweetest Friend...40.00
1978, If I Love You 40.00
1979, My Valentine.............40.00
1980, On a Swing 40.00
1981, Sweet Music 35.00
1982, From My Heart...........40.00
1983, Cherub's Song..........45.00
1984, Love in Bloom...........40.00
1985, Accept These Flowers 40.00
Schmid (Japan)
Christmas, J. Malfertheiner, artist
1971, St. Jakob in Groden, FE 125.00
1972, Pipers at Alberobello....................120.00
1973, Alpine Horn..............375.00
1974, Young Man and Girl 100.00
1975, Christmas in Ireland...90.00
1976, Alpine Christmas 200.00
1977, Legend of Heligenblut........................125.00
1978, Klockler Singers.......175.00
1979, Moss Gatherers 130.00
1980, Wintry Churchgoing 165.00
1981, Santa Claus in Tyrol...................160.00
1982, The Star Singers......160.00
1983, Unto Us a Child Is Born 150.00
1984, Yuletide in the Valley..........................150.00
1985, Good Morning, Good Year 160.00
1986, A Goreden Christmas 75.00
1987, Down from the Alps 175.00
Disney Christmas Series, undisclosed artists, 7-1/2" d
1973, Sleigh Ride, FE........400.00
1974, Decorating the Tree 175.00
1975, Caroling 20.00

1976, Building a Snowman ..35.00
1977, Down the Chimney.....25.00
1978, Night Before
Christmas...........................20.00
1979, Santa's Surprise.........20.00
1980, Sleigh Ride................30.00
1981, Happy Holidays..........18.00
1982, Winter Games............20.00
1987, Snow White Golden
Anniversary 48.00
1988, Mickey Mouse & Minnie
Mouse 60th 50.00
1989, Sleeping Beauty 30th
Anniversary 75.00
1990, Fantasia Relief...........25.00

Disney Mother's Day Series
1974, Flowers for
Mother, FE 80.00
1975, Snow White and the
Seven Dwarfs......................45.00
1976, Minnie Mouse
and Friends 20.00
1977, Pluto's Pals 25.00
1978, Flowers for Bambi......20.00
1979, Happy Feet 25.00
1980, Minnie's Surprise 20.00
1981, Playmates 25.00
1982, A Dream Come True..20.00

Peanuts Christmas Series, Charles
Schulz, artist, 7-1/2" d
1972, Snoopy Guides the
Sleigh, FE 90.00
1973, Christmas Eve at the
Doghouse.........................120.00
1974, Christmas Eve at the
Fireplace 65.00
1975, Woodstock,
Santa Claus 15.00
1976, Woodstock's
Christmas...........................30.00
1977, Deck the Doghouse ...15.00
1978, Filling the Stocking.....20.00
1979, Christmas at Hand 20.00
1980, Waiting for Santa 50.00
1981, A Christmas Wish 20.00
1982, Perfect Performance..35.00

Peanuts Mother's Day Series,
Charles Schulz, artist, 7-1/2" d
1972, Linus, FE...................50.00
1973, Mom?........................45.00
1974, Snoopy and Woodstock on
Parade 40.00
1975, A Kiss for Lucy...........38.00
1976, Linus and Snoopy 35.00
1977, Dear Mom 30.00
1978, Thoughts
That Count 25.00
1979, A Special Letter..........20.00
1980, A Tribute to Mom 20.00
1981, Mission for Mom.........20.00
1982, Which Way

to Mother?...........................20.00
Peanuts Valentine's Day Series,
Charles Schulz, artist, 7-1/2" d
1977, Home Is Where the Heart Is,
FE 25.00
1978, Heavenly Bliss 28.00
1979, Love Match 20.00
1980, From Snoopy,
With Love 24.00
1981, Hearts-a-Flutter..........20.00
1982, Love Patch 18.00
Raggedy Ann Annual Series, undisclosed artist, 7-1/2" d
1980, The Sunshine
Wagon 65.00
1981, The Raggedy
Shuffle.................................25.00
1982, Flying High.................20.00
1983, Winning Streak 20.00
1984, Rocking Rodeo 22.50
U.S. Historical Society (United States),
Stained Glass Cathedral
1978, Canterbury 175.00
1979, Flight into Egypt.......175.00
1980, Washington Cathedral/
Madonna............................160.00
1981, The Magi...................160.00
1982, Flight into Egypt.......160.00
1983, Shepherds at
Bethlehem..........................150.00
1984, The Nativity..............145.00
1985, Good Tidings of Great Joy,
Boston................................125.00
1986, The Nativity from
Old St. Mary's Church,
Philadelphia 165.00
1987, O Come,
Little Children....................160.00
Wedgwood (Great Britain)
Calendar Series
1971, Victorian
Almanac, FE 20.00
1972, The Carousel 15.00
1973, Bountiful Butterfly.......14.00
1974, Camelot 65.00
1975, Children's Games 18.00
1976, Robin 25.00
1977, Tonatiuh....................28.00
1978, Samurai 32.00
1979, Sacred Scarab 32.00
1980, Safari 40.00
1981, Horses 42.50
1982, Wild West..................50.00
1983, The Age of
the Reptiles.........................50.00
1984, Dogs 55.00
1985, Cats 55.00
1986, British Birds...............50.00
1987, Water Birds 50.00
1988, Sea Birds 50.00
Christmas Series, jasper stoneware,

8" d
1969, Windsor
Castle, FE..........................225.00
1970, Christmas in Trafalgar
Square 30.00
1971, Piccadilly Circus,
London................................40.00
1972, St. Paul's Cathedral...40.00
1973, The Tower
of London............................45.00
1974, The Houses
of Parliament 40.00
1975, Tower Bridge 40.00
1976, Hampton Court 46.00
1977, Westminster Abbey ...48.00
1978, The Horse Guards 55.00
1979, Buckingham Palace...55.00
1980, St. James Palace.......70.00
1981, Marble Arch 75.00
1982, Lambeth Palace.........80.00
1983, All Souls,
Langham Palace..................80.00
1984, Constitution Hill..........80.00
1985, The Tate Gallery........80.00
1986, The Albert Memorial ..80.00
1987, Guildhall....................80.00
Mothers Series, jasper stoneware,
6-1/2" d
1971, Sportive Love, FE 25.00
1972, The Sewing Lesson ...20.00
1973, The Baptism of
Achilles 20.00
1974, Domestic
Employment.........................30.00
1975, Mother and Child 35.00
1976, The Spinner 35.00
1977, Leisure Time..............30.00
1978, Swan and Cygnets 35.00
1979, Deer and Fawn 35.00
1980, Birds 48.00
1981, Mare and Foal 50.00
1982, Cherubs with Swing...55.00
1983, Cupid and Butterfly 55.00
1984, Musical Cupids 55.00
1985, Cupids and Doves 55.00
1986, Anemones 55.00
1987, Tiger Lily 55.00

Little Golden Books

Collecting Hints: Little Golden Books offer something for everybody. Collectors can pursue titles according to favorite author, illustrator, television show, film or comic strip character. Disney titles enjoy a special place with nostalgia buffs. An increasingly popular goal is to own one copy of each title and number.

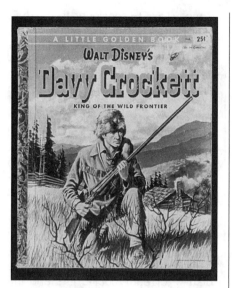

Walt Disney's Davy Crockett King of the Wild Frontier, **told by Irwin Shapiro, pictures by Walt Disney Studio, Adapted by Mel Crawford, Simon and Schuster, NY, 1955, $18.**

Books published in the '40s, '50s and '60s are in the most demand at this time. Books from this period were assigned individual numbers which are usually found on the front cover of the book, except for the earliest titles for which the title must be checked against the numbered list at the back of the book. Although the publisher tried to adhere to a policy of one number for each title during the first 30 years, numbers were reassigned to new titles as old titles were eliminated. Also, when an earlier book was re-edited and/or re-illustrated, it was given a new number.

Most of the first 36 books had blue paper spines and a dust jacket. Subsequent books were issued with a golden-brown mottled spine, which was replaced in 1950 by a shiny gold spine. Early books had 42 pages. In the late 1940s, the format was gradually changed to 28 pages, then to 24 pages in the mid-1950s. Early 42- and 28-page books had no price on the cover. Later the 25¢ price appeared on the front cover, then 29¢, followed by 39¢. In the early 1950s, books were produced with two lines that formed a bar across the top of the front cover. This bar was eliminated in the early '60s.

Little Golden Books can still be found at yard sales and flea markets.

Other sources include friends, relatives and charity book sales, especially if they have a separate children's table. Also attend doll and book shows—good places to find books with paper dolls, puzzles or cutouts. Toy dealers are also a good source for Disney, television and cowboy titles.

Look for books in good or better condition. Covers should be bright with the spine paper intact. Rubbing, ink and crayon markings or torn pages lessen the value of the book. Unless extensive, pencil marks are fairly easy to remove by gently stroking in one direction with an art-gum eraser. Do not rub back and forth.

Within the past two years collecting interest has increased dramatically, thus driving up prices for the most unusual and hard-to-find titles. Prices for the majority of titles are still at a reasonable level.

History: Simon & Schuster published the first Little Golden Books in September 1942. They were conceived and created by the Artists & Writers Guild Inc., which was an arm of the Western Printing and Lithographing Co. More than 1.5 million copies of the initial 12 titles (each 42 pages long and priced at 25¢) were sold within the first five months of publication. By the end of World War II, 39 million Little Golden Books had been sold.

A Disney series was begun in 1944 and Big and Giant Golden Books followed that same year. In 1949, the first Goldencraft editions were introduced. Instead of side-stapled cardboard, these books had cloth covers and were sewn so that they could withstand school and library use. In 1958, Giant Little Golden Books were introduced, most combining three previously published titles into one book. In that same year, Simon & Schuster sold Little Golden Books to Western Printing and Lithographing Company and Pocket Books. The titles then appeared under the Golden Press imprint. Eventually, Western, now known as Western Publishing Co., Inc., bought out Pocket Books' interest in Little Golden Books.

In 1986, Western celebrated the one-billionth Little Golden Book by issuing special commemorative editions

of some of its most popular titles, such as *Poky Little Puppy* and *Cinderella*.

Notes: Prices are based a mint condition book from the first printing. The printing edition is determined by looking at the lower right-hand corner of the back page. The letter found there indicates the printing of that particular title and edition. "A" is the first printing, "B" the next and so forth. Occasionally the letter is hidden under the spine or was placed in the upper right-hand corner, so look closely. Early titles will have their edition indicated in the front of the book.

Any dust jacket, puzzles, stencils, cutouts, stamps, tissues, tape or pages should be intact as issued. If not, the book's value suffers a drastic reduction of up to 80% off the listed price. Books that are badly worn, incomplete or badly torn are worth little. Sometimes they are useful as temporary fillers for gaps in a collection.

References: Rebecca Greason, *Tomart's Price Guide to Golden Book Collectibles*, Wallace-Homestead, 1991; Norman E. Martinus and Harry L. Rinker, *Warman's Paper*, Wallace-Homestead, 1994; Steve Santi, *Collecting Little Golden Books*, 2nd Edition, Books Americana, 1994.

Collectors' Club: Golden Book Club, 19626 Ricardo Ave., Hayward, CA 94541.

Animal Friends, #167, Jane Werner, illus Garth Williams, c1953 .... 10.00
Animal Paint Book, #A4, Hans Welwig, c1955, with paints 18.00
Beany Goes to Sea 12.00
Bugs Bunny Gets a Job, #136, Annie North Bedford, illus Warner Bros., c1952 .... 12.00
Bunny's Magic Tricks, #441, Janet and Alex D'Amato, illus Judy and Barry Martin, c1962, with pages that fold into trucks 10.00
Cars, #251, Kathryn Jackson, illus William J. Dugan, c1956 .... 8.00
Cheyenne 20.00
Christmas Carols 7.50
The Circus ABC, #222, Kathryn Jackson, illus J.P. Miller, c1955 ...... 10.00
The Cold Blooded Penguin 60.00
The Color Kittens, #86, Margaret Wise Brown, illus Alice and Martin Provensen, c1949, with puzzle 35.00
Counting Rhymes, #257, illus Corinne Malvern, c1947 .... 7.50
Dale Evans and the Lost Gold Mine,

#213, Monica Hill, illus Mel
Crawford, c1955 ....12.00

Doctor Dan at the Circus, #399, Pauline
Wilkins, illus Katherine Sampson,
c1960, Johnson & Johnson
Band-Aids 25.00

5 Pennies to Spend, #239,
Miriam Young, illus Corinne
Malvern, c1955 ....12.00

Fun with Decals, #139, Elsa Ruth
Nast, illus Corinne Malvern, c1952,
Meyercord decals 15.00

The Golden Goose 8.00

The Good Humor Man, #550, Kathleen
M. Daley, illus Tabor Gergely, c1964,
Good Humor Ice Cream 15.00

Grandpa Bunny, #D21,
Jane Werner, illus Walt Disney
Studios, c1951 ....20.00

Howdy Doody and Mr. Bluster,
Edward Kean, illus Ellis
Marge, c1954............................20.00

Huckleberry Hound Safety Signs,
#458, Ann McGovern, illus Al White,
c1961 ....12.00

I Can Fly, #92, Ruth Krauss, illus
Mary Blair c1950......................18.00

The Jetsons, #500, Carl Memling,
illus Al White and Hawley Pratt,
7" x 6-1/2", 1962 ....15.00

*The Kitten Who Thought He Was a
Mouse*, #210, Miriam Norton, illus
Garth Williams, c1954 ....12.00

Laddie the Superdog, #185, William P.
Gottlieb, c1954 ....10.00

Little Red Riding Hood,
#A34, illus Sharon Koester,
with paper dolls......................30.00

The Lone Ranger and Tonto, #297,
Charles Spain Verral, illus Edwin
Schmidt, c1957........................15.00

Magilla Gorilla................................12.00

Mickey Mouse Club Stamp Book, #A10,
Kathleen M. Daley, illus Julis Svend-
sen, c1956, with stamps..........30.00

Mister Ed The Talking Horse, #483, Barbara Shook Hazen, illus Mel Crawford, c1962, minor wear...........10.00

My Little Golden Animal Book, #465,
Elizabeth MacPhearson, illus Moritz
Kennel, c1962............................7.50

Old Yeller, #65, Irwin Shapiro, illus
Edwin Schmidt and E. Joseph Mea-
ny, c1957 ....12.00

Our Puppy, #56, Elsa Ruth Nast, illus
Feodor Rojankovsky, c1948....20.00

Peter Potamus, #556, Carl Memling,
illus Hawley Pratt and Bill Lorencz,
c1964..10.00

Prayers for Children, #5,
illus Rachael Taft Dixon,
c1942, dust jacket....................25.00

*Raggedy Ann, Sweet and Dandy Sugar
Candy*, scratch and sniff, 9-1/2" sq,
1976, used 22.00

Rin-Tin-Tin and Rusty, #246,
Monica Hill, illus Mel
Crawford, c1955 ....12.00

The Road To Oz, #144, Peter Archer,
illus Harry McNaught 30.00

Robin Hood, #D38, Annie North Bedford,
illus with scenes from Disney motion
picture, c1955..........................10.00

Roy Rogers and the Mountain Lion,
#231, Ann McGovern, illus Mel
Crawford, c1955 ....12.00

Ruff and Ready, #378, Ann McGovern,
illus Harvey Eisenberg and Al White,
c1949..9.00

Seven Dwarfs Found a House 20.00

The Shy Little Kitten, #23, Cathleen
Schurr, illus Gustaf Tenggren,
c1946, dust jacket 35.00

Steve Canyon, #356, Milton Caniff,
c1959..12.00

Swiss Family Robinson, #95,
Jean Lewis, illus Paul Granger,
c1961..9.00

Tiger's Adventure, #208, William P.
Gottlieb, c1954 ....10.00

Trains Stamp Book, #A26, Kathleen N.
Daley, illus E. Joseph Dreany, with
stamps......................................25.00

Wally Gator, #502, Tom Golberg, illus
Hawley Pratt and Bill Lorencz,
c1963..15.00

*Woody Woodpecker Drawing Fun for
Beginners*, #372, Carl Buettner, illus
Harvey Eisenberg and Norman
McGary, c1959 ....12.00

Little Red Riding Hood

Collecting Hints: Little Red Riding
Hood is a hot collectible. Prices for
many pieces are in the hundreds of
dollars; those for advertising
plaques and baby dishes are in the
thousands.

A great unanswered question at
this time is how many Little Red
Riding Hood pieces were actually
made. Attempts at determining production levels have been unsuc-
cessful. The market could well be
eventually flooded with these items,
especially the most commonly found
pieces. New collectors are advised
to proceed with caution. Undecorat-
ed blanks are commonly found.
Their value is between 25% and
50% less than decorated examples.

History: On June 29, 1943, the U.S.
Patent Office issued design patent
#135,889 to Louise Elizabeth Bauer,

Zanesville, OH, assignor to the A.E.
Hull Pottery Company, Incorporated,
Crooksville, Ohio, for a "Design for a
Cookie Jar." Thus was born Hull's Little Red Riding Hood line, produced
and distributed between 1943 and
1957. The traditional story is that A.E.
Hull only made the blanks. Decoration
of the pieces was done by the Royal
China and Novelty Co., of Chicago.
When decoration was complete, the
pieces were returned to Hull for distribution. Recent scholarship suggests a
somewhat different approach.

Mark Supnick, author of *Hull
Pottery's "Little Red Riding Hood": A
Pictorial Reference and Price Guide*,
believes that A.E. Hull only made the
blanks for early cookie jars and the
dresser jar with a large bow in the
front. These can be identified by the
creamy off-white color of the pottery.
The majority of pieces were made
from a very white pottery, a body
Supnick attributes to The Royal China and Novelty Co., a division of Regal China. Given the similarity in form
to items in Royal's Old McDonald's
Farm line, Supnick concludes that
Hull contracted with Royal for production, as well as decoration.

Many hand-painted and decal
variations are encountered, e.g., the
wolf jar is found with a black, brown,
red or yellow base.

References: Harvey Duke, *Official
Identification and Price Guide to Pot-
tery and Porcelain*, 8th Edition,
House of Collectibles, 1995; Mark E.
Supnick, *Collecting Hull Pottery's
"Little Red Riding Hood,"* L-W Book
Sales, 1989, 1992 value update.

Reproduction Alert: Be alert for a
Mexican-produced cookie jar that
closely resembles Hull's Little Red
Riding Hood piece. The Mexican example is slightly shorter than Hull's
13-inch height.

Bank, standing 495.00
Butter Dish, cov............................400.00
Canister, cov
    Cereal 1,600.00
    Coffee 650.00
    Flour..650.00
    Sugar 650.00
    Tea..650.00
Cookie Jar, cov
    Covered Basket 300.00

Open basket, early 310.00
Creamer
   Pour-through type 315.00
   Side pour.............................135.00
   Tab handle 245.00
Dresser Jar...............................550.00
Lamp 2,195.00
Match Holder, wall type 545.00
Milk Pitcher...............................315.00
Mustard, cov, orig spoon 375.00
Range Shakers, pr 145.00
Salt and Pepper Shakers, pr
   Large 185.00
   Small 100.00
Sugar, cov 450.00
Teapot 365.00
Wall Pocket, Hull 450.00

Lunch Kits

Collecting Hints: The thermos is an integral part of the lunch kit. The two must be present for full value. There has been a tendency in recent years to remove the thermos from the lunch box and price the two separately. The wise collector will resist this trend. Scratches and rust detract from a metal kit's value and lower value by more than 50%.

History: Lunch kits date back to the 19th century when tin boxes were used by factory workers and field hands. The modern children's lunch kit, the form most sought by today's collector, was first sold in the 1930s. Gender, Paeschke & Frey Co., of Milwaukee issued a No. 9100 Mickey Mouse lunch kit for the 1935 Christmas trade. An oval lunch kit of a streamlined train, mkd "Decoware," dates from the same period.

Television brought the decorated lunch box into the forefront. The following are some of the leading manufacturers: Aladdin Company; Landers, Frary and Clark; Ohio Art (successor to Hibbard, Spencer, Bartlett & Co.) of Bryan, Ohio; Thermos/King Seeley; and Universal.

References: Larry Aikins, *Pictorial Price Guide to Metal Lunch Boxes & Thermoses*, L-W Book Sales, 1992, 1996 value update; ——, *Pictorial Price Guide to Vinyl & Plastic Lunch Boxes & Thermoses*, L-W Book Sales, 1992, 1995 value update; Philip R. Norman, *1993 Lunch Box & Thermos Price Guide*, published by

Adam 12, Aladdin Industries, Nashville, TN, 1972, $75.

author, 1992; Allen Woodall and Sean Brickell, *Illustrated Encyclopedia of Metal Lunch Boxes*, Schiffer Publishing, 1992.

Periodical: *Paileontologist's Report*, P.O. Box 3255, Burbank, CA 91508.

Collectors' Club: Step into the Ring, 829 Jackson St. Ext, Sandusky, OH 44870.

Note: Unless noted, prices include the original thermos that accompanied the box. Prices are for items in near mint condition.

Adam 12, 1973.............................75.00
Archies, 1969 ....90.00
Astronauts, dome type, 1960 ......250.00
Baseball Game,
   magnetic pieces, ...25.00
Battle Kit, 1965...........................125.00
Beatles, 1966, no thermos 400.00
Bedknobs and
   Broomsticks, 1972...................90.00
Bionic Woman, 1977 ....60.00
Bonzana, brown rim box, 1963 ...175.00
Captain Kangaroo, vinyl 600.00
Chan Clan, 1973 ....140.00
Cracker Jacks, 1969 ....75.00
Dark Crystal, 1982 ....35.00
Davy Crockett, 1955......................80.00
Deputy Dog, vinyl,
   no thermos, 1964 ....550.00
Dick Tracy, no thermos 150.00
Donnie & Marie, vinyl, 1977 ....130.00
Dr. Seuss, Cat in the Hat, elephant on
   back, metal, Aladdin Industries, Inc.,
   1970, no thermos 140.00
Dukes of Hazzard, 1983................60.00
Emergency!, 1973 ....75.00
Fat Albert, 1973............................60.00
Fireball XL-5, 1964......................270.00
Fritos, generic thermos, 1975 ....90.00
Ghostland, no thermos.................35.00

Green Hornet, 1967 ....525.00
Hanna-Barbera,
   Fantastic World, 1977 ....35.00
Happy Days, 1977 ....60.00
Hogan's Heroes,
   dome top, 1966 ....375.00
Home-Town Airport,
   dome top, 1960 ....1,200.00
Inch-High Private Eye 40.00
James Bond 007, 1966 ....375.00
Jet Patrol, 1957 ....500.00
Jungle Book, 1968 ....125.00
Kewtie Pie, vinyl 180.00
KISS, 1977..................................100.00
Land of the Giants, 1968.............185.00
Land of the Lost, 1975 ....110.00
Mickey Mouse and
   Donald Duck, 1954................450.00
Mickey Mouse Club,
   red rim, sky boat, 1977............45.00
Miss America, 1972 ....85.00
Mod Tulips, dome top, 1975 ....450.00
Mork and Mindy, 1979 ....35.00
Munsters, 1965 ....400.00
Nurse Julia, no thermos, 1969 ....100.00
Paramedics, 1978, no thermos 55.00
Partridge Family, 1971 ....70.00
Peanuts Wienie Roast, 1984 ....25.00
Pink Panther and Sons, 1984 ....55.00
Porky's Lunch Wagon, 1959 ....450.00
Red Paisley, dome top..................50.00
Road Runner, 1970......................90.00
Roy Rogers, Double R Bar Ranch, orig
   thermos, no cup 200.00
Smokey the Bear, 1975 ....550.00
Snoopy, vinyl, 1977......................45.00
Space Explorer, 1960 ....350.00
Space 1999, 1976.........................75.00
Star Wars, 1978 ....55.00
Three Little Pigs,
   no thermox, 1982 ....85.00
Transformers, orig thermos,
   Hasbro 1984, no cup..............18.00
U.S. Space Corps, orig thermos,
   no cup, 1961 ....400.00
Walt Disney School Bus,
   dome, 1968 ....100.00
Wee Pals Kid Power, 1974 ....40.00
Wild Bill Hickok and
   Jingles, 1955 ....240.00
Wild Frontier, magnetic pieces,
   no thermos 40.00
Wizard and the Van, vinyl 100.00
Yankee Doodle, 1975 ....50.00

M

Magazine Covers and Tear Sheets

Collecting Hints: A good cover should show the artist's signature, have the mailing label nonexistent or in a place that does not detract from the design element and have edges which are crisp but not trimmed.

When framing vintage paper, use acid-free mat board and tape with a water-soluble glue base, such as brown-paper gum tape or linen tape. The tape should only be affixed to the back side of the illustration. The rule of thumb is do not do anything that cannot be easily undone. Do not hang framed vintage paper in direct sunlight (causes fading) or in a high-humidity area such as a bathroom or above a kitchen sink (causes wrinkles in both the mat and artwork).

History: Magazine cover design attracted some of America's leading illustrators. Maxfield Parrish, Erte, Leyendecker and Norman Rockwell were dominate in the 20th century. In the mid-1930s, photographic covers gradually replaced illustrated covers. One of the leaders in the industry was *Life*, which emphasized photojournalism.

Magazine covers are frequently collected according to artist-signed covers, subject matter or historical events. Artist-signed covers feature a commercially printed artist's signature on the cover or the artist is identified inside as "Cover by...." The majority of collected covers are in full color and show significant design elements. Black memorabilia is often reflected in magazine covers and tear sheets and it is frequently collected for the positive affect it has on African-Americans. However, sometimes it is a reflection of the times in which it was printed and may represent subjects in an unfavorable light.

Many of America's leading artists also created the illustrations for magazine advertisements. The ads made characters such as the Campbell Kids, the Dutch Girl and Snap, Crackle and Pop world famous.

References: Norman E. Martinus and Harry L. Rinker, *Warman's Paper*, Wallace-Homestead, 1994; Norman I. Platnick, *Coles Phillips*, available from author (50 Brentwood Rd., Bay Shore, NY 11706) 1996; check local libraries for books about specific illustrators such as Parrish, Rockwell and Jessie Wilcox Smith.

Periodicals: *Illustrator Collector's News*, P.O. Box 1958, Sequim, WA 98392; *Paper Collectors' Marketplace* (*PCM*), P.O. Box 128, Scandinavia, WI 54977.

Notes: Prices of covers and complete magazines have remained stable the last few years, but those of tear sheets have declined as more and more magazines have glutted the market. Only a short time ago, magazines were thrown away when attics and garages were cleaned—now these publications are offered for sale. As more and more magazines are destroyed for the tear sheets, complete magazines rise in value proportionate to the decrease in supply. If a magazine is in mint condition, it should be left intact. We do NOT encourage removing illustrations from complete magazines. The complete magazine is the best tool for interpreting a specific historical time period. Editorial and advertising together define the spirit of the era.

Artist Signed
Rolf Armstrong 26.00
Torre Bevans, *Pictorial Review*, April 1920 ....20.00
Howard Chandler Christy 11.00
Grace Drayton (also Weiderseim)
  Paper Dolls
    Large format 20.00
    Small format 10.00
  Tear Sheet, color 4.00
Ruth Eastman, *The Designer*, Aug. 1913 ....10.00
Harrison Fisher, *Ladies' Home Journal*, Dec. 1913 ....29.00
James Montgomery Flagg, color 6.00
Bessie Pease Gutmann 28.00
Hamilton King, Coca-Cola girl illus 15.00
Leyendecker 16.00
Alphonse Mucha
  Century 110.00
  Literary Digest.....................45.00
Rose O'Neill

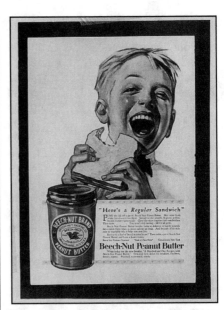

Beech Nut Peanut Butter, Delineator, 1920, unsgd illus, $15.

  Illustrated articles...................6.50
  Kewpies Stories
    Large format, *Woman's Home Companion*, 1911-1912......14.00
    Medium format, *Good Housekeeping*, 1916-1919 ....12.50
    Small format, *Good Housekeeping*, 1914-1916 ....10.00
R.F. Outcault, *Truth*, Feb. 15, 1896..........................18.00
Maxfield Parrish, *Ladies' Home Journal*, rows of soldiers, Nov. 16, 1912 ....50.00
Jessie Wilcox Smith
  Cover, *Good Housekeeping*.....................24.00
  Tear Sheet, Seven Stages of Childhood 17.50
Charles Twelvetrees, *Pictorial Review*
  Large format, pre-1930........17.50
  Small format, pre-1930........12.00
H.E. Wireman, *Woman's Home Companion*, Dec. 1915............14.00
Automobile
  Pre-1918
    Black and white 4.00
    Color 6.50
  1919-1937
    Black and white 2.50
    Color 4.00
  1938-1941
    Black and white 5.00
    Color 5.50
  1942-1955
    Black and white 1.50
    Color 2.50
Aviation

New Perfection Oil Cook Stoves and Ovens, *Designer* and *Woman's Magazine*, sgd Wetteroy illus, June 1920, $8.

Pre-1935	
Black and white	2.50
Color	3.00
Post-1935	
Black and white	1.00
Color	1.00
Beverage	
Beer, identified brand, color	4.00
Coca-Cola	
Pre-1925, color	10.00
1925-1950, color	7.00
Wines and Liquors	2.50
Black Memorabilia	
Covers, personalities	
Louis Armstrong	11.00
Sammy Davis Jr.	7.50
Martin Luther King	10.00
Tear Sheet, adv	
Aunt Jemima	4.50
Cream of Wheat	12.00
Gold Dust Twins	9.00
Cigarettes, Philip Morris, matted and shrink wrapped	15.00
Fashion	
Pre-1930, color	5.50
Post-1930, color	3.00
Food	
Cereal, Cream of Wheat, Li'l Abner graphic, matted and shrink wrapped	15.00
Dairy products	1.75
Gum	2.00
Jell-O	
Animals or children	4.50
Rose O'Neill, sgd, Kewpies, color	17.00
Junket Powder, 1943 ad, matted and shrink wrapped	15.00
Soups, Campbell Kids, large	9.00
Syrup, Karo, features Dionne Quints, matted and shrink wrapped	15.00
Jewelry, color	2.00
Gum, Clark's Teaberry, matted and shrink wrapped	15.00
Movie Stars and Famous People	
Lauren Bacall	7.00
John Wayne	7.00
Toys	
Erector Sets	3.50
Trains, Lionel or Ives	4.00
View-Master, matted and shrink wrapped	15.00
Wagons	2.25

Magazines

Collecting Hints: A rule of thumb for pricing general magazines without covers designed by popular artists is the more you would enjoy displaying a copy on your coffee table, the more elite the publication or the more the advertising or editorial content relates to today's collectibles, the higher the price. *Life* magazine went into millions of homes each week, *Harper's Bazaar* and *Vogue* did not. Upper-class families tended to discard last month's publication, while middle-class families found the art on the *Saturday Evening Post* and *Collier's* irresistible and saved them. The greater the supply, the lower the price.

History: In the early 1700s, general magazines were a major source of information for the reader. Literary magazines, such as *Harper's*, became popular in the 19th century. By 1900, the first photo-journal magazines appeared. *Life*, the most famous example, was started by Henry Luce in 1932.

Magazines created for women featured "how to" articles about cooking, sewing, decorating and child care. Many of the publications were entirely devoted to fashion and living a fashionable life, such as *Harper's Bazaar* and *Vogue*. Men's magazines were directed at masculine interests of the time, such as hunting, fishing and woodworking, supplemented with appropriate "girlie" titles.

References: Ron Barlow and Ray Reynolds, *Insider's Guide to Old Books, Magazines, Newspapers and Trade Catalogs*, Windmill Publishing (2147 Windmill View Rd., El Cajon, CA 92020), 1996; Alan Betrock, *Illustrated Price Guide to Cult Magazines*, Shake Books, 1995; —, *Unseen America*, Shake Book, 1990; David K. Henkel, *Magazines*, Avon Books, 1993; Denis C. Jackson, *Men's "Girlie" Magazines*, 3rd Edition, published by author (P.O. Box 1958, Sequim, WA 98392), 1991; —, *Master's Price & Identification Guide to Old Magazines*, published by author (P.O. Box 1958, Sequim, WA 98392), 1992; Norman E. Martinus and Harry L. Rinker, *Warman's Paper*, Wallace-Homestead, 1994; *1994 Playboy Magazine Price Guide*, Playboy Collectors Association, 1994; *Old Magazine Price Guide*, L-W Book Sales, 1994, 1996 value update; Lee Server, *Danger Is My Business: An Illustrated History of the Fabulous Pulp Magazines*, Chronicle Books, 1993; Gene Utz, *Collecting Paper*, Books Americana, 1993.

Periodicals: *Collecting Cult Magazines*, 449 12th St., #2-R, Brooklyn, NY 11215; *Illustrator Collector's News*, P.O. Box 1958, Sequim, WA 98392; *Paper Collectors' Marketplace* (*PCM*), P.O. Box 128, Scandinavia, WI 54977.

Notes: General magazine prices listed below are retail prices. They may be considerably higher than what would be offered for an entire collection filling your basement or garage. Bulk prices for common magazines such as *Life*, *Collier's* and *Saturday Evening Post* generally range between 50¢ and $1 per issue. Dealers have to sort, protect with plastic covering, discard those that have had items clipped from the interior or have marred covers and make no money on those which they never sell.

African Violet, Sept. 1952	5.00
Airman, Official Air Force Journal, March 1961	3.00
American Childhood, April 1941	5.00
American Golfer, Dec. 1932	10.00
American Heritage, Oct. 1958, Pocahontas cover	6.00
American Motorist, 1916	10.00
Antiques, March 1965	5.00
Arizona Highway	
Aug. 1956, Supailand Waterfall cover	6.00

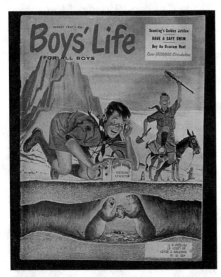

Boy's Life, Creig Flessel cover illus, August 1957, $18.

Dec. 1959, Prickly
Pear in Bloom.............................5.00
July 1960, Navajo portrait 7.00
Atlantic, July 1954,
Churchill cover............................6.00
Aviation, 1928...............................15.00
Better Homes and Gardens,
Dec. 1942 ....6.00
Better Photo, 1913 ....4.00
Boy's Life
June 1955, Boy Scout Statue cover,
Coca-Cola ad 5.00
Jan. 1969, Skiing cover, Bart Starr
article...4.00
Oct. 1970, Bill Bradley cover......6.00
Chatterbox, bound year, 1917,
10" x 7-1/2", 412 pgs 25.00
Children's Play Mate, Nov. 1954.....5.00
Child's Life, 1930.............................4.00
Collier's, Iwo Jima photo cover,
Feb. 18, 1955 ....18.00
Confidential, Aug. 1966, Sammy Davis
cover...8.00
Confidential Confessions,
Aug. 1959 ....3.00
Cosmopolitan, 1910 ....6.00
Dearborn Independent,
Sept. 1926 ....3.00
Delineator, 1904 ....20.00
*Ellery Queen Mystery
Magazine*, 1950s 5.00
Esquire, Sept. 1936.......................12.00
Etude, Nov. 1942, West
Point choir article 5.00
Family Circle, 1954..........................5.00
Farm & Fireside, March 1923,
boy and dog cover 6.00
Farm Journal
Feb. 1923, boy on cover 9.00
Dec. 1927, Santa and

Elves on cover 8.50
April 1928, ducks and
chicks cover 8.60
March 1940, sheep
and lion cover............................5.00
Farm Life, Sept. 1923, cows in pasture
cover...6.00
Friends
Sept. 1955, Girl Eating Apple cover,
Joan Collins article....................5.00
May 1965, NY World's Fair cover,
Errol Flynn article 7.00
Front Page Detective, Aug. 1952....3.00
Golden Book Magazine, 1929, 6 months
bound 35.00
Good Housekeeping, 1965 ....4.00
Hit Parade, Sept. 1947, Jane Greer
cover...7.00
Horticulture, Dec. 1959, poinsettia
cover...3.00
Iron Trade Review Weekly Magazine,
1924, 26 bound issues, Cleve,
900 pgs.....................................35.00
Jack & Jill, 1961 ....10.00
Junior Natural History, April 1954,
goat cover...................................4.00
Ladies Home Journal, June 1970, Tricia
Nixon cover 5.00
Life
Dec. 30, 1940, Britain's Desert
Fighters on cover 7.00
July 13, 1953, Hillary Climb of Mt.
Everest, adv with stars.............12.00
April 21, 1961, Khrushchev and
Gargarin cover, article about Gary
Player...7.00
July 7, 1961, Ike Down on the Farm
cover 10.00
Oct. 12, 1962, Pope
John XXIII cover.........................9.00
Dec. 13, 1963, LBJ in White House
cover, Diligenti Quints story 12.00
March 20, 1964, Lodge in Saigon
cover, Malcolm X story...............6.00
July 10, 1964, Oswald and Diaries
cover, Mark Twain story.............9.00
Oct. 30, 1964, Don Schollander
cover, Herbert Hoover's death
article..10.00
Oct. 15, 1965, Pope Paul VI in Amer-
ica cover, Arthur Ashe article.....9.00
July 17, 1970, Rose Kennedy at 80
cover...7.00
Feb. 12, 1971, Jackie
Onassis cover 7.50
April 23, 1971, Jane Fonda, Rebel
cover, basketball stars article...10.00
Oct. 15, 1971, Disney World Opens
cover, Joan Crawford article 9.00
July 7, 1972, George McGovern
cover, Pandas in DC article 4.00
Literary Digest, May 1, 1937, Princess
Elizabeth cover..........................7.00

Saturday Evening Post, March 21, 1959,
artist sgd, $18.

Look
April 19, 1955, Royal Family cover,
Ed Sullivan article 12.00
Sept. 2, 1958, Ingrid
Bergman cover 15.00
Oct. 9, 1962, Jackie Gleason and
Lucille Ball cover......................17.50
Dec. 8, 1972, Diana Ross cover 7.00
McCall's, 1961, Christmas Make-It
Ideas 4.00
Modern Screen, Aug. 1946,
Gregory Peck cover, Lucy
Ball cover photo 15.00
Motion Picture, Oct. 1959, Sandra Dee
cover, Fabian article................10.00
National Geographic, Aug. 1965,
tribute to Sir Winston Churchill,
137 pgs.....................................45.00
Newsweek, Aug. 19, 1974, Pres Ford
cov, special issue 6.00
Photo Screen, July 1973, Waltons
cover 8.00
Quick, July 24, 1950, Princess Elizabeth
cover 8.00
Redbook, June, 1925.....................5.00
Rexall, June 1939, Nan Gray cover,
Judy Garland article 5.00
Saturday Evening Post
Nov. 5, 1955, Nehru,
Rockwell cover.........................12.00
Jan. 19, 1963, Beverly Hillbillies
cover 30.00
May 2, 1964, Fischer
Quints cover.............................12.00
July 3, 1965, Charleton
Heston cover............................12.00
Scouting, Sept. 1973, Soap Box Derby
cover 3.00
Secrets, Jan. 1959 ....3.00
Silver Screen, June 1973, Bunkers
cover, Brady Bunch article 8.00
Song Hits, March 1953, Janet Leigh cov-
er, Johnnie Ray article 6.00

Story Parade, June 1952................4.00
Successful Farming, May 1941 ....5.00
Time
    Nov. 30, 1942, Halsey cover......6.00
    June 19, 1944,
    Eisenhower cover........................8.00
    Oct. 9, 1972, Pat Nixon portrait..4.00
    Jan. 29, 1973, Nixon Caricature
    cover 5.00
    Dec. 7, 1987, Shirley Maclaine ..3.00
Today's Health, June 1960, Kate Smith
    cover, Civil War article...............4.00
TV Star Parade, Dec. 1972,
    Sonny and Cher cover,
    Shirley Jones article 5.00
Vogue, April 1936...........................10.00
Wee Wisdom, July 1939...................7.50
Women's Day, Oct. 1943,
    cover price 2 cents 7.00
Woman's World, March 1936..........2.00

Marbles

Collecting Hints: Handmade glass marbles usually command higher prices than machine-made glass, clay or mineral marbles. There are a few notable exceptions, e.g., machine-made comic strip marbles were made for a limited time only and are highly prized by collectors. Care must be taken in purchasing this particular type since the comic figure was stenciled on the marble. A layer of glass was to be overlaid on the stencil, but sometimes this process was not completed. In such cases, the stencils rub or wear off.

Some of the rarer examples of handmade marbles are Clambroth, Lutz, Indian Swirls, Peppermint Swirls and Sulphides. Marble values are normally determined by their type, size and condition. Usually, the larger the marble, the more valuable it is within its category.

A marble in mint condition is unmarred and has the best possible condition with a clear surface. It may have surface abrasions caused by rubbing while in its original package. A marble in good condition may have a few small surface dings, scratches and slight surface cloudiness. However, the core must be easily seen and the marble must be free of large chips or fractures.

History: Marbles date back to ancient Greece, Rome, Egypt and other early civilizations. In England,

Good Friday is known as "Marbles Day" because the game was considered a respectable and quiet pastime for the hallowed day.

During the American Civil War, soldiers carried marbles and a small board to play solitaire, a game whose object was to jump the marbles until only one was left in the center of the board. In the last few generations, school children have identified marbles as "peewees," "shooters," "commies," and "cat's eyes." A National Marbles Tournament has been held each year in June since 1922.

References: Robert Block, *Marbles Identification and Price Guide*, Schiffer Publishing, 1996; Everett Grist, *Antique and Collectible Marbles*, 3rd Edition, Collector Books, 1992; ——, *Everett Grist's Big Book of Marbles*, Collector Books, 1993, 1995 value update; ——, *Everett Grist's Machine Made and Contemporary Marbles*, 2nd Edition, Collector Books, 1995; Dennis Webb, *Greenberg's Guide to Marbles*, Greenberg Publishing, 1994.

Collectors' Clubs: Buckeye Marble Collectors Club, 437 Meadowbrook Dr., Newark, OH 43055; Marble Collectors Unlimited, P.O. Box 206, Northboro, MA 01532; Marble Collectors Society of America, P.O. Box 222, Trumbull, CT 06611; National Marble Club of America, 440 Eaton Rd., Drexel Hill, PA 19026; Sea-Tac Marble Collectors Club, P.O. Box 793, Monroe, WA 98272; Southern California Marble Club, 18361-1 Strathern St., Reseda, CA 91335.

Videotape: Elliot Pincus, *Marble World: Video Magazine Issue #1*, Elliot's Marbles, 1994.

Museums: Corning Museum of Glass, Corning, NY; Sandwich Glass Museum, Sandwich, MA; Smithsonian Institution, Museum of Natural History, Washington, DC; Wheaton Village Museum, Millville, NJ.

Reproduction Alert: Comic marbles and some machine-made marbles are being reproduced, as are some polyvinyl packages, mesh packages and original boxes. A complete list and images are shown at http://pages.prodigy.com/marbles/.

Lutz, banded, 3/4" $450.

Notes: Handmade marbles listed below are common examples in mint condition. Unusual examples command prices that are two to 20 times higher. Mint-condition machine-made marbles priced here have a diameter between 9/16 and 11/16 inch, unless otherwise noted.

Advisors: Stanley A. Block and Robert S. Block.

Handmade Marbles

End of Day

Onionskin
    3/4"...35.00
    1-1/2" 200.00
    1-3/4" 200.00
    2"...300.00

Lutz

Banded
    5/8"..100.00
    1"...250.00
    1-1/2" 300.00
    1-3/4" 450.00
End of Day Onionskin
    5/8"..225.00
    3/4".......................................300.00
    1"...750.00
    1-1/2" 1,750.00
Ribbon
    5/8"..300.00
    3/4".......................................400.00
    1"...800.00
    1-1/2" 1,500.00

Mica

5/8"...10.00
3/4"...25.00
1"..100.00
1-1/2"...200.00

Other

Benningtons 1.00
Clays...10
Glazed painted china 10.00
Unglazed painted china 5.00

Sulphide

7/8"	200.00
1-1/4"	125.00
1-1/2"	100.00
2"	125.00

Swirls

Banded

5/8"	10.00
3/4"	15.00
1"	65.00
1-1/2"	140.00

Divided Core

3/4"	18.00
1-1/2"	90.00
1-3/4"	150.00
2"	225.00

Indian

5/8"	75.00
3/4"	125.00
1"	300.00
1-1/2"	1,500.00

Latticinio Core

3/4"	15.00
1-1/2"	75.00
1-3/4"	125.00
2"	200.00

Peppermint

5/8"	65.00
3/4"	125.00
1"	300.00
1-1/2"	1,500.00

Ribbon Core

3/4"	75.00
1-1/2"	200.00
1-3/4"	300.00
2"	500.00

Solid Core

3/4"	25.00
1-1/2"	125.00
1-3/4"	250.00
2"	300.00

Machine-Made Marbles

Akro Agate Co.

Blue oxblood	65.00
Carnelian agate	15.00
Egg Yolk or Carnelian oxblood	80.00
Helmet Patch	2.50

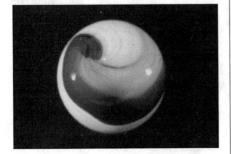

Akro Agate, Popeye corkscrew, blue/yellow $60.

Lemonade corkscrew	15.00
Lemonade oxblood	55.00
Limeade corkscrew	25.00
Limeade oxblood	150.00
Milky oxblood	20.00
Moonstone	10.00
Patch oxblood	7.50

Popeye corkscrew

Blue/yellow	60.00
Green/yellow	18.00
Purple/yellow	60.00
Red/blue	75.00
Red/green	25.00
Red/yellow	18.00
Silver oxblood	30.00
Slag	1.00
Sparkler	50.00
Swirl oxblood	20.00

2 color

Opaque corkscrew

Color matrix	4.00
White matrix	2.00
Transparent or translucent corkscrew	6.00

Christensen Agate Co.

American Agate or Bloodie	45.00
Cobra/Cyclone	750.00
Electric Swirl	75.00

Flame Swirl

2 color	125.00
3 color	300.00
Guinea	350.00
Slag	30.00

M.F. Christensen & Son Co.

Brick, 9-1/16" to 11/16"	60.00
Oxblood Slag	100.00
Slag	3.00

Marble King Co.

Multicolor opaque

Color matrix

Bumblebee/Yellow Jacket (yellow/black)	1.50
Cub Scout (yellow/blue)	5.00
Girl Scout/John Deere (yellow/green)	8.00
Spiderman (blue/red)	250.00
Tiger (orange/black)	25.00
Wasp (red/black)	5.00
Watermelon (red/green)	1,000.00
White matrix	.25
Two-color, white matrix	.10

Master Marble Co.

Patch	1.00

Sunburst

Clear	20.00
Opaque	5.00

Peltier Glass Co.

Peerless Patch	5.00

Marble King, Spiderman (blue/red) $250.

Peerless Patch with aventurine	15.00
Slag	20.00
Sunset, Champion Jr., Muddy, Acme Reeler, Rainbo (new type), Tri-Color, 7-Up, Banana	1.00
Two-color Rainbo, old type	18.00
Two-color Rainbo, old type, with aventurine	50.00

Three-color Rainbo

With aventurine	125.00
Xmas Tree, Patriot, Rebel, Ketchup and Mustard	75.00

Transitional

Creased or pinched pontil transition	10.00
Folded pontil transition	25.00
Melted pontil transition	50.00
Regular, ground or pinpoint pontil transitional	75.00

Unidentified Manufacturers

Bullet mold	15.00
Clearie, Cat's-eye or Chinese Checker	.01
Common patch or swirl	.25
Ravenswood multicolor	10.00

Wire Pull

New	10.00
Old	20.00

Vitro Agate/Gladding-Vitro Co.

All-Red	.25
Blackie	.50
Conqueror	1.00
Hybrid Cat's-eye	2.00
Oxblood patch	7.50
Patch and Brush Transparent	.10
Patch and Ribbon Transparent	.10
Victory	2.00

Original Packaging

Akro Agate Co.

No. 4, Heroes, box of 50	1,500.00
No. 16, cardboard sleeve	125.00
No. 150, tin	350.00
No. 300, cardboard box	600.00
Popeye box, yellow	1,400.00

Christensen Agate Co.

Box of 25 guineas	15,000.00
Box of 100 slags	1,000.00

M.F. Christensen & Son Co.

Box of 8 opaques 1,500.00

Marble King, polyvinyl bag
of 20 Cat's-eyes5.00

Master Marble Co.

Display box of 100 clearies 350.00
No. 5, box of 5 clearies................650.00

Peltier Glass Co., No. 5, box
of 30 comics50.00

Vitro Agate Co.

Mesh bag of 25 Conquerors..........50.00
Polyvinyl bag of 20 Cat's-eyes 5.00

Matchcovers

Collecting Hints: Matchcovers generally had large production runs; very few are considered rare. Most collectors try to obtain unused covers. They remove the matches, flatten the covers and mount them in albums which are arranged by category.

Trading is the principal means of exchange among collectors, usually on a one-for-one basis. At flea markets and shows, beer or pinup art ("girlie") matchcovers frequently are priced at $1 to $5. Actually those interested in such covers would be best advised to join one of the collector clubs and get involved in swapping.

History: The book match was invented by Joshua Pusey, a Philadelphia lawyer, who also was a chemist in his spare time. In 1892, Pusey put 10 cardboard matches into a cover of plain white board and sold 200 of them to the Mendelson Opera Co., which, in turn, hand-printed messages on the front. The first machine-made matchbook was made by the Binghamton Match Co., Binghamton, NY, for the Piso Co., of Warren, PA. The only known surviving cover is now owned by the Diamond Match Co.

Few covers survive from the late 1890s to the 1930s. The modern craze for collecting matchcovers was started when a set of 10 covers was issued for the Century of Progress exhibit at the 1933 Chicago World's Fair. The golden age of matchcovers was the mid 1940s through the early 1960s when the covers were a popular advertising medium. Principal manufacturers included Atlas Match, Brown and Bigelow, Crown Match,

Diamond Match, Lion Match, Ohio Match and Universal Match.

The arrival of throwaway lighters, such as BIC, brought an end to the matchcover era. Today, manufacturing costs for a matchbook can range from less than a penny to 7 or 8 cents for a special die-cut cover. As a result, matchcovers no longer are an attractive free giveaway, and, therefore, many of the older, more desirable covers are experiencing a marked increase in value. Collectors have also turned to the small pocket-type boxes as a way of enhancing and building their collections.

References: Bill Retskin, *Matchcover Collector's Price Guide*, 2nd Edition, Antique Trader Books, 1997; H. Thomas Steele, Jim Heimann, Rod Dyer, *Close Cover before Striking*, Abbeville Press, 1987.

Periodicals: *Match Hunter*, 740 Poplar, Boulder, CO, 80304; *Matchcover Classified*, 16425 Dam Rd #3, Clearlake, CA 95422.

Collectors' Clubs: American Matchcover Collecting Club, P.O. Box 18481, Asheville, NC 28814; Liberty Bell Matchcover Club, 5001 Albridge Way, Mount Laurel, NJ 08054; Long Beach Matchcover Club, 2501 W. Sunflower H-5, Santa Ana, CA

Movies, Janet Gaynor in "A Star Is Born," Diamond Match Co., NYC, 25 cents.

Sports, Forrest McPherson, Philadelphia Eagles, Diamond Match Co., NYC, $1.

92704; Newmoon Matchbox & Label Club, 425 E. 51st St., New York, NY 10022; Rathkamp Matchcover Society, 2920 E. 77th St., Tulsa, OK 74136; Trans-Canada Matchcover Club, P.O. Box 219, Caledonia, Ontario, Canada NOA-1A0; Windy City Matchcover Club, 3104 Fargo Ave., Chicago, IL 60645. There are also many regional clubs throughout the United States and Canada.

Special Covers

Apollo Flights, 8-18, Cameo............5.00
Dwight D. Eisenhower,
    5-Star General.........................17.50
Economy Blue Print, pinup girls,
    set of 6, 1950s.........................48.00
Presidential Helicopter,
    Marine One 12.00
Presidential Yacht, Patricia..........12.00
Pull for Wilkie, Pullquick Match 30.00
Stoeckle Select Beer, Giant,
    Stoeckle Brewery 7.50
Washington Redskins, set of 20 ...40.00

Topics

Airlines 25
Americana...05
Atlas, 4 color 10
Banks 05
Beer and Brewery 75
Best Western, stock design 10
Bowling Alleys....................................05
Cameo's, Universal trademark..........05
Canadian, 4 color...............................10
Chinese Restaurants 05
Christmas..05
Classiques 50
Colleges..05
Contours, diecut.................................20

McCoy Pottery

Collecting Hints: Several marks were used by the McCoy Pottery Co. Take the time to learn the marks and the variations. Pieces can often be dated by according to the mark. Most pottery marked "McCoy" was made by the Nelson McCoy Co.

History: The J.W. McCoy Pottery Co., was established in Roseville, OH, in September 1899. The early McCoy company produced both stoneware and some art pottery lines, including Rosewood. In October 1911, three potteries merged to create the Brush-McCoy Pottery Co. This firm continued to produce the original McCoy lines and added several new art lines. Much of the early pottery is not marked.

In 1910, Nelson McCoy and his father, J.W. McCoy, founded the Nelson McCoy Sanitary Stoneware Co. In 1925, the McCoy family sold its interest in the Brush-McCoy Pottery Co., and started to expand and improve the Nelson McCoy Co. The new company produced stoneware, earthenware specialties and artware.

References: Susan and Al Bagdade, *Warman's American Pottery and Porcelain*, Wallace-Homestead, 1994; Bob Hanson, Craig Nissen and Margaret Hanson, *McCoy Pottery*, Collector Books, 1996; Sharon and Bob Huxford, *Collector's Encyclopedia of Brush-McCoy Pottery*, Collector Books, 1996; ——, *Collectors Encyclopedia of McCoy Pottery*, Collector Books, 1980, 1995 value update.

Periodicals: *NM Express*, 3081 Rock Creek Dr., Broomfield, CO 80020.

Reproduction Alert: Unfortunately, Nelson McCoy never registered his McCoy trademark, a fact discovered by Roger Jensen of Tennessee. As a result, Jensen began using the McCoy mark on a series of ceramic reproductions made in the early

1990s. While the marks on these recently made pieces copy the original, Jensen made objects which were never produced by the Nelson McCoy Co. The best known example is the Red Riding Hood cookie jar which was originally designed by Hull and also made by Regal China.

The McCoy fakes are a perfect example of how a mark on a piece can be deceptive. A mark alone is not proof that a piece is period or old. Knowing the proper marks and what was and was not made in respect to forms, shapes and decorative motifs is critical in authenticating a pattern.

Ashtray, Seagram's VO,
   Imported Canadian
   Whiskey, black, gold letters.....15.00
Baker, oval, Brown Drip, 9-1/4" l...12.00
Bank, sailor, large duffel bag over
   shoulder 20.00
Basket, black and white, emb weave ext,
   double handle..........................25.00
Bean Pot, brown
   #2 ....35.00
   #22 ....60.00
Birdbath....................................28.00
Bowl, 8-1/2" x 3", green 50.00
Casserole, open, Brown Drip 4.00
Center Bowl, 5-1/2" h, Classic Line,
   pedestal, turquoise,
   brushed gold 35.00
Chuck Wagon, El Rancho...........150.00
Coffee Server, El Rancho 125.00
Cookie Jar, cov
   Coffee Grinder 50.00
   Colonial Fireplace 150.00
   Cookstove
      Black....................................35.00
      White 35.00
   Covered Wagon.......................155.00
   Jug, red label with
   Coca-Cola logo 80.00
   Kookie Kettle, black 55.00
   Mr. and Mrs. Owl 155.00
   Oaken Bucket 40.00
   Pontiac Indian 400.00
   Potbelly stove, black 50.00
   Puppy, with sign.....................135.00
   Sad Clown 125.00
   Schoolhouse 225.00
   Strawberry, white 35.00
   Tea Kettle, black 40.00
   Tourist Car 150.00
   Train, black 150.00
   W.C. Fields 400.00
   Woodsey Owl..........................345.00
Creamer
   Brown Drip, 3-1/2" h..................6.00

Soda, Dr Pepper, Universal Match Corp., 85 cents; Beer, Heilman's Old Style Lager, Ohio Match Co., Wadsworth, OH, 75 cents.

Tea set, English Ivy, vine handles, teapot, creamer, and sugar, price for set, $35.

Elsie the Cow 20.00
Custard Cup,
vertical ridges, green 5.00
Decanter, Apollo Mission...............30.00
Dog-Food Dish, emb Scottie 15.00
Flower Arranger, black 15.00
Flower Bowl, Grecian, 12" d, 3" h, 24k
gold marbling 24.00
Hanging Basket, stoneware, mkd
"Nelson McCoy," 1926.............20.00
Jardiniere
6" d
Glossy black, mkd
"McCoy", 6" 65.00
Yellow, 1940s.......................60.00
7" d
Spring Woodline, c1960.......45.00
Swirl, black matte.................38.00
Mug
Surburbia, yellow......................10.00
Willow Ware, brown, c1926......15.00
Pitcher
Brown, Drip, 5" h, 16 oz 9.00
Elephant, figural,
tan glaze, c1940........................32.00
Water Lily, c1935 ....20.00
Planter
Arcature, green and yellow 30.00
Wishing Well 18.00
Reamer, green glaze, 8" d, 1948 ..12.00
Salt and Pepper Shakers, pr, figural,
cucumber and mango, 1954....20.00
Spoon Rest
Butterfly, dark green, 1953.......15.00
Penguin, black,
white and red, 1953..................20.00
Sugar, cov, emb face and scrolls, red
glazed cover 10.00
Teapot
Brown Drip, short spout............20.00
Grecian, 1958...........................30.00
Sunburst Gold, 1957 ....25.00
Vase
Blossomtime............................40.00
Bud, green................................18.00
Double Handles,

green, 8" h, 1948......................50.00
Maroon Gloss, 6" h, 1940s.......35.00
Swan, pink 25.00
Triple Lily, 8-1/2" h, 1950 ....90.00
Wheat, 8" h, 5" d,
yellow, brown tint 45.00

McKee Glass

Collecting Hints: McKee Glass was mass produced in most colors. Therefore, a collector should avoid chipped or damaged pieces.

History: The McKee Glass Co., was established in 1843 in Pittsburgh; in 1852, it opened a factory to produce pressed glass. In 1888, the company relocated to Jeannette, PA, an area that contained several firms that made Depression-era wares. McKee produced many types of glass, including glass window panes, tumblers, tablewares, Depression glass, milk glass and bar and utility objects and continued working at the Jeannette location until 1951 when it was sold to the Thatcher Manufacturing Co.

McKee named its colors Chalaine Blue, Custard, Seville Yellow and Skokie Green. The firm preferred Skokie Green to jadite, popular with other manufacturers at the time. McKee also used these opaque colors as the background for several patterns, including dots of red, green and black and red ships. A few items were decorated with decals. Most of the canisters and shakers were lettered in black indicating the purpose for which they were intended.

Candy dish, orange body, 3/4" gold trim on lid, gold finial, clear base, 7-3/4" h to top of finial, $20.

References: Gene Florence, *Kitchen Glassware of the Depression Years*, 5th Edition, Collector Books, 1995; Ellen T. Schroy, *Warman's Glass*, 2nd Edition, Wallace-Homestead, 1995.

Bowl, 4-1/2" d, Skokie green.........12.00
Butter Dish, red ships on white 27.50
Canister
3-1/2" h, 24 oz, open, red ships on
white 14.00
4" h, ivory, round
Cov 18.00
Open......................................10.00
4-1/2" h, red ships
on white, open 35.00
5-1/2" h, 6" w, cov
Ivory.......................................37.00
Skokie Green, coffee 55.00
6" h, cereal, Seville
yellow, open 47.00
Cordial, Rock Crystal 12.00
Dish, cov, 4" x 5", red ships, white
ground 20.00
Drip Dish, 4" x 5",
cov, Skokie green....................30.00
Eggbeater Bowl, ivory, 1 spout 30.00
Fish Dish, 7" l, oval,
Skokie green 14.00
Flour Shaker,
Chalaine Blue, square...........125.00
Lemon Reamer, Skokie green 30.00
Measuring Cup
Red ships, white ground 28.00
Seville Yellow, 4 cup, ftd........120.00
Pitcher
Dark Skokie green, 16 oz 75.00
Skokie green, 16 oz 37.00
Yutec, Eclipse,
mkd "Presscut".........................45.00
Pitcher, measuring type, beater, Skokie
green 45.00
Range Shakers, pr, 5" h, sq, Skokie
green 27.00
Refrigerator Dish
4" x 5", open, red ships, white
ground......................................7.00
5" x 4-1/2", cov, ivory 23.00
5" x 8"
Cov
Ivory 32.00
Seville Yellow....................47.00
Skokie Green 40.00
Open, red ships,
white ground 9.00
Salt and Pepper Shakers, pr, red ships,
white ground...........................28.00
Shaker, Seville Yellow, sq
Flour..50.00
Plain...25.00
Sugar 50.00
Tom and Jerry Mug, white 5.00

Tumbler
   4" h, flat
      Ivory 12.00
      Sextec, crystal......................20.00
   4-1/2" h, ftd
      Ivory 12.00
      Seville Yellow......................14.00
Water Cooler Set,
   vaseline, orig carton 350.00

Metlox Pottery

Collecting Hints: The choices of patterns and backstamps is overwhelming. Collectors should, therefore, concentrate on one specific line and pattern. Among the most popular Poppytrail patterns are California Ivy, Homestead Provincial and Red Rooster.

The recent cookie jar craze has attracted a number of collectors to Metlox's cookie jar line. Most examples sell within a narrow price range. The Little Red Riding Hood jar is an exception, often selling at two to three times the price of other cookie jars.

History: In 1921, T.C. Prouty and Willis, his son, founded Proutyline Products, a company designed to develop Prouty's various inventions. In 1922, Prouty built a tile plant in Hermosa Beach to manufacture decorative and standard wall and floor tiles.

Metlox (a contraction of metallic oxide) was established in 1927. Prouty built a modern all-steel factory in Manhattan Beach to manufacture outdoor ceramic signs, but the Depression impacted strongly on this type of business. When T.C. Prouty died in 1931, Willis reorganized the company and began to produce a line of solid-color dinnerware similar to that produced by Bauer. In 1934, the line was fully developed and sold under the Poppytrail trademark, chosen because the poppy is California's official state flower. Fifteen different colors were produced over an eight-year period.

Other dinnerware lines produced in the 1930s include Mission Bell, sold exclusively by Sears Roebuck & Co.; Pintoria, based on an English Staffordshire line; and Yorkshire, patterned after Gladding-McBean's Coronado line. Most of these lines did not survive World War II. In the late 1930s Metlox employed the services of Carl Romanelli, a designer of figurines, miniatures and Zodiac vases. He created a line for Metlox called Modern Masterpieces, which featured bookends, busts, figural vases, figures and wall pockets.

During World War II, Metlox devoted its manufacturing efforts to the production of machine parts and parts for the B-25 bombers. When the war ended, Metlox returned to dinnerware production. In 1947, Evan K. Shaw, whose American Pottery in Los Angeles had been destroyed by fire, purchased Metlox. Production of hand-painted dinnerware patterns accelerated: California Ivy was introduced in 1946, California Provincial and Homestead Provincial in 1950, Red Rooster in 1955, California Strawberry in 1961, Sculptured Grape in 1963 and Della Robbia in 1965. In the 1950s, Bob Allen and Mel Shaw, art directors, introduced a number of new shapes and lines, including Aztec, California Contempora, California Free Form, California Mobile and Navajo.

When Vernon Kilns ceased operation in 1958, Metlox bought the trade name and select dinnerware molds and established a separate Vernon Ware branch. Under the direction of Doug Bothwell, the line soon rivaled the Poppytrail patterns.

Artware continued to flourish in the 1950s and 1960s. Harrison McIntosh was one of the key designers. Two popular lines were American Royal Horses and Nostalgia, scale-model antique carriages. Between 1946 and 1956 Metlox made a series of ceramic cartoon characters under license from Walt Disney. A line of planters designed by Helen Slater and Poppets, doll-like stoneware flower holders, were marketed in the 1960s and 1970s. Recent production included novelty cookie jars and Colorstax, a revival solid-color dinnerware.

Management remained in the Shaw family. Evan K. was joined by his two children, Ken and Melinda. Kenneth Avery, Melinda's husband, eventually became plant manager. When Evan K. died in 1980, Kenneth Avery became president. In 1988, Melinda Avery became the guiding force. The company ceased operations in 1989.

References: Susan and Al Bagdade, *Warman's American Pottery and Porcelain*, Wallace-Homestead, 1994; Jack Chipman, *Collector's Encyclopedia of California Pottery*, Collector Books, 1992, 1995 value update; Harvey Duke, *Official Identification and Price Guide to Pottery and Porcelain*, 8th Edition, House of Collectibles, 1995; Carl Gibbs Jr., *Collector's Encyclopedia of Metlox Potteries*, Collector Books, 1995; Lois Lehner, *Lehner's Encyclopedia of U.S. Marks on Pottery, Porcelain & Clay*, Collector Books, 1988.

Antique Grape

Casserole
   1 qt...55.00
   2 qt...75.00
Creamer..18.00
Cup and Saucer............................12.00
Gravy, 1 pt 32.00
Pitcher, water 125.00
Platter
   9" l...32.00
   14" l...40.00
Salad Plate, 7" d...........................10.00
Salt and Pepper Shakers, pr.........20.00
Soup Bowl, 7" d............................12.00
Sugar, cov...................................20.00
Teapot, cov 115.00
Vegetable Bowl
   8-1/2" d, divided 35.00
   9-1/2" d
      Divided..............................37.00
      Undivided...........................35.00

Blue Provincial

Bowl, 11" d 44.00
Bread Server.................................55.00
Coffeepot 100.00
Creamer..24.00
Cup and Saucer............................14.00
Gravy 36.00
Plate
   6" d..8.00
   10" d...14.00
Salt and Pepper Shakers, pr.........55.00
Soup, lug handle 20.00
Sugar, cov....................................28.00

California Confetti

Set, 66 pcs..................................350.00

California Ivy

Bowl, 9" d.....................................36.00
Butter, cov....................................40.00
Coaster...16.00
Creamer..14.00
Cup 9.00
Hors d'ouevre..............................25.00

Plate
  6" d..5.00
  10-1/4" d......................................9.00
Platter, 13" l, oval 36.00
Saucer 1.00
Sugar, cov 17.00
Vegetable, 9-3/4" l, oval, divided...32.00

California Provincial

Bread Server 65.00
Chop Plate.....................................75.00
Coaster...20.00
Cocoa Mug.....................................40.00
Coffee Canister 55.00
Coffeepot, cov 85.00
Condiment Set,
  jam and mustard, lids 65.00
Creamer 22.00
Cup and Saucer 16.00
Gravy, handle, 1 pint 40.00
Mug, 8 oz..65.00
Plate
  7-1/2" d, salad 10.00
  8" d, luncheon 32.00
  10" d, dinner 16.00
Platter, 13-1/2" l...........................45.00
Salt and Pepper Shakers, pr 27.00
Soup, 5" d, lug handle 22.00
Sugar Bowl, cov 28.00
Sugar Canister 70.00
Tea Canister...................................70.00
Vegetable Bowl
  Cov...85.00
  Open, 8-1/2" d,
  round, basket dec...................50.00

California Strawberry

Bowl, 9" d, divided 40.00
Butter, cov 45.00
Creamer 20.00
Cup and Saucer 35.00
Fruit Bowl, 5-1/2" d.......................10.00
Plate
  6" d, bread and butter 6.00
  8" d, salad 10.00
  10" d, dinner..............................15.00
Platter, 13" l, oval 30.00
Salad Bowl 50.00
Soup Bowl, 6-3/4" d.......................15.00
Sugar, cov 20.00
Vegetable Bowl
  Covered......................................35.00
  Round...25.00

Camellia California

Bowl, 6-1/2" d..................................7.00
Plate
  Bread and butter 6.00
  Dinner...10.00
  Salad 8.00
Soup Bowl 15.00
Vegetable Bowl, 10" l, oval...........35.00

Homestead Provincial

Bowl, 6" d 10.00
Butter Dish, cov.............................60.00
Canister Set, 4 pc........................295.00
Casserole, cov 75.00
Coffeepot, cov, blue 125.00
Cookie Jar, cov 90.00
Creamer and Sugar.......................30.00
Cup and Saucer 12.00
Fruit Bowl, 6" d.............................12.00
Gravy Boat, 1 handle 45.00
Matchbox Holder 65.00
Plate, 7" d.......................................7.00
Platter, 14" l................................50.00
Salt and Pepper Shakers, pr 30.00
Tea Kettle, cov 115.00

Miscellaneous

Canister, cov, flour, Colonial
  Homestead 32.00
Canister Set, Four Seasons 200.00
Cookie Jar, cov,
  Colonial Homestead 40.00
Planter
  Mary Jane 45.00
  Papa...45.00
  Pony Cart 45.00
  Santa's Sleigh 55.00
Poppet
  Knight Arthur 95.00
  Princess Grace 65.00
Vase, zodiac, Taurus,
  C. Romanelli............................125.00

Provincial Rose

Bowl, tab handle...........................20.00
Butter, cov 55.00
Coffee Server 75.00
Cookies Canister...........................90.00
Creamer 28.00
Cruet Set, 5 pcs 180.00
Gravy, 2 spouts 28.00
Milk Pitcher....................................38.00
Mug 35.00
Pitcher, large 68.00
Platter
  9-3/8" l.......................................45.00
  14-3/4" l.....................................45.00
Soup, flat 18.00
Vegetable Bowl, cov......................70.00

Red Rooster

Ashtray, large 30.00
Bowl, tab handle...........................15.00
Bread Server 50.00
Butter Dish, cov.............................50.00
Canister Set, 8 pcs......................150.00
Casserole, cov, Kettle 55.00
Cereal Bowl, deep.........................15.00
Chop Plate 40.00
Coaster...20.00
Coffeepot, cov, 6 cup 85.00

Creamer, green.............................15.00
Cruet Set, 8 pcs 150.00
Cup and Saucer 10.00
Fruit Bowl...8.00
Gravy, handle................................30.00
Hen on Nest 90.00
Mug 15.00
Mustard Jar, cov 45.00
Pitcher, figural, 14" h..................695.00
Plate
  Bread and Butter........................6.00
  Dinner 12.00
  Luncheon 10.00
Platter
  Large...45.00
  Small...40.00
Salt and Pepper Shakers, pr, red..12.00
Server, 5 part, divided 100.00
Teapot, cov, 6 cup 80.00
Tumbler, 11 oz 15.00
Turkey Platter...............................200.00
Vegetable Bowl
  7-1/2" d......................................20.00
  Divided, stick handle...............45.00

Sculptured Daisy

Bowl, handle
  7" d...28.00
  8" d...35.00
Cereal Bowl, 7" d 12.00
Creamer 18.00
Cup and Saucer 12.00
Gravy, handle, 1 pint...................32.00
Mug, 8 oz 18.00
Plate
  7-1/2" d..8.00
  10" d...12.00
Set, 24 pcs.....................................75.00
Soup Bowl, 7" d.............................12.00
Sugar, cov......................................24.00
Vegetable Bowl, cov, 1 qt 45.00

Sculptured Grape

Bowl
  8-1/2" d 27.00
  9-1/2" d 30.00
Canister Set, 4 pc 240.00
Cereal Bowl...................................15.00
Creamer and Sugar 45.00
Cup and Saucer 16.00
Fruit Bowl.......................................12.00
Plate
  Dinner 17.00
  Salad, 7-1/2" d 10.00
Platter
  10" l, oval 30.00
  12" l, oval 40.00
Vegetable Bowl 24.00

Sculptured Zinnia

Butter Dish, cov.............................50.00

Cereal Bowl 14.00
Creamer 16.00
Cup and Saucer 14.00
Fruit Bowl 12.00
Plate
    6" d...7.00
    8" d...9.00
    10" d...9.50
    12" d..14.00
Platter, oval
    11" l...28.00
    12" l...38.00
Salad Bowl, 12" d 48.00
Salt and Pepper Shakers, pr 16.00
Sugar, cov 17.50
Vegetable Bowl
    8" d...30.00
    8-1/2" d, divided 28.00
    9-1/2" d, divided 32.00

Militaria

Collecting Hints: Militaria—any item that was used for or relates to the act of warfare, such as tools, clothes or weapons—is found in many different places and in varying quantities. Saving militaria may be one of the oldest collecting traditions. Militaria collectors tend to have their own special shows and view themselves as being outside the normal antiques channels. However, they search small indoor shows and flea markets in hopes of finding additional materials.

History: Wars have occurred throughout recorded history. Until the mid-19th century, soldiers often had to provide for their own needs, including supplying their own weapons. Even in the 20th century, a soldier's uniform and some of his gear are viewed as his personal property, even though issued by a military agency. Conquering armed forces made a habit of acquiring souvenirs from their vanquished foes. They also brought their own uniforms and accessories home as badges of triumph and service.

References: Robert W.D. Ball, *British Army Campaign Medals*, Antique Trader Books, 1996; Thomas Berndt, *Standard Catalog of U.S. Military Vehicles*, Krause Publications, 1993; Gary R. Carpenter, *What's It Worth: A Beginner Collector's Guide to U.S. Army Patches of*

Pistol box, Civil War, "R. Dingee New York" mfg, $185.

WW II, published by author, 1994; W.K. Cross, *Charlton Standard Catalogue of First World War Canadian Corps Badges*, Charlton Press, 1995; ——, *Charlton Standard Catalogue of First World War Canadian Infantry Badges*, 2nd Edition, Charlton Press, 1995; Richard Friz, *Official Price Guide to Civil War Collectibles*, House of Collectibles, 1995; Gary Howard, *America's Finest: U.S. Airborne Uniforms, Equipment and Insignia of World War Two*, Stackpole Books, 1994; Jon A. Maguire, *Silver Wings, Pinks & Greens: Uniforms, Wings, & Insignia of USAAF Airmen in World War II*, Schiffer Publishing, 1994; Jon A. Maguire and John P. Conway, *Art of the Flight Jacket*, Schiffer Publishing, 1995; Ron Manion, *American Military Collectibles Price Guide*, Antique Trader Books, 1995; ——, *German Military Collectibles Price Guide*, Antique Trader Publications, 1995; *North South Trader's Civil War Collector's Price Guide*, 5th Edition, North South Trader's Civil War, 1991; Harry Rinker Jr. and Robert Heistand, *World War II Collectibles*, Running Press, 1993; Ron L. Willis and Thomas Carmichael, *United States Navy Wings of Gold*, Schiffer Publishing, 1995; Richard Windrow and Tim Hawkins, *World War II GI, U.S. Army Uniforms*, Motorbooks International, 1993.

Periodicals: *Cavalry!*, HC3, Box 378A, Rochella, VA 22738; *Men at Arms*, 222 W. Exchange St., Providence, RI 02903; *Military Collector Magazine*, P.O. Box 245, Lyon Station, PA, 19536; *Military Collectors' News*, P.O. Box 702073, Tulsa, OK

74170; *Military History*, 6405 Flank Dr., Harrisburg, PA 17112; *Military Images*, RD1 Box 99A, Henryville, PA 18332; *Military Trader*, P.O. Box 1050, Dubuque, IA 52004; *North South Trader*, P.O. Drawer 631, Orange, VA 22960; *Wildcat Collectors Journal*, 15158 NE 6 Ave., Miami FL 33162.

Collectors' Clubs: American Society of Military Insignia Collectors, 526 Lafayette Ave., Palmerton, PA 18701; Association of American Military Uniform Collectors, P.O. Box 1876, Elyria, OH 44036; Company of Military Historians, North Main St., Westbrook, CT 06498; Imperial German Military Collectors Association, 82 Atlantic St., Keyport, NJ 07735; Orders and Medals Society of America, P.O. Box 484, Glassboro, NJ 08028.

Museums: Battlefield Military Museum, Gettysburg, PA; Liberty Memorial Museum, Kansas City, MO; National Infantry Museum, Fort Benning, GA; Parris Island Museum, Parris Island, SC; Seven Acres Antique Village & Museum, Union, IL; U.S. Air Force Museum, Wright-Patterson AFB, Dayton, OH; U.S. Army Transportation Museum, Fort Eustis, VA; U.S. Horse Cavalry Association & Museum, Fort Riley, KS; U.S. Navy Museum, Washington, DC.

Additional Listings: See Home Front Collectibles, World War I, World War II and *Warman's Antiques and Collectibles Price Guide* for information about firearms and swords.

Revolutionary War

Autograph, Robert T. Paine, partially printed document, bill for Common Pleas Court, 1768, 4" x 6" 290.00
Book
    Battles of the United States, By Sea and Land, Embracing Those of the Revolutionary and Indian Wars, Henry B. Dawson, 2 vols, Johnson Fry, 1858, 530 pgs, steel engravings....................125.00
    History of Maritime Connecticut During the American Revolution 1775-1783 in 2 Volumes, Louis Middlebrook, Salem, 1925, 8vo, 631 pgs, dj 125.00
Newspaper, *The Providence Gazette and Country Journal*, April 4, 1778 ....82.00
Pamphlet, "An Alarm to the Legislature of the Province of New York, Occasioned by the present Political

Disturbances, in North America: Addressed to the Honourable Representatives in General Assembly Convened," printed for James Rivington on Jan. 17, 1775, in NY, 13 pgs 375.00

Sword, British Royal Artillery, iron semi-basket hilt, double side bar, kidney-shaped guard, hand engraved with crowned "RA" motif, 27-1/2" ingle-edged blade 320.00

Civil War

Badge, helmet, brass shield and eagle, company number in center 50.00

Belt, enlisted man's, black leather, brass retaining clips, oval brass "US" buckle 155.00

Book

The Civil War Dictionary, Mark M. Boatner, McKay, NY, 1959, 974 pgs, 1st ed 19.00

Personal Memoirs, Ulysses S. Grant, 2 vol, New York, 1885, 8vo, 1/2 morocco gilt......................170.00

The Photographic History of The Civil War, Francis Trevelyan Miller, ed, 10 vol, New York, 1911, small 4to, publisher's cloth 800.00

R.E. Lee, A Biography, Douglas Southall Freeman, 4 vol, New York, 1934-35, 8vo, 1/2 morocco gilt......................315.00

Reminiscences of Confederate Service, 1861-1865, Capt. Francis W. Dawson, Charleston, 1882, 8vo, orig cloth, 1 of 100 copies printed 4,320.00

Button, brass, U.S. eagle imprint.....9.00

Kepi, Union, brass crossed rifles and "2," torn leather bill and strap 77.00

Magic Lantern Slide, glass

Richard P. Hobson, sank in the Merrimac in Santiago Harbor ...30.00

Robert G. Ingersoll 25.00

John D. Long, , Governor of MA and Secretary of War 25.00

Charles D. Sigsbee, , commander of the *Maine* when it sank at Havana............35.00

Medal, Woman's Relief Corps.......17.00

Pay Voucher, Capt. J. Wilson, CS, 1864 ....50.00

Print, "Camp Huntington, Rome, NY,18" x 24", framed, fair condition 80.00

Sketch, Pvt. Longley, Fredericksburg, 1862......................................145.00

Sword Belt Plate, Union, non-commissioned officer..............75.00

Tintype, Union soldier....................28.00

Indian War

Belt Buckle, Naval officer, brass, stamped "Horstman, Phila."...125.00

Sleeve Patch, U.S. Military, wool, green

Maltese cross, dark blue ground 32.00

Spanish American War

Bayonet, 45-70 Springfield, scabbard mkd "U.S.," front mkd "Rosett"...................................115.00

Book L. Harris and John T. Hilton, Call Printing, Paterson, NJ, 1908, blue cloth binding, gilded edge, photos, 386 pgs, 1st ed 75.00

Canteen, steel, canvas cov, mkd "U.S.," cov dated 1901 ....75.00

Cartridge Box, 45-70 Springfield, McKeever Pat, leather and canvas, loop inserts 75.00

Coat, enlisted man's, 1st sergeant stripes 150.00

Hat, campaign, vented, Banca of Service cord 125.00

Haversack, khaki............................9.50

Holster, leather, black 105.00

Letter, Lt. M. Curry, U.S. Army, Philippine Rebellion, May-Sept. 1900, price for set of 12.........165.00

Medal, campaign, Philippine, U.S. Army, bronze, red and blue ribbon ..155.00

Poster, "Home Support," 1898 ....122.00

Saddle Bags, brown, complete straps and buckles, mkd "US" on both flap tops...................................210.00

Korean War

Ammunition Magazine, 30 round, M1 carbine, black painted steel.......7.00

Coveralls, tanker's, US, olive green, 9th division patch, worn..................30.00

Helmet, M1, US, steel, canvas chin strap, liner...............................26.00

Machete, shoulder, taken from Japanese officer, carved handle, tooled leather sheath..........................62.00

Vietnam War

Book

Vietnam, A History, Stanley Krnow, Viking Press, 1983, small 4to, 750 pgs 9.50

Vietnam II: 3rd Brigade 82nd Airborne Division January 1969 to December 1969, Larry E. Augsber, et al, 1970, 4to, illus, photos, 143 pgs, with box 75.00

Cigarette Lighter, Zippo, mkd "SP/4 L.B. Parker"................................50.00

Crossbow, wood and bamboo, Vietnamese 345.00

Jungle Fatigues, shirt and trousers, large size, Marshall, mkd "US Navy" 255.00

Tunic, U.S. Army, sergeant, green, gold stripes, 5th Division red diamonds insignia....................27.50

Miscellaneous Items

Book

Artillery Through the Ages, Albert Manucy, 1949, 92 pgs 20.00

Famous Battles by Land and Sea, Thomas Bailey Aldrich, ed, Hall & Locke, 1902 ....13.00

A Handbook for Infantry: containing the First Principles of Military Discipline, 9th ed, Philadelphia, 1814, 8vo 80.00

Helmets and Body Armor in Modern Warfare Including World War II Supplement, Bashford Dean, Tuckahoe, Carl J. Pugliese, 1977, 4to, illus, photos, index, 363 pgs.................35.00

The Professional Soldier: A Social and Political Portrait, Morris Janowitz, Macmillan Co., NY, 1964, 8vo, 464 pgs 10.00

Squadron A: A History of Its First Fifty Years, 1889-1939, Herbert Barry et al, NY, 1939, 8vo, photos, illus, 390 pgs, dj 65.00

Broadside, A Complete List of the American Navy, John Russel Jr., Hartford, c1813, 535mm x 630mm, lists names of American and British ships and captured ships 260.00

Cartridge/Belt Plate, brass, eagle and arrows, filled lead back, 2 rusty wire loops..26.00

Catalog

Francis Bannerman Sons, NY, July Wholesale, Export and Retail Price List, Military Goods Catalogue, 1925, 20 pgs, 8-3/4" x 11-3/4" 26.00

Harold M. Bennett, NY, Carl Zeiss Binoculars and Field Glasses, 1920, 46 pgs, 4-3/4" x 7"....................35.00

W. Stokes Kirk, Philadelphia, PA, military goods, guns, carbines, rifles, tents, 1929, 64 pgs, 5-1/4" x 7-1/4" 24.00

Photograph, 9" x 15", Camp McQuade Saratoga Springs, 1857, names of officers, men, cannons, women and horses 125.00

Milk Bottles

Collecting Hints: Many factors influence the price—condition of the bottle, who is selling, the part of the country in which the sale is transacted and how much the buyer wants the bottle. Every bottle does not have universal appeal. A sale in one area does not mean that particular bottle would bring the same amount in another location. For example, a rare Vermont pyro pint would be looked upon as just another ordinary pint in Texas.

Pyroglaze (painted bottles) are becoming more popular than em-

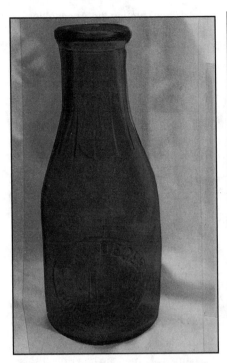

R.M. Deger, Pure Milk, Phoenixville, PA, clear glass, 9-1/2" x 3-3/4", $5.

bossed bottles, possibly because they display better.

History: Hervey Thatcher is recognized as the father of the glass milk bottle. By the early 1880s, glass milk bottles appeared in New York and New Jersey. A.V. Whiteman had a milk bottle patent as early as 1880. Patents reveal much about early milk bottle shape and manufacture. Not all patentees were manufacturers; many individuals engaged others to produce bottles under their patents.

The golden age of the glass milk bottle was from 1910 to 1950. Leading manufacturers include Lamb Glass Co. (Mt. Vernon, OH), Liberty Glass Co. (Sapulpa, OK), Owens-Illinois Glass Co. (Toledo, OH) and Thatcher Glass Co. (NY). Milk bottles can be found in the following sizes: gill (quarter pint), half pint, 10 ounces (third quart), pint, quart, half gallon (two quart) and gallon. Paper cartons first appeared in the early 1920s but were not popular until after 1950. The late 1950s witnessed the arrival of the plastic bottle. A few dairies still use glass bottles, but the era has essentially ended.

References: John Tutton, *Udder Delight*, published by author, 1980.

Periodical: *Cream Separator and Dairy News*, Rte. 3, Arcadia, WI 54612; *Udder Collectibles*, HC73 Box 1, Smithville Flats, NY 13841.

Collectors' Club: National Association of Milk Bottles Collectors, Inc., 4 Ox Bow Rd., Westport, CT 06880.

Museums: Billings Farm Museum, Woodstock, VT; New York State Historical Association and The Farmers Museum, Inc., Cooperstown, NY; Southwest Dairy Museum, Arlington, TX.

Additional Listings: Related items are included in the Farm category.

Alberts Dairy Inc., qt, orange, slogan "Milk for Health" 10.00
Alta Crest Farm, Spencer, MA, qt, round, green glass, emb, cow's head on front 600.00
Baily and Doctor, Wilmington, DE, 1/2 pt, emb 20.00
Ball Dairy, qt, round, clear, emb, baseball emb in slug plate 30.00
Borden, qt, square, amber, white pyro, signature and picture of Gail Borden 15.00
Bucknell University, qt, round, clear, emb 12.00
Butler Dairy, Willimantic, CT, qt 15.00
Capital Dairy, North Dartmouth, MA, qt, round, clear, emb, capital dome emb on front slug plate 15.00
Clover Brand Dairy Products, 1/2 pt, round, clear green pyro, picture of family, large milk bottle and slogan "Follow Road to Health, Drink More Milk" 15.00
Combs Dairy, Aurelia, IA, bucking bronco, qt 80.00
Cream and Sweet Shop, qt, round, clear, emb 27.50
Devine's Dairy, Norwalk, CT, qt, square, amber, white pyro 10.00
Firestone Farms, Columbiana, OH, 1/2 pt, round, clear, Firestone emblem emb in slug plate 28.00
Gettysburg Ice and Storage Co., Gettysburg, PA, qt, round, clear, emb 10.00
Hendricks, qt, square, clear, white pyro 10.00
Maplewood Dairy, Fairhaven, VT and Hudson Falls, NY, qt, amber ... 12.00
Noble Dairy, Baseball Milk Drink for Muscle and Strength 18.00
Orchard Farms Dairy, Dallas, PA, qt, square, clear, red pyro, "Cop the Cream" 25.00
Pennsylvania State University, qt, round, red pyro, tower on back 12.00
Peoples Milk Co., Buffalo, NY, qt, round,

amber, emb 55.00
Pet Milk Co., gal 18.00
Rider Dairy, Danbury, CT, qt, square, clear, red pyro, cream top 14.00
Round Hill Farms Dairy, Greenwich, CT, qt, round, clear, tin top, emb on bottom "AV Whitman" 45.00
St. Joseph's Hospital, Buckhannon, WV, 1/2 pt, round, clear, black pyro 12.00
Springdale Farms, Millington, NJ, qt, cream top 24.00
Sunrise Dairy, 1/2 pt, round, clear, red pyro, war slogan 20.00
Taylor's Dairy, 1/2 pt, square, amber, yellow pyro 40.00
Thompson's Dairy, Washington, DC, qt, squatty round, clear, emb, modern top 10.00
Universal Store Bottle, qt, round, clear, emb 5.00
University of Connecticut, Storrs, CT, 1/2 pt, round, clear, emb 7.50
White Springs Farm Dairy, Geneva, qt, orange pyro 12.00

Model Kits

Collecting Hints: Model kits, assembled or unassembled, are one of the hot collectibles of the 1990s. Even assembled examples, provided they are done well, have value.

In many cases, a kit's value is centered more on the character or object it represents than on the kit itself. The high prices paid for monster-related kits is tied directly to the current monster collecting craze, which means a portion of the value is speculative.

Box art can influence a kit's value. When individual boxes sell in the $40 to $100 range, it becomes clear that they are treated as *objets d'art*, a dangerous pricing trend. The value of the box is easily understood when you place an assembled model beside the lid. All too often, it is the box that is more exciting.

History: The plastic scale-model kit originated in England in the mid-1930s with the manufacture of 1/72 Frog Penguin kits. The concept caught on during World War II when scale models were used in identification training. After the war, companies such as Empire Plastics, Hawk, Lindberg, Renwal and Varney introduced plastic model kits to American hobbyists. The 1950s witnessed the arrival of Aurora and Monogram in the United States, Airfix in the United

Kingdom, Heller in France and Hasegawa and Marusan in Japan.

The 1960s was the golden age of the plastic kit model. Kits featured greater detail and accuracy than the early examples and three scale sizes dominated: 1/48, 1/72 and 1/144. The oil crisis in the 1970s caused a temporary set-back to the industry.

A revival of interest in plastic scale-model kits occurred in the late 1980s. At the same time, collector interest began to develop. The initial collecting focus was on automobile model kits from the 1950s and early 1960s. By the end of the 1980s, interest had shifted to character and monster kits.

References: Paul A. Bender, *1990 Model Car Promotional and Kit Guide*, Brasilia Press, 1990; Bill Bruegman, *Aurora*, Cap'n Penny Productions, 1992; Gordy Dutt, *Aurora: A Collection of Classic Instruction Sheets, Vol. 1, Figures*, published by author (P.O. Box 201, Sharon Center, OH 44274), 1992; ——, *Collectible Figure Kits of the 50's, 60's & 70's*, Gordy's Kitbuilders Magazine (P.O. Box 201, Sharon Center, OH 44274), 1995; *Fantasies in Plastic: Directory of Old and New Model Car Kits, Promotionals and Resin Cast Bodies*, C&C Collectibles, 1991.

Periodicals: *Kit Builders and Glue Sniffers*, P.O. Box 201, Sharon Center, OH 44274; *Model and Toy Collector*, P.O. Box 347240, Cleveland, OH 44134.

Videotape: *Aurora Figure Kit*, Time Machine (P.O. Box 1022, Southport, CT 06490-2022).

Collectors' Clubs: Kit Collectors International, P.O. Box 38, Stanton, CA 90680; Society for the Preservation and Encouragement of Scale Model Kit Collecting, 3213 Hardy Dr., Edmond, OK 73013.

AMT

Budweiser Delivery Van, MIB........35.00
Copperhead Rear Engine Dragster, MIB..........................28.00
Ford Roadster, 1923, Street Rod Series, MIB...........................28.00
Semi-Tractor
    Kenilworth K123 Cabover, #T702, sealed.........................35.00
    Peterbuilt 359 Conventional, #T700,

sealed 35.00
Star Trek Exploration, Phaser, Tricorder and Communicator, 1974......100.00
Star Trek, Mr. Spock, 1968 ....245.00

Aurora

Apollo 11, Columbia and Eagle '72, Young Model Builders Club, MIB...................35.00
Batman, 1964, sealed 350.00
Bat Plane, built 110.00
Black Knight of Aurnberg, MIB......30.00
Chevy Monza GT, box top and instruction sheet only..............10.00
Delta Boeing 747, MIB 35.00
Ferrari Sportster, F scale 35.00
Frankenstein, 1961 ....250.00
Gold Knight of Nice, #475, MIB...175.00
Jaguar XK-E, 1960s, Young Model Builders Club, MIB..................30.00
Military Midgets
    German "A.A." Tank, sealed 20.00
    German "Panther" Tank, sealed 20.00
Old Timers
    Mercer Racer, 1961, MIB.........30.00
    Stutz Bearcat, 1961, MIB.........30.00
Prehistoric Scenes
    Cave Bear, built 30.00
    Flying Reptile, built................30.00
    Jungle Swamp, built................50.00
Ruth, Babe, 1965 ....345.00
Sabertooth Tiger, built..................35.00
Spartacus, 1965 ....250.00
UFO, #813, sealed in box, 1968 .185.00

Billiken, Phantom of the Opera, 1982 ....125.00

Hawk

Sebring Sports Roadster, partially built, 1962, orig box..........................12.00
Travelair Mystery Ship, racing airplane, 1964, MIB 20.00
Wierd-Oh's Davey the Cyclist, built 20.00

Hubley, 1932 Ford Coupe, die-cast metal, built 20.00

IMC

A4E Skyhawk Jet, sealed..............20.00
Dodge Touchtone Terror Pick-Up, MIB 60.00
Cougar II Ford, minor damage to box........................30.00

Lindberg

Butatile Royale Victoria, 19321, MIB 15.00
F-100 Super Saber Jet, motorized version, 1965 ....24.00
Goofy Klock, 1960s, unused, MIB 75.00
Henschel HB-1928, World War I aircraft, 1972, MIB 15.00

Monogram

Bobby Allison's Miller Buick Regal, Grand National Race Car, 1984, MIB...............................30.00
Corvette, 1957 model, 1977, MIB .15.00
Elvira, Mistress of the Dark, 1988, MIB 35.00
Hawker, MB, IB Typhoon aircraft, 1968 ....20.00
Mack Bulldog Tank Truck, Texaco, 1926, 1/24 scale, MIB 50.00
Mercedes-Benz, 1939 540-K Cabriolet, 1963, MIB..............................60.00
The Sizzler, customized dragster, box only...................................20.00
World War II British Fighter, 4-star kit, no instructions 20.00

MPC

Black Spider Camaro Funny Car, 1970 ....40.00
Corvette, custom, built, 1985, sealed..........................12.00
Laser Vette, 1/20 scale, 1979, MIB..............................25.00
Mag II, built 35.00

Revell

Atomic Cruiser, USS Long Beach, Young Model Builders Club, sealed 35.00
Baja Husky Motorcycle, 1976, sealed, MIB...30.00
Corvair, F-102A Supersonic Jet, "S" Kit, 1956, MIB...............................45.00
Don Garlits Dragster, 1974, MIB...50.00
Huey Attack Helicopter, 1969, MIB.......................................25.00
Hunt for Red October, 18 Hornet Jet, MIB...10.00
Kawasaki Cafe Racer, 1976, sealed, MIB...35.00
Mercury Capsule and Atlas Booster, 1969, MIB...........................650.00
PT Boat 211, 1974, Young Model Builders Club, MIB 35.00
U.S. Army Tactical Missile Set, "S" Kit, 1958, MIB..............................45.00

Monsters

Collecting Hints: This is a category rampant with speculative fever. Prices rise and fall rapidly, depending on the momentary popularity of a figure or family group. Study the market carefully before becoming a participant.

Stress condition and completeness. Do not buy any item in less than fine condition. Check carefully to make certain that all parts or elements are present. Since the material in this category is of recent origin, no one is certain how much has survived. Hoards are not uncommon and it is possible to find examples at garage sales. It pays to shop around before paying a high price.

While an excellent collection of two-dimensional material, e.g., comic books, magazines and posters, can be assembled, concentrate on three-dimensional material. Several other crazes, e.g., model kit collecting, cross over into monster collecting, thus adding to price confusion.

History: Collecting monster-related material began in the late 1980s as a generation looked back nostalgically on the 1960s monster television shows, e.g., "Addams Family," "Dark Shadows," and "The Munsters," and the spectacular monster and horror movies of the 1960s and 1970s. Fueling the fire was a group of Japanese collectors who were raiding the American market for material relating to Japanese monster epics featuring reptile monsters such as Godzilla.

It did not take long for collectors to seek the historic roots for their post-World War II monsters and interest in collecting Frankenstein, King Kong and Mummy material was revived. Contemporary items featuring these characters also appeared.

References: Ted Hake, *Hake's Guide to TV Collectibles*, Wallace-Homestead, 1990; Carol Markowski and Bill Sikora, *Tomart's Price Guide to Action Figure Collectibles*, Revised Edition, Tomart Publications, 1992.

Periodicals: *Future News*, 5619 Pilgrim Rd., Baltimore, MD 21214; *G-Fan*, Box 3468, Steinbach, Manitoba, Canada R0A 2A0; *Japanese Giants*, 5727 N. Oketo, Chicago, IL 60631; *Kaiju Review—The Journal of Japanese Monster Culture*, Ste. 5F, 301 E. 64th St., New York, NY 10021; *Monster Attack Team—The Japanese Monster Superhero & Fantasy Fanzine*, P.O. Box 800875, Houston, TX 77280; *Questnews*, 12440 Moorpark St., Ste. 150, Studio City, CA 91604.

Collectors' Club: Club 13, P.O. Box 733, Bellefonte, PA 16823.

Addams Family

Bank, Thing, 1960s, MIB 75.00
Bubble Gum Cards, 1964, complete set
of 66 .... 295.00
Card Game, MIB 60.00
Figure, Uncle Fester, Remco, holding frog in outstretched palm 300.00
Puzzle, The Addams Family Mystery Jigsaw Puzzle, titled "Ghost at Large," 14" x 24", orig box, Milton Bradley, 1965 Filmways TV Productions Inc. 75.00
Record, 33-1/3 RPM, RCA Victor label, 6 orig music themes, 12-1/4" cardboard album with full-cover family photo, 1965 .... 25.00

Attack of the Killer Tomatoes, Halloween costume, Tomato, Collegeville, 1991, orig box 30.00

Alien

Halloween Mask, Ben Cooper, 1979 .... 15.00
Halloween Costume, Ben Cooper, 1979, orig box 150.00
Pulp, magazine, *Amazing Stories,* May, 1931 .... 45.00
Wristwatch, figural, wrap around tail wristband, MIP 15.00

Bride of Frankenstein, model, Aurora, built, 1 minor pc missing 325.00

Creature From The Black Lagoon

Snow Dome, MIB 25.00
Soakie 135.00

Dark Shadows, music box, Josette's, working condition, some minor damage 60.00

Dracula

Action Figure 35.00
Game, Hasbro, incomplete 75.00
Halloween Costume, Ben Cooper, rooted hair on mask, all-vinyl costume, 1978, orig box 15.00
Model, Aurora, 1972, MIB 175.00
Movie, "Dracula and the Son of Frankenstein," Double-Vue Automatic Movie Viewer Cartridge, 5" x 7" card with 2 different film strips, 1978 .... 32.00
Paint Set, Dracula Oil Painting by Numbers, 12" x 16" canvas panel, 14 oil paints, paint brush, orig box, Hasbro, 1963 Universal Pictures Corp. 110.00

Dr. Strange, Halloween Costume, Ben Cooper, 1978, orig box 80.00

Frankenstein

Action Figure, MOC 135.00
Drinking Glass, 1960s 70.00
Halloween Monster, 55" h, jointed, 1960s, MIP 35.00
Head, 5", cast, 1960s 15.00
Makeup Kit, Remco, MIB 110.00
Notebook, 10" x 11", 3-ring binder, vinyl black, full-color illus,

Godzilla, windup walker, sparker, yellow and green, red winder, mkd "Made in Hong Kong," $3.

late 1960s 55.00
Puzzle, Whitman, Frankenstein Jr., 1968 .... 38.00
Soakie 85.00

Ghoul, Halloween Costume, Collegeville, cloth, glows in the dark, orig box 40.00

Godzilla

Cigarette Lighter, MOC 125.00
Figure, 18" h, plastic, dark green, hand fires dart, movable legs and arms, 1977, Mattel 135.00
Game, Godzilla Game, 18-1/2" x 19" playing board, orig box, Ideal, 1963 .... 110.00
Model, Aurora, MIB 995.00
View-Master Reel, set of 3, orig booklet, 1978 Toho Co. Ltd. 25.00

Milton the Monster, game, Milton Bradley, 1966 .... 55.00

Monster

Book, *Monsters*, Wonder Book, 1965, 48 pgs, 8-1/4" x 11" 30.00
Eye Glasses, 6" l, molded plastic, green, black hair, 1 lens vampire, other Frankenstein type monster, c1960 .... 20.00
Game
I Want to Bite Your Finger, 1980s 25.00
Old Maid, Milton Bradley, MIB . 45.00
Learn to Draw Set, Lakeside, 1960s 325.00
Model, Aurora, Monsters of the Movies, Rodan, MIB 350.00
Necklace, black vinyl necklace, molded plastic monster head, orig display bag with header card, 1970s ... 20.00
Pinback Button, Universal, set of six 35.00
Toy, Candle-Making Set, Famous Monsters, plastic molds, orig box

and instructions, Rapco, 1974
Universal Pictures....................32.00

Mummy

Magazine, *Weekly Film Review*,
Dec. 15, 1932, Vol 22, #3, The
Mummy and Boris Karloff adv,
9-1/4" x 12-1/2".........................50.00
Model, Aurora...............................60.00
Puzzle, jigsaw, orig box,
Jaymar, 1963.........................125.00
Soakie, 10" h.................................75.00

Munsters

Book, *The Munsters and the Great
Camera Caper*, Whitman, 1965, 212
pgs, hardcover, 5-1/2" x 8"......20.00
Card Game, MIB...........................60.00
Doll, 1965 Ideal, plastic and vinyl
Herman, 8-1/2" h.....................130.00
Lily, 8" h.................................115.00
Jewelry box, wood, musical,
glossy color photo of Grandpa
on top, plays "King of the Road,"
Presents, 1990, MIB.................45.00
Model, Aurora, Living Room, built,
several pcs missing...............300.00
Sticker Book, Whitman, 1965,
8-1/2" x 12".............................70.00

Nightmare Before Christmas

Badge, NBC video release............12.00
Flip Book, *The Gift*...........................10.00
Gift Bag, NBC, Jack and Zero with Lock,
Shock and Barrel.......................7.00
Hang Tag, NBC, A&W, stickers,
mug offer...................................5.00
Pop-Up Book.................................30.00
Wristwatch, set of four, MIB..........65.00

Nightmare on Elm Street

Doll, Freddy Krueger, talking, pull-string,
MIB...65.00
Halloween Costume, Freddy Krueger,
Collegeville, 1987, orig box.....30.00

Phantom

Doll, dressed, brass knuckles, orig
pistols.....................................275.00
Model, Aurora, MIB......................225.00

Wolfman

Comic Book, *The Wolfman #1*,
June-August, 1963, Dell
Publishing Co............................25.00
Drinking Glass, 1960s...................70.00
Figure, 4" h, plastic, brown, movable
head, blue cloth pants, 1960s..20.00
Model, Aurora, MIB......................275.00
Soakie, 10" h................................75.00

Morton Potteries

Collecting Hints: The potteries of
Morton, IL, used local clay until 1940.
The clay fired out to a golden ecru

color which is quite easy to recognize. After 1940, Southern and Eastern clays were shipped to Morton, but these clays fired out white. Thus, later wares are easily distinguishable from the earlier ones. Few pieces were marked by the potteries. Incised and raised marks for the Morton Pottery Works, the Cliftwood Art Potteries, Inc., and the Morton Pottery Co., do surface at times. Occasionally, the Cliftwood, Midwest, Morton Pottery Co., and American Art Pottery affixed paper labels and some pieces have survived with these intact.

Glazes from the early period, 1877 to 1920, usually were Rockingham types, both mottled and solid. Yellowware also was standard during the early period. Occasionally, a dark cobalt blue was produced, but this color is rare. Colorful drip glazes and solid colors came into use after 1920.

History: Pottery was produced in Morton, IL, for 99 years. In 1877, six Rapp brothers, who emigrated from Germany, began the first pottery, Morton Pottery Works. Over the years, sons, cousins and nephews became involved and the other Morton pottery operations were spin-offs from this original Rapp brothers' firm. When it was taken over in 1915 by second-generation Rapps, Morton Pottery Works became the Morton Earthenware Co. Work at that pottery was terminated by World War I.

The Cliftwood Art Potteries, Inc., which operated from 1920 to 1940, was organized by one of the original founders of the Morton Pottery Works and his four sons. They sold out in 1940 and the production of figurines, lamps, novelties and vases was continued by the Midwest Potteries, Inc., until a disastrous fire in March 1944 brought an end to that operation. By 1947, the brothers who had operated the Cliftwood Art Potteries, Inc., came back into the pottery business. They established the short-lived American Art Potteries. The American Art Potteries made flower bowls, lamps, planters, some unusual flower frogs and vases. Their wares were marketed by florists and gift shops. Production at American Art Potteries was halted in 1961. Of all the wares of the Morton

Morton Pottery Works, Dutch jug, 3 pt, brown Rockingham, $60.

potteries, the products of the American Art Potteries are the most elusive.

Morton Pottery Co., which had the longest existence of all of the potteries in Morton, was organized in 1922 by the same brothers who had operated the Morton Earthenware Co. The Morton Pottery Co., specialized in beer steins, kitchenwares and novelty items for chain stores and gift shops. The firm also produced some of the Vincent Price National Treasures reproductions for Sears Roebuck & Co., in the mid-1960s. The Morton Pottery closed in 1976, thus ending almost 100 years of pottery production in Morton.

Reference: Doris and Burdell Hall, *Morton's Potteries*, *Vol. 2*, L-W Book Sales, 1995.

Museums: Illinois State Museum, Springfield, IL; Morton Public Library (permanent exhibit), Morton, IL.

Advisor: Doris and Burdell Hall.

Morton Pottery Works, Morton Earthenware Co., 1877-1917

Bank, acorn, 3-1/2" h, green, Acorn
Stove Co. adv...........................50.00
Churn, butter, 4 gal,
brown Rockingham...............225.00
Dutch Jug, 3 pt
Brown Rockingham..................60.00
Cobalt blue...............................90.00
Jardiniere, leaf dec, 7" d
Brown......................................30.00
Cobalt blue...............................60.00
Green.......................................45.00
Miniature
Coffeepot, 3-1/2" h, brown
Rockingham............................75.00
Jug, 3" h, brown Rockingham..50.00
Milk pitcher, 3-3/4" h,
cobalt blue..............................60.00

Cliftwood Art Potteries, Inc., console bowl, dolphins base, 6" h, 12" l, matte ivory with Old Rose high gloss int, $100.

Mug, 1 pt, brown Rockingham.......60.00
Pie Baker, 11" d,
    brown Rockingham................100.00
Teapot, acorn shape, 3-3/4" cup,
    brown Rockingham..................80.00
Urinal, shovel shape
    Brown Rockingham..................45.00
    Yellow Rockingham..................60.00

Cliftwood Art Potteries, Inc.,

Cliftwood Art Potteries, Inc., lamp, donut shape with clock insert, 8-1/2" h, Blue Mulberry, $150.

1920-1940

Bookends, tree trunk with woodpeckers,
    6" x 5" x 3-1/2", chocolate brown drip
    glaze, price for pr...................100.00
Compote, 4-dolphin base, 6" h, 8-1/2" d,
    Old Rose high gloss 90.00
Console, 4-dolphin base, 6" h, 12" l,
    matte ivory ext, Old Rose high-gloss
    int...100.00
Figurine
    Billikin doll, 11" h, brown 100.00
    Bulldog, "Nero,"
        11" h, gray drip.........................95.00
    Elephant, trumpeting,
        Blue Mulberry..........................55.00
Lamp
    Boudoir, #16, 6-1/2" h,
        cobalt blue................................24.00
    Desk, elephant figure, 8" h, natural
        colors 80.00
    Donut shape, clock insert, 8-1/2" h,
        Blue Mulberry........................150.00
Vase, 9" h
    Handled, red and white drip over
        white...60.00
    Tree trunk, Herbage Green......70.00

Midwest Potteries, Inc., 1940-1944

Bud Vase, hand, 6-1/2" h
    Flesh color 18.00
    14k gold 25.00
Figurine
    Deer, stylized, 12" h
        Looking back,
            white, gold dec....................25.00
        With antlers, blue-brown spray
            glaze 30.00
    Ducks, 3 in a row, 6-1/2" l, 2-1/2" h,
        white, yellow dec......................18.00
    Tiger, 7" h, 12" l, natural colors 40.00
    Water Bird, 11" h
        Crane, drip colors 35.00
        Heron, blue-yellow spray glaze,
            gold dec 40.00
Miniature
    Frog, 1" h, green drip 10.00
    Rabbit, 1-1/2" h,
        white and pink..........................12.00
    Squirrel, 2" h, brown drip..........12.00
    Swan, 2" h, matte white 12.00
    Turtle, 1" h, green drip 10.00

Morton Pottery Co., 1922-1976

Bank, hen, 4" h, with, hp dec.........35.00
Cookie Jar
    Basket of fruit, green, naturally
        colored fruit 45.00
    Hen, chick finial, white,
        black wash 125.00
    Panda, black and white...........50.00
    Turkey, chick finial
        Brown...............................125.00
        White................................175.00

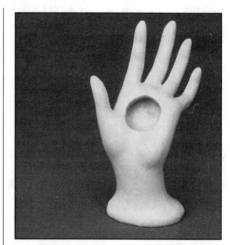

Midwest Potteries, Inc., bud vase, hand, flesh color, $18.

Flowerpot Soaker
    Bird, blue and yellow................18.00
    Calla lily, yellow and green 15.00
    Hound dog, brown and white ...20.00
Night-Light
    Old woman in shoe house, yellow,
        red roof 35.00
    Praying child, prayer in wall hanging
        shadow box...............................35.00
    Teddy bear, brown spray glaze, hp
        dec, heart-shaped nose 40.00
Planter
    Covered wagon, unattached oxen
        team, price for set 55.00
    Davy Crockett as boy, bear beside
        open stump 40.00
    Rabbit, female, with umbrella, beside
        blue egg 18.00
Salt and Pepper Shakers, chick, 1-3/4"
    h, white, black wash, each 50.00
Santa Claus head
    Ashtray....................................15.00
    Mug...18.00
    Nut Cup...................................14.00
    Plate
        8"..40.00
        12" 50.00
    Punch Bowl...........................150.00

Morton Pottery Co., planter, covered wagon with unattached team of oxen, price for set, $55.

American Art Potteries, vase, feather shape, 10-1/2" h, high gray-yellow spray glaze, $30.

Toothpick, chick, 1-3/4" h, white,
    black wash...............................50.00

American Art Potteries, 1945-1961

Console Set, petal design, 10" l x 6-1/2" h bowl, 1-3/4" h candleholders, pink and gray spray glaze, price for 3-pc set..30.00
Creamer, bird, tail is handle, 1 cup, black and green spray glaze.............15.00
Planter, pheasant, 8-1/2" h, 18" l, natural colors, spray glaze...................35.00
TV Lamp
    Afghan hounds, 15" h, black 55.00
    Conch shell, 6" h, yellow and green spray glaze...............................25.00

Midwest Potteries, deer, stylized, looking back, 12" h, white, gold dec, $25.

Double fish planter,
    6" x 9" x 3-1/2" rect base,
    pink-purple spray glaze............25.00
Vase
    Feather shape, 10-1/2" h, gray and yellow spray glaze....................30.00
    Ruffled tulip, 9" h, ivory, pink and blue spray glaze.......................35.00
Wall Pocket
    Apple, 3 leaves, 5" h,
    red and green...........................18.00
    Chrysanthemum blossom, 7-1/2" h, mauve and green spray glaze..22.00

Movie Memorabilia

Collecting Hints: Collectors tend to focus on the blockbuster hits, with "Gone with the Wind" and "Casablanca" among the market leaders. Cartoon images, especially Disney material, are also very popular. Much of the material is two-dimensional and collectors have just begun to look for three-dimensional objects, although the majority of these are related to stars and personalities rather than movies.

The market went crazy with speculation in the mid-1970s. Prices fell in the 1980s as a result of self-discipline compounded by the large number of reproductions, many of European origin, which flooded the market.

History: By the 1930s and into the 1940s, the star system had reached its zenith and studios spent elaborate sums promoting their major stars. Initially, movie studios and their public relations firms tightly controlled the distribution of material such as press books, scripts, preview flyers, costumes and props. Copyrights have expired on many of these items and reproductions abound.

The current interest in Hollywood memorabilia can be traced to the pop-art craze of the 1960s. Film festivals increased the desire for decorative film-related materials and movie posters became a hot collectible. Piracy, which has always plagued Hollywood, is responsible for the release of many items into the market. Today, the home video presents new challenges to the industry.

References: Pauline Bartel, *Complete Gone with the Wind Sourcebook*, Taylor Publishing, 1993; *Big Reel Annual*, Antique Trader Books, 1996; Tony Fusco, *Posters*, 2nd Edition, Avon Books, 1994; John Hegenberger, *Collector's Guide to Movie Memorabilia*, Wallace-Homestead Book Co., 1991; John Kisch, *Movie Poster Price Database*, published by author, 1995; Patrick McCarver, *Gone with the Wind Collector's Price Guide*, Collector's Originals, 1990; Robert Osborne, *65 Years of the Oscar*, Abbeville, 1994; Susan and Steve Raab, *Movie Star Autographs of the Golden Era*, published by authors, 1994; Jay Scarfone and William Stillman, *Wizard of Oz Collector's Treasury*, Schiffer Publishing, 1992; Jon R. Warren, *Collecting Hollywood: The Movie Poster Price Guide*, 3rd Edition, American Collectors Exchange, 1994; Dian Zillner, *Hollywood Collectibles*, Schiffer Publishing, 1991; —, *Hollywood Collectibles: The Sequel*, Schiffer Publishing, 1994.

Periodicals: *Autograph Times*, 2303 N. 44th St., #225, Phoenix, AZ 85008; *Big Reel*, P.O. Box 1050, Dubuque, IA 52004; *Celebrity Collector*, P.O. Box 1115, Boston, MA 02117; *Classic Images*, P.O. Box 809, Muscatine, IA 52761; *Collecting Hollywood*, 2401 Broad St., Chattanooga, TN 37408; *Gone with the Wind Collector's Newsletter*, 1347 Greenmoss Dr., Richmond, VA 23225; *Hollywood & Vine*, P.O. Box 717, Madison, NC 27025; *Hollywood Collectibles*, 4099 McEwen Dr., Ste. 350, Dallas, TX 75244; *Movie Advertising Collector*, P.O. Box 28587, Philadelphia, PA 19149; *Movie Collectors' World*, P.O. Box 309, Fraser, MI 48026; *Movie Poster Update*, 2401 Broad St., Chattanooga, TN 37408; *Poorman's VHS Movie Collectors Newsletter*, 902 E. Country Cables, Phoenix, AZ 85022; *Silent Film Newsletter*, 140 7th Ave., New York, NY 10011; *Spielberg Film Society Newsletter*, P.O. Box 13712, Tucson, AZ 85732; *Under Western Skies*, Rt. 3, Box 263H, Waynesville, NC 28786.

Collectors' Clubs: Emerald City Club, 153 E. Main St., New Albany, IN 47150; Hollywood Studio Collectors Club, 3960 Laurel Canyon Blvd., Ste. 450, Studio City, CA 91604; Manuscript Society, 350 N. Niagara

St., Burbank, CA 91505; Old Time Western Film Club, P.O. Box 142, Siler City, NC 27344; Western Film Appreciation Society, 1914 112 St., Edmonton, Alberta T6J 5P8 Canada; Western Film Preservation Society, Inc., Raleigh Chapter, 1012 Vance St., Raleigh, NC 27608.

Additional Listings: Animation Art, Cartoon Characters, Disneyana, Movie Personalities, Posters.

Advertisement
 "Harvey Girls," Judy Garland....15.00
 "Heat's On," Mae West.............15.00
Almanac, *Motion Picture Magazine*,
 1945...42.00
Book
 Clockwork Orange, Anthony Burgess, 1st ed, hardcover............80.00
 The Emerald City of Oz,
 L. Frank Baum, John R. Neill, illus, 1932, dg............................75.00
Booklet, *Ben Hur*, MGM, 1926 ......20.00
Catalog, McGull's Camera & Film Exchange Inc., New York, NY, c1942, 84 pgs, 4" x 9", catalog of 16mm silent motion picture film library, Victory edition 25.00
Chair, "War of the Worlds," director's chair, Gene Barry 150.00
Christmas Stocking, "ET," cotton...15.00
Cookbook, *Gone With The Wind,* 5-1/2" x 7-1/4", soft-cover, 48 pgs, Pebeco Toothpaste premium, c1939....45.00
Display, stand-up, "Ghostbusters".35.00
Doll
 James Bond 007, Gilbert, 1964, MIB...............................400.00
 Oddjob, Gilbert, 1965, 11" h, orig first issue box 485.00
Film
 "Have Badge, Will Chase," Abbott and Costello, Castle Films No. 850, 50', 8 mm, orig box..................22.50
 "Oh Doctor," Three Stooges, 16 mm, 4" sq box 35.00
 The Fast Getaway," Charlie Chaplin, 16 mm, 2.5" box 25.00
Game, Movie Moguls, Research Games, 1970 ....200.00
Gum Card
 James Bond, Philadelphia Gum Co., 1965, complete set of 66 photo cards 250.00
 Planet of the Apes, Topps, 1967, 24 bubble gum card packs, box ..100.00
Handbill
 "Men Are Not Gods," Miriam Hopkins, 6" x 9", 1930s..........................20.00
 "Spellbound," Gregory Peck and Ingrid Bergmann, 8" x 11", 4 pgs 25.00

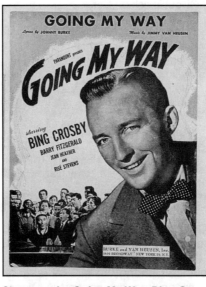

Sheet music, *Going My Way*, Bing Crosby, lyrics by Johnny Burke, music by Jimmy Van Heusen, Burke and Van Heusen, 1944, $10.

Handkerchief, *Gone With The Wind*, 13" sq, Scarlet O'Hara, floral design, yellow, rose, green, black, white and gold, black diecut foil sticker....60.00
License Plate
 Batman, used by Michael Keaton, Gotham City 165.00
 Ghostbusters, "ECTO-1"........165.00
Lobby Card
 Berlin Express, set of 8, RKO Radio Pictures, 1948 ....60.00
 House of Frankenstein, Universal Pictures, 1944 ....255.00
 Miss Tatlock's Millions, Robert Stack, Dorothy Wood, 1948, framed...45.00
 Parade of Comedy, 1964 ....25.00
 Rawhide Rangers, Johnny Mack Brown, Universal......................20.00
 Target, Tim Holt, RKO, 1952 ...20.00
 Yogi Bear, 1964 ....20.00
Model Kit
 Frankenstein, Aurora, 1961 ...250.00
 Phantom of the Opera, Billiken, 1982.......................................125.00
 Spartacus, Aurora, 1965........250.00
 2001: A Space Odyssey, Moon Bus, Aurora, 1969 ....135.00
Movie Folder, *Son of the Sheik*, Valentino 25.00
Paint Set, *Tom Sawyer,* Paramount, 1931 ....32.00
Pistol, used by Bruce Willis for *Die Hard* 500.00
Playbill, *Laffing Room Only,* Olsen and Johnson, 1945..........................10.00
Press Book
 Circus World, John Wayne, 14 pgs 25.00

Girl Happy, Elvis Presley, 1964 ....25.00
Mary Poppins, Julie Andrews ..15.00
The Caine Mutiny, Humphrey Bogart, 18 pgs.....................................35.00
Record, *The Wild One*, orig motion picture soundtrack, Deca, 1954............................135.00
Sheet Music, *As Time Goes By*, "Casablanca," photographs of Humphrey Bogart, Ingrid Bergmann and Paul Henreid on cov 148.00
Souvenir Book
 Gone With The Wind, 1939 ...115.00
 Lawrence of Arabia, Peter O'Toole, colored photos, 2 fold-out double-page maps 18.00
 Since You Went Away, Selznick, 1944, 9" x 12", 20 pgs............25.00
 The Song of Bernadette, 9" x 11-1/2", 20 pgs, 1944 religious movie, full color cov Norman Rockwell illus of Jennifer Jones 40.00
 White Shadows In The South Seas, MGM, 1928 ....40.00
Sword, Klingon, Star Trek 655.00
Textile, James Bond, pillow case, illus of Bond and other characters......70.00
Toy, James Bond Shooting Attache Case, MPC, 1965, orig box 1,165.00
Window Card
 High Noon, Gary Cooper, 14" x 22", 1952...75.00
 On The Waterfront, Marlon Brando, 14" x 22", 1954 ....125.00

Movie Personalities

Collecting Hints: Focus on one star. Today, the four most popular stars are Humphrey Bogart, Clark Gable, Jean Harlow and Marilyn Monroe. Many of the stars of the silent era are being overlooked by the modern collector.

Remember that stars have big support staffs. Not all autographed items were or are signed by the star directly. Signatures should be checked carefully against a known original. Many stars had fan clubs and the fans tended to hold on to the materials they assembled. The collector should be prepared to hunt and do research. A great deal of material rests in private hands.

History: The star system and Hollywood are synonymous. The-2 studios spent elaborate sums of money promoting their stars. Chaplin, Valentino and Pickford gave way to Garbo and Gable.

The movie magazine was a key vehicle in the promotion. *Motion Picture*, *Movie Weekly*, *Motion Picture World* and *Photoplay* are just a few examples of this genre, although *Photoplay* was the most sensational. The film star had no private life and cults grew up around many of them. By the 1970s, the star system of the 1930s and 1940s had lost its luster. The popularity of stars is much shorter lived today.

References: Pauline Bartel, *Complete Gone with the Wind Sourcebook*, Taylor Publishing, 1993; *Big Reel Annual*, Antique Trader Books, 1996; Patrick McCarver, *Gone with the Wind Collector's Price Guide*, Collector's Originals, 1990; Robert Osborne, *65 Years of the Oscar*, Abbeville, 1994; Edward R. Pardella, *Shirley Temple Dolls and Fashions*, Schiffer Publishing, 1992; Susan and Steve Raab, *Movie Star Autographs of the Golden Era*, published by authors, 1994; Jay Scarfone and William Stillman, *Wizard of Oz Collector's Treasury*, Schiffer Publishing, 1992; Jon R. Warren, *Collecting Hollywood: The Movie Poster Price Guide*, 3rd Edition, American Collectors Exchange, 1994; Dian Zillner, *Hollywood Collectibles*, Schiffer Publishing, 1991; ——, *Hollywood Collectibles: The Sequel*, Schiffer Publishing, 1994.

Periodicals: *Autograph Times*, 2303 N. 44th St., #225, Phoenix, AZ 85008; *Big Reel*, P.O. Box 1050, Dubuque, IA 52004; *Celebrity Collector*, P.O. Box 1115, Boston, MA 02117; *Classic Images*, P.O. Box 809, Muscatine, IA 52761; *Collecting Hollywood*, 2401 Broad St., Chattanooga, TN 37408; *Gone with the Wind Collector's Newsletter*, 1347 Greenmoss Dr., Richmond, VA 23225; *Hollywood & Vine*, P.O. Box 717, Madison, NC 27025; *Hollywood Collectibles*, 4099 McEwen Dr., Ste. 350, Dallas, TX 75244; *Movie Advertising Collector*, P.O. Box 28587, Philadelphia, PA 19149; *Movie Collectors' World*, P.O. Box 309, Fraser, MI 48026; *Movie Poster Update*, 2401 Broad St., Chattanooga, TN 37408; *Silent Film Newsletter*, 140 7th Ave., New York, NY 10011; *Under Western Skies*, Rte. 3, Box 263H, Waynesville, NC 28786.

Collectors' Clubs: All About Marilyn, P.O. Box 291176, Hollywood, CA 90029; Emerald City Club, 153 E. Main St., New Albany, IN 47150; Hollywood Studio Collectors Club, 3960 Laurel Canyon Blvd, Ste. 450, Studio City, CA 91604; Manuscript Society, 350 N. Niagara St., Burbank, CA 91505; Old Time Western Film Club, P.O. Box 142, Siler City, NC 27344; Western Film Appreciation Society, 1914 112 St., Edmonton, Alberta T6J 5P8 Canada; Western Film Preservation Society, Inc., Raleigh Chapter, 1012 Vance St., Raleigh, NC 27608.

Additional Listings: Autographs, Magazines, Movie Memorabilia, Posters.

Woody Allen, magazine, *Life*, March 21, 1969 .... 9.00
Fred Astaire
    Magazine, *Life*, Dec. 30, 1940 ... 7.00
    Sheet Music, *My Shining Hour*... 7.50
Lauren Bacall, magazine, *Life*, April 3, 1970 .... 7.00
Brigitte Bardot
    Book, *Brigitte Bardot*, Francoise Sagan, 1976, 100 pgs, 12-1/2" x 9-1/2" 10.00
    Magazine, *Life*, July 28, 1961 .. 15.00
Ingrid Bergmann, magazine
    Life, Oct. 13, 1967 .... 8.00
    Look, Nov. 11, 1958 .... 12.00
Marlon Brando
    Book, *Brando*, Charles Highman, hardcover 10.00
    Magazine, *Life*, Dec. 14, 1962 . 12.00
Charlie Chaplin
    Cartoon Book, *Charlie Chaplin in the Movies*, 1917 .... 65.00
    Figure, 2-1/2" x 8", stuffed leather, full-length portrait image, inked in black on natural tan leather, black felt back, 1920s 72.00
    Pencil Box, 2" x 8", full-figure illus 60.00
Joan Collins, dress, red, strapless, from movie "Bitch" 3,115.00
Jackie Coogan
    Clicker, metal, adv for peanut butter 24.00
    Pencil Box, minor rust 12.00
Bing Crosby
    Box, ice cream 8.00
    Game, Call Me Lucky, Parker Bros., 1954, b&w portrait on box lid, 19-1/2" sq playing board 30.00

Louis Armstrong, plaster statue, full figure, colored, blue clothing, 1939, 15-1/2" h, $160.

    Magazine, *Look*, June 7, 1960, Bing and family cover 13.00
Bette Davis
    Coloring Book, 10" x 13", Merrill, 1942 .... 24.00
    Movie Poster, "Hush Hush Sweet Charlotte," 27" x 41" 35.00
    Press Book, *The Catered Affair*, 20 pgs 30.00
James Dean, scrapbook of press cuttings and photographs, anniversary book and 1955 magazine 82.00
Zsa Zsa Gabor, magazine, *Life*, Oct. 15, 1951 .... 22.50
Jackie Gleason, magazine
    Life, Nov. 2, 1959 .... 15.00
    Look, Nov. 15, 1966, with Art Carney on cover 12.50
Bob Hope, magazine
    Life, Jan. 29, 1971 .... 10.00
    Post, Nov. 9, 1963 .... 16.00
    Time, Sept. 20, 1943 .... 15.00
Grace Kelly, coloring book, Whitman, 1956, few pgs colored 45.00
Laurel & Hardy
    Movie Poster, "Four Clowns," 27" x 41" 45.00
    Salt and Pepper Shakers, pr, 1/2" x 2-1/2" x 4" white china tray, 4" h Laurel with black derby, 3" h Hardy with brown derby, Beswick, England, 3 pcs 115.00
Janet Leigh, magazine, *Motion Picture*, Aug. 1959 .... 10.00
Sophia Loren, magazine, *Life*, Nov. 14, 1960 .... 15.00
Dean Martin, single-breasted blazer, from movie "Cannonball Run II" 325.00
Steve McQueen, magazine, *Life*, July

12, 1963....................................15.00
Midler Bette, magazine, *Time*, March 2,
    1987...3.00
Marilyn Monroe
    Cologne Spray, 1983, MIB.......45.00
    Doll, Tristar, 11-1/2" h 45.00
    Newspaper Supplement, New York,
        Sunday, 1982.........................20.00
Kim Novak, fan-club kit, wallet, photos
    and Christmas card, 1966 ....25.00
Mary Pickford
    Magazine, *Photoplay*,
        Sept. 1914, full-color cover,
        article with photos 45.00
    Photograph, sgd, 1930.............55.00
Robert Redford, magazine, *Argosy*,
    cover story, Aug, 1974...............5.00
Ginger Rogers
    Magazine, *Life*, Nov. 5, 1951 ...15.00
    Photograph, sgd, 5" x 7", color,
        Alhambra Theatre 1940 roster
        on back......................................15.00
Dinah Shore, Emmy 2,460.00
Frank Sinatra, magazine
    Life, April 23, 1965 ....15.00
    TV Guide, May 14, 1954,
        New England edition, full-color
        cover photo 45.00
Barbara Stanwyck, Vita-Sert Chocolate
    Box, 1940s, illus on lid...........150.00
Barbara Streisand, set of 8 lobby
    cards for "Funny Girl," 27 b&w
    stills, "Funny Girl" program,
    2 "Funny Girl" records............125.00
Shirley Temple, cereal box, Quaker
    Puffed Wheat, c1939 ....110.00
Three Stooges, punch-out book, 7-1/2" x
    13", Golden Press, 1962 ....75.00
Mae West, magazine, *Life*, April 18,
    1969...7.00

Music Boxes

Collecting Hints: A music box can be inserted into any figurine or box-shaped object. The objects priced below are only those in which the music box is secondary to the piece. Antique music boxes are covered in *Warman's Antiques and Collectibles Price Guide*.

Some collectors tend to focus on one tune, trying to collect each of the various ways it has been used. Others concentrate on a musical toy form, such as dolls or teddy bears. A popular item is the musical jewel box, prevalent between 1880 and 1930.

History: The insertion of a small music box into toys and other products dates back to the 18th century. Initially, these were primarily given to

Mira, 19" x 25-1/2" x 14", restored and cleaned, 20 discs, $2,900.

children of the aristocracy; but the mass production of music boxes in the late 19th century made them available to everyone.

The music box toy enjoyed greater popularity in Europe than in America. Some of the finest examples are of European origin. After World War II, there was an influx of inexpensive music box toys from the Far East. The popularity of the musical toy suffered as people reacted negatively to these inferior products.

References: Gilbert Bahl, *Music Boxes*, Courage Books, Running Press, 1993; Arthur W.J.G. Ord-Hume, *The Musical Box*, Schiffer Publishing, 1995.

Collectors' Clubs: Musical Box Society International, 1062 Alber St., Wabash, IN 46992; Musical Box Society of Great Britain, The Willows, 102 High St., Landbeach, Cambridge CB4 4DT England.

Museums: Bellms Car and Music of Yesterday, Sarasota, FL; Lockwood Matthews Mansion Museum, Norwalk, CT; Miles Musical Museum, Eureka Springs, AR; Musical Museum, Deansboro, NY; Musical Wonder House Museum, Iscasset, ME.

Ballerina, 9" h, bisque, glass eyes,
    cylinder base, French 300.00
Bank, plastic, Gorham, 7-1/2" h
    Acrobat, green 18.00
    Cyclist, red 18.00
Barrel Organ, 5-1/2" h, Ohio Art......5.00
Bear, hand carved.........................65.00

Bird, figural, ceramic
    Cardinal, 6-1/2" h 18.00
    Dove, 6-1/4" h 15.00
    Owl, 6" h 20.00
Box
    1-1/4" x 4-1/4" x 3-1/2", Thorens
        cylinder, grained-wood case plays
        Bicycle Built for Two 45.00
    2-1/2" h, Santa, white, plays Jingle
        Bells 8.00
    2-1/2" h, snowman and lady, red,
        plays Frosty the Snowman 8.00
    2-1/2" x 3-1/2" x 6-1/2", leather,
        porcelain plaque painting of 5
        mallards on cov.......................70.00
    3" x 3" x 5", Manivelle, 3 tunes, litho
        on cov, children feeding swan, tune
        sheet on bottom, Swiss...........80.00
Children on Merry Go Round, 7-3/4" h,
    wood, figures move, plays Around
    the World in 80 Days...............22.00
Children on Seesaw, 7" h, wood, figures
    move in time to music 20.00
Christmas Tree Stand, revolving,
    Germany 65.00
Church, 4" x 6", tin, hand crank,
    Germany 125.00
Cigar holder, 15" h,
    wood and brass 75.00
Clown, 5-1/2" h, plastic,
    dome, Gorham 18.00
Coffee Grinder shape, 3" h 30.00
Dog, 12" h, Nipper, ceramic..........45.00
Doll
    Drum Major, 15" h, blue uniform,
        plays Cecile 100.00
    Sammy Kay, 11" h, composition,
        sways...65.00
Dove, figural, ceramic 18.00
Easter Egg, tin 15.00
Kitten with ball, 5-1/2" h, ceramic..18.00
Man, leaning against lamp post, cast
    iron, plays How Dry I Am, New York
    City souvenir 18.00
Merry-Go-Round, 3 horses and riders,
    1904 ....45.00
Paddington Bear 45.00
Phonograph, 5-3/4" x 3-1/4" x 3-1/4",
    miniature, upright, windup,
    Swiss...78.00
Powder Box, 3-1/2" x 4-1/4", metal,
    silver, litho cov, c1940.............25.00
Snowball, glass, wood base
    Frosty the Snowman,
        5" h, red base..........................10.00
    Mr. and Mrs. Santa, 5" h,
        green base................................10.00
    Santa and Rudolph, 5" h,
        green base................................10.00

N

Napkin Rings

Collecting Hints: Concentrate on napkin rings of unusual design or shape. This is one collectible that still can be used on a daily basis. However, determine the proper cleaning and care methods for each type of material. Many celluloid items have been ruined because they were stored in an area that was too dry or were washed in water that was too hot.

Napkin rings with an engraved initial or monogram are worth less than those without personalized markings. Many collectors and dealers have these marks removed professionally, if it will not harm the ring.

History: Napkin rings enjoyed a prominent role on the American dinner table during most of the 19th and early 20th centuries. Figural napkin rings were used in upper-class households. The vast majority of people used a simple napkin ring, although these could be elegant. Engraving, relief designs and carving turned simple rings into works of art. When cast metal and molded plastic became popular, shaped rings, especially for children, were introduced. The arrival of inexpensive paper products and fast and frozen foods, along with a faster-paced lifestyle, reduced American's concern for elegant daily dining. The napkin ring has almost disappeared from the dining table.

Brass, 2 elves, dog, dragon and leaf dec,
emb...20.00
Celluloid, grapes, emb...................10.00
China, blue and pink floral dec, white
ground 15.00
Cloisonné
  Dragon, white ground...............25.00
  Floral, dark blue dec,
  white ground...........................50.00
Cut Glass
  Harvard Pattern........................75.00
  Hobstars and Bow Tie Fans.....85.00
Ivory, carved
  Medallions................................38.00
  Openwork.................................20.00
Metal, lady holding stick, c1942 ....15.00
Nippon
  Floral, blue and gold,
  white ground............................35.00

Tennis racquet figural, #98, silver, $145.

  Rose, gold trim,
  cream ground..........................50.00
  Scene, forest and lake,
  beaded trim..............................75.00
Noritake
  Flowers and Butterfly 15.00
  Man, Art Deco design 30.00
  Rose Azalea.............................45.00
Porcelain, owl, seated on ring.......20.00
Sabino Glass, bird, opalescent 40.00
Silver, plated
  Birds and tulips, beaded
  base and ring, Rockford
  Silver Plate Co. 80.00
  Bulldog, Dirigo Boy 125.00
  Cat, arched back....................120.00
  Children and goats, etched......15.00
  Dog, pulling sled,
  emb greyhounds on sides,
  engraved "Sara," Meriden......165.00
  Floral bouquets,
  Victorian, 1-1/2".......................15.00
  Man, nude, running holding torch,
  sq base 150.00
  Oriental Fans, repoussé flowers and
  hummingbird dec 75.00
  Parrot, rect base,
  Rogers Mfg. Co........................50.00
  Ring, etched dogwood branch,
  1-3/4" w..................................20.00
Silver, sterling
  Art Nouveau, girl with flowing hair,
  1-1/2".......................................25.00
  Cherubs, 2 seated....................65.00
  Eagles, two 55.00
  Hen, sgd "Meriden" 195.00
  Koala Bear,
  2" x 3", Australian....................65.00
  Mickey Mouse 75.00
  Nursery rhyme figures.............25.00
  Peacock, standing....................55.00
  Scotty 35.00
  Windham Pattern,

  Tiffany & Co. 70.00
Souvenir
  Grand Rapids, MI, scenic 15.00
  Louisiana Purchase 25.00
  St. Louis World's Fair, 1904,
  enameled 40.00

New Martinsville Viking

Collecting Hints: Before 1935, New Martinsville glass was made in a wide variety of colors. Later glass was only made in crystal, blue, ruby and pink. Look for cocktail, beverage, liquor, vanity, smoking and console sets. Amusing figures of barnyard animals, sea creatures, dogs and bears were produced.

Both Rainbow Art Glass and Viking Glass hand-made their products and affixed a paper label. Rainbow Art Glass pieces are beautifully colored and the animal figures are more abstract in design than those of New Martinsville. Viking makes plain, colored, cut and etched tableware, novelties and gift items. Viking began making black glass in 1979.

History: The New Martinsville Glass Manufacturing Co., founded in 1901, took its name from its West Virginia location. Early products, made from opal glass, were decorative and utilitarian. Later, pressed crystal tableware with flashed-on ruby or gold decorations was made. In the 1920s, innovative color and designs made vanity, liquor and smoking sets popular. Dinner sets in patterns such as Radiance, Moondrops and Dancing Girl, as well as new colors, cuttings and etchings were produced. In the 1940s, black glass was formed into perfume bottles, bowls with swan handles and flower bowls. In 1944, the company was sold and reorganized as the Viking Glass Co.

The Rainbow Art Glass Co., Huntington, WV, was established in 1942 by Henry Manus, a Dutch immigrant. This company produced small, hand-fashioned animals and decorative ware of opal, spatter, cased and crackle glass. Rainbow Art Glass also decorated for other companies. In the early 1970s, Viking acquired Rainbow Art Glass

Co., and continued the production of the small animals.

References: Lee Garmon and Dick Spencer, *Glass Animals of the Depression Era*, Collector Books, 1993; James Measell, *New Martinsville Glass*, The Glass Press, 1994; Naomi L. Over, *Ruby Glass of the 20th Century*, The Glass Press, 1990, 1993-94 value update; Ellen T. Schroy, *Warman's Glass*, 2nd Edition, Wallace-Homestead, 1995; Hazel Marie Weatherman, *Colored Glassware of the Depression Era*, Book 2, Glassworks, 1982.

Ashtray
   Fish, 4" d 10.00
   Skillet, 5" d 15.00
Basket, Janice 65.00
Beer Mug, pink 25.00
Bonbon, Radiance, sky blue, ftd 15.00
Bowl
   9" d,. Prelude,
   3 legs, crimped 50.00
   10" d, Meadow Wreath,
   crimped 35.00
   12" d, Radiance, red,
   crimped, #4212 .... 75.00
Cake Plate, 14" d,
   Hostmaster, amber 35.00
Candlesticks, pr, Florentine 45.00
Candy Dish, cov, 1 lb, 10" d,
   orange, Viking 22.00
Celery Dish, 10" l,
   Meadow Wreath 17.50
Chip and Dip Set, 14" d,
   orange, Viking 27.00
Cigarette Holder, cart shape 20.00
Cordial, Moondrops, 1 oz,
   amber, silver dec 25.00
Creamer, Radiance, red 25.00
Creamer and Sugar, individual size,
   Moondrops, red 35.00
Cup and Saucer
   Fancy Square, jade 15.00
   Hostmaster, ruby 10.00
   Moondrops
      Amber 14.00
      Green 14.00
   Radiance, red 24.00
Decanter
   Crystal, Volksted Pup 75.00
   Green, Nice Kitty 55.00
Figure
   Bear
      Baby, sun colored 35.00
      Mama 225.00
   Chick, baby 45.00
   Dog, 8-1/2" l, orange,
   Viking, #1316 .... 37.50

Duck, 15" l, orange, Viking 50.00
Eagle 60.00
Elephant 80.00
Gazelle 70.00
Hen 60.00
Horse, head up 90.00
Owl, 8-1/2" h, orange,
   Viking 100.00
Piglet, standing 145.00
Rooster, large 80.00
Seal 80.00
Squirrel, base 45.00
Swan, 12" h, Janice 55.00
Wolfhound 70.00
Goblet
   Hostmaster, 6-1/4" h, ruby 15.00
   Mt. Vernon, ruby 17.50
   Prelude, etched 40.00
Marmalade, cov, Janice 20.00
Nappy, Prelude, 5" d, heart shape,
   handle 20.00
Pitcher, orange, Viking 18.00
Plate
   7-1/2" w, Fancy Square, jade 8.00
   8" d, Radiance, red,
   slight wear 13.00
   8-1/2" d, Moondrops, red 20.00
   14" d, Florentine 25.00
Relish, Moondrops,
   3 part, 8-1/2" d, red 40.00
Sherbet, Moondrops, red 20.00
Sugar, ftd, Moondrops, amber 12.00
Vanity Set, cov box, 2 jars with stoppers
   Geneva 65.00
   Shining Star 45.00
Vase
   9" h, Morning Dove 45.00
   12" h, Radiance,
   black, ruffled 295.00
Water Set, Oscar, red, pitcher and
   4 tumblers 175.00
Whiskey, Moondrops,
   cobalt blue 15.00
Wine, Moondrops, 4" h, 4 oz, red .. 25.00

Newspapers

Collecting Hints: All newspapers must be complete with a minimum of chipping and cracking. Post-1880 newsprint is made of wood pulp and deteriorates quickly without proper care. Pre-1880 newsprint was composed of cotton and rag fiber and has survived much better than its wood-pulp counterpart.

Front pages only of 20th-century newspapers command about 60% of the value for the entire issue, since the primary use for these papers is display. Pre-20th-century is-

Man Walks on Moon, *New York Times*, July 21, 1969, $26.

sues are collectible only if complete, as banner headlines were rarely used. These papers tend to run between four and eight pages in length.

Major city issues are preferable, although any newspaper providing a dramatic headline is collectible. Banner headlines, those extending completely across the paper, are most desirable. Those papers from the city in which an event happened command a substantial premium over the prices listed below. A premium is also paid for a complete series, such as all 20th-century election reports.

Twentieth-century newspapers should be stored away from high humidity and out of direct sunlight. Issues should be placed flat in polyethylene bags or in acid-free folders that are slightly larger than the paper.

Although not as commonly found, newspapers from the 17th through the 19th centuries are highly collectible, particularly those from the Revolutionary War, War of 1812, Civil War and those reporting Indian and desperado events. Two of the most commonly reprinted papers are the *Ulster County Gazette*, of Jan. 4, 1800, dealing with Washington's death, and the *N.Y. Herald*, of April 15, 1865, concerning Lincoln's death. If you have either of these papers, chances are you have a reprint.

History: America's first successful newspaper was *The Boston Newslet-*

ter, founded in 1704. The newspaper industry grew rapidly and reached its pinnacle in the early 20th century. Within the last decade, many great evening papers have ceased publication and many local papers have been purchased by the large chains.

Collecting headline-edition newspapers has become popular during the last 20 years, largely because of the decorative value of the headlines. Also, individuals like to collect newspapers related to the great events which they have witnessed or which have been romanticized through the movies, television and other media. Historical events, the Old West and the gangster era are particularly popular subjects.

References: Ron Barlow and Ray Reynolds, *Insider's Guide to Old Books, Magazines, Newspapers and Trade Catalogs*, Windmill Publishing (2147 Windmill View Rd., El Cajon, CA 92020), 1996; Norman E. Martinus and Harry L. Rinker, *Warman's Paper*, Wallace-Homestead, 1994; Gene Utz, *Collecting Paper*, Books Americana, 1993.

Periodical: *Paper Collectors' Marketplace* (*PCM*), P.O. Box 128, Scandinavia, WI 54977.

Collectors' Clubs: Newspaper Collectors Society of America, P.O. Box 19134, Lansing, MI 48901; Newspaper Memorabilia Collectors Network, P.O. Box 797, Watertown, NY 13601.

Advisor: Tim Hughes.

Notes: The following listing concentrates on newspapers of the 20th century. The date given is the date of the event itself; the newspaper coverage usually appeared the following day.

1865, April 14, Lincoln assassinated at Ford's Theater 600.00
1881, July 14, Billy the Kid killed...................350.00
1893, June 1, start of the Lizzie Borden trial...25.00
1898, Feb. 15, Battleship *Maine* sunk 55.00
1901, Sept. 6, President McKinley shot 45.00
1903, Oct. 7, final game of the first "modern" World Series 50.00
1903, Dec., 17, Wright brothers first airplane flight 325.00
1910, April 21, Samuel Clemens (Mark Twain) dies 25.00
1912, April 15, *Titanic* hits an iceberg and sinks 500.00
1913, March 4, President Wilson inaugurated 24.00
1915, May 7, *Luisitania* sinks 275.00
1917, April 6, U.S. enters war 35.00
1918, Nov. 11, Armistice signed ...58.00
1920, Sept. 29, Black Sox convicted for throwing 1919 World Series ..130.00
1923, Feb. 16, King Tut's tomb opened 33.00
1924, Oct. 18, Red Grange scores 4 touchdowns in first quarter 30.00
1925, July 21, Scopes convicted in Monkey Trial...........................35.00
1926, Sept. 23, Tunney-Dempsey fight 26.00
1927, May 21, Lindbergh lands successfully in Paris 75.00
1927, Sept. 30, Babe Ruth hits 60th home run 185.00
1928, June 18, Amelia Earhart crosses Atlantic.......................................78.00
1930, Oct. 13, gangster Legs Diamond shot...35.00
1931, Feb. 27, Al Capone sentenced to 6 months for contempt.............32.00
1931, Oct. 17, Thomas Edison dies.................80.00
1932, March 1, Lindbergh baby kidnapped 57.00
1932, May 12, Lindbergh baby found dead 59.00
1933, Jan. 7, President Coolidge dies 22.00
1933, Jan. 31, Hitler becomes Chancellor of Germany 25.00
1933, July 6, first All Star game 30.00
1933, Sept. 26, Machine Gun Kelley captured in Tennessee...........29.00
1933, Oct. 20, Dillinger robs Indiana bank...28.00
1934, Jan. 20, Bonnie and Clyde rob Texas bank..............................34.00
1934, May 23, Bonnie and Clyde killed in Louisiana 210.00
1934, Oct. 22, Pretty Boy Floyd killed by FBI in Ohio 55.00
1935, April 14, Bruno Hauptman sentenced to death..................25.00
1936, Aug. 3, Jesse Owens captures 100-meter gold at Berlin Olympics............25.00
1937, May 6, *Hindenburg* disaster at Lakehurst, New Jersey...........95.00
1938, July 17, "Wrong Way" Corrigan flies to Ireland 27.00
1939, May 2, Lou Gehrig's consecutive-game streak ends....................68.00
1941, Dec. 7, Pearl Harbor attacked 37.00
1942, June 5, Battle of Midway 17.00
1944, June 6, D-Day invasion of France........35.00
1944, Dec. 16, Battle of Bulge begins 15.00
1945, April 12, President Franklin D. Roosevelt dies........................25.00
1945, May 8, V-E Day, Germany surrenders 36.00
1945, Aug. 9, atomic bomb dropped on Nagasaki, Japan 35.00
1947, Jan. 25, Al Capone dies......34.00
1950, June 28, Korean War begins 22.00
1954, May 6, Roger Bannister breaks 4-minute mile record 18.00
1958, July 1, Alaska joins Union ...18.00
1961, April 20, Bay of Pigs invasion................22.00
1962, Feb. 21, John Glenn orbits Earth 20.00
1963, June 12, Medgar Evers shot in Mississippi.............................24.00
1963, Dec. 22, John F. Kennedy assassinated 25.00
1965, Malcolm X assassinated in New York City................................70.00
1967, Jan. 16, Green Bay Packers defeat Kansas City Chiefs in first Superbowl 20.00
1969, July 21, man walks on the Moon 26.00
1970, May 4, National Guard shooting at Kent State 22.00
1977, Aug. 17, Elvis Presley dies in Memphis................................23.00

Niloak Pottery

Collecting Hints: Mission ware pottery is characterized by swirling layers of browns, blues, reds and cream. Very few pieces are glazed on both the outside and inside; usually only the interior is glazed.

History: Niloak Pottery was made near Benton, AR. Charles Dean Hyten, the founder of this pottery, experimented with the native clay and tried to preserve the natural colors. By 1911, he had perfected a method that produced the desired effect, resulting in the popular Mission ware. The pieces were marked "Niloak," which is Kaolin—the type of fine porcelain clay used—spelled backwards.

After a devastating fire, the pottery was rebuilt and named Eagle Pottery. This factory included enough space to add a novelty pottery line, introduced in 1929. This line continued until 1934 and usually bears the name "Hywood-Niloak." After 1934,

Planter, elephant on circus drum, pink and gray, 6" h, $30.

"Hywood" was dropped from the mark. Hyten left the pottery in 1941; in 1946, the operation closed.

References: Susan and Al Bagdade, *Warman's American Pottery and Porcelain*, Wallace-Homestead, 1994; David Edwin Gifford, *Collector's Encyclopedia of Niloak*, Collector Books, 1993; Ralph and Terry Kovel, *Kovels' American Art Pottery*, Crown Publishers, 1993.

Videotape: Ralph and Terry Kovel, *Collecting with the Kovels: American Art Pottery*, available from producers (P.O. Box 22990, Beachwood, OH 44122).

Collectors' Club: Arkansas Pottery Collectors Society, 12 Normandy Rd., Little Rock, AR 72007.

Ashtray, hat shape, blue 10.00
Bowl, 8" x 3", Mission Ware,
    chocolate brown, tan and
    turquoise swirls 65.00
Candlestick, 12" h, Mission Ware,
    brown, red and cream 75.00
Cornucopia, 3" l, light pink 7.50
Creamer and Sugar, Hywood line,
    rose glaze 35.00
Figure
    Canoe, 7-1/2" l, white matte 35.00
    Frog 25.00
    Polar Bear, white matte 40.00
Paperweight, rabbit,
    orig paper label 40.00
Pitcher
    3-1/2" h, yellow 15.00
    7" h, dark green glaze 16.00
Planter
    Bear, tan 20.00
    Cannon, blue 20.00

Duck, pink and blue 20.00
Fox, red 25.00
Frog, seated on lily pad 40.00
Kangaroo, white,
    brown accents 12.00
Parrot, white, orange accents ..15.00
Rabbit, green 15.00
Swan, light brown 12.00
Toothpick Holder, Mission Ware ...45.00
Vase
    6" h, Hywood line, bud, leaf, blue
    glaze 25.00
    7" h, maroon, handles 18.00
    8" h, gray shaded
    to pink, 4 flowers 30.00
Wall Pocket, 6" l, Mission Ware, brown,
    blue and tan 85.00

Noritake Azalea China

Collecting Hints: There are several backstamps on the Azalea pattern of Noritake China. The approximate dates are:
Prior to 1921: Blue rising sun, printed "Hand painted NIPPON"
1921-1923: Green wreath with M, printed "Noritake, Hand painted, Made in Japan"
1923-1930s: Green wreath with M, printed "Noritake, Hand painted, Made in Japan 19322"
1925-1930s: Red wreath with M, printed "Noritake, Hand painted, Made in Japan 19322"
1935-1940s: Red azalea sprig, printed "Noritake Azalea Patt., Hand painted, Japan No. 19322/252622."

Most of the saucers and underplates do not have a backstamp. Those that do are stamped "Azalea 19322/252622."

Most collectors assemble sets and are not concerned with specific marks. Those concentrating on specific marks, particularly the "NIPPON" one, may pay higher prices. Pieces of Azalea pattern china are available through replacement services.

History: The Azalea pattern of Noritake China was first produced in the early 1900s. Each piece of fine china was hand painted. The individuality of the artists makes it almost impossible to find two pieces with identical painting. In the early 1900s, the Larkin Co., Buffalo, NY, sold many household items to the American public through

its catalog (similar to the Sears Roebuck & Co., catalog). In the 1924 Larkin catalog, a basic Azalea pattern serving set was advertised. The set included the larger coffee cups with the blue rising-sun backstamp.

Two forces came together in the 1920s to make the Azalea pattern of Noritake China one of the most popular household patterns in this century. First, the Larkin Co., initiated its "Larkin Plan," encouraging housewives to sign up to become "Larkin Secretaries." Each Larkin Secretary formed a small neighborhood group of five or more women who would purchase Larkin products. The Larkin Secretary earned premiums based on the volume of orders she obtained and could then exchange these premiums for household items, including Azalea china. Second, many households in the 1920s could not afford to spend all at one time the amount needed to purchase a complete set of fine china. The Larkin Club Plan enabled them to eventually complete sets of the Azalea pattern by buying items one or a few at a time.

Over the years, and to provide more enticements, additional pieces, such as the nut/fruit shell-shaped bowl, candy jar and child's tea set were offered. Glassware, originally classified as "crystal," was introduced in the 1930s but was not well received. It became somewhat of a status symbol to "own a set of Azalea." The Azalea pattern china advertisement in the 1931 Larkin catalog claimed, "Our Most Popular China."

Some Azalea pieces were advertised in the Larkin catalogs for 19 consecutive years, while others were advertised for only four or five years. These latter pieces are scarcer, resulting in a faster appreciation in value. Most serious collectors would like to own the child's tea set, which we believe was advertised in only two Larkin Fall catalogs and the so-called salesmen's samples, which were never advertised for sale. Larkin ceased distribution in 1945.

References: Larkin catalogs from 1916 through 1941.

Notes: The Larkin catalog numbers are given in parentheses behind each listing. If arranged numerically, you will notice gaps. For example, numbers 41 through 53 are missing. Noritake's Scenic pattern, presently called Tree in the Meadow, also was popular during this time period. Many of the missing Azalea numbers were assigned to Scenic pieces.

Basket (193)	125.00
Bonbon Dish, 6-1/4" d (184)	45.00
Bouillon Cup and Saucer, 5-1/4" (124)	20.00
Bowl, shell shape	325.00
Butter Pat (312)	65.00
Butter Tub, insert (54)	45.00
Cake Plate (10)	35.00
Casserole, cov (16)	75.00
Celery Dish (444)	250.00
Cheese Dish, cov (315)	125.00
Coffeepot (182)	500.00
Condiment Set (14)	75.00
Creamer (7)	25.00
Cruet, orig stopper (190)	165.00
Cup and Saucer (2)	17.00
Demitasse Cup and Saucer (183)	125.00
Eggcup (120)	55.00
Grapefruit Bowl (185)	115.00
Gravy Boat (40)	50.00
Jam Jar, cov (125)	110.00
Lemon Tray, handle (121)	27.00
Mayonnaise Set (3)	50.00
Milk Pitcher, quart (100)	165.00
Plate	
Dinner (13)	22.00
Luncheon (4)	12.00
Platter, 12" l (56)	50.00
Relish, 4 sections (119)	110.00
Salad Bowl, 10" d (12)	35.00
Salt and Pepper Shakers, pr	23.00
Spooner (189)	90.00
Syrup, cov (97)	95.00
Teapot (15)	95.00
Toothpick Holder (192)	95.00
Vase, fan-shaped (187)	1,100.00

Vegetable bowl, cov, handles, gold finial, $375.

Nutcrackers

Collecting Hints: The most popular modern nutcrackers are the military and civilian figures which are made in East Germany. These are collected primarily for show and not for practicality.

Nutcracker design responded to each decorating phase through the 1950s. The figural nutcrackers of the Art Deco and Art Nouveau periods are much in demand. Concentrating on 19th-century models results in a display of cast-iron ingenuity. These nutcrackers were meant to be used. Several cast-iron animal models have been reproduced. Signs of heavy use are one indication of age.

History: Nuts keep well for long periods, up to two years, and have served as a dessert or additive to cakes, pies, bread, etc., since the colonial period. Americans' favorite nuts are walnuts, chestnuts, pecans and almonds.

The first nutcrackers were crude hammers or club devices. The challenge was to find a cracker that would crack the shell but leave the nut intact. By the mid-19th century, cast-iron nutcrackers in animal shapes appeared. Usually the nut was placed in the jaw section of the animal and the tail pressed as the lever to crack the nut.

The 19th- and early 20th century patent records abound with nutcracker inventions. In 1916, a lever-operated cracker which could be clamped to the table was patented as the Home Nut Cracker, St. Louis. Perhaps one of the most durable designs was patented on Jan. 28, 1889, and sold as the Quakenbush plated model. This hand model is plain at the top where the grip teeth are located and has twist-style handles on the lower half of each arm. The arms end in an acorn finial.

References: Judith A. Rittenhouse, *Ornamental and Figural Nutcrackers*, Collector Books, 1993; James Rollband, *American Nutcrackers*, Off Beat Books (1345 Poplar Ave., Sunnyvale, CA 94087), 1996.

Alligator, 6", cast iron 32.00

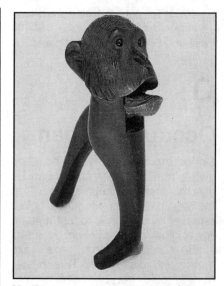

Monkey, carved wood, 6-3/4", $85.

Bear, wood, glass eyes, hand carved, German	100.00
Cat, 4-1/2", brass	50.00
Chicken, head, 7", wood, glass eyes, 1850s	85.00
Dog	
4-5/8", cast iron, old paint	65.00
6", brass	41.00
10" l, 5-1/4" h, brass	60.00
13" l, 6" h, cast iron, SP	75.00
Dragoon, brass	50.00
Elephant, 10" l, 5" h, orig paint, c1920	72.50
Fish, 5", brass	30.00
Gentleman, 9" h, bust, wood, hand carved	64.00
Jester, head, brass	77.00
Lady's Leg, 7", wood	32.00
Lion, head, brass	32.50
Monkey, head, brass	36.00
Parrot, 5-1/2", brass	16.00
Pheasant, bronze, French	110.00
Pliers Type	
Cast iron, Torrington	5.00
Silver, double	28.00
Steel, 5-1/2", adjustable, c1890	11.00
Punch & Judy, figural, brass	95.00
Rabbit, head, wood, glass eyes, hand carved, German	110.00
Ram, 8-1/2", wood, glass eyes	66.00
Sailor and woman, 6-1/4", brass, couple kisses when handles squeeze together	72.00
Skull and Cross Bones, 6", cast iron	88.00
Squirrel	
Bronze, sitting on branch	48.00
Cast Iron, sitting on leaf	47.00
Table Type, Perfection Nut Cracker Co.,	

Waco, TX, pat 1914, clamp-and-turn
buckle 22.00
Twist-and-Screw Type, nickel-plated
cast iron, 5" 12.00

O

Occupied Japan

Collecting Hints: Buyers should be aware that a rubber stamp can be used to mark "Occupied Japan" on the base of objects. Fingernail polish remover can be used to test a mark. An original mark will remain intact since it is under the glaze; fake marks will disappear. This procedure should not be used on unglazed pieces. Visual examination is the best way to identify a fake mark on an unglazed item.

Damaged pieces have little value unless the item is extremely rare. Focus on pieces which are well-made and nicely decorated. There are many inferior examples. From the beginning of the American occupation of Japan until April 28, 1952, objects made in that country were marked "Japan," "Made in Japan," "Occupied Japan," or "Made in Occupied Japan." Only pieces marked with the last two designations are of major interest to Occupied Japan collectors. The first two marks also were used during other time periods.

History: The Japanese economy was devastated when World War II ended. To secure necessary hard currency, the Japanese pottery industry produced thousands of figurines and other knickknacks for export. The variety of products is endless—ashtrays, dinnerware, lamps, planters, souvenir items, toys, vases, etc. Initially, the figurines attracted the largest number of collectors; today many collectors focus on other types of pieces.

References: Florence Archambault, *Occupied Japan for Collectors*, Schiffer Publishing, 1992; Gene Florence, *Price Guide to Collector's Encyclopedia of Occupied Japan*, Collector Books, 1996 (updated prices for five-book series *Collector's Encyclopedia of Occupied Japan*); David C. Gould and Donna Crevar-Donaldson, *Occupied Japan Toys with Prices*, L-W Book Sales, 1993; Anthony Marsella, *Toys from Occupied Japan*, Schiffer Publishing, 1995; Lynette Parmer, *Collecting Occupied Japan*, Schiffer Publishing, 1996; Carole Bess White, *Collector's Guide to Made in Japan Ceramics*, *Book I* (1994), *Book II* (1996) Collector Books.

Collectors' Club: Occupied Japan Club, 29 Freeborn St., Newport, RI 02840; Occupied Japan Collectors Club, 18309 Faysmith Ave., Torrance, CA 90504.

Ashtray
Coal Hod, china,
white, floral dec 10.00
Florida, china, state
shape, state name in
black letters, gold trim 12.00
Pikes Peak, metal,
emb scene, oval 3.00
View of life and times of silk worm,
roaring dragon motif on reticulated
border, 5-5/8" d, mkd "Made in
Occupied Japan" 35.00
Basket, china,
miniature, floral dec 5.00
Bell, chef holding wine bottle and glass,
3" h 24.00
Bookends, pr,
sailing ships, emb wood 75.00
Box, cov, inlaid, dog motif 15.00
Cache Pot, 3-1/2" h, fawn 10.00
Cigarette Box, cov, china, rect, blue
floral dec, gold trim 15.00
Cigarette Set, plated metal,
cov box, Scottie dog dec,
matching lighter 20.00
Clicker, beetle, silver color 5.00
Coaster Set, papier-mâché box, floral
dec, price for 6-pc set 18.00
Compass, pocket-watch shape 20.00
Cornucopia, china, white, pink roses,
gold trim 35.00
Creamer, figural, cow 25.00
Crumb Tray, metal, emb New York
scenes 10.00
Cup and Saucer
Checkered borders,
black and white 6.00
Floral dec, blue 12.50
Demitasse Cup and Saucer, white,
yellow and red flowers 10.00
Dish, china, fish shape 10.00
Doll, celluloid, baby wearing snowsuit,
jointed 40.00
Doll House Furnishings, china
Couch, white, pink roses, 3"l 15.00
Lamp, white base,

Figure, beetle, black top hat, green, white violin, mkd "Made in Occupied Japan," 3", $15

green shade, gold trim 10.00
Figure
3-3/4" h, metal, cowboy on rearing
horse 15.00
4-3/4" h, ballerina, bisque 35.00
5" h, jumping horses 12.00
7-1/2" h, Santa, china 65.00
8" h
Oriental man 20.00
Woman, porcelain, lavender and
yellow dress 20.00
8-1/2" h, lady, china, hp 145.00
Harmonica, Butterfly, orig box.......17.50
Head Vase, Oriental girl, china 18.00
Honey Jar, bee hive, bee finial......25.00
Incense Burner, woman 20.00
Kazoo, litho tin, set of 3, MIB 5.00
Lantern, 4-1/2" h, owl motif 35.00
Mug, china
Boy Handle 14.00
Indian Chief..............................35.00
MacArthur 55.00
Napkins, damask, orig paper labels,
price for set of six 45.00
Necklace, pearls, double strand, orig
paper label 12.00
Nodder, donkey, celluloid..............30.00
Noise Maker, horn, gold................25.00
Parasol, multicolored, 32" d 50.00
Perfume Bottle, glass, blue, 4" h...15.00
Piano Baby, hp..............................65.00
Pincushion, metal, grand-piano shape,
red velvet cushion 15.00
Planter, figural
Baby booties, blue trim 8.00
Cat, sitting up...........................10.00
Dog, with basket 20.00
Donkey Pulling Cart 10.00
Rabbit..12.50

Tea set, miniature, $25.

Plate
    Cabin Scene,
      chickens in yard 18.00
      Cherries, lacy edge 25.00
Platter, Blue Willow pattern,
    oval, 12" l................................35.00
Powder Jar, cov, Wedgwood style, blue
    and white, 3" d........................15.00
Rooster, inflatable, rubber.............20.00
Salt and Pepper Shakers, pr
    Hat, 1 brown, 1 black 15.00
    Pigs, large ears 12.00
Shelf Sitter, Little Boy Blue............15.00
Silent Butler, metal 15.00
Stein, man and woman with dog,
    8-1/2" h 40.00
Tape Measure, figural, pig, flowered
    dec..35.00
Teapot, china,
    colonial couple dec 20.00
Tea Set, miniature,
    china, floral dec 25.00
Toby Pitcher, barkeeper, holding mugs,
    5" h 30.00
Toothpick Holder, puppy in barrel ...6.00
Toy
    Baby Pontiac, windup, litho tin, car,
      orig box 65.00
    Boy on Sled, windup,
      litho tin, MIB 150.00
    Camel, walker,
      celluloid, MIB..........................120.00
    Cherry Cook, windup................90.00
    Dancing Couple,
      celluloid, MIB..........................95.00
    Hopping Dog, windup...............22.00
    Minstrel Monkey,
      celluloid, MIB..........................175.00
    Monkey, windup, plays banjo,
      orig box 75.00
    Trick Seal, windup..................880.00
Tray, rect, papier-mâché, black ground,
    gold floral dec 8.00
Vase, 5-1/4" h, figural, Hummel-type boy
    reading book............................25.00
Wall Plaque,
    Victorian lady, flowers..............18.00
Wall Pocket
    5" h, porcelain, lady with hat,

Art Deco style............................35.00
7-1/4" h, Dutch Girl, mkd "Made in
Occupied Japan"......................12.50

Ocean Liner Collectibles

Collecting Hints: Don't concentrate only on ships of American registry, although many collectors try to gather material from only one liner or ship line. Objects associated with ships involved in disasters, such as the *Titanic*, often command higher prices.

History: Transoceanic travel falls into two distinct periods—the era of the great Clipper ships and the era of the diesel-powered ocean liners. The latter craft reached their golden age between 1900 and 1940.

    An ocean liner is a city unto itself. Most have their own printing rooms to produce a wealth of daily memorabilia. Companies, such as Cunard and Holland-America, encourage passengers to acquire souvenirs with the company logo and ship's name. Word-of-mouth is a principal form of advertising. Certain ships acquired a unique mystic. The *Queen Elizabeth*, *Queen Mary* and *United States* became symbols of elegance and style. Today, the cruise ship dominates the world of the ocean liner.

References: John Adams, *Ocean Steamers*, New Cavendish Books, 1992; Karl D. Spence, *How to Identify and Price Ocean Liner Collectibles*, published by author, 1991; James Steele, *Queen Mary*, Phaidon, 1995.

Collectors' Clubs: Oceanic Navigation Research Society, Inc., P.O. Box 8005, Studio City, CA 91608; Steamship Historical Society of America, Inc., 300 Ray Dr., Ste. 4, Providence, RI 02906; Titanic Historical Society, P.O. Box 51053, Indian Orchard, MA 01151.

Periodical: *Voyage*, P.O. Box 7007, Freehold, NJ 07728.

Museums: Mystic Seaport, Mystic, CT; South Street Seaport Museum, New York, NY; University of Baltimore, Steamship Historical Society Collection, Baltimore, MD.

Ashtray

Everett, Washington, Yacht Club,
    brass 20.00
RMS *Queen Elizabeth I,* Cunard
    Line, wood ship's wheel, glass insert
    over color center photo 30.00
Pacific Far East
    Steamship, china 25.00
Baggage Tag, French
    Line, first class 5.00
Belt Buckle, RMS *Queen Elizabeth II,*
    Cunard Line, chrome-plated solid
    brass, black outline of ship, name in
    red 14.00
Book, *Sinking of the Titanic*, Logan
    Marshal, L.T. Myers, 1912, photos
    and drawings............................20.00
Booklet
    Independence, American
      Export Lines, 1966 Gala
      Springtime Cruise, itinerary and
      deck plan inserts......................20.00
    St. Lawrence Route to Europe,
      Canadian Pacific 1930,
      8" x 11", 16 pgs.........................24.00
Brochure
    Cunard and Anchor-Donaldson Line,
      Canadian Service. The Historic
      St. Lawrence River Route to Europe,
      late 1920s 7.50
    Cunard Line, Getting There is Half
      the Fun, 16 pgs, 1952...............6.00
    Italian Line, Six Cruises to the Medi-
      terranean and Egypt, 1934 ......12.00
Change Tray,
    American Line Ship 100.00
Cigarette Lighter,
    RMS *Queen Mary* 32.00
Coffee Cup, SS *United States* 32.00
Compact, *Empress of Canada*,
    Canadian Pacific Line, Stratton, line
    flag logo, ship's name in enameled
    front medallion.........................40.00
Cruise Book, *Scythia*, 1929...........40.00
Deck Card, Concordia Lines,
    Norway 18.00
Deck Plan
    MV *Westerdaam* 1950,
      multicolored 15.00

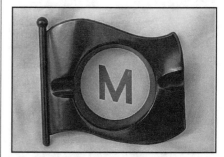

Ashtray, flag shape, green plastic, center with red "M" on white ground, Matson Lines, 4-3/4" w, $25.

RMS *Samaria*, Cunard Line, Plan of Tourist Accommodation 15.00

SS *Hamburg*, 1930, fold out.....35.00

Dish, RMS *Queen Mary*, Cunard Line, ceramic, 5" l, oval, color portrait, gold edge, Staffordshire 35.00

Excursion Announcement, SS *Cuba* 20.00

Goblet, RMS *Queen Elizabeth II*, Cunard Line, souvenir, etched image and name, manufactured by Stuart Crystal, #1305 ....225.00

Landing Arrangements Card, RMS *Caronia*, July 28, 1950...............5.00

Menu

Ile de France, July 12, 1938, dinner.................5.00

RMS *Caronia*, breakfast, Aug. 2, 1950, 1-pg card 6.00

SS *Columbus*, Norddestcher Lloyd Bremen line, 1938, 5-3/4" x 8-1/4", 4 pgs, litho color cover showing German statue 8.00

SS *Manhattan*, United States Lines, 6" x 10", 4 pgs, 1933, dinner, cream-colored cover with Arch of Triumph, deckled edges 7.50

SS *Santa Rose*, Grace Line, dinner, June 18 1964 ....5.00

Newspaper

RMS *Caronia*, *Ocean Times*, Aug. 1, 1950, 4 pgs 8.00

RMS *Queen Mary*, May 10, 1950, 12 pgs 15.00

Note Paper

Cunard *White Star*, blue.............5.00

MS *Osloofjord*, 2 color views of ship...................6.00

RMS *Queen Mary*, beige............6.00

Passenger List

Pitcher, RMSP *Danube*, The Royal Mail Stream Packet Co., White Horse China, c1880, 3" h, $60.

RMS *Aquitania*, full-color illus of ship................50.00

SS *Leviathan*, 1924..................15.00

St. Louis, American Line, eastbound trip, Feb. 10, 1906....................35.00

Passport Cover, Red Star Line, fabric, ship illus..................................25.00

Pencil, mechanical, Cunard liner *Mauretania*, black and white, 5" l, "Right Point," gold metal accent tip, metal clip with b&w illus of passenger ship, name in black and red letters, c1930.....................24.00

Pinback Button

Carnival Cruises.........................3.00

RMS *Queen Elizabeth I*, Cunard Line, 1-3/4", photo, "World's Largest Liner" at bottom.........................8.00

Playing Cards

Alaska Steamship 15.00

Holland American Line, double deck..............................25.00

SS *Badger*, double deck 20.00

SS *Spartan*, double deck 20.00

Swedish American Lines, orig slip case 18.00

Postcard

Andania, Cunard Line 6.00

Aurania, Cunard Line 6.00

Cosulich Lines, 1929..................6.00

Poster, Grace Line, Caribbean, 1949 C. Evers, illus of tourists, ship, cars and boats, 23" x 30" 200.00

Print

Moor-McCormack Lines...........85.00

Titanic, 15" x 22-1/2", b&w, text of sinking, published by Tichnor Bros., Boston.....................................60.00

Program of Events, Cunard Line

RMS *Caronia*, Aug. 1, 1950 ....6.00

RMS *Queen Mary*, May 12, 1950 ....6.00

Puzzle, 1/2" x 1-1/2" x 4", tin frame holding glass over metal playing surface separated by horiz raised bar that shows engraved battleship scene, 2 tin pivot bars to obstruct playing balls, upper compartment titled "Atlantic Ocean," and lower compartment "Pacific Ocean," object is to "Pilot 2 Battleships Pacific to Atlantic, Hold Them There While Piloting Remaining 2 Battleships Atlantic to Pacific," Panama Canal Locks, Poplar Games Co., NY, c1915 ....125.00

Race Card, Cunard White Star

RMS *Caronia* 7.00

RMS *Queen Mary*, some ink marks........................7.00

Razor Towel, Cunard White Star, paper..........5.00

Souvenir Spoon

Cunard White Star, demitasse, SP,

mkd 18.00

Transylvania Anchor Line, SP, twisted handle, blue enameled ring, flag and crest 75.00

Stationery

RMS *Queen Mary*, Cunard Line, note paper, matching envelope, color portrait, line and ship name, 5" x 7"..........................10.00

Royal Mail Steamer, 2 sheets of paper, matching envelope 20.00

Sylvania, Cunard Line, beige, color portrait, line and ship name, 5-1/4" x 6-3/4" 8.00

Steamer Directory, Clyde-Mallory Lines, c1920 ....12.00

Tie Clasp, RMS *Queen Mary*, Cunard Line, gold tone, red, white and blue enameled ship 15.00

Timetable, Monticello Steamship Co., "On the Bay of San Francisco," 1907 ....65.00

Tour Booklet, Anchor Line, United Kingdom Ship, 5-1/4" x 7-1/2", litho color cover of passenger ship going through ocean, 32 b&w pgs of text, points of interest in Ireland, Scotland and England, 1907 ....28.00

Whiskey Bottle, RMS *Titanic*.........60.00

Olympics Collectibles

Collecting Hints: Collectors of Olympic materials should remember that the Olympic Games have been a multi-language event. Collectors may not wish to limit their collections to English-only examples. The other important fact to remember is that the more recent the Olympiad, the greater the number of items that have survived. Items from the 1996 Olympics have not yet reached the secondary market, but things from 1988 are beginning to surface. More collectibles tend to enter the antiques and collectibles marketplace during the years the games are scheduled, creating more interest in this fast-growing field.

History: Organized amateur sports games originated in ancient Greece. The games were held every four years beginning about 776 B.C. At first, running events were the only type held, but many different events have been added over the years. The Olympics as we know them were revived in Athens about 1896. After that date the games were held in a different city around the world every four years. The number of participants, competing nations and events have increased steadily.

Women were first allowed to participate in the games in 1912. The winter games began in 1924 and were held on a four-year schedule until 1992 when they were rescheduled so that they would alternate at a two-year interval with the more traditional summer games.

References: Roderick A. Malloy, *Malloy's Sports Collectibles Value Guide*, Wallace-Homestead, 1994; Michael McKeever, *Collecting Sports Memorabilia*, Alliance Publishing, 1966.

Periodicals: *Sports Collectors Digest*, 700 E. State St., Iola, WI 54990.

Collectors' Clubs: Olympic Pin Collector's Club, 1386 Fifth St., Schenectady, NY 12303.

Badge, 1980 Winter Olympics, 2-1/2" d, celluloid, color image of mascot raccoon as hockey player, white ground, black letters 20.00

Cigarette Lighter, 2-3/4" l, 1984 Winter Olympics, red plastic, silvered metal, Olympic ring symbol, insignia and "Sarajevo, Yugoslavia" in black on one side, black cartoon snowman illus other side..........................15.00

Doll, 1980 Winter Olympics raccoon mascot, Chiquita, 14" h, stuffed cloth, gray, black and white face, blue body, orange gloves, skating boots, separate white vinyl racing bib pullover vest, orig stitched tag with licensing authorization, Chase Bag Co.....................................40.00

Fan, Tenth Olympic Games/1932/Los Angeles, folding paper type, balsa sticks, chapel building illus, Olympic symbol, Japan 40.00

Glass, 5-1/2" h, 1932 Olympics, clear, frosted white picture 50.00

License Plate Holder, 1932, aluminum, 2 athletes holding the world, "Los Angeles" in raised letters 150.00

Magazine, *Sports Illustrated*, Sept. 5, 1960, Rome Olympics Ceremonies 7.50

Map, 1960, Rome Olympics, 6" x 10" folder opens to 10" x 35", 8 color maps on both sides, Automobile Club of Italy sponsor.................15.00

Pin
1964, Innsbruck Winter Olympics, Austrian-made, black, white and red

accent enamels, gold finish......65.00
1980, Moscow Olympics
Figural mascot bear as soccer player, blue, white and brown enamels, gold luster 20.00

Official symbol flanked by deep red porcelain enamel under Russian inscription, gold luster 15.00

1984, Calgary Winter Olympics, official symbol in 5 colors, white ground, double needle post and clutch fasteners.......................8.00

1984, Los Angeles Olympics, Fuji, domed acrylic on metal, symbolic cartoon U.S. eagle holding Olympic torch, needle post and clutch fastener 10.00

1988, Seoul Summer Olympics, domed acrylic, 3 enameled colors, gold luster, needle post and clutch fastener 5.00

1992, Albertville Winter Olympics, CBS, domed acrylic, gold luster, white enamel, tiny Olympic rings in 5 colors 5.00

1996, Atlanta Olympics pre-event promotion pin, cartoon baseball player, 4 colors, gold above bar inscription "Atlanta 1996/1000 Days/October 23, 1993," needle post and clutch fastener.....................2.00

Pin Display, 1988 Olympics, 1-3/4" x 6" x 8" cover box, wood display frame, high-gloss finish, very dark mahogany enamel, frame holds recessed glass over gold luster metal title plate identifying Jeep as official sponsor of U.S. Olympic team, 5 different Jeep pins comprising limited edition set ..30.00

Plate, 7" d, 1968, gold leaf, Mexico and torch dec..................................60.00

Postcard, 1912 Stockholm Olympics, b&w photo 30.00

Stadium Cushion, 11" x 13-1/2", 1956 Summer Olympics, red vinyl, yellow, white and blue Olympics logo 48.00

Stick Pin
1940, sterling-like silvered metal, Helsinki, Finland, torch flame under Olympics rings symbol, above 1940 date 80.00

1980, Moscow Olympics, miniature Gold Olympics rings under miniature image of Soviet flag, dark red porcelain enamel accents 18.00

Toy, 1992 Olympic Bobsled Run, wood replica, 1-1/2" h x 2" w x 8-1/2" l, wire handgrip rail and bumper bar, 2 front skis swivel left and right, driver unit inscribed "U.S.A.," thumbtack steering wheel, Olympic symbols on riding surface......................200.00

Tray, 1976 Olympics, Montreal, litho metal, Coca-Cola adv..............40.00

Owl Collectibles

Collecting Hints: If you collect the "creature of the night" or the "wise old owl," any page of this book might conceivably contain a related object since the owl theme can be found in hundreds of collectible categories, including advertising trade cards, books, buttons and postcards, to name a few.

Don't confine yourself just to old or antique owls. Owl figurines, owl themes on limited edition collectors' plates and handcrafted items from modern artisans are plentiful. There are many examples available in every price range.

History: Owls have existed on earth for over 60 million years. They have been used as a decorative motif since before Christ. An owl and Athena appeared on an ancient Greek coin.

Every culture has superstitions surrounding the owl. Some believe the owl represented good luck, others viewed it as an evil omen. The owl has remained a popular symbol in Halloween material. Of course, the owl's wisdom is often attached to scholarly pursuits. Expanding this theme, the National Park Service uses Woodsey to "Give A Hoot, Don't Pollute."

Reproduction Alert: Wholesalers who sell to antiques and collectibles

Figure, owl standing on book, SS, 1-1/2" h, $125.

dealers have recently offered reproduction fruit crate labels with an owl
motif. These labels are appearing at
flea markets and in shops where
they are being passed off as originals. Westmoreland Glass molds
have been sold to several different
manufacturers. The owl sitting on
two books is being reissued with the
original "W" still on top of the books.
The three-owl plate mold also was
sold. Imperial Glass owl molds have
also found new owners.

Andirons, pr, 14-3/4" h, cast iron, glass
  eye, mkd "407E" 375.00
Bank, 2" x 2-1/2", tin, owl pictured on
  side 50.00
Bell, 4" h, brass, emb feathers and fea-
  tures..45.00
Book
  Lavine, Sigmund,
    Wonders Of The Owl, Dodd,
    Mead & Co., NY, 1971 ....1.50
  Mowat, Farley, *Owls In The Family*,
    Little, Brown & Co., 1961 35
Bookends, pr
  Brass, Frankart.......................135.00
  Bronze, head, sgd "M. Carr"...120.00
  Van Briggle, green,
    matte finish..........................135.00
Book Rack, expanding 55.00
Calendar Plate, 1912, owl on open book,
  Berlin, NE 25.00
Calling Card Tray, 8-1/2" x 7", quadruple
  plate, emb music staff and "Should
  Owl's Acquaintance Be Forgot," 2
  owls sitting on back of tray 85.00
Candy Container, 4-1/8" h, glass, screw
  cap closure 125.00
Clock, 6-1/2" h, wood,
  hand carved...........................100.00
Cookie Jars
  Snow Owl, mkd "Made in Poppytrail
    Calif"....................................40.00
  Winking Owl, mid "856 USA"....32.00
  Woodsey Owl 95.00
Decoy, 13", papier-mâché, double
  faced, glass eyes, brown, small white
  area on chest..........................65.00
Degenhart
  Custard....................................35.00
  Holly Green 20.00
  Red Carnival 80.00
  Vaseline 45.00
Fairy Lamp
  3-3/8" d, 4-1/8" h, double-faced
    figure, pyramid size, frosted cranber-
    ry glass, lavender enameled eyes,
    Clarke base 200.00
  4" h, painted eyes,
    Clarke base 225.00
Figure

**Trade card, diecut, Colburn's Philadel-
phia Mustard, 3-3/8" x 3-1/2", $7.50.**

3" h, carnival glass, Fenton......18.00
4" h, carnival glass, Moser.......20.00
8-1/2" h, orange, Viking..........100.00
9" h, turquoise, Van Briggle 60.00
Humidor, 6-1/4" h,
  octagonal, Nippon 375.00
Inkwell, 8" x 4", brass,
  glass inset, hinged lid, pen tray,
  2" owl figure............................75.00
Lamp, candle, 5-1/4", snow white china,
  owl-shaped shade, stump-shaped
  base, fitted candleholder, mkd "R.S.
  Germany" 225.00
Letter Opener, bronze 30.00
Limited Edition Collector Plate
  1991, Peek-A-Whoo, Screech Owl,
    Baby Owls of North America, J
    Thornburgh 37.00
  1993, Great Gray Owl Family, Family
    Circles, R. Rust 30.00
  1994, Great Horned Owl Family,
    Family Circles, R. Rust 30.00
Mask, papier-mâché, c1915..........90.00
Match Holder
  2-/12" h, dark green, Wetzel Glass
    Co. 8.00
  8" h, 3" w, metal,
    hanging type 18.00
Medal
  Leeds International Exhibition, 1890,
    2-1/4", metal, white bust of Queen
    Victoria on 1 side 25.00
  Natural History Society of Montreal,
    1-3/4", bronze, cast, owl with
    branch in beak 20.00
Mustard Jar, cov, 5" h, milk glass, screw
  top, glass insert, Atterbury.....165.00
Napkin Ring
  Nippon, owl sitting on stump ..225.00
  Silver Plated, owl standing.....145.00
Owl Drug Co.
  Bottle, 3-1/2" h, cork top, clear, Oil of
    Sweet Almond label, 1 oz 4.00
  Shot Glass, clear......................14.00
  Tin, 4-1/4" d, 3" h,

"Theatrical Cold Cream"
  orange ground, black print 24.00
Paperweight, Kosta,
  sgd "D. Lindstrand".................95.00
Pin, blue, green and gold enamel, amber
  eyes with rhinestone eye disks, pearl
  tail feathers..............................18.00
Pitcher
  8" h, 6" d top, pressed glass, owl
    shape 110.00
  9-1/2" h, cov, china, semi-vitreous,
    Edwin M. Knowles China Co. ..37.50
Plate
  China, barn owl, 1976 Wildlife,
    Goebel 38.00
  Milk Glass
    Owl Lovers, 7-1/2" d 40.00
    3 owl heads, 6" d, fluted open work
      edge, gold paint 65.00
Quilt, cigar silks, 5¢ Owls, single-bed
  size 450.00
Ring Tree, 3-1/4" " d, 4" h, shallow brown
  dish, blue lining, brown and tan owl
  perched on back, mkd "Doulton
  Stoneware"..............................325.00
Salt and Pepper Shakers, pr, 3-1/4" h,
  china, brown and white, mortarboard
  hats, scholarly expression, horn rim
  glasses 6.50
Sheet Music
  Beautiful Ohio, owl on cover 3.50
  The Pansy and the Owl 4.50
  The Wise Old Owl.....................3.50
Tape Measure, 1-3/8" h, brass, glass
  eyes, mkd "Germany"..............35.00
Thermometer, 6" h, plaster body...75.00
Toothbrush Holder,
  figural, Syroco 12.50
Valentine, 15" l, girl and boy riding
  balloon, owl sitting on moon above,
  "Nobody's looking but the owl and
  the moon!" 8.00

**Pitcher, yellow shaded to red-orange,
Kanawha Glass, orig label, 5" h, $12.**

P

Paden City Glass

Collecting Hints: Although Paden City glass is often lumped with mass-produced, machine-made wares into the Depression Glass category, Paden City's wares were, until 1948, all hand-made. Its products are better classified as "Elegant Glass" of the era, as it ranks in quality with the wares produced by contemporaries such as Fostoria, New Martinsville and Morgantown.

Paden City kept a low profile, never advertising in consumer magazines of the day. The firm never marked its glass in any way because a large portion of its business consisted of sales to decorating companies, mounters and fitters. The firm also supplied bars, restaurants and soda fountains with glassware, as evidenced by the wide range of tumblers, ice cream dishes and institutional products available in several Paden City patterns.

Paden City's decorating shop also etched, cut, hand painted and applied silver overlay and gold encrustation. However, not every decoration found on Paden City shapes will necessarily have come from the factory. Cupid, Peacock and Rose and several other etchings depicting birds are among the most sought after decorations. Pieces with these etchings are commanding higher and higher prices even though they were apparently made in greater quantities than some of the etchings that are less-known (but just as beautiful).

Paden City is noted for its colors: opal (opaque white), ebony, mulberry (amethyst), Cheriglo (delicate pink), yellow, dark green (forest), crystal, amber, primrose (reddish-amber), blue, rose and great quantities of ruby (red). The firm also produced transparent green in numerous shades ranging from yellowish to a distinctive electric green that always alerts knowledgeable collectors to its Paden City origin.

History: Paden City Glass Manufacturing Co., was founded in 1916 in Paden City, WV. David Fisher, former-ly of the New Martinsville Glass Manufacturing Co., operated the company until his death in 1933, at which time his son, Samuel, became president. A management decision in 1949 to expand Paden City's production by acquiring American Glass Co., an automated manufacturer of bottles, ashtrays and novelties, strained the company's finances, forcing the firm to close permanently in 1951.

Contrary to popular belief and previously incorrect printed references, The Paden City Glass Manufacturing Co., had absolutely no connection with the Paden City Pottery Co., other than their identical locale.

References: Lee Garmon and Dick Spencer, *Glass Animals of the Depression Era*, Collector Books, 1993; Naomi L. Over, *Ruby Glass of the 20th Century*, The Glass Press, 1990, 1993-94 value update; Ellen T. Schroy, *Warman's Glass*, 2nd Edition, Wallace-Homestead, 1995; Hazel Marie Weatherman, *Colored Glassware of the Depression Era 2*, Glassbooks, 1974.

Advisor: Michael Krumme.

Animal, pheasant, blue.................110.00
Bookends, pr, Pouter
  Pigeons, crystal.....................170.00
Bowl
  11" d, #300 Archaic, Peacock and
  Rose etching, pink..................130.00
  13" d, Gazebo
  etching, crystal.....................55.00
Cake Salver, low, ftd, #412 Crow's Foot
  Square, Orchid etching
  Crystal..............................40.00
  Ruby.................................120.00
Candleholders,
  #191 Party Line, dome foot,
  Gypsy cutting, medium blue....25.00
Candlesticks, pr, #300 Archaic, Nora
  Bird etching, amber...............100.00
Cocktail Shaker,
  Speakeasy, green..................45.00
Compote
  Gothic Garden etching,
  yellow, tall.........................45.00
  Party Line, #191,
  pink, ftd, 11".......................35.00
Console Bowl
  7", 3-ftd base,
  #503, amber, cutting...............25.00
  11" sq, Orchid, yellow............115.00
Creamer, #412 Crow's Foot Square,
  Orchid etching, ruby...............40.00
Cream Soup Bowl, #412 Crow's Foot,

amber, ftd.................................9.00
Cup and Saucer,
  #412 Crow's Foot, red............15.00
Finger Bowl, #991,
  Penny Line, ruby....................35.00
Serving Plate, center handle
  #300 Archaic,
  Cupid etching, pink...............160.00
  #411, Mrs. B, pink..................20.00
Sherbet, #991
  Penny Line, ruby, tall..............13.00
Sugar Bowl, #411 Mrs. B, Gothic Garden
  etching, green.......................35.00
Sugar Pourer, #94 bullet-shape, screw-
  on nickel base, green............175.00
Tumbler
  #890 Crow's
  Foot Round, amber.................35.00
  #991 Penny Line, red
    3-1/4" h, red.........................8.00
    4-1/8" h, red.......................10.00
    5" h, cone shape, green.........7.75
    5-1/4" h, red.......................12.00
    5-3/4" h, cone shape
      Green..............................8.75
      Pink...............................10.00
    6-3/4" h, cone
      shape, green......................8.75
Vase
  Fan, #191 Party Line, green....38.00
  10" h, Utopia etching, yellow....85.00

Padlocks

Collecting Hints: Some collectors look for all kinds of old padlocks, which is costly and endless because of the wide variety available. Many collectors specialize in one category, but may buy others that appeal to them. Other collectors look for locks from just one manufacturer.

Just being old and scarce is not always enough; locks must have some kind of appeal. They must be in a category of special interest, have an interesting design or have historical significance. Desirable padlocks are embossed with the name or initials of a defunct company or railroad, a logo, an event, such as an exposition, a scroll or a figural design. Other desirable types have unique construction, unusual size or trick and intricate mechanisms. The more recent and inexpensive logo locks—stamped, incised or embossed with the names or initials of government agencies or petroleum, automobile or other companies—have increased in popularity.

Lever Push Key, Favorite 6-lever, Eagle, Breass 2 1/4" d, $25.

The most competitive and expensive collecting pertains to the intricate and finely made locks of the mid 1800s, the simple earlier locks that can be identified and the embossed brass locks from the now-defunct short-line railroads. The name or initials of the manufacturer is usually stamped on the lock. If marked with the name of a small company from the 1850s, a lock can be worth many times more than a similar one made by a large, prolific manufacturer. There are always exceptions, e.g., Smokies do not have much value no matter how old or scarce.

Locks made by certain manufacturers can be more valuable than similar and even more scarce locks made by others. The round Lever Push Key locks can be several times more valuable than other types with the same embossing. Locks classified as Story are worth many times more than similar locks classified as Warded. The reason for the differences in value is often inexplicable.

Identifying many of the old padlocks is possible using either markings on the lock or old catalogs—for some of the padlocks, this is difficult or impossible. They are not marked and the manufacturer evidently did not publish catalogs. Identical locks can be marked by different manufacturers as a result of one company acquiring another. Dating can also be a problem. Some manufacturers made almost identical locks for more than 50 years and there are Yale models that were made for almost 100 years. A lock can be made the same year as the patent date or the date can be marked on the padlock long after the patent expired.

Original keys can increase the value of locks, but other keys have no value to most collectors. Having a key made can cost more than the value of the lock, Locksmiths who are not familiar with the antique value of old padlocks can do irreparable damage. If you have repairs or a key made, make sure that the locksmith is an expert on old locks. Repairs, cracks, holes, internal damage or appreciable dents can drastically reduce the value of locks.

History: In the 1830s, Elijah Rickard was making screw-key padlocks. He stamped some of them "B&O RR" for the Baltimore & Ohio Railroad. These were the first marked railroad locks. In the 1840s, safe-lock manufacturers were adapting their lever tumbler safe-lock designs to padlocks. Also, in the 1840s, the U.S. Post Office was ordering padlocks with postal markings and the first pin-tumbler padlocks were made in the Yale Lock Shop. In the 1850s, a few companies were making lever-tumbler padlocks that were simpler than the safe-lock designs; after about 1860, companies which had made only cabinet and door locks were adapting their designs to padlocks. Linus Yale Jr., patented the pin-tumbler lock in 1865. In 1860, Wilson Bohannan returned from the California gold fields, patented a simple, reliable, brass-lever padlock and started his lock manufacturing company. The brass-lever and the similar iron-lever padlocks were subsequently manufactured in large quantities by many companies. Wilson Bohannan is still an independent company and the pin-tumbler lock is the worldwide standard medium-security lock.

Padlocks of all shapes and sizes have been made in Europe and Asia since the 1600s. Asian locks can be distinguished from European locks, but it is usually difficult to determine which European country made a lock.

American collectors generally prefer American-manufactured locks.

More than 240 United States padlock manufacturers have been identified. Eight prolific companies were:

Adams & Westlake, 1857-: "Adlake" trademark introduced c1900, made railroad locks after acquisition of Union Brass & Mfg. Co., in 1887.

• *Eagle Lock Co., 1833-1976*: General line of padlocks from 1880, with padlock patent dates from 1867.

• *Mallory, Wheeler & Co., 1865-1910*: Partnership history started in 1834, predominant manufacturer of wrought-iron-lever (Smokies) padlocks.

• *Miller Lock Co. (D.K. Miller from 1870-c1880, Miller Lock Co., to 1930)*: General line of padlocks.

• *Slaymaker Lock Co., 1888-1985*: Dates include name changes, partnership changes and mergers. A general line of padlocks.

• *Star Lock Works, 1836-1926*: Largest manufacturer of Scandinavian padlocks.

• *Wilson Bohannan, 1860-*: Made mostly brass-lever padlocks until the early 1900s, then changed to the pin-tumbler type.

• *Yale & Towne Mfg. Co., 1884-*: Yale Lock Mfg. Co., 1868-1884, started c1840 by Linus Yale, Sr., as the Yale Lock Shop, started producing padlocks c1875.

Padlock Types: Padlocks are categorized primarily according to tradition or use: Story, Railroad, etc. The secondary classification is according to the type of construction. For example, brass-lever locks marked with a railroad name are called Railroad locks and are identified by the name of the company that bought and used them. Scandinavian locks have always been called Scandinavians. The term "story locks" became common in the 1970s; in the 1880s, they were listed in various ways. Those made from about 1880 to 1900 are odd- or heart-shaped cast-iron padlocks and have various decorative or figural embossing.

Governmental agencies and thousands of companies had locks custom made with their names to create logo locks. Logo locks are not to be confused with locks that are embossed with the names of jobbers. This applies particularly to the round six-lever push-key locks. If "6-Lever" is included in the name, it is rarely a logo lock. Since 1827, about 10,000 railroad companies have crisscrossed the United States. Most of these companies used at least two types of locks; some used dozens of types.

References: Franklin M. Arnall, *The Padlock Collector, Illustrations and Prices of 2,800 Padlocks of the Last 100 Years*, 6th Edition, The Collector 1996; Jack P. Wood, *Town-Country Old Tools and Locks, Keys and Closures*, L-W Book Sales, 1990.

Collectors' Clubs: American Lock Collectors Association, 36076 Grennada, Livonia, MI 48154; West Coast Lock Collectors, 1427 Lincoln Blvd., Santa Monica, CA 90401.

Museum: Lock Museum of America, Terryville, CT.

Reproduction Alert: Beware of bargains and know your locks. Be especially cautious of brass story locks, locks from the Middle East, railroad switch locks made in Taiwan and the United States and switch-lock keys made in the United States. Story locks should be embossed cast iron; however, there are excellent iron reproductions of the Skull and Crossbones lock.

Screw-key, trick, iron-lever and brass-lever padlocks are being imported from the Middle East. The Taiwan switch locks are rougher and lighter in color than the old brass ones. The crudely cast new switch keys are obvious. The high-quality counterfeits are expertly stamped with various railroad initials, tumbled to simulate wear and aged with acid. They can be detected only by an expert.

Authentic railroad, express and logo locks will have the name of only one user. The size and shape will be like other locks that were in common use at the time, except for a few modified locks made for the U.S. govern-

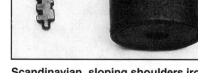

Scandinavian, sloping shoulders iron, 3 1/2" h, $30.

ment. All components of an old lock must have exactly the same color and finish. The front, back or drop of an old lock can be expertly replaced with a reproduced part embossed with the name or initials of a railroad, express company or other user.

Advisor: Franklin M. Arnall.

Note: The prices shown are for padlocks in original condition and without keys.

Brass Lever

2-1/4" h, T. Slaight,
Pat Oct. 14, 1851 ....30.00
2-1/2" h
RFD, Pat 3-17-03.......................5.00
W. Bohannan,
Pat Apr 17, 1860 ....25.00
2-5/8" h, A.E. Dietz 253.................20.00
2-7/8" h, New Champion 6 Lever 2.00
3" h, Yale, emb.............................10.00
3" w, keyhole in bottom 60.00
3-1/8" h,
Anchor 6-Lever 35.00
J.A. Goewey,
Pat Feb. 8, 1869 ....125.00
3-3/4" h, JHW Climax....................25.00
3-3/8" h, Reese 15.00
Winchester, emb raised letters....140.00

Combination

Dot Lock, brass case, 3-1/4" h 40.00
Dudley Lock Corp.,
brass case, 3" h.........................5.00
The Edwards Mfg. Co.,
No-Key, 2-3/4" h 25.00
4 brass lettered dials, 2" w 75.00
J.B. Miller Keyless Lock Co.
Zinc case...................................5.00
Steel..5.00
"No-Key" Lock, brass case, 2" h....70.00
Rochester, Warranted, 2-1/2" h...150.00
Sesamee
Brass or zinc case, 2-1/2" h 15.00
Corbin, brass case, 2-1/2" h.......1.00

Steel case & brass dl, 2-1/2" h........4.00

Commemorative

The "Buffalo Lock,"
brass case, 2" h.....................200.00
Dan Patch, iron, 2" h 175.00
Panama Pacific Exposition,
steel, 3" h 275.00
World's Fair, 1904,
St. Louis, brass plates on s
teel case, 3-5/8" h 600.00

Express

AD EX Co., WD, emb,
brass-lever type.....................900.00
AM EX Co., emb,
brass-lever type.....................450.00
AM RY EX, stamped on shackle and
back, steel, iron-lever type 30.00
RY EX AGY, stamped on back,
steel, iron-lever type...............30.00

Iron Lever (includes steel locks)

Eagle, 2-1/8" h 10.00
Emb dragons, 3-1/4" h 15.00
Five Star, steel, 2-7/8" h...............15.00
Jupiter, 3-1/4" h 15.00
King Korn, 2-7/8" h.......................25.00
Kinglock, Keyproof,
10 lbs, 8-1/2" h 350.00
Merkel & Meyer, 3" h....................40.00
Miller, iron with brass drop,
4-1/2" h...................................30.00
Watch Dog, 2-3/8" h.......................5.00

Lever Push Key

Achilles, steel case, 3-5/8" h 75.00
Yale 635, 3" h.................................5.00
Champion 6-Lever, 2-1/4" d............5.00
Keystone 6-Lever, 2-1/4" d 15.00
Van Camp 6-Lever, 2-1/4" d 130.00

Logo

Chrysler, Best 30.00
Cornell University, emb, 2-1/4" d, lever
push-key type.......................300.00
Diamond Alkali, Best....................15.00
Ordnance Dept., emb cannons.......5.00
Sinclair, Corbin............................25.00
Trenton Prison, Corbin..................40.00
U.S. BIR, brass-lever seal lock 60.00
U.S. Custom House,
Slaymaker 150.00
U.S.N. emb,
several manufacturers.............10.00
University of California, W.B. 20.00
University of Colorado,
emb, Yale 75.00
Western Union Tel Co., brass-lever
type 30.00

Pin Tumbler

Corbin
Brass
1-1/4" to 2" w,

keyhole in bottom 2.00
   3" w, keyhole in bottom........50.00
   Steel case 5.00
Hurd, 3-1/8" h 5.00
OVB, Our Very Best, 3" h...........135.00
Segal
   2-7/8" h......................................5.00
   3-5/8" h, keyhole in front 45.00
Unit, 2-7/8" h 55.00
Yale
   Brass case, emb 2.00
   Iron case, round brass panels....5.00
   Nickel plated, dust cover 25.00

Railroad

General Purpose & Signal
   B&O RR, Yale, emb,
   pin-tumbler type 15.00
   CPRY Signal,
   emb, brass lever.....................75.00
   Illinois Central Signal, emb,
   brass lever..............................15.00
   MP Signal, Yale, emb, pin-tumbler
   type 40.00
   Rock Island Lines, brass,
   Corbin......................................15.00
   SP Co.
      Ames Sword,
      brass lever type....................20.00
      Steel, iron lever type 10.00
   Santa Fe, emb, 2-1/4" d, lever
   push-key type........................ 225.00
   SO RY Signal,
   brass-lever type.......................75.00
   Southern Pacific,
   Keen Kutter, emb 350.00
   Union Pacific CS 21, Roadway &
   Bridge Dept 35.00
Switch
   Brass
      B&M RR, stamped
      on shackle 10.00
      C&A RR, stamped on shackle,
      Union Brass 60.00
      C&S RY, stamped on shackle,
      Prier Brass 100.00
      CM & St. PRR,
      emb in panel 95.00
      DL&W RR, emb in panel......80.00
      Erie RR, emb in panel........150.00
      L&N RR, emb in panel 100.00
      LV RR, stamped on back,
      G W. Nock............................175.00
      MK&T RR, emb in panel,
      Dayton 225.00
      Ohio River Rd.,
      emb in panel 550.00
      P RR, emb across back 165.00
      Rich Conn RR, stamped on
      shackle..................................20.00
      SO PAC Co., emb in panel & on
      drop.......................................80.00

      SP Co., stamped on shackle,
      Adlake....................................25.00
      USY of O, stamped on back,
      Adlake....................................15.00
   Steel
      AT & SF RY, other common
      railroads 5.00
      DSS&A RY,
      stamped on shackle.............20.00
      Frisco, emb brass drop 20.00

Scandinavian

Brass, 2-1/2" h...........................20.00
Iron
   2-1/2" h....................................12.00
   3-1/2" h....................................35.00
JHW Climax, iron, 3-1/2" h 40.00
999, emb, brass, 2-1/2" h..............30.00
Star emb on bottom
   1-1/2" h, iron............................15.00
   3-1/2" h, brass.......................100.00
   3-3/4" h, iron............................55.00
Yale Junior, emb, brass, 2-1/2" h..75.00

6 Lever & 8 Lever

6 Lever
   Eagle, steel 5.00
   Sargent 5.00
   Winchester, steel 90.00
8 Lever
   Electric, steel...........................25.00
   Samson, brass 15.00

Story, emb cast iron

Civil War canteen shape,
   "US" emb 475.00
Floral and scroll emb, shield shape
   2-3/8" h..................................125.00
   3-3/8" h..................................175.00
NH Co. & scrolls, heart shape.....175.00
Skull & Crossbones, emb............250.00

Warded

Army, emb,
   round iron case, 2-1/2" h 10.00
Corbin, emb, brass, 1-1/2" h 10.00
Fordloc, emb, brass case, adjustable
   shackle 25.00
Magic, emb, brass case, 2-3/4" h...5.00
Motor, emb, brass case, 2-1/2" h 4.00
1902, emb, brass case, 2-1/8" h 5.00
Omeco, steel, 3-1/8" h.....................5.00
Ruby, floral on back, emb, brass,
   2-1/8" h 25.00
Star, emb, iron............................15.00
W, emb, brass case, 2-1/2" h........10.00
Winchester, incised, iron case, brass
   panels, 2-3/4" h 110.00

Wrought Iron (Smokies, Smoke House, Shield), brass drop

Bramah's Patent, VR, 4-1/2" h 25.00
DM & Co., 5-1/8" h 25.00
MW & Co., 2-5/8" h 5.00

S & Co., 3-1/2" h 8.00
WW & Co., 3-1/2" h 10.00

Paper Dolls

Collecting Hints: Most paper dolls that are collected are in uncut books, on intact sheets or in boxed sets. Cut sets are priced at 50% of an uncut set, providing all dolls, clothing and accessories are still present.

Many paper doll books have been reprinted. An identical reprint has just slightly less value than the original. If the dolls have been redrawn, the price is reduced significantly.

History: The origin of the paper doll can be traced back to the jumping jacks (pantins) of Europe. By the 19th century, boxed or die-cut sheets of paper dolls were available featuring famous dancers, opera stars, performers such as Jenny Lind and many general subjects. Raphael Tuck began to produce ornate dolls in series form in the 1880s in England.

The advertising industry turned to paper dolls to sell products. Early magazines, such as *Ladies' Home Journal*, *Good Housekeeping* and *McCall's*, used paper doll inserts. Children's publications, like *Jack and Jill*, picked up the practice.

Cardboard-covered paper doll books first appeared and were mass-marketed in the 1920s. Lowe, Merrill, Saalfield and Whitman were the leading publishers. The 1940s saw the advent of paper doll books featuring celebrities drawn from screen and ra-

Three Sisters, designed by Doris Lane Buttler, Whitman Publishing Co., 1942, 12-3/4" x 12-1/2", $20.

dio and later from television. A few comic characters, such as Brenda Starr, also made it to paper doll fame. By the 1950, paper doll books were less popular and production decreased. Modern books are either politically or celebrity oriented.

References: Mary Young, *Collector's Guide to Magazine Paper Dolls*, Collector Books, 1990; Mary Young, *Tomart's Price Guide to Lowe and Whitman Paper Dolls*, Tomart Publications, 1993.

Periodicals: *Celebrity Doll Journal*, 5 Court Pl., Puyallup, WA 98372; *Loretta's Place Paper Doll Newsletter*, 808 Lee Ave., Tifton, GA 31794; *Midwest Paper Dolls & Toys Quarterly*, P.O. Box 131, Galesburg, KS 66740; *Northern Lights Paperdoll News*, P.O. Box 871189, Wasilla, AK 99687; *Paper Doll Gazette*, Route #2, Box 52, Princeton, IN 47670; *Paper Doll News*, P.O. Box 807, Vivian, LA 71082; *Paperdoll Review*, P.O. Box 584, Princeton, IN 47670; *PD Pal*, 5341 Gawain #883, San Antonio, TX 78218.

Collectors' Clubs: Original Paper Doll Artist Guild, P.O. Box 176, Skandia, MI 49885; United Federation of Doll Clubs, 10920 N. Ambassador, Kansas City, MO 64153.

Museums: Children's Museum, Indianapolis, IN; Detroit Children's Museum, Detroit, MI; Kent State University Library, Kent, OH; Margaret Woodbury Strong Museum, Rochester, NY; Museum of the City of New York, New York, NY; Newark Museum, Newark, NJ.

Notes: Prices are based on uncut, mint, original paper dolls in book or uncut-sheet form. It is not unusual for companies to have assigned the same number to different titles.

Alice Faye, uncut............................95.00
Arlene Dahl, Saalfield Publishing Co., 5 dolls, 8 pgs, 1953, uncut..........60.00
Baby Sandy, Merrill Publishing Co., 1941, uncut............................185.00
Barbie's Boutique, Whitman, 1973, uncut......................................10.00
Bedknobs and Broomsticks, 1971, uncut...40.00
Betsy McCall, Biggest Paper Doll, Samuel Gabriel & Sons, 1955, uncut......................................24.00

Walking Paper Doll Family, Ruth Upham, Saalfield #1074, 1934, uncut, $25.

Cinderella, Saalfield Publishing Co., 4 dolls, 4 pgs, uncut 18.00
Dainty Dollies and Their Dresses, E.P. Dutton, uncut..........................48.00
Dean & Son, Dolly's Wardrobe, chlth folder, c1910, uncut.................85.00
Deanna Durbin, Merrill Publishing Co., 1940, uncut...........................245.00
Dennison's Doll & Dresses No. 34, 3 sizes of dolls and patterns for dresses, crepe paper, orig instructions 65.00
Dotty and Danny on Parade, Burton Playthings, #875, 1935, uncut.............................35.00
Fairliner Paper Doll Book, Merrill Publishing Co., 2 dolls, 8 pgs, 1953............................10.00
Forest, Sally, Debby Reynolds and Monica Lewis, double cover, heavy statuette dolls, 1951 ....295.00
Gone with the Wind, Merrill Publishing Co., c1940, uncut 265.00
Haley Mills That Darn Cat, 1965, CPC, cut 55.00
Jack & Jill, Folk Festival, Philadelphia Mummers, Jan, 1951, Janet Smalley, artist, uncut sheet 12.00
Judy Garland................................65.00
Julia, Artcraft #5140, 5 dolls, 4 pgs, 1971, uncut....................25.00
Lennon Sisters, Whitman, 1957, cut 55.00
Let's Play Paper Dolls, McLoughlin, 1938, uncut................................25.00
Lizzie, McLoughlin Bros., 1 doll, c1870 ....165.00
Lucille Ball & Desi Arnez, Whitman,

1953, uncut 80.00
Mamie, 3 outfits, hats, orig paper envelope, late 1800s 40.00
Margy & Mildred, American Colortype Co., 1927, uncut.....................25.00
Mary's Trousseau, Saalfield Publishing Co., c1918, neatly cut 10.00
Mary Poppins, 1973, partially cut 35.00
Mickey and Minnie, partially cut 20.00
Miss America Magic Doll, Parker Bros., 1953, uncut.............................20.00
Moving Eye Dolly, Toddling Tom, Samuel Gabriel & Sons, 1920, uncut...24.00
Nanny and the Professor, Artcraft, #5114, 6 dolls, 4 pgs, 1971 .....24.00
Natalie Wood, Whitman, 1957, cut 80.00
Oliver, Artcraft, #4330, 4 pgs, 1968 ....12.00
Our Gang, Whitman, 1931, clothes uncut 60.00
Our Happy Family, Samuel Gabriel & Sons, uncut 24.00
Playtime Fashions, Stephens Publishing Co., 1946, uncut.....................10.00
Pony Tail, Samuel Gabriel & Sons, uncut 20.00
Roy Rogers and Dale Evans, Whitman, 2 dolls, 1956, uncut 35.00
Sally Dimple, Burton Playthings, 1935, uncut 25.00
Sparkle Plenty, uncut 55.00
This Is Margie, Whitman, 1939 .....45.00
Triplet Dolls, Stephens Publishing Co., c1950, uncut...........................10.00
The Waltons, uncut 35.00
The Wedding Party, Samuel Gabriel & Sons, uncut 35.00
Your Own Quintuplets, Burton Playthings, 1935, uncut.................40.00

Paperback Books

Collecting Hints: For collecting or investment purposes, buy only items in fine or better condition because books of lower-quality are too numerous to be of value. Unique items, such as paperbacks in dust jackets or in boxes, often are worth more.

Most collections are assembled around one or more unifying themes, such as author (Edgar Rice Burroughs, Dashiell Hammett, Louis L'Amour, Raymond Chandler, Zane Grey, William Irish, Cornell Woolrich, etc.), fictional genre (mysteries, science fiction, westerns, etc.), publisher (early Avon, Dell and Popular Library are best known), cover artist

(Frank Frazetta, R. C.M. Heade, Rudolph Belarski, Roy Krenkel, Vaughn Bode, etc.) or books with uniquely appealing graphic design (Dell map backs and Ace double novels).

Because paperbacks still turn up in large lots, collectors need to be cautious. Books that are in fine or excellent condition are uncommon. Currently, many dealers charge upper-level prices for books that are not in correspondingly good condition. Dealers' argument that top-condition examples are just too scarce is not valid, just self-serving.

History: Paperback volumes have existed since the 15th century. Mass-market paperback books, most popular with collectors, were printed after 1938. These exist in a variety of formats, from the standard-size paperback and its smaller predecessor to odd sizes like 64-page short novels (which sold for 10 cents) and 5-1/4-by 7-1/2 inch volumes known as "digests." Some books came in a dust jacket; some were boxed.

Today, there are not as many companies publishing mass-market paperbacks as there were between 1938 and 1950. Books of this period are characterized by lurid and colorful cover art and title lettering not unlike that of the pulp magazines. Many early paperback publishers were also involved in the production of pulps and merely moved their graphic style and many of their authors to paperbacks.

References: Bob and Sharon Huxford, *Huxford's Paperback Value Guide*, Collector Books, 1994; Dawn E. Reno and Jacque Tiegs, *Collecting Romance Novels*, Alliance Publishers, 1995; Lee Server, *Over My Dead Body: The Sensational Age of the American Paperback*, Chronicle Books, 1994; Jon Warren, *Official Price Guide to Paperbacks*, House of Collectibles, 1991.

Periodicals: *Books Are Everything*, 302 Martin Dr., Richmond, KY 40475; *Paperback Parade*, P.O. Box 209, Brooklyn, NY 11228; *Pulp and Paperback Market Newsletter*, 5813 York Ave., Edina, MN 55410.

Buffalo Bills' Spy Shadower, from The Buffalo Bill Stories, Gold Star Books, $20.

Museum: University of Minnesota's Hess Collection of Popular Literature, Minneapolis, MN.

Notes: Prices are given for books in fine condition. Divide by three to get the price for books in good condition; increase price by 50% for books in near mint condition.

Adventure

Edgar Rice Burroughs, *Tarzan and the Lost Empire*, Ace, F-169............5.00

Gardner F. Fox, *Woman of Kali*, Gold Medal, 438........................5.00

Phillip Lindsay, *Sir Rusty Sword*, Harlequin, 141 ....11.00

Frank Yerby, *Captain Rebel*, Cardinal, C249..3.50

Biography

Benvenuto Cellini, *The Autobiography of Cellini*, Boni Book 5.00

B. Donovan, *Eichman—Man of Slaughter*, Avon, T-464........................3.00

Martin and Miller, *The Story of Walt Disney*, Dell, D266.....................4.00

W. Wright, *Life and Loves of Lana Turner*, Wisdom House, 104 .....3.00

Combat

Gregory Boyington, *Baa Baa Black Sheep*, Dell, F88........................3.00

Walt Grove, *The Wings of Eagles*, Gold Medal, 649, tie-in with John Wayne Movie..6.00

Leon Uris, *Battle Cry*, Bantam, F1996..........................4.00

Erotica/Esoterica

Sinclair Drago, *Women to Love*, Novel Library, 16 ....5.00

Hannah Leem, *Yaller Gal*, Handi-Book, 84 ....6.00

Jack Woodford, *The Abortive Hussy*, Avon, 146 ....5.00

Horror

Michael Avallane, *The Coffin Things*, Lancer, 74-942 ....6.00

Robert Bloch, *Firebug*, Regency, 101 ....9.50

Bram Stoker, *Dracula*, Perma Book, M4088, tie-in with Christopher Lee movie...6.00

Humor

Al Capp, *L'il Abner*, Ballantine, 350K, tie-in with movie 5.00

Jimmy Hatlo, *They'll Do It Every Time*, Avon, 366 ....6.00

Harry Hershfield, *Book of Jokes*, Avon, 65 ....12.50

Mystery

Dashiell Hammett, *Hammett Homicides*, Bestseller, B81 ....11.00

William Irish, *Bluebeard's Seventh Wife*, Popular Library, 473.................11.00

Dana Lyon, *I'll Be Glad When You're Dead*, Quick Reader, 132..........6.00

Non-Fiction

Walt Disney, *Our Friend the Atom*, Dell, LB117.............................4.00

Gordon Sinclair, *Bright Path to Adventure*, Harlequin, 288 ....9.00

Romance

Emily Bronte, *Wuthering Heights*, Quick Reader, 122 ....8.00

Walter Edmonds, *The Wedding Journey*, Dell, 6, 10¢ 6.00

Science Fiction

John W. Campbell, *Who Goes There?*, Dell, D-150 ....4.00

Robert A. Heinlein, *Beyond This Horizon*, Signet, 1891...............5.00

L. Ron Hubbard, *Return to Tomorrow*, Ace, S-66 ....7.50

R.A. Lafferty, *Space Chantey*, Ace, H-56, Vaughn Bode cover........5.00

George Orwell, *Animal Farm*, Signet, 1289 ....6.00

Robert Silverberg, *Regan's Planet*, Pyramid, F-986.........................4.00

Sports

Bruce Jacobs (ed), *Baseball Stars of 1955*, Lion Library, LL12 ....6.00

Ray Robinson (ed), *Baseball Stars of 1961*, Pyramid, G605 ....3.00

Bill Stern, *Bill Stern's Favorite Boxing Stories*, Pocket Books, 416.......3.50

Western

Zane Grey, *Nevada*, Bantam, 3.......4.50

Paul Evan Lehman, *Range Justice*,
Star Books, 8............................6.00

Frederick Manfred, *Lord Grizzly*,
ardinal, C192............................5.00

Armstrong Sperry, *Wagons Westward*,
Comet, 1....................................3.00

Patriotic Collectibles

Collecting Hints: Concentrate on one symbol, e.g., the eagle, flag, Statue of Liberty or Uncle Sam. Remember that the symbol is not always the principal attraction; don't miss items with the symbol in a secondary role. Colored material is more desirable than black and white. Many items are two-dimensional, e.g., posters and signs. Seek three-dimensional objects to add balance and interest to a collection.

Much of the patriotic material focuses on our national holidays, especially the Fourth of July; but other holidays to consider are Flag Day, Labor Day, Memorial Day and Veterans' Day. Finally, look to the foreign market. Our symbols are used abroad, both positively and negatively. A novel collection would be one based on how Uncle Sam is portrayed on posters and other materials from Communist countries.

History: Patriotic symbols developed along with the American nation. The eagle, among the greatest of our nation's symbols, has appeared on countless objects since it was chosen to be part of the American seal.

Uncle Sam arrived on the American scene in the mid 19th century and was firmly established by the Civil War. Uncle Sam did have female counterparts—Columbia and the Goddess of Liberty. He often appeared together with one or both of them on advertising trade cards, buttons, posters, textiles, etc. His modern appearance came about largely as the result of drawings by Thomas Nast in *Harper's Weekly* and James Montgomery Flagg's famous World War I recruiting poster, "I Want You." Perhaps the leading promoter of the Uncle Sam image was the American toy industry, aided by the celebration

of the American Centennial in 1876 and Bicentennial in 1976. A surge of Uncle Sam-related toys occurred in the 1930s led by American Flyer's inexpensive version of an earlier lithographed tin, flat-sided Uncle Sam bicycle string toy.

Reference: Gerald Czulewicz, *Foremost Guide to Uncle Sam Collectibles*, Collector Books, 1995.

Periodical: *Pyrofax Magazine*, P.O. Box 2010, Saratoga, CA 95070.

Collectors' Club: Statue of Liberty Collectors' Club, P.O. Box 535, Chautauqua, NY 14722.

Museum: 4th of July Americana & Fireworks Museum, New Castle, PA.

Additional Listings: Flag Collectibles.

Eagle

Architectural Element, snow bird, cast
iron, black................................45.00

Bookends, 5-1/2" l, cast white metal,
worn...50.00

Change Tray, 4" d, Hebbrun House
Coal, eagle in center, holding
banner, wood-grain ground.....50.00

Cookie Cutter, 6-1/2" l, tin.............90.00

Fan, 8" x 9" diecut cardboard, 4" wood
handle, full-color eagle front, b&w
illus text on back for Ontario Drill Co.,
Baltimore, 1908.......................85.00

Figure, 6" h,
pot metal, gold paint................35.00

Pinback Button
Century Tire, celluloid, gold, red,
white and blue..........................55.00
National Cycle, red, white and blue,
star-studded shield...................35.00

Flags and Shields

Fan, 7" x 9" diecut shield, red, white and
blue cardboard, 3-1/2" l wood
handle, titled "America First," sailor
raising deck flag, warships in
background, biplane flying overhead,
back with sponsors' names and
song lyrics...............................40.00

Lapel Stud, Colonial Bicycles, red, white
and blue, shield symbol...........20.00

Match Safe, 1-1/2" x 2-1/2",
celluloid covering silvered
brass, black and white bulldog
standing on American flag as
warships steam in background, inscribed "What We Have We'll Hold,"
reverse with b&w photo of Philadelphia businessman....................90.00

Paper Dolls, 7" x 13", Liberty Fair
Dressing Doll, blue and white box,

Miss Liberty cardboard doll, flags on
wood stick, cut, c1900.............65.00

Paperweight, 3" d, celluloid over
weighted metal, mirror bottom, full
color images of 12 Allied flags, local
sponsor art center...................35.00

Patch, 9" x 9", cloth, Apollo 16, white
background, full color 3-1/2" d astronaut patch in center of red, white and
blue shield, eagle at top against lunar
background, blue and white star border, astronaut names Young,
Matlingly and Duke..................24.00

Pin, 1" x 1-1/4", diecut celluloid,
ed, white and blue shield design,
dark gold eagle, raised flipper
inscribed "Hupmobile The Car of
the American Family on United
America Tour," c1910..............45.00

Pinback Button
AOH Lodge, multicolored,
U.S. and Irish flags beneath
streamer design listing group's
virtues, early 1900s..................60.00
N.A.W.T. (woodworkers) Third
Annual Convention, red, white and
blue shield...............................15.00

Pocket Mirror, Beautifiers of Homes, red,
white and gold patriotic shield shape,
black lettering..........................40.00

Portrait, 5-3/4" x 8", full-color celluloid,
sepia portrait, surrounding flags and
patriotic symbols, inscription "Army
and Navy Forever," single-star
service banner, black velveteen-
over-metal back, wire easel stand,
World War I era........................65.00

Stickpin, 3/4" x 1", diecut celluloid,
red, white and blue American flag
on front, b&w adv text for Artistic
Pianos on reverse, brass stickpin,
early 1900s..............................25.00

Tray, 12" d, Jacob Metzger,
American Brewing Co.,
Indianapolis, IN, trademark on
star in center of flag...............165.00

Watch Fob, 1" d, silvered brass,
shield shape, attached silvered
brass horseshoe, raised eagle
on front, red white and blue
enameled name "American
Badge Co," c1900...................45.00

Liberty Bell
Bank, 4-1/2" h, pot metal and wood,
brown, mkd "USA 1947"..........40.00
Bread Plate, glass, Constitution sign-
ers' names, emb 1776-1876....90.00
Paperweight 6" h, cast iron......60.00
Pinback Button, National Relief
Assurance Co., Philadelphia, multicolored eagle and Liberty Bell, dark
blue ground, c1900..................20.00
Pocket Mirror, Bell's Coffee,
green Liberty bell trademark, mocha
and java specialties, J H Bell & Co.,

Chicago 60.00

Postcard

Independence Hall, Philadelphia, sepia...8.50

Liberty Bell Trolley, insignia on front........................10.00

Sheet Music, *Liberty Bell Time to Ring Again*, 1918 ....10.00

Tape Measure, 1-3/4" d, celluloid case, blue and white design, logo and inscription for Missouri and Kansas telephone company, reverse "When You Telephone, Use the Bell," cloth tape, c1900 ....40.00

Statue of Liberty

Advertising Trade Card, Pratts Astrol Oil, night scene 25.00

Bookmark, silk, Paris, 1878...........75.00

Hat, heavy paper, "Liberty," red, white and blue, picture of Statue, c1918 ....25.00

Lamp, 5-1/2" h, dark copper-finished white metal, holds small electric bulb, wood base, sliding base opens to hold battery, c1920 ....40.00

Playing Cards, "606," U.S. Playing Card Co., Cincinnati, OH, picture of Statue of Liberty and flags of nations, gold edges, complete, orig box 20.00

Statue of Liberty, stamping emblem, KKK, iron, reads "Independent Klan of America," Christian Americanism, Toledo, OH, Statue of Liberty in center.......................................195.00

Tie Slide, 1-1/4" x 2", Boy Scouts, emb brass, detailed raised Statue, scroll banner at base, c1930.............25.00

Uncle Sam

Advertising Trade Card

3-1/2" x 5-1/4", Frank Millers Blacking, Uncle Sam shaving with straight razor, using polished boot as mirror, eagle looking at reflection in another book 25.00

3-1/2" x 6-1/4", Hub Gore, Uncle Sam holding shoe, saying "Hub Gore Makers of Elastic For Shoes... It Was Honored at the World's Fair of 1893"....................................15.00

Bank, Puriton.................................30.00

Magazine Tear Sheet, 5-1/2" x 8-1/2", Uncle Sam Holding a "Health Bill" under his arm, looking at Cream of Wheat adv billboard, 1915.......22.00

Pinback Button

7/8" d, Uncle Sam's Citizenship Training Corps, lieutenant rank, c1920 ....20.00

1" d, Good Teeth, Cincinnati Schools dental-care program, 1930s.....20.00

1-1/4" d, American Traveler Bicycle, Uncle Sam holding bicycle, balloon tires, American B-H-O and Sewing

Machine Co., Philadelphia, PA, solid-tin back, embedded fastener, early 1900s 75.00

Pocket Mirror, *Watertown Times* newspaper 75.00

Puzzle, 4" x 4" box, Uncle Sam's Tar Soap, Uncle Sam's National Puzzle, 10 cards, advertising slogans, c1900...35.00

Salt and Pepper Shakers, pr, 1-1/2" x 2-1/2" x 2", painted plaster, glossy white, black and red accents, red, white and blue top hat 65.00

Sign, 36" x 24", canvas, Uncle Sam selling U.S. Paint, National Sign Co., Dayton, OH, c1910................700.00

Stickpin, 1", diecut, white metal, tinted cherry red trousers and hat, blue coat, marching pose, c1898 ....35.00

Tray, Cascade Beer, San Francisco, Uncle Sam and 5 ethnic people 675.00

Watch Fob, 1-1/4" x 1-1/2", brass, raised profile portrait of Uncle Sam above VFW symbol, inscribed "Dedication Uncle Sam Oakwood Cemetery," 1930s....................45.00

George Washington

Pinback Button, 1-1/4", multicolored, portrait of Washington, dark red shaded to olive green ground, black inscription for Cherry Smash soft drink, c1912 ....45.00

Postcard, multicolored...................50.00

Sheet Music, *Father of the Land We Love*, lyrics and music by George M. Cohan, cover artist James Montgomery Flagg, 1931 ....10.00

Tray, 7-1/2" x 11", porcelain, portraits of George and Martha Washington, Mt. Vernon, titled "Washington's Home, Mt. Vernon, VA," in center, multicolored, enhanced enameling, sq corners, gold trim, mkd "Germany" 75.00

Pennsbury Pottery

Collecting Hints: Concentrate on one pattern or type. Since the wares were hand carved, aesthetic quality differs from piece to piece. Look for those with a strong design sense and a high quality of execution.

Buy only clearly marked pieces. Look for decorator and designer initials that can be easily identified. Pennsbury collectors are concentrated in the Middle Atlantic states. Many of the company's commemorative and novelty pieces relate to businesses and events in that re-gion, thus commanding the highest prices when sold within that area.

History: In 1950, Henry and Lee Below established Pennsbury Pottery, named for its close proximity to William Penn's estate "Pennsbury," three miles west of Morrisville, PA. Henry, a ceramic engineer and mold maker and Lee, a designer and modeler, had previously worked for Stangl Pottery in Trenton, NJ.

Many of Pennsbury's forms, motifs and manufacturing techniques have Stangl roots. A line of birds similar to those produced by Stangl were among the earliest Pennsbury products. The carved-design technique is also of Stangl origin; high bas-relief molds are not.

Most Pennsbury products are easily identified by their brown-wash background. The company also made pieces featuring other background colors so do not make the mistake of assuming that a piece is not Pennsbury if it does not have a brown wash.

Pennsbury motifs are heavily nostalgic, often farm- or Pennsylvania German-related. Among the most popular lines were Amish, Black Rooster, Delft Toleware, Eagle, Family, Folkart, Gay Ninety, Harvest, Hex, Quartet, Red Barn, Red Rooster, Slick-Chick and Christmas plates (1960-1970). The pottery made a large number of commemorative, novelty and special-order pieces.

In the late 1950s, the company had 16 employees, mostly local housewives and young girls. By 1963, at the company's peak, there were 46 employees. Cheap foreign imports cut deeply into the pottery's profits; by the late 1960s, just more than 20 employees remained.

Marks differ from piece to piece depending on the person who signed it or the artist who sculpted the mold. Some initials still have not been identified. Henry Below died on Dec. 21, 1959, leaving the pottery in trust for his wife and three children with instructions that it be sold upon the death of his wife. She died on Dec. 12, 1968; in October 1970, the Pennsbury Pottery filed for bankruptcy. The contents were auctioned off on Dec. 18, 1970. On May 18,

1971, a fire destroyed the pottery and support buildings.

References: Susan and Al Bagdade, *Warman's American Pottery and Porcelain*, Wallace-Homestead, 1994; Lucile Henzke, *Pennsbury Pottery*, Schiffer Publishing, 1990; Mike Schneider, *Stangl and Pennsbury Birds*, Schiffer Publishing, 1994.

Look-Alike Alert: The Lewis Brothers Pottery, Trenton, NJ, purchased 50 of the Pennsbury molds. Although they were supposed to remove the Pennsbury name from the molds, this was not done in all instances. Further, two Pennsbury employees moved to Lewis Brothers when Pennsbury closed, helping to produce a number of pieces that are reminiscent of Pennsbury's products. Many of Pennsbury's major lines, including the Harvest and Rooster patterns, plaques, birds and highly unusual molds, were not reproduced. Glen View, Langhorne, PA, continued marketing the 1970s Angel Christmas plate with Pennsbury markings. The company continued the Christmas plate line into the 1970s, utilizing the Pennsbury brown-wash background. In 1975, Lenape Products, a division of Pennington, bought Glen View and continued making Pennsbury-like products.

Ashtray
    Amish People 25.00
    Don't Be So Doppish, 5" l 20.00
    Doylestown Trust 20.00
    Hex Sign, earth tones 27.50
    Outen the Light 20.00
    Such Schmootzers 20.00
    What Gifts 20.00
Bank, jug, pig, "Stuff Me" 100.00
Bread Tray, rect, wheat motif 45.00
Cake Stand, Amish 75.00
Candleholders,
    pr, Red Roosters 85.00
Canister set, cov, Black
    Rooster dec, 9" h flour and
    sugar, 8" tea and coffee 425.00
Coaster, Shultz 17.50
Cream Pitcher
    Large, Hex Sign 55.00
    Medium, Distilfink 45.00
    Small, Hex Sign 25.00
Cruet, stopper, Amish 40.00
Cup and Saucer
    Black Rooster 15.00

    Red Rooster 17.50
Desk Basket, Exchange Club 40.00
Mug
    Eagle 25.00
    Sweet Adeline 20.00
Pie Plate, Mother serving pie 75.00
Pitcher
    2-1/2" h, Amish man 12.00
    3-3/4" h, Rooster, red 18.00
    4" h, Hex Sign 20.00
    5" h, Amish woman 45.00
Plaque, 4"
    Black Rooster 28.00
    Lafayette, B&O Railroad 50.00
    Pops half et already,
    crimp edge 28.00
Plate
    8" d, Hex Sign 20.00
    10" d
        Black Rooster 15.00
        Hex Sign 20.00
Pretzel Bowl, 8" x 11",
    eagle motif 55.00
Salt and Pepper Shakers, pr, Amish
    heads 60.00
Saucer, 5 leaf design 5.00
Sign, small 350.00
Snack Tray,
    matching cup, red Rooster 25.00
Sugar Lid, Hex Sign 8.00
Vegetable Dish, divided,
    Red Rooster 32.00
Wall Pocket, 10" h, bellows shape, eagle
    motif 50.00

Pens and Pencils

Collecting Hints: Price is lessened dramatically by any defects such as scratches, cracks, dents, warping, missing parts, bent levers, sprung clips, nib damage or mechanical damage. Engraved initials or names do not seriously detract from the price.

History: The steel pen point or "nib," was invented by Samuel Harrison in 1780. It was not commercially produced in quantity until the 1880s when Richard Esterbrook entered the field. The holders became increasingly elaborate. Mother-of-pearl, gold, sterling silver and other fine materials were used to fashion holders of distinction. Many of these pens can be found along with their original velvet-lined presentation cases.

Lewis Waterman invented the fountain pen in the 1880s. Three other leading pioneers in the field were Parker, Sheaffer (first lever-filling ac-

Sheaffer, combination, 1 unit, pencil turns out, pen pulls out, gold-plated point mkd "E.J. Johnson & Co., New York, No. 4," 2-3/8" (plus ring) collapsed, 4-7/8" (plus ring) fully extended, $85.

tion, 1913) and Wahl-Eversharp. The mechanical pencil was patented in 1822 by Sampson Mordan. The original slide-type action developed into the spiral mechanical pencil. Wahl-Eversharp was responsible for the automatic "clic," or repeater-type, mechanism which is used on ball-points today.

The flexible nib that enabled the writer to individualize his penmanship came to an end when Reynolds introduced the ball-point pen in October 1945.

References: Glen Bowen, *Collectible Fountain Pens*, L-W Book Sales, 1992, 1996 value update; George Fischler and Stuart Schneider, *Fountain Pens and Pencils*, Schiffer Publishing, 1990; ——, *Illustrated Guide to Antique Writing Instruments*, Schiffer, 1994; Cliff and Judy Lawrence, *1992 Official P.F.C. Pen Guide*, Pen Fancier's Club, 1991; Jonathan Steinburg, *Fountain Pens*, Running Press, 1993.

Periodicals: *Pen World Magazine*, P.O. Box, 6007, Kingwood, TX 77325; *Pens*, P.O. Box 64, Teaneck, NJ 07666.

Collectors' Clubs: American Pencil Collectors Society, 2222 S. Milwood, Wichita, KS 67213; Pen Collectors of American, P.O. Box 821449, Houston, TX 77282; Pen Fancier's Club, 1169 Overcash Dr., Dunedin, FL 34698.

Conklin
    Endura Model, desk set,
    black marble base, 2 pens,
    side-lever fill, double narrow gold-
    colored bands, mkd "Patent Nov. 17,
    1925," on pen barrel, black-
    brown overlay color 125.00
    Model 20, 5-5/16" l, pen,
    #2 Conklin pint-nib, black crescent
    filler #20, gold clip, narrow gold band
    on cap, pat date May 28, 1918,

stamped on clip 75.00
Model 25P, pen,
ladies filigree cap ribbon, black,
crescent filler, 1923 ....70.00
Model 30, pen, black
hard rubber, 1903.....................75.00
Dunn, pen, black, red barrel, gold-plated
trim, c1920 ....40.00
Epenco, pen, black case, gold-plated
trim.......................................25.00
Eversharp
CA Model, ball-point pen, black,
gold-filled cap, 1946 ....42.00
Doric
Desk pen, gold seal, green marble
cov, lever fill, large adjustable nib,
c1935 ....55.00
Fountain pen, amber threading,
restored 225.00
Pencil, lady's, SP, c1920 ....25.00
Marvel, black chased hard rubber,
eyedropper, 1906 ....75.00
Moore
Desk Set, gray and black marble
base, black pen, 12k nib, side-lever
fill..75.00
Pen, rose color, fancy
band around cap, warranted
nib, side-lever filler 65.00
Ribbon Pen, lady's, black, 3 narrow
gold bands on cap, lever fill,
pat nib #2 ....70.00
Onoto, Ink Pencil Stylographic pen,
black chased hard rubber,
eyedropper, 1924 ....40.00
Parker
Blue-Diamond-51, pen, black, gold-
plated cap, button filled, 1942 ..70.00
Duofold
Deluxe, pen and pencil set,
black and pearl, 3 narrow gold-
colored bands on cap, push-button
fill, 1929..............................575.00
Senior, pen,
Flashing Black, 1923 ....185.00
Streamline, burgundy
and black, double narrow

band on cap, 1932 ....125.00
Lucky Curve, ring pen,
black hard rubber, gold-filled
trim, 19212 ....85.00
Model 48, pen, ring top,
gold-filled barrel and cap,
button filled, 1915...................150.00
Model 51, pen, maroon, stainless
steel cap, chrome-plated trim,
aeromatic filler, 1950................50.00
Vacumatic, gray-black, arrow clip,
arrow design engraved on nib, silver-
colored clip and band on cap,
oversized model, 1932...........125.00
Reynolds, Model 2, pen, orig ball-point,
c1945......................................75.00
Security, pen, check protector, red hard
rubber, gold-filled trim, 1923....85.00
Sheaffer
Strato Writer, ball-point pen, gold-
filled metal mountings, 1948 ....65.00
Triumph Lifetime, desk set, green
marble base, 2 black snorkel-design
pens, c1940 ....95.00
White Dot, pen, green jade, gold-plated trim, lever filled, 1923..........95.00
White Dot Lifetime, pen, classic
torpedo design cap and body, lever
filler on side, 1930..................115.00
Wahl
Lady's, ribbon pen, double narrow
band on cap, 14k #2 nib, lever fill,
1928 ....75.00
Tempoint No. 305A, pen,
gold-filled metal mounted,
eyedropper, 1919 ....145.00
Wahl-Eversharp
Pen, gold seal, black, gold-filled trim,
lever filled, 1930.....................125.00
Pencil, gold filled, metal mounted,
1919 ....35.00
Waterman
Model #12, pen, mottled brow, 14k
gold bands, 1886 ....125.00
Model 42-1/2V, Safety Pen, gold
filigree, retractable screw-action nib,
1906 ....135.00
Model #71, pen, ripple red, hard rub-
ber case, gold-plated trim, white clip,
lever filled, 1925.....................150.00
Taperite, pen, black, gold-filled metal
mounted cap, gold-filled trim, lever
filled, c1949.............................75.00

Pepsi

Collecting Hints: Items advertising Pepsi, Hires and a number of other soft drink companies became hot collectibles in the 1980s, fueled in part by the pricey nature of Coca-Cola items. The Pepsi market is still young and some price fluctuations occur.

Pepsi-Cola enjoys a much stronger market position in many foreign countries than it does in the United States.

Reproductions, copycats and fantasy items are part of the Pepsi collecting scene. Be on the alert for the Pepsi and Pete pillow issued in the 1970s, a 12-inch-high ceramic statue of a woman holding a glass of Pepsi, a Pepsi glass-front clock, a Pepsi double-bed quilt and set of four Pepsi glasses. These are just a few of the suspect items, some of which were done under license from Pepsi-Cola.

History: Pepsi-Cola was developed by Caleb D. Bradham, a pharmacist and drugstore owner in New Bern, NC. Like many drugstores of its time, Bradham provided "soda" mixes for his customers and friends. His favorite was "Brad's Drink," which he began to call "Pepsi-Cola" in 1898. Its popularity spread and in 1902 Bradham turned the operation of his drugstore over to an assistant and devoted all his energy to perfecting and promoting Pepsi-Cola. He sold 2,008 gallons of Pepsi-Cola syrup his first three months and by 1904 was bottling Pepsi-Cola for mass consumption. He sold his first franchise within a short time.

By the end of the first decade of the 20th century, Bradham had organized a network of more than 250 bottlers in 24 states. The company's fortunes sank shortly after World War I when it suffered large losses in the sugar market. Bankruptcy and reorganization followed. Roy Megargel, whose Wall Street firm advised Bradham, helped keep the name alive. A second bankruptcy occurred in 1931, but the company survived.

In 1933, Pepsi-Cola doubled the size of its bottle but held the price at 5¢. Sales soared. Under the direction of Walter Mack, 1938 to 1951, Pepsi challenged Coca-Cola for market dominance. In the 1950s, Pepsi advertising featured slogans such as "Pepsi Cola Hits the Spot, Twelve Full Ounces That's a Lot." PepsiCo., is currently a division of Beatrice. It has a worldwide reputation and actually is the #1 soft drink in many foreign countries.

References: James C. Ayers, *Pepsi-Cola Bottles Collectors Guide*,

Sheaffer, pen and pencil set, white dot, Triumph Valiant, 14k gold pen point, 1948, $85.

published by author (P.O. Box 1377, Mt. Airy, NC 27030), 1995; Ted Hake, *Hake's Guide to Advertising Collectibles*, Wallace-Homestead, 1992; Everette and Mary Lloyd, *Pepsi-Cola Collectibles*, Schiffer Publishing, 1993; Bill Vehling and Michael Hunt, *Pepsi-Cola Collectibles*, *Vol. 1* (1990, 1993 value update), *Vol. 2* (1990, 1992 value update), *Vol. 3* (1993, 1995 value update), L-W Book Sales.

Collectors' Clubs: Ozark Mountain Pepsi Collectors Club, P.O. Box 575631, Modesto, CA 95357; Pepsi-Cola Collectors Club, P.O. Box 1275, Covina, CA 91722.

Museum: Pepsi-Cola Co., Archives, Purchase, NY.

Ashtray, 4" sq, glass, "Pepsi Beats the Others Cold!," 1960s 25.00
Bottle, 32 oz,
    applied color label, c1960........25.00
Bottle Carrier,
    6-bottle type, aluminum 52.50
Bottle Opener, bottle shape.............8.00
Cake Pan.......................................25.00
Calendar, 1955,
    card stock, 12" x 20"..............400.00
Carton, tin.....................................17.50
Cigarette Lighter, 4" l, metal, bottle-cap
    illus on side, 1950s................150.00
Clock, wall type 40.00
Cooler, aluminum 200.00
Door Push, wrought iron, 1960s....65.00
Drinking Cup, 6-1/4" h, plastic, racing-
    car theme, Pepsi 89 Car, "Pepsi Offi-
    cial Soft Drink of the Daytona 500,"
    red plastic cap, reverse side with rac-
    ing flags and their meanings......1.00
Fan, 10" sq, cardboard, wood handle,
    c1940.......................................75.00
Figure, 5-1/2" h, 30th Anniversary,
    pewter, billboard center with bottle
    cap and "Cool" and cat figure leaning
    on it with 1 elbow, feet crossed,
    limited edition of 250................60.00
Letterhead, 8-1/2" x 11",
    Pepsi-Cola Bottling Works,
    Greensboro, NC, 1916 ....100.00
Mileage Chart, tin, framed.............45.00
Napkin, 19" sq, cloth, c1940..........25.00
Notepad, 2-1/2" x 4-1/2",
    cardboard cov, red and
    black logo, 1914 calendar........35.00
Pinback Button, 2" d, I Drank a Pepsi,
    Did You," tin, 1970s 12.00
Push Bar, porcelain, Canadian, French,
    1950s.......................................75.00
Radio, can shape 40.00
Ruler, 12" l, tin, c1950 ....20.00

Sign
    9" d, celluloid and tin, "Ice Cold Pep-
    si-Cola Sold Here," 1930s......295.00
    12" x 8", plastic, "Take
    Home Pepsi," light-up type,
    bottle-cap illus, 1950s 160.00
    18" x 6", porcelain, red,
    white and blue banner,
    double dotted logo, "America's
    Biggest Nickel's Worth"..........300.00
    22" x 7", paper, "Have a
    Pepsi," man, woman and
    bottle-cap illus, 1950s 35.00
    24" x 28", tin, "Drink Pepsi-Cola,"
    bottle-cap illus, 1950s 55.00
Snowdome, soda-can shape.........35.00
Toy
    Delivery Truck, 2-1/2" x
    7-1/2" x 2", white plastic body,
    black wood wheels, red, white and
    blue Pepsi decal, 3 white plastic
    cases with 24 plastic bottles, Marx
    Toys, c1940 ....95.00
    Farm Tractor, 1/16 scale, limited
    edition of 300...........................45.00
Tray
    Bottle-cap shape,
    round, 1940............................325.00
    Coney Island, 1955 ....50.00
Uniform Patch, 7" 15.00
Walkie-Talkie, bottle shape 25.00
Watch, bottle-cap style, Pepsi logo, hot
    pink vinyl band........................25.00

PEZ

Collecting Hints: PEZ became a hot collectible in the late 1980s. Its rise was due in part to the use of licensed cartoon characters as heads on PEZ dispensers. Initially, PEZ containers were an extremely affordable collectible. Generic subjects often sold for less than $5, character containers for less than $10.

Before investing large amounts of money in PEZ containers, it is important to recognize that: 1) they are produced in large quantities—millions, 2) PEZ containers are usually saved by their original buyers, not disposed of when emptied and 3) no collecting category stays hot forever. PEZ prices fluctuate. Advertised price and field price for the same container can differ by as much as 50%, depending on who is selling.

Starting a PEZ collection is simple. Go to a local store that sells PEZ and purchase the current group of products. Your initial cost will be less than $1.50 a unit.

History: Vienna, Austria, is the birthplace of PEZ. In 1927, Eduard Haas, an Austrian food mogul, invented PEZ and marketed it as a cigarette substitute, i.e., an adult mint. He added peppermint oil to a candy formula, compressed the product into small rectangular bricks and named it PEZ, an abbreviation for the German word *Pfefferminz*. Production of PEZ was halted by World War II. When the product appeared again after the war, it was packaged in a dispenser that resembled a BIC lighter. These early 1950s dispensers had no heads.

PEZ arrived in the United States in 1952. PEZ-HAAS received United States Patent #2,620,061 for its "table dispensing receptacle," but the public response was less than overwhelming. Rather than withdraw from the market, Haas repositioned his product to appeal to children by adding fruit flavors. PEZ's success was assured when it became both a candy and a toy combined into one product. In some cases, the shape of the dispenser mimics an actual toy, e.g., a space gun. Most frequently, appealing heads were simply added to the tops of the standard rectangular containers.

PEZ carefully guards its design and production information. As a result, collectors differ on important questions such as dating and numbers of variations. Further complicating the issue is PEZ production outside the United States. A company in Linz, Austria, with PEZ rights to the rest of the world, including Canada, frequently issues PEZ containers with heads not issued by PEZ Candy, Inc., an independent privately owned company which by agreement manufactures and markets PEZ only in the United States. PEZ Candy, Inc., is located in Connecticut.

The American and Austrian PEZ companies use a common agent to manage the production of dispensers. The result is that occasionally the same container is issued by both companies. However, when this occurs, the packaging may be entirely different.

PEZ Candy, Inc., issues generic, seasonal and licensed-character containers. Container design is continually evaluated and upgraded.

The Mickey Mouse container has been changed more than a dozen times. Today, PEZ candy is manufactured at plants in Austria, Hungary, Yugoslavia and the United States. Previously, plants had been located in Czechoslovakia, Germany and Mexico. Dispensers are produced at plants in Austria, China, Hong Kong, Hungary and Slovenia.

References: Richard Geary, *PEZ Collectibles*, Schiffer Publishing, 1994; David Welch, *Pictorial Guide to Plastic Candy Dispensers Featuring PEZ*, Bubba Scrubba Publications, 1991; David Welch, *Collecting Pez*, Bubba Scrubba Publications, 1994.

Periodical: *Positively PEZ*, 3851 Gable Ln. Dr. #513, Indianapolis, IN 46208.

Dispenser

Angel, Christmas, 1960s 5.00
Baloo 15.00
Barney Bear, MGM cartoon character, 1980s 10.00
Baseball Glove, 1960s 110.00
Batman, black, 1985....................40.00
Bouncer Beagle Boy, MOC 5.00
Boy with Hat, Pez Pal, 1960..........10.00
Bride, Pez Pal, 1960...................250.00
Bugs Bunny, 1979, with feet............7.50
Bullwinkle, 1960s........................150.00
Camel, Melody Maker 40.00
Captain America, no feet, MIP 65.00
Captain Hook................................50.00
Casper, diecut, 1960s 100.00
Charlie Brown, frown, MIP..............7.00
Cool Cat, Warner Brothers cartoon character, 1970s...................24.00
Crocodile 5.00
Clown, Melody Maker, MOC 10.00
Dalmatian 20.00
Dog, Melody Maker 25.00
Donald Duck, no feet, MIP 25.00
Donald Duck's Nephew, blue hat 5.00
Donkey, Melody Maker, MOC 10.00
Donkey Kong Jr., premium, 1980s.....................200.00
Droopy Dog 5.00
Dumbo...25.00
Elephant 5.00
Fozzie Bear, Sesame Street, 1991 ....2.00
Frog, Melody Maker 30.00
Goofy, no feet, MIP 25.00
Gyro...5.00
Happy Bear, circus, 1970s 10.00
Hippo..5.00
Hulk, no feet, MIP.........................35.00

Icee 5.00
Indian Chief 150.00
Jerry 5.00
King Louie 15.00
Koala 5.00
Koala, Melody Maker 30.00
Lamb, Melody Maker....................40.00
Lil Wolf 15.00
Lion 5.00
Maharaja 25.00
Mama Giraffe, circus, 1970s 20.00
Mickey Mouse, no feet 5.00
Monkey, Melody Maker 25.00
Moo Moo Cow, Kooky Zoo, 1960s 20.00
Mopsy, Beatrix Potter, Eden, 1972 ....30.00
Mowgli 15.00
Orange, crazy fruit, 1970s.............40.00
Panda, Melody Maker, MOC...........10.00
Panther, Kooky Zoo, 1970s...........40.00
Papa..5.00
Parrot, Melody Maker, MOC 10.00
Penguin, Melody Maker, MOC 10.00
Pineapple, crazy fruit, 1970s.......200.00
Pirate, Pez Pal, 1960 ....25.00
Pluto, no feet, MIP.......................25.00
Policeman, Pez Pal, c1979 ....15.00
Popeye, removable pipe, no feet, MIP 65.00
Practical Pig 25.00
Raven, Kooky Zoo, 1970s.............12.00
Rhino, Melody Maker, MOC..........10.00
Roadrunner, Melody Maker, MOC 10.00
Robot, blue, 3-1/2" h, c1950..........75.00
Santa Claus, painted eyes 5.00
Sheik 35.00
Scrooge McDuck............................5.00
Silly Clown, 1970s........................25.00
Smurf...5.00
Smurfette.......................................5.00
Space Gun 150.00
Spaceman, full body, 1950s..........90.00
Spike 5.00
Stewardess, Pez Pal, 1960 ....40.00
Tiger, Melody Maker, MOC 10.00
Tom 5.00
Truck, "C" Class
  Orange cab
    Black stick 240.00
    Green stick 240.00
  Pink cab, black stick................50.00
  Yellow cab
    Black stick 60.00
    Red stick 90.00
Tuffy 5.00
Webbly, MOC.................................5.00
Whistle, 1980s...............................2.00
Winnie the Pooh............................20.00
Wounded Soldier,

  Bicentennial, 1976.................75.00
Yappy Dog, Kooky Zoo, 1970s 80.00
Yosemite Sam...............................5.00

Outfit

Cowgirl, MOC.................................5.00
Nurse, MOC 5.00
Robin Hood, MOC 5.00
Roman Soldier, MOC.....................5.00
Santa, MOC 5.00
Space Robot, MOC 5.00
Tarzan, MOC 5.00

Phoenix Bird Chinaware

Collecting Hints: Within this particular design of primarily blue and white Japanese chinaware, there are more than 500 different shapes and sizes and more than 100 different factory marks that have been cataloged. The pieces vary greatly, not only in the quality of chinaware itself—from very thick to eggshell thin—but also in design execution, even the shades of blue vary from powder blue to deep cobalt. All of these factors, as well as condition, should be considered when determining prices. Especially important is the border width of the design, "superior" widths are preferred over the more common, narrower border. Another important consideration is that pieces with "Japan" appearing below the cherry blossom mark generally have a better-quality print and also were made in some of the more unique shapes.

Note that the Phoenix Bird's body is facing *forward* while its head is facing *back over its wings*, that is, the head looks opposite the direction the body is facing. Occasionally, on one side of a rounded piece, such as a creamer, sugar or teapot, the phoenix's stance is reversed, but this is not the norm. Note, too, the phoenix always has at least four and no more than seven spots on its chest and its wings are spread out and upward.

Green and white pieces are *very rare*. Do not confuse the Phoenix Bird pattern with the Flying Dragon design that does, in fact, come in either green and white or blue and white. Multicolored Phoenix Bird pieces are also rare and these oddities are generally carelessly painted, not the usual high-quality of the blue and white examples. Another pattern that can be confused with Phoenix Bird is Flying Turkey. The latter design was more often hand-painted while Phoenix Bird was generally decorated by transfer printing. Furthermore, Flying Turkey has a heartlike border with a dot inside each heart. The few pieces of Phoenix Bird with this border, rather than the "cloud & mountain" (C/M) border are referred to as HO-O and rarely have a mark.

Because there are so many different shapes available, buying Phoenix Bird sight unseen can be risky. Insist on a sketch of the shape or a photocopy of the actual piece if at all possible—flat pieces copy well—but a photograph is best. Also ask for the dimensions as well as the mark on the bottom. The latter will sometimes give you a clue as to the quality of the piece.

History: The manufacture of the Phoenix Bird design began in the late 19th century and pieces were marked "Nippon" from 1891 to 1921. Large quantities of this ware were imported into the United States from the 1920s through the 1940s. A smaller amount went into a few European countries and are so marked, each in their own way. The vast majority of Phoenix Bird was of the transfer-print variety; hand-painted pieces with Japanese characters underneath are rare.

The pattern was primarily sold, retail, through Woolworth's stores. It could also be ordered, wholesale, from the catalogs of Butler Brothers and the Charles William Stores in New York. However, only the most basic shapes were offered through the catalogs. The pattern was also carried by A.A. Vantine Co., New York. The products, which were exported by Morimura Brothers, Japan, were known at that time as Blue Howo Bird China. Morimura used two different marks: "Japan" below a convex "M" under two crossed branches or "Made in Japan" beneath a concave "M" inside a wreath with an open bottom.

Phoenix Bird pieces could also be acquired as premiums. A simple breakfast set could be obtained by selling a particular number of sub-

Marmalade jar (#2), attached underplate, heart border, $65.

scriptions to *Needlecraft* magazine. During the early 1900s, two different brands of coffee and tea included a cup and saucer with purchase and some pieces were available as premiums into the 1930s.

While no ads have yet been found, three-piece tea sets (teapot, creamer and sugar) were made at some point in time. To date, six different sets have been cataloged along with small cups, saucers and plates.

There are several other patterns which are considered to be in the phoenix family: Flying Turkey (an all-over pattern that was hand-painted or transfer-printed), Twin Phoenix (a Noritake border-only pattern), Howo (a Noritake allover pattern), Flying Dragon (available in blue and white and green and white and marked with six Japanese characters) and Firebird (the bird's tail flows downward; usually hand-painted and character-marked). Most Japanese potteries were destroyed during World War II making it difficult to trace production of these related patterns.

Two different styles of coffeepots and after-dinner cups and saucers, as well as child-size cups and saucers, have been found marked "Made in Occupied Japan" and/or "Maruta." Myott, Son & Co., copied Phoenix Bird in England around 1936 and named the pattern Satsuma. These earthenware pieces do not have the same intense blue of the Japanese-made wares.

References: Joan Collett Oates, *Phoenix Bird Chinaware*, Books I-IV, 1984-1989, published by author (685 S. Washington, Constantine, MI 49042).

Periodical: *Phoenix Bird Discoveries* (*PBDs*), 685 S. Washington, Constantine, MI 49042.

Museums: Alice Brayton House, Green Animals Topiary Gardens, Newport, RI; Charles A. Lindberg Home, Little Falls, MN; Historic Cherry Hill, Albany, NY; Huntingdon County Historical Society, Huntingdon, PA; Laura Ingalls-Wilder/Rose Lane Historic Home, Mansfield, MO; Majestic Castle (Casa Loma), Toronto, Canada; W.H. Stark House, Orange, TX; Val-Kill Cottage, Hyde Park, NY.

Reproduction Alert: Approximately 20 pieces of Phoenix Bird were produced in the late 1960s; these are now called Post-1970 Phoenix Bird. They are not reproductions, as such, because the pieces are not identical to nor of the same shape as earlier Phoenix Bird. Generally, these later pieces do not have a backstamp, although they did originally come with a "JAPAN" sticker that could be easily removed. Distinguishing characteristics of the newer wares are a milk-white rather than a grayish body, sparsity of design, especially near the bottom and a more brilliant blue color in the designs.

Takahashia Imports, California, created a new style of "Phnx" (their term) that has been on the market since the late 1970s and was featured in gift catalogs in the 1980s. The phoenix itself is different on these blue and white porcelain pieces and the wares have no border design, making it easy to distinguish them from true Phoenix Bird. Phnx is a unique pattern in its own right and has been purchased by many Phoenix Bird collectors as conversation pieces. Some Takahashi pieces come with a blue backstamp, but most were originally marked with a round, gold sticker naming the firm. Collectors call it "T-Bird," for short.

Advisor: Joan Collett Oates.

Note: Since there are several different shapes within some kinds of Phoenix Bird, the various shapes are given a style number in the listings below. This numbering system corresponds to that used in the books by Joan Collett Oates.

Chocolate pot (#1) 135.00
Coffeepot, "A," post-1970 .... 45.00
Cup and saucer

Plate, 6-1/8", $65.

Adult (#3)	10.00
After-dinner (#4)	18.00
Children's	15.00
Chocolate (#1)	25.00
Eggcup, double cup	15.00
Gravy tureen and cov (#2), attached underplate	120.00
Marmalade spoon	12.00

Plate

Dinner, 9-3/4" d	45.00
Grille, sectional	45.00
Luncheon, 8-1/2" d	15.00
Tea/Toast, round, no cup	25.00

Platter, oval, plain edge

14"	95.00
17"	170.00
Soup dish, 7-1/4" d	35.00
Sugar basin, extra-large	85.00

Teapot

#3, fat/squatty	40.00
#4, fat/round	45.00
Toothpick holder (#3)	45.00

Pig Collectibles

Collecting Hints: Bisque and porcelain pig items from late 19th-century European potters are most widely sought by collectors. Souvenir items should have decals which are in good condition; occasionally the gilding wears off from rubbing or washing.

History: Historically, the pig has been important as a source of food and has also been an economic factor in rural areas of Europe and America. It was one of the first animals imported into the American colonies. A fatted sow was the standard gift to a rural preacher on his birthday or holiday.

As a decorative motif, the pig gained prominence with the figurines and planters made in the late 19th century by English, German and Austrian potters. These "pink" porcelain pigs with green decoration were popular souvenir or prize items at fairs and carnivals or could be purchased at five-and-dime stores.

Many pig figurines were banks and by the early 20th century "Piggy Bank" became a synonym for coin bank. When tourist attractions became popular along America's coasts and in the mountain areas, many of the pig designs showed up as souvenir items with gilt decals identifying the area.

The pig motif appeared on the advertising items associated with farm products and life. Movie cartoons introduced Porky Pig and Walt Disney's "Three Little Pigs." In the late 1970s pig collectibles caught fire again. Specialty shops selling nothing but pig-related items were found in the New England area. In a 1981 issue, *Time* magazine devoted a page and a half to the pig phenomena.

Reproduction Alert: Reproductions of three German-style painted bisque figurines have been spotted in the market. They are pig by outhouse, pig playing piano and pig poking out of large purse. The porcelain is much rougher and the green is a darker shade.

Additional Listings: Cartoon Characters, Disneyana.

Advisor: Mary Hamburg.

Advertising

Cutting Board, 14" x 19-1/2", wood, pig shape, mkd "Arnold, Kent Feeds"	22.00
Mirror, 2-1/8" d, Newton Collins Short Order Restaurant, St. Joe, MO, yellow and orange	55.00
Trade Card, "Try Wright's Little Liver Pills," 5 pigs	10.00

Bank

3-1/2" h, front of pink pig sticking out 1 end, back of pig sticking out other end	75.00
3-3/4" h, money bag, pig along side, "My System"	110.00
Heart, green, 2 pigs on each side of sheet music, mkd "Germany"	62.00
Barometer, pig shape	105.00

Bottle, 5-3/4", Benedictine

Liqueur, pig popping out of bottle, orange seal	97.50
Cork, 3", Heidsieck Dry Champagne,	

2 pigs	65.00
Crock, 3" h, orange, pig along side	85.00
Dish, 3-3 dice, pig	110.00

Figure

Canoe, yellow-gold pig inside, c1930	65.00
Car, 3" l, 2-1/4" h, old-fashioned with rumble seat, 2 pigs inside	85.00
Carriage 3-3/4" l, 3" h, mother pig wheeling 2 piglets, incised "Made in Germany," "The Heavenly Twins"	98.00
Lobster, pulling leg of red pig	110.00
Mammy, 4-1/4" h, with spoon and bandanna, pink pig in basket	350.00
Mother and piglet, 2" h, 3" l, "Let Me Also Have Some Mother"	95.00
Fence, 4-1/2" l, 3-1/2" h, black bisque pig jumping over	80.00
Playing cards, 3-1/2" h, 3-3/4", "Hearts Are Trumps"	105.00
Purse, 2-1/4" h, green, black bisque pig sitting on top	80.00

Shoe

One pink pig inside, 4-1/2" l green shoe	78.00
2 pigs inside looking out	80.00
Tree, white, swinging piglet, larger pig looking on, "Mind How You Fall"	
3-3/4" h	100.00
4-3/4" h	110.00
Typewriter, pink pig	95.00
Water pump, 3-3/4" h, piglet inside, mkd "Made in Germany," "Good Old Annual"	100.00
Water trough, 4" l, 3-3/4" h, bisque, surrounded by 4 pigs	110.00
Well, 3" h, orange top, gold pig, souvenir of Chicago, IL, mkd "Made in Germany," 1930s	65.00
Inkwell, 3" h, green, pink pig sitting on top	100.00

Match Holder

5" l, on top of pink bisque pig, "Scratch My Back" on large one, "Me Too" on smaller	110.00
One pig holding flag, 2 black children in boat	350.00

Dish, pig bowling, piglet watching, $105.

Match safe, brass, SP, English, 2" l, $125.

Nodder, china, dressed as man and
    woman.....................................90.00
Pin Dish
    Horseshoe, 5" l, yellow-green,
    "Good Luck," mkd "Made in
    Germany".................................80.00
    Older couple, 4-3/4" l, 3-1/2" h, man
    with top hat and green bow tie,
    woman with umbrella.............135.00
Pitcher, 4" h, figural, dressed in tie and
    tails, brown.............................29.00
Salt Dish
    "Casino Wash," pig with hands
    on flat holder..........................100.00
    One on either side of 4-1/4" tall chef
    pig with shamrocks.................110.00
Stuffed, 2-1/2", velvet, Steiff........115.00
Toothpick Holder, pink pig holding
    camera....................................90.00
Toy
    Squeak, 5" h, papier-mâché,
    painted..................................350.00
    Stuffed, 2-1/2", velvet, Steiff...115.00
    Windup, 8-1/2" litho tin,
    Porky Pig, cowboy outfit,
    yellow hat, Marx, MIB.............200.00
Vase, 7-1/4" h, red devil's arm around
    pink pig, sitting on log.............130.00
Weather Vane, metal...................130.00

Pinball Machines

Collecting Hints: Cosmetic condition is of paramount importance. Graphics are unique to specific models, especially backglass and playfield plastics, making replacements scarce. Because they are complex, graphics are difficult, if not impossible, to repair. Prices in this listing are for games in working condition that are considered cosmetically good and have 95% or more of backglass decoration present.

Some wear is expected in pinballs as a sign that the game was a good one, but bare wood detracts from overall condition. Watch for signs of loose ink on the rear of the glass. Unrestorable games with good cosmetics are valuable because they can be used to help restore other games. A non-working game is worth 30% to 40% less than a working one.

Add 10% if the paper items, such as score card, instruction card and schematic, are present and in good condition. It is fair to suggest that regardless of mechanical condition, a game in good cosmetic condition is worth roughly twice that of the same game in poor cosmetic condition.

Pinball collecting is a new hobby which is still developing. It can be started inexpensively, but requires space to maintain. The tremendous diversity of models made has prevented the market from becoming well developed. There are relatively few people who restore antique pinball machines and then sell them. Expect to buy games in non-working condition and learn to repair them yourself.

History: Pinball machines can be traced back to the mid-1700s. However, it was not until Gottlieb introduced Baffle Ball in 1931, during the Depression, that pinball machines caught on and became a popular and commercial success because people were hungry for something novel and for the opportunity to make money. Pinball machines offered both. The first games were entirely mechanical, cost about $20 and were produced in large numbers—25,000 to 50,000 machines of the same model were not uncommon.

Pinball developments include:
1932: addition of legs
1933: electric, at first using batteries
1936: addition of bumpers
1947: advent of flippers
1950: kicking rubbers
1953: score totalers
1954: multiple players
1977: solid-state electronics

The size of the machines changed over the years. The early countertops were 16 by 32 inches. Later models were freestanding with the base measuring 21 by 52 inches and the back box, 24 by 30 inches. Most pinballs were made in Chicago. Major manufacturers were Gottlieb, Williams and Bally. The total number of pinball models that have been manufactured has not been precisely determined. Some suggest over 10,000 different models from 200-plus makers. After 1940, most models were produced in quantities of 500 to 2,000; occasionally, games had production figures as high as 10,000. Pinball machines have always enjoyed a high attrition rate. New models made the most money and were introduced by several of the major manufacturers at the rate of one entirely new model every three weeks during the mid 1940s and 1950s. Today, new models are introduced at a slower rate, averaging four to six new games per year.

Most pinball owners used the older games for spare parts to repair newer models. Earning life was less than three years in most markets. Many games were warehoused or destroyed to keep them from competing with the newest games. At the very least, the coin mechanisms were removed before the game was sold.

Pinball art is part of the popular culture and the kinetic art movement. The strength of their pinball playfield design made D. Gottlieb & Co., the premier maker through the 1950s and into the 1970s. During the 1960s, their fame grew because of their animated backglasses, which both amused and attracted players. The combination of animation and availability make the 1960s machines a target for collectors.

The advent of solid-state games in 1977, coupled with the video-game boom, dramatically changed the pinball-machine market. Solid-state game production increased as manufacturers attempted to replace all obsolete electromechanical games. Initially, Bally was the predominant maker, but Williams has since attained this position. Although solid-state games made electromechanical ones commercially obsolete, collectors who are rediscovering the silver ball are helping the pinball machine recover some of its popularity.

References: Richard Bueschel, *Collector's Guide to Vintage Coin Machines*, Schiffer Publishing, 1995; Heribert Eiden and Jurgen Lukas,

Pinball Machines, Schiffer Publishing, 1992; Bill Kurtz, *Arcade Treasures*, Schiffer Publishing, 1994; ——, *Slot Machines and Coin-Op Games*, Chartwell Books, 1991; Donald Mueting and Robert Hawkins, *Pinball Reference Guide*, Mead Co., 1979.

Periodicals: *Coin Drop International*, 5815 W. 52nd Ave., Denver, CO 80212; *Coin Slot*, 4401 Zephyr St., Wheat Ridge, CO 80033; *Coin-Op Classics*, 17844 Toiyabe St., Fountain Valley, CA 92708; *Gameroom*, 1014 Mt. Tabor Rd., New Albany, IN 47150; *PinGame Journal*, 31937 Olde Franklin Dr., Farmington Hills, MI 48334; *Pinball Trader*, P.O. Box 1795, Campbell, CA 95009.

Notes: Pinballs are listed by machine name and fall into various classifications: novelty with no awards, replay which awards free games, add-a-ball which awards extra balls instead of games and bingo where players add additional coins to increase the odds of winning. Some payout games made in the mid- to late 1930s paid out coins for achieving scoring objectives. After the first add-a-ball games in 1960, many game designs were issued as both replay and add-a-ball, with different game names and slight modifications to the game rules, but similar art work.

Advisor: Bob Levy.

Bally
    1933, Airway, first mechanical
      scoring.....................................350.00
    1951, Coney Island, bingo 350.00
    1963, Moon Shot, replay........300.00
    1968
    Rock Makers, replay, unusual playfield...300.00
    Safari, replay..........................275.00
    1973, Nip-It, ball grabber........225.00
    1975, Bon Voyage, replay......275.00
    1978, Lost World, electronic...350.00
Chicago Coin
    1948, Spinball,
      spinner action........................175.00
    1974, Gin, replay....................175.00
Exhibit, 1941, Big Parade, patriotic
    theme, classic art..................450.00
Genco
    1937, Cargo 375.00
    1949, Black Gold, replay........325.00
Gottlieb
    1936, Daily Races, 1-ball 375.00
    1948, Buccaneer, replay, mirrored

Gottlieb's Sinbad, D. Gottlieb & Co., 25¢ play, electric, wood case, 22" x 52" top surface, $325.

    graphics 350.00
    1950, Just 21, turret shooter ..325.00
    1955, Duette, replay,
      first 2-player 325.00
    1956, Auto Race, replay 350.00
    1965, Cow Poke,
      animation classic...................475.00
    1967, King of Dinosaurs,
      replay, roto 375.00
    1968, Spin-a-Card, replay......300.00
    1971, Roller Coaster, replay,
      multi-level..............................325.00
    1977, Target Alpha,
      multi-player 350.00
    1981, Black Hole, electronic,
      multi-level..............................475.00
Mills Novelty Co., 1932, Official,
    push-button ball lift 350.00
Pacific Amusement, 1934, Lite-a-Line,
    first light-up backboard 400.00
Rock-Ola
    1932, Juggle Ball, countertop, rod
      ball manipulator.....................295.00
    1935, Flash, early free play....315.00
United
    1948, Caribbean, replay.........225.00
    1951, ABC, first bingo 400.00
Williams
    1948, Yanks, baseball theme,
      animated 300.00
    1953, Army-Navy, replay, reel
      scoring 300.00
    1958, Gusher,
      disappearing bumper 375.00
    1961, Metro, replay 225.00
    1964, Palooka, add-a-ball 400.00
    1967, Touchdown,

    animation 250.00
    1972, Olympic
    Hockey, replay 275.00
    1973, Travel Time,
      timed play 225.00
    1977, Grand Prix, replay........350.00
    1980, Firepower, electronic ...450.00

Pinup Art

Collecting Hints: Try to collect calendars that are intact. There is a growing practice among dealers to separate calendar pages, cut off the date information and sell the individual sheets in hopes of making more money. Buyers are urged not to support this practice.

Concentrate on the work of one artist. Little research has been done on the pinup artists so it is a wide open field. The original art on which calendar sheets and magazine covers are based has begun to appear on the market. High prices are being asked for both the oil paintings and pastel examples, but the market is not yet stabilized—beware!

Pinup material can be found in many other collectible categories. Usually the items are referred to as "girlies." Many secondary pinup items are not signed, but a collector can easily identify an artist's style.

History: Charles Dana Gibson introduced the first true pinup girl when he created the Gibson Girl in the early 1900s. Other artists who followed his example included Howard Chandler Christy, Coles Phillips and Charles Sheldon. The film magazines of the 1920s, such as *Film Fun* and *Real Screen Fun*, developed the concept further. Their front covers featuring minimally clad beauties were designed to attract a male readership. During the 1930s, popular cover artists included Charles Sheldon, Cardwell Higgins and George Petty. Sheldon did calendar art as well as covers for Brown & Bigelow. *Esquire* began in 1933; its first Petty gatefold appeared in 1939.

The golden age of pinup art was 1935 to 1955. The 1940s brought Alberto Vargas (the final "s" was dropped at *Esquire's* request), Gillete Elvgren, Billy DeVorss, Joyce Ballantyne and Earl Moran into the picture. Pinup art appeared everywhere—magazine covers, blotters, souvenir items, posters, punchboards, etc. Many artists besides those mentioned here adopted the style. Photographic advertising and changing American tastes ended the pinup reign by the early 1960s.

References: Denis C. Jackson, *Price and Identification Guide to Alberto Vargas and George Petty*, 2nd Edition, published by author (P.O. Box 1958, Sequim, WA 98382), 1987; ——, *Price and Identification Guide to Coles Philips*, published by author (P.O. Box 1958, Sequim, WA 98382), 1986; Leland and Crystal Payton, *Girlie Collectibles*, Martin's Griffin, 1996; *Pinup Poster Book*, Collectors Press, 1995; Norman I. Platnick, *Coles Phillips*, published by author (50 Brentwood Rd., Bayshore, NY 11706) 1996.

Periodicals: *Glamour Girls: Then and Now*, P.O. Box 34501, Washington, DC 20043; *The Illustrator Collector's News*, P.O. Box 1958, Sequim, WA 98382.

Blotter, 3-1/2" x 6", cardboard, full-color sgd art by Rolf Armstrong, blond nude seated at edge of pond waters, 1935 Brown & Bigelow, unused...................45.00

Box, 4-1/4" x 4-1/4" x 1-3/4", red and white, color graphics of high-heeled smiling girl, bow and arrow, large red heart background, logo "Hit for His Heart," Pioneer Belts, c1940 ...28.00

Calendar
  1942, 8-1/2" x 12", Esquire, Varga Girl, plastic spiral binding, 12 pgs, horiz format, verses by Phil Stack 75.00
  1945, Starlight, Earl Moran, full-color nude blond, dark green drape, black ground 40.00
  1948, 8-1/2" x 12", Esquire Glamour Gallery, paper wall type, full-color pinup art for each month, contributing artists include Ben-Hur Baz, Fritz Willis, Joe DeMers, Al Moore, J. Frederick Smith, Ron Wicks 65.00
  1951
    5-1/2" x 6", Esquire, desk type, Al Moore graphics, 12 pgs 38.00
    5-1/2" x 6-1/4", Esquire, Hargrave Secret Service cardboard frame, dark green top, gold accent lettering, 3-3/4" x 4-1/4" window for inserts, Al Moore graphics 28.00
    11" x 23", paper wall type, full-color art by Rolf Armstrong, bru-

Magazine page, *Esquire*, **Alberto Varga[s], 1941, $20.**

nette model in red and white 2-pc swimsuit, titled "Tip Top," lower part inscribed for Brown & Bigelow, St. Paul, MN, sample type, one month 85.00
  1952, Thompson Studio, sketches, orig envelope 50.00
  1954, 8-1/4" x 11", Petty Girl, 12 pgs, vertical format, verses..............65.00

Calendar Folder, 4" x 9", colored cardboard folder, 2-3/4" x 4-1/4" tipped on b&w glossy photo on front cover, Superior Switchboard & Devices Co., Canton, OH, assortment of jokes and gags printed inside, holed for hanging, Oct. 1955 ....28.00

Card, 3-1/2" x 5", c1940, set of five
  Earl Moran, red ground 25.00
  Zoe Mozert, full color 30.00

Christmas Card, 5-1/2" x 8", tan, red, black and blue, MacPherson ...25.00

Cigarette Lighter, 1-7/8" h, b&w photos, green and red tints 35.00

Coaster, 3-1/4" d, litho tin, full-color pinup art, faint lettering "Ray Raedel," orange rim, from 1960 PA Fireman's Convention, price for 5-pc set.....................75.00

Date Book, 5" x 7", Esquire, color cover, spiral binding, full-color pinup photos, 1943 George Hurrell 35.00

Display Sign, 8-1/2" x 12-1/2", black cardboard insert sign for arcade vending machine, Exhibit Supply Co., Chicago, c1940, 3 brown-tone glossy paper photo samples
  Ava Gardner.............................35.00
  Terry Moore 35.00
  Unidentified Girl 30.00

Glass

5-1/2" h, Playboy Bunny, 3/4" black image profile trademark, c1960.....................18.00
7-1/2" h, fluted beer schooner, 3-1/2" decal of blond woman putting on bikini, different view when viewed from reverse, c1940.................32.00

Hair Pin, orig 4" x 5-1/2" yellow, red, black and white card, Petty, artist sgd, 1948, MOC 25.00

Key Chain, Elvgren insert, 1-1/2" x 2", slotted plastic case, full-color insert, metal key chain, c1950
  A Hitch in Time, girl adjusting stocking as dog looks on 35.00
  Belle Ringer, girl doing laundry, skirt caught in ringer 25.00
  Look What I've Got, leggy girl fishing 25.00
  See-Worthy, leggy girl boating....................25.00

Magazine
  After Hours, 1st issue, 1957, Betty Page centerfold 35.00
  Prevue, Jan. 1953, Marilyn Monroe cover, article 35.00

Mug, 4" d, 5" h, aluminum tankard, clear glass bottom, incised rabbit's-head symbol 15.00

Playing Cards, Elvgren 50.00

Shot Glass, 3" h, Playboy Club, 1-1/4" h image of semi-nude female trademark holding Playboy key, black name around sides, early 1960s.............................28.00

Stationery Kit, Thinking of You, 7-1/2" x 9" cardboard folder album, 3 panel 9" x 23" full-color art of blond model in light green sarong, tropical motifs, upper contour of figure has diecut slash openings which hold set of 50 sheets of plain white note paper, orig 20 envelopes, front cover art of letter writing solider, another panel wing for addresses, early 1940s, unused...............75.00

Strip Illusion Card
  1-1/4" x 3-1/4", Sally of Hollywood and Vine, cardboard folder, 2 plain white cardboard strips to be inserted between acetate layers of picture, evening gown to underwear to nudity, 1940s 38.00
  3-1/2" x 4-1/2", Polly Peel, thin white cardboard, 2 plain white cardboard strips to be separated and inserted between acetate layers of picture, nightgown to underwear to nudity, 1940s, unused 45.00

Tin, 3-1/2" x 8-1/2" x 1-1/2" box, tin litho, Thorn's Toffee, black lid, brass accent sides with 7-1/2" full-color photo of smiling full-figure short-haired blond looking at viewer suggestively, holding martini glass, gold accent skimpy swimsuit, gold accent high heels, worn luster, c1960.........48.00

Viewer, 1" x 1-1/2" x 2", plastic miniature television set, white screen, small circular hole for viewing, 8 views, Hong Kong, c1970

Golden Dreams, classic Marilyn Monroe pose on red drapery....40.00

Jayne Mansfield, Bettie Page, unknown models 70.00

Marilyn Monroe 40.00

Planters

Collecting Hints: Planters are available in a wide array of shapes and colors. Seek out the best examples available. Because many planters were made inexpensively and were meant to be used with dirt, water and growing plants, it is not unusual to find wear and minor interior scratches and damage.

Collectors of modern planters should carefully save any packaging or brochures which illustrate the planter. The brochures issued as sales promotions by florists will become the advertising collectibles of tomorrow. Collectors of specialty planters should check to make sure all decorations are included, e.g., ladies' heads should be complete with original necklaces and earrings. Collectors should be careful to determine that the object is a true planter and not a mismatched canister or vase that has been home to a plant.

History: As soon as houseplants became an important part of interior decoration, planters were created. Some planters are simply vessels given a new lease on life, such as crock or chamber pot. Other items, such as jardinieres, window boxes and hanging baskets were designed specially to hold growing materials. Many manufacturers created these interesting shapes and colors to complement not only the plant but also the interior design of the room where it was placed.

Like cookie jars, wonderful figural planters were created in the 1940s and have continued to present times. Many major companies, such as McCoy and Roseville, created an inexpensive line of planters for use by florists. Some of these same planters are now eagerly sought by collectors. Florists have learned this valuable lesson and today planters issued by organizations like FTD are dated.

Some planters, such as the popular ladies' heads, were made by small firms and were distributed regionally. These charming figural planters give a wonderful perspective on the fashion and colors that were popular at the time of their manufacture.

References: Mike Posgay and Ian Warner, *World of Head Vase Planters*, The Glass Press, 1992; Mary Zavada, *Lady Head Vases*, Revised Edition, Schiffer Publishing, 1994.

Publications: *Head Hunter Newsletter*, Box 83H, Scarsdale, NY 10583.

Figural

Auto, 9" x 4-1/2", ceramic, Birchwood line, McCoy, some wear to yellow trim...................45.00

Bambi, mkd "Walt Disney Productions".......65.00

Birds on a Perch, 4 white, yellow and black birds, brown tree branch, glossy glaze, mkd "Shawnee 502" 35.00

Blackamoor, heavy gold trim.........35.00

Butterfly on Log, brown and white, glossy glaze, mkd "Shawnee USA 524" 10.00

Cactus and Cowboy, natural colors, Morton 15.00

Camel, 3" h, Niloak....................25.00

Cart, blue exterior, yellow interior, glossy glaze, Shawnee, mkd "USA 775" 10.00

Cat, coral glaze, green box, McCoy, c1950......................................12.00

Conch Shell, yellow and green, glossy glaze, Hull..............................35.00

Cradle, pink, McCoy......................10.00

Dachshund, brown, glossy glaze, Hull 75.00

Davy Crockett, baby Davy, foil label reads "Napco, Davy Crockett S90E," 4" x 4-1/2" 75.00

Dog, light green, white accents, McCoy 10.00

Donkey, standing, small Mexican figure sleeping in front of legs, baskets on back, high gloss, white, 6" h 9.00

Elf, sitting on large shoe, multicolored, glossy glaze, mkd "Shawnee 765" 10.00

Fawns, standing pair, 5" x 3-1/2", McCoy, 1957 ....38.00

Giraffe, 9" h, green,

glossy glaze, Hull 35.00

Globe, blue and green, yellow stand, glossy glaze mkd "Shawnee USA" 15.00

Goat, gray, red harness, McCoy ...15.00

Gondola, yellow, McCoy 18.00

Goose, Hull, #80 ....30.00

Guitar, black, semi-gloss, mkd "Red Wing USA #M-1484" 15.00

Lady, 2 wolfhounds, Brayton Laguna, 11" h, 7-1/2" w 175.00

Lamb, white, blue bow, McCoy 10.00

Lion, white, McCoy, c1940............12.00

Log, 7" l, white, Niloak..................18.00

Mallard, ead down, Royal Copley 20.00

Mouse, leaning on cheese wedge, multicolored, glossy glaze, Shawnee, mkd "USA 705".......15.00

Parrot, 5", white, orange accents 18.00

Pelican, turquoise, matte glaze, McCoy, mkd " NM USA" 12.00

Piano, upright, green, glossy glaze, Shawnee, mkd "USA 528".......18.00

Policeman and Donkey, 5", blue, Niloak 35.00

Quail, 9-1/2" h, natural-color spray glaze, American Art Potteries 30.00

Rabbit, with top hat and vest, beside yellow egg, Morton Pottery Co.....18.00

Raggedy Ann, holding baby bottle, 6" h, incised "Relpo 6565" 45.00

Santa Claus, flesh tone, red and white, Morton 25.00

Scottie Dog, Royal Copley 15.00

Shoe, bronzed-type, McCoy 8.00

Skunk, 6-1/2" h, black and white, pastel pink and blue basket, airbrushed, Brush-McCoy, #249 ....35.00

Space Shuttle and Astronaut, Inarco.....................75.00

Stork, McCoy 10.00

Turkey, brown, red wattle, Morton 12.00

Whale, 10" l, black, Freeman McFarlin...................50.00

Wishing Well, 7-1/4" h, dusty rose, Niloak 20.00

Head Types

Baby, 5-3/4" h, blond hair, open eyes, pink cheeks, open mouth, pink ruffled bonnet tied under chin, pink dress, unmkd 18.00

Black Lady, 5" h, young, downcast eyes, yellow turban, red sarong, large gold hoop earrings, 3-strand pearl necklace, Japan.............................45.00

Cowboy, 6" h, brown hair, blue eyes, yellow hat and neckerchief, white shirt, yellow star-shaped badge, unmkd 35.00

Girl, 5-1/4" h, long blond hair, straight bangs, blue flowers at ponytail on top of head, eyes looking right, raised hand, slender neck, blue press, Parma by AAI, Japan, A-222........12.50

Howdy Doody 35.00

Jackie O 350.00

Lady, 7" h, brown hair, downcast eyes, raised right hand, black hat with white and gold ribbon, black dress, white glove with gold accents, pearl drop earrings and necklace, Inarco, C-2322....................................55.00

Nurse, 5-3/4" h, short blond hair, downcast eyes, raised right hand, white cap with Red Cross insignia, white uniform with gold accents, painted fingernails, unmkd 65.00

Miscellaneous

Hedi Schoop, ceramic, abstract comma shape, 3" d, 9" w, white ext with stylized red flowers and green leaves, rose int.....................................65.00

McCoy Pottery, basket shape, yellow and brown..............................35.00

Metlox Pottery, clock, California Provincial pattern 95.00

Weller Pottery, window box, 14-1/2" l, Forest pattern 325.00

Wall Pocket

Acorn, light brown, mkd "Frankoma 190" 25.00

Baby and Diaper, mkd "4921, Japan"...................15.00

Bird on tree trunk, 5-1/2" h, blue and tan spray glaze, American Art Potteries.............18.00

Broom, inverted, mkd "L&C Ceramics Hollywood Hand Made" 25.00

Cocker Spaniel, head, mkd "Royal Copley".........................20.00

Corner, 5-1/2" h, hp underglaze floral dec, Midwest Potteries 20.00

Cowboy Boot, figural, blue and white, speckled, mkd

McCoy, dog figural, light green, white highlights, 7-1/4" h, 7-1/2" l, $10.

"Frankoma 133".......................28.00

Fish, yellow stripes, mkd "Gilner Calif C" 20.00

Geisha Girl 70.00

Grape Cluster, mkd "Royal Haeger R-745 USA" 25.00

Horseshoe, horsehead enter, green 25.00

Peacock, mkd "West Coast Pottery, California, USA-441" 45.00

Sandy and Jean, head type, boy and girl, blue plaid shirts, minor damage, price for pr 75.00

Straw Hat, mkd "Stewart G. McCullock Calif"......................................15.00

Teapot, pink apple dec, Shawnee.........................30.00

Tree Trunk, 8" h, chocolate brown drip, Cliftwood Art Potteries.............90.00

Umbrella, black, white handle, mkd "McCoy USA" 35.00

Planters Peanuts

Collecting Hints: Planters Peanuts memorabilia is easily identified by the famous Mr. Peanut trademark. Items made between 1906 and 1916 have the "Planters Nut And Chocolate Company" logo. Papier-mâché, die-cut and ceramic pieces must be in very good condition. Cast-iron and tin pieces should be free of rust and dents and have good graphics and color.

History: Amedeo Obici and Mario Peruzzi organized the Planters Nut And Chocolate Co., in Wilkes-Barre, PA, in 1906. Obici had conducted a small peanut business for several years and was known locally as the "Peanut Specialist." At first, Spanish salted red skins were sold for 10 cents per pound. Soon after, Obici developed the whole, white, blanched peanut and this product became consumers' favorite.

In 1916, a young Italian boy submitted a rough version of the now-famous monocled and distinguished Mr. Peanut as an entry in a contest held by Planters to develop a trademark. A wide variety of premium and promotional items were soon based on this character. Planters eventually was purchased by Standard Brands, which itself later became a division of Nabisco.

Collectors' Club: Peanut Pals, 804 Hickory Grande Rd., Bridgeville, PA 15017.

Measure, plastic, 1/4, 1/2, and 1 teaspoon, tablespoon, red, $5.

Reproduction Alert.

Ashtray, 6" x 5", emb, silvered metal, 1906-56 ....50.00

Bank, plastic, Mr. Peanut 18.00

Belt Buckle, Dinah Shore Golf Tournament gift, MIB.............140.00

Book, *Presidents*, 7-1/2" x 10-1/2, 32 pgs, soft-cover, multicolor and b&w photo of presidents, 1953........20.00

Booklet, *Peanut Pals*, 3-1/2" x 6, 24 pgs, peanut characters Percy and Peter meet Mr. Peanut at factory, 1927 ....65.00

Bookmark, diecut, cardboard, 1920 ....25.00

Cigarette Lighter, plastic, yellow ...20.00

Coloring Book, 8-1/4" x 11", 32 pgs, orig letter dated June 16, 1928, Planters Nut & Chocolate Co., Wilkes-Barre, PA, letterhead, 9" x 12" envelope, 6 pgs neatly water colored, rest unused...............75.00

Figure, Mr. Peanut, 6" h, flexible, 1991, Planter's Lifesavers Co. 15.00

Jar

    Barrel shape 195.00

    6-sided 75.00

Key Chain, figural, peanut shape, tan 20.00

Lamp, figural, glowing Mr. Peanut 325.00

Mug, figural, 1960s 15.00

Nut Spoon, blue, red, tan and green, price for set 28.00

Paint Book, Mr. Peanut, orig mailer, unused, 1929 ....80.00

Peanut Butter Machine, MIB 50.00

Peanut Butter Spreader, red 6.00

Pencil, lead, white and red, clear tube at top contains floating Mr. Peanut, name in red script on white part, 1940s......................................85.00

Pin, Mr. Peanut

75th Anniversary 1906-1981, enameled 28.00

NY World's Fair, 1-3/4" h, wood, Mr. Peanut resting against Trylon, inscribed "1940 World's Fair," red name on top hat, Perisphere behind crossed legs 110.00

Pinback Button

Planters Golden Jubilee, brown letters, gold litho ground, c1956...80.00

Vote for Mr. Peanut, black, white and red litho, c1940.........................50.00

Punch Board, 2 pcs......................65.00

Serving Spoon, 5-1/4" l, SP, Carlton, c1930..15.00

Shoe Polish, blue, 2-1/4" plastic figural Mr. Peanut charm, Esquire Scuff Kote, orig 2-1/4" x 2-1/4" x 5" multicolored box, c1950...........35.00

Spotlight, Mr. Peanut....................95.00

Straw, figural, Mr. Peanut, green.....8.00

Swizzle Stick, figural.......................4.00

Tab, 1-1/2" d, diecut litho metal, yellow, black and white Mr. Peanut, 1920 ....15.00

Tin, 10-lb size 65.00

Whistle, figural..............................25.00

Plastics

Collecting Hints: Thermoplastic collectibles can be ruined when exposed to heat, flame or a hot-pin test.

History: The term "plastic" is derived from the Greek word "Plastikos," which means pliable. Therefore, any material which can be made pliable and formed into a desired shape, technically falls into the category of plastic. For the collector, two categories of plastics should be recognized: natural and synthetic.

Natural plastics are organic materials which are found in nature. The most common natural plastics are tortoiseshell and cattle horn. They have been used for hundreds of years to make both utilitarian and luxury items. Natural plastics were harvested and cleaned, then softened in hot liquid. Once pliable, they were manipulated into shape by a variety of methods including carving, sawing and press molding.

Semi-synthetic and synthetic plastics are those which are man-made from combinations of organic and/or chemical substances. The most commonly collected plastics in this category include the earliest examples: 1870—Celluloid (pyroxylin plastic), 1890—Casine (milk protein and formaldehyde) and 1907—Bakelite (phenol formaldehyde).

The years between World Wars I and II gave birth to the modern plastics age. Beetleware, a urea formaldehyde plastic with properties similar to Bakelite, was introduced in 1928. Lumarith, a trade name for cellulose acetate plastic, was introduced in 1929 and served as a non-flammable replacement for celluloid.

During the Great Depression, the plastics industry developed at an astounding rate with the introduction of acrylic and polymer plastics: Polystyrene and Poly-vinyl-chloride—PVC (1930), Methylmethacrylic (1934), Melamine (1935) and Polyethylene (1939). Today, all of these plastics are collected in hundreds of forms.

All plastics fall into one of two categories: thermoplastic or thermoset. Thermoplastics are those which are molded by the application of heat and pressure, then cooled. Additional applications of heat will resoften or melt the material. Tortoiseshell, horn, celluloid, cellulose acetate, polystyrene, polyethylene and acrylic fall into this category.

Thermoset plastics are those which are molded by the application of heat and pressure, then upon cooling, permanently hardened. While they are resistant to high temperatures, they are subject to cracking over time. Thermoset plastics include Bakelite, Beetleware and Melmac.

Acrylic Plastic, introduced in 1927 by Rohm & Haas as "Prespex" or "Plexiglas," is used instead of curved glass in airplane cockpits. In 1937, Dupont introduced Lucite, a thermoplastic acrylic resin that could be either crystal clear or opaque, tinted any color and cast, carved or molded.

Bakelite is the registered trade name for the first entirely synthetic plastic. It was developed by Leo H. Baekeland in 1907 using carbolic acid and formaldehyde. Commonly called phenolic resin, Bakelite is a

Ink blotter booklet, 8-1/2" l, 1-1/2" w, wood-grained celluloid, black lettering, "Jennison Co., Engineers & Contractors, Fitchburg, Mass," 1917 calendar, 8" ruler markings, $30.

tough, thermoset plastic that can be cast or molded by heat and pressure.

Celluloid was the first commercially successful semi-synthetic plastic. Introduced as a denture-base material in 1870, it reigned supreme as the most versatile man-made plastic for 40 years.

References: Lillian Baker, *Twentieth Century Fashionable Plastic Jewelry*, Collector Books, 1992; Corinne Davidov and Ginny Redington Dawes, *Bakelite Jewelry Book*, Abbeville Press, 1988; Tony Grasso, *Bakelite Jewelry*, Chartwell, 1996; Bill Hanlon, *Plastic Toys*, Schiffer Publishing, 1993; Lyngerda Kelley and Nancy Schiffer, *Plastic Jewelry*, Schiffer Publishing, 1987, 1994 value update; Jan Lindenberger, *Collecting Plastics*, Schiffer Publishing, 1991; Lyndi Stewart McNulty, *Wallace-Homestead Price Guide to Plastic Collectibles*, Wallace-Homestead, 1987, 1992 value update; Holly Wahlberg, *Everyday Elegance: 1950s Plastic Design*, Schiffer Publishing, 1994; Gregory R. Zimmer and Alvin Daigle Jr., *Melmac Dinnerware*, L-W Book Sales, 1997.

Museum: National Plastic Museum, Leominster, MA.

Advisor: Julie P. Robinson.

Acrylic

Bedside Stand, 3-pc twisted acrylic rod base, round glass top............250.00

Beverage Pitcher, clear acrylic cylinder, designed by Neal Small, 1970 ....45.00

Bracelet, 3/4" bangle, green, opaque, orig tag "Genuine Lucite".........10.00

Brush and Comb, translucent pink set, nylon bristles, mkd "Dupont Lucite," orig box...........................15.00

Business-Card Holder, sea shells suspended in rect base, c1965.......6.00

Four-prong ornamental hair comb, genuine mottled tortoiseshell, all hand-carved fretwork, $85.

Buttons, pearlescent pink squares, metal loop, set of 8 on orig card 4.00
Clock
 Alarm, key wind, Black Forest works, octagonal translucent green case.............25.00
 Electric, chrome and Lucite, cylinder shaped, rotating disc that changes color, pink, yellow, purple and green reflect in face, c1970s 65.00
Compact, 4" sq translucent case, applied sunburst medallion, gold glitter acrylic, Roger & Gallet, mfg by Donmark Creations Co., 1946......150.00
Cufflinks, pr, Krementz, toggle findings, paperweight style, fishing fly suspended in Lucite.................35.00
Drafting Tools, Rohm & Haas Plexiglas, set of 2 rulers, 2 triangles and semicircle, c1940....................20.00
Dress Clips, green opaque Lucite, triangular, chevron design, rim set with rhinestones......................18.00
Etagere, 60" h, freestanding triangular shelf, clear acrylic with 4 mirror shelves, pointed finial 550.00
Hand Mirror, beveled acrylic handle and frame, U-shaped mirror, SS floral ornament, c1946......................55.00
Lamp, chrome cylinder base, 3" d solid Lucite ball top, flickering red, white and blue lights in base reflect through bubbles in acrylic globe, c1976......................................22.00
Napkin Ring, translucent Lucite, sq shape, rounded edges, circular center, c1960, price for 4-pc set....10.00
Paperweight
 2" x 1", rect cube, suspended purple rose 5.00
 3" cube, translucent Lucite, suspended JFK 50¢ pc, c1965 ....8.00
Pin
 Apple, pink Lucite, gold-plated stem and leaf, Sarah Coventry, c1970 ....20.00

Dragonfly, pearlescent green Lucite wings, enamel paint over pot metal, c1960 ....8.00
 Turtle, jelly belly, aqua Lucite center, pot metal, red painted eyes, c1950.................12.00
Purse
 Basketweave chrome, 8" x 4", clear Lucite bottom, black Lucite hinged to and handle, c1955 ....55.00
 Clutch, smoky gray Lucite, camera-case shape, hinge opening, c1950 ....45.00
 Vanity
  4-1/2" x 4-1/2", envelope-type front, white marbleized, Elgin American...........................100.00
  7" x 4" oval, compartmentalized lid, tortoise color, Wilardy Original 145.00
Ring, SS, sq emerald green Lucite jewel, c1960..85.00
Tumbler, 8 oz, clear, octagonal, chevron design, Art Deco revival, Norse Products, price for 4-pc set 25.00
Wall Shelf, 30" x 6", translucent neon pink, 1970s 25.00

Bakelite

Ashtray, 8" d, black and white 45.00
Bar Pin, dangling heart, bright red Catalin 150.00
Bracelet, bangle
 1/2" wide, carved leaf design, red Catalin....................................45.00
 3/4" wide, reverse-carved floral design, translucent amber......150.00
Buckle, 2-1/2" w, rect, carved flower on each end, dark blue.................20.00
Button, 1 large, 4 small, oval, 2 holes, translucent amber and brown swirl, price for 5-pc set......................12.00
Cake Server, green handle 12.00
Chess Set, butterscotch and marbleized brown......................................400.00
Clock, 12" h, Western Electric, Gothic shape, dark brown....................65.00
Crib Toy, amber, green and orange opaque Catalin, shape of female doll, 17 separate pcs strung together................125.00
Corn-Cob Holder, diamond shape, 2 prongs, red or green, price for pr 15.00
Dominoes 65.00
Dress Clip, triangular, chevron grooves, green, price for pr 65.00
Hors-d'oeuvre Pick Set, sq base in shape of die, 6 dice-topped picks 110.00
Manicure Box, Cleopatra, mfg by GE, black and red Art Deco..........165.00
Napkin Ring, figural
 Animal shape, red, green or

butterscotch 45.00
 Trylon and Perisphere, orange, green, red and yellow, price for pr......................................75.00
Pie Crimper, marbleized butterscotch handle 4.00
Pin, figural, cat, yellow Catalin, chrome 95.00
Poker Chips, black, maroon, butterscotch, maroon holder...........130.00
Rattle, bar-bell shape, 5 rings, red, green and butterscotch......................90.00
Ring
 Dome top, floral carving, butterscotch 75.00
 Square, star-burst carving, brown.......................................65.00
Ring Box
 Clam-shell style, streamlined-modern grooves, orange and butterscotch swirl 85.00
 Semicircular, hinged lift top, sq base, mottled green and yellow.........75.00
Salt and Pepper Shakers, pr
 Figural brown bird-shaped holder, amber shakers 120.00
 Gear shape, chrome lids, marbleized caramel, 2" h..........................85.00
Washington Monument souvenir, obelisk shape, cream color 65.00
Serving Tray, oval dark blue with inlaid strips of chrome, Art Deco style........................350.00
Shaving Brush and Stand, deep red, Catalin, c1940 ....35.00
Stationery Box, 7" x 8", molded brown, Art Deco winged horse design, American Stationery Co., 1937 ....75.00
Telephone, Stromberg Carlson, cradle-style, black 50.00
Toothpick Holder, dachshund, green 95.00
Utensil set, knife, fork, spoon, marbleized red and yellow handles....16.00
Yo-Yo, mottled green, mkd "Regal PDC" 30.00

Celluloid

Animal
 Cow, 6", purple, red rhinestone eyes, mkd "Made in Occupied Japan".................22.00
 Dog, 3", black Scottie, mkd "Made in USA" 20.00
 Horse, 7" l, cream color, brown highlights, hp eyes, intertwined VCO mark 45.00
Bar Pin, 2-3/4" l, ivory grained, orange and brown layered pearlesence, hp rose motif 12.00
Bookmark, 4-1/2" l, cream-colored diecut celluloid, poinsettia motif, Psalm 22, printed by Meek Co.15.00

Bracelet, bangle, translucent amber celluloid, double row of green rhinestones 25.00

Collar and Cuff set, Champion brand 25.00

Collar Box, 6" x 6", olive color, emb celluloid with floral motif, picture of beautiful woman on top 45.00

Doll, 5" h, Kewpie type, movable arms, molded clothing and cap, mkd "Made in Japan"..................................22.00

Dresser Set, comb, brush, mirror, tray, powder, box and hair receiver, mkd "Ivory Pyralin," price for 6-pc set......................65.00

Dresser Tray, 8" oval, imitation tortoiseshell rim, glass and lace center 35.00

Fan, 6" w, ivory color, hp floral motif, blue satin ribbon 18.00

Hair Comb, 6" l, pale amber, blue rhinestones, painted blue bird motif 55.00

Ink Blotter Booklet, 8-1/2" l, 1-1/2" w, wood-grained celluloid, black lettering, "Jennison Co., Engineers & Contractors, Fitchburg, Mass," 1917 calendar, 8" ruler markings......30.00

Kewpie, 2-1/4" h, #43660, hp features, blue wings................................40.00

Letter Opener, 8-1/4" l, ivory-grained cream celluloid, black lettering "Smith & Nichols, 141 Milk St., Boston, WAX"..........................25.00

Match Safe, 2-1/4" x 1-1/2", color photo scenes from Atlantic City, NJ...18.00

Necktie Box, 12-1/2" x 3-3/4", reverse-painted Art Nouveau design, cream, brown and coral 48.00

Picture Frame, 8" x 10", oval, ivory-grained celluloid, easel back ...18.00

Pinback Button, 1-1/4" d, dangling 1" celluloid camel, Shriner's logo......55.00

Pocket Mirror, 2-1/2" oval, souvenir of Niagara Falls, printed colored drawing of Falls 18.00

Purse, 4-1/4" d, clam-shell-type, amber colored celluloid, leather strap..............................45.00

Rattle 4" l, blue and white, egg shape,

Easter toy, duck, chick, and big chick, celluloid, $65.

Pocket mirrors, Mennen Talc, celluloid, $40 each.

white handle.............................18.00
4-3/4" l, figural, little girl playing lute, pink 45.00

Toy 2-1/2" d, roly poly, realistic chicken, weighted base..........................35.00
5" h, duck in police uniform, cream and teal blue, movable legs, VCO, USA..............................75.00

Vase, 8" h, conical, weighted base, translucent amber and cream pearlesence............................12.00

Horn

Dressing Comb, 7-1/2" l, raw horn 10.00

Fish Knife, gold-plated blades, stained horn handles with matching golden hue, price for set of 6.............150.00

Letter Opener, 8" l, translucent amber-colored clarified horn, antler handle..............................8.00

Ring, raw horn, sawed from tip of cattle horn, plain band........................5.00

Serving Spoon, amber clarified horn............................15.00

Tumbler, 4 oz, cut from raw horn, clarified translucent base, hp floral motif..........................12.00

TV Lamp, 18" l, fish carved from single horn, light in back, horn fins and tail, gray 45.00

Tortoiseshell

Brooch, 1-1/4" w, shamrock, brad-fastened bindings............30.00

Dressing Comb, 6-3/4" l, even teeth, mottled..................40.00

Hair Comb, ornamental 5 prong, 6" l, blond, carved fan shape 80.00
8 prong, simple curves, mottled, no carving or ornamentation 35.00

Sweater Pin, 1-1/2" l, cursive initial "L" 15.00

Playing Cards

Collecting Hints: Always purchase complete decks in very good condi-

tion. Know the exact number of cards needed for a full deck—an American straight deck has 52 cards and usually a joker; pinochle requires 48 cards; tarot decks use 78. In addition to decks, collectors seek very early uncut sheets and single cards.

Many collectors focus on topics, for instance, politics, trains, World's Fairs, animals, airlines or advertising. Most collectors of travel-souvenir cards prefer a photographic scene on the face. The most valuable playing card decks are unusual either in respect to publisher, size, shape or subject. Prices remain modest for decks of cards from the late 19th and 20th centuries.

History: Playing cards were first used in China in the 12th century. By 1400, playing cards were in use throughout Europe. French cards are known specifically for their ornate designs. The first American cards were published by Jazaniah Ford, Milton, MA, in the late 1700s. United States innovations include upper-corner indexes, classic joker, standard size and slick finish for shuffling ease. Bicycle Brand was introduced in 1885 by the U.S. Playing Card Co., of Cincinnati.

Card designs have been drawn or printed in every conceivable size and on a variety of surfaces. Miniature playing cards appealed to children. Novelty decks came in round, crooked and die-cut shapes. Numerous card games, beside those using the standard four-suit deck, were created for adults and children.

References: Phil Bollhagen (comp.), *Great Book of Railroad Playing Cards*, published by author, 1991; Everett Grist, *Advertising Playing Cards*, Collector Books, 1992.

Collectors' Clubs: American Antique Deck Collectors Club, 204 Gorham Ave., Hamden, CT 06514; American Game Collectors Association, PO Box 44, Dresher Pa, 19205; Chicago Playing Card Collectors, Inc., 1559 West Platt Blvd., Chicago, IL 60626; 52 Plus Joker, 204 Gorham Ave., Hamden, CT 06514; International Playing Card Society, 3570 Delaware Common, Indianapolis, IN 46220; Playing Card Collec-

Souvenir, Canada, published by Canadian Pacific Railroad News Service, Consolidated Lithographing & Mfg. Co., Montreal, Canada, $35.

tors Association, 337 Avelon St. #4, Roundlake, IL 60073.

Museum: Playing Card Museum, Cincinnati Art Museum, Cincinnati, OH.

Notes: The following list is organized by both topic and country. Although concentrating heavily on cards by American manufacturers, some foreign-made examples are included.

Country

Austria

Classic, Piatnik,
1955, 53 cards 25.00
La Provence, Piatnik, 1960,
53 cards 28.00
Belgium, Joyeaux De Beligique
"Sieradan Van Belgie," Royal Belgian coat of arms, 54 cards 27.50
England
Coronation King Edward VIII,
1902, picture on back, 53 cards,
orig box 95.00
Prince of Wales National
Relief Fund, World War I,
De La Rue, 1914, MIB..............40.00
France, The Parlou Sibyl, Grimaud,
1968, 3" x 4-1/2" 52 cards 25.00
Italy, World Bridge, Modiano, 1953,
54 cards....................................35.00
Oriental, Fujitsu, Nintendo, Japan, 1973,
2-1/2" x 3-15/16", orig box 35.00
United States
A Doughtery Triplicate Cards, #18,
1876, 53 cards, MIB.................50.00
Maxfield Parish, limited edition of
1,000 ....40.00
Political, Politcards Corp.,
1971, caricatures of politicians,
54 cards, MIB 35.00

Topic

Advertising
American Red Cross,
1944, unused 20.00
GE Refrigerators 75.00
Heileman's Old

Style Lager Beer 35.00
Hard a Port Cut Plug, buxom
Victorian women, partial
deck of 35 cards....................750.00
Prize Metal Sacks,
Cincinnati, OH.........................15.00
Rocky Mountain Motor Co.,
52 cards, orig box 40.00
Fire Department, One of the Finest, uniformed police inspectors, captains and chiefs of fire departments in the Northeastern states, color litho, c1887, complete set 250.00
Games and Fortune Telling
Games of Poems,
orig box, 1898 ....40.00
H-Bar-O, 32 cards,
instructions..............................20.00
National Club Tourists 1881,
handwritten fortunes 45.00
Nile Fortune Telling Cards, 1897-
1904 ....30.00
Souvenir
Apollo VIII, double deck, lift-off with red borders on one, blue border on other, plastic case 20.00
Black Hills, Coolidge 35.00
Movie Souvenir Card Co., Cincinnati, half-tone portraits of motion picture stars, back design of multicolored reproduction of "The Chariot Race" painting, M.J. Moriarty, 1916, price for pr.............................500.00
Tarot
The New Tarot, Hurley & Horle, 2nd ed, 1974, 2-1/2" x 3-1/2", 78 cards, MIB..........................25.00
Uncut Sheet, 18" x 25", B P Grimaud, c1890, 38 cards 85.00
Transportation
Alaska, Yukon Railroad..........100.00
C&O Railroad, double deck,
unopened 45.00
Frisco Railroad, single deck.....25.00
Furness Lines Steamship,
2 decks, day and night scenes,
boxed, late 1930 ....40.00
Long Island Railroad, The Route of the Dashing Commuter, gold on dark blue background, suede-like box, 52 cards, 1940-50 ....35.00
N&W Railroad, double deck,
unopened45.00
New York Central System, 2 sealed decks, Morning along the Hudson and "Super-Van" pictured on back, suede-like box, 1960s 30.00
Pennsylvania Railroad,
double deck..............................85.00
U.S. and Axis Warplanes, 52 cards, instruction card, orig red, white and blue box, early 1940s 40.00
World's Fairs and Expositions
1901 Buffalo, Pan American, color

design, orig box 40.00
1933 Chicago, Century
of Progress, 52 cards, Sky Ride scene, orig box 35.00
1964, New York World's Fair, Unisphere design, unused 10.00

Pocket Knives

Collecting Hints: The pocket knife collector has to compete with those who collect in other categories. The pocket knife with a celluloid handle and advertising underneath dates back to the 1880s. Celluloid-handled knives are considered much more desirable than the plastic-handled models. Collectors also tend to shy away from purely souvenir-related knives.

History: Pocket knife collectors fall into two main types: 1) those who concentrate on the utilitarian and functional knives from firms such as Alcas, Case, Colonial, Ka-Bar, Queen, Remington, Schrade and Winchester; and 2) those interested in advertising, character and other knives, which, while meant to be used, were sold with a secondary function in mind. These knives were made by companies such as Aerial Cutlery Co., Canton Cutlery Co., Golden Rule Cutlery Co., Imperial Knife Co., and Novelty Cutlery Co.

The larger manufacturing firms also made advertising, character and figural knives. Some knives were giveaways or sold for a small premium, but most were sold in general stores and souvenir shops.

References: Jerry and Elaine Heuring, *Keen Kutter Collectibles*, 2nd Edition, Collector Books, 1990, 1993 value update; Jacob N. Jarrett, *Price Guide to Pocket Knives*, L-W Book Sales, 1993, 1995 value update; Bernard Levine, *Levine's Guide to Knives and Their Values*, 3rd Edition, DBI Books, 1993; ——, *Pocket Knives*, Apple Press, 1993; *Price Guide to Keen Kutter Tools*, L-W Book Sales, n.d., 1993-94 value update; C. Houston Price, *Official Price Guide to Collector Knives*, 10th Edition, House of Collectibles, 1991; Jim Sargent, *Sargent's American Premium Guide to Knives and Razors* 4th Edition, Books Americana, 1995; Roy Ritchie and Ron

Advertising, Old Reading Beer, PA, 1 blade, $15.

Stewart, *Standard Knife Collector's Guide*, 2nd Edition, Collector Books, 1993, 1995 value update; J. Bruce Voyles, *American Blade Collectors Association Price Guide to Antique Knives*, Krause Publications, 1995.

Periodicals: *Blade*, 700 E. State St., Iola, WI 54990; *Edges*, P.O. Box 22007, Chattanooga, TN 37422; *Knife World*, P.O. Box 3395, Knoxville, TN 37927.

Collectors' Clubs: American Blade Collectors, P.O. Box 22007, Chattanooga, TN 37422; Canadian Knife Collectors Club, 3141 Jessuca Ct., Mississauga, ON L5C 1X7 Canada; Ka-Bar Knife Collectors Club, P.O. Box 406, Olean, NY 14760; National Knife Collectors Association, P.O. Box 21070, Chattanooga, TN 37421.

Museum: National Knife Museum, Chattanooga, TN.

Egyptian mummy case, blue, rust, green, white, enamel dec, blade and scissors, 2-1/2" l closed, $25.

Reproduction Alert: Advertising knives, especially those bearing Coca-Cola advertising, have been heavily reproduced.

Note: See *Warman's Antiques and Collectibles Price Guide* for a list of knife prices for major manufacturers.

Advertising
  Anheuser-Busch, red side panels, Stanhope viewer, photo of Busch, knife and corkscrew 145.00
  Cudahy Packing Co., grading and sausage knife, pearl handle 35.00
  Omega Watches, silver watch inlay 35.00
  Purina, 3 blades 20.00
  St. Pauli Girl Beer, nickel plated 35.00
  Westinghouse Coolers, emb handle 32.00
Character
  Buffalo Bill, 3-3/8" l, steel blade, plastic case, c1950 .... 15.00
  Davy Crockett, single blade, hatchet bottle opener, Walt Disney 40.00
  Lone Ranger, 3" l, black grip, white image of Lone Ranger and Silver, knife blade and bottle opener ... 40.00
  Popeye, 3" l, red celluloid sides, King Features Syndicate 90.00
  Tom Mix and Tony, 3" l, b&w celluloid, c1930 .... 30.00
Commemorative, Our Martyred Presidents, Golden Rule Cutlery Co. 165.00
Display, Providence Cutlery Co., 1982 World's Fair, red and white handles, 12 knives on card with key chains 25.00
Figural
  Baseball Bat, celluloid, Sportsman's Price, Fairmont Cutlery 25.00
  Lady's Leg, slim, bone-colored handle, Buck Cutlery 65.00
Masonic 45.00
Scout, 1" l, stag handles, A.E. Wadsworth 75.00
Swiss Army Knife, Victorinox, mkd "Champion" 25.00

Police Collectibles

Collecting Hints: Police-related items are primarily collected by people employed in law enforcement areas. Collectors often base their collection on badges or material from a specific locality. As a result, prices are regionalized, e.g., a California collector is more interested in California material than items from another state.

Condition is critical. Badges were worn everyday so some deterioration is to be expected. The popularity of televised police shows has attracted many non-law enforcement people to the field of police collectibles.

History: The first American colonists appointed one of their own to maintain and enforce the laws of the land. The local sheriff held an important social and political position. The mid-19th century witnessed the development of two important trends: the growth of the professional police force in cities and the romanticizing of the Western lawman. Arthur Conan Doyle's Sherlock Holmes novels popularized police methods. Magazines, such as the *Police Gazette*, kept the public's attention focused on the sensationalism of police work.

The Gangster era of the 1920s and 1930s and the arrival of the "G-Men," glamorized by Hollywood movies, kept police work in the limelight. Television capitalized on the public enthusiasm for police drama with shows such as "Dragnet," "The Untouchables," "Starsky and Hutch," "Hill Street Blues," "Homicide," "Law & Order" and "NYPD Blue."

References: Monty McCord, *Police Cars*, Krause Publications, 1991; Don Stewart, *Collectors Guide: Handcuffs & Restraints*, Key Collectors International, 1993; —, *Collectors Guide: The Yale & Towne Mfg. Co.*, Key Collectors International, 1982.

Periodical: *Police Collectors News*, RR1 Box 14, Baldwin, WI 54002.

Museums: American Police Center & Museum, Chicago, IL; American Police Hall of Fame & Museum, Miami, FL; New York City Police Academy Museum, New York, NY; Suffolk County Police Dept. Museum, Yaphank, NY.

Reproduction Alert: Police badges.

Badge
  Boston Police, city skyline, nickel plated, c1880 .... 100.00
  Cambria County, Special Deputy Sheriff, shield shape 75.00
  Fire Police, silver luster metal, center triangle design, PA Fire Police Association, 1949 .... 34.00

Badge, Railway Police, DL&W Railroad, nickel-plated brass, c1920, $85.

Forest Park, IL,
Chief of Police 35.00
General Electric Patrolman, silver
luster metal, GE trademark initials,
c1930 ....35.00
Lake Ozark MO,
Police Chief 85.00
Buckle, City of New York Police Dept.,
c1900......................................75.00
Cabinet Card, Westerly,
RI, full-uniform policeman,
town name and #3 ....50.00
Emblem, Lieutenant, braided, gold and
silver thread, c1800 ....35.00
Handcuffs, Pratt's
Combination, c1932...............750.00
Helmet, New York City Police Dept, riot
and patrol type, leather..........225.00
Magazine
The Arizona Sheriff,
Dec. 1971, Sheriff Bud Yancey
pictured on front 6.00
The Police Chief, April 1965.......5.00
Night Stick, wood...........................10.00
Patch
Maricopa County Deputy Sheriff,
star center 2.00
San Francisco Police, eagle.......5.00
Pocket Watch, silver, engraved
blade design, Boston Police,
Matthew Mullen, 16th Division,
Waltham, 1880s....................550.00
Sheet Music, *Police Parade March,*
c1917.......................................25.00
Suspenders, mkd "Police," engraved po-
lice club on slides 35.00
Toy
2-1/2" x 4" x 2-1/2", cast-iron
policeman on motorcycle, mkd
"Champion," attached sidecar, orig
white rubber wheels, Champion

Hardware Co., 1930-36..........300.00
3-3/4" l, hard plastic,
motorcycle policeman, yellow
and blue wheels, red 3D policeman,
Renwal, 1950s 25.00
Uniform, pants, vest and coat, wool,
blue, 9 brass buttons, made by Fred
Batchelder Co., Boston 195.00
Wanted Poster, issued by Division of Investigation, U.S. Dept of Justice,
March 12, 1934, for John Dillinger,
mug shots, fingerprints, facsimile signature, physical description, detailed
criminal record, 8" sq.............250.00

Political and Campaign Items

Collecting Hints: Items priced below $100 sell frequently enough to establish firm prices. Items above that price fluctuate according to supply and demand. Many individuals now recognize the value of acquiring political items and holding them for future sale. As a result, modern material has a relatively low market value.

Knowledgeable collectors also keep in touch with Presidential libraries to find out what type of souvenir items they are offering for sale. This information is helpful in determining which items on the market originated at the time of actual campaigns and these are the ones collectors should concentrate on acquiring.

The pioneering work on the identification of political materials has been done by Theodore L. Hake, whose books are listed below. Two books have greatly assisted in the identification and cataloging of campaign materials, especially those from earlier periods: Herbert R. Collins's *Threads of History* and Edmund B. Sullivan's *American Political Badges and Medalets 1789-1892.*

History: Since 1800, the American presidency always has been a contest between two or more candidates. Initially, souvenirs were issued to celebrate victories. Items issued during a campaign to show support for a candidate were actively distributed in the William Henry Harrison election of 1840.

There is a wide variety of campaign items—buttons, bandannas, tokens, pins, etc. The only limiting factor has been the promoter's imagination.

The advent of television campaigning has reduced the quantity of individual items and modern campaigns do not seem to have the variety of materials that were issued earlier.

Modern collectors should be aware of Kennedy material. Much has been reproduced and many items were issued after his death.

References: Herbert Collins, *Threads of History,* Smithsonian Institution Press, 1979; Stan Gores, *Presidential and Campaign Memorabilia with Prices,* 2nd Edition, Wallace-Homestead, 1988; Theodore L. Hake, *Encyclopedia of Political Buttons, United States, 1896-1972,* Americana & Collectibles Press, 1985; ——, *Political Buttons, Book II, 1920-1976,* Americana & Collectibles Press, 1977; ——, *Political Buttons, Book III, 1789-1916,* Americana & Collectibles Press, 1978 (note: Hake issued a revised set of prices for his three books in 1991); ——, *Hake's Guide to Presidential Campaign Collectibles,* Wallace-Homestead, 1992; Edward Krohn, *National Political Convention Tickets and Other Convention Ephemera,* David G. Phillips Publishing Co., Inc. (P.O. Box 611388, No. Miami, FL 33161), 1996; Keith Melder, *Hail to the Candidate,* Smithsonian Institution Press, 1992; James W. Milgram, *Presidential Campaign Illustrated Envelopes and Letter Paper 1840-1972,* David G. Phillips Publishing Co., Inc. (P.O. Box 611388, No. Miami, FL 33161), 1996; Edmund B. Sullivan, *American Political Badges and Medalets, 1789-1892,* Quarterman Publications, 1981; ——, *Collecting Political Americana,* Christopher Publishing House, 1991.

Periodicals: *Autograph Times,* 2303 N. 44th St., #225, Phoenix, AZ 85008; *Political Bandwagon,* P.O. Box 348, Leola, PA 17540; *Political Collector Newspaper,* P.O. Box 5171, York, PA 17405.

Collectors' Clubs: American Political Items Collectors, P.O. Box 340339, San Antonio, TX 78234; Ford Political Items Collectors, 18222 Flower Hill Way #299, Gaithersburg, MD 20879; Indiana Political Collectors Club, P.O. Box 11141, Indianapolis, IN 46201; NIXCO, Nixon Collectors Organization, 975

Maunawili Cr, Kailua, HI 96734; *Rail Splitter* (Abraham Lincoln), Box 275, New York, NY 10044; Third Party Hopefuls, 503 Kings Canyon Blvd, Galesburg, IL 61401.

Museums: Museum of American Political Life, Hartford, CT; Smithsonian Institution, Washington, DC; Western Reserve Historical Society, Cleveland, OH.

Advisor: Ted Hake.

Abraham Lincoln, 1860, 1864

Carte de Visite, 2-1/2" x 4", T.R. Burhman, Boston, photographer, untrimmed, c1864 .... 50.00

Game, Lincoln's Log Cabin Games, 11-1/2" x 11/1/2" black, white and red box, by W.H. Davidheiser, 1924, 11" x 11" x 1/2" tin litho board, illus of young boy reading by fireplace, different bird in each corner, center with circular design of letters and numbers plus metal spinner, cardboard sheet with full-color bird illus, only top and bottom of box remain 60.00

Print, 2-1/2" x 4", President Lincoln and Mary, sepia 35.00

Benjamin Harrison, 1888, 1892

Advertising Card, 2-3/4" x 3" thin paper, adv *Demorest's Family Magazine*, b&w photo illus of Harrison on front, reverse is gift solicitation of "The Only Picture Ever Painted by a President's Wife for the Public," 1888 .... 20.00

Ticket, 3" x 8" b&w ticket for election day, Tuesday, Nov. 6, 1888, Harrison/Morton, from Maryland 45.00

Woodrow Wilson, 1912, 1916

Medal

1-1/2" octagon-shaped bronze medal attached to orange and black striped 1-1/2" x 4" fabric ribbon, reads "Inauguration March 4, '13/Personal Escort/Princeton Univ" 125.00

2-3/4" d, bronze, slight raised image of Wilson on 1 side, 3 flowing garbed women on the reverse surveying war-ravaged background with Cathedral of Notre Dame in very distant horizon, French inscription at bottom, 1919 .... 30.00

Warren G. Harding, 1920

Pinback Button, Harding and Coolidge, red, white and blue litho 10.00

Post Card, brown-tone photo top, encouragement to elect Harding senator in Ohio, light soil, unused, 1915 .... 30.00

Poster, 16" x 21", Harding/Coolidge, paper, sepia portraits, 1920 ..... 65.00

Buttons: Coolidge and Dawes, red, white, and blue, 3/4" d, $12; Harding and Coolidge, white and blue, 5/8" d, $10.

Herbert Hoover, 1928, 1932

Campaign Fabric, 14" x 18", tan chiffon, sepia portrait, bright red, white and blue border, brown facsimile signature, 1928 .... 40.00

Pencil, 8" h, Hoover for President 1928, yellow, Hoover's head as red 3D top, unsharpened 20.00

Franklin D Roosevelt, 1932, 1936, 1940, 1944

Autograph

6" x 7" white-paper typed note of thanks, letterhead reads "Mrs. Franklin D. Roosevelt," bold blue ink Eleanor Roosevelt signature 125.00

8" x 10-1/2" typed letter to former governor of NY thanking him, large bold signature, 1930 .... 300.00

Bust, 4" x 8" x 8", Remember Pearl Harbor, dark brown luster, solid plaster, wearing V emblem on label, complete Pledge of Allegiance text incised on base above "Remember Pearl Harbor" slogan 100.00

Inaugural Puzzle, 3/4" x 8" x 10", red, white, blue and black box inscribed "Souvenir 1933/Over 200 Pieces," 11" x 15" puzzle with interlocking full-color pieces, rounded corners, under caption "Prosperity Ahead," Hoover shows FDR the presidential chair, image of "The Forgotten Man" in foreground, 1 replaced pc 175.00

Newspaper, *Daily Mirror*, April 16, 1945, tabloid size, covers funeral, slightly browned with age 15.00

Pillow Cover, 16" x 18", front with black photo of FDR in wicker chair printed over light peach fabric, pale blue background tint and pink tint on carnation flower he wears, bright orange fabric back, navy blue piping border with bright yellow stitching 40.00

Pinback Button, 3-1/2" d, red, white and blue, b&w photo, attached to 2" x 5" paper on fabric ribbon, 1936 ... 85.00

Sheet Music, 9" x 12", red, white and blue cov, 5" x 7" blue-tone portrait of FDR, 4 pgs, inside front cover has facsimile typed letter dated Jan. 27,

1933, from Roosevelt to music's author saying FDR will consider song "my official march" 15.00

Alfred Landon, 1936

Arm Band, 3-1/4" x 8" l, yellow and brown felt, elastic attachment band, Landon/Knox 20.00

Poster, 11" x 16", Landon for President, paper, brown and white, 1936 . 25.00

Wendell Willkie, 1940

Banner, 9" x 11-1/2", God Bless America/Wendell Willkie, fabric, red, white and blue, 1940 .... 25.00

Matches, 2" x 2-1/4", red, white and blue, blue-tone photo of Willkie on cover with slogan "For President Wendell Willkie," blue matches are held individually by red and white paper covers that have "Pull Quickly" printed on them, back cover reads "Pull for Willkie," 1940 .... 15.00

Pinback Button, Willkie Square Deal, red, white and blue litho 15.00

Sticker, 3-1/2" x 6", diecut foil, silver, blue and red, inscribed "Willkie/The Hope of America" 10.00

Harry S. Truman, 1948

Certificate, 9-1/2" x 11", green, black and white, Truman insert at top, text reads "President Harry S. Truman Forest in Israel Planted by the Mizrachi Women's Organization, In Honor of Mrs. Leah Sklar, Planted by Leah Katz Chamisho Osor B'Shevet/February 1950," framed 60.00

Photographer's Credentials, 3" x 6-1/2" b&w fabric permit for inauguration parade route, Jan. 20, 1949, hand-lettered name, 3" x 5" black on yellow card to permit photographer to stand, 3" x 5" yellow-colored police-pass card, formerly pasted in scrapbook, price for 3-pc set 30.00

Pinback Button, 3-1/2" d, red, white, blue and gold, b&w photo center, 1948 .... 125.00

Dwight Eisenhower, 1952, 1956

Bandanna, 28" sq, red, white and blue silk-like material, "I Like Ike," small hole 20.00

Bobbing Head Figure, 6" h, composition, full color, brown hat, blue coat, gray vest, red tie, gray trousers, black shoes, c1956, Japan 100.00

Bumper Sticker, 4" x 7-1/2", California Ike-Dick, black on orange, 1956 .... 10.00

Pinback Button

1-3/4" d, blue and white, attached blue and white fabric 1-1/2" x 5" ribbon, Vote Ike 30.00

3-1/2" d, red, white and blue, b&w center photo

Eisenhower, Man
of the Hour 35.00
Eisenhower/Nixon, 1952 ......40.00
Ike/Nixon 25.00
Ribbon, 1-1/4" x 3-1/2", We Like Ike!,
Austrian woven silk, black, white and
yellow, image of Ike at top, outline of
NY state at bottom 75.00

Richard Nixon, 1960, 1968, 1972

Bracelet, 2-1/2" d plastic simulated
tortoiseshell, raised blue "Nixon" on
blue plate, c1972 ....15.00
Card, 4-1/2" x 6", full color, VP Nixon
Leaves Washington, black with vice
presidential seal, facsimile signature
and message from Nixon after 1960
election defeat 20.00
Fan, 9" x 12" h including wood handle,
cardboard, blue-tone photo, white
ground, blue design trim, Nixon and
NJ coattail, 1972 ....30.00
Figure, 4" h, 5" l, caricature, elephant
with Nixon head, black slicked hair,
brown eyebrows, blue eyes, pink
lips, glowing white teeth, gray elephant body, blue painted blanket with
large "R" and white "Nixon", 1" hollow
vinyl ball with world's continents in
black sitting on elephant's back, right
front leg is on orange stand with
black letters "GOP," c1972 ......25.00
Inaugural Book, 9" x 12", 100 pgs, The
Spirit of '76, 1st ed, b&w and color
photos, dj, 1973 ....30.00
Jugate Button, 2-1/4" d, Nixon
and Agnew inauguration, red,
white and blue, b&w photos, 2" x 5"
purple fabric ribbon, gold type, Jan.
20, 1969.................................15.00
Pennant, 11" x 29" felt, full color, 6" d paper portrait at left-hand edge ...15.00
Pen Set, pair of 5" l bright gold brushed
metal ball-point pens, black facsimile
signature of Richard and Pat, c1968,
ink dried out 25.00
Photograph, 11" x 14", full color, high
gloss, white facsimile signature at
bottom, no inscription 10.00
Pinback Button
2" d, inauguration, red and white,
blue-tone center photo, 2" x 6" l
yellow fabric ribbon, blue type
reads "Lancaster County,
Pennsylvania"...........................25.00
2-1/2" x 3-1/4", red, white and
blue litho, b&w photos of Nixon
and Lodge 20.00
3-1/2" d, red, white and blue,
b&w center photo 25.00
Playing Cards, 3/4" x 4" x 5" felt-covered
cardboard card-deck holder, 2
decks, Richard Nixon/Air Force One,
light wear on slipcase, 1 deck
unopened...............................100.00

Sign, 12" x 18", metal, inaugural,
red, white and blue "No
Parking," 1969 ....100.00

John F. Kennedy, 1960

Ashtray, 5-1/2" d, ceramic, full-color
painted center portrait, gold accent
rim, c1961..............................25.00
Drinking Glass, 5" h, clear glass,
blue inscription "Vote you Win
in 1960 with Jack Kennedy/Lyndon
Johnson"..................................70.00
Flicker Badge, 3" d, blue-tone
flicker encased in plastic oval, m
etal bar pin..............................70.00
Hat, 3-1/2" h, 14" d rim, plastic, red,
white and blue paper label, "Win with
Kennedy," 4 b&w photos of Kennedy,
6" d b&w paper photo of Kennedy
taped on top 40.00
Jugate Button, 3-1/2" d, red, white and
blue, b&w photo of Kennedy and
Johnson at center....................40.00
Medal, 1" d silver finish,
raised image, Inaugural Ball
Jan. 20, 1961, orig cotton-lined blue
cardboard box 90.00
Pennant, 6-1/2" x 18", red felt, white type
"John F. Kennedy Inauguration," full-
color 5" d paper photo at left, 2 pairs
of 4" long blue felt streamers...25.00
Pinback Button
1-3/4" d, red, white and blue, b&w
photo, attached to 2" x 6-1/4" purple
fabric ribbon, white type 20.00
3-1/2" d, Let's Back Jack,
red, white and blue litho,
white background.....................40.00
Plate, 9" d, full-color photo
illus of JFK and Jackie,
gold accent rim, c1961 ....20.00

**Booklet, Al Smith, National Life Maga-
zine, Vol 1, No 1, 1928, 45 pgs, 8-3/8" x
10-1/2", $20.**

Poster
13" x 18", red, white and blue,
large b&w photo center, "Kennedy for
President" 65.00
16" x 20", official inauguration photo
by Fabian Bachrach, transformed
into memorial poster, full-color heavy
paper, "Ask Not" quote on top left
center, facsimile signature on bottom
right, dates all in white 20.00
Salt and Pepper, 2" h, 2-1/2" d, full-color
photo illus of JFK on one, Jackie on
other, inscriptions read "President
John F. Kennedy," and "Mrs. John F.
Kennedy," orig cork, c1961 .....30.00
Sheet Music, 9" x 12", The
New Frontier, 5" x 7" b&w Fabian
Bachrach photo of Kennedy on
front cover, facsimile signature on
bottom right, red, white and blue flag,
capitol dome on cover 25.00
Trivet, 6" h, 4-1/4" d, ceramic, full-color
painted center and gold painted ac-
cents, "President and Mrs. John F.
Kennedy," c1961 ....30.00

Lyndon Johnson, 1964

Clock, 10" d, red, white and blue metal
block, b&w photo illus of all presidents up to and including Johnson,
5-1/2" d clear plastic dome, blue
background White House dial, white
plastic hands, gold-colored metal
second hand...........................30.00
Hat, 4" x 11", plastic camp
style, red, white and blue
stripes, b&w illus of Johnson on right,
"LBJ for the USA" 10.00
Inaugural Program, 8-1/2" x 11",
48 pgs, white lined paper covered
booklet, gold presidential seal,
Jan. 20, 1965, full-color and
b&w photos and text...............10.00
Jugate Button, 3-1/2" d, red, white and
blue, b&w center photos of Johnson
and Humphrey........................35.00
Pen, give-away, gold presidential
logo, facsimile signature on black
plastic, gold metal top and clip, felt-
tipped pen frayed 15.00
Poster, 14" x 22", black, white and
brown, b&w photos of Johnson,
Humphrey and Robert F. Kennedy
for Senator 60.00

Barry Goldwater, 1964

Pinback Button
4" d, red, white and blue, blue-tone
center photo...........................25.00
6" d, Vote Goldwater in '64, red,
gold and black easel back,
center b&w photo....................20.00
Poster, 13" x 22", red, white and blue,
off-white cardboard, "Goldwater
Victory Rally, Madison Square
Garden," Oct. 26, 1964 ....15.00

Hubert H Humphrey, 1968

Bank, 1-1/2" x 4-1/2" x 4", raised "Humphrey Muskie '68," cast iron, figural, donkey, 1968 ....30.00

Cigar, 4-1/2" x 8" red, white and blue box, flip-open paper on inside with b&w candidate's photo, 25 individually wrapped bubble gum cigars 40.00

Poster, 11" x 14", black paper, b&w photo at top, red and blue type at bottom......................................10.00

Gerald R. Ford, 1976

First Day Cover, autographed 55.00

Pinback Button, For President 1976 Ford, black and white, bright red, white and blue rim 10.00

Jimmy Carter, 1976

Bandanna, 28" sq, Carter-Mondale, white and green, 1980 ....25.00

Pinback Button, 4" d, Trust Me, full-color caricature illus of Carter, GRT Records release 25.00

Poster, 11" x 14" paper, b&w photo at left, green type, white ground, AFL-CIO, Nov. 2, 1976, election day 10.00

Program, U.S. *China Trade*, Kennedy Center, 6-1/2" x 10", 16-pg paper booklet, January 1979, lists performers, printed in Chinese and English..............................10.00

Ronald Reagan, 1980, 1984

Autograph, 8" x 10" vintage 1950s sepia matte-finish photo, inscribed "To Carol Sue, Best Wishes and Good Luck Always From Ronald Reagan" 200.00

Fan, Franklin D. Roosevelt, cardboard, head and shoulders litho portrait, Walter, artist, O.H.K., adv for Boy School, Washington, DC, on back, $35.

Christmas Card, 5-1/4" x 7-1/2", folded, full-color illus of Green Room, The White House, 1983, deckled edge, tissue insert, printed message......................30.00

Greeting Card, 5" x 7", musical, raised image of White House on cover, decked edge, message, facsimile signature, plays "Hail to the Chief"............................25.00

License Plate, Presidential Inauguration, red, white and blue aluminum plates, 1981, price for pr 32.00

Pinback Button, 3-1/2" d, red, white and blue, b&w center photo, Reagan for Governor 25.00

Ribbon Badge, 1-1/2" x 6-1/2", red, white and blue fabric ribbon, brass bar hanger, 1-3/4" d brass inaugural medal, raised image of Capitol dome, gold type, 1981 ....20.00

George Bush, 1980, 1984, 1988

Bumper Sticker, 3-1/2" x 9-1/2", Bush/Quayle '88, red, white and blue.....................................2.50

Cigarette Pack, Bush For President/Dukakis for President, red, white and blue packs, king-size filter cigarettes, unopened, price for pr 15.00

Golf Ball, white, full-color vice presidential seal, orig blue box with gold signature, Wilson.....................35.00

Inaugural Medal, 2-3/4" d, bronze, raised boxed medal, wooden display stand, 1989 ....30.00

Program, 8-1/2" x 11", Republican National Convention, New Orleans, Bush on cover, 97 pgs, 1988...15.00

Bill Clinton, 1992, 1996

Inaugural Program, 8-1/2" x 11", 24 pgs, glossy content pages, full-color photos 15.00

Jugate Button, 3-1/2" full-color button, gold ground, attached 2" x 8" long blue fabric ribbon, gold type, 2" h gold-colored metal saxophone, Inauguration Day, 1993 ....10.00

Postcards

Collecting Hints: Concentrate on one subject area, publisher or illustrator. Collect cards in mint condition, when possible.

The more common the holiday, the larger the city, the more popular the tourist attraction, the easier it will be to find postcards on the subject because of the millions of cards that were originally available. The smaller runs of "real" photo postcards are the most desirable of the scenic

cards. Photographic cards of families and individuals, unless they show occupations, unusual toys, dolls or teddy bears have little value. Stamps and cancellation marks may sometimes affect the value of cards. Consult a philatelic guide.

Postcards fall into two main categories: view cards and topics. View cards are easiest to sell in their local geographic region. European view cards, while very interesting, are difficult to sell in America. It must be stressed that age alone does not determine price. A birthday postcard from 1918 may sell for only 10 cents while a political campaign card from the 1950s may bring $10. The price of every collectible is governed by supply and demand.

Although cards from 1898 to 1918 are the most popular with collectors, the increasing costs of postcards from this era have turned attention to postcards from the 1920s, 1930s and 1940s. Art Deco cards from the 1920-1930 period are the most desirable. The 1940s "linens," so called because of their textured linenlike paper surface, are the most popular cards of that time period.

Cards from the 1950 to 1970 period are called "Chromes" because of their shiny surface.

History: The golden age of postcards dates from 1898 to 1918. Cards printed earlier are collected for their postal history. Postcards prior to 1898 are called "pioneer" cards.

European publishers, especially in England and Germany, produced the vast majority of cards during the golden age. The major postcard publishers are Raphael Tuck (England), Paul Finkenrath of Berlin (PFB-German) and Whitney, Detroit Publishing Co., and John Winsch (United States). However, many American publishers had their stock produced in Europe, hence, "Made in Bavaria" imprints. While some Tuck cards are high priced, many are still available in the "10 cent" boxes.

Styles changed rapidly and manufacturers responded to every need. The linen postcard, which gained popularity in the 1940s, was quickly replaced by the chrome cards of the post-1950 period.

References: Diane Allmen, *Official Price Guide Postcards*, House of Collectibles, 1990; Janet A. Banneck, *Antique Postcards of Rose O'Neill*, Greater Chicago Productions, 1992; Jody Blake and Jeannette Lasansky, *Rural Delivery: Real Photo Postcards from Central Pennsylvania*, Union County Historical Society (Union County Courthouse, Lewisburg, PA 17837), 1996; J.L. Mashburn, *Artist-Signed Postcard Price Guide*, Colonial House, 1993 (**Note**: all Mashburn books are available from Box 609, Enka, NC 28728); ——, *Black Americana Postcard Price Guide*, Colonial House, 1996; ——, *Fantasy Postcards with Price Guide*, Colonial House, 1996; ——, *Postcard Price Guide*, 3rd Edition, Colonial House, 1997; ——, *Super Rare Postcards of Harrison Fisher*, Colonial House, 1992; Frederic and Mary Megson, *American Advertising Postcards*, published by authors, 1985; ——, *American Exposition Postcards*, The Postcard Lovers, 1992; Susan Brown Nicholson, *Antique Postcard Sets and Series Price Guide*, Greater Chicago Productions, 1993; ——, *Encyclopedia of Antique Postcards*, Wallace-Homestead, 1994; *Postcard Collector Annual*, 6th Edition, Antique Trader Books, 1996; Cynthia Rubin and Morgan Williams, *Larger Than Life; The American Tall-Tale Postcard*, Abbeville Press, 1990; Nouhad A. Saleh, *Guide to Artist's Signatures and Monograms on Postcards*, Minerva Press, 1993; Robert Ward, *Investment Guide to North American Real Photo Postcards*, Antique Paper Guild, 1991; Jane Wood, *Collector's Guide to Postcards*, L-W Book Sales, 1984, 1995 value update.

Periodicals: *Barr's Postcard News*, 70 S. 6th St., Lansing, IA 52151; *Gloria's Corner*, P.O. Box 507, Denison, TX 75021; *Postcard Collector*, P.O. Box 1050, Dubuque, IA 52004.

Collectors' Clubs: *Barr's Postcard News* and the *Postcard Collector* publish lists of more than 50 regional clubs in the United States and Canada.

Notes: The following prices are for cards in excellent to mint condition—no sign of edge wear, no creases, untrimmed, no writing on the picture side of the card, no tears and no dirt. Each defect reduces the price given by 10%.

Advertising

Adv on linens, large product image	6.00
Adv on chromes, large product image	2.50
Automobile	
American prior to 1920	20.00
European prior to 1920	12.50
After 1920	5.00
After 1950	1.00
Bulova Watch, government postal back	6.00
Campbell's Soup	
Horizontal format	30.00
Vertical format	100.00
Coca-Cola	
Duster girl in car	450.00
Hamilton King	250.00
Diner, linen era	12.50
Do-Wah-Jack	12.50
DuPont Gun	
Birds	30.00
Dogs	100.00
Zeppelin	150.00
Elgin Watch Co.	6.00
Formica, chrome era	3.00
Frog-in-the-Throat	50.00
Gas Station, linen era	6.00
Heinz, Ocean Pier, Atlantic City, NY, 1910s	5.00
Hotel-Motel	
Chrome	1.00
Early	2.50
Linen era	6.50
Livermore & Knight Publishing	12.50
McDonald's, chrome era	1.00
Michelin Tire Co., featuring Michelin man	30.00
Parker Gun	200.00
Rockford Watch, calendar series	15.00
Seed Co., good images	6.00
Sloppy Joe's Bar, Havana, Cuba, 1930s	25.00
Tupperware, chrome era	3.00
Warner Corset, Mucha	500.00
Yellow Kid, calendars, Outcault	112.50
Zeno Gum, mechanical	35.00

Artist Signed

Atwell, Mabel Lucie	
Early by Tuck	12.50
Regular, comic	6.00
Basch, Arpad, Art Nouveau	125.00
Bertiglia, children	12.50
Boileau, Philip	
By Reinthal Neuman	15.00
By Raphael Tuck	100.00
By other	35.00

F. Earl Christy, "Roses Are Always in Season," $20.

Bompard, art dec	10.00
Boulanger, Maurice, cats	
Large images	25.00
Many in action	12.50
Brill, Ginks, set of 16	12.50
Browne, Tom	
American Baseball series, green background	9.00
English comic series	3.00
Brundage, Frances	
Children	1.00
Early Tuck chlth	30.00
Brunelleschi, Art Nouveau	200.00
Busi, Art Deco	10.00
Caldecott	
Early	10.00
1974 reprints	1.00
Carmichael, comic	3.00
Carr, Gene, comic	12.50
Chiostri, Art Deco	20.00
Christy, Howard Chandler	20.00
Clapsaddle, Ellen Hattie	
Children	15.00
Floral, sleds, crosses	5.00
A Thrilling Halloween, mechanical, pumpkin head moves over child's face	275.00
Unsigned, Wolf Publishing Co.	10.00
Valentine, mechanical	45.00
Corbella, Art Deco	12.50
Corbett, Bertha, sunbonnets	15.00
Curtis, E., children	3.00
Daniell, Eva, Art Nouveau, Tuck	85.00
Drayton/Weiderseim, Grace (Campbell's Kids)	35.00
Dwig	

Comic 5.00
Halloween 15.00
Fidler, Alie Luella, women 6.00
Fisher, Harrison.......................12.50
Gassaway, K., children..................6.00
Gibson, Charles Dana, sepia 6.00
Golay, Mary, flowers.....................1.50
Greenaway, Kate, sgd................350.00
Greiner, M.
Blacks.............................12.50
Children...........................5.00
Molly and Her Teddy 12.50
Griggs, H.B.............................10.00
Gunn, Archie 3.00
Gutmann, Bessie Pease.............12.50
Hays, Margaret.........................10.00
Humphrey, Maud, sgd..................70.00
Innes, John, western 3.00
Johnson, J., children 6.50
Kirchner, Raphael
First period 125.00
Second period 65.00
Third period 50.00
Santa..............................200.00
Klein, Catherine
Floral 2.50
Alphabet..........................9.00
Alphabet, letters X, Y, Z 25.00
Koehler, Mela, early 65.00
Kokoschka,
Weiner Werkstatte 1,500.00
Mauzan, Art Deco........................15.00
May, Phil, English comic series.....10.00
McCay, Winsor, "Little Nemo" 25.00
Mucha, Alphonse
Art Nouveau,
months of the year 200.00
Slavic period, murals................75.00
Women, full-card design 600.00
O'Neill, Rose
Gross Publishing Co. 125.00
Ice Cream adv....................100.00
Kewpies..........................35.00
Pickings from Puck-Blacks.....100.00
Suffrage
Babies.........................200.00
Kewpies 125.00
Opper, Frederick, comic 10.00
Outcault.................................12.50
Parkinson, Ethel, children.............6.00
Patella, women........................15.00
Payne, Harry 15.00
Phillips, Cole, fade-away style.......25.00
Price, Mary Evans 5.00
Remington, Frederic...................35.00
Robinson, Robert 15.00
Rockwell, Norman 35.00
Russell, Charles 9.00
Sager, Xavier............................15.00
Schmucker, Samuel
Halloween greetings.................65.00

New Years 25.00
Silk, any greeting 55.00
St. Patrick's Day greetings.......15.00
Valentine greetings 15.00
Shinn, Cobb 3.00
Smith, Jessie Wilcox,
7 different images...................15.00
Studdy, Bonzo Dog 12.50
Tam, Jean, women........................20.00
Thiele, Arthur
Blacks
Large faces 25.00
On bikes.........................45.00
Cats
In action 15.00
Large heads 20.00
Pigs, large heads 25.00
Twelvetrees, Charles,
comic, children 5.00
Underwood, Clarence 9.00
Upton, Florence,
Golliwoggs, Tuck 35.00
Wain, Louis
Cat 45.00
Dog 25.00
Frog.............................35.00
Paper doll, cat 200.00
Santa and cat 100.00
Wall, Bernhardt, sunbonnets.........15.00
Wood, Lawson 10.00

Exposition

Alaska-Yukon-Pacific 12.50
California Midwinter....................250.00
Cotton States Exposition..............200.00
Hudson-Fulton.........................12.50
Jamestown, mechanical, dressed bear,
144 outfits.........................350.00
Lewis and Clark............................12.50
Pan American
Black and white......................6.00
Color 12.50
Portland Rose Festival 6.50
Portola Festival ....
Poster style 15.00
Views 3.00
Priest of Pallas 12.50
St. Louis, 1904
Eggshell paper 12.50
Hold to light type
General 35.00
Scene inside inn 125.00
Silver background 12.50
Trans-Mississippi
Advertising 125.00
Officials 75.00
World Columbian, 1893
Officials 25.00
Pre-Officials, without seals.....100.00

Greetings

April Fools

American comic 3.00
French litho with fish 12.50
Birthday
Floral.....................................10
Children 50
Christmas
No Santa.....................................25
Santa
Artists signed 15.00
Black face,
Coontown series...............100.00
German, highly emb 15.00
Hold-to-light type 100.00
Installment, unused 100.00
Kirchner 200.00
PFB Publishing Co. 20.00
Red Suits 10.00
Silk Applique 35.00
Suits other than red 12.50
Easter
Animals, dressed 5.00
Chicks or rabbits 2.50
Children 4.50
Crosses...................................25
Fourth of July
Children 5.00
Uncle Sam 10.00
Others 1.50
Ground Hog Day
Early, Lounsbury Publishing ..250.00
After 1930 ....20.00
Halloween
Children 3.00
Children, extremely colorful or
artist sgd 10.00

Cat, German Novelty Art Series #710,
sgd "Arth. Thiele," $20.

Santa Claus, green outfit, relief, red ground, $12.50.

Winsch Publishing	45.00

Labor Day
Lounsbury Publishing	125.00
Nash Publishing	95.00
Leap Year	5.00
Mother's Day, early	5.00

New Year
Bells	25
Children or Father Time	6.50
Winsch Publishing, beautiful women	15.00

St. Patrick's Day
Children	4.50
No children	2.50

Thanksgiving
Children	3.50
No children	50
Uncle Sam	6.50

Valentines's Day
Children, women	6.50
Hearts, comic	1.00
Winsch Publishing, beautiful women	15.00

Patriotic

Decoration Day	6.00
Lincoln	6.50
Patriotic Songs	3.00
Uncle Sam	10.00
Washington	6.50
World War II, linen	2.50

Photographic

Children under Christmas trees	12.50
Children with animals or toys	10.00
Christmas trees	6.50
Circus Performer, identified and

close-up	15.00

Exaggerations
Conrad Publishing, after 1935	10.00
Martin Publishing	12.50
Martin Publishing, U.S. Coin	75.00

Main Streets
Large cities	6.50
Unidentified towns	2.50
With trains or trolleys	12.50

People
Military with flags	5.00
Occupation, American	15.00
Portraits, instant relatives	1.00
Unusual studio backdrops	5.00

Railroad Depots
With trains	12.50
Without trains	10.00

Stores
Exteriors, identified	6.00
Interiors, identified location	25.00

Political and Social History

Billy Possum	15.00
Blacks	10.00

Campaign
1900	100.00
1904	65.00
1908	35.00
Indians	10.00
Jewish, comic	10.00
McKinley's death	6.00
Prohibition	6.00
Roosevelt's African Tour	3.00
Russo-Japanese war	20.00

Suffrage
Cargill publisher Number 111 only	125.00
Other numbers	12.50
Clapsaddle	50.00
General	12.50
Kewpie	125.00
Parades	12.50
Taft, cartoons	12.50
Thomas Edison, Henry Ford, President Calvin Coolidge, others on President's Vermont farm, unused	135.00
Truman, campaign card	25.00
Wilson	6.00

Posters

Collecting Hints: Posters are collected either for their subject and historical value, e.g. movie, railroad or minstrel or for their aesthetic appeal. Modern art historians have recognized the poster as one of the most creative art forms of our times.

Often, a popular film would be re-released several times over a period of years. Most posters for re-releases can be identified by looking at the lower right corner in the white border area. A re-release will usually be indicated with an "R" and a diagonal slash mark followed by the year of the newest release. Therefore, a "R/47" would indicate a 1947 issue.

History: Posters were a critical and extremely effective method of mass communication, especially in the period before 1920. Enormous quantities were produced, some playing a propaganda role during World War I.

Print runs of two million were not unknown. Posters were not meant to be saved; they usually were destroyed once they had served their purpose. The paradox of high production and low survival is one of the fascinating aspects of poster history.

The posters of the late 19th and early 20th centuries represent the pinnacle of American lithography. The advertising posters of firms such as Strobridge or Courier are true classics. Philadelphia was one center for the poster industry.

Europeans pioneered posters that were highly artistic and aesthetic and poster art still plays a key role in Europe. Many major artists of the 20th century designed posters.

References: P. Paret, *Persuasive Images*, Princeton University Press, 1992; *Pin-Up Poster Book: The Elvgren Collection*, Collectors Press, 1995; George Theofiles, *American Posters of World War I*, Dafram House Publishers; Susan Theran, *Leonard's Annual Price Index of Prints, Posters and Photographs*, Auction Index, 1995; ——, *Prints, Posters and Posters*, Avon Books, 1993; Jon R. Warren, *Collecting Hollywood: The Movie Poster Price Guide*, 3rd Edition, American Collector's Exchange, 1994; Bruce Lanier Wright, *Yesterday's Tomorrows*, Taylor Publishing, 1993.

Periodicals: *Collecting Hollywood*, American Collectors Exchange, 2401 Broad St., Chattanooga, TN 37408; *Hollywood Collectibles*, 4099 McEwen Dr., Ste. 350, Dallas, TX 75244; *Movie Poster Update*, Amer-

Columbia Records, color placard, c1924, 18" x 26", $350.

ican Collectors Exchange, 2401 Broad St., Chattanooga, TN 37408.

Reproduction Alert. Many classic film posters are now being reproduced, often in an 18- by 24-inch format. Many French posters by Cappiello, Cheret and others are being well-reproduced, as are varied images of the entertainer Josephine Baker.

Advisor: George Theofiles.

Advertising

Buckwheat Flour, 19" x 10", flour bag shape..25.00
Ceresota Flour, 20" x 24", mother and son illus............................50.00
Chase & Sanborn Coffee, 23" x 20", grocery store, framed..................200.00
Diamond Gloss Starch, 17" x 22", baby illus 55.00
Fatima Turkish Cigarettes, 14" x 17", harem girl's face, yellow, red and green ground, c1910 ....125.00
Henry Clay Habana, 19" x 25", Clay, plant, banded cigars and boxes 500.00
Holsum Bread, 12" x 20" 8.00
Independent Brewing Co., 21" x 11", Maynard Williamson, 1910 ......85.00
International Stock Food, 17-1/2" x 28-1/2", sitting pig, horse and cow, framed 200.00
Pacific Paints, 47" x 62", sailors rowing out to steamship, c1900 ....300.00
Swing with Sinclair, 44" x 28", red car, blue ground, c1938..................85.00
Take Some Home—Independent Brewing Co of Pittsburgh, 21" x 11",

Maynard Williamson, 1910 ......85.00
Wrigley's Gum—Pioneer Women Helped Build Our Great Country, 28" x 11", Otis Shepard, 1943 .....115.00

Causes

American Field Service, Nuyttens, 20" x 30", 1917, man in French helmet leads way for transport under flare-lit sky, light and dark blues........275.00
Be Ready! Keep Him Smiling, United War Work, 21" x 11", smiling Doughboy 95.00
Cleveland—Many Peoples One Language, Board of Education, J.H. Donahey, 11" x 18", 1917, appeal in 6 languages, gives locations of classes 175.00
The Comforter, Gordon Grant, 18" x 24", Red Cross nurse comforts refugee, pinks, blue, red and brown 125.00
Hey Fellows! Your Money Brings the Book We Need, J.E. Sheridan, 20" x 30", 1918, Doughboy holds book high while sailor reads at this side, vivid orange background 75.00
1919 War Chest—Minneapolis, J. Almars, 54" x 40", lists agencies to be financed by campaign 75.00

Movies

One Sheet, 27" x 41"
Adventures of Robin Hood, 1950s, reissue, Errol Flynn 330.00
Beast from 20,000 Fathoms, 1953 ....360.00
Crazy Knights, Monogram, 1944, Three Stooges, Shemp Howard, Billy Gilbert, Maxie Rosenbloom....125.00
Frankenstein Meets the Wolfman, 1949 re-release, Lon Chaney and Bela Lugosi, framed 220.00
Great Plane Robbery, Columbia, 1940, Jack Holt 75.00
Haunted House, Monogram, 1940, Jackie Moran, Marcia Mae Jones 75.00
Laurel & Hardy in the Big Noise, Fox, 1944, Tooker litho 300.00
Midnight Cowboy, 1969, foreign 100.00
One New York Night, MGM, 1935, Franchot Tone, Una Merkel ...110.00
Paleface, Paramount, 1948, Bob Hope, Jane Russell................100.00
Rookie Cop, RKO, 1939, Ace the Wonder Dog, Tim Holt 100.00
Song of Love, MGM, 1947, Katharine Hepburn, Paul Henreid 75.00
Sweet Rosie O'Grady, Fox 1943, Betty Grable, Robert Young, Adolphe Menjou 150.00
Thunderball, 1965, Sean Connery 125.00
Up the River, Fox, 1938, Preston

Foster, Tony Martin................100.00
You'll Never Get Rich, Columbia, 1942, Fred Astaire and Rita Hayworth..............................690.00
3 Sheets, 41" x 81"
An Affair to Remember, 20th Century Fox, 1957, Cary Grant and Deborah Kerr, linen back...................1,495.00
Courtship of Andy Hardy, MGM, 1942, Mickey Rooney, Tooker litho 110.00
Guilty, Monogram, 1944, Bonita Granville, Don Castle.............125.00
Phantom of 42nd Street, PRC, 1945, Dave O'Brien, Kay Aldridge ...100.00
The Three Caballeros, Disney, 1945 ....575.00

Sports

British Empire & Commonwealth Games, Perth, Western Australia, 25" x 40", panorama of city, 1962 ....150.00
Fidass Sporting Goods, 29" x 52", F. Romoli, Italian soccer player, 1946 ....300.00
Grays of Cambridge, 24" x 39", Affiches Marci, large tennis racket bounces "The Light Blue Tennis Ball" toward viewer, c1947 ....225.00
High Diver, 27" x 29", Arthur Albrecht & Co., swimming exhibition, c1910 ....325.00
Let's Go Skiing—Use the New Haven RR Snow Trains, 14" x 22", Sascha Maurer, c1937 ....300.00
Munich Olympics, 1972—Fencing, 33" x 46", Gaebele, posted at Olympics 125.00
Ninth International Students' Games, Paris, 1947, 30" x 46", P. Colin...................................350.00
Philadelphia Sunday Press, 16" x 22", red-haired female tennis player, c1896 ....125.00
Radio Returns of the Louis-Schmeling Fight, 14" x 22", Martin's Scotch Whiskey adv, O. Soglow illus...............100.00
Samson Kina, 20" x 30", Goffart, Brussels, chlth of 2 boxers, c1910.....................275.00
The Saturday Evening Post, 100th Year of Baseball, 22" x 28", Norman Rockwell, 1939 ....175.00
Wrestling, York Beach Casino, Monday, July 8, Pat "Crusher" O'Hara vs. Luke Graham and Diamond Jim Brady vs. Vincent Garabaldi, 4" x 22", cardboard, b&w.........25.00

Theater

Blue Jeans, 40" x 30", Enquirer Co., c1905 ....200.00
Charles A. Gardner in His

USA Bonds, J.C. Leyendecker, 1918, 70" x 30", $300.

New Comedy—The Prize Winner, 42" x 80", Greve Litho Co., Milwaukee, c1900 .... 175.00

Child Slaves of New York, 20" x 30", Strobridge Litho, 1903 .... 165.00

La Glu, 26" x 35", Robert DuPont, 1910 .... 175.00

Lena Horne: The Lady and Her Music, 14" x 22", c1980 .... 35.00

Life's Shop Window, 40" x 80", Ritchey Litho, c1900 .... 210.00

Madame Butterfly—A Grand Opera by Giacomo Puccini, 28" x 42", Enquirer Litho Co., c1900 .... 175.00

Nip and Tuck, Detectives Out of the Window into the Water, 28" x 21", J.M. Jones Co., Chicago, c1880 ... 225.00

Patterson's New York Opera Co—In the Queen's Handkerchief, 13" x 28", Currier Co., Buffalo, c1885 .... 250.00

Penelope, 27" x 35-1/2", George Rochegross 150.00

Rosemarie, 40" x 90", English, c1948 .... 200.00

A Royal Rogue Starring Jefferson De Angelis & Co., 40" x 80", Metropolitan Printing, c1900 .... 175.00

Salisbury's Troubadours— Nelly McHenry, 20" x 30", Strobridge, c1880 .... 225.00

Transportation

Automobile Club Show Old Deer Park, London, 20" x 30", c1905 ...... 600.00

Buick, 25" x 28", Kansas City, black and white, 1921-22 .... 85.00

Chicago, Milwaukee and St. Paul Railway, 24" x 34", c1870 .... 250.00

Favor Cycles, 62" x 47", c1925, linen backing 350.00

Mercedes Benz, 23" x 33", 1955, showroom, brown, blue, black, red and yellow 975.00

National Flying Day, 15" x 23", 1937 .... 100.00

Nice Auto Races—12 June 1949, 25" x 39", J. Ramel, 1949 ...... 350.00

Speed to Winter Playgrounds in Pullman Safety and Comfort, 19" x 27", William Welsh, 1935 .... 300.00

SwissAir, 27" x 39", Herbert Leupin, c1955 .... 250.00

Veritable Vieux Systems, 17" x 23", chlth, drinkers in hot-air balloon gondola, 1890 .... 175.00

Travel

American Airlines, 40" x 30", Arizona, c1955 .... 50.00

Berwick Upon Tweed—It's Quicker by Rail-liner, 25" x 40", Frank Mason, 1935 .... 275.00

Britain in Winter, 29" x 19", Terence Cuneo 50.00

Come to Britain for Racing, 20" x 30", Lionel Edwards, litho, c1948 .... 125.00

Genoa and the Italian Riviera, 27" x 39", Graffonara, 1931 .... 325.00

Montage de France, 24" x 39", Nathan, c1947 .... 125.00

Panama Pacific, New York-California, 27" x 23", white liner passing through Panama Canal, framed 250.00

SS *France*, A New Concept in Luxury for All, launching, 34" x 45", Bob Peak Litho, 1962 .... 225.00

"Apache Rifles" Audie Murphy, Admiral pictures, 1964, $20.

Sunny Ryhl—The Children's Paradise, 25" x 40", Mays, c1946 .... 300.00

TWA, Las Vegas—Fly TWA, 25" x 40", showgirl, casino items and airliner in background, c1960 .... 225.00

World War I

Be a Sea Soldier, 20" x 40", Marine sitting on dock 200.00

Call to Duty, Join the Army for Home and Country, 30" x 40", Army bugler and unfurled banner, 1917 .... 250.00

Columbia Calls—Enlist in the Army, Francis A Halstead, 28" x 40", chlth, Columbia with banner and sword atop globe, sky blue ground .. 200.00

Do Your Duty, Join the Marines, 20" x 30", gun crew loading on deck, c1917 .... 135.00

Earn While You Learn, 19" x 24", machinist illus, purple and white, 1919 .... 95.00

Follow the Flag for Freedom, The Navy Strikes Now, James Daugherty, 14" x 22", stylized Columbia points sword to multicolored horizon as sailor looks on, vivid colors 125.00

He Is Getting Our Country's Signal, Are You? Join the Navy, 20" x 30", Navy signal man waving flag, 1917 .... 300.00

It Protected You, Will You Defend It?, 25" x 35", artillery crew silhouette 225.00

Join the Quartermaster Corps, John W. Sheeres, 18" x 26", 1919, smiling Uncle Sam in doughboy outfit, purple starry heavens 150.00

Keep the American Flag on the Seas, 14" x 22", battleship in rough seas, 1917 .... 175.00

Men Wanted for the Army, 30" x 40", cavalryman on horse blowing bugle, Rocky Mountain background, c1908 .... 975.00

Over There—U S. Navy, 38" x 56", sailor holding banner, 1917 .... 750.00

Register! Tuesday, June 5th, 14" x 22", State of Massachusetts draft, 1917 .... 75.00

Tell That to the Marines, 20" x 40", man taking off suit coat, James Montgomery Flagg, 1918 ...... 375.00

U.S. Marines, Active Service on Land and Sea, 30" x 40", marine marching on pier 275.00

World War II

All Soldiers Can't Be in the Infantry, 17" x 25", charging soldier holding bayonet, 1944 .... 125.00

Be a Marine—Free a Marine to Fight, 28" x 40", woman Marine in uniform, 1943 .... 125.00

Build and Fight in the Navy Seabees, 28" x 42", recruiting

image, 1943...........................300.00

Defend Your Country, 21" x 11",
Uncle Sam rolling up
sleeves, 1940 ....125.00

Dish It Out with the Navy, 28" x 42", gun
crew in battle, 1942 ....135.00

Enlist Now, U S. Marine Corps,
28" x 40", full-color island
setting, 1945 ....200.00

Join the WAC, 22" x 28", WAC sitting on
bunk typing letter, c1942 ....100.00

Let's Hit 'Em with Everything We've Got!,
28" x 41", Naval deck gunner firing,
raging battle, 1942.................150.00

Marines Have Landed, 30" x 40",
Marines wading ashore, James
Montgomery Flagg, 1941.......350.00

Now Is the Time, 25" x 38", army
war jobs, red, mauve, blue and
white, 1942 ....125.00

Proud I'll Say—Join the Waves,
14" x 20", father showing picture of
Wave daughter, 1943 ....100.00

Put the Squeeze on Food Waste,
7" x 10", cartoon image of Navy
kitchens, 1945 ....45.00

Speed Up the Process, 19" x 27",
endless line of Marines with man at
desk, J. Hearne, 1945 ....250.00

Take Your Place in the Ranks, 25" x 38",
recruiting image, 1942...........175.00

Want Action?—Join U S. Marine Corps!,
28" x 41", Marine holding out right
hand, rifle in left hand, James
Montgomery Flagg, 1942.......350.00

We're in the Fight Too!, 14" x 20", farm
woman, blue, red, black and white,
1942.......................................150.00

You Can Build and Fight,
19" x 25", trooper with jack
hammer, 1943 ....135.00

Elvis Presley

Collecting Hints: Official Elvis Presley items are usually copyrighted and many are dated. Learn to differentiate between items licensed during Elvis's lifetime and the wealth of "fantasy" items issued after his death. The latter are collectible but have nowhere near the value of the pre-1977 material.

Also, accept the fact that many of the modern limited edition items are purely speculative investments. It is best to buy them because you like them and plan to live with them

Postcard, color-photo portrait, brown border, 1987 Elvis Presley Ent., Inc., 4" x 6", $8.

for an extended period of time, not because you might realize a profit.

History: As a rock 'n' roll star, Elvis Presley was one of the first singers to target teenagers in his promotional efforts. The first Elvis merchandise appeared in 1956. During the following years, new merchandise was added both in America and foreign countries. After his death in 1977, a vast number of new Elvis collectibles appeared.

References: Pauline Bartel, *Everything Elvis*, Taylor Publishing, 1995; Jerry Osborne, *Official Price Guide to Elvis Presley Records and Memorabilia*, House of Collectibles, 1994.

Collectors' Clubs: Elvis Forever TCB Fan Club, P.O. Box 1066, Pinellas Park, FL 34665; Graceland News Fan Club, P.O. Box 452, Rutherford, NJ 07070.

Museums: Graceland, Memphis, TN; Jimmy Velvet's Elvis Presley Museum, Franklin, TN.

Album/Songbook, *The Elvis Presley Album of Jukebox Favorites*, 9" x 12", soft-cover, 36 pgs, photos, words and music to popular songs, Hill and Range Songs, Inc., 1956.........38.00

Anklet, dog tag, 1956,
mint on card............................35.00

Autograph

8" x 10" b&w "Jailhouse
Rock" movie still, boldly
sgd in blue ball-point pen.......920.00
10-1/2" x 12-1/2", RCA Victor color
promotional photo collage, boldly sgd
in blue ball-point pen, mid-1960s,
matted 1,322.00

Belt, metal, gold colored, intricate mesh,
2 eagle's-head fasteners, "Russian
Double Eagle" 55.00

Book, *My Life With Elvis, Becky Yancey*,
Book Club Edition....................12.00

Button, 2-1/2" d, flasher type,
Love Me Tender, performing
pose, 1956 ....25.00

Calendar, 1963, RCA
premium, unused 75.00

Charm Bracelet, letters read "Loving
You," 1956, MOC 80.00

Credit Card, Elvis's orig American
Express card, dated 6/73
through 5/74 ....41,400.00

Decanter 35.00

Dog Tag/Necklace, 1" x 1-3/4" chrome-
luster metal, image of Elvis with side-
burns, facsimile signature, name,
Arm code and blood type stamped
above signature, 12" l silver-colored
metal necklace, late 1950s......35.00

Handkerchief, black silk, worn by Presley in 1962-63 movie "It
Happened at the World's
Fair," accompanied by photo of Presley with handkerchief in breast pocket, letter of authenticity 575.00

Hat, khaki, Army dress hat, worn by
Presley in Germany, size 7-1/4",
accompanied by photo of Elvis
wearing hat..........................8,100.00

Key Chain, 3" x 4-1/2" orig cellophane
bag, white card holding 1" x 2" thin
metal dog tag, sideburn image of
Elvis, stamped signature beneath his
Army number and blood type, 2" key
chain, unopened, late 1950s...45.00

Lobby Card, 14" x 22", "Fun in
Acapulco" 35.00

Magazine
Life, April 30, 1956...................24.00
Stardom Magazine,
Aug., 1960 ....27.50
TV Guide, May 7, 1960,
Ohio edition.............................45.00

Movie Poster, orig s
tand-up sidewalk marquee,
"Easy Come, Easy Go" 80.00

Newspaper, *Memphis Press*,
Aug. 17, 1977, articles
relating to death 30.00

Pennant, 29" l, felt, blue,
yellow design and lettering,
b&w photo, white "Love, Elvis"
signature, c1960......................45.00

Perfume Bottle, Teddy
Bear, 1957, MIB 220.00

Photo Album, 1950s 85.00

Photograph, color, white plastic frame emb with guitars, musical note and "Love Me Tender" in raised gold letters, issued by Elvis Presley Enterprises, 1956 ....250.00

Pinback Button

1-3/4" d, "I Like Elvis," red and white, c1956 ....15.00

2-1/2" d, Sept. 10, 1978, fan reunion, "Always Elvis," and "V.I.P.," red inscriptions, b&w photo 15.00

3-1/4" d, litho tin, "Sincerely Elvis," color photo of laughing Elvis, facsimile white printed signature, late 1960s..................................35.00

3-1/2" d, Memorial, 1977, 4 b&w photos, red and white inscriptions at top, purple and white bottom......7.50

Postcard, 3-1/2" x 5-1/2", Easter Greetings, Elvis wearing gray tux, red ground, unused 35.00

Poster, 40" x 60", Elvis Presley in Wild in Country Style, large full-color image of Elvis playing guitar with co-stars Hope Lange, Tuesday Weld, Millie Perkins...................................245.00

Program Menu, Sahara Tahoe, 1970s, large............................45.00

Radio, 1-1/4" x 3" x 5", figural, 8" h Elvis in suit, holding microphone, standing on plastic base, mkd "Elvis Presley" on front, c1977, Hong Kong.....35.00

Scarf, 8" x 3", pale blue, stitched border, printed "Sincerely Elvis Presley" signature, orig tag......85.00

Sheet Music, *Love Me Tender* 35.00

Wallet, tan vinyl, blue, pink, white and flesh-tone illus on front cover, blue and gold stars, back "1956 Elvis Presley Enterprises"......165.00

Window Card, 14" x 22", "King Creole," heavy-stock poster, Carolyn Jones and Elvis, 1958 ....165.00

Punchboards

Collecting Hints: Punchboards which are unpunched are collectible. A board which has been punched has little value unless it is an extremely rare design. Like most advertising items, price is determined by graphics and subject matter.

The majority of punchboards sell in the $8 to $30 range. At the high end of the range are boards such as Golden Gate Bridge ($85) and Baseball Classic ($100).

History: Punchboards are self-contained games of chance made of pressed paper that has holes and coded tickets inside each hole. For an

agreed amount, the player uses a "punch" to extract the ticket of his or her choice. Prizes are awarded to the winning ticket. Punch prices can be 1¢, 2¢, 3¢, 5¢, 10¢, 20¢, 50¢, $1 or more.

Not all tickets were numbered. Fruit symbols were used extensively as well as animals. Some punchboards had no printing at all, just colored tickets. Other ticket themes included dice, cards, dominoes and words. One early board featured Mack Sennet bathing beauties. Punchboards come in an endless variety of styles. Names reflect the themes of the boards: Barrel of Winners, Break the Bank, Baseball, More Smokes, Lucky Lulu and Take It Off are just a few.

At first, punchboards winners were awarded cash. As a response to attempts to outlaw gambling, prizes were switched to candy, cigars, cigarettes, jewelry, radios, clocks, cameras, sporting goods, toys, beer, chocolate, etc. The golden age of punchboards was from the 1920s to the 1950s. Attention was focused on the keyed punchboard in the film "The Flim Flam Man." This negative publicity hurt the punchboard industry.

Museum: Amusement Sales, Midvale, UT.

Advisor: Clark Phelps.

Ace High, 13" x 17", deck of cards 45.00

As You Like It, 9" x 9", 1¢ punch, glamour girl...............................20.00

Bars and Bells, 19" x 13", deck of cards as jackpot determinator, fruit-symbol punches 80.00

Beat the Seven, winner needs 8 or better 25.00

Big Bills, 2-bit punch, large thick board......................18.00

Block Buster, 5¢ punch, double jackpot 18.00

Bull's Eye, contains 76 uncirculated 1940s pennies 225.00

Card Game 13, forth deck of cards to make up jackpot 45.00

Double or Nothing, 60% double tickets, 40% nothing 35.00

Five Tens, 10¢ punch, cash board..............................20.00

Full of Tens, 2-bit punch, thick large cash pay 15.00

Gold as Gold, large thick colorful seals 20.00

Home Run Derby, 14" x 10", baseball

Play Basketball, Havana Blend Cigar adv, red, blue, and white, 5¢, 1930s, 7-1/4" x 10", $17.50.

diamond header 45.00

Joe's Special Prize, cash board, writing space for jackpot prize 18.00

Lulu Bell, 5¢ punch, large 15.00

Odd Pennies, flapper-type girl, Lucky Strike greens, old patina 55.00

Professor Charlie, professor overlooks award schedule, 2-bit punch, factory wrapped, price for 2 ....24.00

Pick a Cherry, fruit seals, cash prizes 20.00

Speedy Tens, 10¢ punch, cash board 20.00

Super Bingo, winners match small bingo card 20.00

Take Me Home, small, space for boxed-watch prize 12.00

Purinton Pottery

Collecting Hints: The most popular patterns among collectors are Apple, Intaglio (brown), Normandy Plaid (red), Maywood and Pennsylvania Dutch. Variations, e.g., Intaglio with a green ground, are known for many of these patterns.

Purinton also made a number of kitchenware and specialty pieces. These should not be overlooked. Among the harder-to-find items are animal figurines, tea tiles and the Tom and Jerry bowl and mug set.

History: Bernard Purinton founded Purinton Pottery in 1936 in Wellsville, OH. This pilot plant produced decorative dinnerware and some special-order pieces. In 1940, Roy Underwood, President of Knox Glass Co., approached Purinton about moving his operation to Knox's community, Shippenville. In 1941, the pottery relocated to a newly built plant in Shippenville, PA. The company's first product at the new plant, a 2-cup premium teapot for McCormick Tea Co., rolled off the line on Dec. 7, 1941.

Dorothy Purinton and William H. Blair, her brother, were the chief designers for the company. Maywood, Plaid and several Pennsylvania German designs were among the patterns attributed to Dorothy Purinton. William Blair, a graduate of the Cleveland School of Art, designed the Apple and Intaglio patterns. Initially, slipware was cast. Later, it was pressed using a Ram Press process. Clays came from Florida, Kentucky, North Carolina and Tennessee.

Purinton Pottery did not use decals, as did many of its competitors. Greenware was hand painted by locally trained decorators who then dipped the decorated pieces into glaze. This demanded a specially formulated body and a more expensive manufacturing process. Hand painting also allowed for some of the variations in technique and colors found on Purinton ware today.

Purinton made a complete dinnerware line for each pattern, plus a host of accessory pieces ranging from candleholders to vases. Dinnerware patterns were open stock. Purinton's ware received national distribution and select lines were exported. The plant ceased operations in 1958, reopened briefly and finally closed for good in 1959. Cheap foreign imports were cited as the cause of the company's decline.

References: Pat Dole, *Purinton Pottery*, Denton Publishing, 1990; Harvey Duke, *Official Identification and Price Guide to Pottery and Porcelain*, 8th Edition, House of Collectibles, 1995; Lois Lehner, *Lehner's Encyclopedia of U.S. Marks on Pottery, Porcelain & Clay*, Collector Books, 1988; Susan Morris, *Purinton Pottery*, Collector Books, 1994.

Periodical: Purinton Pastimes, 20401 Ivybridge Ct., Gaithersburg, MD 20879.

Collectors' Club: Purinton Pottery Convention, P.O. Box 9394, Arlington, VA 22219.

Bank, Uncle Sam 30.00
Bean Pot, cov, Normandy Plaid 35.00
Beer Mug
    Maywood..................................60.00
    Normandy Plaid 70.00
Canister
    Flour, Brown Intaglio, square,
    wood lid...................................95.00
    Set
        Apple, 4 pc, wire rack 225.00
        Pennsylvania Dutch 195.00
    Sugar
        Brown Intaglio, square,
        wood lid...............................95.00
        Fruit dec, cobalt blue trim 95.00
Casserole, cov
    Apple, oval 25.00
    Brown Intaglio, 9" d 50.00
Cereal Bowl
    Brown Intaglio 12.00
    Pennsylvania Dutch 15.00
    Normandy Plad 12.00
Chop Plate, 12" d,
    Brown Intaglio..........................40.00
    Normandy Plaid 50.00
Coffee Mug, Plaid...........................1.00
Coffeepot, cov, Apple....................30.00
Cookie Jar, cov
    Apple.......................................40.00
    Normandy Plaid 110.00
    Pennsylvania Dutch 55.00
Creamer
    Apple, double
    spout, 1-1/2" h..........................12.00
    Fruits 10.00
Cruet, Pennsylvania Dutch, jug-shape,
    price for pr 50.00
Cup and Saucer
    Apple.......................................12.00
    Brown Intaglio 9.00
Dessert Bowl, Brown Intaglio 10.00
Drip Jar, cov
    Apple.......................................20.00
    Plaid..20.00
Fruit Bowl
    Intaglio 60.00
Kent Jug
    Apple.......................................15.00
Lazy Susan, Fruits, apple finial,
    painted pear, plum,
    pineapple and cherries 250.00
Marmalade, cov, Maywood 32.00
Meat Platter
    Apple.......................................90.00

Pitcher, Fruits 32.00
Plate
    8" d, Apple 10.00
    9-1/2" d, Fruits 15.00
    9-3/4" d, Plaid 15.00
    10" d, Brown Intaglio...............14.00
    12" d, Apple, grill.....................20.00
Platter
    Brown Intaglio, 11" l, oval 35.00
    Maywood, 12" l, oblong............30.00
Relish Dish, Fruits, divided,
    3 parts, handle 18.00
Roll Tray, Brown Intaglio, 11" l......35.00
Salt and Pepper Shakers, pr, jug shape
    Apple.......................................18.00
    Plaid..10.00
Saucer, Apple 5.00
Sugar, open, Apple 10.00
Tea and jToast Set
    Intaglio 45.00
Teapot, cov, Maywood, 6 cup 35.00
Tumbler
    Normandy Plaid 30.00
Vegetable
    Apple, oval 20.00
    Brown Intaglio, 8-1/2" d............25.00
    Divided, Normandy Plaid 40.00

R

Racing Collectibles

Collecting Hints: This is a field of heroes and also fans. Collectors love the winners; a household name counts. Losers are important only when major races are involved. Pre-1945 material is especially desirable because few individuals were into collecting prior to that time.

The field does have problems with reproductions and copycats. Check every item carefully. Beware of paying premium prices for items made within the last 20 years.

Auto racing items are one of the hot collectible markets of the 1990s. Although interest in Indy 500 collectibles remains strong, the market is dominated by NASCAR collectibles. In fact, the market is so strong that racing collectibles have their own separate show circuit and supporting literature.

Because racing collecting is in its infancy, price speculation is rampant. Market manipulators abound. In addition, copycat, fantasy and contemporary limited edition items are being introduced into the market as fast as they can be created. A shakeout appears years in the future. In the interim, check your engine and gear up for fast action.

There are so many horse racing collectibles that specialization is required from the beginning. Collector focuses include a particular horse racing type or a specific horse race, a breed or specific horse or racing prints and images. Each year there are a number of specialized auctions devoted to horse racing. These range from sporting prints sales at the major New York auction houses to benefit auctions for the Thoroughbred Retirement Foundation.

History: Man's quest for speed is as old as time. Although this category focuses primarily on automobile and horse racing, other types of racing memorabilia are included. If it moves, it will and can be raced.

Plate, black-and-white Dan Patch photo center, scalloped edge, gold trim, "Dan Patch, Champion Harness Horse of the World, Time 1.56," East Liverpool Potteries Co., 8-3/8" d, $60.

Automobile racing began before the turn of the century. Many of the earliest races took place in Europe. By the first decade of the 20th century, automobile racing was part of the American scene. The Indianapolis 500 began in 1911 and was interrupted only by World War II. In addition to Formula 1 racing, the NASCAR circuit has achieved tremendous popularity with American racing fans. Cult heroes such as Richard Petty, Dale Earnhardt and Jeff Gordon have become household names.

The history of horse racing dates back to the domestication of the horse itself. Prehistoric cave drawings illustrate horses racing. The Greeks engaged in chariot racing as early as 600 B.C. As civilization spread, so did the racing of horses. Each ethnic group and culture added its own unique slant.

The British developed the concept of the Thoroughbred, a group of horses that are descendants of three great Arabian stallions—Carley Arabian, Byerley Turk and Goldolphin Arabian. Horse racing received royal sponsorship and became the Sport of Kings.

Horse racing reached America during the colonial period. By the 1800s, 4-mile match-races between regional champions were common. In 1863, Saratoga Race Track was built. The first Belmont Stakes was run at Jerome Park in 1867. As the 19th century ended, more than 300 race tracks operated seasonal cards. By 1908, the number of American race tracks had been reduced to 25 as a result of widespread opposition to gambling.

The premier American horse race is the Kentucky Derby. Programs date from 1924 and glasses, a favorite with collectors, from the late 1930s.

References: Jack Mackenzie, *Indy 500 Buyers Guide*, published by author (6940 Wildridge Rd., Indianapolis, IN 46256), 1996; Roderick A. Malloy, *Malloy's Sports Collectibles Value Guide*, Attic Books, Wallace-Homestead, 1993.

Periodicals: *Collector's World*, P.O. Box 562029, Charlotte, NC 28256; *Racing Collectibles Price Guide*, P.O. Box 608114, Orlando, FL 32860.

Collectors' Clubs: National Indy 500 Collectors Club, 10505 N. Delaware St., Indianapolis, IN 46280; Sport of Kings Society, 1406 Annen Ln., Madison, WI 53711.

Museums: Aiken Thoroughbred Racing Hall of Fame & Museum, Aiken, SC; Harness Racing Hall of Fame, Goshen, NY; Indianapolis Motor Speedway Hall of Fame Museum, Speedway, IN; International Motor Sports Hall of Fame, Talladega, AL; Kentucky Derby Museum, Louisville, KY; National Museum of Racing & Hall of Fame, Saratoga Springs, NY.

Additional Listings: Horse Collectibles.

Air

Game, The New World to
  World Airship Race, Chicago
  Game Co., orig box 95.00
Picture Frame, 20-1/4" x 26", commemorative, title inscription "Winner, Park Service Station, Third Annual Goodyear Dealers Zeppelin Race, July-August 1931," tag at bottom reads "Made of Duralumin Used in Girder Construction of the United States Airship *Akron* Built by the Goodyear Zeppelin Corporation" 110.00
Pinback Button
  American Air Races, mechanic, red
  and cream, 1923 .... 50.00
  Cleveland National Air Races, silver,
  red, white and blue, 1932 .... 50.00
  Los Angeles National Air Races, red
  and white, 1928 .... 75.00

Auto

Autograph
Mario Andretti, 8" x 10" photo ..24.00
Earnhardt Dale, 1/2" scale Good-
wrench racing helmet 170.00
Jeff Gordon, Rainbow DuPont
1/2" scale racing helmet, silvered
on tinted visor 150.00
Ken Schraeder,
8" x 10" photo 24.00
Al Unser, 8" x 10" photo 24.00
Bobby Unser, 8" x 10" photo 18.00
Rusty Wallace, 8" x 10" photo ..30.00
Ashtray, bronze, Indianapolis
Speedway, race car in relief,
mkd "Clabber Girl Special,
Terre Haute, Ind." 350.00
Bumper Sticker, Miller High Life, white
ground, red lettering, black checker-
board flag, green and gold highlights,
mkd "Miller Brewing Co., Milwaukee,
WI," 4" h, 6" l, unused 1.00
Catalog, 501 Fiat and Winners 1925
Autodromo, color Mingossi lithos,
illus, photogravures 190.00
Cigarette Lighter, 2-1/4" l, Mickey
Thompson Speed Equipment, metal,
chrome finish, mid-1960s 25.00
Cracker Jack Prize, spinner disk,
cardboard, 5 facing cars illus,
1940s..25.00
Game
Auto Race Game, Milton
Bradley, multicolored playing
board, 4 metal race cars,
4 spinners, instructions on back box
cov, orig box, c1925 ....95.00
Turbo, Milton Bradley, cased on
Sega arcade game, 1981 Sega En-
terprises, Inc., 3-fold game board,
plastic cars and ambulance 15.00
Glass, 5-1/4" h, Indianapolis Motor
Speedway, white frosted, red face
car, 1950s................................25.00
Golf Badge, 1966 Indianapolis Speed-
way 500 Festival Golf 30.00
Magazine, *Racing Pictorial*, 8-1/2" x 11",
late 1963, 48 pgs 12.00
Media Guide, Indy 500, 1966 ....15.00
Necktie,
Indianapolis 500, 1940s...........40.00
Pinback Button
Indianapolis the Speedway City,
yellow, red and black, 1930s....75.00
Roosevelt Raceway, red, white and
blue, race car image, 1930s.....32.00
Postcard, Eddie Sachs 15.00
Poster
Miller High Life Racing, facsimile sig-
natures of Bobby Allison and Bobby
Billin Jr., biographies and driver and
car specifications on back, Miller
Brewing Co., Milwaukee, WI,

8" x 10".......................................5.00
Soapbox Derby Workshop/Clinic,
14" x 22", cardboard, 1967 ......24.00
Program, Danbury, 1930...............50.00
Record Book, NASCAR, 1953 ......35.00
Ticket, Indy 500, 1963...................25.00
Toy, Formula-1, Texaco, Marlboro, tin
and plastic, orig box 95.00
Tray, 3-1/2" x 4-1/2", Indianapolis
Motor Speedway, metal, bronze
finish, 1950 ....40.00

Horse

Ashtray, 5-1/4" d, china, full-color
thoroughbred racehorse portrait,
Kentucky Derby and Belmont S
takes winner 17.50
Badge, 3" d, Budweiser Million, Second
Running, Aug. 29, 1982, full-color
illus 10.00
Catalog, 1915, 2 pgs of
Dan Patch...............................150.00
Cigarette Lighter, Kentucky Derby,
silver-colored metal, flip top,
1955 ....125.00
Flier, Dan Patch Contest, 10" x 14",
paper, printed in blue on white,
offer of $350 cash award for 35
colts sired by Dan Patch, back with
pictures Dan Patch and 2 descendants, adv text for M.W. Savage,
proprietor of International Stock
Food Co., c1913 ....125.00
Game, Eddie Arcaro Sweepstakes,
1-1/2" x 11" x 17-1/2", 1954,
Lourol Enterprises, 17" x 22"
playing board, 8 miniature plastic
stand-up racehorses with jockeys,
8 charts, 2 horse dice, single traditional die, 40 plastic tokens, unopened playing parts, game
endorsed by Arcaro on lid 75.00
Glass
Belmont, 1980........................130.00
Kentucky Derby winners
1945...................................960.00
1949...................................120.00
1950...................................260.00
1951...................................355.00
1958...................................100.00
1959.....................................70.00
Preakness, 1972 ....435.00
Label, 10-1/4" x 10-1/4", The Derby
Tobacco, framed 150.00
Needle Book, 4-1/2" x 4-3/4",
Steeple Chase, cardboard, full-color
art, 1930s 35.00
Pass, Florida Jockey Club, 1926...30.00
Pennant, 18" l, Derby Day, felt, red,
white lettering, red and white design
with pink accents, 1939 ....20.00
Pinback Button
Dan Patch Days, brown image, white
ground, black letters, 1967 Savage,

MN, commemorative
celebration 25.00
Dan Patch Stock Food, multicolored,
"The World's Champion Dan Patch
Trotter Horse, driven by M.W. Sav-
age, Owner," endorsement for Inter-
national Stock Food, c1905 ...150.00
Portrait of jockey, early 1900s
Barrett, Celebrated English
Jockey, racing colors, yellow cap,
pale blue jacket, American Pepsin
Gum series 30.00
Taral, Celebrated American
Jockey, racing colors, white outfit
with blue dots, Little Jockey
Cigarettes back paper 35.00
Print, 20-1/2" x 16", American
Quarter Horse Racing, Randy
Steffen, 1972...........................20.00
Stickpin, brass, jockey cap over
entwined initials, green and white
enamel accents, dated 1906 ...25.00
Ticket, Kentucky Derby, admission, race
won by Swaps 40.00

Radio Characters and Personalities

Collecting Hints: Many items associated with radio characters and personalities were offered as
premiums. This category focuses
mostly on the non-premium items.
Radio premiums are listed separately in this book.

Don't overlook the vast amount
of material related to the radio shows
themselves. This includes scripts,
props and a wealth of publicity material. Many autographed photographs
appear on the market. Books, especially Big Little Books and similar
types, featured many radio-related
characters and stories. Radio characters and personalities found their way
into movies and television. Serious
collectors exclude the products which
spun off from these other two areas.

Horace Heidt, Tum's Pot-O-Gold adv tin, 2-1/4", $15.

History: The radio show was a dominant force in American life from the 1920s to the early 1950s. "Amos 'n' Andy" began in 1929, "The Shadow" in 1930 and "Chandu the Magician" in 1932. Although many of the characters were fictional, the individuals who portrayed them became public idols. A number of figures achieved fame on their own—Eddie Cantor, Don McNeill of "The Breakfast Club," George Burns and Gracie Allen, Arthur Godfrey and Jack Benny.

Sponsors and manufacturers were quick to capitalize on the fame of the radio characters and personalities. Premiums were offered as part of the shows' themes. However, merchandising did not stop with premiums. Many non-premium items, such as bubblegum cards, figurines, games, publicity photographs and dolls, were issued. Magazine advertisements often featured radio personalities.

Reference: Jon D. Swartz and Robert C. Reinehr, *Handbook of Old-Time Radio*, Scarecrow Press, 1993.

Periodicals: *Friends of Old Time Radio*, P.O. Box 4321, Hamden, CT 06514; *Nostalgia Digest and Radio Guide*, Box 421, Morton Grove, IL 60053; *Old Time Radio Digest*, 4114 Montgomery Rd., Cincinnati, OH 45212.

Collectors' Clubs: Friends of Vic & Sade, 7232 N. Keystone Ave., Lincolnwood, IL 60646; Golden Radio Buffs of Maryland, Inc., 301 Jeanwood Ct., Baltimore, MD 21222; Illinois Old Radio Shows Society, 10 S. 540 County Line Rd., Hinsdale, IL 60521; Manuscript Society, 350 N. Niagara St., Burbank, CA 91505; National Lum & Abner Society, #81 Sharon Blvd., Dora, IL 35062; North America Radio Archives, 134 Vincewood Dr., Nicholasville, KY 40356; Old Time Radio Club, 56 Christen Ct., Lancaster, NY 14086; Old Time Radio Collectors Traders Society, 725 Cardigan Ct., Naperville, IL 60565; Oldtime Radio Show Collectors Association, 45 Barry St., Sudbury, Ontario P3B 3H6 Canada; Pow-Wow, 301 E. Buena Vista Ave., N. Augusta, SC 29841; Radio Collectors of America, Ardsley Circle, Brockton, MA 02402; Society to Preserve & Encourage Radio Drama,

Variety & Comedy, P.O. Box 7177, Van Nuys, CA 91409.

Museum: Museum of Broadcasting, New York, NY.

Additional Listings: Big Little Books, Comic Books, Radio Premiums, Super Heroes.

Jimmy Allen

Bag, 4" x 6", cloth, white, red printing both sides, drawstring reverse Cleo Cola logo, bottle cap and inscription "Listen to the Air Adventures of Jimmie Allen Every Broadcast for Bulletins about Premiums," c1934 ....175.00

Book, *Jimmie Allen Flying Club Stamp Album*, 5" x 6-1/2", red, white and blue cover design, mounted stamps inside, 1936 ....85.00

Flying Pin 20.00

Map, 11" x 25-1/4", full color, printed letter on back, 1934...............115.00

Membership Card, 2-1/4" x 4", Flying Cadet, black printing, red stamped serial number, blight blue airplanes and wing symbols design border, club pledge and airplane border reverse, penciled signature, c1934 ....45.00

Newsletter, 8-1/2" x 11", 4 pgs, red, white and green holiday design and signatures on front cover, b&w photos on back cover 60.00

Amos and Andy

Birthday Card, brown portraits, message includes song title "Check and Double Check," inked birthday note, Rust Craft...20.00

Quiz Kids Game, Whitman Publishing Co., No. 3020, 1941 by Louis G. Cowan, 5" x 6-1/2" x 15/16" box, $20.

Book, *All About Amos 'n' Andy and Their Creators Correll & Gosden*, 6-1/4" x 7-3/4", 126 pgs, illus, 1929......55.00

Exhibit Card, 3-3/8" x 5-1/2", color-tone photos, 1930s, numbered set

Card #1, Ain't That Sumpin......12.00

Card #2, I's Regusted 12.00

Card #4, Amos 'n' Andy As They Talk to You.....................12.00

Card #8, Andy the President of the Fresh Air Taxi Cab Co., Incropulated 12.00

Card #10, Wait a Minute Andy, Don't Rush Me 12.00

Card #12, Amos 'n' Andy In Big Propolition 12.00

Card #13, Amos 'n' Andy in a Friendly Little Game 12.00

Card #14, Amos 'n' Andy In Person Calling On The President........12.00

Card #15, Well I'll Be Dog-on ..12.00

Card #16, The Boys Resting Before Broadcasting...........................12.00

Figure, 4" h, bisque, painted, stamped "Pfeffer Porzellan, Gotha, Germany," registration marks "6495" and "6496," 1920-30, price for pr 325.00

Game, Amos 'n' Andy Shooting Game, Transogram Co., NY, #51, early 1930s, wear............................75.00

Patch, cloth, 4-3/4" d, Check-Double Check, fuzzy texture, embroidered features, 1930s 60.00

Radio Guide, photo, orig envelope...........................30.00

Jack Armstrong

Flashlight, 4-1/2" l, cardboard, red, metal cap ends, c1939 ....25.00

Ped-O-Meter 40.00

Telescope, 10-1/2" l extended, tin, black cover paper, emb "Jack Armstrong Explorer," c1937 ....45.00

Whistle Ring, gold color, Egyptian symbols, includes 3" x 4" illus code sheet, manila ring envelope, orig mailing envelope, c1938 ....120.00

Jack Benny, magazine, *Post*, March 2, 1963, Norman Rockwell cover 15.00

Chandu the Magician, magic trick, Galloping Coin, 3 metal containers, metal case, instruction sheet, orig mailing box and label 90.00

Dick Daring, map and puzzle, 9" x 12" map, orange, blue and white, adventure scenes, matching puzzle, orig 6" x 8" mailing envelope 65.00

Fibber McGee and Molly

Photo, 8-1/4" x 12", b&w glossy, cast members, Fibber and Molly pictured at top, late 1930s 35.00

Record Album, 10-1/4" x 12", contains four 78 RPM records, live broadcasts, colorful Fibber design on cover, 1947 copyright....................55.00

Fireside Seat, ticket, 2-1/4" x 5-1/2", Max Baer vs. Joe Louis, NBC Radio, thin white cardboard, red and black lettering against yellow ground, Sept. 24, 1935, heavyweight fight, held at Yankee Stadium, issued by Buick dealers, with attached rain check..........48.00

Arthur Godfrey, magazine, *Post*, Nov. 5, 1955 ....8.00

Little Orphan Annie

Ashtray, 3-/4" x 4" x 1", glazed ceramic, figural, gold finish, black trim, 2-3/4" h seated white Annie, orange dress, black shoes, 1-3/4" h yellow smiling Sandy, black accents, copyright stamp on reverse "Famous Artists Syndicate" in black letters, underside stamped "Made in Japan," early 1930s............................120.00

Book, James Whitcomb Riley, *The Little Orphan Annie Book*, 1908, illus by Ethel Betts 35.00

Change Purse, 3" x 2", red vinyl, metal clasp, white image of Annie and Sandy, 1930s..........................45.00

Cup, 3" h, Beetleware, Ovaltine premium, ivory color, multicolored decal of Annie holding cup in air, seated Sandy, 1933.................48.00

Decoder, 1940................................45.00

Pinback Button, 1-1/4" d, black, white and flesh tone, *Los Angeles Evening Express* contest 55.00

Lum and Abner

Family Almanac, 6" x 9", 34 pgs, orig mailing envelope, 1936............55.00

Newspaper, 11-1/2" x 16-1/2", *Pine Edge News*, 4 pgs, b&w, Spring 1936, orig mailing envelope.....45.00

Charlie McCarthy

Card Game, Rummy, 1938 ....30.00

Game, Charlie McCarthy's Radio Party, spinner board, 21 diecut stand-up figures, orig envelope with instructions, Chase & Sanborn Coffee issue..............................60.00

Soap, 4" h, figural, Kerk Gild, orig box, c1930 ....75.00

Joe Penner, valentine, 4-1/2" x 7", mechanical diecut, Joe holding duck on shoulder, eyeballs and mouth move back and forth, inscription "I'll Gladly Buy a Duck," c1935 ....25.00

Sgt. Preston

Cereal Premium, game, Sgt. Preston Gets His Man, clipped from box, 6" x 7" playing board, 3" x 5" perforated

spinner board, mid-1950s........32.00

Map, 7-1/2" x 9-1/2", full color illus, stories and territory history on back, c1955 ....40.00

Pouch, 3-1/2" x 4-1/2", paper, tan, leather drawstring, orig mailing box, Quaker Cereal premium, 1955 ....150.00

Melvin Purvis, premium instruction manual, 5" x 7", b&w, 24 pgs, Post Toasties adv, 1938 G.F. Corp.........................65.00

ROA, decoder, 1936 ....18.00

The Shadow

Blotter, 4" x 9", cardboard, orange, blue and white, red silhouette, 1940s 24.00

Figure, 7" h, china, glossy black cloak and hat, dark blue accent hat brim, white base with gold accents and stripes, c1930 ....265.00

Twin Stars, store advertising card, 11-1/4" x 16-1/4", blue, yellow and red thin cardboard, b&w photos of 1937 edition of Twin Stars Friday night radio show, Helen Broderick and Victor Moore, Buddy Rogers and his Orchestra, National Biscuit Co. ...48.00

Uncle Don, pinback button

Taystee Bread..............................50.00

Uncle Don's Ice Cream Club, Borden's, red ground on lower half, portrait of Uncle Don, radio microphone, mkd "Puldin Co. Inc., NYC" 25.00

Ed Wynn, puzzle, promotional, NBC Radio 35.00

Radio Premiums

Collecting Hints: Most collections are centered around one or two specific personalities or radio programs.

History: Radio premiums are nostalgic reminders of the radio shows of childhood. Sponsors of shows frequently used their products as a means of earning premiums, such as saving box tops to exchange for gifts related to a program or personality.

References: Ted Hake, *Hake's Price Guide to Character Toy Premiums*, Collector Books, 1996; Robert M. Overstreet, *Overstreet Premium Ring Price Guide*, Gemstone Publishing, 1995; ——, *Overstreet Toy Ring Price Guide*, 2nd Edition, Collector Books, 1996; Tom Tumbusch, *Tomart's Price Guide to Radio Premium and Cereal Box Collectibles*, Wallace-Homestead, 1991.

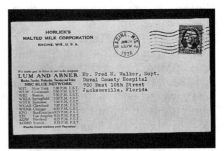

Lum and Abner, envelope, issued by Horlick's Malted Milk Corp., Racine, WI, postmarked Jan. 28, 1936, showing times of radio program on NBC Blue Network, 6-1/2" x 3-5/8", $6.50.

Periodical: *Box Top Bonanza*, 3403 46th Ave., Moline, IL 61265.

Reproduction Alert.

Additional Listings: Radio Characters and Personalities.

Gracie Allen, booklet, 5" x 8", *Gracie Allen's Anniversary Gift to Guy Lombardo*, General Cigar Co., 24 b&w pgs, text and graphics, photo of Burns and Allen with Lombardo, 1933 ....14.00

Jimmie Allen

ID Bracelet, 1935 ....25.00

Whistle, brass, c1936....................28.00

Amos and Andy

Advertising puzzle, Pepsodent, 1931 ....40.00

Map and Letter, Pepsodent premium, full-color "Eagle's View of Weber City, Inc.," orig mailing envelope, 1935........................95.00

Jack Armstrong

Patch, Future Champions of America, cloth, 1943................................20.00

Photo, Jack on his horse Blackster, 1933 ....15.00

Ring, Dragon's Eye, crocodile design, green stone, 1940 ....145.00

Jack Barbour, scrapbook, 8" x 10", soft-cover, white accents, 16 b&w pgs, photos, facsimile newspaper clippings, diary pages, Standard Brands, 1936 ....28.00

Frank Buck

Neckerchief, Frank Buck's Adventurers Club, 1936................................60.00

Pinback Button, Adventurers Club, 1936 ....15.00

Captain Midnight

Decoder, Magni-Matic Code-O-Graph, 1946 ....45.00

Ovaltine Mug, 3-1/8" h, red plastic, colorful decal of Captain saying "Hot Ovaltine-the Heart of a Hearty Breakfast," c1953......65.00

Patch, iron-on, 1948......35.00

Chandu Magic Trick Set, 11" x 14" x 1-1/2" d box, orange, black, white and blue graphics, Chandu gesturing over crystal ball, little girl and dog watching, red diecut insert, mini wood ball trick, black aluminum disappearing scarf trick, safety matchbox, 4 illus black and white boxes, card tricks, coin trick, magic cone trick, billiard ball trick, illus b&w instruction sheet, blue and white White King Soap sponsor adv sheet, red and tan White King coupon, c1933......200.00

Green Hornet, membership card..12.00

Little Orphan Annie

Comic Book, 7" x 10-1/8", full color, 16 pgs, 1938, Popped Wheat......24.00

Costume, premium from Motorola, red paper dress, full-color paper mask, special Motorola Dick Tracy Comic book, Motorola catalog featuring latest TV models, 1953......85.00

Manual, *Radio Orphan Annie's Secret Society*, 1937......40.00

Mask, Annie, 1933......35.00

Lone Ranger

Badge, Chief Scout, 1935......65.00

Certificate, Safety Club, 1938......10.00

Pinback Button, Safety Club, 1934......20.00

Mandrake the Magician, pinback button, Magic Club......55.00

Don McNeill, Breakfast Club, yearbook, orig mailer, 1948......20.00

Tom Mix

Bandanna, checkered border, 1933......40.00

Decoder Button, orig Ralston card, 1936......85.00

Picture, 4-3/4" x 6-7/8", b&w, Mix standing next to Tony, facsimile autograph "To My Straight Shooter Pal From Tom Mix," mid-1930s......35.00

Phantom, Pilot Patrol, membership badge......30.00

Radio Explorers Club, membership certificate, 8-1/2" x 11", white sheet, orange accents, Eastern and Western hemisphere globes, sailing ship with 3/4" d red "Sponsored by American-Bosch Round the World Radio" emb seal at lower left, ink signature of orig member, printed Capt. James Barker at lower right, early 1930s......28.00

Buck Rogers, badge, Solar Scout member, 1935......30.00

The Shadow, rubber stamp......40.00

Superman

Belt and Buckle, 1946......70.00

Certificate, membership, 1940......22.00

Tennessee Jed, mask, paper......20.00

Dick Tracy

Badge, Detective Club Shield......20.00

Manual, Secret Detective Methods & Magic Tricks, 1939......24.00

Don Winslow

Decoder, Golden Torpedo, 1942...65.00

Membership Ring, 1939......50.00

Periscope, 1939......50.00

Radios

Collecting Hints: Radio collectors divide into three groups: those who collect because of nostalgia, those interested in history and/or acquiring radios that represent specific periods and collectors of personality and figural radios. Most collectors find broadcasting and, therefore, broadcast receivers of primary interest.

Broadcast receivers can be divided into these significant categories:

• Crystal sets and battery powered receivers of the early 1920s

• Rectangular electric table models of the late 1920s

• Cathedrals, tombstones and consoles of the 1930s

• Midget plastic portables and wood-cabinet table models built before and after World War II

• Shaped radios with cases made of Bakelite or other plastic

• Personality and figural radios made between the 1930s and the 1960s

Because the prime nostalgic period seems to be the decade of the 1930s, the cathedral-style, socket-powered radios (e.g., the Philco series) have become sought-after items. Recently, young collectors have exhibited interest in the plastic-cabinet radios built between 1945 and 1960.

Newer radio collectors are influenced by novelty, with the outside appearance the most important feature. The radio must play; but, shape, color, decoration and condition of the case far outweigh the internal workings of the set in determining desirability and, consequently, price. Enclosures that resemble things or figures (e.g., Mickey Mouse) command premium prices. The square table models of the later 1930s and the midget sets of the late 1930s and 1940s have recently attracted the attention of collectors.

The value of a radio is directly proportional to its appearance and its operating condition. Minor scratches are to be expected, as is alligatoring of the surface finish, but gouges, cracks and delaminated surfaces adversely affect prices, as will a crack, a broken place where plastic closures belong or missing parts, tubes or components. If major repairs are required to make the set work, the price must reflect this potential expense.

Many collectors specialize in radio-related memorabilia, brand names or in a facet of radio paraphernalia such as loudspeakers, tubes or microphones. As a result, auxiliary and radio-related items are becoming collectibles along with radios themselves.

Very rare radios usually go directly to major collectors, seldom appearing in the general market. Wireless equipment and radios used commercially before World War I are considered rare and are not listed here.

History: The radio was invented more than 100 years ago. Marconi was the first to assemble and employ the transmission and reception instruments that permitted electric messages to be sent without the use of direct connections. The early name for radio was "Wireless," and its first application was to control ships in 1898. Early wireless equipment is not generally considered collectible since its historic value makes it important for museum display.

Between 1905 and the end of World War I, many technical advances, including the invention of the vacuum tube by DeForest, increased communication technology and encouraged amateur interest. The receiving equipment from that period is desired by collectors and historians but is rarely available.

By 1920, radio technology allowed broadcasts to large numbers of people simultaneously and music could be brought directly from concert halls into living rooms. The result was the development of a new art that changed the American way of life during the 1920s. The world became familiar through the radio in an average listener's home.

Radio receivers changed substantially in the decade of the 1920s, going from black boxes—with many knobs and dials—powered by expensive and messy batteries, to stylish furniture, simple to use and operated from the house current that had become the standard source of home energy. During the 1920s, radios grew more complicated and powerful as well as more ornate. Consoles appeared, loudspeakers were incorporated into them and sound fidelity became an important consideration.

In the early 1930s, demand changed. The large expensive console gave way to small but effective table models. The era of the "cathedral" and the "tombstone" began. By the end of the 1930s, the midget radio had become popular. Quality of sound was replaced by a price reduction and most homes had more than one radio. Shortly after World War II, the miniature tubes developed for the military were utilized in domestic radios. The result was further reduction in size and a substantial improvement in quality. The advent of FM also speeded improvements. Plastic technology made possible the production of attractive cases in many styles and colors.

The other development that drastically changed the radio receiver was the invention of the transistor in 1927. A whole new family of radio sets that could be carried in the shirt pocket became popular. Their popularity grew as they became less and less expensive, but their low cost meant that they were frequently thrown away when they stopped working. Today, they are not easy to find in good condition and are, therefore, quite collectible.

References: John H. Bryant and Harold N. Cones, *Zenith Trans-Oceanic*, Schiffer Publishing, 1995; Mar-

Fada, Art Deco, catalin, yellow, red trim, made in USA, 1934, 5-1/2" x 10-1/2" x 6", $600.

ty and Sue Bunis, *Collector's Guide to Antique Radios*, 4th Edition, Collector Books, 1997; ——, *Collector's Guide to Transistor Radios*, Collector Books, 1994; Marty Bunis and Robert F. Breed, *Collector's Guide to Novelty Radios*, Collector Books, 1995; *Evolution of the Radio*, Vol. I (1991, 1994 value update), *Vol. II* (1993), L-W Book Sales; Roger Handy, Maureen Erbe and Aileen Farnan Antonier, *Made in Japan: Transistor Radios of the 1950s and 1960s*, Chronicle Books, 1993; David Johnson, *Antique Radio Restoration Guide*, 2nd Edition, Wallace-Homestead, 1992; David R. and Robert A. Lane, *Transistor Radios*, Wallace-Homestead, 1994; Harry Poster, *Poster's Radio & Television Price Guide*, 2nd Edition, Wallace-Homestead, 1994; ——, *Illustrated Price Guide to Vintage Televisions and Deco Radios*, published by author, 1991; Ron Ramirez, *Philco Radio*, Schiffer Publishing, 1993.

Periodicals: *Antique Radio Classified*, P.O. Box 2, Carlisle, MA 01746; *Antique Radio Topics*, Box 28572, Dallas, TX 75228; *Horn Speaker*, P.O. Box 1193, Mabank, TX 75147; *Radio Age*, 636 Cambridge Rd., Augusta, GA 30909; *Transistor Network*, RR1, Box 36, Bradford, NH 03221.

Videotape: Roger Handy and Eric Wrobbel, *Favorite Transistor Radios*, available from producers (20802 Exhibit Ct., Woodland Hills, CA 91367).

Collectors' Clubs: Antique Radio Club of America, 300 Washington Trails, Washington, PA 15301; Antique Wireless Association, 59 Main St., Bloomfield, NY 14469; New En-

gland Antique Radio Club, RR1 Box 36, Bradford, NH 03221; Vintage Radio & Phonograph Society, Inc., P.O. Box 165345, Irving, TX 75016.

Museums: Antique Wireless Association's Electronic Communication Museum, Bloomfield, NY; Caperton's Radio Museum, Louisville, KY; Muchow's Historical Radio Museum, Elgin, IL; Museum of Broadcast Communications, Chicago, IL; Museum of Wonderful Wireless, Minneapolis, MN; New England Museum of Wireless and Steam, East Greenwich, RI; Voice of the Twenties, Orient, NY.

Advisor: Lewis S. Walters.

Notes: The prices listed are for sets in average to good condition and are based upon an electrically complete receiver that operates when powered.

Admiral, portable
   #33, #35, #37, c1940 .... 25.00
   #218, leatherette, 1958 .... 40.00
   #909, All World, 1960 .... 85.00
Advertising
   Avon Deco, MIB 75.00
   Beanee Weanee, MIB 40.00
   Bud Can, MIB 50.00
   Camus Grand Cognac
   Bottle, MIB 60.00
   Chester Cheetah, MIB 35.00
   Crayola Rocks, MIB 35.00
   4 Seasons Can, MIB 40.00
   Gulden's Mustard Jr., MIB 75.00
   Heinz Ketchup Bottle, MIB 75.00
   Kraft Macaroni &
   Cheese Box, MIB 35.00
   Marlboro Pack, MIB 65.00
   Old Parr Scotch, bottle, MIB 85.00
   Polaroid 600 Plus Film, MIB 50.00
   Scrubbing Bubbles, MIB 50.00
   Tony the Tiger, MIB 30.00
   Tropicana Orange, MIB 35.00
   Welch's, MIB 55.00
Air King, #1946, tombstone, Art Deco,
   plastic, 1935 .... 3,000.00
Arvin
   #522A, ivory metal, 1941 .... 60.00
   Character, Hopalong Cassidy,
   lariatenna 475.00
   Tombstone, #617, Rhythm Maid,
   1936 .... 215.00
Atwater Kent
   Breadboard
      Model 9A 750.00
      Model 10 .... 1,000.00
      Model 10C 900.00
   Cathedral, #80, 1931 .... 380.00
   Table, #55, Keil 225.00

Bulova, clock radio
    #100, 1957 ....40.00
    #120, 1958 ....40.00
Character
    Power Ranger 35.00
    Spiderman................................50.00
Crosley
    Bandbox, #601, 1927 ....75.00
    Gemchest, #609, 1928...........410.00
    Litfella, 1-N cathedral 175.00
    Pup, with box...........................600.00
    Sheraton cathedral, 1933.......290.00
    Showbox, #706, 1928 ....100.00
    Super Buddy Boy,
    #122, 1930 ....325.00
    X Table Radio, 1922 ....175.00
Dumont, RA-346, table, scroll work,
    1956..110.00
Emerson
    Tombstone, Catalin
        #AU-190, 1938.....................1,000
        #BT-245, scalloped dial,
        darker grill 1,000
    #400
        Aristocrat, Catalin, 1940.....600.00
        Patriot, 1940.......................750.00
    #409, Mickey Mouse, wood, black
    and red metal trim 1,300.00
    #411, Mickey Mouse,
    pressed wood, Mickey playing
    instrument, 1933 ....1,400.00
    #570, Memento, picture holder,
    1945 ....110.00
    #640, portable, plastic, flip-up front,
    battery set1950 ....30.00
    #888, Vanguard, transistor,
    portable, 1958 ....60.00
Fada
    Cathedral, #43,
    pressed wood.........................240.00
    Table
        Catalin
        #136, 1941 ....1,000.00
        #252, temple, 1941 ....625.00
        Plastic, #60W 75.00
Federal, table
    #58DX, 1922 ....500.00
    #110, 1924 ....425.00
General Electric
    Clock Radio, # 515
    and # 517, 1950s 30.00
    Console, K-126,
    wood, 1933............................150.00
    Table, #400, #410, #411 and
    #414, all plastic 30.00
Grebe, table
    CR-12, 1923...........................600.00
    MU-1, with chain, 1925 ....200.00
Hallicrafters
    TW-200, World Wide..............100.00
    TW-600, portable, map, whip

antenna, AC/DC
    battery, 1954 ....100.00
Majestic
    Charlie McCarthy, 1938 ......1,000.00
    Console, #92, 1929................125.00
    Treasure Chest, #381, 1934 ..225.00
Motorola
    Jewel Box, #5J1 ....80.00
    Ranger
        #700, 1957 ....45.00
        Portable, leatherette trim 40.00
    Table, plastic, 1950s 35.00
    Transistor
        Jet plane, #7X23E 70.00
        "M" logo, 1960.....................25.00
        Pixie 45.00
Olympic, radio with phonograph,
    lift top, wood 40.00
Paragon, table
    #DA-2, 1921.........................450.00
    #RD-5, 1922 ....600.00
Philco
    Cathedral, #17,
    #20 and #38 ....250.00
    Clock radio, T1000..................80.00
    Console, #40-180, wood 130.00
    Table
        #37-602, Art Deco grill 90.00
        #46-132................................45.00
    Transistor, T-7-126, plastic 65.00
    Transitone, #49-506.................35.00
Radiobar, complete console, glasses,
    decanter 1,300.00
Radio Corp., of America (RCA)
    LaSiesta, 1939 ....300.00
    Radiola
        #18......................................55.00
        #24......................................160.00
        #28, console, highboy........200.00
        #33......................................40.00
    Table, #6X7, plastic, 1956 ....25.00
    Transistor, portable, #8BT-7LE,
    1957 ....35.00
    World's Fair, #40X56, 1939 ...975.00
Silvertone (Sears)
    Cathedral, #1582, wood.........225.00
    Table, #1, 1950 ....75.00
    Tombstone, #1955, 1936 ....135.00
    Transistor, #9205,
    plastic, 1959 ....40.00
Sony, transistor
    TFM-151, 1960 ....50.00
    TR-63, 1958 ....140.00
Sparton, #506, Bluebird, table, round
    blue or peach mirror 3,600.00
Stewart-Warner, table,
    slant, 1938............................175.00
Zenith
    Royal, transistor
        #500, owl eye, 1959...........130.00
        #500D, plastic, 1959............55.00

    #750L, leather case, 1959 ...40.00
    Table, #6D2615, boomerang
    dial, 1942 ....95.00
    Trans-Oceanic 140.00

Railroad Items

Collecting Hints: Most collectors concentrate on one railroad as opposed to one type of object. Railroad material always brings a higher price in the area in which it originated. Local collectors tend to concentrate on local railroads. The highest prices are paid for material from railroads which operated for only a short time. Nostalgia also influences collectors.

    There are many local railroad clubs. Railroad buffs tend to have their own specialized swap meets and exhibitions. A large one is held in Gaithersburg, MD, in the fall each year.

History: It was a canal company, the Delaware and Hudson, which used the first steam locomotive in America. The Stourbridge Lion moved coal from the mines to the canal wharves. Just as America was entering its great canal era in 1825, the railroad was gaining a foothold. The Commonwealth of Pennsylvania did not heed William Strickland's advice to concentrate on building railroads instead of canals.

    By the 1840s, railroad transportation was well-established. Numerous private companies were organized although many remained in business for only a short time. During the Civil War, the effectiveness of the railroad was demonstrated. Immediately following the war, the transcontinental railroad was completed and entrepreneurs such as Gould and Vanderbilt created financial empires.

**China, Northern Pacific, soup bowl, 9",
mkd "Ivory, Lamberton, Scammel,"
$275.**

Mergers generated huge systems. The golden age of the railroad extended from the 1880s to the 1940s.

After 1950, the railroads suffered from poor management, a bloated labor force, lack of maintenance and competition from other forms of transportation. Thousands of miles of track were abandoned. Many railroads failed or merged together. The 1970s saw the federal government enter the picture with Conrail and Amtrak. Today railroads still are fighting for survival.

References: Susan and Al Bagdade, *Warman's American Pottery and Porcelain*, Wallace-Homestead, 1994; Stanley L. Baker, *Railroad Collectibles*, 4th Edition, Collector Books, 1990, 1993 value update; Richard C. Barrett, *Illustrated Encyclopedia of Railroad Lighting*, Railroad Research Publications, 1994; Phil Bollhagen (comp.), *Great Book of Railroad Playing Cards*, published by author, 1991; *Collectible Lanterns*, L-W Book Sales, 1996; David Dreimiller, *Dressel Railway Lamp & Signal Company*, Hiram Press, 1995: Joseph F. Farrell Jr., *Illustrated Guide to Peter Gray Railroad Hardware*, Hiram Press, 1994; Anthony Hobson, *Lanterns That Lit Our World*, Hiram Press, reprinted 1996; Richard Luckin, *Dining on Rails*, RK Publishing, 1994; ——, *Mimbres to Mimbreno*, RK Publishing, 1992; Everett L. Maffett, *Silver Banquet II*, Silver Press, 1990; Douglas McIntyre, *Official Guide to Railroad Dining Car China*, Walsworth Press, 1990; Larry R. Paul, *Sparkling Crystal: A Collector's Guide to Railroad Glassware*, Railroadiana Collectors Association, Inc., 1990; Don Stewart, *Railroad Switch Keys & Padlocks*, 2nd Edition, Key Collectors International, 1993.

Periodicals: *Key, Lock and Lantern*, P.O. Box 65, Demarest, NJ 07627; *U.S. Rail News*, P.O. Box 7007, Huntingdon Woods, MI 48070.

Collectors' Clubs: Chesapeake & Ohio Historical Society, Inc., P.O. Box 79, Clifton Forge, VA 24422; Illinois Central Railroad Historical Society, 14818 Cliron Park, Midlothian, IL 60445; Railroad Enthusiasts, 102 Dean Rd., Brookline, MA 02146;

Railroadiana Collectors Association, 795 Aspen Dr., Buffalo Grove, IL 60089; Railway and Locomotive Historical Society, P.O. Box 1418, Westford, MA 01886; Twentieth Century Railroad Club, 329 W. 18th St., Ste. 902, Chicago, IL 60616.

Museums: Baltimore and Ohio Railroad, Baltimore, MD; California State Railroad Museum, Sacramento, CA; Museum of Transportation, Brookline, MA; New York Museum of Transportation, West Henrietta, NY.

Ashtray, Southern Railroad 17.50
Baggage Check, Texas Central RR,
    1-5/8" x 2", brass, Poole Bros.,
    Chicago 38.50
Blanket, Canadian Pacific 85.00
Blotter, Soo Line, 1920s, unused 5.00
Book
    Locomotive Cyclopedia 1927,
    American Railroad Association,
    1,327 pgs 65.00
    Henry T. Williams, *Pacific Tourist
    Guide over the Continent,* NY,
    1877, 300 pgs 75.00
Booklet
    By the Way of the Canyons, Soo
    Line, 1907 .... 20.00
    Union Pacific RR, 1926 .... 15.00
Brochure
    California Picture Book, ATSF, illus,
    1930s 7.50
    Eastern Summer Trips, B&O 9.00
    French National Fares,
    turbo on cov 7.50
    Holiday Haunts, Adirondacks & 1,000
    Islands, NYC, 1940, 63 pgs 10.00
Calendar
    Chicago, Milwaukee, St. Paul
    Railway, pretty girl illus, Sept./Oct.
    1903, 10" x 14" 75.00
    C&O RR, 1937, Chessie 45.00
    Union Pacific, 1969,
    Centennial 24.00
Catalog, Hibbard Spencer Barlett & Co.,
    Railway and Manufacturer's
    Supplies, 1907, 632 pgs 55.00
Car Inspector's Record, D&RGW,
    Ridway, filled in, 1928 .... 10.00
Cereal Premium,
    tin sign, set of 10 .... 35.00
China
    Bouillon Cup, WP, feather Friver, top
    logo, Shenango 75.00
    Butter Pat, Mimbreno, Syracuse
    China, mkd 30.00
    Celery Dish, Union Pacific, 10" l,
    oval, blue and gold pattern,
    mkd "Scannel China" 40.00
    Coffee Cup, Illinois Central, Coral

    pattern 15.00
    Creamer, B&O Centenary 65.00
    Cup and Saucer
        B&O, Capital 50.00
        NYC, Mercury,
        Syracuse, mkd 55.00
        Southern Pacific 65.00
    Demitasse Cup and Saucer,
    CMSTP&P, Traveler,
    Syracuse, mkd 85.00
    Plate
        Missouri Pacific,
        state flowers 275.00
        NP, dinner, Yellowstone Park Line
        logo, top mkd, Shenango... 145.00
        NYC, dinner, Mohawk, salmon
        pink and black, top mkd 45.00
    Platter
        Southern, Peach Blossom,
        top mkd with logo and
        "Southern Serves the South,"
        Buffalo China 125.00
        Union Pacific, 8" l, oval, Challeng-
        er pattern, top mkd "The Challeng-
        er," mkd Union Pacific RR ... 45.00
    Sauce Dish, NYNH&H, Indian Tree
    pattern, Buffalo China mark 35.00
    Sherbet, PRR, Keystone, Buffalo
    China 65.00
    Soup Plate
        B&O, Capitol,
        Shenango China 85.00
        PRR, Purple Laurel, 6-1/2" d,
        broad lip, Sterling China 40.00
Clothing and Accessories
    Conductor's Suit, CB&Q, 3 pieces,
    dark blue, brass emb buttons .. 95.00

Lamp, stationmaster's, PA RR, $265.

Hat, agent
Boston & Maine, gold finish,
curved top 45.00
Burlington Route 115.00
Lapel Button, Lake Shore & Michigan
Southern, mail-sack shape.......45.00
Patch, coat sleeve type, Santa Fe,
silver bar....................................18.00
Tie Pin, Brotherhood Railroad
Trainmen, 25 years, 10k gold...30.00
Conductor's Report, Wiscasset,
Waterville & Farmington Railway,
filled in, 1920s............................5.00
Freight Receipt, Utica & Black River RR,
1873...5.00
Hat Rack, overhead-type, coach,
wood and brass, 6 brass double-
sided hooks 200.00
Head Rest Cover
PRR, 15" x 18", tan ground, brown
logo, electric train 15.00
Seaboard Coast, 17" x 16",
gold ground, interwoven green
"Seaboard Coast Line Railroad,"
train, palm trees......................10.00
Lamp
Caboose, side, int, C&O Railroad,
c1920, price for pr 350.00
Pullman, brass, early electric, white
Bakelite shade, heavy wall brackets,
7-1/2" h, price for pr 145.00
Lantern
Adams & Westlake, conductor's, car-
bide, nickel over brass 195.00
D&H, clear globe 250.00
Missouri Pacific,
hand, 4" clear globe 75.00
New York Central, bell bottom, red
globe, 6" h, Deitz No. 6, raised
letters 100.00
Southern Railway, red globe ..150.00
Magazine, *Railway Age*, 190, 64 pgs,
9" x 12" 9.00
Map
Atlantic Coast Line, large route,
c1950 ....150.00
Railroad Map of the State of Ohio
1877, O.W. Gray & Son,
27-1/2" x 17-1/2" 30.00
1975, J.A. Caldwell,
26-1/2" x 17" 35.00
Menu
Amtrak, Good Morning, single card,
7" x 11"...3.00
Chicago & North Western Railway,
1958, luncheon, Mt. Rushmore on
cov, issued for Sam Campbell
Alaska Tour 7.50
Lehigh Valley, Black Diamond
Express, dinner, 1927, chef and
train on cov...............................40.00
NYC, Thrift Grill, folder, 1955 .....5.00
Santa Fe, Super Chief, luncheon,

folder, 1971 ....5.00
Nail File, Cotton Belt RR 9.00
Napkin, linen
Burlington Route, 20" sq, white,
woven logo...............................10.00
C&O, blue monogram 8.50
Rio Grande, white,
woven logo...............................12.00
Oil Can, Locomotive Oil 100.00
Padlock, Rock Island, orig key 35.00
Paperweight, 6" x 2" x 2-1/2", General
American Car Co., Modern Milk
Transportation, Refrigerated Glass
lined Tank Car 120.00
Pass
Baltimore and Ohio, 1930s 4.00
Boston and Maine, 1950s 3.00
Fort Smith & Western, 1920s.....6.75
Pennsylvania, 1940s..................3.00
Union Pacific, 1920s 5.00
Wisconsin Central, 1910 ....7.50
Playing Cards
Chessie 20.00
Denver & Rio
Grande Railways......................35.00
EJ&E RR 20.00
Milwaukee Road 15.00
Pocket Calendar,
Santa Fe RR, 1972....................5.00
Postcard, Washington Virginia Railway
Co., scenic, pack 15.00
Rules Book, C&NW, 1929, illus.....15.00
Seal, box car, Wiscasset, Waterville
& Farmington RR, identification
plus serial numbers 7.50
Silver Flatware and Hollowware
Bouillon Spoon, ACL, Zephyr, mkd
"ACL" and "Intl" 25.00
Creamer, PRR, International
Silver Co., soldered, seamless,
"PRR" on bottom 100.00
Dinner Fork, GM&O, Broadway
pattern, International 18.00
Dinner Knife, PRR, Broadway
pattern, mkd "PRR" 10.00
Ladle, New York Central, mkd
"International Silver"................25.00
Soup Spoon,
Southern Pacific.......................20.00
Sugar
Lackawanna, back mkd "Lack-
awanna, International" 145.00
PRR, International Silver Co.,
soldered, keystone mark
on bottom...........................100.00
Tray, 8" l, oval, New Haven RR,
mkd "New Haven RR, International,
1936"......................................35.00
Stamp Set, Jacksonville, FL, freight of-
fice, Atlantic Coast Line, wooddriver,
70 city stamps, c1950............150.00
Step, Pullman RR Station, wood, hand

cut out on top, 21" w, 10" h,
17-1/2" d................................25.00
Stock Certificate, B&O
Railroad, 1920 ....14.00
Tablecloth
California Zephyr, 36" x 42", white,
interwoven oval logo 17.50
Frisco Railway, 36" sq, white,
Frisco emblem 30.00
Illinois Central RR,
banquet size 70.00
Timetable
Erie Railroad, illus, 1907 ....30.00
Hoosier Tunnel Route, 1895....55.00
Lackawanna, Sept. 1952, Phoebe
Snow streamliner on front........10.00
L&N Kansas City Southern,
passenger train, 1955 ....7.50
Norfolk & Western,
employee, 1960s 5.00
Northern Pacific RR, 1927 ....12.00
Southern Pacific RR,
1915, 15 pgs 20.00
Voucher, Union Pacific, Denver and Gulf
Railway, 1890s.........................5.00
Watchman's Station Box, iron.......25.00
Waybill, Kennebec Central, large size,
filled in 7.50

Razors

Collecting Hints: A major revolution
has occurred in razor collecting in
the 1980s. At the beginning of the
decade, almost all collectors focused on the straight razor. By the
late 1980s the collecting of safety razors, their related material and electric shavers has achieved a
popularity that should equal or ex-
ceed that of the straight razor collecting by the 1990s.

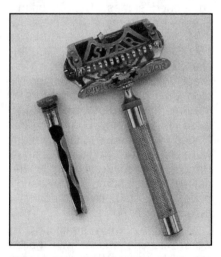

**Safety, Star, Kampee, NY, pat 1900,
built-in strop, 4" l, 2" w, $35.**

Many straight razor collectors focus on the products of a single manufacturer. Value is higher for items associated with certain names, e.g., H. Boker, Case, M. Price, Joseph Rogers, Simmons Hardware, Will & Finck, Winchester and George Wostenholm. The ornateness of the handle and blade pattern also influences value. The fancier the handle or more intricately etched the blade, the higher the price. Rarest handle materials are pearl, stag, sterling silver, pressed horn and carved ivory. Rarest blades are those with scenes etched across the entire front.

Initially, safety razor collectors focused on those razors that were packaged in elaborately lithographed tins from 1890 to 1915. Collectors want the safety razor in a complete kit, i.e., razor, blades, case or tin, instructions, etc. Support items such as blade banks, boxes and sharpeners also attract collectors. The price of many safety razors from the early period already exceeds $50. As a result, new collectors are seeking safety razors from the 1920s through the 1950s because a comprehensive collection can still be assembled at a modest price.

When buying an electric shaver, make certain that it is complete and in working order. Many were originally sold with cleaning kits, most of which have been lost.

History: Razors date back several thousand years. Early man used sharpened stones. The Egyptians, Greeks and Romans had metal razors. Straight razors made prior to 1800 generally were crudely stamped "Warranted" or "Cast Steel," with the maker's mark on the tang. Until 1870, almost all razors for the American market were manufactured in Sheffield, England. Most blades were wedge shaped; many were etched with slogans or scenes. Handles were made of natural materials—various horns, tortoiseshell, bone, ivory, stag, silver or pearl. All razors were handmade.

After 1870, most straight razors were machine made with hollow ground blades and handles of synthetic materials. Razors of this period

usually were manufactured in Germany (Solingen) or in American cutlery factories. Hundreds of molded celluloid handle patterns were produced, such as nude women, eagles, deer, boats and windmill scenes. By 1900, the safety razor was challenging the straight razor for popularity among the shaving community. A wealth of safety razor patents were issued in the first decade of the 20th century. World War I ensured the dominance of the safety razor as American troops abroad made it their preferred shaving utensil. By the 1930s, the first electric shavers appeared, but they did not achieve universal acceptance until the 1950s.

References: Ronald S. Barlow, *Vanishing American Barber Shop*, Windmill Publishing, 1993; Roy Ritchie and Ron Stewart, *Standard Guide to Razors*, Collector Books, 1995; *Safety Razors*, L-W Book Sales, 1995; Jim Sargent, *Sargent's American Premium Guide to Knives & Razors*, 4th Edition, Books Americana, 1995.

Periodical: *Blade Magazine*, 700 E. State St., Iola, WI 54990.

Collectors' Club: Safety Razor Collectors' Guild, P.O. Box 885, Crescent City, CA 95531.

Blade Bank
  2" h, tin, Gem Blades, book shape, gold, red and black 9.00
  2" x 1-1/2" x 1", tin, Ever-ready, treasure-chest shape, orange, black and gold 24.00
  6" h, porcelain, barber-pole shape, red and white stripes, black letters 27.50
Corn Razor
  Bandwagon, Japanese, orig cardboard box 30.00
  Griffon, mkd "Griffin Angle" 35.00
  J.A. Henckels, Twin Works, Germany, rounded and shaped plain bone handle, orig box, silver emb adv 50.00
  Reliance Cutlery Co., 2-colored celluloid handle 75.00
  Rogers & Sons, mkd "Corn Razor" on light colored handle 25.00
Electric Shaver, Schick, black Bakelite, stamped "Model S," orig case and cord 15.00
Razor Hone, Keen Kutter Kombination, fancy emb adv tin, yellow, green, white and black 45.00
Razor Strop, 23-1/2" l, leather strap

mounted on turned wood spools, inscribed "Ono L. Larpy," 19th C 115.00
Safety Razor
  American Can Co., The New Griffon, 2-part handle, interchangeable heads, tin container, patent 1901 .... 235.00
  Curvfit, lady's, orig instructions, orig blue and gold box 10.00
  Devine, ivory handle, double edge, blade guard, leather cov wood case, includes "The Devine Caretaker Chicago USA" adv sharpener 85.00
  Ever-Ready, red and black box, cardboard blade holders 15.00
  Gem Minute Man, metal, wall-mount type, blade holder 30.00
  Gillette, U.S. Service Set, emb metal case, engraved "Stanley J. Lane, Rochester, NY" in shield, fitted metal mirror 35.00
  Henckels Rapide, black and gold, tin box 15.00
  Herbrand, Fremont, OH, orig cardboard box 12.00
  Kampfe Bros., NY, The Star, cylindrical tin container 275.00
  Kewtie Cosmetic Razor, lady's, celluloid handle and case, light blue 30.00
  Laurel, Ladies Boudoir, orig purple tin, cardboard box and instructions 25.00
  Mohican, instructions, orig "Mohican" stamped blade, orig tin 115.00
  Segal, gold plated, blades, instructions, orig box 25.00
  Stahly, windup type, vibrates, orig plastic case 20.00
  Yankee, patent 1903, red and blue tin container, instructions on lid .. 195.00
Straight Razor
  Asco Cutlery Co., imitation ivory handle, Art Nouveau floral design 35.00
  H. Boker & Co., etched "American Lines SS St. Louis" on blade, black handle 15.00
  Crown & Sword, etched "Crown & Sword Manufactory" scene blade, clear horn handle, German silver ends, dated "1873-1898" 35.00
  Holley Mfg. Co., plain black celluloid handle 25.00
  Keen Kutter, etched eagle on blade, emb horn handle 80.00
  Simmons Hardware Co., celluloid handle, twisted bamboo design, blade mkd "Barber's Pet" 90.00
  Wade & Butcher, Sheffield, etched American eagle, "E Pluribus Unum" banner, semi-wedge blade,

bone handle 65.00
Waterville Cutlery Co., CT, black celluloid handle, raised pattern of large oak leaves, scroll with acorns, blade etched "Waterville Hand Forged" 75.00

Reamers

Collecting Hints: Reamers are seldom found in mint condition. Cone and rim nicks are usually acceptable, but cracked pieces sell for considerably less. Ceramic figurals and American-made glass examples are collected more than any other types.

Reamer collecting, which can be an endless hobby, first became popular as a sideline to Depression glass collecting in the mid-1960s. It may be impossible to assemble a collection that includes one of every example made. One-of-a-kind items do exist as some samples were never put into mass production.

History: Devices for getting the juice from citrus fruit have been around almost as long as the fruit itself. These devices were made from all types of material—from wood to glass and from nickel plate and sterling silver to fine china.

Many different kinds of mechanical reamers were devised before the first glass one was pressed around 1885. Very few new designs have appeared since 1940 when frozen juice entered the market. Modern-day ceramists are making clown- and teapot-shaped reamers.

References: Gene Florence, *Kitchen Glassware of the Depression Years*, 5th Edition, Collector Books, 1995, 1997 value update; Mary Walker, *Reamers*, Muski Publishers, out of print (separate price guide); — —, *The Second Book*, Muski Publishers, out of print.

Collectors' Club: National Reamer Collectors Association, 47 Midline Ct., Gaithersburg, MD 20878.

Reproduction Alert: Many glass reamers are being reproduced at this time. Some are American reissues from original molds, while others are made from old reamers in Asia. The Asian reamers are usually easy to spot since they are made from poor-quality glass that feels greasy and is

China, pear, shades of yellow and orange, green leaves, L-39, 4-1/4" x 5", $48.

generally thicker than that used in the originals. Many reproductions are being made in colors which were never used originally, but some of the reamers being made from the original molds are the same colors as the originals making them harder to detect. There are also several new ceramic reamers being made. One even looks like an old piece of flow blue or English china.

An old 5-inch Imperial Glass Co., reamer, originally made in clear glass, was reproduced for Edna Barnes in dark amethyst; 1,500 were made. The reproduction is marked "IG" and "81."

Mrs. Barnes has also reproduced several old 4-1/2-inch Jenkins Glass Co., reamers in limited editions. The reproductions are also made in a 2-1/4-inch size. All Jenkins copies are marked with a "B" in a circle. Collectors should consult Gene Florence's book for information about glass reproductions. Also, the National Reamer Collectors Association keeps its members up to date on the latest reproductions.

Notes: The first book on reamers, now out of print, was written by Ken and Linda Ricketts in 1974. Their numbering system was continued by Mary Walker, although her books are now also out of print. The Ricketts-Walker numbers will be found in the china and metal sections. The numbers in parentheses in the glass section are from Gene Florence's *Kitchen Glassware of the Depression Years*.

Advisor: Judy Smith.

China And Ceramic

Austria, 3-3/4" h, white, pink flowers, green trim (D-106) 75.00
Bavaria, 3-1/2" h, white, red, yellow and green flowers, gold trim, 2 pc (D-119) 50.00
Czechoslovakia, 6" h, orange shape, white, green leaves, mkd "Erphila," 2 pc (L-17) 45.00
England
  3-1/2" h, white, orange and yellow flowers (D-107) 65.00
  3-3/4" h, orange shape, orange body, green leaves, 2 pc (L-20) 35.00
France, 3-1/4" d, white, red, purple and yellow flowers, green leaves, gold trim (D-112) 35.00
Germany
  3-1/2" h, scrolling flow blue dec, white ground (E-60) 75.00
  5" d, Goebel, yellow (E-108) 60.00
Japan
  3" h, saucer-type on pedestal, loop handle fruit dec (D-59) 55.00
  3-1/4" h, hp, white, floral dec, mkd "Nippon," 2 pc 115.00
  3-3/4" h, strawberry shape, red, green leaves and handle, mkd "Occupied Japan," 2 pc (L-38)...........65.00
  4-3/4" h, lemon, yellow, white flowers, green leaves (L-40) 40.00
  5" h, orange, textured orange-peel exterior, yellow, green leaves, white interior (L-39) 48.00
  8-1/2" h, pitcher and tumbler, blue and white windmill dec (P-87)..65.00
United States
  Jiffy Juicer, large bowl, cone center, elongated loop handle, 10 colors known, Pat 1938 (A-5) 60.00
  Red Wing (A-7) 95.00
  United States Ade-O-Matic Genuine, 9" h, green 95.00
  Universal Cambridge (P-104) 155.00
  Zippy, 3-1/4" h, 6-1/2"h hand crank cone, Wolverine Products, Detroit, MI, several colors (A-4)...........80.00

Glass (*Measurements indicate width, not including spout and handle*)

Anchor Hocking Glass Co, 6-1/4" d, lime green, pouring spout (155-4-3).......................20.00
Federal, transparent green, pointed cone, tab handle (149-3-3)......25.00
Fry, 6-5/16" d, opal, pouring spout (149-6-1) 45.00
Hazel Atlas
  Criss-Cross, orange size, pink (153-2-2) 275.00
  Crystal, tab handle, large (153-5-3) 15.00

Glass, Sunkist, yellow milk glass, N-333, $50.

Indiana Glass Co. , green, horiz handle
  (151-5-3)..................................25.00
Jeannette Glass Co.
  Small Delphi,
  Jennyware (159-3-1)................90.00
  Light Jadite, 2 cup,
  2 pc (159-2-3)...........................30.00
McKee
  Vaseline green emb Sunkist
  (162-5-4) 45.00
  White, emb Sunkist
  (163-1-4) 9.00
U.S. Glass Co., light pink, 2-cup pitcher
  set (151-5-3)............................45.00

Metal

Aluminum, Pat, 8" l, 161609,
  Minneapolis, MN.......................5.00
Bernard Rice & Sons, Apollo EPNS,
  3-3/4" h, 2 pc (PM-70) 95.00
Dunlap's Improved, 9-1/2" l, iron hinge
  (M-17).......................................32.00
Gem Squeezer, aluminum,
  crank handle, table model,
  2 pc (M-100) 10.00
Hong Kong, 2-1/2" h, stainless steel, flat,
  2 pc (M-205) 8.50
Kwicky Juicer, aluminum, pan style,
  Quam Nichols Co. (M-97)...........8.00
Nasco-Royal, 6" l, scissors type
  (M-265) 8.00
Presto Juicer, metal stand, porcelain
  juicer (M-112) 70.00
Wagner Ware, 6" d, cast aluminum,
  skillet shape, long rect seed dams
  beneath cone, hole in handle, 2
  spouts (M-96) 18.00
Williams, 9-3/4" l, iron, hinged, glass
  insert (M-60) 45.00
Yates, EPNS, 4-3/4" d,
  2 pc (PM-73)...........................175.00

Records

Collecting Hints: Collectors tend to focus on one particular music field, e.g., jazz, the big bands or rock 'n' roll or on one artist. Purchase records with original dust jackets and covers when possible. Also, check the records carefully for scratches. If the sound quality has been affected, the record is worthless. Proper storage of records is critical to maintaining their value. Keep stacks small. It is best to store them vertically. Place acid-free paper between the albums to prevent bleeding of ink from one cover to the next.

History: The first records—cylinders produced by Thomas Edison in 1877—were played on a phonograph of his design. Edison received a patent in 1878, but soon dropped the project to perfect the light bulb. Alexander Graham Bell, Edison's friend, was excited about the phonograph and developed the graphaphone, which was marketed successfully by 1889. Early phonographs and graphaphones had hand cranks to wind the mechanism and keep the cylinders moving.

About 1900, Emile Berliner developed a phonograph which used a flat disc, similar to today's records. The United States Gramophone Co., marketed his design in 1901. This company eventually became RCA Victor. By 1910, discs were more popular than cylinders.

The record industry continued to develop as new technology improved processes and sound quality. Initially 78-RPM records were made. These were replaced by 45 RPMs, then by 33-1/3 RPMs, and, finally, by compact discs.

References: Steven C. Barr, *Almost Complete 78 RPM Record Dating Guide (II)*, Yesterday Once Again, 1992; Les R. Docks, *American Premium Record Guide, 1900-1965*, 4th Edition, Books Americana, 1992; Steve Gelfand, *Television Theme Recordings*, Popular Culture, 1993; *Goldmine Price Guide to 45 RPM Records*, Krause Publications, 1996; *Goldmine's 1997 Annual*, Krause Publications, 1996; *Goldmine's Price Guide to Alternative Records*, Krause Publications, 1996; Anthony J. Gribin and Matthew M. Schiff, *Doo-Wop*, Krause Publications, 1992; Joe Lindsay (comp.), *Picture Discs of the World Price Guide*, BIOdisc, 1990; Ron Lofman, *Goldmine's Celebrity Vocals*, Krause Publications, 1994; Vito R. Marino and Anthony C. Furfero, *Official Price Guide to Frank Sinatra Collectibles, Records and CDs*, House of Collectibles, 1993; William M. Miller, *How to Buy & Sell Used Record Albums*, Loran Publishing, 1994; Tom Neely, *Goldmine's Price Guide to Alternative Records*, Krause Publications, 1996; Jerry Osborne, *Official Price Guide to Elvis Presley Records and Memorabilia*, House of Collectibles, 1994; ——, *Official Price Guide Movie/TV Soundtracks and Original Cast Albums*, House of Collectibles, 1991; ——, *Official Price Guide to Records*, 11th Edition, House of Collectibles, 1994; ——, *Rockin' Records*, 20th Edition, Antique Trader Books, 1996; Neal Umphred, *Goldmine's Price Guide to Collectible Jazz Albums*, Krause Publications, 1992; ——, *Goldmine's Price Guide to Collectible Record Albums*, 5th Edition, Krause Publications, 1996; ——, *Goldmine's Rock 'n' Roll 45 RPM Record Price Guide*, 3rd Edition, Krause Publications, 1994.

Periodicals: *Cadence*, Cadence Building, Redwood, NY 13679; *DIS-Coveries Magazine*, P.O. Box 1050, Dubuque, IA 52004; *Goldmine*, 700 E. State St., Iola, WI 54990; *Joslin's Jazz Journal*, P.O. Box 213, Parsons, KS 67357; *New Amberola Graphic*, 37 Caledonia St., St. Johnsbury, VT 05819; *Record Collectors Monthly*, P.O. Box 75, Mendham, NJ 07945; *Record Finder*, P.O. Box 1047, Glen Allen, VA 23060.

Collectors' Clubs: Collectors Record Club, 1206 Decatur St., New Orleans, LA 70116; International Association of Jazz Record Collectors, P.O. Box 75155, Tampa, FL 33605.

Note: Prices are for first pressings in original dust jackets or albums.

Additional Listings: Elvis Presley, Rock & Roll.

Alice in Wonderland, Caedmon TC1097
  LB, 3-record album..................20.00
Allen Brothers, Glorious Night Blues,
  Victor, 23707 ....50.00
Louis Armstrong, I'm a Ding Dong
  Daddy, Okeh, 41442, 1930 .....17.50
Chuck Berry, Johnny Bgoode,
  78 RPM, Chess 10.00
Eubie Blake, Sweet Georgie Brown,
  Crown, 3197, 1931 ....12.00
Blue Ridge Mountain Girls, She Came
  Rolling Down the Mountain,
  Champion, 16743 ....12.00
Less Brown, Boogie Woogie, Bluebird,
  7858, 1938 ....7.50

Bye Bye Birdy, Columbia, orig cast,
1960...15.00

Cab Calloway, St. Louis Blues,
Brunswick 4936, 1930 ....7.50

Fiddlin' John Carson & His Virginia
Reelers
Arkansas Traveler,
Okeh, 40108.............................12.00
Times Are Not Like They Used to Be,
Okeh, 45402.............................25.00

Carter Family, I'll Be Home Some Day,
Bluebird, 5911 ....7.50

Chubby Checker, Limbo Party, Parkway,
1962, LP 20.00

Nat King Cole, Early Morning Blues,
Decca, 8541, 1941 ....5.00

Count Basie, Basie Boogie, Okeh,
6330, 1941.................................5.00

Damn Yankees, RCA Victor, orig cast,
green cover, 1955....................30.00

Delmore Brothers, The Frozen Girl,
Bluebird, 5338 ....15.00

Fats Domino, Rolling and Rocking,
Imperial, 5180..........................30.00

Dorsey Brothers, Have a Little Faith in
Me, Banner, 0571, 1930 ....12.00

Duane Eddy, Ring of Fire and Bobbie,
7" x 7" paper slipcover, Jamie
label, 1961 ....12.00

Duke Ellington, Jubilee Stomp, Okeh,
41013, 1938..............................15.00

Gone with the Wind, 1961,
Warner, LP 20.00

Benny Goodman, Wolverine Blues,
Vocalion, 15656, 1928.............45.00

Bobby Hackett, Ain't Misbehavin',
Vocalion, 4877, 1939.................7.50

Bill Haley, Shake, Rattle and Roll,
Decca, 5260 ....35.00

Herman's Hermits, The End of the
World and I'm Henry VIII, I Am,
MGM label, 1965 ....15.00

Woody Herman, Wintertime Dreams,
Decca, 1056, 1936 ....12.00

Buddy Holly, "Words of Love,"
45 RPM, Coral 18.00

Henry James, Two O'Clock Jump,
Brunswick, 8337, 1939 ....9.00

Laurel and Hardy, 7" x 7-3/4", colorful
picture sleeve of Laurel and Hardy
dancing, 45 RPM black vinyl record,
Little Golden Record, 1963 Larry
Harmon Pictures Corp. 18.00

Jerry Lee Lewis, record, Whole Lot of
Shakin' Going On and It'll Be Me,
45 RPM, Sun label, 1956.........20.00

Madame X, Decca, 1966...............15.00

Glenn Miller, Glenn Miller Story, Un-
breakable, Decca, 1954, LP 20.00

Monroe Brothers, Where Is My Sailor
Boy, Bluebird, 6762 ....17.50

New York, New York, United Artists,
1977...7.50

Oklahoma, Decca,

orig cast, 1953.........................40.00

The Palisades, Chapel Bells, Debra,
1003 ....10.00

George Reneau, Wild Bill Jones,
Vocalion, 5058.........................10.00

Roy Rogers, Dale Evans,
family, Jesus Loves Me,
Camden, 1960, LP 20.00

77 Sunset Strip, 6-1/2" x 8",
multicolored sleeves, kids in
hot rod waving at viewer, 6" d
yellow vinyl 78 RPM record,
AA Record's Inc., 1959...........18.00

Shari Lewis Party Record, 6" x 6" b&w
thin cardboard vinyl-coated sheet,
5-3/4" d vinyl record with b&w photo
of Shari, 2 puppets, Allied Creative
Services, Inc., c1950 ....15.00

Muggsy Spanier, Big Butter and Egg
Man, Bluebird, 10417, 1939 ......5.00

Superman, The Movie, 1978,
2-record set, LP.......................20.00

Teardrops, The Stars Are Out Tonight,
Josie, 766 ....32.00

The Three Stooges Christmas Songs, 7"
x 7-3/4" colorful picture sleeve with
Larry, Moe and Curly-Joe dressed in
Santa outfits, Curly pulling sleigh, 45
RPM black vinyl record............20.00

Three Little Pigs, 7" x 7" colorful
sleeve, 6-3/4" d, 45 RPM
black vinyl record, yellow
Disneyland label, c1950 ....18.00

To Kill a Mocking Bird,
Ava, 1963 ....15.00

Fats Waller, Soothin' Syrup Stomp,
Victor, 20470, 1927 ....25.00

Welling & McGhee, Ring the Bells of
Heaven, Champion, 16660......15.00

Bob Wills and His Texas Playboys,
I Ain't Got Nobody, Vocalion,
03206 ....12.00

Loretta Young,
The Littlest Angel, LP 20.00

Red Wing Pottery

Collecting Hints: Red Wing Pottery can be found with various marks and paper labels. Some of the marks include a stamped red wing, a raised "Red Wing U.S.A. #___," or an impressed "Red Wing U.S.A. #___." Paper labels were used as early as 1930. Some pieces were identified only by a paper label that was easily lost.

Many manufacturers used the same mold patterns. Study the references to become familiar with the Red Wing forms.

History: The category of Red Wing Pottery covers several potteries which started in Red Wing, MN. The

Compote, 6-1/4" h, 8-1/8" d, mauve, "M-5008," shaped base and standard, scalloped rim, $35.

first pottery, named Red Wing Stoneware Co., was started in 1868 by David Hallem. The primary product of this company was stoneware. The mark used by this company was a red wing stamped under the glaze. The Minnesota Stoneware Co., was started in 1883. The North Star Stoneware Co., opened a factory in the same area in 1892 and went out of business in 1896. The mark used by this company included a raised star and the words "Red Wing." The Red Wing Stoneware Co., and the Minnesota Stoneware Co., merged in 1892. The new company was called the Red Wing Union Stoneware Co. The new company made stoneware until 1920 when it introduced a line of pottery.

In 1936, the name of the company was changed to Red Wing Potteries Inc. It continued to make pottery until the 1940s. During the 1930s the company introduced several lines of dinnerware. These patterns, which were all hand painted, were very popular and were sold through department stores, Sears Roebuck and Co., and gift stamp centers. The production of dinnerware declined in the 1950s. The company began producing hotel and restaurant china in the early 1960s. The plant was closed in 1967.

References: Susan and Al Bagdade, *Warman's American Pottery and Porcelain*, Wallace-Homestead, 1994; Dan and Gail DePasquale and Larry Peterson, *Red Wing Collectibles*, Collector Books, 1985, 1995 value update; ——, *Red Wing Stoneware*, Collector

Books, 1983, 1994 value update; B.L. Dollen, *Red Wing Art Pottery*, Collector Books, 1996; Ray Reiss, *Red Wing Art Pottery Including Pottery Made for Rum Rill*, published by author (2144 N. Leavitt, Chicago, IL 60647), 1996; Gary and Bonnie Tefft, *Red Wing Potters and Their Wares*, 2nd Edition, Locust Enterprises, 1987, 1995 value update.

Collectors' Clubs: Red Wing Collectors Society, P.O. Box 184, Galesburg, IL 61402; RumRill Society, P.O. Box 2161, Hudson, OH 44236.

Ashtray, horse's head
    Black 75.00
    Ochre 75.00
Basket, white, semi-gloss..............32.00
Bean Pot, cov, Tampico 35.00
Beverage Server,
    cov, Tampico 125.00
Bookends, pr,
    fan and scroll, green 20.00
Bowl
    Cloverleaf, glossy, gray int,
      yellow ext. 32.00
    Spatterware, #4 ....85.00
Butter Dish, rect, Bob White 45.00
Candleholders, pr, Medieval..........50.00
Candy Dish, 3 part, hexagon, gray,
    semi-gloss 15.00
Casserole, cov, Tampico...............25.00
Celery Tray, Random Harvest.......12.00
Cereal Bowl
    Damask......................................7.50
    Pompeii 9.00
Chop Plate, 12" d, Capistrano.......20.00
Compote
    Blue and Brown.........................60.00
    Blue Fleck 45.00
    Orchid Cherub...........................60.00
Console Set, bowl and matching candlesticks, Renaissance Deer 120.00
Cookie Jar, cov
    Katrina, beige.........................125.00
    King of Tarts,
      blue speckled 1,200.00
Creamer and Sugar, Smart Set.....85.00
Crock, 2 gal, birch-leaf dec............50.00
Cruet, Town and Country,
    chartreuse................................25.00
Cup and Saucer
    Bob White.................................18.00
    Capistrano.................................15.00
    Magnolia.....................................7.50
    Tampico 10.00
Custard Cup, Fondos,
    green and pink..........................18.00
Flower Block, Dolphin....................35.00
Fruit Bowl, Lute Song......................9.00

Gravy Boat, Driftwood, blue 19.00
Leaf Dish, 11" x 11", green 60.00
Nappy, Lotus 8.50
Pitcher
    Bob White 35.00
    Brushed Ware, 8-1/4" h..........225.00
Planter
    Birch...25.00
    Loop shape, green and silver...50.00
Plate
    6-1/2" d, bread and butter
      Bob White 7.50
      Pepe 4.00
      Pompeii 5.00
      Random Harvest....................6.00
    10" d, dinner
      Bob White 10.00
      Lotus 8.50
      Town and Country, blue.........9.25
Platter, Town and Country,
    chartreuse 18.00
Relish, Town and Country,
    blue, 7" x 5" 12.00
Salad Bowl, Pheasant,
    blue and green 45.00
Salt and Pepper Shakers, pr
    Bob White 30.00
    Brittany, Provincial 15.00
Shell, ftd, 11" x 9" 80.00
Teapot, yellow rooster, gold trim ...75.00
Trivet, Minnesota Centennial 75.00
Vase
    Calla, blue and yellow 80.00
    Classic shape, 9" h,
    swan handles, cream,
    high glaze, mkd "Rumrill" 75.00
    Fan shape, 7-1/2" h, #892, blue,
    pink int.....................................48.00
Vegetable Bowl
    Lute Song, divided 24.00
    Town and Country,
    chartreuse 15.00
Wall Pocket, Gardenia,
    matte ivory...............................35.00
Warmer, 2 step...............................35.00

Robots

Collecting Hints: Robots are identified by the markings on the robot or box and from names assigned by the trade. Hence, some robots have more than one name. Research is required to learn exactly what robot you have. A leading auctioneer of robots is Lloyd Ralston Toys, Fairfield, CT.

Condition is critical. Damaged lithographed tin is almost impossible to repair and repaint. Toys in mint condition in the original box are the most desirable. The price difference between a mint robot and one in very good condition may be as high as 200%. Working condition is important, but not critical. Many robots never worked well and larger robots stripped their gearing quickly. The rarer the robot, the less important the working condition.

Finally, if you play with your robot, do not leave the batteries in the toy. If they leak or rust, the damage may destroy the value of the toy.

History: Atomic Robot Man, made in Japan between 1948 and 1949, is the grandfather of all robot toys. He is an all-metal windup toy, less than 5 inches high and rather crudely made. Japanese robots of the early 1950s tended to be the friction or windup variety, patterned in brightly lithographed tin and made from recycled materials.

By the late 1950s, robots had entered the battery-powered age. Limited quantities of early models were produced; parts from one model were used in later models with slight or no variations. The robot craze was enhanced by Hollywood's production of movies such as "Destination Moon" (1950) and "Forbidden Planet" (1956). Robby the Robot came from the latter movie.

Many Japanese manufacturers were small and remained in business only a few years. Leading firms include Horikawa Toys, Nomura Toys and Yonezawa Toys. Cragstan was an American importer who sold Japanese-made toys under its own label. Marx and Ideal entered the picture in the 1970s. Modern robots are being imported from China and Taiwan.

The TV program "Lost in Space" (1965-1968) inspired copies of its robot character. However, the quality of the late 1960s toys began to suffer as more and more plastic

Robot driving Mercedes, litho tin, friction, gun sparks, cream color, $350.

was added; robots were redesigned to reduce sharp edges as required by the U.S. government.

Modern robots include R2D2 and C3PO from the Star Wars epics, Twiki, from NBC's Buck Rodgers, and V.I.N.CENT, from Disney's "The Black Hole." Robots are firmly established in American science fiction and among collectors.

References: Teruhisa Kitahara, *Tin Toy Dreams*, Chronicle Books, 1985; Teruhisa Kitahara, *Yesterday's Toys, & Robots, Spaceships and Monsters*, Chronicle Books, 1988; Crystal and Leland Payton, *Space Toys*, Collectors Compass, 1982; Maxine A. Pinksy, *Marx Toys: Robots, Space, Comic, Disney & TV Characters*, Schiffer Publishing, 1996; Stephen J. Sansweet, *Science Fiction Toys and Models*, Starlog Press, 1980.

Periodical: *Robot World & Price Guide*, P.O. Box 184, Lenox Hill Station, New York, NY 10021.

Abbreviations: SH—Horikawa Toys; TM—K.K. Masutoku Toy Factory; TN—Nomura Toys; Y—Yonezawa Toys.

Acrobat Robot, battery operated, SH, Japan, MIB 95.00
Attacking Martian, battery operated, litho tin, flashing light and noise, SH, Japan, MIB 325.00
Cosmic Fighter, battery operated, SH, Japan MIB 275.00
Dynamic Fighter Robot, battery operated, Japan, MIB 175.00
Electro the Robot, 1939 pin............50.00
Fighting Spaceman, 11" h, battery operated, litho tin, walks, blinking light in helmet, SH, Japan......350.00
Flashy Jim, 7" h, remote control, tin, walks, mkd "Ace," MIB........1,750.00
Galaxy Robot, battery operated, SH, Japan, MIB 85.00
Gear Robot, litho tin windup, SH, Japan, MIB 245.00
High Wheel, 10" h, litho tin windup, walks and sparks, mkd "KO, Japan," MIB 195.00
Laughing Robot, 13" h, battery operated, plastic, laughs hysterically, mkd "Waco" 350.00
Lunar Captain, Japan, MIB..........255.00
Magic Action Bulldozer, battery operated, Japan, MIB 185.00
Mechanical Robot, 11-1/2" h, battery operated tin and plastic, bump-and-

go action, flashing lights, noise, mkd "Yonezawa, Japan"..........95.00
Mechanical Sparking Robot, litho tin windup, Japan 145.00
Moon Astronaut Robot, 9" h, litho tin windup, walks, lifts up gun, noise, mkd "Daiya, Japan," MIB....2,500.00
Moon Explorer, 7" l, crank operated, litho tin, walks, spinners in plastic helmet, KO Japan, MIB 1,750.00
Mr. Robot, 11" h, battery operated, tin, bump-and-go action, revolving lights inside clear-plastic dome, Cragston..........425.00
New Space Explorer, 11" h, battery operated, litho tin, walks, SH Japan....................200.00
Piston Robot, SH, Japan, MIB 275.00
Planet Robot, 9" h, litho tin windup, black, red feet and hands, walks and sparks, mkd "KO, Japan," MIB...................195.00
Radar Tractor, 5" l, battery operated, Nomura, antenna missing 395.00
RD-D2, Styrofoam pack 70.00
Robby the Robot, 8-1/2" h, remote control, litho tin, walks, moving pistons in clear dome top, mkd "Nomura, Japan," MIB 950.00
Smoking Engine Robot, battery operated, SH, Japan, MIB 225.00
Space Commander Robot, battery operated, Japan 45.00
Super Robot, SH, Japan, MIB.....155.00
Zoomer the Robot, 8" h, battery operated, litho tin, mechanic type, wrench in hand, Nomura Toys...........575.00

Rock & Roll

Collecting Hints: Many Rock & Roll collections are centered around one artist. Flea markets and thrift shops are good places to look for rock 'n' roll items. Prices depend on the singer or group and works by stars who are no longer living usually command a higher price. Glossy, non-autographed 8-by-10-inch photographs of singers are generally worth $1.

History: Rock music can be traced back to early rhythm and blues. It progressed and reached its golden age in the 1950s. The current nostalgia craze for the 1950s has produced some modern rock 'n' roll which is well received. Rock 'n' roll memorabilia exists in large quantities, each singer or group having had many promotional pieces made.

References: Tony Bacon, *Classic Guitars of the '50s*, Miller Freeman Books (6600 Silacci Way, Gilroy, CA

95020), 1996; Les R. Docks, *American Premium Record Guide*, 4th Edition, Books Americana, 1992; *Goldmine's 1997 Annual*, 6th edition, Krause Publications, 1996; Anthony J. Gribin and Matthew M. Schiff, *Doo-Wop*, Krause Publications, 1992; Fred Heggeness, *Goldmine's Country Western Record and CD Price Guide*, Krause Publications, 1996; David K. Henkel, *Official Price Guide to Rock and Roll*, House of Collectibles, 1992. Karen and John Lesniweski, *Kiss Collectibles*, Avon Books, 1993; Stephen Maycock, *Miller's Rock & Pop Memorabilia*, Millers Publications, 1995; Greg Moore, *Price Guide to Rock & Roll Collectibles*, 2nd Edition, published by author, 1993; Tim Neely, *Goldmine's Price Guide to 45 RPM Records*, Krause Publications, 1996; Jerry Osborne, *Official Price Guide to Elvis Presley Records and Memorabilia*, House of Collectibles, 1994; Michael Stern, Barbara Crawford and Hollis Lamon, T*he Beatles*, Collector Books, 1994; Paul Trynka (ed.), *The Electric Guitar*, Chronicle Books, 1993; Neal Umphred, *Goldmine's Price Guide to Collectible Record Albums*, 5th Edition, Krause Publications, 1996.

Periodicals: *Kissaholics Magazine*, P.O. Box 22334, Nashville, TN 37202; *New England KISS Collector's Network*, 168 Oakland Ave., Providence, RI 02908; *Tune Talk*, P.O. Box 851, Marshalltown, IA 50158.

Collectors' Club: American Bandstand 1950's Fan Club, P.O. Box 131, Adamstown, PA 19501.

Additional Listings: Beatles, Elvis Presley, Records.

Arcade Card, 3-1/4" x 5-1/4", b&w photo, facsimile-printed autograph, Billboard Music Week, c1960
    Paul Anka 2.50
    Frankie Avalon...........................2.50
    Edd Byrnes 2.50
    Joe Dowell 2.50
    Steve Lawrence 2.50
    Bobby Rydell...............................2.50
    Tommy Sands............................2.50
Autograph
    Personality Sheet, 8" x 11", fan card, WABC, New York
        Dan Ingram, photo of Ingram alongside bio, sgd in blue ink.....................25.00

Bruce Morrow, photo of
Cousin Bruce alongside bio,
sgd in blue ink 25.00
Photo, 8" x 10", b&w glossy
Ray Charles 40.00
Chubby Checker, sgd "It Ain't Over
Till It's Over, Keep It Up, Love
Chubby Checker 86" 30.00
Badge, 3" d, Rolling Stones, red metal
rim, flicker image, large-lipped
smiling mouth, flicker tongue,
Vari-Vue, late 1960s 18.00
Belt Buckle, 3-3/4", oval, brass, Kiss
inscription, red, amber and silver,
blue background, 1977 ....15.00
Book
I, James Dean, T.T. Thomas,
Popular Library, 1957, soft-cover,
4" x 7", 128 pgs 120.00
Woodstock 69, Scholastic
Book Services, Joseph J. Sia,
1970, 124 pgs 25.00
Book Cover
10-1/2" x 12" clear plastic bag,
orange and red title paper, 3 b&w
book covers, Pat Boone, Sal Mineo,
1 generic cover, 1958 Cooga Mooga
Products Inc., NY 15.00
13" x 20", paper, full-color
picture of Janis Joplin Cheap Thrills
album, 1969 ....10.00
Bubblegum Cards, Monkees
Complete set, 1960s 85.00
Package, unopened 48.00
Colorforms, Kiss, MIB.....................25.00
Costume, Gene Simmons, Kiss, molded
and diecut plastic mask, vinyl and
fabric costume, boxed, Collegeville
Costumes, 1978 ....25.00
Display Card, 10" x 12", sealed, Kiss,
Mini Self-Adhesive Put-On, color
photo of band in Sprit of '76 style,
Aucion Management Inc. 15.00
Doll, Michael Jackson, 12" h
Beat It.......................................50.00
Grammy Winner 50.00
Thriller 50.00
Figure, 3" h, Dave Clark Five,
3 from set of 5, plastic, 2 with name
tag, mid-1960s.........................50.00
Game
Duran Duran into the Arena, Milton
Bradley, 1985 ....15.00
Kiss on Tour, MIB.....................55.00
Lobby Card, 11" x 14", Bill Haley and His
Comets, Don't Knock the Rock,
Columbia, 1957 ....25.00
Lunch Box, 7" x 8" x 4",
litho metal, thermos, Osmonds,
unused, 1973............................90.00
Magazine, *Life*, July 14, 1972, Rolling
Stones cover article 10.00
Milk Bottle, 1/2 pt, Yasger Farm, Wood-

stock
c1969 ....75.00
c1994 ....10.00
Model, Monkeemobile,
1967, MIB 135.00
Pennant, 7-1/2" x 12", American Bandstand, Dick Clark, paper, adv 5.00
Pinback Button
1-1/4" d, celluloid,
Bob-a-Loo, New York City Disc
Jockey, WABC, b&w photo, name
and "WABC-Go-Go" 65.00
3" d, litho tin, b&w photo of Dick
Clark, dark green ground 10.00
3-1/2" d, Frankie Avalon-Venus,
b&w portrait, bright pink rim 20.00
Playset, Donny and Marie Osmond,
2 figures, MIB 150.00
Poster
Chicago, 22" x 33", album insert,
sepia photos, group name in
shades of blue, Columbia Records,
c1970 ....15.00
The Doors, 24" x 36", white logo,
green border on bottom, Doors
Production Corp., 1968 ....20.00
Janis Joplin,
b&w photo, 1969 ....30.00
Fleetwood Mac, 33" x 46", Jan.
1970 concert, Deutsches Museum,
Munich, West Germany 30.00
Grateful Dead, 14" x 20",
Grateful Dead Fan Club, b&w
photo, gold and blue background,
mkd "The Golden Road to Unlimited
Devotion," late 1960s 50.00
Moody Blues, 18-1/2" x 25-1/2",
April 1, 1970, concert, Terrace
ballroom, Salt Lake City, UT 50.00
Simon & Garfunkel, 22" x 33",
album insert, b&w head photo,
outline body with full-color bridge
and sunset scene, 1968
Columbia Records 15.00
Program
Dave Clark Five Show, Arthur Kim-
brell Presents, 1964, English ...45.00
Rolling Stones Show Concert,
John Smith Production,
Aug. 23-30, 1964 ....100.00
Puppet, 5" h, Mickey
Dolenz, Monkees, plastic torso,
movable arms, molded vinyl head,
brown curly hair, 1970 ....15.00
Record Case, 5" x 8" x 8",
cardboard, full-color photo and
signature of Dick Clark, blue, white
plastic handle, brass closure, holds
45 RPM records 40.00
Scrapbook, 9" x 12",
Bee Gees, 34 pgs....................15.00
Sheet Music, 9" x 12", 4 pgs
It Ain't Me, Babe, Bob Dylan, b&w
photo front cover, 1964 ....15.00

So It Always Will Be,
Everly Brothers, pink-tone photo
on front cover, 1963.................10.00
Thermos, Bee Gees,
plastic, yellow 15.00
Ticket, 2" x 5", Woodstock Music and
Art Fair, orange, red letters, orange
Globe Ticket background, Friday,
Aug. 15, 1969, unused 35.00
Tie Clip, 1-3/4" h, Dick Clark
American Bandstand,
gold-colored metal...................10.00
Toy, musical instrument
Guitar, 20" h, plastic, full-color
diecut paper label with Monkees,
Mattel, 1966 ....75.00
Kizzer Rock Set, colorful 6-1/2" x 12"
header card, graphics resembling
Kiss member, 9-3/4" tan and orange
plastic guitar, 6-3/4" h green and red
plastic flute, Jak Pak Inc., Milsaukk,
WI, late 1970s, MIP 24.00
View-Master Reel, set of 3,
Last Wheelbarrow to
Pokeyville, Monkees 10.00
Watch Fob, The Band-Standers,
jitterbugging couple, Dick Clark,
music notes, mkd "Ajax Belt"...25.00

Norman Rockwell

Collecting Hints: Learn all you can
about Norman Rockwell if you plan
to collect any of his art. His original
artworks and illustrations have been
transferred onto various types of objects by clubs and manufacturers.

History: Norman Rockwell, the famous American artist, was born on
Feb, 3, 1894. When he was 18, he
did his first professional illustrations
for a children's book, *Tell Me Why
Stories*. His next projects were done
in association with *Boy's Life*, the
Boy Scout magazine and after that
his work appeared in many other
magazines. By his death in November 1978, he had completed more
than 2,000 paintings, many of which
were done in oil and reproduced as
magazine covers, advertisements,
illustrations, calendars and book
sketches. More than 320 of these
paintings became covers for the *Saturday Evening Post*.

Rockwell painted everyday people in everyday situations with a little
humor mixed in with the sentimental-
ity. His paintings and illustrations are
well loved because of this sensitive
nature. He painted people he knew
and places with which he was famil-

iar. New England landscapes are seen in many of his illustrations.

Because his works are so popular, they have been reproduced on many objects. These new collectibles, which should not be confused with the original artwork and illustrations, make Norman Rockwell illustrations affordable for the average consumer.

References: Denis C. Jackson, *Norman Rockwell Identification and Value Guide*, 2nd Edition, published by author (P.O. Box 1958, Sequim, WA 98392), 1985; Mary Moline, *Norman Rockwell Collectibles Value Guide*, 6th Edition, Green Valley World, 1988.

Collectors' Club: Rockwell Society of America, 597 Saw Mill River Rd., Ardsley, NY 10502.

Museums: Museum of Norman Rockwell Art, Reedsburg, WI; Norman Rockwell Museum, Northbrook, IL; Norman Rockwell Museum, Philadelphia, PA; The Norman Rockwell Museum at Stockbridge, Stockbridge, MA.

Autograph, TLS, 1 pg 8vo, May 7, 1974, note with initialed postscript...160.00
Bell
    Gorham, 1975,
    Santa's Helper..........................45.00
    Grossman, Dave,
    1975, Christmas, FE 35.00
Figurine
    Gorham
        1976, Saying Grace 150.00
        1982, Jolly Coachman 50.00
        1983, Christmas Dancers 75.00
    Dave Grossman Designs, Inc.
        1973, No Swimming.............45.00
        1978, At the Doctors 125.00
        1982, Doctor and the Doll ..125.00
        1983, The Graduate.............32.00
Lynell Studios, 1980,
    Cradle of Love 85.00
Rockwell Museum
    1978, Bedtime......................50.00
    1979, Bride & Groom 90.00
    1980, Wrapping Christmas
    Presents.............................120.00
    1981, Music Maker...............90.00
    1982, Giving Thanks..........160.00
    1983, Painter........................90.00
Ingot
    Franklin Mint
        1972, Spirit of Scouting, price for
        set of 12 ....275.00
        1974, Tribute to Robert Frost,
        price for set of 12 ....285.00
    Hamilton Mint

Magazine cover, *Saturday Evening Post*, June 7, 1958, $20.

    1975, Saturday Evening Post Covers, price for set of 12 ....210.00
    1977, Charles Dickens.........50.00
Magazine
    American Artist, July, 1976, Self Portrait and article...................15.00
    Country Gentleman, 1979, memorial issue...20.00
    Saturday Evening Post, August, 1977, 250th Edition, Rockwell cov, illus and portfolio.....................25.00
Magazine Cover
    American Boy, April 1920 ....27.50
    American Legion, July 1978.......5.00
    Boy's Life
        Aug. 1915 ....50.00
        Feb. 1947............................45.00
        June 1957 ....42.50
    Colliers, March 1, 1919 ....25.00
    Country Gentleman
        Feb. 9, 1918........................50.00
        May 8, 1920 ....48.00
        March 18, 1922....................45.00
    Family Circle, Dec. 1967, Santa Claus 10.00
    Fisk Club News, May 1917 ......18.00
    Jack and Jill, Dec. 1974 ....5.00
    Literary Digest,
    Dec. 14, 1918.........................30.00
    Look, July 14, 1964..................10.00
    McCall's, Dec. 1974 ....15.00
    Parents, Jan. 1939...................15.00
    Red Cross, April 1918..............25.00
    Saturday Evening Post
        Oct. 14, 1916 ....100.00
        Jan. 26, 1918.......................90.00
        June 19, 1920......................65.00
        Feb. 18, 1922.......................85.00
        March 21, 1945....................70.00
        Nov. 16, 1946 ....25.00

        April 29, 1950 ....80.00
        Aug. 30, 1952 ....40.00
        March 12, 1955....................20.00
        Sept. 7, 1957 ....21.00
        Feb. 13, 1960 ....60.00
        Jan. 13, 1962......................12.00
    Scouting
        Feb. 1934 ....10.00
        Dec. 1944 ....12.00
        Oct. 1953 ....8.50
    TV Guide, May 16, 1970.........15.00
    Yankee, Aug. 1972 ....20.00
Paperweight, River Shore 100.00
Plate
    Franklin Mint
        1970, Bringing
        Home the Tree...................330.00
        1972, The Carolers............165.00
        1974, Hanging
        the Wreath 180.00
    Gorham
        Boy Scout, 1975,
        Our Heritage 60.00
        Christmas Series
            1974, Tiny Tim...................65.00
            1975, Good Deeds.............64.00
            1977, Yuletide
            Reckoning..........................45.00
            1979, Santa's Helpers 20.00
            1981, Santa Plans
            His Visit..............................30.00
            1983, Christmas Dancers ..30.00
    Four Seasons, price for set of 4
        1971, A Boy & His Dog......400.00
        1973, Ages of Love............300.00
        1975, Me & My Pal 200.00
        1979, A Helping Hand 100.00
        1981, Old Timers 100.00
        1983, Old Buddies 115.00
    Grossman Designs, Dave
        Annual Series, bas-relief
            1979, Leapfrog...................50.00
            1981, Dreams
            of Long Ago 60.00
        Christmas Series, bas-relief, 1980, Christmas Trio, FE..............80.00
        Huckleberry Finn Series, 1980, Listening 40.00
        Tom Sawyer Series, 1976, Whitewashing Fence 75.00
    Lynell Studios, Christmas, 1979, Snow Queen 30.00
        Mother's Day, 1980, Cradle of Love 40.00
    River Shore
        1979, Spring Flowers.........120.00
        1980, Looking out to Sea...100.00
        1982, Jennie & Tina.............40.00
    Rockwell Museum
        American Family Series
            1978, Baby's First Step......80.00
            1979, First Prom 30.00

Stein, River Pilot, Rockwell Museum, 5-1/8" h, $15.

American Family II Series
    1980, New Arrival...............40.00
    1981, At the Circus.............96.00
Rockwell Society
  Christmas Series
    1974, Scotty
    Gets His Tree...................160.00
    1976, Golden Christmas 55.00
    1978, Christmas Dream 50.00
    1980, Scotty Plays Santa ...32.00
    1982, Christmas
    Courtship...........................30.00
    1984, Santa in
    His Workshop.....................25.00
  Heritage Series
    1977, Toy maker 260.00
    1979, Lighthouse Keeper's
    Daughter 80.00
    1981, Music Maker.............30.00
    1983, Painter......................25.00
  Mother's Day Series
    1976, A Mother's Love 120.00
    1978, Bedtime..................100.00
    1980, A Mother's Pride.......30.00
    1982, Cooking Lesson 25.00
    1984, Grandma's
    Courting Dress 25.00
  Royal Devon
  Christmas Series
    1975, Downhill Daring........50.00
    1977, The Big Moment.......80.00
    1979, One Present
    Too Many 35.00
  Mother's Day Series
    1975, Doctor
    and the Doll.......................85.00
    1977, The Family 80.00
    1979, Mother's
    Evening Out 35.00
Playing Cards, Four Seasons,
    unopened, orig box..................15.00
Stein
  Gorham, Pensive Pals 37.50
  Rockwell Museum,
  For a Good Boy.......................95.00

Roseville Pottery

Collecting Hints: The prices for Roseville's later commercial ware are stable and unlikely to rise rapidly because it is readily available. The prices are strong for the popular middle-period patterns, which were made during the Depression and produced in limited numbers. Among the most popular patterns from this middle period are Blackberry, Cherry Blossom, Falline, Ferella, Jonquil, Morning Glory, Sunflower and Windsor.

The Art Deco craze has increased the popularity of Futura, especially the more angular-shaped pieces. Pine Cone pieces with a blue or brown glaze continue to have a strong following as do the earlier lines of Juvenile and Donatello. Desirable Roseville shapes include baskets, bookends, cookie jars, ewers, tea sets and wall pockets. Most pieces are marked. However, during the middle period, paper stickers were used. These often were removed, leaving the piece unmarked.

Roseville made more than 150 different lines or patterns. Novice collectors would benefit from reading one of the several books about Roseville and should visit dealers who specialize in art pottery. Collections generally are organized around a specific pattern or shape.

History: In the late 1880s, a group of investors purchased the J.B. Owens Pottery in Roseville, OH, and made utilitarian stoneware items. In 1892, the firm was incorporated and George F. Young became general manager. Four generations of Youngs controlled Roseville until the early 1950s. A series of acquisitions began: Midland Pottery of Roseville in 1898, Clark Stoneware Plant in Zanesville (formerly used by Peters and Reed) and Muskingum Stoneware (Mosaic Tile Co.) in Zanesville. In 1898, the offices also moved from Roseville to Zanesville.

In 1900, Roseville developed its art pottery line—Rozane. Ross Purdy designed a line to compete with Weller's Louwelsa. Rozane became a trade name to cover a large series of lines by designers such as Christian Neilson, John J. Herold and Gazo Fudji. The art lines of hand-decorated underglaze pottery were made in limited quantities after 1919.

The success of Roseville depended on its commercial lines, first developed by John J. Herald and Frederick Rhead in the early decades of the 1900s. Decorating techniques included transfers, pouncing (a method which produced the outline of a pattern which could then be used as the basis for further decorating) and air brushing or sponging over embossed motifs. Dutch, Juvenile, Cameo and Holland are some of the lines from this early period.

George Young retired in 1918. Frank Ferrell replaced Harry Rhead, who had replaced Frederick Rhead, as art director. Ferrell developed more than 80 lines, the first being Sylvan. The economic depression of the 1930s caused Roseville to look for new product lines. Pine Cone was introduced in 1935, made for 15 years and issued in more than 75 shapes.

In the 1940s, a series of high-gloss glazes were used to try to revive certain lines. Other changes were made in response to the fluctuating contemporary market. Mayfair and Wincraft date from this period. In 1952, Raymor dinnerware was produced. None of these changes brought economic success back to Roseville. In November 1954, Roseville was bought by the Mosaic Tile Co.

References: Susan and Al Bagdade, *Warman's American Pottery and Porcelain*, Wallace-Homestead, 1994; John W. Humphries, *Price Guide to Roseville Pottery by the Numbers*, published by author, 1993; Sharon and Bob Huxford, *Collectors Encyclopedia of Roseville Pottery*, 1st Series (1976, 1995 value update), 2nd Series (1980, 1995 value update), Collector Books; Ralph and Terry Kovel, *Kovels' American Art Pottery*, Crown Publishers, 1993; Randall B. Monsen, *Collector's Compendium of Roseville Pottery*, Monsen and Baer (Box 529, Vienna, VA 22183), 1995; Leslie Pina, *Pottery*, Schiffer Publishing, 1994.

Videotape: Ralph and Terry Kovel, *Collecting with the Kovels: American Art Pottery*, available from producers (P.O. Box 22990, Beachwood, OH 44122).

Collectors' Clubs: American Art Pottery Association, 125 E. Rose

Ave., St. Louis, MO 63119; Roseville's of the Past Pottery Club, P.O. Box 656, Clarcona, FL 32710.

Ashtray, Silhouette, brown 35.00
Basket, 10" d
    Clematis, brown 65.00
    Magnolia, green,
    mkd "385-10" 95.00
    Peony, yellow flowers...............95.00
    Pine Cone, mkd "308-10" 215.00
    Rozana, ivory,
    mkd "1-66-2-2" 95.00
Bookends, pr
    Foxglove, blue.........................125.00
    Snowberry, pink 135.00
    Zephyr, brown 115.00
Bowl
    Apple Blossom, 8" d, green......45.00
    Carnelian II, blue and purple 95.00
    Corinthian, 6-1/2" d 55.00
    Magnolia, 10" d, blue 65.00
    Monticello, blue 85.00
    Panel, 5" d, brown 45.00
    Wisteria, blue, 2 handles,
    2-1/2" x 6-1/2" 325.00
Candlesticks, pr
    Baneda, pink, 4-1/2" h............575.00
    Bleeding Heart, blue................95.00
    Clematis, blue, mkd "1158-2" ...85.00
Console Bowl
    Luffa, green, 13" d..................265.00
    Ming Tree, mkd "528-10"..........75.00
    Pine Cone 80.00
Cornucopia
    Bittersweet 50.00
    Ivory II, 8", Art Deco 65.00
    Water Lily, brown 55.00
Creamer and Sugar, Seascape,
    brown dec 140.00
Ewer
    Bushberry, 6" h, blue...............75.00
    Columbine, 7" h, blue..............70.00
    Freesia, 6" h, green.................65.00

Vase, Bleeding Hearts, saucer base, floral extended neck, shaped spout, semi-curved shaped handle, turquoise ground, pink flowers, 6-3/8", $45.

Vase, Cosmos, blue, #649-3, 3", $35.

    Gardenia, 6" h, brown 50.00
    Silhouette, 10" h......................65.00
    Snowberry, 10" h, blue.............95.00
Floor Vase, Velmoss,
    green, 14" h 375.00
Flower Frog, Fuchsia, green 195.00
Hanging Basket, Mock Orange ...265.00
Jardiniere
    Florentine, 8" d, brown.............95.00
    Imperial I, 9" x 9",
    small burst bubble..................175.00
Jug, Cherry Blossom,
    brown, 4" h 265.00
Mug, Pine Cone, 4" h, brown 125.00
Planter
    Artwood, yellow, "1056-10" 125.00
    Earlam, green, 89-8 ....200.00
Soap Dish, Donatello 175.00
Sugar, cov, Snowberry, pink 125.00
Urn, Freesia, 8" h, green 95.00
Vase
    Apple Blossom, pink
    7" h, #382 ....125.00
    8" h, #385 ....165.00
    10" h, #388 ....250.00
    Carnelian II, blue, 8"...............185.00
    Clematis, dark green,
    6" h, #103................................90.00
    Ferrella, 8" h, orange,
    mkd "506-8"............................225.00
    Foxglove, 6" h, blue, double open
    handles, mkd "44-6" 95.00
    Freesia, brown 95.00
    Futura, 6" h 195.00
    Imperial II, 468-5"...................165.00
    Rosecraft, 5" d,
    black, mkd "158-5" 95.00
    Thorn Apple, blue.....................85.00
    Tuscany, gray, 9" 185.00
    Wisteria, brown, 630-6 ....375.00
Wall Pocket
    Corinthian, 12" l.....................225.00
    Donatello, 11-1/2" l.................175.00
    Florane, handle 125.00

    Florentine, 9-1/2" l, brown......135.00
    Imperial II, #1264,
    orange and green 450.00
    Mostique, 9-1/2" l 195.00
    Tuscany, pink.........................125.00
    Wincraft, 5-1/2" l 175.00
Window Box, Ming Tree,
    11-1/2" l, blue 125.00

Royal China

Collecting Hints: The dinnerware has become very collectible and increasingly popular. It can be found at flea markets and antiques malls across the country. Prices are steadily increasing and it is becoming more difficult to find some of the serving pieces.

The backs of pieces usually contain the names of the shape, line and decoration. In addition to many variations of company backstamps, Royal China also produced objects with private backstamps. All records of these markings were lost in a fire in 1970.

The following are some of the items that are considered scarce: the lug soup/cereal bowl in several different patterns, many items with tab handles, coffee mugs and some glasses and pitchers.

History: The Royal China Co., manufactured dinnerware in Sebring, OH, from 1924 to 1986. The original officers were Beatrice L. Miller, William H. Hebenstreit and John Briggs.

The firm produced a large variety of dinnerware patterns, the most popular being the blue and white Currier and Ives. Other patterns made by the company include Bucks County, Colonial Homestead, Fair Oaks, Memory Lane, Old Curiosity Shop and Willow Ware, Gordon Parker, art director at Royal China, was credited with designing the border on the Currier and Ives pattern and some of the other popular dinnerware lines which were made in four basic colors: blue, pink, green or brown.

Royal China was sold through retail department stores, catalog mail-order houses and supermarket chains. Numerous serving pieces as well as advertising and decorative items to compliment the dinnerware were available.

In 1948, Kenneth Doyle developed a new machine, the underglaze stamping machine, that allowed the dinnerware to be mass produced at a very reasonable cost. The company had various owners including the Jeanette Glass Corp., from 1969 to 1976. In 1970, the building and records were destroyed by fire and the operation was moved to the French Saxon China Co., building. In 1976, the company was purchased by Coca-Cola and was operated by them until 1981, when it was sold to the J. Corp. It was sold for the last time in 1984. The new owner, Nordic Capital, filed for bankruptcy in 1986 and ceased production in March of that year.

References: Eldon R. Aupperle, *Collector's Guide for Currier & Ives Dinnerware by Royal China Co.*, published by author (27470 Saxon Rd., Toulon, IL 61483); Susan and Al Bagdade, *Warman's American Pottery and Porcelain*, Wallace-Homestead, 1994; Jo Cunningham, *Collector's Encyclopedia of American Dinnerware*, Collector Books, 1982, 1995 value update; Harvey Duke, *Official Identification and Price Guide to Pottery and Porcelain*, 8th Edition, House of Collectibles, 1995; Lois Lehner, *Lehner's Encyclopedia of U.S. Marks on Pottery, Porcelain & Clay*, Collector Books, 1988.

Collectors' Club: Currier & Ives Dinnerware Collectors Club, RD2, Box 394, Holidaysburg, PA 16648.

Advisor: David J. and Deborah G. Folckemer.

Bucks County: Introduced c1950; prices given are for yellow pieces with a dark brown print.

Dinnerware
Bowl
    Fruit..2.50
    Lug soup/cereal........................20.00
    Oatmeal/cereal...........................8.00
    Rim soup....................................9.00
    Vegetable
        9"...15.00
        10".......................................18.00
Butter Dish, cov, 1/4 lb.................40.00
Casserole, cov, angled handles....70.00
Creamer...4.00
Cup and Saucer..............................3.50
Gravy boat, underplate.................20.00
Gravy Ladle....................................40.00
Plate
    Bread and butter.......................2.50
    Breakfast, 9"............................12.00
    Dinner, 10-1/2".........................4.00
    Grill, 3 sections........................15.00
    Salad, 7-3/8"..............................8.00

Platter
    Lug Meat, 11-1/2"......................20.00
    Oval, 13".................................20.00
    Round
        12".......................................22.00
        13".......................................25.00
Salt and Pepper Shakers, pr.........18.00
Sugar Bowl, cov
    Angled handles.........................20.00
    Tab handles..............................15.00

Accessories
Clock plate.....................................75.00
Glasses, old fashion, juice, 9 oz and
    13 oz, each..............................15.00

Colonial Homestead: Introduced c1950; prices given are for white pieces with a green print.

Dinnerware
Bowl
    Fruit..2.00
    Lug soup/cereal........................20.00
    Oatmeal/cereal.........................10.00
    Rim soup....................................8.00
    Vegetable
        9"...15.00
        10".......................................20.00
Butter Dish, cov, 1/4 lb.................25.00
Casserole, cov
    Angled handles.........................60.00
    Tab handles..............................95.00
Creamer...4.00
Cup and Saucer..............................3.00
Gravy boat, underplate.................22.00
Gravy Ladle....................................40.00
Mug, coffee....................................20.00
Plate
    Bread and butter.......................2.50
    Breakfast, 9"............................12.00
    Dinner, 10-1/2".........................4.00
    Grill, 3 sections........................15.00
    Pie, 10".....................................18.00
    Salad, 7-3/8"..............................8.00
Platter
    Lug Meat, 11-1/2"......................20.00
    Oval, 13".................................20.00
    Round
        12".......................................20.00
        13".......................................30.00
Salt and Pepper Shakers, pr.........20.00
Sugar Bowl, cov,
    angled handles.........................10.00
Teapot, cov....................................85.00

Currier and Ives: Introduced late 1940s; prices given are for white pieces with a blue print. Prices are 20% higher for pieces with a pink print.

Dinnerware
Bowl
    Fruit..3.00
    Lug soup/cereal........................35.00
    Oatmeal/cereal.........................12.00
    Rim soup..................................10.00

Willow Ware, grill plate, 3 sections, $20.

Vegetable
    9"...20.00
    10".......................................25.00
Butter Dish, cov, 1/4 lb
    Fashionable Turnouts..............40.00
    Road Winter..............................30.00
Candle lamp, globe....................100.00
Casserole, cov
    Angled handles.........................75.00
    Tab handles............................145.00
Creamer
    Regular.......................................5.00
    Tall...10.00
Cup and Saucer..............................4.00
Gravy boat, underplate
    Tab handles..............................55.00
Regular handle...............................25.00
Gravy Ladle....................................40.00
Mug
    Coffee......................................25.00
    Train scene..............................30.00
Plate
    Bread and butter.......................3.00
    Breakfast, 9"............................15.00
    Dinner, 10-1/2".........................5.00
    Pie, 10", 9 different scenes......20.00
    Salad, 7-3/8"............................12.00
    Snack, with cup.......................30.00
Platter
    Lug Meat, 11-1/2"....................25.00
    Oval, 13".................................25.00
    Round
        11".......................................25.00
        12".......................................25.00
        13".......................................50.00
Salt and Pepper Shakers, pr.........25.00
Sugar Bowl, cov
    Angled handles.........................15.00
    Handleless................................25.00
Teapot, cov..................................135.00

Accessories
Ashtray..12.00
Beverage set, frosted pitcher, 6 glasses,
    price for set.............................95.00
Clock plate.....................................95.00

Glasses, old fashion, juice, 9 oz and
13 oz, each 12.00
Tidbit
2 tier, wood legs 95.00
3 tier 75.00
Wall plaque...................................50.00

Hostess Set
Cake plate, 10"
Flat 25.00
Footed 60.00
Candy bowl...................................30.00
Dip bowl..20.00
Egg plate 60.00
Pie baker, 11"................................40.00
Serving plate, 7" 12.00

Fair Oaks: Introduced 1960s; prices given are pieces with a multicolored print.

Dinnerware
Bowl
Fruit...3.00
Rim soup 10.00
Vegetable
9"..10.00
10"..20.00
Divided.....................................25.00
Butter Dish, cov, Fashionable Turnouts,
1/4 lb...30.00
Casserole, cov, angled handles 70.00
Creamer 5.00
Cup and Saucer 4.00
Gravy boat, underplate.................22.00
Gravy Ladle....................................40.00
Plate
Bread and butter 3.00
Dinner, 10-1/2"............................4.00
Salad, 7-3/8" 8.00
Platter
Oval
11"...30.00
13"..25.00
Salt and Pepper Shakers, pr 20.00
Sugar Bowl, cov,
angled handles 12.00
Teapot, cov...................................100.00

Accessories
Ashtray 12.00
Beverage set, frosted pitcher, 6 glasses,
price for set..............................85.00
Tidbit, 3 tier...................................40.00
Wall plaque....................................50.00

Memory Lane: Introduced 1965; prices given are for white pieces with a pink print.

Dinnerware
Bowl
Fruit...3.00
Oatmeal/cereal.........................10.00
Rim soup 9.00
Vegetable
9"..20.00
10"..25.00
Butter Dish, cov, Fashionable Turnouts,

1/4 lb...35.00
Casserole, cov, angled handles 75.00
Creamer 5.00
Cup and Saucer 4.00
Gravy boat, underplate.................25.00
Gravy Ladle....................................40.00
Mug, coffee 25.00
Plate
Bread and butter 3.00
Breakfast, 9"..............................12.00
Dinner, 10-1/2" 4.00
Pie, 10".....................................30.00
Salad, 7-3/8" 10.00
Platter
Lug Meat, 11-1/2"......................22.00
Oval, 13" 25.00
Round, 12" 25.00
Salt and Pepper Shakers, pr 25.00
Sugar Bowl, cov,
angled handles 12.00
Teapot, cov 125.00

Accessories
Ashtray 8.00
Glasses, old fashion, juice, 9 oz and
13 oz, each...............................12.00
Serving tray, 19" d, metal 30.00

Old Curiosity Shop: Introduced early 1950s; prices given are for white pieces with a green print.

Dinnerware
Bowl
Fruit...2.50
Lug soup/cereal 25.00
Oatmeal/cereal..........................12.00
Rim soup 10.00
Vegetable
9" 18.00
10"..22.00
Butter Dish, cov, 1/4 lb 30.00
Casserole, cov
Angled handles 65.00
Tab handles 100.00
Creamer 4.50
Cup and Saucer 4.00
Gravy boat, underplate.................25.00
Gravy Ladle....................................40.00
Mug, coffee 30.00
Plate
Bread and butter 3.00
Breakfast, 9"..............................12.00
Dinner, 10-1/2" 4.00
Pie, 10".....................................22.00
Salad, 7-3/8" 10.00
Platter
Lug Meat, 11-1/2".....................22.00
Oval, 13" 22.00
Round
12" 20.00
13" 30.00
Salt and Pepper Shakers, pr 20.00
Sugar Bowl, cov,
angled handles 12.00

Teapot, cov 95.00

Willow Ware: Introduced 1940s; prices given are for white pieces with a blue print.

Dinnerware
Bowl
Fruit...3.00
Lug soup/cereal 25.00
Oatmeal/cereal 12.00
Rim soup....................................10.00
Vegetable
9" 20.00
10"..25.00
Butter Dish, cov, 1/4 lb 25.00
Casserole, cov
Angled handles 75.00
Tab handles 100.00
Creamer 4.00
Cup and Saucer 4.00
Gravy boat, underplate
Regular handle 25.00
Tab handles 50.00
Gravy Ladle....................................40.00
Mug, coffee 20.00
Plate
Bread and butter 4.00
Breakfast, 9" 15.00
Dinner, 10-1/2".............................4.00
Grill, 3 sections 20.00
Pie, 10" 25.00
Salad, 7-3/8" 10.00
Snack, with cup..........................25.00
Platter
Lug Meat, 11-1/2" 20.00
Oval
11" 25.00
13" 25.00
Round
11" 25.00
12" 25.00
13" 40.00
Salt and Pepper Shakers, pr.........25.00
Sugar Bowl, cov
Angled handles 12.00
Handleless 25.00
Tab handles 20.00

S

Salt and Pepper Shakers

Collecting Hints: Collect only sets in very good condition. Make certain the set has the proper two pieces and base, if applicable. China shakers should show no signs of cracking. Original paint and decoration should be intact on all china and metal figurals. All parts should be present, including the closure.

Collectors compete with those in other areas, e.g., advertising, animal groups, Blacks and holiday collectors. Many shakers were stock items to which souvenir labels were later affixed. The form, not the label, is the important element. Black figural shakers are rising in price. The same is true for advertising sets and comic and cartoon characters.

History: The Victorian era saw the advent of elaborate glass and fine-china salt and pepper shakers. Collectors were attracted to these objects by the pioneering research work of Arthur Goodwin Peterson that was published in *Glass Salt Shaker*. Figural and souvenir shakers, most dating from the mid-20th century and later, were looked down upon by this group.

This attitude is slowly changing. More and more people are collecting the figural and souvenir shakers, especially since prices are lower. Many of these patterns were made by Japanese firms and imported heavily after World War II. Some forms were produced for decades; hence, it is difficult to tell an early example from

Praying hands, ceramic, dark brown glaze, gold trim, 3-1/2" h, $15.

a modern one. This is one of the factors that keeps prices low.

References: Gideon Bosker and Lena Lencer, *Salt and Pepper Shakers*, Avon Books, 1994; Larry Carey and Sylvia Tompkins, *1002 Salt and Pepper Shakers*, Schiffer Publishing, 1995; ———, *Salt and Pepper*, Schiffer Publishing, 1994; Melva Davern, *Collector's Encyclopedia of Salt & Pepper Shakers*, 1st Series (1985, 1991 value update), 2nd Series (1990, 1995 value update), Collector Books; Helene Guarnaccia, *Salt & Pepper Shakers*, Vol. I (1985, 1993 value update), Vol. II (1989, 1993 value update), Vol. III (1991, 1995 value update), Vol. IV (1993, 1995 value update), Collector Books; Mildred and Ralph Lechner, *World of Salt Shakers*, 2nd Edition, Collector Books, 1992, 1995 value update; Arthur G. Peterson, *Glass Salt Shakers*, Wallace-Homestead, out of print; Mike Schneider, *Complete Salt and Pepper Shaker Book*, Schiffer Publishing, 1993.

Collectors' Clubs: Antique and Art Glass Salt Shaker Collector's Society, 2832 Rapidan Trail, Maitland, FL 32751; Novelty Salt and Pepper Shakers Club, P.O. Box 3617, Lantana, FL 33465.

Museum: Judith Basin Museum, Stanford, MT.

Advertising

Big Boys, brown hair	350.00
Coca-Cola, ceramic bottles	60.00
Colonel Sanders	75.00
Esso, gas pumps	35.00
Firestone, U.S. Rubber, tires	55.00
Greyhound Buses	80.00
Keebler, Elf and Tee in basket	45.00
Nikolai Vodka Men	195.00
RCA, Nipper, Lenox	65.00
Saf-T-Cups	30.00
Sandeman	125.00
Seagrams Seven	35.00

Depression-Era Glass

Block Optic, green	40.00
Cameo, green	75.00
Cloverleaf, green	35.00
Colonial Knife and Fork, green	145.00
Doric, pink	40.00
English Hobnail, green, round base	85.00
Floral, pink, large	55.00
Florentine #2, green	45.00
Madrid, footed, amber	105.00

Manhattan, pink	50.00
Mayfair, flat, pink	70.00
Miss America, clear	320.00
Newport, amethyst	45.00
Normandie, amber	55.00
Patrician, amber	65.00
Princess, topaz	80.00
Royal Lace, pink	80.00
Sharon, amber	45.00
Tea Room, pink	60.00

Figural

Bears, yellow, snuggle type, Van Tellingen	40.00
Cats, white	40.00
Chicks, yellow chicks hatching from white eggs, Japan	20.00
Corn, standing	55.00
Donkey, gray standing donkey, 2 white jugs over back as shakers, Japan	20.00
Ducks, yellow, snuggle type, Van Tellingen	50.00
Fawns, lying	70.00
Fish	
Gray	45.00
Orange	40.00
Flower, Disney	165.00
Golfer, ball, on tray, Goebel	185.00
Munich Priests	65.00
Pheasants, tall, Rosemeade	38.00
Poodles	38.00
Quail	40.00
Rabbits, yellow, snuggle type, Van Tellingen	40.00
Santa Claus	65.00
Scotties, orange dogs playing instruments	75.00
Teapots, silver-colored metal, small TN souvenir gold-colored plaque on each, orig box	15.00

Santa Claus

Collecting Hints: The number of Santa Claus-related items is endless. Collectors are advised to concentrate on one form (postcards, toys, etc.) or a brief time period. New collectors will find the hard-plastic 1950s Santas easily accessible and generally available at a reasonable price. The current appearance of Santa Claus is directly attributable to the illustrations of Haddon Sundblom for the Coca-Cola Co.

History: The idea of Santa Claus developed from stories about St. Nicholas, who lived about 300 A.D. By the 1500s, "Father Christmas" in England, "Pere Noel" in France and

"Weihnachtsmann" in Germany were well established.

Until the 1800s Santa Claus was pictured as a tall, thin, stately man wearing bishop's robes and riding a white horse. Washington Irving, in *Knickerbocker's History of New York* (1809), made him a stout, jolly man who wore a broad-brimmed hat and huge breeches and smoked a long pipe. The traditional Santa Claus image came from Clement C. Moore's poem "An Account of a Visit from St. Nicholas" (*Troy Sentinel*, NY, 1823) and the cartoon characterizations by Thomas Nast which appeared in *Harper's Weekly* between 1863 and 1886.

References: Ann Bahar, *Santa Dolls*, Hobby House Press, 1992; Polly and Pam Judd, *Santa Dolls and Figurines Price Guide*, Revised, Hobby House Press, 1994; Mary Morrison, *Snow Babies, Santas and Elves*, Schiffer Publishing, 1993; Lissa and Dick Smith, *Christmas Collectibles*, Chartwell Books, 1993.

Reproduction Alert.

Additional Listings: Christmas Items.

Advisor: Lissa Bryan-Smith and Richard Smith.

Advertising Trade Card, "Santa Claus Soap, Gifts for Wrappers," N.K. Fairbanks Co., Chicago, St. Louis, New York, 1899, 3"x 5" 10.00

Bank

   3", hard plastic, red, egg shape with Santa mask, "Firestone Bank, Lisbon, Ohio" 7.00

   4", cardboard, Santa and sleigh, box-shaped sleigh, 1960s 8.00

Santa on Motorcycle, celluloid, red costume, green sack, black lines, orange tones to motorcycle, mkd "Japan," 5-1/4" l, 3-3/4" h, $50.

   6-1/2" h, metal, Santa sleeping in chair 60.00

   11" h, chalkware, Santa sitting on chimney and waving, 1960s.....30.00

Book

   The Night Before Christmas, A Golden Book, Golden Press, Western Publishing Co., Racine, WI, 15" h, 1975 ....7.00

   Night Before Christmas, linenette, Samuel Gabriel Sons & Co., NY, 12" h, 1947 ....18.00

   Santa Claus in Storyland, pop-up, Doehla Greeting Cards Inc., Fitchburg, MA, 11" h, 1950 ......25.00

Candy Box

   3" x 4-1/2" x 1-3/4", Santa face, cotton string handle, USA, 1970s ...5.00

   3" x 6" x 1-3/4", paper handle, Santa Face, Royton Paper Prod., Buffalo, NY 12.00

   3-1/2" x 5-1/2" x 2", "Merry Christmas," picture of Santa and his workshop, cloth handle, USA, 1940s 9.00

Candy Container

   4-1/2", hard plastic, red with green skis, lollipops in open pack on back, USA 10.00

   5-1/2" h, glass, Father Christmas in chimney, metal base, Victory Candy Co. 90.00

   8-1/2" h, papier-mâché, Father Christmas, white mica coat, holding feather tree, early 1900s 500.00

   9" h, papier-mâché, waving, large belly, red coat, 1940s 70.00

Card Holder, cardboard, fold-up, Santa and sleigh with reindeer, Hallmark, 1940s 20.00

Chromolithograph, 10" h, Santa standing, tinsel trim, Germany, 1920s......................45.00

Figure

   2-1/2" h, cotton batting, plaster face, cotton batting reindeer, cardboard sled, 1930s, Japan...................55.00

   3" h, composition face, red chenille body, Japanese.......................12.00

   4" h, hard plastic, Santa on bike, USA, 1960s................................8.00

   4-1/2" h, hard plastic, holding green tree wearing white snowshoes, USA, 1950s 10.00

   6-1/2" h, composition face, skier, red cloth coat, blue pants, wood skis and poles, Japanese................70.00

   7" h, flocked plastic, Mr. and Mrs. Claus, Hong Kong......................7.00

   10" h, cotton batting, white coat, holding foil holly leaf, composition face 110.00

   13-1/2" h, hard plastic, Santa

Pinback, multicolored, 1-1/4" d, $5.

   with small pack in hand, hole for light in back, Union Products, Leominster, MA......................14.00

Game, Santa Claus Ring Toss, 10" h, cardboard, First National Bank of Berwick giveaway................10.00

Greeting Card, Santa riding a plane over the world, "Merry Christmas," 1940s 7.00

Lantern, 5" h, glass and metal, Santa face, battery operated, 1950s 30.00

Light Bulb, 3" h, milk glass, Santa standing..................................35.00

Matches, 2-1/2" h, "Santa Says Join Our Christmas Club," matches make the Santa face, Santa on cover 10.00

Ornament

   3-1/4" h, blown glass, holding tree, German, 1930s 35.00

   6" h

      Blown glass, holding sack with metal clip base, German, 1920s....................55.00

      Cotton batting, paper face, chenille hanger 15.00

Postcard

   "Christmas Greetings," Father Christmas with candlelit tree and toys, German, 1908 ....10.00

   Father Christmas and angel inspecting gift list, German 10.00

Record, "Santa's Surprise," 78 RPM, red with paper label showing Santa and tree...........................8.00

Tin, 4" d, red cov with Santa head surrounded by poinsettias, early 1900s..............................20.00

Toy

   6-1/2" h, hard plastic, cloth coat, walker with string in belly, paper label, German 32.00

   9" h, plastic face and boots, cloth coat, plays hard plastic drum, battery operated, Korean 35.00

   10" h, plastic head and face, metal base and chimney, battery operated, seated on chimney ringing bell,

Japanese..............................60.00
Store Display, 42" h, papier-mâché,
 Santa face, hollow 60.00

Scouting

Collecting Hints: Nostalgia is one of the principal reasons for collecting Scouting memorabilia; individuals often focus on the period during which they themselves were involved in the Scouting movement. Other collectors select themes, e.g., handbooks, jamborees, writings by scout-movement leaders or Eagle Scout material. Jamboree ephemera is especially desirable. The greatest price fluctuation occurs in modern material and newly defined specialized collecting areas.

Scouting scholars have produced a wealth of well-researched material on the Scouting movement. Many of these pamphlets are privately printed and can be located by contacting dealers specializing in Scouting items.

Girl Scout material is about five to 10 years behind Boy Scout material in respect to collecting interest. A Girl Scout collection can still be assembled for a modest investment. While Boy Scout uniforms have remained constant in design throughout time, the Girl Scout uniform changed almost every decade. This increases the number of collectibles.

History: The Boy Scout movement began in America under the direction of William D. Boyce, inspired by a helping hand he received from one of Baden-Powell's English scouts when he was lost in a London fog in 1910. Other American boys' organizations, such as the one organized by Dan Beard, were quickly brought into the Boy Scout movement. In 1916, the Boy Scouts received a charter from the United States Congress. Key leaders in the movement were Ernest Thompson-Seton, Dan Beard, William D. Boyce and James West.

One of Norman Rockwell's first jobs was editor of *Boys' Life* in 1913 and this began the famous American illustrator's lifelong association with the Boy Scouts.

The first international jamboree was held in England in 1920. America's first jamboree was held in 1937 in Washington, D.C. Manufacturers, quick to recognize the potential for profits, issued a wealth of Boy Scout material. Local councils and Order of the Arrow lodges have added significantly to this base, especially in the area of patches. Around the time of the 1950 National Jamboree, everything from patches to lizards were traded.

The Girl Scout movement began on March 12, 1912, under the direction of Juliette Gordon Low of Savannah, GA. The movement grew rapidly; in 1928, the Girl Scout manual suggested cookies be sold to raise funds. The Girl Scout movement received wide recognition for its activities during World War II, selling over $3 million worth of bonds in the fourth Liberty Loan drive.

References: Fred Duersch Jr., *Green Khaki Crimped-Edge Merit Badges*, Downs Printing, 1993; Franck, Hook, Ellis & Jones, *Aid to Collecting Selected Council Shoulder Patches*, privately printed, 1994; R.J. Sayers, *Guide to Boy Scout Collectibles*, published by author, 1992.

Periodicals: *Fleur-de-Lis*, 5 Dawes Ct., Novato, CA 94947; *Scout Memorabilia Magazine*, c/o Lawrence L. Lee Scouting Museum, P.O. Box 1121, Manchester, NH 03105; *Scout Stuff*, P.O. Box 1841, Easley, SC 29641; *Scouting Collectors Quarterly*, 806 E. Scott St., Tuscola, IL 61953.

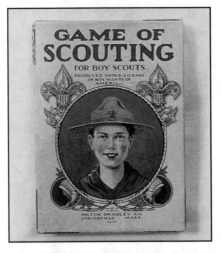

Game of Scouting, Milton Bradley, 52 playing cards, instruction sheet, designed by G. Cornelius Baker, 5-5/8" x 7-1/2" x 1", $75.

Collectors' Clubs: American Scouting Association, P.O. Box 92, Kentfield, CA 94914; International Badgers Club, 7760 NW 50th St., Lander Hill, FL 33351; National Scouting Collectors Society, 806 E. Scott St., Tuscola, IL 61953; Scouts on Stamps Society International, 7406 Park Dr., Tampa, FL 33610.

Museums: Girl Scout National Headquarters, New York, NY; Juliette Gordon Low Girl Scout National Center, Savannah, GA; Lawrence L. Lee Scouting Museum and Max J. Silber Scouting Library, Manchester, NH; Lone Scout Memory Lodge, Camp John J. Barnhardt, New London, NC; Murray State University National Museum of the Boy Scouts of America, Murray, KY; Western Scout Museum, Los Angeles, CA; World of Scouting Museum, Valley Forge, PA; Zitelman Scout Museum, Rockford, IL.

Advisor: Richard Shields.

Reproduction Alert: Boy Scout jamboree patches, rare Council Shoulder patches and rare Order of the Arrow patches.

Boy Scouts

Appreciation Plaque, Onward for God & Country, 1959, laminated 6.00
Armband, Emergency Service, lifesaving ring over Tenderfoot emblem design 35.00
Book
 The Boy Scout Aviators, George Durston, 1921, dj 12.50
 Rolf in the Woods: The Adventures of a Boy Scout with Indian Quonab and Little Dog Skookum, E.T. Seton, Doubleday, Garden City, NY, 1911, gilt cover, 437 pgs, 1st ed 35.00
Canteen, BSA, 1 qt, canvas cov, New York City logo 10.00
Glass, Camp Snoopy, Beagle Scout.............................4.00
Handbook
 Adventuring for Senior Scouts 15.00
 Boy Scout Handbook, 1930, Rockwell cover, 646 pgs..........23.00
 Handbook for Boys, 1940 ....10.00
 Patrol Leaders Handbook, 1962 ....3.00
 Scoutmaster Handbook, 1912, lst ed 200.00
Insignia Strip
 States, red and white, any of the 50 states, each 1.00
 Senior, khaki color 2.00

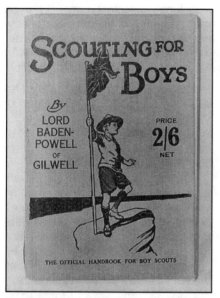

Handbook, *Scouting for Boys*, English, 1935 printing, $15.

Medal
 Duty to God, religious medal,
 Mormon......................................75.00
 Lincoln Pilgrimage,
 Washington, DC.........................6.00
 Scout activities,
 bronze, silver or gold..................4.00
 Scouter's Training Award,
 10k gold.....................................20.00
National Jamboree
 1935, felt, pocket patch,
 no moth holes..........................150.00
 1957, jacket patch.....................45.00
 1964, decal..................................5.00
 1969, Idaho Lumber Industry,
 wooden nickel 1.00
 1973, trading post ticket.............1.00
 1977, sardine can........................5.00
 1981, silver coin 2.00
 1985, towel...................................6.00
Paperweight, silver-colored fleur-
 de-lis, metal 4.00
Patch
 Camp patch, 1970s........................50
 Diamond Jubilee, blue background,
 no words.......................................3.00
 First Class, cut edge,
 brown border..............................2.00
 Gift, BSA Bicentennial.................5.00
 Jubilee Camporee, 1960.............5.00
 Philmont Scout Ranch...............25.00
 Region, 3-cut edge....................12.00
 Sash, 21 twill merit badges 15.00
 Scout Lifeguard,
 diamond-shaped 5.00
 Scoutmaster, gold letters,
 green background, rolled
 edge with title 10.00

Patch, 1950 Jamboree, Valley Forge, canvas, issued prior to Jamboree, $30.

 Southeast Region 8.00
 Ten-Mile River Scout Reservation,
 Indian on cliff, jacket patch.........6.00
Pin, Tenderfoot, safety-pin clasp.....2.00
Plumb Ax, Genuine BSA,
 with sheath 40.00
Registration card, 1930s, in brown
 envelope.....................................3.00
Rope, BSA official commando
 Loose 25.00
 With orig box 50.00
Signaler, BSA,
 2-key set, orig box 40.00

Girl Scouts

Badge, proficiency...............................50
Book
 *The Brownie Scouts at Snow
 Valley*, Mildred Wirt, Cupples &
 Leon, NY, 1949, dj 18.00
 *Girl Scout Badges
 and Signs*, 1990 ....3.00
Can, peanut brittle..........................20.00
Cup, folding, trefoil on lid, metal......8.00
Doll, 1940s, complete.....................50.00
Leaders Nature Guide, 1942.........10.00
Toilet kit, plastic.............................20.00

Dr. Seuss Collectibles

Collecting Hint: Collectors should learn which companies Seuss did advertising work for. People familiar with his drawings will almost always be able to spot his work, even if his name is not on the piece. It is often difficult to determine if one of his children's books is a first edition. Buyers should be aware of the order in which books were published as well as their original prices. Dr. Seuss also wrote under several pseudonyms including Theo. LeSieg (Gei-

sel spelled backwards) and Rosetta Stone. Prices for many Dr. Seuss items are still in a state of flux. The same Coleco plush character can vary in price by as much as $40 in for-sale ads in the same periodical.

History: The collector of Dr. Seuss memorabilia has far more to search for than children's books. Long before the Cat in the Hat first stepped onto the mat, Dr. Seuss had been busy producing cartoons, films and advertising campaigns.

 Dr. Seuss was born Theodor Seuss Geisel in 1904. In the 1920s, he started using his middle name and added the Dr. to the front. He began his career as a freelance illustrator and sent humorous pieces and cartoons to newspapers and magazines. Soon he began to get work in advertising. One of his first accounts was Flit insecticide, a product of Standard Oil of New Jersey. Other advertising work was done for Essolube Motor Oil, Essomarine Products, Ford Motor Co., National Broadcasting Co., Holly Sugar, Narragansett Lager and Ale, Brevo Shaving Cream and Hankey Bannister Scotch Whiskey. Dr. Seuss won Academy Awards for the documentaries *Hitler Lives* in 1946 and *Design for Death* in 1947 and for the animated cartoon *Gerald McBoing-Boing* in 1951. In 1953, *The 5,000 Fingers of Dr. T* was released by Columbia. Seuss wrote the story and those familiar with his work will recognize his characters in the movie.

 Boners was the first book linked with the name Dr. Seuss. Published in 1931, it was a collection of humorous writings by children which Seuss illustrated. His first children's book was *And to Think I Saw It on Mulberry Street*, which was published in 1937 after it had been rejected by 28 publishing houses. *The Cat in the Hat* was published in 1957. Another famous Seuss work, *Green Eggs and Ham*, is the third-largest-selling book in the English language.

 Many of the creatures which would later become famous in his children's works made their first appearance in the advertisements and cartoons that Seuss drew. The forerunner to Horton the kindly elephant

Cartoon drawn for magazine, c1930, $17.

first appeared in a 1929 *Judge* magazine.

Dr. Seuss died in 1991. Most of his children's books are still in print and his characters are still licensed to new products including toys and clothing items.

References: Richard Marschall (ed.), *The Tough Coughs as He Ploughs the Dough*, William Morrow and Co., Inc./Remco World Service Books, 1987; Neil and Judith Morgan, *Dr. Seuss and Mr. Geisel: A Biography*, Random House, 1995; *Dr. Seuss from Then to Now,* a catalog of the retrospective exhibition organized by the San Diego Museum of Art, 1986, Random House, 1986; *The Secret Art of Dr. Seuss*, with introduction by Maurice Sendak, Random House, 1995.

Web sites of interest: Random House has an interactive Dr. Seuss web site where children will find activities and can even write a letter to the Cat in the Hat. Events related to the famous cat and Dr. Seuss are often listed: *http://www.randomhouse.com/seussville*. Another good source is an online listing of the holdings of the University of California, San Diego, Geisel Library, Mandeville Special Collections. The URL is *http://orpheus.ucsd.edu/speccoll/collects/seuss.html*.

Advisor: Connie Swain.

Advertisement, Flit insecticide, b&w, newspaper, 1940s 2.00
Barrettes, 2 barrettes with figural heads, from the 5,000 Fingers of Dr. T, orig card, no mention of Dr. Seuss on the card 35.00
Book, *Cat in the Hat*, autographed 75.00
Doll, Talking Cat in the Hat, 1970, Mattel, 24", talker broken 65.00
Game of Yertle, 1960, Revell, spinner, tumbler, 21 plastic turtles, box corners torn 50.00
Grow Chart, The Cat in the Hat Grow Chart, paper, in orig packaging 15.00
Jack-in-the-Box, Cat in the Hat, 1970, Mattel, metal box shows scenes from The Cat in the Hat, cloth and plastic cat pops up............................100.00
Lunch Box, 1970
  Metal, many Dr. Seuss characters on all sides of box 85.00
  Vinyl, Aladdin, blue, scene from The Cat in the Hat, no thermos, some rust on grommets 225.00
Model, Norval the Bashful Blinket, 1960, Revell, Dr. Seuss Zoo, MIB ...175.00
Pin, pewter, figural, Cat in the Hat 10.00
Record Set, "The 500 Hats of Bartholomew Cubbins," RCA Victor, 2-record set, spine of album detached and taped, cover worn....................18.00
Stuffed Figure, plush, Coleco
  Grinch, 1983, 24", green body, red hat and coat, boxed with orig paper tag showing entire Coleco line of Seuss characters 130.00
  Thidwick, 1983, 12", no box or paper tags............................45.00
Tray, Narragansett Lager & Ale, 12" d, pictures Chief Gansett and a cat....................65.00

Sewing Items

Collecting Hints: Collectors tend to favor sterling silver items. However, don't overlook pieces made of metal, ivory, celluloid, plastic or wood. Before buying anything which is metal-plated, be sure the plating is in very good condition.

Advertising and souvenir items are part of sewing history. Focus on one of these aspects to develop a fascinating collection. Other collectors may specialize in a particular instrument, i.e., tape measures. Figural items of any sort have a high value because of their popularity.

Most collectors concentrate on material from the Victorian era. A novice collector might look to the 20th century, especially the Art Deco and Art Nouveau periods, to build a collection.

History: Sewing was considered an essential skill of a young woman of the 19th century. The wealth of early American samplers attests to the talents of many of these young seamstresses.

During the Victorian era a vast assortment of practical, as well as whimsical sewing devices, appeared on the market. Among these were tape measures, pincushions, stilettos for punchwork and crochet hooks. The sewing birds attached to table tops were a standard fixture in the parlor.

Many early sewing tools, e.g., needle holders, emery holders and sewing boxes, were made of wood. However, the sterling silver tool was considered the height of elegance. Thimbles were the most popular of these, although sterling silver was used in other devices, particularly the handles of darning eggs, stilettos and thread holders.

Needle cases and sewing kits were important advertising giveaways in the 20th century. Plastic sewing items are available, but they have not attracted much collector interest.

References: *Advertising & Figural Tape Measures*, L-W Book Sales, 1995; Elizabeth Arbittier et al., *Collecting Figural Tape Measures*, Schiffer Publishing, 1995; Carter Bays, *Encyclopedia of Early American Sewing Machines*, published by author, 1993; Frieda Marion, *China Half-Figures Called Pincushion Dolls*, published by author, 1974, 1994 reprint; Averil Mathias, *Antique and Collectible Thimbles and Accessories*, Collector Books, 1986, 1995 value update; Dana G. Morykan and Harry L. Rinker, *Warman's Country Antiques & Collectibles*, 3rd Edition, Wallace-Homestead, 1996; Wayne Muller, *Darn It!, History and Romance of Darners*, L-W Book Sales, 1995; James W. Slaten, *Antique American Sewing Machines*, Singer Dealer Museum, 1992; Glenda Thomas, *Toy and Miniature Sewing Machines*, *Book I* (1995), *Book II* (1997) Collector Books; Helen Lester Thompson, *Sewing Tools & Trinkets*,

Needle Book, adv Spud Cigarettes, yellow leaf, $5.

Collector Books, 1996; Gertrude Whiting, *Old-Time Tools & Toys of Needlework*, Dover Publications, 1970; Debra J. Wisniewski, *Antique & Collectible Buttons*, Collector Books, 1997.

Collectors' Clubs: International Sewing Machine Collectors Society, 1000 E. Charleston Blvd., Las Vegas, NV 89104; Toy Stitchers, 623 Santa Florita Ave., Millbrae, CA 94030.

Museums: Fabric Hall, Historic Deerfield, Deerfield, MA; Sewing Machine Museum, Oakland, CA; Shelburne Museum, Shelburne, VT; Smithsonian Institution, Museum of American History, Washington, DC.

Additional Listings: Thimbles.

Advertising Trade Card
   Clarks, ONT Thread,
   boy fishing 9.00
   Domestic Sewing Machine Co., Prize Lincoln Buck Wilton 9.00
   JP Coats, black boy sitting on spool of thread, "We Never Fade" 10.00
   Singer Sewing Machine,
   opens, "The Tea Party, Mothers Helper," 1899 .... 20.00
Bobbin, ivory, Chinese, Victorian carved flowers, price for pr 160.00
Book
   DuBarry Patterns Book, Shortcuts to Sewing Success, 1945, 66 pgs 12.00
   Fabrics and How to Know Them,

   Grace Denny, Lippincott, 1928, 4" x 6-1/2", 151 pgs, dj 9.00
   Singer Sewing Library, 4 volumes, 1930, red marbleized box 45.00
   Wilcox & Gibbs Direction Book, 1900-1920, 48 pgs 25.00
Booklet
   How to Make Children's Clothing, Singer, 1930 .... 10.00
   Spool Cotton Co., Laces & Edgings, No. 199, 24 pgs, 1943 .... 6.50
   Spool Cotton Co., Easy-to-Sew Toys, #S014, 16 pgs, 1944 .... 7.00
   Star Book #22, American Thread, Doilies, 32 pgs, 1940s 7.00
Bookmark, Merrick's Spool Cotton 10.00
Button Hook
   Bone Handle, 2-1/2" l 20.00
   Mother-of Pearl-Handle, natural curvature, 6" l 42.00
Catalog
   Button Sampler, Albert/Adams Grammercy, 1951, 143 pgs 18.00
   Davis Sewing Machine, New York, NY, 1895, 18 pgs 25.00
   Domestic Sewing Machine, New York, NY, 1883, 26 pgs 32.00
   New Home Sewing Machine, New York, NY, 1900, 12 pgs.... 12.00
   Singer Manufacturing Co., NJ, 1900, 8 pgs 24.00
   Wilson Sewing Machine Co., Chicago, IL, 26 pgs 40.00
Chatelaine, silver,
   3 love tokens, 1880s 110.00
Crochet Thread Holder,
   figural, apple, thread through stem, 4" x 3-1/2" 25.00
Darner
   Brass, round egg 45.00
   Oak, 3 part, mushroom, stick and foot form 35.00
Darning Kit, folder, leather, dog on cover 12.00
Embroidery Scissors, black, steel, Germany, orig woven sweet-grass holder 45.00
Fan, hand type, Singer Sewing Machine, 1899 .... 35.00
Grommet Guide, Stimpson Eyelet Selector, 5-1/2" d, paper, center rotates to select size, illus, c1950 .... 18.00
Machine
   Household, treadle, walnut cabinet 175.00
   Singer, Featherweight 375.00
Mending Kit, 3-3/4" h, Bakelite, red and ivory, Bakelite thimble cap 30.00
Needle Book, A Century of Progress, complete 8.00
Needle Case
   Bakelite, doll shape 35.00
   Silver, ribbed 25.00

   Wood, Russian doll type 15.00
Pincushion, figural
   Bird, thimble 15.00
   Doll, arms at head 20.00
   Pyramid, wood 15.00
   Slipper, beaded leather, 5", 1950s 65.00
Pin Holder, advertising
   1-3/4" l, black and white celluloid, silvered-tin frame, "Keystone Boots, Colchester Rubbers," knee-boot illus, name of Philadelphia store, c1880 .... 60.00
   2-1/4" l, multicolored litho tin, slogans "The Success Spreader Fertilizes the Earth" and "Pin Your Faith to Success Spreaders," North and South America on 1 side, reverse with large lion superimposed on globe, c1900 .... 85.00
Program, Bobbin Show, Atlanta, 1985, 32 pgs, Coca-Cola adv 4.00
Rug Hook, wood, cast iron and steel, mkd "Jewel," black and floral dec, dated 1886 .... 125.00
Sample Card, Butler Brothers Shirts, 3 cloth samples, 7" x 11", 1937 .... 6.50
Sewing Bird, brass, emb, orig clamp, pincushion replaced 120.00
Sewing Box, Wheeler & Wheeler, carved lid, logo, 1920s, unused 75.00
Sewing Kit
   American Red Cross, buttons and thread 35.00
   Celluloid, scissors, thimble and thread in case 15.00
   Lydia Pinkham, metal tube 25.00
Table, Singer Sewing Machine, cast-iron base, 1/4" d glass top 125.00
Tape Measure
   Advertising
      Angland's Glory Matches, 1-1/2", celluloid, multicolored, match box illus 85.00
      Colgate's Fab, 1-1/2" d, celluloid, full-color detergent soap box on front, text on back, c1930 .... 45.00

Pincushion, 8 Chinese figures along side, silk, 4-1/2" w, 2-1/2" h, $45.

First National Bank, Sunbury, PA, 1-1/4" d, celluloid multicolored illus of Santa, snow-capped chimney, blue star-filled ground, black celluloid back with red poppy plant, c1920...............85.00

General Electric Refrigerator...........................45.00

Lackawanna Coal, 1-1/2" d, bright orange and black, c1930......25.00

Parisian Novelty Co., 1-1/2" d, blue and white celluloid, adv text, c1920.....................35.00

Portland Cement.................40.00

Stromberg Carburetor..........55.00

Figural

Black Woman, flowers 145.00

Fruit Basket............................50.00

Pig in Shoe...........................85.00

Ship.......................................35.00

Thimble Holder, sweet grass, lid and loop..................................35.00

Thread Box, Coats, wood..............30.00

Thread Winder, ivory.....................20.00

Valentine, 5-1/2", foldout, boy and girl with sewing machine 12.00

Shawnee Pottery

Collecting Hints: Many Shawnee pieces came in several color variations. Some pieces were both painted and decorated with decals. The available literature indicates some, but not all, of the variations. There is not a great deal of interest in either the Shawnee artware or dinnerware lines. These include Cameo, Cheria (Petit Point), Diora and Touche (Liana). New collectors might consider concentrating in one of these areas.

Shawnee pieces were marked "Shawnee," "Shawnee U.S.A.," "USA #___," "Kenwood," or with character names, e.g., "Pat. Smiley" and "Pat. Winnie."

History: The Shawnee Pottery Co., was founded in 1937 in Zanesville, OH. The company acquired a 650,000-square-foot plant that had previously housed the American Encaustic Tiling Co. Shawnee produced as many as 100,000 pieces of pottery a day until 1961, when the plant closed. Shawnee limited its production to kitchenware, decorative art pottery and dinnerware. Distribution was primarily through jobbers and chain stores.

Pitcher, 4-3/4" h, $15.

References: Susan and Al Bagdade, *Warman's American Pottery and Porcelain*, Wallace-Homestead, 1994; Pam Curran, *Shawnee Pottery*, Schiffer Publishing, 1995; Jim and Bev Mangus, *Shawnee Pottery*, Collector Books, 1994, 1996 value update; Mark Supnick, *Collecting Shawnee Pottery*, L-W Book Sales, 1989, 1996 value update; Duane and Janice Vanderbilt, *Collector's Guide to Shawnee Pottery*, Collector Books, 1992, 1996 value update.

Collectors' Club: Shawnee Pottery Collectors Club, P.O. Box 713, New Smyrna Beach, FL 32170.

Bowl

5" d, Corn King, #5....................30.00

8-3/4" l, oval, Corn King, #95.........................45.00

Butter Dish, cov, Corn King, #72...50.00

Casserole, cov

Corn King, 1-1/2" qt...............100.00

Lobsterware, 16 oz, orig stand......................50.00

Cookie Jar

Lucky Elephant, gold trim.......600.00

Muggsy....................................450.00

Owl...175.00

Puss 'n' Boots, gold trim, decals, white bow...........................495.00

Smiley Pig, shamrock trim 325.00

Winnie Pig, blue collar 325.00

Corn Dish, Corn King, oval...........25.00

Creamer

Cat, yellow and green 55.00

Corn King, #70 ....25.00

Elephant...................................35.00

Puss 'n' Boots, green and yellow......................85.00

Creamer and Sugar, Corn King 85.00

Cup, Corn King, #90 ....20.00

Fruit Dish, 6" d, Corn King, #92 ....40.00

Incense Burner, 5" h, Chinaman, blue base, mkd "USA".....................30.00

Lamp, Oriental figures, pr 24.00

Marmalade, cov, Fruits 40.00

Mixing Bowl, Corn King

5" d, #5.....................................40.00

6-1/4" d 45.00

Mug, Corn King, 8 oz, #69 ....45.00

Pitcher

Bo Peep, blue bonnet 145.00

Chanticleer................................110.00

Corn King, #71 ....65.00

Fruits, juice 50.00

Smiley Pig, red flower 145.00

Sunflower, large.......................95.00

Planter

Dog and Jug 22.00

Bull, brown 15.00

Pixie Boot, green, gold trim......15.00

Polynesian Girl, 5-3/4" h, #896.........................35.00

Pup, 3-button shoe, ivory.........18.00

Train, 3 pcs, caboose, coal car and engine 150.00

Wishing Well, Dutch boy and girl...................20.00

Plate

8" d, Corn King.........................40.00

9-1/2" d, Corn King, #68 ....37.50

Platter, 12" l, Corn King, #96.........50.00

Range Shakers, pr

Boy and Girl, 5" h....................50.00

Muggsy 140.00

Pig, green bib...........................125.00

Rooster, 5-1/2" h......................50.00

Relish Tray, Corn King, #79..........40.00

Salad Plate, Corn King, #93..........40.00

Salt and Pepper Shakers, pr

Bo Peep and Sailor..................45.00

Corn King, tall 35.00

Flowerpots 25.00

Fruits, 2-1/2" x 3" 40.00

Muggsy

Large 175.00

Small.................................90.00

Owl, 3-1/2" h, green eyes 65.00

Smiley Pig, 3-1/4" h, pink bib ...70.00

Watering Can, 2-1/4" 45.00

Winnie and Smiley 75.00

Saucer, Corn King, #91.................20.00

Soup Bowl, Corn King, #94...........55.00

Spoon Holder

Flowerpot, pat pending 15.00

Window Box, pat pending 15.00

Sugar, Bowl, cov, Corn King 42.00

Sugar Shaker, White Corn 55.00

Teapot, cov

Corn King 98.00
Granny Anne, peach apron 150.00
Tom the Piper's Son...............115.00
Vase, Bowknot, green 20.00

Sheet Music

Collecting Hints: Pick a theme for your collection: show tunes, songs of World War I, Sousa marches, Black material, songs of a certain lyricist or composer—the list is endless.

Be careful about stacking sheets on top of one another because the ink on the covers tends to bleed. The ideal solution is to place acid-free paper between each cover and sheet. Unfortunately, tape was often used to repair tears in old sheet music, resulting in discoloration. This detracts from value. Seek professional help in removing tape from rarer sheets.

In the late 1980s, mid-19th century sheet music rose rapidly in value. World War I themes and covers featuring Blacks currently enjoy great popularity among collectors.

History: Sheet music, especially piano scores, dates to the early 19th century. The early music contains some of the finest examples of lithography. Much of this music was bound into volumes. The covers of sheet music chronicle the social, political and historical trends of all eras. The golden age of the hand-illustrat-

Barney Google, **Jerome H. Remich & Co., song by Billy Rose and Con Conrad, 1923 by King Features Syndicate, Inc., $18.50.**

ed cover dates to around 1885. Leading artists such as James Montgomery Flagg used their talents to illustrate sheet music. Cover art work was critical to helping a song sell.

Once radio and talking pictures became popular, covers featured the stars. A song sheet might be issued in dozens of cover versions, each picturing a different personality. By the 1950s, piano playing no longer was popular and song sheets failed to maintain a high quality of design.

References: Debbie Dillon, *Collectors Guide to Sheet Music*, L-W Book Sales, 1988, 1995 value update; Anna Marie Guiheen and Marie-Reine A. Pafik, *Sheet Music Reference and Price Guide*, 2nd Edition, Collector Books, 1995.

Collectors' Clubs: City of Roses Sheet Music Collectors Club, 13447 Bush St. SE, Portland, OR 97236; National Sheet Music Society, 1597 Fair Park Ave., Los Angeles, CA 90041; New York Sheet Music Society, P. O. Box 1214, Great Neck, NY 11023; Remember That Song, 5623 N. 64th St., Glendale, AZ 85301; Sheet Music Exchange, 1202 12th St., Key West, FL 33040.

Alexander's Ragtime Band,
Irving Berlin, 1911 ....13.00
All Bound Round with a Woolen String,
Charles Seamon, 1898............15.00
America I Love You, Edgar Leslie

Come Take a Trip in My Air Ship, **lyrics and music by George Evans and Ren Shield, introduced by Edna Wallace Hopper, Charles K. Harris, $20.**

and Archie Gottler, Sophie Tucker
cover photo, 1915 ....25.00
Anything You Can Do, Irving Berlin,
from movie "Annie Get Your
Gun," 1946 ....5.00
At the Devils Ball,
Irving Berlin, 1913 ....12.00
Beautiful Isle of Somewhere,
"As Sung at Funeral of Our
Martyred President William
McKinley," Jessie Brown Pounds
and John S. Fearis, 1923 ....25.00
By the Time I Get to Phoenix,
Jim Webb, cover photo of Glen
Campbell, 1967 ....3.00
Dance of the Fireflies, E.T. Paull ..35.00
Dance of the Kutie Kids, 9-1/4" x 12",
white sample copy, full-color photo
images of 3 figural Kewpie dolls
dressed in swim wear, 4 pgs,
1919 Roat Music Co., second date of
1935, MM Cole Publishing Co.,
Chicago, IL, back cover ad features
Tom Mix, Gene Autry and Ken
Maynard songbooks, inked orig own-
er's name 14.00
Everybody's Doin' It Now,
Irving Berlin, 1911 ....10.00
Everybody Loves A College Girl
Kerry Mills, 1911 ....12.00
For the First Time, I've Fallen in Love,
Charles Tobias and David Knapp,
Kay Kyser photo, 1943..............5.00
Good for Nothin' But Love, William Kernell and Harlan Thompson, from
movie "The Big Party," Sue Carol
and Dixie Lee photo, 1930 ......10.00
*The Harvey Girls, On the Atchison,
Topeka and the Santa Fe*, Judy
Garland, 9" x 12", brown-tone photo,
purple, white and brown art back-
ground, 6 pgs, Judy Garland,
9" x 12" 20.00
Henry's Made a Lady out of Lizzie,
1928 ....15.00
High and Mighty,
John Wayne, 1954 ....20.00
I'll Be Seeing You, Liberace,
blue and white, 9" x 11-3/4",
photo of Liberace at piano, 1938,
Williamson Music, Inc..............12.00
In My Canoe, Isham Jones and
O.E. Story, 1913.........................3.00
In My Harem, Irving Berlin, 1913 ....6.00
Let's Sail to Dreamland,
Harry Kogen, Henry Busse
and Lou Holzer, 1938................5.00
Love Among the Whispering Pines,
Charles B Weston, 1913 ....10.00
Meet Me in St. Louis, Judy Garland,
9" x 12", blue-tone photo, purple,
white and brown art background,
10 pgs, 1944 Leo Feist, Inc.....20.00
My Wubba Dolly, Kay and
Sue Werner, 1939 ....5.00

Just Make It Moxie for Mine, 1904, $18.50.

Over the Rainbow, "Wizard of Oz," 9-1/4" x 12", sepia photos of 1939 feature on right side, color graphics of movie scenes to left, 6 pgs, 1939 Leo Feist, Inc. 48.00

Pickles and Peppers, Adaline Sheperd, 1907............................20.00

Roll Them Cotton Bales 7.50

Russian Rag, Cobb, 1918 ....10.00

Salvation Nell, 1913 ....8.00

The Sidewalks of New York, East Side, West Side, Al Smith's campaign song, 1928 ....15.00

Silver Sleigh Bells, E. T Paull, large folio 50.00

Some Enchanted Evening, Richard Rodgers and Oscar Hammerstein II, from musical "South Pacific," sgd Ezio Pinza cover, 1949 .....10.00

Strike up the Band, 9" x 12", movie music for "Our Love Affair," blue-tone image of Judy Garland and Mickey Rooney, Judy playing snare drums, pink and white accent background, Paul Whiteman Orchestra at bottom, 6 pgs, 1940 Leo Feist, Inc. 24.00

The Subway Glide, 1912 ....12.00

Sunflower Tickle, Benjamin Richmond, 1908..10.00

Tell That to the Marines, 9" x 12-1/4", rotogravure cover, photo of Al Jolson taking off coat preparing to fight, based on James Montgomery Flagg recruiting poster, 4 pgs, 1918 Waterson, Berlin, & Snyder Co. 20.00

That's What Makes a Wild Cat Wild, Norton, 1908..........................25.00

Three Little Words, Amos and Andy 50.00

Umbrella Man, James Cavanaugh, Larry Stock and Vincent Rose, Kay Kyser photo, 1938 ....4.50

Way Down in Borneo-O-O-O, 1916................7.00

Whose Little Heart Are You Breaking Now?, Irving Berlin, 1917 ....7.00

You Great Big Handsome Marine, 10" x 13-1/4", full-color art cover with Marine at attention with rifle, ship and biplane in background, 4 pgs, blue-tone back cover with Marine emblem and explanation of its meaning, 1918 Dixon-Lane Pub Co., St. Louis 24.00

Shelley China

Collecting Hints: The familiar Shelley mark—a script signature in a shield—was used as early as 1910, even though the firm's name was still Wileman & Co. Dainty White was one of the company's most popular shapes and pieces are, therefore, relatively easy to acquire.

History: While the Shelley family has been producing pottery since the mid 1880s, it wasn't until 1925 that the company bore the family name. Joseph Shelley and James Wileman became partners in 1872, operating their pottery under the name Wileman & Co. Joseph's son, Percy, joined the company in 1881 and assumed full control after his father's death in 1896. It was under Percy's direction that the company introduced its most popular shapes—Dainty White, Intarsio, Queen Anne and Vogue.

Percy's three sons became involved in the business following World War I. During the 1920s and 1930s, the pottery produced miniatures, heraldic and souvenir china, Parian busts of military figures, tea wares and nursery items, in addition to its fine dinnerware lines. Percy retired in 1932. After World War II, the company concentrated solely on its dinnerware lines. In 1965, the firm's name was changed to Shelley China Ltd. The Shelley family ties to the company were severed in 1966 when Allied English Potteries took control. Allied merged with the Doulton Group in 1971.

Reference: Susan and Al Bagdade, *Warman's English & Continental Pottery & Porcelain*, 2nd Edition, Wallace-Homestead, 1991.

Cake Plate
    Begonia, 9-3/4" d 95.00

Crochet, handle, yellow 115.00
Cann, Blue Charms.....................175.00
Candy Dish
    Crochet, 4-1/2" d, white, blue trim........................32.00
    Pansy, 4" l 40.00
    Rose, 4" 140.00
Coffee Set
    Dog Roses, Regent 695.00
    Posey Spray, Regent..............795.00
Cream Soup, Duchess, green.......60.00
Cream Soup with Underplate, Regency 75.00
Creamer and Sugar
    Begonia.....................................40.00
    Blue Rock 90.00
    Primrose 45.00
Cup, Campanula 30.00
Cup and Saucer
    Bridal Rose 50.00
    Maytime 125.00
    Melody 120.00
    Old Mill......................................40.00
    Regency....................................35.00
Demitasse Cup and Saucer
    Begonia.....................................50.00
    Georgian 129.00
    Melody 110.00
    Rose 65.00
    Violets 60.00
    Wildflowers 129.00
Eggcup, Primrose 60.00
Hostess Set, 8" d plate and cup
    Campanula 55.00
    Dainty White, gold trim.............45.00
Muffineer, Primrose.....................225.00
Mug and Saucer, Dainty White 40.00
Mustard, 3 pcs, Celadine 85.00
Nappy, Begonia 35.00
Nut Dish, Maytime.........................58.00
Place Setting, 5-pc set, Duchess, green 95.00
Plate
    6" d, bread and butter
        Bridal Rose 24.00
        Primrose 30.00
        Regency 30.00
    8" d
        Dainty Mauve.....................125.00
        Dainty Pink 125.00
        Heather................................30.00
        Melody 125.00
        Regency 75.00
        Summer Glory 125.00
Set, Regency, service for six, creamer and sugar, tray, 2 toothpick holders, price for 32-pc set 1,100.00
Snack Set, Campanula 65.00
Soup Plate, Regency 30.00
Sugar, open, Regency 25.00
Toast Rack, Shamrock................150.00

Trio
Begonia	100.00
Blue Rock	100.00
Dainty Blue	135.00
Vegetable Dish, Wildflower	200.00

Slot Machines

Collecting Hints: Check the laws in your state. Some states permit the collecting of slot machines manufactured prior to 1941, while other states allow the collecting of all machines 25 years old or older, provided that they are not used for gambling. A few states prohibit ownership of any gambling machine.

A complete slot machine is one that is in working order, has no wood missing on the case and no cracked castings. Restoration work to improve appearance can cost from $100 to more than $1,000. The average restoration includes plating of all castings, refinishing the cabinet, repainting the castings to the original colors, rebuilding the mechanism, tuning up the operation of the mechanism and adding new reel strips and award card. A quality restoration will increase the value of a machine by $400 to $800. A guarantee usually is given when a restored machine is purchased from a dealer.

Most collectors stay away from foreign machines, primarily because foreign coins are hard to find. Machines that have been converted to accept American coins frequently jam or do not pay out the correct amount.

Condition, rarity and desirability are all very important in determining the value of a machine. Try to find one that is in as close to new condition as possible since "mint original" machines will resell for at least the same amount as restored machines.

History: The Liberty Bell, the first three-reel slot machine, was invented in 1905 by Charles Fey in San Francisco. Only three of these can be accounted for and one of them is housed at the Liberty Bell Saloon, the inventor's grandson's restaurant in Reno, NV.

In 1910, the classic fruit symbols were copyrighted by Mills Novelty Co. They were immediately copied by other manufacturers. The first symbols still are popular on contemporary

Jennings, Chief, 3 reels, 25¢, $1,300.

casino machines. The wood cabinet was replaced by cast iron in 1916. By 1922, aluminum fronts were the norm for most machines and in 1928 the jackpot was added.

Innovations of the 1930s included more reliable and improved mechanisms with more sophisticated coin entry and advanced slug detection systems. In the 1940s, drill-proof and cheat-resistant devices were added. Electronics, including electronic lighting, were introduced in the 1950s. Although the goosenecks of the 1920s and 1930s often are more intricate and rarer than the models of the 1930s and 1940s, the gimmickry and beauty of machines of the latter period, such as Rolatop, Treasury, Kitty or Triplex, bring more money.

References: Jerry Ayliffe, *American Premium Guide to Jukeboxes and Slot Machines*, 3rd Edition, Books Americana, 1991; Richard M. Bueschel, *Collector's Guide to Vintage Coin Machines*, Schiffer Publishing, 1995; ——, *Lemons, Cherries and Bell-Fruit-Gum*, Royal Bell Books (5815 W. 52nd Ave., Denver, CO 80212), 1995; Bill Kurtz, *Slot Machines and Coin-Op Games*, Chartwell Books, 1991.

Periodicals: *Antique Amusements, Slot Machines & Jukebox*, 909 26th St. NW, Washington, DC 20037; *Chicagoland Program*, 414 N. Prospect Manor Ave., Mt. Prospect, IL

60056; *Chicago Land Slot Machine & Jukebox Gazette*, 909 26th St., NW, Washington, DC 20037; *Coin Drop International*, 5815 W. 52nd Ave., Denver, CO 80212; *Coin-Op Classics*, 17844 Toiyabe St., Fountain Valley, CA 92708; *Coin-Op Newsletter*, 909 26th St., NW, Washington, DC 20037; *Coin Slot*, 4401 Zephyr St., Wheatridge, CO 80033; *Loose Change*, 1515 S. Commerce St., Las Vegas, NV 89102.

Museum: Liberty Belle Saloon and Slot Machine Collection, Reno, NV.

Notes: All machines listed are priced as if they are in good condition, meaning the machine is complete and working. An incomplete or non-working machine is worth only 30% to 70% of the listed price. Machines listed are those which accept nickels or dimes. Quarter and 50-cent-piece machines can run several hundred dollars more. A silver-dollar machine, if you are lucky enough to find one, can cost $400 to $800 more than those listed.

Advisor: Bob Levy.

Buckley
   Bones, countertop, spinning disks roll dice for craps, similar to Bally's Reliance, c1937 .... 4,000.00
Criss Cross, revamp of Mills machine, escalator coin entry, fancy casting around escalator and jackpot, usually has guaranteed jackpot, c1948 .... 950.00
Caille
   Cadet, circular jackpot, escalator moves from bottom up, c1938 .... 700.00
   Detroit Floor Wheel, upright, 1 reel, 6-way play action, bettors pick color wheel will land on, c1899 .... 8,250.00
   Groetchen, Columbia, the size of normal slot machine, club handle, small reels, coins go around in circle behind coin head, 1934 .... 250.00
   Superior, nude woman on front, scroll-work lower casting, coin entry in center above award card, c1928 .... 1,900.00
   Victory Mint, center pull handle, ladies pictured on both sides of handle, c1924 .... 2,750.00
Jennings
   Challenger Console, 48" h, vertical and horiz glass with silk-screen design, reels seen from top of lower glass, plays 2 coin denominations,

usually 5¢ and 25¢, c1946 .....800.00
Duchess, 3 reels, front vendor
with mints or candy displayed behind
windows flanking jackpot, orig
decal, c1934 ....1,050.00
Four Star Chief, Indian
carrying deer on front, large
Indian chief above jackpot,
4 stars on top, 1936 ....1,150.00
Governor, tic-tac-toe theme, Indian's
head above jackpot, 1948 ......750.00
Little Duke, large coin-head
casting on top of machine, classic
Art Deco design, reels spin
concentrically, 1932 ....1,350.00
Sportsman, golf ball vendor, pay card
placed at angle, 1937 ....2,750.00
Standard Chief, chrome
finish, teardrop design on both
sides of jackpot, flat Indian above
jackpot, 1948 ....1,150.00
Sun Chief, Indian bust, illuminated
side panels, c1948 ....2,250.00
Victoria, 3 reels, 2 jackpots, fortune
strips, c1932 ....1,750.00
Victory Chief, wood front,
eagle above jackpot, minutemen
soldiers to right and left of
eagle, 1945 ....1,050.00

Mills
Black Cherry, escalator,
painted silver with black case,
4 applied cherries, bib award-card
front, 1947 ....1,050.00
Diamond Front, escalator,
10 raised diamonds around large bib
award card, 1940 ....1,050.00
Futurity Bell, 3 reels,
5¢, 1936 ....2,000.00
High Top, light colors, strong player,
1946-62 ....1,050.00
Lion Front, gooseneck coin entry,
large lion with mouth open around
jackpot, 3 rows of 6 circles below
reels, 1929 ....1,550.00
Melon Bell, 3 reels, high top, melon
on front, 1948 ....1,350.00

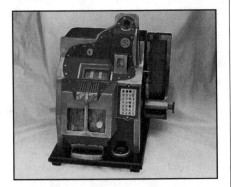

Mills, Firebird, 5-cent side vender, $1,250.

Mystery Front, 3 reels,
26" h, c1932 ....1,350.00
Operator Bell, 23-1/2", 5¢,
3 reels, c1926 ....900.00
Owl, oak cast, upright floor model,
color wheel, c1905 ....5,500.00
Poinsettia, gooseneck coin entry,
flowers on lower casting, Liberty Bell
under coin entry, c1930 ......1,100.00
Silent Golden, 3 reels, Roman's head
on front, 1932 ....2,400.00
Vest Pocket, 3 reels, box shape,
plain design, 1938 ....450.00

Pace
All Star Comet, rotary escalator,
stars and vertical pointed stripes
on front, 1936 ....1,000.00
Bantam, 3 reels, jackpot vendor front,
appealing design, 1932 ....1,250.00

Watling
Blue Seal, gooseneck, twin jackpot,
fancy front, 1930 ....1,000.00
Exchange, 1 wheel, countertop
model, 5-way coin head,
oak case, c1910 ....2,500.00
Gumball Vendor, gooseneck,
ornate casting around reels,
gumball vendors on each side of twin
jackpot, 1¢ only, c1921 ....1,750.00
Rolatop, rotary escalator,
twin jackpot with eagle above,
checkerboard 1,750.00

Snowdomes

Collecting Hints: There are two distinct types of snowdomes: 3- to 4 inch leaded-glass balls set on ceramic, plastic, wood or "marble" bases; and plastic figurals averaging 2-1/2" inches in height, with plastic globes in shapes ranging from simple designs, such as drums, cubes and bottles, to elaborate figurals. There are also two kinds of figurals. In one, the design incorporates the entire object, including the water ball. In the other, a plastic figurine sits on top of the dome.

Either type of snowdome can be collected by any number of subgroups or themes, e.g., Christmas (probably the most familiar), tourist souvenirs, Biblical scenes, Disney and other cartoon characters, commercial advertisements, fairy tales, scenic railroads, famous buildings, sailing ships, geographic regions or states (the goal being to collect one from each of the 50).There are also snowdomes with a variety of novelty features such as battery-powered

flashing lights which illuminate the inner scene, salt and pepper snowdomes, those with perpetual calendars or banks included in the base and pieces that contain water/ring toss games. Some snowdomes have parts that move: a seesaw, bobbing objects attached to strings or small objects that move back and forth on a groove in the bottom of the dome. The objects themselves range from ferries to buses to Elvis Presley figures.

Value rests primarily on the physical condition of the paperweight itself and the condition of the water inside. Make sure there are no cracks in ceramic bases or in the globes themselves, check the condition of the label (if there is one) and the figurine, determine whether the paint has chipped or the colors seem faded and be certain that the scene inside is not obscured by any streaking on the front of the dome.

The most common snowdomes do not have a specific label on the base, but do have a single figurine and a glass, ceramic or Bakelite base. If the only difference between two snowdomes is the existence of a decal on the base identifying one as a "Souvenir of _____," the one with the decal is more valuable because a smaller number of that exact item would have been made. The same figurine was probably used for any number of places and there is often no connection between the object and the place. An incongruous match-up may have value to a particular collector but would not necessarily affect the market price. Of greater value are those snowdomes which were obviously made for a specific place or event, where the object and the decal match, e.g., the ceramic-base snowdome containing a bisque Trylon and Perisphere and a "1939 Worlds Fair" decal.

While mismatched figurines and decals of the glass/ceramic style should not have a higher price than logical match-ups, there are many examples of obvious mistakes in the plastic snowdomes. These are worth more than a perfect one, e.g., a dome with "Milano" printed upside down or a souvenir of a religious shrine with a "Kings Island" plaque.

Left: Sleeping Beauty and Prince Charming, rounded dome, green ground and base, "Made in West Germany," 1970s, $15; Right: Gingerbread House, figural, candies, sweets, and logs on all sides, Hansel and Gretel inside, 1970s, $25.

Generally, early snowdomes (1950s and 1960s) have greater detail and more sophisticated colors than the later snowdomes, which are simpler and have an unrefined, mass-produced appearance

Age can affect a dome's physical deterioration—fading, chipping paint, even bleaching of the words on the plaque must be constantly evaluated by the collector. The plastic snowdomes that were introduced in the 1950s were fragile objects, easily broken and often discarded. It is indeed a challenge to find unusual survivors.

History: A snowdome is a clear globe- or dome-shaped paperweight which is filled with water and loose particles which swirl when the paperweight is turned upside down. A visible figurine and/or decorated panel inside the globe is magnified by the water.

Snowdomes originated during the mid 19th century in Europe. In France, they evolved from round, solid-glass paperweights; by 1878, there were seven French manufacturers of snowdomes. They also were produced in what is now Germany, Austria, Poland and the Czech Republic, often as a cottage industries.

During the Victorian era, snowdomes were very popular as paperweights, souvenirs and toys. Early domes featured religious scenes, tourist sites and children and animals associated with winter or water. A variety of materials were used to create the "snow," ranging from ground porcelain and bone to rice. The figurines inside were made of carved bone, wax, porcelain, china, metal or stone. The bases were made in a variety of shapes and from many materials, including marble, wood, glass and metal.

German companies exported their snowdomes to North America in the 1920s. The bases, which were cobalt blue glass, were occasionally etched with the name of a town or tourist attraction. The first American patent was granted in 1927 for a design of a fish floating on a string among seaweed. The Novelty Pond Co., of Pittsburgh was the original manufacturer of this snowdome, but the idea was soon copied by others. American manufacturers used a black plastic base, either smooth or tiered; Japanese companies used a glazed brown ceramic base.

Italian snowdomes from the late 1940s have a distinctive scallop-shaped base covered with seashells and pebbles and a glass globe containing a flat, rubberized panel with the name of the tourist attraction or a Saint's name written inside a shell on the base.

Three West German companies used plastic to create small cubed or domed snowdomes in the 1950s. Koziol and Walter & Prediger, two of these companies, remain in business manufacturing hand-painted domes with blizzards of white snow. Herr Koziol claims it was the "domed" view of a winter snow scene as seen through the rear window of a Volkswagen that inspired the shape. As a result of court action, Walter & Prediger gained the right to the dome shape and Koziol was restricted to the round shape.

The Atlas Crystal Works was an American firm founded in the early 1940s to fill the void created when the popular glazed style which had been made in Japan became unavailable. Atlas became the giant in the snowdome field, creating hundreds of different designs. Other American firms that made a variety of snowdomes are the Driss Co., of Chicago (1950s) and Progressive Products of Union, NJ (1940s and 1950s)

In addition to an enormous number of figurine designs, either in painted or unpainted bisque, domes also feature Art Deco buildings, saints and snow babies. Another design form consists of a flat, rubberized insert showing a photograph of a tourist attraction, such as Niagara Falls or the Skyline Drive.

The majority of plastic and glass snowdomes made in the 1990s come from the Orient. There are currently no American manufacturers, but rather dozens of large gift companies who design and import an array of styles, shapes and themes. Enesco Corp., Elk Grove Village, IL, is one of the largest.

References: Helen Guarnaccia, *Collector's Guide to Snow Domes*, Collector Books, 1994; Nancy McMichael, *Snowdomes*, Abbeville Press, 1990; Connie A. Moore and Harry L. Rinker, *Snow Globes*, Running Press, 1993.

Collectors' Club: Snowdome Collectors Club, P.O. Box 53262, Washington, DC 20009.

Advisor: Nancy McMichael.

Advertising
  Crown Termite Control, glass ball, oily liquid, brown Bakelite base, 3" w, 4" h, 1950s 65.00
  Jell-O, plastic dome, 1970s, 3-3/4" l, 2-1/2" w, 2-3/4" h 38.00
  Sears Kenmore, America's Largest Selling Washers and Dryers, rect, 1-pc salt and pepper shaker, woman standing next to appliances, 1970s, 3-1/2" x 2-1/2" x 1" 39.00
Amusement Park
  Cedar Point, Sandusky, OH, plastic, 2 dolphins on see-saw, gold printed letters on plaque on waved base, 1970s 14.00
  Coney Island, bathing beauty, scalloped base with sea shells, 1940s, 2" d glass ball 22.00
Ashtray, Yellowstone park, black Bakelite, bisque figure, off-white tiered base, early 1940s, 2-3/4" d glass ball 66.00
Bank, plastic, Mt. Vernon, VA, printed on front, house scene, red base, 1960s, 2-3/4" d ball 11.00
Bottle
  Flat Side, Caverns of Luray, cavern scene, early 1970s, 5" l............ 10.00
  Upright, Mennonite male and female figures, silver, snow, red cap, 1970s, 4-1/2" x 1-1/2", price for pr 14.00
Boxed Set, winter snow scenes, assorted, by Marx, set of 6 small plastic domes, c1960

Sold individually 11.00

Sold as set 110.00

Calendar, plastic, red base with 4 openings where date shows, San Francisco, CA, bridge and city scene, cable car moves on slide, 1970s, 2-3/4" d ball....................7.00

Cartoon Character

Pink Panther, plastic dome, Panther skating around Inspector Clouseau, 1980s 11.00

Popeye, figural, seated, plastic, holds water ball between hands, Olive Oyl, Sweetpea and Wimpy in row boat that moves, King Features Syndicate, 1950s......................66.00

Character

Elvis, singing into microphone, rect shape, figure moves back and forth in front of Graceland mansion panel, Graceland plaque, 1970s 18.00

Lone Ranger, round glass ball, Bakelite base, green, yellow and red, "Lone Ranger: The Last Round-Up" decal, 1950s.............................65.00

Christmas

Boot, clear, 5 pine trees, red house, waving snowman and children, holly trim, 1970s 10.00

Elf, figural, red suit, green jester collar, ball in tummy, snowman, trees and house scene, 1960s..........23.00

Fireplace, child sleeping in pajamas on hearth, Santa in sled on see-saw in dome, mkd "CSA Inc., Curt S. Adler, Inc., NY, NY 10010," 1970s, 3-1/2" x 3-1/4" x 2-1/4" 22.00

Nativity Scene, small plastic dome, 1980s 5.00

Rudolph the Red-Nosed Reindeer, green plastic base, "Rudolph the Red-Nosed Reindeer in the Snow, RLM" decal, 1950s....................44.00

Santa, driving sleigh, 2 reindeer, rect dome with elf sitting under a mushroom 1960s, 5-1/4" x 3-1/2" x 1" 28.00

Figural

Fish, plastic, bright orange, green movable plastic fins, Florida plaque, 4" x 7", 1970s $25.

Church, steeple, plastic, altar, bride and groom, mkd "W. Germany" on bottom, 1980s, 2-1/4" x 2-3/4" x 2-1/2" 18.00

Mickey Mouse, figural, plastic, castle scene, 1960s, hold 2" d ball in lap, 5" h 55.00

Treasure Chest, gold-colored plastic frame, clear sides, Nassau on plaque, red lobster, fish and seaweed, 1970s, 2-1/2" x 3-1/2" x 1-3/4" 8.00

Game, ring toss

Giraffe, plastic dome, 2 giraffes, hoops go over necks, "The Pacifier" decal, 1970s.............................12.00

Lobster, plastic dome, plastic hoops, mkd "Louisiana," early 1980s, 3" x 2" x 1"....................................10.00

General Eisenhower, glass ball, black ceramic base, bisque bust, "General Dwight D. Eisenhower, Commander in Chief, Allied Invasion Forces" decal, mkd "Atlas Crystal Works, Covington, TN, U.S. Patents 231423/4/5," 1940s 65.00

Moving Parts

Champagne, shot and martini glass on strings, naked lady, "The Bar Is Open" bar scene painted backdrop, "This one is on me" plaque, "Las Vegas" on outside, 1960s, 3-3/4" x 2-3/4" x 2-1/2" 10.00

Trolley, Golden Gate Bridge, San Francisco, Chinatown background, small dome, 1970s.....................7.00

Queen Mary, Long Beach, CA, plastic dome, cutout of ship on ocean, printed and town panels, 1970s 14.00

Sailor, glass globe, saluting figure in sailor suit, black ceramic base, 1940s.............................38.00

Salt and Pepper Shaker, Florida's Silver Springs, TV shape, plastic, blue "P," pink "S," boat on seesaw, side compartments, 1970s, 3" x 2-1/4" x 1".............20.00

Sleeping Beauty and Prince Charming, castle, rounded dome, green ground and base, "Made in West Germany," 1970s 15.00

Souvenir

Atlantic City, 4 tiers, painted figure of girl on angled sled, brown ceramic base, 1930s, 4" x 2-1/2" x 2-3/4" 44.00

Dewey Beach, plastic dome, seagull and sea shells, 1960s, 2-3/4" x 2-1/4" x 2" 9.00

Empire State Building, New York City, gold letters, inverted glass cone, black Bakelite base, 1950s, 4-3/4" h 14.00

Expo 67, Montreal Canada, plaque,

fireworks background...............16.00

Ontario, Canada, gold decal, painted, bisque lighthouse, glass top, blue glass base, mkd "Germany," 1920s 40.00

Roy Rogers and Dale Evans Museum, Victorville, CA, plastic dome, barn scene, Trigger moves on slide, 1960s.........................18.00

Terminal Tower Building, Cleveland, OH, plaque, 1970s....................9.00

States

Georgia, The Peach State, bottle, flat sides, plastic, 2 alligators on seesaw, tree and mountain, 1960s, 5" l 11.00

Montana, figural, black bear, plastic, 2 deer on seesaw, state name on chest, mkd "UVC-Inc. 1972" on bottom, 2-1/2" ball, 5" h............20.00

Virginia, small dome, state outline and bird on branch, late 1970s 7.00

World's Fair, New York, 1939, Trylon and Perisphere bisque figurine, brown ceramic base..............100.00

Soda Bottles

History: Soda bottles were made to hold soda water and soft drinks. A beverage manufacturer usually made his own bottles and sold them within a limited area. Coddball stoppers and a stopper perfected by Hutchinson were popular with early manufacturers before the advent of metal or screw-top caps.

References: Ralph and Terry Kovel, *Kovels' Bottles Price List*, 10th Edition, Crown Publishers, 1996; Peck and Audie Markota, W*estern Blob Top Soda and Mineral Bottles*, 2nd Edition, published by authors, 1994; Thomas E. Marsh, *Official Guide to Collecting Applied Color Label Soda Bottles*, *Vol. I* (1992), *Vol. II* (1995), published by author (914 Franklin Ave., Youngstown, OH 44502); Jim Megura, *Official Identification and Price Guide to Bottles*, 11th Edition, House of Collectibles, 1991; Tom Morrison, *Root Beer*, Schiffer Publishing, 1992; Michael Polak, *Bottles*, Avon Books, 1994; Rick Sweeney, *Collecting Applied Color Label Soda Bottles*, published by author (9418 Hilmer Dr., La Mesa, CA 91942).

Mission Beverage, Pioneer Beverages, San Francisco-Oakland, CA, clear, 7 oz, 8-1/4", $6.

Periodical: *Antique Bottle and Glass Collector*, P.O. Box 187, East Greenville, PA 18041.

Collectors' Club: Painted Soda Bottle Collectors Association, 9418 Hilmer Dr., La Mesa, CA 91942.

Additional Listings: Coca-Cola, Pepsi, Soft Drink Collectibles.

Alter & Wilson Mfg., light green applied top, 7" h 20.00
Bacon's Soda Works, light green, blob top, 7" h 9.00
Bryant's Root Beer, This Bottle Makes Five Gallons, amber, applied top, 4-1/2" h 5.00
Cape Arco Soda Works, Marshfield, OR, round, light green, applied top, 7" h....10.00
Deadwood, SD, blob top 125.00
Deamer Grass Valley, aqua, blob top, 7-1/4" hg 7.50
Dr Pepper, Colorado 18.00
English Soda, light green, applied top, 8" h 18.00
Fizz, Southern State Siphon Bottling Co., golden amber, 11" h.........17.50
Hawaiian Soda Works, aqua, emb, 7-1/2" h 9.00
Hippo Size Soda Water, clear, crown top, 10" h..........................6.50
Jackson's Napa Soda, crown cap, 7-1/4" h 7.50
Los Angeles Soda

Works, aqua, 8" h......................5.00
Mendocin Bottling Works, A.L. Reynolds, light green, 7" h 8.00
Mission Dry Sparkling, black 9-3/4" h.............................4.00
Nevada City Soda works, ETR Powell, aqua, applied top, 7" h..............9.00
Orange Crush Co., pat July 20, 1926, light green, 9" h 4.00
Perrier, clear, bowling-pin shape, paper label, 8-1/2" h 3.00
Rapid City Bottling Works, light green, crown cap, 8" h..........................5.00
Ross's Royal Belfast Ginger Gale, green, diamond shape, paper label, 10" h...............................7.50
Sandahl Beverages, clear, 8" h.......5.00
Scott & Gilbert Co., San Francisco, brown, crown top, 10" h.............6.00
Solano Soda Works, aqua, 8" h 6.00
Tahoe Soda Springs Natural Mineral Water, light green, 7-1/2" h......10.00
Union Glass Works, dark blue, blob top...................................20.00
Williams Bros., San Jose, CA 8.00

Soda Fountain Collectibles

Collecting Hints: The collector of soda fountain memorabilia competes with collectors in many other categories—advertising, glassware, ice cream, postcards, food molds, tools, etc. Material still ranges in the 25 cents to $200 range.

When buying a tray, the scene is the most important element. Most trays were stock items with the store or firm's name added later. Always look for items in excellent condition.

History: From the late 1880s through the end of the 1960s, the local soda fountain was the social center of small-town America, especially for teenagers. The soda fountain provided a place for conversation and gossip, a haven to satisfy the mid-afternoon munchies and a source for the most current popular magazines.

References: Douglas Congdon-Martin, *Drugstore and Soda Fountain Antiques*, Schiffer Publishing, 1991; Ray Klug, A*ntique Advertising Encyclopedia, Vol. I* (1978, 1993 value update), *Vol. II*, (1985, 1990 value update), L-W Book Sales; Tom Morrison, *Root Beer*, Schiffer Publishing, 1992.

Collectors' Club: Ice Screamers, P.O. Box 5387, Lancaster, PA 17601;

Hat, felt, Drink Moxie bottled by Yaky's, $6.

National Association of Soda Jerks, P.O. Box 115, Omaha, NE 68101.

Museums: Greenfield Village, Dearborn, MI; Museum of Science and Industry, Finigan's Ice Cream Parlor, Chicago, IL; Smithsonian Institution, Washington, DC.

Reproduction Alert.

Additional Listings: Ice Cream Collectibles.

Ashtray, Richland Snack Bar, tin 5.00
Blackboard, 15" x 30", Squirt 20.00
Can, Abbott's Ice Cream, 1/2 gal, Amish girl, c1940....................15.00
Catalog
Bastian-Blessing Co., Chicago, IL, Soda Fountain Parts & Carbonators, 1955, 65 pgs, 8-1/2" x 11"........30.00
Foot & Jenks, Jackson, MI, c1935, 8 pgs, 5-3/8" x 7", "Start the Season Right with These 3 Proven Winners, Killarn Ginger-Ale, CXC Cherrystone & CXC Lemon & Limes Combined," picture of bottle, return postcard..............14.00
National Licorice Co., New York, NY, early 1900, 19 pgs, 3-1/4" x 6-1/4", licorice specialties, lozenges, penny sticks, cigars, pipes, etc...........65.00
Stanley Knight Corp., Chicago, IL, Soda Fountains, Instructions and Specifications, c1944, 52 pgs, 7" x 10" 32.00
Container, Lutted's S.P. Cough Drops, house shape, name engraved on door, 7" x 7-3/4"...............400.00
Counter Bin, 9" x 13-3/4" x 4-1/4", Quaker Brand Salted Peanuts 42.00
Display Rack
Beech-Nut Chewing Gum, c1920....................................300.00
Lance Candy, 4 shelves 25.00
Dispenser
Hallford's Lemon and Lime Superfine since '69 (1869) 5¢, 8" d, 9" h, hand-blown glass, hp label 50.00
Marble and brass, 9 spouts 4,000.00
Root Beer, Buckeye, tree-trunk

shape, minor chips.................365.00

Hot Plate, commercial, Nestle's
Hot Chocolate, 8" x 12", standing
metal sign, red and white snowman
graphics, late 1940s 95.00

Ice Cream Cup, Borden's, Elsie the Cow,
multicolored illus and logo 35.00

Ice Cream Scoop
Dover, brass............................70.00
Erie, round, size 8,
aluminum...............................180.00
Gilchrist, #30,
size 8, polished 70.00

Jar, Borden's Malted Milk,
glass label.............................175.00

Magazine Cover, *Saturday Evening
Post,* young soda jerk talking to
girls at counter, Norman Rockwell,
Aug. 22, 1953 ....15.00

Malt Machine, Arnold #15............145.00

Milkshake Machine, Hamilton Beach, triple head, green porcelain 500.00

Mirror, Horlicks Malted Milk,
maid with cow 30.00

Paper Cone Dispenser, 11" l, glass tube,
metal holder, "Soda Fountain Drinks
& Ice Cream Served in Vortex," gold
label, wall mount......................40.00

Pinback Button
1" d, Sanderson's Drug Store, blue
and white, soda-fountain glass illus,
"Ice Cream, Soda/Choice Ci-
gars/Fine Candies," 1901-12....28.00
2-1/4" d, Hi-Hat Ice Cream Soda,
10¢, McCrory's, c1940 ....15.00

Postcard, Gunther's Soda Fountain,
Chicago 15.00

Pretzel Jar, 10-1/2" h, Seyfert's Original
Butter Pretzels, glass, orig lid ..60.00

Seltzer Bottle, Sun Shine, 11" h ..150.00

Set, black and chrome, Art Deco styling,
price for 11 pcs 495.00

Sign
12-1/4" x 22", Purity Butter Pretzels,
diecut cardboard, easel back, multicolor, smiling blond boy carrying giant pretzel against black ground,
white-lettered company logo, bright
red and gold ground, Harrisburg,
PA, early 1930s........................68.00
24" x 18", Orange County
Fountain, porcelain on steel,
yellow oval center, blue and white lettering, dark blue ground 100.00
27" h, 13" w, Kayo, Specials Today,
enameled tin, Donaldson Art
Sign Co. 100.00

Straw Jar, glass
Frosted panel 225.00
Green panel 410.00
Pattern glass,
Illinois pattern, orig lid 450.00
Red, metal lid, 1950s..................175.00

Syrup Dispenser Pump, hires 135.00

Tin, Schraft's Marshmallow Topping,
25 lbs..35.00

Tray, 13" x 11", Schuller's Ice Cream, ice
cream sodas and cones 200.00

Soft Drink Collectibles

Collecting Hints: Coca-Cola items have dominated the field. Only recently have collectors begun concentrating on other soft drink manufacturing companies. Soft drink collectors compete with collectors of advertising, bottles and premiums for the same material.

National brands such as Canada Dry, Dr Pepper and Pepsi-Cola are best known. However, regional soft drink bottling plants do exist and their products are fertile ground for the novice collector.

History: Sarsaparilla, a name associated with soft drinks, began as a medicinal product. When carbonated water was added, it became a soft drink and was consumed for pleasure rather than medical purposes. However, sarsaparilla was only one type of ingredient added to carbonated water to produce soft drinks.

Each company had its special formula. Although Coca-Cola has a large market share, other companies provided challenges in different historical periods. Moxie was followed by Hire's, which in turn gave way to Pepsi-Cola and 7-Up.

In the 1950s, large advertising campaigns and numerous promotional products increased the visibility of soft drinks. Regional bottling plants were numerous and produced local specialties such as Birch Beer in Eastern Pennsylvania. By 1970, most of these local plants had closed.

Many large companies had operations outside of the United States and there is a large quantity of international advertising and promotional material. The current popularity of diet soda is a response to the modern American lifestyle.

References: Tom Morrison, *Root Beer*, Schiffer Publishing, 1992; Allan Petretti, *Petretti's Soda Pop Collectibles Price Guide*, Antique Trader Books, 1996.

Hires Mug, Villeroy and Boch, $185.

Collectors' Clubs: Club Soda, P.O. Box 489, Troy, ID 83871; Dr Pepper 10-2-4 Collectors Club, P.O. Box 153221, Irving, TX 75015; Moxie Enthusiasts Collectors Club of America, Route 375, Box 164, Woodstock, NY 12498; National Pop Can Collectors, P.O. Box 7862, Rockford, IL 61126; New England Moxie Congress, 445 Wyoming Ave., Millburn, NJ 07041.

Museums: Clark's Trading Post, North Woodstock, NH; Matthews Museum of Maine Heritage, Union, ME.

Additional Listings: Coca-Cola, Pepsi, Soda Bottles, Soda Fountain Collectibles.

Advertising Trade Card, 3" x 5", Hires Root Beer, smiling young boy holding empty glass saying "Could I Have Another Glass of That Hires Root Beer?" short company history on reverse, 1894 ....14.00

Ashtray, Dr Pepper 7.50

Bank, 7-Up, soda-can shape, white, orange and green, 1950s, 12 oz, flat top, steel............................40.00

Banner, Lime Cola, canvas...........40.00

Battery Operated Toy, Sprite-Lymon, talking, vinyl, MIB 35.00

Beanie, Dr Pepper, orig charms....18.00

Blotter, Nehi Soda, 1930s...............4.00

Booklet, 7-Up
Floats, 8 pgs, foldout type, recipes, 1961 ....4.00
7-Up Goes to a Party, 16 pgs, 1961 ....5.00

Bottle, Moxie, emb name, wire cap..................9.00

Bottle Carrier
Kist Soda, cardboard 5.00
RC Cola, aluminum..................12.00

Bottle Display, 7-Up, 1949..............6.50
Calendar
    Dr Pepper, 1937, Earl Moran art,
      framed......................................150.00
    Nu-Grape, 1941 ....40.00
Can, Dr Pepper, cone top.............20.00
Carton, Squirt, red and white cardboard,
    front says "2 Free Bottles of Squirt
    and Never an afterthirst!" on
    1 side, recipes on reverse, 1959
    Squirt Co., 4" h, 5" w 10.00
Clock, 7-Up, "You Like It, It Likes You,"
    wood frame.............................75.00
Coin, Moxie Bottle Wagon, aluminum,
    detailed image of horse-drawn street
    vending wagon, huge bottle replica
    holding vendor dispensing drink to
    2 children, 3 adults waiting, inscribed
    "Moxie Nerve Food 5¢," reverse
    inscription "Good for One Drink of
    Moxie at the Moxie Bottle Wagon,"
    early 1900s 45.00
Cooler, Squirt, round 95.00
Coupon, Royal Crown,
    free card, 1950s.........................5.00
Door Pull, tin, Drink Hire's 50.00
Fan, cardboard, wood handle
    Dr Pepper...................................40.00
    Goold's Orangeade 25.00
Label, Dr Pepper, paper 12.00
Magazine Advertisement,
    Ladies Home Journal, 1895,
    back page, matted..................45.00
Mechanical Pencil,
    Orange Crush..........................22.00
Menu Board, Orange Crush 55.00
Mug
    Buckeye Root Beer,
      stoneware................................12.50
    Dad's Root Beer.......................12.00
    Graft's Root Beer 100.00
    Hire's Root Beer,
      glass, 12940s.........................12.00
    Hunter's Root Beer.................112.00
    Jim Dandy Root Beer 125.00
    Twin Kiss Root Beer, 3" h 15.00
Pencil Clip, 7/8" d, celluloid
    Orange Crush, black and
      white inscription, orange
      ground, c1930 ....12.00
    7-Up, black, white
      and red logo 10.00
Pinback Button
    Cherry Smash, George
      Washington portrait, dark red
      shaded to olive green ground, black
      inscription, c1911 ....35.00
    Dad's Root Beer, litho,
      bottle cap, yellow, red, blue,
      white and black, c1940.............20.00
    7-Up, Fresh Up Freddie, red, white,
      blue and yellow litho, c1959 .....50.00
Pitcher, Orange Crush,

Tray, Ace-Hy, blue, orange, and white, 13" x 10", $35.

    chrome lid..............................115.00
Playing Cards, Nu-Grape,
    single deck, slide out box 25.00
Push Bar, porcelain
    Nesbitt's, French 75.00
    Pure Spring
    Ginger Ale, 1950s 65.00
    7-Up, bilingual, 1950s 50.00
    Up-Town, lemon-lime,
    French, 1950s 50.00
Sign
    B-1 Lemon Soda, 12" x
    14" x 6",
    light-up 25.00
    Canada Dry, porcelain 40.00
    Dixie Springs Soda, 14" x 20",
    cardboard stand-up, Eskimos
    pulling sled 30.00
    Grapette, 12" x 24",
    tin, emb, 1940s 40.00
    Hires, 5" x 14", tin, emb, some flak-
    ing, 3 small holes 75.00
    Nehi, 14" x 14" Drink Nehi
    Beverages, white and red,
    raised metal 60.00
    Mission Orange of California, 25" h,
    tin, 1950s 90.00
    Nesbitt's Orange,
    48" x 16", tin, 1938.................175.00
    Nu-Grape Soda, tin, yellow and blue,
    dated March 9, 1920 ....125.00
    Orange, Lemon,
    Lime Crush, emb tin...............350.00
    RC
      11-1/2" x 29-1/2", red and white,
      emb letters adv crown, tin....50.00
      12" x 18", Drink Royal Crown,
      Better Taste Calls for RC, diamond
      shape, red and white, raised
      letters 50.00
      42" x 34", Drink Royal Crown Cola,
      Best by Taste Test, red,
      yellow, white, 12" privilege space,

      raised metal, 1954 ....295.00
      51" x 38", Drink Royal Crown Cola,
      red, white and blue, 12" privilege
      space, raised metal 165.00
    Squirt, 8" h, cardboard,
    double sided, c1949................25.00
    Sunrise Orange, tin, bottled by
    Coca-Cola 90.00
Stickpin, Moxie Boy, multicolored diecut
    thin litho tin, short back pin, hanging
    type, c1910.............................75.00
Thermometer, tin
    Crush, 5" x 17", 1960s 65.00
    Nesbitt's, French, 5" x 17".......55.00
Tip Tray, Royal Crown Cola..........40.00
Tray, Hires Root Beer, 1935 ....90.00
Uniform Patch, Dr Pepper, 10" d,
    mkd "Good for Life" 24.00
Watch, 7-Up, promotion for Jerry Lewis
    Telethon, windup, pink border, Cher-
    ry 7-Up, orig box and mailer....30.00
Watch Fob
    Drink Chero-Cola 5¢ 60.00
    Hires Root Beer, octagonal,
    raised "Drink Hires," boy,
    early 1900s 75.00

Soldiers, Dimestore

Collecting Hints: Figures of soldiers are preferred over civilians. The most valuable figures are those which had short production runs, usually because they were less popular with the youthful collectors of the period. O'Brien and Pielin use numbering systems in their books to identify figures. Newcomers to the field should study these books, taking note of the many style and color variations in which these soldiers were made.

    Condition, desirability and scarcity establish the price of a figure. Repainting or the presence of rust severely reduce the value. Auction prices often mislead the beginning collector. While some rare figures have sold in the $150 to $300 range, most sell between $10 and $25.

History: Three-dimensional lead, iron and rubber soldier and civilian figures were produced in the United States by the millions before and after World War II. These figures are called dimestore soldiers because they were sold in the "five and dime" stores of the era and usually cost a nickel or dime. Although American toy soldiers can be traced back to the early 20th century, the golden age of the dimestore soldier lasted from 1935 until 1942.

Four companies—Barclay, Manoil, Grey Iron and Auburn Rubber—mass produced the three-inch figures. Barclay and Manoil dominated the market, probably because their lead castings lent themselves to more realistic and imaginative poses than iron and rubber.

Barclay's early pre-war figures are identifiable by their separate glued-on and later clipped-on tin hats. When these are lost, the hole in the top of the head identifies the piece as a Barclay.

The Manoil Co., first produced soldiers, sailors, cowboys and Indians. However, the younger buyers of the period preferred military figures, perhaps emulating the newspaper headlines as World War II approached. Manoil's civilian figures were made in response to pacifist pressure and boycotts mounted before the war began.

Figures also were produced by such companies as All-Nu, American Alloy, American Soldier Co., Beton, Ideal, Jones, Lincoln Log, Miller, Playwood Plastics, Soljertoys, Tommy Toy, Tootsietoy and Warren. Because most of these companies were short-lived, numerous limited production figures command high prices, especially those of All-Nu, Jones, Tommy Toy and Warren.

From 1942 through 1945, the wartime scrap drives devoured tons of dimestore figures and the molds that produced them. In late 1945, Barclay and Manoil introduced modernized

Indian, kneeling, with bow and arrow, Barkley, $5.50.

military figures, but they never enjoyed their pre-war popularity. Military operations generally were phased out by the early 1950s. Similarly, the civilian figures could not compete with escalating labor costs and the competition from plastic products.

References: Bertel Bruun, *Toy Soldiers*, Avon Books, 1994; Norman Joplin, *Great Book of Hollow-Cast Figures*, New Cavendish Books, 1992; Norman Joplin, *Toy Soldiers*, Running Press, 1994; Richard O'Brien, *Collecting American-Made Toy Soldiers*, No. 3, Krause Publications, 1996; ——, *Collecting Foreign-Made Toy Soldiers*, Krause Publications, 1997.

Periodicals: *Old Toy Soldier*, 209 N. Lombard, Oak Park, IL 60302; *Plastic Figure & Playset Collector*, P.O. Box 1355, LaCrosse, WI 54602; *Plastic Warrior*, 905 Harrison St., Allentown, PA 18103; *Toy Soldier Review*, 127 74th St., North Bergen, NJ 07047.

Reproduction Alert: Some manufacturers identify their newer products; many do not.

Notes: Prices listed are for figures in original condition with at least 95% of the paint remaining. Unless otherwise noted, uniforms are brown.

Advisor: Barry L. Carter.

Civilian Figure

Auburn Rubber
    Baseball 32.00
    Football 32.00
Barclay
    Cowboy
        Mounted, firing pistol 22.00
        With lasso 16.00
    Indian
        Standing, bow and arrow 9.00
        Tomahawk and shield 8.00
    Miscellaneous
        Girl skater 10.00
        Mailman 10.00
        Newsboy 10.00
        Pirate 12.00
        Policeman, raised arm 10.00
        Redcap with bag 15.00
        Santa Claus on skis 45.00
        Woman passenger
        with dog 10.00
Grey Iron
    American Family Series,
    2-1/4" h 5.00-25.00
    Western
        Bandit, hands up 40.00

    Cowboy
        Hold-up man 15.00
        Standing 9.00
Manoil
    Happy Farm Series
        Blacksmith
            Making horseshoes 20.00
            With wheel 21.00
        Farmer, sowing grain 18.00
        Man
            Chopping wood 18.00
            Juggling barrel 30.00
        Man and woman on bench .. 18.00
        Watchman blowing
        out lantern 25.00
        Woman
            Sweeping 20.00
            With pie 25.00
    Western
        Cowboy
            Arm raised 17.00
            One gun raised, flat base ... 14.00
        Cowgirl riding horse 25.00
        Indian with knives 12.00

Military Figure

Auburn Rubber
    Charging with tommy gun 10.00
    Grenade thrower 15.00
    Machine gunner, kneeling 11.00
    Marching with rifle 15.00
    Motorcycle with sidecar 55.00
    Motorcyclist 35.00
    Soldier
        Kneeling with binoculars 12.00
        Searchlight 28.00
Barclay
    Podfoot Series, 2-1/4" h
        Bugler 7.00
        Flag bearer 10.00
        Machine gunner
            Charging 6.00
            Prone 8.00
        Nurse, white 18.00
        Officer, standing 9.00
        Sailor, blue 8.00
        Soldier
            Charging 6.00
            Marching with rifle 7.00
    Post-War, pot helmet
        Flag bearer 15.00
        Machine gunner, prone 15.00
        Officer with sword 15.00
        Rifleman, standing 15.00
    Pre-War
        Anti-aircraft gunner,
        standing 15.00
        Bugler, tin helmet 15.00
        Cameraman,
        kneeling, tin hat 25.00
        Cook in white,
        holding roast 15.00

Dispatcher with dog 35.00
Doctor, white coat,
carrying bag 12.00
Machine gunner,
kneeling, tin hat....................10.00
Marching with rifle, tin hat 12.00
Marine officer, marching, sword,
blue uniform, tin hat 22.00
Nurse, kneeling
with cup, white 15.00
Parachutist.............................15.00
Pilot, standing 15.00
Sailor
  Carrying flag, white 15.00
  Marching, white.................12.00
  Signal flags, white 20.00
Sharpshooter
  Prone 15.00
  Standing 11.00
Signalman with flags 20.00
Soldier
  Crawling, tin hat 18.00
  Lying wounded, tin hat 12.00
  Peeling potatoes 20.00
  Prone with binoculars.........15.00
  Releasing pigeons,
  tin hat.................................18.00
  Running with rifle................18.00
  Searchlight 20.00
  Standing at attention,
  tin hat.................................14.00
  Stretcher bearer 15.00
  Telephone operator,
  tin hat 15.00
  Two-man rocket team 20.00
  Wireless operator,
  antenna, tin hat 28.00
  Wounded
    On crutches........................15.00
    Sitting, arm in sling.............15.00
Grey Iron
  Cavalryman..............................25.00
  Colonial soldier.......................15.00
  Doctor, white, bag 12.00

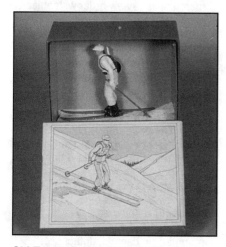

Ski Trooper, No. 2037, $125.

Doughboy
  Crawling....................................15.00
  Marching...................................10.00
  Rifle, kneeling 15.00
  Sentry 10.00
Drum major 17.00
Drummer 15.00
Ethiopian
  Charging 35.00
  Marching 28.00
Flag bearer.............................15.00
Machine gunner
  Kneeling..............................10.00
  Prone 15.00
Nurse, white and blue 12.00
Radio operator 45.00
Sailor, marching
  Blue.....................................14.00
  White...................................12.00
Manoil
Post-War
  Marching with rifle................16.00
  Soldier
    Bazooka.............................20.00
    Mine detector 30.00
  Tommy gunner, standing 22.00
Post-War, 2-1/2", mkd "USA"
  Aircraft spotter 25.00
  Aviator, holding bomb 24.00
  Flag bearer 20.00
  Grenade thrower..................24.00
  Machine gunner, seated 20.00
  Observer with binoculars 27.00
  Soldier with bazooka...........18.00
Pre-War
  Bicycle rider 30.00
  Bomb thrower, 3 grenades ..14.00
  Boxer 65.00
  Cameraman,
  overhead flash 40.00
  Cannon loader 14.00
  Cook's helper with ladle.......30.00
  Deep-sea diver, silver 15.00
  Doctor, white........................12.00
  Firefighter,
  "Hot Papa," gray 75.00
  Flag bearer 18.00
  Hostess, green.....................45.00
  Machine gunner, prone........15.00
  Marching 16.00
  Navy gunner, white, firing
  deck gun 32.00
  Nurse, white, red dish 16.00
  Observer with periscope 20.00
  Radio operator, standing 33.00
  Rifleman, standing...............15.00
  Sailor, white 18.00
  Sharpshooter,
  camouflage, prone 20.00
  Signalman, white, 2 flags.....24.00

Soldier
  At searchlight 18.00
  Charging with bayonet 28.00
  Gas mask and flare gun.....18.00
  Running with cannon 28.00
  Sitting, eating 26.00
  Wounded 15.00
  Writing letter......................50.00
Stretcher carrier,
medical kit...........................17.00

Soldiers, Toy

Collecting Hints: Consider three key factors: condition of the figures and the box, the age of the figures and the box and the completeness of the set. Toy soldiers were meant to be playthings. However, collectors consider them an art form and pay premium prices only for excellent to mint examples. They want figures with complete paint and intact parts, including the moving parts.

The box is very important, controlling 10% to 20% of the price of a set. The style of the box is a clue to the date of the set. The same set may have been made for several decades; the earlier the date of manufacture, the more valuable the set.

Sets have a specific number of pieces or parts. These must all be present for full value to be realized. The number of pieces in each set, when known, is indicated in the listings below. Beware of repainted older examples and modern reproductions. Toy soldiers still are being manufactured, both by large companies and private individuals. A contemporary collection may prove a worthwhile long-term investment, at least for the next generation.

History: The manufacture of toy soldiers began in the late 18th century by individuals such as the Hilperts of Nuremberg, Germany. The early figures were tin, pewter or composition. By the late 19th century, companies in Britain (Britains, Courtenay), France (Blondel, Gerbeau and Mignot) and Switzerland (Gottschalk, Wehrli) were firmly established. Britains and Mignot dominated the market into the 20th century.

Mignot established its French stronghold by purchasing Cuperly, Blondel and Gerbeau who had united to take over Lucotte. By 1950, Mignot

Britains, No. 9265, Camel Corps, $180.

had 20,000 models representing soldiers from around the world. Britains developed the hollow cast soldiers in 1893. Movable arms also were another landmark. Eventually, bases were made of plastic, followed finally by the entirely plastic figures. Production ceased in the 1980s.

Between 1930 and 1950, the English toy soldier was challenged in America by the dimestore soldiers made by Barclay, Manoil and others. Nevertheless, the Britains retained a share of the market because of their high quality. The collecting of toy soldiers remains very popular in the United States.

References: Bertel Bruun, *Toy Soldiers*, Avon Books, 1994; *Elastolin, Miniature Figures and Groups from the Hausser Firm of Germany* (1990), *Vol. 2* (1991), Theriault's; Norman Joplin, *Great Book of Hollow-Cast Figures*, New Cavendish Books, 1993; Norman Joplin, *Toy Soldiers*, Running Press, 1994; Richard O'Brien, *Collecting Toy Soldiers, No. 3*, Krause Publications, 1996; James Opie, *Collecting Toy Soldiers*, Pincushion Press, 1992; ; ——, *Collecting Foreign-Made Toy Soldiers*, Krause Publications, 1997; Joe Wallis, *Armies of the World*, published by author, 1993.

Periodicals: *Old Toy Soldier*, 209 North Lombard, Oak Park, IL 60302; *Plastic Figure & Playset Collector*, P.O. Box 1355, LaCrosse, WI 54602; *Plastic Warrior*, 905 Harrison St., Allentown, PA 18103; *Toy Soldier Review*, 127 74th St., North Bergen, NJ 07047.

Collectors' Club: American Model Soldier Society, 1528 El Camino Real, San Carlos, CA 94070; Military Miniature Society of Illinois, P.O. Box 394, Skokie, IL 60077; Northeast Toy Soldier Society, 12 Beach Rd., Gloucester, MA 09130; Toy Soldier Collectors of America, 6924 Stone's Throw Circle, #8202, St. Petersburg, FL 33710.

Reproduction Alert.

Advisor: Barry L. Carter.

Authenticast, Russian Infantry, advancing with rifles at the ready, 2 officers carrying pistols and swords 65.00

Blenheim

B2, Coldstream Guards Colors, 1812, 2 color bearers, escort of 4 privates, mint, orig excellent box 115.00

B17, Royal Marines, 1923, marching at the slope, officer, sword at carry, mint, orig excellent box 75.00

B63, Royal Co., of Archers Colors, 2 color bearers, escort of 4 privates, mint, orig excellent box 90.00

C13, 17th Lancers, 1879, foreign service order, officer, bugler and trooper with lance, mint, orig excellent box 150.00

U.S. Naval Academy Color Guard, 4 standard bearers, escort of 2 midshipmen, mint, orig excellent box 100.00

Britains, sets only

28, Mountain Gun of the Royal Artillery, with gun, gunners, mules and mounted officer, mint, orig good box.....250.00

33, 16th/5th Lancers, mounted at the halt in review order with officer turned-in-the-saddle, excellent, orig illus box...........170.00

44, 2nd Dragoon Guards, The Queen's Bays, mounted at the gallop with lances and trumpeter, 1 trooper missing, c1940, excellent, good orig Whisstock box........100.00

117, Egyptian Infantry, at attention in review order, c1935, good, orig Whisstock box......................200.00

122, The Black Watch, standing firing in tropical service dress with officer holding binoculars, c1940, good, orig Whisstock box.......................300.00

136, Russian Cossacks, mounted at the gallop with officer, excellent, orig box 170.00

138, French Cuirassiers, mounted at the walk in review order with officer, excellent, orig box 140.00

167, Turkish Infantry, standing on guard in review order, c1935, good/fine, orig Whisstock box.......................130.00

190, Belgian 2nd Regiment Chasseurs a Cheval, mounted in review order with officer, good, orig box 140.00

201, Officers of the General Staff, comprising Field Marshal, General Officer and 2 Aides-de-Camp, good............120.00

216, Argentine Infantry, marching at the slope in review order, c1940, excellent, good orig "Types of the Argentine Army" box 325.00

217, Argentine Cavalry, mounted in review order with lances and officer, excellent, orig box 250.00

1323, The Royal Fusiliers, The Royal Sussex Regiment and the Seaforth Highlanders, marching at the slope with mounted and foot officers, excellent, orig good box.........300.00

1339, The Royal Horse Artillery Khaki Service Order, with 6-horse team, lumber, gun, drivers with whips, 4 mounted outriders on trotting horses and officer on galloping horse, excellent, good orig "Types of the British Army" box with gold and black label 1,700.00

1343, The Royal Horse Guards, mounted in winter cloaks with officer, c1940, good, orig "Armies of the World" box 130.00

1631, The Governor General's Horse Guards of Canada, mounted in review order with officer on prancing horse, mint, orig excellent box...........................110.00

1632, The Royal Canadian Regiment, marching at the slope with officer, c1940, good, fine orig "Soldiers of the British Empire" box ...1,100.00

1935, Argentine Naval Cadets, marching at the slope in review order with officer, 1948-49, excellent, good orig box 1,800.00

1836, Argentine Military Cadets, marching at the slope in review order with officer, c1940, excellent, orig "Armies of the World" box ...3,250.00

2009, Belgian Grenadier Regiment, marching in review order with officer, excellent, orig box 120.00

2028, Red Army Cavalry, mounted at the halt in parade uniform with officer, excellent, orig box..................200.00

2035, Swedish Life Guard, marching at the slope in review order with officer, mint, tied in excellent orig box 200.00

2059, Union Infantry, action poses, with officer holding sword and pistol, bugler and standard bearer, excellent, orig box....................90.00

9217, 12th Royal Lancers, mounted in review order with officer, mint, good orig window box 80.00

9265, Egyptian Camel Corps, mounted on camels, detachable riders, mint, tied in excellent orig

Britains Zoo, $300.

window box 180.00
9291, Arabs of the Desert on Horses, with jezails and scimitars, excellent, good orig window box 80.00
9402, State Open Road Landau, drawn by 6 Windsor Greys, with 3 detachable positions, attendants and Queen Elizabeth and Prince Philip as passengers, mint, tied in excellent orig box 375.00
9407, British Regiments on Parade, comprising General Officer, Royal Horse Artillery at the walk, 17th Lancers in review order on trotting and cantering horses with officer, Life Guards with trumpeter and officer, Royal Norfolk Regiment at the slope with officer, Scots Greys on trotting and walking horses with officer, The Black Watch marching at the slope with piper and officer and a Band of the Line, excellent, orig 2-tray display box 2,500.00

Elastolin/Lineol
Flak Gunner, blue and gray uniform, kneeling with shell, very good 40.00
Medic, walking, helmet, big pack with red cross 35.00
Nurse, attending wounded, kneeling, holds foot of soldier sitting on keg, excellent 40.00
Staff Officer, pointing, field glasses, aristocratic pose 35.00

Heyde
Chicago Police, 1890s, on foot with billy clubs, including policeman with dog, standard bearer and good mounted policeman, very good 225.00
French Ambulance Unit, horse-drawn ambulance, 2-horse team, rider with whip, stretcher bearers, stretchers and casualties, mounted and foot medical officers and medical orderly, very good, fair orig box..........275.00
German Infantry, World War I, attacking with fixed bayonets, officer with extended sword, very good 90.00
Hessian Infantry, 1777, marching at the slope, officers, standard bearer, 4 mounted dragoons, movable reins

on horses, good 375.00
U.S. Army World War I Pontoon Train, 4 horse-drawn pontoon wagons, pontoon boats, engineer detail on foot with mounted officer, very good, poor orig display box....475.00

Mignot
15, French Musketeers Period of King Louis XIII, marching with muskets at shoulder arms, with officer and standard bearer, c1960, excellent, orig box 275.00
17, Infantry of King Louis XIV, marching at the slope with office, standard bearer and drummer, c1950, excellent, orig box 400.00
28/C, Band of Napoleon's Imperial Guard, 1812, marching with full instrumentation and band director with baton, excellent 350.00
36, French Napoleonic Skirmishers of the 17th Line Regiment, 1809, marching in blue and white uniforms faced in red with tall plumed shakos, gloss paint, c1965, mint 4-piece set in excellent orig window box and outer cardboard box.................80.00
39, Italian Light Infantry, Regiment de Beauharnais, 1810, marching at the slope in green uniforms with pale blue facings and plumed shakos, with drummer and officer, excellent 8-pc set in orig box.................275.00
43/H, Austrian Infantry, 1805, standing at attention at shoulder arms with officer, drummer and tandard bearer, limited issue, mint, tied in excellent orig box 225.00
45/A, Bavarian Infantry, 1812, marching at the slope in blue and white uniforms with yellow facings and plumed light infantry caps, with standard bearer and bugler, excellent 8-pc set in orig box.................250.00
200, Ancient Gaul Cavalry, mounted with swords, spears and shields, excellent, orig box 275.00
200/8, Ancient Greek Cavalry, mounted with swords, spears and shields, excellent, orig box.....250.00
231/B, Austrian Cavalry, 1814, mounted in review order, with officer, trumpeter and standard bearer, mint, excellent orig box 250.00
255, Spanish Hussars, 1808, mounted in green uniforms with red facings and tall plumed shakos, with officer, trumpeter and standard bearer, mint, excellent orig box 375.00
1016, Drum Majors of the Empire, drum majors of French Napoleonic regiments including Orphans of the Guard, Marines of the Guard, St. Cyr Academy and arious line infantry regiments,

special limited edition, all mint and in excellent orig boxes 475.00

Militia Models
Gatling Gun Team of 3rd London Rifles, Gatling gun and gunner, 2 ammunition carriers, officer holding binoculars, mint, excellent orig box 90.00
The Pipes and Drums of 1st Battalion Royal Irish Rangers, pipe major and 4 pipers, 2 snare and 2 tenor drummers, drum major, limited edition, mint, excellent orig box 125.00

Nostalgia
1st Gurkha Light Infantry, 1800, red and blue uniforms, marching with slung rifles, officer with sword at the carry, excellent, orig box..........80.00
Kaffrarian Rifles, 1910, gray uniforms, plumed pith helmets, marching at the trail, officer with sword at the carry, mint, excellent orig box...................125.00
New South Wales Irish Rifles, 1900, marching at the trail, officer holding sword at the carry, mint, excellent orig box....................95.00
New South Wales Lancers, 1900, marching carrying lances on the shoulder, khaki uniforms, trimmed in red and plumed campaign hats, officer holding swagger stick, mint, excellent orig box....................85.00

S.A.F.
1358, Royal Horse Guards, 1945, mounted at the halt with officer, mint, excellent orig box............50.00
1761, French Cuirassiers, mounted at the walk, mint, excellent orig box....................85.00
3310, 1st Bengal Lancers, at the halt, mint, excellent orig box 115.00

Souvenir and Commemorative Items

Collecting Hints: Most collectors of souvenir and commemorative china and glass collect items from a region which is particularly interesting to them—their hometown or birthplace or place of special interest such as a President's home. This results in regional variations in price because a piece is more likely to be in demand in the area it represents.

When collecting souvenir spoons be aware of several things: condition, material, subject and any markings, dates, etc. Damaged spoons should be avoided unless they are very rare

Canoe, milk glass, white, red, yellow, green, and black lettering, Cascade Park, New Castle, PA, 3-5/8" l, $30.

and are needed to complete a collection. Some spoons have enamel crests and other decoration. This enameling should be in mint condition.

History: Souvenir and commemorative china and glass date to the early fairs and carnivals when a small trinket was purchased to take back home as a gift or remembrance of the event. Other types of commemorative glass include pattern and milk glass made to celebrate a particular event. Many types of souvenir glass and china originated at the world's fairs and expositions.

The peak of souvenir spoon collecting was reached in the late 1800s. During that time two important patents were issued. One was the Dec. 4, 1884, patent for the first flatware design and it was issued to Michael Gibney, a New York silversmith. The other important patent was the one for the first spoon design which commemorated a place. That patent was given to Myron H. Kinsley in 1881 for his spoon which showed the suspension bridge at Niagara Falls. This was the first of many scenic views of Niagara Falls which appeared on spoons over the years.

Spoons depicting famous people soon followed, such as the one of George Washington which was issued in May 1889. That was followed by the Martha Washington spoon in October 1889. These spoons, made by M.W. Galt of Washington, D.C., were not patented but were trademarked in 1890.

During the 1900s, it became popular to have souvenir plates made to memorialize churches and local events such as centennials and homecomings. These plates were well received in their respective communities. Collectors search for them today because they were made in a limited number. They are especially interesting as an indication of how an area changed architecturally and culturally over the years.

References: Arene Burgess, *Collector's Guide to Souvenir Plates*, Schiffer Publishing, 1996; George B. James, *Souvenir Spoons* (1891), reprinted with 1996 price guide by Bill Boyd (7408 Englewood Ln., Raytown, MO 64133), 1996; Dorothy T. Rainwater and Donna H. Fegler, *American Spoons*, Schiffer Publishing, 1990; ——, *Spoons from around the World*, Schiffer Publishing, 1992; *Sterling Silver, Silverplate and Souvenir Spoons with Prices*, Revised Edition, L-W Book Sales, 1987, 1994 value update.

Collectors' Club: American Spoon Collectors, 7408 Englewood Ln., Raytown, MO 64133; Antique Souvenir Collectors News, Box 562, Great Barrington, MA 01230; Northeastern Spoon Collectors Guild, 52 Hillcrest Ave., Morristown, NJ 07960; The Scoop Club, 84 Oak Ave., Shelton, CT 06484.

Basket, 3" h, pottery, white ground, hp blue bonnets, Myer, Texas......25.00
Book, Follies Bergere, heavy gold-stamped flocked cover, c1950 ....70.00
Booklet
  Cathedral of Commerce, Woolworth Building, 8" x 11", gray soft-cover, relief gold accent lettering, 32 pgs, b&w photos and text, 1917, Broadway Park Place Co. 22.00
  Souvenir of Coney Island, Brighton and Manhattan Beaches, 1904, 40 pgs with b&w illus, 8" x 5" 65.00
  Views of Coney Island, 7-3/4" x 9-3/4", green soft-cover, gold accent title, 32 pgs, photos and text of Luna Park, Dreamland and bathers, 1906, L.H. Nelson Co..............35.00
  Steel Pier, Atlantic City, NJ, summer program, 32 pgs, picturesand ads........................45.00
Bottle Opener, San Diego, 1912 ...25.00
Brochure, Burlington Railroad Chicago Expo Souvenir, 5-1/2" x 8-1/2", black and white, red accent soft-covers, 32 pgs, photo and text, 1933 Century of Progress Expo aerial scene with dirigible 14.00
Calling Card Receiver, Philadelphia, 1907, copper, moose, tree, lake and mountains........................40.00

Card Game, Excursion to Coney Island, Milton Bradley, c1885..............20.00
Cup, china, white
  St. Charles Hotel, New Orleans 15.00
  Souvenir of the Midget's Palace, Montreal, well-dressed male and female midgets illus, late 1800s..65.00
Cup and Saucer, Niagara Falls, mkd "Carlsbad, Austria" 18.00
Demitasse Cup and Saucer, Hotel Roosevelt, New Orleans 35.00
Doll, Luray Caverns, VA, Skookum, boy and girl, 3-1/2" h, price for pr...70.00
Figure, 3-1/2" h, Chinatown, NY, Chinese couple 25.00
Guidebook, 7" x 10", New York, soft-cover, full color, airships and planes flying over city skyline and Statue of Liberty, 64 b&w pgs, 1932 Manhattan Card Co. Publishing Co.....24.00
Hatchet
  6" l, Hazelton, PA, white milk glass, red letters 40.00
  12" l, Washington, Inauguration of President of United States, April 30, 1789, cast iron, c1889 ....85.00
Match Safe, Kennebunkport, ME, celluloid face 45.00
Medal
  Coney Island, steeplechase face, orig ribbon, 1924......................90.00
  Souvenir of Wisconsin, green with gold...................................30.00
Mug
  Hardwick, VT, custard glass, gold trim....................................35.00
  Karlsbad, 1934, multicolored view of colonnade, purple ground, gold filigree trim and handle 65.00
  New Rockford, ND, custard glass...........................35.00
Notebook, George Washington silhouette, mkd "1732-1932 Jamestown, NY," celluloid.......22.00
Paperweight, glass, round
  Brainard, MN, lake scene, 3" d 40.00
  New Salem State Park, 2-3/4" d 35.00
Pennant, felt
  Coney Island, maroon, white title, yellow, green, orange and white scene of Steeplechase Pool, amusement rides, Luna Mill Sky Chaser building, c1930 ....30.00
  Hershey Park, brown ground, white letters, c1950 ....25.00
Photo Album, New Orleans, various scenes, 1885........................45.00
Pinback Button, 1-1/4" d
  Asbury Park, b&w, bathing beauty scene, c1900 ....12.00

Coney Island, multicolored, bathing beauty scene, rim reads "Citizens Committee of Coney Island," c1915 ....35.00

Dreamland, NY, white lettering, red ground, 1900s 10.00

Hershey Park, multicolored, child emerging from cocoa bean, c1905 ....35.00

New Virginia Reel, Luna Park, 2 men and 4 ladies on ride, Bastian Brothers back label 125.00

Wonderland Stamford, CT, multicolored, c1900 ....90.00

Pitcher, Bar Harbor, ME, custard glass, gold trim, beaded base 95.00

Plate

Alabama, state capital in center, blue, Vernon Kilns 22.00

Albany, MN.............................40.00

Along 101 The Redwood Highway, maroon, Vernon Kilns...............25.00

Baltimore & Ohio Railroad, Harpers Ferry, blue and white, 10-1/2" d.................................95.00

Birmingham, AL, The Industrial City, maroon, Vernon Kilns...............22.00

Boston, MA, Filene's, brown, Vernon Kilns............................22.00

Carlsbad Caverns, White's City, New Mexico.............................25.00

Chicago, clock in center, maroon......................................22.00

Daytona Beach, FL, World's Most Famous Beach, maroon, Vernon Kilns............................22.00

Delaware Tercentenary Celebration, 1938, black and white, Spode 35.00

Denver, CO, state capital in center, blue, Vernon Kilns 22.00

Greenville, SC, blue, Vernon Kilns............................22.00

Hollywood, CA, NBC Studios, Hollywood Bowl, Ciro's, Graumann's, Earl Carroll's, Brown Derby, blue, Vernon Kilns 35.00

Jacksonville, FL, Gateway to Florida, maroon 22.00

Laguna Beach, CA, Festival of Arts 25.00

Maine, state capital in center, multicolored, Vernon Kilns 30.00

Mississippi, blue, Vernon Kilns............................22.00

My Old Kentucky Home, 10" d, cobalt blue, Adams..................75.00

Nevada, The Silver State, Hoover Dam in center, brown, Vernon Kilns............................22.00

New Mexico, picture map.........22.00

Northwestern University, multicolored, Vernon Kilns 35.00

Our West, Vast Empire, maroon, Vernon Kilns............................35.00

Portsmouth Virginia Bicentennial, 1752-1952, light brown, Vernon Kilns............................22.00

Saint Augustine, FL, brown, Vernon Kilns............................22.00

San Diego County Fair, Delmar, CA, Don Diego Welcomes You, blue 35.00

SE Missouri State College, Diamond Jubilee, brown, Vernon Kilns ...25.00

Sonoma, CA, Cradle of California, maroon, Vernon Kilns 35.00

South Dakota, state capital in center, maroon, Vernon Kilns 22.00

Spokane, WA, The Inland Empire, blue, Vernon Kilns...................25.00

SS *Grand View Hotel*, A Steamboat in the Allegheny Mountains, 10" d, cobalt blue, Adams 95.00

Statue of Liberty, mkd "Made expressly for James Hill, Bedloe's Island, NY, The New Colossus by Emma Lazarus" on back, blue, Vernon Kilns............................35.00

Vermont, Green Mountain State, brown, Vernon Kilns.................22.00

Washington, state capital in center, brown, Vernon Kilns.................22.00

West Virginia, state capital in center, brown 22.00

Program

Eighth World Championship Rodeo, Boston, *Garden Area Sports News*, Vol. VII, No. 1, c1939 ....25.00

Ice Follies of 1953, Shipstads & Johnson 25.00

Radio City Music Hall Pictorial, 1945 ....20.00

Sonja Henie and Her Hollywood Ice Review, 1940 ....25.00

Spoon, SS

Athens, PA, engraved high school bowl 35.00

Plate, Views of Asbury Park, NJ, Rowland and Marsellus, Heath Novelty Co., Asbury Park, NJ, 8-1/2", $35.

Battle Monument, Trenton, NJ 35.00

Ben Franklin, Philadelphia 55.00

Bethesda Springs, Waukesha, WI 55.00

Bismarck, ND, post office bowl 45.00

Brooklyn, NY, 13th Regiment ..35.00

Calumet, MI, mining, Helco Shaft #2 ....35.00

Chicago, IL, U.S. Government Building, Fort Dearborn...........40.00

Columbus, bust, plated 20.00

Columbus, OH, Lancaster pattern handle 35.00

Cornell University, Art Nouveau woman 75.00

Cuba, Morro castle 50.00

Detroit Skyline.........................70.00

Elgin Watch Factory.................85.00

Eureka, CA, courthouse...........30.00

Fredericton, New Brunswick, spiral handle, gold-wash bowl 60.00

Girard College, Irian pattern handle 45.00

Golden Gate, San Francisco ...45.00

Grant Monument, Chicago.......45.00

Hope, ID.................................30.00

Hot Springs, AK, Indian head, corn 45.00

Inclined Plane, Cincinnati, OH.........................35.00

Kansas City, MO, Convention Hall 45.00

Lake Worth, Palm Beach, FL...65.00

Madison, WI.............................35.00

McDermott Falls, Glacier National Park bowl 45.00

Michigan City, IN, ornate Art Nouveau handle......................50.00

Miles Standish, fruit bowl 75.00

Mt. Vernon 20.00

Old Hickory, Jackson monument.................75.00

Paul Revere, Midnight Ride 95.00

Prairie du Chien, WI.................28.00

Quebec, open-work handle......35.00

Reading, PA, Mt. Penn Tower, demitasse 40.00

Salt Lake City, UT, Mormon Temple handle, demitasse...................45.00

San Francisco, Mission Dolores 1776, bear on dec handle, gold bowl 45.00

Sioux City, IA, Corn Palace, 1891 ....80.00

Springfield, IL, Abraham Lincoln.....................60.00

Statue of Liberty, Tiffany 75.00

Texas, enameled star, demitasse 25.00

Union Station, Dayton, OH,

Spoons, Quakertown, PA, SS, mkd, demitasse, $15; Allentown, PA, Allentown Crockery Co., SP, demitasse, $20.

picture bowl 35.00
Vassar, MI, high school
engraved bowl...........................35.00
Waseca, MN, grape pattern 55.00
Washington's Tomb 30.00
Wilmington, NC, floral handle,
gold-wash bowl, demitasse 35.00
Yellowstone Park, etched falls
bowl, bear, stag's head and
buffalo's head on handle 45.00
Tape Measure, New York City,
celluloid, pig............................25.00
Teapot, Morrison Hotel,
Chicago 35.00
Tip Tray, Hotel Coronado,
china..15.00
Toothpick Holder
Glen Ullen, ND, ruby-stained glass,
gold 35.00
Lewistown, ME, Georgia Gem pattern, custard glass, gold trim 45.00
Providence, Shamrock pattern,
ruby-stained glass 40.00
Trowel, Acme Portland Cement,
engraved eagle, 5-1/2" l 40.00
Vase
Opera House, What Cheer, IA,
china, multicolored scene.........45.00
Red Wing, MN, custard glass,
multicolored scene, c1920 ....95.00
Watch Fob
Magnetic Club, NY,
enameled, 1913 ....45.00
Mormon Temple,
Salt Lake City...........................50.00

Souvenir Buildings

Collecting Hints: Collectors look for rarity, architectural detail and quality of material, casting and finishing. As in real estate, location affects price: European and East Coast buildings are more expensive on the West Coast and vice versa.

History: Small metal replicas of famous buildings and monuments first became popular souvenirs among Victorian travelers returning from a Grand Tour of Europe. In the 1920s and 1930s, metal replicas of banks and insurance company headquarters were made as promotional giveaways to new depositors and clients. In the 1950s and 1960s, Japanese-manufactured metal souvenir buildings were the rage for motorists visiting attractions across America.

Souvenir buildings are still being manufactured and sold in cities and capitals around the world and depict churches, cathedrals, skyscrapers, office buildings, capitols and towers. Most souvenir buildings are made of white (or pot) metal with a finish of brass, copper, gold, silver or bronze. Souvenir buildings are also made of sterling silver, brass, silvered lead, plastic, resin composition and ceramic.

Collectors' Club: Souvenir Building Collectors Society, 25 Falls Rd., Roxbury, CT 06783.

Additional Advisor: Dixie Trainer.

Alamo, San Antonio, TX, 2" x 4" x 3-1/2", copper finish.................17.00
Alder Planetarium, Chicago,
IL, incense burner, 3" x 4" d,
copper finish 44.00
Arc de Triomphe, Paris, 1-3/4" x 1-1/2" x 1", copper finish 6.00
Brandenberg Gate, Berlin,
4" x 3-3/4" x 2", antique
bronze, wood base 38.00
Bunker Hill Monument, Boston, MA,
copper finish 14.00
Capitol, Washington, DC
Jewelry Box, 4-1/4" x 5" x 3-1/2",
gold, mkd "JB" on bottom.........55.00
Souvenir, 2-1/4" x 3-1/2" x 2" 6.00
Coit Tower, San Francisco,
6-1/2" h, 2-1/4" sq base,
antique bronze finish 78.00
Cologne Cathedral, Germany,
4-1/8" x 3-3/4" x 1-1/2", antique
pewter or silver finish...............14.00
Coliseum, Rome, 1-1/2" x 2-1/4" x 2", copper finish......................15.00
Dollar Savings Bank, Pittsburgh,
PA, 3-1/8" x 4" x 3", silvered
lead bank.................................88.00
Easton National Bank, Easton, PA,
4-1/2" x 3-3/4" x 2-1/2", bank,
copper finish 68.00
Eiffel Tower, Paris
3" x 1" x 1", copper, antique brass

or silver finish 8.00
6" x 2-1/2" x 2-1/2", copper, antique
brass or silver finish 13.00
Empire State Building, New York City
Prewar, no spire
3-1/2" x 1-1/2" x 1", antique
brass finish 28.00
5-3/4" x 2-1/2" x 2",
silver finish...........................63.00
Postwar, with radio antenna spire
3-1/2" x 1-1/4" x 3/4",
gold plastic.............................3.00
5" x 1-3/4" x 1-1/4",
antique brass finish................7.00
7-1/2" x 2-3/4" x 1-1/4",
copper finish 14.00
Field Museum of Natural History,
Chicago, IL, 1" x 4-1/4" x 3",
silver or copper finish 33.00
Flatiron Building, New York City,
5-1/2" h, cast iron bank,
silvery finish...........................158.00
Ft. Dearborn, Chicago, IL, 4" x 3-1/8" x 2", green or tan paint, souvenir of 1933 Chicago World's Fair......38.00
General Motors Building, Detroit, MI,
3-3/4" x 6-1/4" x 4", antique
bronze finish 110.00
La Giralda, Seville, Spain, 7-1/2" h,
antique brass, 2-1/4" black
marble base 50.00
Havoline Tower, thermometer,
souvenir of 1933 Chicago World's
Fair, 4-5/8" h
Cast iron, ivory paint 37.00
Plastic, marble base 22.00
Immaculate Conception National Shrine,
Washington, DC, antique
copper finish3" x 3" x 2".............16.00
5" x 5" x 4" 38.00
Ivan's Bell Tower, Moscow, 3-1/2" x 2" x 1-1/4", solid brass,
marble base 91.00
Jefferson Memorial, Washington, DC,
1-1/2" x 2" x 2", copper finish ..16.00
Kraft International Headquarters,
Chicago, IL, 3-1/8" x 2-3/4" x 3-1/4",
silvered lead paperweight, cast by
A.C. Rehberger 80.00
Leaning Tower of Pisa, Italy
3-1/2", silver finish,
metal ashtray 34.00
5" x 1-3/4" d, white alabaster ...28.00
Lincoln Memorial, Washington, DC,
1-1/2" x 3" x 2, copper finish......8.00
Louisiana State Capitol, Baton Rouge,
LA, 7" x 5-1/2" x 2-3/4", antique
copper finish 88.00
Metropolitan Life Insurance Co.,
New York City, 5-1/4" x 3-3/4" x 2-1/4", silver or gold finish 118.00
Miami Beach Federal Savings, Miami,
FL, 5-1/2" x 3-1/2" x 3-1/4", brass
finish, Banthrico Bank 68.00

Mormon Temple, Salt Lake City, UT, 4" x 2-1/4" x 3-3/8", copper finish 30.00
Notre Dame, Paris, 2" x 3" x 1-1/2", bronze finish 16.00
Parthenon, Athens, Greece, 3-1/4" x 6" x 3-1/2", copper, marble base 98.00
Pilgrim Memorial Monument, Provincetown, MA, 4-3/4" h, 2-1/4" d base..............................22.00
Rockefeller Center (RCA Building), New York City
  2-5/8" x 2" x 1", copper finish 27.00
  4-1/4" x 3" x 1-3/8", silver finish 89.00
Sacre Coeur, Paris, 4-1/2" x 4-1/4" x 2-1/2", antique brass...................32.00
Singing Tower, Bok Tower, Lake Wales, FL, 5" h, 1-3/4" d base...............21.00
Space Needle, Seattle, WA, 6" h, revolving turret, silver or copper finish...................................22.00
Statue of Liberty, New York City
  2" h...3.00
  4-1/2" h 5.50
  6" h...8.00
St. Basil's Cathedral, Moscow, 4" x 3-1/2" x 3-1/2" h, solid brass, marble base.....................................300.00
St. Mary's Cathedral, Florence, Italy, 2-1/2" x 3-1/2" x 2-1/2", silver finish 27.00
St. Peter's Cathedral, Rome, 3-1/2" x 3-1/2" x 2-1/2", silver finish 28.00
Syracuse Savings Bank, Syracuse, NY, 5-1/2" x 4" x 3", copper finish...............................68.00
Taj Mahal, Agra, India, 8" x 7" x 7", white marble, night-light..............64.00
United Nations Building, New York City, 3" x 4" x 2-1/2", antique brass 22.00
U.S. Fidelity & Guaranty Co., 5-3/4" x 7-1/4" x 6", building as combination cigar humidor, inkwell and clock, cast by Art Metal Works, NJ, antique bronze finish 190.00
Washington Monument, Washington, DC
  3-1/4" h, silver, salt and pepper set......................27.00
  6" h, copper, thermometer 9.00
Woolworth Building, New York City, 4" x 1-3/4" x 1-1/4", gold finish........26.00
Zembo Museum, Harrisburg, PA, 2-1/2" x 4-1/2" x 1-3/4", antique copper finish 63.00

Space Adventurers and Exploration

Collecting Hints: There are four distinct eras of fictional space adventurers: Buck Rogers, Flash Gordon, the radio and television characters of the late 1940s and 1950s and the Star Trek and Star Wars phenomenon. Because Buck Rogers material is rare, condition is not as much of a factor as it is for the other three areas. Beware of dealers who break apart items, especially games, and sell parts separately.

In the early 1950s, a wealth of tin, battery-operated, friction and windup toys not associated with a specific Space Adventurer were marketed. The popularity of these robots, space ships and space guns is growing rapidly. Trekkies began holding conventions in the early 1970s. They issued many fantasy items which must not be confused with items issued during the years the TV show was broadcast. The fantasy items are numerous and have little value beyond the initial selling price.

The American and Russian space programs produced a wealth of souvenir and related material. Beware of astronaut-signed material; it may have a printed or autopen signature.

History: In January 1929, "Buck Rogers 2429 A.D." began its comic strip run. Buck, Wilma Deering, Dr. Huer and the villain Killer Kane, were the creation of Phillip Francis Nowlan and John F. Dille. The heyday of Buck Rogers material was 1933 to 1937 when premiums were issued in conjunction with products such as Cream of Wheat and Cocomalt.

Flash Gordon followed in the mid-1930s. Buster Crabbe gave life to the character in movie serials. Books, comics, premiums and other merchandise enhanced the image during the 1940s. The use of rockets at the end of World War II and the beginning of the space research program gave reality to space travel. Television quickly capitalized on this in the early 1950s with programs such as "Captain Video" and "Space Patrol." Many other space heroes, such as Rocky Jones, had short-lived popularity.

In the 1950s, real-life space pioneers and explorers replaced the fictional characters as the center of the public's attention. The entire world watched on July 12, 1969, as man first walked on the moon. Although space exploration has suffered occasional setbacks, the public remains fascinated with its findings and potential.

Tom Corbett Danger in Deep Space, Carey Rockwell, Willy Ley, Technical Advisor, Grosset & Dunlap, 1953, illus by Louis Glanzman, 7-5/8" x 5" x 3/4", $17.50.

"Star Trek" enjoyed a brief television run and developed a cult following in the early 1970s. "Star Trek: The Next Generation" has an established corps of watchers. "Star Wars" (Parts IV, V and VI) and "ET" also initiated a wealth of merchandise which already is collectible.

References: Sue Cornwell and Mike Kott, *Official Price Guide to Star Trek and Star Wars Collectibles*, 3rd Edition, House of Collectibles, 1991; Christine Gentry and Sally Gibson-Downs, *Greenberg's Guide to Star Trek Collectibles*, Vols. I-III, Greenberg Publishing, 1992; Stephen J. Sansweet, *Star Wars*, Chronicle Books, 1992; Stuart Schneider, *Collecting the Space Race*, Schiffer Publishing, 1993; Stephen Sansweet and T.N. Tumbusch, *Tomart's Price Guide to Star Wars Collectibles Worldwide*, Tomart Publications, 1994; Jeffrey B. Snyder, *Trekker's Guide to Collectibles with Values*, Schiffer Publishing, 1996; T.N. Tumbusch, *Space Adventure Collectibles*, Wallace-Homestead, 1990; Bruce Lanier Wright, *Yesterday's Tomorrows: The Golden Age of Science Fiction Movie Posters*, Taylor Publishing, 1993.

Periodicals: St*arlog Magazine*, 475 Park Ave. South, New York, NY

10016; *Strange New Worlds*, P.O. Box 223, Tallevast, FL 34270; *Star Wars Collection Trading Post*, 6030 Magnolia, P.O. Box 29396, St. Louis, MO 63139; *Trek Collector*, 1324 Palm Blvd., Dept. 17, Los Angeles, CA 90291.

Collectors' Clubs: Galaxy Patrol, 22 Colton St., Worcester, MA 01610; International Federation of Trekkers, P.O. Box 3123, Lorain, OH 44052; Lost in Space Fan Club, 550 Trinity, Westfield, NJ 07090; Society for the Advancement of Space Activities, P.O. Box 192, Kent Hills, ME 04349; Star Trek: The Official Fan Club, P.O. Box 111000, Aurora, CO 80011; Starfleet, P.O. Box 430, Burnsville, NC 28714; Starfleet Command, P.O. Box 26076, Indianapolis, IN 46226.

Museums: Alabama Space & Rocket Center, Huntsville, AL; International Space Hall of Fame, The Space Center, Alamogordo, NM; Kennedy Space Center, Cape Canaveral, FL.

Additional Listings: Robots, Space Toys.

Space Adventurers

Apollo, Johnny, game, Johnny Apollo Moon Landing Game, Marx, 10" x 16" x 1", clear hard plastic, bagatelle marble game...........................25.00

Battlestar Galactica
    Activity Book, 8-1/4" x 10-3/4", Wonder Books, 1978 Universal City Studios Inc., color photo cover, 64 b&w pgs, unused...................8.00
    Pistol, Lasermatic, Mattel, MIB...............................50.00

Lost in Space
    Comic Album, 7-3/4" x 10-1/4", Space Family Robinson/Lost in Space, stiff cover comic album, English reprints of Western Publishing Co. full-color comic book stories, 1965 by World Distributors Ltd., 64 pgs 18.00

Rogers, Buck
    Badge, Solar Scout..................95.00
    Better Little Book, *Buck Rogers and the Doom Comet*, Whitman #1178, 1935, 432 pgs, hardcover 65.00
    Big Little Book
        Buck Rogers in the City Below the Sea, Whitman, 1934 ....60.00
        Buck Rogers/25th Century A.D., Whitman, 1938, Cocomalt premium 45.00

Gum card wrapper, Man on the Moon, A&B, Topps London affiliate, 1969, $10.

Book, *Bucks Rogers Collected Words of Comics,* hardcover....35.00
Colorforms Set, diecut vinyl figures, box, 1979 ....25.00
Crayon Box, 2" x 5", Buck Rogers Crayon Ship, cardboard, 6 colored pencils, c1930 ....165.00
Holster, 5" x 10", diecut, tan leather, incised inscription, Rogers holding gun, cloud design, Cream of Wheat premium, 1936 ....125.00
Lobby Card, "The Enemy Stronghold," Buster Crabbe, 1938....190.00
Lunch Box, 7" x 8" x 4", litho metal, 6-1/2" h plastic thermos 45.00
Manual, 5" x 7-1/2", Buck Rogers Solar Scouts, 16 pgs, Cream of Wheat premium, 1936............165.00
Matchcover, Popsicle adv 15.00
Paint Book, 11" x 14", 96 pgs, Whitman, 1935........................85.00
Pencil Case, 5" x 8-1/2" x 1/2", cardboard, yellow illus top and bottom, green background, brass snap fastener, American Lead Pencil Co., 1936.....................225.00
Rocket Ship, 4-1/2" l, Venus Duo-Destroyer, die-cast metal, yellow, red, trim, inscription on each side, orig box, 1937 ....150.00

Captain Video
    Decoder, 1-1/2" d, Capt Video Mysto-Coder, brass, plastic wheels, lightning-bolt design 165.00
    Gun, 2-1/2" x 3-1/2", Captain Video Secret Ray Gun, red plastic flashlight, secret message instructions, glow-in-the-dark card, Power House Candy premium........................85.00
    Magazine, *TV Star Parade*, 2-pg photo article, Ideal

Publishing Co., 1953...............20.00
Press Book, 12" x 18", black, white and blue cover, newspaper headline style...........................90.00
Rocket Ship, 4-1/2" l, plastic, metallic lavender, removable cannons, inscription on tail fin, Lido Toy Co., orig box, early 1950s........65.00

Gordon, Flash
    Bank, metal, rocket 35.00
    Better Little Book, *Flash Gordon and the Perils of Mongo*, Whitman, 1940............45.00
    Big Little Book, Whitman
        Flash Gordon and the Tournaments Of Mongo, 426 pgs, late 1930 ....35.00
        Flash Gordon in the Water World of Mongo, 424 pgs, 1937.....50.00
    Book, pop-up, *Tournament Of Death*, Blue Ribbon Press and Pleasure Books, 1935, 20 pgs 145.00
    Coloring Book, 8-1/2" x 11", Whitman, 1952.....................35.00
    Dixie Cup Lid, Buster Crabbe Starring in the Universal Chapter Play Flash Gordon 50.00
    Kite, 7" x 37", plastic, multicolored image, transparent ground, orig pkg, Roalex Co., c1950 ....40.00
    Membership Card, 3" x 4-1/4", Flash Gordon Movie Club, green, black scene and lettering, unused...600.00
    Pinback Button, 1-1/8" d, black, white and red, Flash Gordon Club, Chicago, Herald and Examiner 75.00
    Record, 6-1/2" d, City of Sea Caves, plastic on cardboard, 78 RPM, 1948........45.00
    Telescope, 9" l, Flash Gordon Planet Gazer, plastic, decal portrait, orig display card, unopened plastic bubble, 1970s 125.00
    Wallet, tan vinyl, color illus, zipper edge, unused, 1949 ....45.00
    Water Pistol, 7-1/2" l, blue plastic, whistle mouthpiece, inscribed "Flash Gordon Water Pistol," Marx, orig box, c1950 ....95.00

Space Cadet, Tom Corbett
    Book, *Tom Corbett Space Cadet/Sabotage In Space*, Grosset & Dunlap, hardcover, 212 pgs, dj 15.00
    Decoder, 2-1/2" x 4", Tom Corbett Space Cadet Code, black, white and red cardboard, membership card printed on back 45.00
    Flashlight, 7" l, Space Cadet Signal Siren Flashlight, full-color illus, orig box, c1952 ....65.00
    Lunch Box, 7" x 8" x 4", litho metal, full-color space scene, dark

blue galaxy background, 1954 Rockhill Radio 95.00

Membership Kit Fan Photo, 3-1/2" x 5-1/4", glossy b&w photo, Tom with Space Rangers, facsimile blue ink signature, c1952 ....28.00

Patch, 2" x 4", cloth, Space Cadet, red, yellow and blue, Kellogg's premium 35.00

Photo, 3-1/2" x 5-1/2", b&w glossy, blue signature "Spaceman's Luck/Tom Corbett/Space Cadet," early 1950s 45.00

School Bag, 11" x 14-1/2", plastic, Tom on center flap, rocket designs on side, red plastic handle 45.00

View-Master Reel, set of 3, orig story folder and envelope.................45.00

Wristwatch, orig band.............150.00

Space Patrol

Belt and Buckle, 4" brass buckle, rocket, decoder mounted on back, glow-in-the-dark belt, Ralston premium, early 1950s.............175.00

Coin Album, 3" x 7-3/4", thin cardboard black, white and blue folder, spaceship landing and men rushing toward it, diecut slots for plastic Ralston premium or Schwinn Bicycle dealer coins, c1953 ....175.00

Dart Gun, 9-1/2" l, plastic, red, designs on each side, U.S. Plastic Co., early 1950s 125.00

Flashlight, 12" l, silvered metal body, pointed rubber red top nose, decal inscription on fin Official Space Patrol Rocket Lite and Commander Buzz Corry, Ray-O-Vac Co., orig box, early 1950s 250.00

Handbook...............................165.00

Microscope, orig slides...........195.00

Paper Cup, pkg of 6, rocket ships, stars and planets motif, orig cellophane and company label........70.00

Premium Card, 2-1/2" x 3-1/2", full-color scene on front and back, text, adv for Wheat and Rice Chex Cereal, Rockets, Jets and Weapons Series, 7 cards from 40-card set, early 1950s.........135.00

Space Helmet, diecut cardboard, 6 sided, yellow, green, red design, black top with printed red lightning flashes................................1,230.00

Watch, silvered chrome, stainless steel back, black leather straps, "Space Patrol" inscription on dial, black numerals, U.S. Time, early 1950s.............................165.00

Star Trek

Activity Book, 8" x 11", Whitman, 1979 ....15.00

Bed Sheet, 38" x 785", cotton and polyester, red, blue, yellow, b&w illus,

light blue background, c1970 ...35.00

Book, *Star-Trek, Mission to Horatius*, Whitman TV Adventure Book, #1549, 1968, 210 pgs, 5" x 8" 20.00

Fast Food Meal Box, McDonald's, flattened, 9" x 10-3/4", colorful tin diecut cardboard, movie promotion, 1979 McDonald's Corp., unused

   The Bridge 20.00

   Klingon................................20.00

   Transporter 24.00

   United Federation 20.00

Halloween Costume, Tng-Frengi, Ben Cooper, 1987, orig box 50.00

Model, Star Trek USS *Enterprise*, 8-1/2" x 10" x 2-3/4" box, image of spaceship between planets, gray unassembled plastic pieces, folded b&w instruction sheet, AMT #6676, 1983 ....20.00

Mug, 3-3/4" h, white plastic, color illus, red inscription, 1975 ....15.00

Paint Set, 12" x 16" canvas portrait, Hasbro, 1974, partially used 60.00

Poster, Mr. Spock holding model of Enterprise, Personality Posters 24.00

Tablecloth, 54" x 88", blue, red, yellow, black and white design, white background, unopened plastic pkg, 1976 ....25.00

Trekkie Outfit, worn during filming of TV series, "Star Trek: The Next Generation" 820.00

Utility Belt, phaser, tricorder and communicator, Remco, 1975 ...45.00

Wallet, vinyl, silver, 1979, MOC..............................15.00

Star Wars

Card Set, 12 perforated 3-1/2" x 7-1/2" thin cardboard sheets, 3 color cards on each, Burger King premium, Lucasfilm Ltd., complete set of 36 cards, unpunched 15.00

Clock, alarm, talking.................30.00

Coloring Book, The Empire Strikes Back, 8" x 11", Kenner, 1982 Lucasfilm Ltd., color photo of Darth Vader and 2 Storm Troopers on front and back, 64 pgs, unused..........9.00

Cookie Jar, Darth Vader/C3P0, turn-about type, Sigma...........150.00

Figure

   AT-AT, MIB.........................90.00

   Jawa, vinyl cape, 1977 ...1,400.00

Game, Destroy Death Star, Kenner, 16" sq board, 1977..................35.00

Lunch Box with thermos, King Seeley, 1978 ....55.00

Model, 7" x 9-3/4" x 2", Return of the Jedi, B-Wing Fighter, box with image of fighter flying past planet, Lucasfilm 1983 MPC, unopened 25.00

Mug, 4" h, Return of the Jedi, plastic, white, 1983 ....40.00

Place Mat, 8-1/2" x 11", The Empire Strikes Back, paper, full color, Burger King, 1980.....................7.50

Poster

   15-1/2" x 24", Star Wars, sealed in orig shrink wrap, five 15" x 23" posters, 6 different containers of paint, 2 brushes, Kenner 1977 Universal City Studios, 5 different scenes, MIP.......................24.00

   17-1/2" x 22", 3D Darth Vader, sealed set, Craftmaster, 1978 20th Century Fox Film Corp., large b&w poster sheet to be colored, several illus scenes from film, plus large center Darth Vader image, separate thin diecut parts sheet for assembly of 3D Darth Vader mask that attaches to poster, smaller X-Wing and Tie Fighter attachments, MIP 24.00

Press Kit, first movie 70.00

Puppet, 8" h, Yoda, molded soft rubber, silver hair wisps, 1979 ......25.00

Record Storybook 15.00

Telephone, Darth Vader, figural, speakerphone 125.00

Toy

   Tie Fighter, orig box.............85.00

   X-Wing Fighter, orig box, 1977 ....90.00

Space Exploration

Ashtray, 5-1/2" sq, china, Apollo 11, mission insignia, mkd "Johnson Space Center/Houston, Texas" 30.00

Autograph, envelope, inked Jack Swigert signature on back, Man on Moon stamp, canceled Kennedy Space Center, April 11, 1970 ....50.00

Bank, 4-1/2" h, Freedom 7, plastic, silver, flight details listed on bottom, inscription on base, "Freedom 7 Capsule/Project Mercury/ Redstone Rocket" 45.00

Book

   First American Into Space, Robert Silverberg, Monarch Books, 142 pgs, 1961 ....20.00

   NASA Astronauts Biography Book, NASA, 1968, 8" x 10-1/4", soft-cover.............40.00

Clock, 4" x 4-1/2" x 2", Apollo 11, animated windup, ivory case, red, white and blue diecut, metallic blue dial, Apollo craft illus, gold-colored numerals, brass hands, mkd "Lux Clock Mfg Co." 145.00

Dish, 8" d, Apollo II Commemorative, irid glass, raised design, inscription "One Small Step," 1970s 18.00

Glass

Astronaut Neil Armstrong, 5-1/2" h, clear glass, brown and white graphics of Armstrong wearing suit, gold lettering "Wapakoneta Astronaut Neil Armstrong," list of 1961-1966 manned space flights on reverse 37.00

Columbia Space Shuttle, 4-1/2" h, clear, weighted bottom, b&w facsimile of New York Times, April 15, 1981, Wendy's 15.00

Gyroscope, Gemini, plastic, 1960s, MOC 30.00

Letter Opener, 7" l, Apollo 11, gold-colored metal, insignia on handle, grained black leather-like scabbard.................................30.00

Magazine

Life

1966, July 1, Moon Shot cover...................5.00

1969, July 25, leaving for Moon cover, article on Armstrong..10.00

1969, Aug. 8, on the Moon with flag cover, color photos........12.00

Look, 1960, Feb. 2, The Lady Wants to Orbit, cov article, 6 pgs, Betty Skelton article and photos........17.50

Newsweek

1969, Jan. 6, Apollo, Anders, Lovell, Borman cover 8.00

1969, July 28, Moon Walk cover, b&w...9.00

1969, Aug. 11, Moon Walk cover, color 9.00

Time

1962, March 2, John Glenn cover...................6.00

1962, Aug. 24, Russian Astronauts cover.....................5.00

1969, Jan. 3, U.S. Astronauts cover 5.00

Medal, 1-1/2" d, commemorative, SS, astronaut descending from landing module onto Moon, "One Small Step" inscription, plaque left on Moon on reverse, acrylic case................40.00

Mug, 3" h, china, black St. *Louis Globe-Democrat* newspaper design of July 20, 1969, Moon landing...........35.00

Pennant, 29" l, felt, red and white, blue trim, First Man on Moon...........20.00

Photo, 8" x 10", Apollo 16, NASA, 1972 liftoff and lunar view.................20.00

Pinback Button

1-1/4" d, New Frontier, Man of the Year, Astronaut John Glenn, blue and white 35.00

3" d, Challenger 7, b&w photo, purple background 15.00

3-1/2" d, Gemini 4, b&w photos of McDivitt and White, red, white and blue ground, June 3-7, 1965,

walk-in-space mission 35.00

Plate

7-1/2" d, Apollo 13, glass, brown and tan lunar landscape, white silhouette of astronaut on Moon surface, rim inscribed "General Electric" and "United States Atomic Energy Commission," back and white NASA symbol 40.00

9-1/4" d, John Glenn, white china, b&w illus, stylized gold pattern, Feb. 20, 1962 flight 25.00

Press Pass, 3" x 4-1/4", laminated, ABC News, June 18-24, 1983, Challenger Mission, b&w photos, blue, white and orange design...................60.00

Puzzle, Apollo 11, 1969, MIB........25.00

Record, "America's First Man in Orbit, John Glenn, 33-1/3 RPM, orig envelope......................................35.00

Rug, 19-1/2" x 37-1/2", woven, full-color Moon landing scene, red, white and blue stars and stripes motif border, made in Italy, orig label 60.00

Ruler, 6", Space Shuttle 3D Picture Ruler, blue, red and white, illus 4-1/2" x 7" card, diecut opening, 5 images of space shuttle in flight, Vari-Vue, Mt. Vernon, NY, unopened, orig display bag 8.00

Salt and Pepper Shakers, pr, 3" h, china, blue symbol and Columbia shuttle design, inscription "Johnson Space Center, Houston, TX," early 1980s.......20.00

Tie Clip, 1-1/2", Apollo 11, brass, black accents, raised Moon-landing design, landing date and astronaut names on rim, orig plastic display case............................40.00

Space Related

Bank mechanical, rocket ship, Astro Mfg., 1957 ....50.00

Bank, still, planets circling the sun, orig key and box 125.00

Birthday Card, 6" x 7", 1950s........20.00

Blotter, Bond Bread Rocket to the Moon, 3-1/2" x 6-1/2".................8.00

Book

First Book of Space Travel, 1853 ....25.00

Victory In Space, Otto O. Binder, 1963, 212 pgs, hardcover 20.00

Booklet, Western Electric, *The Space Age*, 32 pgs, 1960 ....4.00

Bubble Bath Set, Space Mates, Watkins, 1960s.........................40.00

Christmas Light, 3" h, figural, spaceman, white, red and brown accents, hands at side, not working, 70% complete paint, early 1950s 15.00

Cigarette Lighter, 6" l, rocket, silvered brass, 2" sq base, mkd "Made in Occupied Japan" 40.00

Coloring Book, Space Ghost, lab scene 60.00

Crayon Box, spaceship, stiff litho cardboard, enameled wood nose cone, diecut openings reveal multiplication tables.................35.00

Distance Wheel, 4-1/4" x 5-1/4", Swift's Space Travel Guide, thin diecut cardboard, color graphics of rocket ship going from Earth to Moon, planet, astronomical sign, temperature, distance from Earth and sun revolution time, c1958...........................14.00

Drink Shaker, 2-3/4" x 2-3/4" x 8-1/2" box, titled "Space Patrol," colorful graphics of kids mixing drinks and manned rocket ship, 2-1/2" d, 8" h, 2-pc translucent deep pink plastic shaker in shape of rocket ship, opaque vinyl straw, Steri-Lite United Plastics Corp., Fitzburg, MA, early 1950s 78.00

Game

Rocket Race to Saturn, Lido Toy, c1950, 9-1/2" x 13" board, 4 plastic rocket playing pcs 50.00

Space Age Math, 1974 ....20.00

Glass, Holder, Sputnik, Brussels World Far, 1958, price for set of four 275.00

Halloween Costume, Andromeda Lady Space Fighter, MIB 30.00

Nodder, 8" h, Space Traveler, 1950s spaceship 250.00

Figure, 3" h, bisque, spaceman 40.00

Pencil Case, Rocket Whiz, 1950s 35.00

Pin, 3" l, Up, Up & Away, rocket shape 15.00

Plaque, 36" x 24", carved, NASA commemorative.......................95.00

Pocket Knife, jet and rocket graphics, 1950s 25.00

Pulp Magazine, *Future Science Fiction*, 1950s 20.00

Rattle, Man in the Moon, winking, celluloid 160.00

Record, "Rocket to the Moon," set, 1950s..............................25.00

Thermos, 8" h

Orbit, lift off, in space and return to Earth images, c1960............65.00

Satellite Vehicle, metal, tan cup, 3 spacecraft over lunar surface, Earth in background, 1950s 40.00

Tin, 6" x 1-1/2", Variety Toffee, Riley Bros., England, boy astronauts point to stars and planets, 1950s 65.00

Space Toys

Collecting Hints: The original box is an important element in pricing, perhaps controlling 15% to 20% of the price. The artwork on the box may differ slightly from the toy inside; this is to be expected. The box also may provide the only clue to the correct name of the toy.

The early lithographed tin toys are more valuable than the later toys made of plastic. There is a great deal of speculation in modern toys, e.g., Star Wars material. Hence, the market shows great price fluctuation. Sales at Lloyd Ralston Toys, Fairfield, CT, are a good barometer of the auction market.

Collect toys in very good to mint condition. Damaged and rusted lithographed tin is hard to repair. Check the battery box for damage. Don't ever leave batteries in a toy when it is not in use.

History: The Hollywood movies of the early 1950s drew attention to space travel. The launching of Sputnik and American satellites in the late 1950s and early 1960s enhanced this fascination. The advent of manned space travel, culminating in the landing on the moon, further increased interest in anything space-related and the toy industries of Japan and America. Lithographed tin and plastic models of astronauts, flying saucers, spacecraft and space vehicles became quickly available. Some were copies of original counterparts; most were the figments of the toy designer's imagination.

During the 1970s, there was less emphasis on the space program and a corresponding decline in the production of space-related toys. The earlier Japanese- and American-made products gave way to less-expensive models from China and Taiwan.

Reference: Maxine A. Pinksy, *Marx Toys: Robots, Space, Comic, Disney & TV Characters*, Schiffer Publishing, 1996; Leslie Singer, *Zap! Ray Gun Classics*, Chronicle Books, 1991.

Periodical: *Robot World & Price Guide*, P.O. Box 184, Lenox Hill Station, New York, NY 10021.

Reproduction Alert.

Additional Listings: Robots, Space Adventurers and Explorers.

Capsule, Friendship 7, litho tin and plastic, red and silver, pilot moves around and handles controls, SH, Japanese, $65.

Astronaut
    7" h, Mark Apollo Astronaut-Movable Spaceman, white vinyl figure, jointed arms, legs and head, 5" x 8" x 2" black, white, blue and orange box, mkd "Marx," 1969 ....125.00
    7-1/2" h, litho tin, wearing space suit, carrying gun in right hand, arms swing as he walks, mkd "AN" 1,500.00
    8" h, litho tin, windup, Mechanical Interplanetary Explorer, mkd "AN, Japan," 1950s 400.00
    12" h, battery operated, NASA Astronaut, plastic, walks, rotating blades spin atop head, mkd "Marx" ...500.00
Bubblegum Card, Topps, 2-1/2" x 3-1/2"
    Return of the Jedi, full-color movie image, blue, yellow, red back, 1983, full set............................45.00
    Space, full-color graphics, cards #19, 20, 28, 37, 38, 44, 48, 49, 68, 79 from set of 88, c1957 ....25.00
Apollo Spacecraft, Japan, battery operated, MIB.......................250.00
Cap Gun
    Jet Jr. Space, chrome, MIB....425.00
    Strato Gun, chrome, mint.......465.00
Chalk, rocket ship illus, Creston....10.00
Colored Pencils, Dixon, space graphics 25.00
Eagle Lunar Module, Daishin, Japan, battery operated, 1969, MIB..............300.00
Figure
    Astronaut, 6" h, Marx, set of 6 different poses 100.00
    Space Alien, 11" l, suction cup walker 40.00
    Space Man, A-OK, 3-1/2" h, clear helmet, 1950s, MOC 10.00
    Space Woman, A-OK, 3-1/2" h, clear helmet, 1950s, MOC 10.00
Flying Saucer
    Atomic Jet, Flying-O-Saucer, 1950s, orig instructions 20.00

Jupiter, litho tin, clear dome, sparks, mkd "K, Japan" 45.00
King, tin, battery operated, MIB 140.00
Litho tin, friction powered, tin astronaut sitting behind steering wheel, 7" d, MIB......................55.00
Space Patrol X-16, 8" d, 5" h, metallic green, multicolored details, battery operated, mkd "Modern Toys, Japan"....................................125.00
Game, Black Hole Space Alert, Whitman, 1979 ....30.00
Helmet, Space Patrol, cardboard, 1950s....................................220.00
Helmet and Walkie-Talkie Playset, Johnny Seven OMA 135.00
Jet Car, litho tin, friction powered, 7" l, MIB.....................................60.00
Mobile Space TV Unit, 10-1/2" l, litho tin, battery operated, space tank with trailer, astronaut sitting on top operates TV camera, lights up and shows lunar landscape, mkd "TN, Japan," MIB........................2,500.00
Moon Explorer, 4-1/2" x 8" x 7-1/2", tin and plastic, remote control, NASA symbols, 8-1/2" l rocket shaped blue box, mkd "Yone, Japan" 400.00
Moon Globe Orbitor, Japan, MIB 225.00
Passenger Space Rocket, friction powered, blue, MIB 55.00
Pinball Game, Bagatelle Space Travel, 1950s, sealed 40.00
Pistol, 5" l, Atomic, Newalls, red plastic, 1950s 65.00
Play Money, Spaceman, sealed in orig pkg, 1960s............................25.00
Playset, Apollo Exploration 75.00
Postcard Book, Close Encounters....................25.00
Project Yankee Doodles, some pcs missing, good condition box..125.00
Ray Gun
    Laser, plastic,

Battlestar Galactica game, Parker Brothers, 1978, Universal City Studios, Inc., $10.

Tim-Me, 10" l, sealed 55.00
Popper, 1950s.........................30.00
Sparkler, Japan,
mint in orig bag........................50.00
Rocket
Apollo/Saturn V, desk model,
14" h, plastic.............................35.00
Battery operated, automatic docking
and separating actions, orig
antenna, 17" l, Daiya, MIB 285.00
Friction, 8" h, 1950s 50.00
Moon Rocket, 9" l, battery operated,
litho tin, bump-and-go action, outside
revolving astronaut, flashing colored
lights, mkd "MT. Japan"..........140.00
Sand Crawler, Dune 50.00
Satellite Rocker, Rarles, water
powered, 1950s........................35.00
Space Capsule, Friendship 7
Blow-Up, Purolator advertising,
1960s 45.00
Tin, rotating astronaut, friction
powered 210.00
Space Capsule and Parachute,
Apollo, 10" l, 1960s...................20.00
Space Copter, 2 spin-off copters, plastic,
die cast, Japan, 1970s, MIB 45.00
Space Dog
6" l, litho tin, windup, runs,
wiggles ears, moves mouth and
eyes, mkd "KO Japan" 395.00
10-1/2" l, Astro Dog, black and white,
standing, bubble dome helmet, holding briefcase and American flag,
walks, wags tail and barks,
Yonezawa Toys, MIB 750.00
Space Gun
Electronic,
mkd "Remco," MIB 50.00
Friction powered, MIB 40.00
Space Rocket Missile Launcher, 1960s,
sealed in box 20.00
Space Scooter, 8" l, battery
operated, litho tin and plastic,
bump-and-go action, headlight,
engine noise, boy astronaut steers,
mkd "MT, Japan" 200.00
Spaceship
Burger Blaster,
Heinz Catsup, MIB 125.00
X-7, battery operated, 8" d,
Modern Toys, MIB..................195.00
Space Station, Pilgra Observer, MIB,
sealed 25.00
Space Tank, tin, battery operated,
9" l, Gama, MIB 225.00
Spinner, 3" d,
Space Patrol, 1950s 20.00
Tank
Robo Tank Z, 10-1/2" l,
battery operated, litho tin,
half robot, half tank, bump-and-
go action, flashing dome light,

noise, mkd "TN, Japan"..........500.00
Space Explorer Bump 'n' Go Vehicle
X-8, multicolored litho tin, crank,
6" l, KO, Japan 300.00
Space Patrol, 8-1/2" l,
battery operated, litho tin,
flashing light, cockpit opens and
closes, Yonezawa, MIB 250.00
Space Tank, 6" l, battery operated, litho
tin, bump-and-go action, antennae,
mkd "SH, Japan" 300.00
Top Flite Junior Rocket Booster, 30-1/2"
h, 1-1/2" d heavy cardboard, silver,
blue and red foil covering, black
plastic top, upper 5-1/2" is
removable, Top Flite Models, Inc.,
Chicago, IL, early 1960s..........65.00
Universe Car, litho tin,
China, MIB............................125.00
Voice Control Astronaut Base,
Remco, MIB...........................180.00
Zeriod Command
Action Set, Ideal, MIB............200.00
Zoom Outer Space
Projector, unused 28.00

Sports Collectibles

Collecting Hints: The amount of material is unlimited. Pick a favorite sport and concentrate on it. Within the sport, narrow collecting emphasis to items associated with one league, team, individual or era or concentrate on one type of equipment. Include as much three-dimensional material as possible.

Each sport has a hall of fame. Make a point to visit it and get to know its staff, an excellent source of leads for material that the museum no longer wants in its collection. Induction ceremonies provide an excellent opportunity to make contact with heroes of the sport, as well as with other collectors.

History: Individuals have been saving sports-related equipment since the inception of sports. Some material was passed down from generation to generation for reuse. The balance occupied dark spaces in closets, attics and basements.

In the 1980s, two key trends brought collectors' attention to the sports arena. First, decorators began using old sports items, especially in restaurant decor. Second, card collectors began to discover the thrill of owing the "real" thing. Although

Tennis, inkwell, bronze, figural player, porcelain well, 7-1/4" x 4-1/2" x 5-1/2", $280.

the principal thrust was on baseball memorabilia, by the beginning of the 1990s, all sport categories were collectible, with automobile racing, boxing, football and horse racing especially strong.

References: Mark Allen Baker, *All Sport Autograph Guide*, Krause Publications, 1994; James Beckett, *Official Price Guide to Basketball Cards*, 6th Edition, House of Collectibles, 1996; ——, *Official Price Guide to Football Cards*, 16th Edition, House of Collectibles, 1996; ——, *Official Price Guide to Hockey Cards*, 6th Edition, House of Collectibles, 1996; David Bushing, *Sports Equipment Price Guide*, Krause Publications, 1995; *Charlton Standard Catalogue of Canadian Baseball & Football Cards*, Charlton Press, 1996; *Charlton Standard Catalogue of Hockey Cards*, 7th Edition, Charlton Press, 1996; Jeanne Cherry, *Tennis Antiques & Collectibles*, Amaryllis Press (Box 3658, Santa Monica, CA 90408), 1996; Duncan Chilcott, *Miller's Soccer Memorabilia*, Millers Publications, 1994; Ralf Coykendall Jr., *Coykendall's Complete Guide to Sporting Collectibles*, Wallace-Homestead, 1996; Roderick A. Malloy, *Malloy's Guide to Sports Cards Values*, Wallace-Homestead, 1995; ——, *Malloy's Sports Collectibles Value Guide*, Wallace-Homestead, 1994; Michael McKeever, *Collecting Sports Memorabilia*, Alliance Publishing, 1996; *Standard Catalog of Football, Basketball & Hockey Cards*, 2nd edition, Krause Publications, 1996.

Periodicals: *Boxing Collectors Newsletter*, 59 Bosson St., Revere, MA 02151; *Olympic Collectors Newsletter*, P.O. Box 41630, Tucson, AZ 85717; *Sports Collectors Digest*, 700 E. State St., Iola, WI 54990.

Additional Listings: Baseball Collectibles, Golf Collectibles, Racing Collectibles.

Boating

Catalog, Thompson Bros. Outboard Motor Boats, Canoes, Motor Boats, 1929, 32 pgs, 8" x 10-3/4" 25.00
Magazine, *Sports Illustrated*, Sept. 6, 1954, sailing 17.50
Pinback Button
1-3/4" d, Devil's Lake Regatta, blue and white, speedboat races, July, 1934 ....15.00
2-1/8" d, Outboard Regatta, black lettering, tan ground, 1930s 15.00

Bowling

Game, Bowling: A Board Game, Parker Bros., orig box, 1896 ....60.00
Magazine, *Sports Illustrated*, March 28, 1955, Steve Nagy 10.00
Nodder, 6" h, "You're Right Down My Alley," composition, man holding bowling ball, mounted on woodblock base 50.00
Pencil Sharpener, 1-1/4" x 1-3/4" x 2", green hard plastic, portable-TV shape, full-color flicker as screen, Kohner Products, c1950 ....25.00
Pinback Button
American Bowling Congress, 1932, 32nd Annual Tournament, Detroit, silver-dollar size, red, blue and blue, large luxury car in center..........80.00
Dallas Turnverein Bowling Club, "There's No Use Crying Baby Houston, You Can't Have This Cup," blue, white and black, 1901-10 ....40.00

Hockey

Autograph, photograph
Harold Ballard 90.00
Phil Esposito 15.00
Moose Goheen........................100.00
Claude Lemieux 25.00
Mario Lemieux...........................45.00
Eric Lenders.............................45.00
Harry Oliver..............................100.00
Henry Richard 15.00
Jersey, game used
Alain Cote, Montreal Canadiens, home, white, 1990..................400.00
Wayne Gretzky, Rangers, autographed...........................415.00
Pittsburgh Penguins, 1996, auto-graphed, 24 signatures 300.00
Silvain Turgeon, Montreal Canadians, home, white, 1990..........400.00
Magazine, *Sport Revue*, Quebec publication, Feb. 1956, Bert Olmstead, Hall of Fame cover 15.00
Program
1937-38 Boston Bruins, Sports News, each player sgd by picture........................250.00
1967, Montreal Canadians vs. Rangers, action shot cover 20.00
1969
Jan., Rangers vs. Red Wings, action shot cover..................12.00
Nov., Boston vs. Blues, Phil Esposito cover 12.00
1982, Jan., Edmonton Oilers vs. Colorado 8.00
Stick, game used
Jason Arnott, Easton................95.00
Peter Bondra, Sherwood, autographed.............................90.00
John Cullen, Easton..................35.00
Glenn Healy, Cooper, goalie....75.00
Dimitri Khristivch, Victoriaville..............................75.00
Mario Lemieux, black Koho Revolution stick, stamped "Lemieux" on side 350.00
Eric Lindros, Bauer Supreme......................295.00
Mike Richter, Stanley Cup championship, 1994-95..........350.00
Sergei Zubov, Easton 75.00
Yearbook, Hall of Fame
1971-72, 84 pages 40.00
1978, 100 page 35.00

Marbles, cabinet photo, 4-1/4" x 6-1/2", sepia tone, blond-haired young boy in dress suit and necktie, aiming shooter marble at 5 others, reverse with pencil inscription "Landon's boy," photographer Landon, Allentown, PA, late 1800s 95.00

Pan Am Games, pin, Penthalon.....3.00
Skating, autograph, Katarina Witt, photograph 40.00

Tennis

Autograph
Andre Agassi, photograph 40.00
John McEnroe...........................40.00
Martina Navratilova 40.00
Fred Perry, canceled check 50.00
Gabriella Sabatina 40.00
Magazine
Life, Nov, 1971 ....7.50
Sports Illustrated, July 15, 1974, Jimmy Connors and Chris Evert....10.00
Pinback Button, 2-1/8", U.S. Open Tennis Championship, 1975 ....15.00
Poster, Play Helps Study, colorful tennis motif, 1924 ....30.00
Program, United States Lawn Tennis Championships, 9" x 12", official souvenir program, men's singles, women's singles, mixed doubles, Sept. 1947, West Side Tennis Club, Forest Hills, NY, 56 pgs, photos and player profiles, adv 40.00
Tennis Racket, 27" l, Maureen Connolly, full-color portrait on handle, Wilson Sporting Goods, 1950s 20.00

Wrestling, magazine, 8-1/2" x 11", Vol. 1, #4, May 1951, full-color action photo featuring Gene Stanlee, 52 pgs, articles, photos 30.00

Stangl Pottery

Collecting Hints: Stangl Pottery produced several lines of highly collectible dinnerware and decorative accessories, including the famed Stangl birds. The red-bodied dinnerware was produced in distinctive shapes and patterns. Shapes were designated by numbers. Pattern names include Country Garden, Fruit, Tulip, Thistle and Wild Rose. Special Christmas, advertising and commemorative wares also were produced.

Bright colors and bold simplistic patterns make Stangl pottery a favorite with Country collectors. Stangl sold seconds from a factory store long before outlet malls became popular. Large sets of Stangl dinnerware currently command high prices at auctions, flea markets and even antiques shops.

As many as 10 different trademarks were used. Dinnerware was marked and often signed by the decorator. Most birds are numbered; many are artist-signed. However, signatures are useful for dating purposes only and add little to value.

Several of the well-known Stangl birds were reissued between 1972 and 1977. These reissues are dated on the bottom and are worth approximately half as much as the older birds.

History: The origins of Fulper Pottery, the predecessor to Stangl, are clouded. The company claimed a date of 1805. Paul Evans, a major American art pottery researcher, suggests an 1814 date. Regardless of which date is correct, by the middle of the 19th century an active pottery was located in Flemington, NJ. When Samuel Hill, the pottery's founder, died in 1858, the pottery was acquired by Abraham Fulper, a nephew. Abraham died in 1881 and the business continued under the direction of his sons, Edward, George W. and William.

In 1910, Johann Martin Stangl began working at Fulper as a chemist and plant superintendent. He left Fulper in 1914 to work briefly for Haeger Potteries. By 1920, Stangl was back at Fulper serving as general manager. In 1926, Fulper acquired the Anchor Pottery in Trenton, NJ, where a line of solid-color dinnerware in the California patio style was produced. William Fulper died in 1928, at which time Stangl became president of the firm. In 1920, Johann Martin Stangl purchased Fulper and Stangl Pottery was born. During the 1920s, production emphasis shifted from art pottery to dinner and utilitarian wares. A 1929 fire destroyed the Flemington pottery. Rather than rebuild, a former ice cream factory was converted to a showroom and production facility. By the end of the 1930s, production was concentrated in Trenton with the Flemington kiln used primarily for demonstration purposes.

Stangl's ceramic birds were produced from 1940 until 1972. The birds were made in Stangl's Trenton plant, then shipped to the Flemington plant for hand painting. During World War II, the demand for these birds and Stangl pottery was so great that 40 to 60 decorators could not keep up with it. Orders were contracted out to private homes. These pieces were then returned for firing and finishing. Different artists used different colors to decorate these birds.

On Aug. 25, 1965, fire struck the Trenton plant. The damaged portion of the plant was rebuilt by May 1966. On Feb. 13, 1972, Johann Martin Stangl died. Frank Wheaton Jr., of Wheaton Industries, Millville, NJ, purchased the plant in June 1972 and continued Stangl production. In 1978, the Pfaltzgraff Co., purchased the company's assets from Wheaton. Production ceased. The Flemington factory became a Pfaltzgraff factory outlet. One of the original kilns remains intact to commemorate the hard work and to

Thistle plate, 9-1/8", cream ground, mkd "Stangl Pottery, Trenton, N.J.," $12.

demonstrate the high temperatures involved in the production of pottery.

References: Susan and Al Bagdade, *Warman's American Pottery and Porcelain*, Wallace-Homestead, 1994; Harvey Duke, *Stangl Pottery*, Wallace-Homestead, 1993; Mike Schneider, Stan*gl and Pennsbury Pottery Birds*, Schiffer Publishing, 1994.

Collectors' Club: Stangl/Fulper Collectors Club, P.O. Box 538, Flemington, NF 08822.

Additional Listings: See *Warman's Antiques and Collectibles Price Guide* for prices of bird figurines.

Amber Glo, platter, 13" l 15.00
Brittany, plate, 10-1/2" d 125.00
Blue Rooster
    Coffeepot 85.00
    Creamer 25.00
    Platter, 14" l 36.00
    Salt and Pepper Shakers, pr 16.00
    Vegetable Dish,
      divided, handle 48.00
Country Garden
    Butter Dish 40.00
    Cake Stand 30.00
    Casserole, 8" d 50.00
    Creamer, individual size...........15.00
    Cup and Saucer 17.50
    Eggcup 15.00
    Gravy Boat 20.00
    Plate
      7" d 9.00
      11" d 36.00
    Server, center handle...............12.00
Daisy, #1870, 1935
    Candleholders, pr, blue...........55.00
    Creamer and Sugar, green 24.00
    Cup and Saucer, green...........20.00

Plate
    6" d, bread and butter, blue ...9.00
    8" d, salad, red.....................12.00
    10" d dinner, yellow 24.00
    Salad Bowl, red........................30.00
    Vegetable Bowl, oval, blue 27.50
Fruit
    Salad Bowl 75.00
    Server, center handle 12.00
Garden Flowers, plate, 12" d 20.00
Golden Blossom,
    creamer and sugar 25.00
Golden Grapes
    Bowl, 11-1/2" d........................15.00
    Server, center handle 9.00
Goldfinch, cigarette box 80.00
Granada, candy,
    2 part, gold, 1800D.................22.00
Harvest
    Carafe, wood handle...............60.00
    Chop Plate, 14" d 40.00
    Cup and Saucer.......................20.00
    Fruit Dish, 6" d 12.00
    Plate
      7" d, salad...........................12.00
      9" d, luncheon.....................17.50
      10" d, dinner 24.00
    Teapot, cov 75.00
    Vegetable Bowl, oval 36.00
Kiddieware
    Bowl, ABC...............................95.00
    Child's Feeding Dish, 3
    compartments
      Kittens...............................125.00
      Our Barnyard Friends 100.00
    Cup
      ABC 40.00
      Ginger Cat 180.00
      Indian Campfire 100.00
      Little Boy Blue.....................40.00
    Plate
      Circus Clown, pink...............80.00
      Fairy, pink 145.00
      Little Quackers,
        whiteware 110.00
      Peter Rabbit.......................145.00
    Plate and Cup
      Little Bo Peep, pink...........175.00
      Little Quackers...................175.00
Lyric, server, center handle...........11.00
Magnolia
    Coffeepot, individual size.........40.00
    Creamer and Sugar 45.00
    Cup 5.00
    Fruit Bowl 9.00
    Plate
      Bread and butter 6.00
      Dinner 12.00
    Salt and Pepper Shakers, pr....22.50
    Saucer 3.50

Vegetable, round

  8" d.....................................24.00

  10" d....................................28.00

Miscellaneous

  Ashtray

    Flying Duck 45.00

    Pink Elephant......................265.00

  Candy Dish, 2 part, handle,
  gray and green 14.00

  Canister, Milk Pail,
  butterscotch...........................110.00

  Clock, Dogwood 65.00

  Coffee Warmer, chartreuse......15.00

  Vase, 4" h, matte green,
  tulip shape.................................12.00

Morning Glory, plate, 15" d...........27.00

Orchard Song

  Mug..25.00

  Plate, 8" d..................................6.00

  Server, center handle...............12.00

Pheasant, cigarette box, cov.........85.00

Sculptured Fruit, snack set, 10" d plate
  with indent, cup.........................12.00

Terra Rose

  Ashtray, #3242 ....37.50

  Butter Dish, cov........................20.00

  Cake Stand 20.00

  Casserole, 6" d..........................15.00

  Cereal Bowl, 5-1/2" d 12.00

  Gravy and Liner.........................20.00

  Plate

    8" d, salad 10.00

    9" d, luncheon 12.00

    10" d, dinner..........................14.00

  Salt and Pepper Shakers, pr.....15.00

  Server, center handle, green
  speckled 24.00

Thistle

  Coffeepot, cov 25.00

  Cup and Saucer 12.00

  Eggcup......................................15.00

  Fruit Dish...................................12.00

  Gravy Boat 20.00

  Pitcher.......................................35.00

  Plate

    6" d, bread and butter 7.50

    10" d, dinner..........................17.50

    Platter, oval 40.00

Town and Country

  Bowl, brown

    7-3/4" d 50.00

    10" d......................................50.00

  Butter Dish, cov, brown............60.00

  Candlesticks, pr,
  7-1/2" h, brown.........................50.00

  Coffeepot, yellow......................85.00

  Creamer, brown 20.00

  Cup and Saucer, brown 20.00

  Flowerpot, 4-3/4" d, brown.......25.00

  Jell-O Mold, brown 35.00

Mug, blue 20.00

Plate, brown

  Bread and Butter....................8.00

  Dinner, 10-1/2" d.................18.00

  Salad, 8-1/2" d 12.00

Platter, 11-1/2" l, oval, brown...60.00

Salt and Pepper Shakers,
pr, brown 18.00

Spoon Rest, brown 25.00

Sugar, cov, brown...................35.00

Tumbler, 3-3/4" h,
8 oz, brown 25.00

Wash Pitcher and Basin,
blue 150.00

Water Lily, box, cov.......................65.00

Stereo Viewers

Collecting Hints: Condition is the key to determining price. Undamaged wooden-hood models are scarce and demand a premium price if made of bird's-eye maple. The presence of all-original parts increases the value. Plentiful engraving adds 20 to 30%.

Longer lenses are better than smaller ones. Lenses held in place by metal are better than those shimmed with wood. Because aluminum was the same price as silver in the late 19th century, aluminum viewers often are the more collectible.

History: There are many different types of stereo viewers. The familiar table viewer with an aluminum or wooden hood was jointly invented in 1860 by Oliver Wendell Holmes and Joseph Bates, a Boston photographer. This type of viewer also was made in a much scarcer pedestal model. Three companies—Keystone, Griffith & Griffith and Underwood & Underwood—produced hundreds of thousands of hand viewers between 1899 and 1905.

In the mid-1850s a combination stereo viewer and picture magnifier was developed in France and eventually was made in England and the United States. The instrument, which was called a Graphascope, usually consisted of three pieces and could be folded for storage. When set up, it had two round lenses for stereo viewing, a large round magnifying lens to view cabinet photographs and a slide, often with opaque glass, for viewing stereo glass slides. The height was adjust-

Hand-held viewer, $65; price varies for cards.

able. A rotary or cabinet viewer was made from the late 1850s to about 1870. Becker is the best-known maker. The standing floor models hold several hundred slides; the table models hold 50 to 100.

From the late 1860s to 1880s, there were hundreds of different viewer designs. Models had folding wires, collapsible cases (Cortascope), pivoting lenses to view postcards (Sears' Graphascope) and telescoping card holders. The cases, which also became ornate, were made of silver, nickel or pearl and were trimmed in velvets and rosewood.

Reference: John Waldsmith, *Stereo Views*, Wallace-Homestead, 1991.

Collectors' Clubs: National Stereoscopic Association, P.O. Box 14801, Columbus, OH 43214; Stereo Club of Southern California, P.O. Box 2368, Culver City, CA 90231.

Corte-Scope, folding
  aluminum or metal, came
  in box with views, c1914 ....50.00

Hand, common maker

  Aluminum hood,
  folding handle 65.00

  Bird's-eye maple hood,
  folding handle 85.00

  Walnut, screw-on handle,
  velvet hood 85.00

  Wide hood for people who
  wear glasses, dark brown
  or green metal.........................80.00

Hand, scissor device to
  focus, groove and wire
  device to hold card 120.00

Pedestal

  Foreign, French or English, nickel
  plated with velvet hood 300.00

  Keystone, school and
  library type, black
  crinkle-metal finish with light 85.00

Sculptoscope, Whiting, counter-top style, penny operated 500.00

Stand, Bates-Holmes, paper or wood hood 150.00

Stereographascope, Sears Best, lens rotates to allow viewing of photos or postcards 90.00

Telebinocular, binocular style, black crinkle-metal finish, excellent optics, came with book-style box 50.00

Stock and Bond Certificates

Collecting Hints: Some of the factors that affect price are: *date* (with pre-1900 more popular and pre-1850 most desirable), *autographs of important persons* (Vanderbilt, Rockefeller, J.P. Morgan, Wells and Fargo, etc.), *number issued* (most bonds have the number issued noted in text) and *attractiveness of the vignette.*

Stocks and bonds are often collected for the appeal of their graphics or as a record of events or people which have impacted American history, such as gold and silver mining, railroad development and early automobile pioneers.

History: The use of stock to raise capital and spread the risk in a business venture began in England. Several American colonies were founded as joint-venture stock companies. The New York Stock Exchange on Wall Street in New York City traces its roots to the late 18th century.

Stock certificates with attractive vignettes date to the beginning of the 19th century. As engraving and printing techniques developed, so did the elaborateness of the stock and bond certificates. Important engraving houses which emerged include the American Bank Note Co., and Rawdon, Wright & Hatch.

References: Norman E. Martinus and Harry L. Rinker, *Warman's Paper*, Wallace-Homestead, 1994; Gene Utz, *Collecting Paper*, Books

Chenango Canal, Rawdon, Wright, Hatch & Co., NY, engravers, 1837, 9-3/4" x 7-1/8", $90.

Americana, 1993; Bill Yatchman, *Stock & Bond Collectors Price Guide*, published by author, 1985.

Periodical: *Bank Note Reporter*, 700 E. State St., Iola, WI 54990.

Collectors' Club: Bond and Share Society, 26 Broadway, New York, NY 10004.

Airline, stock, Hornell Airways Inc., issued and canceled, NY, 2 women and sun rising over mountains vignette, 1920s............................65.00

Automobile, stock
 Cole Motor Car, 1909-25, man with woman feeding flame vignette
  Green, not sgd and sealed ..25.00
  Orange, sgd, corporate seal 35.00
 Kelly-Springfield Motor Truck Co., issued and canceled, 1910-20, seated woman, anvil and gears vignette, green or purple, American Bank Note Co. 35.00
 Willys Corp., issued, 1921
  Brown..................................15.00
  Orange...............................15.00

Business, Stock
 American Express Co., issued and canceled, 1860s, bulldog vignette, sgd "Henry Wells" and "William Fargo" 750.00
 Broadway Joe's, issued and canceled, green or blue border, sports figure's restaurant 10.00
 F.W. Woolworth Co., eagle over 2 hemispheres vignette, brown 4.00
 General Foods, issued and canceled, green, brown or orange, engraved, vignette scene on right...............2.50
 International Business Machines Corp., issued, brown 5.00
 International Immigration & Colonization Association, HI, 1911, issued, not canceled, map vignette 100.00
 Uncas National Bank of

Norwich, 1900, green, gray and white, Indian, blacksmith and sailing ship vignette 15.00
 Wells Fargo Bank & Union Trust, 1940s, issued and canceled, green pony express ride vignette.......25.00

Canal, bond, Pennsylvania Canal Co. issued and canceled, 1870, canal and surrounding area vignette, 2 revenue stamps..................125.00

Industrial, stock
 Colorado Milling & Elevator Co., issued and canceled, gold border, company buildings vignette
  1890s...................................25.00
  1920s...................................15.00
 Edison Portland Cement Co., issued and canceled, engraved, rust or green, Thomas Edison vignette
  1890s.....................................28.00
  1900s.....................................35.00
 Gray Manufacturing Co., issued and canceled, orange, dial pay telephone vignette 15.00
 Jantzen Knitting Mills, 1930s, issued and canceled, engraved, swimmer vignette, orange or green.........20.00
 Sentinel Radio Corp., issued and canceled, green or brown, goddess and 2 radio towers vignette........5.00
 Waikea Mill Co., unissued, 1889, black and white sugar mill........45.00

Mining
 Bond, Sovereign Gold Mining, issued and canceled, $5,000, Canadian, 1903, peach borders, coupon 10.00
 Stock
  Industry Gold & Silver Mining, 1870s, unissued, fancy design, mining vignette 20.00
  Isabella, Gold Mining Co., CO, 1890s, issued and canceled, engraved, eagle vignette 8.00
  Sheba Gold & Silver Mining, Humboldt County, NV, issued, not canceled, 3 mining vignettes, gold seal 20.00
  Sun-Hope Mining Co., CO, unissued, 3 mining vignettes........2.50
  Syndicate Mines, Inc., NV, unissued, brown, mining vignette, V-cut cancel...........................3.50

Railroad
 Bond
  Cairo & Norfolk RR Co., KY, 1908, issued, not canceled, orange, speeding train vignette, coupons 45.00
  New York, New Haven & Hartford, 1920, $10,000, issued and canceled, engraved, electric train vignette 48.00

Sacramento & Woodland RR, CA, 1911, issued, not canceled, rust-brown, logo around capitol building vignette, coupons 165.00
Union Pacific RR, 1946, $1,000, issued and canceled, 2 engraved angels and company logo 15.00

Stock

Cambridge Railroad Co., MA, 1880s, unissued, b&w.............8.00
Gulf, Mobile & Ohio, issued and canceled, engraved, blue or brown, 2 women and diesel train vignette 3.50
Illinois, Central, issued and canceled, engraved, orange or brown, diesel train vignette 3.50
Nashville & Decatur, 1880s, issued and canceled, green border, train vignette 25.00
Raleigh & Gaston, 1870s, issued and canceled, 2 vignettes 65.00

Railways (Trolley)

Bond

Chicago & Wisconsin Valley Street Railways Co., 1912, $1,000, issued and canceled, first mortgage gold, b&w 25.00
New Paltz, & Highland Electric RR, 1893, $500, issued and canceled, trolley car vignettes, gold seal, 2 pages of coupons.................95.00
Southern Indiana, 1908, $1,000, issued and canceled, green 28.00

Stock

California Street Cable RR Co., San Francisco, CA, 1884, unissued, cable car vignette 35.00
Omaha & Council Bluffs Street Railway, 1906, issued and canceled, blue, green or pink.....20.00
Rochelle & Southern, IL, 1900, unissued, b&w......................12.00
Rock Island & Eastern, IL, 1900, b&w, curved company name 15.00

Utility

Bond

Columbus & Southern Ohio electric Co., issued and canceled, blue, engraved 7.50
Consolidated Edison Co., NY, $1,000, issued and canceled, engraved, blue or purple........8.00
Long Island Lighting Co., issued and canceled, orange, engraved, woman, child, generator and light vignette ...7.50

Stock

Communications, Satellite Corp., 1960s, issued and canceled, green or blue, space vignette........................4.00
International Telephone & Telegraph, 1930s, blue, engraved, goddess and globe vignette ...8.00
Maryland Telecommunications, issued and canceled, green, drawn 1957 TV and TV camera vignette 8.00
Philippine Long Distance Telephone Co., 1950s, issued and canceled, blue, engraved, woman on 2 globes vignette..............5.00
Tuolumne County Water Co., 1850s, issued and canceled, mining methods vignette......75.00

Stuffed Toys

Collecting Hints: Collectors tend to focus on one type of animal and to collect material spanning a long time period. The company with the strongest collector following is Steiff. Collectors are mainly interested in items in very good to mint condition. Often stuffed toys had ribbons or clothing. All accessories must be intact for the toy to command full value.

History: The stuffed toy may have originated in Germany. Margarete Steiff GmbH of Germany began making stuffed toys for export beginning in 1880. By 1903, the Teddy Bear had joined Steiff's line and quickly worked its way to America. The first American Teddy Bears were made by the Ideal Toy Corp. Not much is known about earlier manufacturers since companies were short-lived and many toys have lost their labels.

The stuffed toy has always been an American favorite. Some have music boxes inserted to enhance their appeal. Carnivals used stuffed toys as prizes. Since the 1960s, an onslaught of stuffed toys have been imported to America from Japan, Taiwan and China. These animals often are poorly made and are not popular among serious collectors.

References: Dottie Ayers and Donna Harrison, *Advertising Art of Steiff*, Hobby House Press, 1990; Kim Brewer and Carol-Lynn Rössel Waugh, *Official Price Guide to Antique & Modern Teddy Bears*, House of Collectibles, 1990; Pauline Cockrill, *Teddy Bear Encyclopedia*, Dorling Kindersley, 1993; Margaret and

Steiff, cat, standing, blue ribbon, glass eyes, pink nose, paw marks, 7" l, 5-3/4" h, $65.

Gerry Grey, *Teddy Bears*, Courage Books, 1994; Pam Hebbs, *Collecting Teddy Bears*, Pincushion Press, 1992; Dee Hockenberry, B*ear Memorabilia*, Hobby House Press, 1992; ——, *Big Bear Book*, Schiffer Publishing, 1996; ——, *Enchanting Friends: Collectible Poohs, Raggedies, Golliwogs & Roosevelt Bears*, Schiffer Publishing, 1995; Margaret Fox Mandel, *Teddy Bears and Steiff Animals*, 1st Series (1984, 1993 value update), 2nd Series (1987, 1992 value update), 3rd Series (1990), Collector Books; Terry and Doris Michaud, *Contemporary Teddy Bear Price Guide*, Hobby House Press, 1992; Linda Mullins, *American Teddy Bear Encyclopedia*, Hobby House Press, 1995; Linda Mullins, *4th Teddy Bear and Friends Price Guide*, Hobby House Press, 1993; ——, *Teddy Bears Past & Present*, Vol. II, Hobby House Press, 1992; Sue Pearson and Dottie Ayers, *Teddy Bears: A Complete Guide to History, Collecting and Care*, McMillan, 1995; Christel and Rolf Pistorius, *Steiff*, Hobby House Press, 1991; Cynthia Powell, *Collector's Guide to Miniature Teddy Bears*, Collector Books, 1994; Gustav Severin, *Teddy Bear*, Running Press, 1995; Carol J. Smith, *Identification & Price Guide to Winnie the Pooh Collectibles*, Hobby House Press, 1994.

Periodicals: *National Doll & Teddy Bear Collector*, P.O. Box 4032, Portland, OR 97208; *Teddy Bear and Friends*, 6405 Flank Dr., Harrisburg, PA 17112; *Teddy Bear Review*, 170 Fifth Ave., New York, NY 10010.

Collectors' Clubs: Collectors Club for Classic Winnie the Pooh, 468 W. Alpine #10, Upland, CA 91786; Good Bears of the World, P.O. Box 13097, Toledo, OH 43613; Steiff Collectors Club, P.O. Box 798, Holland, OH 43528; Teddy Bear Boosters Club, 19750 SW Peavine Mountain Rd., McMinnville, OR 97128.

Alligator, 9-1/2" l, vinyl, green and brown, glass eyes, c1950 ....35.00
Beaver, mohair, brown, Steiff 45.00
Boa Constrictor, plush, multicolored, felt eyes and tongue, c1958 ....12.00
Camel
   4-1/2" h, leather, tan, single hump, straw saddle, c1955 ....12.00
   8" h, plush, tan, single hump, glass eyes, c1950 ....65.00
Cat
   4" h, Tabby, orig bell, Steiff 60.00
   5" l, Snurry, sleeping 105.00
   5-1/4" h, mohair, green plastic eyes, movable head and legs, Steiff, c1950 ....45.00
   11" h, Diva, long white fur, sitting, orig Steiff tag and button 110.00
Cow, 5-1/2" h, felt, brown and white, glass eyes, wood wheels 65.00
Deer, 15" h, Bambi, plush, Gund, c1953 ....60.00
Dog
   4-1/2" h, Scottie, cotton, plaid, embroidered features and collar, hand made, c1950 ....5.00
   6" h, Boxer, Steiff 75.00
   7" h, Dalmatian, sitting, mohair, swivel head, orig collar, Steiff..........75.00
   8" h, plush, amber, swivel neck, oversized head, milk glass and amber bead eyes, embroidered nose and mouth, stitched tail and ears, early 20th C 75.00
   8-1/2" h, Poodle, pink, standing, glass eyes 18.00
   9" h, Beagle, plush, glass eyes.....................25.00
   10" h, Snoopy, black and white 15.00
   11" h, Terrier, white plush, black spots, swivel head, white muzzle, yellow glass eyes, embroidered features, red ribbon, c1925 ....50.00
   12" h, Poodle, curly, gray, plaid coat, hat and boots, c1960................15.00
   16" h, Huckleberry Hound 14.00
Donkey
   11" h, plush, gray, brown glass eyes, brown yarn mane, gray tail, wheeled base, c1950 ....100.00
   13" l, amber velvet body, glass eyes,

black mohair tail, mane, wood base, tin wheels 300.00
Duck
   4" h, calico, blue, yellow and pink, embroidered wing and eye, hand made, c1950 ....10.00
   8" h, plush, standing, yellow, straw hat, blue suspender pants........45.00
Elephant
   4" h, gray mohair, black glass eyes, red saddle, Steiff, c1953 ....100.00
   6-1/2" h, standing, gray, red suspender pants 65.00
Fish, 25" l, Steiff, Steiff button with remnants of yellow tag in top fin, excellent condition.................400.00
Frog, 9" h, green velvet back, white satin underside, c1960 ....12.50
Giraffe, 42" h, plush, yellow, brown spots, brown button eyes, brown yarn tail, c1957 ....20.00
Goat, 6-1/2" h, standing, white, brown felt horns, Steiff 50.00
Hedgehogs, 22" h, Micky & Mecky, vinyl swivel heads, pressed mask face, tan, squinting eyes, smiling mounts, bristly hair, felt bodies sewn on shoes, checkered costumes, c1950, price for pr 475.00
Hen, 7" h, gold and black spotted feathers, yellow plush head, felt tail, black button eyes, Steiff, c1949........75.00
Hippo, plush, purple, plastic eyes and teeth, c1962...........................18.00
Horse, 15" h, amber hopsacking, straw stuffing, reinforced stitching, pale yellow underbelly, amber glass eyes, stitched smiling mouth, applied ears, black fur mane, horsehair tail, velvet and leather saddle and harness, c1890 ....85.00
Kangaroo, 11" h, plush, glass eyes, 2 plastic Joeys, Steiff button in ear mkd "Linda" 65.00
Lamb, 9" h, white, fluffy, glass eyes, embroidered features, bell, flowers and ribbon at neck, paper label 90.00
Leopard, 15" l, silver button, Steiff.................185.00
Llama, 11" h, standing, white, brown spots, Steiff.................100.00
Monkey
   11" h, mohair, jointed, felt paws and face, Steiff 85.00
   36" h, Curious George, plush, yellow knitted sweater, red cap, c1975 ....45.00
Mother Goose, 22" h, muslin, white, yellow felt feet, white cotton bonnet, blue floral apron, c1962...........30.00
Owl, 10" h, Steiff...........................70.00
Owl, 8-1/2" h, Steiff Wittie Owl, Marguerite Steiff's nephew's signature on bottom of foot......70.00

Panda, 47" h, plush, black and white, jointed, humpback, pie-shaped eyes, straw filled 225.00
Parrot, 9" h, Lora, glass eyes, Steiff 75.00
Penguin, 10" h, black and white, black plastic wings, c1960 ....10.00
Pig, 6" h, plush, pink, pink felt cork screw tail, black and white felt eyes ..20.00
Rabbit
   6-1/2" h, mohair, jointed, Steiff 100.00
   12" h, plush, glass eyes, embroidered features, jointed body, paper label 70.00
   15" h, felt, eating carrot, Lenci 24.00
Raccoon, 6" h, Raccy, plush, glass eyes, Steiff 45.00
Seal, 10" h, fur, black, glass eyes 85.00
Squirrel, plush, Perri, Steiff 42.00
Teddy Bear
   4" h, plush, dark brown, jointed 40.00
   5" h, plush, standing, swivel head, "Character" label 40.00
   6" h, plush, jointed, fully dressed orig clothes, "Berg" label.................65.00
   9" h, plush, blond, black shoe-button eyes, shoulder hump, small tail, straw filled, c1905 ....165.00
   9-1/2" h, 13-3/4" l, brown curly hair, bear on all fours, mohair, early 20th C, unjointed, glass eyes...... 1,380.00
   11" h, brown woven mohair, black shoe-button eyes, embroidered features and claws................115.00
   12" h
      Mohair, blond, c1910, black shoe-button eyes, fully jointed 275.00
      Plush, amber, swivel head, jointed arms and legs, stitched-on ears, felt paws, functioning grower, straw filled, c1915 ....200.00
   14" h
      Knickerbocker, 1950s 26.00
      Zotty, Hermann, platinum frosted mohair....................155.00
   15" h, mohair, brown, black shoe-button eyes, black embroidered nose, mouth and claws, fully jointed, label "Bruin Mfg. Co.," c1907..........250.00
   16" h, Steiff
      Molly Koala bear, gray and tan......................135.00
      1903 Anniversary Bear, 1980s, #3026, yellow mohair, peach felt pads, certificate, orig box...275.00
   17" h
      Mohair, blond, 1910, black steel eyes 515.00
      Plush, brown, tan paws, molded

muzzle, Ideal Toy 50.00
18" h, gold mohair, unmkd, brown glass eyes, applied ears, felt pads on paws 375.00
20" h, mohair, brown, jointed, flat face, Knickerbocker 100.00
24" h, mohair, brown, glass eyes, black cloth nose, fully jointed, c1925 ....600.00
25" h, Ideal, light yellow mohair, c1905, black shoe-button eyes...............13,800.00
Tiger
6" h, plush, Steiff 60.00
8" h, Tony, Esso Tiger, orange and black, felt trim 45.00
13" h, plush, Shere Khan, black-green eyes, 8" l tail, button in ear, Steiff 175.00
Turtle, 5-1/2" l, plush and felt, Steiff 40.00
Walrus, pink, Gund 22.00
Weasel, 7-5/8" h, Steiff, 1970s, "Wiggy," synthetic white winter fur, black plastic eyes, ear button and chest tag 258.00
Zebra, 7" h, black and white, button in ear, Steiff 75.00

Super Heroes

Collecting Hints: Concentrate your collection on a single super hero. Because Superman, Batman and Wonder Woman are the most popular, new collectors are advised to focus on other characters or on one of the modern super heroes. Nostalgia is the principal motivation for many collectors; hence, they sometimes pay prices based on sentiment rather than true market value.

Comics are a fine collectible but require careful handling and storage. An attractive display requires inclusion of a three-dimensional object. Novice collectors are advised to concentrate on these first before acquiring too much of the flat paper material.

History: The super hero and comic books go hand in hand. Superman made his debut in 1939 in the first issue of *Action Comics*, six years after Jerry Siegel and Joe Shuster conceived the idea of a man who flew. A newspaper strip, radio show and movies followed. The popularity of Superman spawned many other super heroes, among them Batman, Captain Marvel, Captain Midnight, The Green

Hornet, The Green Lantern, The Shadow and Wonder Woman.

These early heroes had extraordinary strength and/or cunning and lived normal lives as private citizens. A wealth of merchandising products surround these early super heroes. Their careers were enhanced further when television chose them as heroes for Saturday morning shows as well as for prime time broadcasts.

The Fantastic Four—Mr. Fantastic, The Human Torch, The Invisible Girl and The Thing—introduced a new type of super hero, the mutant. Other famous personalities of this genre are Captain America, Spiderman, The Hulk and The X-Men. Although these characters appear in comic form, the number of secondary items generated is small. Television has helped to promote a few of the characters, but the list of mutant super heroes is close to a hundred.

References: John Bonavita, *Mego Action Figure Toys*, Schiffer Publishing, 1996; Bill Bruegman, *Superhero Collectibles*, Toy Scouts (137 Casterton Ave., Akron, OH 44303), 1996; Joe Desris, *Golden Age of Batman*, Artabras, 1994; Alex G. Malloy and Stuart W. Wells III, *Comic Collectibles & Their Values*, Wallace-Homestead, 1995; Paris & Susan Manos, *Collectible Action Figures*, 2nd Edition, Collector Books, 1996; Jeff Rovin, *Encyclopedia of Super Heroes*, Facts on File Publications, 1985.

Collectors' Clubs: Air Heroes Fan Club, 19205 Seneca Ridge, Gaithersburg, MD 20879; Batman TV Series Fan Club, P.O. Box 107, Venice, CA 90291.

Additional Listings: Action Figures, Comic Books, Radio Characters and Personalities.

Aquaman

Action Figure, MOC 35.00
Bathtub Toy, Burger King Kids Meal premium 12.00
Costume, Ben Cooper, 1967.......200.00
Glass, 1973...................................15.00
Puzzle, Whitman, action scene, 1967 ....40.00
Tattoo, 1967, unused, orig wrapper 50.00

Batman

Superman, wallet, leather and plastic, made in Hong Kong, 1976, $24.

Animation Art
Batman, Warner Bros., 1992, full-moon background 40.00
Batwoman, knee-up pose, profile, exiting to right of cel, hand out of picture, matted, framed............50.00
Arcade, Batman and Joker, 1966 ....325.00
Bag, 8-3/4" x 18-1/4", Batman Bread, thin plastic bag, design on both sides, black, white, blue and yellow, 1966 National Periodical Publications, many characters illus 20.00
Battery Operated
Batmobile, black, red trim, ASC, Japan 400.00
Talking Batmobile, Palitoy, MIB...........................300.00
Book, Famous First Editions, reprint of *Detective #27*, dj 120.00
Charm Bracelet, child's, gold metal, Batman, Robin, Joker, Penguin, Riddler charms, 3 colors, 1966.....50.00
Coin, Transogram, 1966, MOC.....85.00
Coloring Book, 1966, 6 pgs lightly colored 25.00
Con-Tact Paper, 96" x 18" roll, images of Batman, Robin and other characters, 1970s, unused........................25.00
Doll, 12" h, Mego, MIB 95.00
Drinking Cup, 3" h, 2-3/4" d, glazed white ceramic, color graphic of bat signal at left, Batman head at right set against burgundy red background, black cityscape with yellow accepts, 1982 DC Comics Inc., "Made in England" in relief on bottom...........................15.00

Game, Batman/Superman Super Powers, The Justice League of American Skyscraper Caper, 3D, Parker Brothers, 1984, MIB 40.00

Glass

Batman, 16 oz, Pepsi, 1978, minor paint loss 15.00

Robin, 6 oz, National Periodical Publications, 1960s 25.00

Halloween Costume

Batgirl, mask, cape and skirt, DC Comics, 1977, box damaged ...40.00

Batman, DC Comics, 1976, factory-sealed in pkg 45.00

License Plate, 2-1/4" x 4", tin litho, red art image, yellow lettering, green ground, Marx, National Periodical Publications Inc. 28.00

Lobby Card, 11" x 14", "Batman—The Wizard's Challenge, Chapter 13," Batman, Robin, Wizard, 2 bad guys, 1949...165.00

Magazine

Life, March 11, 1966 ....35.00

TV Guide, March 26, 1966, #67, Pow cover, Batman throwing punch, article "Batty over Batman".......48.00

Mask

Bat shape, felt, 1960s 45.00

Head and shoulders, latex, black and yellow, adult size, 23" l.............75.00

Milk Mug, Robin.............................20.00

Puppet, hand, vinyl head, plastic body, Batman 55.00

Shopping Bag, 15" x 18", vinyl, white, full-color illus of Batman and Robin, 1970s 25.00

Soakie 75.00

Toy, Batcopter, battery operated, Remco, 1977, MIB.................100.00

Wristwatch, animated, 1974..........30.00

Bionic Woman

Bank, figural, wearing running suit, pile of rocks base.....................42.00

Card Set, 44 color cards, colorful wrapper with Jamie..................40.00

Model, Repair Kit, Jamie on operating table, computerized medical equipment, Oscar Goldman, snap together, 1976 ....30.00

Buck Rogers

Action Figure, 12" h, Mego, NRFB 30.00

Rubber Stamp Kit, MIB.................35.00

Space Ship, Marx.........................350.00

View-Master Set, Battle of the Mon, cartoon version, 1978, MIP......24.00

Captain Action

Doll, red shirt, fully dressed, complete accessories, orig box.............225.00

Outfit, cap, chains.........................95.00

Captain America

Action Figure, 12" h, Mego, MIB...................125.00

Badge, Sentinel of Liberty, copper, 1941-43 ....325.00

Doll, 8" h, Super Baby, vinyl head, white hair, stuffed body, uniform, shield, gloves, Amsco, 1970s, orig box...........85.00

Game, Captain America game, Milton Bradley, 1966...............60.00

License Plate, 2-1/4" x 4", metal, full-color graphics, green back- ground, 1967 Marvel Comics Group, Louis Marx & Co., Japan 28.00

Transfer Sheet, 11" x 12-1/4", white sheet, colorful day-glow image, 1971 Marvel Comics Group.....18.00

Tricycle, worn 95.00

Wristwatch, figural, digital, MIP 30.00

Captain Marvel

Balloon Whistle, 4-1/2" l, red and yellow, 1941 ....40.00

Beanie, felt, 1944 ....145.00

Comic Book, 5" x 5", issue #11, Might Midgets Comics series, 1942 Fawcett Publications Inc..........35.00

Membership Button, tin litho, 1941 ....30.00

Pennant, felt, blue, 1944 ....85.00

Standup Figure, Rocket Raider, cardboard, Reed, 1940, unpunched, orig envelope........................110.00

Captain Midnight

Decoder...50.00

Stamp Album, Air Heroes, Skelly Gas premium 70.00

Electra Woman, Halloween costume, Ben Cooper, 1976, orig box 45.00

Fantastic Four

Action Figure, Mego, set of 4 figures, MOC 200.00

Puzzle, Marvel, 1970s.................120.00

Green Hornet

Autograph, color photo Van Williams, Hornet with Kato 25.00

Wende Wagner, Miss Case 25.00

Bendie 45.00

Book, *Disappearing Doctor*, 1966...........................25.00

PEZ Candy Container, 1966 ....325.00

Postcard, Green Hornet with Kato and car, Dexter Press, 1966...........35.00

Record, 12-1/4" sq, green art accent sleeve, black vinyl record, 10 songs by The Bus Lines, Diplomat Records, c1967 ....24.00

Ring, rubber, licensed 35.00

Spoon, emb Green Hornet figure on handle, 1955...........................18.00

Toy, Black Beauty Corgi, missile and rocket 275.00

T-Shirt, Hornet logo, 1966.............40.00

Incredible Hulk

Action Figure, 12" h, Mego, MIB...................75.00

Con-Tact Paper, 96" x 18" roll, 1978, 4 color images.........................65.00

Gum Card Set, complete set, 1978 ....25.00

Record, 4 action adventure stories, unused 18.00

Switch-Plate Cover, glow in the dark, hp, 3D Hulk image, MIP 21.00

Toy, truck, Corgi, NRFB................95.00

Wall Clock, multicolored...............45.00

Wallet, white stitching, 1978, unused 18.00

Invisible Man, comic book, Classics Illustrated, No. 153, Nov. 1959.................................27.00

Jet Man, Halloween costume, Ben Coo- per, 1950, goggles, cape, body suit, orig box 75.00

Six Million Dollar Man

Book

Six Million Dollar Man and the Bionic Woman, Scholastic, 1976, col- or photo of Lee and Lindsay 17.50

Six Million Dollar Man, The Secret of Bigfoot Pass, MCA, 1976.........16.00

Coloring Book, Saalfield, cover illus of Steve in bathing suit coming out of ocean, unused.........................20.00

Thermos, plastic, Aladdin, 1974....21.00

View-Master Set, 3 reels, story booklet, orig envelope..........................32.00

Spiderman

Action Figure, 9-1/2" x 14-3/4", diecut card, Spiderman on rope, red, blue and black costume, Fly-Away Action version sticker, Mego, 1979 Marvel Comics, MOC 90.00

Halloween Candy Container, plastic, black and white eyes, A.J. Renzy Corp., Leominster, MA, 1979 Marvel Comic 20.00

Doll, 12" h, Mego, MIB 95.00

Patch, iron-on, set of 6 different poses, Marvel 5.00

Race Car, Ricochet, 1974.............85.00

Sign, adv Spiderman comic strip in Bee Comics, autographed by Stan Lee, 1977 ....150.00

Toy, Helicopter, NRFB 95.00

Wrist Watch, figural, digital, MIP ...35.00

Superman

Action Figure, Super Powers, Kenner, 1983, MOC 35.00

Animation Art, cel, Superman with 3 lava monsters, flying to left, matted and framed 300.00

Catalog, Superman at the
Gilbert Hall of Science, toy
catalog, Superman cover, illus,
8-1/2" x 5-1/2", 1948...............175.00

Coloring Book, Saalfield,
11" x 15", 1940, 52 pgs,
some colored 120.00

Comic Book, *The Amazing
World of Superman*, 1973,
map of Krypton 8.00

Comic Book Offer, Nestle Quick
1-lb container, front with small
picture of Superman, back with
colorful graphics, offers Action
#1 reprint and Quick Bunny
Superman comic.......................25.00

Doll, wood and composition,
Ideal, 1940s........................1,250.00

Game, 9" x 14" x 1-3/4", Electronic
Question and Answer Game,
lid with graphics of Superman flying
past angry dictator on telephone,
green plastic and silver foil insert,
4 diecut 8-1/2" x 10" colorful tin
cardboard cards, holes for insertion
of green plastic pens, Lisbeth Whiting Co., 1966 National Periodical
Publications Inc. 38.00

Hair Brush, 2-1/4" x 4" x 1-1/2" tan
wood brush, curved top surface,
black and brown bristles, 1-1/4" x 2"
red and dark blue image of flying
Superman carrying red, white and
blue stars and stripes banner reading
"Superman America," gold
background, c1942 ....90.00

Horseshoes, Official Junior Rubber
Horseshoe Set, red, white and
blue box top, 3 rubber horseshoes,
black and green bases with stars,
wood pegs, 1950s 60.00

Movie Viewer, 5-1/4" x 7"
diecut card, image of Superman
punching through brick wall,
2-3/4" red and black plastic viewer,
2 boxed films, Chemtoy Co.,
Chicago 1965, MOC................25.00

Nutcracker, 11" h, wood figure, turn
head to crack nut, 1979 ....35.00

Pinback Button, 7/8" d, Action
Comics, multicolored 350.00

Play Suit, vinyl mask, cloth suit
and cape, Ben Cooper, 1972,
orig bright yellow box...............45.00

Postcard, sent as thank you for
entering contest, green printing,
Superman and Tim, 1943 ......125.00

Scrapbook, Saalfield,
10-1/2" x 15", spiral bound, 1940,
some pages used 95.00

Toy, car, Corgi,
Supermobile, NRFB.................95.00

Thor

PEZ Candy Container, 1960s........95.00

Walking Figure, 5" h, mechanical, plastic, Marx, 1966, orig box 75.00

Wonder Woman

Action Figure, MOC.....................25.00

Animation Art, cel, Wonder Woman
and Firestore, 3/4 poses, matted
and framed 50.00

Book and Record Set, 33-1/3 RPM,
Peter Pan, 16-pg comic story, 1977,
orig cardboard sleeve..............20.00

Coloring and Fun
Activity Book, mask 12.00

Doll, 12" h, Steve Trevor, orig box
with small tape tear 75.00

Drinking Cup, Burger King Kid's
Meal premium........................12.00

Puzzle, 15 pc..............................8.00

Skates 20.00

Sticker, 3D, unused sheet 3.00

Sunglasses...................................4.00

Swankyswigs

Collecting Hints: Ideally, select glasses whose pattern is clear and brightly colored. Rarer patterns include Carnival, Checkerboard and Texas Centennial. Look-alike patterns from other manufacturers include the Rooster's Head, Cherry, Diamond over Triangle and Circus. The look-alike patterns date from the 1930s to the 1960s.

History: Swankyswigs are decorated glass containers that were filled with Kraft Cheese Spreads. The first Swankyswigs date from the early 1930s. Production was discontinued during the last days of World War II because the paint was needed for the war effort. After the war, production resumed and several new patterns were introduced, including Posy or Cornflower No. 2 (1947), Forget-Me-Not (1948) and Tulip No. 3 (1950). The last colored pattern was Bicentennial Tulip (1975).

In the mid-1970s, several copy-cat patterns emerged. These include Wildlife Series (1975) and Sportsman Series (1976)—most likely Canadian varieties—Rooster's Head, Cherry, Diamond over Triangle and Circus. Kraft Cheese Spread is still available but is sold in crystal-type glass.

Swankyswigs were very popular with economy-minded ladies of the Depression era. After the original contents had been consumed, the containers, which could be used as

Posy pattern, Cornflower No. 2, dark blue, $2.

tumblers or to store juice, served as perfect companions to Depression glass table services. Their cheerful designs helped to chase away the Depression blues.

The first designs were hand applied. When the popularity of Swankyswigs increased, more intricate machine-made patterns were introduced. Designs were test marketed and those that did not achieve the desired results are hard to identify and find. The lack of adequate records about Swankyswigs makes it very difficult to completely identify all patterns. Since 1979, quite a few look-alikes have appeared. Although these glasses were similar to the originals, only Kraft glasses are considered Swankyswigs.

References: Gene Florence, *Collectible Glassware from the 40's, 50's, 60's*, 2nd Edition, Collector Books, 1994; Ian Warner, *Swankyswigs*, Revised, The Daze, 1988, 1992 value update.

Periodical: *The Daze*, P.O. Box 57, Otisville, MI 48463.

Advisor: M.D. Fountain.

Notes: If a Swankyswig retains its original label, add $4 to the value of the glass.

Antique, 3-3/4" h
    Black, coffeepot and trivets........4.25
    Brown, coal bucket and clock 4.00
    Orange, crib and butter churn....2.25
Bands, black and red 3.00

Bicentennial, 1938-type tulip,
red, yellow or green, coin-dot
design, 1975 ....10.00
Bustlin' Betsy, 3-3/4" h 2.25
Carnival, 3-1/2" h, fired on
Fiestacolors, dark blue, orange,
yellow and light green................7.50
Checkerboard, 3-1/2" h, green, red
and dark blue...........................25.00
Daisies, red daisies on top row, white in
middle, green leaves 3.00
Dots & Circles,
black, blue, green or red...........4.50
Kiddie Cup or Animal, 3-3/4" h
Black, pony and duck.................2.25
Blue, pig and bear......................2.00
Brown, deer and squirrel............2.00
Dark blue, pig and bear..............2.25
Green, kitten and bunny.............2.00
Orange, puppy and rooster 2.00
Red, bird and elephant...............2.00
Modern Flowers, dark and light blue, red
or yellow
Cornflower, 3-1/2" h 3.00
Forget-me-not, 3-1/2" h..............3.00
Jonquil, yellow, green leaves 3.00
Tulip, dark and light blue, red or yel-
low flowers
No. 1, 3-1/2" h, 1937,
white leaves 6.00
No. 2, 1938, green leaves, 6
molded bands around top 20.00
No. 3, 3-3/4" h, green leaves,
4 molded bands around top ...3.00
Sailboat, red, green or dark blue, racing
or sailing 20.00
Star, 3-1/2" h, black, dark blue, green or
red 5.00
Texas Centennial, cowboy, riding
bucking horse on 1 side, Texas State
Seal on other, black, dark blue,
green and red 9.00

Swarovski Crystal

Collecting Hints: Sophisticated design and custom fabricated components of the clearest crystal are
some of the criteria that distinguish
Swarovski crystal from other collectible crystal figurines. The most popular array of Swarovski items falls
within the Silver Crystal line, which
has included animals, candlesticks,
paperweights and decorative accessories since 1977. Most items are
marked and this is helpful to collectors. The first mark for Silver Crystal
items was a block style "SC," sometimes accompanied by the word
"Swarovski." Since 1989, an impres-
sionistic swan has been used as the

Swarovski symbol. The logo accompanied by a small copyright symbol
indicates that the piece was manufactured for the American market.

Other items produced by the
Swarovski company are also of interest to collectors and these include
Trimlite, Savvy, Swarovski Selec-
tions, Daniel Swarovski Collection,
Ebeling & Reuss and Giftware Suite
assortments.

Swarovski crystal collecting has
attracted a worldwide following, with a
vigorous secondary market. New collectors will find the Swarovski company's Product Listing leaflet very helpful
as a beginning checklist of retired and
current items. Condition is critical
when contemplating an item for resale
and presence of original packaging
with enclosures, where applicable, is
important. Also desirable is an artist's
autograph, occasionally found on the
underside of a figurine. Some figurines were produced in more than one
version and the pursuit of various con-
figurations of a design is one type of
collection pursued by some Swarovski
enthusiasts.

Some crystal figurines have
metal trim, usually in one of two colors: shiny silvertone is called "Rhodium" and usually predates the
goldtone version of the same item.
Examples include the In Flight series
of Bee, Butterfly and Hummingbird,
which were produced with both
types of trim.

In addition to stunningly clear
crystal, color appears in some
Swarovski items. For a number of
years, paperweights were produced
in assorted colors, few of which were
sold at retail in the United States.
These paperweights, which were
colored by applying a vaporized
chemical coating to the bottom, have
sparked interest among collectors.
Recently, the company has introduced several figurines with integral-
ly colored glass.

Few Swarovski pieces are serially numbered and the items that are
numbered have attracted considerable interest. In 1995, the Eagle was
produced in an edition of 10,000
pieces. In 1995 and 1996, the company collaborated with perfume
makers to create serially numbered
perfume flacons in limited quantities.

History: The Swarovski family has
been perfecting the glassmaker's art
in Wattens, Austria, since 1895 and
is responsible for many technical advances in the glass industry. For decades, this company has been a
leading producer of colored and faceted stones for the costume jewelry
and fashion industry and also is
widely respected for its industrial
abrasives and quality optics.

Silver Crystal collectible figurines and desk accessories were introduced in 1977, with the creation of
a sparkling crystal mouse, followed
soon after with a spiny crystal hedgehog. Formed of crystal with lead content of at least 30%, these crystal
critters have unmistakable sparkle
and were immediately popular.

The Swarovski Collectors Society, which was formed in 1987, ex-
tends exclusive offers to members to
purchase annual limited editions.
The first SCS series, called Caring
and Sharing, features three different
pairs of birds. The second series,
entitled Mother and Child, focuses
on three sets of sea mammals with
their young. The third SCS series,
with the Inspiration Africa theme, offers three different African wildlife
figurines. A new series, called Fabulous Creatures, was launched in
1997 and the first offering is a Unicorn. All SCS figurines are limited to
one per member during the year it is
offered and each piece comes with
special packaging and a certificate
of authenticity.

References: Swarovski, *Swarovski,
The Magic of Crystal*, Harry N.
Abrams, 1995; Jane and Tom Warner, *Warner's Blue Ribbon Book on
Swarovski Silver Crystal*, 3rd Edition
(separate pocket guide included),
published by authors (7163 W. Fred-
erick-Garland Rd., Union, OH
45322), 1996.

Periodical: *Swarovski Collector*,
General Wille Strasse 88, SH-8706,
Feldmeilien, Switzerland.

Collectors' Clubs: Swan Seekers,
9740 Campo Rd., #134, Spring Valley, CA; Swarovski Collectors Society, 2 Slater Rd., Cranston, RI
02920.

Reproduction Alert: Nefarious reproductions haven't been a problem, but copycats are widespread. Collectors who are alert to correct proportions and quality material rarely are mistaken about a piece of Swarovski crystal and the presence of the maker's mark and correct packaging make acquisition almost foolproof. Replica mouse, replica hedgehog and replica cat were issued by the company in 1995. Although similar to early figurines, these reissues are clearly marked with the swan logo and also have design distinctions that will keep collectors from becoming confused.

Advisor: Maret Webb.

Notes: All prices shown are approximate retail replacement cost for items in perfect condition with correct original packaging and enclosures. Deduct 15% for missing boxes or certificates.

Accessories

Apple, photo, apple hinged at side, photograph revealed when top tilted back
    King size, 60mm d, SC logo
        #7504nr060, gold 400.00
        #7504nr060R, rhodium 450.00
    Large size, 50mm d
        #7504nr050, gold, SC or swan logo 180.00
        #7504nr050R, rhodium, SC logo 225.00
    Small size, 30mm d
        #7504nr030, gold, SC or swan logo............................180.00
        #7504nr030R, rhodium, SC logo 225.00
Ashtray, #7461nr100, 3-3/8" d, sculpted crystal, SC or swan logo........225.00
Bell, large, #7467nr071000, 5-3/4" h, SC or swan logo 125.00
Blush Brush, prototype, black bristles, row of rhinestones around ferrule, crystal-ball handle, large SC logo on other end 1,000.00
Candleholder
    #7600nr116, holds 5 candles, with sockets or prickets, SC logo 1,200.00
    #7600nr130, holds 4 candles, sockets or prickets, SC logo 1,050.00
    #7600nr131, 15/16" h, small, pricket, SC logo, price for set of six 350.00
    #7600nr1360002, rhodium foliage, pineapple, SC logo.................500.00
Christmas Ornament

1981, undated, crystal snowflake, hexagonal metal trim ring and neck chain, ring stamped "SC" at top back, orig blue velour pouch, silver logo box 400.00

1987, dated, Giftware Suite, etched baroque teardrop shape, unmkd 240.00

1991, dated, Giftware Suite, star/snowflake series 145.00

Cigarette Holder, #7463nr062, 2-3/8" h, sculpted crystal, SC or swan logo 130.00

Grapes, large, #7550nr30015, cluster of 30 1-1/8" d clear grapes, clear stem, SC logo, USA only..............1,000.00

Lighter, #7462nr062, 3-12/" h, chrome lighter in crystal base, SC or swan logo 250.00

Paperweight

    Atomic, 2-3/4" h, hexagonal facets, SC logo (often unmkd or with paper label on felt bottom)

        Clear, #7454nr60095 ......1,000.00

        Vitrail, medium color, #7454nr600.....................1,700.00

    Barrel, 2-5/8" h, rect facets vertically aligned, SC logo (often unmkd or with paper label on felt bottom)

        Bermuda Blue, #7453nr60088, shades from dark to light blue 400.00

        Clear, #7453nr60095.........240.00

    Carousel, 2-3/4" h, flared sides, vertical facets, SC logo (often unmkd or with paper label on felt bottom)

        Clear, #7451nr60095 ......1,200.00

        Vitrail, medium color, color strongest viewed from top, shades from lime green to fuschia.......1,200.00

    Cone, 3-1/8" h, facts spiral around cone, SC or swan logo

        Clear, #7452nr600878 ....240.00

        Vitrail, medium color, color strongest viewed from top, shades from line green to fuschia...........240.00

        Volcano color, #7452nr600.........................450.00

    SCS dealer, 50mm d, SCS edelweiss logo in blue.............................225.00

    SCS member gift, 40mm d, SCS edelweiss logo in blue..............80.00

Perfume Bottle, Lancome Tresor, 1994 ed of 5,000 serially numbered,

Renewal Gift, 1988, cactus, approx 1" h, $225.

    full, with box 425.00
Picture Frame
    Oval, #7505nr75G, 3" h, gold trim, SC or swan logo 400.00
    Sq, #7506nr60, gold or rhodium trim, SC or swan logo 250.00
Pineapple, rhodium foliage
    Large, #7507nr105002, 4-1/8" h, SC logo 400.00
    Small, #7507nr060002, 2-1/2" h 130.00
Salt and Pepper Shakers, pr, #7508nr068034, 2-3/8" h, rhodium screw-off tops, SC logo 300.00
Schnapps Glass, #7468nr039000, approx 2" h, SC or swan logo
    European, set of three 180.00
    USA, set of six 250.00
Treasure Box, cov
    Butterfly on removable lid
        Heart shape, #7465nr52/100, SC or swan logo 250.00
        Oval, #7466nr063100, SC logo.............................300.00
        Round, #7464nr50/100, SC logo.............................250.00
    Flowers on removable lid
        Heart shape, #7465nr52, SC logo.............................275.00
        Oval, #7466nr063000, SC or swan logo 275.00
        Round, #7464nr50, SC or swan logo 200.00
Vase, #7511nr70, 2-7/8" h, sculpted crystal, 3 frosted crystal flowers, SC or swan logo....................140.00

Figurines

Bear
    Giant, #7636nr112, 4-1/2" h, SC mark only, USA only, SC logo 2,200.00
    King size, #7637nr92, 3-3/4" h, USA only, SC logo 1,250.00
    Mini, #7670nr32, 1-1/8" h, SC logo...................200.00
Bee, crystal and metal bee feeding on crystal lotus flower, 4" w, SC logo

#7553nr100,
gold metal bee.....................1,500.00
#7553nr200,
silver metal bee.................2,100.00

Butterfly
1" h, mini, #7671nr30, crystal,
metal antennae, no base, USA only,
SC logo 120.00
4" w, crystal and metal butterfly feeding on crystal lotus flower, SC logo
#7551nr100,
gold metal butterfly..........1,000.00
#7551nr200,
silver metal butterfly........2,200.00

Cat
Large, #7634nr70, 2-7/8" h,
SC or swan logo.....................100.00
Medium, #7634nr52, 2" h, flexible
metal tail, SC logo 500.00
Mini, #7659, 1-1/4" h, flexible
metal tail, SC or swan logo 75.00

Chicken, mini, #7651nr20, 7/8" h,
conical metal beak and metal fee,
SC logo.....................................80.00

Dachshund, metal tail
Large, #7641nr75, 3" l,
rigid, limp or gently arched,
SC or swan logo.....................120.00
Mini, #7672nr42, 1-1/4",
SC logo 150.00
Dog, Pluto (name on European list),
SC or swan logo.....................130.00

Duck
Large, #7653nr75, 3" l, crystal beak,
USA only, SC logo 275.00
Medium, #7653nr55, 2-1/8" l, silver
beak, USA only, SC logo........135.00
Mini, #7653nr45, 1-7/8" l, silver beak,
SC logo 80.00

Eagle, #7607nr000001, 1995,
ed of 10,000 serially numbered,
gray train-case-type box, wood
display pedestal..................8,000.00

Elephant
Dumbo
#7640nr100, 1990, black eyes,
clear hat, ed of 3,000, most have
swan logo, few unmkd 1,100.00
#7640nr100001, 1993, blue eyes,
frosted hat, swan logo and
Disney copyright 375.00
Large
#7640nr40, 2" h, frosted tail, swan
logo 100.00
#7640nr55, 2-1/2" h, flexible
metal tail, SC logo..............180.00

Falcon Head
Large, #7645nr100, 4" h, SC or
swan logo 1,300.00
Small, #7645nr45, 1-3/4" h, SC
or swan logo...........................130.00

Frog, #7642nr48, clear crown
Black eyes,

SC or swan logo......................180.00
Clear eyes, usually found with
SC logo 300.00

Hedgehog, silver whiskers
King, #7630nr60, 2-3/8" h
including spines, 60mm body,
SC logo, USA only 650.00
Large, #7630nr50, 2" h including
spines, 50mm body, SC logo,
worldwide distribution............250.00
Medium, #7630nr40, 1-3/4" h including spines, 40mm body, SC mark,
worldwide distribution............180.00
Small, #7630nr30, 1-1/4" h including
spines, 30mm body, SC logo,
USA only 475.00

Hummingbird, crystal and metal
hummingbird feeding on crystal lotus
flower, 4"w, SC logo
#7552nr100, gold metal
hummingbird, green stones
on wings...............................1,500.00
#7552nr200, silver metal humming-
bird, red stones on wings 2,500.00

Mallard, #7647nr80, 3-1/2" l, frosted
beak, SC or swan logo 160.00

Mouse, silver whiskers, metal coil tail
King, #763nr60, 3-3/4" h to
top of ears, 60mm body, sq base,
USA only, SC logo 750.00
Large, #763nr50, 2-7/8" h to top
of ears, 50mm body, sq base,
USA only, SC mark 300.00
Mini, #7655nr23,
13/16" h, SC logo 90.00
Small, #763nr30, 1-3/4" h to top
of ears, 30 mm body, octagonal
base, SC or swan logo...........125.00

Pig, large, #7638nr65, 1-3/4" l, crystal
J-shaped tail, SC logo 225.00

Rabbit, ears lay flat on top of head, SC
logo
Large, #7652nr45, 1-1/2" h 250.00
Mini, #7652nr20, 1" h.............100.00

Sparrow, silver metal open beak
Large, #7650nr32,
1-1/4" h, SC logo....................150.00
Mini, #7650nr20, 3/4" h,
SC or swan logo.......................65.00

Swan, mini, #7658nr27, 1" h, delicate
crystal neck connected to body,
2 wings, tail, SC logo.............125.00

Turtle, king size, #7632nr75, 3" l, green
eyes, SC logo 400.00

Swarovski Collectors Society Items

Anniversary Figurine, 1991, birthday
cake for SCS 5th anniversary, #003-
0168678, cake on pedestal, 1 candle
in center, SCS swan logo 160.00

Limited Edition Figurine
1987, Togetherness,
lovebirds, #do1x861, SCS
edelweiss mark 4,200.00

1988, Partnership,
woodpeckers, #d01x881,
SCS edelweiss mark...........1,500.00
1989, Amour, turtledoves,
#d01x891, SCS swan mark ...850.00
1990, Lead Me,
dolphins, #d01x901,
SCS swan mark 1,100.00
1991, Care for Me, seals,
#d01x911, SCS swan mark ...500.00
1992, Save Me, whales,
#d01x921, SCS swan mark ...500.00
1993, Inspiration Africa,
elephant, #d01x931, SCS
swan mark 1,300.00
1994, Inspiration Africa, lion,
#d01x941,SCS swan mark 400.00

T

Taylor, Smith, Taylor

Collecting Hints: Collector interest focuses primarily on the Lu-Ray line, introduced in 1938 and named after Virginia's Luray Caverns. The line actually utilized forms from the Empire and Laurel lines. Lu-Ray was made from the 1930s through the early 1950s in coordinating colors, which has encouraged collectors to mix and match sets.

Pieces from the Coral-Craft line are very similar in appearance to pink Lu-Ray. Do not confuse the two. Vistosa, introduced in 1938, is another example of the California patio dinnerware movement that featured bright, solid-color pieces. Unfortunately, the number of forms was restricted. As a result, many collectors shy away from it.

Pebbleford, a plain colored ware with sandlike specks, can be found in gray, dark blue-green, light blue-green, light tan and yellow. When in production, it was the company's third most popular line, but it is only moderately popular among today's collectors.

Taylor, Smith and Taylor (TST) used several different backstamps and marks. Many contain the company name as well as the pattern and shape names. A dating system was used on some dinnerware lines until the 1950s. The three-number code identifies month, year and crew number.

History: W.L. Smith, John N. Taylor, W.L. Taylor, Homer J. Taylor and Joseph G. Lee founded TST in Chester, WV, in 1899. In 1903, the firm reorganized and the Taylors bought Lee's interest. In 1906, Smith bought out the Taylors. The firm remained in the family's control until it was purchased by Anchor Hocking in 1973. The tableware division closed in 1981.

TST started production with a nine-kiln pottery. Local clays were used initially; later only southern clays were used. Both earthenware and fine-china bodies were produced. Several underglaze print patterns, e.g., Dogwood and Spring Bouquet, were made. These prints, made from the copper engravings of ceramic artist J. Palin Thorley, were designed exclusively for the company. During the 1930s and through the 1950s, competition in the dinnerware market was intense. Lu-Ray was designed to compete with Russel Wright's American Modern. Vistosa was TST's answer to Homer Laughlin's Fiesta.

References: Susan and Al Bagdade, *Warman's American Pottery and Porcelain*, Wallace-Homestead, 1994; Jo Cunningham, *Collector's Encyclopedia of American Dinnerware*, Collector Books, 1982, 1995 value update; Harvey Duke, *Official Identification and Price Guide to Pottery and Porcelain*, 8th Edition, House of Collectibles, 1995; Lois Lehner, *Lehner's Encyclopedia of U.S. Marks on Pottery, Porcelain & Clay*, Collector Books, 1988; Kathy and Bill Meehan, *Collector's Guide to Taylor, Smith & Taylor Lu-Ray Pastels U.S.A.*, Collector Books, 1995.

Lu-Ray: Produced from the late 1930s until the early 1950s. Available in five pastel colors: Chatham Grey, Persian Cream, Sharon Pink, Surf Green and Windsor Blue.

Berry Bowl, Chatham Grey 14.00
Bowl, c1936
    Persian Cream 60.00
    Surf Green 60.00
    Windsor Blue 60.00
Cake Plate
    Persian Cream 110.00
    Sharon Pink 110.00
Casserole, cov
    Sharon Pink 150.00
    Surf Green 140.00
    Windsor Blue........................... 140.00
Chop Plate, 14" d, Sharon Pink..... 30.00
Cream Soup and Underplate
    Persian Cream 125.00
    Sharon Pink 125.00
    Windsor Blue........................... 125.00
Demitasse Creamer,
    Sharon Pink............................. 50.00
Demitasse Cup and Saucer,
    Persian Cream 20.00
Eggcup
    Persian Cream 20.00
    Surf Green 20.00
    Windsor Blue............................ 20.00
Epergne

Sharon Pink 145.00
Windsor Blue 145.00
Fruit Bowl, Persian Cream 8.00
Gravy Boat, attached underplate,
    Windsor Blue.......................... 50.00
Juice Pitcher, Windsor Blue 225.00
Juice Tumbler
    Persian Cream 70.00
    Sharon Pink 70.00
Nappy, Sharon Pink 15.00
Nut Dish, Surf Green................. 125.00
Pickle Dish, Persian Cream 45.00
Pitcher, Sharon Pink 65.00
Plate
    6" d, Windsor Blue 6.00
    8-1/2" d, Sharon Pink.............. 20.00
    10" d, dinner
        Sharon Pink 20.00
        Surf Green 20.00
    Grill
        Persian Cream.................... 30.00
        Surf Green 30.00
Platter, 12" l, Surf Green 20.00
Salad Bowl, Sharon Pink 45.00
Salt and Pepper Shakers, pr,
    Persian Cream 18.00
Sauceboat, underplate,
    Persian Cream 18.00
Soup, flat, Windsor Blue 15.00
Teapot, Sharon Pink 50.00
Tidbit Tray, Chatham Grey............ 80.00
Tumbler, Windsor Blue 90.00
Vase, bud, Surf Green 150.00
Vegetable, 8" d, Windsor blue....... 17.50

Vistosa: Solid-colored dinnerware similar to Homer Laughlin's Fiesta. Vistosa pieces have piecrust edges and were produced from 1938 until the early 1940s. Vistosa pieces are available in four colors: Cobalt Blue, Deep Yellow, Light Green and Mango Red.

Bowl
    8" d, Cobalt Blue 65.00
    12" d, ftd, Mango Red 115.00
Chop Plate, 11" d, Light Green 80.00
Creamer and Sugar,
    Light Green 40.00
Salt and Pepper Shakers, pr,
    Mango Red............................. 20.00
Sauceboat, Light Green 145.00
Soup, flat, Deep Yellow................ 20.00
Teapot, Deep Yellow.................... 75.00
Water Jug, Deep Yellow 75.00

Teapots

Collecting Hints: Most collectors focus on pottery, porcelain or china examples. Much attention has been given recently to the unglazed pottery teapots referred to as Yixing. These teapots are small in size and feature earthy designs such as lotus flowers, handles of twig and insects shaped on the body or lid finial. Yixing (traditionally Vis-Hsing or I Hsing) is a Chinese province that has been known for these artistic wares since the 16th century. Since they are still being produced, collectors need to learn to differentiate the antique from the modern.

History: The origin of the teapot has been traced back to the Chinese province of Yixing in the late 16th century. The teapots, similar to ones still being produced today, were no bigger than the tiny teacups used at that time.

By the 17th century, tea drinking had spread throughout the world. Every pottery or porcelain manufacturer from the Asia, Europe and America has at one time produced teapots. Forms range from the purely functional, such as the English Brown Betty, to the ornately decorative and whimsical, such as individual artist renditions or popular figurals depicting shapes of people, animals or things. The majority of teapots available in today's market date from 1870 to the present.

References: Edward Bramah, *Novelty Teapots*, Quiller Press (available from John Ives, 5 Normanhurst Dr., Twickenham, Middlesex, TW1 1NA, London, England), 1992; Tina M. Carter, *Teapots*, Running Press (available from author, 882 S. Mollison Ave., El Cajon, CA 92020), 1995; Robin Emmerson, *British Teapots and Tea Drinking*, distributed by Seven Hills, 1996.

Periodicals: *Tea Talk*, P.O. Box 860, Sausalito, CA 94966; *Tea Time Gazette*, P.O. Box 40276, St. Paul, MN 55104.

Museum: Arthur Wood Teapot Showroom, Los Angeles, CA; Greater Gibson County Area Chamber of Commerce, P.O. Box 464, Trenton, TN 38382, sponsors an annual Teapot Festival.

Reproduction Alert: Watch out for new Yixing teapots mimicking older ones. Modern versions of the Granny teapot have been made by sever-

Morton Pottery Works, acorn shape, 3-3/4 cup, brown Rockingham, $48.

al companies. Teapots marked "Made in China" are not antique but may resemble 1920s and 1930s examples, especially figural shapes.

Advisor: Tina M. Carter.

American

Coorsite, cobalt blue, 2-pc 22.00
Monterey, CA, pink,
    speckled glaze.........................42.00

Chinese

Floral, tiny spout, unmkd 25.00
Set, teapot and 2 cups, in padded
    basket, mkd "China" 100.00

English

Abrams, cosy pot, pitcher shape,
    patents....................................50.00
Ellgreave, Wood & Sons, floral 32.00
Portmeirion, Meridian,
    speckled glaze.........................28.00
Sadler, floral, raised mark 30.00
Wade, majolica style,
    basket and fruit.......................35.00
Wedgwood, jasperware,
    6 cup, 20th C 175.00

Figural

Auto, silver details, Carlton Ware,
    English....................................350.00
Cat, beckoning,
    paper label, German................55.00
Dickens characters,
    Beswick, English 75.00
House, Cottage Ware,
    Price Kensington, English 32.00
Sherlock Holmes, 12" h,
    Hall China, 1988.....................125.00
Snow White, 6" h, musical, dwarfs in
    relief, Walt Disney Prod...........95.00

German

Large, chocolate pot,
    scroll handle, ftd 85.00
Small, hp china, Royal Hanover....75.00

Glass, Pyrex

Etched flowers, c1920...................85.00
Stove top, chrome and
    lass handle, c1950 ....30.00

Japan

Brown, raised dots (coralene type),
    flowers....................................14.00
Brown lustre, sq, 2 cup 12.00
Buff sharkskin, bisque, orange-peel
    glaze, unmkd..........................30.00
Cube shape, hp, c1930................22.00
Violets, china, c1950....................18.00

Pewter

1 cup, copper-wrapped bail handle,
    mkd "M.H. Japan"...................22.00
6 cup, mkd "Pewter"......................28.00

Porcelain

Lipton's Tea
    Fraunfelter,
    ribbed body, c1930 ....30.00
    Hall China, various colors 35.00
Mermaid, Eliza Hurdle, modern ..350.00
Simple Yet Perfect, teapot on side,
    floral 185.00

Pottery

Brown, 2 cup, mkd "U.S.A." 18.00
Brown Betty, colored rings, various
    sizes 28.00
Frankoma, autumn yellow,
    warming stand........................45.00
Granny Ann, Shawnee,
    mkd "U.S.A.".............................80.00
Granny Woods, English 40.00
Green glaze, crude, unmkd...........15.00
Torquay, motto ware, small,
    Watcombe, English 38.00

Yixing

Gourd shape, chop mark under cov,
    leaves and insects dec..........125.00
Miniature, silver-chased dec,
    dragon 48.00
Modern, fixed bail handle, Chinese
    writing all over 50.00

Television Personalities and Memorabilia

Collecting Hints: Collectors of television memorabilia fall into two categories. One includes those who specialize in acquiring items from a single television series. "Star Trek," "Hopalong Cassidy," "Howdy Doody," "Roy Rogers," or "Leave It To Beaver" are the most popular series. The other category of collector specializes in TV memorabilia of one type such as *TV Guides*, model kits, films or cards.

There have been more than 3,750 series on television since 1948. Therefore, an enormous number of ar-

Bonanza, cup, litho tin, mkd "Ponderosa Ranch, Nevada, U.S.A.," 2-5/8 " h, 3-1/2" d, 1960s, $15.

tifacts and memorabilia relating to television are available. Premiums from the early space shows and cowboy adventure series are eagerly sought by pop-culture collectors. As a result, these items are beginning to command high prices at auction.

Systematic scheduling of television programs developed a new type of publication called *TV Guide*. The early guides are avidly sought. The first schedules were regional and include titles such as *TV Today in Philadelphia*, *TV Press in Louisville* and *Radio-Television Life in Los Angeles*. The first national *TV Guide* was published on April 3, 1953. Collectors enjoy these older magazines because they are good sources for early stories about the stars of the time.

History: The late 1940s and early 1950s was the golden age of television. The first TV programming began in 1948. Experimentation with programming, vast expansion and rapid growth marked the period. Prime-time live drama series were very successful and provided the start for many popular stars, such as Paul Newman, Steve McQueen, Rod Steiger, Jack Lemmon and Grace Kelly. The stars signed autographs and photographs to promote the dramas. These items, plus scripts and other types of articles, have become very collectible.

When the period of live drama ended, the Western assault began. In 1959, there were 26 Western series, many of which were based on movie or radio heroes. The Western era continued until the early 1960s when it was replaced by the space adventure series and science fiction.

The 1970s are remembered for their situation comedies, including "All In The Family" and "M*A*S*H*." The collectibles resulting from these series are numerous.

References: Ted Hake, *Hake's Guide to TV Collectibles*, Wallace-Homestead, 1990; John P. Holms and Ernest Wood, *Game Show Almanac*, Wallace-Homestead, 1995; David Inman, *TV Encyclopedia*, Perigee Book, 1991; Jack Koch, *Howdy Doody*, Collector Books, 1996; Brian Paquette and Paul Howley, *Toys from U.N.C.L.E.*, Entertainment Publishing, 1990; Maxine A. Pinksy, *Marx Toys: Robots, Space, Comic, Disney & TV Characters*, Schiffer Publishing, 1996; Neil Summers, *Official TV Western Book, Vol. 4*, Old West Shop Publishing, 1992; Ric Wyman, *For the Love of Lucy*, Chronicle Books, 1995; Alan Young, *Mister Ed and Me*, St. Martin's Press, 1994; Dian Zillner, *Collectible Television Memorabilia*, Schiffer Publishing, 1996.

Periodicals: *Autograph Times*, 2303 N. 44th St., #225, Phoenix, AZ 85008; *Big Reel*, P.O. Box 1050, Dubuque, IA 52004; *Celebrity Collector*, P.O. Box 1115, Boston, MA, 02117; *Collecting Hollywood*, 2401 Broad St., Chattanooga, TN 37408; *Norm's Serial News*, 1726 Maux Dr., Houston, TX 70043; *Television History Magazine*, 700 E. Macoupia St., Staunton, IL 62088; *TV Collector*, P.O. Box 1088, Easton, MA 02334.

Collector's Club: TV Western Collectors Fan Club, P.O. Box 1361, Boyes Hot Springs, CA 95416.

Museum: Smithsonian Institution, Washington, DC.

Additional Listings: Cowboy Heroes, Space Adventurers & Explorers, Super Heroes, Western Americana.

Activity Book, Soupy Sales, 8-1/4" x 11", photo of Soupy on cover, 64 b&w pages, some color on text, games and art, Treasure Books, 1965 Soupy Sales 12.00
Activity Box Kit, Captain Kangaroo, 1956, shoe-box type 60.00
Autograph
  Check, Elizabeth Montgomery, Sept. 1974, personal check to Pacific Telephone 150.00

Photograph, sgd by cast
  Gilligan's Island 275.00
  Lost in Space 370.00
Bandanna, Howdy Doody 8.00
Bank, Romper Room, Do-Bee, 5" plastic, figural, Hasbro, early 1960s 55.00
Big Little Book, *Lassie Adventure in Alaska*, Whitman #2004, 3-3/4" x 5", 248 pgs, 1967 .... 12.00
Book
  I *Spy, Message From Moscow*, Whitman, Robert Culp and Bill Cosby on cover, hardcover, 1966 .... 20.00
  TV's Top Ten Shows and Their Stars, Peggy Herz, Scholastic Book Service, 1976, paperback 8.00
  You're Never Too Young, Lawrence Welk, autographed 15.00
Card Game, Howdy Doody, Russell, slide-out box, 1950s 45.00
Card Set
  Dukes of Hazzard, 1983 .... 24.00
  Gomer Pyle, b&w photos, 1960 .... 90.00
Cigar Band, Hawaii Five-O, full color, 1970s, price for set of 12 .... 25.00
Chalk, 2-3/4" x 3-1/2" x 1", features 3 Chipmunks on front, used pieces of chalk, Creston Crayon & Toy Co., c1980 .... 12.00
Colorforms, Daniel Boone, Fess Parker, 1964, unused 85.00
Coloring Book, unused
  Beverly Hillbillies, Whitman, 1963, 8" x 11" 20.00
  Flying Nun, 1968 .... 40.00
  Gilligan's Island, Whitman, 1965, 128 pages 132.00
  Howdy Doody, Whitman, 1957, 7" x 7", soft-cover 25.00
  Johnny Quest, 1965 .... 85.00
Coloring Set
  Bonanza, Foto Fantasticks Photo, Eberhard Faber, 1965, unused 100.00
  Lassie and Timmy, pictures to color, paints, crayons, plastic palette, Standard Toykraft, 1960s, minor use 45.00
Cookbook, *Buffy's Cookbook*, Jody Cameron, Family Affair, Buffy rolling out dough illus on glossy color cover, Berkeley Medallion 14.00
Comic Book, *I Love Lucy*, Dell, #3, 1954 .... 135.00
Dog Training Kit, Lassie Trick Trainer, Mousley, 1956, orig training devices, picture album, photo cards of Lassie and trainer Rudd Weatherwax, orig box 275.00
Doll
  Capt. Kangaroo, 21", Baby Barry

Toys, c1965, orig box.............385.00

Cher, 12" h, posable, plastic and vinyl, Mego, orig box, 1970s.......50.00

Farrah Fawcett, 1977, MIB.......25.00

Honey West, 12" h, posable plastic, Gilbert, 1965, orig box............370.00

I Dream of Jeannie, Libby Majorette Doll Co., Barbara Eden, c1966, 18" h, orig box 2,437.00

Man from U.N.C.L.E., Gilbert, 1965, orig box

    Ilya Kuryakin 385.00

    Napoleon Solo 385.00

M.C. Hammer, boom box, MIB 20.00

Oscar Goldman, MIB................25.00

Shaun Cassidy, from Hardy Boys, MIB...................................20.00

Six Million Dollar Man, 1973, MIB...............................35.00

Toni Tennelle, 1977, MIB.........25.00

Fan Club Pack, Richard Diamond, Private Detective, David Janssen, c1959 ....130.00

Game

    Adventures of Lassie, Lisbeth Whiting Co., 1955.....................50.00

    Flying Nun, Milton Bradley, 1968, sealed...........................200.00

    F Troop, Ideal, 1965...............165.00

    Have Gun Will Travel, Parker Bros., 1959 ....75.00

    Howdy Doody...........................75.00

    Ironside Game, Ideal, 1967....185.00

    Lost in Space 180.00

    Mod Squad, Remco, 1968 .....200.00

    Name That Tune 25.00

    NBC Peacock, Selchow & Righter, 1966, sealed..........................200.00

    Rin-Tin-Tin, Transogram, 1955....................40.00

    Road Runner, Milton Bradley, Warner Bros., 1968 ....65.00

    Route 66, Transogram, travel type, 1962 ....225.00

    Twelve O'Clock High, Milton Bradley, 1965, deck of 40 oversized playing cards 100.00

Glass, Dick Van Dyke Show, 7-1/2" h, white design, studio spotlight shows title on center of light, derby on top, cane resting on spotlight's pole, 1960s 135.00

Gum Card, complete 55 card set

    Land of the Giants, 1968........220.00

    Man from U.N.C.L.E., Topps, 1965, orig box 550.00

Gum Card Box, McHale's Navy, Fleer, 1965, illus pop-open diecut lid 115.00

Gum Card Wrapper

    Beverly Hillbillies,

Tic-Tac Dough game, Transogram Co., Inc., Jack Barry/Dan Enright Production, No. 3866398, 2nd ed, $20.

    Topps, 1963 ....85.00

    Hogan's Heroes, Fleer, 1965.............................100.00

Halloween Costume

    Flipper, cloth, black velvet trim, crack in mask 40.00

    Fred Flintstone, cloth, Ben Cooper, orig box 40.00

    Howard the Duck, Collegeville, 1986, orig box 45.00

    Lambchop, Shari Lewis, Halco, 1961, orig box 35.00

    The Fonz, Happy Days, Ben Cooper, 1976, orig box 30.00

Jewelry, Captain Video, secret seal ring, c1950..150.00

Kerchief, Howdy Doody, 18" sq, red, blue, green and orange, Howdy at the rodeo, 1950s 65.00

Kit, M*A*S*H Make Your Own Dog Tag, 2 steel chains, Tristar, 1981, unused 18.00

Lamp, figural, sitting Howdy Doody 175.00

Lunch Box

    Gunsmoke, Aladdin, 1959, metal box 150.00

    Munsters, 1965, lunch box and thermos, various scenes and portraits 400.00

    S.W.A.T., plastic, Thermos, King Seeley, 1975, blue, multicolored images, thermos missing 95.00

Magazine

    Confidential, Aug. 1966, Sammy Davis cover 8.00

    Life

        Oct. 30, 1970, Dick Cavett.....7.00

        March 26, 1971, Walter Cronkite cover 8.00

        May 7, 1971, Germaine Greer cover, Howdy Doody article.........8.00

        Dec. 10, 1971, Cybil Shepard cover, Today Show article 6.00

    Look

        Nov. 11, 1958, Ozzie & Harriet cover 12.00

        March 23, 1971, Marcus Welby cover..................................10.00

    Post, Dec. 4, 1965, Bonzana cover........................15.00

    TV Guide

        April 3, 1953, Lucille Ball's newborn baby 400.00

        Feb. 3, 1973, Bill Cosby 7.50

        July 5, 1975, Tony Orlando & Dawn 6.50

        Aug. 6, 1981, Archie Bunker, O'Conner 6.00

        Jan. 9, 1982, Michael Landon 7.00

    TV Mirror, 1963, March, Vince Edwards........................4.00

    TV Star Parade, 1973, July, Lawrence Welk cover, Rock Hudson article 4.00

Magic Drawing Slate

    Dr. Kildare, Lowe, 1962 ....50.00

    Flipper, Lowe, 1963 ....45.00

    Popeye, Eraso, MIB................85.00

Magnet, Josie & the Pussycats, 2" x 3"..4.00

Marionette, Howdy Doody, Summer, Fall, Winter & Spring, orig necklace with 4-seasons charms 225.00

Medic Kit, M.A.S.H. 30.00

Mug, 3-1/2" h, Dennis the Menace, molded plastic, painted, early 1950s 15.00

Night-Light, Flintstones, Fred and Barney 25.00

Nodder, Dr. Kildare, Lego, 7" h, ceramic, Richard Chamberlain 125.00

Paint Set

    Flipper Stardust, Hasbro, 1966, missing 1 picture and vial of paint ...50.00

    Flying Nun, Hasbro, 1967, sealed 140.00

Pennant, Howdy Doody, felt 85.00

Pinback Button

    1-3/4" d, Mighty Mouse color image, light blue ground, unofficial use of character, "Maryland Needs a Mighty Muse," c1960 ....15.00

    3-1/2" d

        Ben Casey, white, blue letters 15.00

        Fonz, "Sit On It," red and yellow, large color photo of Fonz giving thumbs up, 1974..................15.00

    Sesame Street

        Ice Follies, Ernie and Bert, yellow ground, red lettering, 1974 Muppets Inc.........................6.00

        Tennis Is A Ball, color photo image of Rolf playing tennis, green ground, Hallmark, c1980 ......6.00

Wouldn't You Rather Vote for Kermit, full-color photo image of Kermit, Henson Associates, 1980, Hallmark Cards.........12.00

Planter, 2-3/4" x 6-1/4" x 4-1/2" h, glazed ceramic, Lawrence Welk, lime green, flared accordion design, name in relief on 1 side, musical notes and bubbles on reverse, 1950s 48.00

Play Suit, Rifleman, Play-Master, 1959, mint condition, orig photo box...............................250.00

Poster Put-Ons, Charlie's Angels, self-adhesive picture posters, Bi-Rite Enterprises, Chicago, IL, 1977, MIP 24.00

Premium

Lassie, Giant Picture Premium, Best-in-Children's Books, 1961 ......110.00

Sgt. Preston, framed color portrait, Quaker Oats, 1950.................200.00

Prototype Toy, Man from U.N.C.L.E. Projector Gun, Marx, 1965, battery-operated film projector in shape of gun...................1,560.00

Shooting Arcade, Marx, 1966, hand-lettered box 650.00

Puppet, hand

Gumby and Pokey, 1964, price for pr 42.00

Howdy Doody, Mr. Bluster, Princess, Clarabelle, Dilly Dally, multicolored, plastic, figural, boxed set........175.00

Lambchop, plastic face, plain blue body 65.00

Mr. Ed, Mattel, talking, 12" h, vinyl, 1962 ....220.00

Puzzle

Ben Casey, 13-1/2" x 24", Milton Bradley, 1962 ....25.00

Family Affair, Whitman, 10 pcs, Uncle Bill sitting in chair with cast and sling, Buffy and Jody attending, 1970................25.00

Happy Days, Fonz....................15.00

Howdy Doody..........................25.00

Voyage to the Bottom of the Sea, Milton Bradley, 1964, 4 tray puzzles, orig box 450.00

Record

Addams Family, 12-1/4" sq orig cardboard slip case, 33-1/3 RPM record with 6 TV music themes, RCA Victor label, 1965.............25.00

Get Smart, United Artists, Don Adams on cover, LP, orig jacket, 1960s 25.00

Howdy Doody and the Air-O-Doodle, RCA, Little Nipper, 2 yellow 78 RPM records, foldout paper jacket, 6-pg story book about Air-O-Doodle, 1950s.........................45.00

Theme from Dr. Kildare, MGM Studios, 45 RPM, 1960s 10.00

Robot, Lost in Space, 12" h, plastic, Remco, 1966, metallic blue body, red arms, near mint condition, orig box 850.00

Shampoo Bottle, Farrah Fawcett, Faberge, 1977, 7" h, plastic.........170.00

Slide Show, Mr. Ed Give-A-Show, Kenner, 1962 ....15.00

Thermos, Beverly Hillbillies, 6-1/2" h, litho metal, red plastic cap, full-color scene, Aladdin, c1962 ....75.00

Towel, Queen for a Day, contestant dressing-room type, NBC, c1956 ....140.00

Toy

Gun

Man from U.N.C.L.E.

Napoleon Solo, Ideal, 1965, orig window box 1,200.00

Secret Service, Ideal, 1965, orig box 650.00

T.H.E. Cat, Hide-a-Way Gun, Ideal, 1966, boxed set of cap pistol, 7" stiletto and wrist scabbard.....................500.00

Motorcycle, CHiPs, removable rider, Fleetwood Toys Inc., 1978 Metro Goldwyn Mayer, MOC..............28.00

Talking, 14-1/2" h, Sesame Street Count, stuffed, purple and black, white shirt, red and yellow stripe, white bow tie, black cloth cape, says "Count My Fingers" when string is pulled, Sesame Street Muppets Inc., Knickerbocker, c1970 ....20.00

Walking Toy, 7" h plastic figure, hands raised, suction cups on back, red, white and blue open-faced box, 1950s.....................75.00

T-shirt, Josie & the Pussycats, cotton 17.00

TV Kit, Winky Dink & You, Super Magic TV Kit, Standard Toycraft, 1968 ....235.00

View Master Reel, orig envelope, 16-pg illus story booklet

Lost in Space, Sawyers, 1967 ....165.00

Star Trek GAF, 1969.............110.00

Wallet, CHiPs, orig display card, MGM, MOC 18.00

Waste Can, Laugh-In, 13" h, oval, litho metal, color photos on 1 side, "Sock It to Me" slogan on reverse, 1968 ....42.00

Whistle, Dragnet...........................15.00

Wristwatch

Howdy Doody, 1971, orig band 95.00

Tammy, half face is blue, other is white, blue band, 1960s.........125.00

Yo-Yo, 2-1/4" d, Official Pee Wee

Herman Brand, white plastic, colorful image of Pee Wee, name in different colors, image repeated on both sides, late 1980s 12.00

Thermometers

Collecting Hints: These are collectibles we can all identify. Ranging from the small ones kept in the medicine cabinet, to the readily found color advertising examples, thermometers are plentiful and represent a hot collectible.

Thermometer collectors divide their collections into advertising, science/medicine, souvenir types and miscellaneous. Souvenir types are especially numerous since many were produced. Some are unusual and whimsical. Science/medicine thermometers range from industrial usage models to the type often tucked away in the medicine cabinet.

History: The first practical thermometer was invented by Galileo about 1593. It wasn't until the Celsius and Fahrenheit scales were accepted that measurement became standardized; early Americans had used as many as 18 different scales to measure temperature. New Englanders used devices with alcohol, rather than expensive mercury. Southerners were known to favor a bi-metallic spring device. Thermometers are found mounted on metal, wood, silver and gold, but brass seems to have been the favorite.

Thousands of advertising thermometers were made, running the gamut of products from beverages to home heating contractors. One of the more unusual types of thermometers is the kind known as a bathtub floater. Long before the advent of hot water and indoor plumbing it was used to check the bath-water temperature. Desk and more decorative room thermometers became an important home accessory.

Collector's Club: Thermometer Collectors Club of America, 6130 Rampart Dr., Carmichael, CA 95608.

Museum: Richard Porter's Thermometer Museum, Box 944, Onset, MA 02558-0944.

Braun's Bread, Town Talk, tin, painted, 38-3/4", $40.

Reproduction Alert: Reproduction advertising thermometers exist. Many of these counterfeits use a paper label, whereas the original was painted and has the maker's name stamped on the back in ink. Modern metal thermometers lack the natural aging resulting from long exposure to the weather.

Advisor: Warren Harris.

A.J. Dodge, Peterboro, NH, wall, wood frame, brass F scale, blue spirit, 8" x 1-1/2", 1900 .... 650.00

American Thermometer Co., St. Louis, wall, porcelain-on-steel frame, porcelain F scale, red spirit, 8-1/2" x 2", 1920 .... 100.00

B.T. Co., NY, wood with green enamel, wood F scale, red spirit, 7-1/2" x 1-3/4", 1910 .... 150.00

Bradley & Hubbard, wall, brass-on-cast-iron frame, cast-iron F scale, mercury, 12" x 3", 1890 .... 850.00

Bullock & Reynolds, London, wall, wood frame, wood F scale, mercury, 9-1/2" x 1/2", 1900 .... 500.00

C.J.T., cottage barometer, wall, tin frame, brass F scale, blue spirit, 8" x 2-1/2", 1895 .... 450.00

C.M. Mfg Co., NY, wall, cast-iron frame, iron F scale, 13" x 13-1/2", 1890 .... 400.00

C.P. Scott, Buffalo, cottage barometer, wall, wood frame, spirit, 8" x 3" 250.00

Carl Leidig, Nurnberg, wall, wood frame, ivory R&C scale, mercury, 8" x 1-1/2" 450.00

Charles Doran, Rochester, wall, tin frame, tin F scale, red spirit, 7-3/4" x 1-3/4", 1895 .... 300.00

Charles Wilder, Troy, NY, wall, brass frame, brass F scale, mercury, 7" x 1-3/4", 1885 .... 1,200.00

Chas. E. Large, Brooklyn, wall, tin frame, tin F scale, red spirit, 9" x 2-3/4", 1895, rare 750.00

David Leeds, England, wall, wood frame, wood F scale, mercury, 6" x 4", 1895 .... 650.00

Diamond, wall, wood frame, brass F scale, mercury, 7-3/4" x 1-3/4", 1900 .... 450.00

Dollond, London, wall, mahogany frame, SS F scale, mercury, 22" x 3", 1870 .... 1,900.00

Fairbanks & Co., wall, brass frame, enamel dial F scale, 9" d, 1890 .... 650.00

J.M. Schmidt, Amsterdam, wall, mahogany frame, brass F scale, red spirit, 9-1/2" x 2", 1890 .... 95.00

J. Waldstein, Wien, German, wall, wood frame, SS R scale, mercury, 10-1/2" x 1-3/4", 1890 .... 100.00

L.C. Tower, Weather Prognosticator, wall, wood frame, brass F scale, 9" x 3" 450.00

Maixi Facien, France, wall, wood frame, wood R & C scale, spirit, 10-1/2" x 2-1/4", 1880 .... 1,100.00

Moeller Instrument Co., wall, brass frame, black enameled metal F scale, red spirit, 12" x 1", 1895 .... 300.00

Motometer, Long Island, desk, brass frame, brass F scale, round dial, 11" x 14", 1910 .... 350.0

P. Harris & Co., LTD, Birmingham, wall, wood frame, wood C&R scale, 8" x 12", 1905 .... 650.00

Pool, cottage barometer, wall, wood frame, tin F scale, amber spirit, 8" x 3" 300.00

Moxie, litho tin, 12" x 9-9/16", $750.

R. Klaasesz en CR, German, wall, glass frame, glass C&F scale, mercury, 10" x 2-1/2", 1895, very rare 1,200.00

Standard Thermometer Co., Peabody, MA, wall, round brass frame, dial with picture of Newbury Bridge, 8" d, 1900 .... 400.00

Taylor Bros., wall, wood frame, brass F scale, mercury, 11" x 2", 1905 .... 450.00

Taylor, Rochester,
    Candy, wood frame, brass F scale, mercury, 8" x 1-1/2", 1910 .... 60.00
    Storm Guide, wall, 1900
        8" x 2", japanned metal frame, black enamel F scale, mercury 450.00
        9-1/2" x 3-3/4", wood frame, brass F scale 350.00
    Wall, wood frame
        7-1/2" x 2", brass F scale, red spirit, 1920 .... 125.00
        9-1/2" x 2-1/4", black enamel on F scale, mercury, 1900 ...... 350.00

Tycos
    Chandelier, brass frame, brass F scales on 3 sides, red spirit, 8-1/2" x 2-1/2", 1885, very rare 1,650.00
    Hygrometer, wall, wood frame, brass F scale, mercury, 8-1/2" x 4-1/2", 1910 .... 600.00
    Min-max, wall, brass frame, brass F scale, mercury, 9-1/2" x 2-1/4", 1910 .... 300.00

Unknown maker
    English, wall, wood "battle ax" frame, iron R&C scale, mercury, 18" x 10", 1920 .... 180.00
    Wall
        Brass frame mounted on deer leg, brass F scale, mercury, 15" x 2", 1915.................................. 100.00
        Wood tramp art frame, wood F scale, spirit, 15" x 6", 1925 .... 150.00

W.B. Loveday Co., wall, cast-iron frame, white enamel dial, 5" d, 1895 .... 850.00

Watertown Thermometer Co., Watertown, NY, wall, wood frame, brass F scale, 8-3/4" x 2-1/4", 1895 .... 550.00

White & Westall, Lewiston, ME, wall, wood frame, porcelain F scale, mercury, 7-1/2" x 1-1/2", 1880, rare 770.00

Toys

Collecting Hints: Condition is a critical factor. Most collectors like to have examples in very fine to mint condi-

Chein, Ferris Wheel, Hercules, windup, litho tin, yellow and red, $150.

tion. The original box and any instruction sheets add to the value. Sophisticated collectors concentrate on the tin and cast iron toys of the late 19th and early 20th centuries. However, more and more collectors are specializing in products made between 1940 and 1970, including those from firms such as Fisher-Price.

Many toys were characterizations of cartoon, radio and television figures. A large number of collectible fields have some form of toy spin-off. The result is that the toy collector is constantly competing with the specialized collector.

History: The first cast iron toys began to appear in America shortly after the Civil War. Leading 19th-century manufacturers include Hubley, Dent, Kenton and Schoenhut. In the first decades of the 20th century, Arcade, Buddy L, Marx and Tootsie Toy joined these earlier firms. Wooden toys were made by George Brown and other manufacturers who did not sign or label their work.

Nuremberg, Germany, was the European center for the toy industry from the late 18th through the mid-20th centuries. Companies such as Lehman and Marklin produced high-quality toys.

References: Linda Baker, *Modern Toys*, Collector Books, 1985, 1993 value update; William M. Bean and Al M. Sternagle, *Greenberg's Guide to Gilbert Erector Sets, Vol. 1, 1913-1932*, Greenberg Publishing, 1993; John Bonavita, *Mego Action Toys*, Schiffer Publishing, 1996; Raymond V. Brandes, *Big Bang Cannons*, Ray-Vin Publishing, 1993; Steve Butler and Clarence Young, *Autoquotes, The Complete Reference for: Promotions, Pot Metal & Plastic with Prices*, Autohobby Publications, 1993; *Cartoon & Character Toys of the 50s, 60s, & 70s*, L-W Book Sales, 1995; Wallace M. Chrouch, *Mego Toys*, Collector Books, 1995; John A. Clark, *HO Slot Car Identification and Price Guide*, L-W Book Sales, 1995; *Collector's Digest Price Guide to Pull Toys*, L-W Book Sales, 1996; *Collector's Digest Tops and Yo-Yos and Other Spinning Toys*, L-W Book Sales, 1995; Christopher Cook, *Collectible American Yo-Yos*, Collector Books, 1997; Gael de Courtivron, *Collectible Coca-Cola Toy Trucks*, Collector Books, 1995; Don Cranmer, *Collectors Encyclopedia: Toys-Banks*, L-W Book Sales, 1986, 1994-95 value update; Henry René D'Allemagne, *Antique Playing Cards*, Dover, 1996; Don and Barb DeSalle, *Collector's Guide to Tonka Trucks 1947-1963*, L-W Book Sales, 1996; Charles F. Donovan Jr., *Renwal, World's Finest Toys*, published by author (11877 U.S. Hwy. 431, Ohatchee, AL 36271), 1994; Elmer Duellman, *Elmer's Price Guide to Toys, Vol. 1* (1995), *Vol. 2* (1996), L-W Book Sales; James L. Dundas, *Collecting Whistles*, Schiffer Publishing, 1995;

Arcade, Road Construction Set, No. 431, red and green toys, yellow, red, and green signs, Arcade Mfg. Co., Freeport, IL, c1935, $795.

Evolution of the Pedal Car, Vol. 1 (1996 values), *Vol. 2* (1993 values), *Vol. 3* (1992 values), *Vol. 4* (1997 values); Edward Force, *Classic Miniature Vehicles: Made in Italy*, Schiffer Publishing, 1992; ——, *Corgi Toys*, Schiffer Publishing, 1984, 1991 value update; ——, *Dinky Toys*, 3rd Edition, Schiffer Publishing, 1996; ——, *Lledo Toys*, Schiffer Publishing, 1996; ——, *Solido Toys*, Schiffer Publishing, 1993; Tom Frey, *Toy Bop*, Fuzzy Dice Productions, 1994; Christine Gentry and Sally Gibson-Downs, *Motorcycle Toys*, Collector Books, 1994; David C. Gould and Donna Crevar-Donaldson, *Occupied Japan Toys with Prices*, L-W Book Sales, 1993; Jeffrey C. Gurski, *Greenberg's Guide to Cadillac Models and Toys*, Greenberg Publishing, 1992.

Bill Hanlon, *Plastic Toy*; Morton Hirschberg, *Steam Toys*, Schiffer Publishing, 1996; Jay Horowitz, *Marx Western Playsets*, Greenberg Publishing, 1992; Don Hultzman, *Collecting Battery Toys*, Books Americana, 1994; Ken Hutchison & Greg Johnson, *Golden Age of Automotive Toys*, Collector Books, 1996; Charles M. Jacobs, *Kenton Cast Iron Toys*, Schiffer Publishing, 1996; Dana Johnson, *Matchbox Toys*, 2nd Edition, Collector Books, 1996; Douglas R. Kelly, *Die Cast Price Guide*, Antique Trader Books, 1997; Lisa Kerr, *American Tin-Litho Toys*, Collectors Press, 1995; Raymond R. Klein, *Greenberg's Guide to Tootsietoys 1945-1969*, Greenberg Publishing, 1993; David Longest, *Antique & Collectible Toys*, Collector Books, 1994; ——, *Toys*, Collector Books, 1990, 1995 value update; Charlie Mack, *Lesney's Matchbox Toys, Vol. 1* (1992), *Vol. 2* (1993), *Vol. 3* (1993), Schiffer Publishing; Jack Matthews, *Toys Go to War: World War II Military Toys, Games, Puzzles & Books*, Pictorial Histories Publishing, 1994; Neil McElwee, *McElwee's Collector's Guide #1: Smith-Miller*, published by author, 1994; ——, *McElwee's Collector's Guide #3: Tonka Toys*, published by author, 1992; ——, *McElwee's Collector's Guide #5: Postwar Buddy "L,"* published by author, 1992; ——, *McElwee's Collector's Guide #6: Ny-*

Hubley, airplane, yellow, orange wings, landing gear goes up, clear plastic cover slides back, 10" l, 11" wingspan, $20.

Lint, published by author, 1993; ——, *McElwee's Collector's Guide #7: Big Ertl, Cast Commercial Trucks & Construction Vehicles*, published by author, 1993; ——, *McElwee's Collector's Guide #8: Gasoline Company Toys...Trucks & Automotive*, published by author, 1994; ——, *McElwee's Collector's Guide #9: Structo*, published by author, 1993; ——, *McElwee's Collector's Guide #10: Postwar Big Metal Classics*, published by author, 1994; ——, *McElwee's Small Motor News Annual*, published by author, 1994.

John J. Murray and Bruce Fox, *Fisher-Price*, 2nd Edition, Books Americana, 1991; *1997 Toys & Prices*, 4th Edition, Krause Publications, 1996; Richard O'Brien, *Collecting Toy Cars & Trucks*, Books Americana, 1994; ——, *Collecting Toys*, 7th Edition, Books Americana, 1995; Robert M. Overstreet, *Overstreet Toy Ring Price Guide*, 2nd Edition, Collector Books, 1996; Bob Parker, *Hot Wheels*, 2nd Edition, Schiffer Publishing, 1996; John Ramsay, *British Diecast Model Toys*, 6th Edition, available from Tim Arthurs (109 Glover Ave., Norwalk, CT 06850), 1996; David Richter, *Collectors Guide to Tootsietoys*, Collector Books, 1990, 1993 value update; *Riding Toys*, L-W Book Sales, 1992, 1996 value update; Harry L. Rinker, *Toy Price Guide*, Antique Trader Books, 1996; Nancy Schiffer (comp.), *Matchbox Toys*, Revised, Schiffer Publishing, 1995; *Schroeder's Collectible Toys*, 3rd Edition, Collector Books, 1996; Carole and Richard Smith, *Pails by Comparison*, published by authors (P.O. Box 2068, Huntington, NY 11743), 1996;

Ron Smith, *Collecting Toy Airplanes*, Books Americana, 1995; Bruce and Diane Stoneback, *Matchbox Toys*, Chartwell Books, 1993; Glenda Thomas, *Toy and Miniature Sewing Machines*, Collector Books, 1995; Sharon Korbeck (ed), *Toy Shop 1998 Annual Directory*, 6th edition, Krause Publications, 1996; Tom Tumbusch, *Tomart's Price Guide to Hot Wheels*, Tomart Publications, 1993; Carol Turpen, *Baby Boomer Toys and Collectibles*, Schiffer Publishing, 1993; Gerhard C. Walter, *Metal Toys from Nuremberg* Schiffer Publishing, 1992.

Periodicals: *Action Toys Newsletter*, P.O. Box 31551, Billings, MT 59107; *Antique Toy World*, P.O. Box 34509, Chicago, IL 60634; *Canadian Toy Mania*, P.O. Box 489, Rocanville, Saskatchewan S0A 3L0 Canada; *Collecting Toys*, P.O. Box 1989, Milwaukee, WI 53201; *Die Cast & Tin Toy Report*, P.O. Box 501, Williamsburg, VA 23187; *Die Cast Digest*, P.O. Box 12510, Knoxville, TN 37912; *Matchbox USA Newsletter*, 62 Saw Mill Rd., Durham, CT 06422; *Model and Toy Collector Magazine*, 137 Casterton Ave., Akron, OH, 44303; *Plane News*, P.O. Box 845, Greenwich, CT 06836; *Plastic Figure & Playset Collector*, Box 1355, La Crosse, WI 54602; *Spec-Tacular News*, P.O. Box 324, Dyersville, IA 52040; *Toy Cannon News*, P.O. Box 2052-N, Norcross, GA, 30071; *Toy Collector and Price Guide*, 700 E. State St., Iola, WI 54990; *Toy Collector Marketplace*, 1550 Territorial Rd., Benton Harbor, MI 49022; *Toy Farmer*, HC 2, Box 5, LaMoure, ND 58458; *Toy*

Fisher-Price, Squeaky the Clown, 1958, $35.

Shop, 700 E. State St., Iola, WI 54990; *Toy Tractor Times*, P.O. Box 156, Osage, IA 50461; *Toy Trader*, P.O. Box 1050, Dubuque, IA 52004; *Toybox Magazine*, 8393 E. Holly Rd., Holly, MI 48442; *Tractor Classics*, P.O. Box 191, Listowel, Ontario N4H 3HE Canada; *Turtle River Toy News & Oliver Collector's News*, RR1, Box 44, Manvel, ND 58256; *U.S. Toy Collector Magazine*, P.O. Box 4244, Missoula, MT 59806; *Wheel Goods Trader*, P.O. Box 435, Fraser, MI 48026; *Yo-Yo Times*, P.O. Box 1519, Herndon, VA 22070.

Videotape: David Pressland, *Magic of the Tin Toy* Toy World.

Collectors' Clubs: A.C. Gilbert Heritage Society, 594 Front St., Marion, MA 02738; American Game Collectors Association, 49 Brooks Ave., Lewiston, ME 04240; American International Matchbox Collectors & Exchange Club, 532 Chestnut St., Lynn, MA 01904; Anchor Block Foundation, 980 Plymouth St., Pelham, NY 10803; Antique Engine, Tractor & Toy Club, 5731 Paradise Rd., Slatington, PA 18080; Antique Toy Collectors of America, Two Wall Street, 13th Fl., New York, NY 10005; Capitol Miniature Auto Collectors Club, 10207 Greenacres Dr., Silver Spring, MD 20903; Diecast Exchange Club, P.O. Box 1066, Pineallas Park, FL 34665; Ertl Collectors Club, Hwys. 186 & 120, Dyersville, IA 52040; Farm Toy Collectors Club, P.O. Box 38, Boxholm, IA 50040; Fisher-Price Collector's Club, 1442 N. Ogden, Mesa, AZ 85205; Girder and Panel Collectors Club, P.O. Box 494, Bolton, MA, 01740; HO Slot Car Collecting & Racing Club, 284 Willets Ln., West Islip, NY 14795; Majorette Diecast Toy Collectors Association, 1347 NW Albany Ave., Bend, OR 97701; Matchbox Collectors Club, P.O. Box 278, Durham, CT 06422; Matchbox International Collectors Association, 574 Canewood Crescent, Waterloo, Ontario N2L 5P6 Canada; Miniature Piano Enthusiast Club, 633 Pennsylvania Ave., Hagerstown, MD 21740; San Francisco Bay Brooklin Club, P.O. Box 61018, Palo Alto, CA 94306; Schoenhut Collectors Club, 45 Louis Ave., West Seneca, NY

14224; Schoenhut Toy Collectors, 1916 Cleveland St., Evanston, IL 60202; Southern California Meccano & Erector Club, 9661 Sabre Ave., Garden Grove, CA 92644; Southern California Toy Collectors Club, Ste 300, 1760 Termino, Long Beach, CA 90804.

Museums: American Museum of Automobile Miniatures, Andover, MA; Eugene Field House & Toy Museum, St. Louis, MO; Evanston Historical Society, Evanston, IL 60201; Forbes Magazine Collection, New York, NY; Hobby City Doll & Toy Museum, Anaheim, CA; Margaret Woodbury Strong Museum, Rochester, NY; Matchbox & Lesney Toy Museum, Durham, CT; Matchbox Road Museum, Newfield, NJ; Museum of the City of New York, New York, NY; Smithsonian Institution, Washington, DC; Spinning Top Exploratory Museum, Burlington, WI; Toy & Miniature Museum of Kansas City, Kansas City, MO; Toy Museum of Atlanta, Atlanta, GA; Washington Dolls' House & Toy Museum, Washington, DC; Western Reserve Historical Society, Cleveland, OH.

Additional Listings: Battery Operated Automata, Cartoon Characters, Disneyana, Dolls, Games, Paper Dolls, Radio Characters, Dimestore Soldiers, Toy Soldiers, Toy Trains and many other categories.

Alps: Alps Shoji LTD, located in Tokyo, was founded in 1948. The company manufactured windup and battery-powered toys made from tin and plastic. Toys are marked "ALPS."

Baby in Walker, cloth and vinyl baby, metal walker, shakes litho tin rattle, 10" h, orig box 75.00

Bar-X Cowboy, litho tin windup, full-figure cowboy on horse, twirls metal lariat, horse with leather tail and ears, 6-1/2" l, 1950s, orig box.........145.00

Bozo the Clown, litho tin windup, plays drums, 8" h 500.00

Combination Sink and Stove, metal, battery operated, 6" x 7", MIB.......90.00

Cubby, Reading Bear, holds and turns tin book pages, MIB.................95.00

Fire Chief Car, tin friction, 8" l, worn box...........................60.00

Lester the Jester, litho tin windup, fabric clothing, 9" h, orig box...........395.00

Porsche, 911 Carrera #19, East African Safari, battery operated,

9-1/2" l, MIB............................325.00
Race Car, Chaparral, battery operated, flashing lights, 11" l, MIB 185.00
Sea Wolf, litho tin windup, peg-legged pirate with spy glass, 7" h......275.00
Strutting Parade, litho tin windup, cowboy duck, twirls lariat, quacks, 8" h, orig box.................................110.00

A.M.T.

Promo Car, plastic

T-Bird, red convertible, white int, gold accents, chrome-colored bumpers, black metal undercarriage, 7-1/4" l.....................120.00
Thunderbird, white, gold int, chrome accent bumpers, beige plastic hubcaps, black rubber wheels, black metal undercarriage, 1957, plate stamped "Birmingham, Mich," 2-3/4" x 7" x 1-3/4" h 100.00
Slot Car, AC Cobra Body, 1/24 scale, tan, MIB 95.00

Arcade: The Arcade Manufacturing Co., first produced toys in 1891. In 1919, the firm began to make the yellow cabs for the Yellow Cab Co., of Chicago. The exclusive advertising rights were sold to the cab company with Arcade holding the right to make toy replicas of the cabs. This idea was popular and soon was used with Buick, Ford, etc., and McCormack and International Harvester farm equipment. The company remained in business until 1946 when it was sold to Rockwell Manufacturing Co., of Pittsburgh.

Airplane, cast iron, red, silver wings, 7-1/4" wingspan.....................225.00
Bus...110.00
Ford, Model A, sedan..................400.00
Horse and Sulky...........................95.00
Pickup Truck, cast iron, 5" l.........225.00
Showboat 225.00
Tractor, cast iron, 1930s 115.00

Bandai Co.: Bandai, one of the many toy manufacturers that began production in Japan after World War II, started with tin toys and later changed to plastic and steel. Bandai Toys have friction action or are battery operated. They are often marked "Bandai Toys, Japan." Bandai still produces toys and is a major Japanese exporter to the U.S. and other foreign countries.

Aircraft Carrier and Helicopter, T15 Bay Carrier, 7" l, litho tin friction, orig box 165.00
Cadillac, litho tin friction, 1959 convertible, blue 350.00
Chevy Camaro SS, battery-operated litho tin, 13" l, MIB..................225.00

Hubley, Bell Telephone truck, white metal, painted olive green, $45.

Harbor Patrol, battery-operated tin, boat, 9" l 150.00
MG Racer, litho tin friction, tin steering wheel, scalloped plastic windshield, "Winner 1956 Overland Race" on trunk, spare tire, chrome detail, engine noise, 8" l, orig box........365.00
Silver Pidgeon Motor Scooter, litho tin friction...................................425.00
Volkswagen Sedan, battery-operated tin litho, MIB 325.00

Buddy L: Buddy L Co., was founded in 1921 by Fred Lundahl. It produced high-quality, finely detailed toys. Many were large enough to ride on. Production changed from steel to lighter-weight, smaller toys in the 1930s. A limited number of wooden toys were made during World War II. The firm still operates today.

Air Mail Truck, 1932, 24" x 7-1/4" x 8".....................365.00
Airplane, orange wings, 2" d aluminum propeller, decals, c1930 ....95.00
Baggage Truck...........................165.00
Dairy Transport Truck, Duo-Tone slant design paint, red and white, opens in back, decal, 26" l 75.00
Coke Truck..................................225.00
Dump Truck, seat and handle missing, 1948 ....110.00
Emergency Auto Wrecker, #3317, red and white bed........................185.00
Fast Freight Truck, pressed steel, white cab, orange truck, black rubber tires, c1940, 20" l 145.00
Greyhound Bus, litho tin windup, 16" l..........................350.00
Ice Truck, black front and hood, yellow cargo, natural canvas cov imprinted "Buddy L Ice Delivery," imitation ice, tongs, orig decals, 1933, 26-1/2" l 125.00
Merry Go Round Truck 95.00
Steam Shovel, orig red and black panel, orig decals.............................150.00
Towing Service "Fix My Flat" with dome light, white and light blue.......145.00

Chein: The Chein Co., was in business from the 1930s through the 1950s.

Most of its lithographed tin toys were sold in dimestores. Chein toys are clearly marked.

Barnacle Bill, litho tin windup, wearing barrel, c1930 ....300.00
Broadway Trolley, litho tin momentum, red and green, c1930 ....325.00
Carousel, tin pump toy 60.00
Checker Cab, litho tin momentum, 1924, 8" l 525.00
Donald Duck, litho tin windup 65.00
Dump Truck, litho momentum, Mack style, lever dumping action, 9" l 95.00
Happy Hooligan 600.00
Helicopter, litho tin windup, 12" l, MIB 230.00
Hercules Ferris Wheel, litho tin windup, 17" h, orig box 375.00
Mechanical Turtle #145, litho tin windup, native riding back, 7" l, orig box 325.00
Pianola, player piano, 6 rolls 325.00
Sand Pail, litho tin, fish in the fun ..35.00
Sand Shovel, litho tin, 14" l 45.00
Skin Diver, litho tin windup, plastic flippers, 11" l, orig box 145.00
Waddling Duck, litho tin windup, c1935, 4" h 75.00

Corgi: Playcraft Toys introduced Corgi miniature vehicles in 1956. This popular line soon became Corgi Toys. The first cars were made on a scale from 1:45 to 1:48. Corgi cars were the first miniature cars to have clear-plastic windows. Other design features included doors that opened and interiors. In 1972, the scale of 1:36 was introduced. This scale was more durable for play but less desirable to collectors. Finally, the company added other types of cars and trucks, including character representations.

Astin Martin Competition Model, MIB 100.00
Barney Rubble's Car, MOC 25.00
Charlie's Angels Chevy Van, MIB 60.00
Chevrolet Caprice, MIB 60.00
Chrysler Imperial, MIB 85.00
Ford Consul Classic 315, MIB 80.00
Ford Dragster, Glow Worm, white, #163, MIB 85.00
Ford Escort 13GL, MIB 30.00
Fred Flintstone's Car, MOC 25.00
Hillman Husky, MIB 160.00
Hot Roadster, #28, yellow 25.00
James Bond Moonraker Shuttle, MIB 90.00
Jerry's Banger 15.00
Kojak's Buick, MIB......................100.00
Marlin, #263, red and black, 1/43 scale, MIB 100.00
Mercedes-Benz 240D, MIB 45.00

KO, F-50 fighter, battery operated, litho tin and plastic, stop-and-go and mystery action, lighted engine, 11" l, 6" h, Japanese, orig box, $150.

Midland Bus, MIB 270.00
Oldsmobile Super 88, MIB 130.00
Rover 2000 TC, MIB 65.00
Simon Snorkel Fire Engine, MIB ...75.00
Spiderman's Spiderbike, MIB......100.00
Super Stock Car, silver and yellow, Castrol trim 25.00
Triumph TR3 Sports Car, MIB.....130.00
Vegas Ford T-Bird, MIB 90.00

Courtland: Courtland Manufacturing Co., was founded by Walter Reach in 1944. Originally located in Camden, NJ, the firm later moved to Philadelphia. The company closed in 1951.

Circus Truck, litho tin, truck pulls revolving cylinder with litho lion, bear, tiger and elephant, 9" l...................125.00
Coal Truck, litho tin windup, coal chute, crank, activates scissors-dumping action, 1950s, 11" l, orig box..........................145.00
Dairy Semi-Truck 195.00
Fire Dept. Truck, litho tin windup, ladder raises, 9" l, orig box 225.00
Modern Bakery Truck, #4000, litho tin windup, panel body, red and yellow, 7" l, orig box...............150.00
State Police 175.00

Dinky: Dinky Toys, made by the Meccano Toy Co., of England, were first created by Frank Hornby in 1933. The Dinky series of die-cast cars and trucks continued until World War II precluded the use of metal for toys. In 1945, production of die-cast metal toys again began with the introduction of a military line, as well as new cars and trucks. Production continued in factories in England and France until competition from Corgi, Tootsietoy and Matchbox caused a decline in sales. The Dinky line was discontinued in 1979.

Austin Taxi, MIB 75.00
Beach Buggy, MIB 30.00
Citrone Dyuane, MIB.....................40.00

Climax Ford Lift Truck, MIB 100.00
Chrysler New Yorker, MIB 150.00
Corvette Stingray 30.00
Euclid Dump Truck, #965..............50.00
Ford Ambulance, MIB 50.00
Ford Sedan Military 100.00
Four-Berth Caravan, MIB.............100.00
Hay Rake 45.00
Hudson Hornet Sedan, MIB 120.00
Jeep, #153A, restored...................50.00
Mercedes-Benz 600, MIB 120.00
MGB Sports Car, MIB 120.00
Morris Pick-Up, MIB 50.00
Opel Kapitan, MIB 100.00
Panhard Esso Tanker, MIB.........140.00
Pontiac Parisienne, MIB 120.00
Race Car......................................100.00
Rolls Royce Silver Shadow, MIB............................70.00
Studebaker Land Cruiser, MIB....110.00
Tractor, Aveling-Barford, red and green, 1950s....................50.00
Triumph Vitesse, MIB....................50.00
USA Police Car, MIB 120.00

Ertl: Fred Ertl Sr., founded Ertl in 1945. Blueprints obtained from companies such as John Deere and International Harvester were used as patterns, thus insuring a high level of similarity to the originals. Ertl produces a fill line of wheeled vehicles and is recognized as the world's largest manufacturer of toy farm equipment.

Airplane, Wings of Texaco
#2, Gamma 27.95
#3, Biplane...............................25.95
Bell Truck, Bell Telephone Pioneer, NY 20.00
Campbell Soup Truck 30.00
Coke Truck, #1 ....100.00
Majorette Mercedes 500L Roadster, MIB 25.00
Pickup, Bell Systems 20.00
Promo Vehicle, plastic, 3-1/4" x 7-3/4" x 2-3/4" orig white box
1990 Beretta GTZ, #6037 ....10.00
1991 Geo Storm GSI 10.00

Fisher Price: Fisher-Price Toys was founded in East Aurora, NY, in 1930. The original company consisted of Irving L. Price, retired from F.W. Woolworth Co., Herman G. Fisher, who was associated with the Alderman-Fairchild Toy., in Churchville, NY, and Helen M. Schelle, a former toy store owner. Margaret Evans Price, wife of the company president, was the company's first artist and designer. She had been a writer and illustrator of children's books. The company began with 16 designs. Herman Fisher resigned as president in 1966. In 1969, the company was acquired by the Quaker Oats Co. Black and white rectangular logos appeared on all toys prior to 1962. The first plastic part was used after 1949. Mattel bought Fisher-Price a few years ago.

Bunny Cart, #10, 1940, 9" l 50.00
Cackling Hen, #120 ....60.00
Chatter Monk, #798......................45.00
Doctor Kit, 1977............................15.00
Donald Duck, #765......................100.00
Mickey Mouse Safety
  Patrol, #733 ....160.00
Peter Pig.....................................50.00
Pluto Pop-Up, #440 ....125.00
Popeye, spinach drum, pull top ...550.00
Radio, #759, wood 30.00
Snoopy, #181 ....55.00
Space Blazer, #750.....................200.00
Tailspin Tabby, #400 ....85.00

Hasbro: Hasbro Industries, Inc., an American toy manufacturer, is well known for several lines. One of the most popular toys produced by this company is Mr. Potato Head. It was introduced in 1948 and is still being made today. Another popular Hasbro line is GI Joe along with all the accessories made for this series of action figures.

Digger the Dog, plastic, vinyl tail
  and ears, orig yellow hat and
  leash string, 13-3/4" l 15.00
Mickey Mouse Talking Telephone, battery operated, 1964, MIB 175.00
Mr. Potato Head, 7-1/2" x 10" x 2" box,
  2-1/4" d Styrofoam ball head,
  plastic accessories, orig color
  illus instruction sheet, #2000,
  c1950, orig box 40.00
Scooter the Tooter, plastic,
  clown, flexible vinyl arms,
  bluebird on hat........................10.00
Weebles Haunted House, plastic
  furniture, glow-in-the-dark Ghost
  Weeble, Witch Weeble, Boy
  Weeble and Girl Weeble..........20.00

Hot Wheels: Made by Mattel beginning in 1968. Redline-wheel cars were made until 1977, after which black-wall-wheel cars were made.

Backwoods Bomb, #7670, light blue,
  1979, MOC 125.00
Bronco 4-Wheeler, Toys R Us,
  1981, MOC 120.00
Cadillac Seville, gold, French, Real
  Rider, 1983, MOC...................95.00
Custom Mustang, red, redlines 25.00
Deora, aquamarine,
  surfboards, MOC 225.00
Double Header, #5880, 1968 ....60.00
El Rey Special, green,
  1974, MOC 70.00

Evil Weevil, #6471, 1971, MOC 85.00
Hi Tail Hauler, orange, black bikes,
  MOC 25.00
Otis 442, red...............................165.00
T-Bird, 1957, yellow,
  red lines, MOC 135.00
Whip Creamer, yellow,
  red lines, MOC 45.00

Hubley: The Hubley Manufacturing Co., was founded in 1894 in Lancaster, PA, by John Hubley. The first toys were cast iron. In 1940, cast iron was phased out and replaced with metals and plastic. By 1952, Hubley made more cap pistols than any other type of toy. Gabriel Industries bought Hubley in 1965.

Airplane
  American Eagle, 11" wingspan,
    all metal, MIB 150.00
  DO-X, cast iron, gray, red wings,
    4" wingspan............................500.00
  Low Wing, cast iron, orange, nickel-
    plated wings, 1930s
      3-5/8" wingspan 140.00
      5" wingspan 160.00
  TAT NC-491, green, cast iron,
    nickel-plated wings.................185.00
Baby Speedboat, cast iron, emb "Baby"
  on side, 4-1/2" l........................85.00
Buick Convertible, die cast, black rubber
  tires, nickel-plated windshield,
  1940s, 7" l, orig box...............125.00
Crash Car......................................65.00
Ice Wagon 45.00
Mare, foal, cast iron,
  wood base 125.00
Pickup, die cast, 11" l...................45.00
Pistol, Colt 45,
  orig holsters, price for pr........575.00
Racer, die cast 165.00

Ideal: The Ideal Toy Co., was owned by Lewis David Christie. It was located in Bridgeport, CT. Among the toys it produced were dolls, cars, trucks and even a line of toy soldiers produced for a short time span in the 1920s.

Betty Crocker Junior Baking Kit,
  1952, MIB 90.00
Electric Food Center,
  1950s, MIB 35.00
Hot Dog Wagon, MIB 315.00
Satellite Launcher, 3 satellites, orig
  instructions, 1950s Ideal catalog,
  box fair..................................125.00
Slot Car, TCR, Dirt Modified Mustang,
  blue and yellow, MIB 25.00
The Big Press, printing press 45.00

Japanese, Post War: Following World War II, a huge variety of toys produced in Osaka and the Koto District

Sun Rubber Co., truck, #14, red and yellow, 4-3/4" l, $50.

of Japan flooded the American market. The vast majority of these toys are marked only with the country of origin and a trademark, usually consisting of a two- or three-letter monogram. It is virtually impossible to trace these trademarks to a specific manufacturer. Also, many toys were assembled from parts made by several different factories. To make matters even more confusing, names found on boxes are often those of the agent or distributor, rather than the manufacturer. The following toys are listed by their trademarks. When possible, the toy's manufacturer and/or distributor are also identified. Also see specific listings for other Japanese toy companies.

ATC, Asahi Toy Co.
  Champion Race Car, 8" l, tin, ATC
    and Mobil Oil sponsors 275.00
  Mary Open Television Co.,
    litho tin friction, 1953, 7" l.........85.00
  Subaru Sedan, litho tin friction,
    detailed int, emb "Subaru" under
    front grill, 1950s, 6" l 285.00
Cragston
  Airplane, circus jet, battery-operated
    tin, MIB..................................225.00
  Car, 3" x 7-3/4" x 2-1/2", plastic
    friction, GTO race car, lime green,
    red int, chrome-colored racing
    scoop in hood, mkd "Made in
    Hong Kong"............................35.00
  Dump Truck, trailer,
    side dump, all tin 120.00
  Rock and Roll Monkey,
    battery operated.....................225.00
Honey, Van, John Cool Volkswagen Ice
  Cream, 1:43 die cast, MIB.....100.00
K
  Cycling Quacky, litho tin windup,
    duck riding tricycle, quacks,
    7" l, orig box 150.00
  Ford Skyliner, litho tin friction,
    hardtop convertible, Ford hubcaps,
    1958 model, 10" l, orig box 350.00
  Walking Circus Elephant, plush
    windup, celluloid native sitting on
    trunk, 7" l, orig box 225.00
KO, Kanto Toys

Ack Ack Jeep, tin friction, full-figure soldier driver, black rubber spare tire, firing guns, 7" l, orig box...........65.00

Togo Gigio, tin windup, bumper-type car, 6" l..............185.00

Kyoe
Ford, pulling U-Haul, all tin.....145.00
Steam Roller, tractor, piston action...............145.00

Mikuni, roaring bull, boy holding tail, windup, 9-1/2" l, MIB 350.00

Modern Toys
Combat Car, tin friction, sparking, sealed, MIP 55.00
Jack-O-Panda, litho tin windup, bear on horse, MIB.........................150.00

TCO
Lufthansa D-ACOH Aeroplane, friction, 12-1/2" wingspan, MIB ...725.00
Sabena Saboo Plane, friction, 16-1/2" wingspan, MIB...........875.00

TN Co., Nomura Toys
Fire Truck, ladder, battery operated, 13" l, MIB.............................250.00
Highway Patrol Helicopter, tin, 16" l 100.00
Jet Plane, tin friction, ejecting pilot, 11" l, MIB...........................250.00
Soldier with machine gun, litho tin windup, 6" l..............................65.00
USAF Jet, tin friction, flint sparkler, 14" l 175.00

Unknown maker
Airplane, American Airlines, tin friction, 13" l wingspan 135.00
Alligator, animated tin windup, snapping.................................190.00
Boy on Tricycle, celluloid windup, rings bell, orig paper label on foot 125.00
Car, 2-3/4" x 7-1/2" x 2-3/4" h, litho tin friction, limousine, black, pink roof, beige and black striped int, black rubber tires, metal hub caps, "N-1929 made in Japan" lettered in black on white front license plate, pink, black and white attached spare tire ...45.00
Hydraulic Dump Trick, tin friction, 89" l, MIB 150.00
Moving Van, World Wide Van Lines, box of 12 trucks, different adv

Tootsietoy, car, convertible, yellow, rubber wheels, $12.

slogans, MIB 180.00
Tow Truck, 5" x 12" x 4-3/4" illus box, red and white metal truck, red metal crane, metal chain for moving vehicles, black rubber wheels, mkd "MKK #S-1139 made in Japan," c1960 ....145.00

Y Co., Yonezawa Toys, airplane, friction, rockets missing, 13" l.............165.00

Line Mar (Linemar): Line Mar is a subsidiary of Marx. Linemar toys are manufactured in Japan.

Army Radio Jeep, 7-1/4", white body, orig drawer, worn box............195.00
Banjo Cowboy, litho tin windup, 5-1/2" h 175.00
Casper Flipover Tank, litho tin windup......................300.00
Chevy Police Car, battery-operated tin, 9" l.....................................100.00
Concrete Mixer, battery-operated tin, 9" l, MIB................................240.00
Dick Tracy Police Car, remote-control battery-operated tin, Dick Tracy shield on doors, policeman driver, Chevy hubcaps, flashing roof light, siren noise, 1949, 9" l, orig box................................425.00
Honeymoon Express, MIB 230.00
Pluto the Drum Major, litho tin windup, 6" l, orig box...........................615.00
Popeye Turnover Tank, litho tin windup, 4" l............................425.00
Power Shovel, tin friction, 8" l......100.00
Sand Loader, yellow, MIB 35.00
Snow Plow, tin friction, 7" l............50.00
Violin Player, litho tin windup, red, white and blue tuxedo, 5-1/2" h 200.00
Wilma Flintstone on Tricycle, litho tin windup, celluloid Wilma, rings bell, 1962, 4" l...............425.00

Marx: Louis Marx founded the Marx Toy Co., in 1921, stressing high quality at the lowest possible price. His popular line included every type of toy except dolls. The company was sold to Quaker Oats Co., who sold it in 1976 to the European company of Dunbee-Combex-Marx.

Action Truck, late 1960s, MIB

Cement Truck 30.00
Dump Truck 30.00
Fire Truck................................35.00
Garbage Truck.........................35.00
Stake Truck.............................30.00
Tow Truck 30.00

Airplane
Pressed steel, silver gray, 9-1/2" wingspan................................140.00
Stunt plane, pilot, all tin, MIB.....................250.00

Army Set, 20 flat soldiers,

tin windup tank, tin cannon, wood bullets 200.00
Bulky Mule, litho tin windup, post-war 165.00
Bulldozer Climbing Tractor, litho tin windup, mkd "Caterpillar," engine noise, piston spring action plow, c1940, 10" l, orig box.............195.00
Dick Tracy Squad Car No. 1 ....250.00
Disneyland Express Train, 1950, MIB..............................200.00
Doll House, tin, Mickey and Friends 145.00
Driver Training Co., litho tin windup, plastic roof, non-fall action, 1950s, 6-1/2" l, orig card 160.00
Drum Major, litho tin windup, moving eyes, c1940 ....175.00
Dump Truck, 7" l 95.00
Farm Set, mechanical tractor and mower, 1940s, orig 6-1/2" x 8-1/2" x 2-1/4" box.................265.00
Flashy Flickers, orig box 150.00
Flintstone Pals on Dino, litho tin windup, Fred with vinyl head, 8" l, orig box 675.00
Give-a-Show Projector, 23 reels, MIB 35.00
Hometown Movie Theatre, litho tin, orchestra in front, lobby and ticket booth on sides, litho paper movie on winding rods, c1930, 5" x 2" orig box 450.00
Jocko, litho tin climbing monkey, orig box 120.00
Jumpin' Jeep, litho tin windup 185.00
Locomotive, die cast, smoking, freight cars, c1950 ....48.00
Lone Ranger, litho tin, riding rearing Silver, rotating lasso, moving arm holds gun, dated 1939..........395.00
Marvel the Mustang Kid's Riding Horse, 1960s................90.00
Merrymakers Band, violin player 1,075.00
Playset, Air-Sea Power, 1940s, orig box....................400.00
Race Car, plastic, friction, 6" l.......45.00
Ramp Walker, jockey and horse ...50.00
Roaring Lion, windup, orig box ...120.00
Rollover Tank No. 3 ....190.00
Sam the Gardner, figure pushing wheelbarrow, 2 orig garden tools, MIB 275.00
Shoot the Chutes, skill ball, pinball bagatelle, 1950s, orig box.......60.00
Target Game, Lone Ranger, litho tin, standing target, orig box, 17-1/4" x 11-1/2", 1939..........175.00
Tiger on Trike, windup, MIB 135.00
Tinytown, Spear's London, Bavaria graphics, telegraph office 250.00
Tractor, tin, painted silver, tractor, trailer, driver, c1930, orig box...........195.00

Truck, Hi-Way Express,
blue cab 215.00
U.S. Tank Co. #4, tin
windup, 6" l 100.00
Western Tricycle, litho
tin windup, MIB 100.00

Matchbox: Matchbox cars were first manufactured by Lesney Products, an English company founded in 1947 by Leslie Smith and Rodney Smith. Their first die-cast cars were made in 1953 on a scale of 1:75. The trademark "Matchbox" was registered in 1953. In 1979, Lesney Products Corp. made more than 5.5 million toys a week. The company was sold to Universal International in 1982.

Ambulance,
Mercedes, K-6, MIB................22.00
Berkeley cavalier
Trainer, 23B-1..........................35.00
Big Tipper, SK-4, MIB...................22.00
Bus, Londoner, SK-15, MIB...........25.00
Cattle Truck, 37-C2 ....20.00
Diesel road Roller, 1C-2................30.00
Earth Mover, #9, MOC 20.00
Ford Cortina, 25-D1......................10.00
Highway Express, vehicle set, 5-3/4" x 11-1/2" x 4-1/2" orig box, attached illus header card, cellophane-cov diecut window displaying "NASA Countdown" vehicles, 2-1/2" Space Shuttle Command Center, Winnebago, two 6" l trucks with white plastic NASA rockets, 1982 Lesney Products Corp., NJ 38.00
Hydraulic Excavator, SK-1, MIB....18.00
Lambourghini, K-24, MIB...............22.00
Lincoln Continental, 31-C2 ....10.00
Mercedes Truck, 1-E1 ....15.00
Mercury Commuter Station Wagon,
#73, green 25.00
Merry Weather Fire Truck, 9C-1....40.00
Quarry Truck, 6A-1.......................45.00
Road Roller, 18-1 ....65.00
Scammel Tripper Truck,
K-19, MIB................................30.00
School Bus, #47, MOC..................20.00
Snow-Trac Tractor, #35, red 20.00
Stake Truck, 20A-2.......................45.00
Studebaker Station
Wagon, 42-B2.........................20.00
Toll Truck, SK-11-AA, MIB 20.00
VW 1600 TL, 67-B1......................15.00

Mattel: Mattel, formed by Harold Mattson and Ruth and Elliot Handler in 1945, originated in a garage in Los Angeles. From its humble beginnings as a manufacturer of picture frames, the company evolved into making dollhouse furniture, burp guns and eventually the Barbie doll, its most-famous product.

Car, 8-1/4" l, hard-plastic
friction, experimental, yellow
and silver, SS wheel................75.00
Crackers, The Talking
Parrot, MIB 165.00
Farmer in the Dell, litho tin, musical,
c1953, 9-1/2" x 9-1/2" x 7".......90.00
Guitar, cowboy, orig box 40.00
Machine Gun, air cooled, MIB.....200.00
Moon Base Space 1999, Star Flash
Computer Kit 50.00
Top, Whizzer, 1969, MIB..............35.00
Whistling Train Station,
litho tin, MIB...........................65.00

Miscellaneous Companies

Arnold
Gas Pump, Shell, worker,
4" h, MIB 495.00
Pontiac, replaced tires,
orig paint, 6" l 450.00
Doepke, road grader, Adams,
#2006, orange, professionally
restored 125.00
Dunwell, auto wrecker, red,
blue bed, restored 85.00
Dyna Mite, Derringer gun,
orig box..................................20.00
General Toy of Canada, Racer,
#3, litho tin windup.................125.00
Hess
Tanker
1988...................................75.00
1989...................................60.00
1990...................................50.00
1991...................................35.00
1992...................................35.00
1994...................................25.00
Training Van..........................250.00
Truck and racer, 1991, 4" x 14" x 3-1/4" orig box, green and white plastic truck, friction race car, MIB 35.00
Kenner, Super Show Projector, cartoon shoes, Flintstone, Popeye, Mr. Ed and other character finger puppets, 1962, MIB 165.00
Keystone, target game, Davy Crockett Indian Target Set, 22-1/2" x 12-1/4", c1949....................................175.00
Knickerbocker
Camel, blue, wrinkled knees,
replaced red harness 95.00
Marionette, Raggedy Ann 85.00
Metalcraft, Spirit of St. Louis,
kit, orig instruction book,
parts box, MIB 225.00
Ny-Lint, U-Haul set......................245.00
Playskool, Underdog
Airplane..................................40.00
Boat...40.00
Car 40.00
Underdog 60.00
Renwal

F9F Navy Panzer Jet, plain,
7" x 7-3/4" x 101/2", red accent
name, insignia and wheels,
#162, c1960 ....15.00
The Invisible Man,
c1959, MIB..............................125.00
Simplex, toy typewriter, 1970s
Practical No. 1, MIB 40.00
Special Demonstration
Model B, MIB 50.00
Steelcraft
Bus, inter-city, green,
orange wheels, professionally
restored, 24" l.......................545.00
Truck, City Delivery
Closed truck........................395.00
Open truck, 1930s 575.00
Structo, ready-mix concrete
truck, green, black drum,
orange bed 130.00
Topper, car, 5-3/4" x 6", Johnny Lightning Mako Shark, 2-3/4" l die-cast metal, lime metallic Corvette-type car, late 1960s, MOC 28.00

Ohio Art: In 1907, Harry S. Winzeler founded The Ohio Art Co., in Archbold, OH. Originally, the company produced metal picture frames; toy production began in 1912. In 1969, Ohio Art purchased Emenee Industries. Ohio Art is noted for colorful lithographed tin toys.

Coney Island Roller Coaster,
windup, litho vacuform plastic,
roller coaster above carnival scenes,
two 3" l litho tin cars, 15" x 21"
base, orig box........................225.00
Ferris Wheel, litho tin 275.00
Mangasticks, orig box 25.00
Mickey Mouse Sand Pail, litho tin, Mickey, Minnie, Donald and Pluto in rowboat illus, 1930s, 5-1/2" h......350.00
Sprinkling Can, litho tin 25.00

Remco: Remco Industries, Inc., was founded by Sol Robbins and was the first company to advertise its products on television. A unique aspect of the firm was that many of its products were related to television and promotional character dolls. The company closed in January 1974.

Movie Land Drive-In
Theater, MIB 95.00
Rifle, Screaming Mee-Mee, 38-1/2" x
15", orig box 250.00
Slide Projector, Doctor Doolittle Ugly
Mugly, 1968............................40.00
Speedrail Monorail, 1969, MIB....125.00

Schuco

Beach Buggy, worn orig box 175.00
Dump Truck, orig key.................120.00
Elektro Delfino 5411 Navico, boat,
accessories, 14" l, MIB.........325.00

Elektro 3112U Truck,
red and gray, MIB 175.00
Gas Pump, Shell, 4" h 295.00
Porsche 917, battery operated,
1970, MIB 175.00
Radio 412 Car, built-in music box,
maroon 300.00
Variantus, bus, maroon, litho tin,
1950s, MIB 185.00

Sun Rubber: The Sun Rubber Co., was located in Barberton, OH. During the 1930s, it produced a number of character dolls and Disney items in addition to a general line. It was forced to cease production during World War II because of the scarcity of rubber. Production was revived after World War II and continued through the 1950s.

Car, 4-door limousine type, white rubber
wheels, 4" l, 1-1/2" h
Blue 15.00
Red..15.00
Donald Duck and Pluto, red car 85.00
Porky Pig, multicolored molded rubber,
c1950, orig box 95.00
Race Car, silver body, white rubber
wheels, 2" x 4" x 1" 45.00
Tank 25.00
Truck, streamlined design, green paint,
white rubber tires, c1930,
2" x 4-1/2" x 1-1/2" 45.00

Tonka: In 1946, Mound Metal Crafts Inc., Mound, MN, manufactured the first Tonka Toys. The name Tonka was derived from the firm's proximity to the banks of Lake Minnetonka. The company introduced a full line of trucks in 1949. In 1956, it changed its name to Tonka Toys.

Car Carrier, c1960 ....45.00
Corvette, tin 50.00
Dump Truck, #180, green bed,
professionally restored 175.00
Farm Truck 85.00
Fire Pumper, 1964.........................95.00
Road Grader...................................75.00
Service Truck, #01, medium blue,
professionally restored 125.00
Winnebago 70.00
Wrecker, c1960 ....85.00

Tootsietoy: The first Tootsietoys were made in 1911, although the name was not registered until 1924 and it was not until after 1930 that the name appeared on the toys. Tootsie was an early manufacturer of prizes for Cracker Jack. Production of real vehicles began in 1914 and continued until World War II. After the war, cars were made as toys rather than models.

Airplane, Red Baron,

tri-wing, #3260 ....75.00
Army Gun Truck, F-700, 6" l..........50.00
Best Vette, #1765,
5" l, 1963, MIB 65.00
Fire Truck 60.00
MG Roaster, 6" l 30.00
Porsche 30.00
Sedan, Ford, #0111, 1935,
replaced tires 75.00
Service Station Set #5710,
eight 3" l vehicles, gas station
island, 4 traffic signs, car lift,
orig box, fitted insert 475.00
Station Wagon, #238,
replaced tires 65.00
Stack Truck, Ford,
F-700, 6" l, 1955 ....75.00
Train Cars, PA RR
Engine.......................................45.00
Passenger Car 25.00
Truck
#4639, Mack, coal,
gold metal wheels 95.00
#4640, Mack, oil,
gold metal wheels 95.00

Unidentified Maker

Ambulance, 1-1/2" x 4-3/4" x 1-1/2" h,
painted cast white metal, blue accent
cross on each side, orig white paint,
mkd "Made in USA," 1920s 25.00
Fire Chief Car, 3" x 8" x 2",
plastic, friction, red and white,
1958 Chevy, helmet, black and white
tires, metal underside, 1958 on
front bumper, "USA" on back
bumper, siren sound................48.00
Highway Patrol, 2-1/2" x 5-1/2" x 1-3/4"
h, tin litho friction, black and white,
2-door, dark red, blue int accents,
license plate dated 1969, trunk mkd
"Police Dept. No. 1," hood mkd "Plymouth," orig rubber tires 24.00
Promo Plastic Car, 2-1/2" x 7-1/4" x 2" h,
Mercury Comet, silver, gray int,
whitewalls, front and rear license
plates stamped "1960"............45.00
Steam Roller, 5" x 11-1/2" x 7" h,
litho tin windup, brown metal
rolled roof, silver luster tin body,
front 3-1/4" wide roller, standing
driver, c1920.........................250.00
Thomas Taxi, plastic, 4-1/2" l,
1-1/2" h, green, black rubber wheels,
yellow and red checkered
paper sticker on each side, maker's
logo and black, white and silver
accent paper label on roof, mkd
"Made in USA," c1950 ....35.00

Unique Art: Unique Art Manufacturing Co., was located in Newark, NJ. The firm was in business by 1916 and operated until about 1952.

Artie, litho tin windup, clean driving car,
7" l 365.00

Baggage Handler 275.00
Bamboo the Monk,
litho tin windup 285.00
Capital Hill Racer, litho tin windup,
orig box 160.00
Gertie Goose,
litho tin windup, 9" l 160.00
Lil' Abner Band............................575.00
Lincoln Tunnel, litho tin windup, cars
and buses travel on expressway,
Lincoln Tunnel on 1 end, New York
other end, policeman in middle,
24" l, orig box 575.00
Rodeo Joe Crazy Car,
litho tin windup 425.00
Sky Ranger, orig box 550.00

Wolverine: The Wolverine Supply & Manufacturing Co., was founded in 1903 and incorporated by Benjamin F. Bain in 1906. The first type of toys they produced were lithographed tin sand toys. The firm began to make girls' housekeeping toys and action games by the 1920s. Production of toys continued and expanded in 1959 to include children's appliances, known as "Rite-Hite." The name was changed to Wolverine Toy Co. in 1962. The company was originally located in Pittsburgh, but relocated to Booneville, AR, in 1970 after being acquired by Spang and Co.

Diving Submarine,
litho tin windup, 13" l 195.00
Drum Major, 13-1/4" h,
round base, #27, c1930 ....225.00
Gee Whiz Racehorse Game, 15" l,
1930s 125.00
Icebox, tin....................................50.00
Kitchen Cabinet, No. 280, 1949, toy
groceries, orig box.................185.00
Merry-Go-Round, musical, 4 planes,
4 flags, 1930s 625.00
Refrigerator, No. 186, Frigidaire, pink,
toy groceries, orig box...........175.00
Sand Toy, Cap't Sandy Andy,
orig box 195.00
Shooting Gallery, orig box...........165.00
Sunny Andy Street Car, pull toy, litho tin,
c1935, 13" l, orig box.............210.00
Sunny Suzy,
electric iron, orig box 15.00

Wyandotte: All Metal Products Co., located in Wyandotte, MI, was in business by the early 1920s. The company, better known as Wyandotte Toys, originally produced wood and steel toy weapons. In 1935, it introduced an innovative line of streamlined wheeled vehicles. The firm ceased operations in 1956.

Airplane, Boeing Stratocruiser, pressed
steel, red, blue wings, some chipping
to decals, 13" wingspan 225.00

Air Speed Coupe, rubber wheels, 5-5/8"
l, good......................................40.00

Ambulance, 6-1/4", white, pressed
steel.......................................100.00

Army Corps Engineer Corp. Truck, wood
wheels, 17-1/2" l.....................150.00

Battleship, rubber wheels, 6" l.......65.00

Coast to Coast Push Lines, rubber
wheels, 21" l...........................325.00

Coupe, 5" l, 1932...........................75.00

Dairy Wagon, Sunshine Dairy, orig box,
1 flap missing...........................65.00

Gasoline Service Station, Shell,
2 vehicles...............................550.00

Gasoline Truck, 22" l, pressed steel, rear
gate missing, poor paint........300.00

Rocket Ship, 6-1/2" l,
pressed steel, red, orange
tail, green body, 1930s..........165.00

Sand Hopper Set,
orig shovel, 7" h.......................35.00

Stack Truck,
wood wheels, 6-3/4" h...........150.00

Truck
#50, red cab, green bed, white rubber
wheels, electric lights, 15-1/4" l,
professionally restored...........110.00
#53, red cab, green bed, wood
wheels, 12-1/2" l, professionally
restored....................................75.00

Zephyr Racer, 10" l, mint.............150.00

Trains, Toy

Collecting Hints: Prices do fluctuate—those from mail order houses and stores generally are higher than those found at train swap meets, such as the large one held in York, PA, each year.

Condition is critical. Items in fair condition (scratched, chipped, dented, rusted or warped) and below generally have little value to the collector. Restoration is accepted and can enhance the price by one or two grades, provided it has been done accurately. Spare parts are actively traded and sold among collectors to assist in restoration efforts. Exterior condition often is more important than operating condition. If you require a piece that works, you should test it before you buy it.

Collecting toy trains is a very specialized field and collectors tend to have their own meets. A wealth of literature is available but only from specialized book, railroad or toy-train dealers. Novice collectors should read extensively before buying.

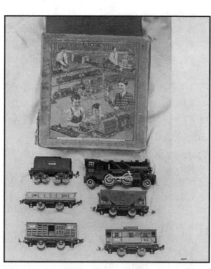

Lionel, No. 233, O-gauge, engine #262, hopper car #803, gondola #902, cattle car #806, caboose #802, $260.

History: Railroading has always been an important part of childhood, largely because of the romance associated with the railroad and the prominence of toy trains.

The first toy trains were cast iron and tin; windup motors added movement. The golden age of toy trains was 1920 to 1955, when electric-powered units and high-quality rolling stock were available and names such as Ives, American Flyer and Lionel were household words. The advent of plastic in the late 1950s resulted in considerably lower quality.

Toy trains are designated by a model scale or gauge. The most popular are HO, N, O and standard. Narrow gauge was a response to the modern capacity to miniaturize. Its popularity has decreased in the last few years.

Periodicals: *Classic Toy Trains*, P.O. Box 1612, Waukesha, WI 53187; *Lionel Collector Series Marketmaker*, P.O. Box 1499, Gainesville, FL 32602; *O Scale Railroading*, P.O. Box 239, Nazareth, PA 18064; S. *Gaugian*, 7236 Madison Ave., Forest Park, IL 60130.

Collectors' Clubs: American Flyer Collectors Club, P.O. Box 13269, Pittsburgh, PA 15243; Lionel Collector's Club of America, P.O. Box 479, La Salle, IL 61301; Lionel Operating Train Society, 18 Eland St., Fairfield, OH 45014; Marklin Club-North America, P.O. Box 51559, New Berlin, WI 53151; Marklin Digital Special

Interest Group, P.O. Box 51319, New Berlin, WI 53151; The National Model Railroad Association, 4121 Cromwell Rd., Chattanooga, TN 37421; Toy Train Operating Society, Inc., 25 W. Walnut St., Ste 308, Pasadena, CA 91103; Train Collector's Association, P.O. Box 248, Strasburg, PA 17579.

Note: All prices given are for items in very good condition, meaning that the piece shows some signs of use but all parts are present and any damage is minor.

American Flyer O Gauge

Set
Burlington Zephyr Streamliner, passenger, #9900 power car, coach, baggage car, #9900 tail car...700.00
Freight, 2-6-4 locomotive, 8-wheel tender, flat-bed car, box car, derrick car, tank car, gondola, caboose, 1930s....................450.00
Passenger, #253 locomotive, 2 #610 cars, #612, dark green, maroon inserts, 1924............295.00

American Flyer S. Gauge

Accessories
Billboard, #566, whistling, 1951-55....................20.00
Eureka Diner, #275, 1952-53.........................45.00
Gabe the Lamplighter, #23780, controller, orig decal, 1958..........585.00
Hotel, #168, roof re-attached, 1953...........225.00
Log Loader, #164, gray, vermilion roof, controller, wiring bad, 1940....400.00
Magnetic Crane, #165, 1940......................................600.00
Station and Terminal, #795, 1954..........................400.00
Truss Bridge, #571, 1955-56.....7.50
Locomotive
#303, 4-4-2, Atlantic, 1954-56, steam....................................25.00
#316, 4-6-2, K-5, Pennsylvania, 1946, steam...........................45.00
#345, 4-6-2, Pacific, 1954, steam............................50.00
#405, Silver Streak, 1952, Alco PA.........................85.00
#499, New Haven, 1956-57, GE Electric.............................150.00
#21551, Northern Pacific, 1958, Alco PA...................................110.00
Rolling stock
Box Car, #24047, GN, plug door.........................85.00
Caboose

#607 ....10.00
#907 ....18.00
#24526, 1957 ....15.00
Coal Car, #752, Seaboard,
3-button controller, 1946 ....475.00
Flat Car, #24516, New Haven,
1957-59 ....10.00
Gondola, #24125, Bethlehem Steel,
3 rails, 1960 ....40.00
Hopper and Dump Car
  #719, CB&Q, 1950-54..........30.00
  #940, Wabash, 1953-56.......15.00
Passenger Car
  #653, Pullman, 1946-53.......25.00
  #662, Vista dome,
  1950-52 ....27.50
  #961, Jefferson, 1953-58.....30.00
  #24773, Columbus,
  1957-58 ....45.00
Reefer, #24191 Canadian National,
1958 ....250.00
Tank Car
  #24313, Gulf, 1957-60 ....20.00
  #24330, Baker's Chocolate,
  1961-72 ....25.00
Set
  American Legion LTD, #4019 locomotive, #4040 box car, American
  pullman, Pleasant View observation
  car, maroon litho and roofs 660.00
  Century, #9915, locomotive, integral
  tender, 2 #3178 coaches, #3179
  observation car......................850.00
  Eagle, #21920 MP Alco PA,
  #24856 combine, 24863
  vista dome, 24866 observation car,
  1963, MIB..............................1,600.00
  Minnie Ha-Ha, locomotive,
  3 coaches, orange and gray,
  minor wear 295.00
  Nation Wide, #1093 locomotive,
  green and black, brass trim,
  combine and coach 575.00
  Passenger, #21927 engine,
  #24773, #24813, #24833 cars,
  1960 ....450.00
  Washington, #21089 locomotive
  and tender, #24055 box car, #24565
  flat-bed car with replica cannon,
  #24750 coach..........................600.00

Ives

Accessories
  Bridge, 91, O gauge,
  1912-30 ....25.00
  Platform, cov,
  119, 1905-14 ....100.00
Locomotive
  #17, 0-4-0, 1908....................300.00
  #1118, 0-4-4, 1913-14............275.00
  #1661, 2-4-0, steam, 1932.....125.00
  #3218, 0-4-0,1917..................125.00
Rolling stock
  #52, Passenger Car, 1915-25 ..45.00

#57, Lumber,
O gauge, 1915-30 ....40.00
#121, Caboose, 1929...............75.00
#130, Buffet, 1930....................75.00
#136, Observation,
1926-30 ....40.00
#198, Gravel Car, 1930..........200.00
#1813, Baggage, 1931-32 ....20.00

Lionel O Gauge

Accessories
  Block Signal, red base,
  #99N, 1932 ....200.00
  Catalog, Lionel Train Accessories,
  1954, 64 pgs 20.00
  Diesel Fueling Station, #415,
  1955-57, MIB 250.00
  Light Tower, 11" h 110.00
  Milk Car Platform 75.00
  Power Station, #435, mustard, terra-
  cotta and green, 1926 ....275.00
  Railroad Crossing Station 125.00
  Street Sign, Main Street/Broadway,
  7" 60.00
Locomotive
  #60, Lionelville, trolley type,
  aluminized-paper reflector,
  1955-58 ....175.00
  #203, 0-6-0, steam,
  1940-42 ....325.00
  #212, U.S. Marine Corps, Alco A,
  1958-59 ....50.00
  #665, 41-6-4, steam,
  1954-59 ....75.00
  #706, 0-4-0, Electric,
  1913-16 ....250.00
  #3927, Lionel Lines,
  1956-60 ....65.00
Rolling stock
  #530, Observation, 1926-32 ....17.50
  #605, Pullman, 1925-32...........65.00
  #801, Caboose, 1915-26 ....17.50
  #638-2361, Van Camp's Pork &
  Beans, 1962............................20.00
  #1007, Lionel Lines, SP Die 3,
  1948-52 ....17.50
  #1514, Baby Ruth 35.00
  #1717, gondola, 1933-40.........25.00
  #1887, flat car, fence and horses,
  1959 ....125.00
  #2400, Maplewood,
  reen and gray 25.00
  #2454, Sunoco
  tank car, 1946 ....10.00
  #2816, hopper and
  dump car, 1935-42...................50.00
  #3356, Santa Fe Railway Express,
  1956-60 ....35.00
  #3360, Burro Crane,
  1956, MIB................................275.00
  #3413, Mercury Capsule Launching,
  1962, MIB................................325.00
  #3444, Erie,
  gondola, 1957-59 ....30.00

#3461, flat car, log,
dump, 1949-55 ....25.00
#3494-150, MoPac, box car,
1956, MIB 300.00
#6025, Gulf,
tank car, 1956-57 ....10.00
#6464-400, B&O Timesaver, box car,
metal tracks, 1956 ....125.00
Set
  Blue Streak, #265, #265WX,
  #617 coach, #618 observation
  car, #619, 1936 ....700.00
  City of Denver, #636W locomotive,
  2 #617 coaches, #618 observation
  car, 1936................................550.00
  Flying Yankee, #616 locomotive, 3
  #617 coaches, #618 observation car,
  gunmetal and chrome, 1935 ..275.00
  Hiawatha, #250E
  locomotive, #250W tender,
  #782 coach, #783 coach, #784
  observation car, 1935 ....1,250.00

Lionel S Gauge

Accessories, station
#115, 1935 ....300.00
#122, 1920 ....325.00
Locomotive, #1912, square cab, 1910-
  12 ....250.00
Rolling stock
  Box Car, #214, yellow and orange,
  1926 ....350.00
  Tank Car, #215,
  pea green, 1927 ....450.00
Set
  Freight, #33, #35, #36, olive green,
  1920 ....350.00
  Freight, #41, #38 locomotive, #114
  box car, #112 Lakeshore gondola,
  #113 stock car, #116 hopper, #117
  caboose, 1913-24 ....325.00
  Passenger, #352E, #10E locomotive,
  #332 baggage car, #339 coach, #341
  observation car, 1926, orig box, minor fatigue to locomotive........500.00

N Gauge

Atlas
  Locomotive, EMD E8, diesel,
  Santa Fe 25.00
  Rolling Stock
  Box Car, #2204,
  Great Northern..........................5.00
  Pullman, #2601, Santa Fe 9.00
Lone Star
  Locomotive, EL-65,
  F-7, Kansas City 17.50
  Rolling Stock
    EL-70, coach, B
    ritish Main Line 5.00
    El-141, caboose,
    Canadian Pacific....................7.50
Tyco, locomotive, car,
Santa Fe................................100.00

U

Uhl Pottery

Collecting Hints: Collector interest in this pottery is rapidly expanding beyond its Midwest origins. Some Uhl Pottery pieces are marked "Uhl Pottery, Huntingburg, Inc." in a circle. Another mark is the same name in block letters arranged in a circle with no border, while still another mark is an acorn with the name "Acorn Wares/Uhl Pottery."

History: Uhl Pottery was founded as a pottery in Vanderburgh County, near Evansville, IN, in 1854, by August Uhl and his brother. In 1879, the pottery became Benninghof, Uhl and Co. About 1891, the name was changed to Uhl Pottery Co., and the firm moved from Evansville to Huntingburg, allowing easier access to clay. While no definitive records exist, it is believed the pottery existed until the early 1940s.

The principal production was stoneware kitchen items. The company made crocks of every size, from one quarter to 60 gallons, as well as covered churns, milk pans, mixing bowls, covered casseroles, bean pots and so on. Interesting items, such as wren houses, were made in dull glazed ceramics or terra-cotta. Other glazed pottery items for outdoor use included birdbaths, sundials and flowerpots.

Collectors' Club: Uhl Pottery Collectors Society, 801 Poplar St., Boonville IN 47601.

Acorn Ware
  Ashtray, black.........................210.00
  Churn, 4 gal.............................85.00
  Crock, 1 gal.............................37.50
  Harvest Jug, brown and white, bail
    handle....................................110.00
  Jug, shoulder
    1/2 gal..................................95.00
    1 gal.....................................35.00
    5 gal.....................................50.00
Advertising
  Full Size
    Ashtray,
    Cannelton Sewer Tile.........140.00
    Ashtray, 4", Acorn Ware,
    mkd "Rustic Tavern, Jasper,
    Ind.," c1930........................660.00
    Pitcher, Hill-Top Gift Shop,
    Canmer, KY, Lincoln, 1 pt, blue,

    repaired handle..................175.00
  Miniature
    Jug
      Cumberland Falls,
      brown and white, double
      handle, bellied.................200.00
      Dalton, OH, 1932, brown,
      white shoulders...............350.00
      H. Sonneman, yellow, sq...60.00
      Schoepfling Christmas
      Greetings, shoulder..........115.00
    Mug, Compliments Meyer &
    Danzinger, barrel shape....175.00
    Perfume Bottle, Botay, Camp
    Pendleton...........................180.00
    Pitcher, Hill-Top Gift Shop,
    Canmer, KY, pink..............145.00
    Prunella Jug, N.J. Wilhems,
    double handle....................270.00
Baked Beans Pot, Boston.............25.00
Bank, pig, white..........................210.00
Bowl, #119, white tulip...............100.00
Butter Crock, Sullivan,
  blue and white..........................60.00
Christmas Jug
  Believe It or Not, Filled
  with Best Wishes from Uhl
  Pottery Co., Huntingburg, IN, white
  canteen, c1936.....................605.00
  Christmas Cheer from
  Uhl Pottery Co., 1933, brown
  demijohn miniature, message
  flanked by 2 Santas..............370.00
  Greetings from Uhl Pottery Co.,
  Huntingburg, IN, brown over white
  miniature Prunella, c1938......360.00
  Merry Christmas 1937, brown
  over white globe....................350.00
Collectors Club Commemorative
  1987, blue miniature stein,
  sold with orig mold.................460.00
  1989, large white football.......150.00
  1991, white hand-turned
  ashtray..................................100.00
  1992, beater jar.......................95.00
  1993, miniature
  Evansville crock......................80.00
  1994, miniature blue and white
  shoulder jug, Dillsboro logo....100.00
Doorstop, flattened
  globe shape, white................170.00
Footwear
  Baby Shoes
    Blue, price for pr...............250.00
    Pink, price for one..............85.00
    White, price for pr.............110.00
  Dutch, large
    Peach, price for pr..............90.00
    Pink, price for one..............35.00
  Military Boots
    Blue, price for pr...............100.00
    Green, price for pr.............145.00
  Slippers, price for pr

    Black....................................140.00
    Blue.......................................90.00
Grandpa Meier Jug
  Miniature, brown over white...145.00
  1 gal, orig paper label............370.00
  Pt...100.00
Jug, bellied, #176
  Blue......................................27.50
  Pink......................................37.50
Logo, disc, brown.......................220.00
Miniature
  Baseball, Meier's label, tan......80.00
  Cookie Jar
    Globe, blue.........................330.00
    Standard shape, blue........180.00
  Football..................................40.00
  Jug, figural
    Canteen, pink and green...100.00
    Cat
      Black..............................95.00
      Peach............................105.00
    Elephant
      Black..............................60.00
      Blue...............................85.00
      Peach............................80.00
      Tan................................100.00
      White..............................75.00
      Yellow............................90.00
    Globe, blue.........................120.00
    Horse's Head
      Blue...............................335.00
      Yellow............................325.00
    Ring
      Peach............................260.00
      Yellow............................130.00
  Stein, barrel shape,
  3 oz, brown............................110.00
Mug, barrel shape, blue, corked hole
  just under the handle.............130.00
Pitcher
  Grape, blue,
  squatty, orig lid.....................375.00
  1 gal, blue and white sponged
  dec, faint Uhl mark................510.00
  Pinched spout, blue,
  hand turned..........................500.00
Planter, figural
  Cat, white...............................75.00
  Elephant, white......................140.00
  Rabbit
    Blue....................................175.00
    Yellow.................................180.00
Souvenir
  Dutch Shoe, Fort Harrod,
  KY, yellow...............................60.00
  Vase, Souvenir of Red Rolling
  Springs, peach......................130.00
Soup Bowl, green, small chip........35.00
Sugar, cov, hand turned
  Green, glaze defects.............100.00
  Light blue..............................310.00
Utilitarian Ware

Churn, 3 gal, Evansville 80.00
Jug, 5 gal, Evansville 115.00
Vase, bud
   Pink 120.00
   Rose...55.00
Vase, 8" h, black 10.00
Water Cooler, Polar Bear, black
   and green, 2 gal....................230.00

Universal Pottery

Collecting Hints: Not all Universal pottery carried the Universal name as part of the backstamp. Wares marked "Harmony House," "Sweet William/Sears Roebuck and Co.," and "Wheelock, Peoria" are part of the Universal production. Wheelock was a department store in Peoria, IL, that controlled the Cattail pattern on the Old Holland shape. Like many pottery companies, Universal had many shapes or styles of blanks, the most popular being Camwood, Old Holland and Laurella. The same decal might be found on several different shapes.

The Cattail pattern had many accessory pieces. The 1940 and 1941 Sears Roebuck & Co., catalogs listed an oval wastebasket, breakfast set, kitchen scale, linens and bread box. Calico Fruits is another pattern with accessory pieces. Because the Calico Fruits decal has not held up well over time, collectors may have to settle for less-than-perfect pieces.

History: Universal Potteries of Cambridge, OH, was organized in 1934 by The Oxford Pottery Co. The firm purchased the Atlas-Globe plant properties. The Atlas-Globe operation was a merger of the Atlas China Co. (formerly Crescent China Co., in 1921, Tritt in 1912 and Bradshaw in 1902) and the Globe China Co. Even after the purchase, Universal retained Oxford ware, made in Oxford, OH, as part of its dinnerware line. Another Oxford plant was used to manufacture tiles. The plant at Niles, OH, was dismantled.

The most popular Universal lines were Ballerina and Ballerina Mist. The company developed a detergent-resistant decal with permacel, a key element in keeping a pattern bright. Production continued until 1960, when all plants were closed.

References: Susan and Al Bagdade, *Warman's American Pottery and Porcelain*, Wallace-Homestead, 1994; Jo Cunningham,

Collector's Encyclopedia of American Dinnerware, Collector Books, 1982, 1995 value update; Harvey Duke, *Official Identification and Price Guide to Pottery and Porcelain*, 8th Edition, House of Collectibles, 1995.

Bittersweet

Drip Jar, cov 20.00
Mixing Bowl 30.00
Platter..32.00
Salad Bowl 20.00
Stack Set..35.00

Calico Fruit

Custard Cup, 5 oz 5.00
Milk Jug, 3 qt.................................25.00
Plate, 6" d.......................................5.00
Refrigerator Set, 3 jars,
   4", 5" and 6" d..........................45.00
Salt and Pepper Shakers, pr.........17.50
Utility Pitcher, cov.........................40.00
Utility Plate, 11-1/2" d....................20.00

Cattails

Bread Box, double compartment...30.00
Butter Dish, cov, 1 pound..............40.00
Canteen Jug...................................30.00
Casserole, cov, 8-1/4" d................17.50
Cookie Jar, cov 45.00
Gravy Boat......................................20.00
Milk Pitcher, 1 qt............................20.00
Pie server.......................................20.00
Platter, oval 20.00
Range Set, 5 pcs............................40.00
Tea Set, 4 pcs 27.50

Rambler Rose

Gravy Boat......................................10.00
Milk Pitcher.....................................20.00
Plate, 9" d..7.50
Salt Shaker......................................5.00
Soup Bowl, flat 5.00

Woodvine

Creamer and Sugar, cov 20.00
Cup and Saucer 9.00
Gravy Boat......................................10.00
Plate, 9" d..5.00
Utility Jar, cov................................20.00
Vegetable Bowl, oval.......................9.50

V

Valentines

Collecting Hints: Unless the design is unique, the very simple, small penny cards given by school children are not of interest to collectors. Most collectors tend to specialize in

one type of card, e.g., transportation theme cards, lacy or honeycomb.

Condition of the card is very important—watch out for missing parts, soil, etc. Keep cards out of direct sunlight to prevent fading and to keep them from becoming brittle. Store them in layers with acid-free tissue between each one and use moth crystals or silverfish packets to protect them from insect infestation.

History: Early cards were often handmade and included both handwritten verses and hand-drawn design or border. Many cards also had some cutwork and hand-colored designs.

Among the prettiest collectible cards found today are the early handdone lace paper valentines made between 1840 and 1900. Lace paper cards are folded in half, the front is covered with one or more layers of lace paper—either white, silver or gold—with colored scraps or lithos filling the center. A printed verse is found inside and the card may come in a matching embossed lacy envelope. The older the paper-lace, the fine the quality of the paper. The period from 1840 to 1860 is considered the golden age of lace paper valentines.

Most collectible valentines found today were made between 1900 and 1914 and are freestanding and consist of layers of die cuts. These include pull-downs, pullouts, pop-ups and foldouts. Pull-downs are made of cardboard die cut into fancy, lacy, colored shapes that create multi-dimensional images such as boats, ships, cars, planes or gardens. Early examples pulled down from the middle; later pieces, which are not quite as elaborate as their predecessors, come down from the front.

Animated, sailor boy, World War II, 5" x 8", $15.

Honeycomb tissue was used a great deal on pullouts, which open out and are free standing on a honeycomb base or easel back. Some of these open to form a whole circular design. The most valuable ones are those with a center column and a honeycomb base and canopy top. Tissue used on the early pieces was usually white, soft pink, blue or green; during the 1920s red or soft red tissue was used.

Along with tissue-paper valentines, we see lots of mechanical cards from the 1920s. Mechanicals have moving parts that are set in motion by pulling at tabs or moving wheels that are part of the card. Two other popular styles are flats and hangers. Flats—easy to find and among the most reasonable to collect—often have fancy die-cut borders, embossing and an artist-designed center of a pretty girl. Hangers are cards with silk ribbon at the top for hanging. A string of pretty die-cuts on a ribbon is called a charm string.

Bitter comic valentines were made as early as 1840, but most are from the post-1900 period. These cards make fun of appearance, occupation or personality and also embraced social issues of the day. Comic character valentines feature comic strip characters or the likes of Snow White, Mickey Mouse, Superman or Wonder Woman.

References: Dan and Pauline Campanelli, *Romantic Valentines*, L-W Books, 1996; Katherine Kreider, *Valentines with Values*, Schiffer Publishing, 1996.

Collectors' Club: National Valentine Collectors Association, P.O. Box 1404, Santa Ana, CA 92702.

Advisor: Evalene Pulati.

Animated
    World War II sailor
      boy in boat, 5" x 8" 15.00
    World War II soldier
      boy standup.............................15.00
    1920s, children
      with bear, seesaw 18.00
    1920s, girl playing piano, 6" 12.50
    1923, small walking doll, 4" 14.00
Comic
    McLoughlin
      4" x 6", 1900..........................7.50
      8" x 10", sheet,
        sgd CJH, 1914 ....8.50

      10" x 15", sheet,
        occupational........................18.00
    Unknown maker, 8" x 10",
      sheet, 1925 ....5.00
Diecut, small
    Artist sgd
      Brundage 9.00
      Clapsaddle..........................10.00
    Heart shapes, girls 5.00
Flat
    Art Nouveau
      3" x 5", emb girls...................5.00
      4" x 4", emb, fancy................7.50
    Heart Shape, child, 1920s..........3.50
Folder
    Fancy borders, birds, 1914 ....9.50
    Lacy cutwork edges, verse 10.00
    Tied with silk ribbon, 1920 ....7.50
Hanger and String
    Hanger
      3" x 4", cutwork edge,
        litho, 1910 ....9.50
      5" x 5", Art Nouveau,
        heart, silk ribbon 10.00
      8" x 8, fancy,
        artist sgd, 1905 ....15.00
    String
      4 pcs, 3" x 3", artist sgd 35.00
      5 pcs, 2" x 4",
        sweet children.....................45.00
Honeycomb Tissue
    Beistle
      Early 1920s, pale red...........15.00
      1926, honeycomb
        base and top, red................10.00
    Temple Love
      Honeycomb base only 18.00
      Honeycomb base and top....25.00

Honeycomb, children playing house, German, 1920s, 5" x 8", $25.

    Wide-eyed children
      playing house..........................25.00
Paper Lace
    American
      1890, McLoughlin,
        layered folder.....................20.00
      3" x 5", c1900,
        orig envelope 25.00
      6" x 9", 2 added
        lace layers 25.00
      8" x 10", c1910, 2 layers 35.00
      Boxed, fancy scraps,
        ribbons 45.00
      Early, hand-done,
        scraps, ribbons 55.00
      c1870, 5" x 7",
        simple lace folder....................20.00
      c1885, simple lace folder.........12.50
Pull-Down
    1910, horse-drawn wagon 165.00
    c1910, auto, layered,
      very large 125.00
    Pre-World War I, German
      auto, 5" x 8" 65.00
    1920s
      Auto, cute children...............75.00
      Dollhouse, elaborate............85.00
      Floral, children, 4 layers 55.00
      Garden, layered, fancy 75.00
      Three layers
        Artist die cut 45.00
        Flowers 18.00
    1930s
      Children
        Fancy background 27.50
        2 layers 20.00
        Windmill background 25.00
        Hearts 65.00
Pullout
    Flowers in vase,
      opens out, 1920s 20.00
    Garden scene,
      children, 7" x 10" 55.00
    Gondola, children, honeycomb base,
      1930s......................................35.00
    Lighthouse,
      opens out, 1920s 25.00
    Sea plane, opens out, 1920s ...25.00
    Ship, 7" x 12",
      honeycomb base 75.00
    Tunnel of Love
      Honeycomb base.................28.00
      Honeycomb base and top....35.00
Silk Fringed
    Prang
      3" x 5", double-sided,
        1880s.................................15.00
      5" x 7", fancy
        padded front 25.00
    Tuck
      3" x 5", double-sided,
        c1900.................................12.50
      5" x 7", artist sgd, c1890......20.00

Unmarked, small, 1900 ....7.50
Standup with Easel Back
  Airport scene,
    children traveling 18.00
  Automobile,
    windows open, small 10.00
  Cherub with heart 5.00
  Children
    Die cut, fancy 12.50
    Dollhouse, 1925 ....15.00
    Figural 5.00
    Sledding, flat 7.50
  Fancy, silk inserts,
    10" x 14", 1900 ....9.50
  Flat, flapper, 8", c1920s 7.50
  Flower basket
    Cherub 15.00
    Pasteboard, 1918 ....7.50
  Layered parchment,
    5" x 8", c1910 ....15.00
  Schoolroom scene,
    children at desks 18.00
  Sports figures, 7" h....................7.50
  World War I doughboy, 6" h 9.50
  World War II soldier and
    sailor boys, 8" h..........................9.50
Victorian Novelty
  Animated, doll,
    head reverses, large 85.00
  Diecut
    Children, fancy, boxed 25.00
    Musical instrument, large 55.00
Parchment
  Children, umbrella................75.00
  Layered, ribbons 55.00
  Silk, cherubs 75.00
Wood, telephone,
  small, boxed 75.00

Vending Machines

Collecting Hints: Since individual manufacturers offered such a wide range of models, some collectors choose to specialize in a particular brand of machine. Variations are important. Certain accessories, porcelain finish, colors or special mechanical features on an otherwise common machine can add greatly to value.

Original paint is important, but numerous machines, especially peanut vendors with salt-damaged paint, have been repainted. Most vendors were in service for 10 to 20 years or more. Repainting normally was done by the operator as part of routine repair and maintenance. Repaints, recent or otherwise, if nicely done, do not necessarily lessen the value of a desirable machine. How-

ever, original paint should be retained if at all possible.

Decals add substantially to the appearance of a vendor and often are the only means of identifying it. Original decals, again, are the most desirable. Reproduction decals of many popular styles have been made and are a viable alternative if originals are not available.

Some reproduction parts also are available. In some cases, entire machines have been reproduced using new glass and castings. Using one or two new parts as a means of restoring an otherwise incomplete machine is generally accepted by collectors.

Collecting vending machines is a relatively new hobby. It has increased in popularity with other advertising collectibles. Previously unknown machines constantly are being discovered, thus maintaining the fascination for collectors.

History: Some of us still remember the penny gumball or peanut machine of our childhood. Many such vendors still survive on location after 30 years or more of service, due in part to the strength and simplicity of their construction.

The years between 1910 and 1940 were the heyday of the most collectible style of vendor, the globe-type peanut or gumball machine. Throughout this period, machine manufacturers invested a great deal of money in advertising and research. Many new designs were patented.

The simple rugged designs proved the most popular with the operator who serviced an established route of vendors as a means of making a living. Many operators made their fortunes "a penny at a time," especially during the Depression when dollars were hard to come by. Fifty years later, the vendors that originally cost between $4 and $15 command a much higher price.

In addition to the globe-style variety of vendor, cabinet-style machines were also made. These usually incorporate a clockwork mechanism and occasionally mechanical figurines to deliver the merchandise. The earliest examples of these were produced in the 1890s.

References: Richard M. Bueschel, *Collector's Guide to Vintage Coin Machines*, Schiffer Publishing, 1995; ——, *Lemons, Cherries and Bell-Fruit-*

Gum, Royal Bell Books, 1995; Richard Bueschel and Steve Gronowski, *Arcade 1*, Hoflin Publishing, 1993; Herbert Eiden and Jurgen Lukas, *Pinball Machines*, Schiffer Publishing, 1992; Bill Enes, *Silent Salesmen Too, The Encyclopedia of Collectible Vending Machines*, published by author (8520 Lewis Dr., Lenexa, KS 66227), 1995; Eric Hatchell and Dick Bueschel, *Coin-Ops on Location*, published by authors, 1993; Bill Kurtz, *Arcade Treasures*, Schiffer Publishing, 1994.

Periodicals: *Antique Amusements Slot Machines & Jukebox Gazette*, 909 26th St. NW, Washington, DC 20037; *Around the Vending Wheel*, 5417 Costana Ave., Lakewood, CA 90712; *Coin Drop International*, 5815 W. 52nd Ave., Denver, CO 80212; *Coin Machine Trader*, 569 Kansas SE, P.O. Box 602, Huron, SD 57350; *Coin-Op Classics*, 17844 Toiyabe St., Fountain Valley, CA 9270; *Coin-Op Newsletter*, 909 26th St., NW, Washington, DC, 20037; *Coin Slot*, 4401 Zephyr St., Wheat Ridge, CO 80033; *Gameroom*, 1014 Mt. Tabor Rd., New Albany, IN 47150; *Loose Change*, 1515 S. Commerce St., Las Vegas, NV 89102; *Pin Game Journal*, 31937 Olde Franklin Dr., Farmington, MI, 48334; *Scopitone Newsletter*, 810 Courtland Dr., Ballwin, MO 63021.

Museum: Liberty Belle Saloon and Slot Machine Collection, Reno, NV.

Advisor: Bob Levy.

Aspirin, Winthrop Metal Products, 10¢,
  c1940 ....40.00
Cigar, Malkin Phillies, steel metal,
  10¢, c1930 ....75.00
Cigarette, Row Mfg. Co.,
  6 columns, glass and metal,
  15¢ pkg, c1935.....................250.00
Collar Button, Zeno Machine, metal and
  glass, marquee, c1905..........375.00
Combs, Advance machine,
  Model #4, 10¢, c1950..............40.00
Condoms, Harmon Mfg., 25¢ pkg,
  c1962 ....75.00
Food, Horn & Hardart Automat,
  metal and marble, glass doors,
  4 units, complete, c1902 ....1,500.00
Gum
  Adams, stick gum, Tutti-Frutti, wood
    upright case, 1¢, c1890 ....700.00
  Advance, stick gum, metal upright
    case, c1925 ....75.00
  Atlas, ball gum, aluminum with tray,

c1950 ....85.00
Becker, ball gum, "Ring Ding Clown,"
plastic vendor, c1950 ....45.00
Caille Bros., ball gum, cast iron, claw
feet, etched globe, c1909....2,000.00
Columbus, ball gum,
cast iron and round globe,
Model "A," c1915.....................200.00
Dugreiner, 4-column
gum tab, stainless case,
Adams decal, c1934.................75.00
Ford, gum ball, 1¢,
chrome, c1947 ....45.00
Kayum, stick or pack gum,
metal case, Adams or Beechnut
decal, c1947...........................195.00
Masters, gum ball, aluminum
with porcelain base and lid,
#2, c1925 ....200.00
Penny King, ball gum,
Art Deco chrome design,
4 sections, c1935 ....550.00
Pulver, stick gum, Too Choos and
Joy Mint, red porcelain case with
policeman, c1930 ....400.00
Victor, gum ball, plastic top,
"Topper," c1950........................40.00
Zeno, stick gum, yellow porcelain
case, black lettering, 1908 .....300.00
Hot Nuts, Cebco Products, cast
aluminum, c1930 ....175.00
Lotion, National Dispenser, 1¢,
Jergens, c1938 ....50.00
Matches, Kelley Mfg.,
boxes, 1¢ c1920 ....200.00
Peanut, Oak Mfg., Acorn, c1947 ...35.00
Pens, Victor Vending, revolving,
25¢, c1962...............................55.00
Perfume, Mercury Tool, "Perfumatic,"
c1950......................................225.00
Postcard, Exhibit Supply,
1¢, novelty, c1930 ....125.00
Stamps, Postage Stamp Machine Co.,
metal, 5¢ and 10¢, c1948........40.00

Vernon Kilns

Collecting Hints: Vernon Kilns used 48 different marks during its years of operation. Collect examples which are in very good condition and concentrate on the specialty items rather than dinnerware.

History: During the Depression, many small potteries flourished in southern California. One of these, Poxon China, which was founded in Vernon, CA, in 1912 was sold to Faye G. Bennison in 1931. It was renamed Vernon Kilns and also was known as Vernon Potteries, Ltd. Under Bennison's direction, the company became a leader in the pottery industry.

High quality and versatility made its wares very popular. Besides a varied dinnerware line, Vernon Kilns also produced Walt Disney figurines and advertising, political and fraternal items. Their popular historical and commemorative plates were made in several different series featuring scenes from England, California missions and the West.

Vernon Kilns survived the Depression, fires, earthquakes and wars. However, it could not compete with the influx of imports. In January 1958, the factory was closed. Metlox Potteries of Manhattan Beach, CA, bought the trade name and molds along with the remaining stock.

References: Susan and Al Bagdade, *Warman's American Pottery and Porcelain*, Wallace-Homestead, 1994; Maxine Feek Nelson, *Collectible Vernon Kilns*, Collector Books, 1994; Leslie Pina, *Pottery, Modern Wares 1920-1960*, Schiffer Publishing, 1994.

Periodical: *Vernon View*, P.O. Box 945, Scottsdale, AZ 85252.

Brown-Eyed Susan: Montecito shape. Yellow daisies and green leaves on ivory ground, 1946-58.

Creamer 5.00
Mug 25.00
Pitcher, 2 qt, ice lip........................40.00
Plate, 6" d.......................................5.00
Platter, 12" d, round 12.00
Salt and Pepper Shakers, pr 15.00
Teapot..45.00
Tumbler, 4 oz 18.00

Gingham: Montecito shape. Green and yellow plaid with green border, 1949-58.

Carafe 30.00
Casserole, handle 25.00
Cup...7.50
Pitcher, ice lip................................45.00
Plate, 10-1/2" d, dinner...................7.50
Salt and Pepper Shakers, pr 35.00
Serving Bowl, 9" d 17.50
Soup Bowl, 8-1/2" d.......................15.00
Syrup Pitcher.................................85.00
Teapot..20.00

Hawaiian Flowers: Ultra shape. Designed by Don Bladding. Lotus flower transfer in pink, blue, maroon or mustard; 1938.

Chop Plate, 14" d, blue 40.00
Coffeepot, blue............................125.00
Creamer and Sugar, blue..............50.00
Cup and Saucer 60.00

Child's Feeding Dish, Golliwog decal, white ground, mkd "Vernon China, Vernon, Cal," $48.

Dinner Service,
maroon, 91 pcs 850.00
Plate
6" d, bread and butter, pink......20.00
8" d, luncheon, maroon............24.00
9" d, dinner, blue......................30.00

Miscellaneous

Bellaire, teapot 55.00
Bird Pottery, hp flowers
Demitasse Cup 20.00
Saucer, 6-1/4" d 8.00
Cinnamon, set, 83 pcs 250.00
Coral Reef, Salt and Pepper
Shakers, pr 65.00
Hibiscus, teapot 65.00
Honolulu, cup and saucer 65.00
Mayflower
Coffeepot 50.00
Teapot.....................................45.00
Mission, plate, 8-1/2" d, 4 color
San Gabriel.............................35.00
Santa Barbara.........................35.00
Plaid, creamer...............................22.50
Raffia, coffee server.....................65.00
Salamina, plate, 10" d 195.00

Moby Dick: Ultra shape. Transfer whaling scenes in blue, brown, maroon and orange; 1939.

Chowder, blue...............................30.00
Creamer, brown 15.00
Cup and Saucer, brown 20.00
Fruit Bowl, blue 25.00
Plate, luncheon, maroon 40.00
Sauceboat, brown 25.00
Sugar, cov, brown 30.00

Organdie: Monticeto shape. Brown and yellow plaid; 1940-58.

Bowl, 7-1/4" d..................................5.00
Butter Dish, cov.............................35.00
Cake Plate, 12" d 15.00
Chop Plate, 12" d 15.00
Creamer...5.00
Cup and Saucer 7.50
Eggcup...24.00
Mug, 9 oz 15.00

Plate, 10-1/2" d, dinner................10.00
Platter, 12-3./4" l, oval..................10.00
Salt and Pepper Shakers, pr.........15.00
Tea Set, round cov teapot, creamer,
  sugar.......................................45.00
Tidbit Tray, 2 tiers........................25.00

Tam O'Shanter: Monticeto shape.
  Chartreuse, green and rust plaid with
  green border; 1949-58.

Eggcup...30.00
Pitcher, 2 quart.............................95.00
Platter, 12" l................................17.50
Ramekin, cov.................................25.00
Tidbit Tray, 3 tiers, wood handle...40.00
Tumbler, 14 oz..............................15.00

Winchester 73: Western scene transfer
  with hand-tinted accents on cream-
  colored ground, 1950.

Chop Plate, 14" d.........................200.00
Demitasse Cup and Saucer..........65.00
Mug...250.00
Platter, 12-1/2" l, oval.................130.00
Salt Cellar and Pepper Mill..........125.00
Set, service for 8.......................1,200.00
Tumbler......................................250.00

View Master Products

Collecting Hints: Condition is the
key price determinant. Because this
collecting category is relatively new
and large quantities of material were
made, viewers and reels in mint or
near-new condition can still be found.
Original packaging is sought by collectors. Many viewers and reels were
removed from boxes and envelopes,
used excessively and damaged.

History: The first View-Master viewers and reels were made available in
1939. Invented by William Gruber,
View-Master products were manufactured and sold by Sawyer's, Inc.,
of Portland, OR. The early growth of
View-Master was cut short by World
War II. Shortages of film, plastic and
paper would have crippled the operation and possibly ended the existence
of View-Master had not the Army and
Navy recognized the visual training
potential of this product. Between
1942 and the war's end, about
100,000 viewers and five to six million
reels were ordered by the military.

After the war, public demand for
View-Master products soared. Production barely satisfied the needs of
the original 1,000-dealer network.
The Model C viewer, introduced in
1946, was practically indestructible,

making it the most common viewer
found by collectors today. In October
1966, General Aniline & Film Corp.
(GAF) bought Sawyer's and re-
vamped the View-Master line. GAF
introduced new 2-D projectors and
the 3-D Talking View-Master.

In late 1980, GAF sold the
View-Master portion of their company to a limited partnership headed by
businessman Arnold Thaler. Further
acquisition resulted in the purchase
of Ideal Toys. Today, the 3-D viewers and reels are manufactured by
View-Master Ideal, Inc.

Reference: Roger T. Nazeley, *View-
Master Single Reels*, published by au-
thor, 1987; John Waldsmith, *Stereo
Views*, Wallace-Homestead, 1991.

Collectors' Club: Many View-Master
collectors are members of the National Stereoscopic Association, P.O.
Box 14801, Columbus, OH 43214.

Alaska, 49th State, Sawyers.........15.00
Barnaby in Space, 1972, GAF......20.00
Birds of the World, 1968, GAF......15.00
Bedknobs and Broomsticks, 1971,
  Disney, sealed pack.................20.00
Bon Voyage, Charlie Brown,
  1980, GAF..............................10.00
Bonanza, 1964, GAP....................30.00
Brady Bunch, Grand Canyon Adventure,
  1960s, GAF.............................30.00
Buck Rogers, 1960s, GAF............10.00
Casper, 1961, GAF......................25.00
The Christmas Story, Sawyers,
  sealed pack.............................10.00
Daktan, 1968, GAF......................35.00
Disneyland, 1962, Sawyers
  Frontierland............................25.00
  Tomorrowland.........................25.00
Donald Duck, 1960s, Sawyers......25.00
Flintstones, View-Master International,
  1980, MOC..............................15.00
France, Sawyers, sealed pack......15.00
Frankenstein, 1976, GAF.............15.00
Germany, GAF, sealed pack.........15.00
GI Joe Adventures, GAF..............20.00
Grotto of Redemption, West Bend,
  IA, GAF...................................10.00
Gunsmoke, 1972, GAF.................30.00
Hopalong Cassidy
  No. 955, Hopalong Cassidy and
    Topper, 1950..........................12.00
  No. 956, The Cattle
    Rustler, 1950..........................12.00
Incredible Hulk, 3 reels, booklet,
  envelope, GAF View-Master Cartoon
  Favorites, J26, 1981................12.00
Iowa, Sawyers.............................15.00
Italy, Sawyers, sealed pack..........15.00
Jetson's, 1981, sealed pack.........24.00

Julia, 3 reels, story booklet,
  no envelope, 1969...................40.00
Lassie and Timmy, 1958, GAF.....20.00
Lassie Look Homeward,
  1965, GAF..............................20.00
Laugh-In, 3 reels,
  orig envelope, 1968.................45.00
Man from U.N.C.L.E., 3 reels, story
  booklet, no envelope, 1965.....36.00
Mexico, 1973, GAF,
  sealed pack.............................15.00
Modern Aircraft Boeing and Concorde,
  1969.......................................15.00
Monkees, Last Wheelbarrow to
  Pokeysville, 1967, MIP............60.00
Monkey Jungle,
  Miami, FL, GAF.......................13.00
Mount Rushmore, 1966, GAF.......15.00
Popeye, 1962, Sawyers...............20.00
Quick-Draw McGraw,
  1961, Sawyers........................25.00
Road Runner, 1967, GAF.............20.00
The Rookies, 1975, GAF,
  sealed pack.............................20.00
San Diego Zoo.............................15.00
Scenic USA, GAF, sealed pack....15.00
Silver Dollar City, 1971...............15.00
Space Mouse, 1964, Sawyer.......25.00
Space: 1999, 1975, GAF.............28.00
Star Trek, Mr. Spock's Time Trek,
  1974, GAF..............................20.00
Strange Animals of the World,
  1958, GAF..............................18.00
Tarzan, 3 reels, 3 story booklets,
  color photo on envelope,
  Sawyers, 1950........................45.00
The Time Tunnel,
  1966, Sawyers........................55.00
20,000 Leagues under the Sea,
  1962, Sawyers........................30.00
U.S. Spaceport, GAF...................15.00
Universal Studios Scenic Tour,
  1974, GAF, sealed pack..........25.00
Voyage to the Bottom of the Sea,
  1966, Sawyers........................30.00
Walt Disney
  The Love Bug,
    1968, GAF............................25.00
  Mickey Mouse in Clock Cleaners,
    1971, GAF............................20.00
  World Adventureland, GAF......20.00
Washington, DC, Sawyers,
  sealed pack.............................15.00
Water Ski Show,
  Cypress Gardens....................15.00
Welcome Back Kotter,
  3 reels, story booklet,
  color-photo cover, 1977..........24.00
Wild Animals of Africa,
  1958, GAF..............................15.00
Wild Animals of the World,
  1958, GAF..............................12.00
Yellowstone, Sawyer...................15.00

W

Watch Fobs

Collecting Hints: The most popular fobs are those related to old machinery, either farm, construction or industrial. Advertising fobs are the next most popular group.

The back of a fob is helpful in identifying a genuine fob from a reproduction or restrike. Genuine fobs frequently have advertising or a union trademark on the back. Some genuine fobs have blank backs, but a blank back should be a warning to be cautious.

History: A watch fob is a useful and decorative item that attaches to a man's pocket watch by a strap and assists him in removing the watch from his pocket. Fobs became popular during the last quarter of the 19th century. Companies such as The Greenduck Co., in Chicago, Schwabb in Milwaukee and Metal Arts in Rochester, N.Y., produced fobs for companies that wished to advertise their products or to commemorate an event, individual or group.

Most fobs are made of metal and are struck from a steel die. Enamel fobs are scarce and sought after by collectors. If a fob was popular, a company would order restrikes. As a result, some fobs were issued for a period of 25 years or more. Watch fobs still are used today in promoting heavy industrial equipment.

Reference: John M. Kaduck, *Collecting Watch Fobs*, Wallace-Homestead, 1973, 1995 value update.

Collectors' Clubs: Canadian Association of Watch Fob Collectors, P.O. Box 787, Caledonia, Ontario, N0A IAO Canada; International Watch Fob Association, Inc., RR5, P.O. Box 210, Burlington, IA 52601; Midwest Watch Fob Collectors, Inc., 6401 W. Girard Ave., Milwaukee, WI 53210.

Reproduction Alert.

Advertising
Biston's Golden Grain Coffee, brass, coffee-bean shape 115.00
Brown Gin and Liquors, 1-1/2" d, brass, raised moose head, reverse "Sold by H. Obernauer & Co.,

Roosevelt and Cox, brass, 1920, $100.

Pittsburgh, PA" 60.00
Caterpillar Construction Equipment, silvered metal, tread-tractor earth mover, reverse inscribed with dealer's name, orig strap 25.00
Chapman Drug Co., White Lion Drugs, Knoxville, silvered metal 35.00
Engeman-Matthew Range, diecut range 85.00
Evening Gazette, baseball shape, scorecard back, 1912 .... 95.00
Gardner-Denver Co., jackhammer, silvered brass, tool replica, symbol and name on back, c1950 .... 25.00
General Motors Diesel Engine, bronze-luster metal, detailed engine image, block inscription "GM/General Motors Diesel Power," block logo on back, engraved dealer's name 15.00
Green River Whiskey 45.00
Huntingdon Pianos, dark white metal, 7/8" black, white, blue and gold celluloid with Paderewski, inscription "Paderewski Bought One," early 1900s 65.00
Ingersoll-Rand, bronze luster, construction worker using pneumatic jackhammer beside "IR" logo, name and "Carset Jack Bits" on back 25.00
Joliet Corn Shellers 150.00
Kellogg Switchboard & Supply Co./The Service of the Telephone Proves the Worth of the Line, dark copper luster brass, raised image of candlestick phone with receiver off the hook, "K" circular logo, 1920s 60.00
Kelly Springfield Tires, 2" d, white metal, raised illus of female motorist, "Kelly Springfield Hand Made Tires" on back 75.00
Lima Construction Equipment, copper luster, large excavation

tractor, world continents background, inscribed "Lima/Move the Earth with a Lima," back text for shovels, draglines, clamshells and cranes 25.00
Lorain Construction Equipment, silvered brass, truck crane used to fill bed of pickup truck, inscribed "Loraine Cranes-Shovels/Draglines/Moto-Cranes," back inscribed "Freeland Equipment Co., Baltimore, orig strap 30.00
Martin-Senour Paints, 1-1/2" d, silvered brass, 1" d multicolored celluloid insert, hand holding dripping paint brush, text on back 65.00
Old Dutch Cleanser, porcelain center with Dutch lady 75.00
Porter Hay Carrier, scrolled shield 150.00
Red Goose Shoes, enameled red goose 95.00
Rosenthal Bros., NY, Adamant Suit, boy holding knickers, sitting on box holding extra pants 40.00
Schramm Tractors 60.00
Studebaker, nameled tire design 50.00
Ward's Fine Cakes, white porcelain, bluebird, silvered beaded rim 45.00
Zeno Means Good Chewing Gum, brass 95.00
American Legion, Cleveland State Convention, 1946, diecut brass 30.00
Beaded, hand worked, black, blue, yellow, red and white beads, 2 American flags and date 1936, 5-3/4" l 85.00
Elk's Tooth, gold filled 65.00
Political
Bryan, Our Next President 40.00
Democratic National onvention, Baltimore, 1912, silvered brass, center shield with eagle standing atop 20.00
Charles E. Hughes, 1908, silvered brass, head-and-shoulder portrait, from governor's campaign 60.00
Republican National Convention, brass, 1920, bust of Lincoln 40.00
Taft, brass, figural, padlock, "White House Lock, Taft 1908/Holds the Key" 50.00
Princeton University, brass, 1908 .... 45.00
Rally Day, 1-1/2" x 1-3/4", white metal, 7/8" bright multicolored celluloid insert, c1920 .... 35.00
World Championship Rodeo Contest, Chicago 45.00

Watt Pottery

Collecting Hints: Since Watt pottery was hand painted, there is a great deal of variation in patterns. Look for pieces with aesthetically pleasing designs which have remained bright and cheerful.

Watt had a strong regional presence in New England and New York, where more than 50% of its production was sold. Little of the output made its way west. Beware of placing too much emphasis on availability as a price consideration when buying outside the New England and New York areas.

Watt made experimental and specialty advertising pieces. These are eagerly sought by collectors. In addition, Watt made pieces to be sold exclusively by other distributors, e.g., Ravarino & Freschi Company's "R-F Spaghetti" mark.

History: Watt Pottery traces its roots back to W.J. Watt who founded the Brilliant Stoneware Co., in 1886 in Rose Farm, OH. Watt sold his stoneware company in 1897. Between 1903 and 1921, Watt worked at the Ransbottom Brothers Pottery owned by his brothers-in-law. In 1921, he purchased the Crooksville, OH, Globe Stoneware Co. (known as the Zane W. Burley Pottery between 1919 and 1921) and renamed it Watt Pottery Co. Watt was assisted by Harry and Thomas, his sons, C.L. Dawson, his son-in-law, Marion Watt, his daughter and numerous other relatives.

Between 1922 and 1935, the company produced a line of stoneware products manufactured from clay found in the Crooksville area. The company prospered, exporting some of its wares to Canada. In the mid 1930s, Watt introduced a kitchenware line with a background of off-white and tan earth tones. This new ware was similar in appearance to dinnerware patterns made by Pennsbury, Pfaltzgraff and Purinton. It also can be compared to English Torquay.

Most Watt dinnerware featured an underglaze decoration. On pieces made prior to 1950, decoration was relatively simple, e.g., blue and white banding. Patterns were introduced in 1950; the first was a pansy motif. Red Apple began in 1952 and Rooster in 1955. Floral series, such as Starflower and Tulip variations, were made. New patterns were introduced yearly.

Watt sold its wares through large chain stores such as Kroger's, Safeway and Woolworth and grocery, hardware and other retail merchants. Most of its output was sold in New England and New York. The balance was sold in the Midwest, Northwest and South. In the early 1960s, Watt was grossing more than $750,000. Future prospects were promising, but on Oct. 4, 1965, fire destroyed the factory and warehouse. The pottery was not rebuilt.

References: Susan and Al Bagdade, *Warman's American Pottery and Porcelain*, Wallace-Homestead, 1994; Harvey Duke, *Official Identification and Price Guide to Pottery and Porcelain*, 8th Edition, House of Collectibles, 1995; Sue and Dave Morris, *Watt Pottery*, Collector Books, 1993; Dennis Thompson and W. Bryce Watt, *Watt Pottery*, Schiffer Publishing, 1994.

Periodical: *Watt's News*, P.O. Box 708, Mason City, IA 50401.

Collectors' Club: Watt Pottery Collectors USA, Box 26067, Fairview Park, OH 44126.

Reproduction Alert: A Japanese copy of a large spaghetti bowl marked simply "U.S.A." is known. The Watt example bears "Peeddeeco" and "U.S.A." marks.

Apple

Bean Pot	195.00
Bowl	
#6, ribbed, adv	70.00
#8	50.00
#63	60.00
#66	85.00
#601, cov, ribbed 3 leaves	125.00
Canister, cov, #72	260.00
Casserole, cov, individual size, 2 leaves, hairline	100.00
Cereal Bowl	20.00
Cookie Jar, #503	375.00
Creamer, #62	170.00
Ice Bucket	295.00
Mug	65.00
Pie Plate	145.00
Pitcher, advertising	85.00
Salad Bowl, #73	65.00
Spaghetti Bowl, #39	150.00
Vegetable Bowl, cov	50.00

Autumn Foliage, baker, cov | 90.00

Banded, creamer, brown, #62 | 550.00

Bleeding Heart

Bean Pot	125.00
Bowl, #7	30.00
Creamer	75.00
Pitcher, #15	55.00

Cherry

Berry Bowl, #4	25.00
Bowl, #89	50.00
Pitcher, #15	60.00
Platter	150.00
Salt Shaker	50.00
Spaghetti Bowl, #39	50.00

Dutch Tulip, creamer, #62 | 225.00

Eagle 73, salad bowl | 225.00

Flower, 5-star, red, pitcher, #16 | 75.00

Greenbriar, bowl, #55 | 95.00

Nassau, cruet | 85.00

Pansy

Creamer, 3-1/2" h	100.00
Pie Plate, #33, adv	60.00
Pizza Plate	275.00
Spaghetti Bowl, #39	80.00

Rio Rose, mixing bowl, #9 | 80.00

Rooster

Bowl, adv	55.00
Creamer, #62	225.00
Ice Bucket	125.00
Refrigerator Pitcher, #69, adv	595.00
Salt Shaker, adv	50.00
Vegetable Bowl, adv	55.00

Starflower

Bowl, #15, 4-petal flower	95.00
Casserole, cov, #67	110.00
Mixing Bowls, nesting, set of four, #4, #5, #6, #7	185.00
Mug, #501	95.00
Pitcher, #15	50.00
Salt and Pepper Shakers, pr, barrel	160.00
Tumbler	300.00

Tulip

Bowl, #73	115.00
Casserole, cov, #600	125.00
Cookie Jar, #503	375.00
Mixing Bowl, #602	65.00
Pitcher, #17	295.00

Weller Pottery

Collecting Hints: Because pieces of Weller's commercial ware are readily available, prices are stable

Ewer, Cameo, salmon and white, 9-3/4", $40.

and unlikely to rise rapidly. Forest, Glendale and Woodcraft are the popular patterns in the middle price range. The Novelty Line is most popular among the lower-priced items.

Novice collectors are advised to consider figurals. There are more than 50 variations of frogs and many other animal shapes also are available. Pieces made during the middle production period are usually marked with an impressed "Weller" in block letters or a half-circle ink stamp with the words "Weller Pottery." Late pieces are marked with a script "Weller" or "Weller Pottery." Many new collectors see a dated mark and incorrectly think the piece is old.

There are well over 100 Weller patterns. New collectors should visit other collectors, talk with dealers and look at a large range of pieces to determine which patterns they like and want to collect. Most collections are organized by pattern, not by shape or type.

History: In 1872, Samuel A. Weller opened a small factory in Fultonham, near Zanesville, OH, where he produced utilitarian stoneware, such as milk pans and sewer tile. In 1882, he moved his facilities to Zanesville. In 1890, Weller built a new plant in the Putnam section of Zanesville along the tracks of the Cincinnati and Muskingum Railway. Additions to this plant followed in 1892 and 1894. In 1894, Weller entered into an agreement

with William A. Long to purchase the Lonhuda Faience Co., which had developed an art pottery line under the guidance of Laura A. Fry, formerly of Rookwood. Long left in 1895, but Weller continued to produce Lonhuda under the new name "Louwelsa." Replacing Long as art director was Charles Babcock Upjohn who—along with Jacques Sicard, Frederick Hurten Rhead and Gazo Fudji—developed Weller's art pottery lines.

At the end of World War I, many prestige lines were discontinued and Weller concentrated on commercial wares. Rudolph Lorber joined the staff and designed lines such as Roma, Forest and Knifewood. In 1920, Weller purchased the plant of the Zanesville Art Pottery and claimed to produce more pottery than anyone else in the country. Art pottery enjoyed a revival when the Hudson Line was introduced in the early 1920s. The 1930s saw Coppertone and Graystone Garden wares added. However, the Depression forced the closing of the Putnam plant and one on Marietta Street in Zanesville. After World War II, inexpensive Japanese imports took over Weller's market. In 1947, Essex Wire Co., of Detroit took control through stock purchases; however, operations ceased early in 1948.

References: Susan and Al Bagdade, *Warman's American Pottery and Porcelain*, Wallace-Homestead, 1994; Sharon and Bob Huxford, *Collectors Encyclopedia of Weller Pottery*, Collector Books, 1979, 1994 value update; Ralph and Terry Kovel, *Kovels' American Art Pottery*, Crown Publishers, 1993.

Collectors' Club: American Art Pottery Association, 125 E. Rose Ave., St. Louis, MO 63119.

Note: For pieces in the middle and upper price ranges, see *Warman's Antiques and Collectibles Price Guide*.

Ashtray
    Coppertone, frog seated
    at end 95.00
    Roma, 2-1/2" d........................35.00
    Woodcraft, 3" d 75.00
Basket
    Melrose, 10" 145.00

    Sabrinian.................................165.00
    Silvertone, 8".........................350.00
Batter Bowl, Mammy...................895.00
Bowl
    Cameo, 6" d, 3-1/4" h,
    all-over crazing 85.00
    Claremont 325.00
    Claywood, 4" d........................40.00
    Fleron, 3", all green.................80.00
    Knifewood, swans,
    dark ground...........................255.00
    Marbleized, 5-3/4" d, 1-5/8" d,
    shades of rose, pink
    and mauve 55.00
    Sabrinian, 6-1/2" x 3" h 240.00
Candlesticks, pr
    Euclid, 12-1/2" h,
    orange luster...........................85.00
    Lorbeek, 2-1/2" h, shape #1...125.00
    Pumila......................................65.00
Feeding Dish, Strutting Duck 125.00
Milk Pitcher, 4" h, Zona 75.00
Plate, Zona, 7" d 70.00
Cigarette Holder, figural, frog,
    Coppertone 200.00
Compote, Bonito, 4" h 75.00
Console Bowl, Warwick,
    10-1/2" d..................................75.00
Cornucopia
    Softone, light blue 45.00
    Wild Rose 75.00
Ewer
    Cameo, 10" h, white rose, blue
    ground......................................65.00
    Louwelsa, red and orange clover dec,
    5-1/2" h, artist sgd.................190.00
    Panella.....................................55.00
Figure
    Brighton Kingfisher 350.00
    Elephant, bug-eyed,
    Cactus line, yellow 145.00
    Turtle, Coppertone, 5-1/2" l......95.00
Flask, Take a Plunge 135.00
Flower Frog, figural
    Muskota 125.00
    Silvertone, 1928....................100.00
    Woodcraft, figural lobster,
    c1917 ....120.00
Hanging Basket
    Marvo, 7"...............................145.00
    Woodcraft, 9" 225.00
Jardiniere
    Claywood, 8",
    cherries and trees 95.00
    Ivory, 5"...................................45.00
    Marvo, rust, 7-1/2" 85.00
Jug, Louwelsa, small...................140.00
Mug
    Claywood,
    star shaped flowers.................65.00
    Ivory, brown accents,

cream ground 55.00

Pitcher

Bouquet, 6" h, ruffled top,
lavender flower, white ground,
artist sgd "M" 60.00

Pansy, 6-1/2" h........................110.00

Pierre, 5" h 50.00

Zona, 8" h, kingfisher dec,
green glaze, c1920.................140.00

Planter

Blue Drapery 60.00

Klyro, small..............................45.00

Sabrinian, 5" x 5"...................170.00

Woodrose, 9" h 60.00

Teapot, cov, pink, 5-1/2" h,
gold trim, all-over crazing 75.00

Tumbler, Bonito, multicolored
flowers, 4-1/4" h.......................70.00

Umbrella Stand, Ivory, 20" h 225.00

Vase

Art Nouveau, 9-3/4" h.............225.00

Bonito, blue flowers,
2 small handles, 5" h................70.00

Burntwood, pin-oak dec,
11" h.......................................150.00

Claremont, 5" h, 2 handles.......60.00

Coppertone, 8-1/2" h.............265.00

Fan, 7" h, small flake...............60.00

Floretta, 7-1/2" h,
grapes dec,
high-gloss glaze 175.00

Forest, 6" h.............................165.00

Glendale Thrush.....................250.00

Hudson, floral dec, 7" h

Sgd "D England" 200.00

Sgd "Timberlake" 375.00

Knifewood, 5-1/2" h,
canaries, high glaze,
nick on inside rim 125.00

Louwelsa, 10" h.....................210.00

Marbleized, 6" h 80.00

Muskota, boy fishing,
c1915, 7-1/2" h.....................200.00

Oak Leaf, 7" h, double bud type,

green and brown accents,
blue ground 85.00

Paragon, gold, base chip,
6-3/4" h...................................145.00

Roma, grape, dec, 6" h

Scenic 65.00

Suevo, 7" h.............................115.00

Tutone, 4" h, 3-legged
ball shape................................75.00

Woodcraft, 1917, smooth
tree-trunk shape, molded
leafy branch around rim,
purple plums, 12" h 195.00

Wall Pocket

Roma 195.00

Sabrinian...............................475.00

Suevo....................................195.00

Sydonia, blue 225.00

Woodcraft

9" h, tree-trunk shape,
molded leaves,
purple plus 400.00

10" h, conical,
molded owl's head in
trunk opening 300.00

Woodrose, lilac 85.00

Western Americana

Collecting Hints: Western Americana is a relatively new collecting field. The initial emphasis has been on books, prints and paper products. The barbed wire craze of the early 1970s drew attention to three-dimensional objects.

Texas material is the most sought after. All collectors tend to focus on the 19th century rather than modern material. Within the last decade, Indian materials have moved to the level of sophisticated antique collecting.

Collectors should pick a theme or subject. The military west, exploration accounts and maps and early photography are a few of the more popular focuses. The collecting field now has progressed to the point where there are more than a half-dozen dealers specializing solely in western materials.

History: From the Great Plains to the Golden West and from the mid-19th century to the early 20th century, the American west was viewed as the land of opportunity by settlers. Key events caused cataclysmic changes: the 1848 Gold Rush, the opening of

the Transcontinental railroad, the silver strikes in Nevada, the Indian massacres and the Oklahoma land rush. By 1890, the West of the cowboy and cattle was dead; Indians had been relocated onto reservations.

The romance did not die. Novels, movies and television, whether through the Ponderosa or Southfork, keep the romance of the West alive. Oil may have replaced cattle, but the legend remains.

References: Warren R. Anderson, *Owning Western History*, Mountain Press Publishing, 1993; Robert W.D. Ball, *Western Memorabilia and Collectibles*, Schiffer Publishing, 1993; Robert W.D. Ball and Edward Vebell, *Cowboy Collectibles and Western Memorabilia*, Schiffer Publishing, 1991, 1993 value update; James Lynn Bartz, *Company Property of Wells, Fargo & Co.'s Express 1852-1918*, Westbound Stage Co., 1993; Judy Crandall, *Cowgirls*, Schiffer Publishing, 1994; *Cowboy Clothing and Gear: The Complete Hamley Catalog of 1942*, Dover Publications, 1995 reprint; Michael Friedman, *Cowboy Culture*, Schiffer Publishing, 1992; R.C. House, *Official Price Guide to Old West Collectibles*, House of Collectibles, 1994; William C. Ketchum Jr., *Collecting the West*, Crown Publishers, 1993; ——, *Western Memorabilia*, Avon Books, 1993; Hunter and Shelkie Montana, *Cowboy Ties*, Gibbs Smith, 1994; Joice I. Overton, *Cowbits and Spurs*, Schiffer Publishing, 1997; Richard C. Rattenbury, *Packing Iron*, Zon International Publishing, 1993; Jim Schleyer, *Collecting Toy Western Guns*, Krause Publications, 1996.

Periodicals: *American Cowboy*, P.O. Box 12830, Wichita, KS 67277; *Boots*, Lone Pine Rd., P.O. Box 766, Challis, ID 83226; *Cowboy Collector Newsletter*, P.O. Box 7486, Long Beach, CA 90807; *Cowboy Guide*, P.O. Box 47, Millwood, NY 10546; *Texas Monthly*, P.O. Box 7088, Red Oak, IA 51591; *The Westerner*, P.O. Box 5253, Vienna, WV, 26105; *Wild West*, 6405 Flank Dr., Harrisburg, PA 17112; *Yippy Yi Yea Magazine*, 8393 E. Holly Rd., Holly, MI 48442.

Collectors' Club: American Barb Wire Collector's Society, 1023 Bald-

Vase, Atlas, mkd with script "Weller Pottery/since 1872", 7-1/6", $40.

win Rd., Bakersfield, CA 93304; National Bit, Spur & Saddle Collectors Association, P.O. Box 3098, Colorado Springs, CO 80934; Western American Collectors Society, P.O. Box 620417, Woodside, CA 94062.

Museums: Cowboy & Gunfighter Museum, Craig, CO; Gene Autry Western Heritage Museum, Los Angeles, CA; National Cowgirl Hall of Fame & Western Heritage Center, Hereford, TX; Pony Express Museum, St. Joseph, MO; Rockwell Museum, Corning, NY; Wells Fargo History Museum, Los Angeles, CA; Round Up Hall of Fame & Museum, Pendleton, OR 97801; Seven Acres Antique Village & Museum, Union, IL; Texas Ranger Hall of Fame & Museum, Waco, TX.

Additional Listings: Cowboy Heroes/ and Horses.

Advertising
  Banner, 19-1/2" x 29",
  Winchester, horse-and-rider
  center, "Headquarters for
  Winchester Rifles & Shotguns,"
  fringed hem, wood rod 150.00
  Sign, Moccasin Agency,
  fierce Indian with full
  headdress, emb tin...................50.00
Artwork
  Buffalo Bill, drawn and
  burnt by Albert J. Seigfried,
  Seneca Falls, NY, 1907 ....120.00
  Wells Fargo Depot and
  Office Building, Moron Taft,
  CA, 1910, orig ink drawing,
  20" x 30", framed....................400.00
Autograph, photo, "Louise Getchell

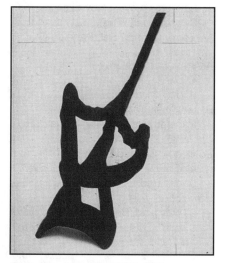

Branding iron, 16-1/2" l, $42.

from W.F. Cody, Cauifro Bonito,
Feb. 20, 1906"....................1,430.00
Bit
  J.F. Echaverria, silver inlay,
  spade bit, full engraving of
  kissing-birds design, minor
  restoration 1,870.00
  G.S. Garcia, silver inlaid
  high-port style, curved-
  snake cheeks, large 2"
  domed conchos..................1,320.00
  Phillips and Gutierrez, #20,
  engraved silver eagle
  shank style, sgd
  "Blake Miller" 5,610.00
  Jesus Tapia, half-breed,
  eagle and shield engraved
  design, c1916.....................7,700.00
  Unmarked, CA spade,
  silver overlay on brass,
  narrow mouth, 1850s 3,300.00
Bolo, 3" d, found, filigreed
  and engraved SS,
  ruby-eyed steer in yellow, pink
  and green gold, 1930 ....1,540.00
Book
  Elizabeth B. Custer, *Tenting
  on the Plains*, 1893 ....20.00
  McKenney-Hall, *History of the
  Indian Tribes of North America*,
  Grant, 1934, 123 color plates,
  3-vol set 125.00
Cabinet Card, W.F. Cody, Woodbury-
  type card, wood frame........1,375.00
Chaps
  Bohlin, batwin style, brown,
  tooled billet (belt), engraved
  SS buckle, mounted with eight
  1878 silver dollars...............1,980.00
  Hamley, wide, over 1,000
  metal studs, c1919..............4,510.00
Clothing Rack, Tales of Wells Fargo,
  1-1/2" x 20" x 20", wood rack,
  2 metal hanger loops at top,
  light oak finish, brown lettering
  across top, 6 attached black-
  finished metal horseshoe hangers,
  1959 Overland Products, 2 wood
  pegs missing 90.00
Cuffs, shirt type, tooled leather,
  c1915....................................500.00
Figure, cowboy, Stetson...............35.00
Gun Belt and Holster, Bohlin,
  2-tone floral carved, large
  engraved SS buckle 1,260.00
Headstall (bridle) and bit
  Keystone Bros., scalloped,
  engraved SS horsehead
  conchos trimmed in gold,
  1930s, bit missing 550.00
  Visalia, silver mounted,
  round silver-ferruled cheeks,
  star-face drop matching silver-
  mounted spade bit 1,925.00

Holster and Gun
  Fast draw, Colt SA 38-40
  revolver, used by stunt man
  Mark Swain 2,200.00
  Visalia, .38-caliber Smith &
  Wesson revolver, made for
  Alamedo County Sheriff's
  Posse, 1930s 3,850.00
Magic Lantern Slides, set of 60,
  "Colorado by a Tenderfoot,"
  railroad, mining towns,
  Pikes Peak, waterfalls,
  Denver, c1907 ....225.00
Newspaper Adv, Dr. Carver's,
  illus, 1883 ....30.00
Parade Outfit, Bohlin, silver mounted
  c1937, Cottam model, made for
  Eleanor Montana 16,700.00
  c1950, black, silver mounted, wool
  corona roll, matching breast collar
  and bridle 29,700.00
Party Set, covered wagon bean pot,
  ceramic coffeepot, beverage
  barrel, chip-and-dip bowl with
  cowboy hat lid, tan, ranch
  scenes, McCoy Pottery,
  price for set 1,045.00
Pinback Button
  Niagara County Pioneers
  Association, multicolored
  Indian portrait, c1918 ....90.00
  Redpath Chautauqua Indian,
  multicolored illus, red ground,
  c1907-20 ....80.00
Poster
  Levi's, Round-Up of Cowboy Lore,
  by Joe Mora, 1930 ....395.00
  101 Ranch Wild West Show,
  1915, 28" x 42" 2,200.00
Program, 101 Ranch Wild West
  Show 330.00
Saddle
  20" l, rawhide and tooled
  tanned leather, brass fittings,
  wood stirrups, some wear and
  damage 165.00
  Bohlin, youth, 11" seat,
  small silver diamond-shaped

Conestoga wagon, orig condition, needs restoration, $750.

spots, 1920s.........................5,500.00
Tibercio Carlos, loop, slick fork
working style, large sq skirts,
minor restoration 4,100.00
Child's, unknown maker,
c1950 ....400.00
J.C. Higgins, black silver-
trimmed parade, 15" seat,
factory floral stamping.........1,100.00
Mexican, stock, tapaderos
and exposed wood tree,
floral carved and buck stitched,
raised leather flowers, silver
thread trim, tooled bull-roping
scene, c1900.......................3,850.00
Texas Ranger, stock, floral
stamped, Cheyenne roll cantle,
nickel horn, double rigging,
1930s 1,100.00
Saddle Bags, pr, R.T. Frazier,
woolly angora trim 1,870.00
Saddle Blanket 225.00
Saddle Stand..............................100.00
Spittoon
  Brass and iron turtle,
  Victorian 935.00
  Copper, 13" d, saloon-type,
  1870s 275.00
Spurs, silver mounted
  Bohlin/Hollywood, McChesney,
  #125-2, tooled leather Bohlin
  straps 3,400.00
  Cox, John, Canon City, prisoner
  #4307, 4" l shanks, fancynickel-spot-
  ted leather straps by R.T. Frazier
  Saddlery Co., CO 13,200.00
  Garcia, G.S., #44, early mark,
  14-point rowels....................7,150.00
  Eddie Hulbert, Montana,
  Cheyenne-style heel band,
  engraved button design, 2-1/4"
  18-point rowels..................11,600.00
  Mike Morales, CA-style,
  engraved shield, snowshoes
  and eagle motif...................5,500.00
  Phillips & Gutierrez,
  eagle bit.............................5,610.00
  Qualey Bros., fully engraved,
  card-suit design, raised silver
  buttons, tooled leather
  straps 12,100.00
  L.D. Stone, mkd "1900," silver-
  mounted drop shank, engraved
  button heel band, silver inlaid rowels,
  orange 2-1/4" domed-button beaded
  conchos, basketweave leather
  straps 6,050.00
  Jesus Tapia, c1916...........23,650.00
  Wauley Bros.....................12,100.00
Thermometer, Dr. Cox's Barbed Wire
  Liniment................................225.00
Toy Chest, cowboy and Indian
  motif, burnt-wood designs,

1950s.........................350.00
Trunk, Miller Bros., rawhide cov,
"101" and "MB" in brass
nailheads, from Cody's 1
01 Ranch Show 1,650.00
Vase, 7" h, 7-1/2" h, green fan,
paper label, blue stamp
"Alamo Pottery, San Antonio,
Texas" 35.00
Watch Band, Bohlin, SS filigree, 1
0k and 18k yellow and pink gold,
rubies..................................4,400.00

Westmoreland Glass Company

Collecting Hints: The collector should become familiar with the many lines of tableware produced. English Hobnail, made from the 1920s to the 1960s, is popular. Colonial designs were used frequently and accessories with dolphin pedestals are distinctive.

The trademark, an intertwined "W" and "G," was imprinted on glass beginning in 1949. After January 1983, the full name, "Westmoreland," was marked on all glass products. Early molds were reintroduced. Numbered, signed, dated "Limited Editions" were offered.

History: The Westmoreland Glass Co., was founded in October 1899 at Grapeville, PA. From the beginning, Westmoreland made handcrafted high-quality glassware. During the early years the company processed mustard, baking powder and condiments to fill its containers. During World War I, candy-filled glass novelties were popular.

Although Westmoreland is famous for its milk glass, other types of glass products were also produced. During the 1920s, Westmoreland made reproductions and decorated wares. Color and tableware appeared in the 1930s; but, as with other companies, 1935 saw production return primarily to crystal. From the 1940s to the 1960s, black, ruby and amber objects were made.

In May 1982, the factory closed. Reorganization brought a reopening in July 1982, but the Grapeville plant closed again in 1984.

References: Lorraine Kovar, *Westmoreland Glass, Vols. I and II*, The

Candlestick, double, Della Robia, price for pr, $55.

Glass Press, 1991; Ellen T. Schroy, *Warman's Glass*, 2nd Edition, Wallace-Homestead, 1995; Hazel Marie Weatherman, *Colored Glassware of the Depression Era, Book 2*, Glassbooks, Inc., 1982; Chas. West Wilson, *Westmoreland Glass*, Collector Books, 1996.

Collectors' Clubs: National Westmoreland Glass Collectors Club, P.O. Box 372, Westmoreland City, PA 15692; Westmoreland Glass Collectors Club, 2712 Glenwood, Independence, 64052; Westmoreland Glass Society, 4809 420th St. SE, Iowa City, IA 52240.

Museum: Westmoreland Glass Museum, Port Vue, PA.

Animal, covered-dish type, white milk
  glass
  Camel, kneeling 75.00
  Cat, blue eyes.........................75.00
  Chick on eggs, iridized............85.00
  Fox, brown eyes, lacy base 75.00
  Swan, raised wing.................115.00
Appetizer Canapé Set, Paneled Grape,
  milk glass 80.00
Ashtray, Beaded Grape
  4" d...12.00
  5" d...15.00
Basket, milk glass
  Paneled Grape, 6-1/2" l, oval...25.00
  Pansy.......................................20.00
Bowl, cov, Beaded Grape
  4" d, ftd...................................16.00
  5" d, flared...............................55.00
Bowl, open, milk glass
  9" w, sq, ftd, Beaded Grape.....55.00
  9" d, 6" h, ftd, Paneled Grape ..45.00
  10-1/2" d, ftd,
  Paneled Grape.......................100.00
  11" l, oval, lipped, skirted pedestal

base, Paneled Grape 110.00
Butter Dish, cov, 1/4 lb, milk glass
   Old Quilt 28.00
   Paneled Grape 24.00
Cake Salver, Paneled Grape, milk glass,
   skirted 85.00
Candlesticks, pr
   Old Quilt, milk glass 16.00
   Paneled Grape, milk glass,
   4" h..25.00
   Ring & Petal 22.00
Candy Dish, cov
   Beaded Bouquet, blue
   milk glass 35.00
   Beaded Grape, 9" d, ftd 40.00
   Paneled Grape, milk glass,
   3 legs, crimped.........................35.00
   Wakefield, crystal, low..............45.00
   Waterford, ruby stained, 9" d ...35.00
Cheese, cov,
   Old Quilt, milk glass.................52.00
Children's Dishes
   Creamer, File & Fan,
   ruby carnival.............................20.00
   Pitcher, Flute, cobalt blue,
   white floral dec 40.00
   Sugar, cov, File & Fan,
   ruby carnival.............................30.00
   Table Set, cov butter, creamer,
   cov sugar, File & Fan,
   milk glass 45.00
   Tumbler, Flute, green,
   white floral dec 15.00
Compote, cov, 7" d
   Paneled Grape,
   Golden Sunset 40.00
   Roses and Bows, green...........65.00
Compote, open, ftd
   6" d, crimped, Paneled Grape,
   milk glass 40.00
   7" d, milk glass
      Old Quilt, bell-shape 26.00
      Paneled Grape, orig label 20.00
   7" sq, Beaded Grape...............17.00
   8" d, Dolphin, milk glass..........45.00

Plate, Ring & Petal, No. 1875, milk glass, $12.

9" d, Paneled Grape, milk glass,
   clear foot 75.00
9" sq, Beaded Grape................30.00
Creamer, 6-1/2 oz, Paneled Grape,
   milk glass, orig label 16.00
Creamer and Sugar on Tray,
   individual size, Paneled Grape,
   milk glass.................................27.00
Cruet, stopper, milk glass
   Old Quilt....................................30.00
   Paneled Grape.........................30.00
Cup and Saucer, Paneled Grape,
   milk glass.................................22.00
Dish, heart shape, handle,
   Della Robia, stained 70.00
Epergne, 8-1/2" h, Paneled Grape,
   milk glass.................................70.00
Flowerpot, Paneled Grape,
   milk glass.................................48.00
Fruit Cocktail, Paneled Grape,
   milk glass.................................25.00
Fruit Cocktail Underplate, Paneled
   Grape, milk glass......................9.00
Goblet, 8 oz
   Della Robia, stained................40.00
   Paneled Grape, milk glass.......18.00
Gravy Boat and Underplate, Paneled
   Grape, milk glass.....................58.00
Honey, cov, 5" d, Beaded Grape,
   milk glass, roses and garland
   dec..45.00
Jardiniere, Paneled Grape,
   milk glass, 6-1/2" h, ftd 42.00
Jelly, cov, Paneled Grape,
   milk glass.................................30.00
Pitcher, milk glass
   Old Quilt....................................40.00
   Paneled Grape
      16 oz...................................45.00
      32 oz...................................35.00
Planter, 5" x 9", Paneled Grape, milk
   glass...48.00
Plate
   6" d, Beaded Edge......................5.00
   7" d, Beaded Edge
      Goldfinch center...................13.00
      Red edge 10.00
   8" d, Princess Feather,
   crystal......................................15.00
   Salad, Della Robia,
   dark stain 22.00
Puff Box, cov, Paneled Grape,
   milk glass.................................30.00
Punch Bowl Base, Paneled Grape,
   milk glass...............................115.00
Punch Cup, Fruits, milk glass..........6.00
Punch Set, milk glass
   Fruits, 12 pc set 150.00
   Paneled Grape, red hooks
   and ladle, 13" d, 15-pc set 595.00
Rose Bowl, 4" d, Paneled Grape, milk
   glass, ftd 30.00

Salt and Pepper Shakers, pr
   Della Robia, stained................70.00
   Old Quilt, milk glass 25.00
   Paneled Grape, milk glass.......25.00
Sauceboat and Underplate, Paneled
   Grape, milk glass 70.00
Saucer, Paneled Grape,
   milk glass 8.50
Sherbet, 10-3/4" h, Della Robia,
   light stain 26.00
Slipper, figural, almond
   milk glass 20.00
Spooner, Old Quilt, milk glass,
   6-1/2" h....................................28.00
Sugar, milk glass
   Beaded Grape,
   individual size 10.00
   Old Quilt, large, open...............15.00
Torte Plate, 14" d, Della Robia,
   light stain 125.00
Tumbler, flat
   Della Robia, dark stain, 8 oz....28.00
   Paneled Grape, milk glass.......12.50
Vase
   6" h, ftd, bell-shape,
   Paneled Grape, milk glass.......15.00
   7" h, horn-shape,
   Lotus, #9 ....35.00
   9" h, bud, Roses and Bows......30.00
   9" h, ftd, bell-shape,
   Paneled Grape, milk glass.......25.00
   10" h, bud, Paneled Grape,
   milk glass, orig label 30.00
   15" h, swing-type, Paneled Grape,
   milk glass 20.00
Water Set, 1776 Colonial, amber,
   flat water pitcher, 6 goblets,
   price for 7-pc set 70.00
Wedding Bowl, cov, 10" d,
   ruby stained.............................40.00
Wine, Paneled Grape, milk glass,
   2 oz 22.00

Whiskey Bottles, Collectors' Special Editions

Collecting Hints: Beginning collectors are advised to focus on bottles of a single manufacturer or to collect around a central theme, e.g., birds, trains or Western. Only buy bottles that have a very good finish (almost no sign of wear), no chips and intact original labels.

    A major collection still can be built for a modest investment, although some bottles, such as the Beam Red Coat Fox, now command over $1,000. Don't overlook miniatures if you are on a limited budget. In many states, it is against the law to sell liquor without a license; hence, collectors tend to focus on empty bottles.

History: The Jim Beam Distillery began the practice of issuing novelty (collectors' special edition) bottles for the 1953 Christmas trade. By the late 1960s, more than 100 other distillers and wine manufacturers followed suit. The Jim Beam Distillery remains the most prolific issuer of the bottle. Lionstone, McCormick and Ski Country are the other principal suppliers today. One dealer, Jon-Sol, Inc., has distributed his own line of collector bottles.

The golden age of the special edition bottle was the early 1970s. Interest waned in the late 1970s and early 1980s as the market became saturated with companies trying to join the craze. Prices fell from record highs and many manufacturers dropped special-edition bottle production altogether.

A number of serious collectors, clubs and dealers have brought stability to the market. Realizing that instant antiques cannot be created by demand alone, they have begun to study and classify their bottles. Most importantly, collectors have focused on those special-edition bottles which show quality workmanship and design and which are true limited editions.

References: Hugh Cleveland, *Bottle Pricing Guide*, 3rd Edition, 1988, 1993 value update; Ralph and Terry Kovel, *Kovels' Bottles Price List*, 10th Edition, Crown Publishers, 1996; Jim Megura, *Official Price Guide Bottles*, House of Collectibles, 1991; Michael Polak, *Bottles*, Avon Books, 1994.

Collectors' Clubs: Cape Codders Jim Beam Bottle & Specialty Club, 80 Lincoln Rd., Rockland, MA 02370; Hoffman National Collectors Club, P.O. Box 37341, Cincinnati, OH 45222; International Association of Jim Beam Bottle & Specialties Clubs, 5013 Chase Ave., Downers Grove, IL 60515; National Ski Country Bottle Club, 1224 Washington Ave., Golden, CO 80401; Space Coast Jim Beam Bottle & Specialties Club, 2280 Cox Rd., Cocoa, FL 32926.

Museum: American Outpost, James B. Beam Distillery, Clermont, KY.

Aesthetic Specialties, Inc., World's Greatest Hunter, 1979.............34.00

ALPA, Warner Bros. Characters

Bugs Bunny, 1977.........................10.00
Tweety Bird, 1978.........................20.00

Anniversary, Lincoln, 1973..........15.50

Ballantine

Golf Bag, 1969...............................9.50
Mallard, 1969.................................18.00
Zebra, 1970....................................14.00

Jim Beam

Beam Clubs and Conventions
Akron, Rubber Capital, 1973.........24.00
    Conventions
        First, Denver, 1971..............16.00
        Fifth, Sacramento, 1975......14.00
        Thirteenth, St. Louis, 1983...48.00
Evergreen State Club, 1974..........15.50
Twin Bridges Club, 1971...............50.00
Beam on Wheels
    Cable car, 1983......................66.00
    Caboose, 1980........................39.00
    Ernie's Flower Car, 1976.........35.00
    Stutz Bearcat, yellow, 1977.....38.00
Casino Series
    Barney's Slot Machine, 1978...20.00
    Harolds Club, Covered Wagon, green, 1969................................6.00
Centennial Series, first issued 1960
    Alaska Purchase, 1966.............9.00
    Civil War, 1961, South.............53.00
    Hawaii, 200th, 1978.................20.00
    Reidsville, 1973.......................7.50
    San Diego, 1968.......................7.00
Clubs and Organizations
    Ahepa, 1972.............................5.00
    BPO Does, 1971.......................5.00
    Ducks Unlimited, #5, 1979.......22.00
    Pennsylvania Dutch Club, 1974.......................................12.00
    Shriners, Western Association, 1980.......................................30.00
Customer Specialties
    Armanetti, fun shopper, 1971.....7.50
    Katz Cat, black, 1968..............13.00
    Ralph's Market, 1973...............13.00
    Zimmerman, vase, brown, 1972.......................................20.00
Executive Series, first issue 1955
    1957, Royal DiMonte..............73.00
    1960, Blue Cherub..................120.00
    1969, Sovereign......................14.00
    1972, Regency.........................14.00
    1982, Executive.......................30.00
Foreign Countries
    Australia, Sydney Opera, 1978.........................22.50

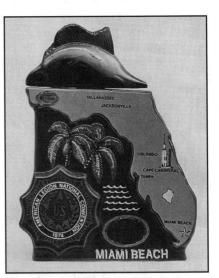

Ezra Brooks, Heritage China, American Legion National Convention, 1974, Miami Beach, $15.

Thailand, 1969...........................5.00
People Series
    Cowboy, 1981.........................15.50
    Emmet Kelly, Kansas autograph, 1973.......................68.00
    John Henry, 1972....................72.00
    Paul Bunyan, 1970..................10.00
    Viking, 1973............................12.00
Political Series
    Kansas City Convention Elephant, 1976.......................14.00
    Spiro Agnew Elephant, 1970.................2,200.00
Regal China Series
    Green China Jug, 1965.............7.00
    Las Vegas, 1969......................5.00
    London Bridge, 1971................5.50
    New Hampshire Golden Eagle, 1971................44.00
Sports Series
    Fiesta Bowl, 1970....................13.00
    Hawaiian Open, golf ball, 1983.......................16.00
    Kentucky Derby, 100th, 1974.......................10.00
    Louisiana Superdome, 1975......9.00
State Series
    Colorado, 1959........................33.00
    New Hampshire, 1968...............7.00
    New Jersey, blue, 1963...........68.00
    Ohio, 1966..............................14.00
    South Carolina, 1970.................7.50
Trophy Series
    Bird, pheasant, 1960...............30.00
    Coho Salmon, 1976.................12.00
    Dog, poodle, gray, 1970............7.00
    Horse, brown, 1967-68............21.50
    Rabbit, 1971............................13.50

Beneagle
Barrel, thistle 4.50
Chess Pawn, John Knox, black,
    miniature.................................12.00
Bischoff
Chinese Boy, 1962 ....36.00
Grecian Vase, 1969.....................15.50
Pirate...20.00
Ezra Brooks
Animal Series
    Elephant, Big Bertha, 1970 ....8.00
    Hereford, 1971 ....14.00
    Panda, 1972..............................18.00
Automotive/Transportation Series
    Motorcycle, 1971 ....13.50
    Ontario Racer, #10, 1970.........21.00
    Train, Iron Horse, 1969 ....12.00
Fish Series, trout and fly, 1970......10.00
Heritage China Series, silver dollar,
    black base, 1969 ....9.00
Institutional Series
    Bucket of Blood, 1970 ....8.00
    Club Bottle #1,
      Distillery, 1970.........................12.50
    Iowa Farmers Elevator, 1978 ...36.00
    Wichita Centennial, 1970 ....7.50
People Series
    Clown with balloons, 1973 ....22.00
    Max "The Hat"
      Zimmerman, 1976.....................32.00
    Mr. Merchant, 1970 ....10.00
    Oliver Hardy, 1976 ....17.50
    Stonewall Jackson, 1974 ....32.00
Sports Series
    Basketball Players, 1974..........10.00
    Casey at Bat, 1973..................16.00
    Go Big Red #3, Rooter, 1972...14.00
    Greensboro Open,
      cup, 1975 ....50.00
Collector's Art
Bird Series, cardinal, miniature 30.00
Cattle Series, Texas
    Longhorn, 1974 ....35.00
Dog Series, miniature
    Basset Hound...........................25.50
    Poodle, white............................21.00
Cyrus Noble
Animal Series
    Buffalo Cow & Calf,
      Nevada ed, 1977.....................88.00
    Moose & Calf, 2nd ed, 1977.....80.00
Carousel Series,
    pipe organ, 1980.....................45.00
Mine Series, mine shaft, 1978.......35.00
Sea Animals
    Harp Seal, 1979 ....50.00
    Sea Turtle, 1979......................50.00
J.W. Dant
Boeing 747 ....14.00
Field Birds, 1969, #4,
    mountain quail 9.00

Patrick Henry, 1969.........................5.00
Double Springs
Bicentennial Series
    Iowa 50.00
    Washington, DC........................14.00
Car Series
    Mercedes Benz, 1975 ....28.00
    Rolls Royce, 1971 ....40.00
Early Times, 1976
Cannon Fire
    Delaware..................................22.00
    Nevada.....................................22.00
    New Mexico 28.00
Drum and Fife
    Florida......................................17.00
    Kansas.....................................20.00
Minuteman
    Alaska 35.50
    Oklahoma.................................24.00
Paul Revere, Arizona 21.00
Washington Crossing the Delaware,
    South Dakota...........................17.00
Famous Firsts
Airplane Series, Winnie Mae,
    large, 1972 ....88.00
Animal Series
    Bears, miniature, 1981..............36.00
    Hippo, baby, 1980....................50.00
    Panda, baby, 1980...................50.00

Grenadier, Civil War Series, Jeb Stuart, Oct. 1970, Arnart Imports, Inc., $20.

Car/Transportation Series
    Balloon, 1971 ....65.00
    Corvette, 1963 Stingray, white,
      miniature, 1979 ....13.50
    Porsche Targa, 1979 ....44.00
Miscellaneous
    Fireman, 1980..........................53.50
    Hurdy Gurdy,
      miniature, 1979 ....15.50
    Phonograph, 1969 ....36.00
    Sewing Machine, 1979 ....35.00
Garnier (France)
Christmas Tree, 1956 ....67.00
Locomotive, 1969.........................14.00
Soccer Shoe, 1962 ....37.00
Grenadier
American Revolution Series
    Second Maryland, 1969...........37.50
    Third New York, 1970 ....22.00
British Army Series, Kings African Rifle
    Crops, 5th, 1970.....................20.00
Civil War Series, General Robert E.
    Lee, 1/2 gal, 1977 ....150.00
Miscellaneous
    Jester Mirth King, 1977 ....56.00
    San Fernando
      Electric Mfg Co., 1976 ....66.00
Napoleonic Series,
    Eugene, 1970 ....21.00
Hoffman
Aesop's Fables Series, music,
    6 types, 1978...........................30.00
Band Series, Accordion player,
    miniature, 1987 ....13.50
Bird Series, eagle,
    open wing, miniature, 1979 .....18.00
Cheerleaders, Rams,
    miniature, 1980 ....20.00
Mr. Lucky Series, music
    Barber, 1980 ....38.00
    Cobbler, 1973 ....25.00
    Fiddler, 1974............................25.00
    Mailman, miniature, 1976 ....12.50
School Series
    Kentucky Wildcats,
      football, 1979 ....38.00
    Tennessee Volunteers.............28.00
Wildlife Series,
    doe & fawn, 1975 ....50.00
Japanese Firms
House of Koshu
    Geisha,
      chrysanthemum, 1969 ....23.50
    Sake God, white, 1969 ....14.00
Kamotsuru, treasure tower, 1966..18.00
Kikukawa
    Eisenhower, 1970 ....17.00
    Royal couple, pr......................32.00
Kentucky Gentleman
Confederate Soldier, 1969 ....13.00
Union Soldier, 1969 ....13.00

W.A. Lacey

Log Animal, raccoon,
1980, miniature.........................21.50
Tun Tavern, 1975..........................14.00

Lewis and Clark

Clark, miniature, 1971 ....15.50
General Custer, 1974.....................71.00
Lewis, 1971 ....88.00
Troll Family,
grandmother troll, 1979 ....29.00

Lionstone

Bird Series,
dove of peace, 1977 ....40.00
Car/Transportation Series
Stutz Bearcat,
miniature, 1978 ....15.00
Turbo Car STP, red, 1972.........25.00
Clown Series, #6, Lampy, 1979 ....34.00
European Workers Series, 1974, 6
types, each 24.00
Firefighter Series, fireman, #8, fire
alarm box, 1983........................57.00
Old West Series
Bartender, 1969 ....30.00
Dance Hall Girl, 1973 ....67.00
Indian, squaw, 1973.................25.00
Riverboat Captain, 1969 ....14.00
Telegrapher, 1969....................20.00
Sports Series
Baseball Player, 1974 ....27.50
Hockey Player, 1974 ....20.00
Tennis Player, male, 1980 ....45.00

Luxardo

Apple, figural 14.00
Bizantina......................................26.00
Babylon, 1960 ....
Calypso Girl, 1962.........................15.50
Frog, miniature 15.00
Tower of Flowers, 1968.................18.00
Zodiac, 1970.................................31.50

McCormick

Bicentennial Series, Betsy Ross,
miniature, 1976.........................48.00
Bull Series
Brahma, 1973............................40.00
Texas Longhorn, 1974 ....36.50
Entertainment Series, Jimmie
Durante, 1981 ....50.00
Football Mascots
Drake Bulldogs, 1974...............23.00
Indiana Hoosiers, 1974 ....17.00
Frontiersmen Series,
Kit Carson, 1975......................15.00
Great American Series
Ulysses S. Grant, 1976 ....29.00
Mark Twain, 1977.....................32.00
Sports Series
Air Racy Pylon, 1970................14.00
Nebraska Football
Player, 1972.....................24.00

Train Series, wood tender, 1969 ...22.00
Warrior Series, Centurion, 1969....20.00

OBR

Caboose, 1973..............................21.00
River Queen, 1967 ....10.00
W.C. Fields, top hat, 1976.............16.00

Old Bardstown, bulldog, 1980.....80.00

Old Crow, crow, 1974...................14.00

Old Commonwealth

Apothecary Series, North Carolina
University, 1979.......................30.00
Coal Miners
#3, with shovel, 1977 ....41.50
#5, coal shooter, 1983 ....44.00
Fireman Series, modern, #5,
Lifesaver, 1983........................72.50
Miscellaneous
Indian Chief Illini, University of
Illinois, 1979 ....60.00
Lumberjack, old time, 1979......20.00
Kentucky
Thoroughbreds, 1977...............39.00

Old Fitzgerald

America's Cup, 1970.....................27.00
Blarney, Irish toast, 1970 ....16.00
Davidson, NC, 1972.....................40.00
Hospitality, 1958...........................9.00
Rip Van Winkle, 1971....................34.50
West Virginia
Forest Festival, 1973..............22.00

Old Mr. Boston

Concord Coach, 1976 ....17.00
Deadwood, SD, 1975....................16.00
Hawk, 1975 ....18.00
Nebraska, #1, gold, 1970.............20.00
Paul Revere, 1974 ....15.50
Town Crier, 1976..........................10.00

Pacesetter

Camaro, Z28, yellow, 1982 ....42.00
Corvette, red, 1975 ....40.00
Tractor Series, No. 2, Big Green

Wild Turkey, No. 6, Striding, $85.

Machine, International
Harvester, 1983......................66.00
Vokovich, #2, 1974 ....30.00

Pancho Villa, Pancho
on horse, 1975 ....40.00
Potters
Clydesdale, 1978, miniature 20.00
Pirate, 1973.................................48.00

Ski Country

Christmas Series, Ebenezer Scrooge,
1979, miniature 24.00
Circus Series
Clown, bust, 1974, miniature ...17.00
Ringmaster, 1975, miniature....26.50
Customer Specialties
Eagle, paperweight 190.00
Mill River Country
Club, 1977 ....44.00
Submarine, 1976, miniature.....29.00
Domestic Animal Series
Bassett, miniature, 1978 ....20.00
Labrador with mallard, 1977,
miniature 49.00
Indian Series, Cigar
Store Indian, 1974...................40.00
Waterfowl Series, duck, mallard,
1973, miniature 40.00
Wildlife Series
Antelope, pronghorn 70.00
Jaguar, miniature 33.00
Koala, 1973..............................42.00
Mountain Lion,
1973, miniature 30.00
Woodpecker, ivory bill, 1974....66.00

Wild Turkey

Crystal Anniversary, 1955........2,000.00
Mack Truck 20.00
Series #1
2, female, 1972 ....150.00
5, with flags, 1975...................40.00
8, strutting, 1978 ....45.00
Turkey Lore Series
#1, 1979..............................65.00
#4, 1982..................................50.00

Women's Causes

Collecting Hints: Collecting with a theme or special emphasis is important. Focus on one individual, one kind of activity (women's firsts, explorers, artists, journalists, teachers, etc.) or a particular time period.

The list below deals with material by and about women. However, a collection of how women have been portrayed through history can be assembled by concentrating on other collectible fields—advertising, comic books, cookbooks, magazine tear sheets, paper dolls, photographs, postcards, toys, etc. The possibilities are endless. Study and look before you build your collection.

History: The accent on women's rights is not new—in 1792, Mary Wollstonecraft published *A Vindication of the Rights of Women*. But the First Woman's Rights Convention, in Seneca Falls, NY, wasn't held until 1848. By the late 19th century and into early 20th century, there was a major thrust to give women the right to vote. The suffrage movement, after decades of work, saw its efforts rewarded when the 19th amendment was ratified in 1920.

Women's involvement in World War II broke down more barriers. However, it was Betty Friedan's *The Feminine Mystic*, that heralded the modern women's liberation movement. In addition to concern about their own rights, many women in the 19th century were also conscious of injustices to others and became involved in the abolition and social reform movements. Women pioneers wrote and published accounts of their role in settling the American West, became involved in American industrial growth and explored foreign lands.

References: Eleanor Flexner, *Century of Struggle: The Woman's Rights Movement in the United States*, Revised Edition, Belknap Press, 1975; *Notable American Women*, 4 vols., Belknap Press, 1971-1980.

Autograph, Clara Barton, Civil War nurse, founder of American Red Cross, ALS, 4-pg small 8vo, Glen Echo, MD, May 5, 1906, to Miss Kensel, regarding organizational business and praise of 2 younger women who are enthusiastic and devoted to first-aid work 485.00

Book

American Feminists, Robert E. Riegel, University of Kansas Press, 1963, 233 pgs 28.00

Marking A Trail, Texas Women's University Press, hardcover,

orig dust jacket 20.00
The Female Spy of the Union Army, 1864 ....35.00
Fan, Women's Christian Temperance Union 10.00
Lapel Stud, 7/8" l, I Am for Allison Are You, b&w, 1896 ....10.00
Photo, woman on motorcycle, 4" x 5" 25.00
Pin, Angela Davis, gold-finished brass, black image, red letters "Libertad Para," inscribed "Hecho En Cuba" 50.00
Pinback Button
Don't Let Us Suffer, b&w cigarette premium, Rube Goldberg cartoon of woman singing 50.00
Equality, b&w litho, c1960........20.00
Equal Suffrage, 6 stars, 3/4" d, black letters, dark gold ground 85.00
Frances Willard, softly tinted sepia, c1900............................40.00
Gave My Blood for the Equal Rights Amendment, 1-3/4" d, bright red on white..25.00
I Vote Dry, purple type, purple diamond design, white ground......20.00
Mamie/Pat, 3-1/2" d, red, white and blue, b&w photos, 1952 ....30.00
Opposed to Woman Suffrage, black and white, red center 20.00
President Carter/Barbara Walters, 3-1/2" d, white, yellow, b&w portraits, Balloon coming from Walters' head that says "Be Wise with Us…Be Good to Us," Dec. 1976 ....15.00
Take Delmar Garden Cars to Camp Lewis, City of Tents and Woman's Magazine Building, cel 35.00
Time for Repeal, dark blue on gold ground, Liberty Bell, designed as clock face 15.00
United Nations Decade for Women, white lettering, dark blue ground, peach dove and female symbols, dated 1976-1986............................25.00
Vote No for My Sake, prohibition, young girl, faded red rim 10.00
Votes for Women
Black letter, gold ground......40.00
Red, white and blue sunburst, 1915 ....150.00

Stickpin, Woman's Benefit Association Peace Jubilee, oval, 1-1/2" x 5/8", 1919, $25.

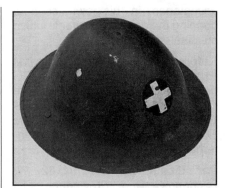

Helmet, World War I, American, divisional helmet, orig liner, $50.

World War I Collectibles

Collecting Hints: Be careful. Uniforms and equipment from World War I were stockpiled at the end of the war and reissued in the early years of World War II. Know the source of the items before you buy and scrutinize all materials. Some research and investigation might be necessary to correctly identify an item as an actual war artifact.

Collectors' clubs and re-enactment groups are among the best sources of information. These groups also are very knowledgeable about reproductions, copycats and fantasy items.

History: Power struggles between European countries raged for hundreds of years. As the 20th century dawned, leading European countries became entangled in a series of complex alliances, many sealed by royal marriages and a massive arms race. All that was needed to set off the powder keg was a fire. The assassination of Austrian Archduke Franz Ferdinand by a Serbian national ignited the fuse on June 28, 1914. Germany invaded Belgium and moved into France. Russia, England and Turkey joined the war. Italy and the United States became involved by mid-1917.

In 1918, Germany sued for peace. A settlement was achieved at the Versailles Conference, January-June 1919, during which time the United Sates remained in the background. President Wilson's concept for a League of Nations failed to gain acceptance in his own country, opening the door to the events which culminated in World War II.

References: W.K. Cross, *Charlton Price Guide to First World War Canadian Infantry Badges*, The Charlton Press, 1995; *Windrow & Greene's MilitariaDirectory and Sourcebook* 1994, Motorbooks International, 1994.

Periodicals: *Men at Arms*, 222 W. Exchange St., Providence, RI 02903; *Military Collector Magazine*, P.O. Box245, Lyon Station, PA, 19536; *Military Collectors' News*, P.O. Box 702073, Tulsa, OK 74170; *Military History*, 6405 Flank Dr., Harrisburg, PA 17112; *Military Trader*, P.O. Box 1050, Dubuque, IA 52004; *Wildcat Collectors Journal*, 15158 NE 6 Ave., Miami FL 33162.

Collectors' Clubs: American Society of Military Insignia Collectors, 526 Lafayette Ave., Palmerton, PA 18701; Association of American Military Uniform Collectors, P.O. Box 1876, Elyria, OH 44036; Company of Military Historians, North Main St., Westbrook, CT 06498; Orders and Medals Society of America, P.O. Box 484, Glassboro, NJ 08028.

Museums: Liberty Memorial Museum, Kansas City, MO; National Infantry Museum, Fort Benning, GA; The Parris Island Museum, Parris Island, SC; Seven Acres Antique Village & Museum, Union, IL; U.S. Air Force Museum, Wright-Patterson AFB, Dayton, OH; U.S. Army Transportation Museum, Fort Eustis, VA; U.S. Navy Museum, Washington, DC.

Advertising, drawing book, Old Reliable Coffee, patriotic ed 8.00
Badge, American Red Cross-Military Welfare, cap, enamel...............20.00
Bayonet, orig case........................20.00
Belt, web....................................254.00
Book

Britain's Clandestine Submarines 1914-1915, Gaddis Smith, Yale University Press, New Haven, 1964, 155 pgs, 1st ed, dj....................22.00

History of the 101st Machine Gun Battalion, P.S. Wainwright, ed, Hartford 101st Machine Gun Battalion Association, 1922, 8vo, 327 pgs...................35.00

History of the Great War, The

British Campaign in France and Flanders, 1918, July to November, Arthur Conan Doyle, 6 vol, George H. Doran, 1920, 325 pgs..........30.00

Without Censor, New Light on Our Greatest World War Battles, Thomas M. Johnson, Bobbs-Merrill, 1928, 8vo, photos, maps, dj.....18.00

Candleholder, Germany, sword handle fits into candleholder, silver inlay reads "To Mom & Dad from Gordon" just above handle, no blade 85.00
Canteen, Army 15.00
Flip Book, 2" x 2-1/2" x 1/4", soldier, sailor and Uncle Sam presenting the colors, pledge of Allegiance, Liberty Bond promotion, 1917 ....30.00
Gas Mask, carrying can, shoulder strap, canister attached to bottom, German 50.00
Handkerchief, 11" sq, "Remember Me," soldier and girl in center, red, white and blue edge 20.00
Helmet, U.S., 3rd Army insignia 65.00
Key-Chain Fob, Kaiser Bill's Bones, 1-1/4" l replica of shell casing holding miniature celluloid die set, inscription on firing cap end of brass cartridge, removable silver-bullet head, loop for key chain 72.00
Medal, Iron Cross...........................45.00
Paperweight, weighted celluloid, full-color image of 12 "Flags of the Allies—United for the Cause of Liberty," white center, black letters, mirror base 40.00
Pinback Button
  Australia Day
    1916, light sepia portrait of English naval officer Lord Kitchener, white ground, blue letters, 1916 Unley event.........20.00
    1918, red, white, blue and black, aborigine young woman puffing pipe, wearing red bandanna, blue and black rim depiction of tiny boomerangs 40.00
    Lloyd George, black and gray portrait of British Prime Minister,

Recognition certificate, 18" x 12", issued in Bellevue, PA, $20.

Welsh rim inscription................30.00
On Active Service, multicolored image of English bulldog staunchly positioned on national flag, blue lettering 30.00
Our Heroes Welcome Home, blue letters, white bordered by red victory wreath 20.00
Port Pirie Repatriation, black cat on lower yellow ground, shaded blue top, black lettering, Australian, c1916 ....35.00
78th Division, red, white and blue, Welcome Home, issued for "The Fighting Demons"............35.00
World Peace, multicolored, Allied flags around white dove carrying olive branch 60.00
Pin Holder, 2-1/4" d, celluloid, full-color image of 12 Allies flags around white center, blue letters, perimeter ring holds glass mirror...................35.00
Postcard, 3-1/4" x 5-1/4", Chicago Daily News War Postals, b&w photos of war scenes, lettered title on front, tiny printed stamp from Chicago Daily News, white reverse printed "Chicago Daily News G.J. Kavanaugh War Postal Card Dept.," unused, lot of 20..........48.00
Ribbon, 2" x 5", Welcome Home 26th Division....................................25.00
Tobacco Jar, cov, 6-1/2" h, ceramic, brown glaze, General Pershing 145.00
Uniform, U.S. Army, Engineer, coat, belt, pants, cap, canvas leggings, wool puttees and leather gaithers, canteen 400.00
Watch Fob, flag on pole, USA, beaded, blue 45.00
Yard Long, framed, USS *Siboney* Arriving at U.S. Naval Base, Aug. 8, 1919..........................165.00

Silk, Greetings from Our Camp, white and black, maroon border, 15" x 15", 16-1/2" x 16-1/2" frame, $25.

World War II Collectibles

Collecting Hints: To the victors go the spoils or so World War II collectors would like to think. Now that the Soviet Block has fallen, a large number of dealers are making efforts to import Soviet Block World War II collectibles into the United States. Be careful when buying anything that has a new or unused appearance. Many Soviet countries continued to use stockpiled World War II equipment and still manufacture new goods based on World War II designs.

The Korean Conflict occurred shortly after World War II. The United States and other armed forces involved in this conflict used equipment and uniforms similar to those manufactured during World War II. Familiarize yourself with model styles, dates of manufacture and your buying sources.

If you locate a World War II item, make certain to record all personal history associated with the item. This is extremely important. Collectors demand this documentation. If possible, secure additional information on the history of the unit and the battles in which it was engaged. Also make certain to obtain any extras that are available, such as insignia or a second set of buttons.

History: With the rise of the German Third Reich, European nations once again engaged in a massive arms race. The 1930s Depression compounded the situation. After numerous compromises to German expansionism, war was declared in 1939 following Germany's Blitzkrieg invasion of Poland. Allied and Axis alliances were formed. Although neutral, Americans were very supportive of the Allied cause. The Dec. 7, 1941, Japanese attack on the U.S. Naval Station at Pearl Harbor, Hawaii, forced America into the war. It immediately adopted a two-front strategy.

From 1942 to 1945, the entire world was directly or indirectly involved in the war. Virtually all industrial activity was war related. The resulting technological advances guaranteed that life after the war would be far different from prior

years. Germany surrendered May 7, 1945. Japan surrendered on Aug. 14, 1945, after the atomic bombing of Hiroshima on Aug. 6, 1945 and Nagasaki on Aug. 9, 1945.

References: Thomas Berndt, *Standard Catalog of U.S. Military Vehicles*, Krause Publications, 1993; Stan Cohen, *V for Victory*, Pictorial Histories Publishing, 1991; Robert Heide and John Gilman, *Home Front America: Popular Culture of the World War II Era*, Chronicle Books, 1995; Jon A. Maguire, *Silver Wings, Pinks & Greens: Uniforms, Wings, & Insignia of USAAF Airmen in World War II*, Schiffer Publishing, 1994; Jack Matthews, *ToysGo to War: World War II Military Toys, Games, Puzzles & Books*, Pictorial Histories Publishing, 1994; Walton Rawls, *Disney Dons Dogtags*, Abbeville Publishing, 1992; Richard Windrow and Tim Hawkins, *World War II GI*, Motorbooks International, 1993; *Windrow & Greene's Militaria Directory and Sourcebook 1994*, Motorbooks International, 1994.

Periodicals: *Men at Arms*, 222 W. Exchange St., Providence, RI 02903; *Military Collector Magazine*, P.O. Box 245, Lyon Station, PA, 19536; *Military Collectors' News*, P.O. Box 702073, Tulsa, OK 74170; *Military History*, 6405 Flank Dr., Harrisburg, PA 17112; *Military Trader*, P.O. Box 1050, Dubuque, IA 52004; *Wildcat Collectors Journal*, 15158 NE 6 Ave., Miami FL 33162.

Collectors' Clubs: American Society of Military Insignia Collectors, 526 Lafayette Ave., Palmerton, PA 18701; Association of American Military Uniform Collectors, P.O. Box 1876, Elyria, OH 44036; Company of Military Historians, North Main St., Westbrook, CT 06498; Imperial German Military Collectors Association, 82 Atlantic St., Keyport, NJ 07735; Orders and Medals Society of America, P.O. Box 484, Glassboro, NJ 08028.

Museums: Liberty Memorial Museum, Kansas City, MO; National Infantry Museum, Fort Benning, GA; The Parris Island Museum, Parris Island, SC; Seven Acres Antique Village & Museum, Union, IL; U.S. Air Force Museum, Wright-Patterson

Postcard, Seabees, June 15, 1943, $3.

AFB, Dayton, OH; U.S. Army Transportation Museum, Fort Eustis, VA; U.S. Navy Museum, Washington, DC.

Arm Band., Civilian Defense Air Raid
    Warden, 4" w, white, 3-1/2" blue
    circle, red and white diagonal
    stripes within triangle 10.00
Better Little Book, *Fighting
    Heroes Battle for Freedom*,
    #1401, 1942, 1943 .... 18.00
Binoculars, Army, M-17, field type,
    7-1/2" l, olive drab, 7" x 50 power,
    clear, fixed optics 95.00
Book
    Guadalcanal Diary, Richard Tre-
    gaskis, Random House, 1943, illus,
    official USMC photos, 263 pgs .. 7.50
    My Life, Grand Admiral Erich Raeder,
    U.S. Naval Institute, 1950, photos,
    430 pgs, 1st ed, dj 22.00
    *Pearl Harbor, Story of the Secret
    War*, George Morgenstern,
    Devin-Adair, 1947, 425 pgs 15.00
    *The "Last" Nazi: The Life and
    Times of Dr. Joseph Mengele*,
    Gerald Astor, Donald I Fine,
    NY, 1985, illus, 305 pgs 9.00
    *World War II in Headlines
    and Pictures*, Philadelphia
    Evening Bulletin, 16-1/2" x 14",
    soft-cover, 1956 .... 35.00
    *World War II Prisoner of War
    Scrip of the United States*,
    Albert I. Dunn, Krause, Iola, WI,

Game, Trap the Jap, marble puzzle, 4 blue, 4 white, 1 red marble, 4-1/2" sq, Modern Novelties Inc., Cleveland, OH, $10.

1970, 8vo, 112 pgs...................25.00
Calendar, 6-3/4" x 10",
   Co-Operative Elevator Co.,
   Gen. Douglas MacArthur, 1943,
   cream-colored diecut sheet, red and
   blue sword design at center, brown-
   tone portrait of general 45.00
Cap, AAF Officer's, 50-Mission, crash
   cap, small gilded eagle, front and
   back straps, soft bill, gabardine, mkd
   "Fighter by Bancroft, O.D." 95.00
Cover
   3-1/2" x 6-1/2", Let's Go,
   envelope with blue and red graphics
   at left showing Uncle Sam rolling up
   sleeves, Hawaii lying on ground,
   knife in back, "Remember Pearl
   Harbor," postmarked 1944, typed
   address 18.00
   3-3/4" x 6-1/2", Remember Pearl
   Harbor First Anniversary, emb
   green image of wounded serviceman
   being helped by Navy and Marine es-
   corts and nurses, snake, rat and
   skunk in foreground with faces of
   Axis powers, postmarked Dec. 7,
   1942, typewritten address 28.00
Flight Suit, Army Air Force, Type A-4,
   olive drab gabardine, matching belt,
   zipper front...............................95.00
Glass, 4-1/2" h, flying white eagle, blue
   and red V symbol.....................24.00
Helmet, MI, olive drab sand finish,
   olive drab chin strap, orig liner,
   thin mesh helmet net 145.00
Jacket, A-2 Army Air Force,
   leather, cowhide, light brown,
   name tag.................................495.00
Knife, Camillus USN Mark 5
   Sheath, black finish blade, light
   scabbard wear, USN and name mkd
   on guard, gray web belt loop, gray
   fiber scabbard..........................65.00
Magazine
   Life, Occupation of Germany,
   Feb. 10, 1947 ....9.00
   Pin-Up Parade, 8-1/2" x 11", b&w
   photo cov, purple and yellow accents,
   48 pgs, full-page b&w pinup photos of
   Hollywood stars such as Lucille Ball,
   Barbara Stanwyck, Lana Turner,
   Ginger Rogers centerfold, 1944
   Bond Publishers 40.00
   War Planes, Dell, 8-1/4" x 11", full-
   color cov, 28 b&w pgs, 1942....35.00
Mirror and Thermometer Premium Pic-
   ture, 4-1/2" x 9-3/4", cream-colored
   cardboard mat, diecut opening, blue
   accent mirror, full-color 3" oval art of
   Gen. MacArthur, 2-1/4" diecut open-
   ing with thermometer, c1943 ...48.00
Patch, AAF, cloth, bombardier wings,
   embroidered silver and gray, tan
   cotton, unused 15.00
Pin, Axe the Axis, hatchet shape,

inscription on blade, mkd
   "Sterling Silver".........................85.00
Pinback Button
   Battleship USS *Washington,* green
   on gold, June 1, 1940, launch from
   Philadelphia Navy Yard............45.00
   Eat to Beat the Devil, red, white and
   blue litho, image of clenched fist
   belting head of devil 55.00
   Gen. Douglas MacArthur, 2-1/2" d,
   red, white and blue, blue-tone
   portrait......................................60.00
   Gen. MacArthur Welcome Home,
   red, white and blue, blue-tone
   portrait......................................60.00
   Gopher Ordnance Works, full-color
   war production cartoon of
   determined gopher....................35.00
   Mothers of World War II, blue
   and white image.......................40.00
   Pabst Breweries Bond Buyer, red,
   white and blue, 10% salary
   contributor 30.00
Postcard, 3-1/2" x 5-1/2", Just a Little
   Something to Remember Pearl Harbor, full-color cartoon showing Navy
   ship firing on and sinking Japanese
   ship, 1942 cancellation 18.00
Shovel, fox-hole type.....................15.00
Sweater, sleeveless,
   V-neck, olive drab....................45.00

World's Fairs and Expositions

Collecting Hints: Familiarize yourself with the main buildings and features of the early World's Fairs and
Expositions. Much of the choicest
china and textiles pictured an identifiable building. Many exposition
buildings remained standing long after the fairs were over and souvenirs
proliferated. Prices almost always
are higher in the city or area where
an exposition was held.

There have been hundreds of
local fairs, state fairs, etc., in the last
100 years. These events generally
produced items of little value today,
except to local collectors.

History: The Great Exhibition of
1851 in London marked the beginning of the World's Fair and Exposition movement. The fairs generally
featured exhibitions from nations
around the world displaying the best
of their industrial and scientific
achievements.

Many important technological
advances have been introduced at

world's fairs, including the airplane,
telephone and electric lights. Ice
cream cones, hot dogs and iced tea
were first sold by vendors at fairs. Art
movements were often closely associated with fairs and exhibitions. The
best works of the Art Nouveau artists
were assembled at the Paris Exhibition in 1900.

References: Robert L. Hendershott,
1*904 St. Louis World's Fair Memen-
tos and Memorabilia,* Kurt R. Krueger Publishing (5438 N. 90th St.,
Ste. 309, Omaha, NE 68134), 1994;
Frederick and Mary Megson, *American Exposition Postcards,* The Postcard Lovers, 1992; *New York
World's Fair Licensed Merchandise,*
World of Tomorrow Co. (P.O. Box
229, Millwood, NY 10546), 1996.

Periodical: *World's Fair,* P.O. Box
339, Corte Madera, CA 94976.

Collectors' Clubs: 1904 World's
Fair Society, 529 Barcia Dr., St. Louis, MO 63119; World's Fair Collectors' Society, Inc., P.O. Box 20806,
Sarasota, FL 34276.

Museums: Atwater Kent Museum,
History Museum of Philadelphia, Phil-
adelphia, PA; Buffalo & Erie County
Historical Society, Buffalo, NY; Califor-
nia State University, Madden Library,
Fresno, CA; 1893 Chicago World's
Columbian Exposition Museum, Co-
lumbus, WI; Museum of Science & In-
dustry, Chicago, IL; Presidio Art
Museum, San Francisco, CA; The
Queens Museum, Flushing, NY.

**1893, Chicago, The Columbian Expo-
sition**

Book, *Harper's Chicago and the
   World's Fair,* Julian Ralph, NY,
   Harper and Brothers, 1893, cloth-
   bound, 244 pgs, 70 illus 45.00
Brochure, Mammoth Redwood
   Plank, Owned by the Berry Bros.,
   Ltd., 4 pgs, 4" x 5" 25.00
Crumb Tray and Scraper, SP........30.00
Folder, 5-1/2" x 9-3/4", views 40.00
Playing Cards...............................45.00
Souvenir Book, *Official Guide to the
   World's Columbian Exposition,*
   5" x 7", 192 pgs 50.00
Tablecloth, 11" sq, Machinery Hall,
   fringed border, small stain and
   damage 70.00

**1894, California Mid-Winter Exposi-
tion,** souvenir spoon, bowl with
drawing of ornate pavilion, SP, mkd

"AMN Sterling Co." 25.00

1901, Pan Am Exposition, Buffalo

Bandanna, 20" sq, silk, Electrical
Tower illus 195.00
Match Holder, hanging type 25.00
Souvenir Spoon
4-1/2" l, SP, Machinery & Transportation Building on bowl 13.00
6" l, SP, buffalo sitting on earth on top
of handle, waterfalls on bowl....15.00

1904 St. Louis, Louisiana Purchase Exposition

Bowl, Grant log cabin 165.00
Coffee Tin, Hanley & Kinsella........30.00
Letter Opener, emb
buildings on handle.................45.00
Souvenir Book, *Souvenir Book of the
Louisiana Purchase Exposition,*
day-and-night scenes, published by
the Official Photographic Co.,
11" x 8-1/2" 45.00

1915, San Francisco, Panama-Pacific International Exposition

Booklet, Panama-Pacific International
Exposition, compliments of Reming-
ton Typewriter, 30 pgs,
7-1/4" x 11" 40.00
Handbook, *The Sculpture &
Murals of the Panama-Pacific
International Exposition,* Stella S.
G Perry, 1915, 104 pgs, 5" x 6-3/4",
ex-library copy 45.00
Tray, 3-1/2" x 5-1/2,
hammered metal, bear figural, emb
"Towe of Jewels, Panama Pacific
International/San Francisco,
Cal 1915," dark finish...............45.00
Watch Fob, brass, orig black leather
strap......................................95.00

1934 Chicago Century of Progress

Automobile Accessory, rear-view mirror,
no glare, orig box.....................90.00
Bracelet, copper, scenic 35.00
Brochure
Baltimore and Ohio Railroad World's
Fair Exhibit 1934, 20 pages,
4-1/2" x 9-3/4" 25.00
57 at the Fair, Heinz 57 Exhibit,
Agricultural Building, 16 pgs.....22.00
How! And Where! At Chicago and the
World's Fair, Chicago and
Northwestern (Railroad) Line,
16-pg guide to Chicago 20.00
Official Pictures, Reuben H. Donnelly,
b&w, 7" x 10" 35.00
Sky-Ride, See the Fair from the Air,
4 pgs, 3-1/2" x 5-3/4" 12.00
The Why-What-and When of a Century
of Progress, 10 pgs 10.00
Certificate of Attendance, Closing Day,
Oct. 31, 1934, 3" x 5-1/4" 15.00
Coffee Mug, Stewart's...................50.00

Coin, flattened
1-3/8" l, Fort Dearborn 15.00
1-1/2" x 3/4", General
Motors Exhibit 15.00
Good Luck Key, 2" l, Master Lock,
pavilions on shank...................20.00
Handkerchief, 11" sq, painted silk,
small stains..............................40.00
Magazine, *Marshall Field & Co.,*
9-1/2" x 13", 44 pgs, photos
and articles 20.00
Map, City of Chicago and
Century of Progress
fairgrounds, Shell Oil 16.00
Needle Case, 6-3/4" x 4-1/2",
A Century of Progress 27.00
Playing Cards, gold-leaf edges,
orig red leather case................30.00
Pocket Mirror................................25.00
Puzzle, 16-1/2", aerial view of fair
opening, 300 pcs 50.00
Snowdome 50.00
Souvenir Book
*1933 Century of Progress Souvenir
Book,* 8-1/2" x 11-1/2" 20.00
Official Guide Book of the Fair,
foldout map and Firestone
olored adv insert 25.00
Souvenir Spoon, SP
Electrical Group on bowl, Fort Dear-
born on handle, dated 1934 .....10.00
Travel & Transport on bowl,
Hall of Science on handle,
dated 1933 ....8.00
Tray, Hall of Science, emb buildings,
bridge 30.00
View Book, 9" x 12", A Century
of Progress Exhibition Official Book
of Views, watercolor views and
painting reproductions, published by
Donnelly 30.00
Wings 25.00

1939, New York, New York's Fair

Ashtray, 3" x 3-1/2", Trylon
and Perisphere, Almar,
Point Marian, PA 60.00
Banner, 10" x 8", multicolored

**1934, Chicago, puzzle, Marshall Field
Co., Electrical Building, basswood,
3-1/2" x 5-9/16", $20.**

paint on blue felt.....................45.00
Belt Buckle, goldtone, enameled
Trylon and Perisphere............20.00
Bookends, pr, alabaster, figural, Trylon
and Perisphere......................110.00
Booklet
General Motors Highway &
Horizons, 20 pgs.....................24.00
The Foods of Tomorrow,
Birdseye...................................8.00
Bowl, spring, Homer
Laughlin Pottery......................55.00
Brochure, 12 pgs, foldout, Trylon
and Perisphere........................16.00
Cake Knife 45.00
Cane, 34" l, wood, blue,
round wood knob, Trylon and
Perisphere decal 85.00
Clock, travel, 1-2/ x 1-1/4" x 1-1/2",
chrome-silver case, Trylon,
Perisphere and fair buildings
on cover, blue and orange
enamel accents 125.00
Coin, flattened, World of Tomorrow,
Trylon and Perisphere............13.00
Commemorative Plate 150.00
Compact, 2-3/4" d, metal, full-color
celluloid insert, ivory white
enameling................................40.00
Cuff Links, pr, Trylon and
Perisphere..............................45.00
Cup 25.00
Glass, 4-1/4" h
Business Administration
Building, dark blue top and center,
orange base, "NYWF 39" and
row of stars at base 20.00
Textile Building, yellow top and
center, green base, center
shows building 20.00
Guide Book, *Official Guide to World of
Tomorrow,* first ed, 1939 ....25.00
Hat, employee, wool, navy, orange
Trylon and Perisphere and "1940"
on front 42.00
Hot Plate, silver,
engraved fair scenes...............15.00
Identification Check,
Greyhound Bus, Sightseeing
Bus Trip Thru Grounds.............7.50
Kerchief, 20" sq, deep blue,
cluttered yellow, green and
red artwork of Fair buildings, Trylon
and Perisphere........................65.00

**1939, New York, spoon, SP, Oneida
Community, 4-3/8", $10.**

Key Ring.................................20.00
Magazine, *Life*, Trylon and Perisphere
    on cover................................30.00
Map, Transit Map of Greater
    New York, Compliments of Franklin
    Fire Insurance Co. 25.00
Match Case, 1-1/2" x 2", leather, Trylon
    and Perisphere 35.00
Music Box...................................65.00
Night-Light, ceramic, oval base with
    Trylon and Perisphere, ivory white
    finish, gold accents 100.00
Photo, 25" x 20", American Jubilee,
    dry mounted............................55.00
Pin
    I Have Seen the Future 25.00
    Shield-shaped logo, 5/8" h, 3/8" w,
    1-1/2" chain to "39" on smaller shield,
    blue enamel on brass..............25.00
Plate
    7-1/4" d, Joint Exhibit of Capital & La-
    bor, The American Potter, New York
    World's Fair, 1940, National Brother-
    hood Cooperative Potteries......45.00
    9" d, Homer Laughlin Pottery,
    potter, turquoise 38.00
    10" d, Cronin, crazed 85.00
Playing Cards, 2 decks, orig box, U.S.
    Playing Card Co. 50.00
Postcard, set of 10 double-faced cards,
    orig folder, unused...................18.00
Postage Stamps, 54 licensed stamps in
    orig envelope, unused 25.00
Potholder, 7-1/2" x 8-1/2", woven terry
    cloth, blue and white design, in-
    scribed "Macy's Pot Holder" 50.00
Program, Opening Day,
    April 30, 1939 ....150.00
Ring, 5/8" d, 3/8" x 5/8" top with Trylon
    and Perisphere, SS 45.00
Rug, 9" x 13", woven Oriental type,
    image of Trylon and Perisphere
    surrounded by flowers, shades of
    green, yellow, red and orange
    highlights, Italian......................95.00
Salt and Pepper Shakers, pr, figural,
    Trylon and Perisphere,
    range and blue........................25.00
Scarf, 18" x 17", white, orange, yellow
    and maroon, blue ground, trees and
    buildings, Trylon and Perisphere
    around edge, clouds center 45.00
Souvenir Spoon, SP, Trylon
    and Perisphere on handle,
    different exhibit on bowl,
    Wm. Rogers, set of 12...........240.00
Table Mat, 11" x 21", red felt,
    yellow, green and white graphics,
    Statue of Liberty, Fair Administration
    Building, Empire State Building,
    Trylon and Perisphere 95.00
Tape Measure, 2-1/2" w, egg
    shape, metal, blue finish, bee figure
    on both sides, orange Trylon and

1964, New York, game, The Official World's Fair Game, Milton Bradley, Springfield, MA, 1964-65, $15.

Perisphere on 1 side, mkd "New York
    World's Fair 1939"...................60.00
Teapot, white glazed china, blue Trylon
    and Perisphere 50.00
Thermometer, 8-1/4" l, key shape,
    aerial view 32.00
Thermos, 10" h, steel, threaded alumi-
    num cap, orange Trylon and Peri-
    sphere, Universal Thermos ...100.00
Ticket, 3" x 4", b&w photo, starched
    black fabric holder 45.00
Tie Clip, 2-3/4" w, brass,
    raised center emblem of Trylon
    and Perisphere 25.00
Valet Holder, clothes-brush holder
    and tie rack, sirocco, raised Trylon
    and Perisphere, orig brush......50.00
View-Master, set of 3 reels, orig
    booklet and envelope 40.00

1939, San Francisco, Golden Gate International Exposition

Ashtray, 1939 Golden Gate Expo,
    Homer Laughlin Pottery.........125.00
Handkerchief, 12-1/2" sq, Treasure
    Island, minor stains 40.00
Label, luggage type, Greyhound,
    3-1/2" d.................................15.00
Matchcover, Golden Gate Bridge
    scenes, pr................................25.00
Pinback Button, 1-1/4" d, yellow, blue
    and white 25.00
Plate, 10" d, Homer Laughlin 125.00
Ticket
    Elephant Train Ticket,
    3-1/2" x 2", slight glue and
    paper on back 15.00
    General Admission,
    3-1/2" x 2-1/4", slight glue
    and paper on back 15.00

1962, Seattle, Century 21 Exposition

Glass, set of eight 80.00
Pinback Button, 1-1/4" d, red, white and
    blue, Space Needle scene 17.50
Token, gold 10.00
Tray, metal, Space
    Needle scene 12.00

1964, New York, New York World's Fair

Ashtray
    4" x 5", glass, white, orange
    and blue graphics, 2 Fair Kids,
    Unisphere, 1964 ....25.00
    5" h, ceramic,
    Unisphere shape......................35.00
Backpack, vinyl 15.00
Bank, dime register, orig card 40.00
Change Tray 12.00
Coaster, 4" d, plastic, white,
    emb gold Unisphere, title and date,
    price for 4-pc set 32.00
Comic Book, Flintstones 20.00
Envelope, Unisphere as Christmas tree
    ornament, unused 10.00
Flash Card Set, New York World's Fair
    Attractions
    Full Size, 3-1/2" x 6",
    28 cards...................................25.00
    Miniature Size, 24 cards 20.00
Fork and Spoon Display, 11" l,
    mounted on wood plaque, Unisphere
    decals on handles 45.00
Hat, black felt, Unisphere emblem, white
    cord trim, feather, name "Richard"
    embroidered on front...............25.00
Mug, 3-1/4" h, milk glass,
    red inscription 17.50
Place Mat, 11" x 17-1/2", plastic, full-
    color illus, Swiss Sky Ride and Lunar
    Fountain, price for pr 25.00
Postcard, 10 miniature pictures,
    20 natural color reproductions,
    unused 20.00
Salt and Pepper
    Shakers, pr, figural 12.00
Souvenir Book, *Official Souvenir
    Book of the New York World's
    Fair*, 1965 ....25.00
Stein, 6" h, ceramic, blue, German-style,
    emb Unisphere, German village
    scene, beer drinkers................25.00
Thermometer, 6" x 6", diamond shape,
    metal and plastic, full-color fair
    buildings and attractions 25.00
Ticket
    Belgian Village 7.50
    General Admission,
    adult, unused 20.00
    Pavilion of American Interiors,
    unused prepaid ticket, courtesy of
    International Silver Co. 15.00
    Travelers Pavilion, The Travelers
    Insurance Companies stockholders'
    courtesy card 12.00

Tray, 10-1/2" x 11-1/2", oval, plastic,
raised fair attractions 42.00

Tumbler, Science Hall, 6-1/2" h.....17.50

1967, Montreal, Montreal Expo

Lapel Pin, brass, repeated motif
around edge, threaded post fastener
on back 12.00

Tab, 1-1/2" l, litho tin, blue and white,
U.S. Pavilion, Compliments of
Avis Car Rental.........................6.00

1982, Knoxville, World's Fair

Glass, 5-1/2" h, clear, tapered,
Energy Turns the World theme,
trademark for McDonald's and
Coca-Cola.................................8.00

Sailor Cap, black and red inscription
on brim.......................................5.00

Russel Wright

Collecting Hints: Russel Wright worked for many different companies in addition to creating material under his own label, American Way. Wright's contracts with firms often called for the redesign of pieces which did not produce or sell well. As a result, several lines have the same item in more than one shape.

Wright was totally involved in design. Most collectors focus on his dinnerware; however, he also designed glassware, plastic items, textiles, furniture and metal objects. He helped popularize bleached and blonde furniture. His early work in spun aluminum often is overlooked as is his later work in plastic for the Northern Industrial Chemical Co.

History: Russel Wright was an American industrial engineer with a passion for the streamlined look. His influence is found in all aspects of domestic life. Wright and his wife, Mary Small Einstein, wrote *A Guide To Easier Living* to explain their concepts.

Russel Wright was born in 1904 in Lebanon, OH. His first jobs included set designer and stage manager under the direction of Norman Bel Geddes. He later used this theatrical flair for his industrial designs, stressing simple clean lines. Some of his earliest designs were executed in polished spun aluminum. These pieces, designed in the mid-1930s, include trays, vases and teapots. Wright garnered many awards, among which were those he re-

ceived from the Museum of Modern Art in 1950 and 1953.

Chase Brass and Copper, General Electric, Imperial Glass, National Silver Co., Shenango and Steubenville Pottery Co., are some of the companies that used Russel Wright designs. In 1983, a major exhibition of his work was held at the Hudson River Museum in Yonkers, NY, and at the Smithsonian's Renwick Gallery in Washington, DC.

References: Susan and Al Bagdade, *Warman's American Pottery and Porcelain*, Wallace-Homestead, 1994; Ann Kerr, *Collector's Encyclopedia of Russel Wright Designs*, 2nd Edition, Collector Books, 1997; Leslie Pina, *Pottery, Modern Wares 1920-1960*, Schiffer Publishing, 1994.

American Modern: Made by the Steubenville Pottery Co., 1939-1959. Originally issued in Bean Brown, Chartreuse Curry, Coral, Granite Grey, Seafoam Blue and White. Later color additions were Black Chutney, Cedar Green, Cantaloupe, Glacier Blue and Steubenville Blue. The Ideal Toy Co., made a set of miniature dishes, which was distributed to Sears, Roebuck.

Baker, small, Chartreuse Curry.....25.00

Butter, cov

   Black Chutney.........................285.00

   Chartreuse Curry 285.00

   Coral 285.00

Carafe, Granite Grey.................175.00

Casserole, cov, stick handle,
   Seafoam Blue..........................40.00

Celery

   Bean Brown............................24.00

   Granite Grey 20.00

Chop Plate

   Chartreuse Curry 20.00

   Coral 20.00

   Granite Grey 25.00

   Seafoam Blue..........................25.00

Coaster, White 24.00

Cocktail, 2-3/4" h, 2-1/2 oz,
   Seafoam Blue, glass 17.00

Creamer

   Coral 9.00

   Granite Grey 8.50

Creamer and Sugar,
   Chartreuse Curry.....................20.00

Cup, Seafoam Blue........................9.00

Cup and Saucer

   Coral 8.00

   Glacier Blue 28.00

   Granite Grey 12.00

Demitasse Cup

Chartreuse Curry 8.00

Granite Grey 17.00

Demitasse Cup and
   Saucer, coral 20.00

Demitasse Pot, cov

   Coral 70.00

   Granite Grey 80.00

   Seafoam Blue........................150.00

Dinner Service,
   Seafoam Blue, 74 pcs 600.00

Fruit Bowl, lug handle

   Bean Brown............................19.00

   Chartreuse Curry 8.00

   Coral 12.00

Hostess Plate

   Chartreuse Curry 75.00

   Granite Grey 85.00

Iced Tea Tumbler, 5" h, Coral,
   glass, slight use......................24.00

Pickle

   Chartreuse Curry 12.00

   Granite Grey 13.00

Pitcher

   Chartreuse Curry 65.00

   Coral 120.00

   Seafoam Blue..........................85.00

Plate

   6" d, bread and butter

      Bean Brown...........................9.00

      Chartreuse Curry 4.00

      Glacier Blue 11.00

   8" d, salad

      Coral 15.00

      Granite Grey 12.00

   10" d, dinner

      Bean Brown.........................17.00

      Cedar Green........................10.00

      Chartreuse Curry 8.00

      Coral 8.00

      Granite Grey 10.00

      Seafoam Blue......................10.00

Platter, oval

   Chartreuse Curry 17.00

   Coral 20.00

Refrigerator Dish, cov

   Coral 225.00

   Granite Grey 175.00

Relish

   Chartreuse Curry, rosette 145.00

   Seafoam Blue..........................24.00

Salad Bowl

   Coral 75.00

   Granite Grey 85.00

   Seafoam Blue..........................85.00

Salt and Pepper Shakers, pr

   Chartreuse 12.00

   Coral 12.00

   Granite Grey 12.00

   Seafoam Blue..........................15.00

Sauceboat, liner, Coral 45.00

Sherbet, 5 oz,
　　Seafoam Blue, glass...............20.00
Soup Bowl
　　Bean Brown, lug handle..........24.00
　　Coral...........................15.00
　　Granite Grey, lug handle.........15.00
Stack Server, Cedar Green........250.00
Sugar, cov
　　Cedar Green 12.00
　　Chartreuse Curry.................20.00
　　Seafoam Blue.....................12.00
Teapot, Granite Grey...................75.00
Tumbler
　　Black Chutney 65.00
　　Cedar Green 72.00
　　Coral............................60.00
　　Granite Grey.....................65.00
Vegetable Bowl
　　Chartreuse Curry.................15.00
　　Coral............................20.00
　　Granite Grey.....................22.00
　　Seafoam Blue.....................20.00
Vegetable Bowl, divided,
　　Chartreuse Curry.................80.00

Iroquois Casual: Made by the Iroquois China Co., and distributed by Garrison Products, 1946-1960s. Initially issued in Ice Blue, Lemon Yellow and Sugar White. Later colors produced were Aqua, Avocado Yellow, Brick Red, Cantaloupe, Charcoal, Lettuce Green, Oyster, Nutmeg Brown, Parsley Green (later called Forest Green), Pink Sherbet and Ripe Apricot.

Butter, cov
　　Avocado Yellow...................65.00
　　Ice Blue 85.00
　　Lemon Yellow.....................54.00
　　Pink Sherbet.....................75.00
　　Ripe Apricot.....................85.00
　　Sugar White 85.00
Carafe
　　Avocado Yellow...................90.00
　　Ripe Apricot....................175.00
Casserole, cov, 2 qt
　　Avocado Yellow...................35.00
　　Oyster...........................20.00
Cereal Bowl, 5-1/4" d
　　Cantaloupe.......................15.00
　　Ice Blue 8.00
　　Oyster...........................10.00
Chop Plate, 13" d
　　Ripe Apricot.....................24.00
　　Sugar White 30.00
Coffeepot, cov
　　Ice Blue 135.00
　　Nutmeg Brown 125.00
Coffee Service, Nutmeg Brown,
　　10-pc set........................135.00
Creamer and Sugar, cov, stacking

　　Avocado Yellow 15.00
　　Ice Blue 12.50
　　Sugar White 27.50
Cup and Saucer
　　Charcoal.........................10.00
　　Ice Blue, ear handle 8.00
　　Lemon Yellow......................8.00
　　Pink Sherbet 8.00
　　Sugar White 10.00
Demitasse Pot, cov
　　Avocado Yellow 65.00
　　Nutmeg Brown 75.00
Demitasse Cup and Saucer
　　Avocado Yellow 150.00
　　Ice Blue 150.00
Fruit Bowl
　　Avocado Yellow 4.00
　　Oyster............................4.50
Gumbo
　　Ice Blue 35.00
　　Pink Sherbet 30.00
Hostess Plate, Ice Blue 85.00
Mug, Ripe Apricot......................75.00
Plate
　　6-1/2" d, bread and butter
　　　　Avocado Yellow 4.00
　　　　Ice Blue.......................3.00
　　　　Ripe Apricot 3.50
　　　　Sugar White 6.50
　　7-3/8" d, salad
　　　　Ice Blue.......................6.00
　　　　Lemon Yellow 7.00
　　　　Oyster 8.00
　　　　Sugar White 10.00
　　9" d, luncheon
　　　　Avocado Yellow 5.00
　　　　Ice Blue.......................6.00
　　　　Oyster 8.00
　　10" d, dinner
　　　　Avocado Yellow 8.00
　　　　Charcoal 8.00
　　　　Lemon Yellow 8.50
　　　　Lettuce Green 9.00
　　　　Oyster 10.00
Platter, 14" l, oval, Ice Blue 20.00
Salt and Pepper Shakers, pr, stacking
　　Oyster 15.00
　　Sugar White 17.50

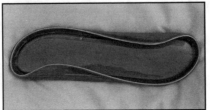

Celery, American Modern, chartreuse, $10.

Vegetable
　　8" d, open
　　　　Avocado Yellow 15.00
　　　　Ice Blue......................15.00
　　　　Nutmeg Brown 15.00
　　　　Pink Sherbet 17.50
　　10" d, cov
　　　　Chartreuse, pinch lid, 2 pt....30.00
　　　　Nutmeg Brown 55.00
　　　　Pink Sherbet 50.00

Iroquois Casual, Redesigned: In 1959, Iroquois Casual dinnerware was produced in patterns and offered in 45-piece sets. Cookware in the redesigned style was a later addition.

Cup, Charcoal 8.00
Cup and Saucer, Ice Blue 10.00
Gravy, Ice Blue 220.00
Mug
　　Apricot Yellow 80.00
　　Ice Blue................................75.00
　　Lemon Yellow 75.00
　　Pink Sherbet 70.00
　　Ripe Apricot 70.00
　　Sugar White, Christmas dec 85.00
Set, Pink Sherbet, 24 pcs 125.00
Teapot, Lemon Yellow 185.0

Index

Warman's Americana & Collectibles
8TH EDITION

Everybody's a Collector!

Everybody's a collector, whether you realize it or not. Collecting is one of the biggest American hobbies. Bet if you look around your home, you'll find small (or perhaps large) piles of things that constitute a collection. Remember those magazines and catalogs under the sofa? Right, a collection! Add to that those toys too much fun to give away. Remember those records you no longer listen to—bet they are in the back of the entertainment center. Now, think about all the other things you collect, whether conscientiously or not. Beginning to see the piles? Bet you are! Now have some fun and look them up in the 8th edition of *Warman's Americana & Collectibles* and find out what your collections are really worth. While you're reading, you might find some new places to acquire even more collectibles to enhance your life.

The American viewpoint of collectibles is constantly changing and Warman's responds to that by adding and enhancing categories with every edition.

New this year are:

◆ Boxing Collectibles ◆ Basketball Collectibles
◆ Bookends ◆ Chintz China ◆ Hunting Collectibles
◆ Olympics Collectibles ◆ Planters ◆ Dr. Seuss
◆ Thermometers ◆ Uhl Pottery

As always, we rely on the wisdom of our Advisors and have added several new names to our Board. We've also increased our reference sections and added addresses for hard-to-find small publishers. We've increased the size of the book and the size of the type and even added more photographs. *Warman's Americana & Collectibles* is a great value for your collecting dollar.

WARMAN'S ENCYCLOPEDIA OF ANTIQUES AND COLLECTIBLES
Your Place to Start for What You Want to Know

Warman's Encyclopedia of Antiques and Collectibles is dedicated to providing reference information, detailed descriptions and accurate pricing in a number of specialized areas to auctioneers, collectors, dealers and anyone else interested in antiques and collectibles. These user-friendly guides will answer your questions or point you towards other sources that will. Each volume in the Warman's Encyclopedia contains these features:

◆ Histories—Historical developments, manufacturer profiles and socioeconomic factors which influenced production runs.

◆ References and museums and other important information—listed right where they belong—within each category. This information will tell you where to look it up in print or see it in person.

◆ Reproductions—Who's making them and how to tell the originals from the reproductions.

◆ Dozens of categories, hundreds of photographs and marks and thousands of items make each volume the most valuable guide of its kind in the field.

From the same experts who bring you
Warman's Antiques & Collectibles Price Guide

About the Author

Ellen T. Schroy is a nationally recognized antiques and collectibles expert. Besides lecturing and researching antiques and collectibles, Ellen's new column, "What's New At Warman's," appears monthly in *Warman's Today's Collector*. You'll find Ellen at all kinds of antiques and collectibles events, from garage sales to auctions, flea markets, to antique shows. Or she can be found quietly observing what's going on in the vast field of collecting through the Internet!

ISBN: 0-87069-752-8

$17.95 U.S.
$24.95 CAN

51795>

9 780870 697524